BANKING LAW AND REGULATION

Banking Law and Regulation

IRIS H-Y CHIU

AND

JOANNA WILSON

OXFORD
UNIVERSITY PRESS

Great Clarendon Street, Oxford, OX2 6DP,
United Kingdom

Oxford University Press is a department of the University of Oxford.
It furthers the University's objective of excellence in research, scholarship,
and education by publishing worldwide. Oxford is a registered trade mark of
Oxford University Press in the UK and in certain other countries

Published in the United States of America by Oxford University Press
198 Madison Avenue, New York, NY 10016, United States of America

British Library Cataloguing in Publication Data
Data available

Library of Congress Control Number: 2018964749

ISBN 978–0–19–878472–2

Printed in Great Britain by
Bell & Bain Ltd., Glasgow

To all our students, past, present, and future

Preface

The UK banking industry has developed at a rapid pace in recent years, particularly since the onset of the global financial crisis in 2007, which has resulted in a proliferation of public regulation and has meant that transactional issues such as consumer protection measures and banking services have been subject to greater scrutiny.

This book offers a one-stop shop for students interested in both the transactional and regulatory aspects of banking. In particular, it aims to offer an accessible but comprehensive coverage of banking regulation to emphasise the rise in global importance in the public governance of banking as a multi-faceted activity. Chapters 2, 3 and 4 of the book examine the traditional areas of transactional and private law issues, focusing in particular on the bank-customer relationship, and the legal regimes that apply to payment methods and various lending facilities. Recent developments in the banking industry are also analysed including innovations in lending, such as peer-to-peer lending, and the rise in third-party, non-bank payment service providers, such as FinTechs. The remainder of the book explores banking regulation, which has increased in recent decades, and exponentially since the 2007–9 global financial crisis. We first offer a comprehensive discussion of the policymakers and bank regulators at a global level, the European level and of course, in the UK. Although the UK's departure from the EU would have new repercussions for its financial sector, it remains important for us to appreciate the highly global developments in banking regulation. In relation to substantive topics, we explore the principally 'law and economics' approach taken towards micro-prudential regulation, the public-interest led approach in bank crisis management and the UK's structural reforms, as well as salient topics for bank regulation in corporate governance, individual responsibility regimes and anti-money laundering.

This book is intended to provide both undergraduate and postgraduate students with an in-depth understanding of banking law and regulation. Each chapter contains a series of boxes and diagrams which incorporate key lists and important information. Key takeaways are provided at the end of each section in a chapter as well as a key bibliography, directing students to primary legislation, case law sources, and secondary resources for further reading. In addition, the end of each chapter features a series of questions for thought, with brief answer tips.

We are grateful and would like to give thanks to all those who provided us with advice and assistance, the anonymous referees who read earlier drafts, and our editors at Oxford University Press, in particular Tom Young and Lucy Hyde. The law is correct as of 31 May 2018.

Professor Iris H-Y Chiu   Dr Joanna Wilson
August 2018

Acknowledgements

We would like to thank the following people for their invaluable contributions during the development of this title:

Dr Olufemi Amao, Senior Lecturer in Corporate Law, University of Sussex

Andrew Baker, Senior Lecturer, Liverpool John Moores University

Professor Andrew Campbell, Emeritus Professor of International Banking and Finance Law, University of Leeds

Dr Jay Cullen, Reader in Banking Law and Financial Regulation, University of Sheffield

Michael Derks, Lecturer, University of West London

Dr Shabir Korotana, Lecturer, Brunel University London

Dr David McIlroy, Visiting Professor, CCLS, Queen Mary University of London

Dr Ricardo Pereira, Senior Lecturer in Law, Cardiff University

Dr Radek Stech, Founder of SFLS Network, Lecturer in Law, University of Exeter

Dr Yog Upadhyay, Senior Lecturer in Construction Law, Liverpool John Moores University

Dr Steven Vaughan, Associate Professor, University College London

Dr Matteo Zambelli, Senior Lecturer, University of West London

Outline Contents

Detailed Contents

Table of Cases

Table of Primary Legislation

Table of Secondary Legislation

Other Jurisdictions Legislation

US

EU Secondary Legislation

Table of International Treaties and Conventions

Treaty on the Functioning of the European Union

Introduction to banking law and regulation

1.1 What this book covers

This book addresses both the private commercial law influences on the development of the banking industry, as well as the explosion of public regulation. Chapters 2, 3, and 4 deals with transactional banking, focusing in particular on the duties that a bank owes its customer, as well as the legal parameters and regulatory regimes that apply to different payment methods and various lending facilities. Next, we explore the increasingly complex landscape of bank regulation. Chapters 5 and 6 deal with the regulatory institutions and architecture at the international and UK levels. Chapter 7 examines how bank regulation has become an increasingly centralised area of policymaking and regulatory activity at the EU level. Chapters 8 and 9 discuss extensively micro-prudential regulation, which is a key regulatory technique in overseeing bank risk management. Chapter 10 is dedicated to discussing a unique regulatory regime of structural reforms in the UK, where large banks are required to ensure that their retail operations are safely separate from other financial activities. Chapters 11 and 12 look at regulatory reach into bank organisation, governance and individual responsibility and liability. Chapter 13 explores the post-crisis regime for public powers in managing and resolving bank crises. Finally, Chapter 14 deals with the regulatory regime for anti-money laundering and banks' responsibilities for combatting financial crime.

1.2 What is banking law and regulation?

Banking law and regulation covers private commercial law developed through banking custom, standards of good practice, and the common law, which together have a long history of shaping and refining the rights and obligations of banks and their customers. Since the 1980s, public regulatory law for banks has also emerged, in order to introduce standards for banks in managing their risks prudently, so as to prevent failure. In particular in the post-2007–9 financial crisis landscape, public interest demands greater oversight by public authorities over financial sector activities, resulting in a proliferation of public regulation relating to prudential issues, financial crime, and conduct of business and market behaviour.

1.3 The nature of the banking business

Banks have evolved from historic houses that provided intermediation services in relation to creating and circulating money.[1] Banks' roles form the basis of modern capitalism[2] as banks are key actors that facilitate the investment, transfer and circulation of money to facilitate economic activities.

The provision of custodial services by the goldsmiths of London was an early form of 'banking' service. The goldsmiths of London in the sixteenth century provided custodial services that allowed safe storage of value such as gold,[3] and issued instruments that evidenced such value, which could be used for withdrawal and exchange purposes. These early instruments fulfilled the function of money, and the goldsmiths' role was a forerunner of what we recognise today as 'deposit' services, a key function of banks. The deposit service is essential to basic financial management for most ordinary citizens. Most of the population in the UK has a basic current deposit account, which allows money to be stored and payments to be made and received.[4] It is estimated that only less than 1 per cent of the UK population is 'unbanked' as at 2018,[5] that is, without a basic current deposit account at a bank.

The deposit service provided by banks is seen to form the basis for another fundamental banking service, that is, the creation of credit (i.e. lending), a phenomenon known as 'fractional reserve banking'. Fractional reserve banking means that banks only keep a fraction of deposits so that they can lend the rest. This is a historical perception of how banking operates but, over time, banks no longer create credit on the basis of deposits alone, and lend on the basis of other forms of funding they raise, such as in 'shadow banking' markets, which will be introduced shortly. The Bank of England does not implement a fractional reserve policy for UK banks.

Banks 'create' money[6] by creating credit or making loans in order to finance an undertaking that a customer is not able to pay for in full immediately. This is immensely important to facilitating productive economic activities and trade. The needs of sovereigns from the medieval era, largely in connection with financing wars, resulted in the first systems of borrowing.[7] Monarchs borrowed from citizens in order to finance expensive wars, and private business and merchants involved in international trade also needed access to lending facilities. Early financiers[8] provided the essential services of

---

[1] Richard Hildreth, *The History of Banks* (1837, rep CreateSpace Independent Publishing Platform, 2017).

[2] Christine Desan, *Making Money: Coin, Currency and the Coming of Capitalism* (Oxford: OUP 2015).

[3] British Banking History Society, 'A History of English Clearing Banks' (2010) at https://www.banking-history.co.uk/history.html.

[4] These aspects of banking services and the legal framework are dealt with in Chapters 2 and 3.

[5] http://www.financialinclusioncommission.org.uk/facts.

[6] By creating credit, the amount of money is multiplied in a system, and private banks play a key role in this, see Mary Mellor, *The Future of Money* (Pluto Press 2010) chs 1 and 2.

[7] See Niall Ferguson, *The Ascent of Money* (London: Penguin 2012), ch 2 'Of Human Bondage'; and Hildreth, *The History of Banks*, ch III.

[8] Such as the services of country banks and later joint stock banks in industrial England, see British Banking History Society, 'A History of English Clearing Banks' at https://www.banking-history.co.uk/history.html; and the discussion on the Medici bankers of Florence, in Ferguson, *The Ascent of Money*, ch 1 'Dreams of Avarice'.

lending by evidencing this debt in the form of instruments such as bonds or bills (i.e. bills of exchange)[9] and ultimately turning such debt obligations[10] into financial 'assets' that could be used for exchange or realisation into cash.[11] Banks have been essential financial intermediaries in the creation and circulation of money and **capital** for facilitating productive economic activities and trade.

1.4 Types and scope of banking business

Today, retail, commercial and investment banks perform a range of financial services for the same purposes as have been outlined. In Box 1.1, we introduce the common terms associated with today's banking business. There is some 'overlap' between the terms as many 'clearing banks' are also 'retail banks', and retail banks engage in commercial business and, subject to the structural requirements discussed in Chapter 10, may be involved in investment business. Further 'shadow' banks may refer to one of the recognisable banks mentioned above, and relate to the nature of 'shadow banking activities' they engage in. We also introduce the term 'challenger banks' in recognition of the UK regulators' policy of encouraging new banks to be introduced to the UK market in order to improve the market competition.

Box 1.1 Types of banks

Retail banks: full range of customer payment, savings, borrowing, and even investment services, more limitedly see section 1.4.1.1 on *building societies and credit unions*.

Clearing banks: mainly retail banks that have membership in the Bank of England's payment clearing systems to effect large and small payments between individual and business users.

Commercial banks: services for businesses such as deposits, payments and borrowing, issuing negotiable instruments, and letters to finance international trade.

Investment banks: services for corporations in terms of raising finance, such as securities offerings, syndicated lending (see Chapter 4), project finance such as for building infrastructure, investment services, etc.

Financial supermarkets: financial institutions that conduct a range of financial services including banking, commercial, and investment services, providing a one-stop shop for many customers. Many *universal banks* are financial supermarkets, which are large financial groups with global footprint.

---

[9] Bills of exchange are notes issued by banks that are recognised by other banks for payment to the presenter (either as named or bearer, where the instrument is negotiable) of the note. These were developed for the purposes of facilitating international trade. See s3, Bills of Exchange Act 1882.

[10] The moneyness of financial assets is ultimately a legal creation, as the law provides the framing of rights and obligations in them, which has given them attributes of enforceability and moneyness, see Christine Desan, 'Money as a Legal Institution' (2015) at https://papers.ssrn.com/sol3/papers.cfm?abstract_id=2321313.

[11] Financial assets can be realised into cash in markets such as securities or bond markets today, or can be 'discounted' at face value by a discount house or broker willing to advance cash to the holder before the maturity of the financial instrument.

Shadow banks: is arguably a misnomer in some cases as the term refers more to activities that produce similar economic effects as banking activities but not necessarily regulated in the same manner. For example, the Financial Stability Board[12] refers to 'repo transactions' carried out by banks (i.e. the aforementioned type of **banks**) as 'shadow banking', because repo transactions involve the use of banks' assets as collateral to borrow from other banks and financial institutions, usually on a short-term basis, in order to fund banks' lending. This has far overtaken deposits as a source of funding for bank lending. However, repo transactions were largely unregulated, compared to the deposit market, until after the global financial crisis of 2007–9. Shadow 'banks' also include financial institutions that perform economic functions like banks but are not regulated in the same manner, for example, money market funds.[13]

Challenger banks: largely referring to new banks that have come to the market after the 2007–9 global financial crisis, as regulators welcome more competition.[14] The arrival of these banks is partly due to regulatory policy that promotes competition, and the revolutions in technological innovation that have changed the face of financial services.[15]

1.4.1 **Retail and clearing banks**

Retail banks are the most recognisable banks to members of the public, as they, along with building societies and credit unions, provide a wide footprint of individual and household deposit, lending, and payment services. The key retail banks in the UK are also clearing banks. The clearing banks evolved from joint stock banks that, since the industrial revolution in Britain, were formed as private companies, many of which have merged over the years and become the concentrated sector of 'high street' household names in the UK today: Barclays, Lloyd's, HSBC, and National Westminster. The small coterie of clearing banks used to have a stranglehold on the payments and clearing systems in Britain, as they processed payments, largely **cheque** payments, to ensure the smooth running of the economy. Government interventions over the years have forced the privatisation of clearing services and the widening of clearing membership. Today, payments clearing is supported by the UK Payments Administration,[16] a private company that is the umbrella organisation providing services for all forms of payments, from cheques, interbank transfers, and credit cards to digital payments using devices such as mobile phones.[17] Not only do a wider range of British banks (including Scottish

---

[12] FSB, *Policy Framework for Strengthening Oversight and Regulation of Shadow Banking Entities* (2013) ch 2.2ff. See also Erik Gerding, 'The Shadow Banking System and its Legal Origins' (2012) at https://papers.ssrn.com/sol3/papers.cfm?abstract-id=1990816.

[13] FSB, *Policy Framework* ch 2.1; see Viktoria Baklanova and Jo Tanega, 'Money Market Funds' in Iris H-Y Chiu and Iain MacNeil (eds), *Research Handbook on Shadow Banking* (Cheltenham: Edward Elgar 2018).

[14] See PRA and FCA, *New Bank Start-up Unit Guide* at https://www.bankofengland.co.uk/prudential-regulation/new-bank-start-up-unit.

[15] Much of this is discussed in Chapter 3.

[16] See https://www.ukpayments.org.uk/our-clients/.

[17] Payment services are discussed in Chapter 3 generally.

banks) participate directly in clearing but foreign banks do so too.[18] The UK clearing banks, however, still maintain a reputation for their high street presence and wide footprint for retail services in the UK.

1.4.1.1 Building societies and credit unions

Building societies and credit unions are dedicated to retail banking services in the UK. A building society is a mutual organisation that focuses on deposit-taking and mortgage lending to individuals and households,[19] and generally stands out as being able to offer better savings rates as it does not have to pay dividends to shareholders. The building society sector has sought to become more competitive by demutualisation and mergers with banks over the last decades (such as the acquisition of Abbey National by Santander UK, the demutualisation of Alliance and Leicester and subsequent acquisition by Santander, and demutualisation of Bradford & Bingley). The numbers of building societies have declined over the years, now standing at 51 members of the Building Society Association for the entire UK. The largest building society in the UK and the world is Nationwide, which is also a clearing member. Credit unions are also membership-based organisations for local communities for the purposes of savings and loans. They are not for profit by nature and their remit is limited by legislation,[20] but they may offer a locally available service especially if a financing need is not met by a bank. There are about 450 credit unions in the UK with about 1.7 million members.[21]

1.4.2 Commercial banking

Commercial needs, such as in international trade and now globalisation, have led to developments in **commercial banking**.[22] Commercial banking involves banks intermediating the processes of international trade, such as in payments, currency exchange, and managing price risks. For example, commercial banks developed financing instruments such as documentary credits for international commodities trading, where banks pay against documents issued by other banks in reliance of the underlying physical trade that the documents embody.[23] Banks also developed business lines to help customers hedge against fluctuations in commodities value or in foreign exchange by taking on commodities or foreign exchange exposures themselves. Banks make markets such as in foreign exchange and commodities, oiling the wheels of international trade while earning significant returns in trading arbitrage.

---

[18] For example, the membership of CHAPS, the same-day clearing service overseen by the Bank of England that comprises of UK and foreign banks such as Bank of America, Bank of China, and key European banks. See https://www.bankofengland.co.uk/payment-and-settlement/chaps. CHAPS is further discussed in Chapter 3, section 3.4.

[19] Their business remit is defined and limited by the Building Societies Act 1986.

[20] Credit Unions Act 1979 now superseded by the Co-operative and Community Benefit Societies Act 2014.

[21] Numbers obtained from https://www.moneysavingexpert.com/banking/credit-unions.

[22] SD Chapman, *The Rise of Merchant Banking* (London: Harper Collins 1992).

[23] Peter Ellinger and Dora Neo, *The Law and Practice of Documentary Credits* (Oxford: OUP 2010).

1.4.3 **Investment banking**

Further, the needs of ***corporate finance*** have also played an important part in bank business development, giving rise to ***investment banks***.[24] Investment banks serve the needs pertaining to the raising of finance by corporations from investment markets, such as in securities. For example, investment banks undertake underwriting services for corporations that seek to issue securities to the investment market. In such an arrangement, the bank advises the corporation and also guarantees to take up all of the securities in the offer if there is insufficient public uptake. Investment banks earn significant fees in corporate finance advisory work, and become exposed to markets. Investment banking has further developed into other business lines of market exposures, such as in ***proprietary trading*** where the bank itself trades securities directly as principal in order to generate market gains, and ***securitisation*** where investment banks attempt to transform otherwise illiquid assets such as bank loans into securities-like products.[25]

The diversification in the banking business reflects the dynamism of changing economic needs, and introduces new risks for banks in the different markets they are now intermediating. In particular, banks have become more exposed to ***currency risk***, ***commodities risk***, and ***market risk*** in various types of investment instruments.[26]

1.4.4 **Financial supermarkets**

The growth of modern banks into ***financial supermarkets*** has been accelerated by liberalisation forces that have been driving change in the global banking market since the early 1990s; when the conglomeration of banks started to take place at an unprecedented pace. This is largely due to the repeal in 1999 of the Glass–Steagall Act in the US, which used to prevent retail banks serving the deposit and loans markets from taking on merchant and investment banking activities.[27] This legislative liberalisation unleashed a wave of bank conglomeration in the US, as many banking outfits, such as JP Morgan Chase Manhattan and Citigroup, merged to become powerful one-stop shops for various banking services. Although universal banking has always been practised in Europe, and Credit Suisse, for example, is the Swiss counterpart to the aforementioned successful American investment bank, the growth of European universal banks

---

[24] David P Stowell, *Investment Banks, Hedge and Private Equity Funds* (Elsevier Academic Press 2013) ch 1.

[25] Erik Gerding, 'The Shadow Banking System and Its Legal Origins' (2011) at http://ssrn.com/abstract=1990816.

[26] These have been increasingly addressed as matters for prudential regulation, see Chapters 8 and 9.

[27] Discussed in Arthur E Wilmarth Jnr, 'The Transformation of the Financial Services Industry: 1975–2000, Competition, Consolidation and Increased Risks' (2002) *University of Illinois Law Review* 215. It may be argued that as there are economies of scale and synergies in the fusion of different lines of banking and finance business, US banking businesses have for a long time devised structures to avoid the Glass–Steagall Act anyway, prompting its repeal to be seen as timely.

has been in response to the increasing global profile of their American counterparts.[28] Further, American investment banks have taken the lead in financial innovation such as securitisation.[29] The conglomeration in banking services has caused structural change in the financial sector, allowing banks to establish extensive global footprints. These banks have become global financial powerhouses on their own, sometimes known as 'Too Big to Fail' banks.[30] These global banks may give rise to *systemic risk*, which is the risk of instability and contagion in the financial sector as a result of the failure or stresses of a particular important bank.[31]

1.4.5 **Shadow banking**

This relates to financial activities or transactions that perform similar economic functions to banking services but are structured differently, therefore attracting different regulatory treatment. For example, in order for banks to lend, they source short-term funding from other financial institutions in *wholesale markets*, often structured as the sale of an asset to be repurchased in the short term. Financial institutions that 'purchase' an asset from a bank in order to advance the short-term lending can often engage in further resale and repurchase transactions with other counterparties. The reuse of the asset as in fact collateral for the funding transactions is known as 'rehypothecation' or 'repo' transactions. Repo transactions allow banks and financial institutions to access short-term funding and create credit, but the reuse of collateral poses risks in the case of defaulting counterparties. This area is known as shadow banking as it was unregulated prior to the global financial crisis of 2007–9. The lack of regulation facilitated the tremendous growth of this market.

However, problems in the wholesale markets were fundamental to the development of the global financial crisis. Banks widely used securitised assets in repo transactions and, as discussed in section 1.5.3 (Box 1.3), the credibility of a group of securitised assets was crucial to the development of the crisis. When confidence in this group of securitised assets fell in the wholesale markets in about mid-2007, banks experienced marked difficulties in obtaining short-term funding in wholesale markets: a phenomenon known as the 'credit crunch'. The credit crunch was an early sign of and preceded the global financial crisis. The wholesale markets are now subject to a regulatory regime that improves transparency

---

[28] Suzanne McGee, *Chasing Goldman Sachs: How the Masters of the Universe Melted Wall Street Down and Why They'll Take us to the Brink Again* (New York: Crown Business 2010).

[29] Gerding, 'The Shadow Banking System and its Legal Origins' and Richard E Mendales, 'Collateralized Explosive Devices: Why Securities Regulation Failed to Prevent the CDO Meltdown, and How to Fix it' (2009) *University of Illinois Law Review* 1359.

[30] This issue is discussed in detail in Chapters 10 and 13.

[31] Again, a phenomenon of increasing public interest that regulation has begun to address since the global financial crisis, in terms of prudential regulation see Chapters 8 and 9, structural reforms see Chapter 10, and bank crisis management and resolution see Chapter 13.

in repo transactions.[32] Wholesale market participants are also given guidance on how to behave more prudently in relation to accepting collateral and creating credit.[33]

Shadow banking extends to a wider range of activities than repo transactions (which banks are extensively engaged in) and is discussed in detail elsewhere.[34]

1.4.6 Challenger banks

In the aftermath of the global financial crisis, banks recovering from the crisis and subject to new regulation faced constraints in their ability to lend, and financial innovation, coupled with technological breakthroughs, has arisen to fill market gaps and exploit new efficiencies. The UK regulators actively promote innovation and competition, and challenger banks are encouraged to enter the market. As the UK retail banking market is dominated by a handful of high street names, challenger banks have always been welcome and are not a new concept. The Co-operative bank, Virgin Money, the building societies, and TSB (which is now spun off Lloyd's) are all regarded as existing challenger banks. Further, a new high street bank Metro Bank has arrived to challenge the incumbent retail banks. However, a new generation of challenger banks is beginning to emerge that adopt new business models and interfaces.

The New Bank Start up Unit[35] is a joint initiative by UK regulators and provides a platform for early stage advice and engagement with entrepreneurs who plan to start a new bank. Prospective new banks would then have to go through pre-application discussions to ensure that they have a viable business plan, that they understand the regulatory requirements for being authorised as a bank, and are able to put in process the requirements for regulatory compliance. A special regime of mobilisation would apply to them as they roll out their operations during a testing period of 6–12 months. They are advised and overseen by the regulators to become fully compliant and able to be authorised as banks at the end of the testing period. A number of new banks have been authorised since the launch of this initiative, and the majority of them are innovative banks, such as Atom Bank and Monzo Bank. They provide innovative interfaces with customers such as mobile phone app-only user interfaces. Although online-only banks, such as First Direct (owned and operated by HSBC), are not new, the new generation of innovative banks try to distinguish themselves by offering novel services including competitive rates for transactions made in foreign currency (Revolut, Monzo), more user-friendly financial data management such as tracking one's purchases (Starling), or appealing to the unbanked (Monese, for foreigners and immigrants to the UK).

---

[32] The EU Securities Financing Transactions Regulation 2015/2365.

[33] FSB, *Regulatory Framework for Haircuts on Non-Centrally Cleared Securities Financing Transactions* (2015) at http://www.fsb.org/wp-content/uploads/SFT_haircuts_framework.pdf.

[34] For example, see Iris H-Y Chiu and Iain MacNeil (eds), *Research Handbook on Shadow Banking* (Cheltenham: Edward Elgar 2018).

[35] http://www.bankofengland.co.uk/pra/nbsu/Pages/default.aspx.

1.5 Objectives of banking law and regulation

Banking law and regulation has been developed in private commercial law and public regulation over the years to address issues of certainty in rights and obligations, banks' parameters of responsibility, and their public interest profiles. The need for consumer protection has developed profoundly in private commercial law as well as in public regulation. Public regulation has become most pronounced in dealing with the 'safety and soundness' of banks and in combatting financial crime. UK banks are **dual-regulated** by the Prudential Regulation Authority, which focuses on their safety and soundness, and by the Financial Conduct Authority, concentrating on their conduct of business, market behaviour, and roles in combatting financial crime.[36]

1.5.1 Conduct of business, market behaviour, and consumer protection

Consumer protection lies at the heart of many banking law and regulatory initiatives, which often seek to address or rebalance the superior bargaining position of banks in the bank–customer relationship. While we now have a comprehensive piece of legislation in place in the form of the Consumer Rights Act 2015, which protects the interests of consumers in relation to the fairness of contract terms, the common law has also played an important role in developing and defining a bank's obligations to its customer. For example, as discussed further in Chapter 2, a bank owes its customer a duty of confidentiality,[37] a duty of care,[38] and it can find itself subject to a claim of undue influence, both directly and indirectly.[39]

More recently, as part of the ongoing package of public regulatory interventions that have characterised the post-1980s landscape, banks have been subject to a series of 'conduct of business' regulations, which concern, among other things, how a bank treats its clients and customers. These initiatives stem from the 'consumer protection' regulatory objective of the former Financial Services Authority,[40] and now the Financial Conduct Authority (FCA).[41] In pursuing this objective the FCA expects banks to adhere to a general principle of 'treating customers fairly',[42] which is both generally applied as well as specifically elaborated in a number of areas.[43] The FCA also carries out market-based

---

[36] Discussed extensively in Chapter 6.

[37] *Tournier v National Provincial and Union Bank of England* [1924] 1 KB 461.

[38] *Barclays Bank v Quincecare Ltd* [1992] 4 All ER 363; *Lipkin Gorman v Karpnale Ltd* [1989] 1 WLR 1340.

[39] *Royal Bank of Scotland v Etridge (No.2)* [2002] 2 AC 773. Undue influence is an equitable ground of restitution that applies where the defendant (or a third party in the case of tri-party cases) has a relationship of influence with the claimant and they abuse that influence in order to induce the claimant to enter into a contract that benefits the defendant or third party in some way. If successfully pleaded, the claimant will be entitled to have the contract set aside.

[40] Former s2(2), Financial Services and Markets Act 2000.

[41] Financial Services and Markets Act 2000, s1C, inserted by s6, Financial Services Act 2012.

[42] FCA Handbook, PRIN 2.1.1 at principle 6. 'A firm must pay due regard to the interests of its customers and treat them fairly.'   [43] See Chapters 2, 3, and 4.

studies of structurally disadvantageous or uncompetitive features in various banking markets, such as in relation to bank accounts[44] and overdrafts,[45] in order to recommend policy and regulation.

The FCA, as part of its general consumer protection mandate, enjoys extensive powers to intervene in consumer redress in a collective manner, introducing new dimensions to dispute resolution for consumers other than under private litigation. In large-scale cases where misconduct is widespread, the FCA can institute rules to compel financial services providers to pay compensation,[46] or institute redress schemes that allow consumers to resolve complaints directly with their service providers.[47] For individual cases, the FCA works alongside the Financial Ombudsman, an independent and informal resolution body established in 2000 for consumers who wish to bring grievances against a financial sector service provider in respect of amounts less than £150,000.[48] The Financial Ombudsman provides a cost-effective service to resolve disputes with binding effect upon FCA's regulated persons, without necessarily applying the law or incurring legal representation cost.[49] In the context of payment services and the provision of credit, consumers are protected by the Consumer Credit Act 1974 and the new Payment Services Regulations 2017, which together provide a comprehensive regime to safeguard the rights of consumers in relation to issues such as the misuse of a payment instrument, the obligations of the paying and receiving banks in relation to the electronic **transfer of funds**, and the banks' duty of disclosure in the context of loan agreements.[50]

Finally, the FCA also provides a consumer education service to complement its supervision and enforcement powers.[51] These roles are fleshed out in further detail in Chapter 6.

1.5.2 The 'safety and soundness' of banks

Banks provide a full intermediation business that involves maturity transformation. What this means is that banks act as middlemen to allocate their funds to productive use in economic needs, by lending to households, businesses, and governments.

---

[44] FCA, *Cash Savings Market Report* (January 2015) at https://www.fca.org.uk/publications/market-studies/cash-savings-market-study; FCA, 'Our Response to the CMA's Final Report on its Investigation into Competition in the Retail Banking Market' at https://www.fca.org.uk/publications/corporate-documents/our-response-cma-investigation-competition-retail-banking-market (3 November 2016).

[45] Following consumer research into the overdrafts market in 2014 and 2015, the FCA is of the view that consumers are paying too much for overdrafts and the £8 billion market is somewhat uncompetitive, therefore prompting the FCA to consider policy reform: for example, see 'Bank overdraft cap could be re-examined', *BBC News* (3 November 2016).

[46] FCA Handbook, DISP APP 1 and APP 3 on special resolution procedures for mortgage endowment and payment protection insurance mis-selling complaints.

[47] S404A, Financial Services and Markets Act. The scheme has been used for resolving the mis-sold investors in Arch Cru funds in 2015 and card identity protection insurance in 2014.

[48] Part XVI, Financial Services and Markets Act 2000 setting up the Ombudsman scheme.

[49] For example, see *R. (on the application of IFG Financial Services Ltd) v Financial Ombudsman Service Ltd* [2005] EWHC 1153.

[50] See Chapters 3 and 4.   [51] See https://www.moneyadviceservice.org.uk/en.

Banks' funds come from borrowing from a range of sources including other financial institutions and depositors.[52] Banks' borrowing may be short term, such as subject to return on demand by depositors or overnight borrowing in wholesale markets, or may be longer term, such as 3, 6, or 12 months or exceeding 12 months.

In this process of full intermediation, banks encounter a maturity mismatch as their *assets* (i.e. the lending they make) generally take a longer time to mature than their *liabilities* (what banks owe), a phenomenon we often call 'borrowing short and lending long'. For example, banks that lend to households to purchase homes may allow repayments over 25 years but some of their liabilities may mature in 12 months! We can see that the business model of full intermediation entails two key risks. One is that banks may face a *liquidity risk* if they have to repay a significant amount of liabilities (e.g. if depositors turn up in significant numbers to withdraw cash) while they are still committed to long-term loans that have not yet matured. The other is that banks may face a *solvency risk* if their borrowers turn out to be uncreditworthy and default on their borrowing.[53]

Solvency and liquidity risks are to be expected in the nature of the banking business, but if these risks materialise and cause a bank to fail, the repercussions of disruption for other banks, financial institutions, and economic participants can in general be significant. These repercussions are likely to be more severe with banks that have significant economic footprint and globally so.

In 1974, Herstatt Bank in Germany became insolvent, which led to knock-on effects in international banking.

Box 1.2 Contextual insight: Herstatt's failure

Herstatt Bank had excessive exposures to the US dollar. When the dollar fell, the losses suffered by Herstatt made it insolvent and its banking licence was withdrawn by the German authorities. The withdrawal of the banking licence meant that it could no longer conduct banking business, although pending transactions such as international payments were left stranded. At a higher level, Herstatt's failure raised questions as to whether the nature of banking business, such as exposures to various **market risks** including currency risks, was adequately supported by banks' own risk management. If not, there could be a case for regulatory standards to address such deficiencies.

The failure of Herstatt Bank in Germany in 1974 (see Box 1.2) sowed the seeds for the development of international bank regulation for the *prudential* control of bank activities, that is, regulation that controlled banks' risk-taking in order to prevent

---

[52] Savers usually have rights of immediate return of their cash, as opposed to the longer-term commitments banks make to their borrowers in terms of repayment, see *Foley v Hill* (1848) 2 HLC 28, 9 ER 1002, discussed in Chapter 2.

[53] The consequences of these risks and their public interest has increasingly led to public regulation of banks to manage such risks, the regimes are discussed in Chapters 8 and 9.

failure.[54] In the UK, the failure of Johnson Matthey Bank in 1984, which was due to defaults on loans made by the bank, was key to the end of self-regulation by banks and brought in the beginnings of a comprehensive regulatory regime.[55]

At a more fundamental level, banking regulation may be regarded as a requirement for the protection of public interest in the economic function of banking. Banks perform an important economic function of lending to the wider economy but lending is risky and banks need to judge their risks well and manage them. Banks may not manage their range of *risks* adequately or may be insufficiently motivated to do so where profitmaking through risk-taking is an immediate incentive. Protecting the economically useful function of banking involves not just bank regulation in terms of standard-setting, but in the state underwriting to some extent the cost of banking when it fails (*the public backstop*). Thus, the imposition of regulatory standards can be regarded as an exchange for the institution of public sector support for banking, in the forms of *lender of the last resort* (introduced shortly and discussed in Chapter 6) and *the deposit guarantee scheme* (Chapter 13).

A bank may face a liquidity crisis if levels of depositor withdrawal are above what is expected and bank assets have yet to mature (the liquidity mismatch problem discussed earlier). In this situation, the central bank could extend emergency liquidity facilities known as '**lender of last resort**'[56] to the bank challenged by its liquidity needs. This is usually on the basis of the expected solvency of the bank in the long term, and the bank may access such facilities on a cost-effective basis by posting acceptable collateral with the central bank.[57] Further, there is a need to provide a scheme to support depositor confidence so that depositors may not abandon the banking system in view of its risks. It is therefore socially beneficial to provide a state-backed guarantee system[58] for deposits in the event of bank failure.[59] The *lender of the last resort facilities* and the *deposit guarantee scheme* are backbones provided by the public sector that support market confidence in the banking system. Hence it is arguable that banks should be subject to certain regulatory standards designed to protect their solvency.

Micro-prudential regulation for banks has been developed internationally since the 1980s (see Chapters 8 and 9) and has been implemented in many banking jurisdictions

---

[54] International bank regulation is discussed in Chapter 5, while the prudential regulatory standards are discussed in Chapters 8 and 9.

[55] In the form of the Banking Act 1987, see Chapter 6, section 6.1.2.

[56] See Esther Jeffers, 'The Lender of Last Resort Concept: From Bagehot to the crisis of 2007' (Revue de la regulation 2010) at https://regulation.revues.org/8903; X Freixas et al, 'Lender of Last Resort: What Have We Learned since Bagehot?' (2000) 18 *Journal of Financial Services Research* 63.

[57] The role of the UK central bank, the Bank of England, as lender of last resort will be discussed in Chapter 6.

[58] The regime for the UK's deposit guarantee scheme will be discussed in Chapter 13.

[59] DW Diamond and PH Dybvig, 'Bank Runs, Deposit Insurance, and Liquidity' (1983) 91 *Journal of Political Economy* 401–19. But some argue that a deposit guarantee scheme fosters moral hazard, see Patricia A McCoy, 'The Moral Hazard Implications of Deposit Insurance: Theory and Evidence' (IMF Working Paper 2007) at https://www.imf.org/external/np/seminars/eng/2006/mfl/pam.pdf.

of the world. Further, European legislation has adopted these standards as harmonising legislation applying across the European Economic Area in order to provide a strong basis for developing the Internal Market for banking services, that is, to develop increasing levels of cross-border banking activities (see Chapter 7). This area of regulation has been significantly ramped up in the wake of the 2007–9 global financial crisis.

1.5.3 The impact of the global financial crisis

The global financial crisis of 2007–9 is often regarded as not only a turning point for the banking sector but also a turning point for the trajectory of financial regulation.[60] Box 1.3 summarises how the crisis unfolded.

Box 1.3 How the financial crisis of 2007–9 began

The crisis started slowly in mid-2007 with the onset of the 'credit crunch' when BNP Paribas reported difficulties in borrowing in wholesale markets. In the UK, the first signs of the crisis appeared when Northern Rock asked the Bank of England for emergency lending facilities in September 2007 due to severe stresses suffered during the credit crunch. The crisis, however, only became fully blown with the near-failure of US investment bank Bear Stearns in March 2008.

In the years leading up to the crisis, Bear Stearns, along with many banks in the US, had been heavily involved in a type of financial innovation known as securitisation. Banks transformed illiquid bank loans such as home mortgages into securities products with income streams from the long-term repayment of underlying loans. These securities were not only created with creditworthy mortgages but also with sub-prime mortgages. Sub-prime mortgages are mortgages of a less creditworthy nature as borrowers are often of a riskier profile. It was believed that the mixture of creditworthy and less creditworthy underlying loans in a packaged bundle of securities could improve the risk profile of such securities overall, making them attractive to investors. Securitisation allowed banks to sell off these illiquid assets, freeing them up for more lending, such credit creation being seen as beneficial to the economy. However, the growth of the securitisation markets also introduced perverse incentives to generate more mortgages despite sub-prime quality.[61] The securitisation market grew on the weak foundations of dubious quality in underlying loan assets, but banks all over the world started to originate and also hold these securities.

The case of Northern Rock illustrated how popular and attractive these securitised products were for banks: banks engaged in securitisation so that they could lend more, and held securitised assets in order to use them as collateral to obtain short-term funding in wholesale markets to generate more lending. This was a euphoric time of growth and profitability for banks.

However, when sub-prime borrowers started to default in the US from the beginning of 2007, the weak foundations of securitised assets began to show. The value of such assets plummeted

---

[60] Mads Andenas and Iris H-Y Chiu, *The Foundations and Future of Financial Regulation* (Oxford: Routledge, 2014) chs 1 and 2.
[61] Gillian Tett, *Fool's Gold* (London: Abacus Books 2010).

significantly, leading to losses for holders of such assets. Where such assets were used as collateral by banks for their own borrowing, banks had to top up collateral values when the securitised assets started to plummet in value.

That was the context leading up to the failure of Northern Rock in the UK in late 2007 and early 2008, followed by Bear Stearns in the US, which had held vast quantities of such 'toxic assets' and was bought out by JP Morgan in March 2008. Other affected banks were revealed, including Lehman Brothers, which failed in September 2008, and the UK's the Royal Bank of Scotland, which became afflicted due to the large quantities of toxic assets held by its major Dutch acquisition ABN-AMRO.[62] In the EU, BNP Paribas suffered severe losses from its holdings of toxic assets, though it was Fortis and Swiss Bank UBS that had to be rescued due to their vast exposure to the same toxic assets. The UK bank Halifax Bank of Scotland also came close to failure at the same time, although for a different reason: its corporate lending had been aggressive and imprudent, and high levels of default during the time of crisis then threatened to make the bank insolvent.[63]

As a financial crisis of this scale had not been experienced since the Great Depression of the 1930s, regulators and governments around the world scrambled to rescue their afflicted banks, using vast amounts of taxpayers' money to bail out banks in order to prevent their insolvency. National debt was raised to cover such expenditure. Bank crisis **resolution** had become socially very costly, hence there was both social appetite and political will to reform bank regulation in order to address the gaps in regulation that contributed to the crisis.[64]

Although bank regulation in prudential safety and soundness has been internationally promoted since the 1980s, there has been a marked move since the 2000s towards less regulatory intervention. Bank regulators have stepped back to allow banks to develop sophisticated risk management products,[65] forgetting that banks generally have every incentive to under-estimate their risks in the face of immediate commercial prospects and profitability. Post-crisis regulation therefore resurrects the public interest rationale in prudential regulation, and this has allowed regulators to introduce highly interventionist forms of prudential regulation internationally[66] and in the EU.[67] These

[62] FSA, 'The Failure of the Royal Bank of Scotland: Financial Services Authority Board Report' (December 2011) at http://www.fsa.gov.uk/static/pubs/other/rbs.pdf.

[63] House of Commons and House of Lords, Parliamentary Commission on Banking Standards, *An Accident Waiting to Happen: The Failure of HBOS* (4 April 2013).

[64] See, for example, reform policies urged in MK Brunnermeier et al, *The Fundamental Principles of Financial Regulation* (Geneva Reports on the World Economy, London: Centre for Economic Policy Research 2009).

[65] Notably in the Basel II Capital Accord regime, discussed in Chapter 8; also see Charles Goodhart et al, *Financial Regulation: Why, How and Where Now?* (Oxford: Routledge, 1998).

[66] The Basel III reforms to capital adequacy, liquidity, and leverage ratio, and the Total Loss Absorbing Capacity reforms, see Chapters 8 and 9.

[67] Most notably the Capital Requirements Directive and Regulation 2013, but see range of institutional and substantive reforms recommended in J De Larosière and others, *Report by the High Level Group on Financial Supervision in the EU* (Brussels, 25 February 2009) at http://ec.europa.eu/internal_market/finances/docs/de_larosiere_report_en.pdf, most of which are implemented.

are in the form of standards far exceeding the pre-crisis levels,[68] as well as increased discretion for regulators to supervise banks[69] and exercise pre-emptive powers, such as in **macro-prudential regulation** discussed in Chapter 6, section 6.4

1.5.4 **Combatting financial crime**

As banks are essential financial intermediaries for the global movement of money and capital, they may be used as channels for money laundering, the movement of criminal moneys, and terrorist financing. As such, an important objective in bank regulation is to combat financial crime. As will be discussed in detail in Chapter 14, banks are subject to regulatory standards compelling them to institute certain systems and procedures in order to combat money laundering and to report financial crime. These have been developed from international and European legislation.

1.6 Sources of law in banking regulation

In recent decades, public regulatory sources of law in banking regulation have become multi-layered and complex, ranging from international to European and national regulation. This section will first set out the sources of law in the realm of the private commercial law of banking, followed by a mapping of the public regulatory sources.

1.6.1 **Commercial law sources**

The banking industry has long been the subject of commercial law developed through common law, trade practice, international custom, and more recently standards of good practice. The common law has traditionally played a crucial role in developing and defining the obligations that a bank owes its customer and it continues to refine and scrutinise the rights and responsibilities that arise in the bank–customer relationship. The various common law and contractual duties are discussed in detail in Chapters 2, 3, and 4.

Another important source of law in the banking industry is trade practice and international custom. A trade practice or custom is the settled practice of a trade or profession that has obtained the force of the law. As such, evidence of a trade practice or custom can be used by the courts to imply a term into a commercial contract or as an aid to the construction of a contract. For example, for a long time it was the trade practice of banks to provide customer references to third parties on the ground that their customers had given their implied consent to it. However, this was examined by the Court of

---

[68] See Chapters 8 and 9. Also see reforms unique to the UK in Chapter 10.
[69] Such as in stress testing, discussed in Chapter 9, section 9.6.

Appeal in *Turner v Royal Bank of Scotland*[70] where it was held not to be an implied term as the custom was not sufficiently notorious and well known to the bank's customers. In reaching this decision the court emphasised the distinction between banking practice that operates as 'no more than a private agreement between banks' and such practice that constitutes an established usage contractually binding on a bank's customer even if the customer is unaware of it.[71] Accordingly, when giving a credit reference, the bank must first obtain the consent of the customer.

In international financial transactions, documentary letters of credit[72] are governed by the 'Uniform Customs and Practice for Documentary Credits' (known as the UCP 600), a set of rules published by the International Chamber of Commerce that has been adopted by traders and bankers across the world.[73] It has been described as 'the most successful harmonizing measure in the history of international commerce.'[74] While, in the strictest sense, the UCP 600 has no legal force except when it is incorporated into the contract between the parties,[75] some commentators such as Professor Goode recognise that the UCP embodies usages that have gained international acceptance among bankers meaning that 'even when they have no contractual force they are strong evidence of banking custom and practice, which themselves will readily be treated by the court as impliedly incorporated into the various documentary credit contracts as established usage.'[76]

Finally, in recent decades the bank–customer relationship has been governed by voluntary codes adopted by the banking industry. The first of these, the Banking Code, was published in January 2001 and introduced voluntary standards of best practice to the sector in the context of personal customers. This was accompanied in March 2002 by the Business Banking Code, which applied similar standards in relation to small business customers. These codes were succeeded in 2011 by the Lending Code,[77] which itself was replaced in July 2016 by the Standards of Lending Practice (personal customers), and in March 2017 by the Standards of Lending Practice (business customers).[78] These documents establish standards of good practice in relation to credit card,

---

[70] [1999] 2 All ER (Comm.) 664.   [71] Per Sir Richard Scott VC at 671.

[72] A letter of credit is a letter issued by a bank promising the seller of goods that payment will be made against the presentation of specific documents (including a bill of lading, commercial invoice, insurance policy, etc.).

[73] Note that international finance, including Documentary Letters of Credit, falls outside the scope of this book.

[74] Roy Goode, 'The New ICC Rules on Demand Guarantees' (1992) *Lloyds Maritime and Commercial Law Quarterly* 190.

[75] See Article 1 of UCP 600 itself.

[76] Roy Goode, *Commercial Law* (London: Penguin Books 2010) p 1077.

[77] Revised most recently in September 2015, https://www.lendingstandardsboard.org.uk/wp-content/uploads/2016/06/The-Lending-Code-Mar-2011-revised-2015-1.pdf

[78] The standards for personal customers are available at https://www.lendingstandardsboard.org.uk/wp-content/uploads/2016/07/Standards-of-Lending-Practice-July-16.pdf. The standards for business customers are available at https://www.lendingstandardsboard.org.uk/wp-content/uploads/2017/03/standards-of-lending-practice-business.pdf.

overdraft, and unsecured loan products provided to customers across the lifecycle from the product design phase to the initial offering of the product through to dealing with customers who find themselves in financial difficulty.[79]

Private law sources are often most applicable where banks' transactional relations with their customers are concerned, but regulatory sources are becoming increasingly important in consumer protection as Chapters 2 and 3 discuss in greater detail. Next, we examine the public regulatory sources of bank regulation.

1.6.2 Public regulatory sources

UK bank regulation, as has been discussed, deals with the public interest in bank risk management and solvency. Bank regulation is a body of standards for banks that impose limits on their activities and hence their risk-taking, as well as regulatory powers that can be exercised over banks. Bank regulation is drawn from a number of sources.

First, there are internationally convergent standards applicable to prudential regulation of banks and the crisis management and resolution regime. These are based on the work of the Basel Committee and the Financial Stability Board, both groups set up under the auspices of the Bank for International Settlements.[80]

Next, the UK has during its years of membership in the EU, been obliged to give effect to European legislation in relation to the banking sector. Much of the UK's bank regulation in prudential regulation[81] and regulation to combat financial crime[82] has come from EU legislation. Further, conduct of business and market behaviour regulation has also been harmonised in the EU.[83]

The UK has had a profound influence upon EU banking and financial regulation although it has, as an EU member state, adopted and transposed all EU level legislation, however opposed it may be to certain policies.[84] In light of the referendum vote on 23 June 2016 for the UK to leave the EU, the withdrawal of membership has of course severe implications for the future of UK banking regulation. There is every incentive for the UK to remain convergent in its bank regulatory regime with the EU in order to remain a regulated jurisdiction that can be recognised for *equivalence* with EU member states, hence continuing to attract European flows of capital into the UK's banking and investment sectors. However, the UK's own competitive and financial stability

---

[79] See Chapter 4.

[80] See Chapter 5. The FSB was first introduced as the Financial Stability Forum in 1997 to deal with the implications of the Asian financial crisis in the late 1990s. However, after the global financial crisis of 2007–9, the Financial Stability Forum has been elevated to a more permanent institution with its own remit, especially in research and policymaking in financial stability protection.

[81] Chapters 8 and 9.   [82] Chapter 14.

[83] Markets in Financial Instruments Directive 2004, recast in 2014 as both a Regulation and Directive. Also regulations pertaining to market behaviour, such as derivatives trading under the EMIR 2009, short selling in Regulation (EU) No 236/2012 of the European Parliament and of the Council of 14 March 2012 on short selling and certain aspects of credit default swaps; and the EU Benchmarks Regulation 2016.

[84] Such as in the bonus cap introduced in Article 90, Capital Requirements Directive 2013. A challenge was mounted in the ECJ in 2013 but later withdrawn, see Case C-507/13 *United Kingdom v Parliament and Council*.

needs may take it into divergent directions.[85] The PRA and Bank of England would have greater latitude to shape bank regulation policy, but regulators also face pressure to maintain a regulatory regime that is competitive in the eyes of the banking sector.

1.6.2.1 Bank regulation as 'public law'

Bank regulation is an area that demonstrates the rise of the regulatory state in response to the needs of both freedom and protection in the economy. Hence, much of this area of law is 'public law', reflecting the relationship between the regulators and the regulated. Statutory law takes pre-eminence in this context, from primary **acts** of parliament to secondary legislation such as **regulations** and **orders**, and the PRA's **Rulebook**. Many enforcement decisions contain the application and interpretation of regulatory law. Judicial jurisprudence may be found where the Upper Tribunal has had an opportunity to review a regulatory enforcement decision referred to it.[86]

Figure 1.1 provides an overview of the levels and sources of statutory law in bank regulation, excluding enforcement decisions and case law as the other corpus of source

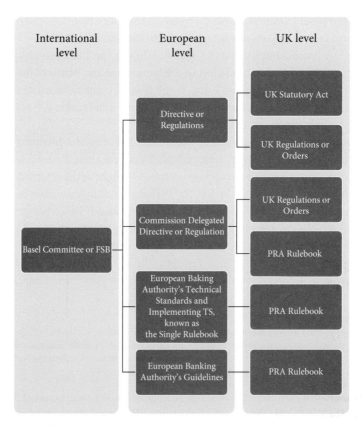

Figure 1.1 Sources of Bank Regulation

[85] See Mads Andenas and Iris H-Y Chiu, 'Financial Stability and Legal Integration in Financial Regulation' (2013) *European Law Review* 335.   [86] Section 130, Financial Services and Markets Act 2000.

of law. The figure maps how international, European, and national bank regulation are related in terms of implementation in the UK.

The key takeaways of this chapter will now be sumarised, followed by a key bibliography and questions with answer guides relating to the issues that have been discussed in this chapter. The rest of the book will proceed with this structure, providing a summary of key takeaways at the end of each substantive section with key bibliography details, and a sample of questions and answer guides at the end of each chapter.

Key takeaways

- Banks engage a range of financial services, crucially deposit-taking, payments, and credit creation, which are fundamentally important to the economy.
- Retail, commercial, and investment banking have developed over the years, exposing banks to solvency, liquidity, and various market exposure risks.
- Banking law and regulation covers the private commercial law of banking that deals with banks' and customers' rights and obligations as well as the increasingly comprehensive regulatory law.
- Bank regulation deals with customer protection, protecting bank solvency and liquidity, bank conduct of business and market behaviour, and combatting financial crime.
- The global financial crisis of 2007–9 has had a massive impact upon bank regulation, increasing the extensive scope of regulation for public interest reasons.
- This chapter maps the sources of banking law and regulation, which include international and domestic origins for the private commercial law of banking and international, European, and UK bank regulatory sources and standards.

Key bibliography

Armour, J, et al. *The Principles of Financial Regulation* (Oxford: OUP 2016)

Andenas, M and Chiu, I H-Y *The Foundations and Future of Financial Regulation* (Oxford: Routledge 2014)

de Larosière, J et al., *Report by the High Level Group on Financial Supervision in the EU* (Brussels, 25 February 2009) http://ec.europa.eu/internal_market/finances/docs/de_larosiere_report_en.pdf

Ferguson, N, *The Ascent of Money* (London: Penguin 2012)

FSA, 'The Turner Review: A Regulatory Response to the Global Banking Crisis' (March 2009) http://www.fsa.gov.uk/pubs/other/turner_review.pdf

Hildreth, R, *The History of Banks* (1837, rep CreateSpace Independent Publishing Platform, 2017)

Moloney, N, 'Reform or Revolution? The Financial Crisis, EU Financial Markets Law, and the European Securities and Markets Authority' (2011) 60 *International and Comparative Law Quarterly* 521

Questions

1. **Can banking regulation prevent crises?**

   Answer tips You should discuss the preventive nature of some aspects of bank regulation, for example, prudential regulation and its limitations in terms of catching up with banks' business risks and the development of modern banking. Consider whether the context for bank regulation, that is, crises and international will, is sufficient for preventive purposes. You should then look at the global financial crisis and regulatory responses to carefully assess whether regulation addresses past problems or is indeed capable of preventing problems. This question is broad in nature and would need to be answered with detail from other chapters in the book, such as Chapters 5, 6, 7, 8, 9, and 13.

2. **'There is excessive regulatory law for the banking sector'. Do you agree?**

   Answer tips This is a much more open-ended question and you can take it in different directions. You may look at the range of banking regulation, from prudential, financial stability-based regulation to market and client conduct regulation and assess whether these are necessary. You may also look at it from the point of view that regulatory institutions engage in law-making to 'consolidate' their turf and their powers, an idea known as 'public choice theory', and consider if EU regulation is an example of such excessive law-making for the single market project.

2

The banker–customer relationship

2.1 Introduction

The banking industry has evolved extensively from its traditional roots in the nineteenth century when the relationship between a bank and its customer was much more intimate, with only a handful of private banks accepting deposits and making loans to a selective group of affluent businessmen and members of the upper classes. In stark contrast, banking is now a mass market activity with the majority of the UK's adult population maintaining some form of account. In 1986 the Jack Committee reported that 90 per cent of the adult population maintained an account with a bank.[1] This figure had increased to 95 per cent by 2004,[2] and by 2016, the Competition and Markets Authority reported that there were 70 million active personal current accounts in the UK, equating to a 97 per cent take up by adults in the UK.[3]

This banker–customer relationship is governed by principles of contract law, although it is rarely based on a single contractual document. Rather, it is more usual for it to be subject to a variety of written terms, including those derived from standard-form contracts,[4] and accompanied by terms implied by law and voluntary codes of banking practice.[5] The first of these codes, the Banking Code, was published in January 2001 and introduced voluntary standards of best practice to the sector in the context of personal customers. This was accompanied in March 2002 by the Business Banking Code, which applied similar standards in the context of small business customers. They were succeeded by the 2011 Lending Code,[6] which itself was replaced in July 2016 by the Standards of Lending Practice (personal customers) and in March 2017

---

[1] Review Committee on Banking Services Law, *Banking Services: Law and Practice* (1989) para 2.20.

[2] Association for Payment Clearing Services, *Yearbook of Payment Statistics* (2004) p 6.

[3] Competition and Markets Authority, *Retail Banking Market Investigation: Final Report* (9 August 2016) p iii, at https://assets.publishing.service.gov.uk/media/57ac9667e5274a0f6c00007a/retail-banking-market-investigation-full-final-report.pdf.

[4] Which will be subject to the relevant provisions on 'unfairness' in the Consumer Rights Act 2015.

[5] See, for example, FCA, *Banking: Conduct of Business Sourcebook* (BCOBS) at https://www.handbook.fca.org.uk/handbook/BCOBS.pdf, which includes the 'fair, clear and not misleading rule' in Section 2.2.

[6] Revised most recently in September 2015, https://www.lendingstandardsboard.org.uk/wp-content/uploads/2016/06/The-Lending-Code-Mar-2011-revised-2015–1.pdf.

by the Standards of Lending Practice (business customers).[7] Accordingly, a customer has to rely on a range of different sources, including the common law, statute, and these voluntary codes to determine his or her relationship with their bank. Further, regulatory standards have also been introduced by the Financial Services and now Financial Conduct Authority (FCA) to govern the banker–customer relationship. These will be discussed where applicable.

This chapter begins by looking at the definition of a 'bank' and its 'customer' before focusing on the corresponding common law and regulatory duties that arise between those two parties. It will also analyse the circumstances in which a bank will be subject to further fiduciary duties and, finally, it will consider the doctrine of undue influence and the implications this will have on the ability of a bank to enforce a guarantee or other form of **security**.

2.2 What is a bank?

The ability to identify a corporate entity as a 'bank' is fundamental for a number of reasons, not least for the purposes of regulation but, more importantly to us here, because in law it is only a bank or 'banker' that will be subject to certain rights and duties including, for example, the duty of confidentiality, as will be discussed. In the UK there is no single comprehensive legal definition of a bank but there are different pieces of legislation that refer to the terms 'bank', 'banker', or 'banking' for their own purposes, which could be useful; and there have been some attempts by the judiciary to define the business of banking.

2.2.1 Statute

A traditional, and at first glance unhelpful, statutory definition can be found in the Bills of Exchange Act 1882, which defines a banker to include 'a body of persons whether incorporated or not who carry on the business of banking.'[8] Despite its apparent circularity, this definition usefully indicates that it is for the court to analyse the activities undertaken by the institution in order to determine whether it does in fact carry on the business of banking.[9]

Other pieces of legislation contain their own definitions of a bank. For example, the Banking Act 2009 defines a bank as a 'UK institution which has permission under Part 4 of the Financial Services and Markets Act 2000 to carry on the regulated activity of accepting deposits'[10] and, from a European perspective, the Capital Requirements Regulation 2013 defines a 'credit institution' as 'an undertaking the business of which is to take deposits or

---

[7] The standards for personal customers are available at https://www.lendingstandardsboard.org.uk/wp-content/uploads/2016/07/Standards-of-Lending-Practice-July-16.pdf. The standards for business customers are available at https://www.lendingstandardsboard.org.uk/wp-content/uploads/2017/03/standards-of-lending-practice-business.pdf.   [8] Bills of Exchange Act 1882, s2.
[9] See section 2.2.2.   [10] Banking Act 2009, s2.

other repayable funds from the public and to grant credits for its own account.[11] These definitions are similar in the sense that they turn on the fundamental services being provided by the institution. This is something that has been further explored by the courts as they attempt to define the nature, scope, and breadth of the 'business of banking'.

2.2.2 **Common law**

Over time a number of definitions of the business of banking have emerged from the common law but the most authoritative of these comes from the decision of the Court of Appeal in *United Dominions Trust Ltd v Kirkwood*.[12] United Dominions Trust (UDT) was a finance house and it lent the sum of £5,000 to Lonsdale Motors Ltd to enable them to buy cars. When Lonsdale Motors Ltd, went into liquidation, UDT sued the defendant, the Managing Director of Lonsdale Motors Ltd to recover the loan. The defendant used the defence that UDT was an unregistered moneylender and the loan was therefore illegal as it contravened the Moneylenders Act 1900. UDT claimed that it was a banker, not a moneylender. The key question was whether UDT was bona fide carrying on the business of banking. To answer that question Lord Denning MR established that:[13]

> There are, therefore, two characteristics usually found in bankers today: (i) They accept money from, and collect cheques for, their customers and place them to their credit; (ii) They honour cheques or orders drawn on them by their customers when presented for payment and debit their customers accordingly. These two characteristics carry with them also a third, namely: (iii) They keep current accounts, or something of that nature, in their books in which the credits and debits are entered.

After assessing the evidence, Lord Denning MR stated that firstly, while UDT did receive money on deposit, these were short-term investments repayable on agreed dates and were not repayable on demand, and that, secondly, there was no evidence that UDT collected cheques on behalf of customers. However, he went on to say that while UDT did not have the usual characteristics of a banker, there are other characteristics that are important, namely 'stability, soundness and probity', and he argued that in the case of doubt one should 'look at the reputation of the firm amongst ordinary intelligent commercial men. If they recognise it as carrying on the business of banking, that should turn the scale.'[14] Based on this fourth characteristic of 'reputation' Denning concluded that because UDT was recognised in the City as a 'bank' it should therefore be considered as such and excluded from the provisions of the Moneylenders Act 1900. This conclusion, he thought, was justified on the basis of clear policy grounds, and the need to avoid the reversal of millions of pounds worth of transactions that would result from a finding that UDT was not a bank and had failed to comply with the terms of the Moneylenders Act 1900.[15]

---

[11] Regulation (EU) No 572/2013 on prudential requirements for credit institutions and investment firms, Article 4. [12] [1966] 2 QB 431.

[13] At 447.   [14] At 455.   [15] Ibid.

In similar vein to Lord Denning MR, Diplock LJ considered that the core characteristics of the business of banking centred on (1) accepting money from and collecting cheques for customers, (2) honouring cheques, and (3) maintaining current accounts.[16] Having reviewed the facts, Diplock LJ held that UDT did carry on a limited banking business in that some customers used current accounts for the payment or collection of cheques. However, he disagreed with Lord Denning's policy-based conclusion that the reputation of UDT could tip the scales in case of doubt, instead arguing that the importance of UDT's reputation here was that it provided *prima facie* evidence of the nature of the financial transactions the institution engaged in.[17] Dissenting, Harman LJ argued that the central feature of the business of banking was the maintenance of current accounts and that, based on the evidence presented, UDT did not satisfy this criteria and nor could it rely on its reputation that 'alone is not enough. There must be some performance behind it.'[18]

Accordingly, the common law definition of the business of banking, in terms of the objective or usual characteristics that such an activity encompasses, is tied to the collection and honouring of cheques and the running of current accounts through the entry of credits and debits in a written bank ledger. However, this definition must be considered in context, as discussed in Box 2.1.

Box 2.1 Banking in context

When considering the common law definition of the business of banking, as derived from *Kirkwood*, it is important to be alert to the fact that this case was decided on the basis of how banks operated in 1966. Fast forward over 50 years and it is clear that the world of banking has changed dramatically; cheques are increasingly becoming obsolete and have been replaced by the **transfer of funds** through other plastic and electronic means including debit cards, ATM machines, and internet and telephone banking.[19] As such, we have to view this decision and the definition it gives of banking in the context within which it was decided and recognise that the definition should be flexible enough to reflect the continual development of modern banking practices. In particular, we should not tie the definition too closely to the particular means through which money is paid in and out of current accounts. This sentiment is reflected in the Privy Council decision of *Bank of Chettinad Ltd of Colombo v Commissioner of Income Tax, Colombo*[20] where it was recognised that the words banking and banker 'may bear different shades of meaning at different periods of history, and that their meaning may not be uniform today in countries of different habits of life and different degrees of civilization.'[21]

---

[16] At 465:

> Accordingly it is, in my view, essential to the business of banking that a banker should accept money from his customers upon a running account into which sums of money are from time to time paid by the customer and from time to time withdrawn by him by cheque, draft or order … the banker must also undertake to pay cheques drawn upon himself (the banker) by his customers in favour of third parties up to the amount standing to their credit in their 'current accounts' and to collect cheques for his customers and credit the proceeds to their current accounts.

[17] At 462 and 474.   [18]At 461.   [19] See Chapter 3.   [20] [1948] AC 378 (PC).
[21]At 383.

> **⮕ Key takeaways**
>
> - It is important to define the business of banking, not only for regulatory purposes, but also because in law it is only a 'bank' or 'banker' that will be subject to certain rights and duties.
> - Some of the statutory definitions turn on the fundamental services being provided by the institution, that is, deposit-taking and the granting of credit.
> - The common law definition, derived from *UDT v Kirkwood*, ties the business of banking to a number of key characteristics including the collection and honouring of cheques and the running of current accounts through the entry of credits and debits in a written bank ledger. However, given the passage of time since the *Kirkwood* decision we should recognise that the definition should be flexible enough to reflect the continual development of modern banking practices.

> **Key bibliography**
>
> **Legislation**
>
> Banking Act 2009.
> Regulation (EU) No 572/2013 on prudential requirements for credit institutions and investment firms.

2.3 Who is a customer?

Many statutes use the term 'customer' without providing any further definition of the term[22] and, in the context of the banker–customer relationship, certain obligations, such as the bank's duty to obey the customer's **mandate**, and the contractual duty of care, will only arise when it is a customer that is involved. Since there is no definitive statutory definition we must turn to the common law and analyse the judicial attempts that have been made to determine the scope and circumstances under which someone will be deemed to be a customer.

2.3.1 The opening of an account

Traditionally, it was held that in order for a person to become a customer of a bank, the bank would have to habitually perform services for that person, meaning that simply opening an account would be insufficient to confer the status of customer.[23] This requirement was subsequently questioned, and later overruled.[24] Accordingly, upon the

---

[22] See, for example, the Bills of Exchange Act 1882, s75.
[23] *Matthews v Brown & Co.* (1894) 10 Times Rep. 386.
[24] *Lacave & Co. v Crédit Lyonnaise* [1897] 1 QB 148; *Ladbroke & Co. v Todd* (1914) 30 Times Rep. 433.

opening of an account, a person will be deemed to have become a customer of the bank and there is no requirement for a habitual course of dealings.

This was clearly demonstrated in *Taxation Commissioners v English, Scottish and Australian Bank*.[25] On 6 June, Mr Friend wrote a cheque, placed it in an envelope and addressed it to the Commissioners of Taxation. This cheque was stolen by a thief who, on 7 June, entered the respondent bank and opened an account in the name 'Stuart Thallon'. The next day the thief paid the stolen cheque into the account and, after it had cleared, drew cheques on the proceeds over the following days. No more was ever seen of Thallon; no person of that name lived at the address he had given the bank and it was assumed that the name was fictitious. Accordingly, the Commissioners of Taxation brought an action against the bank for **conversion**[26] and the success of the bank's statutory defence (under the Bills of Exchange Act 1909, s88) turned on whether the thief had become a customer of the bank by virtue of this single transaction. Lord Dunedin summarised the position well:[27]

> The word 'customer' signifies a relationship in which duration is not of the essence. A person whose money has been accepted by a bank on the footing that they undertake to honour cheques up to the amount standing to his credit is, in the view of their Lordships, a customer of the bank in the sense of the statute, irrespective of whether his connection is of short or long standing ... Thallon was, therefore, a customer, though one of short standing.

Thus, a person becomes a customer of a bank when he or she opens an account; there is no need for longevity or a habitual course of dealings between the two parties.

In terms of the specific time at which the banker–customer relationship comes into play, the courts clarified in *Woods v Martins Bank*[28] that you will become a customer of a bank as soon as you agree to open an account with the bank, even though the formalities may not yet have been completed. In this case the plaintiff, a young man with little business experience, inherited a considerable sum of money from his father. He met with the manager of the defendant bank on a number of occasions in April and early May of 1950 to discuss potential investments in a particular company, which resulted in the plaintiff investing £5,000 in the company on 9 May 1950. On that same day the plaintiff instructed the defendant bank to collect the balance of an account that he maintained with another financial institution and use those funds to make the investments suggested and to credit any remaining sums to a new account to be opened at the defendant bank. On 1 June, the bank opened a current account for the plaintiff. Relying on further advice from the bank manager, the plaintiff invested a further £6,800 in shares in the company and made them a loan of £3,000. Further, in February 1952, the plaintiff signed a guarantee of the overdraft of another company, based on advice from the manager that they too were financially sound.

---

[25] [1920] AC 683 (PC).

[26] See Chapter 3, section 3.2.5.1 for more information on a collecting bank being subject to claim in conversion.   [27] At 687.

[28] [1959] 1 QB 55.

It became apparent that there were no grounds on which the bank manager could have advised the plaintiff of the financial stability of the first company: in fact, at all times, the first company held a substantial overdraft with the bank, which the district head office had been pressing the bank manager to reduce. Nor was there any reasonable ground to give advice in relation to the second company. The plaintiff lost all the money invested in the first company and was called upon to pay £990 under guarantee for the second company's overdraft. The plaintiff claimed these sums back from the bank and its manager on the grounds of negligence.

At the time the initial advice was given, during their meetings in April and early May 1950, the plaintiff did not have a current account with the defending bank. The question therefore arose as to the point in time when the claimant became a customer of the bank. Salmon J held that on 9 May, when the bank accepted the plaintiff's instructions to invest the money and open the account, the relationship of banker–customer did exist between the two parties despite the fact that that account was not strictly opened on that date. He held that although the claimant had no account with the bank when the advice was originally given, when the plaintiff decided to act on that advice he concurrently advised the bank to open an account in his name and, because the investment advice was repeated on that occasion, the bank had failed to observe the contractual duty of care that arose from the banker–customer relationship. He concluded:[29]

> In my view the defendant bank accepted the instructions contained in this letter as the plaintiff's bankers, and at any rate from that date the relationship of banker and customer existed between them. It is true that the express advice was in the first place given before the 9th May, but it was implicitly repeated on that day.

Accordingly, although the account was not formally opened until a later date, the court here clarified that the banker–customer relationship arose on the 9 May, when the instructions were received by the bank to open the account.[30]

2.3.2 The opening of an account by a fraudster

Even when an account has been opened it is sometimes difficult to identify the bank's customer and this problem tends to arise in the context of fraud. Where someone fraudulently impersonates another, it is generally the case that that person will become the customer of the bank (and not the person he or she is impersonating) if it can be shown that the bank intended to deal only with the person present and not the person the rogue was impersonating.

---

[29] At 63.

[30] Note, the only action available to the plaintiff here was for breach of the contractual duty of care, which required him to show that the banker–customer relationship had come into play; the decision pre-dated the tortious action for negligent misstatement, which was later developed in the case of *Hedley Byrne & Co. Ltd v Heller & Partners Ltd* [1964] AC 65.

For example, in *Stoney Stanton Supplies (Coventry) Ltd v Midland Bank Ltd*,[31] a man named Fox forged the signature of the directors of the plaintiff company on documents requesting that an account be opened with the defendant bank in the plaintiff company's name. Unbeknown to the plaintiff company, the account was duly opened and money was paid into the account. By forging the signature of the plaintiff company's directors, Fox then drew cheques on the account to the value of £9,000. When the plaintiff company went into liquidation, the liquidator sought to recover those sums from the defendant bank, alleging that there was a banker–customer relationship between the plaintiff company and the defendant and as such the defendant had a contractual duty to take reasonable care which it had failed to do. It was held that no banker–customer relationship arose between the two parties with the result that the bank did not owe the company any contractual duty of care. Lord Denning MR summarised:

> As to the claim against the Bank for breach of duty, that too fails for the simple reason that there was never any relationship of banker and customer. As far as the opening of the account was concerned, it was not taken out by the company but by Fox, who forged all the documents. The company did not authorise it at all. It is quite impossible to hold that there is any relationship of banker and customer between this company and the bank ... Where a person opens an account in the name of another person without any authority to do so, it is quite plain there is no relationship of banker and customer and so no question of breach of duty arises.

This makes sense in light of the basic contract law principle that there must be a meeting of minds between the two relevant parties to give rise to contractual relations. We can, however, contrast this with decisions such as *Rowlandson v National Westminster Bank Ltd*[32] where the court used the law of agency to find that the person named on the account implicitly consented to its opening either before or after the event has occurred. In *Rowlandson*, a grandmother deposited a cheque as a gift into an account that she opened at the bank in her grandchildren's joint names. The guardians of the grandchildren were given the right to draw proceeds from the account though they were never explicitly notified of the opening of the account. When funds were later misappropriated by one of the guardians the court held that the bank had breached its fiduciary duty of care to the grandchildren. In analysing the decision, Ellinger argues that, 'Presumably, a banker–customer contract came into existence between the defendant bank and the grandchildren as a result of the guardians' subsequent tacit approval of the account's opening.'[33]

From the above discussion, it is clear that the opening of an account is the hallmark indicator of a customer. Historically, this was important because, for example, it determined whether or not a bank could be afforded protection under the Bills of Exchange

---

[31] [1966] 2 Lloyd's Rep. 373.   [32] [1978] 1 WLR 798.

[33] Peter Ellinger, Eva Lomnicka, and Christopher Hare, *Ellinger's Modern Banking Law* (Oxford: OUP 2011) 119.

Act 1882 and then s4 of the Cheques Act when it collected a cheque on behalf of a fraudulent customer who had a defective title.[34] However, the concept of a customer is broader than this, denoting anyone who deals with a bank in relation to banking services, including borrowers who do not maintain an account with the bank, and those who use the bank for financial advisory services. While maintaining an account with a bank will give rise to certain obligations within that contractual relationship, many of the legal issues discussed here, such as the duty of confidentiality, and the fiduciary obligations owed by a bank, are not confined to those who hold an account with the bank.

> ### ➜ Key takeaways
>
> - The opening of an account is the hallmark indication that someone has become a customer of a bank; there is no requirement for a consistent course of dealings between the two parties.
> - The banker–customer relationship comes into play as soon as the customer has instructed the bank to open an account in his or her name.
> - The opening of an account in another party's name without their authority does not, in general, establish the banker–customer relationship between the bank and that other party.
> - While the opening of an account is an important indicator, the concept of a 'customer' is broader than that, describing anyone who deals with a bank in relation to a banking service.

2.4 Duties of the bank in the banker–customer relationship

While we now have a comprehensive piece of legislation in place in the form of the Consumer Rights Act 2015 to protect the interests of customers in relation to the fairness of contract terms, it is the judiciary that has been at the forefront of developing and defining the fundamental obligations owed by a bank to its customer. This section will analyse the development of some of these duties including the bank's duty to obey the customer's *mandate* and *countermand*, the duty of confidentiality, and the duty of care in contract and tort.

2.4.1 To repay an on-demand deposit

The relationship between a bank and its customer is best understood as a *debtor–creditor* type contract; when the customer is in credit he or she is the creditor and the bank is the debtor. The opposite is true when the customer's account is overdrawn. When the customer deposits money, the bank owes a duty to repay that sum, either on demand in the case of a current account or savings account, or at a pre-determined date

---

[34] See Chapter 3, section 3.2.5.2.

in the case of a fixed deposit.[35] This principle is best demonstrated by Lord Cottenham in *Foley v Hill*[36] who said:[37]

> Money, when paid into a bank, ceases altogether to be the money of the principal … it is then the money of the banker, who is bound to return an equivalent sum to that deposited with him when he asked for it … The money placed in the custody of the banker is, to all intents and purposes, the money of the banker, to do with as he pleases.

The essence of the contract then is that the bank has the right to use the money so deposited for its own purposes and it undertakes to repay an amount equal to that paid in, on demand. This is interesting because in the context of a *normal* creditor–debtor relationship it would be the debtor's duty to seek out the creditor in order to repay the money. Lord Cottenham emphasised here that this position is reversed in the context of a banker–customer relationship where it is the customer, as creditor, who seeks out the debtor bank and demands repayment.

2.4.2 To obey the customer's mandate

One of the most fundamental obligations a bank owes to its customer is that it must conform to the customer's mandate. This means, for example, that when the customer instructs the bank to make payments from or receive payments into his or her account, the bank is under a duty to obey those instructions. This is demonstrated in *Sierra Leone Telecommunications Co. Ltd v Barclays Bank Plc*[38] by Cresswell J who stated that:[39]

> It is a basic obligation owed by a bank to its customer that the bank will honour on presentation a cheque drawn by the customer on the bank … where the bank honours such a cheque or other instructions it acts within its mandate, with the result that the bank is entitled to debit the customer's account with the amount of the cheque or other instruction.

Traditionally these payment instructions would have been made in the form of a cheque, but in modern practice they are more commonly received in the form of electronic instructions through debit card payments and online banking transactions.[40] In the context of an account, generally the mandate will specify who can draw money against the account balance and, where more than one signature is required, the identity of each signatory. The mandate therefore embodies the agreement between the bank and its customer and the terms under which it must act.

While the bank has a positive duty to obey its customer's mandate, there is a corresponding negative duty not to act in a way that exceeds its customer's mandate. For example, where a customer's signature is forged on a cheque, the payment is clearly

---

[35] A fixed deposit, such as an ISA (Individual Savings Account), will mature at a pre-determined time meaning that the amount will become repayable on a designated day rather than on demand.
[36] (1848) 2 HLC 28.   [37] At 36.   [38] [1998] CLC 501.   [39] At 505.   [40] See Chapter 3.

outside the customer's mandate. In fact, under s24 of the Bills of Exchange Act 1882 the instruction is wholly inoperative, meaning that the bank has no authority to make the payment and is not entitled to debit the customer's account where it has acted on the forged document.[41] Similarly, where a cheque is materially altered, for example, the figures or the name written on the cheque are changed, according to s64 of the Bills of Exchange Act 1882, the cheque is void, meaning again that the bank has no authority to make the payment and is not entitled to debit the customer's account where it has acted on the basis of the altered cheque.[42]

2.4.2.1 When can a bank refuse to honour its customer's mandate?

While the most fundamental duty of a bank is to honour its customer's payment instruction, that duty is subject to a number of limitations and exceptions.

Insufficient funds and no overdraft facility

Where there are insufficient funds available in the customer's bank account and no agreed **overdraft** facility, the bank's duty to honour its customer's mandate is overridden. This is confirmed by Cresswell J who argues that a bank will only be obliged to obey its customer's instruction 'provided that there are sufficient funds in the customer's account to meet the cheque or the bank has agreed to provide the customer with overdraft facilities sufficient to meet the cheque.'[43]

The alternative option available for the bank is to view the payment instruction as an offer from the customer to the bank to extend credit to the customer on the bank's usual rates of interest and charges, that is, an offer from the customer to the bank to extend an overdraft facility which is accepted by the bank when it decides to honour the cheque.[44] In such a situation the bank is entitled to charge the customer at a higher unauthorised overdraft rate of interest rather than at the standard rate for an authorised overdraft.[45]

---

[41] Which reads: 'where a signature on a bill is forged or placed thereon without the authority of the person whose signature it purports to be, the forged or unauthorised signature is wholly inoperative, and no right to retain the bill or to give a discharge therefor or to enforce payment thereof against any party thereto can be acquired through or under that signature'. However, it is important to note that the customer could be estopped from asserting this if it is discovered that the customer had knowledge of the fraud and did not inform the bank immediately; *London Joint Stock Bank Ltd v Macmillan & Arthur* [1918] AC 777, discussed further in section 2.5.

[42] Section 64 reads: 'Where a bill or acceptance is materially altered without the assent of all parties liable on the bill, the bill is avoided'.

[43] *Sierra Leone Telecommunications Co. Ltd v Barclays Bank Plc* [1998] CLC 501, 505. See also Goff J in *Barclays Bank Plc v W.J.Simms & Cooke (Southern Ltd)* [1980] 1 QB 677, 699.

[44] *Lloyds Bank Plc v Voller* [2000] 2 All ER (Comm) 978, 982; *Emerald Meats (London) Ltd v AIB Group (UK) Ltd* [2002] EWCA Civ 460, [12].

[45] Ibid. These higher charges were challenged recently for being unenforceable under the (then) Unfair Terms in Consumer Contracts Regulations 1999. However, in the case of *Office of Fair Trading v Abbey National Plc* [2010] 1 AC 696 it was held that these bank fees were core terms relating to price or remuneration under the contract and could not therefore we assessed for fairness under the Regulations (see Regulation 6(2)). See Chapter 4, section 4.2.2.

Ambiguity in instructions

The customer's payment instruction to the bank must be unambiguous otherwise the bank will be entitled to reject the instruction. This is unlikely to be the case in relation to electronic methods of payment, but it could arise in the context of a cheque payment, meaning that if the cheque is not properly drawn the bank can refuse to honour it. This point was stressed in *London Joint Stock Bank Ltd v Macmillan*[46] where Lord Haldane stated that 'the banker as a mandatory has a right to insist on having his mandate in a form which does not leave room for misgiving as to what he is called on to do.' Accordingly, if the cheque is illegible or there is some irregularity in the mandate, such as a disparity between the words and the figures that denote the amount to be paid, the bank is entitled to disobey the order.

Out of date

It has become a matter of practice for banks to dishonour cheques that are out of date or 'stale'. Usually a cheque is treated as such if it is presented for payment more than six months from the date written on it.[47]

If the bank has reasonable grounds for believing that the mandate is not authorised

If the bank believes that there is a real possibility that a payment instruction has been given without the authority of the customer such that the customer is being defrauded, then they will be entitled to refuse to honour the instruction. In fact, the bank would be in breach of its contractual duty of care to the customer if, without inquiry, it proceeded with the instruction.[48]

Where the bank's duty to pay is abrogated by court order or statute

There are a number of situations in which the duty of a bank to honour its customer's payment instruction is abrogated by court order or statute. These situations include (but are not limited to) where the customer's account is frozen under the relevant provisions of the Proceeds of Crime Act 2002; where the customer's account is served with a **third-party debt order** or **freezing injunction**; where a corporate customer is wound up; and where an individual customer is declared bankrupt. Each will be examined in turn.

As discussed in more detail in Chapter 14, if a bank becomes aware or has reasonable grounds to believe that its customer is committing a money laundering offence or funding terrorism, the bank has a duty to make an authorised disclosure of that information to the relevant authority and freeze the customer's account until the appropriate

---

[46] [1918] AC 777, 816. See also Lord Blackburn in *Cunliffe, Brook & Co. v Blackburn and District Benefit Building Society* (1884) 9 App. Cas. 857, 864 who argues that banks are only 'bound to pay cheques properly drawn'.

[47] See, for example, *Commissioner of Inland Revenue v Thomas Cook (NZ) Ltd* [2003] 2 NLR 296, [38]: 'there is in New Zealand a term implied by custom and usage that banks are not bound to pay a cheque, presentment of which takes place more than six months after its date.'

[48] *Lipkin Gorman v Karpnale & Co.* [1989] 1 WLR 1340. See section 2.4.5.1.

consent is obtained.[49] In fact, s328 of the Proceeds of Crime Act 2002 provides that a person commits an offence if he or she enters into or becomes concerned in an arrangement which he or she knows or suspects facilitates (by whatever means) the acquisition, retention, use, or control of criminal property by or on behalf of another person. Accordingly, a bank would be liable for this offence unless, according to s328(2), it makes an authorised disclosure to the relevant authority that the property was criminal property and obtained consent to deal with the account.[50]

A bank may also be precluded from honouring its customer's payment instructions as a result of the proceeds in his or her account being subject to a third-party debt order. This is issued pursuant to Part 72 of the Civil Procedure Rules 1998, which allows the court to grant to a judgment creditor of the customer an order that attaches to funds held by a third party (i.e. a bank).[51] What happens in practice is that the judgment creditor will apply to the court to attach the order to funds held by the bank in its customer's account. The court will first grant an interim order meaning that the bank must refuse to honour any payments that would reduce the customer's balance to an amount below that specified in the order.[52] Following a final hearing, a final third-party debt order can be granted, meaning that the bank will have to pay over the amount specified in the order to the judgment creditor.[53] Compliance by the bank with this order has the effect of discharging the bank from its indebtedness to the customer.

Similarly, a bank's duty to obey its customer's instructions in the payment or transfer of money can be abrogated by the imposition of a freezing injunction. This order, which was formerly known as a 'Mareva injunction',[54] was recognised in s37 of the Supreme Court Act 1981 and is now governed by Rule 25.1(f) of the Civil Procedure Rules 1998.[55] As suggested by its name, a freezing injunction freezes the customer's assets with the aim of preventing him or her from otherwise dispersing the proceeds of the account in order to avoid the execution of a judgment that has been made against them. Unlike a debt relief order, a freezing injunction does not attach itself to a customer's assets and require the bank to pay over the sum that makes up the order but rather, it is simply designed to prevent the customer from defeating a judgment that has been made against him or her by dissipating the customer's assets. A freezing injunction therefore

---

[49] Proceeds of Crime Act 2002, s335.   [50] See Chapter 14, section 14.4.

[51] Civil Procedure Rules r.72.1(1) 'This Part contains rules which provide for a judgment creditor to obtain an order for the payment to him of money which a third party who is within the jurisdiction owes to the judgment debtor.'

[52] Ibid, r.72.4(2)(b). 'The judge may make an interim third party debt order … directing that until that hearing the third party must not make any payment which reduces the amount he owes the judgment debtor to less than the amount specified in the order.'   [53] Ibid, r.72.2 and 72.9.

[54] After the first case that attempted to define it: *Mareva Campania Naviera SA v International Bulk Carriers SA (The 'Mareva')* [1975] 2 Lloyd's Rep. 509.

[55] Section 37(3): 'The power of the High Court under subsection (1) to grant an interlocutory injunction restraining a party to any proceedings from removing from the jurisdiction of the High Court, or otherwise dealing with, assets located within that jurisdiction shall be exercisable in cases where that party is, as well as in cases where he is not, domiciled, resident or present within that jurisdiction.'

does not create any proprietary interest, only a form of personal relief.[56] As soon as the bank has notice of the freezing injunction, this will suspend the bank's duty to honour its customer's mandate.

Upon the presentation of a petition for the winding up of a company, a bank no longer owes a duty to obey its corporate customers' instructions. In fact, by virtue of s127 of the Insolvency Act 1986, any disposition of the company's property made after the commencement of the winding up is void.[57] Similarly, according to s278(a) of the same Act a bank will no longer have the authority to pay against a customer's payment instructions when the bankruptcy of an individual commences. In similar vein to the position in relation to the winding up of a company, by virtue of s284(1) any disposition of property made will be void.[58]

2.4.2.2 Customers' remedies for wrongful dishonour of a payment instruction

The above discussion highlights the fundamental duty owed by a bank to its customer and some of the inroads or limitations to that duty. This poses the question: what are the implications for the bank if it fails to honour its customer's mandate and none of the aforementioned limitations apply?[59] The short answer is that the bank will be liable for breach of contract and in certain circumstances the customer may also be able to bring an action in defamation.

In terms of an action for breach of contract, where a bank wrongfully refuses to honour its customer's mandate the customer will be entitled to recover damages from the bank provided that he or she has sustained some sort of loss. Traditionally, the amount one could be awarded depended on whether one was a trader. Traders would be able to recover substantial damages for injury to their credit and reputation regardless of showing any actual loss[60] whereas a non-trader could recover only nominal damages, unless he or she could prove actual loss.[61] This reflected the belief that as a trader one

---

[56] See, for example, *Customs and Excise Commissioners v Barclays Bank Plc* [2007] 1 AC 181.

[57] Section 127(1): 'In a winding up by the court, any disposition of the company's property, and any transfer of shares, or alteration in the status of the company's members, made after the commencement of the winding up is, unless the court otherwise orders, void.'

[58] Section 284(1): 'Where a person is adjudged bankrupt, any disposition of property made by that person in the period to which this section applies is void except to the extent that it is or was made with the consent of the court, or is or was subsequently ratified by the court.'

[59] For a discussion of the bank's defences for wrongful payment of a cheque see Chapter 3, section 3.2.4.

[60] *Wilson v United Counties Bank Ltd* [1920] AC 102, 112 per Lord Birkenhead:

> The defendants undertook for consideration to sustain the credit of the trading customer. On principle the case seems to me to belong to that very special class of cases in which a banker, though his customer's account is in funds, nevertheless dishonours his cheque. The ratio decidendi in such cases is that the refusal to meet the cheque, under such circumstances, is so obviously injurious to the credit of a trader that the latter can recover, without allegation of special damage, reasonable compensation for the injury done to his credit.

Also see *Mazetti v Williams* (1830) 1 B & Ad 415; *Rolin v Stewart* (1854) 14 CB 595.

[61] *Gibbons v Westminster Bank* [1939] 2 KB 882, 888 per Lawrence J: 'In my opinion … a person who is not a trader is not entitled to recover substantial damages for the wrongful dishonour of his cheque, unless the damage which he has suffered is alleged and proved as special damage.'; '*Evans v London and Provincial Bank*', *The Times*, 1 March 1917.

had more at stake and more to lose in terms of one's creditworthiness and reputation if a bank dishonoured a payment instruction. However, this traditional view, which saw a distinction drawn between traders and non-traders, was abolished by the Court of Appeal in the case of *Kpohraror v Woolwich Building Society*.[62]

Kpohraror, who described himself as a self-employed importer/exporter, had a current account at the defendant bank and he drew a cheque for £4,550 in favour of a third party who had agreed to supply him with goods for resale in Nigeria. The next day, the cheque was wrongfully dishonoured by the bank and, although payment was eventually made, the delay meant that the goods were shipped late and Kpohraror consequently lost his sub-buyer in Nigeria. The plaintiff accordingly brought an action against the bank for breach of contract claiming (1) general damages for injury to credit and reputation and (2) special damages for loss of profit. Evans LJ in the Court of Appeal took this opportunity to emphasise that it could no longer be the case that only tradesmen were affected in terms of their credit rating and reputation when in fact these issues now affected every customer no matter whether they are traders or private individuals. He said:[63]

> It is abundantly clear, in my judgment, that history has changed the social factors which moulded the rule in the nineteenth century. It is not only a tradesman of whom it can be said that the refusal to meet his cheque is 'so obviously injurious to his credit' that he should 'recover, without allegation of special damage, reasonable compensation for the injury done to his credit' ... The credit rating of individuals is as important for their personal transactions, including mortgages and hire purchase as well as banking facilities, as it is for those who are engaged in trade ... I would have no hesitation in holding that what is in effect a presumption of some damage arises in every case, in so far as this is a presumption of fact.

The effect of this decision is that in every case, no matter whether the individual is a trader or not, there is an irrebuttable presumption of fact that the party suffers some injury to his credit and reputation when a cheque is wrongfully dishonoured. Although the decision has been subject to scrutiny in terms of its legality,[64] it has also been praised for abolishing what was a difficult distinction to apply in practice and for recognising explicitly that the wrongful dishonour of a cheque can have similarly grave consequences for both traders and non-traders in terms of the availability of credit.[65]

A bank that wrongfully dishonours its customer's payment instruction may face an additional action in defamation and the context in which this arises surrounds the wording used by the bank on the back of the cheque when it is returned to the payee. Generally speaking, there will be no issue if the bank marks on the cheque that it is being returned because there is a discrepancy in the wording and the figures used or where the cheque does not bear all the required signatories. Where a bank may face

---

[62] [1996] CLC 510.   [63] At 513.

[64] See, for example, Nelson, after Enonchong 'Contract Damages for Wrongful Dishonour of a Cheque' (1997) 60 *Modern Law Review* 412, who argues that the case is unfounded both in terms of authority and principle.

[65] Richard Hooley, 'Remedies for Wrongful Dishonour of a Cheque–Injury to Credit and Reputation' (1996) 55(2) *Cambridge Law Journal* 189.

an action in defamation is where the wording on a returned cheque makes reference to a supposed lack of funds on the part of the customer, something which clearly has the potential to damage the reputation of the customer when it is read by the payee. In *Jayson v Midland Bank*[66] it was accepted that the words 'refer to **drawer**' suggested that the customer had insufficient funds to honour the cheque and this was capable of lowering the customer's reputation and therefore defamatory if untrue.[67] The safest course of action for a bank in this situation is probably not to give any reason for the non-payment of the cheque. Indeed, in *Frost v London Joint Stock Bank Ltd*[68] the defendant bank returned a cheque stamped 'reason not stated' and it was held that this was not a defamatory statement because the wording, while possibly being understood as defamatory, was equally capable of having an innocent meaning.

2.4.3 **To obey the customer's countermand**

The next core duty of a bank in relation to its customer, and one that runs converse to its duty to obey its customer's mandate, is that it must also obey its customer's *countermand*. What is meant by countermand is the revocation of a previous instruction; so, although the bank has a duty to obey its customer's mandate, this may be superseded by a countermand instruction that directs the bank not to pay. In the case of cheques, this obligation is defined by statute under s75 of the Bills of Exchange Act 1882, which provides that 'The duty and authority of a banker to pay a cheque drawn on him by his customer are determined by (1) countermand of payment'.

In order to be effective, this countermand must satisfy three requirements: it must be clear and unambiguous such that the bank can identify the instruction being countermanded; it must be brought to the actual knowledge of the bank; and the instruction must be made in time.

The general rule in relation to ambiguity is that provided the bank acts in accordance with what it honestly believed were the customer's intentions, it is entitled to debit its customer's account with the amount of the cheque. In *Westminster Bank v Hilton*[69] the customer drew a cheque on 31 July that bore the serial number 117285 and it was post-dated to 2 August. On 1 August the customer telegraphed his bank to stop payment of that cheque, citing the incorrect cheque number (117,283) but otherwise correctly stating the details on the cheque in terms of the payee and the amount. When cheque 117,285 was duly presented for payment by the **holder**, the bank honoured it in the (albeit mistaken) belief that it was a replacement for revoked cheque number 117,283. In honouring this cheque, the customer's account was exhausted of funds meaning that another cheque was subsequently dishonoured. The House of Lords dismissed the customer's action

---

[66] [1968] 1 Lloyd's Rep. 409.

[67] The same conclusion was reached in *Pyke v Hibernian Bank Ltd* [1950] IR 195 where the words 'refer to drawer' were also used and in *Baker v Australia and New Zealand Bank Ltd* [1958] NZLR 907 where the words 'present again' were used.   [68] (1906) 22 TLR 760.

[69] (1926) 43 TLR 124.

for damages, holding that the customer's instruction was ambiguous, and the bank had made a reasonable inference. However, if the ambiguity is patent, the bank should contact the customer to verify the payment instruction, before acting on it.[70]

The second requirement is that the bank must have actual notice of the countermand, meaning that the instruction must be brought to the attention of a bank employee who has the authority to act on that instruction before the payment is made. In *Curtice v London City and Midland Bank*[71] the plaintiff drew a cheque on his account payable to a third party on 31 October. On the same day, he changed his mind and so, after business hours, telegraphed the defendant bank to countermand payment of this cheque. The instruction was delivered on the evening of the same day by the Post Office and, it being after office hours, was placed in the letter-box of the bank. By an oversight this telegram was not brought to the notice of the bank manager until two days later on 2 November. By this time, the cheque had been presented and paid. In bringing an action against the bank, the Court of Appeal held that the cheque had not been successfully countermanded by the plaintiff because actual notice of the instruction was required.[72] Cozens-Hardy MR stated:[73]

> Countermand is really a matter of fact. It means much more than a change of purpose on the part of the customer. It means, in addition, the notification of that change of purpose to the bank. There is no such thing as a constructive countermand in a commercial transaction of this kind. In my opinion, on the admitted facts of this case, the cheque was not countermanded

In similar vein, Farwell LJ argued that 'the duty and authority of a banker to pay a cheque drawn on him by his customer may be countermanded on notice being given to him. In my opinion that must be actual notice brought to his attention.'[74] What the court were emphasising here was the fact that a countermand will not become effective until the bank has received actual notice of it. Accordingly, there is no room for 'constructive countermand', meaning that, in order to be effective, the countermand must be brought to the notice of a bank employee who has the authority to act upon the instruction.[75]

A final requirement of an effective countermand is that it must be made in time. Generally speaking, any countermand received *after* the original payment instruction had been fully executed by the bank would be ineffective.[76] Further, in light of the modern and more expeditious means of effecting payment transfers through, for example,

---

[70] *European Asian Bank AG v Punjab and Sind Bank (No.2)* [1983] 1 WLR 642; *Patel v Standard Chartered Bank* [2001] Lloyd's Rep. (Bank.) 229; *Cooper v National Westminster Bank* [2009] EWHC 3035.

[71] [1908] 1 KB 293.

[72] Clearly here the bank would have been liable in negligence for failing to ensure that the letter-box was emptied, but that was not pleaded in the case itself.   [73] At 298.

[74] At 301.   [75] *Giordano v Royal Bank of Canada* [1973] 3 OR 771, 775.

[76] A cheque will only be considered 'paid' and the countermand therefore out of time when its proceeds are unconditionally made available to the payee, that is, at the end of the cheque clearing cycle. See *Capital Associates Ltd v Royal Bank of Canada* (1970) 15 DLR (3d) 234. For a discussion of the cheque clearing cycle see Chapter 3, section 3.2.3.

CHAPS where payments are instantly credited,[77] a customer will be unable to counter-mand once the bank has received the customer's payment instruction.[78]

2.4.4 **Confidentiality**

A bank owes its customer a legal duty of confidentiality. The basis for this is the fact that a customer, who places confidential financial information in the hands of another, should be entitled to some legal assurance that such information will not be revealed to anyone. The duty of secrecy owed by a bank was emphasised by Diplock LJ in *Parry Jones v Law Society*[79] where he argued that:[80]

> Such a duty exists not only between solicitor and client, but, for example, between banker and customer, doctor and patient and accountant and client. Such a duty of confidence is subject to, and overridden by, the duty of any party to that contract to comply with the law of the land. If it is the duty of such a party to a contract, whether at common law or under statute, to disclose in defined circumstances confidential information, then he must do so, and any express contract to the contrary would be illegal and void.

2.4.4.1 Scope of the duty of confidentiality

The bank's duty of confidentiality takes the form of a term implied into the banker–customer contract. The necessity of implying such a term and the scope and duration of that duty was examined extensively in the leading case of *Tournier v National Provincial and Union Bank of England*.[81] Tournier was a customer of the defendant bank whose account was heavily overdrawn. A cheque was drawn by another customer of the bank in favour of Tournier but, rather than paying it into his own account, Tournier indorsed[82] it over to a third-party bookmaker. Upon realising that this had occurred, the branch manager of the defendant bank telephoned Tournier's employer to ascertain his address and, in the course of the conversation, disclosed to the employer that Tournier was indebted to them and was sending money to a bookmaker. As a result of this disclosure, Tournier's employer failed to renew his contract upon its expiration and so Tournier brought an action against the bank claiming damages for breach of the implied term in his banker–customer contract that the bank would not disclose to third persons any information regarding his account.

The Court of Appeal held that the bank had breached its duty of confidentiality and awarded damages to the customer. In reaching this conclusion the court had to deal with the issue of whether the bank's duty extended to information received by it from sources other than the customer himself or his account; clearly the information the

---

[77] Discussed more in Chapter 3, section 3.4.3.

[78] See Payment Services Regulations 2017, Regulation 83(1), 'a payment service user may not revoke a payment order after it has been received by the payer's payment service provider.'

[79] [1969] 1 Ch. 1.   [80] At 9.   [81] [1924] 1 KB 461.

[82] Traditionally, cheques could be transferred from one holder to another by being indorsed (i.e. signed) by the holder and delivered to the indorsee.

bank received here regarding the indorsed cheque came not from Tournier himself but from the chequing operations of the drawers account, that is, the third party that had originally written him the cheque. In this regard Bankes LJ stated:[83]

> The case of the banker and his customer appears to me to be one in which the confidential relationship between the parties is very marked. The credit of the customer depends very largely upon the strict observance of that confidence. I cannot think that the duty of non-disclosure is confined to information derived from the customer himself or from his account.

Accordingly, he held that the duty of non-disclosure extended to any information, regardless of its source, that was acquired 'in the character of a banker'. In similar vein, Atkin LJ held that this duty related not only to information derived from the account itself, but also to 'information obtained from other sources than the customer's actual account, if the occasion upon which the information was obtained arose out of the banking relations of the bank and its customers.'[84] Scrutton LJ expressed a contrary view, arguing that the duty of confidentiality should not apply to 'knowledge derived from other sources during the continuance of the relation.'[85] Regarding this point the courts have subsequently emphasised the correctness of the majority decision in *Tournier*.[86]

Furthermore, in relation to *when* the duty applies, the information gathered during the relationship remains confidential after it has terminated, but there is no duty of confidentiality in relation to information acquired before or after the termination.[87] This former point was discussed by Atkin LJ who stated that:[88]

> it must, I think, extend beyond the period when the account is closed, or ceases to be an active account. It seems to me inconceivable that either party would contemplate that once the customer had closed his account the bank was to be at liberty to divulge as it pleased the particular transactions which it had conducted for the customer while he was such.

Banks should, however, exercise some caution in relation to information they obtain before the commencement of the banker–customer relationship because this information could subsequently be reiterated by the customer and therefore fall within the scope of the duty. Additionally, information obtained by the bank, though not subject to the bank's implied duty of confidentiality could nevertheless be subject to the general law of confidences as set out in *Attorney-General v Guardian Newspapers Ltd (No.2)*.[89]

In summary, the duty of confidentiality is an implied term in the banker–customer contract, meaning that a bank must abstain from disclosing information to third

[83] At 474.   [84] At 485.   [85] At 481.
[86] See *Lipkin Gorman v Karpnale Ltd* [1989] 1 WLR 1340; *Barclays Bank v Taylor* [1989] 1 WLR 1066 per Lord Donaldson MR at 1070: 'The banker–customer relationship imposes upon a bank a duty of confidentiality in relation to information concerning its customer and his affairs which it acquires in the character of his banker.'
[87] As suggested by Scrutton LJ in *Tournier v National and Provincial Bank of England* [1924] 1 KB 461, 481 and 485.   [88] At 485.
[89] [1990] 1 AC 109.

parties. This obligation extends to all information acquired by the bank during its performance of that role and the duty continues beyond the period when the account is
closed. Where a bank discloses information in breach of this duty, the customer can
bring an action for damages.

2.4.4.2 Alternative sources of the duty

Before turning to consider the qualifications to the bank's duty of confidentiality it is
important to consider whether the duty has been bolstered by other initiatives and
sources.

While the bank's duty of confidentiality is currently implied into the banker–customer contract, there have been several calls to strengthen the duty through statutory codification. This was the view of the Jack Committee in 1989, which was commissioned
to conduct a review on banking services in the UK.[90] They recognised that the duty of
confidentiality was something that lay at the heart of the banker–customer relationship
and warned of loss of confidence in the banking system if there was any uncertainty
on the part of customers as to the application of that duty. Despite their recommendation, the UK government rejected the option of statutory codification, arguing that it
was unnecessary and would likely introduce new difficulties and confusion.[91] Instead a
Banking Code was written in 2001 that introduced voluntary standards of best practice
to the sector when dealing with customer information and confirmed the existence
of the bank's duty as well as its exceptions. This was replaced by the *Lending Code* in
2009,[92] which was a similar guide to best banking practice and provided as one of its
key commitments that 'personal information will be treated as private and confidential'.
Most recently the *Lending Code* was replaced by the *Standards of Lending Practice* in
July 2016, which fails to explicitly refer to the requirement of banks to treat personal
information as private and confidential, instead only mentioning that '*Firm's will maintain the security of customer's data*'.[93]

Although the Jack Committee's proposal to put the duty of confidentiality on a statutory footing was ultimately rejected, there are other statutory sources that have an
impact on the use of customers' information by a bank that could serve to bolster the
duty.

First, there is the General Data Protection Regulation (GDPR), which has had direct
effect in EU member states since 25 May 2018.[94] Its predecessor, the European Directive

---

[90] Review Committee on Banking Services Law, *Banking Services: Law and Practice* (1989).
[91] See *White Paper on Banking Services: Law and Practice* (1990, London Cm.1026).
[92] Revised most recently in September 2015, https://www.lendingstandardsboard.org.uk/wp-content/up-
loads/2016/06/The-Lending-Code-Mar-2011-revised-2015–1.pdf.
[93] The July 2016 publication relates to the voluntary standards for personal customers, available at https://
www.lendingstandardsboard.org.uk/wp-content/uploads/2016/07/Standards-of-Lending-Practice-July-16.
pdf. The same phrase is contained in the March 2017 standards for business customers, available at https://
www.lendingstandardsboard.org.uk/wp-content/uploads/2017/03/standards-of-lending-practice-business.
pdf.   [94] General Data Protection Regulation (EU) 2016/679.

on the Protection of Individuals with regard to the Processing of Personal Data and on the Free Movement of such Data,[95] which was implemented in the UK via the Data Protection Act 1998, was introduced in the context of computerisation and the advent of the internet, which allowed for large volumes of information to be stored, accessed, and processed, bringing with it a concern as to how institutions such as banks should handle such information. The new Regulation is designed to reflect technological developments, to harmonise data privacy laws across Europe, to enhance the protection of EU citizens' data privacy, and to reshape the way organisations approach data privacy.[96]

While the UK was still part of the EU when the GDPR came into force, the uncertainty in light of Brexit led the UK Department of Digital, Culture, Media and Sport to publish a Statement of Intent on 7 August 2017 in which it outlined the policy and objectives behind a new Data Protection Bill that would enshrine the EU standards in the UK.[97] This Bill was introduced in Parliament on 13 September 2017 and it is currently making its way through the House of Lords and House of Commons. The Bill subjects most processing of data to the GDPR and applies a broadly equivalent regime to certain types of processing to which the GDPR does not apply. Some of the key developments in the Bill are as follows:

- The definition of 'personal data' contained in the UK Data Protection Act 1998 has been broadened to reflect the growth and development of technology in recent decades. For example, personal data now encompasses IP addresses and internet cookies.[98]

- A number of data subject rights have been introduced and enhanced including; the right to be notified by the controller or processor of a data breach;[99] the right to obtain confirmation from the data controller with respect to whether data concerning them is being processed, where, and for what purpose (responses must be given within a month, generally without charge, and with additional information, such as data retention periods);[100] the right to request, and in some cases require, companies to delete their personal data (this could include e.g. the right to request that media platforms delete all of someone's posts).[101]

- Higher financial penalties can now be imposed up to €20 million or 4 per cent of a company's global turnover (whichever is higher).[102]

---

[95] Council Directive 95/46.   [96] https://www.eugdpr.org/

[97] Department for Digital, Culture, Media and Sport, *A New Data Protection Bill: Our Planned Reforms Statement of Intent* (7 August 2017) at https://assets.publishing.service.gov.uk/government/uploads/system/uploads/attachment_data/file/635900/2017–08–07_DP_Bill_-_Statement_of_Intent.pdf

[98] Data Protection Bill (HL) s3(2) and (3). An IP address is a unique string of numbers separated by full stops that identifies a device using the internet. An internet cookie is a small piece of data that is generated by a website and saved by your web browser, the purpose of which is to remember information about you.

[99] Ibid, s68.   [100] Ibid, s45.   [101] Ibid, s47–8.

[102] Ibid, s154. Previously the Information Commissioner could only impose fines up to £500,000, see Information Commissioner's Office *Data Protection Act 1998: Information Commissioner's guidance about the issue of monetary penalties prepared and issued under section 55C (1) of the Data Protection Act 1998* (December 2015) at https://ico.org.uk/media/for-organisations/documents/1043720/ico-guidance-on-monetary-penalties.pdf.

Second, there is the Human Rights Act 1998 (HRA), which incorporates the European Convention for the Protection of Human Rights and Fundamental Freedoms (ECHR) into English law. While the HRA does not give private individuals a direct horizontal right of action against one another for breaches of ECHR rights, it does make it unlawful for a 'public authority' to Act in in a way that is incompatible with the ECHR.[103] What this means is that the HRA has an indirect horizontal effect in relation to the manner in which the courts (as a 'public authority'[104]) deal with proceedings between private individuals. Because of this, the ECHR will undoubtedly influence the exercise of judicial discretion and the development of the common law in actions between private individuals.[105]

2.4.4.3 Qualifications to the duty

The duty of confidentiality is not absolute and in *Tournier* itself, Bankes LJ recognised four qualifications to the duty:[106]

> At the present day I think it may be asserted with confidence that the duty is a legal one arising out of contract, and that the duty is not absolute but qualified ... On principle I think that the qualifications can be classified under four heads: (a) Where disclosure is under compulsion by law; (b) where there is a duty to the public to disclose; (c) where the interests of the bank require disclosure; (d) where the disclosure is made by the express or implied consent of the customer.

Each of these qualifications will be discussed in turn.

Compulsion by law

Recent years have seen an increasing number of inroads into the duty of confidentiality as a result of statutory or judicial intervention that compels a bank to disclose otherwise confidential information. In the Report published by the Jack Committee in 1989, 19 statutes were identified under which disclosure could be compelled[107] and this list has continued to grow, particularly in the context of money laundering provisions, which means that there are now major inroads into a bank's duty of confidentiality.[108] In fact, Arora has gone so far as to say that 'in modern UK banking law, the duty of confidentiality has, in fact, been so eroded that the obligation now is to make disclosure and the duty of confidentiality exists only as an exception.'[109] Similarly, Wadsley argues that, as

---

[103] Section 6(1) of ECHR.   [104] Section 6(3) of ECHR.

[105] For a discussion of the merits of bolstering the duty of confidentiality through recourse to human rights principles see Robert Stokes, 'The Banker's Duty of Confidentiality, Money Laundering and the Human Rights Act' (2007) *Journal of Business Law* 502.   [106] At 473.

[107] Review Committee on Banking Services Law, *Banking Services: Law and Practice* (1989), paras 4.04, 6.23 and 16.10–16.12.

[108] See Howard Johnson, 'Confidentiality Diminished' (1995) *International Banking and Finance Law* 98: 'It is now generally accepted that the implied duty of confidentiality as enunciated by the Court of Appeal in Tournier v National Provincial and Union Bank of England [1924] 1 KB 461 is being reduced in scope almost by the day as new and more draconian measures are introduced to stop bank accounts being used for money laundering, fraud, tax evasion and a variety of other misdemeanours.'

[109] Anu Arora, *Banking Law* (Pearson, 2014) p 263.

a result of this erosion, if customers want to ensure that their financial affairs remain confidential, they would be best advised to 'keep their money under their mattresses in future'.[110]

The most common examples of legislation compelling banks to disclose information usually involve regulatory or investigatory authorities being allowed access to the confidential information held by a bank about its customers. For example, a bank may be ordered to produce information for the purposes of a criminal investigation by virtue of the Police and Criminal Evidence Act 1984; a bank can be compelled to disclose information about the affairs of insolvent customers by virtue of the Insolvency Act 1986; and laws relating to money laundering and terrorism under the Proceeds of Crime Act 2002 and Terrorism Act 2000 make it an offence for a bank to fail to disclose information to the police when there is suspicion or knowledge of an offence (see Chapter 14).

Compulsion by law also arises in the context of a court order for disclosure. This is part of the pre-trial process that enables each party in litigation to discover information about the other side. In this context a bank can be compelled to disclose confidential information regarding its customer to enable a third party to bring legal proceedings against that customer. The means by which this is done is for the claimant to ask the court to exercise its *Norwich Pharmacal* jurisdiction, a name which derives from the case of *Norwich Pharmacal Co v Customs and Excise Commissioners*.[111] Here Lord Reid established that a court may order someone, including a bank, who has become mixed up in the wrongful acts of others to disclose all the relevant information and identify the wrongdoer.[112] A successful application of this can be found in *Bankers Trust Co v Shapira*[113] where a bank was ordered to disclose confidential customer information in order to assist the victim of fraud trace funds. The Court of Appeal here recognised that it was 'a strong thing to order a bank to disclose the state of its customer's account and the documents and correspondence relating to it'[114] but in these circumstances an order would be granted because there was clear evidence that the claimant had been fraudulently deprived of their funds.

Duty to the public

The second qualification to the duty of confidentiality, as recognised by Bankes LJ in *Tournier*, relates to the duty of a bank to disclose information when it is in the public interest to do so. Lord Finlay in *Weld-Blundell v Stephens*[115] spoke of the scope of the second qualification in terms of cases in which 'some higher duty is involved' including, for instance, where 'danger to the State or public duty may supersede the duty of the agent to his principal'.[116] An obvious example of this would be the situation where a

---

[110] Joan Wadsley, 'Bank Confidentiality: A Much Reduced Duty' (1990) *Law Quarterly Review* 204, 207.

[111] [1874] AC 133.

[112] At 175: 'if through no fault of his own a person gets mixed up in the tortious acts of others so as to facilitate their wrong-doing he may incur no personal liability but he comes under a duty to assist the person who has been wronged by giving him full information and disclosing the identity of the wrongdoers.'

[113] [1980] 1 WLR 1274.   [114] At 1282.   [115] [1920] AC 956.   [116] At 965–6.

bank was required to disclose information in relation to an alien enemy during a time of war or national state of emergency.

In the majority of cases where disclosure may be considered to be in the public interest, it is required by statute, the most obvious example being those pieces of legislation that relate to money laundering or financing terrorism.[117] This fact has led to the questioning of whether this 'duty to the public' is required as a standalone exception to the duty of confidentiality.[118] Indeed, because of the apparent overlap between the first two qualifications, the Jack Committee recommended the abolition of this second exception in order to bring clarification and certainty to the duty of confidentiality.[119] The Government rejected this proposition arguing that, while the statutory route *requires* disclosure, this route simply *permits* disclosure and so should be kept.[120] Further, as Cranston et al highlight:[121]

> Just because legislation now requires the disclosure of information by bankers in a range of circumstances does not mean that the public-interest qualification is redundant. There is a need for a long stop to deal with other situations, those not covered by statutory provision but especially those which are unanticipated.

There have been few instances where the courts have had to adjudicate on the application of this second qualification but the need to retain it as an independent ground for justifying disclosure was confirmed in the case of *Price Waterhouse v BCCI Holdings (Luxembourg) SA*.[122] This case concerned disclosure by accountants of confidential information concerning their clients BCCI to the 'Bingham Inquiry', which was a non-statutory inquiry established by the Chancellor of the Exchequer and the Governor of the Bank of England to investigate the central bank's performance of its statutory supervisory functions in relation to the BCCI Group. As a non-statutory inquiry, there was no statutory duty compelling Price Waterhouse to disclose so they applied to the court to determine whether they could legally provide the confidential information required.

Millet J held that the situation fell within the second *Tournier* qualification because it was in the public interest to disclose information regarding the performance of the Bank of England to the Bingham Inquiry. He emphasised that the context in which this second exception should apply need not be limited to situations that are designed to detect and prevent wrongdoing, but should also include the interest that exists in ensuring the effective regulation and supervision of banking institutions by the central bank and the protection of depositors.[123]

---

[117] As discussed earlier in relation to the first qualification.

[118] Indeed, this exception has been described as the 'least easily comprehended of the *Tournier* exceptions.' *R v Curtis* (NZCA, 3 December 1993).

[119] Review Committee on Banking Services Law, *Banking Services: Law and Practice* (1989) paras 5.30 and 5.41.

[120] *White Paper on Banking Services: Law and Practice* (1990 London Cm.1026) p 15.

[121] Ross Cranston, Emilios Avgouleas. Kristin van Zwieten, Christopher Hare and Theodor van Sante, *Principles of Banking Law* (3rd Edn, Oxford: OUP 2017) p 264.

[122] [1992] BCCLC 583. Although this case concerned disclosure by accountants it was accepted that the same principle would apply to banks.   [123] At 596.

The *Price Waterhouse* case has been commended for breathing fresh life into the second *Tournier* exception,[124] thereby demonstrating the need to retain it as a separate and independent qualification to the duty of confidentiality. The later case of *Pharon v Bank of Credit and Commerce International SA (in liquidation)*,[125] which also stemmed from the collapse of BCCI, demonstrated that the second exception from *Tournier* can be applied not only in the context of disclosure to a public or regulatory body, but also in the context of disclosure to a private person. Here Rattee J held that the duty of confidentiality could be overridden by some greater public interest in making confidential documents available to private parties in foreign proceedings where there was alleged fraud involving an international bank.

Interests of the bank

The third qualification from *Tournier* relates to the situation where disclosure is required because it is in the interests of the bank itself to do so. The most obvious application of this qualification is where the bank commences proceedings against its customer to recover, for example, an unpaid loan or overdraft facility and it has to disclose in the proceedings details regarding the customer's account. However, one could argue that this situation could equally fall within the second exception, where disclosure is in the interests of the public, as has been discussed.

The potential for this exception to be interpreted too liberally in favour of the bank was demonstrated in *Sunderland v Barclays Bank*[126] where the defendant bank dishonoured a married woman's cheques, not only because the account had insufficient funds but also because the bank had knowledge that the cheques were being drawn in relation to gambling debts. During a telephone conversation between the bank manager and the plaintiff, the plaintiff's husband intervened to complain on behalf of his wife and the bank manager disclosed to him that his wife had been drawing cheques in favour of bookmakers. The plaintiff thereby brought an action against the bank for breach of the duty of confidentiality, but her claim was dismissed by Du Parcq LJ, who held that the bank's reputation was clearly under threat and so it was justified in disclosing the confidential information to the husband. It was further held that the plaintiff had given her implied consent to the disclosure of facts to her husband by allowing him to join in the telephone conversation.

The decision could be criticised on the ground that, in order to protect its reputation, the bank manager need only have disclosed to the husband that his wife had insufficient funds in her account to meet the payment instructions; it was unnecessary and therefore not justified for the bank to also reveal the wife's gambling activities. Indeed, Cranston et al have argued that the correct interpretation of the third exception from *Tournier* is that disclosure of confidential information to protect the reputation of a

---

[124] Ruth Chastney and Mark Reed, 'PW v BCCI: The Public Interest Exception to Duties of Confidentiality' (1992) *Journal of International Banking Law* 72, 74.   [125] [1998] 4 All ER 455.
[126] (1938) 5 LDAB 163.

bank should only ever be justified when it is in the interests of the public, not simply because it is in the private interest of the bank.[127] Fear of this potential for abuse led the Jack Committee to recommend legislation in favour of confining the ambit of this qualification to three specific situations: firstly, disclosure in the event of legal action to which the bank is a party; secondly, disclosure between banking companies within the same group; and thirdly, disclosure for the purposes of or in connection with the proposed sale of the bank itself or a substantial part of its undertaking.[128] Despite the criticism of *Sunderland* and the view of the Jack Committee and academics such as Cranston, the existence of the third qualification has been confirmed and upheld in subsequent cases.[129]

Customer's consent

The final qualification that may justify disclosure is where it is made with the express or implied consent of the customer. Express consent is simply a matter of fact,[130] but what is more difficult to establish is where the customer has given his or her implied consent for the bank to disclose the confidential information. Bankes LJ in *Tournier* itself gave the example of a customer authorising the disclosure by the bank of confidential information for the purpose of providing a credit reference[131] and it became the trade practice of banks to provide references on the ground that their customers had given their implied consent to it.

However, this trade practice was examined by the Court of Appeal in *Turner v Royal Bank of Scotland*[132] where it was held not to be an implied term as the custom was not sufficiently notorious and well known to the bank's customers. In this case, Turner held personal and business accounts with the defendant bank, which responded unfavourably to eight status enquiries made by another bank regarding Turner's creditworthiness. Accordingly, Turner brought an action against the bank contending a breach of its implied duty of confidentiality and the bank argued that it was the general practice of banks to respond to status enquiries from other banks by giving information about the creditworthiness of their customers. However, the Court of Appeal rejected the bank's argument and emphasised the distinction between banking practice that operates as 'no more than a private agreement between banks' and such practice that constitutes an established usage contractually binding on a bank's customer even if the customer is unaware of it.[133] If a practice is to bind the customer it must be 'notorious, certain and reasonable and not contrary to law'.[134] This practice was deemed not to be sufficiently notorious in *Turner* and so was not to be considered an implied term. Therefore, when

---

[127] Cranston et al, *Principles of Banking Law*, p 261.

[128] Review Committee on Banking Services Law, *Banking Services: Law and Practice* (1989) paras 31.3, 35.6.

[129] See, for example, *El Jawhary v Bank of Credit and Commerce SA* [1993] BCLC 396; *Christofi v Barclays Bank Plc* [1999] 2 All ER (Comm.).

[130] An example of express consent is where the customer has ticked a box saying that information can be shared with selected third parties. [131] At 473.

[132] [1999] 2 All ER (Comm.) 664. [133] Per Sir Richard Scott VC at 671.

[134] *Cunliffe-Owen v Teather and Greenwood* [1967] 1 WLR385,391.

> **Box 2.2. At a glance: the duty of confidentiality**
>
> The duty of confidentiality is an implied term in the banker–customer relationship as demonstrated in the leading case of *Tournier*.
> - In terms of scope, the duty of non-disclosure extends to any information obtained by the bank regardless of its source; information remains confidential after the account is closed.
> - There are other sources that serve to bolster the duty including *The Standards of Lending Practice, 2016 and 2017*; *the Human Rights Act 1998*; and the *GDPR 2016*.
> - There are four qualifications to the duty of confidentiality: (1) compulsion by law; (2) duty to the public; (3) interests of the bank; and (4) customer's consent.

giving a credit reference, the bank must first obtain the consent of the customer. The duty of confidentiality is summarised in Box 2.2

2.4.5 Duty of care and other regulatory duties

A bank has a duty to its customer to exercise reasonable care and skill in conducting its banking business. This duty may be implied into the banker–customer contract as a result of the common law rules established by the court or by virtue of s49 of the Consumer Rights Act 2015.[135] This duty of care may also arise concurrently in tort. Banks also owe certain regulatory duties. Each of these will be discussed in turn.

2.4.5.1 Contract

As mentioned, it is an implied term of the contract between a bank and its customer that the bank will exercise reasonable care and skill when executing its customer's orders.[136] Often this can create a conflict between the bank's duty to honour its customer's mandate[137] and its duty to exercise reasonable care and skill in relation to the execution of that instruction. It is the resolution of this conflict that is the subject of the two leading cases in this area, *Barclays Bank v Quincecare Ltd*[138] and *Lipkin Gorman v Karpnale Ltd.*[139] In the former case, under consideration was the question of whether a bank, when executing a payment order given to it by the chairman of its corporate customer, had been put on inquiry that the chairman was actually acting fraudulently and for his own purposes. In delivering judgment, Steyn J recognised that there were countervailing policy considerations that, on the one hand, required that the law should

---

[135] Which replaces s13 of the Supply of Goods and Services Act 1982 in the context of business to consumer contracts: s49(1): every contract to supply a service is to be treated as including a term that the trader must perform the service with reasonable care and skill.

[136] See, for example, *Westminster Bank Ltd v Hilton* (1926) 43 TLR 124 where Atkin LJ said 'it is the duty of the bank, arising out of the contract, to exercise reasonable care and skill in dealing with the communications which the customer sends to [him] in relation to his banking business.'

[137] As discussed in Section 2.4.2.   [138] [1992] 4 All ER 363.   [139] [1989] 1 WLR 1340.

not put too onerous an obligation on bankers and, on the other hand, required the law to safeguard against the facilitation of fraud. In balancing those interests he concluded that the sensible compromise should be that:[140]

> a banker must refrain from executing an order if and for as long as the banker is put on enquiry in the sense that he has reasonable grounds (although not necessarily proof) for believing that the order is an attempt to misappropriate the funds of the company ... the external standard of the likely perception of an ordinary prudent banker is the governing one.

On the facts it was held that there was nothing that would have put the bank on inquiry. This decision was followed shortly after by *Lipkin Gorman* where again the court had to consider whether the bank had breached its contractual duty of care to the customer. A man, Cass, was a partner in the plaintiff firm of solicitors and he had the authority to operate and draw cheques on the firm's client account at the bank with his signature. He was also an addicted gambler who fraudulently withdrew cash amounting to £200,000 from the client account by making cheques out for cash and sending the firm's cashier to cash them. He then used that money to fund his gambling addiction at the defendant club. Importantly, the branch manager of the solicitor's bank was aware of Cass's gambling addiction but still allowed him to draw a total of 63 cheques. The manager did not inform the claimant firm's senior partners that Cass was gambling or that large sums were being withdrawn from the client account under Cass's authority, and made no inquiry as to the propriety of those withdrawals.

The issue for the court was whether, in executing those payment instructions, the bank had breached its duty of care to the customer and was therefore liable for the sums drawn. In answering this question, May LJ began by emphasising that the principal obligation of a bank is to honour its customer's cheques in accordance with its mandate or instructions. He argued that any implied term requiring the banker to exercise care must be limited to the extent that when a bank is presented with a cheque that has been drawn in accordance with the mandate, the banker must honour it, save in 'exceptional circumstances'.[141] Importantly, he went on to formulate a test to determine when a bank should be put on inquiry:[142]

> Having in mind the vast numbers of cheques which are presented for payment every day in this country, whether over a bank counter or through the clearing bank, it is, in my opinion, only when the circumstances are such that any reasonable cashier would hesitate to pay a cheque at once and refer it to his or her superior, and when any reasonable superior would hesitate to authorise payment without inquiry, that a cheque should not be paid immediately on presentation and such inquiry made.

Parker LJ concurred with May LJ, arguing that although a bank's primary obligation was to honour its customer's mandate, this was not absolute and, in certain circumstances, if a bank was to honour such a payment, it would be guilty of a breach of

---

[140] At 379.   [141] At 1356.   [142] Ibid.

contract. Those circumstances and the standard of care to be met were formulated by Parker LJ as follows:[143]

> The question must be whether, if a reasonable and honest banker knew of the relevant facts, he would have considered that there was a serious or real possibility, albeit not amounting to a probability, that its customer might be being defrauded, or, in this case, that there was a serious or real possibility that Cass was drawing on the client account and using the funds so obtained for his own and not the solicitors' or beneficiaries' purposes. That, at least, the customer must establish. If it is established, then in my view a reasonable banker would be in breach of duty if he continued to pay cheques without inquiry.

On the evidence, it was held that the bank had had no reason to believe that there was such a possibility and therefore it was not guilty of breaching its duty of care. Furthermore, it was recognised that because the bank was only aware of Cass's gambling addiction through the operation of his own personal account with them, any disclosure by the bank to the solicitors of their suspicions would have breached the bank's duty of confidentiality to Cass.[144]

It would appear that the decisions in both the aforementioned cases adequately strike a balance between the protection of banks from extensive litigation, given the infinite number of transactions they are involved in, and the requirement of customers to safeguard their own interests rather than rely on the bank to do so.

While this clarifies the law in relation to a bank's duty of care in the context of honouring payment instructions, a contentious issue that has been subject to litigation is whether a bank owes a duty to advise a customer of the risks of a proposed business transaction. This relates to the situation where a customer applies to the bank for a loan or an overdraft facility in order to pursue a particular business venture and the question of whether there is an implied contractual duty on the party of the bank to advise the customer of the commercial viability of that project. The general rule is that a bank is under no duty to warn a customer of the risks of a particular transaction when that customer approaches the bank for financial assistance. This was confirmed by Scott LJ in *Lloyds Bank v Cobb*[145] who stated that:

> the ordinary relationship of customer and banker does not place on the bank any contractual or tortious duty to advise the customer on the wisdom of commercial projects for the purpose of which the bank is asked to lend.

This general position was also confirmed by the case of *Williams & Glyns Bank Ltd v Barnes*,[146] which concerned an experienced businessman who held both personal and corporate accounts with the claimant bank. The defendant personally borrowed money from the bank to invest in his company, which was also heavily indebted to the bank

---

[143] At 1378.
[144] *Tournier v National Provincial and Union Bank of England* [1924] 1 KB 461, discussed in Section 2.4.4.
[145] (Unreported) 18 December 1991.   [146] [1981] Com LR 205.

and when the company collapsed the defendant argued that the bank had breached their duty of care to him in failing to warn him of the unsound nature of his proposed investments. In rejecting this argument, it was held that the law does not impose any duty on a bank either to consider the prudence of the lending from the customer's point of view or to advise with reference to it. Accordingly, when a bank examines a borrowing proposal to decide whether or not to lend, it does so for its own purpose and does not assume any responsibility in relation to the commercial soundness of the proposed transaction. The effect of this general rule in practice is that it insulates banks from claims that they have failed to take sufficient steps to warn or advise customers of the commercial wisdom of their transactions.[147]

However, in exceptional circumstances it may be the case that the bank has gone further and assumed the role of the borrower's financial adviser. In such a case the bank may be liable in negligence and this was successfully pleaded in *Verity and Spindler v Lloyds Bank Plc*.[148] Here the claimants, who were a teacher and acupuncturist, wished to renovate a property in order to resell it at a profit and so they approached the defendant bank to take advantage of its advertised financial advisory service. The branch manager of the bank, after physically inspecting the two properties in contention, encouraged the claimants to purchase one in particular, claiming that it would be the better investment. The bank accordingly granted them the loan to do so. The investment failed because the refurbishment took longer and cost more than they anticipated, and, paired with a slump in the property market, meant that they made a loss on their investment. When the bank demanded repayment of the loan, the claimants resisted on the ground that the bank had breached its contractual and tortious duties to them by tendering negligent advice.

The High Court held in favour of the plaintiffs, arguing that the bank had voluntarily assumed responsibility to the borrowers to advise them with reasonable care and they were in breach of that duty. The key issues that informed the court's decision were: firstly, the fact that the claimants were unexperienced financially; secondly, the fact that the branch manager had inspected the properties and encouraged them to buy a particular property; and finally, the importance of the terms of the bank's advertisements offering advice. Accordingly, it was held that the bank had assumed the role of the borrower's financial adviser and was under a duty to take reasonable care in performing that role, which they didn't do here as they had been negligent in giving that advice.[149]

2.4.5.2 Tort

The duty of the bank to exercise reasonable care and skill arises concurrently in tort, meaning that a bank can be held liable for negligent misstatements to those with

[147] The reluctance of the courts to impose a duty in this context has been demonstrated in a number of Australian cases including; *Lloyd v Citicorp Australia Ltd* (1986) 11 NSWLR 286; and *McEvoy v ANZ Banking Group Ltd* [1988] ATR 80.   [148] [1995] CLC 1557.
[149] Compare this to *Bankers Trust International PLC v PT Dharmala Sakti Sejahtera* [1995] Bank LR 381 where no duty of care was found where the relationship between the two parties was not a conventional banker–customer relationship, but rather a commercial one where the buyer in question had held himself out as being experienced and capable of understanding the implications of the complex swap transactions.

whom they do not necessarily have a contractual relationship. The key to establishing this tortious duty is to find a 'relationship of proximity' between the two parties in question.

In *Hedley Byrne & Co. Ltd v Heller and Partners Ltd*[150] the bank gave a negligent reference regarding the customer's creditworthiness to a third party who then incurred substantial losses. In bringing an action against the bank to recover those losses, the House of Lords held that the bank owed a duty of care to the enquirer on the basis of a voluntary assumption of responsibility to that third party by the bank.[151] While the test from this case was restricted to instances of negligent advice and misstatements, *Henderson v Merrett Syndicate Ltd*[152] established that it also applied in the context of pure economic loss suffered as a result of the negligent provision of services. Further, Lord Goff in that case confirmed that what a claimant was required to show was that there had been a voluntary assumption of responsibility on the part of the bank, paired with reliance by the claimant, although he recognised that liability could still be imposed even if reliance could not be proven as long as the conduct of the bank caused economic loss.[153] For example, in *White v Jones*[154] the House of Lords held that a solicitor who had accepted instructions to draft a will owed a duty of care to the beneficiary of a will, despite the fact that the beneficiary had no knowledge that the solicitor had been employed for such a task and therefore could not be said to have relied on the solicitor for that purpose.

While it is accepted that this 'assumption of responsibility' is now the leading test, an alternative three stage test, as established in the case of *Caparo Industries Plc v Dickman*,[155] is sometimes applied by the courts instead.[156] Here the House of Lords established that in order to bring an action to claim damages for economic loss, it had to be shown that: firstly, the loss was foreseeable; secondly, that there was a relationship of proximity between the two parties; and thirdly, that it was fair, just, and reasonable to impose a duty of care. In *Caparo* itself, the claimants owned shares in a public company and after receiving the year's audited accounts for the company they purchased more shares, before eventually taking over the company. However, the auditors had been negligent, meaning that the accounts were misleading, so the claimants brought an action against the auditors and the question for the court was whether the auditors owed the claimants a duty of care. It was held that in order for a relationship of proximity to exist between the maker of the statement and the enquirer who relies on it, the adviser must at the time when the advice is given know (1) the identity of the person to whom the advice is to be communicated, (2) the purpose for which that person is to be provided with that advice, and (3) that the person to whom the advice is given is likely to rely on it for the known purpose. Lord Bridge doubted whether a statement that is put into

---

[150] [1964] AC 465.
[151] Although note that, on the facts, the bank had a disclaimer and therefore avoided liability.
[152] [1995] 2 AC 145.   [153] At 180.   [154] [1995] 2 AC 207.   [155] [1990] 2 AC 605.
[156] See, for example, *Customs and Excise Commissioners v Barclays Bank Plc* [2004] EWHC 122.

general circulation, such as these audited accounts, could give rise to a duty of care on the part of the auditors. He said:[157]

> To hold the maker of the statement to be under a duty of care in respect of the accuracy of the statement to all and sundry for any purpose for which they may choose to rely on it is not only to subject him, in the classic words of Cardozo C.J. to 'liability in an indeterminate amount for an indeterminate time to an indeterminate class:' … is also to confer on the world at large a quite unwarranted entitlement to appropriate for their own purposes the benefit of the expert knowledge or professional expertise attributed to the maker of the statement.

Accordingly, he concluded that there was no relationship of proximity such that the auditors of the company's accounts could owe a duty of care to members of the public who relied on those accounts when deciding to buy shares in the company.[158]

2.4.5.3 Regulatory duties

The FCA Handbook, as inherited and subsequently developed from the previous Financial Services Authority (FSA) Handbook, contains a number of regulatory duties that banks are subject to.[159] This is relevant to the banker–customer relationship as banks can be the subject of enforcement by the regulator if regulatory duties are breached, and private persons (including customers) are able to bring an action in damages against banks directly for the breach of a regulatory duty under s138D of the Financial Services and Markets Act.[160]

These regulatory duties include the fair, clear, and not misleading rule[161] and regulatory duties relating to bank–customer communications such as the appropriate information rule[162] and the distance marketing disclosure rules.[163] Perhaps the most fundamental regulatory duty, which emanates from an earlier FSA initiative,[164] is the 'Treat Customers Fairly' (TCF) principle. The Handbook provides in its *Principles* (PRIN) section that 'a firm must pay due regard to the interests of its customers and treat them fairly'.[165] This means that all firms have to be able to show consistently that fair treatment of customers is at the heart of their business model. In separate guidance, the FCA

---

[157] At 621.   [158] At 623.   [159] Available at https://www.handbook.fca.org.uk/handbook.

[160] Section 150(1): 'A contravention by an authorised person of a rule is actionable at the suit of a private person who suffers loss as a result of the contravention'. See also, FCA, *Banking: Conduct of Business Sourcebook* (BCOBS), Schedule 5 at https://www.handbook.fca.org.uk/handbook.

[161] Which applies in the context of communication with banking customers and financial promotions, see *Banking: Conduct of Business Sourcebook* (BCOBS) 2.2.   [162] BCOBS 4.4.1.

[163] BCOBS 3 generally.

[164] See, for example, FSA, 'Treating Customers Fairly After the Point of Sale' (June 2001); FSA 'Treating Customers Fairly: Progress Report' (2002); FSA 'Treating Customers Fairly—Progress and Next Steps' (2004); FSA 'Treating Customers Fairly—Building on Progress' (2005); FSA 'Treating customers fairly—Towards fair outcomes for consumers' (2006); FSA 'Treating Customers Fairly Initiative: Progress Report', (2007).

[165] PRIN 2.1 (Principle 6).

> ### Box 2.3 *FCA Fair Treatment of Customers: Consumer Outcomes*
>
> - **Outcome 1:** consumers can be confident they are dealing with firms where the fair treatment of customers is central to the corporate culture.
>
> - **Outcome 2:** products and services marketed and sold in the retail market are designed to meet the needs of identified consumer groups and are targeted accordingly.
>
> - **Outcome 3:** consumers are provided with clear information and are kept appropriately informed before, during, and after the point of sale.
>
> - **Outcome 4:** where consumers receive advice, the advice is suitable and takes account of their circumstances.
>
> - **Outcome 5:** consumers are provided with products that perform as firms have led them to expect, and the associated service is of an acceptable standard and as they have been led to expect.
>
> - **Outcome 6:** consumers do not face unreasonable post-sale barriers imposed by firms to change product, switch provider, submit a claim, or make a complaint.

highlights that there are six consumer outcomes that firms should strive to achieve to ensure the fair treatment of customers, as set out in Box 2.3.[166]

This duty is re-emphasised in the context of mortgage arrears. The *Mortgages and Home Finance: Conduct of Business Sourcebook* (MCOB) states that the TCF principle applies in respect of the information and service provided to customers who have payment difficulties or face a sale shortfall.[167] For example, MCOB 13.3 stipulates the policies and procedures that banks must have in place when dealing with a shortfall including the fact that:[168]

> Where a customer has a payment shortfall … a firm must not attempt to process more than two direct debit requests in any one calendar month … Where a firm's direct debit request … has been refused, on at least one occasion in each of two consecutive months, due to insufficient funds, the firm must: (a) consider whether the method of payment remains suitable for the customer; (b) make reasonable efforts to contact the customer to discuss whether the method of payment remains suitable for the customer; and (c) not pass on any costs to the customer which were incurred as a consequence of presenting direct debit requests during this period of consideration.

The FCA Handbook is clear that banks must ensure that their communications with customers are fair, clear, and not misleading. Banks promoting sales of products to

---

[166] FCA, *Fair Treatment of Customers: Consumer Outcomes* (12 May 2015) at https://www.fca.org.uk/firms/fair-treatment-customers?field_fcasf_sector=221&field_fcasf_page_category=unset.

[167] See generally, Mortgages and Home Finance: Conduct of Business Sourcebook (MCOB) 13: Arrears, payment shortfalls and repossessions: regulated mortgage contracts and home purchase plans.

[168] MCOB 13.3.1A.

customers have to make sure that any promotion is fair and balanced, not obscuring any relevant information and not exaggerating any benefits of such promotion.[169] Banks should provide 'appropriate information' to existing customers about a retail banking service and any deposit made in relation to that retail banking service (1) in good time, (2) in an appropriate medium, and (3) in easily understandable language and in a clear and comprehensible form; so that the banking customer can make decisions on an informed basis.[170] Further, in distance marketing contracts, banks need to ensure that their communications are comprehensive and unambiguous and customers should have the right to request paper copies of communication.[171] Customers also have the right to cancel the provision of retail banking services within 14 calendar days.[172]

Key Takeaways

- The fundamental duty of a bank is to obey its **customer's mandate**, although there is an extensive list of circumstances in which this duty can be abrogated. If a bank wrongfully dishonours its customer's mandate it can face an action in damages for breach of contract as well as an action for defamation.

- In order for a customer to successfully **countermand** a previous payment instruction that countermand must be (1) clear and unambiguous and (2) brought to the actual notice of the bank, and (3) made in time.

- A bank owes an implied duty of **confidentiality** but there are four qualifications to that duty (compulsion of law, duty to the public, the interests of the bank, and the express of implied consent of the customer) which could undermine its strength.

- A bank owes its customer a contractual **duty of care**. This duty arises concurrently in tort, which requires a 'relationship of proximity' between the two parties in question. Banks also owe a series of regulatory duties, as derived from the FCA Handbook.

Key Bibliography

Reports and Codes

Review Committee on Banking Services Law, *Banking Services: Law and Practice* (1989)
Standards of Lending Practice, July 2016 https://www.lendingstandardsboard.org.uk/wp-content/uploads/2016/07/Standards-of-Lending-Practice-July-16.pdf
White Paper on Banking Services: Law and Practice (1990 London Cm.1026)

Articles

Enonchong, N 'Contract Damages for Wrongful Dishonour of a Cheque' (1997) 60 *Modern Law Review* 412

---

[169] BCOBS 2 generally.   [170] BCOBS 4.4.1.   [171] BCOBS 3 generally.   [172] BCOBS 6.1 ff.

Hooley, R, 'Remedies for Wrongful Dishonour of a Cheque- Injury to Credit and Reputation' (1996) 55(2) *Cambridge Law Journal* 189

Houghton, J, 'Bank's duty of confidentiality—recent developments' (1990) *Journal of International Banking Law*, 40

Stokes, R, 'The Banker's Duty of Confidentiality, Money Laundering and the Human Rights Act' (2007) *Journal of Business Law* 502

2.5 Duties of the customer in the banker–customer relationship

In contrast to the duties of a bank to its customer, the scope of the duties owed by a customer to its bank are well defined and narrow. Indeed, the purpose of the implied duties is to ensure that the customer's account is not subject to any fraudulent activity or loss that could otherwise have been prevented by the customer. If a customer fails to adhere to one of these duties, it may prevent them from asserting any claim they would otherwise have against the bank. To put this into context, a payment made by a bank in excess of the customer's mandate is an unauthorised payment and the bank will not be entitled to debit the customer's account for that amount. Similarly, if a payment is made on a cheque, for example, that has been materially altered by a third party, that instrument is void under s64 of the Bills of Exchange Act, meaning that the bank has no authority to debit its customer's account for that amount. In these circumstances, if a customer's account is debited, the customer will be able to bring an action against the bank *unless* it can be shown that the customer has failed to comply with one of the two duties owed to the bank, namely, the duty not to draw cheques so as to facilitate fraud or forgery and the duty to inform the bank of any fraudulent activity as soon as the customer has actual notice of it.

Each of these two duties will be dealt with in turn, followed by a discussion of whether a customer should be subject to a wider duty of care in the management of his or her account.

2.5.1 Duty not to draw cheques so as to facilitate fraud or forgery

This duty was confirmed and upheld in the case of *London Joint Stock Bank Ltd v Macmillan*.[173] The defendant firm engaged in the practice of allowing a clerk to prepare and present cheques to a partner of the firm ready for their signature. The clerk duly presented a cheque for signature that had no text written in the space for providing the amount in writing and only the figure £2 written in the space intended for digits. The partner signed the cheque, believing that it was being drawn for the purposes of petty

---

[173] [1918] AC 777.

cash. The clerk subsequently added the words 'one hundred and twenty pounds' in the space left for words and wrote the figures '1' and '0' respectively on each side of the figure '2', which had been so placed as to leave room for the addition of these figures. The clerk presented the cheque for payment at the firm's bank, obtained payment of £120 out of the firm's account, and duly absconded. The question for the House of Lords was whether the bank was entitled to debit the firm's account for that sum. It was held that the bank was so entitled because the customer firm had breached its duty to take care in the mode of drawing cheques and the alteration of the amount on the cheque was a direct result of that breach of duty. Lord Finlay summarised the position as follows:[174]

> It is beyond dispute that the customer is bound to exercise reasonable care in drawing the cheque to prevent the banker being misled. If he draws the cheque in a manner which facilitates fraud, he is guilty of a breach of duty as between himself and the banker, and he will be responsible to the banker for any loss sustained by the banker as a natural and direct consequence of this breach of duty.

It is a question of fact whether the behaviour of the customer will amount to negligence such that he will be estopped from claiming that the bank has wrongfully debited his account. For example, in *Slingsby v District Bank*[175] it was held that not every blank space or incomplete detail on a cheque will lead to a finding that the customer has been negligent. Here the customer left a blank space after the payee's name and before the words 'or order', which enabled a fraudulent third party to add the words 'per C&P'. It was held that the customer had not been negligent here and was therefore able to dispute the debiting of his account with the bank, Scrutton J arguing that the drawing of a line in the blank space after the payee's name was not a 'usual precaution' that customers were required to take.[176]

It should be noted that this duty of care is relatively narrow and relates only to the transactional aspect of the process, that is, the carelessness or negligence of the customer in the actual drawing of the cheque itself; there is no wider duty to, for example, take reasonable care not to lose your cheque book or to take care in hiring an honest clerk. Accordingly, the lack of care must arise from the transaction itself – from the way the cheque is written – to enable banks the protection afforded by the *Macmillan* case. This was confirmed in *Bank of Ireland v Evans' Trustees*[177] where the House of Lords stated that a bank would not be entitled to debit a customer's account if a cheque was drawn on it as a result of the customer losing his or her cheque book, or neglecting to lock up the desk in which it is kept such that it fell into the hands of a fraudulent third party.[178] Similarly, in *Lewes Sanitary Steam Co. Ltd v Barclay & Co Ltd*[179] a bank was held not to be entitled to debit their customer's account even though that customer had hired a

---

[174] At 789. The House of Lords here were applying the principles as established in *Young v Grote* (1827) 4 Bing 253, a case factually similar to *Macmillan* where it was held that a bank is entitled to debit its customer's account in circumstances where that customer has allowed an agent to complete an incomplete cheque.
[175] [1932] 1 KB 544.   [176] At 559.   [177] (1855) 5 HLC 389.   [178] At 410–11.
[179] (1906) 95 LT 444.

secretary who had been convicted of forgery, and made them a joint signatory on the company's chequebook.

2.5.2 Duty to inform the bank of forgery as soon as customer has actual notice

A customer must inform the bank of any forgeries as soon as they have actual notice of such forgery. As with the first duty, this is also narrowly defined and was discussed at length in the case of *Greenwood v Martins Bank Ltd*.[180] Mr Greenwood had an account with the defendant bank and his wife fraudulently withdrew sums from his account by forging his signature. When Mr Greenwood became aware of this, his wife persuaded him not to inform the bank. When he later discovered that his wife's explanation for withdrawing the funds was false, he threatened to disclose the information to the bank resulting in his wife committing suicide. Mr Greenwood subsequently brought an action against the bank to recover the sums paid out of his account on cheques to which his signature had been forged. The House of Lords held that Mr Greenwood owed a duty to the defendants to disclose the forgeries as soon as he became aware of them and so enable the defendants to take steps towards recovering the money wrongfully paid on the forged cheques. Accordingly, because he had breached this duty in waiting eight months to inform the bank, he was estopped from asserting that the signatures to the cheques were forgeries and was not entitled to recover the funds.[181]

A more explicit example of estoppel is demonstrated in the case of *Brown v Westminster Bank*.[182] Here the servants of an elderly customer forged her signature on cheques that were drawn on her current account over a number of years. During this time the branch manager of the defendant bank enquired on several occasions about the genuineness of the cheques and was reassured on each occasion by the customer that all of the cheques had been genuinely drawn. It was held that because of the reassurances she gave to the bank manager, she was estopped from later asserting that the cheques had been forged and her account should be re-credited.

2.5.3 A wider duty of care?

While the duties owed by a customer to its bank are currently limited to those discussed earlier, the question has been raised as to whether customers should be subject to a wider duty to take care when managing their accounts. This issue was addressed in *Tai Hing Cotton Mill Ltd v Liu Chong Hing Bank Ltd*[183] where the three defendant banks had honoured some 300 cheques worth HK$5.5 million drawn fraudulently on the plaintiff customer's account over a six-year period. On first appearances the cheques appeared to have been drawn by the company's managing director who was one of the company's

---

[180] [1933] AC 51.   [181] See Lord Tomlin at 57–8.   [182] [1964] 2 Lloyd's Rep 187.
[183] [1986] AC 80.

authorised signatories, but they had in fact been forged by an accounts clerk employed by the company. The issue to be decided in the case was upon whom the loss should fall and, more importantly, the nature and extent of any duty of care owed by the customer to his bank in relation to the operation of his current account.[184] The defendant banks contended that the customer owes a wider duty to take reasonable care in the operation of his account and, more specifically, a duty to take such steps to check his periodic (in this case, monthly) bank statements to enable him to notify the bank in a timely manner of any debit items in the account that he has not authorised. The Privy Council, however, rejected this argument. Lord Scarman concluded that the customer's duty in relation to forged cheques is limited to those two duties as recognised in *Macmillan* and *Greenwood*.[185] Accordingly, the decision confirmed that a customer is not bound by a wider duty of care that involves employing a careful management system and checking monthly bank statements. Here the banks were therefore ordered to reverse the debit entries and pay interest on the sums involved.

The decision of the Privy Council has been met with extensive academic critique. For example, Professor Ogilvie delivered a scathing response to the decision, arguing that Lord Scarman was biased against the banks and this clouded his judgment. She argued that Lord Scarman's assertion that one side should take all the risks (i.e. the bank) was questionable and as long as courts treat banks as insurers there is no incentive for a customer to adapt and utilise reasonable accounting procedures to reduce the incidents of forgery by dishonest employees. She posited that a more appropriate policy goal would be to recognise that, in cases where customers have unsound office procedures that contribute to their loss, they should be expected to bear that loss in proportion to their causation of it. Finally, she argued that it is irrational to restrict the duties owed by a customer to those established in *Macmillan* and *Greenwood*.[186]

Sealy and Hooley raise three justifications in defence of the decision. Firstly, they argue that a bank is usually in a far better position to absorb losses than its customer and, accordingly, the Privy Council were correct in refusing to impose a wider duty that would likely affect the position of the customer in a detrimental way. Secondly, they claim that as it stands the law remains clear and certain – we currently have two clearly defined duties arising from *Macmillan* and *Greenwood*, by introducing a wider and more general duty of care we would be injecting uncertainty and increasing instances of litigation in this area. Thirdly, they argue that banks are always at liberty to include a verification clause in their

---

[184] Per Lord Scarman at 101: 'the question is whether English law recognises today any duty of care owed by the customer to his bank in the operation of a current account beyond, first, a duty to refrain from drawing a cheque in such a manner as may facilitate fraud or forgery, and, secondly, a duty to inform the bank of any forgery of a cheque purportedly drawn on the account as soon as he, the customer, becomes aware of it'.
[185] At 108.
[186] Margaret Ogilvie, 'Bank Accounts and Obligations' (1986) *Canadian Business Law Journal* 220. For further critique see, for example, Benjamin Geva, 'Allocation of Forged Cheque Losses—Comparative Aspects, Policies and a Model for Reform' (1998) *Law Quarterly Review* 250; Alfred Silvertown, 'Fraudulent Cheques—Time for Changes in the Law?' (1986) *International Banking Law* 158; Jonathan Fisher, 'Bank and Customer Relations: Fraud' (1986) *Journal of International Banking Law* 47.

bank–customer contract to provide them with protection.[187] What this means is that a bank can include a term in its contract that extends the duties of the customer to say, for example, that the customer must scrutinise their bank statements and complain within a certain period of time of any errors or they will lose the right to challenge the payment. However, such a term will have to be expressly drafted and unambiguous. There was indeed such an express term in the *Tai Hing* case itself that required the customer to scrutinise statements and complain within a fixed period or lose the right of challenge, but it was held to be ambiguous and therefore construed against the bank (based on the **contra proferentum** rule).[188] Such clauses may also be unenforceable as a result of the Consumer Rights Act 2015 if the term was deemed to be unfair.

Whatever the viewpoint, it is clear that as it stands, the judiciary have rejected the possibility of incorporating a wider duty of care into the banker–customer relationship such that the only two duties owed by a customer to his or her bank are those set out in *Macmillan* and *Greenwood*.

 Key Takeaways

- A customer owes a bank two narrowly defined duties:

  - A duty not to draw cheques so as to facilitate fraud or forgery as discussed in *Macmillan*. This duty relates only to the transactional aspect of drawing the cheque itself; there is no wider duty to, for example, take care not to lose one's cheque book.

  - A duty to inform the bank of any forgery as soon as the customer has actual notice of it as discussed in *Greenwood*.

- If a customer breaches one of the above duties, they will be estopped from asserting the bank has wrongfully debited their account.

- Despite academic criticism to the contrary, the judiciary have forcefully maintained that a customer is *not* subject to a wider duty to take care in the management of his or her accounts.

Key bibliography

Articles

Fisher, J, 'Bank and Customer Relations: Fraud' (1986) *Journal of International Banking Law* 47.

Geva, B, 'Allocation of Forged Cheque Losses—Comparative Aspects, Policies and a Model for Reform' (1998) *Law Quarterly Review* 250.

Ogilvie, M, 'Bank Accounts and Obligations' (1986) *Canadian Business Law Journal* 220.

Silvertown, A, 'Fraudulent Cheques—Time for Changes in the Law?' (1986) *International Banking Law* 158.

---

[187] Leonard Sealy and Richard Hooley, *Commercial Law* (4th edition, Oxford: OUP 2009) p 707.

[188] See, for example, *University of Keele v Price Waterhouse* [2004] EWCA Civ 583.

2.6 The fiduciary nature of the banker–customer relationship

2.6.1 Definition of 'fiduciary'

Although the relationship between a bank and its customer is primarily governed by contract law, there may be circumstances in which the bank undertakes additional obligations, thereby taking the relationship beyond the remit of contract law such that the bank becomes subject to fiduciary duties of trust and loyalty.

The classic case from which the definition of the term 'fiduciary' derives is *Bristol and West Building Society v Mothew*.[189] This concerned a claim by a building society against a solicitor who had failed to inform the building society that a purchaser, to whom the building society was advancing sums for the acquisition of a property, had borrowed further sums secured by way of a second mortgage on the property. When the purchasers defaulted and the house was sold for less than the mortgage, the building society brought an action against the defendant solicitor alleging breach of contract, negligence, and a breach of trust. The Court of Appeal held that while the actions of the solicitor constituted a breach of contract, there was no breach of any fiduciary duty because the building society had authorised the solicitor to act on behalf of both themselves and the purchasers and at all times the solicitor had served each of those parties loyally and faithfully. In identifying who would qualify as a fiduciary, Millet LJ stated that:[190]

> A fiduciary is someone who has undertaken to act for or on behalf of another in a particular matter in circumstances which give rise to a relationship of trust and confidence. The distinguishing obligation of a fiduciary is the obligation of loyalty. The principal is entitled to the single-minded loyalty of his fiduciary. This core liability has several facets. A fiduciary must act in good faith; he must not make a profit out of his trust; he must not place himself in a position where his duty and his interest may conflict; he may not act for his own benefit or the benefit of a third person without the informed consent of his principal. This is not intended to be an exhaustive list, but it is sufficient to indicate the nature of fiduciary obligations. They are the defining characteristics of the fiduciary.

At the heart of this definition is the fact that a fiduciary is expected to promote the interests of his or her principal above their own. In the context of the banking industry, clearly banks are commercial parties that are pursuing their own business interests ahead of their customers and, accordingly, the courts have often stressed the fact that the core deposit-taking and lending functions of a bank are confined to principles of contract law rather than being fiduciary in nature.[191] While this is easily understandable

---

[189] [1998] Ch 1.   [190] At 18.

[191] See, for example, *Foley v Hill* (1848) 2 HLC; *Bank of Scotland v A Ltd* [2001] EWCA Civ 52, per Lord Woolfe at [25]: 'on the face of it the relationship between a bank and its customer is not a fiduciary relationship.' However, the more complex services offered by banks such as investment portfolio management or acting as the trustee of an estate may well extend beyond contractual duties and impose additional fiduciary duties on the part of the bank. See, for example, '*Ata v American Express Bank Ltd, The Times*', 26 June 1998; *Bartlett v Barclays Trust Co. Ltd* [1980] Ch 515.

in relation to commercial customers,[192] the courts have still been reluctant to impose fiduciary duties on banks in relation to their dealings with more vulnerable personal customers. This was evidenced in the case of *Wright v HSBC Plc*[193] where the claimant brought an action against the defendant bank contending that it had breached its fiduciary duty to her when they advised her to enter into a settlement agreement with them following the death of her husband. Despite her apparent vulnerability here,[194] Jack J held that the bank had not assumed any fiduciary obligations to the claimant, particularly since they had advised her to seek independent legal advice and had ultimately left her to make her own decision as to whether to enter into the agreement.[195] There are, however, certain circumstances where the courts have accepted that a bank may be subject to fiduciary duties. Two such specific circumstances will now be dealt with in turn, followed by a discussion of how a bank can avoid its liability as a fiduciary.

2.6.2 Imposing fiduciary obligations where the customer executes a guarantee, charge, or other security in relation to the loan or overdraft of another customer

The first context in which the courts have imposed fiduciary obligations relates to the situation where a customer is asked to execute a guarantee, **charge**, or some other form of security in relation to a loan or overdraft that is being extended to another customer of the bank. Cleary where the surety is a relation of the customer such as an elderly parent or spouse, there is scope for some influence to be exerted over that person. In those circumstances, where a bank seeks to enforce a claim against the surety, the action may well be defeated because of the fiduciary relationship that arises between the bank and the surety.[196] The leading case in which this was successfully pleaded by a surety is *Lloyds Bank Ltd v Bundy*,[197] which centred on the defendant, Mr Bundy, and his son who were both customers of the plaintiff bank. Here, Mr Bundy's son's company ran into some financial difficulty and so Mr Bundy guaranteed the company's overdraft and charged his farm as security. The bank failed to suggest that Mr Bundy seek independent legal advice before agreeing to the charge and they also failed to disclose the full extent of the financial difficulties of his son's company. In determining whether the bank owed Mr Bundy a fiduciary duty Sir Eric Sachs established that a fiduciary relationship could arise in the following circumstances:[198]

> Such cases tend to arise where someone relies on the guidance or advice of another, where the other is aware of that reliance and where the person upon whom reliance is placed obtains, or may well obtain, a benefit from the transaction or has some other interest in it being concluded. In addition, there must, of course, be shown to exist a vital element which in this judgment will for convenience be referred to as confidentiality.

---

[192] *JP Morgan Chase Bank v Springwell Navigation Corporation* [2008] EWHC 1186.
[193] [2006] EWHC 930.   [194] As discussed at [61].   [195] At [61]–[63].
[196] It could also be defeated as a result of the doctrine of undue influence, discussed in Section 2.7.
[197] [1975] QB 326.   [198] At 341.

The Court of Appeal found that, on the facts, a fiduciary relationship had clearly arisen and by failing to advise Mr Bundy to seek independent legal advice they were in breach of their fiduciary duty, meaning that the guarantee could be set aside.

However, there are a number of reasons why the courts should exercise caution when applying the fiduciary line of reasoning from *Bundy* to future cases. First, it is recognised that *Bundy* is a decision that is rather peculiar in terms of its facts.[199] Secondly, while the Court of Appeal held in favour of the defendant unanimously, their reasoning all differed and it was only Sir Eric Sachs who decided the case on the grounds of a breach of fiduciary duty.[200] Thirdly, Sir Eric Sachs was of the opinion that the conflict of interest between the bank, Mr Bundy, and his son was an important consideration in deciding to classify the bank as a fiduciary but the importance of this factor has since been doubted because it has been recognised that there will always be a conflict in this type of three-party case.[201] Finally, the decision in *Bundy* must now be understood in light of the later decision of *National Westminster Bank Plc v Morgan*[202] where the House of Lords doubted the route used by the Court of Appeal in *Bundy* arguing that the sole focus should have been on undue influence rather than the question of whether the bank was subject to fiduciary obligations.

In *Morgan*, the customer of a bank, who had defaulted on a loan from a building society that was secured upon the matrimonial home that he owned jointly with his wife, sought to refinance the loan with the applicant bank. The bank agreed to a short-term bridging loan on the basis that it would be subject to a legal charge over the matrimonial home. Morgan duly signed the charge and the manager of the bank visited the customer's home in order to obtain the wife's signature. During his visit it was clear that the atmosphere was tense and the wife was concerned about the effect of the charge. While she duly signed the required paperwork, the bank manager failed to fully explain the nature of the charge to her and nor did he recommend that she seek independent legal advice. When the defendant failed to repay the loan, the bank sought to enforce the charge. In concluding that the charge should not be set aside, Lord Scarman revisited *Bundy*, arguing that while Sir Eric Sachs got the decision 'absolutely right' he preferred to use the language of 'undue influence' when determining the availability of relief for the surety, rather than that of 'breach of fiduciary duty'.[203] On the facts, Lord Scarman found that the branch manager had not exercised undue influence over the wife and therefore the bank was not obliged to suggest that the wife seek independent legal advice.

Accordingly, in the litigation that has ensued post *Morgan*, the courts have made their decisions on the basis of whether the bank has notice of any undue influence that may have been exerted by the debtor over the guarantor.[204]

---

[199] Indeed, this was recognised in the case itself, Cairns LJ commenting that the circumstances were 'very unusual' (at 340) and Sir Eric Sachs recognising that the case involved 'special facts' (at 347).

[200] Cairns LJ, found in favour of the defendant on the grounds of undue influence, as did Lord Denning.

[201] See *Susilawati v American Express Bank Ltd* [2008] 1 SLR 237.   [202] [1985] AC 686.

[203] At 708 and 707–9.   [204] This is considered fully in section 2.7.

2.6.3 Imposing fiduciary obligations where the bank assumes the role of financial adviser

The second context in which the courts have found that a bank may owe fiduciary obligations to its customer is where the bank assumes the role of a financial adviser by giving the customer investment advice. The leading example of this type of case is *Woods v Martins Bank*.[205] Here, the branch manager of the defendant bank persuaded their (inexperienced in business) customer to invest substantial sums of money in a company that was also a customer of the bank. The branch manager failed to disclose to the claimant that the company in question was heavily overdrawn and an ongoing concern for the bank. Following the loss of his entire investment the claimant brought an action against the bank based on the grounds that, firstly, as a customer of the bank the bank owed him an implied contractual duty to exercise reasonable care and skill and, secondly, that the bank had become the claimant's fiduciary after agreeing to act as his financial adviser. While the claimant was successful on the first ground, Salmon J nonetheless held that even if this contractual duty didn't exist, liability could be imposed as a result of a breach of fiduciary duty on the part of the bank. This conclusion rested on three key factors:

1. In emphasising the financial expertise of the bank during conversations with the claimant, the bank manager had, in effect, agreed to act as the claimant's financial adviser.

2. The claimant had been given a leaflet that advertised the bank as an expert in furnishing business and financial advice.

3. The branch manager had advised the claimant to invest in the company in question without disclosing the conflict of interest that this gave rise to by virtue of the fact that the company was heavily indebted to the bank and by investing in the company, the claimant would be reducing the extent of that indebtedness.

A similar conclusion was found in the Canadian case of *Standard Investments Ltd v Canadian Imperial Bank of Commerce*.[206] Here, the claimant customers of the defendant bank sought to acquire a controlling interest in another company, Crown Trust (also a customer of the bank), and the bank offered them the necessary guidance and advice in relation to the takeover. The bank was subsequently held to be in breach of their fiduciary duty to the claimant because they failed to disclose the fact that another officer of the bank had already agreed to assist in blocking the claimant's attempted takeover and, in fact, at the request of one of the bank's directors who had a personal interest in Crown Trust, the bank had already agreed to purchase shares in the company in order to counter the takeover bid. In fact, those shares were subsequently sold to another organisation, which then acquired a controlling interest in Crown Trust. The Court of Appeal found in favour of the claimant, arguing that the bank had never informed

---

[205] [1959] 1 QB 55. Discussed in section 2.3.1.   [206] (1985) 22 DLR (4th) 410.

them of the clear conflict of interest that arose meaning that the bank had effectively proceeded with 'a course of action to achieve a purpose which [the bank] had already decided to thwart.'[207]

2.6.4 **Avoiding liability as a fiduciary**

While it is clear that in certain circumstances a bank may find itself liable as a fiduciary, it could avoid liability by making full disclosure to the client of any conflict of interest or by including a term in the banker–customer contract that purports to exclude or modify any obligations of a fiduciary nature.

In terms of disclosure, if a bank fully and frankly discloses any potential conflict of interest it might have between the claimant and a third party, and in doing so obtains the customer's informed consent to continue to deal with the parties in the agreed manner, then they may escape liability for breach of fiduciary duty if later pleaded by the claimant.[208] However, while advanced disclosure may be sufficient to avoid liability in certain circumstances, this will not be the case in every situation as demonstrated in *Commonwealth Trading Bank of Australia v Smith*.[209] Here, the branch manager of a bank introduced the claimants, who were both customers of the bank, to other customers of the bank who were selling their hotel business, something the claimants had an interest in acquiring. In line with the bank's duty of confidentiality, the manager informed the claimants that, as the vendors were also their customers, they couldn't disclose any information to them regarding their accounts with the bank. However, rather than advising the claimants to seek independent legal advice, the branch manager instead informed them that the proposed sale was favourable and any attempt to negotiate a lower price would be futile. The bank manager failed to disclose the contents of a valuation report submitted as part of the claimant's mortgage application that valued the business at considerably below the asking price.

The Australian Federal Court held that the bank in question had become a fiduciary because it had assumed the position of 'investment' adviser to the claimants.[210] Moreover, the court emphasised that the bank had not discharged its fiduciary duty simply by informing the claimants that there existed a conflict of interest; they held that as this conflict and the duty of confidentiality precluded the bank from disclosing certain information, it should have either encouraged the claimants to seek independent legal advice, or refrained from advising the claimants at all.

It is also possible for a bank to include in its contract with the customer a clause that purports to exclude or limit their liability for breach of any fiduciary duty. This approach has been recognised and approved by both the Privy Council in *Kelly v Hooper*[211] and

---

[207] Per Goodman JA at 431.
[208] *Australian Securities and Investments Commission v Citigroup Global Markets Australia Pty Ltd (No.4)* (2007) 241 ALR 705, [293]–[296]; *Ratiu v Conway* [2006] 1 All ER 571, [99]–[102]; *Forsyth-Grant v Allen* [2008] EWCA Civ 505, [40].   [209] (1991) 102 Aust. L. Rep. 453.
[210] At 476.   [211] [1993] AC 205, 214–15.

the House of Lords in *Henderson v Merrett Syndicates Ltd*[212] However, the ability to rely on such a clause will depend on a number of factors including whether the clause passes the test of 'fairness' in the Consumer Rights Act 2015, whether the clause is clearly worded such that it avoids the ***contra proferentum*** rule,[213] and whether there was a pre-existing fiduciary relationship between the two parties and the claimant did not give his or her consent to the inclusion of a clause that modified or excluded those fiduciary obligations.[214]

 Key takeaways

- Generally speaking, the courts have been reluctant to impose additional fiduciary obligations in the context of the banker–customer relationship, recognising that banks are commercial parties who pursue their own business interests.

- There are, however, two contexts in which the courts have recognised the fiduciary nature of the relationship:
  - Where a customer is asked to execute a guarantee, charge, or some other form of security in relation to a loan or overdraft that is being extended to another customer of the bank (although it is recognised that these cases will now normally be dealt with under the equitable doctrine of undue influence).
  - Where the bank assumes the role of financial adviser.

- Banks can avoid liability as a fiduciary either by ensuring that they make full disclosure of any conflict of interest or by including a contractual term that excludes or modifies their fiduciary obligations.

---

[212] [1995] 2 AC 145, per Lord Browne-Wilkinson at 206:

> the extent and nature of the fiduciary duties owed in any particular case fall to be determined by reference to any underlying contractual relationship between the parties. Thus, in the case of an agent employed under a contract, the scope of his fiduciary duties is determined by the terms of the underlying contract. Although an agent is, in the absence of contractual provision, in breach of his fiduciary duties if he acts for another who is in competition with his principal, if the contract under which he is acting authorises him so to do, the normal fiduciary duties are modified accordingly … The existence of a contract does not exclude the co-existence of concurrent fiduciary duties (indeed, the contract may well be their source); but the contract can and does modify the extent and nature of the general duty that would otherwise arise.

[213] Which tells us that any ambiguity in the wording of a clause will be construed against the party seeking to rely on it; *University of Keele v Price Waterhouse* [2004] EWCA Civ 583.

[214] See David Hayton, 'Fiduciaries in Context: An Overview' in P.B.H Birks, ed *Privacy and Loyalty* (Oxford, 1997), 300; however, this principle was unsuccessfully invoked in *Australian Securities and Investments Commission v Citigroup Global Markets Australia Pty Ltd (No.4)* (2007) 241 ALR 705.

Key bibliography

Articles

Breslin, J 'Banks as Fiduciaries' (1998) 5 *Commercial Law Practitioner* 47.
Clayton, N, 'Banks as Fiduciaries: the UK Position' (1991) *Journal of International Banking Law* 315.
Ogilvie, M, 'Banks, Advice-Giving and Fiduciary Obligations' (1981) 17 *Ottowa L Rev* 263.

2.7 Undue influence

Undue influence is an equitable ground of restitution, which applies where the defendant (or a third party in the case of three-party cases) has a relationship of influence with the claimant and they abuse that influence in order to induce the claimant to enter into a contract that benefits the defendant or third party in some way. Undue influence is therefore concerned with the reality of the consent that one gives when entering into a contract. If successfully pleaded, the claimant will be entitled to have the contract set aside.

Since the decision in *National Westminster Bank Plc v Morgan*,[215] where Lord Scarman shifted the focus away from fiduciary obligations to undue influence where vulnerable sureties have been presented to banks, the law surrounding the equitable doctrine of undue influence has developed at a rapid pace. The discussion that follows will start by defining the different categories of undue influence (see Box 2.4) and the shift away from the requirement that the transaction has to be at the 'manifest disadvantage' of the claimant. Then it will look at how banks might be affected by undue influence, particularly in three-party cases.

2.7.1 Categories of undue influence and the requirement of 'manifest disadvantage'

In *Bank of Credit and Commerce International v Aboody*[216] the Court of Appeal set out the different categories of undue influence as follows:[217]

1. Actual Undue Influence' (Class 1): Here the claimant will have to affirmatively prove on the evidence that the wrongdoer exerted undue influence on him and this induced him to enter into the transaction in question. An example of this is demonstrated in the *Aboody* case itself, which concerned the question of whether a charge over the claimant's property could be set aside on the ground that her husband had exercised actual undue influence. The claimant was an Iranian national who had moved to the UK under an arranged marriage. Her husband, who owned his own business, sought a business loan from the bank which in turn required that a charge be placed over the matrimonial home as security. When the claimant met with the bank manager to discuss the implications of the charge, her husband burst into the room and shouted at them, reducing the claimant to tears and forcing her to sign the document. The

---

[215] [1985] AC 686.   [216] [1990] 1 QB 923.   [217] Per Slade LJ at 953.

Court of Appeal held that this was a clear case of actual undue influence; the claimant had not entered into the transaction based on her own free will.

2. Presumed Undue Influence' (Class 2): Here the claimant will have to show only that there was a relationship of trust and confidence between themselves and the wrongdoer. This will raise a presumption of undue influence and it will then be for the wrongdoer to rebut that presumption by bringing evidence to show that the claimant in fact entered into the transaction freely. Class 2 is sub-divided into two further categories. Class 2A relates to protected relationships and establishes that in certain contexts, including doctor and patient, solicitor and client and parent and child, the courts will presume the existence of undue influence.[218] Class 2B relates to all the other relationships not covered by 2A including husband and wife and banker and customer, and here the complainant will have to bring evidence to show that there was a relationship of trust and confidence between themselves and the wrongdoer.

Importantly, these categories were revisited and redefined in the seminal case of *Royal Bank of Scotland v Etridge (No.2)*.[219] Here, Lord Nicholls criticised the classification of Class 2 presumed undue influence, arguing that there had been a misunderstanding in terms of the evidential presumption that it gave rise to.[220] He stressed that the presumption in Class 2 related only to the existence of influence *not* the existence of undue influence. In recasting the parameters of this second class, Lord Nicholls established a two-stage test. First, the claimant must establish that there was a relationship of trust and confidence between themselves and the wrongdoer- for those relationships falling within Class 2A this is irrefutably presumed- for all the other relationships falling within Class 2B this has to be proven. This will give rise to a presumption of influence.[221] Second, whether or not that influence was undue required the complainant to prove that the transaction was one that called for an explanation. Only if it did would the presumption of undue influence arise and the burden shift to the wrongdoer to prove that in fact no undue influence took place.

So, following *Etridge*, it is the combination of these two elements (a relationship of trust and confidence and a transaction that calls for explanation) that gives rise to the rebuttable presumption that undue influence has been exerted.

This second prerequisite is a modern reformulation of the previous requirement deriving from *National Westminster Bank Plc v Morgan*,[222] which required the claimant to prove that the transaction was to their 'manifest disadvantage.' In *Morgan* itself, this proved fatal to the wife's claim, with the court recognising that she had entered into the transaction in the hope that it would save the matrimonial home and therefore she would benefit from it. In revisiting this requirement in *Etridge*, Lord Nicholls recognised that the label had been 'causing difficulty' because it could be interpreted in

---

[218] See, for example, *Bullock v Lloyds Bank Ltd* [1955] Ch 137 which concerned a father and daughter; and *Allcard v Skinner* (1887) 36 Ch D. 145, which concerned a spiritual adviser and disciple.

[219] [2002] 2 AC 773.

[220] At [17]. See also Lord Clyde at [92], Lord Hobhouse at [98] and [105]–[107] and Lord Scott at [157] and [161].

[221] At [14] and [18].   [222] [1985] AC 686.

a number of ways.[223] First, if a narrow perspective was utilised it could be argued that whenever a wife offers her matrimonial home as security for her husband's business debts this would be to her manifest disadvantage as she risks losing her home. However, Lord Nicholls recognised that this gave an 'unrealistically blinkered view of such a transaction' and so the wider perspective would be to recognise that there are inherent reasons why such a transaction may benefit a wife. He argued that the financial interests of a husband and wife are often bound together and the husband's business may be the source of the family income meaning that the wife has an interest in supporting that business, which may well including charging the matrimonial home to secure a business related loan or overdraft.[224] In addressing the question of which approach would be best to adopt, Lord Nicholls held that 'The answer is neither' and the preferred approach would be to discard of a label which gives rise to such ambiguity and instead simply ask whether the transaction is one that calls for an explanation.[225] Accordingly, the phrase 'manifest disadvantage' is no longer the substantive test, although in practice it does still have evidential value as one of the factors to be taken into consideration when determining the question of whether the transaction is one that calls for an explanation.[226]

Box 2.4 At a glance: the categories of undue influence

Class 1: actual undue influence

The claimant will have to bring evidence to affirmatively prove both the **influence** and the fact that it was **undue**.

Class 2: presumed undue influence

Class 2A: Protected relationships: **influence** will be irrebuttably presumed because of the protected relationship; the question of whether it was **undue** will have to be **proved** by the claimant showing that the transaction is one that calls for an explanation. This gives rise to a presumption of **undue influence** at which point the burden will shift to the wrongdoer to show that the claimant entered into the transaction with full knowledge.

Class 2B: Other relationships: The claimant will have to **prove** they are in a relationship of trust and confidence and this will give rise to a presumption of **influence**; the question of whether it was **undue** will have to be **proved** by the claimant showing that the transaction is one that calls for an explanation. This gives rise to a presumption of **undue influence** at which point the burden will shift to the wrongdoer to show that the claimant entered into the transaction with full knowledge.

2.7.2 **Banks and undue influence**

Since the cases of *Bundy* and *Morgan* discussed in section 2.6.2, it has been relatively rare for a surety to seek to rely on this equitable doctrine to show that a bank *itself* has exerted undue influence over them in order to enforce a guarantee or other form of

---

[223] At [26].   [224] At [28].   [225] At [29].

[226] Edwin Mujih, 'Over ten years after Royal Bank of Scotland v Etridge (No.2): is the law on undue influence in guarantee cases any clearer?' (2013) *International Company and Commercial Law Review* 57.

security.[227] Accordingly, the type of cases in which banks become wound up in litigation are three-party cases where the enforcement of a charge by a bank is resisted on the ground that the claimant was unduly influenced into entering the transaction by a third party. Frequently, it is a wife claiming that her husband has unduly influenced her to sign her interest in the matrimonial home over to a bank or other creditor in order to secure a loan for the husband's business debts. What generally happens is the business fails and the bank seeks repossession of the property, but the wife resists the claim on the ground that her consent was vitiated as a result of the undue influence of the husband.

The circumstances in which a bank's interest will be affected by the undue influence of a third party was considered at length in *Barclays Bank Plc O'Brien*[228] and then reconsidered and reformulated in *Royal Bank of Scotland Plc v Etridge*.[229] In *O'Brien*, a wife signed a charge over her family home to secure a guarantee that her husband had given to the bank in respect of his company's debts. Various misrepresentations had been made by the husband regarding his finances to coerce the wife into signing this agreement with the bank and, when she attended the bank's premises to sign the relevant paperwork, she was not advised to seek independent legal advice and nor was she given the opportunity to read the documents or clarify that she understood the nature of the transaction. The House of Lords held that the husband had unduly influenced his wife and, because the bank had notice of this, she was entitled to have the transaction set aside.

Importantly, Lord Browne-Wilkinson in *O'Brien* set out the principles to determine when a bank will be put on notice (actual or constructive), and the steps that it has to take in order to avoid being fixed with that notice such that they cannot resist a claim that the transaction be set aside. In terms of *when* a bank will be put on notice he said:[230]

> a creditor is put on inquiry when a wife offers to stand surety for her husband's debts by the combination of two factors: (a) the transaction is on its face not to the financial advantage of the wife; and (b) there is a substantial risk in transactions of that kind that, in procuring the wife to act as surety, the husband has committed a legal or equitable wrong that entitles the wife to set aside the transaction.

Further, Lord Browne-Wilkinson established that a bank can avoid being fixed with notice if it takes 'reasonable steps to satisfy himself that the wife's agreement to stand surety has been properly obtained.'[231] He states that these 'reasonable steps' simply mean that the bank needs to 'take steps to bring home to the wife the risk she is running by standing as surety and to advise her to take independent advice.'[232] If the bank fails to do this, they will be fixed with notice and the wife will be able to avoid the transaction.

These principles were re-examined in the seminal case of *Royal Bank of Scotland v Etridge*.[233] Here, the House of Lords heard eight appeals in which the wife had agreed to a charge over her interest in the family home as security for her husband's personal or business debts. In all cases the husbands had defaulted on the loans and the banks

---

[227] For a case in which it was pleaded, but ultimately failed, see *National Wesminster Bank Plc v Waite* [2006] EWHC 1287.   [228] [1994] 1 AC 180.
[229] [2002] 2 AC 773.   [230] At 196.   [231] Ibid.   [232] Ibid.   [233] [2002] 2 AC 773.

were seeking repossession and in all cases the wives resisted on the basis that they only entered into transactions as a result of the undue influence of their husbands. The House of Lords here reiterated that a bank will be affected by the undue influence of a third party and therefore the contract will be set aside only where the bank has notice and it has failed to take the necessary steps to avoid being fixed with that notice. However, Lord Nicholls reformulated the principles from the earlier case of *O'Brien*.

First, he set out that the correct interpretation of Lord Browne-Wilkinson's two stage test to determine *when* a bank is put on notice is that, quite simply, 'a bank is put on inquiry whenever a wife offers to stand as surety for her husband's debts.'[234] Accordingly, post-*Etridge*, the circumstances in which a lender will be deemed to be put on notice is much more easily satisfied. There is no need to look at whether the transaction was disadvantageous to the wife or not, it is now simply the case that whenever a wife agrees to act as surety for her husband's debts, or in fact whenever the relationship between the surety and the debtor is non-commercial,[235] the bank will be deemed to be put on notice.

In terms of the steps a bank has to take in order to avoid being fixed with that notice, whereas Lord Browne-Wilkinson in *O'Brien* determined that a bank simply had to have a meeting with the wife to explain the risks of the transaction and urge her of to seek independent advice, Lord Nicholls in *Etridge* established a much more comprehensive step by step process that banks must now follow:

Box 2.5 Steps a bank must take to avoid being fixed with notice following *Etridge*

1. The bank must take steps to ascertain the name of the solicitor the wife wishes to act for them [79(1)]. Interestingly, Lord Browne-Wilkinson recognised that the solicitor acting for the wife may be the family solicitor, which could bring into question how independent the advice is when the solicitor is also acting for her husband [72]–[74].

2. The bank must provide the solicitor with all the financial information it needs for the purpose of advising the wife. Lord Browne-Wilkinson admitted that the information required to be sent will be fact dependent but as a general rule, banks will be required to send over all information regarding the purpose for which the proposed facility is being requested, the amount of the husband's indebtedness, the amount of the husband's overdraft facility, and the amount and terms of any new facility [79(2)].

3. In the exceptional case that a bank has reason to believe or suspects that the wife has been subject to undue influence by her husband, the bank must inform the solicitors of the facts that gave rise to that belief or suspicion [79(3)].

4. The bank must, in every case, obtain from the wife's solicitor a written confirmation that advice has been given to her and understood [79(4)].

5. The bank must communicate with the wife the reason that the bank requires written confirmation from her solicitor that she understands the practical implications of the transaction, that is, so that she cannot then later claim that her consent was vitiated when agreeing to enter into the transaction [79(1)].

---

[234] At [44].   [235] At [87].

In practice, the impact of the decision is that it shifts the responsibility for protecting vulnerable sureties away from the bank, towards the solicitor. Post-*Etridge*, as long as the bank follows the step by step process, as established by Lord Nicholls, they will have the assurance that their security will be enforced, thereby leaving wives with no option but to pursue their solicitor for redress. Academic reaction to the decision has been mixed. Muiji argues that 'Etridge was heralded as a victory for wives, seen as imposing an onerous burden on solicitors and accorded a warm reception by banks.'[236] While it is true that wives have been placed in a better position in terms of the information they receive from their solicitor, and there has been a clear decline in the number of cases since *Etridge* of wives asserting an undue influence claim in three-party contexts, it is difficult to imagine that wives are simply no longer being subject to undue influence. Indeed, Auchmuty argues that the decision in *Etridge* acts as 'the protector and defender of commerce itself against women trying to get mortgages set aside.'[237] Even in instances where solicitors do competently fulfil their role, there may be circumstances in which women still feel that they have no option but to consent to a charge being placed over their home.

Key takeaways

- Undue influence is an equitable doctrine that, if successfully claimed, will entitle the claimant to have the transaction in question set aside.

- There are two categories of undue influence, Actual (Class 1) and Presumed (Class 2), and each have differences in terms of what has to be proven by the claimant and what is presumed.

- While it is rare for a customer to assert that a bank itself has exercised undue influence over him, banks have frequently been involved in three party cases where the enforcement of a charge by a bank is resisted on the ground that the customer was unduly influenced into entering into the transaction by a third party.

- The case of *Etridge* is seminal for not only did Lord Nicholls reformulate the categories of undue influence, he also re-examined the law relating to three-party cases and the circumstances in which a bank will be put on notice, as well as the steps the bank will have to take to avoid being fixed with that notice.

Key bibliography

Articles

Auchmuty, R, 'Men Behaving Badly: An Analysis of English Undue Influence Cases' (2002) 11 *Social and Legal Studies* 257.

---

[236] Edwin Mujih, 'Over ten years after Royal Bank of Scotland v Etridge (No.2): is the law on undue influence in guarantee cases any clearer?' (2013) *International Company and Commercial Law Review* 57, 96–7.
[237] Rosemary Auchmuty, 'Men Behaving Badly: An Analysis of English Undue Influence Cases' (2002) 11 *Social and Legal Studies* 257, 277.

Enonchong, N, 'Presumed Undue Influence: Continuing Misconceptions' (2005) 121 *Law Quarterly Review* 29.

Mujih, E, 'Over Ten Years after Royal Bank of Scotland v Etridge (No.2): is the Law on Undue Influence in Guarantee Cases Any Clearer?' (2013) 2 *International Company and Commercial Law Review* 57.

Questions

1. 'Banking confidentiality is an important part of one's private life and as such warrants protection. It is lamentable that this fact has been diluted in recent years by the erosion of the common law duty of confidentiality.' Robert Stokes (2007). Discuss.

   Answer tips You should demonstrate your understanding of the rationale behind the duty of confidentiality as well as the decision of the courts in Tournier. *Most importantly you should engage with the wider literature in order to critically analyse the extent to which the four qualifications from* Tournier *undermine and erode the duty of confidentiality. In particular, you could explore the significant inroads to the duty posed by the various statutory duties that banks now have to disclose information, as well as the contentious issue of whether a bank should ever be entitled to disclose because it is in its personal interests to do so. You might also want to consider the other initiatives that serve to bolster the duty.*

2. 'In Lord Scarman's judgment [In *Tai Hing Cotton Mill Ltd v Liu Chong Hing Bank Ltd*], there is much disheartening news for the laws of banking' Ogilvie (1986). Discuss in relation to the customers duty of care in the banker–customer relationship.

   Answer tips You should evaluate the decision of the Privy Council in Tai Hing Cotton Mill *and critically engage with the issue of whether a customer should be subject to a wider duty to take care in the management of their accounts. You should consider arguments from both the bank and customer perspectives and ultimately, you should make a judgment call on whether you agree with the decision in* Tai Hing Cotton Mill.

3. The case of *Royal Bank of Scotland plc v Etridge (No 2)* is described by Andrew Burrows as, 'by far the most important case in English Law on undue influence. Its impact is on both the law of undue influence generally and the specific problems raised by undue influence in … three-party cases' (2009). Discuss.

   Answer tips This requires you to demonstrate your understanding of the impact that Etridge *has had on the application of both two and three-party cases of undue influence. You should analyse the pre-Etridge position from the likes of* Aboody *and* O'Brien *and engage with how Lord Nicholls re-evaluated the law in this area. You might want to consider in particular whether the court here struck a fair balance between the need for the bank to extend finance with confidence in the strength of its security and the need to protect vulnerable sureties by ensuring that they enter into security transactions with full and informed consent.*

3

Payment methods

3.1 Introduction

Payment methods refer to the mechanisms, procedures, and organisations that are used to enable parties to discharge their payment obligations. They sit at the heart of the economy, allowing money to continually flow between individuals and businesses. Payment methods enable individuals to, among other things, withdraw money from a cash machine, pay a deposit on a house, pay a mobile phone bill by *direct debit*, write a cheque to a charity, receive a monthly salary directly into a personal account, and send money using a mobile banking app. In 2016, these payment systems were used to process more than 22 billion transactions worth around £75 trillion.[1] From 1 April 2015, retail payment systems became subject to regulatory oversight by the new Payment Services Regulator (PSR), a subsidiary of the Financial Conduct Authority (FCA), created by the Financial Services (Banking Reform) Act 2013. The PSR is tasked with regulating a range of entities involved in the payment process, as discussed briefly in section 3.5.

While there are a vast range of different payment mechanisms, this chapter focuses on three of the most common methods, namely cheques, payment cards, and the electronic transfer of funds. The legal parameters of each of these payment methods is considered, as well as how they are regulated. The chapter closes by looking at recent innovations in the payment services industry relating to third-party providers.

3.2 Cheques

3.2.1 Introduction

The Bills of Exchange Act 1882 defines a *cheque* as a written order from an account holder instructing their bank to pay a specified sum of money to one or more named beneficiaries.[2] Accordingly, the primary function of a cheque is as a payment instruction from an account holder to his or her bank, requesting it to transfer funds held in their account to a third party. Traditionally, cheques were also transferable and negotiable

---

[1] See https://www.psr.org.uk/payment-systems/payment-systems-explained.
[2] Bills of Exchange Act 1882, ss73 and 3(1).

meaning that they could be passed from one holder (i.e. the person in possession of the cheque) to another. A bearer cheque[3] is transferred simply by delivery of the cheque by the holder to the new holder. An order cheque,[4] on the other hand, is transferred by being indorsed (i.e. signed) by the holder and delivered to the indorsee. However, by virtue of the Cheques Act 1992, it is now the practice of banks that cheques are 'crossed' and therefore not transferable or negotiable. On a crossed cheque the words 'account payee only' or 'a/c payee only' are written between two parallel vertical lines in the middle of the cheque. This means that the cheque is non-transferable and non-negotiable and therefore cannot be indorsed and paid into the account of anyone other than the named recipient.[5]

Box 3.1 Cheques: facts and figures

- In 2017 a total of 405 million cheques were used to make payment and acquire cash. This is a 15 per cent decline from 2016.

- In 2017, on average, 1.2 million cheques were cleared each day by the Cheque and Credit Clearing Company, with an average daily total value of around £1.4 billion. (cheque volumes peaked in 1990 at 11 million per day).

- The average value of a cheque cleared by the Cheque and Credit Clearing Company in 2017 was £1,217, up 5 per cent from £1,161 in 2016.

- In research undertaken in spring 2017: 87 per cent of charities said they had either made or received a payment by cheque in the past month; 53 per cent of charities said they receive donation income by cheque; 29 per cent of charities said they receive over half their donation income by cheque; 75 per cent of UK businesses said that they had either made or received a payment by cheque in the past month; 55 per cent of UK personal account holders said that they had either made or received a payment by cheque in the past year.

- It is forecast that by 2026, only 156 million cheques will be written.

The past three decades have seen a clear downward trend in the use of cheques as a payment method by both business and consumers.[6] Card payments and electronic fund

---

[3] A bearer cheque simply requires the sum to be paid to the holder of the cheque, that is, the person with possession of the cheque.

[4] An order cheque requires the sum to be paid to a specific person (the payee) or to their order, that is, to the person they indorse (sign) the cheque over to.

[5] This is confirmed in s81A Bills of Exchange Act 1882: 'Where a cheque is crossed and bears across its face the words "account payee" or "a/c payee", either with or without the word "only", the cheque shall not be transferable, but shall only be valid as between the parties thereto.'

[6] In fact, in 2009 the (then) Payments Council voted in favour of abolishing the use of cheques as a means of payment and set a target date of 31 October 2018 to close the central cheque clearing system. However, in July 2011, following lobbying from the charity sector and criticism from the Treasury Committee, the Payments Council took a U-turn, announcing that cheques will continue for as long as customers need them. The previous 2018 closure deadline was cancelled. See The Treasury Committee, *The Future of Cheques* (18 July 2011) at https://publications.parliament.uk/pa/cm201012/cmselect/cmtreasy/1147/114702.htm.

transfers are increasingly being used where previously a cheque may have been written. Despite this trend, cheques are still valued by those who use them, and they continue to provide a convenient and secure method of transferring funds, particularly where customers do not have the recipient's bank account details. Furthermore, the new cheque imaging system, discussed in section 3.2.3.2, has dramatically improved the clearing of cheques, providing a more efficient and timely system that utilises modern technology. Box 3.1 offers some key statistics on the use of cheques in 2017.[7]

3.2.2 Terminology and contractual relationships

The party that writes and signs the cheque is known as the ***drawer*** of the cheque.[8] They complete the cheque and then deliver it to the ***holder*** who is the intended recipient of the cheque—that is, the person who is identified on the cheque and in whose favour it is drawn.[9] The holder will present the cheque at his or her own bank, known as the ***collecting bank*** for payment; it is for the holder's bank to collect the amount on the cheque by presenting it to the ***paying bank***—that is, the bank at which the drawer holds an account.

There are therefore four contractual relationships that come into play when a cheque is used as a payment method, as demonstrated in Figure 3.1.

First, there is the relationship between the drawer of the cheque and the paying bank on which the cheque is drawn. This relationship will be governed by the banker–customer rules, as discussed in Chapter 2, which include the duty of a bank to honour its customers mandate (provided, among other things, that there are sufficient funds in the customer's account). By paying the amount of the cheque, the paying bank acts as the drawer's agent to discharge the payment obligation.[10] If the paying bank fails to act

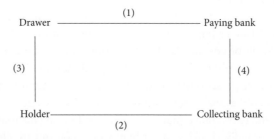

Figure 3.1 The contractual relationships created through use of a cheque

---

[7] See https://www.chequeandcredit.co.uk/information-hub/facts-and-figures and Payments UK, *UK Payment Markets—Summary* (2017) at https://www.ukfinance.org.uk/wp-content/uploads/2018/01/PUK-UK-Payments-Markets-2017-Summary-AW-Online.pdf.

[8] Sometimes the drawer is referred to as the payer.   [9] Sometimes the holder is referred to as the payee.

[10] The law of agency is an area of commercial law which concerns a person, known as an agent, that is authorised to act on behalf of another, known as the principal, to create legal relations with a third party.

in accordance with the mandate, it will be unable to debit the drawer's account, unless it can establish a defence.[11]

The second relationship is that between the holder of the cheque and the collecting bank. Since the holder will generally have an account at the collecting bank this relationship is also governed by the rules surrounding the bank and its customer. In collecting the amount of the cheque from the paying bank, the collecting bank acts as agent for the holder. The collecting bank is under a duty to take reasonable steps to obtain payment from the paying bank and if the paying bank refuses to honour the cheque, the collecting bank must notify the holder.

Third, there will often be an underlying contractual relationship between the drawer and the holder of the cheque, for example, where payment is being made to pay for goods and services. Finally, there is a relationship between the paying and collecting banks, which is governed not only by the common law, but also by banking practice in terms of clearance, as discussed in section 3.2.3.

3.2.3 **Clearing**

3.2.3.1 **The clearing process**

The process through which a cheque moves from the bank at which it is deposited (the collecting bank) to the bank at which it is drawn (the paying bank), and the movement of money in the opposite direction, is known as clearing. Before cheque imaging took over in late 2018, discussed in section 3.2.3.2, cheques, as paper items, have been physically transferred between banks, meaning that the cheque clearing process is non-instantaneous and takes several days.[12] The cheque clearing process is managed by the Cheque and Credit Clearing Company, a non-profit making industry body funded by its members. The process involves the physical exchange of items and the settlement of payments, as outlined in Box 3.2.

In November 2007, an industry-wide agreement, known as 2-4-6 (for current accounts) and 2-6-6 (for savings accounts), was introduced to set the maximum timescales for the clearing of customer's cheques.[13] Pursuant to the 2-4-6 commitments, customers must start earning interest on money paid into their account no later than two working days after presenting a cheque for payment. After four working days the money has to be made available for withdrawal, and by the end of six working days the customer has the reassurance that the cheque will not be dishonoured. The 2-6-6 commitments are broadly similar, except banks only commit to allowing customers to withdraw funds from the account from the sixth working day following the cheque being presented.

---

[11] Discussed in section 3.2.4 and in Chapter 2, section 2.4.2.

[12] Some information is, however, transferred electronically; see Box 3.2.

[13] For a useful video which explains this process, see https://www.chequeandcredit.co.uk/information-hub/history-cheque/original-2-4-6-video.

Box 3.2 The clearing process

- At the end of each working day, each branch of each collecting bank physically transports all the cheques paid in by customers to a central clearing exchange centre.

- The clearing exchange centre processes the cheques through its machines, which capture the value of the cheque and the code line containing the customer's account number, sort code, and the cheque serial number. That data is converted into encrypted digital files and transferred across a secure network (known as the Inter-Bank-Data-Exchange (IBDE)) to the relevant paying banks.

- Banks input their bilateral pay and charge figures onto a secure browser-based application, which then calculates the multilateral net figures that must be paid to or received from each bank. The Settlement Service Provider (SSP) is the Bank of England. Society for Worldwide Interbank Financial Tele-Communication (SWIFT) messaging is used to transmit the figures directly into a *real time gross settlement system* **(RTGS)** at the Bank of England for final settlement (this process is discussed in section 3.4.3.3).

- The cheques are then physically transferred using a courier service to the paying bank—that is, the bank on which the cheque is being drawn—so that they can determine if there are any irregularities.

These industry-wide timescales have provided a common set of expectations regarding the timeliness of the clearing process and they provide customers with the assurance that by the end of the sixth working day following presentation of the cheque the funds are theirs and they will be protected from loss even if the cheque subsequently bounces. These are maximum timescales and, in practice, banks can and often do compete by offering to accrue interest or allow funds to be drawn earlier than the two, four, or six working days.

3.2.3.2 Cheque imaging

In recognition of the need to improve the speed and efficiency of the cheque clearing process, in 2013, the Cheque & Credit Clearing Company began extensive research to find a method of clearing cheques that utilised modern technology. This research culminated in the introduction of an image-based method of clearing cheques, which was launched on 30 October 2017 on a phased-out basis.[14] Accordingly, by late 2018 the paper-based system becomes obsolete, and all cheques are processed by the image-based system. This new 'image clearing system' enables the images of cheques to be exchanged between banks, rather than having to physically transfer the paper-based

---

[14] This new system is given a statutory footing by Part 1, s13 Small Business, Enterprise and Employment Act 2015, which adds a new Part 4A into the Bills of Exchange Act 1882, eliminating the need for cheques to be physically transported and allowing for the presentment of instruments by electronic means.

cheque. Cheques are still written out by the drawer as before, but when they are presented by the holder to the collecting bank, the collecting bank will create an image of the cheque and transfer it electronically to the paying bank.

Interestingly, customers may be offered new ways of presenting a cheque for payment. If the collecting bank offers this service, personal or small business customers can image cheques they receive themselves using a secure imaging tool accessed via a mobile banking app and then upload the images for processing by the collecting bank. Businesses and charities can scan cheques to create images and then upload them for processing.

Cheques processed through this new system will clear much quicker than the previous paper-based system. When a customer presents a cheque for payment, they will be able to withdraw the funds by 23.59 the following working day. Again, this is a maximum timescale, so it may be the case that banks will allow customers to access their funds before this time.

The introduction of cheque imaging is a welcome and much needed change. The new system means that funds can be transferred in a more timely manner. Importantly, customers can still present cheques in the same way as before, via a branch, by post, or at an automated teller machine (ATM) but it also provides customers with new options for paying in cheques that are in line with modern technological developments.

3.2.4 **Paying bank's liability for wrongful payment**

As discussed in Chapter 2, section 2.4.2, one of the fundamental duties of a bank is to obey its customer's mandate. In this context, a paying bank must act in accordance with the customer's payment instructions, as embodied on the cheque. If the paying bank acts outside that mandate, for example, by wrongfully paying a cheque that was not in fact authorised by the customer, it will not be entitled to debit its customers account. There are, however, a series of common law defences, an equitable defence, and a series of statutory defences that may be available to a paying bank that has been accused of wrongfully paying over a cheque in excess of its mandate.

3.2.4.1 **Common law defences**

When a bank executes a payment instruction embodied on a cheque, it does so as agent for the account holder. Accordingly, the following common law defences that can be raised by an agent who disobeys his principal will be available to a paying bank who wrongfully pays a cheque.

Estoppel

As discussed in Chapter 2, section 2.5, a customer owes a duty to the bank not to draw cheques so as to facilitate fraud or forgery,[15] and a duty to inform the bank of any fraudulent activity as soon as it has actual notice of it.[16] If the customer fails to adhere to

---

[15] *London Joint Stock Bank Ltd v Macmillan* [1918] AC 777.   [16] *Greenwood v Martins Bank* [1933] AC 51.

either of these duties, he or she will be estopped from asserting that the bank has wrongfully debited his or her account.

Ratification

Where the paying bank, as agent, exceeds its authority in paying an unauthorised cheque for example, that act can be ratified (i.e. approved or adopted) by the customer as principal. Where a customer ratifies the actions of the paying bank, he or she is precluded from claiming that the paying bank had no right to debit the customer's account.

The context in which this issue normally arises is where the cheque is drawn and signed solely by a director as agent of a company who is authorised only to draw on the company's account jointly with the signature of other officers. In *London Intercontinental Trust Ltd v Barclays Bank*[17] the claimant company authorised the bank to honour cheques provided that they were signed by two officers. Two cheques totalling £195,000 were signed by the director of the company in favour of a stockbroker and honoured by the defendant bank. The stockbroker subsequently went into liquidation and when the board of directors (which embody the company as principal) met to discuss the issue, there was no suggestion that the money had been deposited without authority and no action was taken against the bank. The claimant company brought an action against the liquidator and also a claim, which was rejected, against the Stock Exchange Compensation Fund. Subsequently, the claimant company brought an action against the bank alleging that it had acted in breach of its mandate.

The court held in favour of the bank for a number of reasons. First, Slynn J held that the director had the actual authority[18] from the board to transfer the amounts on his own and the bank was therefore entitled to act on the director's instruction. The payment was therefore not invalidated by the fact that there was a mandate requiring two signatures. His Lordship observed that 'The bank, as a result of its failure to observe the discrepancy took a risk in honouring the cheque that the director was not authorised. In the case of both these cheques … he was so authorised.'[19] Secondly, Slynn J held that, on the facts, the transaction had been approved and therefore ratified at the board meeting. Finally, he held that in pursuing the claim against the Stock Exchange on the basis that the stockbroker had validly received the money, the claimant company could not then claim that the transaction was invalid.

This case demonstrates that ratification can be pleaded in two instances by a bank; first, where the principal expressly ratifies the unauthorised payment and, second, where the conduct of the principal indicates that he or she has adopted their agent's act. It is important to note that this defence is only available when it concerns the relationship between an agent and their principal. It will not apply where a cheque is signed by someone who has no authority. A forgery cannot be ratified.[20]

---

[17] [1980] 1 Lloyd's Rep. 241.

[18] Actual authority refers to specific powers, expressly conferred by a principal to an agent to act on the principal's behalf.

[19] At 249.   [20] See *Brook v Hook* [1870–1] L.R. 6 Ex. 89.

Customer's ambiguous instructions

A general principle of agency law is that an agent will not be liable for disobeying the principal's intended instruction if it was so ambiguous as to mislead a reasonable person.[21] In the banker–customer context the paying bank is entitled to debit the customer's account as long as it acts on what it honestly believes is the customer's intention. This principle will only apply if the ambiguity is not apparent—where there is a clear ambiguity the bank is entitled to dishonour.[22] In *Cunliffe Brook & Co v Blackburn and District Benefit Building Society*[23] it was held that a bank is only obliged to obey its customers instruction if they are clearly expressed on the cheque.[24]

3.2.4.2 Equitable defence

Where a payment is made in excess of the banks mandate but the customer benefits from it because it discharges a debt owed by the customer to a third party, it may be that the paying bank can raise an equitable defence based on subrogation against any claim that the customer's account was wrongfully debited.[25] This is known as the *Liggett* doctrine, taking its name from the case of *Liggett (Liverpool) Ltd v Barclays Bank Ltd.*[26] In this case the paying bank honoured a cheque drawn on the company's account even though it only had one signature, and the mandate required two. The cheque was made in favour of tradesmen for amounts due to them for the supply of goods to the company. Accordingly, the payment discharged the company's debt to the tradesmen. In addressing the question of whether the bank was entitled to debit the company's account, the court held that the legal position was that the bank had acted outside of its mandate and would therefore have to restore the customer's account. However, it was held that the bank had an equitable defence because the payment had conferred a benefit on the customer by discharging the company's debt to the tradesman. Wright J noted:[27]

> The equitable principle has been applied beyond question over and over again to cases where an agent not having the authority of his principal has borrowed money as on behalf of his principal. Under those circumstances at common law the principal cannot be sued and cannot be made to repay the amount so borrowed, but in equity it has been held that to the extent that the amount so borrowed has been applied in payment of the debts of the principal, the quasi lender is entitled to recover from the quasi borrower ... The ground is sometimes put in this way, that the lender or the quasi lender is subrogated to the rights of the creditor who has been paid off.'

---

[21] See Chapter 2, section 2.4.2.1; *London Joint Stock Bank Ltd v Macmillan* [1918] AC 777 per Lord Haldane, 'the banker as a mandatory has a right to insist on having his mandate in a form which does not leave room for misgiving as to what he is called on to do.'

[22] In practice, this might be where the handwriting is illegible or where there is a difference between the words and figures on the cheque. See *European Asian Bank AG v Punjab and Sind Bank (No.2)* [1983] 1 WLR 642.

[23] (1844) 9 App. Cas. 857.

[24] Per Lord Blackburn at 864, banks are only 'bound to pay cheques properly drawn.'

[25] Subrogation is a term describing the legal right of someone to assume the legal rights of another. Here it means that the bank can step into the shoes of the customer's creditor and recover the sum from the customer.

[26] [1928] 1 KB 48.   [27] At 60.

Accordingly, the bank, which has paid off the debt of the customer, is entitled to recover those sums from the customer by debiting their account even though, at law, the bank has no right to do this. In essence, the bank is taking over, that is, being subrogated to, the creditors remedies against the customer. In the same way the creditor would be able to recover the sums from the customer, the bank is able to do so.

However, the subsequent case of *Crantrave v Lloyds Bank plc*[28] revisited the circumstances in which Liggett might be applied and took a more restrictive view. The bank in this case transferred funds being held in its corporate customer's account upon the service of an interim third-party debt order.[29] Before the interim order was made final by the court, the corporate customer was wound up. The liquidators subsequently claimed that that the bank had wrongfully and without authority debited the company's account and it was therefore entitled to repayment of the sums paid out to the judgment creditors. In response, the bank contended that the company suffered no loss since the payment partially discharged an existing debt. The Court of Appeal found in favour of the liquidator, ordering the bank to repay the sum debited and suggesting that the bank pursue an action against the recipient on the basis of payment by mistake of fact. Pill LJ argued that 'in the absence of authorisation or ratification by the company of the bank's payment to the third party, the "mere fact" that the bank's payment enured to the benefit of the company does not establish an equity in favour of the bank against the company.'[30] Moreover, he stated that 'in order to establish the equity, the bank would have to show that the payment discharged (at least partially) a legal liability of the customer.'[31] On the facts it was held that the bank had not established that the company's liability to the creditor had been discharged: the bank had simply made a mistake.

It is difficult to see why the debt was discharged in *Liggett*, but not in *Crantrave*. One possible explanation is the fact that in *Liggett*, although the cheque bore only one of the two necessary signatures, the signing director did have authority to deal with the company's trade debts. Conversely in *Crantrave*, the bank acted in mistake on an interim court order and there was no question of the implied authority being given by the customer.

3.2.4.3 Statutory defences

The statutory defences available to a paying bank mainly arise in the context of liability resulting from the forged indorsement of a cheque. The rationale for these defences is that a bank is not ordinarily in a position to know whether or not an indorsement on a cheque was made by the original holder or a subsequent third-party indorsee. In the absence of

---

[28]   [2000] 3 WLR 877.

[29]   A third-party debt order is issued pursuant to Part 72 of the Civil Procedure Rules 1998, which allows the court to grant to a judgment creditor of the customer, an order which attaches to funds held by a third party (i.e. a bank). What happens in practice is that the judgment creditor will apply to the court to attach the order to funds held by the bank in its customer's account. The court will first grant an interim order meaning that the bank must refuse to honour any payments that would reduce the customer's balance to an amount below that specified in the order. Following a final hearing, a final third-party debt order can be granted, meaning that the bank will have to pay over the amount specified in the order to the judgment creditor.

[30]   At 923.   [31]   Ibid.

these statutory provisions, which apply only to forged indorsements, not to forgeries or material alterations on the original cheque, the paying bank would be strictly liable. The effect of the provisions, if they apply, is that the bank will have a defence against a claim brought against it by the customer for wrongfully debiting his or her account, and also against any potential action by a third party. As already mentioned, given that banks in the UK have chosen to take advantage of the provisions in the Cheques Act 1992, which enables them to pre-print cheque books with the words 'account payee only' or 'a/c payee only', in practice, cheques are no longer transferable and so the statutory provisions are inapplicable. As such they will only be outlined in brief here.

Payment in due course

Section 59 of the Bills of Exchange Act 1882 provides that a bill is discharged by payment in due course by or on behalf of the drawee bank. 'Payment in due course' is defined as 'payment made at or after of the bill to the holder thereof in good faith and without notice that his title to the bill is defective.' In these circumstances payment of the cheque is discharged, and the customer of the bank cannot claim that his or her account should not have been debited.

Payment in the ordinary course of business

Section 60 of the Bills of Exchange Act 1882 provides that where a bank, in good faith and in the ordinary course of business, pays a cheque on which an indorsement is later found to be forged or not authorised, the payment will be treatment as having been made in due course. This means that, where s60 applies, the bank is not obliged to make a second payment to the true owner of the cheque.

Payment without negligence

Section 80 of the Bills of Exchange Act 1882 provides that where a bank, in good faith and without negligence, pays a crossed cheque in accordance with the instructions of the crossing, then the paying bank is placed in the same position as it would have been had payment of the cheque been made to the true owner. This is a complementary defence to s60 of the Bills of Exchange Act, which applies specifically to crossed cheques, where the phrase 'in the ordinary course of business' is replaced with the phrase 'without negligence'.

Irregularity in or absence of indorsement

Section 1 of the Cheques Act 1957 provides that where a bank, in good faith and in the ordinary course of business, pays a cheque that has not been indorsed or is irregularly indorsed,[32] it does not, in doing so, incur any liability by reason only of the absence of, or irregularity in, the indorsement, and is deemed to have paid in due course.

---

[32] An indorsement is irregular when it differs materially from the description of the person indorsing it. For example, if a company indorses a cheque and omits the word 'Ltd' it will be irregular. See *Arab Bank Ltd v Ross* [1852] 2 QB 216.

3.2.5 Collecting bank's liability for wrongful payment

3.2.5.1 Action in conversion

If a collecting bank collects a cheque and deals with the proceeds of the cheque on behalf of its customer, but the customer's title to that cheque is defective, the collecting bank could face an action against the true owner of the cheque who has an interest in those proceeds. This was explained by Rix J in *Honourable Society of Middle Temple v Lloyds Bank and Sekerbank*:[33]

> It seems to me that there is an important distinction to be made between the case where the agent is in breach of some duty vis-à-vis the party which requests him to act, and the case where the agent is in breach of some duty to a third party.

In this context, the customer of the bank may him or herself be at fault and liable to the third-party true owner, but that third party is more likely to target the collecting bank, who will have greater resources and will therefore be more likely to satisfy the judgment. The action a collecting bank could face, which does not require that the bank retain the proceeds of the cheque, is an action in **conversion**. Conversion is a tortious action that occurs when one person interferes with the property rights of another. Interestingly, an action in conversion cannot be brought in relation to the misappropriation of money. Accordingly, the common law developed a cause of action relating to the conversion of the cheque itself where the amount of damages awarded is based on the face value of the cheque.[34] Liability for conversion is strict, meaning that the absence of any knowledge of wrongdoing by the collecting bank or the absence of any negligence on the part of the collecting bank will be no defence. As expressed by Diplock LJ in *Marfani & Co Ltd v Midland Bank Ltd*:[35]

> At common law, one's duty to one's neighbour who is the owner, or entitled to possession, of any goods is to refrain from doing any voluntary act in relation to his goods which is a usurpation of his proprietary or possessory rights in them ... it matters not that the doer of the act of usurpation did not know, and could not by the exercise of any reasonable care have known, of his neighbour's interest in the goods. The duty is absolute; he acts at his peril. A banker's business, of its very nature, exposes him daily to this peril. His contract with his customer requires him to accept possession of cheques delivered to him by his customer, to present them for payment to the banks upon which the cheques are drawn, to receive payment of them, and to credit the amount thereof to his own customer's account, either upon receipt of the cheques themselves from the customer or upon receipt of actual payment of the cheques from the banks upon which they are drawn. If the customer is not entitled to the cheque which he delivers to his banker for collection, the banker, however innocent and careful he might have been, would at common law be liable to the true owner of the cheque for the amount of which he receives payment ... as damages for conversion.

---

[33] [1999] CLC 664, 700.

[34] See *OBG v Ltd v Allan* [2008] AC 1, where the House of Lords confirmed that the availability of an action in conversion in the context of a cheque is a 'legal fiction' where the document recording the debt or obligation is treated as having the same value as the debt or obligation.   [35] [1968] 1 WLR 956, 970–1.

3.2.5.2 Defence under Section 4 Cheques Act 1957

If the customer of a collecting bank deposits a cheque regarding which he or she has no title, the common law position, based on conversion, is that the collecting bank will be liable to the true owner of the cheque for damages regardless of its innocence. In recognition of the harsh effect of the common law, s4 of the Cheques Act 1957 was passed to provide the collecting bank with a defence that enables it to avoid liability provided it has acted in good faith and without negligence. Section 4 provides:

> (1) Where a banker, in good faith and without negligence, (a) receives payment for a customer of an instrument to which this section applies; or (b) having credited a customer's account with the amount of such an instrument, receives payment thereof for himself; (2) and the customer has no title, or a defective title, to the instrument, the banker does not incur any liability to the true owner of the instrument by reason only of having received payment thereof.

This can only be relied on as a defence to an action being brought in conversion where the cheque is a valid payment order; a cheque that bears a forged signature, and is therefore wholly inoperative, will not be a cheque for the purposes of s4 and neither will a cheque that has been materially altered.

In order to benefit from the protection of s4 the collecting bank must show that it received the payment 'in good faith and without negligence'. Section 90 of the Bills of Exchange Act 1882, which is applied to the construction of the Cheques Act 1957 by s6(1) of the 1957 Act, provides that 'A thing is deemed to be done in good faith … where it is in fact done honestly, whether it is done negligently or not.' While this is relatively straightforward,[36] it is the requirement that the bank acts without negligence that has given rise to extensive litigation. The discussion that follows will look at the general standard of negligence and then some specific examples of negligence.

General standard of negligence

Section 4 essentially imposes a statutory duty of care on the part of the collecting bank, enabling it to avoid the liability it would otherwise face under the common law. In interpreting this statutory duty of care the courts have formulated general tests to determine whether, objectively speaking, the collecting bank (and its officers) have discharged the required standard of care. Fundamentally, this standard of care is based on what is considered expedient in terms of general banking practice.

In *Marfani & Co ltd v Midland Bank Ltd*[37] Diplock LJ argued that:[38]

> the usual matter with respect to which the banker must take reasonable care is to satisfy himself that his own customer's title to the cheque delivered to him for collection is not defective, i.e., that no other person is the true owner of it. Where the customer is in possession of the cheque

---

[36] In fact there has only been one reported case where the bank's good faith was questioned, and the bank was successful; the bank must simply deny actual knowledge or any suspicion in the defective title of the cheque: *Lawrie v Commonwealth Trading Bank of Australia* [1970] Qd. R. 373.

[37] [1968] 1 WLR 956.   [38] At 972.

at the time of delivery for collection and appears upon the face of it to be the 'holder,' i.e., the payee or indorsee or the bearer, the banker is, in my view, entitled to assume that the customer is the owner of the cheque unless there are facts which are, or ought to be, known to him which would cause a reasonable banker to suspect that the customer was not the true owner. What facts ought to be known to the banker, i.e., what inquiries he should make, and what facts are sufficient to cause him reasonably to suspect that the customer is not the true owner, must depend upon current banking practice, and change as that practice changes. Cases decided 30 years ago, when the use by the general public of banking facilities was much less widespread, may not be a reliable guide to what the duty of a careful banker in relation to inquiries, and as to facts which should give rise to suspicion, is today.

Diplock LJ concluded by formulating a simple question that the court must ask itself, namely, 'were those circumstances such as would cause a reasonable banker possessed of such information about his customer as a reasonable banker would possess, to suspect that his customer was not the true owner of the cheque?'[39]

Similarly, in *Architects of Wine Ltd v Barclays Bank*,[40] Rix LJ explained that every inquiry is fact sensitive, and current banking practice is highly relevant to the issue of negligence. He argued that the relevant test of negligence is 'Notice of what is so out of the ordinary course of events as to arouse doubts in a banker's mind or put him on enquiry.'[41]

It is for the collecting bank to show that they have acted without negligence, which makes sense in light of the fact that s4 affords the bank with protection against strict liability. This was emphasised in *Marfani & Co ltd v Midland Bank Ltd*[42] where Diplock LJ highlighted that:

The only respect in which this substituted statutory duty differs from a common law cause of action in negligence is that, since it takes the form of a qualified immunity from a strict liability at common law, the onus of showing that he did take such reasonable care lies upon the defendant banker.[43]

There are some well-defined circumstances in respect of which a bank can be found to be negligent and these relate to the carelessness of the bank at the time the account was opened, and their carelessness more directly in relation to the cheque that is presented for payment. Both will now be discussed further.

Negligence in opening an account

A bank may lose the protection of s4 of the Cheques Act 1957 if it was negligent in opening the customer's account, particularly where that account was specifically opened to facilitate the fraud. Under money laundering regulations[44] and the FCA

---

[39] At 973.   [40] [2007] 2 Lloyd's Rep. 471.   [41] At paragraph 12.
[42] [1968] 1 WLR 956.   [43] At 972.
[44] See Part 3 (Regulation 27–45) Money Laundering, Terrorist Financing and Transfer of Funds (Information on the Payer) Regulations 2017 SI 2017/692 which implement the Fourth Money Laundering Directive EU 2015/849.

rules,[45] banks must satisfy certain 'customer due diligence' measures. Accordingly, before a bank 'establishes a business relationship'[46] with a customer such as opening an account, the bank is required to identify and verify the customer 'on the basis of documents or information in either case obtained from a reliable source which is independent of the person whose identity is being verified'[47] and assess, and where appropriate obtain information on, the purpose and intended nature of the business relationship.[48] Further, where the customer is a corporate entity, the bank must obtain and verify the name of the company, its company number or other registration number, and the address of its registered office.[49] These rules and regulations provide the standards against which the reasonableness of the banks actions will be measured.

Negligence in the collection of the cheque

Litigation has arisen frequently in relation to the situation where an employee or agent presents for payment into their personal account cheques that originally named their employer or principal as the payee, or cheques that have been drawn on the employer's or principal's account. Before discussing each type of case in turn, it should be noted that the general principle in relation to these scenarios is that whenever a bank is aware that an employer or principal has some interest in the cheque presented by an employer or agent, the bank is put on inquiry.[50]

Cheques owned by employer or principal

Here, the employee or agent pays, to the credit of their own personal account, a cheque that was originally payable to his employer or principal. This generally involves a forged indorsement (meaning that it is no longer applicable in practice, as already discussed), but the case of *Bute (Marquess) v Barclays Bank*[51] demonstrates how else this situation can arise. Here, McGaw was appointed as the manager of three farms in Scotland belonging to the claimant. Part of his duties involved applying to the Department of Agriculture for Scotland for hill sheep subsidies in respect of the farms. After leaving the claimant's employment, McGaw received three payment warrants marked in favour of 'Mr D. McGaw, Kerrylamont, Rothesay, Bute £133 10s in respect of Hill Sheep

---

[45] See FCA Handbook, SYSC 6.3, at https://www.handbook.fca.org.uk/handbook/SYSC/6.pdf. This area is discussed in Chapter 14.
[46] Money Laundering, Terrorist Financing and Transfer of Funds (Information on the Payer) Regulations 2017 SI 2017/692, Regulation 27(1).   [47] Ibid Regulation 28(18)(a).
[48] Ibid Regulation 28(2).   [49] Ibid Regulation 28(3).
[50] See, for example, *Lloyds Bank Ltd v Savory & Co* [1933] AC 201 per Buckmaster at 212:

> There is also a rule, not reduced into writing but said to be a well known banking understanding, familiar to cashiers from their ordinary experience, the effect of which is stated in the evidence, in terms accepted by the appellants, as follows: 'Banks do not take payments in, without inquiry, of cheques drawn by a firm in favour of a third party, and paid in by a person, other than the payee, who is known or ought to be known to be an employee of the drawing firm.'

[51] [1955] 1 QB 202.

Subsidy, 1949 for the Marquess of Bute.' McGaw subsequently opened an account with the defendant bank, who collected the warrants and credited his account with the proceeds. In an action in conversion against the bank, the court held that the defendant had been negligent because the instructions clearly indicated that he was to receive the money as an agent for the farm here, not in a personal capacity. McNair J concluded that the warrants:[52]

> Bore the clear indication at the lowest that McGaw was to receive the money as agent or in a fiduciary capacity, and it is elementary banking practice that such documents should not be credited to a personal account of the named payee without inquiry.

Cheques drawn on employer or principal

Here, the employee or agent abuses their authority to draw cheques on their employer's or principal's accounts or they forge or materially alter a cheque that was drawn by the employer or principal in favour of a third party so that it can be paid into their personal account. In *Lloyds Bank Ltd v E.B. Savory & Co*[53] a number of bearer cheques, which were drawn by the employer company in favour of creditors, were misappropriated by the company's clerk and paid into his own account. The creditors brought an action against the bank in conversion. On the question of whether the bank should have been put on inquiry Wright J said that:[54]

> The most obvious circumstances which should put the banker on his guard (apart from manifest irregularities in the indorsement and such like) are where a cheque is presented for collection which bears on its face a warning that the customer may have misappropriated it, as for instance where a customer known to be a servant or agent pays in for collection a cheque drawn by third parties in favour of his employer or principal. Such a case carries even a clearer warning if the cheque is indorsed per pro. the employer or principal by the servant or agent.

Accordingly, the defendant bank was held to be negligent in not inquiring about the payee's title to the cheque.

Another case that demonstrates the principles in this context is *Lloyds Bank Ltd v Charted Bank of India, Australia and China.*[55] Here, the chief accountant of the claimant bank had express authority to draw cheques on an account that the claimants had with another bank. In abusing this authority, the accountant drew cheques on this account and forwarded them for collection to the defendant bank with written instructions to place the cheques to the credit of his account with them. It was held that the defendant bank was liable in conversion and could not rely on s1 of the Cheques Act 1957 because they had been negligent in collecting the cheques without inquiry. In reaching this conclusion, Sankey LJ emphasised the fact that the defendants knew the accountant was an employee of the claimants and that he was transferring large sums of money from the claimant's bank, which should have put them on inquiry.[56]

---

[52] At 214.   [53] [1933] AC 201.   [54] At 229.   [55] [1929] 1 KB 40.   [56] At 72–4.

> **⮕ Key takeaways**
>
> - The core function of a cheque is as a payment instruction from an account holder to his bank, requesting it to transfer funds held in their account to a third party. Traditionally, cheques were also transferable and negotiable meaning that title to the instrument could be passed from one holder to another. Given the widespread practice of crossing cheques, the latter function is no longer utilised in practice.
> - While there is a clear downward trend in the use of cheques, they remain important as a payment method, particularly in light of the new cheque imaging clearing system that was introduced in 2017.
> - A paying bank may face liability for the wrongful payment of a cheque in excess of its mandate unless it can successfully raise one of the common law defences, the equitable defence, or one of the statutory defences.
> - A collecting bank may face liability in the tort of conversion against the true holder of a cheque unless it can successfully raise the defence under s4 of the Cheques Act 1957.

Key bibliography

Reports

The Treasury Committee, *The Future of Cheques* (18 July 2011) at https://publications.parliament.uk/pa/cm201012/cmselect/cmtreasy/1147/114702.htm

Websites

Cheque and Credit Clearing Company: https://www.chequeandcredit.co.uk/
UK Finance: https://www.ukfinance.org.uk/

3.3 Payment cards

3.3.1 Introduction

Payment cards—small pieces of plastic that are used in financial transactions—have revolutionised the way that we pay for goods or services. The oldest form of payment card is the store card, which was distributed by department stores to enable clients to purchase goods.[57] Here, the card was used to charge the client's account with the issuer

---

[57] In fact, the first 'store card' existed as a credit voucher, produced in 1880 in the UK by the Provident Clothing Group; customers were issued with vouchers that they could spend in a variety of shops from an approved list and a Provident Clothing rep would then call at the customer's home at a late date to collect payment. See http://www.theukcardsassociation.org.uk/history_of_cards/index.asp.

and the customer would settle the bill at a later date. Although these traditional store cards were limited in terms of where they could be used, modern plastic cards are now used practically everywhere for a variety of banking transactions.

There are five different types of plastic card, although commonly a single card will serve multiple functions: credit cards, charge cards, debit cards, ATM or cash cards, and, most recently, digital cash cards. A sixth type of plastic card, known as a cheque guarantee card, provided a guarantee to the retailer that the issuing bank would honour the cheque drawn by the customer up to the amount specified on the card whatever the state of his account at that time.[58] Given the recent decline in the use of cheques, in December 2009 the UK Payments Council announced that cheques would be phased out by October 2018. While the Council ultimately reversed this decision, arguing that cheques still had an important role to play as a payment method,[59] the UK Cheque Guarantee Card Scheme was closed at the end of June 2011.[60] Box 3.3 provides some interesting facts and figures on card usage in the UK.[61]

While the use of cheques as a payment method continues to fall, in 2016 it was reported that, for the first time, debit card payments have overtaken cash.[62] Credit cards remain important for purchasing goods at a distance and where cash is required for

---

Box 3.3 Plastic cards: UK facts and figures

- On June 29 1966 Barclaycard launched the first credit card in the UK.

- At the end of 2016 there were 99.6 million debit cards and 64 million credit and charge cards in circulation.

- The total number of plastic card purchases in 2016 was 14.8 billion. This is a 10.6 per cent growth from 2015.

- Spending on plastic cards in 2016 amounted to £647.2 billion. This is a 4.3 per cent growth from 2015.

- As of April 2017, there were a total of 108.4 million contactless cards in circulation.

- There were 2.9 billion contactless payments made in the UK during 2016.

- Debit card payment volumes are forecast to increase more than any other payment method, growing by 57 per cent to 18.2 billion payments in 2026.

- Credit card payment volumes are expected to reach 3.7 billion payments in 2026.

---

[58] The use of the cheque guarantee card gave the payee a direct contractual right against the bank for the amount in the transaction. See Millet J in *Re Charge Card Services* [1987] Ch 150.

[59] See https://www.gov.uk/government/news/frequently-asked-questions-on-the-closure-of-the-cheque-system.

[60] See http://www.consumercouncil.org.uk/news/payments-council-announces-the-end-of-the-cheque-guarantee-scheme/.

[61] See http://www.theukcardsassociation.org.uk/contactless_contactless_statistics/; www.theukcardsassociation.org.uk/wm_documents/Quarterly%20Market%20Trends%20Q1%202017.pdf.

[62] See British Retail Consortium (BRC), *Payments Survey* (2016) at https://brc.org.uk/media/179489/payment-survey-2016_final.pdf.

Box 3.4 Payment card fraud statistics

- Fraud losses on UK issued cards totalled £618 million in the UK in 2016.

- 2016 saw the fifth consecutive year of increase in fraud losses which surpassed the previous peak of £609.9 million in 2008.

- In real terms, however, overall card fraud losses as a proportion of the amount being spent has fallen from 8.4p per £100 spent in 2015 to 8.3p per £100 in 2016 (in 2008 it was 12.4p for every £100 spent). This shows that although the value of payment card fraud is increasing, it is doing so at a much lower proportional rate than in 2008.

- Seventy per cent of card fraud is attributed to card details being obtained fraudulently through methods, such as unsolicited emails or telephone calls, or digital attacks, such as malware and data hacks, where the card details are then used to undertake fraudulent purchases over the internet, phone, or by mail order.

---

purchases, ATM cards, which are often combined with debit cards, provide the means to do so. One of the biggest problems posed by the use of these plastic cards is fraud, as demonstrated by the statistics in Box 3.4.[63]

A number of steps have been taken to improve the security of payment card transactions in recent years in order to reduce these figures. Most prominently, we have seen a move away from the use of a signature to authenticate a transaction, in favour of a smart chip, which has allowed for authentication by a secret four-digit personal identification number (PIN). The addition of security numbers printed on the back of the card on the signature strip was also introduced as a further security measure. This was designed to reduce fraud by requiring the user to have the card physically present with them when, for example, purchasing goods online.

As the use of plastic cards has proliferated, so have the rules and regulations that govern their use. Card issuers will have to comply with the relevant terms of the Consumer Rights Act 2015 (for consumers) and the Unfair Contract Terms Act 1977 (for businesses). They must also abide by the Standards of Lending Practice, which set out standards of good practice in relation to credit cards,[64] and the relevant aspects on the FCA's *Consumer Credit Sourcebook* (CONC).[65] The main sources of statutory regulation, which overlap in some respects, are the Consumer Credit Act 1974 and PSR 2017. The following sections will analyse the different card types and the contractual relationships they involve before focusing in detail on the regulations that govern their usage.

---

[63] See Financial Fraud Action UK, *Fraud: The Facts 2017. The Definitive Overview of Payment Industry Fraud* (2017) At https://www.financialfraudaction.org.uk/fraudfacts17/.

[64] The standards for personal customers were published in July 2016, at https://www.lendingstandardsboard.org.uk/wp-content/uploads/2016/07/Standards-of-Lending-Practice-July-16.pdf. The standards for business customers were published in March 2017, at https://www.lendingstandardsboard.org.uk/wp-content/uploads/2017/03/standards-of-lending-practice-business.pdf.

[65] At https://www.handbook.fca.org.uk/handbook/CONC.pdf.

3.3.2 **Credit cards**

With a credit card transaction, when the cardholder presents his or her card for payment, the card issuer will make payment to the merchant and then obtain reimbursement from the cardholder of the amounts spent on a periodical basis. Generally, the customer will have the option to either repay the balance in full every month, or pay at least a minimum monthly amount. In contrast, with a debit card transaction, discussed in section 3.3.4, when the cardholder presents his or her card for payment, the cardholder's account with the card issuer is debited at the time the transaction takes place.

Credit card transactions, and the contractual relationships that they give rise to, are summarised by Gloster J in *OFT v Lloyds TSB*:[66]

> Credit card issuers operate under the Visa, Mastercard and American Express international network schemes, of which they are members. This membership permits them to print the respective trademarks 'Visa', 'MasterCard' and 'American Express' on their cards issued to cardholders under their credit agreements. The networks have comprehensive rules governing the operation of the respective schemes. In particular the rules provide that suppliers are recruited only by a limited number of members of the networks, who are given the status of 'merchant acquirers'. A supplier enters into a contract with a merchant acquirer, which contract obliges the supplier to accept all cards bearing a trademark of the relevant network as payment for goods or services supplied by them to such cardholders. In return, the merchant acquirer agrees to pay the supplier for any such transaction, less a discount. The merchant acquirer recoups his payment to the supplier from the card issuer through a settlement system organised by the network, together with a fee representing a proportion of the discount. The card issuer in turn is paid the supply price in full by the card holder pursuant to the credit card agreement. A credit card transaction of this nature is referred to in the industry as a 'four-party transaction' with debtor, creditor, merchant acquirer and supplier involved. It is contrasted to the 'three-party transaction' where the card issuer also 'acquires' the merchant.

Figure 3.2 depicts the credit card payment cycle in a four-party context.

In summary, the cardholder presents their card at the point of sale and enters their PIN. The card details are then sent to the merchant acquirer who processes the transaction and forwards it on to the relevant card issuer for authorisation and settlement via the relevant card scheme. A card scheme is an organisation that manages and controls the operation and clearing of card payment transactions according to its rules. The card scheme passes the card transaction details from the acquirer to the card issuer and they pass payment back to the acquirer who in turn pays the merchant. In the UK the card schemes that operate are American Express, Diners Club, JCB, Maestro, UnionPay International, Mastercard, and Visa.

In these four-party cases the suppliers are recruited by 'merchant acquirers' who pay the supplier (minus a fee) and then seek reimbursement from the card issuer (minus a fee). Visa and Mastercard operate on a four-party basis. Credit card transactions can also be three-party in nature. The card issuer will enter into a 'merchant agreement'

---

[66] [2004] EWHC 2600 (Comm) at 271.

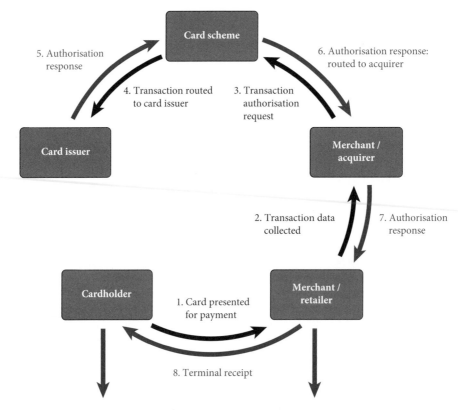

Figure 3.2 Credit card payment cycle[67]

directly with the supplier who undertakes to accept the issuer's cards as payment. American Express operates on a three-party basis.

The following discussion will describe the contractual relationships that arise between the parties in more detail.

3.3.2.1 Cardholder and supplier

This is the underlying contract of sale between the supplier and the cardholder. This contract will be governed by normal principles of contract law as set out in the Consumer Rights Act 2015 (for consumer contracts) and the Sale of Goods Act 1979 and the Supply of Goods and Services Act 1982 (for business contracts). The legal implications of using a credit card are that once the card is presented and payment is made, the cardholder is absolutely discharged from their payment obligation. This point was stressed by Millet J in *Re Charge Card Services*[68] where it was held that payment by credit card was *not* a conditional payment and the cardholder would not become liable to fulfil

---

[67] From the UK Cards Association at http://www.theukcardsassociation.org.uk/getting_started/card-payment-cycle.asp#content_1232.   [68] [1987] Ch 150.

the payment obligation directly to the supplier in the event that the card issuer did not make payment. He summarised: [69]

> The card-issuing company is liable to pay the supplier very shortly after the receipt of the sales vouchers and claim form, but is entitled to deduct its commission; while the customer is liable to pay the full face value of the voucher, but is entitled to much longer credit. If the customer is liable to pay the supplier on the failure or default of the card-issuing company, it is on terms more onerous than either, for he must be liable to make immediate payment of the full face value of the voucher. It is difficult to find any justification for imputing to the customer an intention to undertake any such liability.

3.3.2.2 Cardholder and card issuer

Under this contract the card issuer undertakes to make immediate payment to the supplier (minus any commission) for purchases made by the cardholder within a specified credit limit and in return the cardholder undertakes to make periodical payments to the issuer upon the presentation to the cardholder of monthly statements in the prescribed manner, which may include the payment of interest charges. This contract will be governed by the standard terms of the issuer as well as the relevant pieces of legislation, which are discussed in section 3.3.7.

3.3.2.3 Supplier and card issuer/merchant acquirer

The third contract is between the supplier and the card issuer if it is a three-party transaction, or between the supplier and the merchant acquirer if it is a four-party transaction. Either way the relationship between the two parties will be governed by a 'master agreement' that sets out the standard terms and conditions agreed between the two parties relating to things such as payment card acceptance, authorisation, and settlement. It also sets out the fees and charges that the supplier will pay and any floor limits or transaction limits that might apply.

3.3.2.4 Card issuer and merchant acquirer

Under this contract the merchant acquirer will recoup their payment to the supplier from the card issuer through a settlement system organised by the network, together with a fee.

3.3.3 Charge cards

Charge cards are similar to credit cards in the sense that they both operate on a line of unsecured credit that has been extended by the card issuer. However, unlike credit cards, cash withdrawals are not available with charge cards and the cardholder is required to settle their account in full upon receipt of their periodic statement. Accordingly, a charge cardholder cannot roll their balance over from month to month like a credit cardholder can.

---

[69] At 169.

3.3.4 **Debit cards**

Debit cards can be used by a cardholder to purchase goods or services. At the point of sale, the debit card electronically transfers funds directly from the cardholder's account to the merchant's account. This can either be done when the cardholder is present, and he or she enters their four-digit pin or, in the case of distance purchases such as those made online, by the cardholder entering his or her card number and other security details. These debit card transactions are processed through a system known as Electronic Funds Transfer at Point of Sale (EFT-POS). When the cardholder presents his or her card at the payment terminal the information encoded on it is sent to a central processing point where the validity of the card is authenticated. The transaction is then authorised by the cardholder who enters their PIN, following which the cardholder's account is debited and the supplier's account is credited automatically.

A recent innovation in the payment services industry is the introduction of contactless payment cards. This allows cardholders to use their cards to pay for purchases up to the value of £30 without having to enter their PIN. Contactless is designed specifically to provide a quick and convenient way to pay in any environment where the speed of the transaction is essential for cardholders. Contactless cards contain an antenna, allowing the cardholder to simply touch their card against the contactless reader to allow the relevant information to be transferred securely across.[70]

3.3.5 **ATM or cash cards**

ATM cards or cash cards allow holders to withdraw funds from their bank account at an ATM (or cashpoint, as they are more commonly known in the UK). ATM cards operate under the standard terms of the card issuer. Through entering a PIN, the cardholder can withdraw cash up to a daily maximum amount, provided their account is in credit to that sum or it is within their overdraft limit.

Most banks have entered into master agreements to allow their customers to use other bank's ATM facilities to withdraw money using their cash card. While the precise contractual relationships between a bank, its customer, and the bank at which they withdraw funds is yet to be judicially determined, it could be argued that a unilateral contract arises between the cardholder and that bank, or that the other bank simply acts as an agent of the cardholder's bank when dispersing the money.

3.3.6 **Digital cards**

Digital cash cards can serve as a replacement not only for credit and debit cards, but also for cash itself. These cards are loaded with monetary value in the form of digital information, which can be instantaneously transferred from the cardholder to the supplier

[70] For further information see http://www.theukcardsassociation.org.uk/contactless_consumer/what_is_contactless.asp.

to satisfy a payment obligation. Essentially, the customer is using his or her own money, but in digital form. Digital cash systems are privately run. An 'originator' issues digital cash to participating banks who then re-issue it to their customers in the form of electronic purses. However, only merchants who have an agreement with an originator can accept payment by way of these prepaid cards.

3.3.7 The regulation of payment cards

The use of payment cards is regulated by two pieces of, sometimes overlapping, legislation: the Consumer Credit Act 1974 (CCA) and the more recent PSR 2017. Each will be discussed in turn, paying particular attention to how they apply when a card has been misused.

3.3.7.1 The Consumer Credit Act 1974

Application

The provisions of the CCA apply to 'credit tokens' and 'credit-token agreements'. Section 14(1) defines the term 'credit token' as a card, check,[71] voucher, coupon, stamp, form, booklet, or other document or thing. For the provisions of the CCA to apply, the credit token must have been issued to an individual rather than a company or partnership of more than three members[72] and it must have been issued by someone who carries on a 'consumer credit business', that is, someone who is in the business of making regulated consumer credit agreements.[73]

It further provides that for the provisions to apply the issuer must supply cash, goods, or services 'on credit'[74] or, where a third party provides cash, goods, or services against the production of the token, the issuer will pay the third party for them.[75] The first scenario simply covers two-party agreements where the issuer themselves provides cash, goods, or services on credit. On its face, there seems to be no express requirement of credit in the second scenario, but s14(3) provides that whenever a third party supplies cash, goods, or service the issuer is taken to provide credit. There are differing views as to whether a credit requirement is implicit, with s14(3) simply informing us when and by whom the credit is provided. It would seem that, if a credit requirement was not implicit, a credit token would arise in this second scenario even if there was no express undertaking to provide credit because s14(3) would deem the credit to arise.[76] However, the weight of academic

---

[71] Not the same as a 'cheque', rather, 'checks' are documents that entitle the holder to purchase goods from particular shops. The holder then repays the issuer their face value, plus interest, in instalments.

[72] section 14(1) CCA 1974. For a definition of 'individual' see s189(1).   [73] Section 189(1):

'consumer credit business' means any business be-herwise his being a creditor, under regulated consumer credit agreements.

[74] section 14(1)(a).   [75] section 14(1)(b).

[76] See S.A Jones, 'Credit Cards, Card Users and Account Holders' (1988) *Journal of Business Law* 457, 471–2.

[77] Roy Goode, *Consumer Credit Law and Practice* (London, loose-leaf, 1999).

opinion seems to be that credit **is** a requirement of the second alternative in s14(1)(b).[77] The absence of any explicit reference to the word 'credit' in the section can be explained on the basis that at the time the CCA was passed, the only form of tripartite card was the credit card, which always involved a deferred payment and therefore the provision of credit. This means that cards that do not give rise to credit will not be deemed a 'credit token' and will not therefore be subject to the provisions of the CCA.

Clearly credit cards fall within the ambit of the CCA, as do charge cards.[78] Electronic purses, or digital cash cards, are not subject to the provisions of the CCA and neither were cheque guarantee cards when they were in circulation. What is more difficult, however, is whether debit cards or ATM cards are covered by the Act. The problem with this question is that debit cards were not established until 1987, over a decade after the Act was introduced, and so the extent to which they are covered is uncertain. On one hand, it is argued that debit cards are simply modern payment mechanisms equivalent to cheques, meaning that they are not 'credit tokens' and therefore not subject to the provisions of the Act. It is submitted that this is the case for debit or ATM cards that are used in relation to an account that cannot go overdrawn. However, if the account does have an overdraft facility, meaning the account can go into debit, then it is arguable that the card could fall within s14(1)(b) of the Act and be construed as a credit token.

A 'credit-token agreement' is a regulated agreement for the provision of credit in connection with the use of the credit token.[79] Accordingly, not every agreement involving a credit token will be a credit-token agreement and subject to the provisions of the CCA: only those where the card is issued under a regulated agreement.[80]

The credit-token agreement

The credit-token agreement, made between the cardholder and the issuer, is a regulated consumer credit agreement, meaning that the issuer is obliged to satisfy various requirements relating to the disclosure of pre-contractual information[81] and the form and content of the agreement itself.[82] For example, the Act specifies that the agreement must be in writing and signed by the prospective debtor cardholder and creditor card issuer.[83] Furthermore, the debtor must be made aware of the rights and duties conferred or imposed on him or her by the agreement, the amount and rate of the total charge for credit, and the protection and remedies available to him or her under the Act.[84] If the card issuer fails to comply with any of these requirements, the agreement will not be deemed to have been properly executed and the issuer will only be able to enforce the agreement on an order of the court.[85]

---

[78] Note that before the implementation of the Consumer Credit Directive 2008/48/EC, charge cards gave rise to 'exempt agreements' and so the cards were not deemed to be 'credit tokens' for the purposes of the Act. Such exemptions were later found to be incompatible with the Consumer Credit Directive and so they now fall within s14 CCA. These cards are, however, exempt from s75 CCA.

[79] Section 14(2).   [80] See Section 8(3).   [81] Sections 55–9.   [82] Sections 60–6.
[83] Section 61(1).   [84] Section 61(2).   [85] Section 65.

Misuse of card by third parties

As discussed in the introduction, payment cards are vulnerable to fraud and the policy under the Consumer Credit Act 1974 is, for the most part, to transfer the risk of loss to the creditor—that is, the card-issuing bank. The general rule can be found in s83(1) of the Act, which tells us that 'The debtor under a regulated consumer credit agreement shall not be liable to the creditor for any loss arising from use of the credit facility by another person not acting, or to be treated as acting, as the debtor's agent.' However, s84 provides an exception to this general rule in the context of credit tokens. It provides that, in this context, s83 does not prevent the debtor:

(a) From being made liable for up to £35 of the loss arising from the unauthorised use of the card while it was not in his possession.[86]

(b) From being made liable for any losses sustained from the use of the card by a person who acquired it with the cardholder's consent.[87]

These two exceptions are themselves subject to a number of restrictions, as follows:

(c) The provisions in (a) and (b) above do not apply to any use of the credit token after the creditor has given notice that it has been lost or stolen.[88] This means the creditor cannot impose liability on the cardholder in relation to any losses that occur after notice is given either orally or in writing.[89]

(d) The provisions in (a) and (b) above do not apply in relation to distance contracts, that is, those entered into over the phone, internet, by mail order, and so on.[90] In this context, the general rule in s83 will apply, that is, no liability will be imposed on the cardholder.

(e) The provisions in (a) and (b) above do not apply unless the agreement provides details of the person or body to be contacted if the card is lost or stolen.[91]

---

[86] Section 84(1): 'Section 83 does not prevent the debtor under a credit-token agreement from being made liable to the extent of [£35] (or the credit limit if lower) for loss to the creditor arising from use of the credit-token by other persons during a period beginning when the credit-token ceases to be in the possession of any authorised person and ending when the credit-token is once more in the possession of an authorised person.'

[87] Section 84(2): 'Section 83 does not prevent the debtor under a credit-token agreement from being made liable to any extent for loss to the creditor from use of the credit-token by a person who acquired possession of it with the debtor's consent.'

[88] Section 84(3): 'Subsections (1) and (2) shall not apply to any use of the credit-token after the creditor has been given oral or written notice that it is lost or stolen, or is for any other reason liable to misuse.'

[89] See also section 84(5): 'Notice under subsection (3) takes effect when received, but where it is given orally, and the agreement so requires, it shall be treated as not taking effect if not confirmed in writing within seven days.'

[90] Section 84(3A): 'Subsections (1) and (2) shall not apply to any use, in connection with a distance contract (other than an excepted contract), of a card which is a credit-token.'

[91] Section 84(4): 'Subsections (1) and (2) shall not apply unless there are contained in the credit-token agreement in the prescribed manner particulars of the name, address and telephone number of a person stated to be the person to whom notice is to be given under subsection (3).'

Connected lender liability

Section 75 Consumer Credit Act 1974 introduces the notion of 'connected lender liability'. In a credit card transaction there is a connection between the supplier and the card issuer, which stems from the fact that the debtor is only able to use his or her card where the card issuer has entered into a contract with the supplier either directly (as in three-party-cases) or through a merchant acquirer (as in four-party cases). Connected lender liability means that if a cardholder has a claim against a supplier based on misrepresentation or breach of contract he or she will have a 'like claim' against the card issuer.[92] It provides that the cardholder can bring an action against the supplier and card issuer on a joint and several basis and it will be for the supplier to reimburse the card issuer.[93] The cardholder has this right even if the debtor, in entering into the transaction, has exceeded their credit limit or otherwise contravened any term of the agreement.[94] However, s75 is not limitless in terms of scope. First it does not apply to non-commercial agreements, meaning that private consumer–consumer contracts are excluded from its remit.[95] Further, s75 only applies to transactions involving a cash price of more than £100 but less than £30,000.[96]

In *Office of Fair Trading v Lloyds TSB Bank plc*[97] the House of Lords dealt with the question of whether connected lender liability applied in the context of international transactions, or if it was limited only to domestic transactions. This was an important point considering the rise in the use of credit cards abroad. It was held that liability does apply in relation to domestically issued cards that are used to finance transactions with a foreign supplier.[98]

3.3.7.2 The Payment Services Regulations 2017

The first PSR 2009 were introduced to give effect to the EU Payment Services Directive 2007/64 EC (PSD). The first PSD set up common rules on payments across Europe and provided that, among other things, payment service providers must give adequate information to consumers, ensure fast and efficient service, and compensate the consumer if services are not provided correctly. Following a period of review by the European Commission, in December 2015 the second PSD (PSD2) was published.[99] This came into force in January 2016, replacing the first PSD and bringing with it further clarifications, enhancements, and protections, as well as incorporating technological innovation in the sector. The UK has implemented the directive as the PSR 2017.

---

[92] Section 75(1).   [93] Section 75(1) and (2).   [94] Section 75(4).
[95] Section 75(3)(a).   [96] Section 75(3)(b)   [97] [2008] 1 AC 316.
[98] For an interesting discussion on the notion of connected lender liability and whether it should extend to modern four-party credit card transactions see Christopher Bisping, 'The Case Against s.75 of the Consumer Credit Act 1974 in Credit Card Transactions' (2011) *Journal of Business Law* 457, and Janice Montague 'Case Comment Consumer Law: Consumer Credit Act 1974 s.75—Liability of Credit Card Companies' (2007) *Coventry Law Journal* 63.   [99] Directive (EU) 2015/2366.

Application

For the purposes of the Regulations, the cardholder is known as the 'payment service user' and the card issuer is known as the 'payment services provider'. The PSR apply to 'payment instruments' issued under a 'payment services contract'. Regulation 2(1) defines 'payment instruments' widely to include any personalised device or set of procedures used to initiate a payment transaction by a payment services provider. Most of the cards considered in this chapter fall under the definition of a 'payment instrument'.[100] Those cards are therefore subject to the consumer protection measures contained in Part 6, which relates to information provision, and Part 7, which relates to the rights and obligations of the parties. Some of these provisions can be contracted-out unless the payment service user is a consumer, a micro-enterprise, or a charity.[101]

Where a payment card is issued under a 'regulated agreement' within the meaning of the CCA 1974, the relevant consumer protection measures of the PSR are excluded in so far as they would otherwise duplicate the provisions of the CCA.[102]

Information provisions

Card agreements are deemed to be 'framework contracts' for the purposes of the PSR and so the relevant 'information' provisions found in Part 6 of the Regulations will apply. For example, pre-contractual information must be supplied to the cardholder 'in good time' before he or she is bound by the contract;[103] the cardholder has the right to obtain certain information during the period of the contract;[104] and there are provisions concerning the notification of any variations in the contract[105] and the cancellation of the contract[106] that must be adhered to.

Misuse of cards by third party

Like the CCA the PSR provide a comprehensive liability framework in relation to the misuse of payment cards that fall within their remit.

First though, express obligations are imposed on cardholders under Regulation 72, which provides that cardholders must use the payment instrument in accordance with the terms and conditions governing its use[107] and they must notify the payment service provider as soon as they become aware of the loss, theft, misappropriation, or

---

[100] Except cheque guarantee cards (although they are now redundant), store cards issued by a retailed for use in that particular store, and electronic purses that can only be used in certain outlets. See Schedule 1 Para 2 for a list of instruments that are excluded.

[101] Regulation 40(7) and 63(5). See Regulation 2(1) for definitions.

[102] See Regulations 41 and 64.

[103] Regulation 48. The information that must be given is listed in Schedule 4.

[104] Regulation 49.   [105] Regulation 50.   [106] Regulation 51.

[107] 72(1) The previous regime simply stated that the cardholder must use the instrument in accordance with the terms and conditions governing its use (Payment Services Directive 2007/64 EC Article 56(1)(a); Payment Services Regulations 2009 57(1)(a). The new PSD2 and PSR add a further layer of protection for the cardholder in Regulation 72(2), which stipulates that those terms and conditions must be objective, non-discriminatory, and proportionate.

unauthorised use of the payment instrument. Furthermore, cardholders must take all reasonable steps to keep safe personalised security credentials[108] relating to a payment instrument. These obligations apply even if the card is deemed a 'credit token' and therefore governed by the CCA 1974.

There are corresponding obligations placed on card issuers under Regulation 73, which provides that card issuers must ensure, for example, that the personalised security features of a card are not accessible to other persons and they must ensure that the appropriate means are available at all times for the cardholder to give notification of any misuse of the card. An additional obligation for card issuers that was introduced in the new PSR is that they must provide cardholders with the option to make a notification of misuse free of charge and they must ensure that any costs charged are directly attributed to the replacement of the card.[109]

In terms of liability and who bears the risk of loss, the Regulations are similar, but not identical to the provisions of the CCA. The starting point is Regulation 76, which provides the general rule that that card issuer must refund transactions that are not authorised and, where applicable, restore the debited payment account to the state it would have been in had the unauthorised payment transaction not taken place.[110] This refund must be provided as soon as practicable, and in any event no later than the end of the business day following the day on which the payment service provider becomes aware of the unauthorised transaction.[111] This is broadly equivalent to s83 of the CCA, although the CCA makes no reference to when the refund should take place. In similar vein to the CCA, the Regulations go on to provide certain exceptions to this general principle so that the cardholder is liable in certain circumstances:

(a) Cardholders will be liable up to £35 for any losses incurred in respect of unauthorised payment transactions arising from the use of a lost or stolen payment instrument, or from the misappropriation of a payment instrument.[112] The corresponding provision in the CCA refers to the card not being in the cardholders 'possession'.

(b) Cardholders will be liable for all losses where they have acted fraudulently or where the cardholder has, with intent or gross negligence, failed to comply with their obligations in Regulation 72 (discussed earlier).[113] Under the CCA cardholders are only liable for all the losses if they consent to someone else having their card and they misuse it.

---

[108] Personalised security credentials are defined in Regulation 2(1) as personalised features provided by a payment service provider to a payment service user for the purposes of authentication.
[109] Regulation 73(1)(e).   [110] Regulation 76(1).
[111] Regulation 76(2). Under the previous regime, (Payment Services Directive 2007/64 EC Article 60; Payment Services Regulations 2009 Regulation 61) if there was an unauthorised transaction, card issuers were required to immediately refund the amount to the cardholder. The new PSD2 and PSR have therefore added further clarity to this requirement.
[112] Regulation 77(1).   [113] Regulation 77(3).

As with the CCA, these two exceptions are themselves subject to a number of restrictions, provided that the cardholder has not acted fraudulently:

(c) The cardholder is not liable for any losses that have arisen after notification is made under Regulation 72(1)(b).[114]

(d) The cardholder is not liable for any losses where the card issuer has failed at any time to provide, in accordance with Regulation 73(1)(c), appropriate means for notification.[115]

(e) The cardholder is not liable for any losses where Regulation 100 (authentication) requires the application of *strong customer authentication*,[116] but the payer's payment service provider does not require strong customer authentication.[117]

(f) The cardholder is not liable for any losses where the card is used in connection with a distance contract.[118]

It is clear that PSR 2017 has improved the existing rules by bolstering the protection and rights of cardholders. As such, PSD2 and the new PSR in the UK are a welcome change in strengthening the position of consumers, particularly when it comes to the misuse of their payment instruments. PSD2 has also introduced a number of other changes that relate to improved market efficiency and integration as well as increased competition and choice.[119] Some of the security measures that are being strengthened will be discussed later, in the context of the electronic transfer of funds.[120]

Key takeaways

- Payment cards are small pieces of plastic that are used to pay for goods and services. The most common type are credit and debit cards but there are also charge cards, ATM or cash cards, and digital cash cards.

- Payment card transactions are regulated by two core pieces of legislation: the Consumer Credit Act 1974 and the PSR 2017 both of which provide comprehensive consumer protection regimes, particularly in the context of misuse.

---

[114] Regulation 77(4)(a).   [115] Regulation 77(4)(b).   [116] Defined in Regulation 2(1) as:

authentication based on the use of two or more elements that are independent, in that the breach of one element does not compromise the reliability of any other element, and designed in such a way as to protect the confidentiality of the authentication data, with the elements falling into two or more of the following categories—(a) something known only by the payment service user ('knowledge'); (b) something held only by the payment service user ('possession'); (c) something inherent to the payment service user ('inherence').
See section 3.4.4.1.

[117] Regulation 77(4)(c).   [118] Regulation 77(4)(c).
[119] See section 3.5. For an overview of the changes introduced by PSD2 see Jonathan Rogers and Talia Carman 'PSD2 and the Payment Services Regime: What's Changing, What's New and What You Need to Do' (2016) 5(6) *Compliance & Risk* 2.   [120] See section 3.4.4.1.

Key bibliography

Articles

Bisping, B, 'The Case Against s. 75 of the Consumer Credit Act 1974 in Credit Card Transactions' (2011) *Journal of Business Law* 457

Jones, SA, 'Credit Cards, Card Users and Account Holders' (1988) *Journal of Business Law* 457

Montague, J, 'Case Comment Consumer Law: Consumer Credit Act 1974 s. 75—Liability of Credit Card Companies' (2007) 12(2) *Coventry Law Journal* 63

Rogers, J and Carman, T, 'PSD2 and the Payment Services Regime: What's Changing, What's New and What You Need to Do' (2016) 5(6) *Compliance & Risk* 2

Reports and codes

The Standards of Lending Practice: Personal Customers, July 2016 https://www.lendingstandards-board.org.uk/wp-content/uploads/2016/07/Standards-of-Lending-Practice-July-16.pdf

The Standards of Lending Practice: Business Customers, March 2017 https://www.lendingstandardsboard.org.uk/wp-content/uploads/2017/03/standards-of-lending-practice-business.pdf

Websites

The UK Card Association: http://www.theukcardsassociation.org.uk/

3.4 Electronic transfer of funds

3.4.1 Introduction

The ***transfer of funds*** refers to the movement of a credit balance from one account to another, which occurs by adjusting the balances of the respective party's accounts; the debt owed by the bank to the payer (assuming he is in credit) is reduced by the amount of the transfer, and the debt owed by the bank to the payee is increased by the amount of the transfer.[121]

Traditionally, fund transfers were only paper based, and known as the bank ***giro system***. The word 'giro' comes from the Greek word for circle and, in this context, represents the cyclical process of transferring credit balances between accounts. The bank giro system, as an alternative to the settlement of accounts by cheque,[122] became

---

[121] It should be noted that there is no physical transfer of coins or banknotes as a result of this transaction, it is simply an adjustment of the separate property rights (i.e. the choses in action). Accordingly, the word 'transfer' is slightly misleading. See *Libyan Arab Foreign Bank v Bankers Trust Co* [1989] QB 728, per Staughton J at 750.

[122] There are three fundamental differences between the cheque system and the giro system. (1) Theoretically, cheques can be transferred from the original payee to a third party holder (although in practice cheques are non-transferable, having been pre-printed with 'account payee only'), whereas under the giro system a transfer can only be made to the specified payee. (2) Cheques allow for the collection of payment by the payee (or holder) from the payee's account at any bank whereas a giro transfer can be made only to the payee's account at the bank specified in the instruction. (3) Cheques can be cashed by the payee over the counter of their bank whereas the payee of the giro transfer must receive payment through a bank account.

fully operational in the UK in the 1960s and was run by the Post Office. The system works through the physical transfer of a money transfer order from the payer's bank to the payee's bank. They are commonly found in the form of tear-off strips at the bottom of utility, telephone, and other regular bills. In 2016, 22 million bank giro credits were cleared worth over £15 billion. That amounts to around 87,000 credits per day with an average daily value of £60 million or £687 per item. Around 90 per cent of these were for bill payments.[123] Taking the paper-based bank giro and cheque clearing systems together, giro payments constituted 6 per cent of the volume and 3.6 per cent of the value of transactions that passed through clearing.[124] The rationale for the introduction of this system was to allow for the rapid transmission of funds in a safe and secure way.[125]

While all bank transfers are known collectively as 'giro transfers' in recent years we have seen the development of electronic fund transfer systems, the main ones being Bankers Automated Clearing Services (BACS) and Clearing House Automated Paying System (CHAPS) transfers. The interbank communication of this payment instruction is conducted through electronic means. The original payment instruction can still be embodied in paper form but the communication between the two banks in effecting the transfer will be through electronic means. The remainder of this section will analyse the distinction between credit and debit transfers, before outlining the various ways of clearing giro transfers and the obligations of the paying and receiving banks under the PSR 2017.

3.4.2 Credit and debit transfers

The transfer of funds can be classified as either a credit or debit transfer depending on the way the payment order is communicated to the payer's bank. A *credit transfer* involves a communication from the payer to his or her bank, instructing it to credit the account of the payee. It therefore involves a push of funds from the payer to the payee. This can take place on a one-off basis as in the case of a bank giro credit or CHAPS (discussed in section 3.4.3.3) or it can take place on a recurring or periodical basis as in the case of a standing order. A *standing order* is an instruction given by a payer to his or her bank for the bank to make regular fixed payments to a payee. The payer will have completed a standard pro forma setting out the payee's account details and the dates and frequency of payments to be made. When the bank receives the instruction from the payer (subject to the account having sufficient funds or an overdraft facility) it will debit the

---

[123] Cheque and Credit Clearing Company, *Annual Review* (2016) at https://www.chequeandcredit.co.uk/sites/default/files/cccc_annual_review_2016_0.pdf.   [124] Ibid.

[125] The giro system was designed to reduce the opportunities for fraud involved with cheque payments. Thus, giro forms are generally sent first to the transferring bank and not the payee, meaning that there is no opportunity for them to fraudulently alter the amount on the cheque. Furthermore, the system reduces the possibility of dishonoured payment instructions since the money transfer form is initially processed by the payer's bank, rather than in the cheque clearing system where the payee's account is credited before the cheque is transmitted for payment at the payer's account.

payer's account with the amount specified and forward the payment instruction to the payee's bank who will credit the payee's account accordingly. Standing order payments are effected through the CHAPS Faster Payments Service, discussed in section 3.4.3.4.

In contrast, a ***debit transfer*** involves a communication from the payee to the payer's bank, instructing it to transfer funds from the payees account. It therefore involves a pull of funds by the payee from the payer. These instructions can be initiated by the payer him or herself and then passed to the payee, as in the case of cheque payments, or they can be initiated directly by the payee pursuant to the payer's authority,[126] as in the case of a ***direct debit***. With a direct debit, the payer signs a mandate that authorises the bank to pay the amounts requested by the payee—there is no need to require separate authorisation on each occasion the payee requests funds. When the bank receives the instruction from the payee, it will provisionally credit the payee's account with the amount to be collected and then forward the payment instruction to the payer's bank who will debit the payer's account accordingly. The credit will become final when the debit to the payer's account is irreversible. The attraction of the direct debit system is that it allows the payee to collect regular and varied payments from the payer for things like mobile phone contracts where the amount owed can vary on a month by month basis. Payment of direct debits are effected through the BACS system, discussed in more detail in section 3.4.3.2.

As part of the BACS Direct Debit Guarantee Scheme, the payee must give the payer a minimum of ten working days' notice of the amount and date of the first direct debit and of any subsequent changes to those details.[127] The scheme further provides that if an error is made in the payment of a direct debit, the payer is entitled to a full and immediate refund of the amount. This error could be a payment that is made after the payer has cancelled their authorisation, or payment of an incorrect amount or on the incorrect day.[128]

3.4.3 Clearing giro transfers

The process of exchanging payment orders between participating banks is known as clearing. There are currently four main clearing methods when funds are transferred— a paper-based method and three electronic methods—namely, BACS, CHAPS Sterling, and CHAPS Faster Payment Service. Each will be discussed in turn.

3.4.3.1 Manual clearance

In a paper-based transfer system the piece of paper embodying the payment instruction is physically transferred from one bank to another, either directly through a courier or at a centralised clearing house. The procedure is therefore fundamentally the same

---

[126] For example, when a customer sets up a direct debit to pay their mobile phone bill, they will sign a mandate authorising their bank to pay the amounts demanded every month by the payee mobile phone company.

[127] For the wording of the Direct Debit Guarantee Scheme see https://www.fca.org.uk/publication/forms/fca-direct-debit-mandate.pdf

[128] Note, if payment is to be made through the direct debit scheme, and the payer subsequently cancels the direct debit, he or she could be liable to the payee for breach of contract. See *Esso Petroleum Co Ltd v Milton* [19978] 1 WLR 938.

as that used for the clearance of cheques.[129] The payer will present to his or her bank a bank giro credit accompanied by a cheque or a withdrawal form. The payer's bank will then enter the relevant information on the form in magnetic ink[130] and debit the payer's account. The bank giro credit is then sent to the clearing office of the payer's bank and on the following day the form is transferred to the clearing office of the payee's bank. In some cases, the amount involved will be credited to the payee's account and the form will then be forwarded to the branch of the payee's bank where the account is held. In other cases, the payee's account is credited by the relevant branch. This manual clearing process is relatively slow, with the ordinary cycle taking three banking days.

3.4.3.2 BACS

This form of clearing began in 1971 when the London and Scottish clearing banks created a company—BACS—with a view to providing a more cost-efficient service for the interbank clearance of payments. While the process still takes three banking days, as with manual clearing, the transfer of payments is executed electronically using BACS as a centralised agency. This extinguishes the need to physically transfer documents. In practice, BACS is used for high-volume low-value funds transfers, particularly direct credits, which are payments initiated by the payer,[131] and direct debits, which are initiated by the payee.[132] Member banks have direct access to BACS and banks can also sponsor non-member banks and building societies, as well as corporate customers who can submit their own data to BACS.

Box 3.5 sets out the BACS clearing process.

Given this three-day clearing cycle, BACS transfers cannot be considered as an immediate transfer of funds because the system requires that a payment instruction must be made at least two days before the actual payment date. For example, if a customer has a direct debit set up to pay their mobile telephone bill on the twentieth of each month, the payment instruction will be sent by the customer's provider at least two days before that date.

BACS uses a *deferred net settlement clearing system* (as opposed to a *RTGS*, discussed in section 3.4.3.3) where settlement takes place across members' accounts with the Bank of England on a daily basis. While this reduces the liquidity needs of the member banks, it means that members are exposed to settlement risk in the period between settlement cycles.

---

[129] As discussed in section 3.2.3.

[130] Sometimes the payee will provide pre-printed credits with the payee's account details already encoded on it so that the payer's bank need only add on the amount of the transfer.

[131] The most common type of payment in this context is wages and salaries: in 2017 over 364 million payroll related direct credit payments were made. See BACS, *Annual Processing Statistics* (2017) at https://www.bacs.co.uk/DocumentLibrary/Bacs_annual_processing_stats_2017.pdf.

[132] The most common types of payment in this context are household bills and subscription payments. For example, in 2017 over 578 million mobile phone bills and over 107 million charity donations were paid via direct debit. See BACS, *Annual Processing Statistics* (2017) at https://www.bacs.co.uk/DocumentLibrary/Bacs_annual_processing_stats_2017.pdf.

> ### Box 3.5 The BACS clearing process
>
> - **Day 1**: payment instructions are submitted via electronic file to BACS via BACSTEL-IP, a telecommunications service that offers direct communication to the BACS processing centre. This information must be received by 22.30 so that it can be processed overnight. Input data is recorded and validated by BACS and an input report is sent to the user.
> - **Day 2**: by 06.00, BACS sorts the data and produces a series of credit and debit instructions, known as output data, for each member bank.
> - **Day 3**: by 09.30 member banks will have processed the output data received on day two and ensure that the debits and credits are applied to the customer's accounts. Any interbank obligations that arise are settled with the Bank of England.

BACS is by far the largest payment system in the UK in terms of volume. In 2016 there were over 6.2 billion payments effected through the BACS system with a value of over £4.7 trillion.[133] While this constitutes a 2.3 per cent and 4.1 per cent rise in terms of volume and value respectively from 2015, the alternative CHAPS Faster Payments system, for example, is experiencing a much steeper rise; in 2016 payments through this method rose 14.4 per cent and 14.2 per cent in volume and value respectively.[134]

3.4.3.3 CHAPS Sterling

CHAPS clearing began on 9 February 1984 as a same-day electronic sterling credit system and is run by the CHAPS Clearing Co Ltd. Since 1996, CHAPS has used an enhanced RTGS system meaning that each individual payment is settled in real time across its participants' accounts with the Bank of England. In 2016, 39 million payments were effected through the CHAPS Sterling system with a value of over £75 trillion making it by far the largest payment method in the UK in terms of value.[135] Most of the value processed by CHAPS is from wholesale transactions but it is most commonly known in the UK as being the payment method for property purchases. The system is used by 26 direct banking participants and over 5,000 other participants who process the payments through agency arrangements with the direct participants.

Unlike BACS, CHAPS is not a central clearing system. Instead, members communicate directly with one another using the SWIFT network. SWIFT is an interface that allows financial institutions across the globe to send and receive information to one another in a secure way. Accordingly, credit transfer messages are sent to and from member banks via the SWIFT interface. Traditionally, the system operated between

---

[133] Cheque and Credit Clearing Company, *Quarterly Statistical Report* (2017 Q1) at https://www.chequeandcredit.co.uk/sites/default/files/quarterly_statistical_report_2017_q1.pdf Payments.

[134] Although their respective values are much lower; in 2016 1,426 billion payments were made with a value of £1,189 trillion. Ibid.   [135] Ibid.

06.00 and 16.20[136] but as of 20 June 2016 the hours extended to 06.00—18.00, providing a new deadline of 17.40 for customer-to-customer payments, and 18.00 for bank-to-bank payments. Customers can use a variety of means to communicate the instructions to their bank to issue a CHAPS payment including the telephone or in writing. The customer provides the bank with the name and account details of the payee, details of the account against which the payment is to be debited, and the amount to be transferred. Each CHAPS member will hold a Sterling Settlement Account at the Bank of England. When a payment instruction is made it is settled in real time across the members' accounts at the central bank. This means that the Bank of England will debit the sending bank's account with the value of the transfer, and credit the receiving bank's account, provided that the sending bank has sufficient funds. The instruction, and a confirmation that the accounts have been settled, is then sent, via the SWIFT interface, to the receiving bank. Upon receipt of this communication, the receiving bank then sends a positive 'user acknowledgement' (known as a UAK) to the sending bank. Box 3.6 provides a summary of the CHAPS Sterling clearing process.

This system is effective because it eliminates **credit risk** between banks; as soon as the receiving bank receives the instruction and confirmation from the Bank of England, it has the assurance that the amount in question has been credited to its settlement account. However, in order for this system to be effective member banks need to maintain sufficient liquidity in their respective settlement accounts. If they do not, the system could become gridlocked, because a member must defer settlement until they have received sufficient credits from other participants.

To address this issue, in April 2013, the central bank introduced a Liquidity Saving Mechanism (LSM) to reduce the amount of liquidity member banks had to maintain in their accounts for the purposes of making real-time CHAPS payments.[137] Under this mechanism, which utilises offsetting algorithms, banks can now submit their payment instructions to the Bank of England without settling them immediately. These

---

Box 3.6 Summary of the CHAPS Sterling clearing process

- Customer at the sending bank requests a CHAPS transfer.
- Instruction is sent, via SWIFT to the Bank of England.
- Using the RTGS system, the Bank of England settles the payment in real time by debiting the sending bank's account and crediting the receiving bank's account.
- Instruction, as well as confirmation of the settlement, is sent via SWIFT to the receiving bank.

---

[136] There was a deadline of 16.00 for submitting customer payments with a further 20 minutes for interbank payments.

[137] See Bank of England, 'How has the Liquidity Saving Mechanism Reduced Banks Intraday Liquidity Costs in CHAPS' (2014) *Quarterly Bulletin* Q2, 180.

payments are referred to as 'queued'. Once payments are queued in the system, banks are able to use a queue management programme called the 'central scheduler' to control when payments are settled. The longer a payment queues in the central scheduler the more time there is for another member bank to submit a payment that could offset the queued payment and therefore reduce the amount of liquidity the bank requires. This system therefore creates a trade-off between liquidity savings and payment delay.

If a member bank wishes to make a payment immediately, rather than allowing it to queue, it can mark the instruction as 'urgent', which means it will settle with minimal delay. Every 120 seconds the system briefly suspends the immediate processing of urgent payments so that non-urgent payments can be dealt with. These payments are settled in 'matching cycles' that last just over 20 seconds. During this cycle, an algorithm attempts to find groups of broadly offsetting payments from different member banks. At the end of the cycle all payments that have been identified as eligible by the algorithm are settled at the same time. If any non-urgent payments remain unsettled at the end of this cycle they will simply remain in the queue until the start of the subsequent cycle.

A year after it was introduced, it was reported that this mechanism had reduced member banks' daily liquidity requirements by 20 per cent, or £4 billion.[138] This is achieved because successfully matched payments are settled at exactly the same time meaning that a member bank only needs to fund the difference between the payments sent and received in that cycle, rather than the gross value of its sent payments. Most importantly, this means that UK financial stability has been enhanced because, under stress conditions, it is less likely that banks will be unable to settle CHAPS payments because of liquidity shortfalls.

CHAPS subjects member banks to a number of obligations, which are found in the CHAPS Reference Manual, the most recent version of which was published 5 January 2018.[139] The Manual performs two principle functions: first, it forms a core part of the legal basis for the Bank of England's operation of the CHAPS system; and, second, it aims to provide a clear and comprehensive description of the rules, requirements, and key procedures relevant to the Bank of England's operation of the CHAPS system in a document that is publicly disclosed.[140]

The Manual is split into four substantive sections: Overview (Chapter I); CHAPS Rules (Chapter II); CHAPS Participation Requirements (Chapter III); and CHAPS Procedures (Chapter IV). The CHAPS Rules, for example, set out the participation and access criteria for members,[141] the rights and duties of participants,[142] and rules surrounding payment, including that payment made through CHAPS Sterling must be unconditional.[143] Another obligation is that participants must 'accept and give same day value to all payments denominated in sterling received within the timeframes set out in the CHAPS Timetable.'[144] It could therefore be argued that a payee who was due

---

[138] Ibid.

[139] At https://www.bankofengland.co.uk/-/media/boe/files/payments/chaps/chaps-reference-manual.pdf?l a=en&hash=7E5E1353D9B19B63CA1DD936160C2F8954675932.   [140] Ibid, p 14.

[141] Paragraph 2.   [142] Paragraph 3.   [143] Paragraph 4.1.2.   [144] Paragraph 3.2.3.

to receive a payment though CHAPS could have an action for breach of contract if his or her bank failed to give them same-day access to the funds as required by the rules. This is based on the argument that the CHAPS Rules represent the reasonable usage of bankers and as such constitute an implied term in the payee's contract with his or her bank.

This was confirmed in *Tayeb v HSBC Bank plc*[145] where, without its customer's consent, the receiving bank returned funds that had been sent to it via CHAPS because it was suspicious of the origin of those funds. It was held that, once the customer's account had been credited, the bank was indebted to the customer for that sum. Importantly, Colman J held that when a customer opens an account with a bank, which is available to receive CHAPS transfers, the bank is promising that it will accept those transfers in compliance with the CHAPS Rules. He stressed that, although the CHAPS Rules contained specific information on the return of transfers made in error, because it was silent on the reversal of credit entries in any other context there was a 'very strong implication that following application to the customer's account, in the absence of error, the banking practice in relation to CHAPS transfers is that they are made ordinarily irreversible'.[146] Accordingly, it is argued that the CHAPS Rules are incorporated in the banker–customer relationship, meaning that if a bank fails to adhere to the rules it could face an action for breach of contract.

In any event, most CHAPS Sterling transfers will now fall within the scope of Part 7 of the PSR 2017, which tells us, for example, that a payer cannot revoke his or her payment instruction once the bank has received it,[147] and a payee will have an action for breach of statutory duty if the payee bank fails to credit his or her account on the same day as the CHAPS transfer.[148]

3.4.3.4 **CHAPS Faster Payment Service**

In May 2008 CHAPS launched the Faster Payment Service, which was intended to provide same-day clearing of high-volume, low-value sterling denominated credit transfers. This is the system that bank customers utilise to transfer funds from their accounts 24 hours a day, seven days a week. Normally funds are transferred immediately, but it can take up to two hours. Depending on the bank or building society, the amount customers can transfer in a single day is limited to somewhere between £10,000 and £250,000.[149] This service covers three types of payment instruction: standing orders,

---

[145] [2004] 4 All ER 1024.   [146] Ibid, at [60].   [147] Regulation 83(1).   [148] Regulation 89:

(1) The credit value date for the payee's payment account must be no later than the business day on which the amount of the payment transaction is credited to the account of the payee's payment service provider ... (3) The payee's payment service provider must ensure that the amount of the payment transaction is at the payee's disposal immediately after that amount has been credited to that payment service provider's account.

[149] For example, the personal transaction limits for one-off online transfers are: £25,000 for HSBC and Halifax; £50,000 for Barclays; £20,000 for Royal Bank of Scotland and NatWest; and £10,000 for M&S Bank. Information correct as of 12 April 2018, see http://www.fasterpayments.org.uk/about-us/personal-transaction.

> ### Box 3.7 The CHAPS Faster Payment Service clearing process for single immediate payments
>
> - Payer instructs the bank to make the payment and provides the payee's account details and the amount of the transfer.
> - After carrying out the necessary verification procedures and checking that the payer has sufficient funds, the bank generates a message and sends this to the messaging platform provided by IPL.
> - This message is then forwarded to the payee's bank.
> - The payer and payee's accounts are debited and credited.
> - The payee's bank generates a return message confirming that the payee's account has been credited.
> - Members' accounts are settled three times a day using a net settlement system. At the end of each cycle IPL will calculate the net position of each bank based on the messages transmitted. IPL forwards this information to the Bank of England, which then adjusts the members' accounts as necessary.

which are instructions given by a payer to his or her bank for the bank to make regular fixed payments to a payee; single immediate payments, which are one-off credit transfers that are sent straightaway; and forward dated payments, which are one-off credit payments sent at a future date.

The service operates using a messaging platform provided by Immediate Payments Ltd (IPL). Settlement takes place across members' accounts with the Bank of England three times per working day using a net settlement service, rather than a RTGS service as employed by the CHAPS Sterling system.

Box 3.7 sets out a step-by-step guide to the clearing process of a single immediate payment.

The benefits of the CHAPS Faster Payment Service are clear. One-off or recurring fund transfers can be effected within a few hours rather than three days under the alternative BACS system. Furthermore, unlike BACS and CHAPS Sterling, single immediate and forward dated payments can be transferred around the clock, although standing order payments are limited to banking days between midnight and 06.00. Most importantly, unlike CHAPS Sterling, the Faster Payment Service operates under a net settlement system rather than an RTGS system, which reduces the liquidity requirements of members, thereby enhancing financial stability. Finally, imposing a daily limit of £250,000 (although in practice for personal customers the limit is much less) mitigates the potential increased risk of fraud given the immediacy of the transfer and places a limit on interbank settlement risk.

Box 3.8 provides a summary of the four different clearing systems that have been discussed.

> **Box 3.8 At a glance: a summary of the four main clearing systems**
>
> - The manual clearing of bank giro credits is very similar to cheques. It involves a three-day process and is often used for the payment of household bills.
> - BACS deals with high-volume, low-value fund transfers, including direct debits and credits. It involves a three-day clearing cycle.
> - CHAPS Sterling is an instantaneous transfer of funds effected through the SWIFT network. Settlement takes place using an RTGS system. Often used for higher value fund transfers such as property purchases.
> - CHAPS Faster Payments Service deals with same-day high-volume, low-value fund transfers. Settlement takes place using a net settlement system.

3.4.4 The Payment Services Regulations 2017

Although the law relating to the electronic transfer of funds is entrenched in the rules of contract and agency law, the PSR 2017 also confer a series of rights and obligations in respect of transfers that fall within its remit. This section will look at this statutory regime as it applies to the paying and receiving banks.

3.4.4.1 The paying bank

Information requirements

Part 6 of PSR 2017 establishes certain minimum requirements in relation to the information that the paying bank must provide to the payer. Where the payer is a consumer, micro-enterprise, or charity that information is mandatory, but outside those contexts it can be displaced by contrary agreement.[150] The information that has to be provided depends on whether the payer makes a one-off request for a transfer of funds where there is not necessarily a continuing commercial relationship (known as a single payment service contract)[151] or where the payment request is made in the context of an ongoing contractual or account relationship (known as a framework contract).[152] It is likely that most single payment service contracts will be business–business transactions, whereas most consumer contracts, which usually stem from a current or savings account, will be a framework contract.

For example, in the context of a single payment service contract, the paying bank must make available to the payer, either before the contract is concluded or immediately after the execution of the payment transaction by means of distance communication, certain information including: the information or unique identifier that has to be provided by the payer in order to effect the transfer; the maximum time it will take to effect the transfer; the charges payable by the payer; where applicable, the actual or

---

[150] Regulation 41.   [151] Governed by Regulations 43–7.   [152] Governed by Regulations 48–54.

reference exchange rate to be applied to the transfer; and any information specified in Schedule 4 that is relevant to single payment service contracts.[153] When the paying bank has received the payment order, it must immediately make available the following information: a reference enabling the payer to identify the transfer; the amount and currency of the transfer; the amount of any charges payable by the payer; where the exchange rate used differs from the rate originally quoted, details of the actual rate used and the amount of the payment after conversion; and the date when the paying bank received the transfer instruction.[154] For framework contracts, the paying bank must provide the payer with all the information specified in Schedule 4,[155] which includes, for example, the name and address of the paying bank; a description of the service to be provided; details of charges payable; the means of communication for the transmission of information between the parties; details about the payer's liability; and the conditions for the payment of any refund. There is also a series of common provisions including, for example, that information provided must be accessible, in an easily understandable language, in a clear and comprehensible form, and in English or any other agreed language.[156] The payer will also have the right to request a hard copy of any information the paying bank is required to disclose[157] and to receive that information free of charge.[158]

Rights and obligations

Part 7 of the Regulations sets out the rights and obligations of the parties. While there is no explicit distinction in the Regulations between single payment service contracts and framework contracts, the distinction is still important because where a payer has an account with the paying bank (and therefore a framework contract) the paying bank is more likely to provide the payer with a device, password, or other set of procedures to initiate the payment transaction. This is significant because such a device, password, or set of procedures could amount to a 'payment instrument' under the Regulations,[159] which brings with it additional responsibilities on the part of the paying bank (and the payer).[160]

---

[153] Regulation 53.   [154] Regulation 45.   [155] Regulations 48 and 49.
[156] Regulation 55.   [157] Regulation 55(1)(b).   [158] Regulation 46(1).
[159] Regulation 2(1): 'payment instrument' means any (a) personalised device; or (b) personalised set of procedures agreed between the payment service user and the payment service provider, used by the payment service user in order to initiate a payment order.
[160] Regulation 73. For example, the paying bank must: ensure that the personalised security credentials are not accessible to persons other than the payment service user; not send an unsolicited payment instrument; ensure that appropriate means are available at all times to enable the payment service user to notify the payment service provider of the loss or misuse of a payment instrument; on request, provide the payment service user at any time during a period of 18 months after the alleged date of notification with the means to prove that such notification to the payment service provider was made; provide the payment service user with an option to make a notification free of charge, and ensure that any costs charged are directly attributed to the replacement of the payment instrument; and prevent any use of the payment instrument once such notification has been made.

Consent

In relation to the authorisation of the transaction, the paying bank will only execute a transfer when the payer has given his or her consent.[161] Such consent must be given before or, if agreed between the parties, after the execution of the transfer.[162]

Limits on the use of payment instruments

The payer and its payment service provider may agree on spending limits for any payment transactions executed through a particular payment instrument.[163] Where a payment instrument is used to initiate a transfer, the paying bank can stop the use of the instrument on reasonable grounds relating to the security of the payment instrument, the suspected unauthorised or fraudulent use of the payment instrument, or, in the case of a payment instrument with a credit line, a significantly increased risk that the payer may be unable to fulfil its liability to pay.[164] Before the paying bank carries out any measures to stop the use of the payment instrument it must inform the payer of its intention to stop the payment instrument and give reasons for doing so.[165] Where it is not possible for the paying bank to inform the payer beforehand, it must inform them immediately afterwards.[166] However, these notification requirements do not apply where it would be unlawful.[167] Finally, the paying bank must allow the use of the payment instrument or replace it with a new payment instrument as soon as practicable after the reasons for stopping its use cease to exist.[168]

Unauthorised payment transactions

If the payer's bank executes a payment order that has not been authorised, it must refund the amount of the unauthorised payment to the payer and, where applicable, restore the payer's account to the position it would have been in had the unauthorised transaction not taken place.[169] This refund must be provided as soon as practicable, and in any event no later than the end of the business day following the day on which the payment service provider becomes aware of the unauthorised transaction.[170] However, the payer must notify the paying bank of the unauthorised transaction without undue delay, or in any event no later than 13 months after the date the account was debited.[171] This notification requirement is waived if the payer's bank fails to comply with the information requirements contained in Part 6 of PSR 2017.[172] The paying bank will bear the burden of proving that the payment was in fact authorised.[173] The mere fact that the payer's bank can produce evidence to show that the payment instrument was used to initiate the transaction is not in itself necessarily sufficient to prove that the payment transaction was authorised by the payer.[174]

---

[161] Regulation 67(1). [162] Regulation 67(2). [163] Regulation 71(1).
[164] Regulation 71(2). [165] Regulation 71(3). [166] Regulation 71(4).
[167] Regulation 71(5). [168] Regulation 71(6). [169] Regulation 76.
[170] Regulation 76(2). Under the previous regime, (Payment Services Directive 2007/64 EC Article 60; Payment Services Regulations 2009 Regulation 61) if there was an unauthorised transaction, card issuers were required to immediately refund the amount to the cardholder. The new PSD2 and PSR has therefore added further clarity to this requirement.
[171] Regulation 74(1). [172] Regulation 74(3). [173] Regulation 75(1). [174] Regulation 75(2).

Liability

There are limited circumstances in which the paying bank can pass some of the losses resulting from an unauthorised transaction to the payer.[175] These have already been discussed at length in section 3.3.7.2 in relation to card payments and will not be repeated here. In the case of a direct debit transaction, the payer may be entitled to a refund even in circumstances where the transaction was authorised. This is available where the payer did not specify the exact amount of the payment transaction when the direct debit was initially authorised, and the amount of the payment transaction exceeded the amount that the payer could reasonably have expected, taking into account the payer's previous spending pattern, the conditions of the framework contract, and the circumstances of the case.[176]

Execution of payment transactions

The PSR 2017 imposes certain time limits, which the paying bank must comply with when executing a payment instruction. These time limits run from the 'time of receipt' of the payment order, which is defined as the moment when the instruction is received by the paying bank, either directly from the payer (as in the case of a credit transfer), or indirectly from the payee (as in the case of a direct debit).[177] Where it is agreed that the payment order should be executed on a specific day (as in the case of a standing order), then the 'time of receipt' will be treated as the agreed date.[178]

The paying bank cannot refuse to execute a payment order that complies with the relevant framework contract unless that execution is unlawful.[179] Where the paying bank refuses to carry out the payment instruction it must notify the payer of the refusal, the reasons for the refusal and any additional steps that the payer needs to take to rectify any factual errors in the instruction.[180] This notification has to be given at the earliest opportunity, but generally no later than the end of the business day following the time of receipt of the payment order.[181] The paying bank can charge the payer for issuing a notification provided that the bank's refusal is reasonable.[182]

The Regulations provide that a payer cannot revoke an instruction after it has been received by the paying bank.[183] More specifically, in the case of a credit transfer, which is initiated by the payer, the payer cannot revoke the payment order after they have given consent to execute the payment transaction to the payee.[184] In the case of a direct debit, which is initiated by the payee, the payer cannot revoke the payment order after the end

---

[175] See Regulation 77.

[176] Regulation 79. The payer must apply for a refund within 8 weeks of the date on which the funds were debited: Regulation 80(1).

[177] Regulation 81(1) and (2). Unless the time of receipt of the payment order is a non-business day, in which case the payment order is deemed to have been received on the first business day thereafter; Regulation 81(3).

[178] Regulation 81(5). Unless the agreed date is a non-business day, in which case the payment order is deemed to have been received on the first business day thereafter; Regulation 81(6).

[179] Regulation 82(5).   [180] Regulation 82(1).

[181] Regulation 82(2) read in conjunction with Regulation 86(1).

[182] Regulation 82(3).   [183] Regulation 83(1).   [184] Regulation 83(2).

of the business day preceding the day agreed for debiting the funds.[185] Similarly, in the case of a standing order, the payer cannot revoke the payment order after the end of the business day preceding the agreed day.[186] When these time limits have passed, the payment order can only be revoked if, in the case of a credit transfer, it is agreed between the payer and the paying bank, and, in the case of a direct debit, it is agreed between the payer, paying bank, and payee.[187]

Incorrect unique identifiers

Where the payer has supplied the paying bank with a 'unique identifier' for the payee (such as a sort code and account number),[188] a payment made in accordance with that unique identifier is deemed to have been properly executed.[189] Where the unique identifier provided is incorrect, the paying bank will not be liable for the non-execution or defective execution of the transaction.[190] However, the paying bank must make reasonable efforts to recover the funds involved in the payment transaction and may, if agreed in the framework contract, charge the payment service user for any such recovery.[191]

The 2017 Regulations introduce further guidance on what is expected of the payer and payee banks in this context. Thus, it provides that the payee's payment service provider must co-operate with the payer's payment service provider in its efforts to recover the funds, in particular by providing to the payer's payment service provider all relevant information for the collection of funds.[192] Further, it provides that if the payer's payment service provider is unable to recover the funds it must, on receipt of a written request, provide to the payer all available relevant information in order for the payer to claim repayment of the funds.[193] A practical insight into the relationship between unique identifiers and banking practice is considered in Box 3.9.[194]

To complement the regulatory regime relating to mistaken payments, a voluntary code of best practice has been developed by the banking industry. Announced in January 2016, this regime, which is known as the Credit Payment Recovery Process, supports customers in the recovery of funds that have been paid over in error via BACS of Faster Payments. According to this regime, customers can expect the following:[195]

- When a customer notifies his or her bank or building society that they have made an electronic payment to the wrong account, the customer's bank will commence action on their behalf within a maximum of two working days.

---

[185] Regulation 83(3).   [186] Regulation 83(4).   [187] Regulation 83(5).

[188] 'Unique identifier' is defined in Regulation 2(1) as 'a combination of letters, numbers or symbols specified to the payment service user by the payment service provider and to be provided by the payment service user in relation to a payment transaction in order to identify unambiguously one or both of (a) another payment service user who is a party to the payment transaction; (b) the other payment service user's payment account.'

[189] Regulation 90(1).   [190] Regulation 90(2).   [191] Ibid.
[192] Regulation 90(3).   [193] Regulation 90(4).

[194] For an interesting discussion of this case see Holly Powley, 'Tidal Energy Ltd v Bank of Scotland plc [2014] EWCA Civ 1107' (2015) 44(4) *Common Law World Review* 231.

[195] See http://www.fasterpayments.org.uk/press-release/new-help-customers-recover-payments-sent-error.

> ## Box 3.9 Banking in practice: the role of unique identifiers
>
> In *Tidal Energy Ltd v Bank of Scotland plc* [2014] EWCA Civ 1107 the claimant gave an instruction to the defendant bank to pay a sum of money to a creditor via a CHAPS transfer form. The transfer form contained four boxes that needed to be completed (each box representing a different unique identifier) depicting the beneficiary's account number, sort code, bank and branch, and name. After the funds were sent, Tidal Energy realised they had been tricked by a fraudster meaning that although they had correctly named the intended beneficiary, the account number and sort code it had been given were false and the designated receiving account belonged to a different entity. Accordingly, the claimant sought a declaration that they were entitled to have the funds re-credited to their account.
>
> The Court of Appeal held that by instructing the bank to make a CHAPS payment, the claimant had agreed that the payment was to be made in accordance with the usual banking practice that governed CHAPS transactions. In order to meet the short timescale that was the hallmark of CHAPS, all of the major UK clearing banks processed and routed CHAPS payments on the basis of sort code and account number alone, not account or beneficiary name. Accordingly, the transfer form completed by the claimant authorised the defendant bank to debit the claimant's account when the sort code and account number matched the information on the transfer form. The defendant bank was therefore not liable to re-credit the claimant's account with the sum transferred.
>
> It is clear that customers are responsible for making sure that the unique identifiers they enter on CHAPS transfer forms correspond with both the account and the intended beneficiary. Given the importance placed on banking practice in this case, it is suggested that banks should ensure that customers are aware of the approach taken by banks when they analyse unique identifiers.

- Where the customer's bank finds clear evidence of a genuine mistake, they will contact the receiving bank on the customer's behalf with a request to prevent the money being mistakenly spent. As long as the recipient does not dispute the customer's claim, the customer will subsequently receive a refund of the protected funds within 20 working days from when the customer is notified by the bank.

- In cases where the circumstances of the claim are not clear cut, the customer's bank will still contact the receiving bank on his or her behalf. The recipient will be contacted by their bank to ask for consent to debit their account. No funds would be removed without the consent of the receiving customer.

- If it is not possible to reclaim a payment the customer has sent in error—for instance, if the recipient disputes its return—the customer will be notified of the outcome within 20 working days from the point of his or her inquiry and in many cases much sooner.

- If funds cannot be recovered through the standard central process the customer's bank will give the customer clear and accurate information on the options the customer has available—such as court action against the recipient.

- The industry procedures do not change the legal rights and responsibilities of the customer, his or her bank, or the recipient of the funds. Anyone that intentionally spends money that does not belong to them is committing a crime, which can be reported to the police.

- If the customer does not get the service expected under the new procedures the customer can firstly follow his or her provider's formal complaints procedure. If the customer is not happy with the outcome, the customer's bank will provide them with information on how to take their complaint to the independent Financial Ombudsman Service.[196]

Strong customer authentication

A new feature of the 2017 regime, which was introduced in response to the need to reduce the risk of fraud in electronic payment services, is the requirement of *strong customer authentication* (SCA).[197] SCA is a new mandatory method of authenticating online payments or verifying a customer's identity before accepting an online payment. PSR defines SCA as:[198]

> authentication based on the use of two or more elements that are independent, in that the breach of one element does not compromise the reliability of any other element, and designed in such a way as to protect the confidentiality of the authentication data, with the elements falling into two or more of the following categories–(a) something known only by the payment service user ('knowledge'); (b) something held only by the payment service user ('possession'); (c) something inherent to the payment service user ('inherence').

PSR stipulates that a bank must apply SCA whenever a customer accesses its account online, initiates an electronic payment transaction, or carries out any action through a remote channel, which may imply a risk of payment fraud or other abuses.[199] More specifically, it provides that whenever a payer initiates a remote payment transaction, it must apply SCA that includes elements that dynamically link the transaction to a specified amount and a specific payee.[200]

A paying bank may face liability if it fails to require SCA. For example, if the payer's account is subject to an unauthorised transaction, and the payer's bank does not require SCA, then, unless the payer has acted fraudulently, the bank will be liable for the losses.[201] Further, if a bank becomes liable for non-executed, defective, late, or unauthorised payment transactions because another bank has not used SCA, the other bank must compensate the first bank for any losses incurred or sums paid.[202]

The European Banking Authority (EBA) was charged with drafting Regulatory Technical Standards (RTS) on the meaning and application of SCA.[203] They launched their consultation in August 2016 and on 23 February 2017 the EBA published their

---

[196] See Chapter 7.   [197] Directive (EU) 2015/2366, Article 97.   [198] Regulation 2(1).
[199] Regulation 100(1).   [200] Regulation 100(2).   [201] Regulation 77(4)(c).
[202] Regulation 95.   [203] Directive (EU) 2015/2366, Article 98.

final Draft RTS.[204] The Draft RTS was submitted to the European Commission, who officially adopted it, with changes, on 27 November 2017.[205] Following a three-month period of scrutiny by the European Parliament and Council, it was officially published on 13 March 2018.[206] The RTS will be effective from September 2019, giving the payment industry 18 months to implement the measures.

One of the features of the new RTS is the introduction of an exemption from the application of SCA for low-value transactions. According to Article 16, where the payer initiates a remote electronic payment transaction, SCA will not apply provided that a number of conditions are met: first, the amount of the remote electronic payment transaction does not exceed EUR30; second, the cumulative amount of previous remote electronic payment transactions initiated by the payer since the last application of SCA does not exceed EUR100; or, third, the number of previous remote electronic payment transactions initiated by the payer since the last application of SCA does not exceed five consecutive individual remote electronic payment transactions. The RTS also introduces an exemption in the case of transactions that are identified by the bank as posing a low level of risk.[207] This is based on a 'transaction risk analysis', the conditions for which are detailed in the RTS.[208]

3.4.4.2 The receiving bank

Information requirements

Much like the paying bank, the receiving (or payee) bank is subject to certain information disclosure requirements. Where the payee holds an account with the receiving bank and that account is used to receive funds transfers (as in the case of direct debits), the bank will have to satisfy the information requirements for a 'framework contract'.[209] Where the payee doesn't hold an account, but rather they initiate the transfer by approaching the receiving bank and requesting it to act and receive the funds on their behalf (as in the case of a debit transfer), the bank will have to satisfy the information requirements of a 'single payment service contract'.[210]

Rights and obligations

Once that information has been provided to the payee (either under a framework contract or a single payment service contract), the receiving bank will send the payment instruction to the payer's bank unless there is some reason why it refuses to do so, in which case it will have to notify the payee of its reasons for refusing.[211]

---

[204] European Banking Authority 'Final Report: Draft Regulatory Technical Standards on Strong Customer Authentication and common and secure communication under Article 98 of Directive 2015/2366 (PSD2)' 2017.
[205] At http://ec.europa.eu/finance/docs/level-2-measures/psd2-rts-2017-7782_en.pdf.
[206] Commission Delegated Regulation (EU) 2018/389.   [207] Article 18.
[208] These exemptions have been implemented in the Payment Services Regulations 2017 via Article 100(5), which provides that: 'Paragraphs (1), (2) and (3) are subject to any exemptions from the requirements in those paragraphs provided for in regulatory technical standards adopted under Article 98 of the payment services directive.'   [209] Regulations 48–54, as discussed in section 3.3.4.1.
[210] Regulations 43–47, as discussed in section 3.3.4.1.   [211] Regulation 82(1).

In the case of a direct debit instruction, the receiving bank must send the payment instruction within the time limits agreed with the payee.[212] When the funds have been transferred to the receiving bank, it must credit the payee's account with the amount in question.[213] Once the account has been credited, those funds must be made immediately available to the payee[214] and interest must begin to accrue by the end of the business day on which the bank received the funds.[215] Accordingly, the receiving bank must ensure that the full amount is credited to the payee and no charges have been deducted unless previously agreed.[216] If charges other than those agreed are deducted from the amount transferred, and the payee has initiated the transfer, the receiving bank will be liable to reimburse the payee.[217] On the contrary, where it is the payer that has initiated the transfer, it is the paying bank that will be liable to reimburse the payee.[218]

When the payment instruction has been executed, the receiving bank must supply the payee with further information including; a reference enabling the payee to identify the payment transaction and, where appropriate, the payer; the amount of the payment transaction; the amount of any charges; where applicable, the exchange rate used in the payment transaction; and the credit value date.[219]

Liability for a defective payment or the non-execution of a payment instruction will turn on whether it was the payee or the payer who initiated the payment instruction. Where the payer initiates the transfer—for example, in the case of a CHAPS transfer— the payer's bank is liable for correctly executing the instruction unless it can prove that the payee's bank received the amount of the payment transaction in accordance with the Regulations.[220] In circumstances where the payer's bank can demonstrate that the funds have been transferred correctly, responsibility then transfers to the receiving bank who must immediately make available the amount of the payment transaction to the payee and, where applicable, credit the corresponding amount to the payee's account.[221]

Conversely, where the payee initiates the transfer—for example, in the case of a direct debit—the payee's bank is liable for correctly executing the instruction.[222] If the payee initiated instruction is transmitted defectively, or not at all, the receiving bank must immediately re-transmit the payment order in question to the payer's bank.[223] Further, the receiving bank must, on request, make immediate efforts to trace the payment transaction and notify the payee of the outcome.[224] Where the receiving bank can demonstrate that it correctly transmitted the payment order, responsibility then transfers to the payer's bank who must immediately refund the payer and restore the debited payment account to the state in which it would have been had the defective payment transaction not taken place.[225]

---

[212] Regulation 86(5).
[213] Regulation 86(4).
[214] Regulation 87(1) and (2) and 89(3).
[215] Regulation 89(1).
[216] Regulation 84(1).
[217] Regulation 84(3)(b).
[218] Regulation 84(3)(a).
[219] Regulations 46 and 54.
[220] Regulation 91(2).
[221] Regulation 91(5).
[222] Regulation 92(2).
[223] Regulation 92(3).
[224] Regulation 92(5).
[225] Regulation 92(6).

Although in general the receiving bank will be liable for a defective transaction, they can escape this liability if they can show that the payee failed to notify them of the defect without undue delay, or in any event no later than 13 months after the account was debited.[226] This notification requirement is waived if the receiving bank fails to comply with the information requirements contained in Part 6 of PSR 2017.[227]

Key takeaways

- The electronic transfer of funds reduces the debt owed by the bank to the payer and correspondingly increases the debt owed by the bank to the payee by the amount of the transfer.

- There are four main clearing methods involved in the transfer of funds; a paper-based method and three electronic methods: BACS, CHAPS Sterling, and CHAPS Faster Payment Service.

- The PSR 2017 provides a comprehensive scheme in terms of the rights and responsibilities of the parties involved in an electronic transaction.

- Part 6 of PSR provides a series of information requirements that both paying and receiving banks must adhere to. These rules vary depending on whether there is a 'single service contract' (Regulations 43–7) or 'framework contract' (Regulations 48–54).

- Part 7 of PSR establishes the rights and responsibilities of the respective parties including rules surrounding the authorisation of payment transactions (Regulations 67–80); the execution of payment transactions (Regulations 81–4); the execution time and value date (Regulations 85–9); and liability (Regulations 90–6).

Key bibliography

Articles

Rogers, J and Carman, T, 'PSD2 and the Payment Services Regime: What's Changing, What's New and What You Need to Do' (2016) 5(6) Compliance & Risk 2.

Legislation

Commission Delegated Regulation (EU) 2018/389 of 27 November 2017 supplementing Directive (EU) 2015/2366 of the European Parliament and of the Council with regard to regulatory technical standards for strong customer authentication and common and secure open standards of communication.

---

[226] Regulation 74(1) [227] Regulation 74(2).

3.5 Innovation in the payment services industry: open banking and third-party providers (TPPs)

The past decade has seen a fundamental change in the landscape of payment services, with customers demanding real-time, personalised, and more streamlined payment experiences. This demand has been met by a rise in third-party, non-bank, payment service providers (such as FinTechs)[228] who offer specific payment solutions or services to customers.[229] The PSD2,[230] which has been transposed into the UK via the PSR 2017, has responded to these demands by mandating the opening of banks' payment infrastructures to third parties and bringing these new forms of payment institutions within the remit of the updated regulatory regime. In doing so, PSD2 has removed market entry barriers, which should result in increased competition from new players who offer cheaper payments solutions. These TPPs are subject to the same regulatory regime as the more traditional payment service providers including authorisation requirements and supervision by the new Payment Services Regulator (PSR), a subsidiary of the FCA. The PSR is tasked with regulating the operators of traditional payment systems, as well as the new TPPs discussed in this section. It has three statutory objectives: to promote effective competition in the markets for payment services; to promote the development of, and innovation in, payment systems in the sector; and to ensure that payment systems are operated and developed in a way that takes account of, and promotes, the interests of those who use, or are likely to use, services provided by payment systems.[231]

PSD2 extends the definition of a 'payment institution' by introducing two types of third-party payment service provider: *Payment Initiation Service Providers* **(PISP)** and *Account Information Service Providers* **(AISP)**. In addition, PSD2 introduces the *Account Servicing Payment Services Provider* **(ASPSP)**, which identifies and distinguishes the provider (normally a bank) where the customer's payment account is held. Customers can use PISPs and AISPs where their account is accessible online,[232] and where they have given express permission for their account details to be passed to them.[233] The success of PISPs and AISPs turns on the cooperation of the ASPSP in providing the customer's account information so that the TTPs can collate data or initiate a transaction. PSD2 requires ASPSPs to provide these TPPs access to their customers' accounts[234] and this is achieved through an open Application Program Interface (API).

---

[228] A FinTech is a company that uses new technology and innovation to compete with more traditional methods in the delivery of financial services.

[229] For a general discussion see Iris H-Y Chiu, 'A New Era in FinTech Payment Innovations? A Perspective from the Institutions and Regulation of Payment Systems' (2017) *Law, Innovation and Technology* 190 at http://dx.doi.org/10.1080/17579961.2017.1377912. See also Lerong Lu, 'Financial Technology and Challenger Banks in the UK: Gap Fillers or Real Challengers?' (2017) 39(7) *Journal of International Banking Law and Regulation* 273.

[230] Payments Services Directive (EU) 2015/2366.

[231] Financial Services (Banking Reform) Act 2013 ss50–2.

[232] Payments Services Directive (EU) 2015/2366 Article 66(1).

[233] Ibid, Article 64; Payment Services Regulations 2017 Regulation 67.

[234] For PISPs see Payments Services Directive (EU) 2015/2366 Article 66, Payment Services Regulations 2017 Regulation 69. For AISPs see Payments Services Directive (EU) 2015/2366 Article 67, Payment Services Regulations 2017 Regulation 70.

3.5.1 **Payment initiation service providers (PISPs)**

PSD2 defines a payment initiation service as a 'service to initiate a payment order at the request of the payment service user with respect to a payment account held at another payment service provider.'[235] PISPs are therefore concerned with customer interfaces for payment, where the online service accesses a customer's payment information in order to initiate a transfer of funds. A PISP can allow users to initiate online payments directly from their bank account, as discussed in Box 3.10, but it can also take the form of an interface that stores the user's credit or debit card information and enables them to initiate payment while protecting their privacy. For example, Apple Pay allows users to initiate a payment through their mobile phone interface, which stores their credit or debit card information in its digital wallet.[236] Similarly PayPal, which originally arose to support eBay purchases and can now be used at an increasing number of online merchant outlets, allows users to initiate a payment using only their email address. Another type of PISP is a mobile payment services app, which, for example, allows users to initiate a payment to certain other people within a closed group. A recent example of this is Paym, (discussed in Box 3.12), which allows users to make payment using mobile phone numbers as initiators and recipients.

PSD2 provides a comprehensive framework for the allocation of responsibilities between users and providers, most of which has already been discussed in sections 3.3 and 3.4. In relation to PISPs specifically, the Directive provides, for example, that where a payment order is initiated through a PISP, immediately after initiation the PISP must

---

Box 3.10 Banking in practice: credit cards v PISPs in online merchant transactions

Ordinarily, when a customer purchases goods online, they enter their payment details into the merchant's website (such as Amazon) and the funds are transferred via several intermediaries. For example, if a credit card is used, once the payment details are entered, the card details are then sent to the merchant acquirer (the bank that signs up merchants to accept certain cards) who processes the transaction and sends it on to the relevant card issuer (such as Barclays) for authorisation and settlement via the relevant card scheme (such as Visa). The card scheme passes the card transaction details from the acquirer to the card issuer and they pass payment back to the acquirer who in turn pays the merchant (see section 3.3.2).

Under the new PSD2 regime, third-party PISPs initiate online payments to a merchant directly from the payer's bank account, without the use of intermediaries by creating a software 'bridge' between the two accounts. PISPs allow customers to 'push' credit payments from their bank accounts to merchants. These services are not yet offered extensively in the UK, but they are used widely in other European countries. Established online payment systems include: in Germany, Sofort Überweisung; in the Netherlands, IDeal; and in Sweden, Trustly. PISPs integrate their service with the merchant's online checkout process giving consumers greater choice as to how they conduct their online transactions. As these services roll out across the UK, customers should expect to see new, alternative logos for making payment alongside card symbols at online checkouts.

---

[235] Article 4. See also Payment Service Regulations 2017, Regulation 2.

[236] See Mark Edwin Burge, 'Apple Pay, Bitcoin, and Consumers: The ABCs of Future Public Payments Law' (2016) 67 *Hastings Law Journal* 1493.

provide and make available to the payer the following data: confirmation of the successful initiation of the payment order with the payer's account servicing payment service provider; a reference enabling the payer and the payee to identify the payment transaction and, where appropriate, the payee to identify the payer, and any information transferred with the payment transaction; the amount of the payment transaction; and, where applicable, the amount of any charges payable to the payment initiation service provider for the transaction and, where applicable, a breakdown of the amounts of such charges.[237] Further, PSD2 provides that following the initiation of a payment order, the PISP must make available to the payer's ASPSP the reference of the payment transaction.[238]

Interestingly, PSD2 provides that where payment is initiated through a PISP but the payment was not authorised, the user's ASPSP must refund the user the amount of the unauthorised payment immediately, and in any event no later than the following business day, and, where applicable, restore the debited payment account to the state in which it would have been had the unauthorised payment transaction not taken place.[239] If, however, the PISP is liable for the unauthorised payment transaction, it must compensate the ASPSP for the losses incurred or sums paid as a result of the refund to the user.[240] The burden is on PISP to prove that:[241]

> within its sphere of competence, the payment transaction was authenticated, accurately recorded and not affected by a technical breakdown or other deficiency linked to the payment service of which it is in charge.

Similar provisions apply in the case of the non-execution, defective, or late execution of a payment transaction. Thus, where an order is initiated by a PISP, the ASPSP must refund to the user the amount of the non-executed or defective payment transaction and, where applicable, restore the debited payment account to the state in which it would have been had the defective payment transaction not taken place.[242] The burden is on the PISP to prove that the payment order was received by the ASPSP and that, as in relation to unauthorised payments, the transaction was authenticated, accurately recorded, and not affected by a technical breakdown.[243] If the PISP is liable for the non-execution, defective, or late execution of the payment transaction, it must compensate the ASPSP.[244]

3.5.2 **Account information service providers (AISPs)**

An account information service is defined in PSD2 as 'an online service to provide consolidated information on one or more payment accounts held by the payment service user with either another payment service provider or with more than one payment

---

[237] Article 46; Payment Services Regulations 2017 Regulation 44(1).
[238] Article 47; Payment Services Regulations 2017 Regulation 44(2).
[239] Article 73(2); Payment Services Regulations 2017 Regulation 76(5).   [240] Ibid.
[241] Article 72(1); Payment Services Regulations 2017 Regulation 75(2).
[242] Article 90(1); Payment Services Regulations 2017 Regulation 93(2).
[243] Article 90(1) Payment Services Regulations 93(3)(b).
[244] Article 90(2); Payment Services Regulations 2017 Regulation 93(4).

service provider.'[245] It includes such a service whether information is provided '(a) in its original form or after processing; (b) only to the payment service user or to the payment service user and to another person in accordance with the payment service user's instructions.'[246] This change reflects the trend towards customers having relationships with multiple account providers and allows those customers to have a consolidated view of their finances, enabling them to analyse their spending patterns and assess their financial needs more easily. For example, customers can categorise their spending across their accounts according to different groups (food, bills, etc.) thereby helping them with budgeting. During the consultation process regarding the implementation of PSD2, the UK government highlighted that an account information service could include, but was not limited to:[247]

- dashboard services that show aggregated information across a number of payment accounts;

- price comparison and product identification services;

- income and expenditure analysis, including affordability and credit rating or credit worthiness assessments; and

- expenditure analysis that alerts users to consequences of particular actions, such as breaching their overdraft limit.

In the UK, an example of an AISP is Money Dashboard, a service that allows users to view their finances across all their online accounts and provides personal financial assistance. When an account is linked to Money Dashboard, transaction types are categorised into various tags such as electricity and groceries. This information is then converted into graphs so that users can clearly see their incomings and outgoings according to each category. Their budget planner shows how much disposable income users have, and how much they can realistically put away in savings. Established in 2010, by May 2018 more than 150,000 people have signed up to the service.[248] The *Financial Times* recently conducted a survey on four AISPs—Moneybox, Chip, Emma, and You Need A Budget—to determine how useful they were at enabling users to save and manage their money more effectively.[249]

3.5.3 **Analysis**

The introduction of PSD2 has signalled a shift in the dynamics of payment services away from a monopolised industry characterised by traditional 'banking' service providers to one where new non-banking TPPs can enter the market and offer innovative payment services. An example of this is Revolut, discussed in Box 3.11.

---

[245] Article 4.   [246] Electronic Money Regulations 2011, Regulation 2.
[247] HM Treasury, *Implementation of the revised EU Payment Services Directive II* (February 2017) para 6.29.
[248] See https://www.moneydashboard.com/.
[249] For the results see 'Millennials and the Smartphone Savings Revolution' *Financial Times* (25 May 2018).

> **Box 3.11 A case study: Revolut**
>
> Revolut is a UK-based FinTech that launched in July 2015. It is a digital banking alternative that offers a prepaid Mastercard debit card, currency exchange and budgeting services.
>
> As of May 2018, Revolut has over 1.5 million customers that have made over 70 million transactions worth over $10 billion.
>
> Operating from a mobile banking app, Revolut allows users to send fast, free, and secure money transfers to bank accounts in over 120 countries using the Interbank Exchange Rate. It supports spending and ATM withdrawals in over 120 currencies and it offers a budgeting service through which customers can set up a monthly budget and track their progress in real time.

By forcing banks to open their payment infrastructures to third parties through APIs, PSD2 has opened the doors to competition and exposed traditional banks to uncertainty regarding the future of the traditional payment methods they offer. This evolving landscape, which means that customers will have easy access to potentially cheaper and more efficient products from new competitors, poses two core problems for banks: loss of revenue from traditional card-based transactions and loss of ownership control of customers.[250]

First, despite the capping of interchange fees[251] in card-based transactions in recent years,[252] the revenue generated from such transactions remains a valuable source of income for traditional retail banks. By bringing PISPs within the regulatory remit of PSD2, a simplified payment system is being contemplated (as discussed in Box 3.10), which fully disintermediates the payment process in, for example, online merchant transactions. This means that any interchange fees previously received by the issuing bank (and the other parties to the transaction) could be fully displaced.

Second, the introduction of PSD2 has the potential to fundamentally change the customer ownership and insight that traditional banks currently enjoy. In particular, it may reduce the ability of banks to use their existing current account relationships with customers as a gateway to sell other financial products and services. Moreover, by mandating the opening of bank's payment infrastructures through an API to third parties, banks face the prospect of losing a direct relationship with their customers and instead becoming a simple utility-type service. The advent of AISPs and PISPs means

---

[250] See, for example, Accenture, *Seizing the Opportunities Unlocked by the EU's Revised Payment Services Directive* (July 2017) at https://www.accenture.com/t00010101T000000Z__w__/gb-en/_acnmedia/PDF-19/Accenture-Banking-Opportunities-EU-PSD2-v2.pdf#zoom=50.

[251] An interchange fee is the fee paid from a merchant's bank to a card user's bank for transactions when a card payment is made.

[252] A result of the Interchange Fee Regulation (EU) 2015/751, which was transposed into UK law by The Payment Card Interchange Fee Regulations (SI) 2015 No.1911. Where the caps apply, the interchange fee is limited to 0.2 per cent of the value of the transaction for consumer debit cards, and 0.3 per cent of the value of the transaction for consumer credit cards.

> ### Box 3.12 A case study: Paym
>
> Paym is an industry-lead mobile payment system, launched by the UK Payments Council in conjunction with 15 participating banks and building societies in April 2014. It is now run by an independent company made up of these participating financial institutions that offer the Paym service directly to their customers.
>
> More than 3 million people have registered with the service already and it is available to more than 40 million customers, representing more than 90 per cent of current accounts.
>
> Accessed via a mobile banking app on an Android or iOS device, Paym allows users to transfer money using just a mobile number. This means that no sort codes or account numbers need to be exchanged, although users can check the name of the recipient before confirming the payment. Once a user has registered their mobile number with the current account they want to use, they can send and receive payments.
>
> In practice, users simply enter the recipient's mobile phone number, confirm the recipient, check the amount to be sent, and complete the transaction. The user's bank will send a payment conformation by text. The money will appear in the recipient's account within two hours.

that customers can potentially fulfil all of their banking needs, such as viewing their transaction history, checking their account balances, and initiating payments through third parties, with no engagement at all with their bank.

However, PSD2 also presents lucrative opportunities for banks to extend their reach and boost their income stream by developing their own payment initiation and account information services. Paym is an example of the banking industry seizing such an opportunity, as discussed in Box 3.12.[253]

As well as developing technology to transfer funds between users in new and innovative ways, banks could also develop their own payment initiation products to be used in the context of online merchant transactions (as discussed in Box 3.10). This product could be offered to merchants so that funds can be transferred directly from their customer accounts, without the need for the intermediaries involved in traditional card payments. Banks could charge a fee for this service, thereby creating the potential for a new source of revenue. This would appeal to merchants as the service charge they would otherwise pay in a card transaction would be greatly reduced.

In summary, it is clear that PSD2 will accelerate the digital disruption that is currently reshaping the payment services industry. While this changing landscape will threaten traditional banks' payment revenues and the ownership of their customers, it will also drive strategic and innovative developments, as banks strive to maintain their share of the market.

In terms of drawbacks, one of the most obvious issues raised by this emerging landscape is the increase in exposure to cyber risk: by passing account information to TPPs

---

[253] See http://www.paym.co.uk and http://www.paymentsuk.org.uk/projects/past-projects/paym.

via APIs, banks are opening themselves up to a significantly greater risk of cyber-attack. AISPs, which will hold aggregated customer data relating to user's transactions and balances, will be particularly vulnerable. It also raises public concerns over the privacy of personal data, although under PSD2 data can only be shared with a customer's explicit consent.

 Key takeaways

- PSD2 has opened up the banking sector by introducing two new types of TPPs that satisfy the definition of a payment institution: PISP and AISP.
- PSD2 requires banks to provide these TPPs with access to their customer's accounts and this is achieved through an open AIP.
- This new environment poses two core problems for banks: loss of revenue from traditional card-based transactions, and loss of ownership control of customers. It also raises key risks relating to cyber-attacks and data protection.

Key bibliography

Articles

Burge, ME, 'Apple Pay, Bitcoin, and Consumers: The ABCs of Future Public Payments Law' (2016) 67 *Hastings Law Journal* 1493

Chiu, I H-Y, 'A New Era in Fintech Payment Innovations? A Perspective from the Institutions and Regulation of Payment Systems' (2017) *Law, Innovation and Technology* 190 at: http://dx.doi.org/10.1080/17579961.2017.1377912

Lu, L, 'Financial Technology and Challenger Banks in the UK: Gap Fillers or Real Challengers?' (2017) 39(7) *Journal of International Banking Law and Regulation* 273

Rogers, J and Carman, T, 'PSD2 and the Payment Services Regime: What's Changing, What's New and What You Need to Do' (2016) 5(6) *Compliance & Risk* 2

Questions

1. **The UK Payments Council erred when it reversed its decision to phase out cheques. They have no place in modern society. Discuss.**

   Answer tips You should demonstrate your understanding of the role and function of cheques as a method of payment. You could compare their relative strengths and weaknesses with other methods of payment such as card payments and electronic fund transfers, particularly in light of the new cheque imaging system that was rolled out in October 2017. Reference could be made, for example, to the 2011 Treasury Committee report, which looked at the arguments for and against the abolition of cheques.

2. The liability regime imposed by the Consumer Credit Act 1974 s75 should not extend to credit cards. Discuss.

> **Answer tips** *You should demonstrate your understanding of connected lender liability and how it works in practice. Answers should focus on the tension between protecting consumers and imposing costs on credit card providers and evaluate the policy reasons in favour and against the application of s75 to credit cards. You might consider, for example, who ultimately bears the burden in terms of cost, and whether the regime makes sense in light of its intended historical application to three-party rather than four-party cases.*

3. Alan sells his car to Bob for £10,000. Bob instructs his bank at 10.00 on Monday to transfer funds via CHAPS Sterling to Alan. Alan's account it not credited until Wednesday, as a result of which he has to use his overdraft and he incurs charges. What action, if any, could Alan take against his bank?

> **Answer tips** *You should discuss the fact that Alan could bring an action under two headings (presuming that Alan's bank was at fault in delaying crediting his account):*
>
> - *Breach of contract—Alan's bank may have failed to abide by the CHAPS Reference Manual, which is incorporated into the banker–customer relationship (Tayeb v HSBC Bank plc).*
> - *Breach of statutory duty under the PSR 2017 because his bank failed to credit the account on the same day as the CHAPS transfer (Regulation 89).*

4

Banks and finance

4.1 Introduction

Alongside taking in deposits from customers, the other core function of banking business is lending. Indeed, the Capital Requirements Regulation 2013 defines a 'credit-institution' (including a bank) as an 'undertaking the business of which is to take deposits or other repayable funds from the public and to grant credits for its own account.'[1] This chapter analyses the operation and regulation of a number of traditional forms of lending including overdrafts, *fixed-term loans*, and *syndicated loans*. It also considers lender liability and the different forms of security a bank can use to realise the repayment of a loan in the event of default by the borrower. It closes by addressing recent innovations in the lending market that offer a competitive alternative to traditional bank lending, including payday lending and peer-to-peer lending.

4.2 Overdrafts

An *overdraft* generally involves an extension of credit by a bank to its customer via the customer's current account. Often an express agreement is entered into between a bank and its customer with agreed terms and conditions. However, an overdraft facility can also be offered on an ad hoc basis without prior agreement and this tends to happen when the customer presents a payment instruction to the bank that, if honoured, would result in his or her account becoming overdrawn. This payment instruction, issued by a customer who has insufficient funds to meet the obligation, can be construed by the bank as an implied request for an overdraft facility on the bank's standard terms and conditions. The bank is under no obligation to accept this request, and it would be acting within its rights if it chose to dishonour the payment instruction.[2] However, if the bank did honour the mandate, it would be accepting the customer's request to extend to them an overdraft facility, and the consequence would be that the customer's debt to the third party would be discharged and the bank would be entitled to repayment from the customer as their creditor. This position was confirmed by Wall J in *Lloyds Bank Plc v Voller:*[3]

---

[1] Capital Requirements Regulation 575/2013 Article 4(1). [2] See Chapter 2, section 2.4.2.1.
[3] [2000] 2 All ER (Comm) 978, 982.

If a current account is opened by a customer with a bank with no express agreement as to what the overdraft facility should be, then, in circumstances where the customer draws a cheque on the account which causes the account to go into overdraft, the customer, by necessary implication, requests the bank to grant the customer an overdraft of the necessary amount, on its usual terms as to interest and other charges. In deciding to honour the cheque the bank, by implication, accepts the offer.

4.2.1 Legal nature of an overdraft

From a legal perspective, an overdraft is a loan granted by the bank to its customer such that the bank is the *creditor* and the customer is the *debtor* for the amount of the credit balance in the customer's account. When an account goes overdrawn, whether by express agreement or otherwise, the role of the banker and its customer, as explained in *Foley v Hill*,[4] is therefore reversed. When a customer deposits money, the bank owes them a duty, as their debtor, to repay that sum. The opposite is true when the account becomes overdrawn: the customer becomes the debtor, and the bank the creditor. Once the customer's account is overdrawn, any amounts deposited by the customer will pay off the overdraft until it is extinguished, and the customer's account returns to a credit position. The nature of the contractual obligations that arise in the context of a pre-arranged overdraft facility was explained by Cresswell J:[5]

It is a basic obligation owed by a bank to its customer that the bank will honour on presentation a cheque drawn by the customer on the bank provided that there are sufficient funds in the customer's account to meet the cheque or the bank has agreed to provide the customer with overdraft facilities sufficient to meet the cheque. Where the bank honours such a cheque or other instructions it acts within its mandate, with the result that the bank is entitled to debit the customer's account with the amount of the cheque or other instruction.

Just as the funds standing to the credit of a customer's account are repayable to him or her on demand,[6] at common law an overdraft is also repayable on demand, unless the bank has agreed to an alternative repayment arrangement. In *Rouse v Bradford Banking*[7] Lord Herschell said:[8]

It may be that an overdraft does not prevent the bank who have agreed to give it from at any time giving notice that it is no longer to continue, and that they must be paid their money. This I think at least it does; if they have agreed to give an overdraft they cannot refuse to honour cheques or drafts, within the limit of that overdraft, which have been drawn and put

---

[4] (1848) 2 HLC 28. Per Lord Cottenham at 35: 'Money, when paid into a bank, ceases altogether to be the money of the principal … it is then the money of the banker, who is bound to return an equivalent sum to that deposited with him when he asked for it … The money placed in the custody of the banker is, to all intents and purposes, the money of the banker, to do with as he pleases.' See Chapter 2, section 2.4.1.

[5] *Sierra Leone Telecommunications Co. Ltd v Barclays Bank Plc* [1998] CLC 501, 505. See also Goff J in *Barclays Bank Plc v W.J.Simms & Cooke (Southern Ltd)* [1980] 1 QB 677, 699.

[6] See Chapter 2, section 2.4.1.   [7] [1894] AC 586.   [8] At 596.

in circulation before any notice to the person to whom they have agreed to give the overdraft that the limit is to be withdrawn.

Accordingly, the bank owes no duty to the customer to ensure that any demand for repayment is made in sufficient time to allow the customer a reasonable opportunity to raise the funds owed. Despite this, it has been held that the customer should be given reasonable notice of the withdrawal of the facility, although this notice period is limited only to the time necessary to make the payment, and does not extend to any time to raise the money if it is not there to be paid.[9] Given the speed with which money can be now be transferred, any notice period is therefore likely to be very short.

Where a customer receives a demand for the repayment of an overdraft facility and they have no means of satisfying this demand, the bank can legally treat the customer as being in default and can act as appropriate to enforce their rights as creditor. However, where the overdraft facility is accompanied by an agreement that it will remain open for a particular time or purpose, the bank's right to demand repayment may be revoked. For example, in *Titford Property v Cannon Street Acceptances Ltd*[10] a letter written from the bank to the customer stipulated that the bank was extending to the customer an overdraft facility in the maximum sum of £248,000 for a period of 12 months in order to assist the customer to purchase and develop property. It was held that in these circumstances, where an overdraft is extended for a fixed time and for a specified purpose, the bank could not demand repayment, because this would have frustrated the object of the transaction and left the customer in a disastrous position.

4.2.2 **Interest and charges**

The interest charged on an overdrawn account will be calculated at either an agreed rate or based on the bank's current published lending rate. Interest is charged at a daily compound rate,[11] although the amount debited from the account may be periodical.[12] Thus, in *Yourell v Hibernian Bank Ltd*[13] Lord Atkinson considered that charging compound interest was 'a usual and perfectly legitimate mode of dealing between banker and customer'[14] and in *National Bank of Greece SA v Pinios Shipping Co (No 1)*[15] the House of Lords held that this method of charging interest was 'well established as the ordinary usage prevailing between bankers and customers'.[16]

Where an account becomes overdrawn without prior agreement, or where a customer exceeds his or her overdraft limit without the bank's consent, the bank can charge the customer higher rates of interest and also additional bank charges. These practices have been challenged in recent years in a series of high-profile cases. In *Office of Fair Trading v Abbey National plc*[17] the Office of Fair Trading (OFT) challenged the standard-form

---

[9] See *Bank of Baroda v Panessar* [1987] Ch 335 per Walton J at 348. Discussed in more detail in section 4.5.2.
[10] Unreported, QBD, 22 May 1975.
[11] Compound interest is interest that is charged not only on the original sum borrowed, but also on the accumulated interest of previous periods. [12] Normally quarterly, or half yearly.
[13] [1918] AC 372. [14] At 385. [15] [1990] 1 AC 637. [16] At 683. [17] [2010] 1 AC 696

provisions in current account agreements that permitted banks to impose additional charges on their customers for incurring an unauthorised overdraft on their account. In particular, the OFT sought a declaration that the standard terms and charges in question were not excluded from an assessment for fairness[18] under the Unfair Terms in Consumer Contracts Regulations 1999 (UTCCR).[19] The banks argued that the charges were the price or remuneration they received for the services offered and therefore could not be subject to an assessment of fairness, as stipulated in Regulation 6(2)(b).[20] The Court of Appeal[21] held that while Regulation 6(2)(b) excluded the essence of the price from any assessment of fairness, it did not exclude ancillary terms, and the charges in question were ancillary rather than essential terms. On appeal, the Supreme Court held in favour of the banks, concluding that a more restrictive interpretation should be taken meaning that any price or remuneration will naturally fall within the language of Regulation 6(2)(b). The relevant charges here were construed as part of the monetary consideration for the package of banking services supplied to current account customers and therefore fell squarely within Regulation 6(2)(b).[22]

In May 2018 the FCA announced that it would be putting forward proposals that would change the way that banks operate and charge for overdrafts.[23] Some of the immediate proposals, which are designed to increase consumer awareness of how they are using their overdrafts and how the facility works, include: mobile phone alerts linked to overdrafts, improvements in the visibility and content of key information, and online tools to allow consumers to quickly get an indication of their eligibility for an overdraft.[24] The FCA is also considering the case for more interventionist measures such as directly intervening in how firms structure their prices (including a ban on the use of fixed fees), price capping,[25] and measures to ensure that companies take active steps to address repeat overdraft use.[26]

It is clear that intervention is required in this context. Although widely used, the FCA has reported that overdrafts are poorly understood, with low levels of consumer engagement and weak competition.[27] In 2016, firms made an estimated £2.3 billion in revenues from overdrafts, of which around 30 per cent was from unarranged overdrafts.[28] The proposals put forward by the FCA would go some way to addressing the issues, making it easier for customers to manage their accounts, and making bank charges more equitable.

---

[18] For the purposes of the Regulation, a term is 'unfair' if it has not been individually negotiated and, contrary to the requirement of good faith, it causes a significant imbalance in the parties' rights and obligations arising under the contract, to the detriment of the consumer. See Regulation 5.

[19] Which implemented the EU Unfair Terms in Consumer Contracts Directive 93/13/EC. On 1 October 2015 the UTCCR's were replaced by the Consumer Rights Act 2015.

[20] 'In so far as it is in plain intelligible language, the assessment of fairness of a term shall not relate … (b)to the adequacy of the price or remuneration, as against the goods or services supplied in exchange.'

[21] [2009] 2 WLR 1286.

[22] See, for example, the judgment of Lord Walker at [42] and [51]. For a short case note on the decision see Janice Montague 'Office of Fair Trading v Abbey National Plc: Contract—Bank Levies Unfair Terms—Office of Fair Trading' (1999) *Coventry Law Journal* 44. See also Anu Arora 'Unfair Contract Terms and Unauthorised Bank Charges: A Banking Lawyer's Perspective' (2012) *Journal of Business Law* 44.

[23] FCA, *High-Cost Credit Review: Overdrafts* (May 2018) at https://www.fca.org.uk/publication/consultation/cp18–13.pdf.   [24] Ibid, Section 3.

[25] Ibid, Section 4.   [26] Ibid, Section 5.   [27] Ibid, p 3.   [28] Ibid.

> ### Box 4.1 The aftermath of *Abbey National*
>
> The Supreme Court's decision in *Abbey National* was immediately labelled by the media as 'sensational' and 'shocking' and as providing further evidence of the protected status of banks' profits. Millions of customers who eagerly anticipated refunds from incurring costs of up to £39 a day for unauthorised overdrafts were left disappointed and frustrated. However, the Supreme Court was not ruling that these charges were acceptable, rather, from a legal perspective, they simply could not be challenged in this way under the Regulations. The OFT ultimately decided not to pursue any further court challenges against the banks in respect of these charges, preferring to concentrate instead on persuading the banks to unilaterally change their practice or otherwise to lobby for new legislation to address the issue.
>
> While the former Financial Services Authority and the OFT continued to conduct research in this area, emphasising the need to treat customers fairly, most recently, in July 2017 the Financial Conduct Authority (FCA) published its report on *High-Cost Credit* (FS17/2) concluding that they had 'significant concerns about how unarranged overdrafts operate.' They found that 'Charges are high, complex and potentially harmful.' Accordingly, the FCA believes that 'there is a case to consider fundamental reform of unarranged overdrafts and consider whether they should have a place in any modern banking market.' Following a further period of review, in May 2018 the FCA concluded that there was a case for intervention in this area. This was discussed further earlier in the chapter.
>
> It should also be noted that the decision in *Abbey National* was one of the key drivers behind the introduction of the Consumer Rights Act 2015, which now provides that core terms will only be excluded from an assessment of fairness if it is 'transparent and prominent' (s64(2)). The Act also introduces a standalone requirement that all written terms must be transparent (s68).

4.2.3 Regulation of overdrafts

4.2.3.1 Standards of good practice and obligations from the FCA handbook

Both the *Standards of Lending Practice*[29] and the FCA's *Consumer Credit Sourcebook (CONC)*[30] provide standards of good practice and obligations that arise on the part of banks in relation to the provision of overdrafts. For example, where the customer can overdraw their account without a pre-arranged overdraft, or where they can exceed their pre-arranged overdraft limit, the current account agreement must contain information pertaining to the rate of interest charged, any conditions applicable to that rate, any reference rate on which that rate is based, information on any changes to that rate of interest, and any other charges payable by the customer under the agreement.[31] If a current account customer wishes to opt out of an unarranged overdraft, the *Standards of Lending Practice* provide that banks should enable customers to exercise this option

---

[29] *Standards of Lending Practice: Personal Customers* (July 2016) at https://www.lendingstandardsboard.org.uk/wp-content/uploads/2016/07/Standards-of-Lending-Practice-July-16.pdf.

[30] FCA, *Consumer Credit Sourcebook (CONC)* at https://www.handbook.fca.org.uk/handbook/CONC.pdf.

[31] Ibid, paragraph 4.7.2. This information has to be provided in writing, at least annually: CONC paragraph 6.3.3.

and inform them of the effect this will have on the operation of their account.[32] Where a customer overdraws on their account without a pre-arranged overdraft, or they exceed their pre-arranged overdraft limit for a period of more than one month, and the amount of the overdraft or the excess is significant,[33] the bank must inform the customer in writing of: [34]

- The fact that the account is overdrawn or in excess of the agreed limit.
- The amount of the overdraft or excess.
- The rate of interest charged on it.
- Any other charges payable by the customer in relation to it (including any penalties and any interest on those charges).

Further, banks are required to inform their customers of any changes to the interest rates and fees on their overdraft. To help the customer to compare costs, banks must include details of the previous interest rates and fees in the information provided.[35] Finally, banks are encouraged to monitor customers' overdraft limits to ensure they are not exhibiting signs of financial stress and, where relevant, offer appropriate support.[36]

4.2.3.2 The Consumer Credit Act 1974

As discussed in Chapter 3, the Consumer Credit Act 1974 (CCA) applies protective measures in the context of 'regulated agreements', which apply if credit[37] is extended to an individual.[38] A bank overdraft falls within the definition of an unrestricted use[39] running-account credit,[40] even if the overdraft is unauthorised.[41] Originally, most overdrafts were excluded from the documentation and cancellation provisions found in Part V CCA,[42] but the implementation of the Consumer Credit Directive[43] resulted in the imposition of certain requirements. For these purposes, the Act distinguishes between 'authorised business overdrafts' and 'authorised non-business overdrafts'.[44] In both contexts, the rules relating to antecedent negotiations,[45] the form and content of the agreement,[46] and the

---

[32] *Standards of Lending Practice: Personal Customers* (July 2016) 'Account maintenance and servicing' paragraph 6 at https://www.lendingstandardsboard.org.uk/wp-content/uploads/2016/07/Standards-of-Lending-Practice-July-16.pdf.

[33] The amount of the overdraft or excess is significant if: (a) the account holder is liable to pay a charge for which he or she would not otherwise be liable; (b) the overdraft or excess is likely to have an adverse effect on the customer's ability to receive further credit (including any effect on the information about the customer held by a credit reference agency); or (c) it otherwise appears significant, having regard to all the circumstances. CONC paragraph 6.3.4(3).   [34] CONC paragraph 6.3.4.

[35] *Standards of Lending Practice: Personal Customers* (July 2016) 'Account maintenance and servicing' paragraph 6 at https://www.lendingstandardsboard.org.uk/wp-content/uploads/2016/07/Standards-of-Lending-Practice-July-16.pdf.   [36] Ibid, 'Money management' paragraph 3.

[37] Section 9: '"credit" includes a cash loan, and any other form of financial accommodation.'

[38] Section 8.   [39] Section 11.   [40] Section 10(1).   [41] See Schedule 2, example 17.

[42] Section 74.

[43] 2008/48/EC. The Directive was transposed in the UK by a series of implementing regulations that came into force on 1 February 2011.

[44] See Section 74(1B)–(1C), inserted by The Consumer Credit (EU Directive) Regulations 2010 (SI 2010/1010), Regulation 17(2).   [45] Section 56.   [46] Section 60.

duty to provide a copy of the overdraft agreement[47] apply. In the context of non-business overdrafts further rules relating to disclosure of information[48] and the duty to provide a copy of the consumer credit agreement apply.[49]

Under Part VI CCA, the bank has a duty (following payment of a £1 fee) to give certain information to the debtor under a running-account agreement including the state of the account, the amount, if any, currently payable under the agreement by the debtor to the creditor, and the amounts and due dates of any payments that, if the debtor does not draw further on the account, will later become payable under the agreement by the debtor to the creditor.[50] The bank must also provide periodic statements.[51] Further, CCA provides that in the case of all overdraft facilities, except if certain conditions are met,[52] the bank must notify the debtor of any increases in the rate of interest charged.[53]

Part VII CCA contains provisions relating to default and termination. While the bank is normally required to give seven days' notice before terminating the agreement,[54] this only applies if the credit is extended for a fixed period.[55] Accordingly, CCA preserves the bank's right to demand repayment of the overdraft without notice; while new rules were introduced on the termination of agreements with no fixed duration,[56] these do not apply to overdrafts.[57] However, if repayment is demanded because the customer has defaulted in some way, the bank must provide the customer with a default notice.[58]

⊙ Key takeaways

- An overdraft is an extension of credit by a bank to its customer via the customer's current account. It can be entered into by express agreement, or by implication when a customer instructs the bank to make a payment but there are insufficient funds in their account to satisfy it.

- Where an account is overdrawn, the customer becomes the debtor and the bank becomes the creditor. The bank can demand repayment without notice.

- Overdrafts are a regulated credit agreement and therefore banks must satisfy certain protective measures under the Consumer Credit Act 1974. Banks are also subject to certain standards of good practice and obligations from the *Standards for Lending Practice* and the FCA's *CONC*.

---

[47] Section 61(B), inserted by The Consumer Credit (EU Directive) Regulations 2010 (SI 2010/1010), Regulation 9.   [48] Section 55.

[49] Section 55C, inserted by The Consumer Credit (EU Directive) Regulations 2010 (SI 2010/1010), Regulation 6.   [50] Section 78.   [51] Section 78(4).

[52] Section 78A(2), inserted by The Consumer Credit (EU Directive) Regulations 2010 (SI 2010/1010), Regulation 27. Including, for example, where the agreement provides that the rate of interest is to vary according to a reference rate, where the reference rate is publicly available, and where information about the reference rate is available on the premises of the creditor.

[53] Section 78A(4) and (5), inserted by The Consumer Credit (EU Directive) Regulations 2010 (SI 2010/1010), Regulation 27.   [54] Section 98(1).

[55] Section 98(2).

[56] Section 98A, inserted by The Consumer Credit (EU Directive) Regulations 2010 (SI 2010/1010), Regulation 38.

[57] Section 98A(8), inserted by The Consumer Credit (EU Directive) Regulations 2010 (SI 2010/1010), Regulation 38.   [58] Section 87.

Key bibliography

Articles

Arora, A, 'Unfair contract terms and unauthorised bank charges: a banking lawyer's perspective'
(2012) *Journal of Business Law* 44

Montague, J, 'Office of Fair Trading v Abbey National Plc: contract—bank levies unfair terms—
Office of Fair Trading' (1999) 14(2) *Coventry Law Journal* 44

Reports

FCA, *High-Cost Credit* (July 2017) FS17/2 at https://www.fca.org.uk/publication/feedback/fs17-02.pdf

Codes

Standards of Lending Practice: Personal Customers (July 2016) at https://www.lendingstandards-
board.org.uk/wp-content/uploads/2016/07/Standards-of-Lending-Practice-July-16.pdf

Standards of Lending Practice: Business Customers (October 2017) at https://www.lendingstand-
ardsboard.org.uk/wp-content/uploads/2017/10/Standards-of-Lending-Practice-Business-
27-Oct.pdf

4.3 Fixed-term loans

A *fixed-term loan*, as the name suggests, is a loan made for a fixed period of time. It
can be made to an individual consumer or to a business. This distinction is important
because there are separate standards of good practice that apply to lending, depending
on whether the loan is made in favour of a consumer[59] or business.[60] The object of a
loan can vary hugely, from a personal loan for the purposes of home improvements, to
large loans extended to a corporation to enable them to finance a new business venture.
The loan agreement normally specifies the purpose for which the loan is being drawn.
Banks tend to make loans to consumers and smaller businesses for a term of up to five
years, and larger companies for longer periods of up to ten years, although this will
ultimately depend on the financial condition of the company and the intended use of
the loan facility. Larger-term loans made to multinational companies are often made by
a syndicate of banks who share the cost of borrowing in agreed proportions (discussed
in section 4.4). The conditions of the loan agreement relating to security[61] will depend
on who the borrower is and the object of the loan (see section 4.6). Loans to individual
consumers will often be unsecured. The interest charged will depend on a number of
factors including the bank's assessment of the risk, the period of time over which the

---

[59] *Standards of Lending Practice: Personal Customers* (July 2016) at https://www.lendingstandardsboard.org.
uk/wp-content/uploads/2016/07/Standards-of-Lending-Practice-July-16.pdf.

[60] *Standards of Lending Practice: Business Customers* (October 2017) at https://www.lendingstandardsboard.
org.uk/wp-content/uploads/2017/10/Standards-of-Lending-Practice-Business-27-Oct.pdf.

[61] Security generally relates to some form of proprietary or possessory right in the borrower's (or a third
party's) property that a bank can exercise in order to enforce repayment of the loan facility.

loan is extended, and any security that has been furnished. The rate of interest paid will vary with the market rate during the lifetime of the loan.

Initially, the bank will review the transaction to determine the viability of the proposal made by the borrower. If the bank agrees to lend, the loan facility will follow a standard form, especially if it is a consumer transaction, in which case it will have to comply with the provisions of the CCA 1974.

4.3.1 **Reviewing the transaction**

When deciding whether to enter into a lending transaction, the bank will consider a number of factors in order to safeguard its interests. For example, the bank will need to consider the income of the borrower, the source of the repayments and the nature of the repayments (i.e. whether the loan will be repaid in fixed equal payments,[62] whether the repayments will increase over the loan period,[63] or whether the repayments will all be made in one single payment at the end of the loan period[64]). In determining the nature of the repayments, the bank may consider the purposes for which the loan is sought.[65] For example, if the loan is needed in order to set up a business, the bank will appreciate that the borrower may be unable to repay the capital in the early stages and might therefore offer a facility whereby only interest is charged for an initial amount of time. The bank will also have to consider whether the facility should be available to be drawn down in one single transaction or by successive instalments. Finally, they will need to determine when the sums will be repayable, which is usually monthly, quarterly, bi-annually, yearly, or in a single sum on an agreed date.

4.3.2 **Terms of the loan facility**

The detailed terms of a loan facility may vary but each will contain similar core provisions. There has been some attempt to standardise loan documentation. In October 1999, the Loan Market Association (LMA), the Association of Corporate Treasurers, and some of the major city law firms introduced recommended standard forms of primary loan documentation in the syndicated lending market.[66] Commercial loan agreements typically contain (1) *conditions precedent* in relation to the availability of the loan, (2) a series of representations, warranties and *covenants* provided by the borrower, and (3) a series of default clauses to protect the interests of the bank. Each will be discussed in turn.

---

[62] Known as amortised repayments.   [63] Known as balloon repayments.
[64] Known as a bullet repayment.
[65] LMA, *Multicurrency Term and Revolving Facilities Agreement*, 18 July 2017, Clause 3.1 Available to LMA members via http://www.lma.eu.com. © Loan Market Association. Whilst the LMA has consented to the quotation of, and referral to, parts of its documents to the purpose of this publication, it assumes no responsibility for any use to which its documents, or any extract from them, may be put. The views and opinions expressed in the publication are the views of the authors and do not necessarily represent those of the LMA. Furthermore, the LMA cannot accept any responsibility for any error or omission.   [66] Ibid.

4.3.2.1 **Conditions precedent**

Conditions precedent[67] are terms that have to be complied with before the borrower can draw down the funds from the bank. They are used by the lender as a mechanism to ensure that the borrower provides certain documents and that certain factual circumstances exist. The borrower will normally be required to provide certain documentation such as, in the case of a corporate borrower, a copy of the company's constitutional documents, a copy of the board's resolution approving the loan, most recent financial information, and, where there is a cross-border element, confirmation from the relevant foreign lawyers of the loan's validity.[68] Before a loan is made, the bank will usually require confirmation that any representations and warranties given by the borrower remain accurate and no event of default is outstanding or would result from making the loan.[69]

4.3.2.2 **Representations, warranties, and covenants**

Representations and **warranties** fall within two core categories:[70] those relating to legal issues such as the legal status, power, and authority of the borrower and the validity of the documents, and those relating to commercial issues such as the credit standing and financial position of the borrower. Accordingly, representations and warranties perform an investigative function and are used by the bank to obtain information on the borrower and the project being financed. Borrowers will be required to represent, for example, that their accounts are accurate and they have not suffered any material adverse change,[71] and that they are not subject to any legal proceedings that could affect their ability to repay the loan.[72] The core purpose of a representation or warranty from the bank's perspective, and something that is normally specified in the loan agreement, is that any inaccuracy in a representation or warranty will be treated as an event of default, enabling the bank to cancel the agreement and accelerate repayment.[73]

Covenants are undertakings given by the borrower to the bank, which give the bank a degree of control over the conduct of the borrower's business to ensure that the borrower preserves his or her financial standing. The covenants found in a loan agreement will depend on a number of factors including the size and duration of the loan, the financial state of the borrower, whether the agreement is standard or has been negotiated, and the existence of competition from other banks.[74] The main covenants normally required of a corporate borrower include: the provision of financial information including statements and management accounts;[75] the maintenance of certain financial

---

[67] See generally, ibid, Clause 4.   [68] Ibid, Clause 4.1 and Schedule 2, Part I.   [69] Ibid, Clause 4.2.
[70] See generally, ibid, Section 8.   [71] Ibid, Clause 19.10 and 19.11.   [72] Ibid, Clause 19.13.
[73] Ibid, Clause 23.4.
[74] See, for example, Peter Taylor and Judy Day, 'Evidence on the Practices of UK Bankers in Contracting for Medium-Term Debt' (1995) 9 *Journal of International Banking Law* 394 and Peter Taylor and Judy Day 'Bankers' Perspectives on the Role of Covenants in Debt Contracts' (1996) 5 *Journal of International Banking Law* 201.
[75] LMA, *Multicurrency Term and Revolving Facilities Agreement*, 18 July 2017, Clause 20. Available to LMA members via http://www.lma.eu.com.

ratios, for example, the maintenance of a certain minimum net worth;[76] restrictions on the disposal of assets;[77] restrictions on the granting of security to other lenders[78] (known as a negative pledge clause[79]); and an undertaking that the borrower's obligations under the loan agreement will rank at least equally with other unsecured obligations[80] (known as a *pari passu* clause[81]). Failure to comply with one of these covenants will usually be treated as an event of default, entitling the bank to cancel the agreement and accelerate repayment.[82]

4.3.2.3 Default clauses

All lending agreements will contain a clause that specifies certain events of default, which will give the bank the option of accelerating repayment of the loan and terminate its commitment to make any further advances.[83] The loan agreement must specify explicitly the event of default. It is unlikely that the courts will ever imply an event into the contract.[84] The rights the bank has under the loan agreement run alongside their common law rights, which are triggered if the borrower breaches their obligations under the loan agreement.[85] Typical events of default include a failure to repay any capital or interest as it falls due, the bankruptcy of the customer, the appointment of an official receiver or the company being wound up.[86] Banks often include a cross-default clause, which means that any event of default by the borrower to another lender will be treated as a default under the loan agreement.[87] Further, any 'material adverse change' (MAC) in the borrower's financial position could be considered as a defaulting event.[88]

---

[76] Ibid, Clause 21. As this is a complex area, a blank space is left to be filled in by the parties.

[77] Ibid, Clause 22.4.   [78] Ibid, Clause 22.3.

[79] A negative pledge clause is a clause in a loan agreement that prevents the borrower from granting any security interests in their property. The purpose is to ensure that the property of the borrower will be available to satisfy any claim made by the bank in the event of the borrower defaulting on its payment obligations. See generally, Philip Woods, *International Loans, Bonds, Guarantees, Legal Opinions* (London: Sweet and Maxwell 1995).

[80] LMA, *Multicurrency Term and Revolving Facilities Agreement*, 18 July 2017, Clause 19.12. Available to LMA members via http://www.lma.eu.com.

[81] The rationale for such a clause is to ensure that the borrower cannot incur obligations to other lenders that rank legally senior to the loan agreement. See Philip Woods, *International Loans, Bonds, Guarantees, Legal Opinions* (London: Sweet and Maxwell 1995); and Vanessa Finch, 'Is pari passu passe?' (2000) *Insolvency Lawyer* 194.

[82] LMA, *Multicurrency Term and Revolving Facilities Agreement*, 18 July 2017, Clause 23.2 and 23.3. Available to LMA members via http://www.lma.eu.com.   [83] Ibid, Clause 23.

[84] For example, in *Cryne v Barclays Bank plc* [1987] BCLC 548 it was held that, in the absence of a contractual right to do so, a bank could not appoint a receiver (and therefore enforce repayment) on the grounds that their security was in jeopardy.

[85] If the borrower defaults on a payment, and this is construed as a breach of a condition, the bank will be entitled to repudiate the contract.

[86] LMA, *Multicurrency Term and Revolving Facilities Agreement*, 18 July 2017, Clause 23. Available to LMA members via http://www.lma.eu.com.

[87] Ibid, Clause 23.5. This is designed to protect the interests of the bank, who would want to be on an equal footing with other lenders who may have started enforcement proceedings against the borrower.

[88] Ibid, Clause 23.12. The section is left bank so that parties can individually agree upon the wording.

Historically there has been limited litigation on MAC clauses in loan agreements,[89] but they were subject to review in two recent cases.

In *Cukurova Finance International Ltd v Alfa Telecom Turkey Ltd*,[90] ATT lent CFI the sum of $1.352 billion. Clause 17 of the facility agreement set out the defaulting events, which, according to clause 17.18, would entitle ATT to obtain immediate repayment of the loan together with accrued interest. Such an event included, by Clause 17.16, a circumstance that 'in the opinion of ATT had, or was reasonably likely to have, a material adverse effect on the financial condition, assets or business of CFI'. When an arbitration award was made against CFI for breaching an agreement with a third party that ordered specific performance but subsequently, in lieu, awarded damages, ATT argued that there had been a MAC, and sought immediate repayment of the loan. In determining whether a defaulting event had occurred within the meaning of Clause 17.16, the Privy Council held that despite the subjective nature of the clause, an objective approach must be taken such that the court 'has to be convinced by admissible evidence that ATT did in fact form the requisite opinion, as well as being convinced that that opinion was honest and rational'.[91] The Privy Council found that the arbitration award, which amounted to a 'very substantial order for damages against ATT' was unquestionably 'reasonably likely to have a material adverse effect on CFI's financial condition'[92] and, on the facts, it was established that ATT had formed the requisite opinion. Accordingly, the arbitration award constituted a defaulting event.

In *Grupo Hotelero Urvasco SA v Carey Value Added SL*[93] the loan agreement contained a clause that required the borrower (GHU), at specified times, to make representations to the absence of any MAC in their financial condition. When the lender, CVA, ceased trading, GHU brought a claim for damages. CVA denied breaching the agreement and in turn brought a counterclaim against GHU, contending that there had been a MAC regarding which GHU had made a false representation, thereby amounting to a defaulting event. Although on the facts the court held that there had been no breach of the representation, they did offer some general guiding principles on the interpretation of MAC clauses as set out in Box 4.2.

A breach of any of the defaulting events will not necessarily lead to an automatic default under the loan agreement. In practice, borrowers may be allowed a certain grace period. In the context of corporate loans, there is no statutory control on the ability of a lender to exercise its discretion to invoke its remedies under an event of default clause. Previously, consumers could rely on the UTCCR 1999, which required terms to pass a test of 'fairness'. This has now been replaced by the Consumer Rights Act 2015, which applies a similar test of 'fairness'.[94]

---

[89] For example, in *BNP Paribas SA v Yukos Oil Company* [2005] EWHC 1321 the court held that a MAC had clearly occurred when YOC became subject to a special enquiry by the Russian Ministry of Natural Resources, the Chief Executive of the company was arrested and resigned, Standard and Poor's downgraded Yukos' credit rating, YOC was given a tax bill of $3.3 billion, and they announced in a press release that they may have to consider bankruptcy.   [90] [2016] AC 923.

[91] At 950.   [92] Ibid.   [93] [2013] EWHC 1039.

[94] Section 62(4): 'A term is unfair if, contrary to the requirement of good faith, it causes a significant imbalance in the parties' rights and obligations under the contract to the detriment of the consumer.'

> **Box 4.2 Guiding principles on interpreting MAC clauses**
>
> • If a bank is trying to argue that there has been a MAC based on a change in the company's 'financial condition' this will be determined by analysing the company's financial statements at the relevant date (para 351). As a matter of ordinary language, 'financial condition' does not encompass other matters such as the prospects of a company or external economic or market changes. Such an interpretation would render the enquiry wide ranging and imprecise (paras 348 and 351). However, the enquiry may not necessarily be limited to financial information if there is other 'compelling evidence' such as the fact that the borrower has ceased paying its bank debts (para 352).
>
> • Unless the adverse change in its financial condition significantly affects the borrower's ability to perform its obligations, and in particular its ability to repay the loan, it is not a material change (para 357).
>
> • If a state of affairs at the time of drawdown was already subsisting at the date of the loan agreement, and the lender was aware of this, it will not give rise to a MAC (paras 358–62).
>
> • In order to be material, any change must not merely be temporary (para 363).
>
> • The burden of proof is on the lender to prove that there has been a MAC (para 363).

In *Director General of Fair Trading v First National Bank plc*[95] the defendant bank included a term in its loan agreement stipulating that, should the borrower default on his or her repayments, interest would continue to be payable at the contractual rate until any judgment obtained by the bank was discharged. The House of Lords determined that this term could be scrutinised under the UTCCR because it concerned neither the main subject matter of the contract nor the adequacy of the price or remuneration for the goods or services provided.[96] In assessing the clause for fairness, the House of Lords held that the term was not 'unfair' as it did not 'cause a significant imbalance in the parties' rights and obligations under the contract to the detriment of the consumer in a manner or to an extent which is contrary to the requirement of good faith.'[97] On the contrary, their Lordships held that the main purpose of the clause was 'to ensure that the borrower does not enjoy the benefit of the outstanding balance after judgment without fulfilling the corresponding obligation which he has undertaken to pay interest on it as provided for in the contract.'[98]

---

[95] [2002] 1 AC 481.

[96] Both of which are excluded from the test of fairness: Regulation 6(2). A similar exclusion applies in the Consumer Rights Act 2015, s64(1). However, according to s64(2) of the 2015 Act, these terms will be excluded from an assessment of fairness only if they are transparent and prominent.

[97] Per Lord Bingham of Cornhill, at 497.

[98] Per Lord Hope of Craighead, at 502.

4.3.3 **Regulation**

As well as adhering to the relevant provisions in the *Standards for Lending Practice*[99] and the FCA's *Consumer Credit Sourcebook (CONC)*[100] banks must also comply with the extensive provisions of the Consumer Credit Act 1974 (CCA). Importantly, Part V of the CCA applies in its entirety to loans, unlike overdrafts, which are subject to a series of concessions (discussed in section 4.2). Section 60 of the Act empowers the Treasury[101] to make regulations as to the form and content of documents embodying regulated agreements. The Consumer Credit (Agreements) Regulations,[102] which were passed pursuant to that power, must be strictly adhered to, otherwise the loan will be unenforceable by the bank in the absence of a court order. Similarly, the pre-contractual information requirements contained in the Consumer Credit (Disclosure of Information) Regulations[103] must be given in the prescribed form before the contract is concluded otherwise, as above, the agreement will be unenforceable without a court order.

The Consumer Credit (Agreements) Regulations require certain information to be contained in the agreement,[104] prescribing, for example, that the agreement bears a heading that makes clear reference to the fact that it is an agreement regulated by the CCA 1974,[105] that it contains notices advising the borrower of their rights under the Act,[106] and that the signature of the borrower must be executed in a prescribed form.[107] In terms of the information to be provided, the Agreement Regulations require the lender to provide, for example: the duration of the agreement; the amount of credit or the credit limit; a statement indicating how and when the credit to be advanced under the agreement is to be drawn down; the rate of interest payable; the total amount repayable; information about the annual percentage rate (APR); the timing of repayments; and the amount of the repayments.[108] Additionally, any charges must be listed, as well

---

[99] *Standards of Lending Practice: Personal Customers* (July 2016) at https://www.lendingstandardsboard. org.uk/wp-content/uploads/2016/07/Standards-of-Lending-Practice-July-16.pdf; *Standards of Lending Practice: Business Customers* (October 2017) at https://www.lendingstandardsboard.org.uk/wp-content/ uploads/2017/10/Standards-of-Lending-Practice-Business-27-Oct.pdf.

[100] Financial Conduct Authority, *Consumer Credit Sourcebook (CONC)* at https://www.handbook.fca.org. uk/handbook/CONC.pdf.

[101] As amended by The Financial Services Act 2012 (Consumer Credit) Order 2013, SI 2013/1882, Article 7(3)(a)(i), previously it was the Secretary of State.

[102] There are two sets of regulations; The Consumer Credit (Agreements) Regulations 1983, SI 1983/1553 (as amended by SI 2004/1482) which applies to agreements secured on land unless the lender has 'opted into' the newer regime; and The Consumer Credit (Agreements) Regulations 2010, SI 2010/1014.

[103] 2004, SI 2004/1481.

[104] A comprehensive list can be found in Schedule 1 of both The Consumer Credit (Agreements) Regulations 1983 SI 1983/1553 (as amended by SI 2004/1482) and The Consumer Credit (Agreements) Regulations 2010, SI 2010/1014.

[105] Ibid.   [106] Ibid, Schedule 2.

[107] The Consumer Credit (Agreements) Regulations 1983 SI 1983/1553 (as amended by SI 2004/1482), Regulation 6; The Consumer Credit (Agreements) Regulations 2010, SI 2010/1014, Regulation 4.

[108] Ibid, Schedule 1.

as the rate of interest for late payments and details of the borrower's right of withdrawal under s66A of the CCA 1974.[109] In the event that an agreement is modified, including, for example, where a further advance is made under an existing agreement, the modification must comply with the terms of the Regulations.[110]

Where the loan agreement is secured on land (except in the case of agreements that fall within s58(2) CCA 1974), the CCA contains certain special provisions. For example, the bank is required to send the borrower an advance copy of the agreement and then allow them seven days to consider whether they wish to withdraw from the transaction. At the end of this period, the bank then has to send the borrower the agreement for signature, allowing the customer a further seven-day 'consideration period' during which the bank is refrained from approaching the borrower.[111] The objective of these elaborate provisions is to allow the borrower plenty of time, free from any pressure from the bank, to make up his or her mind and to ensure that the borrower does not rush into the transaction.

Even after the agreement has been executed, the bank continues to have duties relating to disclosure. For example, the bank is obliged to provide periodic statements of account[112] and, upon request (and after payment of a £1 fee), the bank must provide the borrower with certain information relating to the total sum paid under the agreement by the borrower, the total sum that has become payable under the agreement by the borrower but remains unpaid, and the total sum that is to become payable under the agreement by the borrower.[113] Further, if the bank wishes to make any unilateral variations to the agreement, notice must be given to the borrower,[114] and that notice must be in writing if the variation relates to interest rates.[115]

Part VII CCA deals with default and termination. In the event that the borrower defaults in payment, the CCA provides that the bank must give him or her at least 14 days' notice before it can terminate the agreement, demand earlier repayment, or enforce any security.[116] The default notice must be in a particular form and specify the following: the nature of the alleged breach; if the breach is capable of remedy, if so, what action needs to be taken by what date; and, if the breach is not capable of remedy, the sum (if any) to be paid as compensation for the breach and the date before which it has to be paid.[117] The notice must also advise the borrower that if the arrears are duly paid, no further action will be taken against them.[118] The bank must also serve notice in non-default cases where, for example, they want to call in the loan,[119] or terminate the agreement because of bankruptcy.[120]

---

[109] Ibid.

[110] The Consumer Credit (Agreements) Regulations 1983 SI 1983/1553 (as amended by SI 2004/1482), Regulation 7 and Schedule 8; The Consumer Credit (Agreements) Regulations 2010, SI 2010/1014, Regulation 5.

[111] See ss58(1) and 61.

[112] Section 77A inserted by Consumer Credit Act 2006, s6. These statements must be provided free of charge: s77A(3).   [113] Section 77.

[114] Section 82.

[115] Section 78A inserted by The Consumer Credit (EU Directive) Regulations 2010 (SI 2010/1010), Regulation 27.   [116] Section 87.

[117] Section 88(1).   [118] Section 89.   [119] Section 76(1).   [120] Section 98.

Key takeaways

- A fixed-term loan is a loan made to either an individual consumer or business for a fixed period of time.
- Commercial loan agreements typically contain (1) conditions precedent in relation to the availability of the loan, (2) A series of representations, warranties, and covenants provided by the borrower, and (3) a series of default clauses to protect the interests of the bank.
- Banks must adhere to the *Standards of Lending Practice*, the FCA's *Consumer Credit Sourcebook (CONC)*, and the relevant provisions of the Consumer Credit Act 1974, which details, for example, the information that must be provided to borrowers both before and after the execution of the agreement as well as the rights and responsibilities of both parties in the event of default.

Key bibliography

Articles

Finch, V, 'Is pari passu passe?' (2000) *Insolvency Lawyer* 194

Taylor, P and Day, J, 'Bankers' Perspectives on the Role of Covenants in Debt Contracts' (1996) 5 *Journal of International Banking Law* 201

Taylor, P and Day, J, 'Evidence on the Practices of UK Bankers in Contracting for Medium-Term Debt' (1995) 9 *Journal of International Banking Law* 394

Codes

Standards of Lending Practice: Personal Customers (July 2016) at https://www.lendingstandards-board.org.uk/wp-content/uploads/2016/07/Standards-of-Lending-Practice-July-16.pdf

Standards of Lending Practice: Business Customers (October 2017) at https://www.lendingstand-ardsboard.org.uk/wp-content/uploads/2017/10/Standards-of-Lending-Practice-Business-27-Oct.pdf

---

4.4 Syndicated loans

A *syndicated loan* involves two or more banks that each contributes towards making a single loan to a borrower. A loan syndicate is commonly used where an individual bank is unable or unwilling to offer the full amount of the loan or to take on the entire risk of advancing the loan. Rather than entering into a series of bilateral loans, each with different terms and conditions, a syndicated loan agreement simplifies the process as the borrower has a single agreement covering the whole group of lenders. It therefore creates savings in terms of money and time because the borrower can deal with one agent bank and one set of documents. Large corporations are usually the borrowers for this type of loan where the funds are used for things such as acquisitions or expansion projects. Similarly, sovereign countries may utilise a syndicated loan facility to fund large infrastructure projects.[121]

4.4.1 Mechanics of the loan syndication

The process of setting up a loan syndication is initiated by the borrower, who grants a mandate to a single bank (known as the 'arranger') to arrange the loan. The arranging bank, who will often already have an established relationship with the borrower, is responsible for advising the borrower on the facilities it requires and then negotiating the terms of those facilities. The main function of the arranging bank is to put together the loan and it will do so by sending out 'term sheets' to selected banks to solicit their interest. These term sheets will contain a brief description of the borrower and details of the proposed financing structure including, for example, the type of facility,[122] the facility amounts, the pricing, and the terms of the loan. While potential participants are being approached, the arranging bank will work with the borrower to produce a more detailed document called an 'information memorandum' (IM), which will be used to market the loan to the banks that have expressed an interest. It will contain a more detailed description of the borrower's business, management and accounts, and the proposed loan facility.

To facilitate the administration of the loan once the facility has been executed, one bank from the syndicate is appointed as an agent.[123] This is often, although not always, the arranging bank. This bank (that acts as agent for the other participating banks, not the borrower) has a number of important administrative functions, as detailed in Box 4.3.

Any decisions of a material nature (e.g. waiving a breach of covenant, amending a term, or deciding whether or not to trigger a MAC clause) must usually be taken by the majority, if not the entire, syndicate.[124] However, the loan agreement may confer some discretionary powers on the agent bank including, for example, the power to request financial information from the borrower, or the power to accelerate the loan on default without confirmation of the views of the other participating banks in certain urgent circumstances. While the agent bank will be subject to the standard duties and responsibilities of any agent under English law, the facility agreement will normally contain a number of provisions to limit the scope of the agent bank's relationship with the other

---

[121] For example, the construction of the Eurotunnel was financed by a syndicate of over 200 banks. See Michael Grant, 'Financing Eurotunnel' (1997) *Japan Railway and Transport Review* 46.

[122] Generally, there are two types of facility: a term loan facility where the bank provides a certain sum over a fixed period of time (i.e. the term), which is repayable either in instalments (amortising) or in one payment at the end of the facility (bullet); or a revolving loan facility that provides the borrower with a certain sum over a specified period of time, which can be drawn down, repaid, and re-drawn again during the term of the facility.

[123] LMA, *Multicurrency Term and Revolving Facilities Agreement*, 18 July 2017, Clause 26.1. Available to LMA members via http://www.lma.eu.com.

[124] These decisions requiring unanimous consent relate to things such as extending payment dates, varying the amounts due, and releasing any security.

> ### Box 4.3 Functions of an agent
>
> - **Point of contact**: the agent will be responsible for maintaining contact with the borrower and representing the views of the other syndicate participants.
> - **Monitor**: the agent will be responsible for monitoring the compliance of the borrower with the terms of the loan facility.
> - **Record-keeper**: the agent will receive any notices from the borrower.
> - **Paying agent**: the agent will receive the funds from the participating banks and disperse them to the borrower. Similarly, the agent will receive all payment of interest and capital from the borrower under the loan agreement. They are responsible for passing this money back to the participating banks.
> - The terms of the loan agreement provide that the agent bank will be paid a fee in exchange for performing these functions.

parties, including, for example, a disclaimer that no fiduciary duty exists in relation to the other participating banks.[125]

4.4.2 Terms

In October 1999, the LMA, the Association of Corporate Treasurers, and some of the major city law firms, introduced recommended standard forms of primary loan documentation. Some of the core provisions of the LMA's *Multicurrency Term and Revolving Facilities Agreement* have already been considered, in section 4.3, so the focus here will be on those provisions that relate specifically to the syndicated nature of the loan facility. The agreement will set out the party's rights and obligations including that:[126]

- Each party's obligations are several.
- Failure of one party to perform their obligations does not affect the obligations of the other party's.
- No party is responsible for the obligations of any other party.
- The rights of each party are separate and independent.
- Each party may separately enforce its rights.

---

[125] LMA, *Multicurrency Term and Revolving Facilities Agreement*, 18 July 2017, Clause 26.5. Available to LMA members via http://www.lma.eu.com. See also; Leo Clarke and Stanley Farrar, 'Rights and Duties of Managing and Agent Banks in Syndicated Loans to Government Borrowers' (1982) *University of Illinois Law Review* 229 at 234; and David Halliday and Rhodri Davies, 'Risks and Responsibilities of the Agent Bank and the Arranging Bank in Syndicated Credit Facilities' (1997) *Journal of International Banking Law* 182.

[126] LMA, *Multicurrency Term and Revolving Facilities Agreement*, 18 July 2017, Clause 2.3. Available to LMA members via http://www.lma.eu.com.

The divided nature of each bank's rights reinforces the fact that every separate loan is owed to each bank individually. Whilst the bank's rights are generally separate, with respect to the administration of the loan, including, for example, the right to accelerate the loan in the event of default, the syndicate usually agrees to abide by a decision of the majority.[127] A majority is defined as a 'Lender or Lenders whose Commitments aggregate more than 66⅔% of the Total Commitments.'[128] A syndicated loan agreement will also normally contain a pro-rata (sharing) clause, which essentially obliges the agent bank receiving payment from the borrower to share it with the other participants in proportion to the amount of each participant's outstanding debt.[129]

4.4.3 Legal nature

While there is some uncertainty regarding the legal nature of the relationships between the members of a loan syndicate, it is generally accepted that, because there is no sharing of net profit by the members, it is not a partnership arrangement.[130] A partnership arrangement would give rise to fiduciary obligations between the members of the syndicate as well as other consequences including the banks having joint liability for each other's actions. Participants to a loan syndication often want to find that there is a fiduciary relationship because of the duty of disclosure that fiduciaries traditionally owe. Participants may want to argue that the arranging bank failed to disclose certain material information that would have affected their decision to participate in the syndicate.

Despite the fact that loan syndicates are not considered a partnership agreement, there is some English authority that supports the proposition that the arranging bank may owe a fiduciary duty to the other lenders in the syndicate. In *UBAF Ltd v European American Banking Corporation (The Pacific Colocotronis)*,[131] the defendant arranging bank sent the claimant a term sheet and other material stating that the loans were 'attractive financing of two companies in a sound and profitable group.' In reliance on these statements the claimant bank decided to participate in the loan. When the borrowers later defaulted on the loans, the claimant bank alleged that the defendant was liable for deceit, misrepresentation, and negligence. On the question of the arranging bank's relationship with the other banks in the syndicate, Ackner LJ remarked (obiter) that:[132]

> quite clearly the defendants were acting in a fiduciary capacity for all the other participants. It was the defendants who received the plaintiffs' money and it was the defendants who arrange for and held, on behalf of all participants, the collateral security for the loan. If, therefore, it was within the defendants' knowledge at any time whilst they were carrying out their fiduciary duties that the security was, as the plaintiffs allege, inadequate, it must, we think, clearly have been their duty to inform the participants of that fact and their continued failure to do so would constitute continuing breach of their fiduciary duty.

[127] Ibid, Clause 23.13.   [128] Ibid, Clause 1.1.   [129] Ibid, Clause 28.
[130] Partnership Act 1890, s1, which defines a partnership as a 'relation which subsists between persons carrying on a business in common with a view of profit.'
[131] [1984] QB 713.   [132] At 728.

While this case has been cited as authority for the assertion that the arranging bank may owe a fiduciary duty,[133] this should be treated with caution. First, the fact that the arranging bank also became the agent bank and the security trustee seems to have led the court to the conclusion that it owed a fiduciary duty. However, this analysis also invites the view that, had the bank only acted as arranger, it might not have been seen as a fiduciary. Second, it is arguable that Ackner J's view was influenced by the fact that the syndicated loan was drawn to repay an existing loan, which had originally been advanced by the arranger, and that this may have led the arranging bank to take personal responsibility for representations that the borrower was 'a sound and profitable group'. Finally, the case was an interlocutory appeal on a jurisdictional point, meaning that the court did not have the opportunity to hear full arguments on the question of whether the arranging bank owed a fiduciary obligation. Accordingly, it could be argued that something more than the standard relationship between the arranging bank and the syndicate participants should be required before a finding of a fiduciary duty is found.[134] In any event, most loan agreements now expressly provide that the arranging bank is not to be considered a fiduciary[135] and the lenders have not been induced to enter into the contract by any representation.[136]

In the absence of a fiduciary relationship, non-disclosure by the arranging bank will not generally amount to a misrepresentation or breach of the common law duty of care. In *IFE Fund SA v Goldman Sachs International*,[137] an acquisition was partly financed by a syndicated bond facility that was arranged by GSI. It was alleged that between the date of the IM being given, and IFE investing in the syndicate, GSI had received two reports disclosing information showing that the statements about the target of the acquisition's finances in the IM were, or might have been, incorrect in a material way, and GSI had failed to disclose this information. The IM contained disclaimers providing, among other things, that the arranging bank had not independently verified the information, meaning that no representation, express or implied, as to its accuracy was made and that the distribution of the IM did not constitute a representation that the information it contained would be updated.

---

[133] See, for example, Yuzuo Yao, 'A Legal Snapshot of the Rand responsibilities in Arranging a Syndicated Loan' (2010) 25(3) *Journal of International Banking Law and Regulation* 148.

[134] Indeed, this is the approach in the US where the courts have been reluctant to find any fiduciary obligation unless there is 'unequivocal contractual language' to that effect in the loan agreement: *Banque Arabe et Internationale d'Investissement v Mayland National Ban*, 819 F.Supp. 1282 (SDNY 1993).

[135] LMA, *Multicurrency Term and Revolving Facilities Agreement*, 18 July 2017, Clause 26.5. Available to LMA members via http://www.lma.eu.com.

[136] *Welven Ltd v Soar Group Ltd* [2011] EWHC 3240 (Comm) at [110]):

> The contracting party acknowledges that it has not been induced to enter into this Agreement by any representation, warranty, promise or assurance by [the other party] or any other person, save for those contained in this Agreement, and agrees that (except in respect of fraud) it shall have no right or remedy in respect of any other representations, warranties, promise or assurance save for those contained in this Agreement.

[137] [2007] 2 Lloyd's Rep 449.

> **Box 4.4 Example of a clause in an IM protecting the arranging bank**
>
> The contents of this Information Memorandum have not been independently verified. No representation, warranty or undertaking (express or implied) is made, and no responsibility is accepted as to the adequacy, accuracy, completeness or reasonableness of this Memorandum or any further information, notice or other document at any time supplied in connection with the Facility. This Memorandum is being provided for information purposes only and is not intended to provide the basis of any credit decision or other evaluation and should not be considered as a recommendation that any recipient of this Memorandum should participate in the Facility. Each potential participant should determine its interest in participating in the Facility based upon such investigations and analysis as it deems necessary for such purpose. No undertaking is given to assess or keep under review the business, financial condition, prospects, creditworthiness, status or affairs of the Company, the Borrower or any other person now or at any time during the life of the Facility or (except as specifically provided in the Facility Agreement) to provide any recipient or participant in the Facility with any information relating to the Company, the Borrower or otherwise.
>
> From *Raiffeisen Zentralbank Osterreich AG v Royal Bank of Scotland plc* [2010] EWHC 1392 (Comm) at [65]

When the target became insolvent, IFE brought an action against GSI claiming misrepresentation and negligence. The Court of Appeal held that the existence of any duty of care was inconsistent with the express language of the IM and that there was no implied representation from GSI that the IM was, or continued to be, accurate. Gage LJ argued that the only implied representation made by GSI arising out of the IM was one of good faith. Accordingly, he concluded that it was only if GSI 'actually knew that it had in its possession information which made the information in the IM misleading that it could be liable for breach of the representation of good faith, provided the necessary intention was proved. In effect this would amount to an allegation of dishonesty.'[138]

This approach was supported in *Raiffeisen Zentralbank Osterreich AG v Royal Bank of Scotland plc*,[139] where the participant sought to convert the arranging bank's failure to disclose certain information into an implied representation. The IM in question contained a protecting clause for the arranging bank, similar to that in *Goldman Sachs*, as set out in Box 4.4.

In rejecting the claim, Clarke J held that:[140]

> If sophisticated commercial parties agree, in terms of which they are both aware, to regulate their future relationship by prescribing the basis on which they will be dealing with each other and what representations they are or are not making, a suitably drafted clause may properly be regarded as establishing that no representations (or none other than honest belief) are being made or are intended to be relied on. Such parties are capable of distinguishing between

---

[138] At 155.   [139] [2010] EWHC 1392 (Comm).   [140] At [314].

statements which are to be treated as representations on which the recipient is entitled to rely, and statements which do not have that character, and should be allowed to agree among themselves into which category any given statement may fall.

Accordingly, unless it can be shown that there was deliberate concealment or a deliberate failure to disclose some positive misrepresentation, or an assumption of responsibility to the participating bank to disclose that information, the arranging bank will not be liable for failing to disclose certain details in the IM.

This 'assumption of responsibility' might provide the most satisfactory explanation for the imposition of liability on the arranging bank in *NatWest Australia Ltd v Tricontinental Corp Ltd*.[141] The arranging bank, TC, invited NatWest to participate in a loan syndicate and answered various questions put directly by NatWest about the existence of guarantees. TC was aware and failed to disclose that the borrower had given third-party guarantees supporting company obligations (in fact, one such guarantee benefited TC itself). TC knew that NatWest would not have participated in the syndicate if it had known of the guarantees. When the borrower subsequently went into receivership, NatWest brought an action against TC, claiming that it had failed to disclose the borrower's liabilities. The Supreme Court of Victoria held that TC had assumed personal responsibility for the information supplied and owed a duty of care, which it had breached, causing loss to NatWest.

This case is important because, unlike the arranging banks in *IFE Fund* and *Raiffeisen*, *Tricontinental* deals with the situation where the arranging bank has gone above and beyond its usual role in preparing the IM and specifically assumed responsibility to a certain participant in the syndicate. While the general position of the arranging bank is that it will not be subject to wider duties beyond the scope of the IM or loan agreement, the fact that there may be a voluntary assumption of responsibility was recognised in *Sumitomo Bank Ltd v Banque Bruxelles Lambert SA*.[142] Here it was held that the arranger assumed responsibility for making disclosures under mortgage indemnity guarantee policies that had been obtained for the benefit of the lenders, and had breached its duty of care to the lenders by failing to make those disclosures.

4.4.4 Distinguishing syndicated loans and loan participation

As already discussed, a syndicated loan involves two or more banks each making separate loans to a borrower on common terms. This is distinct from a loan participation, where one lead bank enters into the loan agreement with the borrower and then sells all or part of its interest in the loan to other participant banks. Even in the context of a syndicate, while many banks will retain their interest in the loan to maturity, often they will want the option of transferring that interest to another party, which may or may not already be a member of the syndicate.

---

[141] (1993) ATPR (Digest) 46.109. See Dan Marjanovic and Jeffrey Goss, 'Case comment: Australia- syndicated loans: duty to disclose' (1993) 8 *Journal of International Banking Law and Regulation* N203.

[142] [1997] 1 Lloyd'sRep 487.

Loan participation is attractive to banks because they can avoid the time and effort it takes to set up a loan syndicate, but they can still diversify their portfolio and avoid excessive exposure to a single borrower. Regulation is another motive. The size of a bank's loan book is restricted by the size of their capital base, the idea being that the bank should have sufficient capital to absorb any losses.[143] Accordingly, a bank that participates in a loan may wish to transfer all or part of its interest in the loan so that it is free under the regulations to engage in further lending and has the funds to do so because of the proceeds it receives from the new lender. There are a number of ways to effect such a transfer including **assignment**, **novation**, and **sub-participation**.

4.4.4.1 Assignment

An assignment involves the outright transfer of the original lending bank's (the assignor) rights to all or part of its interest in the loan to the other participating banks (the assignees). The effect of an assignment is that the participant acquires a proprietary interest in the chose in action,[144] that is, the right to enforce the loan. An assignment will only transfer the rights of the original bank, it will not transfer their obligations.[145] Accordingly, where the funds have not been drawn down in their entirety, or where the loan is revolving in nature, the original lending bank retains the responsibility to the borrower for performing these obligations, even though the right to repayment has been transferred to another participant.

A term in the loan agreement may contain a no-transfer clause that prohibits the assignment of the loan by the original lending bank or makes the assignment subject to certain pre-conditions. In such circumstances any purported assignment may be void.[146] An assignment can either be statutory or equitable in nature.

Statutory assignment is governed by s136(1) Law of Property Act 1925, the operative part of which reads as follows:

> Any absolute assignment by writing under the hand of the assignor (not purporting to be by way of charge only) of any debt or other legal thing in action, of which express notice has been given to the debtor, trustee or other person from whom the assignor would have been entitled to claim such debt or thing in action, is effectual in law (subject to equities having priority over the right of the assignee) to pass and transfer from the date of such notice: (a) the legal right to such debt or thing in action; (b) the legal and other remedies for the same; and (c) the power to give a good discharge for the same without the concurrence of the assignor

The requirements of s136(1) are listed in Box 4.5.

---

[143] See Chapters 8 and 9.

[144] A chose in action is a proprietary right to possession of something that can only be obtained or enforced through bringing legal action. In this context, it is the transfer of the right to bring an action to enforce the loan.

[145] See *Tolhurst v Associated Portland Cement Manufacturers (1900) Ltd* [1902] 2 KB 660.

[146] *Linden Gardens Trust Ltd v Lenesta Sludge Disposals Ltd* [1994] 1 AC 85.

Box 4.5 Requirements of a statutory assignment

- Statutory assignment must be absolute, that is, there can be no statutory assignment where only part of the debt has been assigned (*Williams v Atlantic Assurance Co* [1933] 1 KB 81). However, the nature of the syndicated loan contract structure means that the transfer of one lender's entire participation could be undertaken by statutory assignment.

- It must be in writing. However, there is no stipulation in the Act as to what the writing must contain. Presumably it must make clear the intention to assign and the identity of the subject matter and, perhaps, the identity of the assignee, although this may only be required in the notice to the borrower.

- Express notice must be given to the borrower, which may come from either the assignor (original bank) or the assignee (participating bank) (*Holt v Heatherfield Trust* [1942] 2 KB 1).

- Notice does not have to be given to the debtor at the time of the assignment as long as it is given before an action on the assignment is brought (*Re Westerton, Public Trustee v Gray* [1919] 2 Ch 104).

- The Act is silent as to the contents of the notice to the borrower. It must make the subject matter of the assignment and the identity of the assignee clear so that the reasonable borrower would know what to pay and to whom. Accordingly, a mere request by the bank that the debtor pay a third party will not constitute notice because it is ambiguous (*Talcott Ltd v John Lewis & Co Ltd and North American Dress Co Ltd* [1940] 3 All ER 592).

- No consideration is required for effective assignment (*Re Westerton, Public Trustee v Gray* [1919] 2 Ch 104).

- A statutory assignee can bring an action in his or her own name against the borrower.

As the consent of the borrower is not required, this can be a cause of concern for the borrower, who may prefer not to deal with certain parties such as non-financial companies or who may have a good business relationship with the original lending bank (the assignor). In practice therefore, many loan contracts impose restrictions on transfers.[147]

As most loan participations involve the transfer of only part of the loan, it will usually fall outside the requirements of statutory assignment and therefore it will take effect in equity. At common law (with limited exceptions), it is not possible to transfer a chose in action, because they are seen as personal rights that can only be enforced by the party to whom they were granted (i.e. the original lending bank). They are, however, recognised in equity. An equitable assignment need not take any prescribed form and notice does

---

[147] See Philip Rawlings, 'Restrictions on the Transfer of Rights in Loan Contracts' (2013) 9 *Journal of International Banking and Financial Law* 543.

not have to be given to the borrower. This form of assignment, which is often labelled 'silent assignment', is useful because it enables a bank to transfer its interest in a loan without the borrower knowing, meaning that any concern over the impact of the transfer on the future relationship they have with the borrower is avoided. In this context, the assignor will collect funds on behalf of the assignee.

One of the problems with equitable assignment is that the assignee (i.e. the participating bank to whom the rights are transferred) cannot bring an action to enforce a right against the borrower in his own name; they must join the assignor (i.e. the original lending bank) in bringing proceedings against the borrower. This means that equitable assignment does not bring about privity of contract between the borrower and the assignee, for if it did, it would permit direct, two-party proceedings.

4.4.4.2 Novation

The best way for a bank to transfer its interest in a loan from a legal and regulatory view is **novation**. This is because it allows the transfer of both the rights that the bank has against the borrower, and the obligations that the bank owes the borrower. As has been discussed, the transfer of obligations is not possible with assignment.[148] Accordingly, novation is desirable because it means that, where funds have not been fully drawn down or where there is a revolving facility in place, the bank's obligation to lend can be transferred.[149]

Strictly, however, novation is not a transfer because it involves cancelling the original contract and replacing it with a new contract on the same terms (except with a new lender). The consideration for the termination of the original contract, and the creation of the new one, is that the borrower and the original lending bank relinquish their rights and obligations in exchange for the new rights and obligations arising under the new contract.

Unlike assignment, discussed in section 4.4.4.1, novation requires the consent of all the parties to the original and new contracts, including the borrower. The means that novation can be a cumbersome procedure. It also provides the opportunity for the borrower and the new lenders to attempt to extract concessions in exchange for their agreement to the new contract. These difficulties can be avoided where the loan agreement contains a term permitting transfers. Under these provisions all parties agree that the lender is entitled to assign any of its rights or transfer by novation any of its rights and responsibilities. This provision is construed as an offer to the entire world, which is accepted and thereby turned into a contract by the conduct of the offeree.[150] In practice, this means that all the parties to the loan make an offer to all those institutions that fall within a particular category, as defined in the agreement, that they will cancel the original contract and enter into a new one. This offer is accepted by the new lender when

[148] For a comparison between novation and assignment see *The Argo Fund Ltd v Essar Steel Ltd* [2005] EWHC 600.
[149] See, for example, the Australian decision of *Goodridge v Macquarie Bank Ltd* [2010] FCA 67.
[150] As per the decision in *Carlill v Carbolic Smoke Ball Co* [1983] 1 QB 256.

they follow the procedure for transfer established in the agreement. Some contracts will, however, contain a restriction on novation, which obliges the lender to obtain the borrowers consent, unless, for example, the new lender falls within a certain category, such as a bank.[151]

4.4.4.3 Sub-participation

Sub-participation can be distinguished from assignment and novation in the sense that it does not have any effect on the underlying contract between the original lending bank and the borrower. Instead, it creates separate contracts between the original lending bank and the participants. In the case of sub-participation, a contractual arrangement is made (separate from the loan contract), which transfers the credit risk from the lending bank (known as the grantor or seller) to a third party (known as the grantee or buyer). The right of the grantee is to receive from the lending bank a sum equivalent to that received from the borrower. The sub-participation contract is separate from the loan contract and creates purely contractual obligations and rights between the grantor and grantee that mirror the performance under the loan contract. Accordingly, sub-participation does not give the grantee direct contractual rights against the borrower.[152] As sub-participation does not affect the original contract, the borrower's consent is not required and nor is the bank required to give the borrower notice of the transaction. The sub-participation agreement may take many different forms, but there are two broad types: funded sub-participation and risk sub-participation.

Funded sub-participation

With a funded sub-participation, the participant places a deposit with the original lending bank for the amount of its participation and the original lending bank agrees to pay to the participant a share of the repayments they receive from the borrower. The relationship between the original lending bank and the participant is therefore one of debtor and creditor and allows recourse to the deposit made by the participant, limited by reference to the performance of the borrower. What this means is that if the borrower later defaults, the original lending bank will retain a part of the deposit equivalent to the amount of the default. The original bank's obligation under this second contract then is not simply to pass on the payments it receives from the borrower, but to pay the participant according to the borrower's performance under the loan contract. Box 4.6 shows how this works in practice.

Risk sub-participation

There are two types of risk sub-participation. In the first, funding is not provided by the participant at the outset, rather, it contracts to make payment in the future. For

---

[151] *Essar Steel Ltd v The Argo Fund Ltd* [2006] EWCA Civ 241; see also *Barbados Trust Co Ltd v Bank of Zambia* [2007] EWCA Civ 148 (although this case involved an assignment).

[152] *Lloyds TSB Bank plc v Clarke & Chase Manhattan Bank Luxembourg SA* [2002] UKPC 27; *British Energy Power & Trading Ltd v Credit Suisse* [2008] EWCA Civ 53.

> ### Box 4.6 Funded sub-participation in practice
>
> If the original lending bank enters into a loan transaction with the borrower for £100 million and enters into a subsequent funded sub-participation with a third party for the entire amount, the third party will deposit £100 million with the original bank on terms that repayment of the deposit will be made as and when the borrower makes payment to the original lending bank.
>
> The participant is therefore running a double credit risk. First, there is the risk that the borrower will go into liquidation and default, which means the original lending bank has no obligation to pay the participant. Second, there is the risk that, having received payment from the borrower, the original lending bank then goes into liquidation before payment is made to the participants, which means that the payment will fall into the pool of assets to be distributed to all the unsecured creditors. Increasingly however, the practice is for funded sub-participation to be secured in order to protect against the insolvency of the original lending bank.

example, if the borrower is yet to draw down the funds under the loan agreement, the lending bank might enter into a sub-participation agreement under which the participant agrees to make payment to the original lending bank if and when the borrower draws down the funds. The second, more common, form of risk sub-participation is where the participant agrees to make payments only if the borrower fails to pay the interest or capital on the loan. In exchange for this promise the participant receives a fee, typically based on the interest payments due under the loan.[153]

In contrast to funded sub-participation, it is the original lending bank that runs the risk of the participants insolvency, which would leave the bank's obligation to the borrower uncovered.

> ### Key takeaways
>
> - A syndicated loan involves two or more banks who each contribute towards making a single loan to a borrower.
> - Each lender's rights and obligations are several.
> - While there is some authority to suggest that the arranging bank may owe a fiduciary duty to the other lenders in the syndicate, generally most loan agreements expressly provide that the arranging bank is not to be considered a fiduciary.
> - Syndicated loans must be distinguished from loan participation where one lead bank enters into the loan agreement with the borrower and then sells all or part of its interest in the loan to other participant banks. Banks can transfer their interest via novation, assignment, and sub-participation.

---

[153] *Lloyds TSB Bank plc v Clarke* [2002] 2 All ER 992.

Key bibliography

Articles

Clarke, L and Farrar, S, 'Rights and Duties of Managing and Agent Banks in Syndicated Loans to Government Borrowers' (1982) 12(5) *University of Illinois Law Review* 229

Halliday, D and Davies, R, 'Risks and Responsibilities of the Agent Bank and the Arranging Bank in Syndicated Credit Facilities' (1997) *Journal of International Banking Law* 182.

Rawlings, P, 'Restrictions on the Transfer of Rights in Loan Contracts' (2013) 9 *Journal of International Banking and Financial Law* 543.

Yao, Y, 'A Legal Snapshot of the Lead Bank: The Position and Responsibilities in Arranging a Syndicated Loan' (2010) 25(3) *Journal of International Banking Law and Regulation* 148.

4.5 Lender liability

Lender liability refers to the body of law that covers a range of liabilities based on a range of legal doctrines that a lending bank can be subject to. Indeed, Cranston describes it as an 'elastic term' that can arise in a variety of circumstances including where 'a bank gives negligent advice, does not exercise reasonable care and skill, [or] is liable in knowing receipt or dishonest assistance.'[154] While some of these causes of action have already been dealt with in Chapter 2, this section will explore three specific forms of liability that may arise out of commercial lending, which relate to pre-contractual negotiations, the management and termination of the loan facility, and the insolvency of the borrower.

4.5.1 Pre-contractual negotiations

As discussed in Chapter 2, section 2.4.5, when a bank gives investment advice to a borrower it assumes a contractual duty of care and, if there is an assumption of responsibility, a tortious duty to third parties.[155] Accordingly, when a bank takes on the role of financial adviser, it must exercise reasonable care and skill when executing that role. However, it is clear from the litigation that, as a general rule, a bank owes no duty to advise the borrower of the commercial viability or soundness of a project regarding which he or she is seeking a loan.[156] In *Williams & Glyns Bank Ltd v Barnes*,[157] an experienced businessman held both personal and corporate accounts with the claimant bank. He personally borrowed over £1 million from the bank to invest in his company, which was also heavily

---

[154] Ross Cranston, Emilios Avgouleas, Kristin van Zwieten, Christopher Hare and Theodor van Sante, *Principles of Banking Law* (3rd Ed, Oxford: OUP 2017) p 302.

[155] *Hedley Byrne v Heller Partners Ltd* [1964] AC 465.

[156] See, *Lloyds Bank v Cobb* (Unreported) 18 December 1991, per Scott LJ: 'the ordinary relationship of customer and banker does not place on the bank any contractual or tortious duty to advise the customer on the wisdom of commercial projects for the purpose of which the bank is asked to lend.'

[157] [1981] Com LR 205.

indebted to the bank. When the company later collapsed the defendant argued that the bank had breached its duty of care in failing to warn him of the unsound nature of his proposed investments. In rejecting this argument, Ralph Gibson J held that:[158]

> no duty in law arises upon the bank either to consider the prudence of the lending from the customer's point of view, or to advise with reference to it. Such a duty could only arise by contract, express or implied, or upon the principle of the assumption of responsibility and reliance stated in *Hedley Byrne* or in cases of fiduciary duty. The same answer is to be given to the question even if the bank knows that the borrowing and application of the loan, as intended by the customer, are imprudent.

Merely granting a loan to a borrowing customer will not therefore involve any assumption of responsibility on the part of the bank, nor will it impose any fiduciary duty, and, in the absence of an express term, any contractual duty is unlikely to be implied. Accordingly, when a bank examines a borrowing proposal to decide whether or not to lend, it does so for its own purpose and does not assume any responsibility in relation to the commercial soundness of the proposed transaction. The position of the courts here represents sound business policy. Banks, which have no control over external events that could affect the viability of a project, should be insulated from such claims being brought against them.[159]

While this general rule prevents the imposition of liability on lending banks who haven't taken steps to advise the borrower of the prudence of their investment, there may be circumstances where a bank goes above and beyond their normal role, thereby voluntarily assuming responsibility. In such a case the bank may be liable in negligence and this was successfully pleaded in *Verity and Spindler v Lloyds Bank Plc.*[160] Here the claimants, who were a teacher and an acupuncturist, wished to renovate a property in order to resell it at a profit and so they approached the defendant bank to take advantage of its advertised financial advisory service. The branch manager of the bank, after physically inspecting the two properties in contention, encouraged the claimants to purchase one in particular, claiming that it would be the better investment. The bank accordingly granted them the loan to do so. The investment failed because the refurbishment took longer and cost more than they anticipated, which, paired with a slump in the property market, meant that they made a loss on their investment. When the bank demanded repayment of the loan, the claimants resisted, contending that the bank had breached its contractual and tortious duties to them by tendering negligent advice.

---

[158] At 207. See also *National Commercial Bank (Jamaica) v Hew* [2003] UKPC 51 where Lord Millet observed, at [22], that 'the viability of the transaction may depend on the vantage point from which it is viewed; what is a viable loan may not be a viable borrowing. This is one reason why a borrower is not entitled to rely on the fact that the lender has chosen to lend him money as evidence, still less as advice, that the lender thinks that the purpose for which the borrower intends to use it is sound.'

[159] The reluctance of the courts to impose a duty in this context has been demonstrated in a number of Australian cases including; *Lloyd v Citicorp Australia Ltd* (1986) 11 NSWLR 286; and *MeEvoy v ANZ Banking Group Ltd* [1988] ATR 80.   [160] [1995] CLC 1557.

The High Court held in favour of the claimants, arguing that the bank had voluntarily assumed responsibility to advise them with reasonable care and they were in breach of that duty. The key issues that informed the court's decision were: the financial inexperience of the borrowers; the fact that the branch manager had inspected the properties and encouraged them to buy a particular property; and, finally, the importance of the terms of the bank's advertisements offering advice. Accordingly, it was held that the bank had assumed the role of the borrower's financial adviser and was under a duty to take reasonable care in performing that role, which they didn't do here as they had been negligent in giving that advice.[161]

It seems that the financial experience of the borrower is a key consideration that the court will assess when deciding whether or not to impose liability in relation to the advice given by the bank. In *Barnes*, where no duty was found, the borrowing customer was an experienced businessman of full age and competence, whereas in a case such as *Woods v Martins Bank*,[162] where the court imposed a fiduciary duty of care, Salmon J was influenced by the fact that the borrower was young and inexperienced in business. This means that banks should take care when advising financially inexperienced borrowers, and should make it clear that they are acting for their own interests, and not the borrower's.

4.5.2 Management and termination of a loan facility or overdraft

In the context of a loan facility, the lending bank must act in accordance with the terms of the loan agreement. If required, the courts will construe those terms to give effect to the intention of the parties and it is only in rare circumstances that they will imply a term into the contract that exposes the lending bank to additional duties.[163] If the bank fails to act in accordance with the terms of the loan agreement the borrower may be able to raise a case of estoppel or waiver.[164]

While the courts have no power to consider the fairness of terms imposed on corporate customers,[165] consumer borrowers had the protection of the UTCCR 1999, which has now been replaced by the Consumer Rights Act 2015. Under the UTCCR the courts had the power to set aside a term in a contract that had not been individually negotiated

---

[161] Compare this to *Bankers Trust International PLC v PT Dharmala Sakti Sejahtera* [1995] Bank LR 381 where no duty of care was found where the relationship between the two parties was not a conventional banker–customer relationship, but rather a commercial one where the buyer in question had held himself out as being experienced and capable of understanding the implications of the complex swap transactions.

[162] [1959] 1 QB55.

[163] For example, a duty to increase the loan facility or a duty to give adequate notice of the bank's refusal to increase the facility; see *Williams & Glyns Bank Ltd v Barnes* [1981] Com LR 205.

[164] For example, in *Emery v UCB Corporate Services Ltd* [2001] EWCA Civ 675 the claimants contended that the bank should be estopped from enforcing its security and appointing receivers without further notice to them following an interim agreement between them to reschedule the payments on a weekly basis. However, on the facts, the CA held that the claimants had not acted in reliance and to their detriment on the representations made by the bank to accept the new payment arrangement. Accordingly, the argument failed.

[165] Although there is some relief available for harsh bargains in relation to things such as penalty clauses.

'if, contrary to the requirement of good faith, it causes a significant imbalance in the parties' rights and obligations arising under the contract, to the detriment of the consumer.[166] The Consumer Rights Act broadly retains this test,[167] but it removes the caveat that a term could not be deemed to be unfair if it was individually negotiated, meaning that even if a term is specifically negotiated by the two parties, it can still be subject to the test of fairness.[168]

In, *Director General of Fair Trading v First National Bank*,[169] (discussed in section 4.3.2.3) the House of Lords considered the fairness of a term providing that, in the event of default, interest would continue to be payable at the contractual rate until any judgment obtained by the bank was discharged. The House of Lords held that the term was not unfair and, in fact, operated to prevent an imbalance against the lending bank. Lord Hope of Craighead concluded that the main purpose of the clause was 'to ensure that the borrower does not enjoy the benefit of the outstanding balance after judgment without fulfilling the corresponding obligation which he has undertaken to pay interest on it as provided for in the contract.'[170]

Where the contract provides for the lender's right to terminate the loan facility, the courts will not readily interfere with the exercise of that right. However, in exceptional cases, it may be found that the lender has acted in such a way that it will be estopped from withdrawing the loan facility without providing reasonable notice, or the bank may have waived its right to do so, or, if the language used in the agreement is ambiguous then, based on the notion of *contra proferentum*,[171] the court may impose an obligation on the lending bank to give reasonable notice.

This issue has arisen most commonly in relation to overdraft and other on-demand facilities. In this context, the courts have been reluctant to impose any obligation on a lending bank to give reasonable notice either before it refuses further lending[172] or, more importantly, before it demands repayment of the overdraft facility. There are sound commercial reasons for adopting this approach, as expressed by Gibson J in *Williams & Glyns Bank Ltd v Barnes*:[173]

> A bank which lent on an overdraft might find urgent need for the funds so lent because of commercial misfortunes or other demands and had to be free to call for repayment as and when the terms of the loan permitted it to do so.

---

[166] Regulation 5(1).   [167] Section 62(6).

[168] While this is conceptually a significant extension of the regime, in practice it is unlikely to make much difference since most consumer loan facilities are entered into on a banks standard terms.

[169] [2002] 1 AC 481   [170] Per Lord Hope of Craighead, at 502.

[171] The *contra proferentum* rule essentially tells us that any ambiguity in a clause should be construed/interpreted against the person attempting to rely on it, which, in the context of a loan or overdraft facility, would be the bank. In the context of consumer contracts, the contra proferentum rule is now reflected in s69(1) of the Consumer Rights Act 2015, which stipulates that 'If a term in a consumer contract, or a consumer notice, could have different meanings, the meaning that is most favourable to the consumer is to prevail.'

[172] See *Socomex Ltd v Banque Bruxelles Lambert SA* [1966] 1 Lloyd's Rep 156.

[173] [1981] Com LR 205, at 209.

In any event, the maximum time the borrower will be given to repay an on-demand facility such as an overdraft is a reasonable time to make the payment. This does not extend to a period of time to raise the money if it is not there to be paid, rather it is restricted to the short amount of time it takes for the mechanics of payment to be put in place. Accordingly, in *Bank of Baroda v Panessar*[174] it was held that the bank was entitled to appoint a receiver within one hour of demanding repayment of all monies due to them under the overdraft facility. Walton J, commented that:[175]

> Money payable 'on demand' is repayable immediately upon demand being made ... Nevertheless, it is physically impossible in most cases for a person to keep the money required to discharge the debt about his person. He may in a simple case keep it in a box under his bed; it may be at the bank or with a bailee. The debtor is therefore not in default in making the payment demanded unless and until he has had a reasonable opportunity of implementing whatever reasonable mechanics of payment he may need to employ to discharge the debt. Of course, this is limited to the time necessary for the mechanics of payment. It does not extend to any time to raise the money if it is not there to be paid.

This 'mechanics of payment' test was followed by the court in *Sheppard & Cooper Ltd v TSB Bank plc*,[176] where it was held that the bank was entitled to appoint a receiver within 30 minutes of demanding repayment of £600,000 from the debtor. In reaching this conclusion, Blackburne J offered some general guidance on the application of this test, as set out in Box 4.7.[177]

Most recently in *Lloyds Bank plc v Lampert*[178] it was argued that the 'mechanics of payment' test should be reconsidered to determine whether or not the more liberal approach adopted in Canada and Australia,[179] which gives the borrower a reasonable time to raise money from alternative sources, should be adopted. What is meant by a 'reasonable time' to repay the overdraft facility was discussed in the Canadian case of *Whonnock Industries Ltd v National Bank of Canada*.[180] In that case, at first instance it was held that seven days' notice was insufficient. However, on appeal, the court reversed the decision, holding that:

> The Canadian law demonstrated in the decisions does not contemplate more than a few days and cannot encompass anything approaching 30 days. In the decisions noted nothing approaching the seven days permitted here has been classed as unreasonable. The cases in which the requirement for reasonable notice evolved deal with notices of an hour or less.

[174] [1987] Ch 335.   [175] At 348.   [176] [1996] BCC 965.   [177] At 969.   [178] [1999] BCC 507.
[179] For the Canadian approach to the issue see, for example, *Ronald Elwyn Lister Ltd v Dunlop Canada Ltd* (1982) 135 DLR (3d.) 1 (SCC); *Whonnock Industries Ltd v National Bank of Canada* (1987) 42 DLR (4th) 277 (OCA); *Kavcar Investments Ltd v Aetna Financial Services Ltd* (1989) 62 DLR (4th) 277 (OCA); *Royal Bank of Canada v W.Got Associates Electric Ltd* (2000) 178 DLR(4th) 385 (SCC); *Royal Bank of Canada v Profor Kedgwick Ltd* [2008] NBQB 78. For the Australian approach see, *Bunbury Foods Pty Ltd v National Bank of Australasia Ltd* (1984) 153 CLR 491 (HCA) and *Iaconis v Pynt* [2008] NSWSC 781. Some Australian cases have, however, favoured a more narrow approach; *Bond v Hong Kong Bank of Australia Ltd* (1991) 25 NSWLR 286 (NSWCA) and *Commonwealth Bank of Australia v Renstel Nominees Pty Ltd* (VSC, 8 June 2001).
[180] (1987) 42 DLR (4th) 277 (OCA).

None of them holds that a notice of more than one day was inadequate and none refers to the need for a notice of more than a few days.

Box 4.7 Guidance on the 'mechanics of payment' test

- The question of how much time must elapse after demand before a debtor can be said to be in default is essentially a practical one, which will depend on the circumstances of the case.

- If the sum demanded is of an amount that the debtor will be likely to have in a bank account, the time permitted must be reasonable in all the circumstances to enable the debtor to contact his or her bank and make the necessary arrangements for the sum in question to be transferred from the debtor's account to the creditor.

- If the demand is made out of banking hours, the period of time is likely to be longer (involving waiting until banks reopen) than if the demand is made during banking hours.

- If the debtor has made it clear to the creditor that the necessary moneys are not available, then, provided a proper demand has been made, the creditor need not allow any further time to elapse before treating the debtor as in default.

In rejecting the argument that a more liberal approach should be adopted in the UK, Kennedy LJ in *Lloyds Bank plc v Lampert*[181] argued that the approach adopted in the Commonwealth should not be overstated and, upon review of the relevant authorities, the position in Canada was actually that where the amount to be repaid is very large, Canadian law requires that the lenders should be given 'at least a few days' to meet the demand, but otherwise, reasonable notice can range from a few days to no time at all. In any case, Kennedy LJ argued that the issue was irrelevant, since it was clear on the facts of the case that, even if the borrower had been given a few days, he would not have been able to raise the amount necessary to pay off the overdraft.[182]

As it stands, the 'mechanics of payment' test adopted in the UK provides commercial certainty for banks. To alter the test to one that gave the borrower a 'reasonable time' to repay the overdraft facility would put the bank in the difficult position of having to determine how long they should wait before they can enforce the security; if they don't wait long enough, the borrower could bring an action against them, and if they wait too long, their security could be jeopardised.

4.5.3 **Insolvency of the borrower**

Where the borrower is facing financial difficulty, it may be in the bank's interest to assist them by setting up an alternative repayment plan, rather than exercising its contractual rights under the agreement and enforcing any security it may have. Banks are now encouraged to explore the possibility of saving a customer's business rather than

---

[181] [1999] BCC 507.   [182] At 512.

prematurely withdrawing financial support. In this regard, banks are required to follow the *Standards of Lending Practice*[183] for business customers, which sets out the best
banking practice to follow when a corporate customer is in financial difficulty.[184] Some
of these practices are set out in Box 4.8.

While banks are encouraged not to call in a lending facility too early, they must also
ensure that their actions do not operate to the detriment of the borrower's other creditors, and that it does not take undue advantage of the borrower's financial position to
improve its own position over the borrower's other creditors. The Insolvency Act 1986
will allow a liquidator to challenge and ultimately reverse any transactions that benefited the bank relating to an undervalue,[185] voidable preferences,[186] and certain floating charges.[187] These provisions also apply in the context of 'connected persons', which
include a company's 'shadow directors'.[188]

The question this raises is whether a bank could ever be considered a shadow director
of a corporate customer. This would have implications, not only in terms of the bank's
liability under the aforementioned provisions, but also in determining the liability of
the bank under the wrongful trading provisions of the Act.[189] The wrongful trading
provisions apply where a director (including a shadow director),[190] who knew or ought

---

Box 4.8 Standards of lending practice: financial difficulty

- The overarching customer outcome is that 'business customers in financial difficulty, or
  in the early stages of the collections process, will receive appropriate support and fair
  treatment, in order to help them deal with their debt(s) in the most suitable way.'

- Banks should have triggers and processes in place to enable them to identify
  customers who might be in financial difficulty and are expected to act promptly and
  efficiently to address the situation with the customer.

- If a bank is aware, or suspects, that a customer is in financial difficulty but is able to
  uphold their borrowing commitments to the firm, the customer should be given the
  opportunity to act to turn around the business.

- Banks should work with and support a customer's turnaround plan where they believe
  that it has a good chance of succeeding.

- If a bank is unable to support a turnaround plan, the customer should be notified of
  the reasons why and given a reasonable period of time to consider the options open
  to them.

---

[183] *Standards of Lending Practice: Business Customers* (October 2017) at https://www.lendingstandards-
board.org.uk/wp-content/uploads/2017/10/Standards-of-Lending-Practice-Business-27-Oct.pdf.

[184] Similar standards apply in the context of a consumer customer, see, *Standards of Lending Practice: Personal Customers* (July 2016) at https://www.lendingstandardsboard.org.uk/wp-content/uploads/2016/07/
Standards-of-Lending-Practice-July-16.pdf.   [185] Section 238.

[186] Section 239.   [187] Section 245.   [188] Section 249.   [189] Section 214.

[190] Section 214(7).

to have concluded that there was no reasonable prospect that the company would avoid going into insolvent liquidation,[191] fails to take every step to minimise the potential loss to the company's creditors that he or she ought to have taken,[192] having regard to the general knowledge, skill, and experience that may reasonably be expected of a person carrying out the same functions as are carried out by that director in relation to the company, and the general knowledge, skill, and experience that that director actually has.[193] In these circumstances the shadow director may find themselves liable to contribute to the company's assets in the event that they go into liquidation.

A 'shadow director' is defined in s251 of the Companies Act 2006, s22(5) of the Company Directors Disqualification Act 1986, and, for the purposes of 'wrongful trading' liability, s251 of the Insolvency Act 1986. The latter provision establishes that a shadow director is:

> a person in accordance with whose directions or instructions the directors of the company are accustomed to act (but so that a person is not deemed a shadow director by reason only that the directors act on advice given by him in a professional capacity).

In *Re a Company (No. 005009 of 1987)*[194] the borrowing company had an unsecured overdraft with the bank. When the company ran into financial difficulty the bank commissioned a report on their financial affairs, which made various recommendations that were ultimately implemented by the company. When the company was subsequently liquidated, the liquidator argued that, because the company had implemented the recommendations, the bank had become a shadow director and was therefore liable for wrongful trading. When the bank applied to strike out the claim it was refused, Knox J arguing that it was a triable issue. However, the judge declined to give any reasons for reaching this conclusion, and when the claim did in fact go to trial[195] the allegation that the bank was a shadow director was 'rightly abandoned',[196] suggesting that the judge was not persuaded by the argument.

These decisions raised the concern that in order to avoid any allegation that a bank had become a shadow director, they would be quick to withdraw financial support for their corporate customers, rather than supporting them through their financial problems. To rebut this concern, and writing extrajudicially, Millet J emphasised that in order to be caught as a 'shadow director' a bank would have to go beyond its traditional banker–customer relationship.[197]

Subsequently, in *Re Hydrodan (Corby) Ltd*[198] Millet offered some general guidance on when a defendant will be identified as a 'shadow director'. He held that it would be necessary to prove the following: (1) who the directors of the company are, whether de facto or de jure; (2) that the defendant directed those directors how to act in relation to

---

[191] Section 214(2).   [192] Section 214(3).   [193] Section 214(4).   [194] [1988] 4 BCC 424.
[195] [1990] BCC 78,   [196] At 79.
[197] Sir Peter Millet, 'Shadow Directorship – A Real or Imagined Threat to Banks' (1991) *Insolvency Practitioner* 14.   [198] [1994] BCC 161.

the company or that he or she was one of the persons who did so; (3) that those directors acted in accordance with such directions; and (4) that they were accustomed so to act.[199] Accordingly, he argued that what is need is:[200]

> first, a board of directors claiming and purporting to act as such; and, secondly, a pattern of behaviour in which the board did not exercise any discretion or judgment of its own, but acted in accordance with the directions of others.

In *Re Unisoft Group Ltd (No.2)*[201] Harman J argued that in the case of a multi-member board, unless the whole, or at least the governing majority, of the board are accustomed to acting on the directions of the third party, that third party cannot be a shadow director.[202] Further, he stated that there must be evidence of an ongoing course of conduct rather than a single isolated event.[203] However, the subservience or surrender of any discretion on the part of the board need not be shown. As stated by Morritt LJ in *Secretary of State for Trade and Industry v Deverell*:[204]

> What is needed is that the board is accustomed to act on the directions or instructions of the shadow director. As I have already indicated such directions and instructions do not have to extend over all or most of the corporate activities of the company; nor is it necessary to demonstrate a degree of compulsion in excess of that implicit in the fact that the board are accustomed to act in accordance with them.

Bringing these principles together, it is clear that a standard lending relationship between a bank and its borrower would not typically constitute the bank a 'shadow director' of the corporate borrower. The negotiations that lead to the loan agreement, where the borrower makes certain warranties and covenants and further conditions precedent are imposed on them, do not amount to directions or instructions on how the borrowing company should act. Rather, they are simply the terms on which the lending bank is willing to provide and continue with the loan facility, which the borrower is at liberty to reject or accept. However, the risk of a bank being held liable as a shadow director is heightened when the borrower defaults because, in these circumstances, the bank will seek to renegotiate the terms of the loan facility and, while it will want to support the borrower, it will also want to protect its own interests. In this context, a bank must be careful that it doesn't become too closely involved in the rescue package of the borrower.

In *Re PFTZM Ltd*,[205] Judge Baker QC rejected the allegation that the lenders had become shadow directors even though it was agreed that the lender could attend the borrower's weekly management meetings, that all the borrower's revenue should be paid into the lender's account and that lender's approval was required for all payments made by the borrower. He emphasised that the lender was not acting as shadow director, but simply in defence of its own interests, and it was not the case that the directors

---

[199] At 163. [200] Ibid. [201] [1994] BCC 766. [202] At 775.
[203] Ibid. [204] [2001] Ch 340, at 355. [205] [1995] BCC 280.

of the company were accustomed to acting in accordance with the lender's instructions. He concluded that this was a case 'where the creditor made terms for the continuation of credit in the light of threatened default' and, most importantly, 'The directors of the company were quite free to take the offer or leave it.'[206]

This was echoed in *Ultraframe (UK) Ltd v Fielding*,[207] where Lewison J emphasised that 'A lender is entitled to keep a close eye on what is done with his money, and to impose conditions on his support for the company.'[208] He went on to say that the imposition of these conditions 'does not mean he is running the company or is emasculating the powers of the directors, even if (given their situation) the directors feel that they have little practical choice but to accede to his requests.'[209] More recently, it has been argued that if there is 'doubt whether the acts of a person were referable to an assumed directorship or to some other capacity such as a shareholder ... the person in question must be entitled to the benefit of the doubt.'[210]

There may, however, be some circumstances where it is more difficult to draw the line between a lender that is simply advising the borrower how to act, and a lender that is instructing or directing the borrower, thereby constituting themselves a shadow director. For example, where a lending bank commissions a report on the borrowing customer's affairs, which the borrower then implements, it could be argued that this amounts to taking direction from a shadow director. In such circumstance, the lending bank should make it clear that the proposals in the report are conditions for the lender continuing to provide financial support. In reality, while the borrower will have no option but to implement the proposals, the legal position will be that the borrower did in fact have a choice to either implement the proposals or have its liabilities to the lender accelerated. This choice is enough to negate any claim that the lender is acting as a shadow director. Another situation in which the lending bank could face liability as a shadow director is where the lender appoints a representative on the borrower's board. In practice, however, this should not be an issue since this will not give the lender control of the entire, or majority of, the board, as required for a shadow directorship.[211]

Royal Bank of Scotland (RBS) may find themselves subject to some form of lender liability following the results of a recent independent review that called into question their conduct in treating business customers fairly when they were experiencing financial distress. In November 2013 Dr Lawrence Tomlinson published a report titled *Banks' Lending Practices: Treatment of Businesses in distress*,[212] which made serious allegations against RBS over the treatment of small and medium-sized enterprises (SMEs) that had been transferred to their Global Restructuring Group (GRG) in the five years following the financial crisis. In January 2014, the FCA appointed Promontory Financial Group (UK) Ltd as a Skilled Person under s166 of the Financial Services and Markets Act 2000 (FSMA) to conduct an independent review of RBS's treatment of SME customers transferred to GRG

[206] At 292.　[207] [2005] EWHC 1638.　[208] At 1268.　[209] Ibid.
[210] *Re Mea Corporation Ltd* [2007] BCC 208, at 307.
[211] *Re Unisoft Group Ltd (No.2)* [1994] BCC 766.
[212] At www.tomlinsonreport.com/docs/tomlinsonReport.pdf.

between 2008 and 2013. The resulting Skilled Person's Report was finalised in September 2016.[213] In November 2016 the FCA published a summary of the main findings and conclusions of the report.[214] This was followed by an interim summary[215] in October 2017 and a final summary[216] in November 2017. Essentially, while the most serious allegations in Dr Tomlinson's report were not upheld by the independent review, they did identify significant concerns about SME customer treatment by RBS, which, for example, arose from:[217]

- A failure to support SME businesses in a manner consistent with good turnaround practice.
- Placing an undue focus on pricing increases and debt reduction without due consideration to the longer-term viability of customers.
- A failure to document or explain the rationale behind decisions relating to pricing following transfer to GRG.
- A failure by RBS to adopt adequate procedures concerning the relationship with customers and to ensure fair treatment of customers.
- A failure to identify customer complaints and handle those complaints fairly.
- A failure to place appropriate weight on turnaround options in its handling of SME customers in distress.
- Undue focus on pricing increases without due consideration of the longer-term viability of customers.

In summary, the independent review identified what it regarded as instances of inappropriate treatment on the part of RBS and GRG in 86 per cent of the 207 cases it reviewed.[218] While RBS has taken some remedial action – in November 2016 they set up a complaints procedure and gave an automatic refund of complex fees[219] paid by SMEs that were customers of GRG in the relevant time period[220] – it is clear that this report may well foreshadow some form of lender liability.[221]

---

[213] The report itself has not been published as it would require the consent of all the institutions and individuals covered by the report.

[214] At https://www.fca.org.uk/news/press-releases/review-royal-bank-scotland-treatment-customers-referred-global-restructuring-group.

[215] FCA 'Interim Summary: A report on an independent review of Royal Bank of Scotland Group's treatment of small and medium-sized enterprise customers referred to the Global Restructuring Group' (October 2017) at https://www.fca.org.uk/publication/corporate/interim-summary-independent-review-rbs-grg.pdf.

[216] FCA 'Final Summary: A report on an independent review of Royal Bank of Scotland Group's treatment of small and medium-sized enterprise customers referred to the Global Restructuring Group' (November 2017) at https://www.fca.org.uk/publication/corporate/final-summary-independent-review-rbs-grg.pdf.

[217] Ibid, pp 12–13.   [218] Ibid, pp 13–14.

[219] Complex fees include: facility fees, excess fees, commitment fees, covenant waiver/breach fees, and security fees.   [220] See https://www.rbs.com/rbs/news/2016/11/GRG.html.

[221] Indeed, a group action is being led by the RBS–GRG Business Action Group, a group of individuals and businesses, all of whom claim to have suffered at the hands of GRG. The objective of the group is to bring a case based on an 'Unlawful means conspiracy' by RBS–GRG against its customers. It is also their intention to bring an action against individual directors personally who instigated and directed the conspiracy. See http://www.rbs-grgbusinessactiongroup.org/.

> ## ➡️ Key takeaways
>
> - Lender liability is an elastic term that refers to the range of liabilities under a number of different legal doctrines that a lending bank might be subject to.
> - As a general rule, a bank owes no duty to advise the borrower of the commercial viability or soundness of a project regarding which he or she is seeking a loan. However, where a bank goes above and beyond their duty in advising the borrower, particularly where that borrower is inexperienced in business, it may be that they voluntarily assume responsibility, meaning they could face liability if their advice was negligent.
> - A lending bank must act in accordance with the terms of the agreement. Where the lender has a right under the contract to terminate the facility, the courts will not lightly interfere with the exercise of that right. However, in some circumstances, the lender may have acted in such a way that they are estopped from withdrawing the facility without providing reasonable notice.
> - Upon the insolvency of a borrower a bank could face liability as a shadow director, but the threshold is high, requiring evidence that the whole, or at least the governing majority of, the board of the corporate borrower are accustomed to acting on the directions of the lender.

Key bibliography

Articles

Millet, P, Sir, 'Shadow Directorship – A Real or Imagined Threat to Banks' (1991) 1 *Insolvency Practitioner* 14.

Codes

Standards of Lending Practice: Personal Customers (July 2016) at https://www.lendingstandardsboard.org.uk/wp-content/uploads/2016/07/Standards-of-Lending-Practice-July-16.pdf

Standards of Lending Practice: Business Customers (October 2017) at https://www.lendingstandardsboard.org.uk/wp-content/uploads/2017/10/Standards-of-Lending-Practice-Business-27-Oct.pdf

4.6 Security

When lending, banks will often require the borrower to provide *security*, which will give the bank some form of proprietary or possessory right in the borrower's (or a third party's) property that it can exercise in order to enforce repayment of the loan or overdraft facility. In *Bristol Airport v Powdrill*,[222] Brown-Wilkinson V-C accepted the following description of security:[223]

---

[222] [1990] Ch 744. [223] At 760.

Security is created where a person (the creditor) to whom an obligation is owed by another (the debtor) by statute or contract, in addition to the personal promise of the debtor to discharge the obligation, obtains rights exercisable against some property in which the debtor has an interest in order to enforce the discharge of the debtor's obligation to the creditor.

The main objective of the security is to protect the bank in the event that the borrower is unable to repay the loan. It is most valuable where the borrower becomes insolvent, because it means that the secured lending bank will have priority for repayment over any other unsecured creditors and, where the security is proprietary in nature, the lender can recover what is owed to them against the secured assets.

Securities can be classified as proprietary, possessory, or personal in nature, and each will now be considered in turn.

4.6.1 **Proprietary security**

Proprietary security is concerned with arrangements where the borrower grants to the bank a proprietary right in the relevant property that gives the bank the right to seize the property in the event of default or the insolvency of the borrower. The bank can then satisfy the debt from the proceeds of selling the property. The most common forms of proprietary security are mortgages of chattels and land and a charge over the assets of a company. Both of these will be discussed in turn.

4.6.1.1 **Mortgage over land**

A mortgage has been defined as:[224]

a conveyance of land or an assignment of chattels as a security for the payment of a debt or the discharge of some other obligation for which it is given. This is the idea of a mortgage: and the security is redeemable on the payment or discharge of such debt or obligation, any provision to the contrary notwithstanding.

Accordingly, a mortgage involves the transfer of ownership of property from the borrower (known as the mortgagor) to the bank (known as the mortgagee) as security for a debt. When the loan is repaid, and the land becomes free of the mortgage, the mortgagor is said to have 'redeemed' the land.

When offering land as security, the lending bank will need to determine the nature of the borrower's interest in the land. First, it must ascertain whether the borrower has a freehold or leasehold interest. A freehold interest is permanent and indefensible although its value can be affected by issues such as leases and third-party rights in the property. By contrast, a leasehold interest gives the holder the right of occupation for only a limited amount of time, although leases are often given for extensive terms of 99 or 999 years. On the expiry of the lease term, possession or occupation will revert

---

[224] Per Lindley MR in *Santley v Wilde* [1899] 2 Ch 474, at 474.

back to the freeholder. The bank will also want to consider a number of other factors including: whether the proprietary interest is subject to any adverse interests such as leases; whether the value of the property could be affected by extrinsic factors such as developments taking place in the vicinity; and any other interest that could be binding on the lending bank even though it is not on the register (e.g. the interests of someone in actual possession).[225] Finally, in the case of unregistered land, the lending bank will need to arrange for a search of the deeds and a search of the register, which would disclose details of any adverse rights and interests not disclosed in the deeds.

In the event of default, the mortgagee will have a number of remedies including a statutory power of sale,[226] the power to appoint a receiver,[227] and the power to take possession (although, in practice, the bank is unlikely to exercise this power, unless they want to ensure vacant possession or to preserve the property ready for sale).[228] Finally, the mortgagee has the right to foreclose the mortgage. This requires a court order, which extinguishes the right of the mortgagor to redeem the land and conveys the land to the mortgagee.

There are three types of security that can be given over land: legal mortgage, equitable mortgage, and equitable charge.

Legal mortgage

A legal mortgage confers a legal right on the mortgagee and therefore can only be granted by a mortgagor who has legal title in the land in question. Under the Law of Property Act 1925 a legal mortgage can be created (1) by granting the mortgagee a lease in the legal estate (known as a mortgage by demise) or (2) by conferring a charge by deed expressed to be by way of legal mortgage over the estate (known as a mortgage by charge).[229] In the case of a mortgage by demise, the mortgagee becomes the owner of the land until the loan is repaid over a term of years (this process is called redemption). Accordingly, the property is conveyed to the mortgagee, with a condition that it will be returned on redemption. This method is now relatively obsolete, with the mortgage by charge being more common. In this context, the mortgagee is in the same position as if he or she had been granted a mortgage by demise, but there is no conveyance of the land to the mortgagee, meaning that the mortgagor remains vested in the estate rather than having a reversionary interest. Instead of conveying the land, the mortgagor grants a charge by way of a legal mortgage where the value of the loan is secured by the charge. In the case of registered land, legal mortgages can only be created by way of charge, and not by demise.

Equitable mortgage

An equitable mortgage confers an equitable interest on the mortgagee. This can be granted by a mortgagor who has legal title to the land in question, and it can also be granted by a mortgagor who has only an equitable interest in land (e.g. where he or she is the

---

[225] See Land Registration Act 2002, ss11 and 12.   [226] Law or Property Act 1925 s101(1)
[227] Ibid, s101(1)(iii).   [228] *Four-Maids Ltd v Dudley Marshall Properties Ltd* [1957] Ch 317.
[229] Law of Property Act 1925 s85(1) (for freeholds) and 86(1) for leaseholds.

beneficiary under a trust). In the latter case, the equitable mortgage is created by assigning the mortgagor's interest to the mortgagee with a proviso that the interest is reassigned on redemption. Where the mortgagor has legal title to the land, this method may be preferred over a legal mortgage because there is less formality. Usually the deeds, or in the case of registered land the land certificate, are deposited with the mortgagee. However, the Law of Property (Miscellaneous Provisions Act) 1989 introduced a requirement that the agreement be in writing.[230] Accordingly, to be effective, an equitable mortgage requires a deposit of deeds accompanied by a written contract. In practice, banks use a standard-form contract to secure an equitable mortgage. They are used most commonly in the context of short-term loans. In the event of default, an equitable mortgagee has no inherent right to possession but often such a right is expressly reserved under the agreement. If the mortgage is under seal, the mortgagee has the right to appoint a receiver or sell the land.[231] Otherwise such rights must be provided for in the agreement.

Equitable charge

An equitable charge will confer an equitable interest on the chargee but with more limited rights than an equitable mortgage. It can be created by an agreement between the borrower and the lending bank where the equitable interest is appropriated to the discharge of a debt. In the event of default, an equitable chargee has no right of possession nor to foreclose. If the charge is by deed then the statutory powers of sale and appointment of a receiver are available. If not, the chargee must apply to court for an order.

4.6.1.2 Charges over a company's assets

The most common form of security used to secure loans to a corporate entity is a charge. In the event of default, a charge gives the lending bank the power to apply to the court to realise the property subject to the charge in priority to other creditors.

The most valuable assets of a company are normally their trading stock, their book debts,[232] or their plant machinery. Companies often use these assets to raise finance by granting the lender a fixed or floating charge over them. However, at common law, it was not possible to create a security over future property, and nor could a mortgage be created over trading stock because the mortgagor would need the consent of the mortgagee every time it sold its stock or assets. Equity therefore intervened to address these issues. First, in *Holroyd v Marshall*[233] the mortgagor mortgaged mill machinery to secure his indebtedness and the mortgage deed contained a covenant that all machinery placed in the mill in addition to, or in substitution for, the original machinery should be subject to the mortgage. On the question of whether the mortgagee had an interest in respect of the new machinery purchased and introduced after the date of the deed, the House of Lords held that there was an equitable mortgage over the existing and any new machinery purchased.

---

[230] Section 2. See also *United Bank of Kuwait v Sahid* [1997] Ch 107.
[231] Law of Property Act 1925 s101(1)(i) and (iii).
[232] Which is the debts due or owed to the borrowing company in the course of its business.
[233] (1862) 10 HL Cas 191.

The second device created by equity was the floating charge. In *Re Panama, New Zealand and Australian Royal Mail Company*[234] the debtor company charged its 'undertaking and all sums of money arising therefrom'. It was held that the word 'undertaking' signified not merely the income of the business but also present and future property of the company and that, while by the terms of the charge the holder could not interfere in the running of the company and its dealings with its assets until the winding up of the company, the occurrence of the event entitled the holder to realise its security over the assets, and so assert its charge in priority to the general creditors.

Fixed and floating charges

The availability of charges covering future property has led to the development of two separate categories of charge, namely, the fixed (or specific) charge and the floating charge. There have been many judicial attempts to define these two terms. For example, Lord Macnaghton in *Illingworth v Houldsworth*[235] said that:[236]

> A specific charge, I think is one that without more, fastens on ascertained and definite property or property capable of being ascertained or defined; a floating charge, on the other hand, is ambulatory and shifting in its nature, hovering over and so to speak floating with the property which it is intended to affect until some event occurs or some act is done which causes it to settle and fasten on the subject of the charge with its reach and grasp.

Alternatively, Buckley LJ in *Evans v Rival Granite Quarries*[237] said that:[238]

> A floating security is not a future security, it is a present security, which presently affects all the assets of the company expressed to be included in it. On the other hand, it is not a specific security; the holder cannot affirm that the assets are specifically mortgaged to him. The assets are mortgaged in such a way that the mortgagor can deal with them without the concurrence of the mortgagee. A floating security is not a specific mortgage of the assets, plus a licence to the mortgagor to dispose of them in the ordinary course of his business, but is a floating mortgage applying to every item comprised in the security, but not specifically affecting any item until some event occurs or some act on the part of the mortgagee is done, which causes it to crystallise into a fixed security.

Accordingly, a fixed (or specific) charge is a charge created over property that prevents the debtor dealing with it without first repaying the loan or obtaining the chargee's consent. A fixed charge can cover future assets and will attach as soon as the debtor acquires them. In contrast, a floating charge hovers over a changing fund of assets, including assets acquired by the seller after the creation of the charge. A floating charge allows the debtor to deal with the assets subject to the security in the ordinary course of

---

[234] (1870) LR 5 Ch App 318.   [235] [1904] AC 355.   [236] At 358.
[237] [1910] 2 KB 979.   [238] At 999.

> ## Box 4.9 Fixed v floating charges: why it matters
>
> - Property subject to a fixed charge cannot be dealt with without the consent of the lending bank. However, the debtor under a floating charge may deal with the assets in the ordinary course of business without consent.
> - A floating charge holder has a low ranking in the priority order of creditors – it ranks below preferential creditors (Insolvency Act 1986 s40).
> - A floating charge created in the 12 months prior to the debtor company's liquidation or administration may be subject to avoidance under s245 of the Insolvency Act 1986.
> - All floating charges are required to be registered; some fixed charges are not.
> - A floating charge is subordinated to the costs and expenses of administration and liquidation (Insolvency Act 1986 Schedule B1, paras 70–99 and s176ZA).
> - On insolvency, a portion of floating charge (but not fixed charge) asset realisations must be set aside to pay the company's unsecured creditors (Insolvency Act 1986 s176A).

his or her business.[239] Only when a certain event happens, such as the appointment of a receiver, will the floating charge 'crystallise' and fix on the assets subject to the charge. At that point the debtor has no further right to deal with the charged assets.

The floating charge can be regarded as an English legal innovation, which serves the profoundly important purpose of promoting a form of commercial finance that allows businesses to maintain flexibility in the use of their assets. However, there is a trade-off between strong security rights for the lender and business flexibility for the borrower. The rights that flow from fixed and floating charges differ, as Box 4.9 illustrates.

Lenders tend to prefer charges to be 'fixed' but borrowers may not be able to offer security on such clear terms. Accordingly, charges are often created in a manner that pose challenges for their characterisation as either 'fixed' or 'floating'. For example, future property (i.e. property thath does not exist or in which the debtor has no proprietary interest at the time of giving the security) can be subject to both a fixed and floating charge. Lord Millet in *Agnew v Commissioner of Inland Revenue*[240] explained that:

> In deciding whether a charge is a fixed charge or a floating charge, the court is engaged in a two-stage process. At the first stage it must construe the instrument of charge and seek to gather the intentions of the parties from the language they have used. But the object at this stage of the process is not to discover whether the parties intended to create a fixed or a floating charge. It is to ascertain the nature of the rights and obligations which the parties intended to grant each other in respect of the charged assets. Once these have been ascertained, the

---

[239] This has been recognised as the most essential characteristic of a floating charge: *Re Yorkshire Woolcomber's Association Ltd* [1903] 2 Ch 284, at 295; *Agnew v Commissioner of Inland Revenue* [2001] 2 AC 710, at [13].

[240] [2001] 2 AC 710.

court can then embark on the second stage of the process, which is one of categorisation. This is a matter of law. It does not depend on the intention of the parties. If their intention, properly gathered from the language of the instrument, is to grant the company rights in respect of the charged assets which are inconsistent with the nature of a fixed charge, then the charge cannot be a fixed charge however they may have chosen to describe it.

Book debts

One issue that has been subject to litigation in recent years is whether a book debt can be subject to a fixed charge. Book debts are debts owing to the borrower in the course of business. Although they are an asset, they are inherently subject to change in terms of amounts owing or collected at any one time. Banks have tried to take fixed charges over book debts in order to improve their security rights. However, much litigation has ensued in order to clarify the strength of a bank's security rights in this context.

In *Siebe Gorman & Co Ltd v Barclays Bank*[241] a charge, which was described as a 'first fixed charge', was taken over the current and future book debts of the company. It required the company to pay the proceeds of the book debt into a designated account with the lending bank and undertake not to charge or assign the proceeds to any other person without the consent of the bank. The company was free to use those funds in the course of business. Slade J held that the charge was fixed because the restrictions placed on the company's power to deal with the proceeds gave the bank a degree of control making it fixed, rather than floating in nature. In *Re New Bullas Trading*[242] a company granted what was expressed as a fixed charge over the company's uncollected book debts, which then converted into a floating charge once the proceeds were collected and placed in a designated account. The Court of Appeal held that there were commercial advantages for both parties in using these arrangements and that they were free to agree such terms. Accordingly, it upheld the wording of the charge instrument as having the effect of making the charge over the uncollected debts a fixed charge. However, the decision was subsequently subject to criticism. For example, Goode argued that there could not be a separate security interest over a debt and its proceeds, rather, there could only be one single and continuous security interest. He said:[243]

The crystallisation of a floating charge does not bring a new security interest into existence, nor does the decrystallisation of a fixed charge. All that happens is that in the former case the debtor's power to deal with the collateral free from the security interest is determined and in the latter the restriction on his dealing power is removed. The security interest is still a single and continuous interest.

He concluded that to treat the security interests as separate and distinct would be highly artificial and it would offend the concept of security in future property as a

---

[241] [1979] 2 Lloyd's Rep 142.   [242] [1994] 1 BCLC 465.
[243] Roy Goode, 'Charges over Book Debts: A Missed Opportunity' (1994) 110 *Law Quarterly Review*, 592, at 604.

present security. Professor Worthington argued that the issue with the decision was not that the uncollected debts and their collected proceeds should be treated as indivisible assets, but that the security arrangement left the borrower free to deal with the charged assets without the consent of the lender, which is inconsistent with the character of a fixed charge.[244]

Both *Siebe Gorman* and *Re New Bullas Trading* were later overruled by the House of Lords in *National Westminster Bank v Spectrum Plus Ltd.*[245] Here, Spectrum Plus opened a current account with the claimant bank with an overdraft facility of £250,000, which they secured by way of a fixed charge over the company's book debts. When Spectrum Plus collected the book debts, they paid them into their current account and drew on them as they wished for business purposes. When the company went into liquidation, the issue for the courts was whether the charge over the book debts was fixed or floating in nature.[246] The House of Lords focused on the freedom of the company to deal with the assets in the ordinary course of business and concluded that where the borrower can deal with the charged assets without the lending bank's consent it must be a floating charge. Lord Hope held that the question to ask was:[247]

> Was the account one which allowed the company to continue to use the proceeds of the book debts as a source of its cash flow or was it one which, on the contrary, preserved the proceeds intact for the benefit of the bank's security? Was it, putting the point shortly, a blocked account?

He went on to say that, in this case, the borrowers right to withdraw funds whenever it wished within the agreed overdraft limits was 'wholly destructive of the argument that there was a fixed charge.'[248] Similarly, Lord Scott argued that where the borrower is free to deal with the charged assets without first obtaining the lender's permission, the charge must be categorised as floating. Accordingly, in order for a book debt to be subject to a fixed charge, the lending bank must entirely restrict the borrower's freedom to deal with the assets, so that they are maintained for the benefit of the lender.[249]

Registration of charges

The Companies Act 2006 (Amendment of Part 25) Regulations 2013 came into force in April 2013, thereby replacing the previous system of registering security interests

---

[244] Sarah Worthington, 'Case Comment: Fixed Charges over Book Debts and other Receivables' (1997) 113 *Law Quarterly Review* 563, at 567–8.

[245] [2005] 2 AC 680.

[246] The implications being that, if the charge was construed as floating, Spectrum Plus' creditors were entitled to have their debt paid out of the proceeds in priority to the banks; if it was fixed, the bank would be entitled to the entire proceeds.   [247] At [55].

[248] At [61].

[249] For a discussion of the decision see, for example, Ken Baird and Paul Sidle, 'Case Comment: Spectrum Plus: House of Lords decision – A Cloud with a Silver Lining? (2005) *Insolvency Intelligence* 113 and Katy Anderson, 'Case Comment: The Spectrum Plus Case' (2005) *International Company and Commercial Law Review* 405.

created by UK companies over their assets. The former system had been criticised for a number of years, prompting the Department of Trade and Industry to ask the Law Commission to consider the case for reforming the law on company charges. In their resulting report, the Law Commission explained the problem with the system as follows:[250]

> The scheme for registering company charges dates back to 1900 and is now inappropriate to modern needs. It is particularly inefficient in two ways. First, it requires charge documents to be submitted in paper form, although the register of company charges maintained at Companies House is electronic. Secondly, registry staff must check the particulars submitted against lengthy legal documents before the registrar issues a conclusive certificate of registration. This requires a significant number of staff and is, in our view, unnecessary and impossible to justify. A system of electronic on-line registration, with the party filing being responsible for ensuring that the information registered is accurate, would be far more efficient.

The new regulations provide a comprehensive scheme for the registration, alteration, and satisfaction of all charges created by UK companies, clarifying many of the issues of the previous system. Some of the changes are as follows:

- There is now a single UK-wide scheme covering all UK registered companies instead of two separate schemes for England and Wales and Northern Ireland, and Scotland.

- Rather than a paper-based system, electronic filing of a charge is now possible. This can be done in one of two ways: 'software filing' for bulk filing of charges and web filing where presenters upload pdf versions of the charge documents.

- Instead of providing a list of registerable charges as per the previous system, all charges are now required to be registered, unless they fall within one of the exceptions. These exceptions are: rent security deposits; Lloyd's trust deeds; and any charge that is excluded from registration requirements by other legislation.[251]

- There is no longer a statutory obligation to register, and the criminal sanctions (for companies and their officers in default) for failure to comply have been removed.

- Under the new regime, a UK company will no longer have to maintain a register of charges at its registered office, but they are required to keep copies of charge instruments available for inspection.[252]

- Once a charge is registered, it will be given a 12-digit Unique Reference Code (URC), which will be displayed on the charge registration certificate and will enable members of the public to track the charge, including when it is partially or fully satisfied.[253]

---

[250] Law Commission, 'Company Security Interests' (Law Com No 296, 2002) paragraph 1.5.

[251] Companies Act 2006 Section 859A(6), inserted by Schedule 2 Companies Act 2006 (Amendment of Part 25) Regulations 2013.

[252] Ibid, s859P, inserted by Schedule 2 Companies Act 2006 (Amendment of Part 25) Regulations 2013.

[253] Ibid, s859I(2)(a), inserted by Schedule 2 Companies Act 2006 (Amendment of Part 25) Regulations 2013.

- The particulars to be delivered to the registrar must include the following: whether the instrument contains a floating charge and, if so, whether it covers all the property and undertaking of the company; and whether any of the terms of the charge prohibit or restrict the company from creating further security that will rank equally with or ahead of the charge (i.e. a negative pledge clause).[254] This is important because it will mean that a registered floating charge will be less vulnerable to subsequent security interests because a later security provider will have constructive notice of the negative pledge clause.

- The provisions relating to registration of enforcement of security have been clarified by setting out the information that must be provided to the registrar following the appointment of a receiver.[255]

While a number of changes have therefore been made to the regime, some aspects of the previous system remain. For example, the time period for the registration of a charge remains at 21 days, starting with the day after the creation of the charge.[256] This time limit can only be extended by court order.[257] If a charge is not registered within the 21-day period, it will be void against the liquidator, administrator, or receiver[258] and the money secured becomes immediately repayable. Further, when a charge becomes void the money secured by it immediately becomes payable.[259]

4.6.2 Possessory security

Possessory security is concerned with arrangements where the lender acquires possession of property that serves as collateral. The nature of this form of security can present problems for banks: goods may be perishable; storage costs may be very expensive; and the price of a particular commodity may be unstable. This means that it may be difficult or costly for a bank to enforce their security by selling the goods. Common forms of possessory security are the pledge and banker's lien, which will both now be discussed in brief.

4.6.2.1 Pledge

A legal pledge is created when the goods in question are delivered to the bank as creditor, giving it a legal right to possession until the debt is paid. Although strictly speaking the bank (known as the pledgee) has no proprietary interest in the goods, a pledge confers an implied right for the pledgee to realise the security by selling the goods in his or her possession. A pledge is therefore a contract of bailment where the pledgee acquires not only possession of the goods, but also certain rights in them, including

---

[254] Ibid, s859D(1)(b) and (c), inserted by Schedule 2 Companies Act 2006 (Amendment of Part 25) Regulations 2013.

[255] Ibid, s859K, inserted by Schedule 2 Companies Act 2006 (Amendment of Part 25) Regulations 2013.

[256] Ibid, s859A(4), inserted by Schedule 2 Companies Act 2006 (Amendment of Part 25) Regulations 2013.

[257] Ibid, s859F(3), inserted by Schedule 2 Companies Act 2006 (Amendment of Part 25) Regulations 2013.

[258] Ibid, s859H(3), inserted by Schedule 2 Companies Act 2006 (Amendment of Part 25) Regulations 2013.

[259] Ibid, s859H(4), inserted by Schedule 2 Companies Act 2006 (Amendment of Part 25) Regulations 2013.

a power of sale.[260] In *The Odessa*[261] the Privy Council, however, emphasised that the pledgee's only power on default was to sell the goods, and this was not a property right but simply a 'special interest'.[262] Accordingly, it is clear that the property interest in the goods remains vested with the borrower (known as the pledgor). A pledge ranks somewhere between a mortgage (which confers a property right) and a lien (which is purely possessory) although, on the view taken by the Privy Council in *The Odessa*, it is clearly closer to a mortgage.

In practice, a bank will rarely effect a pledge over goods themselves[263] but they will take possession of documents of title to goods, which will amount to constructive possession of the goods themselves.[264] An example is where the goods are on a ship and the bank has possession of the bill of lading, which embodies the title to the goods and enables the transfer of property in the goods.[265] Further, a negotiable instrument and marketable security transferable by delivery can also be the subject of a pledge. They qualify because they are a special category of property, being not only choses in action (meaning that they confer a right to the proceeds to the holder), but also choses in possession.

4.6.2.2 Lien

A lien is a right to hold property belonging to the borrower, until their debt has been discharged. There is therefore no need for any express agreement to bring a lien into existence.[266] A general lien will arise as a result of the general dealings between the parties, where property that becomes the subject matter of the lien is part of the transaction. A general lien will secure a borrower's entire indebtedness at any one time, unless there is an express or implied agreement to the contrary. Thus, in *Re Bowes*,[267] a customer deposited a policy of life assurance with his bank, accompanied by a memorandum of charge to secure overdrafts up to £4,000. In these circumstances, where there was an express agreement, North J held that the lien did not secure any amounts beyond the stipulated figure.

More specifically, a banker's lien arises over commercial paper, which the bank acquires in the ordinary course of business. For example, an issuing or confirming bank under a letter of credit is entitled to retain possession of the shipping documents that embody title to the goods (including the bill of lading), as security for the amount paid. A special feature of a banker's lien is that, unlike other common law liens, it carries with it the right to sell the security to realise the debt.[268] Accordingly, a banker's lien is more akin to a pledge, and has been referred to as an 'implied pledge' by the courts.[269] The banker's lien extends to all classes of negotiable and semi-negotiable instruments of exchange

---

[260] *Re Hardwick, ex p, Hubbard* (1886) 17 QBD 690.   [261] [1916] 1 AC 145.   [262] At 158–9.
[263] It would be cumbersome to do so; banks do not have the necessary storage facilities, nor would it make sense for them to take possession of, for example, plant equipment that the borrower will clearly need.
[264] *Lickbarrow v Mason* (1787) 2 TR 63.   [265] See, for example, *Sewell v Burdick* (1884) 10 App Cas 74.
[266] *Brandao v Barnett* (1846) 12 Cl & F 787.   [267] (1886) 3 Ch D 586.
[268] *Rosenberg v International Banking Corporation* (1923) 14 Ll L Rep 344.
[269] See *Brandao v Barnett* (1846) 12 Cl & F 787.

including bills of exchange, cheques, promissory notes, and bonds. It will not, however, attach to documents that evidence mere choses in action. In *Wylde v Radford*[270] it was held that a deed concerning a conveyance of land could not be the subject of a banker's lien, but in *Re Bowes*[271] a lien was recognised over a life insurance policy.

4.6.3 Personal security

Guarantees, which are sometimes referred to as a form of 'personal security', arise where one party (known as the guarantor) undertakes a personal obligation to repay a loan in the event that the borrower (the principal debtor) defaults or becomes insolvent. The guarantor is therefore assuming secondary liability. In the context of corporate borrowing, a partner or director of a company can give a personal guarantee, as can parent companies in respect of a loan made to a subsidiary company. A guarantee has been described as:[272]

> an accessory contract by which the promisor undertakes to be answerable to the promise for the debt, default or miscarriage of another person, whose primary liability to the promisee must exist or be contemplated.

What this means is that the borrower will remain primarily liable to repay the debt and the guarantor's secondary liability will only arise if the borrower defaults. The lending bank will enter into a contract with the borrower under which the bank agrees to extend the funds in exchange for the borrower's primary obligation to repay. In addition, either under the same contract or in a second contract, the third-party guarantor will undertake a secondary obligation to repay in the event of default by the principal debtor. Clearly, a principal debtor cannot guarantee his own obligations,[273] and nor can a lending bank stand as guarantor for monies owed to him.[274]

Since a guarantor might find themselves liable not only for the principle debt but also any interest flowing from the primary debtor's default, the *Standards of Lending Practice* provide for a number of safeguarding principles, as set out in Box 4.10.[275]

In addition to these standards, a number of formal requirements have to be complied with to ensure that the guarantee is enforceable. For example, the guarantee must be executed in writing and signed by the guarantor or his or her agent. Failure to do so will not render the guarantee void, but it will be unenforceable.[276] A contract of guarantee must be supported by consideration, unless it is under seal or the agreement takes effect as a deed. This requirement is often constituted by the creditor's action in entering into the transaction with the principal debtor, that is, in exchange for the guarantee the bank provides the loan facility to the borrower.

---

[270] (1863) 33 LJ Ch 51.   [271] (1886) 3 Ch D 586.

[272] *Halsbury's Law of England*, 'Guarantees and Indemnity' paragraph 101.

[273] *Lakeman v Mountstephen* (1874) LR 7 HL 17.   [274] *Re Hoyle* [1893] 1 Ch 84.

[275] *Standards of Lending Practice: Business Customers* (October 2017) at https://www.lendingstandards-board.org.uk/wp-content/uploads/2017/10/Standards-of-Lending-Practice-Business-27-Oct.pdf.

[276] Statute of Frauds 1677, s4.

Box 4.10 Standards of lending practice: guarantees

- If an individual or a business agrees to be a guarantor, the bank should make the individual/business aware of their obligations under the agreement and that they have the option to seek legal advice, should they wish to do so.

- Banks should not accept unlimited guarantees from an individual/business unless it is to support a customer's liabilities under a merchant agreement (defined as a contract between a business and a credit card service provider); however, other forms of unlimited third-party security may be taken, if available.

- Banks should ensure that where an individual provides a guarantee they are able to request information regarding their current level of liability, as long as the customer gives their permission and confidentiality is not breached.

Key takeaways

- Security is some form of proprietary, possessory, or personal right that a lender has that will enable them to realise repayment of a loan in the event of default by the borrower.

- Proprietary security gives the bank a proprietary right in the relevant property, allowing the bank to seize it in the event of default. The most common forms of proprietary security are mortgages of chattels and land, and a charge over the assets of a company.

- Possessory security gives the bank possession of property to serve as collateral. Common forms of possessory security are the pledge (which gives the bank the right to sell the property) and banker's lien.

- Guarantees, a form of personal security, arise where a third-party guarantor gives a personal obligation to repay a loan in the event that the borrower defaults or becomes insolvent. The guarantor is therefore assuming secondary liability.

Key bibliography

Articles

Anderson, K, 'Case Comment: The Spectrum Plus Case' (2005) 16(10) *International Company and Commercial Law Review* 405

Baird, K and Sidle, P, 'Case Comment: Spectrum Plus: House of Lords Decision – A Cloud with a Silver Lining?' (2005) 18(8) *Insolvency Intelligence* 113

Goode, R, 'Charges over Book Debts: A Missed Opportunity' (1994) 110 *Law Quarterly Review* 592

Worthington, S, 'Case Comment: Fixed Charges over Book Debts and other Receivables' (1997) 113 *Law Quarterly Review* 563

Reports

Law Commission, *Company Security Interests* (Law Com No 296, 2002)

4.7 Innovation in lending

In the wake of the 2007–9 financial crisis, the UK's unsecured lending market contracted. Banks reduced lending as they were recovering from the excesses of lending and investment prior to the crisis. The impact of regulatory reforms that exerted greater control over bank lending (see Chapters 8 and 9) also resulted in lending contraction. This gap in the market has been exploited by non-traditional banks such as FinTech[277] lenders who have increased their market share by quickly adapting to the lending demands of a digital market place.[278] Two innovations in particular, namely, payday lending and peer-to-peer (P2P) lending will be discussed in this section with a particular emphasis on how these emerging facilities have been regulated.

4.7.1 Payday lenders

One of the innovations of the post-crisis lending landscape is the payday loan, which is characterised as a form of high-cost short-term credit (HCSTC).[279] The use of payday loans has risen dramatically from their initial introduction to the market in 2006, up until 2013 where, at their peak, they were offered by 400 firms, servicing 1.6 million customers, and 10 million loans with a market value of £2.5 billion.[280] Payday loans are typically used for borrowing a small amount of money (up to £500), which is then repaid, with interest, on the customers next payday, or in short-term monthly instalments.[281] Unlike traditional secured or unsecured lending, payday loans are seen as a short-term borrowing solution aimed at those who cannot access an overdraft or credit card facility and need to cover an immediate or emergency expense. Payday lenders, such as Wonga, QuickQuid, and Money Shop have become dominant in the short-term lending market from around 2012 onwards. With a strong backing from private equity firms, these tech-savvy payday lenders use technology to make rapid lending decisions (normally within 24 hours) at low costs, meaning that the sector has grown rapidly and reaped excellent returns.

---

[277] A FinTech is a company that uses new technology and innovation to compete with more traditional methods in the delivery of financial services.

[278] For an in-depth discussion of the rise in digital challenger banks see Lerong Lu, 'Financial Technology and Challenger Banks in the UK: Gap Fillers or Real Challengers?' (2017) 39(7) *Journal of International Banking Law and Regulation* 273.

[279] An HCSTC is broadly defined as an unsecured regulated credit agreement which has an annual percentage rate of charge (APR) of at least 100 per cent and is due to be repaid (or substantially repaid) within one year. See FCA Handbook at https://www.handbook.fca.org.uk/handbook/glossary/?starts-with=H.

[280] Citizens Advice, *Payday Loans: An Improved Market?* (March 2016), p 4.

[281] The Competition and Markets Authority (CMA) defines a payday loan as 'the provision of small sum loans marketed on a short-term basis, not secured against collateral, including (but not limited to) loans repayable on the customer's next payday or at the end of the month, and specifically excluding home credit loan agreements, credit cards, credit unions and overdrafts.' CMA, *Payday Lending Market Investigation* (February 2015) p 32 at https://assets.digital.cabinet-office.gov.uk/media/54ebb03bed915d0cf7000014/Payday_investigation_Final_report.pdf.

However, because lending decisions are made so quickly, customers often fail to understand the implications of the loan facility, particularly the excessive interest and fees being charged. This has led to a widespread series of complaints to the Financial Ombudsman service. In turn, the industry has come under severe criticism,[282] with consumer bodies arguing that payday loans have caused harm to vulnerable consumers. As a result of this, and in line with their aim to put the spotlight on high-risk products, the FCA has introduced a series of rules to regulate the market and make it fairer for borrowers.

In 2013 the FCA launched a consultation process, which aimed to help consumers most at risk by ensuring that HCSTC lenders pay more attention to responsible lending. Chief concerns of the FCA were: [283]

- The need to stop payday loans spiralling endlessly through repeat rollovers.[284]
- The lack of incentive for lenders to carry out robust affordability assessments, and the unfair treatment of customers experiencing difficulties because lenders are given unlimited access to borrower's accounts through 'continuous payment authorities'(CPA).[285]
- The fact that advertising often made borrowing look easy when, in reality, paying back the loan will be difficult.

In February 2014, following a period of consultation, the FCA published a policy statement setting out detailed rules for consumer credit firms, including conduct rules for HCSTC.[286] The new rules apply from 1 July 2014. First, payday lenders and other firms offering HCSTC must now limit the extension of loans to two rollovers and, before rolling over a loan, lenders will have to give the borrower an information sheet that explains where and how to get free debt advice. This approach balances the need to prevent customers from incurring an unsustainable debt burden, with the recognition that in some circumstances rolling over can offer flexibility and might be in the customer's best interests (e.g. where they are paid late). Second, there is now a limit of two unsuccessful attempts to seek payment using a CPA, and lenders cannot use a CPA to take a part-payment. This can be reset only subject to strict conditions. According to the FCA this restriction enables lenders to use this flexible payment method while

---

[282] See, for example, John McDermott 'We are now all part of the Wonga Economy' (5 November 2013) *Financial Times* at http://www.ft.com/cms/s/0/c80def50–4646–11e3-a0c0–0144feabdc0.html#axzz43kWMQ0Qc.

[283] See FCA, *Detailed Proposals for the FCA Regime for Consumer Credit* (October 2013) CP13/10 at https://www.fca.org.uk/publication/consultation/cp13-10.pdf.

[284] A loan is rolled over if the period over which loan repayments are to be made has been extended, or if the due date for any loan repayment has been moved to a later date.

[285] A CPA (which is also known as a recurring payment) is where a business has permission to take an unlimited series of payments from a customer's debit or credit card. Payday lenders often use CPAs to claim repayments and the FCA found that some firms were using them as a debt collection method, leaving borrowers facing difficulty in paying for essentials such as food.

[286] FCA, *Detailed Rules for the FCA Regime for Consumer Credit Including Feedback on FCA QCP 13/18 and 'Made Rules'* (February 2014) PS14/3 at https://www.fca.org.uk/publication/policy/ps14-03.pdf.

ensuring that customers maintain control.[287] Finally, lenders offering HCSTC must now include a prominent risk warning on all financial promotions as follows: 'Warning: Late repayment can cause you serious money problems. For help, go to moneyadviceservice.org.uk'. This risk warning had to be included in electronic communications from 1 April 2014 (where it was easier to introduce the warning), and on all other promotions including print, TV, and radio promotions from 1 July 2014.

Next, in order to secure an appropriate degree of protection from excessive charges for borrowers of HCSTC, the FCA has introduced a price cap.[288] The cap has three components:

- **An initial cost cap**: When loans are taken out or rolled over, the interest and fees charged must not exceed **0.8 per cent per day** of the amount borrowed. Lenders can structure their charges under this cap in any way they choose, for example, a portion could be upfront or rollover fees.

- **A cap on default fees and interest**: If borrowers default, fees must not exceed £15. Firms can continue to charge interest after default but not above the initial rate.

- **A total cost cap**: Borrowers must never have to pay more in fees and interest than **100 per cent** of what they borrowed.

The effect of this is that from 2 January 2015, customers taking out HCSTC will never need to pay back more than twice what they borrowed, and someone drawing down a loan over a standard 30-day period will not pay more than £24 per £100 borrowed, providing they repay on time.[289] While these limits seem fairly liberal (they can e.g. still result in an APR of over 1,000 per cent) they still constitute a significant reduction in comparison to the previous exorbitant prices some lenders charged.[290] In July 2017, the FCA published a feedback statement following a review of the HCSTC price cap.[291] In concluding that the cap should remain at its current rate, the FCA commented that:[292]

> We have found improved outcomes for consumers since setting the cap. Consumers pay less, repay on time more often and are less likely to need help with HCSTC products from debt charities. Debt charities have also indicated that consumers are presenting themselves earlier and with lower debts, suggesting that underlying problems are being addressed sooner.

Further, the FCA stated that, on the evidence, there had been a growth in lenders offering longer-term multiple instalment loans, which allows consumers to spread

---

[287] Ibid, paragraph 5.21.

[288] FCA, *Consumer Credit Sourcebook (CONC)*, Section 5A 'Cost cap for high-cost short-term credit' at https://www.handbook.fca.org.uk/handbook/CONC/5A/?view=chapter.

[289] FCA, *Detailed Rules for the Price Cap on High-Cost Short-Term Credit Including Feedback on CP14/10 and Final Rules* (November 2014) PS14/16 at https://www.fca.org.uk/publication/policy/ps14-16.pdf.

[290] In its review of high-cost consumer credit, the OFT found that payday lenders were charging an APR of as much as 4,438 per cent. See OFT, *Review of High-Cost Credit: Final Report Annexe E: Competition and Profitability* (June 2010) OFT1232, p 78.

[291] FCA, *High-Cost Credit Including Review of the High-Cost Short-Term Credit Price Cap* (July 2017) FS17/2 at https://www.fca.org.uk/publication/feedback/fs17-02.pdf.   [292] Ibid, p 4.

repayments over time, and that consumers who had been turned down for HCSTC products were not generally turning to other forms of high-cost credit or illegal money lending. Another review of the price cap will be conducted in 2020.

Finally, from 26 May 2017, as a result of an investigation conducted by the Competition and Markets Authority (CMA) in 2015,[293] payday lenders must now advertise on at least one price comparison website.[294] Lenders are also required to display prominently a link on their own websites to a price comparison website.[295] The CMA concluded that these new rules would:[296]

- Allow customers to identify the best value loans and compare loans more easily.

- Increase customer awareness of late fees and other additional charges, making it easier to establish the real cost of missing a repayment.

- Reduce barriers to entry and expansion that are linked to problems with raising customer awareness of different supplier's offers.

- Lower reputational barriers to entry by giving more credibility to the payday lending price comparison market and by encouraging the involvement of normal price comparison website operators.

In terms of impact, it is clear that this series of regulations and restrictions has created a market with better borrowing conditions, which will protect consumers from incurring an unsustainable and escalating debt burden. Product regulation and the imposition of responsible lending rules will improve the reputation of payday lenders and lead to a more efficient and well-resourced industry.[297] However, these changes have also had a direct impact on the dynamics of the industry, with the FCA reporting that in November 2014, just 6 months after the core regulatory changes were introduced, the volume and value of lending had reduced by around 35 per cent. This represents a 20 per cent reduction in application volumes and a 50 per cent reduction in acceptance rates.[298] By March 2016 Citizens Advice reported that 38 per cent of firms had exited the market since the regulations were introduced and that they had witnessed a significant reduction in the number of clients coming to them with payday loan related issues.[299] Citizens Advice argue that 'these reductions point to a society less tolerant of these products and firms tightening up their lending practices.'[300]

---

[293] CMA, *Payday Lending Market Investigation, Final Report* (24 February 2015) at https://assets.publishing. service.gov.uk/media/54ebb03bed915d0cf7000014/Payday_investigation_Final_report.pdf.

[294] CMA, *Payday Lending Market Investigation Order 2016* at https://www.gov.uk/government/uploads/system/uploads/attachment_data/file/453433/Payday_Lending_Market_Investigation_Order_2015.pdf.

[295] Ibid.

[296] CMA, *Payday Lending Market Investigation, Final Report* (24 February 2015) pp 287–90 at https://assets. publishing.service.gov.uk/media/54ebb03bed915d0cf7000014/Payday_investigation_Final_report.pdf.

[297] See Anu Arora, 'Payday Loans: Filling the Gaps in the Short-Term Loan Market' (2017) *Company Lawyer* 172.

[298] FCA Press Release, 'FCA confirms price cap rules for payday lenders' 11 November 2014 at https://www. fca.org.uk/news/press-releases/fca-confirms-price-cap-rules-payday-lenders.

[299] Citizens Advice, *Payday Loans: An Improved Market?* (March 2016) p 23.

[300] Ibid, p 4. For further discussion see Anu Arora, 'Payday Loans: Filling the Gaps in the Short-Term Loan Market' (2017) *Company Lawyer* 172.

4.7.2 **Peer-to-peer (P2P) lending**

In response to the demand for alternatives to personal and small business loans made by banks, non-traditional financial institutions such as FinTech companies and digital banks have taken advantage of technology innovation to create new P2P lending[301] platforms. Unlike traditional unsecured lending where a consumer approaches a bank and applies for a loan, with P2P lending borrowers lend directly from investors via an online lending platform. P2P platforms are among the fastest growing segment in the financial services industry. In the UK, Zopa began offering P2P services in March 2005, and it was joined by FundingCircle and RateSetter in 2010, at which point the market saw explosive growth. Since 2010, the P2P market has grown exponentially, with total lending in the sector between Q3 2014 and Q4 2017 amounting to over £8 billion.[302]

The attraction of P2P lending for borrowers is that it cuts out the banking middleman, thereby offering attractive interest rates. Similarly, the attraction for investors is that they can earn a higher return through P2P lending than through other savings vehicles, such as savings accounts, and the stock market. P2P lending does, however, attract certain risks. Aside from the obvious, such as the risk of borrower default or the risk of not being able to access the capital invested within a short time, there is also the risk that the company operating the lending platform becomes insolvent. These issues are exacerbated by the fact that the FCA decided that P2P platforms should not be included within the remit of the Financial Services Compensation Scheme, meaning that an investor's money isn't protected in the same way it would be if it was in a savings account.[303]

From 1 April 2014, when the FCA took over the regulation of consumer credit from the OFT, P2P platforms became a regulated activity.[304] Firms with a valid OFT licence on 31 March 2014 were given interim permission to carry on their consumer credit activities until they become fully authorised.[305] Of the 'big three' P2P lending platforms in the UK, Zopa and FundingCircle received full authorisation in May 2017, and RateSetter received full authorisation in October 2017.

The FCA has imposed a number of regulatory rules on P2P lending platforms. These relate to mandatory disclosure of information to investors,[306] client money protection rules,[307] dispute resolution rules, and a requirement for platforms to take reasonable steps to ensure existing loans continue to be administered if the platform goes out of

---

[301] Also known as loan-based crowd funding.   [302] See http://p2pfa.info/data.

[303] FCA, *The FCA's Cto crowdfunding over the Internet, and the Promotion of Non-Readily Realisable Securities by Other Media: Feedback to CP13/13 and Final Rules* (March 2014) PS14/4, pp 17–18 at https://www.fca.org.uk/publication/policy/ps14-04.pdf.

[304] The Financial Services and Markets Act 2000 (Regulated Activities) Order 2001 s36H, inserted by The Financial Services and Markets Act 2000 (Regulated Activities) (Amendment) (No.2) Order 2013 s4.

[305] By 1 April 2016 all firms with interim permission should have been granted, or at least applied for, full permission.   [306] FCA, *Consumer Credit Sourcebook (CONC)* 4.3.4.

[307] Found in the *Client Assets Sourcebook* (CASS).

business.[308] Lending platforms are also subject to *capital adequacy* rules, which have the effect of keeping in check the amounts of lending that can be created, as higher amounts attract greater risk to investors and platforms. Between 1 April 2014 and 31 March 2017, P2P lenders were subject to a fixed minimum regulatory capital amount, which was the higher of £20,000 or:

- 0.2 per cent of the first £50 million of total value of loaned funds outstanding; plus
- 0.15 per cent of the next £200 million of total value of loaned funds outstanding; plus
- 0.1 per cent of the next £250 million of total value of loaned funds outstanding; plus
- 0.05 per cent of any remaining balance of total value of loaned funds outstanding above £500 million.

From 1 April 2017 the fixed minimum amount was replaced with a figure of £50,000. These minimum prudential requirements are not effective until a firm becomes fully authorised.

In March 2016 the FCA published an additional policy statement,[309] which finalised rules on the segregation of client money[310] and made advising on P2P agreements a regulated activity[311] subject to certain Handbook rules including, for example, rules on assessing suitability providing that firms must take reasonable steps to ensure that personal recommendations in relation to P2P lending are suitable for their clients.[312] Further, and most importantly, the policy statement introduced the Handbook provisions relating to the Innovative Finance ISA (IFISA), which is available from 6 April 2016. Essentially, via an amendment to the Individual Savings Account Regulations 1998, P2P agreements can be held within a tax efficient ISA wrapper. What this means is that the IFISA allow savers to use some or part of their annual ISA investment allowance (£20,000 in the first year) to receive tax-free interest and tax-free capital gains on funds

---

[308] See FCA, *The FCA's Regulatory Approach to Crowdfunding over the Internet, and the Promotion of Non-Readily Realisable Securities by Other Media: Feedback to CP13/13 and Final Rules* (March 2014) PS14/4 at https://www.fca.org.uk/publication/policy/ps14-04.pdf.

[309] FCA, *Policy Statement: FCA Handbook Changes Regarding the Segregation of Client Money on loan-Based Crowdfunding Platforms, the Innovative Finance ISA, and the Regulated Activity of Advising on Peer-to-Peer Agreements* (March 2016).

[310] In particular, the rules will:

> allow firms that hold money in relation to both P2P and B2B agreements to be able to elect to hold all lenders' monies in relation to this business under CASS 7 if they wish to do so. Firms may then hold P2P and B2B monies together, but segregated from the firm's money, without breaching CASS 7 … where a firm holds money that has not yet been invested for a client, this should be client money held under the CASS rules, unless the circumstances are such that it could never be money held in relation to a P2P agreement.

FCA, *Policy Statement: FCA Handbook Changes Regarding the Segregation of Client Money on loan-Based Crowdfunding Platforms, the Innovative Finance ISA, and the Regulated Activity of Advising on Peer-to-Peer Agreements* (March 2016) p 10. See also FCA, *Client Assets Sourcebook (CASS)*.

[311] The Financial Services and Markets Act 2000 (Regulated Activities) Order 2001 s53(2), as inserted by The Financial Services and Markets Act 2000 (Regulated Activities) (Amendment) Order 2016 s2.

[312] See FCA, *Conduct of Business Sourcebook (COBS)* 9.

Box 4.11 P2PFA High-Level Principles

Competence: platforms will manage all their business activities with technical and professional competence.

Honesty: platforms will communicate to customers and other stakeholders in a way which is open, clear, truthful and unambiguous.

Integrity: platforms commit to promoting and serving the interests of their customers, both lenders and borrowers.

Transparency: platforms pledge to be open, transparent and honest in disclosing information relating to the business transacted and performance achieved in the origination of loans, credit risk assessment and management, delivery of returns for investors and other key information that allows the public to judge their performance.

---

lent through P2P lending platforms. To offer IFISA's, P2P lending platforms must be fully authorised by the FCA. This development demonstrates the commitment of the FCA to the growing P2P sector, particularly as ISA is an established brand with broad, mass market appeal.

Alongside the regulatory regime, in 2011 Zopa, FundingCircle, and RateSetter founded the Peer-to-Peer Finance Association (P2PFA) as a self-regulatory body for the sector to promote high standards of conduct and consumer protection. The three main objectives of the Association are:[313]

- to seek to secure public policy, regulatory and fiscal conditions that enable the UK-based peer-to-peer finance sector to compete fairly and grow responsibly;

- to ensure that Members demonstrate high standards of business conduct, to demonstrate leadership and to promote confidence in the sector; and

- to raise awareness and understanding of the benefits and risks of peer-to-peer finance.

The P2PFA subjects its members to a series of operating principles.[314] Accordingly, members must commit to abide by the High-Level Principles, set out in Box 4.11, in the conduct of their business.

The financial crisis and the advent of new digital technology has facilitated the emergence of this growing industry. P2P lending has brought much-needed new competition and choice to the lending market in providing an alternative source of funds for individuals and businesses.[315] Traditional banks are left with the option to either collaborate with these emerging firms or compete directly with them by offering better deals.[316] The

---

[313] See http://p2pfa.info/about-p2p-finance.   [314] See https://p2pfa.org.uk/operating-principles/.

[315] For an interesting discussion of the challenges posed by P2Ps of certain fundamental assumptions, objectives, and frameworks of consumer protection law and policy, see Onyeka Osuji and Ugochi Amajuoyi 'Online Peer-to-Peer Lending: Challenging Consumer Protection Rationales, Orthodoxies and Models?' 2015 *Journal of Business Law* 484.

[316] See Anu Arora and Ewan Hutton, 'The Regulation of Crowdfunding in the UK' (2017) *Company Lawyer* 368.

FCA continues to monitor developments[317] in this industry as the regulatory framework is still very skeletal at this stage. In particular, pertinent issues are: whether the mandatory disclosure to investors is adequate; whether the advice industry is meeting investors' expectations; and whether P2P lending platforms are competently managing risk. Further, although the leading P2P lending platforms set up investor protection funds in order to help investors manage borrower defaults, it remains open to question how robust such provision is when risks materialise or if situations of stress occur more widely in the market (such as a wave of borrower defaults).

➡ Key takeaways

- The 2007–9 financial crisis, which resulted in the contraction of credit from traditional lenders, paired with the growth of digital technology, has led to the development of new and innovative means of lending money.

- Payday loans, which are classified as a type of HCSTC provide a mechanism for borrowing a small amount of money, which is then repaid, with interest, on the customer's next payday, or in short-term monthly instalments.

- Payday lenders have been subject to extensive criticism for their irresponsible lending practices, resulting in an influx of regulation designed to protect consumers.

- P2P lending cuts out the banking middleman by allowing borrowers to lend directly from investors via online lending platforms.

- P2P lending is now a regulated activity meaning that lending platforms are subject to a number of the FCA Principles relating to, for example, disclosure, client money protection, dispute resolution, and capital adequacy.

Key bibliography

Reports

Citizens Advice, *Payday Loans: An Improved Market?* (March 2016)

CMA, *Payday Lending Market Investigation, Final Report* (24 February 2015) at https://assets.publishing.service.gov.uk/media/54ebb03bed915d0cf7000014/Payday_investigation_Final_report.pdf

FCA, *Detailed Proposals for the FCA Regime for Consumer Credit* (October 2013) CP13/10 at https://www.fca.org.uk/publication/consultation/cp13-10.pdf

FCA, *Detailed Rules for the Price Cap on High-Cost Short-Term Credit Including Feedback on CP14/10 and Final Rules* (November 2014) PS14/16 at https://www.fca.org.uk/publication/policy/ps14-16.pdf

FCA, *High-Cost Credit Including Review of the High-Cost Short-Term Credit Price Cap* (July 2017) FS17/2 at https://www.fca.org.uk/publication/feedback/fs17-02.pdf

---

[317] FCA, *Interim Feedback to the Call for Input to the Post-Implementation Review of the FCA's Crowdfunding Rules* (Dec 2016) at https://www.fca.org.uk/publication/feedback/fs16-13.pdf.

Articles

Arora, A, 'Payday Loans: Filling the Gaps in the Short-Term Loan Market' (2017) 38(6) *Company Lawyer* 172

Arora, A and Hutton, E, 'The Regulation of Crowdfunding in the UK' (2017) 38(12) *Company Lawyer* 368

Lu, L, 'Financial Technology and Challenger Banks in the UK: Gap Fillers or Real Challengers?' (2017) 39(7) *Journal of International Banking Law and Regulation* 273.

Osuji, O and Amajuoyi, U, 'Online Peer-to-Peer Lending: Challenging Consumer Protection Rationales, Orthodoxies and Models?' (2015) *Journal of Business Law* 484

Questions

1. The decision of the Supreme Court in *Office of Fair Trading v Abbey National* [2010] was disappointing. Reform is required in relation to the interest and charges imposed for unauthorised overdraft facilities.

   Answer tips *You should analyse the decision of both the Court of Appeal and the Supreme Court in the* Abbey National *case and consider whether, although disappointing, the decision was legally correct. You may wish to comment on the subsequent work of the OFT and the former FSA in terms of the 'treat customers fairly' campaign, and you should critically analyse the FCA's report on 'High-Cost Credit' (FS17/2) before concluding whether reform is required in this area.*

2. Critically examine the options available to a bank to manage its risk exposure when lending.

   Answer tips *You should start by discussing the reasons a bank may want to limit its exposure when lending before broadly analysing the difference between loan syndication and loan participation. In particular the advantages and disadvantages of the various methods of loan participation should be considered, focusing on which method best satisfies the banks commercial need for transferring their interest in the loan.*

3. Critically analyse the circumstances in which a bank may face liability as a shadow director of a corporate borrower.

   Answer tips *You should start by setting the context to the question, highlighting why a bank might face liability as a shadow director under the provisions of the Insolvency Act 1986. You should then critically analyse the evolution of the case law in this area and the guidance offered by the courts as to what will have to be shown to render a bank a shadow director of its corporate customer. Lord Millet's extrajudicial comments could also be considered.*

5

International banking supervision and regulatory architecture

5.1 Issues in international banking

Banks and banking activity are not confined to national borders. The post-World War II era has seen the rapid globalisation of financial markets,[1] meaning that the amount of banking business that crosses national boundaries, and the interconnections between the financial systems of different countries, have grown rapidly in recent decades. While these trends present enormous financial opportunities for banks, they also increase the risk that problems experienced in one country can spread to other countries, as demonstrated by the financial crisis that emerged in 2007. Supervisors also face difficulties in imposing effective controls in relation to these international risks because their jurisdiction is limited to their national borders.[2]

5.1.1 International banks

A coterie of multinational banks, for example, HSBC and Citigroup, have footprints in many parts of the world. Banks have spread their operations into other countries by, for example, the acquisition of, or merger with, a foreign bank, or the provision of services beyond national boundaries either through agencies in other countries or the internet. This interdependence of banks across the world means that problems can resonate beyond national boundaries. In particular, the connections between international banks means that the failure of one bank can bring down banks in other jurisdictions and with them their financial systems. The likelihood of these difficulties occurring has increased as the result of a number of factors including; the spread of banks with branches and subsidiaries in other countries; the interdependence of banks and countries; advances in technology that allows the rapid transfer of funds across the world; and the changes in regulation that have allowed banks to engage in a broader range of business than simply deposit-taking and lending.

---

[1] Discussed in section 5.2.1.1.
[2] See generally, Duncan Alford, 'International Financial System Risks: A Current Assessment' (2005) 20(1) *Journal of International Banking Law and Regulation* 40.

Box 5.1 Casualties of the financial crisis 2007–9

Northern Rock (NR): NR was a bank that specialised in mortgage lending in the UK. They relied on securitisation[3] and the interbank lending market to run their day to day operations. Accordingly, when the interbank market contracted in 2007, NR found themselves unable to fund their day to day operations and they had to turn to the Bank of England for financial assistance (which extended to £27 billion by the end of 2007). NR was ultimately nationalised in February 2008 and in January 2012 it was sold at a loss to Virgin Money.[4]

Lehman Brothers (LB): LB was a truly multinational bank with an extensive global footprint. They had pursued for many years an aggressive policy of growth and investment in risky and illiquid assets such as commercial property, hedge funds, and securitised assets. Accordingly, when the financial crisis hit, LB reported huge losses and eventually filed for bankruptcy in the US on 15 September 2008.[5]

Bear Stearns (BS): BS was a US investment bank that held huge quantities of mortgage-backed securities or 'toxic assets'. In March 2008, despite emergency funding assistance from the Federal Reserve Bank of New York, BS was bought out by JP Morgan Chase.

This risk of contagion was demonstrated by the 2007–9 financial crisis.[6] While the crisis had its roots in the US housing market, the uncertainty that ensued led to the freezing-up of the interbank lending market through which various banks financed their businesses. The crisis led to a number of casualties, some examples of which are given in Box 5.1.

Furthermore, in addition to the risks faced by ordinary banks such as credit risk, market risk, and *operational risk*,[7] international banks are exposed to two additional risk-related problems. First, international banks must deal with currency risk, that is, the risk that changes in foreign exchange rates will affect the bank, and, second, they are subject to country risk, that is, the risk that conditions (political, economic, and legal) in their country of operation will change and cause the bank to incur losses.

A further issue raised by the internationalisation of the banking industry is that some banks may become too important to be allowed to fail because of the impact it would have on international markets. This 'too big to fail' phrase was coined following the 1984 rescue of Continental Illinois National Bank, which was the seventh largest bank in America. While its problems were largely domestic and related to the impact on its

---

[3] Securitisation is the packaging or bundling of usually loan assets into securities based on their underlying income streams, to be sold to investors in the market such as institutional investors.

[4] See Chapter 13 for more detailed information on the failure of Northern Rock. See also: Maximilian Hall, 'The Sub-Prime Crisis, the Credit Squeeze and Northern Rock: The Lessons to be Learned' (2008) 16(1) *Journal of Financial Regulation & Compliance* 19; and David Llewellyn, 'The Northern Rock to Happen (2008) 16(1) *Journal of Financial Regulation & Compliance* 35.

[5] See, for example, Amirsaleh Azadinamin, 'The Bankruptcy of Lehman Brothers: Causes of Failure & Recommendations Going Forward' (2012) at http://ssrn.com/abstract=2016892.

[6] See Chapter 1.   [7] See Chapter 8.

US borrowers of a decline in oil prices, it had borrowed heavily on the international interbank market and its dependence on foreign funding led regulators to fear that should it be allowed to fail, there might be a loss of international confidence in US banks, which could affect the global financial system.

The recent financial crisis added a number of other banks to this category of 'too big to fail' including Citigroup in the US and Royal Bank of Scotland in the UK, which both received government support. The problem with this too big to fail policy is that it distorts the market and may encourage the bank and/or its customers to take excessive risks in the belief that they will not suffer loss. In the wake of the 2007–9 financial crisis, a new regulatory regime for crisis management and resolution has emerged that aims to put an end to this too big to fail mentality.[8]

5.1.2 Supervision of international banks

From a supervisory perspective, the size and complexity of international financial conglomerates and the fact that supervisors are bound by national borders raises a number of difficulties.

National supervisors can suffer from a lack of oversight of the entirety of a bank's operations. In order to get a full picture of a bank's operations and its financial health, information from abroad must be collected and interpreted. This can be hampered by local laws on bank secrecy and variations in the way data is produced in different countries. Further, while losses incurred by a bank established in one country may create difficulties for that bank (and indeed other banks) in another host country, the supervisor in the host country may be powerless to foresee or prevent such problems from arising because it lacks information on the problems with the bank's operations in the country of establishment. An example to demonstrate this issue is the failure of the UK Barings Bank in 1995 as a result of the activities of a single trader working in the bank's Singapore office.[9] This trader, Nick Leeson, sustained enormous losses by making unauthorised and excessive bets on Nikkei futures indices (a stock market index for the Tokyo Stock Exchange), which wiped out the assets of the bank. Leeson managed to deceive the bank's management so the home supervisor, the Bank of England, were not aware of any issues.

Further, the supervision of huge and complex international financial conglomerates raises a number of concerns and questions. For example, which country's supervisor should take control of the international entity that potentially operates across multiple sectors in multiple jurisdictions? Moreover, which country's rules should apply? Those of the home country—**home country control**—where the head office is located? Or those of the host country where the activities are taking place? Finally, how should crisis management be managed? Should the country in which the problem arises take the lead, that is, the host state? Or should it be the country in which the bank has its head office?

---

[8] See Chapter 13. See also Chapter 9, which discusses the FSB's annual list of systemically important banks.
[9] See Chapter 6.

These issues culminated in the introduction of an international financial architecture that has been established since 1975. This chapter focuses on the mechanisms and efficacy of this architecture.

 Key takeaways

- Recent decades have seen the rapid globalisation of financial markets and banking activity.
- This interdependence of banks across the world raises the likelihood of contagion, where the failure of one bank can bring down banks in other jurisdictions and with them their financial systems.
- The size and complexity of international financial conglomerates means that national supervisors can suffer from a lack of oversight of the entirety of a bank's operations.

Key bibliography

Articles

Hall, M, 'The Sub-Prime Crisis, the Credit Squeeze and Northern Rock: The Lessons to be Learned' (2008) 16(1) *Journal of Financial Regulation & Compliance* 19

Llewellyn, D, 'The Northern Rock Crisis: A Multi-Dimensional Problem Waiting to Happen (2008) 16(1) *Journal of Financial Regulation & Compliance* 35

5.2 International financial architecture

The solution to the problems outlined in section 5.1 has been the development of procedures that seek to encourage coordination or cooperation between national supervisors. This has been facilitated by the creation of international organisations that have allowed large numbers of countries to discuss, agree, and promote not only supervisory standards, but also regulatory rules. Together, these organisations constitute the international financial architecture that seeks to ensure financial stability by addressing a number of different issues, including bank supervision and regulation, accounting standards, transparency in financial systems and transactions, corporate governance, and combating money laundering/terrorist finance. This section will introduce two of the key bodies in international banking regulation, namely, the Basel Committee on Banking Supervision (BCBS) and the Financial Stability Board (FSB). It will then look briefly at the broader international architecture within which those bodies sit.

5.2.1 The Basel Committee on Banking Supervision

The origins of international standard setting in the context of the global financial sector can be traced to the establishment in 1974 of a small club of central bankers that met in Basel at the Bank for International Settlements. The group, which were originally known as the G10 Committee on Banking Regulations and Supervisory Practices, later became known as the BCBS. The Committee was designed as 'a forum for regular cooperation between its member countries on banking supervisory matters' and its main aim was to 'enhance financial stability by improving supervisory knowhow and the quality of banking supervision worldwide.'[10] The Committee's first meeting took place in February 1975, and they have been held three or four times a year since. The work of the BCBS has been expansive, including the Basel Concordat and *Core Principles*, which will be discussed in this chapter, and the landmark accords on capital adequacy, known a Basel I, Basel II, and Basel III, which are discussed in Chapters 8 and 9. This section will look in more detail at what prompted the formation of the Basel Committee in 1974, as well as the legal character of the group.

5.2.1.1 The birth of the BCBS

The BCBS was formed in response to a number of issues, including the globalisation of the financial services industry, the collapse of the Bretton Woods system of fixed exchange rates, and the failure of two international banks, Bankhaus Herstatt and Franklin National Bank.

Globalisation

The post-World War II era saw the rapid globalisation of financial markets and banking activity. This growth occurred at a steady pace as exchange controls and other restriction on financial controls were removed, and as international communication improved.[11] The emergence of the global economic system was due in part to the development of the Euromarkets in the 1950s and 1960s, which gave a renewed energy to capital flows and prompted an explosion in international banking activity.[12] The Eurodollar market, for example, related to dollars that accumulated in European banks as a result of US regulation which capped the interest rates paid on bank deposits.[13] This market provided credit on a worldwide scale, mainly in the context of interbank deposits and the financing of international trade and by 1973 it was worth more than $130 billion.[14]

Similarly, this era saw the emergence and rapid growth of the Eurobond market, which provided an alternative source of funding in the form of tradable debt.[15] This market was initially stimulated by the imposition of the Interest Equalisation Tax in the US in 1963, which intended to put the brakes on the export of capital. The effect of this measure was that the cost of foreign bond issues in America increased, making

---

[10] BCBS, *History of the Basel Committee* (December 2016) at https://www.bis.org/bcbs/history.htm.
[11] Charles Goodhart, *The Basel Committee on Banking Supervision: A History of the Early Years* (Cambridge: Cambridge University Press 2011) 10.
[12] George Walker, *International Banking Regulation: Law, Policy and Practice* (London: Kluwer Law International 2001) 20. [13] Known as Regulation Q.
[14] Yousef Cassis, *Capitals of Capital: A History of International Financial Centres 1780-2005* (Cambridge: Cambridge University Press 2006) 220–1. See also George Walker, *International Banking Regulation* 18–20.
[15] Ibid, p 21.

Eurobonds the more attractive option.[16] Growth in the Eurobond market was substantial and by 1988 the total value of new issues was $175.8 billion.[17]

Finally, this period witnessed the emergence of the global interbank market, which – according to Walker – 'represented a natural extension of the traditional practice of banks placing deposits with or extending credits to each other from the national to the international arena.'[18] This short-term international market was used by banks to adjust their liquidity mis-matches on a day to day basis.

While financial markets became increasingly international in nature, the regulation of those markets and the supervision of international banks remained national, demonstrating a need to open communication channels between national regulators so that common issues could be discussed, and policies converged.

The collapse of the Bretton Woods system of fixed exchange rates

The need for cooperation between regulators was exacerbated by the collapse of the Bretton Woods system of fixed exchange rates in the early 1970s. This system, which was established in 1944 as part of the broader Bretton Woods Agreement, sought to amend the difficulties caused by the use of floating exchange rates in the 1930s by introducing a regime where nations agreed to fix the value of their currencies to a particular weight in gold. It encouraged free trade and international investment because it eliminated the problems caused by currency and exchange rate risk. However, after suffering a crisis of confidence in relation to the US dollar in the early 1960s, the Johnson and then Nixon administrations refused, as was required of them, to devalue the dollar or alter their domestic policies.[19] In 1971, during a televised speech, President Nixon formally announced that the US would no longer back the dollar with gold and instead, a return to a system of floating exchange rates would prevail.[20]

The collapse of the Bretton Woods system of fixed exchange rates in the early 1970s meant that international settlements were once again made in the context of floating exchange rates, determined by the supply and demand of various currencies. Although the industry exploited the opportunities arising from these new risks,[21] it meant that banks were exposed to further sources of instability. This fear, together with the failure of two international banks, prompted concerns about the strength of the international financial system.

International bank failures

One casualty of this new foreign exchange exposure was Franklin National Bank, which at the end of 1973 had been the twentieth largest bank in the US with total assets in excess of $5 billion and extensive international operations. In May 1974 the bank suffered a series

---

[16] Cassis, *Capitals of Capital* 222.   [17] Walker, *International Banking Regulation* 21, footnote 16.

[18] Ibid, 23.

[19] Michael Trebilcock and Robert Howse, *The Regulation of International Trade* (New York: Routledge 2005) 156.

[20] Gianni Toniolo, *Central Bank Cooperation at the Bank for International Settlements, 1930–1973*, (Cambridge: Cambridge University Press 2005) 434.

[21] For example, by the use of spot and forward foreign exchange contracts. See Walker, *International Banking Regulation* 23.

of deposit runs and a sharp confidence crisis, which was triggered by substantial losses in foreign exchange trading. After an extended support operation that included Federal Reserve assistance of over $1.7 billion, the bank eventually closed on 8 October 1974.[22]

There were a large number of other banks that suffered foreign exchange losses but the most spectacular failure as a result of the change of trading conditions was that of Bankhaus Herstatt in Germany in June 1974. Having suffered heavy foreign exchange losses, the Bundesbank stopped clearing payments for Herstatt's accounts at 16.00 on 26 June 1974 and its licence was withdrawn. Due to the size of its foreign exchange operations, the effect of this sudden closure was that it left uncompleted a huge number of payment commitments that had been entered into in the previous days. In particular, a number of banks in the US had released payment of Deutsch Marks to Bankhaus Herstatt, believing that they would receive US dollars in exchange later that day. However, after 16.00 in Germany, and 10.00 in New York, Herstatt stopped all dollar payments to counterparties, leaving the US banks unable to collect payments due.

This exposed the US banks to a serious liquidity crisis, which arose because there was uncertainty as to the extent and type of losses at Herstatt and it was unclear which institutions were affected. As a result, the interbank markets froze as banks became unwilling to lend (or only at higher rates of interest) to those that might have been affected by the Herstatt failure, directly or indirectly. This threatened to bring about the collapse of the entire US payments system and a global financial crisis.[23]

The culmination of these factors was the imposition of political pressure on the central bank governors to put in place mechanisms and procedures to bolster the stability of the international financial system. From this pressure, the BCBS was born.

5.2.1.2 The legal nature of the BCBS

Member countries are represented on the BCBS by either their central bank or the public body responsible for prudential regulation (see Box 5.2 for an overview of the BCBS). The Committee formulates standards and guidelines and recommends sound practices in the expectation that they will be implemented by national authorities. However, the BCBS was not set up by treaty. It has no formal legal authority, meaning that its standards and recommendations are categorised as 'soft law' that have no legal force except when individual countries choose to implement them through their national processes.[24] Ghosh describes the BCBS in the following terms:[25]

> [It] is not an international organisation and its constituents are not member states, but representatives of their respective supervisory organisations and central banks. It has no legal standing, lacks a formal character of incorporation, cannot enforce its contracts and its decisions do not have legal backing.

---

[22] See generally, Ibid, 26–30.   [23] Ibid.

[24] See, for example, Emily Lee, 'The Soft Law Nature of Basel III and International Financial Regulations' (2014) *Journal of International Banking Law and Regulation* 603.

[25] Sailbal Ghosh, 'Evolving International Supervisory Architecture: Design, Rationale and Policy Reform' (2005) 6 *Journal of Banking Regulation* 248–9.

> ### Box 5.2 At a glance: the BCBS
>
> - The BCBS was established in 1974 at the Bank for International Settlements by the G10 central bankers and regulators. Its membership now derives from 28 countries.
> - The creation of the BCBS was prompted by a number of factors including the increasing globalisation of banks, the collapse of the Bretton Woods system of fixed exchange rates, and the collapse of two international banks.
> - The BCBS has become a forum for regular cooperation in relation to banking supervision and regulatory matters. The work of the Committee has been expansive, focusing originally on international cooperation between banking supervisors, and more recently on regulatory standards such as capital adequacy rules.
> - The BCBS is a soft-law body whose recommendations and standards have no legal authority. Despite this fact, they have been implemented into national regimes across the globe.
> - From 2012 the BCBS has monitored and assessed the implementation of its standards through its RCAP.

Given that the BCBS has no legal authority, one might ask why their work has been so widely observed. The recommendations of the Committee are produced by a body whose membership is drawn from the richest and most powerful countries in the world; the implementation of the recommendations by those countries influences the behaviour of other countries, either because those countries are convinced of the value of the recommendations, or because they recognise that they cannot afford to ignore the opinions of the most powerful nations. Accordingly, the reach of the BCBS extends far beyond the economies of its member countries; developing countries face pressure from the market to comply with the Basel standards even though they are not themselves members of the club.

The soft-law nature of the Basel recommendations is a more politically sensitive form of governance that works well in the context of financial regulation. Standards are developed among like-minded individuals via an informal negotiating process rather than in a formal treaty-making way. This model is effective because it provides incentives for compliance, while preserving the benefits of speed, flexibility, and expertise, which are crucial in an ever-changing market.[26] Through the auspices of the BCBS, banking regulators have been able to cooperate informally and successfully to maintain effective regulatory control over international banks without compromising national responsibility.[27] While there is no sanction for a country that fails to implement the BCBS recommendations, other bodies such as the FSB and the International Monetary Fund (IMF) (discussed in section 5.2.2) conduct compliance reviews and results are published with recommendations for improvements. This provides an effective soft-law tool to encourage compliance.

---

[26] Lee, 'The Soft Law Nature of Basel III and International Financial Regulations' 607.   [27] Ibid.

In light of the financial crisis, which demonstrated the inadequacy of the Basel capital standards[28] the Committee has undergone a dramatic transformation. While it was originally a G10 body, its membership was expanded in 2009 and again in 2014 such that it is now represented by 45 institutions across 28 member countries. The BCBS now also reports to the Group of Governors and Heads of Supervision (GHOS), an oversight body comprised of central bank governors and (non-central bank) heads of supervision form the Committee's members. The GHOS endorses the major decisions of the BCBS.

In 2012, the BCBS also began to monitor and assess the implementation of its standards through its Regulatory Consistency Assessment Programme (RCAP).[29] The RCAP consists of two distinct but complementary workstreams. First, the transposition of the Basel III regulatory standards into domestic regulation is monitored on a semi-annual basis based on information provided by each member in a monitoring report. Second, the Committee evaluates the consistency and completeness of the adopted standards, including the significance of any deviations from the Basel III regulatory framework. These consistency assessments are carried out on a jurisdictional and thematic basis. Jurisdictional assessments review the extent to which domestic regulations are aligned with the minimum Basel requirements agreed by the Committee and help identify material gaps in such regulations. Thematic assessments examine the implementation of the Basel requirements at the individual bank level and seek to ensure that prudential ratios are calculated consistently by banks across jurisdictions to improve comparability across outcomes. This monitoring and assessment action has 'harden[ed] the edges of its status as a soft law body.'[30]

5.2.2 The Financial Stability Board

One of the key post-financial crisis developments was the emergence of the FSB, which replaced the Financial Stability Forum (FSF).

The FSF was established in 1999 by the G7 finance ministers and Central Bank governors following recommendations by Hans Tietmeyer, President of the Deutsche Bundesbank. These recommendations followed a series of crises, particularly in South-East Asia in the late 1990s, which had affected worldwide stock prices, and that highlighted the poor lending decisions that were being made across the globe and the weak regulation that accompanied it. The FSF was comprised of representatives from central banks and regulators from the G7 countries as well as members of the IMF, World Bank, and the BIS. It was created to enable the exchange of information between key international institutions and national authorities and to encourage cooperation in the development of policies that would foster stability and reduce systemic risk in the international financial system.[31]

In November 2008, the G20 countries called for increased membership to the FSF and a broad consensus emerged towards placing the body on a stronger institutional ground.

---

[28] See Chapters 8 and 9.   [29] See https://www.bis.org/bcbs/implementation.htm.
[30] Ross Cranston et al, *Principles of Banking Law* (Oxford: Oxford University Press 2017) 21.
[31] See FSB, *Our History* at www.fsb.org/about/history/.

It was argued that this would strengthen its effectiveness as a mechanism for national authorities, standard-setting bodies, and international financial institutions (IFIs) to address vulnerabilities and to develop and implement strong regulatory and supervisory policies in the interest of financial stability.[32] Accordingly, at the London summit of the G20 in April 2009, it was announced that the FSF would be reconstituted as the FSB, with an increased membership and broadened mandate to promote financial stability.

Membership of the FSB is, accordingly, much wider than its predecessor, consisting of representatives from 24 countries (plus the EU), all the major IFIs including the BIS, World Bank, IMF, and the Organisation for Economic Co-operation and Development (OECD), and all the major standard-setting bodies including the BCBS, the International Association of Insurance Supervisors (IAIS), the International Accounting Standards Board (IASB), and the International Organization of Securities Commissions (IOSCO).[33] As obligations of membership, members of the FSB commit to pursue the maintenance of financial stability, maintain the openness and transparency of the financial sector, implement international financial standards, and to undergo periodic peer reviews. According to the FSB:[34]

> FSB members' adherence to international standards is essential to reinforce the credibility of the FSB's efforts to strengthen adherence by all countries and jurisdictions. Their commitment to implementing international financial standards and disclosing their level of adherence reflects their intent to lead by example. The FSB will foster a race to the top, wherein encouragement from peers motivates all countries and jurisdictions to raise their level of adherence to international financial standards.

In similar vein to the BCBS, the work of the FSB is not legally binding on its members. Instead, the FSB operates by moral suasion and peer pressure, in order to create globally agreed policies and minimum standards that its members commit to implementing within their respective jurisdictions.[35]

The FSB inherited some of the FSF's original mandate, which include the task of assessing vulnerabilities affecting the global financial system and identifying and reviewing the regulatory supervisory and related actions that are needed to address them, and promoting coordination and information exchange among authorities responsible for financial stability. It has also been assigned a number of key additional tasks,[36] as set out in Box 5.3.

The work of the FSB has been extensive since its inception. For example, it has set guidance on the key attributes of resolution regimes,[37] on the requirements for additional loss absorbing capacity,[38] and on the enhanced supervision of systemically

---

[32] Ibid.   [33] See section 5.2.3 for more information on some of these organisations.

[34] FSB, *About the FSB* at www.fsb.org/about/.   [35] Ibid.   [36] Ibid.

[37] See FSB, *Key Attributes of Effective Resolution Regimes for Financial Institutions* (October 2014) at http://www.fsb.org/wp-content/uploads/r_141015.pdf. Discussed in Chapter 13.

[38] See FSB, *Principles on Loss-Absorbing and Recapitalisation Capacity of G-SIBs in Resolution Total Loss-Absorbing Capacity (TLAC) Term Sheet* (November 2015) at http://www.fsb.org/wp-content/uploads/TLAC-Principles-and-Term-Sheet-for-publication-final.pdf. Discussed in Chapter 9.

Box 5.3 Core tasks of the FSB

- Monitoring and advising on market developments and their implications for regulatory policy.

- Monitoring and advising with regard to best practice in meeting regulatory standards.

- Undertaking joint strategic reviews of the international standard-setting bodies and coordinating their respective policy development work to ensure this work is timely, coordinated, focused on priorities, and addresses gaps.

- Setting guidelines for establishing and supporting **supervisory colleges**.

- Supporting contingency planning for cross-border crisis management, particularly with regard to systemically important firms.

- Collaborating with the IMF to conduct early warning exercises.

- Promoting member jurisdictions' implementation of agreed commitments, standards, and policy recommendations, through monitoring of implementation, peer review, and disclosure.

---

important financial institutions (SIFIs).[39] The FSB also conducts peer reviews to determine regulatory compliance. It began a regular programme of reviews in 2010, focusing on the implementation and effectiveness of international financial standards developed by standard-setting bodies and of policies agreed within the FSB. Reviews can either be thematic, focusing on the implementation of international financial standards in a particular area across all FSB members, or country based, focusing on the implementation and effectiveness of regulatory, supervisory, or other financial sector policies in achieving the desired outcomes in a specific FSB member jurisdiction.[40] Cranston comments that the work of the FSB 'has been nothing short of impressive, leading in most cases to the worldwide implementation of its standards.'[41]

5.2.3 Other institutions

The BCBS and the FSB sit within a much broader international financial architecture, consisting of numerous international organisations that, among other things, allow a large number of countries to discuss, agree, and promote regulatory and supervisory practices.

---

[39] The FSB defines SIFIs as 'financial institutions whose distress or disorderly failure, because of their size, complexity and systemic interconnectedness, would cause significant disruption to the wider financial system and economic activity.' See FSB, *Intensity and Effectiveness of SIFI Supervision Recommendations for Enhanced Supervision* (November 2010) at www.fsb.org/wp-content/uploads/r_101101.pdf?page_moved=1. Discussed in section 5.3.6.

[40] See FSB, *Peer Reviews* at http://www.fsb.org/what-we-do/implementation-monitoring/peer_reviews/.

[41] Ross Cranston et al, *Principles of Banking Law* (Oxford: Oxford University Press 2017) 22.

5.2.3.1 **International Monetary Fund**

The IMF was established at a UN conference in Bretton Woods, New Hampshire, US, in July 1944. The 44 countries at that conference sought to build a framework for economic cooperation to avoid a repetition of the competitive currency devaluations that had contributed to the Great Depression of the 1930s. The primary objective of the IMF is to ensure the stability of the international monetary system – that is, the system of exchange rates and international payments that enables countries (and their citizens) to transact with each other.

The IMF pursues this objective in three ways. First, it oversees the global economy and the economies of its 189 member countries, an activity known as surveillance. This process, which takes place at national, regional, and global levels, requires the IMF to identify potential risks to stability and recommend appropriate policy adjustments needed to sustain economic growth and promote financial and economic stability. Second, the IMF lends money to countries experiencing balance of payment difficulties. This financial assistance enables countries to rebuild their international reserves, stabilise their currencies, continue paying for imports, and restore conditions for strong economic growth, while undertaking policies to correct underlying problems. Finally, the IMF conducts capacity development, or technical assistance and training, to help member countries design and implement economic policies that foster stability and growth by strengthening their institutional capacity and skills.

The IMF's mandate was updated in 2012 to include all macroeconomic and financial sector issues that bear on global stability.[42] The IMF develops and monitors international standards in areas relevant to this mandate. In collaboration with other standard-setting bodies, it has developed international standards for data dissemination and transparency practices in fiscal, monetary, and financial policies,[43] and has contributed to the development of international standards for banking, as well as for insurance and securities supervision.[44]

In addition, the IMF, in cooperation with the World Bank, conducts comprehensive and in-depth assessments of a country's financial sector through its Financial Sector Assessment Programme (FSAP). Established in 1999, FSAPs analyse the resilience of the financial sector, the quality of the regulatory and supervisory framework, and the

---

[42] See generally, http://www.imf.org/en/About.

[43] See *IMF Standards for Data Dissemination* at www.imf.org/en/about/factsheets/sheets/2016/07/27/15/45/standards-for-data-dissemination. The Special Data Dissemination Standard (SDDS) was established in 1996 to guide members that have, or might seek, access to international capital markets in providing their economic and financial data to the public. The General Data Dissemination System (GDDS) was established in 1997 for member countries with less developed statistical systems as a framework for evaluating their needs for data improvement and setting priorities. In 2012, the SDDS Plus was created as an upper tier of the IMF's Data Standards Initiatives to help address data gaps identified during the global financial crisis. In 2015 the enhanced GDDS (e-GDDS) replaced the GDDS. More than 97 per cent of IMF member countries participate in the e-GDDS, SDDS, or SDDS Plus.

[44] For example, the IMF collaborated with the BCBS in the production of the *Core Principles for Effective Banking Supervision*, and with the FSB in the production of recommendations relating to the *Intensity and Effectiveness of SIFI* Supervision, both discussed later.

capacity to manage and resolve financial crises. Based on its findings, FSAPs produce recommendations of a micro- and macro-prudential nature, tailored to country-specific circumstances.[45]

5.2.3.2 World Bank

The World Bank, established in 1944 at the same time as the IMF, provides low-interest loans, zero- to low-interest credits, and grants to developing countries to support investment in key areas such as education, health, public administration, infrastructure, financial and private sector development, agriculture, and environmental and natural resource management.[46]

As part of its mandate to promote financial sector development, the World Bank develops international standards in areas of direct operational relevance. In collaboration with other standard-setting bodies, it has developed international standards for insolvency and creditors rights,[47] financial infrastructure including credit reporting systems,[48] and public debt management.[49] The World Bank, in cooperation with the IMF, also assesses compliance with core financial sector standards through the FSAP programme, as already discussed.

5.2.3.3 Committee on the Global Financial System

The Committee on the Global Financial System (CGFS) is a forum for central banks from advanced and emerging economies to monitor and examine broad issues relating to financial markets and systems.[50] The Committee articulates policy recommendations aimed at improving market functioning and promoting stability. More specifically, the Committee's primary objectives are as follows:[51]

- To seek to identify and assess potential sources of stress in the global financial environment through a regular and systematic monitoring of developments in financial markets and systems, including through an evaluation of macroeconomic developments.

- To further the understanding of the functioning and underpinnings of financial markets and systems through a close monitoring of their evolution and in-depth analyses, with particular reference to the implications for central bank operations and broader responsibilities for monetary and financial stability.

---

[45] See http://www.imf.org/external/np/fsap/fssa.aspx.

[46] See http://www.worldbank.org/en/about/what-we-do

[47] See, for example, The World Bank, *Principles for Effective Insolvency and Creditor/Debtor Regimes* (2015) at http://pubdocs.worldbank.org/en/919511468425523509/ICR-Principles-Insolvency-Creditor-Debtor-Regimes-2016.pdf.

[48] See, for example, The World Bank, *General Principles for Credit Reporting* (2011) at www.worldbank.org/en/topic/financialsector/brief/credit-reporting.

[49] The World Bank and the IMF, *Revised Guidelines for Public Debt Management* (April 2014) at http://documents.worldbank.org/curated/en/539361468170971115/Revised-guidelines-for-public-debt-management.

[50] For a list of member institutions see https://www.bis.org/about/factcgfs.htm?m=3%7C15%7C82.

[51] https://www.bis.org/cgfs/mandate.htm?m=3%7C15%7C81.

- To promote the development of well-functioning and stable financial markets and systems through an examination of alternative policy responses and the elaboration of corresponding policy recommendations.

The Committee cooperates closely with other institutions with responsibilities for pursuing related objectives including the BCBS and the Committee on Payment and Market Infrastructures, discussed in section 5.2.3.4.

5.2.3.4 Committee on Payments and Market Infrastructures

The Committee on Payments and Market Infrastructures (CPMI) (formerly known as the Committee on Payment and Settlement Systems) is an international body that promotes, monitors, and makes recommendations about the safety and efficiency of payment, clearing, settlement, and related arrangements, thereby supporting financial stability and the wider economy.[52] It also serves as a forum for central bank cooperation in related oversight, policy, and operational matters, including the provision of central bank services.[53]

The CPMI carries out its mandate through the following activities:[54]

- Monitoring and analysing developments to help identify risks for the safety and efficiency of arrangements within its mandate as well as resulting risks for the global financial system.

- Sharing experiences related to arrangements within its mandate, to the performance of oversight functions, and to the provision of central bank services in order to promote common understanding, and developing policy advice or common policies for central banks.

- Establishing and promoting global standards and recommendations for the regulation, oversight, and practices of arrangements within its mandate, including guidance for their interpretation and implementation, where appropriate.

- Monitoring the implementation of CPMI standards and recommendations with the purpose of ensuring timely, consistent, and effective implementation.

- Supporting cooperative oversight and cross-border information-sharing, including crisis communication and contingency planning for cross-border crisis management.

- Maintaining relationships with central banks which are not members of the CPMI to share experiences and views and to promote the implementation of CPMI standards and recommendations beyond CPMI member jurisdictions, either directly or by supporting regional bodies as appropriate.

- Coordinating and cooperating with other financial sector standard setters, central bank bodies, and IFIs.

---

[52] For a list of member institutions see https://www.bis.org/cpmi/membership.htm.
[53] https://www.bis.org/cpmi/about.htm?m=3%7C16%7C29.
[54] https://www.bis.org/cpmi/charter.htm.

5.2.3.5 Joint Forum

The Joint Forum was established in 1996 under the auspices of the BCBS, the IOSCO, and the IAIS (known collectively as the 'Parent Committees') to deal with issues common to the banking, securities, and insurance sectors, including the regulation of financial conglomerates.

The objective of the Joint Forum is to support banking, insurance, and securities supervisors in meeting their regulatory and supervisory objectives and, more broadly, to contribute to the international regulatory agenda, particularly where there are risks common to all three sectors, or gaps between them. In order to achieve this objective, the Joint Forum carries out the following activities:[55]

- Addresses and promotes understanding of issues common to the banking, securities, and insurance sectors, including the supervision of financial conglomerates.

- Analyses cross-sectoral market and regulatory developments.

- Examines cross-sectoral gaps and conflicts in regulation and supervision.

- Develops guidance and principles and/or identifies best practices on cross-sectoral technical, regulatory, and/or policy issues to encourage cross-sectoral consistency and alignment where appropriate, and reduce opportunities for regulatory arbitrage.

- Facilitates cooperation, coordination, and information sharing among banking, insurance, and securities supervisors (or representatives of the Parent Committees) and further supports the Parent Committees by identifying synergies or duplication in their work efforts.

5.2.3.6 Financial Stability Institute

The Financial Stability Institute (FSI) was founded in 1998 by the BCBS and the BIS to provide assistance to supervisors in strengthening financial systems. As such, the FSI provides supervisors with the latest information on market products, practices, and techniques to help them adapt to rapid innovations in the financial sector. It also helps supervisors develop solutions to their multiple challenges by sharing experiences in seminars, discussion forums, and conferences.[56]

5.2.3.7 Financial Action Task Force

Established in 1989, the Financial Action Task Force (FATF) is an intergovernmental body whose objectives are to set standards and promote effective implementation of legal, regulatory, and operational measures for combating money laundering, terrorist financing, and other related threats to the integrity of the international financial system. This body is discussed in detail in Chapter 14.

---

[55] https://www.bis.org/bcbs/jfmandate.htm.   [56] https://www.bis.org/fsi/index.htm?m=3%7C17.

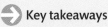 **Key takeaways**

- The international financial architecture consists of a series of international organisations that facilitate coordination and cooperation between national supervisors. These organisations bring together a large number of countries to discuss, agree, and promote not only supervisory standards, but also regulatory rules.

- The BCBS and the FSB have taken the lead in creating global standards and recommendations that seek to enhance cooperation, harmonise regulation, and promote financial stability.

- A number of other international bodies play a key role in the overall international financial architecture including the IMF, the World Bank, the CGFS, the Committee in Payments and Market Infrastructure, the Joint Forum, the FSI, and the FATF.

Key bibliography

Articles

Ghosh, S, 'Evolving International Supervisory Architecture: Design, Rationale and Policy Reform' (2005) 6 *Journal of Banking Regulation* 246

Lee, E, 'The Soft Law Nature of Basel III and International Financial Regulations' (2014) 29(10) *Journal of International Banking Law and Regulation* 603

Books

Goodhart, G, *The Basel Committee on Banking Supervision: A History of the Early Years* (Cambridge: Cambridge University Press 2011)

Walker, G, *International Banking Regulation: Law, Policy and Practice* (London: Kluwer Law International 2001)

5.3 Supervision of international banks

While the BCBS is most well renowned for its work on harmonising regulatory standards (see Chapters 8 and 9), it has also provided extensive guidelines on the effective supervision of international banks. From its inception, one of the most important aims of the Committee's work was to close gaps in international supervisory coverage so that (1) no banking establishment would escape supervision and (2) supervision would be adequate and consistent across member jurisdictions.[57] A first step in this direction was the Basel Concordat, which was published in 1975 and later revised in 1983. Later supplements to the Concordat were issued, as well as the Basel *Core Principles for Effective Banking Supervision* in 1997. Most recently, following the 2007–9 financial crisis, the BCBC has developed guidelines in the context of supervisory colleges and the FSB has

---

[57] BCBS, *History of the Basel Committee* (December 2016) at https://www.bis.org/bcbs/history.htm.

issued recommendations on the intensity and effectiveness of systemically important financial institution (SIFI) supervision. Each of these will be discussed further.

5.3.1 **Basel Concordat 1975**

The expansion of cross-border banking in the decades following World War II meant that national regulators had to address issues concerning the allocation of supervisory responsibility for international banks, that is, whether the home or host regulator should be responsible for supervising bank branches and subsidiaries across borders. The first substantive piece of work completed by the BCBS to address this issue is the Basel Concordat, which established guidelines for the cooperation of national supervisory authorities in relation to the supervision of banks' foreign establishments.[58] The Concordat stipulates that each country has a duty to ensure that foreign banks in its territory are supervised, and also that this supervision is adequate, judged by the standards of both home and host authorities.

The Concordat distinguishes three different types of foreign banking establishment, as set out in Box 5.4.[59]

The Concordat goes on to recognise that banking supervision in this context is considered from three key angles: liquidity (meaning the ability of the bank to meet its financial obligations as they come due), solvency (meaning the degree to which your assets exceed your liabilities), and foreign exchange operations and positions. While recognising that it would be difficult to draw-up any clear-cut rules on the division of responsibilities for supervision, the BCBS agreed on a number of general guidelines, as set out in Box 5.5.[60]

Finally, the Concordat suggests a number of ways to facilitate cooperation between national authorities.[61] First, home and host authorities should directly transfer information between themselves. For example, parent authorities may wish to obtain copies of reports submitted to host authorities and, when circumstances so warrant it, host authorities should be permitted to directly transfer copies of such reports,

---

Box 5.4 Types of foreign banking establishment

1. Branches: integral parts of a foreign parent bank.

2. Subsidiaries: legally independent institutions incorporated in the country of operation and controlled by one foreign parent bank.

3. Joint ventures: legally independent banks incorporated in the country of operation and controlled by two or more parent institutions, most of which are foreign and not all of which are necessarily banks.

---

[58] Committee on Banking Regulations and Supervisory Practices, *Report to the Governors on the Supervision of Banks' Foreign Establishments* (September 1975) at https://www.bis.org/publ/bcbs00a.pdf.

[59] Ibid, 1.   [60] Ibid, 3–4.   [61] Ibid, 4–5.

> **Box 5.5 guidelines on the division of responsibility**
>
> **Liquidity**: *generally*, responsibility for supervising liquidity rests with the host authority, since banks rely heavily on local practices and compliance with local regulations in managing their liquidity. In the case of a foreign *branch*, liquidity cannot be judged in isolation from that of the whole bank to which it belongs, meaning that the liquidity of foreign branches is also a matter of concern for the home authority. In relation to a foreign *subsidiary* or *joint venture*, while the host authority will take the lead in supervising liquidity, there may be some instances when the home authority including, for example, where the parent company provides standby facilities.
>
> **Solvency**: for foreign *subsidiaries* and *joint ventures* primary responsibility rests with the host authority, but home authorities must take account of the exposure of their domestic banks' foreign subsidiaries and joint ventures because the parent banks will have a moral commitment to them. For foreign *branches* solvency is indistinguishable from that of the parent bank as a whole, meaning that it is essentially a matter for the home authority.
>
> **Foreign exchange positions**: banks' foreign exchange positions are supervised partly for prudential reasons, partly for balance of payment reasons, and partly for the purpose of maintaining orderly market conditions. So far as concerns prudential supervision, the considerations set out in the previous paragraph govern the division of responsibility, while the other matters are by definition the concern of the host authorities.

notwithstanding banking secrecy laws.[62] Second, home authorities should be able to directly inspect their domestic banks' foreign establishments. The Concordat recognises that this function is particularly important for the purposes of solvency control and, as such, steps should be taken to facilitate such inspections, if necessary by the amendment of legislation. Third, home authorities should be able to indirectly inspect their domestic banks' foreign banking establishments through the agency of host authorities. Thus, where host authorities do not allow for direct inspections, they should give favourable consideration to carrying out, at the request of the home authority, specific inspections of foreign banks operating in their territory and subsequently report their findings.

5.3.2 **Revised Concordat 1983**

While the Basel Concordat seemed to provide relatively simple guidelines on the division of responsibility of a bank's foreign establishments, in practice the split of responsibility between home and host authorities created some confusion as regulators interpreted the Concordat differently. Shortcomings were highlighted by the collapse in 1982 of the Italian bank Banco Ambrosiano (BA).[63] BA failed after its Chairman, Roberto

---

[62] The issue of bank secrecy laws as a barrier to international supervisory cooperation was discussed in a later document: Committee on Banking Regulations and Supervisory Practices, *Banking Secrecy and International Cooperation in Banking Supervision* (August 1981) at https://www.bis.org/publ/bcbs00f.pdf.

[63] See Charles Goodhart, *The Basel Committee on Banking Supervision: A History of the Early Years* (Cambridge: Cambridge University Press 2011) 104–7.

Calvi, was found dead in London under suspicious circumstances (it was later concluded that he had been murdered, although no convictions were forthcoming). While the Bank of Italy launched a rescue operation allowing a new bank to take over BA's business in Italy, there remained a difficulty regarding the rescue of Banco Ambrosiano Holdings (BAH), which was based in Luxembourg. BA owned 69 per cent of BAH, which was also facing collapse because the difficulties at BA had led depositors in BAH to withdraw their money. The Bank of Italy and the Luxembourg Banking Commission disputed their responsibility for the supervision of BAH and both refused to provide funds to support it. As a result, BAH also failed.

This episode suggested that the Basel Concordat was not working. Despite the guidelines there was uncertainty over whether the home or host authority should supervise BAE and there was the additional concern of whether the home or host central bank should take on the responsibility of lender of last resort. This confusion led to the revised 1983 Concordat, which replaces the earlier version.[64] The aim of the new guidelines is to provide a more sophisticated approach to monitoring a banks' foreign establishments. As such, it reformulates some of the provisions of the 1975 Concordat, most particularly to give effect to the principle that banking supervisory authorities cannot be fully satisfied about the soundness of individual banks unless they can examine the totality of each bank's business worldwide through the technique of consolidation.

The 1983 revision starts by setting out general principles governing the supervision of banks' foreign establishments.[65] For example, it recognises that effective cooperation between host and parent authorities is a central prerequisite for the supervision of banks' international operations. As such, the Concordat offers two basic principles that are fundamental to such cooperation, namely, that that no foreign banking establishment should escape supervision and that the supervision should be adequate. In giving effect to these principles, the Concordat recognises that home and host authorities should inform each other immediately of any problems that arise in a parent bank, or parent banks' foreign establishment.[66]

Further, the Concordat provides that while there should be a presumption that host authorities are in a position to fulfil their supervisory obligations adequately with respect to all foreign bank establishments, this may not always be the case. Accordingly, in cases where the supervision of the host authority is deemed to be inadequate, the home authority should either extend its supervision, as far as is practicable, or it should discourage the parent bank from continuing to operate the establishment in question.[67] Conversely, the Concordat states that where the host authority considers that supervision of the parent institutions of foreign bank establishments operating in its territory is inadequate or non-existent, it should, if possible, forbid the operation in its territory of such foreign establishments. Alternatively, the host authority could impose specific

---

[64] BCBS, *Principles for the Supervision of Banks' Foreign Establishments* (May 1983) at https://www.bis.org/publ/bcbsc312.pdf.   [65] Ibid, 2–4.

[66] Ibid, 2–3.   [67] Ibid, 3.

conditions governing the conduct of the business of such establishments.[68] Finally, the Concordat emphasises the principle of consolidated supervision, which means that:[69]

> parent banks and parent supervisory authorities monitor the risk exposure - including a perspective of concentrations of risk and of the quality of assets - of the banks or banking groups for which they are responsible, as well as the adequacy of their capital, on the basis of the totality of their business wherever conducted ... the implementation of the principle of consolidated supervision presupposes that parent banks and parent authorities have access to all the relevant information about the operations of their banks' foreign establishments.

The Concordat then considers the supervision of banks' foreign establishments from the perspective of solvency, liquidity, and foreign exchange operations and positions. In relation to **solvency**, the Concordat provides that for foreign *branches*, solvency is indistinguishable from that of the parent bank, so while there is a general responsibility on the host authority to monitor the financial soundness of foreign branches, the supervision of solvency is primarily a matter for the home authority. For foreign *subsidiaries*, the supervision of solvency is the joint responsibility of both host and home authorities. While host authorities retain primary responsibility, home authorities, in the context of the consolidated supervision of parent banks, need to assess whether the parent bank's solvency is being affected by the operations of their foreign subsidiaries. For foreign *joint ventures*, supervision will rest primarily with the host authority. However, banks that are shareholders in consortium banks may have commitments to their joint ventures, for example, through comfort letters, and these commitments should be considered by the home authorities of the shareholder banks when supervising their solvency. Where a bank is a dominant shareholder in a joint venture, the supervision of their solvency should be the joint responsibility of both the home and host authorities.[70]

In relation to **liquidity**, the Concordat stipulates that in *general*, the host authority has responsibility for monitoring the liquidity of the foreign bank's establishments in its country and the home authority has responsibility for monitoring the liquidity of the banking group as a whole. For foreign branches, primary responsibility rests with the host authority, which will have knowledge of local practices and regulations and the functioning of their domestic money markets. Simultaneously, the liquidity of all foreign branches is a matter of concern for home authorities and this is because a branch's liquidity is often controlled directly by the parent bank and so should not be viewed in isolation from the entire bank. Importantly, home and host authorities should communicate if there are any doubts regarding the allocation of responsibility for supervising the liquidity of foreign branches. For foreign subsidiaries, primary responsibility rests with the host authority, but home authorities should monitor any standby facilities or other commitments such as comfort letters made by the parent banks to these foreign establishments. Further, where the host authority has difficulty supervising the liquidity of a foreign subsidiary, it will be expected to communicate this to the home authority

---

[68]   Ibid.   [69]   Ibid, 4.   [70]   Ibid, 5–6.

so that arrangements can be made to ensure adequate supervision. Similarly, for joint ventures, primary responsibility rests with the host authority, but home authorities of shareholders in joint ventures should monitor any standby facilities or other commitments such as comfort letters by shareholder banks to those foreign establishments. Finally, the Concordat provides that host authorities have a duty to ensure that the home authority is immediately informed of any serious liquidity inadequacy in a parent bank's foreign establishment.[71]

In relation to **foreign exchange operations and positions** the Concordat provides that the host and home authorities are jointly responsible for the supervision of all foreign establishments. In particular, parent banks should have systems for monitoring the group's overall foreign exchange exposure and home authorities must in turn monitor those systems. Host authorities should monitor the foreign exchange exposures of foreign establishments in their territories and make themselves aware of the nature and extent of the supervision of these establishments being undertaken by the home authorities.

The division of responsibility according to the 1983 Concordat is summarised in Box 5.6.

Box 5.6 At a glance: division of responsibility 1983 Concordat

Solvency

- For foreign branches supervision is primarily the responsibility of the home authority.
- For foreign subsidiaries supervision is the joint responsibility of both the home and the host authorities.
- For foreign joint ventures supervision is the joint responsibility of both the home and the host authorities.

Liquidity

- For foreign branches supervision is the joint responsibility of both the home and host authorities. These authorities should communicate if there are any doubts regarding the allocation of responsibility.
- For foreign subsidiaries supervision is the joint responsibility of both the home and host authorities. The host authority should communicate with the home authority if they are having any difficulties supervising liquidity.
- For joint ventures supervision is the joint responsibility of both the home and the host authorities.

Foreign exchange operations and positions

- For all foreign establishments supervision is the joint responsibility of both the home and host authorities.

---

[71] Ibid, 6–7.

It is clear from this discussion that the revised Concordat provides more detailed rules on the monitoring of solvency, liquidity, and foreign exchange operations and positions for foreign branches, subsidiaries, and joint ventures. Further, it places greater emphasis on the importance of consolidated supervision, highlighting – in particular – the key role that home authorities play in supervising a bank's entire global operations. Interestingly, despite the revised Concordat being prompted by the failure of BA, discussed in earlier in this section, it did not tackle the central issue of whether the home or host country should provide lender of last resort facilities.[72] This is because this facility is political in nature, involving the use of public money, typically by the central bank, and is therefore regarded as being outside the realm of international bank regulation.

5.3.3 Further BCBS publications on international banking supervision

Many of the themes in the 1975 Concordat and its revision were subsequently developed by the BCBS. The Committee has published various papers on information flow between home and host supervisors, and this remains an important theme of much of their work. For example, in April 1990, a supplement to the 1983 Concordat was published that offered guidance on possible ways to facilitate the flow of prudential information between bank supervisors.[73] More recently, in 2006, the BCBS published guidance on home–host information sharing to ensure the effective application of Basel II.[74]

Following the collapse of Bank of Credit and Commercial International (BCCI) in 1991,[75] the BCBS realised that while the principles of the Concordat and its supplement were still sound, greater effort was needed to ensure that the principles could be applied in practice. BCCI had created a complex structure and obtained authorisation in two countries (Luxembourg and the Cayman Islands), neither of which had the capacity to supervise the bank, while the centre of its operations was in a third country (the UK), which did not actively engage in its supervision. In response, the BCBS reformulated some of the principles of the Concordat and published them as minimum standards on the supervision of international banking groups.[76] These minimum standards, which are expected to be observed by BCBS members, are set out in Box 5.7.

---

[72] In fact, the Concordat explicitly states that it 'deals exclusively with the responsibilities of banking supervisory authorities for monitoring the prudential conduct and soundness of the business of banks' foreign establishments. It does not address itself to lender-of-last-resort aspects of the role of central banks.' Ibid, 1.

[73] BCBS, *Information Flows between Banking Supervisory Authorities* (April 1990) at https://www.bis.org/publ/bcbsc313.pdf.

[74] BCBS, *Home-Host Information Sharing for Effective Basel II Implementation* (June 2006) at https://www.bis.org/publ/bcbs125.pdf.   [75] Discussed in Chapter 7.

[76] BCBS, *Minimum Standards for the Supervision of International Banking Groups and their Cross-Border Establishments* (July 1992) at https://www.bis.org/publ/bcbsc314.pdf.

> **Box 5.7 Minimum standards for the supervision of international banking groups and their cross-border establishments**
>
> - All international banking groups and international banks should be supervised by a home country authority that capably performs consolidated supervision.
>
> - The creation of a cross-border banking establishment should receive the prior consent of both the host country supervisory authority and that of the bank and, if different, banking group's home country supervisory authority.
>
> - Supervisory authorities should possess the right to gather information from the cross-border banking establishments of the banks or banking groups for which they are the home country supervisor.
>
> - If a host country authority determines that any one of the foregoing minimum standards is not met to its satisfaction, that authority could impose restrictive measures necessary to satisfy its prudential concerns consistent with these minimum standards, including the prohibition of the creation of banking establishments.

In 1994, a working group comprised of members of the BCBS and the Offshore Group of Banking Supervisors[77] was set up to consider a number of issues relating to the implementation of the 1992 *Minimum Standards*.[78] In October 1996, the resulting report was published, which presents a number of proposals for overcoming the impediments experienced by banking supervisors in conducting effective supervision of the cross-border operations of international banks.[79] The recommendations relate to two core issues, namely, improving the access of both home and host supervisors to information necessary for effective consolidated supervision and effective host supervision respectively, and ensuring that all cross-border banking operations are subject to effective home and host supervision. This report played a vital role in the formulation of the BCBS's *Core Principles*, discussed in section 5.3.4.

5.3.4 Basel *Core Principles for Effective Banking Supervision* and *Core Principles Methodology*

In 1997 the Basel Committee published the *Core Principles for Effective Banking Supervision* (BCPs). They are viewed as the de facto minimum standards for sound prudential regulation and supervision of banks and banking systems across the globe.

---

[77] The Offshore Group of Banking Supervisors changed its name to the Group of International Finance Centre Supervisors (GIFCS) on 1 April 2011. It is comprised of banking supervisors representing smaller overseas centres such as Guernsey, Mauritius, Bahamas, and the Cayman Islands.

[78] Although, because of the group's composition, the discussions focused principally on the supervision of offshore banking, its conclusions are applicable to all home and host supervisory relationships and have been framed as such in the resulting report.

[79] BCBS and the Offshore Group of Banking Supervisors, *The Supervision of Cross-Border Banking* (October 1996) at https://www.bis.org/publ/bcbs27.pdf.

While the principles were influenced by the 1996 report on the supervision of cross-border banking, they were directly prompted by discussions at the G7[80] Summit in Lyon a year earlier, where concern had been expressed about the strength of financial systems following a series of problems, particularly in South-East Asia. This led the G7 finance ministers to call for the effective supervision of all major financial markets, including those in emerging economies.

The BCPs were produced through a collaboration between Basel Committee members, the IMF, World Bank, and a number of other non-G10 supervisory authorities, namely Chile, China, the Czech Republic, Hong Kong, Mexico, Russia, and Thailand. Nine other countries (Argentina, Brazil, Hungary, India, Indonesia, Korea, Malaysia, Poland, and Singapore) were also closely associated with the work.

5.3.4.1 The principles

The BCPs comprised of 25 basic principles that needed to be in place for a supervisory system to be effective.[81] In 1999, in order to encourage consistency, a methodology was introduced that was designed as a tool to enable an objective assessment of a country's implementation of the BCPs and, specifically, to allow an assessment of the adequacy of the regulatory framework (the rules and structures) and the effectiveness of bank regulation.[82] The principles and methodology were revised in 2006,[83] and again in 2012, where they were combined into a single comprehensive document.[84]

The revised set of 29 principles have been reorganised to foster their implementation through a more logical structure, highlighting the difference between what supervisors do and what they expect banks to do. Principles 1–13 address supervisory powers, responsibilities, and functions, focusing on effective risk-based supervision and the need for early intervention and timely supervisory actions. Principles 14–29 cover supervisory expectations of banks, emphasising the importance of good corporate governance and risk management, as well as compliance with supervisory standards.

Some of the *Core Principles* are set out in Box 5.8.[85]

The BCPs should be applied by national authorities in the supervision of all banking organisations within their jurisdictions. As they are minimum standards, it is recognised that individual countries, particularly those with advanced markets and banks, may expand upon the principles in order to achieve best supervisory practice. The BCBS is of the opinion that a high degree of compliance with the BCPs should foster overall financial system stability.

---

[80] G7 members include Canada, France, Germany, Italy, Japan, the UK, and the US.

[81] BCBS, *Core Principles for Effective Banking Supervision* (Sep 1997) available at https://www.bis.org/publ/bcbs30a.pdf.

[82] BCBS, *Core Principles Methodology* (Oct 1999) available at https://www.bis.org/publ/bcbs61.pdf.

[83] BCBS, *Core Principles for Effective Banking Supervision.* on Banking Supervision, *Core Principles Methodology.*   [84] BCBS, *Core Principles for Effective Banking Supervision.*f

[85] Ibid, para 41.

> **Box 5.8 Examples of the BCPs**
>
> **Principle 1 – Responsibilities, objectives, and powers**: an effective system of banking supervision has clear responsibilities and objectives for each authority involved in the supervision of banks and banking groups. A suitable legal framework for banking supervision is in place to provide each responsible authority with the necessary legal powers to authorise banks, conduct ongoing supervision, address compliance with laws, and undertake timely corrective actions to address safety and soundness concerns.
>
> **Principle 2 – Independence, accountability, resourcing, and legal protection for supervisors**: the supervisor possesses operational independence, transparent processes, sound governance, budgetary processes that do not undermine autonomy and adequate resources, and is accountable for the discharge of its duties and use of its resources. The legal framework for banking supervision includes legal protection for the supervisor.
>
> **Principle 3 – Cooperation and collaboration**: laws, regulations, or other arrangements provide a framework for cooperation and collaboration with relevant domestic authorities and foreign supervisors. These arrangements reflect the need to protect confidential information.
>
> **Principle 12 – Consolidated supervision**: an essential element of banking supervision is that the supervisor supervises the banking group on a consolidated basis, adequately monitoring and, as appropriate, applying prudential standards to all aspects of the business conducted by the banking group worldwide.
>
> **Principle 13 – Home–host relationships**: home and host supervisors of cross-border banking groups share information and cooperate for effective supervision of the group and group entities, and effective handling of crisis situations. Supervisors require the local operations of foreign banks to be conducted to the same standards as those required of domestic banks.

5.3.4.2 Assessment methodology

The BCPs and methodology have been used by countries as a benchmark for assessing the quality of their supervisory systems and for identifying future work to be done to achieve a baseline level of sound supervisory practices.

To assess compliance with a principle, the BCBS methodology proposes a set of essential and additional assessment criteria for each principle. An example is given in Box 5.9.

The default position is that the essential criteria are the only elements on which compliance with the BCPs is determined and graded. The additional criteria are suggested best practices that countries having advanced banks should aim for. However, countries can opt to be assessed and/or graded against the additional criteria in order to identify areas in which it could enhance its regulation and supervision further and benefit from the assessors' commentary on how it could be achieved.[86]

The methodology establishes a four-grade scale, as set out in Box 5.10.[87]

In addition to the four-grade scale, a principle may be considered 'not applicable' when, in the view of the assessor, the principle does not apply given the structural, legal,

---

[86] Ibid, para 59.   [87] Ibid, para 61.

Box 5.9 Principle 4: permissible activities

The permissible activities of institutions that are licensed and subject to supervision as banks are clearly defined and the use of the word 'bank' in names is controlled.

- **Essential criteria 1**. The term 'bank' is clearly defined in laws or regulations.

- **Essential criterial 2**. The permissible activities of institutions that are licensed and subject to supervision as banks are clearly defined either by supervisors or in laws or regulations.

- **Essential criteria 3**. The use of the word 'bank' and any derivations such as 'banking' in a name, including domain names, is limited to licensed and supervised institutions in all circumstances where the general public might otherwise be misled.

- **Essential criteria 4**. The taking of deposits from the public is reserved for institutions that are licensed and subject to supervision as banks.

- **Essential criteria 5**. The supervisor or licensing authority publishes or otherwise makes available a current list of licensed banks, including branches of foreign banks, operating within its jurisdiction in a way that is easily accessible to the public.

Box 5.10 Four-grade scale of compliance

- **Compliant**. A country will be considered compliant with a principle when all essential criteria applicable for this country are met without any significant deficiencies.

- **Largely compliant**. A country will be considered largely compliant with a principle whenever only minor shortcomings are observed that do not raise any concerns about the authority's ability and clear intent to achieve full compliance with the principle within a prescribed period of time. The assessment 'largely compliant' can be used when the system does not meet all essential criteria, but the overall effectiveness is sufficiently good, and no material risks are left unaddressed.

- **Materially non-compliant**. A country will be considered materially non-compliant with a principle whenever there are severe shortcomings, despite the existence of formal rules, regulations, and procedures, and there is evidence that supervision has clearly not been effective, that practical implementation is weak, or that the shortcomings are sufficient to raise doubts about the authority's ability to achieve compliance.

- **Non-compliant**. A country will be considered non-compliant with a principle whenever there has been no substantive implementation of the principle, several essential criteria are not complied with, or supervision is manifestly ineffective.

Box 5.11 A case study: UK compliance with BCPs

The most recent IMF assessment of the UK's compliance with the BCPs, conducted in 2016 in the context of the FSAP, found that the supervisory regime was compliant with 20 of the principles and largely compliant with the remaining nine.[90] A series of recommendations were made to improve compliance with the BCP framework. For example, in relation to principle 8 (supervisory approach), it was recommended that the UK evaluate the adequacy of supervision, especially of less systemically important firms, and whether current arrangements provide sufficient testing to ensure that all firms are operating safely and soundly and in compliance with laws, regulations, and supervisory expectations, and in relation to Principle 14 (corporate governance), it was recommended that the UK should promote efforts to make managers in financial institutions more accountable for actions or inactions and ensure that corporate governance is appropriately supervised in firms beyond the largest and most systemically important, including through the implementation of recently released supervisory guidance.

---

and institutional features of a country.[88] For example, in the case of a country whose banking activities are embryonic or immaterial in certain respects, an assessment of 'not applicable' could be given rather than 'non-compliant'. Box 5.11 offers a case study of UK compliance with BCPs).

The methodology can be used in a number of different contexts including: self-assessment performed by banking supervisors themselves; reviews conducted by private third parties such as consulting firms; peer reviews conducted, for example, within regional groupings of banking supervisors; and reviews by the IMF and World Bank in the context of their FSAP (see section 5.2.3.1).[89]

5.3.5 Supervisory colleges

As the financial crisis deepened in late 2008, governments around the world recognised the need to increase the supervisory cooperation of the largest global banks. As such, at its summit in Washington in November 2008, the G20 noted the important role that could be played by colleges of supervisors in enhancing cooperation between supervisors. In their declaration the G20 leaders concluded that:[91]

> supervisors should collaborate to establish supervisory colleges for all major cross-border financial institutions, as part of the efforts to strengthen the surveillance of cross-border firms. Major global banks should meet regularly with their supervisory college for comprehensive discussions of the firm's activities and assessments of the risks it faces.

---

[88] Ibid, para 62.   [89] Ibid, para 56.

[90] IMF, *United Kingdom: Financial Sector Assessment Program – Basel Core Principles for Effective Banking Supervision-Detailed Assessment Report* (June 2016) at https://www.imf.org/en/Publications/CR/Issues/2016/12/31/United-Kingdom-Financial-Sector-Assessment-Program-Basel-Core-Principles-for-Effective-43977.

[91] G20, *Declaration, Summit on Financial Markets and the World Economy* (November 15 2008) at https://www.treasury.gov/resource-center/international/g7-g20/Documents/Washington%20Nov%20Leaders%20Declaration.pdf.

The BCBS define a ***supervisory college*** as 'multilateral working groups of relevant supervisors that are formed for the collective purpose of enhancing effective consolidated supervision of an international banking group on an ongoing basis.'[92] These colleges, which are established for each global systemically important institution, 'enhance information-sharing among supervisors, help the development of a common understanding of risk in financial groups, promote a shared agenda for addressing risks and vulnerabilities, and provide a platform for communicating key supervisory messages among college members.'[93] Although they started out as a tool for addressing cross-border supervisory coordination issues related to Basel implementation, supervisory colleges now serve the broader objectives of supervisory cooperation and coordination.

5.3.5.1 Principles for effective supervisory colleges

In October 2010, the BCBS published its *Good Practice Principles on Supervisory Colleges*,[94] which provided a set of principles that could be used as a basis for continuing to improve the operation of supervisory colleges. The principles are designed to help both home and host supervisors ensure that they work as effectively as possible by clearly outlining expectations in relation to college objectives, governance, communication, and information, as well as potential areas for collaborative work. This was replaced in June 2014 by the *Principles for Effective Supervisory Colleges*.[95] The revised *Principles* build on the 2010 *Principles* and retain their key features. They provide more clarity on the relationship between home and host supervisors and reflect more realistic expectations of how colleges typically function based on past experiences. In particular, the revised *Principles* underscore the importance of continuous collaboration and information-sharing outside the formal college meetings.

The seven principles will now be discussed in turn

Principle 1: college objectives

The first principle provides that supervisory colleges should enhance, on an ongoing and confidential basis, information exchange and cooperation among supervisors to support the effective supervision of international banking groups. Colleges should enhance the mutual trust and appreciation of needs and responsibilities on which supervisory relationships are built. Accordingly, the overarching objective of a supervisory college is to assist its members in developing a better understanding of the risk profile and vulnerabilities of an international banking group and to provide a framework for identifying and addressing key issues. This objective should be pursued on an ongoing basis, not just during the official meetings of the colleges.

---

[92] BCBS, *Good Practice Principles on Supervisory Colleges* (October 2010) footnote 1, at https://www.bis.org/publ/bcbs177.pdf.

[93] BCBBS, *Principles for Effective Supervisory Colleges* (June 2014) 1, at https://www.bis.org/publ/bcbs287.htm.

[94] BCBS, *Good Practice Principles on Supervisory Colleges* (October 2010) at https://www.bis.org/publ/bcbs177.pdf.

[95] BCBS, *Principles for Effective Supervisory Colleges* (June 2014) at https://www.bis.org/publ/bcbs287.htm.

Principle 2: college structures

Principle 2 provides that colleges should be structured in a way that enhances effective oversight of international banking groups, considering the scale, structure, and complexity of the banking group, its significance in host jurisdictions, and the corresponding needs of its supervisors.

While specific terminology to describe college structures may vary across jurisdictions, such structures might include: single college structures, that is, a single general college used where there are a small number of supervisors involved, each with a material role in the supervisory oversight of the banking group; core and universal colleges where there is a 'core' college of key supervisors with responsibility for the primary risk-taking entities within the banking group, and a further 'universal college' with a wider supervisory membership aimed at broader information sharing; and variable structures, which may be appropriate because of the peculiar structures and risks posed by the banking group. For example, the BCBS states that the banking group might have specific risks requiring more intensive engagement between particular supervisors. Box 5.12 offers some insights on the structure of supervisory colleges for the major cross-border banks established in the UK.[96]

Box 5.12 Supervisory college structures for UK banks

The UK regulator, the Prudential Regulation Authority, has established supervisory colleges for the four UK banking groups with material cross-border operations, namely HSBC, Standard Chartered Bank, Barclays, and RBS.

For these large banks there are multiple colleges as follows:

1. Core college: key supervisors. Meets twice a year and have quarterly teleconferences.

2. General college: comprises core college members plus other EU regulators. Meets annually and has additional teleconferences for discussion of issues such as stress test results.

3. Global college: consists of regulators from all jurisdictions in which a firm operates. Meets annually.

4. Regional core colleges: for regulators of the most important branches and subsidiaries of the firm in the region.

Principle 3: information sharing

The third principle provides that college members should do their best to promptly share appropriate information with respect to a banking group's principal risks, vulnerabilities, and risk management practices. Mutual trust and willingness to cooperate are key for effective two-way information sharing. To facilitate this process, supervisory colleges should strive towards confidentiality agreements among college members, such as those contained in memoranda of understanding (MoUs).

---

[96] See IMF, *United Kingdom: Financial Sector Assessment Program-Basel Core Principles for Effective Banking Supervision-Detailed Assessment Report* 7

Principle 4: communication channels

Principle 4 provides that communication channels within a college should ensure the efficiency, ease of use, integrity, and confidentiality of information exchange. The home supervisor should make sound communication channels available to the college and host supervisors should use them appropriately and regularly.

A range of communication channels are required for effective functioning of colleges including: physical meetings, video conferences, online communication tools, email, and letters. The BCBS highlight that some home supervisors have developed secure web-based communication channels, including secure websites, in order to keep all college members informed of college matters.

Principle 5: collaborative work

The fifth Principle provides that supervisory colleges should promote collaborative work among members, as appropriate, to improve the effectiveness of the oversight of international banking groups. Collaborative work should be by agreement among supervisors and should recognise national legal constraints.

Here, the BCBS recognise that there are likely to be specific work streams that could be undertaken collaboratively to improve the effectiveness of the consolidated supervision of international banking groups. To this end, college members should ensure they can, where appropriate, share and allocate work in the pursuit of college objectives.

Collaborative work may focus on one or more group entities (domestic and foreign), the banking group as a whole, or specific aspects of the group's or an entity's functions. Examples of areas in which colleges have already undertaken collaborative work include risk assessment and stress testing, and internal model review and approval.

Principles 6: interaction with the institution

Principle 6 provides that interaction between the college members and the banking group should complement the interaction that individual supervisors (both home and host) have with the specific entity they supervise.

In particular, the college must agree on the feedback that should be communicated to the banking group (e.g. purpose and findings of the college, sharing/delegation of tasks agreed, planned supervisory activities, supervisory risk assessment findings, etc.). In terms of the participation of the banking group at college meetings, this principle provides that the banking group may be invited to attend some college meetings to provide forward-looking information on its strategy, risk appetite, risk profile and vulnerabilities, and financial outlook.

Principle 7: crisis preparedness

The final principle provides that supervisory colleges are distinct from but complementary to crisis management and resolution structures. The work of a banking group's supervisory college should contribute to effective crisis management planning.

While the supervisory college is primarily responsible for supervisory information-sharing and cooperation among supervisors when the banking group is operating as a going concern, and it is for crisis management groups (CMGs)[97] to manage supervisory relationships when a banking group becomes non-viable, the point at which the home supervisor determines that responsibility should shift from the supervisory college to the CMG is not necessarily clear. This timing will likely depend on the relevant facts and circumstances of a banking group's condition. As a result, both colleges and CMGs have a key role to play in crisis preparedness, which broadly includes any steps taken to limit the risk of significant problems at a banking group and to facilitate rapid action by supervisors, other relevant authorities, and the bank in the event that such problems arise.

5.3.5.2 Implementation of the *Principles*

The BCBS monitors the implementation of the *Principles* and reviews the effectiveness of colleges. The Committee published their first progress report in July 2015, based on information from two sources: (1) a brief questionnaire on the existence of colleges and (2) a case study approach to promote more in-depth discussion of current and leading practices and issues in colleges.[98] The report concluded that:[99]

> Broadly speaking, the monitoring indicated considerable progress in the functioning of supervisory colleges in recent years, and supervisors intend to continue enhancing the effectiveness of colleges and addressing remaining challenges going forward.

Some of the key findings of the case study presentations are as follows:[100]

- Colleges play a key role in assisting supervisors by giving both home and host supervisors a comprehensive view of risks and vulnerabilities to a firm and identifying emerging risks on a timely basis. Sharing multiple perspectives on risk helps supervisors to paint a picture of a firm's global risk profile.

- Colleges have evolved to be key forums for rigorous discussion of broader issues that enhance supervision of global firms and contribute to the planning of supervisory assessments.

- A wide range of college structures have been developed by home supervisors to reflect the differing size, complexity, and global reach of internationally active banks, and home supervisors have tried to be more sensitive to host supervisor concerns in developing criteria for college membership.

---

[97] One of the key developments in recent years has been the establishment of crisis management groups (CMGs) that address issues related to recovery and resolution planning at G-SIBs and other systemically important banks. In October 2011 the FSB published its *Key Attributes of Effective Resolution Regimes for Financial Institutions*, which sets out 12 essential features of resolution regimes that are relevant for all jurisdictions (see Chapter 13). Key Attribute 8 provides guidance for CMGs.

[98] BCBS, *Progress Report on the Implementation of Principles for Effective Supervisory Colleges* (July 2015) at https://www.bis.org/bcbs/publ/d329.pdf.

[99] Ibid, 2.   [100] Ibid, 3–4.

- Legal and institutional arrangements are important contributors to successful colleges and have been enhanced in recent years, but trust and mutual understanding among members are equally important, if not more so.
- The collaborative work among college members contributes to improving the effectiveness of the oversight of cross-border banking groups.

The case studies also identified three particular home–host challenges. First, in relation to information sharing (principle 3), while it was clear that information sharing among college members had been enhanced, there were some noted challenges, primarily attributed to issues such as confidentiality concerns as well as the size and composition of college structures.[101]

Second, in relation to collaborative work, including coordinated risk assessments (principle 5) a number of ongoing challenges were cited that related to the following: availability of expertise and resources; operational challenges in organising participation and involvement in joint activities (e.g. language barrier, confidentiality constraints); meeting deadlines that serve the supervisory cycle of another authority; and understanding the supervisory practices across regions and translating and sharing supervisory assessments and outcomes, including differences in definitions used by supervisory authorities.[102]

Finally, in relation to crisis preparedness (principle 7), while some progress had been made since the *Principles* were first introduced, crisis preparedness posed a greater challenge in terms of implementation than any of the other principles. There are two core reasons for this. First, in practice, many supervisors noted that following a coordinated approach in addressing an emergency situation faced by the parent entity of the group or any of its entities, or even keeping college members informed on actions taken individually to deal with an emergency situation, is challenging, given the need to act promptly and to safeguard the confidentiality of information. Second, the division of tasks and responsibilities between supervisory colleges and other structures, including CMGs differs within and among jurisdictions with various legal requirements, and the role of colleges in crisis management and resolution has in some cases become less clear as CMGs have gained heightened prominence.[103]

Since 2015, the BCBS has examined these topics in greater detail and, in December 2017, the Committee published its second progress report on the implementation of the *Principles*.[104] The report was based on solicited information and suggestions from member jurisdictions via detailed surveys.

In general, the survey findings were positive regarding the implementation of principles 3, 5, and 7. Members noted clear progress towards enhanced information sharing as well as in coordinated risk assessment activities in supervisory colleges.

---

[101] Ibid, 8–10.   [102] Ibid, 12–14.   [103] Ibis, 17–18.
[104] BCBS, *Progress Report on the Implementation of Principles for Effective Supervisory Colleges* (December 2017) available at https://www.bis.org/bcbs/publ/d430.pdf

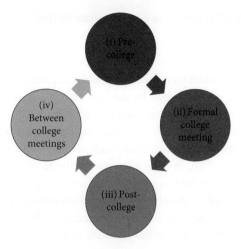

Figure 5.1 College meeting cycle

In addition, it was clear that there had been progress in colleges' contribution to crisis preparedness.[105] Despite this progress, supervisors continue to face challenges in relation to a number of college activities. These include legal constraints on information sharing, absence of formal protocols among different crisis preparedness forums, resource constraints, and expectation gaps between home and host supervisors.[106]

To overcome these challenges, the report identifies a set of sound practices to further strengthen the effectiveness of supervisory colleges. The practices are mapped to a cycle of college meetings, as demonstrated in Figure 5.1.

The report offers practical advice in relation to each stage of the meeting cycle. For example, at the pre-college stage, the report recognises that active participation by college members in the planning process would help to alleviate resource constraints faced by home supervisors in organising the meetings. At the formal college meeting stage, home and host supervisors could present key developments, their risk assessments of the bank's operations in their respective jurisdictions, and their supervisory plans. This would promote a shared understanding of the banking group's risk profile. At the post-college meeting stage, the home supervisor could share the key outcomes and salient points of discussions from the college meetings with all host supervisors. Finally, at the between college meetings stage, the report recommends that information exchange and cooperation among supervisors should take place on an ongoing basis and not just during physical meetings. The cycle highlights the importance of the work outside the in-person college meetings.

---

[105] Ibid, Section 2.   [106] Ibid, Section 3.

5.3.6 **Intensity and effectiveness of SIFI supervision**

The 2007–9 financial crisis revealed that some supervisors were not achieving an appropriate risk assessment/capital requirement balance. As such, in the aftermath of the crisis, the FSB and G20 leaders identified as a priority the need to increase the intensity and effectiveness of the world's largest banks, known as SIFIs. In particular it was recognised that the level of supervision applied by national authorities must be commensurate with the potential destabilisation risk that such firms pose to their own domestic financial systems, as well as the broader international financial system.

In November 2010 the FSB, in consultation with the IMF, released a report on the *Intensity and Effectiveness of SIFI Supervision*, which set out 32 recommendations for making the supervision of financial institutions more intense, effective, and reliable. While these recommendations are primarily aimed at SIFIs, they do contain lessons for the supervision of financial institutions more generally.[107] The recommendations are split into ten core areas, namely, mandates, independence, resources, supervisory powers, improved techniques, group-wide and consolidated supervision, continuous and comprehensive supervision, supervisory colleges, macro-prudential surveillance, and the use of third parties.

The FSB has published a series of progress reports on the implementation of the recommendations, most recently in April 2014.[108] The report noted that advancements had been made in a number of key areas including:

- More effective supervisory interactions, particularly with the board. In particular, a best practice has emerged that supervisors be made aware of board and senior management appointments in advance and have an opportunity to raise any concerns.

- Greater focus on risk governance, including the development of an institution's risk appetite framework and the assessment of its risk culture, which has been supported by new guidance and principles that aim to strengthen the dialogue with the board and senior management.

- Higher expectations for risk identification and measurement.

- Increased understanding of institutions' business models and the key drivers of revenue, as an approach to understanding an institution's prospective vulnerabilities and risks.

- More robust stress testing.

- Stronger resolution planning, which has helped to identify new sources of risk and impediments to resolution, such as the complexity of organisational and funding structures, higher operational risk than previously apparent, and complex booking and collateral management practices.

---

[107] FSB, *Intensity and Effectiveness of SIFI Supervision Recommendations*.1
[108] FSB, *Supervisory Intensity and Effectiveness: Progress Report on Enhanced Supervision* (April 2014) at http://www.fsb.org/wp-content/uploads/r_140407.pdf.

- Increased oversight of financial market infrastructures (FMIs). The risks posed by FMIs have been reviewed with concerns expressed about the need to focus on the quality of supervision of FMIs.

Despite the advancements made, the report recognised that more work is needed in a number of areas including:

- Strengthen risk management and measurement. Supervisors need to continue to impress upon institutions the importance of strengthening risk management and measurement.

- Improve models. BCBS work has revealed issues with bank capital models, which are partly due to poor internal models, variations in implementation of the BCBS standards, and inconsistent supervisory attention on ongoing monitoring of such models.

- Enhance stress testing. Supervisors need to advance further the implementation of the BCBS *Principles* for sound stress testing practices and supervision as a survey by the BCBS showed that very few countries do this well. Discussions suggest that there is a need for continued focus and creativity in stress test scenarios to ensure they sufficiently challenge assumed outcomes, and a need to ensure a strong relationship between supervisors and macroeconomists in developing those scenarios.

- Strengthen resources. Supervisors need to continue to strengthen their resources. The need for talent at supervisory agencies is affected by greater interaction with boards on issues such as risk appetite and risk culture, more focus on stress testing, supervisory intervention in capital models, and better oversight and analysis of data collected from financial institutions.

- Assess supervisory effectiveness. Supervisors need to develop methods to judge supervisory effectiveness in light of the changes implemented within supervision so far. This includes the related assessment of whether all the supervisory focus on boards and risk governance is paying off and institutions are becoming more effective in their risk governance.

- Define supervisory risk appetite. Supervisory authorities will need to focus on the risk appetite of supervisors (how much risk supervisors are prepared to tolerate) and on ways of ensuring that supervisors have reliable mechanisms in place to understand and discuss acceptable versus unacceptable risks.

Moving forward, the FSB recognise that the work ahead will need to focus on the measurement of supervisory effectiveness, including the search for proper input and output metrics.[109]

Further, where SIFIs are concerned, crisis management is a key issue and a special architecture is needed for effective cross-border crisis management. As such, the FSB in their *Key Attributes for Effective Resolution Regimes* has recommended that national

---

[109] Ibid, 15.

authorities of SIFIs should form specialist CMGs and establish the procedures to be applied in order to coordinate cross-border resolution.[110] This is discussed more fully in Chapter 13, section 13.4.

> ### ➡ Key takeaways
>
> - The BCBS has produced extensive guidelines on the effective supervision of international banks.
> - The *Basel Concordat* (1975, revised 1983) establish guidelines for the cooperation of home and host supervisory authorities in relation to the supervision of banks' foreign establishments.
> - The *Basel Core Principles* (1997, revised 2006 and 2012) provide 29 principles, which are viewed as minimum standards for sound prudential regulation and supervision of banks and banking systems across the globe.
> - Supervisory colleges enhance the consolidated supervision of an international banking group. The BCBSs *Principles for Effective Supervisory Colleges* (2014) are used as a basis for continuing to improve the operation of supervisory colleges.
> - The FSB report on the *Intensity and Effectiveness of SIFI Supervision* sets out 32 recommendations for making the supervision of financial institutions more intense, effective, and reliable.

Key bibliography

Reports and recommendations

Basel Committee on Banking Supervision, *Core Principles for Effective Banking Supervision* (Sep 2012) at https://www.bis.org/publ/bcbs230.pdf

Basel Committee on Banking Supervision, *Principles for Effective Supervisory Colleges* (June 2014) at https://www.bis.org/publ/bcbs287.htm

Basel Committee on Banking Supervision, *Principles for the Supervision of Banks' Foreign Establishments* (May 1983) available at https://www.bis.org/publ/bcbsc312.pdf

Financial Stability Board, *Intensity and Effectiveness of SIFI Supervision Recommendations for enhanced supervision* (November 2010) at www.fsb.org/wp-content/uploads/r_101101.pdf?page_moved=1

Books

Goodhart, C, *The Basel Committee on Banking Supervision: A History of the Early Years* (Cambridge: Cambridge University Press 2011)

---

[110] Key Attribute 8 of the 2014 version at http://www.fsb.org/what-we-do/policy-development/effective-resolution-regimes-and-policies/key-attributes-of-effective-resolution-regimes-for-financial-institutions/#1scope.

5.4 **A global regulator?**

The proliferation of international banking in recent decades, and the need to ensure that banking supervision takes place on a consolidated basis, has led to calls for the creation of a single global regulator.[111] Alexander, for example, argues that:[112]

> The globalisation of financial markets and the limited competence of national authorities over such markets necessitate the establishment of a global supervisor whose domain would be international and who would be responsible for generating regulatory standards and coordinating their implementation by national authorities.

The following discussion looks at the different forms that a global regulator could take. It then considers the advantages of having an international supervisor, in particular that it would provide a solution to the problem of lack of oversight. Finally, it explores the problems inherent in creating a worldwide supervisory authority, including the reluctance of national regulators to relinquish control over the regulation of their own banking sectors.

5.4.1 **Different models**

A global financial regulator can take a number of different forms, with each varying in terms of their intervention in the affairs of individual nations, and the degree to which it impacts on sovereignty. Bollen suggests four different models, based on the functional aspects of the international body.[113] These are set out in Box 5.13 and expanded on thereafter.

The first and most simple model of international regulation is to have one or more international standard-setting bodies. These bodies, such as the BCBS and the FSB, bring together a group of national regulators to discuss standards, exchange information, and

---

Box 5.13 Bollen's four models of global regulation

- International standard-setting bodies.
- International coordination of activities.
- A body supervising and coordinating national authorities.
- An international body that directly regulates the financial system.

---

[111] See, for example, Vanessa Blackmore and Esther Jeapes, 'The Global Financial Crisis: One Global Financial Regulator or Multiple Regulators? (2009) 4 *Capital Markets Law Journal* 113.

[112] Kern Alexander, 'The Role of a Global Supervisor for International Financial Markets' (2001) 8(3) *Journal of Financial Crime* 241.

[113] Rhys Bollen, 'The International Financial System and Future Global Regulation' (2008) *Journal of International Banking Law and Regulation* 458.

coordinate policies. This approach is advantageous given its speed and informality, and it is less likely to offend national sovereignty. However, given the soft-law nature of these bodies, in order to be effective, this model relies on the internationally agreed standards being implemented into member jurisdictions through national processes.[114]

The next model relates to the international coordination of activities. Here, regulators coordinate their work through international organisations such as the BIS, or through other channels such as the creation of colleges of supervisors. These colleges, discussed earlier, serve as a useful tool for enhancing information sharing and cooperation between the supervisors of a particular banking group.[115]

A third approach suggests the adoption of a body that supervises and coordinates national regulators. Bollen argues that this is a combination of the previous two approaches because it presupposes that there are international standards and agreed cooperative processes. As a form of federal approach, this involves a central body supervising and potentially directing national supervisors. This 'weak-form' global regulator is more aptly labelled as a 'global coordinator'.[116] We have seen the introduction of this model in some ways in the context of the **Banking Union** in the Eurozone.[117] While regulation and supervision has been centralised at the hands of the European Central Bank (ECB), it is only responsible for directly supervising 'significant institutions'.[118] However, the ECB has indirect control over all banks within the Eurozone through its power to issue regulations, guidance, and general instructions to the national authorities.[119]

The final approach advocated by Bollen is the creation of an international body that directly regulates participants in the financial system. The major functions of such a body could cover a number of regulatory aspects including: the authorisation of financial institutions, the collection of information, and the surveillance of markets and institutions; cooperation and coordination with national authorities; and enforcement.[120] While we have seen this at regional level in the context of the ECB and its direct supervision of significant institutions in the Eurozone, we do not have such activity taking place yet at a global level.[121]

---

[114] Ibid, 463.   [115] Ibid, 464.   [116] Ibid.   [117] See Chapter 6.

[118] Defined in Article 6(4) of Regulation 1024/2013 as those with assets of more than EUR30 billion, those representing more than one-fifth of a member state national output, or those that have requested/received public assistance from European Financial Stability Facility or the European Stability Mechanism.

[119] Article 6(5) of Regulation 1024/2013.

[120] Kern Alexander, 'The Role of a Global Supervisor for International Financial Markets' (2001) 8(3) *Journal of Financial Crime* 241–4.

[121] Rhys Bollen, 'The International Financial System and Future Global Regulation' 464–5. For further discussion on the creation of a 'World Financial Authority' see John Eatwell and Lance Taylor, *Global Finance at Risk: The Case for International Regulation* (The New Press: New York 2000) chapter 7. Other possibilities for a more limited global regulatory architecture could include an international market liquidity provider of last resort (see e.g. Steven Schwarcz 'Keynote Address: The Case for a Market Liquidity Provider of Last Resort' (2009) *NYU Journal of Law and Business* 346, or a centralised resolution regime for multinational banks (see e.g. Barry Eichengreen 'Out of the Box Thoughts about the International Financial Architecture' (May 2009) IMF Working Paper No. WP/09/116 at https://www.imf.org/external/pubs/ft/wp/2009/wp09116.pdf.

5.4.2 **The advantages of a global regulator**

One of the core benefits of having a global regulator is that it gives effect to, and reflects, the global nature of the marketplace. As Bollen argues, 'global firms need a global regulator'.[122] Given the increasingly interrelated and cross-border nature of banking, it makes sense that regulation and supervision should follow suit and be conducted on a unified and international basis. An extract from an article in *The Economist*, published in 2002, articulates the issue well:[123]

> Who regulates Citigroup, the world's largest and most diverse financial institution? With its operations in over 100 countries, selling just about every financial product that has ever been invented, probably every financial regulator in the world feels that Citi is, to some degree, his problem. America alone has the Federal Reserve, the Securities and Exchange Commission, the Commodities and Futures Trading Commission, the New York Stock Exchange, 50 state insurance commissioners and many others. Yet in a sense nobody truly regulates Citi: it is a global firm in a world of national and sometimes sectoral watchdogs. The same is true of AIG, General Electric Capital, UBS, Deutsche Bank and many more.

Accordingly, since global banking groups now operate across increasingly seamless financial markets, the effective supervision of those banks on a global level requires an international supervisor whose regulatory domain reflects that of the banks it supervises.[124] This will lead to fewer gaps in multinational regulation and enable consolidated supervision on a more streamlined basis.

Further, even in relation to less interventionist models of globalisation such as international standard-setting bodies (e.g. BCBS) and international coordination of activity (e.g. colleges of supervisors), greater harmonisation of regulatory standards will likely be achieved. With a global regulator, the risk of national divergencies being created in relation to the implementation of harmonised global standards is minimised.

Importantly, the introduction of a global regulator will lead to less national competition between regulators, thereby reducing the likelihood of a regulatory 'race to the bottom'. It has been well documented that regulators try to attract global firms by offering lower or more lenient levels of regulation. If a global regulator was introduced, these disparate levels of regulation, which encourage riskier activities in less stringent jurisdictions, would be minimised. According to Bollen, 'This benefits all, as a race to the bottom is likely to result in sub-optimal regulatory settings.'[125]

5.4.3 **Barriers and issues**

While a global regulator might be considered the most appropriate option to oversee international financial markets and institutions, there are a number of practical and political issues to achieving that goal.

---

[122] Ibid, 466.   [123] *The Economist*, 'The Regulator Who isn't There' (16 May 2002).
[124] See Kern Alexander, 'The Role of a Global Supervisor for International Financial Markets' (2001) 8(3) *Journal of Financial Crime* 234.
[125] Bollen, 'The International Financial System and Future Global Regulation' 465.

First, although there is some consensus on the need for reform, there are sovereignty and adoption issues. Countries tend to guard their sovereignty, that is, their ability to independently determine their own laws and policies. Financial regulation is closely linked to monetary and macroeconomic policy and it has a direct impact on issues such as the creation of credit. As these functions are performed by public authorities within respective states, and they are peculiar to the conditions in particular jurisdictions, it is not likely that governments will cede power to a global financial regulator.[126] As Bollen argues, 'The most difficult issue is not so much whether an international regulator would be beneficial, but whether in the practical realities of world politics national governments are likely to subscribe to it.'[127] Given the vast differences in political regimes and national interests across the globe, it would be seemingly impossible to reach an international agreement to transfer power to a global organisation, with all the relinquishing of sovereignty and autonomy that that would imply.[128]

Second, it is argued that in order for a global regulator to function effectively, it would need to be able to enforce and implement an internationally harmonised set of rules. While this has been achieved in relation to certain prudential issues such as capital adequacy, 'for the large part many financial institutions operate within a complex matrix of local and national rules and regulations which by their very nature may be difficult to harmonise.'[129] In rebuttal to this point, lessons can be learnt from the structure adopted by the Banking Union in the context of the Eurozone where regulation has been centralised at the hands of the ECB, but only in relation to key prudential issues and requirements.[130] Other aspects of regulation, including conduct of business regulation, are outside the ECBs remit. A similar approach could be adopted on a global scale.

Even if these practical and political hurdles were overcome, the introduction of a global financial regulator raises a number of issues. First, there would be an issue of accountability. National regulators are accountable to their respective ministers, government departments, or parliaments and this serves as an important measure to ensure that the regulator operates with the public interest in mind and that it is subject to the appropriate checks and balances.[131] While accountability can be ensured by, for example, subjecting the body to judicial oversight, appointing senior management, setting budgets through a political system, and making the body accountable to an elected government, some of these are not possible for a global regulator.[132]

Further, a system of regulation led by a single global regulator would suffer from a lack of competition, which would ordinarily keep a regulator accountable, dynamic, and flexible.[133] Although this goes against the earlier argument raised concerning a 'race

---

[126] Blackmore and Jeapes, 'The Global Financial Crisis' 116–7.
[127] Bollen, 'The International Financial System and Future Global Regulation' 467.
[128] Vanessa Blackmore and Esther Jeapes, 'The Global Financial Crisis' 115.   [129] Ibid, 116.
[130] See Chapter 6.   [131] Bollen, 'The International Financial System and Future Global Regulation' 466.
[132] Ibid.   [133] Ibid, 467.

to the bottom', a variety of regulatory regimes allows countries to compete for financial firms and investors, thereby encouraging creative competition. A single regulator would bring with it a harmonised system of regulatory rules, thereby eradicating the potential for regulatory competition to improve the rules.

 Key takeaways

- Given that financial markets and institutions are now global in nature, it makes sense that there should be a global regulator to oversee the system.

- A global regulator can take various forms, ranging from a less interventionist model of international standard setters, to an all-encompassing international financial supervisor, responsible for a range of regulatory issues including authorisation, surveillance, and enforcement.

- A global regulator would eliminate the issue of a lack of supervisory oversight, lead to greater harmonisation, and eradicate the 'race to the bottom'.

- However, there are practical and political barriers to achieving the goal of a global supervisor, particularly the reluctance of nations to relinquish their sovereignty.

Key bibliography

Articles

Alexander, K, 'The Role of a Global Supervisor for International Financial Markets' (2001) 8(3) *Journal of Financial Crime* 234.

Blackmore, V and Jeapes, E, 'The Global Financial Crisis: One Global Financial Regulator or Multiple Regulators? (2009) 4 *Capital Markets Law Journal* 112.

Bollen, R, 'The International Financial System and Future Global Regulation' (2008) *Journal of International Banking Law and Regulation* 458.

Questions

1. **As a body with no legal standing, the effectiveness of the BCBS in setting global standards is limited. Discuss.**

    Answer tips You should demonstrate your understanding of the legal nature and character of the BCBS as a soft-law body. You should discuss the advantages of soft law and the reasons why, despite this fact, the work of the BCBS has been so widely adopted. Also consider the use of compliance reviews (both by the BCBS, and other bodies such as the IMF and FSB) and their impact on the effectiveness of the work of the BCBS.

2. Critically analyse the extent to which the BCBS and FSB have created an effective framework for the supervision of international banks.

> *Answer tips* *You should critically analyse the body of work created by the BCBS and FSB in this area, including the Basel Concordat, 1973, the Basel Core Principles, 2012, the Principles for Effective Supervisory Colleges, 2014, and the work of the FSB on the Intensity and Effectiveness of SIFI Supervision, 2010. You should consider how effective this work has been in terms of implementation.*

3. The supervision of international banks remains fragmented and unsatisfactory. We need a consolidated World Financial Authority to achieve adequate supervision of international banks. Do you agree?

> *Answer tips* *You should consider the development of international banking and the work of the BCBS on facilitating the supervision of international banks (including, for example, the Basel Concordat, Basel Core Principles, and more recently their good practice principles on colleges of supervisors). You should then consider whether we need to have a global regulator to ensure the most effective supervision of cross-border institutions and any barriers there might be to achieving that goal. In the alternative you should consider the advantages of a move towards regional supervision, using, for example, the Banking Union in the Eurozone as a case study.*

6

UK banking supervision and regulatory architecture

6.1 The development of UK bank regulation

Bank regulation in the UK became formalised in the late twentieth century although banking business has existed in England since the seventeenth century,[1] predating the establishment of the Bank of England in 1694. The banking sector had for a long time been regarded as a self-regulatory sector. In this chapter we discuss why self-regulation gradually eclipsed and how bank regulation developed since 1979. Over the years, the scope and intensity of regulation increased, with periods of acceleration observed in the early 2000s and after the global financial crisis 2007–9. UK bank regulation began modestly, and had been driven to become more comprehensive and prescriptive. This development was first attributed to the need to transpose European legislation on bank regulation, at about the same time as major changes were introduced for the supervision of banks by the Labour government that assumed power in 1997. After the global financial crisis, further changes were made to bank regulation as well as the regulatory architecture in the UK for bank regulation.

6.1.1 Self-regulation

Until the Banking Act 1979, the banking sector in the UK was not formally regulated. There existed a skeletal legislative framework that dealt with unsavoury financial conduct. Illegal money lending (Moneylenders Act 1900) on a commercial basis was prohibited unless such activity took place within the scope of exceptions. Fraudulent financial conduct could be caught under the Theft Act 1968 if financial property was dishonestly cheated out of individuals who became permanently deprived of their property.

---

[1] On early history of goldsmiths acting as 'deposit takers' of gold and issuers of notes, see RD Richards, *The Early History of Banking in England* (Oxford: Routledge 2012, reprinted from the 1929 version); Roger Outing (British Museum), 'An Introduction to English Banking History' at http://www.britishmuseum.org/research/publications/online_research_catalogues/paper_money/paper_money_of_england__wales/english_banking_history.aspx.

The self-regulatory nature of the banking sector was remarked in the case of *United Dominions Trust Ltd v Kirkwood*.[2] The case was heard in 1966, and courts had to determine if a car finance company was a 'bank'. In that case, the car finance company United Dominions Trust wished to enforce against a director of an insolvent company, as he had provided a personal guarantee for the company's borrowing. The director argued that the guarantee was not enforceable as the loan was void for illegality. United Dominions Trust was alleged to have engaged in illegal money lending by carrying out its business of financing car purchases. Under the Moneylenders Act, the business of United Dominions Trust could be so regarded unless it showed that it fell within the Act's exceptions, one of which was the carrying on of 'banking business'. It was argued that the company was a 'bank', but as 'bank' was not defined in the Act, the court had to determine if the company was indeed a 'bank'. The court did not think that United Dominions Trust carried on the same type of banking business as most banks did. It had no deposit-taking or payment business, services typically offered by banks on the High Street, and focused only on lending for car purchases. However, based on expert opinion from banking institutions in the City of London that regarded United Dominions Trust as a peer-level institution, the court ultimately found that it was a 'bank' exempt from the Moneylenders Act 1900. This approach showed judicial acceptance of the opinion of the banking sector in terms of what constituted banking business, and reflected the self-regulatory nature of the sector. Nevertheless, in response to the above-mentioned case, the Board of Trade in 1967 began to issue certificates to institutions genuinely carrying on a banking business that allowed them to be exempt from the Moneylenders Act. This, however, was not a system of formal regulation.

The self-regulatory nature of the banking sector did not mean that there was a complete lack of interaction between banking business and public bodies. Indeed, the Bank of England always maintained an informal relationship of oversight with the banks in the City of London, as banks kept their reserves of gold in the Bank of England, regarding the Bank as a bankers' bank. Further, the Bank of England played a significant role in mitigating the panic of 1866 after 'bill broker' Overend, Gurney & Co failed,[3] and established a role of extending emergency lending to banks if necessary.

Overend, Gurney & Co was a 'bill broker', that is, a house that purchased negotiable and endorsed debt (by previous resellers). It held high levels of such risky money market instruments and from 1857 was showing signs of crisis. It failed in 1866. Although the Bank of England did not lend to Overend to avert its failure, it carried on lending to the banking sector on the basis of their bills but increased the discount rate for the face value of the bills of up to 10 per cent. The continued lending by the Bank helped the banking sector to recover and this episode became known as foundational to the role of the central bank's lender of last resort role to banks. The discount facility offered

---

[2] [1966] 2 QB 431.
[3] See Marc Flandreau and Stefano Ugolini, 'The Crisis of 1866' (2014) at http://repository.graduateinstitute.ch/record/285126/files/Flandreau_HEIDWP10–2014.pdf.

by the Bank of England allowed it to monitor the financial situation of banks that used the facility and the Bank was able to spot and deal with early signs of crises, such as relating to Barings Bank in 1890. This soft form of supervision through lending conditions later evolved into a type of moral suasion that the Bank exerted over the self-regulatory banking sector in England, and the Bank of England developed itself as an informal supervisor of banks.

In its informal role, the Bank of England was only able to have a picture of the most-established sections of the banking sector, such as High Street banks Barclays, Lloyd's, Midland, and National Westminster, which had access to the Bank's lending facilities. A little watched section in the banking business, the **secondary banks**, was being propelled into crisis from the early 1970s. This crisis was the catalyst for bringing about a formal bank regulation regime for the first time.

6.1.2 **Early stages of bank regulation 1979–2000**

The secondary banking sector comprised of small deposit-taking and credit institutions that grew since the 1950s to meet needs in business lending and residential mortgages.[4] These needs were often not met by the more well-established High Street banks as borrowers were generally of riskier profiles. The advent of secondary banks was welcomed by policymakers as they saw secondary banks playing a useful part in the general post-war development of the UK economy. However, in order to allay public concern that such institutions were subject to little public accountability, the Protection of Depositors Act 1963 was brought into force to require them to adhere to certain obligations in financial transparency.

However, in the early 1970s, house prices – which had been on a rising trajectory in the UK – started to fall, partly due to a general global economic downturn since 1973.[5] The decline in economic sentiment hit the secondary banking sector. A number of secondary banks that had been over-extended in risky loans started to fail as their borrowers defaulted. By November 1973, the London and County Securities had approached the Bank of England for emergency lending, and through 1974–5, many secondary banks were near insolvency. A secondary bank crisis was on the hands of policymakers.[6] The Bank of England was forced into intervening over several years in order to avert widespread panic, and reportedly spent over £100 million in rescuing over 30 secondary banks. As Lambert remarked,[7] the resolution of this episode behind the closed doors of the Bank of England averted wider panic, but policymakers wished to avoid a repeat of this crisis and increasingly saw the need for a formal regime for bank

---

[4] See Bank of England Quarterly Bulletin (April 1978) 230.

[5] Following the OPEC oil crisis of 1973. The crisis resulted from OPEC countries collectively raising the price of oil in retaliation for American aid to Israel.

[6] Margaret Reid, *The Secondary Banking Crisis, 1973–5* (London: Macmillan 1982).

[7] Richard Lambert, 'A Tale of Two Banking Crises', *Financial Times* (2 December 2008).

regulation. However, such a regime would be politically unpopular as it would affect commercial freedoms in the banking sector.

The introduction of European legislation provided the political will needed to usher in a formal bank regulation regime in the UK. In 1977, European legislation required member states to formally authorise their credit institutions so that these institutions can enjoy the rights of cross-border establishment in the EEA banking market.[8] The UK therefore sought to introduce for the first time a formal bank authorisation and regulation regime under the Banking Act 1979. The Bank of England also became a formal bank regulator, graduating from its hitherto informal but increasingly visible role.

6.1.2.1 Recognised and licensed banks

The Banking Act 1979 had a modest scope of application, and avoided introducing regulation across the entire banking sector. It only introduced licensing for banks that were 'not recognised'. Recognised banks were banks defined as carrying on a wide range of deposit and credit business and enjoying 'a high reputation and standing in the financial community'.[9] These banks were outside of the scope of the Act, and remained free to carry on business in their commercial wisdom. Recognised banks were treated as peer-level institutions by the Bank of England and hence not subject to formal regulation. The Act's scope therefore covered 'not recognised' banks, largely secondary banking institutions, which had to be subject to the Bank of England's formal oversight. In this way the Act's treatment showed significant deference to the industry leaders of the banking sector. It could be argued that these banks were not implicated in the secondary banking crisis and it would have been disproportionate to extend regulation to them. Moreover, they maintained close and informal relationships with the Bank of England, making it less necessary to subject them to regulation.

Banks that had not attained the 'recognised' stature had to be licensed. Licensed banks were subject to the Bank of England's licensing conditions and ongoing oversight. This policy response sought to assure the public that the widespread failure of banks seen in the secondary banking crisis would not be repeated, as the Bank of England would have all licensed banks under its watch. The Act also established for the first time a Deposit Protection Fund overseen by a new statutory body the Deposit Protection Board to provide a guarantee for depositors if their banks failed. The level of protection was set at £10,000 per depositor/institution.

Shortly after the Banking Act 1979 regime came into force, a crisis erupted in the 'recognised bank' sector, forcing the UK to extend its formal bank regulation to all banks.

---

[8] Banking Coordination Directive of 1977, as referred to in Tom Bingham, 'Inquiry into the Supervision of the Bank of Credit and Commerce International' (1992) at https://www.gov.uk/government/uploads/system/uploads/attachment_data/file/235718/0198.pdf, a report that took comprehensive stock of the state of bank regulation up to the 1990s.   [9] Article 1, Schedule 2.

6.1.2.2 Failure of Johnson Matthey Bank, and the Banking Act 1987

The Bank of England found a new crisis on its hands in 1984 when Johnson Matthey Bank (JMB) became stricken with severe loan losses. JMB was formed by major gold bullion company Johnson Matthey, which traced its origins to 1817. JMB was a member of the London Gold Fixing Group, a closed club of banks that had the rights to determine the price of gold each business day. It had, however, made large concentrated loans to a few borrowers who turned out to have deceived it with regard to their assets and who eventually became insolvent. The size of the losses exceeded the JMB's capital and, on 30 September 1984, the Bank of England arranged to rescue JMB in order to avert wider market panic that could entail due to the JMB's membership of the London Gold Fixing Group.[10] The Bank of England purchased JMB for £1 and thereafter arranged to sell most of its assets to Mase Westpac.

The failure of JMB highlighted the gap in the Banking Act 1979 in omitting to formally regulate and supervise the recognised bank sector. This episode gave rise to the Leigh Pemberton Committee, which was instituted to study bank regulation reform in the UK. Their recommendations then culminated in reform, extending formal regulation and supervision by the Bank of England to the entire banking sector in the UK.[11] The Banking Act 1987 was introduced to replace the Banking Act 1979.

The banking sector and the Bank of England had by that time accepted that such formal regulation was inevitable. This was because of strong international trends that were developing at the same time to support bank regulation. From the early 1980s, the Basel Committee of Banking Supervision under the auspices of the Bank for International Settlements (see Chapter 5) had been championing internationally harmonised regulatory standards for banks in order to prevent bank failures, such as Herstatt in 1974, which resulted in international disruptions.[12] By the time the Banking Act 1987 was introduced, the first Basel Capital Accord (see Chapter 8) was also about ready for international adoption. The requirements in the Accord provided the backbones for the regulatory standards introduced in the Banking Act 1987.

The Banking Act 1987 required all deposit-taking institutions in the UK to be authorised by the Bank of England.[13] Authorised institutions were subject to conditions that the Bank of England may impose by written notice, such as in relation to their levels of capital and restrictions of business. Authorised institutions were also required to report **large exposures** to the Bank, that is, lending to customers in excess of 10 per cent of the bank's capital.[14] This measure was presumably in response to the lessons learnt in relation to Johnson Matthey Bank.

---

[10] The Johnson Matthey crisis was discussed in Marlene Havranek, 'The Bank of England and Bank Failures' (2000) 2 *Insolvency Intelligence* 73.

[11] See a summary of their recommendations in Bingham, 'Inquiry into the Supervision of the Bank of Credit and Commerce International'.   [12] Discussed in Chapters 5 and 8.

[13] Section 3.   [14] Section 38. Large exposures are now regulated, see Chapter 9.

The Bank of England could exercise significant supervisory powers over banks including vetting controlling shareholders, requiring information disclosure, carrying out investigations, and ordering authorised institutions to comply with its notices of action. It also had the power to revoke authorisation granted earlier to banks.

However, during the formative stages of the Bank of England's role as bank regulator and supervisor, it was observed that the Bank did not swiftly embrace the new and unfamiliar powers. The Bank of England continued to prefer its mode of informal oversight in the form of peer-level discussions with the banking industry. The style of supervision, known as 'moral suasion', came to be regarded as inadequate and ineffective.

6.1.2.3 Moral suasion and bank failures in the 1990s

Shortly after the introduction of the Banking Act 1987, the Bank of England was to reckon with another bank crisis, which had significant impact in the UK. In 1991 the Luxembourg-domiciled bank BCCI (Bank of Credit and Commerce International), which had extensive private banking and commercial operations in the UK, failed. BCCI was a global private bank that focused on taking large deposits from wealthy clientele and also carried out extensive commercial lending. However, its clientele included drug traffickers and money launderers and its extensive loan portfolios included significant loans to controlling shareholders. Internal documentation and operations in BCCI were fraught with fraud and opaque practices. Many of BCCI's connected loans performed poorly and it suffered significant losses, often unexplained. After undercover operations in BCCI led by the US Customs Services successfully uncovered BCCI's extensive involvement in money laundering, global regulators forced the Luxembourg court to declare BCCI to be insolvent in mid-1991. Global regulators then shut down all BCCI branches worldwide. About a million depositors in the UK were affected by the insolvency of BCCI including local government authorities that had placed significant deposits in BCCI.

A public inquiry was instituted to look into whether the Bank of England had acted appropriately in supervising BCCI prior to BCCI's failure. Although BCCI was a Luxembourg-domiciled bank, its extensive footprint in the UK should have alerted the Bank of England to a need to ensure that UK depositors and customers were adequately protected. The Bingham report[15] provided a detailed study of the 19 years the Bank of England dealt with BCCI and pointed out various flaws in its relationship with BCCI. The Bank of England had received reports of BCCI's questionable expansion since 1982 and was concerned about its financial statements in 1984, but internal communication failed to reach the attention of the highest levels at the Bank and no supervisory action ensued. The Bank had also realised that BCCI used its London office as a *de facto* headquarters and significant business was carried out from there. In spite of visits to BCCI and investigative meetings, the Bank did not bring its authority to bear on BCCI

---

[15] Bingham, 'Inquiry into the Supervision of the Bank of Credit and Commerce International'.

and relied extensively on other bank regulators to decide upon any course of action. Indeed by 1989, although BCCI's responses to more intensive Bank questioning were not totally satisfactory, the Bank somehow did not wish to rock the boat and impose supervisory measures on BCCI, preferring to carry on in 'open relations' with BCCI. Even in the face of qualified financial statements from BCCI's auditors in 1990 and discovery of non-performing large exposures, the Bank only required more documentation from BCCI and did not exercise more robust supervisory powers such as ordering the removal of management. The report seemed genuinely puzzled at the Bank's inertia in extending effective oversight over BCCI.

McGuire[16] argued that the Bank, used to a moral suasion framework for supervision, believed excessively in behind-closed-doors dialogue and persuasion vis-à-vis the banking industry. This practice could be effective where the moral force of persuasion was high within a closely-knit group, but changes in the banking industry, especially with the advent of foreign banks such as BCCI, could pose a challenge to the force of moral suasion. International banks such as BCCI were structured to be opaque from regulators and aimed at evading supervisory oversight instead of cooperating with regulators. Moral suasion would be ineffective in such circumstances. The Bank's stature as bank regulator was damaged in this episode, and this was highlighted by the civil litigation that ensued against the Bank for compensation due to its supervisory failure.[17]

In 1995, another major bank failure in the UK occurred. Although this failure was not directly attributed to the Bank's failure in supervision, the Bank's supervisory stature became further damaged. Barings Bank was an old merchant bank in the UK established since the eighteenth century. It had global operations and its ultimate failure was caused by unchecked activities on the part of a single trader, Nick Leeson, in the Singapore branch. Leeson carried out futures trades, some of which suffered losses. In order to hide his losses, he made unauthorised and excessive bets on Nikkei futures indices hoping to make large and quick profits. However, the earthquake in Kobe in February 1992 caused the Index to plunge and Leeson caused the bank to sustain almost $2 billion in losses. These losses exceeded the banking group's capital but the Bank of England was unable to mount such a large-scale rescue. The Bank became insolvent in February 1995, and its assets and liabilities were ultimately sold to ING Bank for £1.

The Board of Banking Supervision in the Bank of England reported[18] on the causes for the failure of Barings and the state of the supervisory regime. It considered that the Bank was the main supervisor for the Barings group but detailed insights into foreign branches would be difficult to obtain. The Bank was satisfied that the Group on the whole had informal but effective **internal control**, and maintained open relations with

---

[16] Ken McGuire, 'Emergent Trends in Bank Supervision in the United Kingdom' (1993) 56 *Modern Law Review* 669.

[17] Discussed further in section 6.3.4.

[18] Board of Banking Supervision, Bank of England, *Inquiry into the Circumstances of the Collapse of Barings* (18 July 1995) at https://www.gov.uk/government/uploads/system/uploads/attachment_data/file/235622/0673.pdf.

the Bank. Leeson's trading freedoms were in part attributed to favourable exemptions that the Bank earlier gave to Barings from regulatory restrictions in large exposures. The Bank's supervision seemed informal and minimal, but the Group's lack of robust and formal internal control was more directly causal for its failure.[19] The cumulative effect of the Bank's lacklustre supervisory record paved the way for the new Labour government – elected in 1997 – to institute regime change in banking and financial services supervision.

6.1.3 Single financial regulator 2000–13

In 1997 a new Labour government was elected, replacing a Conservative government that had been in place since 1975. The new government ushered in major institutional reform in the regulation and supervision of financial services, including banking, insurance, and investment services. Financial services would be regulated and supervised by a single financial services regulator, the Financial Services Authority (FSA).

The creation of the FSA took a few years of consultation and deliberation but the measure was largely unopposed. This could be explained by the confluence of a number of factors ranging from changes in the financial services industry to policy and social appetite for changes in regulation and supervision.

6.1.3.1 Context and drivers for change to single regulator

By the early 1990s, the global financial services sector had been undergoing structural change. Financial institutions started to undertake a range of cross-sectoral activity – that is, business activities outside of their traditional sector. For example, banks started taking on investment services, and non-banks stepped into the space for lending such as in trade finance and forms of personal finance. The growth of cross-sectoral activity allowed 'financial supermarkets' to grow, that is, financial services institutions that offered many business lines under a 'one-stop' umbrella.[20] There was a perceived need for regulation and supervision not to be confined to sectoral divisions, and should 'match' developments in the global financial services industry.

The single financial services regulator would be an improvement over the hitherto fragmented regulatory regimes that existed for banks, insurance, and investment services in the UK.[21] The banking sector was not seen to be well-regulated by the Bank of

---

[19] *Re Barings plc* (No 5) [2000] 1 BCLC 523.

[20] See also Arthur E Wilmarth Jnr, 'The Transformation of the Financial Services Industry: 1975–2000, Competition, Consolidation and Increased Risks' (2002) *University of Illinois Law Review* 215; Eilis Ferran and Charles Goodhart, 'Regulating Financial Services and Markets in the Twenty-First Century: An Overview' and Amelia C Fawcett, 'Examining the Objectives in Financial Regulation: Will the New Regulator Succeed? A Practitioner's View' in Eilis Ferran and Charles Goodhart (eds), *Regulating Financial Services and Markets in the Twenty First Century* (Oxford: Hart Publishing 2001) chs 1 and 4.

[21] Howard Davies, 'Reforming Financial Regulation: Progress and Priorities' in in Eilis Ferran and Charles Goodhart (eds), *Regulating Financial Services and Markets in the Twenty First Century* (Oxford: Hart Publishing 2001) ch 2.

England and, in 1998, the Cruickshank Report, which dealt with the state of competitiveness in banking services in the UK, was of the view that the sector was uncompetitive, static, and inefficient.

Further, the investment sector had largely been self-regulatory and was seen not to be well-regulated either.[22] Investment services firms were members of powerful trade bodies that provided fragmented forms of supervisory oversight.[23] For example, personal investment advisors were members of one trade body while investment management firms were members of another. There were five powerful trade bodies overseeing firms specialising in different investment-related services. After the government commissioned the Wilson Committee to look into the state of the financial services industry and whether it was meeting economic needs, the conclusions for improvement of the sector led to the commission of the Gower Committee to examine the state of regulation at play, especially in relation to investor protection and the need to be consistent with looming European Economic Community (EEC) regulation. The Gower Committee preferred more robust regulatory oversight by an independent body over investment services, but given the existing state of self-regulation, it ultimately recommended that existing trade bodies be made more robust in their disciplining roles, but they should be subject to the broad oversight of an independent statutory body. This resulted in the establishment of the Securities and Investments Board in 1986.[24] The Board oversaw the trade bodies, which were streamlined from five to three, but the trade bodies remained at the forefront of setting standards and supervision, maintaining a volatile relationship with the Board. This system was criticised by Davies who referred to the self-regulatory bodies as 'dogs that did not bark'.[25] The system reflected the powerful state of industry lobbying and their hold on the power to self-regulate. It persisted until institutional change with the advent of the single financial regulator.

The political appetite for institutional change in financial services regulation was based on the expectation that a stronger and more unified regulatory regime would be good for the market in driving beneficial commercial change.[26] Further, at the same time, policy changes in Europe were also afoot in reforming financial services regulation to boost the single market for financial services. The developments in the UK were very much aligned with the needs of that time.

A single financial services regulator would be able to have oversight of the financial services industry as a whole and not suffer from information 'gaps' that would exist under a sectoral regulatory structure. The single regulator would also be more able to

---

[22] Mis-selling scandals involving investment products were discussed in the Gower Report 'Review of Investor Protection' (1982), commented on by S House, 'Editorial Review' (1984) *Business Law Review* 57.

[23] This is another story, but see Julia Black, *Rules and Regulators* (Oxford: Clarendon Press 1993) chs 2 and 3.

[24] Established by the Financial Services Act 1986.

[25] Davies, 'Reforming Financial Regulation: Progress and Priorities'.

[26] Colin Mayer, 'Regulatory Principles and the Financial Services and Markets Act 2000' in Eilis Ferran and Charles Goodhart (eds), *Regulating Financial Services and Markets in the Twenty First Century* (Oxford: Hart Publishing 2001) ch 3.

introduce consistent regulatory standards across different financial services firms and benefit from economies of scale in administering its functions.[27] The regulatory model of the single regulator in financial services had also attained a level of international popularity.[28] The institution of the single financial services regulator was to be a separate and different body from the existing regulatory bodies, that is, the Bank of England for banks and investment trade associations for investment services. The FSA would combine all financial services regulation and supervision under one outfit and replace the existing fragmentary bodies that were also perceived as inadequate, therefore replacing the Bank of England in bank regulation and supervision.

Figures 6.1 and 6.2 show the regulatory architecture for financial services in the UK before and after the institution of the FSA.

The FSA was instituted in 2000 as the single regulator responsible for multiple objectives: maintaining confidence in the financial system, promoting public understanding of the financial system, consumer protection, and reducing financial crime.[29] It became an amalgamation of the bank supervisory division of the Bank of England and the regulatory policy divisions of the self-regulatory trade associations that were involved in rule making. It was made subject to extensive channels of accountability, so that its newly conferred powers could be kept in check. It entered into a Tripartite Memorandum of Understanding with the Treasury and the Bank of England in order to clearly delineate each body's responsibilities so that overlaps and duplication were avoided. This Tripartite Memorandum of Understanding related more to boundary drawing between

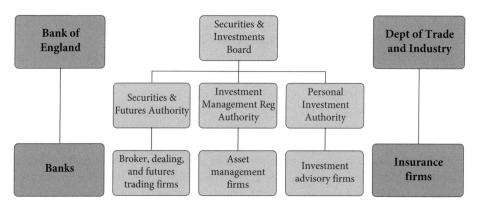

Figure 6.1 Regulatory architecture for banking, investment, and insurance services separated by sectoral lines

---

[27] Eilis Ferran, 'Examining the UK's Experience in Adopting a Single Financial Regulator Model' (2003) 28 *Brooklyn Journal of International Law* 257.

[28] Richard A Abrams and Michael W Taylor, 'Issues in the Unification of Financial Sector Supervision' (IMF Working Paper 2000); Marc Quintyn and Michael W Taylor, 'Regulatory and Supervisory Independence and Financial Stability' (IMF Working Paper 2002).

[29] Set out in the Financial Services and Markets Act 2000 (these have subsequently been amended).

Figure 6.2 Regulatory architecture for all financial services
firms after reform and setting up the FSA

the bodies than to the continuing or cooperative relationship amongst the three bodies. In hindsight, the flawed Tripartite Memorandum of Understanding failed to put in place a system for coordinated work and information sharing among the three bodies, which would have been useful in managing the UK banking crisis 2007–9 (discussed in Chapter 1). The approach in the Memorandum at the time was nevertheless understandable as the FSA was newly created and there was anxiety to ensure that its mandates were clear and that it would not be interfered with by the government and its predecessors. Although the policy move to institute the FSA was largely unopposed, commentators did query whether the removal of the Bank of England's supervisory power completely was a right and optimal move.

Importance of the central bank to the banking sector

Although the Bank of England was perceived to have been a weak bank regulator and supervisor, as the central bank, it continued to be the bankers' bank, it administered the large value payment system for clearing banks in the UK by reconciling banks' accounts at the Bank of England (Chapter 3), and it would remain the lender of the last resort for banks. A number of commentators[30] were of the view that bank supervision was intimately connected with the Bank's role especially as lender of the last resort, and removing bank supervision from the Bank of England completely was not optimal. For example, Goodhart[31] warned that central bank functions could be undermined by the single regulator structure if supervisory information regarding banks would no longer go to the central bank but to the single regulator. Central banks would have less information and a weakened basis to extend the lender of the last resort function to UK banks, and this could jeopardise banks' line to emergency lending by the Bank.

---

[30] Charles AE Goodhart, 'The Organisational Structure of Banking Supervision' (Financial Stability Institute Occasional Papers 2000); Rosa Lastra, 'The Governance Structure for Financial Regulation and Supervision in Europe' (2003) 10 *Columbia Journal of European Law* 49.

[31] Goodhart, 'The Organisational Structure of Banking Supervision'.

There were other cautions raised by commentators in relation to the single regulator structure. For example, a single regulator tasked with multiple objectives may not be able to accomplish all of them equally well. Certain objectives could be compromised if conflicts of objectives occurred.[32] To an extent this concern became real in the FSA's role leading up to the global financial crisis 2007–9. We turn now to examine the FSA's regulatory policy and approach.

6.1.3.2 Functional approach

The FSA required that regulatory approval should be obtained if any natural and legal persons wished to carry out certain prescribed financial services activities.[33] Such regulatory approval would be given on the basis of the FSA being satisfied that certain conditions, known as 'threshold' conditions, being met. These related to capital requirements for banks (discussed in Chapters 8 and 9) and the soundness of persons directing the business.[34] Individuals carrying out significant functions in the financial business were also to be individually approved (discussed in Chapter 11).[35] The authorisation and approval systems introduced a form of *ex ante* vetting. This regulatory approach had moved financial services regulation and supervision far from the incremental regulatory approach earlier described.

The FSA's authorisation framework reflected a 'functional' approach to financial regulation. The functional approach meant that a financial business was authorised based on the economic functions or services it wished to carry out. A financial business could obtain multiple authorisations for different types of financial business, distinguishing from a sectoral approach that would authorise an institution as a 'bank', 'insurer', or 'investment broker', and assuming that such institutions would carry out only certain lines of business that they have always engaged in. The functional approach ensured that each type of financial service business was regulated and overseen in relation to its nature and risks. This meant that financial firms could engage in different lines of business, even if they were cross-sectoral, as long as each financial activity they carried out was authorised. Further, the functional approach applied one consistent set of eligibility criteria to all businesses seeking authorisation. The functional approach is reflected in the case of *FSA v Anderson & Ors*,[36] discussed in Box 6.1.

The case in Box 6.1 showed that the FSA enjoyed a wide berth of powers over all forms of financial services that had the prescribed economic functions. Such powers were not sectorally limited. Financial service businesses traditionally found within a particular sector could be validly carried out by a non-traditional institution as long as

---

[32] E Wymeersch, 'The Structure of Financial Supervision in Europe: About Single, Twin Peaks and Multiple Financial Supervisors' at http://papers.ssrn.com/sol3/papers.cfm?abstract_id=946695; Joseph J Norton, 'Global Financial Sector Reform: The Single Financial Regulator Model Based on the United Kingdom FSA Experience – A Critical Reevaluation' (2005) 39 *International Lawyer* 15.

[33] Section 19, Financial Services and Markets Act 2000, and Schedule 2.

[34] To be of good repute and sufficient experience, in FSA Handbook (until 30 April 2013) COND module.

[35] Section 59, Financial Services and Markets Act 2000.   [36] (2010) EWHC 599 Ch.

> **Box 6.1 Case illustrating the application of the functional approach to regulation and supervision**
>
> The case of *FSA v Anderson & Ors*[37] illustrates very well the implications of the functional approach to authorisation. In that case, Anderson and Peacock (A&P) solicited among wealthy friends and contacts to place sums of money with them, which they then lent to businesses for a short term at a high interest rate. A&P's customers were promised an 8 per cent annual return with guaranteed return of their capital, while they lent to small businesses at a rate of 15–18 per cent annual percentage rate (APR). The difference between what A&P earned as interest from their borrowers and what they needed to repay their 'customers' was their profit. Although no fraud or scam was involved, the FSA took enforcement action to shut down A&P's scheme as an illegal unauthorised deposit-taking scheme. The FSA reasoned that the placement of money for the purposes of a safe and fixed return was equivalent to taking a deposit, and deposit-taking businesses had to be authorised. A&P did not obtain such authorisation but tried to argue unsuccessfully that their scheme was not commercial in nature. The court to which A&P referred the case (the role of the Upper Tribunal, discussed in section 6.3.4) agreed with the FSA.

the FSA authorised it. The functional approach broke new ground in regulatory policy as well as commercial opportunities for financial services.

6.1.3.3 Risk-based approach

As the FSA was managing multiple regulatory objectives, it became imperative to develop a systematic approach to allocating regulatory and supervisory resources in an appropriate manner. Since the early 2000s, the FSA adopted a risk-based approach to determining its regulatory priorities. This meant that the FSA would determine the level of risk posed by each regulated firm in order to decide on how intensively it would be supervised. This approach was also important in unifying the disparate supervisory approaches brought into the FSA by the different sectoral divisions at the start of the FSA's organisational life (referred to earlier). The FSA developed the ARROW (Advanced, Risk-Responsive Operating Framework) approach to supervise financial services firms under its supervision.[38]

In applying ARROW, the FSA considered the adverse possible scenarios that could be generated by each firm, and measured (a) the impact of each scenario multiplied by (b) the probability of the scenario occurring.[39] This methodology yielded for the FSA

---

[37] (2010) EWHC 599 Ch.

[38] Julia Black, 'The Development of Risk-based Regulation in Financial Services: Canada, the UK and Australia- a Research Report' (London: ECRC Centre for the Analysis of Risk and Regulation, LSE 2004) at https://www.lse.ac.uk/collections/law/staff%20publications%20full%20text/black/risk%20based%20regulation%20in%20financial%20services.pdf.

[39] See http://www.fsa.gov.uk/Pages/About/What/Approach/Assessment/index.shtml and https://www.superfinanciera.gov.co/SFCant/seminarios/RISK%20BASED%20REGULATION%20IN%20THE%20UK%20-%20FSA.ppt.

comparable risk profiles for each regulated firm. The FSA would adjust the risk profiles for each firm by considering their mitigating factors, such as the existence of firms' internal control systems (this is dealt with in detail in Chapter 12). The final adjusted score yielded for each firm provided the basis for the FSA's determination in terms of supervisory intensity with the oranisation. The FSA dedicated more supervisory resources to firms with high overall risk scores.

Black[40] had earlier warned that even though the risk-based approach in financial services regulation seemed popular and was adopted elsewhere, there remained dangers in trusting the framework too much. The determination of risk impact and probability need not be accurate, and the FSA tended to neglect low-probability risks, which could result in severe negative impact. These unfortunately materialised in the global financial crisis of 2007–9.[41]

The risk-based approach also meant that the FSA needed to engage closely with financial services firms to accurately evaluate their profile. The relational closeness between the FSA and the industry led to a return to informal forms of supervision, as the FSA refrained from scaling up supervisory actions unless necessary,[42] preferring to have dialogue with financial services firms on an informal basis in order to change behaviour. Such an approach was less threatening to the industry but contributed to the longer-term regulatory failure of the FSA, which came about in the wake of the global financial crisis.

6.1.3.4 Shortfalls of the Financial Services Authority

The major test for the FSA came about when Northern Rock approached the Bank of England for emergency lending facilities in September 2007, an episode discussed in greater detail in Chapter 13. Northern Rock was a significant deposit taker and mortgage lender in the UK but relied on an innovative form of financing that had a low probability risk of failing. However, severe negative impact would occasion if the risk materialised. Northern Rock, being a listed company, was required by listing regulation to publicly disclose that it had sought the Bank of England's lending facilities. Public confidence in the bank plummeted after the disclosure was made and queues of ordinary savers rushed to withdraw their deposits. The UK government subsequently guaranteed all deposits in Northern Rock in order to stem panic, and ultimately nationalised the bank in February 2008. The bank had essentially failed under the watch of the FSA.

The FSA's internal review[43] of its approach to Northern Rock in March 2008 revealed flaws in the application of ARROW, which eventually resulted in inadequate supervision

---

[40] Black, 'The Development of Risk-based Regulation in Financial Services'.

[41] Robert Baldwin and Julia Black, 'When Risk-Based Regulation Aims Low: Approaches and Challenges' (2012) 6 *Regulation and Governance* 2.

[42] Samuel McPhilemy, 'Formal Rules versus Informal Relationships: Prudential Banking Supervision at the FSA Before the Crash' (2013) 18 *New Political Economy* 748.

[43] FSA Internal Audit Division, *Northern Rock: A Lessons Learnt Review* (March 2008) at https://www.fca.org.uk/publication/corporate/fsa-nr-report.pdf.

of Northern Rock. Northern Rock's risks were assessed as 'low probability' although it was acknowledged that severe negative impact would ensue if they materialised. The supervisory team did not maintain complete records of Northern Rock's supervisory information, and also did not require risk mitigation by Northern Rock. There was a lack of ongoing review and this level of supervision was inadequate even according to the ARROW approach. Junior staff were assigned to supervise the bank and lacked experience in discerning signs of risk. As a result of the internal review, several senior resignations took place at the FSA, including Clive Briault formerly of the Bank of England. However, as the crises involving Halifax Bank of Scotland and Royal Bank of Scotland (RBS) started to unfold in October 2008 after the collapse of Lehman Brothers in the US (discussed in Chapter 1), Lord Adair Turner was appointed to become Chairman of the FSA and to investigate into the causes of the crises and the regulator's role.

The Turner Review

The Turner Review[44] identified important aspects of supervisory weaknesses at the FSA. The FSA's approach to supervision was described as 'light touch', an approach of restrained intervention. This was based on an erroneous belief that markets were self-correcting and that firms could be trusted with their internal systems and controls overseen at senior levels. The FSA had placed excessive faith in the regime for approving individuals in significant functions and became blinded from discerning firm-wide and sector-wide risks and problems. The deficient application of ARROW and inadequate supervisory findings of FSA staff were also not subject to adequate critical scrutiny by the FSA's senior management.[45] Further, *The Turner Review* also revealed that the FSA had systemically under-dedicated resources to supervising banks' capital levels. It had prioritised regulatory objectives of investor and consumer protection and focused much more on regulating firms' conduct vis-à-vis their customers. The FSA had not managed its multiple objectives well and the above-mentioned shortcomings were acknowledged by the FSA in its own internal reviews of regulatory failure after the failures of HBOS and RBS.[46]

Indeed, the FSA's excessive trust in the senior management and internal control at banks echoed the earlier days of the Bank of England's approach to BCCI. In hindsight, the FSA's internal reviews revealed the supervisory culture to be intensely flawed. Where HBOS was concerned, the FSA's ARROW assessment of HBOS was superficial, reflecting

---

[44] FSA, *The Turner Review: A Regulatory Response to the Global Banking Crisis* (March 2009) at http://www.fsa.gov.uk/pubs/other/turner_review.pdf.

[45] FCA and PRA, *A Report by the Financial Conduct Authority (FCA) and the Prudential Regulation Authority (PRA) on the Failure of HBOS Plc* (Nov 2015) 247ff at http://www.bankofengland.co.uk/pra/Documents/publications/reports/hbos.pdf.

[46] FCA and PRA, *A Report by the Financial Conduct Authority (FCA) and the Prudential Regulation Authority (PRA) on the Failure of HBOS Plc* (November 2015) 8, 33 at http://www.bankofengland.co.uk/pra/Documents/publications/reports/hbos.pdf for example; FSA Board Report, *The Failure of the Royal Bank of Scotland* (December 2011) 10, 11, and 254, at http://www.fsa.gov.uk/pubs/other/rbs.pdf.

excessive and misplaced trust in the bank's internal control (which, as Chapter 12 discusses, was extensively discredited after the crisis). Supervisory focus was instead placed on sales practices and conduct of business. Where RBS was concerned, a similar story emerged in the FSA's internal review. The FSA[47] realised that it had excessively trusted in bank senior management and internal control, and the supervisory team at the FSA lacked experience and resources to raise meaningful questions.

The criticisms against the FSA did not mean that the FSA had to be dismantled. Ferran argued powerfully[48] that the FSA had learnt plenty of lessons and it remained possible to address weaknesses, improve on the supervision of financial sector risks and bank capital, and ensure adequate attention to all of the FSA's objectives. However, in 2010 a Coalition government of the Conservative Party and Liberal Democrat Party was formed after an indecisive election result, and regime change became imminent for the FSA, which was regarded as an unsuccessful relic of the previous Labour government. It was opined[49] that the dismantling of the FSA was not necessarily efficient and was politically motivated.

The Coalition government, after consultation, determined to reform the financial services regulatory architecture to bring back the Bank of England as a dedicated regulator for the solvency of banks and insurers. The FSA's failure to carry out the regulatory objective of scrutinising bank capital levels and their risk-taking was seen as fatal to the single regulator concept that had attempted to bring too many regulatory objectives under one institution. The Bank of England was regarded as the more appropriate body to understand and monitor banks' risk-taking and the level of prudential supervision that was required. Other regulatory functions in relation to regulating the conduct of financial services firms, regulating financial markets, and making them competitive would be retained in what was left of the FSA, renamed as the Financial Conduct Authority (FCA). In 2012, the Financial Services Act 2012 was introduced to institute a new regulatory architecture. The Prudential Regulation Authority (PRA), a subsidiary of the Bank of England, would regulate and supervise some 2,000 banks, insurers, and investment firms that could cause significant impact to financial stability in the UK if they went insolvent. The FCA would focus on conduct and market regulation for all financial services, including the banks, insurers, and investment firms subject to the PRA's supervision.

Section 6.2 turns to the current regulatory architecture.

Key takeaways

- Banks enjoyed no formal system of regulation until 1979 after the occurrence of the secondary banking crisis.
- After the failure of Johnson Matthey Bank in 1984, the Banking Act 1987 extended formal bank regulation to all banks.

---

[47] Ibid, 257–92.

[48] Eilis Ferran, 'The Break-up of the Financial Services Authority' (2011) *Oxford Journal of Legal Studies* 455.

[49] Ibid.

- The Bank of England's regulatory role was non-interventionist and based on moral suasion. This proved inadequate in the wake of BCCI's failure in 1991.

- After the failure of Barings in 1995 and the election of a Labour government in 1997, reform was introduced in the financial services regulation architecture in the UK. The Bank of England lost its regulatory role and a new single regulator, the FSA, was instituted.

- The FSA was tasked with multiple regulatory objectives and determined a risk-based approach to allocating its resources.

- The single regulator approach in the FSA was unopposed but a number of commentators sounded caution as to the removal of bank supervision from the central bank to an entirely new body. The neglect of the synergies between central banking functions and bank regulation and supervision would prove to become a major problem in the global financial crisis of 2007–9.

- The FSA's risk-based approach was, however, poorly applied and it failed to monitor looming problems in a number of important UK banks. This culminated in the failure of Northern Rock and the near failure of HBOS and RBS in 2007–8.

- Although the FSA undertook extensive internal reviews and identified lessons learnt, a regime change in 2010 led to the dismantling of the FSA in April 2013.

Key bibliography

Legislation

The Financial Services and Markets Act 2000, amended by the Financial Services Act 2012

Official papers and reports

Bingham, T, 'Inquiry into the Supervision of the Bank of Credit and Commerce International' (1992) at https://www.gov.uk/government/uploads/system/uploads/attachment_data/file/235718/0198.pdf

FCA and PRA, *A Report by the Financial Conduct Authority (FCA) and the Prudential Regulation Authority (PRA) on the Failure of HBOS Plc* (Nov 2015) at http://www.bankofengland.co.uk/pra/Documents/publications/reports/hbos.pdf for example.

FSA, *The Turner Review: A Regulatory Response to the Global Banking Crisis* (March 2009) at http://www.fsa.gov.uk/pubs/other/turner_review.pdf.

FSA Board Report, *The Failure of the Royal Bank of Scotland* (Dec 2011) at http://www.fsa.gov.uk/pubs/other/rbs.pdf

FSA Internal Audit Division, *Northern Rock: A Lessons Learnt Review* (March 2008) at https://www.fca.org.uk/publication/corporate/fsa-nr-report.pdf.

Articles

Black, J, 'The Development of Risk-based Regulation in Financial Services: Canada, the UK and Australia- a Research Report' (London: ECRC Centre for the Analysis of Risk and Regulation, LSE 2004) at https://www.lse.ac.uk/collections/law/staff%20publications%20full%20text/black/risk%20based%20regulation%20in%20financial%20services.pdf

Ferran, E, 'The Break-up of the Financial Services Authority' (2011) 31 *Oxford Journal of Legal Studies* 455

Goodhart, CAE, 'The Organisational Structure of Banking Supervision' Financial Stability Institute
  Occasional Papers 2000
McGuire, K, 'Emergent Trends in Bank Supervision in the United Kingdom' (1993) 56 *Modern Law
  Review* 669

Books

Ferran, E and Goodhart, C (eds), *Regulating Financial Services and Markets in the Twenty First
  Century* (Oxford: Hart Publishing 2001)

6.2 The 'twin peaks' regulatory architecture

The regulatory architecture introduced in April 2013 to replace the FSA is characterised as 'twin peaks', that is, having two main agencies that are responsible for different
regulatory objectives. The PRA is responsible for 'prudential' objectives – that is, the
solvency and financial soundness of financial institutions – while the FCA is responsible for conduct of business and market regulation, including promoting competition.

This model is similar to the one adopted in Australia.[50] The UK model is not strictly
speaking, 'twin peaks'. The PRA is the body that authorises banks, insurers, and investment firms that are important to overall financial stability. The PRA supervises the
above firms in relation to the safety and soundness of their risk-taking and management, but the FCA continues to supervise the solvency requirements of smaller firms
that have little impact on financial stability, numbering about 18,500 in 2013. Hence,
only the supervision of significant banks, insurers, and investment firms have been
carved out to the PRA. This architecture benefits from clearly articulating the objectives that each regulator should be responsible for, avoiding the problem of flawed prioritisation carried out by the FSA. Ferran[51] queried if the reforms would lead to a loss
of economies of scale and a holistic view of the financial services sector. This has to an
extent been addressed by formal coordination mechanisms between the PRA and FCA
and other bodies, as will be discussed.

Figure 6.3 shows how the structure of regulation in financial services has changed
from the FSA to the 'twin peaks' architecture in 2013.

6.2.1 Prudential Regulation Authority

The PRA was established on 30 April 2013 by legislation in the Financial Services
Act 2012 that amended the Financial Services and Markets Act 2000.

---

[50] See Giorgio Di Giorgio and Carmine Di Noia, 'Financial Market Regulation and Supervision: How Many
Peaks for the Euro Area?' (2003) 28 *Brooklyn Journal of International Law* 463.
[51] Eilis Ferran, 'The Break-up of the Financial Services Authority' (2011) *Oxford Journal of Legal Studies* 455.

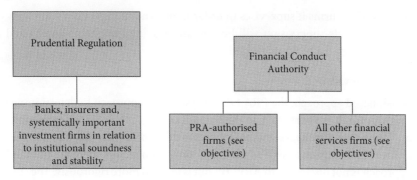

Figure 6.3 The regulatory architecture of the FSA in relation to financial services firms

6.2.1.1 Objectives and structure

The PRA has a strategic objective of contributing to the financial stability of the UK, with an operational objective of ensuring the safety and soundness of PRA-authorised persons.[52] The PRA was initially established as an independent subsidiary of the Bank of England. This was largely due to concerns that the Bank of England could become an extremely powerful body responsible for both financial and monetary stability. Further, the Bank had a poor track record of bank regulation and the PRA also represented a clean slate for commencing its responsibilities. By 2015 the PRA has gained credibility for its supervisory approach and it is now merged back into the Bank of England. The PRA is now the function of the Prudential Regulation Committee of the Bank of England.[53]

The Prudential Regulation Committee comprises of the Governor of the Bank of England, three Deputy Governors of the Bank of England (Financial Stability, Markets and Banking and Prudential Regulation), the Chief Executive of the FCA, a member appointed by the Governor approved by the Chancellor of the Exchequer, and at least six other members appointed by the Chancellor of the Exchequer. This composition[54] ensures that the PRA is provided with relevant insight by the FCA in relation to financial services markets as a whole. The high numbers of chancellors' appointees on the Committee is aimed at ensuring due accountability to the government.

6.2.1.2 Approach to regulation and supervision

The PRA now has a single objective to focus on the sound and safe risk management by the banks, insurers, and investment firms it supervises, in order to protect overall financial stability in the UK. The PRA's approach to banking supervision is set out to be risk-based and judgment-based.[55] The PRA employs a methodology to map the

---

[52] Sections 2B–2D, Financial Services and Markets Act 2000 as amended by the Financial Services Act 2012.
[53] Bank of England and Financial Services Act 2016 ss12–15.
[54] See s30A, Bank of England Act 1998 as amended by the Bank of England and Financial Services Act 2016.
[55] PRA, *Our Approach to Banking Supervision* (October 2012) at http://www.fsa.gov.uk/static/pubs/other/pra-approach-banking.pdf.

risk profiles of the firms it supervises in order to determine supervisory intensity and action. However, its supervision will be forward-looking (judgment-based) and not reactionary (which the FSA was alleged to be).

Risk-based supervision

On its risk-based approach, the PRA takes a systematic approach to determining each firm's risk profile. It purports to map the potential events of failures for each bank onto potential impact on financial stability. It then considers how external contextual factors would affect such impact, as well as what risk mitigation factors there are in each firm. This approach is not dissimilar to ARROW but is applied more rigorously. The supervisory intensity for each firm is determined according to its risk profile.

Judgment-based supervision

The PRA applies a judgment-based approach that is forward-looking in nature. This means that the PRA aims to identify, based on its risk assessments, vulnerabilities in firms with regard to their risks that may threaten their solvency. The PRA develops ongoing supervisory monitoring of firms with regard to those vulnerabilities, and also aims to take supervisory action at an early stage to reduce the probability of a firm's disorderly failure. Such an approach allows pro-active action to be taken at early signs of threats or vulnerabilities. This approach is most clearly seen in the PRA's supervisory actions taken against banks after unfavourable stress test results, discussed in Chapter 9.

Principles-based regulation

The PRA adopts a principles-based regulation regime,[56] which means that regulatory rules are built upon and fundamentally derived from broad principles. The meaning of 'principles-based' regulation has been subject to evolution and change from prior to the global financial crisis to post its aftermath. The principles-based regulatory regime has existed since the days of self-regulation in securities and investment markets (discussed in section 6.1). The trade bodies that have just been discussed applied bodies of principles to the members they oversaw. This regime was absorbed by the FSA. Despite the criticisms against the self-regulatory trade bodies outlined earlier, the FSA saw the adoption of the principles-based regulatory regime as able to provide both flexible and effective regulation.[57] Black et al.[58] explained that regulation by broadly-framed principles focusses on the 'outcomes' firms achieve and therefore allow them greater flexibility in complying with the 'spirit of the law'. This could promote an environment of mutually supporting and cooperative regulatory relationships between the FSA and regulated entities. Detailed and prescriptive rules could encourage creative and

---

[56] FSA, *Principles-Based Regulation: Focussing on the Outcomes that Matter* (April 2007) at http://www.fsa.gov.uk/pubs/other/principles.pdf.
[57] Julia Black, Martyn Hopper, and Christa Band, 'Making a Success of Principles-based Regulation' (2007) *Law and Financial Markets Review* 191.   [58] Ibid.

cosmetic compliance. Nevertheless, principles-based regulation could lack clarity for firms and compliance may then not be robust. After the onset of the global financial crisis, the question was raised as to whether principles-based regulation had failed.[59]

For principles-based regulation to succeed, it cannot descend into 'lax regulation'. Its substitution for detailed rules may be its fatal flaw when regulated entities interpret the lack of detailed rules in their favour. Hence, as Black argues,[60] principles-based regulation may only be successful if paradoxically flanked by sufficient specific rules that provide guidance to the regulated. Further, the regulated entities must already be strong and robust in their compliance and can be trusted.

In post-crisis reforms, principles-based regulation is retained but, instead of substituting for detailed rules, it now underpins and supports detailed and prescriptive regulation, and is used to fill in gaps where no detailed rules may exist. Principles-based regulation has evolved into a broader net of regulatory discretion instead of the 'simple and flexible rulebook' from the days of old. The PRA now carries on principles-based regulation by instituting a set of broadly-framed principles called 'Fundamental Rules' for its regulated firms, while the FCA provides the Principles of FCA Regulation.

This regime now allows the PRA not only to implement and enforce against specific breaches of regulatory rules but, in cases where there may be a gap in specific regulatory rules, a principle can be applied to determine if bank conduct has fallen below the standard in the principle.[61] In this manner, the regulator is not hamstrung in being able to discipline the firms subject to its supervision. There are eight Fundamental Rules as set out in Table 6.1.

We now turn to the other regulatory bodies and the PRA's relationship with them.

6.2.2 Other institutions in the regulatory architecture

The PRA works alongside a number of other bodies in the regulatory architecture, notably the FCA and the Financial Policy Committee of the Bank of England, which has been empowered with specific statutory responsibilities.

6.2.2.1 Financial Conduct Authority

The FCA has the strategic objective of protecting and enhancing confidence in the UK's financial system, and its operational objectives are consumer protection, protecting the

[59] Hector Sants, the chief executive of the FSA during the crisis stated that 'the limitations of a pure principles-based regime have to be recognised. I continue to believe the majority of market participants are decent people; however, a principles-based approach does not work with individuals who have no principles'. The lack of detail and rules in principles-based regulation may be crucially taken advantage of by those who wish to avoid regulation, and the need for support from more prescriptive rules and clearer articulation of the regulator's expectations is highlighted.

[60] Julia Black, 'Forms and Paradoxes of Principles-Based Regulation' (2012) 75 *Modern Law Review* 1037.

[61] *R (British Bankers Association) v FSA and others* [2011] EWHC 999 held that the principles instituted by the FSA constituted the basis for more detailed rules and can themselves form the basis of enforcement.

Table 6.1 Fudamental rules

A firm must conduct its business with integrity.
A firm must conduct its business with due skill, care and diligence.
A firm must act in a prudent manner.
A firm must at all times maintain adequate financial resources.
A firm must have effective risk strategies and risk management systems.
A firm must organise and control its affairs responsibly and effectively.
A firm must deal with its regulators in an open and cooperative way and must disclose to the PRA appropriately anything relating to the firm of which the PRA would reasonably expect notice.
A firm must prepare for resolution so, if the need arises, it can be resolved in an orderly manner with a minimum disruption of critical services.

integrity of the UK's financial markets, and promoting competition in financial markets.[62] This remit is similar to much of what the FSA had focused upon.

The FCA has supervisory remit over PRA-authorised firms in relation to their conduct visàvis customers and in marketplaces. The FCA's regulatory regime is based on 11 high-level principles and specific conduct regulation that largely originates from EU investment firm regulation. Such investment firm regulation deals with a range of investment conduct such as brokerage, underwriting, investment advice, and portfolio management. These business lines are not covered specifically in this book, but are discussed generally as an indication of the changing nature of banking business to a more universalist or 'financial supermarket' model, as discussed in Chapter 1. The 11 principles of regulation are set out in Table 6.2 and show that the FCA deals with banks' conduct where they interface with customers and markets in relation to investment-type business lines.

Besides, the FCA is the enforcement authority for banks if they engage in customer-facing or market misconduct. For example, between 2012 and 2017, evidence of banks manipulating an interest rate benchmark began to emerge. The London Interbank Offered Rate (LIBOR) is a benchmark that is used to price financial contracts with variable interest rates. For example, if a homeowner took out a mortgage tied to a variable interest rate, that could be tied to LIBOR, which changes on a daily basis. LIBOR is determined by a panel of UK banks submitting the notional interest rate they would charge other banks that were to borrow from them. The panel's submissions are aggregated according a best practice maintained by the British Bankers' Association in order to produce the daily LIBOR. However, submitting banks started to manipulate their submissions according to their trading interests and exposures in financial contracts, so as to influence the ultimate LIBOR rate of the day. This systematic malpractice came

---

[62] Sections 1B–1E, Financial Services and Markets Act 2000 amended by the Financial Services Act 2012.

to light in an international effort to enforce against benchmark manipulation, including the US, European, and UK authorities. The FCA, based on the banks' breach of principle 5 in Table 6.2, fined a large number of banks significant sums in order to deter future conduct. Affected banks include Barclays, Lloyd's, RBS, HSBC, UBS, Deutsche Bank, JP Morgan, Citibank, and Rabobank,[63] and individuals were also prosecuted where personal responsibility could be found. Tom Hayes,[64] former trader at UBS and Citigroup was sentenced to imprisonment and fined, while many other individuals were fined.

The FCA's enforcement powers can also be exercised in the form of ordering a 'consumer redress scheme' to be set up.[65] A consumer redress schemes may be ordered to

Table 6.2 Principles of FCA regulation, FCA Handbook PRIN 2.1

1 Integrity	A firm must conduct its business with integrity.
2 Skill, care and diligence	A firm must conduct its business with due skill, care and diligence.
3 Management and control	A firm must take reasonable care to organise and control its affairs responsibly and effectively, with adequate risk management systems.
4 Financial prudence	A firm must maintain adequate financial resources.
5 Market conduct	A firm must observe proper standards of market conduct.
6 Customers' interests	A firm must pay due regard to the interests of its customers and treat them fairly.
7 Communications with clients	A firm must pay due regard to the information needs of its clients, and communicate information to them in a way which is clear, fair and not misleading.
8 Conflicts of interest	A firm must manage conflicts of interest fairly, both between itself and its customers and between a customer and another client.
9 Customers: relationships of trust	A firm must take reasonable care to ensure the suitability of its advice and discretionary decisions for any customer who is entitled to rely upon its judgment.
10 Clients' assets	A firm must arrange adequate protection for clients' assets when it is responsible for them.
11 Relations with regulators	A firm must deal with its regulators in an open and cooperative way, and must disclose to the FCA appropriately anything relating to the firm of which that regulator would reasonably expect notice.

---

[63] A consolidated view of benchmark manipulation enforcement is at https://www.fca.org.uk/markets/benchmarks/enforcement.

[64] 'Tom Hayes and how he was caught in the Libor web', *Financial Times* (4 April 2017).

[65] Sections 404 and 404A, Financial Services and Markets Act 2000.

be set up by the FCA in respect of any authorised firm, if there is a widespread and regular failure in compliance. Such a redress scheme would be a means of forcing firms to compensate their customers without having adjudicated the issue. The safeguard for the exercise of the FCA's power in this regard is mandatory consultation with the industry and stakeholders prior to establishing the scheme. Firms will be required to investigate complaints, contact customers individually, publicise the scheme to customers and provide concrete remedies and redress for customers. The FCA will specify a start and end date for the operation of the scheme. Examples of two such schemes are in Box 6.2.

The FCA has the remit of overseeing financial conduct generally, and it also administers a large structure of offices that fulfil different specific roles in consumer protection and promoting competition.

Financial Ombudsman Service

First, the FCA administers the independent office of the Financial Ombudsman Service. The Financial Ombudsman Service is a mechanism for consumer redress against financial services providers, for amounts less than £150,000. If a consumer seeks the jurisdiction of the Ombudsman to resolve a dispute with a financial services firm, the Ombudsman has 'compulsory jurisdiction' over the firm if the firm is an authorised

---

Box 6.2 Consumer redress schemes

Credit Card Protection Redress Scheme 2013

A number of banks, in selling credit card products to consumers, mis-sold them an add-on product of identity protection or card protection insurance. The insurance product was meant to protect consumers against theft of their card information and unauthorised use of their credit cards. However, consumers are already protected under the law for unauthorised use of their cards and they would not be liable for such use (see Chapter 3, section 3.3.7). Customers were given misleading and unclear information about the policies so that they either bought cover that was not needed or to cover risks that had been greatly exaggerated. The FCA included 13 banks in the scheme to provide compensation for affected customers.

Arch Cru Consumer Redress Scheme 2014

Arch Financial LLP was an investment management firm that managed two UK funds and 22 Guernsey-based companies in which the two UK funds invest. The funds' investments were made in highly risky and concentrated areas, such as in private companies and in companies in which the founder of the investment firm had interests. The funds were mis-sold to investors by a number of financial advisers as being well diversified and balanced in risks, a misleading picture from the true nature of their investments. In the FCA's words, 'Arch cru funds were high-risk products that typically invested in non-mainstream assets such as private equity and private finance. Advisers should only have recommended the funds to investors who fully understood – and were willing to accept – the risks.' The financial advisers involved were enrolled into the scheme and paid out over £30 million in compensation to investors by 2014.

person by the PRA or FCA,[66] or a payment or electronic money services or consumer credit provider overseen by the FCA or any other organisation under the FCA's umbrella (this will be discussed further; see also Figure 6.3). This means that the firm must subject itself to the Ombudsman's jurisdiction if the consumer seeks to resolve the dispute in this manner. Although the Ombudsman is overseen by the FCA, it is also useful for customers of PRA-regulated persons, and forms part of the dual-supervision framework that is in place for PRA-regulated persons. The FCA looks to extending the Ombudsman Service to small businesses too.[67] This is in light of the revelations of bank mis-selling of complex interest-rate hedging products to small businesses who have loan facilities from banks.[68] The extension of the Ombudsman Service to such businesses would help them achieve dispute resolution without needing to face the high costs of accessing the courts for justice.

The Ombudsman is established as a separate body corporate, but the FCA appoints its Board and Chairman. The ombudsmen themselves are appointed by the office of the Ombudsman. The Ombudsman has its own separate budget, procedure, rules, and fees, and reports annually to the FCA. The Ombudsman is able to provide a cost-effective service for dispute resolution as dispute resolution does not involve formal legal processes. There is usually no physical hearing or representation required, and ombudsmen can make decisions based on standards of fairness and reasonableness that are not legal norms. The ombudsmen are free to apply legal principles too, and even such application is subject only to fairness and reasonableness notions and not to any substantive legal framework. In the case of *R. (on the application of IFG Financial Services Ltd) v Financial Ombudsman Service Ltd*,[69] the ombudsman had applied a substantive principle in contract law to determine the dispute but did not apply the legal rules with regard to award of damages. The decision was challenged in judicial review (see the discussion in section 6.3), but the court held that such apparent 'inconsistency' is acceptable as the Ombudsman was not bound to apply any principles of law anyway.

Ombudsmen's decisions are subject to judicial review if errors were made or where unfairness or unreasonableness was alleged. In *The Queen on the Application of Kenneth Green (Trading as Green Denman & Co.) v Financial Ombudsman Service Ltd*[70] a couple were mis-sold a personal pension product and the wife therefore missed out on taking out her employer's pension scheme, which could have benefited the couple more. The ombudsman found for the couple and made an error in quantifying the benefit the couple should have enjoyed if not mis-sold. On judicial review, the error was held to be

---

[66] Section 226 and 226A, Financial Services and Markets Act 2000.

[67] Defined as 'businesses with fewer than 50 employees, annual turnover below £6.5 million and an annual balance sheet (i.e. gross assets) below £5 million'. FCA, *Consultation on SME access to the Financial Ombudsman Service and Feedback to DP15/7: SMEs as Users of Financial Services* (22 January 2018).

[68] See https://www.fca.org.uk/consumers/interest-rate-hedging-products, which sets out the FCA's review of these sales and findings that resulted in a voluntary agreement between certain banks and the FCA to review their sales and address customers' grievances if mis-selling had occurred.

[69] [2005] EWHC 1153.   [70] [2003] EWHC 338.

immaterial. In *Financial Ombudsman Service v Heather Moor & Edgecomb Limited,*[71] the ombudsman found in favour for the consumer complainant but levied a £1,000 case fee on the successful party. The consumer challenged the case fee decision in judicial review and succeeded.

The Ombudsman Service is an extremely useful dispute resolution mechanism for financial consumers in relatively small sums. A question that could arise is whether a consumer could use the Ombudsman Service to gain compensation up to £150,000 and therefore have tested the strength of his or her claim before suing for any sums above £150,000 in a civil court. In *Clark v In Focus Asset Management & Tax Solutions Lt,* the first instance court initially held that this was possible. The Court of Appeal overturned the decision and held that if a consumer had chosen to pursue dispute resolution before the Ombudsman, then *res judicata* applies upon obtaining the resolution.[72] A consumer cannot bring the same legal claim over in the civil court even if the damages pursued are in excess of the £150,000 limit that the Ombudsman can award. It may be argued that *res judicata* should not apply as the Ombudsman is not a formal tribunal as such and consumers who choose subsequently to sue in a civil court would be applying legal principles and arguments for the first time. Financial consumers should therefore weigh their options carefully in pursuing dispute resolution.

An alternative proposal has been made by Samuel[73] in relation to the establishment of a financial services tribunal. This would be a different tribunal from the Upper Tribunal (in section 6.3). Samuel argues that between the Ombudsman Service and the point where it would be economical to launch a civil claim (where compensation sought is significant and usually in millions of pounds), there is no middle ground. Some consumers and small and medium-sized enterprises (SMEs) have claims that exceed £150,000 but it would not be economical to launch a civil suit. For example, in a number of cases that affected SMEs against interest rate swaps mis-sold to them by banks, the compensation claimed could exceed £150,000. These usually involved SMEs that had a loan facility with a bank that involved a variable interest rate. The bank had then suggested that the businesses could take out an interest rate swap that meant 'exchanging' the variable interest rate for a fixed interest rate, therefore minimising uncertainty of interest rate changes to the claimant. The swap contained exorbitant cancellation fees and in effect locked the businesses into the arrangement. After the global financial crisis of 2007–9, the Bank of England revised interest rates to historic lows and so businesses paying on their swapped fixed interest rates were paying much more for their loans than necessary. Yet they could not terminate the arrangements as cancellation fees were significant. Although the FCA entered into agreements with nine banks to compel them

---

[71] [2008] EWCA Civ 643.

[72] This means that the issue has been decided in a competent forum of dispute resolution and must not be opened by the same parties.

[73] Richard Samuel, 'Tools for Changing the Banking Culture: FCA Are You Listening?' (2016) 11(2) *Capital Markets Law Journal* 129–44; 'Tools for Culture Change: FCA Now You Are Listening!' (2016) 12(3) *Capital Markets Law Journal* at https://doi.org/10.1093/cmlj/kmw029.

to review if they have mis-sold the instruments and to make appropriate compensation to their customers,[74] these cases would have fallen into the middle ground between the Ombudsman's limits and commencing civil proceedings. Further, in *MTR Bailey Trading Ltd v Barclays*,[75] the claimant was a small private company and was held not to have standing to sue the bank, as suits against financial services providers based on breaches of regulatory duties to customers can only be mounted by 'private persons', that is, private individuals.[76] Samuel argues that there is a need for a tribunal that would be less formal and cost-effective, like the Employment Services Tribunal that could take on civil cases in smaller amounts in excess of the Ombudsman's limit.

Consumer education

The FCA also maintains the consumer financial education body, which is called the Money Advice Service on the www.moneyadviceservice.org website for general information that may be helpful for financial consumers.[77] Being responsible for protecting financial consumers, the FCA is to engage with other consumer protection bodies such as Which and is responsible for investigating complaints brought by such bodies on behalf of consumers.[78]

Financial Services Compensation Scheme

The FCA is responsible for the Financial Services Compensation Scheme, a guarantee scheme that compensates financial services retail customers for losses up to certain prescribed amounts if their deposit-taking firm, insurer, or investment services firm becomes insolvent. The deposit guarantee scheme is seen as an important pillar for depositor protection as well as financial stability, as deposit guarantee is regarded as having an effect of preventing bank runs, which can be very damaging for market confidence and financial stability. The deposit guarantee scheme is discussed in greater detail in Chapter 13 (section 13.3) in terms of the role it plays to support financial stability in the UK. In brief, depositors are protected up to £85,000 per institution. Where investors have placed money with investment firms, and such firms become insolvent, investors are protected under the Compensation Scheme for up to £50,000 per investor/firm.

The FCA administers the independent Payment Services Regulator, which protects consumer interests in using payment services offered by banks and non-bank financial institutions. It ensures compliance by payment services firms with the relevant regulations, an area discussed in Chapter 3.

---

[74] https://www.fca.org.uk/consumers/interest-rate-hedging-products.

[75] [2015] EWCA Civ 667.

[76] Section s138D, Financial Services and Markets Act 2000.

[77] The independence of the Money Advice Service was established in agreement with the Treasury but the FCA retains residual oversight to ensure that the Service is able to perform the statutory responsibilities envisaged. See 'Money Advice Service, Financial Conduct Authority and HM Treasury Framework Document' at https://www.fca.org.uk/publication/mou/mas-fca-hmt-framework-document.pdf.

[78] Section 234B–D, Financial Services and Markets Act 2000 amended by the Financial Services Act 2012.

Listing authority

In terms of maintaining market integrity, the FCA is the UK Listing Authority for rule-setting and enforcing discipline for listed companies on the London Stock Exchange. The FCA also ensures that financial markets are free from abusive practices and enforces against market abuse by imposing fines and penalties. The FCA also works with the Crown Prosecutions Service if such cases are criminally prosecuted. The FCA supervises financial services firms in terms of their anti-money laundering obligations (discussed in Chapter 14) and works with the National Crime Agency if criminal liability is to be implicated. Finally, the FCA, in administering its competition promotion objective, is now responsible for investigating into competition issues across the wholesale and retail financial sectors, taking over the relevant functions from the Office of Fair Trading.

Figure 6.4 illustrates the FCA's internal structure for its objectives of consumer protection, maintaining market confidence, and promoting competition.

The PRA maintains a close relationship with the FCA, as PRA-regulated firms are also regulated and supervised by the FCA. The regulators' responsibilities may be more effectively discharged if they coordinate in important areas such as ensuring that no information gaps exist. Further, the exercise of either regulator's powers may have implications for the other's regulatory relationship with the firm concerned. We turn to discuss the formal coordination mechanisms between the PRA and FCA shortly.

6.2.2.2 Financial Policy Committee

Despite the FSA being a single regulator for financial services in the UK, it took an approach focusing on individual regulated firms and failed to piece together a picture of overall market risks and vulnerabilities. A key reform made after the crisis is the introduction of a body with responsibility for monitoring risks in the financial systems

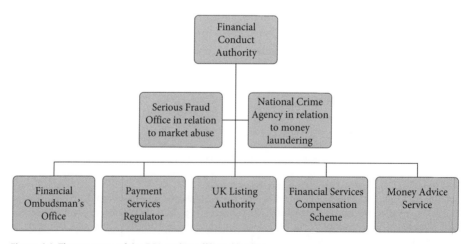

Figure 6.4 The structure of the FCA and its affiliated bodies

and markets as a whole. Such a body is to recommend pre-emptive action if necessary. In the UK, the Financial Policy Committee,[79] which is a Committee of the Court of Directors of the Bank of England, is created for this purpose. This role is to be known as macro-prudential supervision, discussed in greater detail in section 6.4.

The Financial Policy Committee's membership comprises of the Governor of the Bank of England, the Banks' four Deputy Governors (for financial stability, prudential regulation, markets and banking and monetary policy), the Chief Executive of the FCA, one person appointed by the Governor after consultation with the Chancellor of the Exchequer, one person representing the Treasury, and four other persons appointed by the Chancellor of the Exchequer. The Committee's composition reflects the need for all relevant financial regulators and policy officials to be able to participate in the macro-prudential supervision process.

The objective of the Financial Policy Committee is to protect financial stability in the UK by monitoring the development of systemic risks. Systemic risks are defined as including (a) risks attributable to structural features of financial markets, such as connections between financial institutions, (b) risks attributable to the distribution, such as whether there are concentrations of risk within the financial sector, and (c) unsustainable levels of debt, such as borrowing by households or businesses.[80] The responsibilities and powers of the Committee are elaborated upon in section 6.4.

6.2.2.3 Bank of England

The Bank of England houses the PRA as one of its committees, but the PRA performs its tasks independently of the Bank. The Bank is, however, designated the resolution authority in the UK, not the PRA. This relates to the responsibility for carrying out intervention in a bank under conditions of crisis (discussed in Chapter 13). The Financial Services Act 2012 explicitly empowers the Bank of England and Treasury to work together in order to resolve financial crises in the UK.[81]

The Bank is established as an independent body of the government and is principally accountable to its Court of Directors.[82] Its Court of Directors comprises of the Governor of the Bank, all its Deputy Directors, and nine directors appointed by the Queen. These directors are to be non-executive and ensure adequate monitoring and accountability by the executive directors in the Court. Other than its accountability to the Court of Directors, the Bank is essentially protected from outside and governmental interference. This is in order to safeguard its independence in its important function in relation to monetary policy (which is chiefly performed by the Bank's Monetary Policy Committee). As the Bank has in essence assumed more responsibilities after the

---

[79] Section 9A–V, Bank of England Act 1998 as amended by the Financial Services Act 2012.
[80] Section 9C, Bank of England Act 1998 as amended by the Financial Services Act 2012.
[81] Section 58, Financial Services Act 2012.
[82] Sections 1–2 of the Bank of England Act 1998 and amendments by the Financial Services Act 2012 and Bank of England and Financial Services Act 2016.

global financial crisis, shifts have been made in its accountability structures, such as the composition of the Prudential Regulation Committee, which is the PRA and the Financial Policy Committee discussed earlier.

6.2.2.4 Mandatory coordination mechanisms

Statutory-backed formal coordination mechanisms for the PRA and FCA are now in place, perhaps to allay fears that the breaking up of the FSA would result in loss in information and supervisory coordination. The development of formal coordination mechanisms could also in part be due to the failure of the Tripartite arrangement between the FSA, Bank of England, and Treasury earlier discussed. The Tripartite arrangement focused on clarifying the boundaries of responsibility for the three bodies and lacked provision for their coordination. This resulted in an absence of information sharing and pro-active conversation among the three bodies. This also explained why when Northern Rock sought emergency liquidity facilities from the Bank of England response was slow and policymakers were unsure of leadership in the situation. The Bank of England did not have the benefit of supervisory information relevant to Northern Rock, while the Treasury was brought in at a late stage when Northern Rock's woes had been publicised over the media. Hence, the lessons learnt influenced the new framework for coordination, which involves the PRA's and FCA's formal coordination on an ongoing basis and the establishment of a crisis management group between the Bank of England and Treasury to provide leadership in times of crises.

The PRA's and FCA's coordination mechanisms

The PRA and FCA are mandated to coordinate with each other in specified circumstances. Further, they have entered into a formal Memorandum of Understanding (which is renewable) in order to facilitate their coordination.

The PRA and FCA must coordinate with each other in areas of common regulatory interest, to share information relevant to their expertise and to prevent material adverse impact upon each other in the pursuit of their respective regulatory objectives.[83] First, the PRA must consult the FCA before giving permission to any person to be authorised to carry out financial services provision under its remit. This is because all firms are subject to the FCA's supervision too.[84] The FCA must also consult the PRA before authorising any applicant who may be a member of a group authorised by the PRA.[85] The PRA and FCA must also consult each other where there is variation or cancellation of authorisation, unless the authorised person concerned is an FCA-regulated only entity.[86] The need to coordinate between the regulators for authorisation, variation, or cancellation of authorisation allows

---

[83] Section 3D, Financial Services and Markets Act 2000 amended by the Financial Services Act 2012.

[84] Section 55F, Financial Services and Markets Act 2000 amended by the Financial Services Act 2012.

[85] Section 55E, Financial Services and Markets Act 2000 amended by the Financial Services Act 2012.

[86] Sections 55H, 55I, and 55J, Financial Services and Markets Act 2000 amended by the Financial Services Act 2012.

information sharing on the suitability of persons authorised to carry on financial services business, and can assist in more informed decisions by either regulator.

Next, the PRA and FCA need to consult each other before making rules for which they are empowered. Such consultation must take place in relatively early stages before a formal draft of rules is published for public consultation.[87] The authorities are, however, exempted from the need for consultation if the making of new rules may be unduly delayed and adversely impacts on either authority's statutory objectives (i.e. prejudicial to consumers in the case of the FCA, or prejudicial to the safety and soundness of PRA-regulated entities). The PRA and FCA must also consult each other before the acquisition of any authorised person.[88] The PRA and FCA are able to formally agree to provide services to each other.[89]

The PRA and FCA are to work together in consolidated supervision of financial groups and may direct each other to carry out appropriate actions or powers in accordance with the other's scope of powers.[90]

In extraordinary cases, the PRA may intervene in the FCA's enforcement decisions. This is because the FCA has the wider enforcement remit of the two authorities over financial services firms authorised in the UK. The PRA may direct that the FCA refrains from taking enforcement action against a PRA-regulated entity if such an enforcement action may threaten the financial stability of the UK or result in the failure of a PRA-regulated entity in such a way that threatens UK financial stability. The FCA would have to comply with the request unless it is incompatible with an international obligation.[91]

The above-mentioned framework provides clarity and specificity in key moments that require the authorities' coordination. The authorities have also entered into a formal Memorandum of Understanding to provide for further details of coordination[92] and to review the Memorandum each calendar year. The first Memorandum set out the authorities' commitment to share information regularly and enter into early consultations with each other. It also set out a dispute resolution process between the authorities, to resolve conflicts at the highest management levels. This Memorandum has worked well in the first two years and has been amended in 2015 to include the new Payment Services Regulator (discussed in Chapter 3) within the coordination and consultation framework.

Other coordination mechanisms

Formal coordination mechanisms have also been set up involving the Bank of England and Treasury, relating to recovery and resolution planning and crisis management

---

[87] Sections 138I and 138J, Financial Services and Markets Act 2000 amended by the Financial Services Act 2012.

[88] Sections 187A and 187B, Financial Services and Markets Act 2000 amended by the Financial Services Act 2012.

[89] Section 3R, Financial Services and Markets Act 2000 amended by the Financial Services Act 2012.

[90] Section 3M, Financial Services and Markets Act 2000 amended by the Financial Services Act 2012.

[91] Section 3I, Financial Services and Markets Act 2000 amended by the Financial Services Act 2012.

[92] Section 3E, Financial Services and Markets Act 2000 amended by the Financial Services Act 2012.

(discussed in Chapter 13). In brief, although the PRA makes rules on recovery and resolution planning, it must consult the Bank of England (as resolution authority) and the Treasury.[93] Further, if there is a crisis where the Deposit Guarantee Scheme may be called upon or recourse to the Treasury is envisaged, the Bank of England must inform the Treasury without undue delay.[94] The Bank of England, PRA, and Treasury are to put in place a memorandum generally with regard to how they would manage financial crises, and coordinate with third-country regulators.[95]

> ### ⮕ Key takeaways
>
> - The regulatory architecture established after the dismantling of the FSA comprises a number of regulatory bodies with statutorily specified functions.
>
> - The PRA authorises and supervises institutions that may have an impact on the UK's financial stability. It has the operational objective to ensure the safety and soundness of PRA-regulated institutions.
>
> - The FCA is responsible for authorising all other financial services firms. It continues to carry on the remainder of the FSA's objectives in relation to conduct of business, market supervision, and promoting competition. It supervises all PRA-authorised firms in relation to those objectives.
>
> - The Financial Policy Committee under the Bank of England is established for the purposes of macro-prudential supervision (see section 6.4).
>
> - The PRA, initially a subsidiary of the Bank of England, merged back into the Bank in 2016 and is administered by its Prudential Regulation Committee.
>
> - The PRA and FCA are compelled to coordinate with each other in defined ways under legislation and to adopt a formal memorandum of understanding that governs their coordination.
>
> - Other formal mechanisms involving the Bank of England, PRA, and Treasury have been put in place for crisis management, in order to avoid the problems posed by the failed tripartite memorandum of arrangement that existed between the FSA, Treasury, and Bank of England.

Key bibliography

Legislation

Financial Services Act 2012

Official Papers and Reports

PRA, *Our Approach to Banking Supervision* (Oct 2012) at http://www.fsa.gov.uk/static/pubs/other/pra-approach-banking.pdf

---

[93] Sections 137J and 137K, Financial Services and Markets Act 2000 amended by the Financial Services Act 2012.

[94] Section 58, Financial Services and Markets Act 2000 amended by the Financial Services Act 2012.

[95] Sections 65 and 66, Financial Services Act 2012.

Articles

Killick, M, '"Twin Peaks" – A New Series or a New Chimera? An Analysis of the Proposed New Regulatory Structure in the UK' (2012) 33 *Company Lawyer* 366

6.3 Power and accountability of the regulators

The PRA and FCA enjoy a wide berth of rule-making and enforcement powers, much of which has been conferred earlier upon the FSA. We provide an overview below. This section then discusses the accountability regime for the regulators.

6.3.1 Rule-making and enforcement powers

The PRA is expressly conferred rule-making powers pursuant to its objectives. Its rules relate to conditions for authorisation, including the scope of activities for incoming foreign branches.[96] The **PRA Rulebook** provides for micro-prudential regulation rules (see Chapters 8 and 9), rules for corporate governance and internal control of banks (Chapter 12), remuneration rules for bank personnel[97] (Chapter 12), and individual responsibilities and liability (Chapter 11).[98] The **Rulebook** also provides for rules relating to crisis avoidance, such as recovery and resolution planning rules (Chapter 13).[99]

The PRA has powers to require regulated firms to produce information,[100] even confidential information relevant to the needs for financial stability.[101] The PRA can appoint investigators to assume its investigative powers, including entry into premises for seizure of documents under a justice of the peace's warrant.[102] The PRA may also appoint a skilled person to make a report to the PRA.[103] The skilled person is usually an expert such as an auditor who can carry out technical investigations in order to provide information to the PRA. Such a skilled person has statutory backing to require all reasonable assistance from the regulated firm. Skilled person reports usually provide the first substantive insights of issues that require supervisory actions or even enforcement decisions by the PRA.

---

[96] Section 137G, Financial Services and Markets Act 2000 amended by the Financial Services Act 2012.

[97] Section 137H, Financial Services and Markets Act 2000 amended by the Financial Services Act 2012.

[98] PRA Rulebook generally at http://www.prarulebook.co.uk/.

[99] Sections 137J–N, Financial Services and Markets Act 2000 amended by the Financial Services Act 2012.

[100] Section 165, Financial Services and Markets Act 2000.

[101] Such as information pertaining to financial instruments ownership or the management of or provision of services to investment funds, Section 165A, Financial Services and Markets Act 2000 amended by the Financial Services Act 2012.

[102] Sections 168 and 170–6, Financial Services and Markets Act 2000.

[103] Section 166, Financial Services and Markets Act 2000.

The PRA has extensive enforcement powers, from public censure to financial penalties (unlimited). It can also restrict or suspend an authorised person's scope of activities.[104] There is a prescribed procedure for enforcement decisions to be addressed. A warning notice is first sent to the firm before formal enforcement is taken by way of a decision notice.[105] Approved individuals may also be subject to withdrawal of approval[106] and prohibition orders with regard to future involvement in financial services activities.[107]

As the PRA performs the functions of both police and judge vis-à-vis regulated firms, its powers are subject to judicial scrutiny. In addition, its rule-making and policy-making powers are also subject to certain checks and balances. We now turn to the accountability regimes for the PRA.

6.3.2 Accountability relationships with government and parliament

The Bank of England's functions are exercised by its Court of Directors, which comprise the Governor, all its Deputy Governors, and not more than nine non-executive directors appointed by the Queen on the government's recommendation. There used to be an oversight committee on the Court that is responsible for calling to account the exercise of powers and functions by the executive members of the Court. This was abolished in 2016 after the PRA merged back into the Bank. The oversight functions are now part of the Court's functions as a whole. In particular, the non-executive directors are empowered to arrange for reviews to be conducted of the exercise of functions or power by any person tasked by any of the directors. The findings of such reviews are to be reported to the Court.[108]

The PRA is itself subject to government input and accountability. The Treasury is able to write to the PRA with recommendations as to how the PRA's objectives should be advanced in light of economic policy. This must be done at least once in each parliament, laid before parliament and publicly published.[109] As discussed earlier, the Chancellor is able to appoint six representatives to the Prudential Regulation Committee, and also has the power to approve of a Governor-appointed representative to the Committee. This ensures that the Chancellor has some influence over the appointment of seven persons out of the 12-strong Committee, providing a form of check and balance in terms of policymaking at the PRA. The Chancellor and the Governor must also meet twice a year for high-level policy discussions.[110]

---

[104] Sections 205–6A, Financial Services and Markets Act 2000.
[105] Sections 207–9, Financial Services and Markets Act 2000.
[106] Section 63, Financial Services and Markets Act 2000.
[107] Section 56, Financial Services and Markets Act 2000.
[108] Section 2, Bank of England Act 1998 amended by the Financial Services Act 2012 and the Bank of England and Financial Services Act 2016.
[109] Section 30A, Financial Services and Markets Act 2000 amended by the Bank of England and Financial Services Act 2016.
[110] Section 9X, Financial Services and Markets Act 2000 amended by the Financial Services Act 2012.

6.3.2.1 **Efficiency review**

The PRA's and the Bank's use of resources may be subject to audit in order to determine if resources have been used efficiently. The Bank maintains a memorandum of understanding with the Comptroller and Auditor-General in relation to achieving efficient use of resources.[111] The PRA can be specifically subject to independent reviews commissioned by the Treasury regarding the use of its resources.[112] These powers ensure that although independent, the Bank and PRA remain accountable and transparent as to their use of resources, and can be subject to scrutiny in relation to the achievement of their objectives.

6.3.2.2 **Independent inquiries**

The Treasury has the power to order inquiries and investigations into the PRA or FCA. The Treasury has the power to do so under one or more of the following three situations:

(a) Events in relation to a ***collective investment scheme***[113] that pose threats to the UK's financial stability or significant damage to consumers' interests.

(b) Events in relation to a listed company that pose threats to the UK's financial stability or significant damage to consumers' interests.

(c) Events in relation to a recognised clearing house or interbank payment system that pose threats to the UK's financial stability or confidence in the UK's financial system, or significant damage to business and other interests.

These events, if occasioned by serious failure in the regulatory system, would warrant the Treasury's commission of independent inquiries into the FCA or PRA.[114] Such inquiries are to be carried out under the Treasury's terms and supported by statutorily-backed investigative powers. The recommendations are to be publicly published. The inquiry into the failure of BCCI led by Sir Thomas Bingham (as he then was) is an example. It is, however, to be noted that no independent inquiries have been commissioned for events during the global financial crisis of 2007–9. The closest to an independent inquiry carried out after the events of the global financial crisis is by the Joint Committee of the Joint Houses of Parliament, which has made findings of fact and recommendations for reform.[115]

---

[111] Sections 7D and 7E, Financial Services and Markets Act 2000 amended by the Bank of England and Financial Services Act 2016.

[112] Section 7F, Financial Services and Markets Act 2000 amended by the Bank of England and Financial Services Act 2016.

[113] A collective investment scheme is a scheme where investors participate by contributing monies to be pooled together and managed centrally by a 'manager'. This manager is expected to account for investment returns to the participants on a periodic basis, see definition in s235, Financial Services and Markets Act 2000.

[114] Section 68, Financial Services and Markets Act 2000 amended by the Financial Services Act 2012.

[115] House of Lords and House of Commons, *Changing Banking for Good* (2013) Vols I and II.

6.3.2.3 Internal reviews of other regulatory failures

In other circumstances where there may be regulatory failure, the Treasury may direct the PRA or FCA to undertake regulatory inquiries.[116] In relation to the FCA, these could relate to an FCA-regulated firm or a collective investment scheme that has caused detriment to consumer protection, market integrity, or competition.[117] In relation to the PRA, these could relate to the use of public funds in relation to a PRA-regulated firm.[118] These inquiries are only to be warranted if there is serious failure in the regulatory systems. The regulator is obliged to undertake these inquiries with a view to making recommendations for change and must report to the Treasury.[119] The Treasury must publish the report and recommendations but may withhold material that is subject to confidentiality, or for the purposes of avoiding adverse implications.[120] The FSA's internal reviews into the bank failures at Northern Rock, HBOS, and RBS, as discussed earlier, are examples of such inquiries.

Finally, the PRA and FCA have to publish annual reports of their activities every financial year pursuant to their regulatory objectives, and such reports are to be laid before parliament for critical scrutiny.[121] It may, however, be argued that parliamentary scrutiny is likely to be superficial as many such annual reports are laid before parliament yearly and this has become a formality rather than a real opportunity for problems to be discovered.

6.3.3 Relationships with stakeholders and the public

It is important for regulators to engage with stakeholders and the public so that regulatory rules and policy can be appropriately determined. The PRA is required under legislation to establish a stakeholder panel, and is under *a duty to consult* the panel and consider their representations.[122] The FCA is required to establish four stakeholder panels representing different groups of stakeholders in the financial services industry and consumers.[123]

The due discharge of the 'duty to consult' has been explained in the *Couglan* principles[124] to mean the conduct of a 'proper consultation', viz:

> To be proper, consultation must be undertaken at a time when proposals are still at a formative stage; it must include sufficient reasons for particular proposals to allow those consulted to give intelligent consideration and an intelligent response; adequate time must be given for this purpose; and the product of consultation must be conscientiously taken into account when the ultimate decision is taken.

---

[116] Section 77, Financial Services and Markets Act 2000 amended by the Financial Services Act 2012.

[117] Section 73, Financial Services and Markets Act 2000 amended by the Financial Services Act 2012.

[118] Section 74, Financial Services and Markets Act 2000 amended by the Financial Services Act 2012.

[119] Sections 78–9, Financial Services and Markets Act 2000 amended by the Financial Services Act 2012.

[120] Section 82, Financial Services and Markets Act 2000 amended by the Financial Services Act 2012.

[121] See Schedule 1ZB, s19, Financial Services and Markets Act 2000 amended by the Financial Services Act 2012.

[122] Sections 2L–2N, Financial Services and Markets Act 2000 amended by the Financial Services Act 2012.

[123] Sections 1M–1Q, Financial Services and Markets Act 2000 amended by the Financial Services Act 2012.

[124] *R. v North & East Devon Health Authority Ex p. Coughlan* [2001] QB 213.

In *Rusal (Jud Review) v LME*[125] the question was raised as to whether the non-inclusion of certain policy options in the consulting body's document was in breach of the duty to consult. The consulting body in that case, the London Metal Exchange, provided certain options for reform in its consultation document but omitted the course of reform most favoured by the claimants who brought the judicial review proceedings. The first instance court held that the duty to consult was not breached. The consultation document had fulfilled the conditions set out in *Couglan*, setting out proposals and their reasons at a formative stage and providing a reasonable time for response. There was no need for the document to explore every viable option and reasons for their inclusion or otherwise. A consulting body should, however, not omit clearly material matters or consequences of certain policy actions.[126]

The PRA and FCA are under a duty to consider their stakeholder panels' representations. This means that the regulators must conscientiously take the representations into account in determining their decisions, and failure to do so may be regarded as procedurally improper. In the case of *Skyscanner Ltd v Competition and Markets Authority (Skoosh International Ltd and others intervening)*[127] the court found that the Competition and Markets Authority failed to consider a material representation by a consultee, as the Authority's published response to the consultation did not mention its consideration of the representation at all. The omission to consider rendered the Authority's decision procedurally improper and therefore *ultra vires*.

The PRA also has a duty to consult the public in respect of its annual report. Upon the publication of its annual report, it must invite the public to make representations on how it has discharged its functions and whether it has achieved its objectives. The PRA is also required to publicly publish a report on the consultation responses and feedback within 4 months of the closure of consultation.[128] Unlike the FCA, the PRA is not required to hold a public meeting in relation to its annual report.[129]

We now turn to the judicial avenues of oversight in relation to the PRA and FCA.

6.3.4 The Upper Tribunal for finance

The PRA's and FCA's enforcement powers can be held in check by the Upper Tribunal, a specialist court that hears references from complainants who are aggrieved by the regulators' decisions.

---

[125] [2014] EWCA Civ 1271.

[126] *R (Parents for Legal Action Ltd) v Northumberland County Council* [2006] BLGR 646; *R (Madden) v Bury Metropolitan Borough Council* [2002] EWHC 1882 (Admin).

[127] [2015] Bus. L.R. 1318.

[128] Sections 20 and 21, Schedule 1ZB, Financial Services and Markets Act 2000 as amended by the Financial Services Act 2012.

[129] Section 12, Schedule 1ZA, Financial Services and Markets Act 2000 as amended by the Financial Services Act 2012.

Initially the tribunal was established as the Finance and Markets Tribunal but it was merged with the Upper Tribunal in 2010, which also hears references by persons aggrieved by decisions of the tax authorities.

The Upper Tribunal may hear any reference which is the subject of a decision of the Bank of England (including the PRA's decisions) or the FCA.[130] These include decisions such as the refusal to authorise or approve a person and enforcement decisions against firms and individuals. The Upper Tribunal is a judicial body overseen by the Lord Chancellor's office independent of the regulators. The Tribunal is subject to Tribunal Procedure Rules and is usually presided by a qualified judge. It has the power to hear the matter of reference afresh and consider all evidence before it. It may then make an order in relation to the appropriate action that the regulator must take and remit the decision back to the regulator. The order can include specific directions to the regulator. The order has effect as if it were a county court order. If a regulator's decision has been referred to the Upper Tribunal, the regulator must suspend the effect of the decision pending the outcome at the Upper Tribunal.[131] This protects aggrieved persons from having to first comply with the decision.

The Upper Tribunal has heard a number of cases where individuals have been aggrieved by regulators' decisions. As will be discussed in Chapter 11, the regulators set standards of individual responsibility and conduct for a wide range of financial sector employees, such as integrity, care, and diligence, and can fine and disqualify individuals for being in breach of those standards. In the cases in Box 6.3, several individuals have been fined and/or disqualified by the FSA or FCA and have brought proceedings in the Tribunal to challenge their punishments. In Pottage's case,[132] the Upper Tribunal has reversed the FSA's punishment by finding that there was no breach of the standards of conduct, while in Burns' case, the Tribunal confirmed the FCA's decision. The case of Asset LI shows how a firm had tried to challenge the FCA's decision that it had operated an unauthorised collective investment scheme, and the FCA's decision had been affirmed at the levels of the Tribunal and subsequently the Court of Appeal and Supreme Court.

In practice, the regulators usually give a discount (30 per cent) to persons subject to monetary penalties imposed in a decision, if such persons settle early with the regulator and do not proceed further. This may give rise to an incentive for persons not to challenge the regulator in the Tribunal. On the one hand, early settlements save the regulator from expending more resources on a particular enforcement action, but, on the other hand, this may prevent interesting issues of law from

---

[130] Section 133, Financial Services and Markets Act 2000, amended by The Transfer of Tribunal Functions Order 2010 (S.I. 2010/22) and the Banking (Special Provisions) Act 2008.

[131] Section 133A Financial Services and Markets Act 2000, amended by The Transfer of Tribunal Functions Order 2010 (S.I. 2010/22) and the Banking (Special Provisions) Act 2008.

[132] *John Pottage v FSA* [20 April 2012] at http://www.tribunals.gov.uk/financeandtax/Documents/decisions/John_Pottage_v_FSA_decision.pdf. See more detailed discussion in Chapter 11, section 11.2.

Box 6.3

John Pottage v FSA [20 April 2012]

Pottage assumed position as Chief Executive at a time when he was aware of risk management and control deficiencies at UBS. He instituted an overhaul review, made new appointments and installed systems, and had personal engagement with issues via discussion in frequent meetings. However, the then-FSA alleged that the continued failings of UBS were to be attributed to Pottage's inadequate oversight. The Upper Tribunal agreed with Pottage that he had done sufficiently as was required to address the problems brought to his attention and had instituted reforms in processes and systems. The failure of ground implementation could not fully be attributed to Pottage, as a failure in his standard of conduct relating to diligence and care in oversight.

Angela Burns v FCA [2017] EWCA Civ 2140

Burns was appointed as a non-executive director at MGM, as Chair of its investment committee that would advise the Board on investment strategies that the company could pursue. Burns got in touch with Vanguard, a global leading asset management company with which she had previous contact, to actively solicit for consultancy work, therefore putting herself in a position of conflict of interest. The FCA fined and disqualified her for breaches of directors' duties and breach of regulatory conduct standards. She challenged the decision unsuccessfully in the Upper Tribunal and later at the Court of Appeal.

Asset Land Investment Plc v The Financial Conduct Authority [2016] UKSC 17

Asset LI managed a land-banking scheme whereby they identified plots of land suitable for residential development and solicited investors to buy notional parts of the plot in order to gain from future development permission for the plot and a potential sale to property developers. Although the transactions were structured as individual plot sales, the sales 'patter' offered to investors a centrally managed scheme by Asset LI that would seek development permission from the local council and the ultimate sale to a property developer. The FCA closed down the scheme as an unauthorised collective investment scheme but Asset LI challenged the characterisation of the land sales as falling within the definition of a collective investment scheme. Asset LI was unsuccessful in the Upper Tribunal, in the Court of Appeal and subsequently the Supreme Court which provided a definitive characterisation of the land-banking scheme and why it met the requirements of the definition of 'collective investment scheme'.

---

being resolved at the Upper Tribunal. The enforcement decisions of the regulator are not always the most clearly and well-reasoned in terms of application of law.[133] The Upper Tribunal's role is therefore of crucial importance to the development of jurisprudence in financial regulation.

---

[133] See, for example, the role of the Upper Tribunal in clarifying what due diligence means in the oversight expectations of senior management responsibility, in *John Pottage v FSA* [20 April 2012]

6.3.5 **Judicial review**

The judicial review remedy is a general remedy in administrative law available to persons aggrieved by the improper exercise of powers by the government and statutory authorities. It is seen as a necessary safeguard in response to the growth of public sector bodies, which are able to impose obligations and mete out administrative penalties without the need for a judicial order. Judicial review proceedings can be carried out to examine if a public sector body concerned has acted in excess of its jurisdiction or powers, or has indeed abused its powers by acting 'unreasonably', 'irrationally', or having considered irrelevant considerations.[134]

The PRA and FCA can in principle be subject to judicial review for their exercise of powers. However, to date, no judicial review proceedings (including against their predecessor the FSA) has succeeded. This is largely because the scheme of reference to the Upper Tribunal would more often than not provide a comprehensive remedy for persons affected by the authorities' decisions. If judicial review proceedings are carried out before reference to the Upper Tribunal is made, this is generally regarded as premature. This position was upheld in *R (on the application of Christopher Willford) v Financial Services Authority*.[135] In that case, the claimant sought judicial review of the FSA's decision to disqualify and fine him £100,000 for having failed to act with due care, skill, and diligence in his position. Wilford was alleged to have failed to adequately advise the Board of Bradford & Bingley Plc as group finance director. Wilford took issue with the failure of the FSA to explain why it had rejected his earlier submissions, and commenced judicial review proceedings. At the first instance, the review proceedings succeeded as the judge agreed that inadequate reasons were given by the FSA. On appeal, however, the FSA's appeal was allowed, as the statutory scheme for remedy, which is reference to the Upper Tribunal, had not been exhausted. The Upper Tribunal would require a rehearing of the case and the claimant would be able to call the FSA to account in addition to being fully heard. Judicial review proceedings could exceptionally be available if a reference to the Upper Tribunal would not provide an adequate remedy. The Court of Appeal in *Wilford* was of the view that this would be extremely rare.

Further, judicial review proceedings are highly unlikely to succeed against the regulators as the PRA and FCA enjoy a wide berth of discretionary powers, making it difficult for claimants to show that they have exceeded their powers or exercised their powers unreasonably. In *R (Davies and Ors) v FSA*[136] the FSA issued penalty notices against two members of the London Metal Exchange who were alleged to have breached rules of conduct issued by the self-regulatory body, the Securities and Futures Association, before it was merged into the FSA in 2000. The merger took place after the SFA had started but before concluding disciplinary proceedings. The FSA took over the enforcement actions, and decided to issue penalty notices to disqualify the two individuals

---

[134] *Associated Provincial Picture Houses Limited v Wednesbury Corporation* [1948] 1 K.B. 223; *R (Galaxy Land Ltd) v Durham County Council* [2015] EWHC 16 (Admin).
[135] [2013] All ER (D) 114.   [136] [2004] 1 W.L.R. 185.

right away. The aggrieved individuals alleged that the FSA had issued them with penalty notices in circumvention of the procedures for disciplinary proceedings and the exercise of powers was *ultra vires*. The Court of Appeal was convinced that the FSA had good reason to truncate the procedure and it was not restricted in its exercise of powers to disqualify inappropriate persons from working in the financial services industry. In another case, where the FSA would have been time-barred in carrying out its enforcement powers if it followed through a longer process of disciplinary procedures, the court agreed that the FSA was not acting *ultra vires* in imposing a warning notice on an individual right away.[137]

The boundaries of the FSA's powers were challenged in the seminal case of *British Bankers' Association v FSA*,[138] but again without success.

That case concerned the FSA's amendments to regulatory rules regarding how banks should deal with customer complaints in relation to the mis-selling of payment protection insurance. Payment protection insurance referred to insurance cover intended to help a borrower pay off an outstanding loan if the borrower fell into adverse circumstances. Banks and financial services firms that extended credit regularly added the product onto their loan agreements with consumers, often without consent. Such mis-selling of payment protection insurance took place over many years and the FSA finally set up a scheme to redress consumers' grievances. The FSA was of the view that as mis-selling was systemic in the financial services sector, firms should not only compensate the customers who have come forward with complaints. Firms were given guidance to undertake a 'root and branch' analysis of their selling procedures of payment protection insurance. Where there is doubt that customers had been 'treated fairly', firms should try to identify all affected customers to make compensation to them, whether or not individual complaints were received.[139]

The British Bankers Association, on behalf of its member banks, challenged the rules as being *ultra vires*. The Association alleged that the compensation rules were made pursuant to expectations of conduct that had not existed before, and in any case were contrary to the powers of the FSA under s404 of the Financial Services and Markets Act. Under this section, the FSA could order firms to set up consumer redress schemes, but it would require the FSA to show that there was widespread and regular failure in a certain financial activity. Further, a proposal to set up the redress scheme would require public consultation for at least 3 months and be supported by either a Queen's Counsel opinion or court approval. Once a redress scheme had been set up, consumers would have to file their claims within a certain time period. The FSA's redress rules for the mis-selling of payment protection insurance were alleged to have avoided compliance with s404. The court, however, disagreed that the rules were made on the basis of new notions of conduct, as all financial services firms were subject to the high-level principle

---

[137] *R (Griggs) v FSA* [2008] EWHC 2587.   [138] [2011] EWHC 999.
[139] FSA, *Policy Statement 10/12: The Assessment and Redress of Payment Protection Insurance Complaints* (2010) at https://www.fca.org.uk/publication/policy/ps10_12.pdf.

of 'treating customers fairly', which had binding effect.[140] The mis-selling fundamentally contravened the principle even if there were no specific conduct rules. Further, the court also found that the FSA was not limited by the consumer redress scheme in s404 in terms of how it wished to make rules for consumer redress. The s404 scheme was only one such route for consumer redress. The court was of the view that the rules in relation to payment protection mis-selling were less draconian and controlled than under section 404, and served its distinct purpose. The British Bankers Association failed in these proceedings.

6.3.6 Civil liability

There is very little scope in holding government and statutory authorities to civil liability, and the PRA and FCA are no exceptions. A question of civil liability may arise, for example, if the PRA or FCA has been found to be negligent in their supervision of regulated firms, and such regulatory failure contributes to defaults or failures on the part of regulated firms leading to losses suffered by investors or consumers. The PRA and FCA benefit from legislative immunity, which is a statutory provision safeguarding the body, its officers and employees, and any persons for which the body would be vicariously responsible from being sued for civil compensation in damages in relation to any act or omission in the discharge of their functions.[141]

Aggrieved customers or investors may wish to be able to call regulators to civil compensation if the defaulting firm is already insolvent, making their causes of action against the firm relatively worthless, and where regulatory failure is present. The statutory immunity for the PRA and FCA protects the authorities from such actions, subject to the exception of bad faith on the part of the regulator or if the regulator's act or omission constitutes a breach of the Human Rights Act 1998.[142]

In *Melton Medes v Securities and Investments Board*[143] the Board was sued in a civil action for breach of confidentiality, but Lightman J held that the private action could not succeed as the Board benefited from statutory immunity. Such immunity could only be lifted if bad faith was shown on the part of the Board within the meaning of the tort of misfeasance in public office. The requirements of the tort of misfeasance in public office were explained in greater detail in the case of *Three Rivers DC v Bank of England (No3)*.[144] That case dealt with a preliminary ruling to explain the requirements of the tort, in a protracted series of proceedings led by Three Rivers District Council on behalf of 6,000 claimants against the Bank of England. The Bank of England was sued for regulatory failure in supervising BCCI, as highlighted in the

---

[140] This is part of the PRIN module in the FCA Handbook, imposing high-level principles that can be enforced against regulated firms where there may be gaps specific rules. The principles regime is discussed in Chapter 11.
[141] Section 33, Schedule 1ZB, Financial Services and Markets Act 2000 amended by the Financial Services Act 2012.   [142] Ibid.
[143] [1995] 3 All ER 880.   [144] [2000] 2 WLR 1220.

Bingham report (discussed earlier in section 6.1). Three Rivers District Council had substantial deposits at BCCI and became the lead claimant to seek compensation from the Bank of England since recovery prospects from the liquidation of BCCI were remote.

In clarifying what the claimants had to prove in establishing the tort of misfeasance in public office, the preliminary ruling held that the claimants had to establish that a public officer had acted or omitted to do an act, knowing that he or she had no power to do so, and that the claimant would probably be injured. The establishment of the tort required proof of state of mind as well as proximity with the claimant. On state of mind, the court clarified that 'bad faith' meant either (a) the public officer in question did not have an honest belief that his/her act or omission was lawful or (b) the public officer in question was recklessly indifferent as to whether the act or omission was lawful and carried it out anyway. These states of mind had to be proved on a subjective basis. Further, the claimants needed to show that the public officer had subjective knowledge of the proximity with the claimants, that is, that his or her act or omission would have probably damaged the claimants' interests.

The thresholds for proving the tort of misfeasance in public office are high. Although the claimants endeavoured to bring a claim against the Bank of England on the basis of reckless indifference in exercising its functions, it soon became clear that such an argument would unlikely succeed in court, as the Bingham report's findings of the Bank of England's conduct would not necessarily amount to 'reckless indifference'. The Bank was reactive, slow to act, and trusted excessively in the self-regulatory capacity of bank management, but it would be difficult to frame such a supervisory style as being recklessly indifferent. By 2006 the claimants abandoned their claim.

Regulatory failures are treated as issues of public interest and primary accountability lies to the government. Civil liability for public authorities and officers is not designed to cope with the collective consequences of damage for private individuals.

Key takeaways

- The PRA and FCA are conferred a wide range of rule-making and enforcement powers.

- The PRA and FCA are subject to accountability relationships with the government such as in relation to appointments to its governing body. Inquiries may be required in relation to failures of certain regulated firms and in cases of regulatory failure.

- The PRA is generally subject to the oversight mechanisms in the Bank of England's structure.

- The PRA and FCA have a duty to consult its stakeholder panel and is obliged to consider its representations.

- Any person aggrieved by decisions of the PRA or FCA may refer the matter to the Upper Tribunal.

- The Upper tribunal is a specialist and independent court that is able to hear all matters afresh and make an order directing the regulator to take appropriate action as it requires.

- In view of the Upper tribunal's reference role, judicial review of the PRA's or FCA's actions is likely very limited in scope.
- There is also little scope for bringing civil actions against regulators for compensation due to supervisory deficiencies.

Key bibliography

Legislation

Financial Services and Markets Act 2000 as amended by Financial Services Act 2012 and Bank of England and Financial Services Act 2016

Articles

Andenas, A and Fairgrieve, D, 'Misfeasance in Public Office, Governmental Liability and European Influences' (2002) 51 International and Comparative Law Quarterly 757 also at https://lra.le.ac.uk/bitstream/2381/3015/1/Misfeasance%20in%20public%20office,%20governmental%20liability,%20and%20European%20influences.pdf

Lomnicka, E, 'Making the Financial Services Authority Accountable' [2000] *Journal of Business Law* 65

Steyn LJ, Hope LJ, Hutton LJ, Hobhouse LJ, and Millett LJ, 'Three Rivers District Council v Governor and Company of Bank of England' (2001) 9 *Journal of Financial Regulation and Compliance* 279

6.4 Macro-prudential supervision

We now turn to explore in greater detail 'macro-prudential' supervision, an area of financial policymaking introduced in the wake of the global financial crisis of 2007–9. The responsibility for macro-prudential supervision is reposed in the Financial Policy Committee discussed in section 6.2.

Wolf defines macro-prudential supervision as 'oversight of the financial system as a whole'[145] and as different from the chiefly 'micro-prudential' approach[146] taken in financial regulation up until the global financial crisis. Pre-crisis, banking and financial regulation focused on maintaining individual institutional soundness, so that individual institutions may not fail and cause adverse implications for the wider financial system. This 'micro-prudential' approach is now regarded as inadequate[147] as financial stability

---

[145]   Martin Wolf, 'Seven Ways to Fix the System's Flaws' *Financial Times* (London, 23 January 2012).

[146]   See Chapters 8 and 9.

[147]   FSA, *The Turner Review: A Regulatory Response to the Global Banking Crisis* (March 2009) http://www.fsa.gov.uk/pubs/other/turner_review.pdf, *viz* 'The lack of such a [macroprudential] perspective, and the failure to specify and to use macro-prudential levers to offset systemic risks, were far more important to the origins of the crisis than any specific failure in supervisory process relating to individual firms. Getting macro-prudential analysis and tools right for the future is vital.'

problems can arise not only from the failure of individual institutions. Financial stability problems can arise from weak linkages between financial institutions or market developments that are sub-optimal. The UK has recognised a need for overall supervisory perspective of the build-up of risks in the financial system as a whole. Macro-prudential supervision, providing a bird's eye view of the financial system as a whole, [148] is a necessary companion to micro-prudential regulation that is focused on individual institutions, in order to support the regulatory pursuit of financial stability.[149]

6.4.1 Oversight of financial system risks

The FPC's role is to maintain oversight of the risks in the UK's financial system generally. To that end, the Committee is required to produce two half-yearly reports on financial stability.[150] These are usually published in July and November each year setting out the key issues the Committee has monitored and its policy thoughts. The FPC also publishes its quarterly 'record of meeting' as a consolidated report in order to provide transparency as to its policy thinking and any directions or recommendations (discussed later).

In order to maintain meaningful oversight of the risks in the UK financial system, the Committee must be able to obtain adequate information at the levels of individual firms and the markets they transact in, as well as in relation to general economic conditions in the UK and beyond. Information transparency obligations for banks have increased exponentially[151] since the global financial crisis. Box 6.4 sets out a summary of the range of information returns that banks have to make. These constitute the information matrix available to the Bank of England (including the PRA and FPC) in order to carry out the surveillance needed for macro-prudential oversight.

6.4.2 Powers of the Financial Policy Committee

The FPC may exercise binding powers as against the PRA and FCA, as well as make recommendations that are persuasive though not binding.

The FPC may direct the PRA or FCA to implement certain industry-wide policies where relevant, but such a power is not to be directed at any individual regulated

---

[148] G30 Working Group on Macroprudential Policy, *Enhancing Financial Stability and Resilience: Macroprudential Policy, Tools and Systems for the Future* (Washington, DC: Group of Thirty 2010); Claudio Borio, 'Towards a Macroprudential Framework for Financial Supervision and Regulation?' (February 2003) BIS Working Paper at http://papers.ssrn.com/sol3/papers.cfm?abstract_id=841306; Committee on the Global Financial System (Bank of International Settlements), 'Macroprudential Instruments and Frameworks: A Stocktaking of Issues and Experiences' (May 2010) CGFS Paper No 38 at http://www.bis.org/publ/cgfs38.pdf.

[149] European Union Committee, *The Future of EU Financial Regulation and Supervision* (HL 2008–09, 106-I) para 22.

[150] Sections 9G and 9W, Financial Services and Markets Act amended by Financial Services Act 2012.

[151] Iris H-Y Chiu, 'Transparency Regulation in Financial Markets – Moving into the Surveillance Age?' (2011) 3 *European Journal of Risk and Regulation* 303.

Box 6.4 Information transparency obligations for banks (note that many of these are discussed under their respective substantive chapters in the book)

- Micro-prudential information
  - Internal capital adequacy assessment (Chapter 8, Box 8.8)
  - Internal liquidity adequacy assessment (Chapter 9, section 9.2.3)
  - Supervisory information for Pillar 2 purposes (Chapter 8, section 8.5.4.2)
  - *Reverse stress testing* results (Chapter 9, section 9.6)
  - Regulator stress test results (Chapter 9, section 9.6)
- Corporate governance information
  - Statements of responsibilities for individual senior persons (Chapter 11, section 11.2.1)
  - Certified persons register (Chapter 11, Box 11.3)
  - Remuneration reporting (Chapter 12, section 12.4.4)
- Recovery and resolution planning
  - *Recovery plans* (Chapter 13, section 13.2.1)
  - *Resolution plans* (Chapter 13, section 13.2.2)
  - *Resolution colleges* and crisis management planning (Chapter 13, section 13.4)
  - Structural reform plans (Chapter 10, section 10.1.2.4)
- Investment fund disclosures not covered in this book, see resources under Key bibliography
- Market trade data not covered in this book, see resources under **Key bibliography**

---

entity.[152] One example of such power is that the FPC may set the certain micro-prudential requirements. The FPC has been given direct powers to set a particular micro-prudential requirement – the *counter-cyclical buffer* rate in the UK.[153] This power is not directed at the PRA or FCA, hence, the FPC is able to set the rate without the PRA's intervention. The FPC is also able to direct the PRA to implement a micro-prudential requirement in the form of the systemic risk buffer for ring-fenced banks.[154] The

---

[152] Section 9H, Financial Services and Markets Act 2000 amended by Financial Services Act 2012.

[153] Discussed in Chapter 8, section 8.5. Capital Requirements (Capital Buffers and Macro-prudential Measures) Regulations 2014, Regulations 10–12.

[154] See Chapter 8, section 8.5.3; ss34F and 34G, Capital Requirements (Capital Buffers and Macro-prudential Measures) Regulations 2014, as amended by The Capital Requirements (Capital Buffers and Macroprudential Measures) (Amendment) Regulations 2015. See also the Bank of England, *The Financial Policy Committee's Framework for the Systemic Risk Buffer* (May 2016) at http://www.bankofengland.co.uk/financialstability/Documents/fpc/srbf_cp260516.pdf; PRA, *The PRA's Implementation of the Systemic Risk Buffer* (July 2016) at http://www.bankofengland.co.uk/pra/Documents/publications/cp/2016/cp2716.pdf.

PRA, however, reserves judgment to deviate this requirement if there are exceptional circumstances.

In June 2014, the FPC has also acquired powers to guard against financial stability risks arising from the housing market.[155] This is possibly in response to the lessons learnt in the global financial crisis. House prices can rise to inflated levels in part due to uncontrolled lending by banks. The FPC is expressly given powers that it can exercise to direct the PRA or FCA to require regulated lenders to place limits on residential mortgage lending in both the owner-occupied and buy-to-let sectors. Such limits can be placed in terms of loan-to-value ratios, which means that lenders can only lend partially to meet the full purchase price of houses. Loans that require little funding from home purchasers (i.e. high loan-to-value ratios) are seen as more susceptible to the risk of default risk. This is because home purchasers are more likely to commit to mortgage repayments if they have themselves funded the purchase in a substantial amount. Restricting the proportion of high loan-to-value ratio loans can moderate lender behaviour towards more prudent and less risky loans, avoiding other negative effects such as housing price 'bubbles'. The FPC also has the power to direct the PRA or FCA to place limits on lending in buy-to-let markets using the debt-to-income ratio tool. The debt-to-income ratio is the ratio of the borrower's outstanding debt to his or her annual income. Where debt-to-income ratio is high, such as debt being more than five times annual income, borrowers are more likely to struggle in terms of servicing the debt, heightening default risk. While the FPC has not exercised such powers yet, the existence of these powers may cause banks to review and moderate their lending behaviour so as to avoid the imposition of formal restrictions.

The FPC has set out a suite of possible tools it can use in macro-prudential supervision. They include micro-prudential tools in relation to individual banks, tools in relation to managing asset bubbles in certain markets, such as the housing market, tools for increased disclosure, and tools for changing market practices such as requiring central counterparties for certain transactions or for imposing more onerous conditions for the trading of certain risky financial instruments.[156] The FPC's directions, if any, would be communicated to the PRA and/or FCA, and where such has taken place, transparency would be made in the FPC's quarterly record of meetings which is publicly available.

Next, the FPC has extensive powers to make recommendations to the PRA, FCA and the Bank of England generally. In relation to the Bank of England, these may relate

---

[155] Bank of England, *The Financial Policy Committee's powers over Housing Tools: A Policy Statement* (July 2015) at http://www.bankofengland.co.uk/financialstability/Documents/fpc/policystatement010715.pdf.

[156] Bank of England and FSA, 'Instruments of Macro-prudential Policy' (December 2011) Bank of England Discussion Paper at http://www.bankofengland.co.uk/publications/Documents/other/financialstability/discussionpaper111220.pdf.

[157] See Chapter 3.   [158] See Chapter 13.

to its oversight of interbank payment systems,[157] crisis management and resolution,[158] and other matters affecting macro-prudential supervision. The FPC may also make recommendations regarding financial assistance requests from firms to the Bank of England.[159] In relation to the FCA these may relate to financial markets, product sales and distribution (including product intervention[160]), and the designation and scope of regulated activities. One of the key recommendations the FPC has made to date is in response to the Chancellor's request in 2014[161] to review the need or otherwise for the introduction of a *leverage ratio* for banks.[162]

The FPC has used its powers of recommendation sparingly. The caution on the part of the FPC may be due to the forward-looking nature of macro-prudential supervision. As the FPC is required to pre-emptively judge certain risks before they materialise, such judgment needs to be exercised carefully.

In sum, the UK's regulatory architecture for banks is substantially re-concentrated in the Bank of England after the global financial crisis of 2007–9. The Bank has undergone significant reform in terms of its structures and objectives, and its Committee structures and responsibilities have become more clarified and transparent.

⊙ Key takeaways

- Macro-prudential supervision has risen in importance since the lessons learnt in the global financial crisis of 2007–9.

- The FPC of the Bank of England has responsibility for overseeing risks in the UK financial system in general.

- The FPC has powers to direct the PRA and/or FCA in relation to certain micro-prudential requirements and residential mortgage lending matters.

- The FPC has extensive powers in principle to make recommendations in all areas of regulated activities and may direct these recommendations to the FCA and Bank of England generally.

- The FPC provides transparency through its publication of quarterly meeting records and bi-annual Financial Stability reports.

---

[159] Sections 9O–9R, Financial Services and Markets Act 2000 amended by Financial Services Act 2012.

[160] Product intervention refers to powers to ban or control the distribution of certain financial products on an *ex post* basis. These powers are not used for vetting the utility of financial products in general but may be used to prevent foreseeable mis-selling harms. See s137D inserted into the Financial Services and Markets 2000 by the Financial Services Act 2012.

[161] Ibid and Bank of England, *The Financial Policy Committee's Review of the Leverage Ratio* (Oct 2014) at http://www.bankofengland.co.uk/financialstability/Documents/fpc/fs_lrr.pdf.

[162] Discussed in Chapter 9, section 9.4.

Key bibliography

Official papers and reports

G30 Working Group on Macroprudential Policy, *Enhancing Financial Stability and Resilience: Macroprudential Policy, Tools and Systems for the Future* (Washington, DC: Group of Thirty 2010)

Bank of England, *The Financial Policy Committee's Framework for the Systemic Risk Buffer* (May 2016) at http://www.bankofengland.co.uk/financialstability/Documents/fpc/srbf_cp260516.pdf

Bank of England, *The Financial Policy Committee's powers over Housing Tools: A Policy Statement* (July 2015) at http://www.bankofengland.co.uk/financialstability/Documents/fpc/policystatement010715.pdf

Bank of England and Financial Services Authority, *Instruments of Macro-prudential Policy* (December 2011) Bank of England Discussion Paper http://www.bankofengland.co.uk/publications/Documents/other/financialstability/discussionpaper111220.pdf

Articles

Chiu, IH-Y, 'Transparency Regulation in Financial Markets—Moving into the Surveillance Age?' (2011) 3 *European Journal of Risk and Regulation* 303

Garicano, L and Lastra, R, 'Towards a New Architecture for Financial Stability: Seven Principles' (2010) 13 *Journal of International Economic Law* 597

Hanson, SG, Kashyap, AK, and Stein, JC, 'A Macroprudential Approach to Financial Regulation' (November 2010) Chicago Booth Research Paper No 10-29 http://papers.ssrn.com/sol3/papers.cfm?abstract_id=1708173

Books

Andenas, M and Chiu, IH-Y, *The Foundations and Future of Financial Regulation* (Oxford: Routledge 2014) Part 4.

Questions

1. **Critically review if the UK's post-crisis reforms to its regulatory architecture will meet its regulatory objectives for banks.**

   Answer tips You may wish to briefly discuss the FSA structure with its multiple objectives and the failings on the part of the FSA during the global financial crisis of 2007–9. This sets the context for introducing the reforms and evaluating what the reforms achieve. You should discuss the UK's new regulatory architecture and regulatory objectives of bank regulation. You should critically unpick the relevant features in the new architecture that are relevant to delivering the objectives of firm safety and soundness, and overall financial stability.

2. Has the Bank of England become too powerful in financial services regulation?

> **Answer tips** *You may wish to discuss the structure and responsibilities of the Bank of England, and the mechanisms that check and balance its powers. You should refer to both ex ante mechanisms as well as ex post mechanisms, and provide examples as to how they worked. You should discuss judicial mechanisms for checking and balancing the exercise of the Bank's powers and what you think they achieve.*

3. What is macro-prudential supervision and how does this fit in with the rubric for UK bank regulation?

> **Answer tips** *You should discuss the key aim of macro-prudential supervision as having oversight of financial system risks and discuss the role and powers of the Financial Policy Committee. You should critically discuss the pre-emptive or forward-looking nature of this tool and critically evaluate the FPC's work to date.*

7

European banking supervision and regulatory architecture

7.1 Evolution of the single market and banking regulation

The introduction of European policy and law in bank regulation is for the purpose of building a single market in financial services, to give effect to the freedom of movement of capital. Bank regulation has been harmonised in the EU in a gradual manner since the 1970s but has increased in intensity with international harmonisation in the Basel I and II Accords.[1] The pace and intensity of EU bank regulation has accelerated in an unprecedented manner after the global financial crisis of 2007–9. The crisis has provided an opportunity for EU bank regulation to embrace multiple goals instead of focusing only on forging the single market,[2] and has also paved the way for the establishment of new regulatory and supervisory powers by EU-level agencies.

As EU bank regulation has been transposed in the UK, UK bank regulation has been significantly shaped by EU regulation. The existence of a formal bank regulation regime in the UK from 1979 is to a large extent attributed to the needs for complying with the First Banking Directive discussed in this chapter. Further, the mainstay of substantive bank regulation, which is the regulation of capital adequacy (see Chapter 8), has been harmonised at the EU from the start of international harmonisation in those standards. The UK has also transposed the suite of bank regulation reforms introduced in the EU since the 2007–9 global financial crisis, including capital adequacy (Chapter 8, section 8.5) and other microprudential regulation (Chapter 9), bank crisis management and resolution (Chapter 13), and regulation dealing with the qualitative aspects of internal risk management and corporate governance in banks (Chapter 12). Further, the UK has also transposed EU regulation that deals with various aspects of services and transactions that are undertaken by the banking sector, though not exclusively, such as

---

[1] Discussed in Chapter 8, sections 8.2, 8.3 and 8.4.

[2] Mads Andenas and Iris H-Y Chiu, 'Financial Stability and Legal Integration in Financial Regulation' (2013) 38 *European Law Review* 335.

in relation to investment services[3] and consumer protection (see aspects dealt with in Chapters 2 and 4), payment services (Chapter 3), and combatting financial crime such as money laundering and terrorist financing (Chapter 14). Although EU bank regulation is the key source of much of regulation that applies to banks, UK bank regulation maintains its uniqueness in terms of its chosen regulatory architecture (Chapter 6), which is a 'twin peaks' structure that is not the same as in other member states. For example, Germany's financial services regulator, the BaFin, is a single regulator, and so are a number of financial services regulators in the Nordic member states. The UK also continues to maintain certain unique standards that are not harmonised in the EU, such as its individual liability and *senior managers regime* for a range of responsible persons in banks and financial institutions (Chapter 11).

The UK also maintains its own standards in respect of financial products and services that are offered only in the UK, that is, not marketed or marketable in the EU single market. For example, the EU has harmonised a set of rules for retail collective investment funds that can be marketed across the EU, called UCITs or Undertaking in Collective Investments in Transferable Securities, but the UK Financial Conduct Authority (FCA) may authorise collective investment funds that are UCITs and non-UCITs to be offered in the UK, many of which are distributed through banking networks. Non-UCITs funds do not meet the criteria in the EU regime largely because they deal in a scope of investment assets that are not covered in the harmonising legislation. The UK also maintains its own rules for the rights to market financial products and the standards of conduct for such,[4] for how investment advice should be charged,[5] and for how financial innovation should be treated,[6] these policies and regulatory regimes affecting also banks' conduct of business in the relevant areas. Essentially, although EU bank regulation has become increasingly comprehensive, it is not all-pervasive, and the regulatory regimes that apply to UK banks in relation to all of their activities continue to be sourced from both EU regulatory transposition and the financial regulators' own reforms.

7.1.1 The First Banking Directive 1973

Since 1973, the liberalisation of banking services across the European Economic Community (EEC) had been promoted. The 1973 Directive provided for European banks the right of establishment in any member state as well as to provide cross-border

---

[3] Much of this is dealt with in the Markets in Financial Instruments Directive 2014/59/EU, which pertains to investment services firms. Banks providing such services are to adhere to standards of conduct stipulated in the Directive, which is transposed in UK law in the FCA's Handbook. The book does not deal in detail with investment services regulation.

[4] FCA Handbook COBS 4.1, and s21, Financial Services and Markets Act 2000 and the Financial Promotions Order 2005.

[5] FCA Handbook COBS 6.1A, implementing the Retail Distribution Review, which concluded in 2006.

[6] Such as the Regulatory Sandbox initiative for engaging with financial innovation with a view to helping them become fully compliant and authorised to operate.

banking services.[7] The First Banking Directive[8] further fleshed out the framework for the freedom of establishment so that European banks had the right to establish branches in another member state. As the First Banking Directive provided that banks had to be authorised in a member state of its incorporation, this provided an important context for the formal establishment of bank regulation in the UK under the Banking Act 1979.[9]

The promotion of freedom of establishment and cross-border bank branching in the European Economic Area (EEA) was not matched by extensive harmonisation of bank regulation in the EU. The Directive envisaged that bank branches set up in other member states outside of its home jurisdiction had to be authorised by the host member state as well. Although in principle host member states were not to put up barriers to entry to other member states' bank branches, the co-authorisation framework could allow host authorities to impose conditions upon bank branches and make it costly for cross-border branching to occur.

The modest achievement of the First Banking Directive was sought to be improved upon. A framework was needed that made it comfortable for member state regulators to allow cross-border branching and provision of services much more easily. International developments in the harmonisation of prudential regulation for banks at the Basel Committee helped tremendously,[10] as the international standards could provide the basis for harmonised bank regulation in the EEC. With harmonised bank regulation, member states would be less uncomfortable about promoting cross-border banking services as all EEC banks would be subject to similar regulatory standards.

7.1.2 The Second Banking Directive 1989

The Second Banking Directive[11] in conjunction with a number of other directives, sought to provide the basis for cross-border bank '***passporting***' and ***mutual recognition*** by member states. All EEC banks would be authorised and supervised by their home authorities based on a set of minimum but harmonised bank regulation. This allowed member states to mutually recognise each other's authorised entities and avoided the need for a separate authorisation from the host states. Banks thus obtained a 'passport' for providing cross-border services or establishing cross-border branches on the basis of their home state's regulation and supervision.

In light of the objectives of the single market for banking services, European policy-makers pursued increasing legal harmonisation in bank regulation in order to ensure that cross-border banking was made easy on a level playing field. The suite of minimum harmonised bank regulation included capital adequacy,[12] regulation of ***large***

---

[7] Directive 73/183/EEC [1973] OJ L194/1 (superseded).
[8] First Banking Directive 77/780/EEC [1977] OJ L32/30.
[9] Discussed in Chapter 6, section 6.1.   [10] See Chapter 8, section 8.1 and Chapter 5 generally.
[11] Second Banking Directive 89/646/EEC [1989] OJ L386/1.
[12] Solvency Ratio Directive 89/647/EEC and Capital Adequacy Directive (CAD) 93/6/EEC. Capital adequacy is discussed in Chapter 8, sections 8.2, 8.3, and 8.4.

exposures,[13] the definition of capital,[14] and the requirement for all member states to establish deposit guarantee schemes.[15] These areas of harmonisation were important as they were perceived to underpin bank safety, hence crucial to depositor confidence.

The Second Banking Directive effectively introduced a 'single banking licence' to operate in the EEA,[16] in respect of core banking services such as deposit-taking and payments, but also in relation to corporate finance, portfolio management, and advisory and brokerage services, significant aspects of investment services. A bank that wished to establish a branch or provide cross-border services under the Directive's freedoms needed to notify its home regulator who would notify the relevant host regulator. The bank would be subject to 'home country control', which means that the home member state that authorises the bank would remain responsible for supervising its compliance with regulatory capital and microprudential rules. However, the host member state could require the bank to comply with its standards of conduct of business, as part of *general good* exceptions. 'General good' exceptions subject banks to complying with standards that are not part of harmonised regulation, and could be seen as barriers to entry, except that they are allowed only if they are imposed for the purposes for protecting the host member state's consumers, confidence, and reputation of financial markets.[17]

From the 1990s, European policymakers were keen to 'complete' the single market,[18] and in 1998 the Financial Services Action Plan[19] tabled by the Commission was welcomed by policymakers. Although the Plan related mostly to financial services other than banking, such as securities, investment funds, pension funds, insurance, and payment services, the overall importance of the Single Market for financial services as a whole could not be understated. The Plan recommended key actions in legal harmonisation of relevant regulatory rules in order to motivate financial services firms to explore cross-border business, on the basis of one set of compliance rules. This was supported by the Lamfalussy Report, which recommended a fast-track legislative procedure for law-making in EU financial regulation.[20] Legal harmonisation was seen to be instrumental for bringing into effect the policy goal of achieving the Single Market

---

[13] Large Exposures Directive 92/121/EEC. See discussion in Chapter 9, section 9.5.

[14] Own Funds Directive 89/299/EEC, and also see the development of this discussed in Chapter 8, sections 8.2, 8.3, 8.4, and 8.5.

[15] Deposit Guarantee Directives 87/63/EEC, see discussion in Chapter 13, section 13.3.

[16] Philip Woolfson, 'European Union: Banking: Second Banking Directive' (1996) *International Insurance Law Review* 110; Paul Phillips, 'Banking Regulation: Implementing the EC Second Banking Directive in the United Kingdom' (1993) *Journal of International Banking Law* 121.

[17] *Alpine Investments BV v Minister van Financiën* (1995) C-384/93.

[18] This was largely due to incremental enlargement of the Community, rising from the original six in 1957 to 12 by 1986. The Single European Act signed in 1987 envisaged completion of the Single Market by end 1993, see http://eur-lex.europa.eu/legal-content/EN/TXT/?uri=URISERV%3Axy0027.

[19] Commission, 'Financial Services Action Plan: Implementing the Framework for Financial Markets' (Communication) COM (1999) 232.

[20] The Lamfalussy procedure, its legacy and how it has changed law-making in EU banking and financial regulation is discussed in greater detail in section 7.2.2.2.

for financial services, especially with dramatic enlargement of the Community, which became the Union of 25 members by 2004, and 28 members by 2013. It became imperative that all member states operated on the basis of harmonised laws in order to support cross-border liberalisation of economic and financial services. The processes of accelerated legal integration are discussed shortly in section 7.3. For the purposes of achieving legal integration in bank regulation, bank regulators across member states came together to form an informal Committee of European Bank Supervisors (CEBS) in order to advise the Commission on legislative initiatives.

The initiatives to promote cross-border banking and other financial services spurred an increased level of cross-border activity. For example, a number of significant cross-border bank mergers and acquisitions occurred. The UK building society Abbey National was acquired by the large Spanish bank Santander in 2004, although Santander incorporated a UK subsidiary to own and rebrand Abbey National. 'Offensive' takeovers were carried out for example by Deutsche Bank. In 1990 Deutsche Bank took over the UK merchant bank Morgan Grenfell and the Spanish Banco Commercial Transatlantico.[21] After the Treaty of Nice, which provided for institutional changes in view of European enlargement incorporating ten new member states, banks in more economically mature jurisdictions such as Germany expanded their business into the new member states, such as Commerzbank into Poland and Hungary. Nordic banks have also taken advantage of new opportunities in Baltic member states.

It was, however, far from simple to ensure that cross-border bank branches were adequately supervised. The home authority of the bank had responsibility for supervising the bank and all of its branches, even the foreign branches, but this was not always an optimal situation as home authorities would be less aware of the activities carried out in foreign branches. Under the Second Banking Directive, host authorities were given powers to impose 'general good' obligations and to supervise branch liquidity, in order to protect depositors within its jurisdiction. As Chapter 5 discussed in relation to international banking, the coordination between home and host authorities for supervising foreign branches was not always optimal and gaps persisted. The failure of BCCI in 1991, a Luxembourg-authorised bank with extensive operations in the UK, exposed the gaps in home–host supervisory relations for cross-border banks.[22] Often the home authority would have little motivation and lacked resources to supervise the foreign branches of banks, while the host authority could have misplaced reliance on the assumed effectiveness of the home authority's supervision.[23] Although legal harmonisation ensured that the regulatory standards for banks were made similar across the EEA, it was another matter to ensure that home and host authorities supervised cross-border banking in a coordinated and adequate manner. This issue was not given much

---

[21] Discussed in Franco Grilli Cicilioni, 'Europeanisation of EC Banks through Cross-Border Mergers' (1994) *Journal of International Business Law* 419.

[22] Discussed more extensively in Chapter 6, section 6.1.2.

[23] Eva Lomnicka, 'The Home Country Control Principle in the Financial Services Directives and Case Law' (2000) 11 *European Business Law Review* 324.

emphasis as European policymakers continued to push for more legal harmonisation to facilitate the development of the Single Market. Supervisory coordination was devolved to the voluntary efforts taken by CEBs. This blind spot had significant implications during the global financial crisis of 2007–9 when a number of European banks failed. Eventually post-crisis bank regulation included reforms to the supervisory architecture in the EU that would better cope with the realities of the Single Market for bank services.

7.1.3 The Capital Requirements Directive 2006, legal and market integration up to the 2007–9 global financial crisis

A key piece of legal harmonisation for the EU banking market came in the form of the 2006 Capital Requirements Directive.[24] The Directive provided a comprehensive framework for bank authorisation and extensive substantive regulation of banks in terms of microprudential regulation. The latter was made possible due to the completion of the Basel II Accord at the international level for harmonising capital adequacy regulation worldwide.[25] The 2006 Directive provided a 'passport' system for banking services. Upon authorisation by a member state, home authorisation provided a passport for the bank to establish a branch or provide services in other member states, simply upon notification by the home authority to the host authority. The Directive continued to support the coordination between home and host regulators for the supervision of banks, but the home regulator maintained a larger proportion of the responsibility while host country regulators were required to assist in information sharing and supervisory actions. Host country regulators also had powers to require informational returns from 'passported' branches and could also undertake precautionary measures. Precautionary measures could be taken by host regulators to protect their depositors if it had informed the home regulator of the need for a supervisory measure and the home regulator had not provided such adequately. Despite the policy agenda to remove barriers to cross-border banking, home and host regulators were challenged by the growth of 'passporting' activity by banks and the needs for coordinated supervision. The European Court of Justice (ECJ) had also upheld home regulators' imposition of restrictions upon their regulated firms if certain cross-border services could be harmful in host jurisdictions.[26]

Continued success of the single market for banking was perceived as large banking groups in Europe grew to expand their footprint in most member states, such as Deutsche Bank and ING. From 2005, several Icelandic banks – Kaupthing Singer Friedlander, Icesave, and Glitnir banks – also expanded aggressively into mature banking markets such as the UK and Germany, capturing a significant share of deposits by luring depositors with high-savings accounts interest rates.

---

[24] Capital Requirements Directive 2006/48/EC.   [25] Chapter 8, section 8.4.

[26] *Alpine Investments BV v Minister van Financiën* (2005) preliminary reference, at http://eur-lex.europa.eu/smartapi/cgi/sga_doc?smartapi!celexplus!prod!CELEXnumdoc&lg=en&numdoc=61993J0384.

Up to 2007, the impetus for developing EU bank regulation had been for the purpose of facilitating market integration in banking services. A turning point came as the global financial crisis of 2007–9 unfolded and affected many banks in Europe.[27] ABN-AMRO, BNP Paribas, UBS, Commerzbank, and Fortis, to name a few, were all affected by the crisis. Many of these banks had held excessive levels of the 'toxic' assets or collateralised mortgage-based debt obligations that originated from the US. In particular, banks that had a cross-border footprint posed great difficulties for coordinated solutions. Chapter 13 discusses in greater detail how the failure of 'passported' Icelandic banks in the UK and Germany resulted in uncoordinated supervisory actions, and European policymakers had to reckon with the general challenge of the lack of a pan-European supervisory and crisis management framework. The cracks in the pan-European framework began to show and reform was called for.

Since the onset of the global financial crisis, the rationale for bank regulation in the EU started to be framed in terms of new public interest objectives. This led to legislative reform and new institutionalisation in the regulatory and supervisory architecture in the EU, which is discussed in detail in section 7.2.

The reforms took place in two phases. In the first phase, new regulatory reform and institutional changes took place. Regulatory reforms first dealt with microprudential regulation as following in the footsteps of the Basel Committee that quickly introduced reform to international standards in microprudential regulation. These reforms are covered in Chapters 8, 9, and 12. In parallel, institutional reforms were also carried out on the basis of the de Larosière report to be discussed in section 7.2. This ushered in a new era of bank regulation policymaking at the EU level, and directed national regulators to work with these European-level bodies and become accountable to them.

The global financial crisis, however, had lingering effects in the EU. It exposed further weaknesses in European banks that had been ignored for a long time. European banks had been heavily exposed to lending to their national governments or the national governments of member states. Such debt was perceived not to be risky as national governments were seen to be subject to fiscal discipline as part of the conditions of their adoption of the euro as their national currency. However, a number of national governments were not so disciplined and had borrowed in excess of prudence. They were then forced to raise their national debt further when bank bailouts were mounted for banks stricken during the global financial crisis. This then led to a further round of reforms focused on bank crisis management and resolution, that are discussed in Chapter 13, and new institutional reforms in the form of the Banking Union in 2013. The Banking Union is discussed in detail in section 7.3. We now turn to these developments.

---

[27] See Chapter 1 for the discussion of the global financial crisis of 2007–9.

➡ Key takeaways

- Bank regulation in Europe has always been based on the need for market integration in banking services.
- Early directives focused on explicitly providing rights of establishment for bank branches and freedom to provide cross-border services.
- Cross-border banking raised issues of providing a level playing field for banks, and adequate home and host supervision. Legal harmonisation was embarked upon to address both issues.
- Prudential regulation was harmonised on the basis of the development of the Basel I and II Accords.
- The supervisory structure adopted was that of home country control while host member states had limited powers to impose additional requirements to meet their legitimate public interests.
- Cross-border banking has resulted in a number of bank mergers and acquisitions, and allowed the largest national banks to become multinational banking enterprises.
- An early institutional development was the formation of CEBS, the Committee for European Bank Supervisors, which played a key part in advising on legal integration and supervisory coordination.

Key bibliography

Legislation

Single European Act 1987, at http://eur-lex.europa.eu/legal-content/EN/TXT/?uri=URISERV%3Axy0027Banking Coordination (Second Council Directive) Regulations 1992 (SI 1992 3218)

Official Papers

Commission, 'Financial Services Action Plan: Implementing the Framework for Financial Markets' (Communication) COM (1999) 232

Articles

Cicilioni, FG, 'Europeanisation of EC Banks through Cross-Border Mergers' (1994) 9 *Journal of International Banking Law* 419

Lomnicka, E, 'The Home Country Control Principle in the Financial Services Directives and Case Law' (2000) 11 *European Business Law Review* 324

Zimmermann, GC, 'Implementing the Single Banking Market in Europe' (1995) 3 *Federal Reserve Bank of San Francisco Economic Review* 35

Books

Walker, G, *European Banking Law—Policy and Programme Construction: 6* (Sir Joseph Gold Memorial) (BIICL, 2006)

7.2 The de Larosière Report and the European system of financial supervision

In the midst of the global financial crisis, in 2008, the European Commission established a high-level group of experts chaired by Jacques de Larosière to recommend a blueprint for financial supervision in the EU going forward.

The de Larosière Report provided a comprehensive analysis of the weaknesses in the financial sector in the EU and recommended stronger regulatory governance in many areas. These included bank microprudential regulation, reforms to bankers' remuneration policies, and bank corporate governance amongst other measures that dealt with market trading and investment firms. The Report also saw the need for expanding the scope of financial regulation to capture hitherto unregulated areas that had proved to be inadequately self-regulated, such as the oversight of credit rating agencies and then-unregulated hedge and private equity funds. In terms of improving crisis management in the EU financial sector, the Report recommended instituting macroprudential supervision at the EU level so that an effective early warning system could be developed to enable member state regulators to take preventive action against undesirable build-up of financial risks.[28]

The Report recommended even greater levels of legal harmonisation as being inevitable to redress the regulatory weaknesses above. In addition to securing market integration, these regulatory rules were also seen to be able to serve the important objective of protecting financial stability in the EU financial markets. The Report explained that a single financial market could not function properly if national rules and regulations were significantly different, as such diversity was bound to result in competitive distortions and difficulties in managing crises with cross-border implications.[29] In sum, the Report envisaged *more comprehensive* forms of legal harmonisation not only to continue to support the Single Market for financial services but to address the management of problems so that effective collective solutions can be found. Moloney,[30] however, warned that by adopting an approach towards 'more Europe' as a means of fighting trouble, more risks could be incurred. If a 'collective solution' imposed at the EU level were incorrect, this would have amplified effects across many markets.

EU policymakers adopted the Report and embarked upon significant legislative reforms. A comprehensive prudential regulatory regime under the Capital Requirements Directive IV and Capital Requirements Regulation was introduced,[31] and transposed into the UK. The Bank Recovery and Resolution Directive 2014 was also introduced for crisis management, and transposed in the UK.[32] As these

---

[28] Jacques de Larosière et al., *Report by the High Level Group on Financial Supervision in the EU* (Brussels, 25 February 2009) at http://ec.europa.eu/internal_market/finances/docs/de_larosiere_report_en.pdf, 39, 46.

[29] Ibid, 27. http://ec.europa.eu/internal_market/finances/docs/de_larosiere_report_en.pdf, 27.

[30] Niamh Moloney, 'EU Financial Market Regulation after the Global Financial Crisis: "More Europe" or more Risks?' (2010) 47 *Common Market Law Review* 1317.

[31] Both of which are discussed in Chapters 8 and 9.   [32] Discussed in Chapter 13.

substantive developments are discussed in Chapters 8, 9, 12, and 13, this chapter will focus instead on the institutional reforms at the EU level to ensure that banking regulation is developed, implemented, and supervised well in all member states. Indeed, the key highlight of the de Larosière Report was the recommendation to reform the institutional structures at the EU level that generate banking regulation policy and reform and oversee the implementation, supervision and enforcement at member state level, that is, the pan-European framework above the national regulatory architecture.

7.2.1 **Reform of EU institutional architecture for banking regulation**

The Report recommended that in order to achieve the multiple objectives of building the Single Market and making it resilient and stable, more institutions needed to be established at the EU level to drive these objectives. The Report proposed the institution of a *European System of Financial Supervision* **(ESFS)**.[33]

The System would comprise of institutions that would oversee member state regulators at the pan-European level, in the sectors of banking, securities and investments, and insurance and occupational pensions. These pan-European agencies would be formed by elevating informal Committees such as CEBS, alongside with CEBS' counterparts in securities regulation and insurance and occupational pensions regulation, to the stature of formal regulatory authorities. They would have supervisory powers over member state regulators to an extent and could demand member state regulators to account to them. They, however, would not have direct supervisory powers over financial institutions. The ESFS would also include a Joint Committee of the pan-European agencies and a body responsible for macroprudential supervision. This body was envisaged to be a 'European Systemic Risk Council'[34] best placed under the auspices of the European Central Bank (ECB).

On the basis of the Report's recommendations, the ESFS has indeed been introduced by European legislation in 2010.[35] The System comprises the European Banking Authority (EBA, which evolved from CEBS),[36] the European Securities and Markets Authority (ESMA),[37] the European Insurance and Occupational Pensions Authority

---

[33] Jacques de Larosière et al. and others, *Report by the High Level Group on Financial Supervision in the EU* 49.

[34] Jacques de Larosière et al., *Report by the High Level Group on Financial Supervision in the EU* 49–56.

[35] See account and analysis by Eddy Wymeersch, 'Europe's New Financial Regulatory Bodies' (2011) 11 *Journal of Corporate Law Studies* 443; Niamh Moloney, 'The European Securities and Markets Authority and Institutional Design for the EU Financial Market – A Tale of Two Competences: Parts 1 and 2' (2011) 12 *European Business Organisation Review* 43 and 178.

[36] European Parliament and Council Regulation (EU) 1093/2010 of 24 November 2010 establishing a European Supervisory Authority (European Banking Authority), amending Decision No 716/2009/EC and repealing Commission Decision 2009/78/EC [2010] OJ L331/12 (EBA Regulation 2010).

[37] European Parliament and Council Regulation (EU) 1095/2010 of 24 November 2010 establishing a European Supervisory Authority (European Securities and Markets Authority), amending Decision No 716/2009/EC and repealing Commission Decision 2009/77/EC [2010] OJ L331/84 (ESMA Regulation 2010).

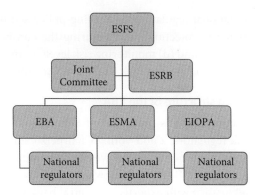

Figure 7.1 The institutional structure of the ESFS after the Implementation of the de Larosière Report

(EIOPA),[38] a Joint Committee of the three Authorities devoted to specific cross-sectoral responsibilities such as consumer protection and financial crime, and the European Systemic Risk Board[39] (ESRB, part of the ECB). The introduction of the Banking Union in 2013 has resulted in some adjustment on the part of the ESFS.

The evolution of the European financial regulatory architecture has proceeded from minimalist legislation and peer-level coordination by member states regulators to increasing legal harmonisation and supranational authority above the member state regulators. The ESFS has now attained institutional stature, and its mandates and powers are turning it into an architecture that achieves a significant extent of pan-European authority over banking and financial services policy and law. We now turn to examine the ESFS in detail.

7.2.2 **The European Banking Authority**

The European Banking Authority (EBA) is a regulator that ***does not deal*** directly with regulated banks. Banks remain primarily accountable to their national regulator. The EBA is a pan-European body that oversees national regulators in their implementation of EU banking regulation and their supervision of the regulated banking sector within the scope of their jurisdiction. Further it has distinct powers in developing banking regulation and policy at the EU level.

The EBA's responsibilities as set out in its establishing legislation include: (a) assisting with law-making and having limited powers to make certain binding rules to pursue legal harmonisation in bank regulation; (b) fostering supervisory coordination and

---

[38] European Parliament and Council Regulation (EU) 1094/2010 of 24 November 2010 establishing a European Supervisory Authority (European Insurance and Occupational Pensions Authority), amending Decision No 716/2009/EC and repealing Commission Decision 2009/79/EC [2010] OJ L331/48 (EIOPA Regulation 2010).

[39] European Parliament and Council Regulation (EU) 1092/2010 of 24 November 2010 on European Union macro-prudential oversight of the financial system and establishing a European Systemic Risk Board [2010] OJ L331/1 (ESRB Regulation 2010).

convergence amongst national regulators; (c) leading policy setting in specific areas such as consumer financial protection[40] and ensuring the consistent application of financial guarantee schemes;[41] and (d) monitoring risk levels in financial systems in the EU and assisting the European Systemic Risk Board in its macroprudential oversight.

7.2.2.1 Composition and structure of the EBA

The EBA's decision-making organ is the Board of Supervisors, which comprises of all member states' bank regulators, a non-voting Chairperson, and other non-voting observer members. These are: one representative of the European Commission, one representative of the Supervisory Board of ECB (who may be accompanied by a further non-voting ECB representative with expertise in central banking), one representative of the ESRB, and one representative each of ESMA and EIOPA.[42]

The EBA is assisted by a Stakeholder Panel that should meet four times a year, but meets with the Board of Supervisors twice a year.[43]

The Board of Supervisors makes decisions on all key matters in relation to the EBA's responsibilities, as will be discussed further. Decisions are made by a simple majority voting system with each member state having one vote. Voting members are to act independently of member state interests and consider the interests of the EU as a whole.[44] The voting system has, however, been adjusted with the advent of the Banking Union, to be discussed later. Certain decisions[45] can only be taken with a qualified majority voting procedure. This means that a simple majority of the class of member states that are Banking Union members must be achieved alongside a simple majority of the class of member states that are not members of the Banking Union. If, in the class for members not belonging to the Banking Union, the number of voting members is four or less, only one vote is needed from that class for the purposes of the qualified majority voting procedure.[46]

In order to carry out day-to-day operational tasks, the EBA is managed by a Management Board. The Management Board comprises of a Chairperson,[47] who is an independent full-time individual appointed by the Board of Supervisors, and six other members elected from the Board of Supervisors who shall hold office for two and a half years with the possible extension of a further term. After the advent of the Banking Union, safeguards are introduced to ensure that the composition of the Management Board reflects the interests of the Union as a whole and is proportionate reflecting the interests of Banking Union and non-Banking Union members. In particular, two

---

[40] EBA Regulation, Article 9.   [41] EBA Regulation, Article 26.

[42] EBA Regulation, Article 40, as amended in 2013 by Regulation (EU) No 1022/2013 of the European Parliament and of the Council of 22 October 2013 amending Regulation (EU) No 1093/2010 establishing a European Supervisory Authority (European Banking Authority) as regards the conferral of specific tasks on the European Central Bank pursuant to Council Regulation (EU) No 1024/2013.

[43] EBA Regulation, Article 37, amended in 2013.   [44] EBA Regulation, Article 42.

[45] That relate to rule-making and the exercise of emergency powers by the EBA.

[46] EBA Regulation, Article 44, amended in 2013.   [47] EBA Regulation, Articles 48 and 49.

members of the Management Board must be from non-Union member states at any one time. Members of the Management Board are to act independently and the Board has the following responsibilities:[48]

(a) to propose, for adoption by the Board of Supervisors, an annual and multi-annual work programme;

(b) to exercise budgetary powers;

(c) to adopt the Authority's staff policy plan and the necessary implementing measures;

(d) to provide for rights of access to the documents of the Authority;

(e) to propose an annual report on the activities of the Authority, including on the Chairperson's duties, to the Board of Supervisors for approval;

(f) to adopt and make public its rules of procedure; and

(g) to appoint and remove the members of the Board of Appeal (to be discussed).

7.2.2.2 The Single Rulebook

The EBA is expressly tasked to pursue regulatory harmonisation and market integration, in order to weed out differences between national regimes that can be taken advantage of by regulated financial institutions. The policy direction remains firmly entrenched in market integration and legal harmonisation continues to be perceived as the key means for achieving that. The EBA has an important role in assisting in the production of regulatory rules. It also has the power to make certain regulatory rules.

In financial services regulation, the EU has adopted institutional reforms for different levels of rule-making since 2001, in the form of the Lamfalussy procedure. This procedure was borne out of the Lamfalussy report,[49] which recommended a system for rule-making that would be efficient for the needs of market integration in financial services. The Lamfalussy report recommended that legal harmonisation required to support the completion of the single market for banking and financial services should be carried out in a fast-track legislative procedure. This procedure would overcome some of the slowness in traditional law-making in the EU but also contained certain safeguards. The Lamfalussy procedure introduced two levels of law-making, one level of supervisory convergence and one level of enforcement action to ensure that member states would give effect to EU laws. Box 7.1 illustrates what the procedure entails, which is explained shortly.

The Lamfalussy procedure sought to introduce fast-track law-making by leaving to the Commission the discretion to fill in details in legislation. Hence, primary legislation was to be drafted with skeletal principles only and passed quickly as binding regulations on member states. This proposal was viewed with suspicion by member states and

---

[48] EBA Regulation, Articles 45 and 46, amended in 2013.

[49] Final Report of the Committee of Wise Men on European Securities Markets (Lamfalussy Report) (2001) at http://ec.europa.eu/internal_market/securities/docs/lamfalussy/wisemen/final-report-wise-men_en.pdf.

Box 7.1   The Lamfalussy procedure

1. **Level 1 legislation** – regulations that set out general principles for financial regulation. These can be passed without much controversy by the Council and European Parliament.

2. **Level 2 legislation** – delegated law-making powers to the European Commission to 'fill in the details' left by the principles in the primary Regulations, in the form of binding secondary Directives or Regulations.

3. **Level 3 legislation** – Committee of European Banking Supervisors and equivalent committees in securities/insurance would ensure that convergence is achieved in implementing the Levels 1 and 2 legislation.

4. **Level 4 legislation** – the Commission can refer member states who fail to give effect to Level 1 and/or 2 legislation to the ECJ for enforcement.

---

hence Level 1 was initially not implemented in the way envisaged by the Lamfalussy Report. In the early days of the Lamfalussy procedure, a number of Level 1 legislation were introduced as directives and not regulations and contained significant amounts of detail.[50] However, the Commission undertook to draft Level 2 legislation alongside the finalisation of Level 1 legislation so that the entire process of law-making was comprehensive and wasted no time. The Lamfalussy procedure managed to achieve its fast-track effect, and has been credited as the start of law-making reforms in the EU generally. Indeed the Commission's powers to make delegated legislation (Level 2 legislation) is now enshrined in Article 290 of the TFEU, although it is subject to revocation by the Council of the European Union (comprising all Heads of State in EU member states) or European Parliament.

The smooth outworking of fast-track legislative procedure under Levels 1 and 2 from 2004 onwards has continued to support efficient law-making after the global financial crisis. However, a marked increase in Level 1 regulations has been observed, such as the Capital Requirements Regulation 2013, the European Market Infrastructure Regulation 2011, Market Abuse Regulation 2014, the Benchmarks Regulation 2016, and the Prospectus Regulation 2017, indicating greater willingness on the part of member states to accept binding regulation at the EU level in respect of financial services, without the need for national transposition. Indeed many Level 2 legislation are also promulgated as 'regulations' that are directly binding on member states.

The Commission seeks assistance in the drafting of Level 2 legislation from two committees. One is the committee comprising of all member states' finance ministers, and the other is the committee represented by member state regulators in the relevant sector. In the area of bank regulation, CEBS used to be the relevant committee that assists the Commission in drafting Level 2 legislation. Indeed the EBA has evolved from CEBs

---

[50] Niamh Moloney, 'The Lamfalussy Legislative Model: A New Era for the EC Securities and Investment Services Regime' (2003) 52 *International and Comparative Law Quarterly* 499.

Box 7.2 Levels of regulatory rules in the EU – post-crisis

1. Primary legislation – directive or regulation
2. Commission legislation (delegated in Primary legislation) – directive or regulation
3. Implementing Technical Standards (EBA to supplement 1 or 2 but not to introduce any new standard or obligation)
4. Non-binding Guidelines (EBA)

---

to become the producer of the first drafts of Level 2 legislation, known as 'Technical Standards', discussed later.

The EBA is now responsible for developing the 'Single Rulebook' for bank regulation. The Single Rulebook includes the EBA's role in assisting in legislation drafting, as well as issuing lower level rules, greatly expanding the original vision for law-making in the EU. Law-making in the EU now includes three levels of binding rules: traditional legislation-making by the Council and Parliament; the Commission's delegated legislation-making role and the European Supervisory Agencies' (EBA/ESMA/EIOPA) lower level rule-making powers.

Box 7.2 sets out the different levels of laws and rules applicable as EU-level legislation that member states have to implement.

Although primary legislation remains firmly in the hands of the Commission and the primary law-making bodies, the Council and Parliament in the EU, the EBA is arguably central to law-making for financial services.

The EBA's role in making regulatory rules

First, the EBA is tasked with drafting **Technical Standards** for consideration by the Commission in order to assist the Commission in drafting Level 2 legislation. The Technical Standards drafted by the EBA are publicly published and submitted to the Commission.[51] The Commission may deviate from the EBA's proposals with reasons.[52] Parliament and the Council of the European Union have the ultimate discretion to adopt the Commission legislation.[53]

Next, the EBA may introduce **Implementing Technical Standards** to support Level 2 legislation.[54] Level 2 legislation are passed after the Commission considers and amends the EBA's draft Technical Standards and issues such legislation in the form of a regulation or directive. The EBA may then introduce supportive rules for such Level 2 legislation. These supportive rules, that is, Implementing Technical Standards, involve no strategic or policy decisions and are of supplemental utility only. The EBA must carry out consultation on proposed implementing technical standards and also consult its Bank Stakeholder Panel. The implementing technical standards are submitted to the

---

[51] EBA Regulation, Article 10.   [52] EBA Regulation, Article 14.
[53] EBA Regulation, Articles 10 and 13.   [54] EBA Regulation, Article 15.

Commission for endorsement, and do not come into effect until such endorsement is obtained. Parliament and Council are to be notified of the implementing technical standards, and they must be published in the Official Journal of the European Union. Implementing technical standards have the status of law as they are binding upon member states to implement them.[55]

Finally, the EBA is also responsible for issuing *guidelines and recommendations.* These are for the purposes of securing efficient and convergent supervisory practices in the EU, to be discussed further.

The many layers of rule-making powers enjoyed by the EBA ensure that the EBA is poised to be the key rule developer in EU banking regulation. Its lower level rule-making powers can pertain to rather detailed matters of interpretive and implementation practice by member states. The Single Rulebook is a highly authoritative development in the EU.

7.2.2.3 Supervisory convergence

Moving on, the EBA has the important role of securing supervisory convergence in the EU. This means minimising supervisory differences between member states and achieving better coordination between them in relation to cross-border establishment of banking services. Supervisory convergence is seen as a necessary counterpart to legal harmonisation. member states are encouraged to implement the harmonised laws in a consistent and convergent manner with each other, and not to introduce vast differences in their supervisory and enforcement styles. Such convergence would reduce any gaps and differences in the 'law in action' in member states and mitigate opportunities for financial institutions to take advantage of those gaps and differences. Further, supervisory convergence can promote closer coordination between member state regulators, improving their cooperation with each other as home and host regulators for cross-border banking groups.

Supervisory convergence has been promoted since the days of CEBS (or CESR/CEIOPS) before the institution of the EBA. CEBS has designed many mechanisms to foster convergence in the interpretation and implementation of the primary legislation among member states, such as by issuing guidelines for interpretation, and databases of Q&As for various directives in order to clarify issues raised by member states. These resources are intended to foster a common approach to interpreting directive provisions. Some of these informal guidelines have evolved into more binding instruments such as Technical Standards or Implementing Technical Standards discussed earlier.

Further, the EBA is empowered to make non-binding but highly persuasive guidelines and recommendations to foster supervisory convergence. Although these are not strictly binding, the guidelines and recommendations are to be notified to the Commission, Parliament, and Council. Each member state is required to state within two months of the issuance of the guideline or recommendation whether it intends to comply and to what extent. If a member state contemplates non-compliance, reasons must be given to the EBA. The EBA will publish the extent of compliance and, where

---

[55] EBA Regulation, Article 17.

relevant, reasons for non-compliance, by each member state.[56] The EBA is also required to consult widely on such draft guidelines and recommendations including consulting the Bank Stakeholder Panel.

Next, the EBA is responsible for organising groups of supervisors to jointly oversee cross-border banking establishments,[57] which we call 'colleges'.[58] This is important as cross-border financial and banking services need to be supervised adequately by home and host authorities, an issue we discussed in section 7.1. The EBA has powers to oversee that colleges function coherently and consistently, ensuring that there is optimal cooperation within colleges such as sharing of sufficient information (as facilitated by the EBA),[59] fostering consistency in supervisory practices, and developing agreements on supervisory and enforcement actions against financial institutions.

In order to promote supervisory convergence, whether in a college context or otherwise, the EBA is committed to fostering a common supervisory culture.[60] This is intended to encourage supervisors to learn from each other and in time adopt consistent and similar styles. For example, the EBA introduces common templates for the collection of supervisory information by member state regulators. This template is known as the 'Supervisory Review and Evaluation Procedure' or SREP. The SREP is a common template that member state regulators send to their regulated banks in order to collect information on key issues such as capital and liquidity adequacy. The promotion of a common information template is intended to promote comparability of supervisory considerations and decisions. This facilitates regulatory learning amongst member states and allows the EBA to discern similarities and differences in supervisory emphases and styles. Such information templates also cover areas such as bankers' remuneration reporting, discussed in Chapter 12, section 12.4.4.

Another example of the EBA's informal mechanisms to promote a common supervisory culture is in the form of enforcement decisions databases for key compliance issues. These information repositories contain key enforcement decisions across member states and provide a one-stop resource for member state regulators to consult. It is intended to foster learning amongst member state regulators, hopefully promoting best practices in a convergent manner.[61] The EBA may also perform peer reviews of member state regulators regularly in order to determine their progress in supervisory convergence.[62]

Further, the EBA also performs the crucial role of settling disagreements among member state regulators so as to remove obstacles to supervisory convergence. member state regulators who fail to agree on a matter for joint decision or coordination may refer the matter to the EBA. The EBA will facilitate conciliation between the disagreeing regulators. If conciliation fails, the EBA is in a position to address a decision to resolve

---

[56] EBA Regulation, Article 16.   [57] EBA Regulation, Article 21.

[58] More in Chapter 13, section 13.4 and Chapter 5, section 5.3.5.

[59] EBA Regulation, Article 31.   [60] EBA Regulation, Article 29.

[61] These are discussed in Iris H-Y Chiu, *Regulatory Convergence in EU Securities Regulation* (The Hague: Kluwer Law International 2008), with special reference to ESMA but the EBA's mandate would have been similar.

[62] EBA Regulation, Article 30.

the conflict.[63] This is improved from the former position developed under CEBS, which promoted mediation amongst disagreeing regulators. The former mediation process did not allow CEBS to impose a decision on disagreeing regulators, due to CEBS' lack of institutional status and formal powers.

7.2.2.4 Systemic risk-related roles and powers

The EBA is tasked with the responsibility to identify and monitor signs of 'systemic risk' in the EU.[64] 'Systemic risk' relates to risks arising from financial markets, or the inter-connections between financial institutions that could amplify and threaten financial stability if they materialise. As the EU comprises of many clusters of interconnected financial institutions, national and regional markets, systemic risks may arise in parts of the EU and not necessarily affect the whole of the EU's financial systems. Nevertheless, systemic risks concentrated in certain regions or markets would likely be regarded as sufficiently important threats as it is uncertain how their adverse footprint may spread.

The EBA monitors market developments and publishes a 'Risk Dashboard' on a yearly basis. It also carries out stress testing of banks (discussed in Chapter 9, section 9.6), almost every two years.[65] The EBA's work feeds into the ESRB's role in monitoring and making recommendations regarding systemic risks in EU financial markets. The EBA collects and relays systemic risk-related information to the ESRB for its systemic risk recommendations and warnings. The EBA has the role to follow up on the ESRB's warnings if any are issued.[66]

Further, as the EBA is expected to have a 'permanent capacity to respond to systemic risks',[67] it enjoys a key power to intervene in the mitigation of systemic risk materialisation. The EBA is able to determine that an 'emergency' has arisen, and address an emergency decision to national regulators. [68] This power can be exercised *in the case of adverse developments that may seriously jeopardise the orderly functioning and integrity of financial markets or the stability of the whole or part of the financial system in the Union.*[69] By issuing such a top-down decision to national regulators, the exercise of this power threatens to undermine national regulators' authority. Hence the power can only be exercised subject to safeguards.

First, if the EBA is of the view that the circumstances of an emergency has arisen, it may refer this to the Council. The EBA is not the only body that may make such a reference – the Commission or the ESRB may do so too of their own accord. The Council must consult with the Commission and the ESRB in order to determine if an emergency situation has indeed occurred. If so, this determination would be addressed to the European Supervisory Authorities. The determination has to be reviewed monthly by the Council to consider whether it should be renewed. The lack of a decision to renew would make the determination of 'an emergency situation' expire at the end of the relevant month.

---

[63] EBA Regulation, Article 19.   [64] EBA Regulation, Article 23.   [65] EBA Regulation, Article 32.
[66] EBA Regulation, Articles 35 and 36.   [67] EBA Regulation, Article 24.
[68] EBA Regulation, Article 18.   [69] EBA Regulation, Article 18.

Upon securing the Council's decision to determine that an emergency situation has arisen, and only if coordinated action by national authorities is required to avert adverse developments that may jeopardise the functioning and integrity of EU financial markets, the EBA may address individual decisions to such authorities to require them to take certain actions and coordinate with each other. If member state regulators do not apply the EBA's individual decisions including imposing on or enforcing against their regulated entities, the EBA has the right to address individual decisions directly to the regulated entities concerned.

The emergency powers allow the EBA in exceptional circumstances to directly impose EU-level decisions against regulated entities, substituting for member state regulators' exercise of authority. These situations are likely to be rare but we have now created a formal set of EU-level institutions with direct power to impose pan-European objectives and powers upon regulators and, sometimes, the regulated entities directly. This direct assumption of powers has further been extended in the Banking Union discussed in section 7.3. These developments allow us to question whether a form of stealthy centralisation of regulatory authority is taking place in the EU, and what implications this raises for member state regulators. We return to this point shortly in section 7.2.3.

7.2.2.5 Relationships with third countries and Brexit

Finally, the EBA enjoys a key power that allows it to treat a third country's regulatory system as equivalent[70] for purposes of determining if a third-country banking institution can be established in a member state or enjoy certain privileges in the Single Market. Financial institutions outside of the EU may wish to enter the EU market, and they can only do so if they are regarded as being authorised and supervised in a manner that is equivalent to the regime in the EU, and would not undermine the legal harmonisation and supervisory convergence sought to be achieved in the EU. The EBA is the gatekeeper for harmonised rules and implementation and may revoke any 'equivalency' decision with a month's notice.

Upon the UK's withdrawal from the EU, the UK's practical access to the Single Market in relation to banking and financial services would depend largely on a new trade deal, or the European supervisory agencies' assessment of the UK's 'equivalence' in regulatory standards and implementation. The UK would be dealing with the EBA as a 'third country' and such equivalence can be revoked with a month's notice, which is a position not highly satisfactory to the UK banking sector having operations in the UK.[71] In line with a general commitment to 'regulatory alignment' agreed between the UK and EU

---

[70] EBA Regulation, Article 33.

[71] See, for example, in depth discussions of possibilities in a Brexit special Issue of the *European Business Law Review* 2016, Matthias Lehmann and Dirk Zetzsche, 'Brexit and the Consequences for Commercial and Financial Relations between the EU and the UK' (2016) *European Business Law Review* 113; Alan Brener, 'No-Man is an Island: UK and EU Banking Engagement after "Brexit"' (2016) *European Business Law Review* 143; Francisco de la Peña, 'Gentle Brexit, a Very British Exit: EEA Membership as the Most Optimal Mechanism to Secure Financial Services Passports' (2016) *European Business Law Review* 171.

in negotiations,[72] the UK is likely to maintain a high level of legal harmonisation as this is also seen as consistent with more broadly the global nature of banking and financial services.[73] Further, the EU–UK negotiations have secured a transitional period up to the start of 2021, which provides some relief to the financial services sector to organise their post-Brexit activities.

In view of Brexit, many financial institutions based in the UK may seek a new 'European base' in order to carry on enjoying access to the Single Market. The EBA is wary of financial institutions that may set up a minimal presence in the EU in order to enjoy 'passporting' rights, and carry out most of their operations from the UK. The EBA has issued an Opinion in October 2017[74] to clarify its expectations as to how financial institutions may re-organise themselves. The EBA warns that financial institutions wishing to be established in an EU member state must meet the full conditions of authorisation and carry out substantive operations in order to benefit from the rights of participation in the Single Market. The EBA eschews 'letter-box' entities expressly and warns member state regulators to implement their authorisation and supervisory regimes robustly.

Further, European banks and financial institutions would need to seek authorisation in the UK. The PRA has issued consultations to gather views on the way forward for authorising foreign financial firms as well as incoming foreign branches. The PRA envisages that such authorisations will be based on assessment of equivalent regulatory regimes and close supervisory relationships that the PRA maintains with the foreign regulator. The PRA envisages to maintain close supervisory relationships with European regulators and the European institutional bodies.[75]

7.2.3 Other institutions in the European System of Financial Supervision

The ESFS also comprises a number of other agencies, the ESMA, overseeing matters in relation to securities markets, investment funds and other trading markets for financial instruments; the EIOPA, responsible for overseeing the prudential requirements for insurers and developing the single market in insurance and occupational pensions products; the Joint Committee of the three European Supervisory Authorities and the ESRB.

---

[72] Para 49 of the Joint report of the EU-UK negotiations published on 8 December 2017 indicating the UK's willingness to maintain full alignment with the rules of the Internal Market and Customs Union, see https://ec.europa.eu/commission/sites/beta-political/files/joint_report.pdf.

[73] 'UK aims to keep financial rules close to EU after Brexit', *Financial Times* (16 February 2018)

[74] *EBA Opinion on Brexit Issues* (October 2017) at https://www.eba.europa.eu/documents/10180/1756362/EBA+Opinion+on+Brexit+Issues+%28EBA-Op-2017-12%29.pdf.

[75] PRA, *The Bank of England's Approach to the Authorisation and Supervision of International Banks, Insurers and Central Counterparties* (20 December 2017) at https://www.bankofengland.co.uk/news/2017/december/approach-to-authorisation-and-supervision-of-international-banks-insurers-central-counterparties; *International banks: The Prudential Regulation Authority's Approach to Branch Authorisation and Supervision* (March 2018) at https://www.bankofengland.co.uk/-/media/boe/files/prudential-regulation/policy-statement/2018/ps318.pdf?la=en&hash=E83AC495359333506CF4AC036784D793CEC06888.

7.2.3.1 European Securities and Markets Authority

The Regulations establishing the EBA, ESMA, and EIOPA have mirror provisions on the roles, functions, and powers of these bodies.[76] Hence, ESMA has similar tasks as the EBA in terms of (a) supporting Level 2 legislation and issuing lower level rules like the EBA, (b) achieving supervisory convergence, and (c) systemic risk-monitoring roles and maintaining a relationship with the ESRB in this regard. All three European Supervisory Authorities have common mandates in protecting financial stability, consumer protection, and instituting financial guarantee schemes in all member states. ESMA also has powers to determine third-country equivalence in relation to securities markets, other trading markets, and investment funds.

ESMA, unlike the EBA, enjoys a greater extent of direct supervisory powers as it has oversight of certain pan-European entities such as clearinghouses and credit rating agencies[77] whose markets are not nationally confined. Further, ESMA enjoys some direct powers of interventions such as powers of product intervention or issuing short-selling prohibitions. Under the Markets in Financial Instruments Regulation,[78] ESMA is able to issue temporary restrictions or prohibitions on the marketing, distribution, or sale of certain financial instruments or financial instruments with certain specified features; or any type of financial activity or practice. This power can be exercised if ESMA is of the view that there is significant investor protection concern or threats to the orderly functioning of any financial markets or the financial system in the EU as a whole, and that existing regulation does not address the issue. This power can be exercised if no member state regulator has addressed the threat adequately.

In relation to issuing temporary prohibitions on short-selling, short-selling is an activity where financial instruments may be sold before they are actually bought by the selling party, in anticipation of the price of these instruments declining in the future. However short-selling may also carry predictive power for the markets in that market prices *will decline* in view of the signals of short-sellers, and may cause financial instrument prices to spiral downwards.[79] ESMA enjoys the power under the Regulation on Short-Selling to require mandatory disclosure of short sales positions in particular financial instruments and/or to temporarily prohibit short sales in particular financial instruments.[80] ESMA may exercise the above powers if there is a threat to the orderly functioning of financial

---

[76] See analysis in Niamh Moloney, 'The European Securities and Markets Authority and Institutional Design for the EU Financial Market – A Tale of Two Competences: Parts 1 and 2' (2011) 12 *European Business Organisation Review* 43 and 178 respectively.

[77] Regulation (EU) No 513/2011 of the European Parliament and of the Council of 11 May 2011 amending Regulation (EC) No 1060/2009 on credit rating agencies.

[78] Article 40, Regulation (EU) No 600/2014 of the European Parliament and of the Council of 15 May 2014 on markets in financial instruments and amending Regulation (EU) No 648/2012.

[79] Avgouleas criticises intervention in short-selling as interfering with price efficiency mechanisms in the market and that long sellers can equally create that effect, see Emilios Avgouleas, 'A New Framework for the Global Regulation of Short Sales: Why Prohibition is Inefficient and Disclosure Insufficient' (2010) 15 *Stanford Journal of Banking and Financial Law* 376.

[80] Article 28, Regulation (EU) No 236/2012 – Short selling and certain aspects of credit default swaps.

markets or to the financial system in the EU as a whole, and that member state regulators have not addressed the threat adequately. ESMA is also required to consider risks of liquidity to markets and regulatory arbitrage risks in exercising that power.

ESMA's more powerful profile has not been accepted easily without challenge. The UK challenged[81] ESMA's power to prohibit short-selling on the basis that such a power involves a large measure of discretion akin to intervening in economic policy and falls foul of the *Meroni* doctrine.[82] The doctrine may be understood in brief as restricting the types of powers that EU-level agencies can exercise. Basically, EU member states have delegated powers to the EU level and one cannot presume that any such powers can, in turn, be delegated to an EU agency without an explicit basis. If delegated, they cannot be 'discretionary' to such an extent that the 'wide margin of discretion' might enable the 'execution of actual economic policy'. The latter would mean an illegal transfer of responsibility altering the balance of powers between member states and EU institutions, that is, 'institutional balance'. The UK alleged that ESMA's power to issue short-selling bans is too discretionary and is the type of power that cannot be delegated to an EU agency. The challenge failed on this head as the ECJ is of the view that ESMA's powers are of a technical nature of expertise in making a judgment about a threat to the orderly functioning of financial markets or systems, and can only be exercised if national regulators have not addressed the threat adequately. Hence it is not overly discretionary. The UK's alternative heads of challenge regarding the power as being incompatible with ESMA's founding legislation also failed, and ESMA's power is ruled not to be outside of the harmonisation objectives for the internal market.

There is also discussion that ESMA's direct regulatory and supervisory authority can be further extended to pan-European investment funds, for example.[83]

It is perceived to be more efficient for a centralised regulator to be instituted at the pan-European level for entities that actually have such a footprint. ESMA's direct regulatory and supervisory capacity has been building up with its experience with credit rating agencies, for example. It has to date carried out supervisory reviews and investigations against credit rating agencies, including a general criticism of the Big Three rating agencies (S&P, Moody's, and Fitch) for an industry-wide downgrade of European banks' solvency prospects in 2012. ESMA found the downgrade unjustified due to flawed methodology and assumptions.[84] Further, it issued a public censure of S&P for its erroneous downgrade of French sovereign debt in 2014.[85]

---

[81]   *UK v Parliament and Council* Case C-270/12 decided in 2014.

[82]   *Meroni & Co., Industrie Metallurgiche, SpA v High Authority of the European Coal and Steel Community* Case 9–56.

[83]   European Commission, 'Creating a stronger and more integrated European financial supervision for the Capital Markets Union' (Press Release, 20 September 2017).

[84]   'ESMA Criticises Agencies Rating Methods', *Financial Times* (18 March 2013) at https://www.ft.com/content/7dd71cc8-8fca-11e2-9239-00144feabdc0.

[85]   'ESMA Censures Standard & Poor's for Internal Control Failings' (3 June 2014) where S&P's organisational failings caused the publication of a downgrade statement for French sovereign debt although there has been no such decision. See https://www.esma.europa.eu/sites/default/files/library/2015/11/2014-596_esma_censures_standard_u_poors_for_internal_control_failings.pdf.

7.2.3.2 European Insurance and Occupational Pensions Authority

EIOPA focuses on the insurance and occupational pensions sectors. Like EBA and ESMA, its roles and powers are similar, relating to maintaining a single rulebook for the insurance and occupational pension sectors, securing supervisory convergence, monitoring systemic risks and maintaining a relationship with the ESRB, and determining third-country equivalence as already discussed.

EIOPA's main focus is securing regulatory convergence in relation to the Solvency II Directive[86] and the accompanying Commission legislation and EIOPA's standards and guidelines. This Directive provides harmonised prudential regulation for insurers, which is a bespoke regime different from banks due to the different risks that insurers face. Like the EBA it has no direct supervisory powers over regulated entities, except the same exceptional powers in an 'emergency situation' as has been discussed.

7.2.3.3 Joint Committee of the European Supervisory Agencies

The Joint Committee of the European Supervisory Authorities comprises of the Chairpersons and Executive Directors of each Authority. A representative from the Commission and ESRB respectively would be observers at the meetings of the Joint Committee.[87] The Joint Committee is established to ensure cooperation and cross-sectoral consistency in policy areas such as financial conglomerates, accounting and auditing, microprudential analyses, risks and vulnerabilities for financial stability, retail investment products, anti- money laundering policies (see Chapter 14), and working with the ESRB.[88] In particular, the Joint Committee may establish sub-committees dedicated to any of the above areas, but a mandatory sub-committee on Financial Conglomerates must be established.[89]

The Joint Committee has formed increasing numbers of sub-committees over the years, suggesting that they are expanding their leadership in policy development. Besides the mandatory Financial Conglomerates sub-committee, the Joint Committee has established a sub-committee on Cross-sectoral Developments, Risks and Vulnerabilities, a sub-committee on Money Laundering, and a sub-committee on Consumer Protection and Financial Innovation, which has further formed three sub-groups to deal specifically with different consumer conduct issues.[90] The Joint Committee also often sees it as efficient to undertake joint analyses of topical issues as

---

[86] Directive 2009/138/EC of the European Parliament and of the Council of 25 November 2009 on the taking-up and pursuit of the business of Insurance and Reinsurance (Solvency II).

[87] EBA, ESMA and EIOPA Regulations, Article 55.

[88] EBA, ESMA and EIOPA Regulations, Article 54.

[89] EBA, ESMA and EIOPA Regulations, Article 57.

[90] Such cross-selling (i.e. selling of financial products with different sectoral features, such as banking and insurance, insurance and investment etc.) and complaints-handling, product development and oversight, and technical standards for packaged retail investor products (PRIPs Regulation 2014 on disclosure formats). See Joint Committee, *Joint Committee Consultation Paper on Guidelines for Cross-Selling Practices* (22 December 2014) at http://www.esma.europa.eu/system/files/jc_cp_2014_05_consultation_paper_on_cross_selling.pdf. Joint Committee Work Programme 2013, at http://www.esma.europa.eu/sk/system/files/jc-2013-002.pdf.

they arise,[91] so that policy development can be made on the basis of joined-up thinking not confined to sectoral perspectives.

Although the Joint Committee does not assume the position of a centralised financial services regulatory body in the EU, its expanding remit and role in providing technical analyses of financial sector issues are noted as features that approximate the stature of such a body. Although the Joint Committee represents the three European Supervisory Authorities whose Boards of Supervisors comprise ultimately of all member state regulators, making each Authority fully representative of all member states, the Joint Committee is set up as a distinct body and its executive body is no longer fully representative. The perception of it being 'centralised' and 'top-down' is, however, mitigated by the consensus procedure taken for decision-making at the Joint Committee. The Joint Committee is the forum for joint decisions to be adopted by consensus among the three Authorities.[92] It has established a procedure of decision-making that involves consensus of the three Chairpersons.[93] Disagreements would result in reconsiderations of issues which would then be subject to decision-making again. The consensus procedure fosters inter-agency transparency, sharing, learning and negotiation and arguably overcomes gaps that may arise from the sectoral divisions between the three Authorities.[94]

7.2.3.4 The Board of Appeal

One of the institutions established by the Joint Committee is the Board of Appeal, a first instance redress mechanism for any natural or legal person affected by any of the European Supervisory Authorities' decisions.

The Board of Appeal consists of six members and six alternates. The three European Supervisory Authorities appoint four representatives each (two members and two alternates) from their Management Boards to the Board of Appeal. Other experts are openly recruited to the Board of Appeal.[95] Every member is expected to act impartially and independently in deciding any appeal, with interested members abstaining from sitting on the appeal.[96] The Board of Appeal should provide resolution in an expeditious manner[97] and must make its procedures and its reasoned decisions publicly accessible.[98]

---

[91] Such as reviewing the extent of mechanistic reliance in EU legislation on credit ratings, and the review of benchmark setting and regulation of the relevant processes. Benchmarks refer to certain indices established for the determine of variable price in contracts, such as the use of the London Interbank Offered Rate (LIBOR) for determining the interest rate for mortgage transactions that are based on a variable rate. See *Joint Consultation Paper on Mechanistic References to Credit Ratings* (November 2013), *Final Report* (February 2014). Joint Committee, *Letter on Possible Framework for the Regulation of the Production and Use of Indices Serving as Benchmarks in Financial and other Contracts* (November 2013).

[92] EBA, ESMA and EIOPA Regulations, Article 56.

[93] Decision of the Joint Committee of the European Banking Authority, European Insurance and Occupational Pensions Authority, and European Securities and Markets Authority adopting the Rules of Procedure of the Joint Committee of the European Supervisory Authorities (21 June 2011).

[94] Joint Committee Work Programme 2013, 2014.

[95] EBA, ESMA and EIOPA Regulations, Article 58.

[96] EBA, ESMA and EIOPA Regulations, Articles 58 and 59.

[97] Within two months of lodging an appeal.   [98] EBA, ESMA and EIOPA Regulations, Article 60.

The Board's decisions are subject to appeal to the ECJ. Access to the Court is also available under Article 263 of the TFEU where an Authority's decision cannot be appealed[99] to the Board of Appeal.[100]

There have not been many appeals to the Board of Appeal and no cases from the Board to the Court of Justice to the European Union (CJEU) to date.

We discuss an example decided by the Board of Appeal. The first decision of the Board of Appeal concerns a complaint made by SV Capital Oü against the EBA.[101] In this case, SV Capital raised a matter to the EBA regarding the suitability of persons directing the Estonian branches of Finnish Bank Nordea in Estonia. A Nordea branch in Estonia froze a particular business account due to money laundering concerns. The freezing action was reviewed by an Estonian court and determined to be illegal. However, the Estonian financial services regulator did not act against the directors of the branch in question. SV Capital was of the view that the Estonian financial regulator ought to have removed two governors of the Nordea branch since their credibility had been doubted in court. The Estonian authority explained that this decision for removal ought to be exercised by the Finnish home authority for Nordea. The Finnish home authority then rejected SV Capital's complaint. SV Capital then complained to the EBA, alleging that the Finnish authority had breached Union law by not removing unsuitable persons from directing the Nordea branch in Estonia. The EBA declined to determine the complaint because it regarded itself as having no jurisdiction to intervene in matters of corporate governance for banks reserved to the home regulator of the bank.

On appeal to the Board of Appeal, the Board considered that the EBA had interpreted its remit too narrowly. The EBA could intervene in matters regarding member states' supervisory decisions over the corporate governance of key branches such as the Estonian branch of Nordea. The matter was remitted to the EBA. However, the EBA ultimately decided not to investigate into the matter as a breach of Union law as it considered the Finnish regulator's explanation of its supervisory decision to be adequate. The Finnish regulator refused to remove the two governors targeted in the complaint as they were not regarded as key function holders in the branch. SV Capital raised another appeal to the Board regarding the EBA's decision. It alleged that the EBA had refused to investigate the matter due to its fears of damaging relations with national regulators, and that it was not pursuing its responsibilities robustly. The Board of Appeal reviewed the EBA's decision and was of the view that the decision not to investigate was based on a reasoned reliance on the Finnish home authority's supervisory assessment.[102]

---

[99] EBA, ESMA and EIOPA Regulations, Article 61.

[100] However, Pieter Van Cleynenbreugel, 'Judicial Protection against EU Financial Supervisory Authorities in the Wake of Regulatory Reform' (2012) at http://ssrn.com/abstract=2194172 criticises that the judicial accountability is too narrow as being confined to persons directly affected by agency decisions and that the grounds in Article 263 may not encompass all possible grievances against the agencies.

[101] Decision of the Board of Appeal in SV Capital Oü v EBA (Frankfurt, 24 June 2013).

[102] Decision of the Board of Appeal in *SV Capital Oü v EBA* (Frankfurt, 14 July 2014).

The two appeals brought by SV Capital against the EBA provided opportunities for high-level scrutiny of the EBA's understanding of its remit, its relations with national regulators and the division of regulatory responsibilities between them. This case demonstrated the EBA's reluctance to intervene in a matter they saw as essentially 'national' in character. The conclusion made by the Board of Appeal in interpreting the EBA's remit in overseeing corporate governance matters has helped to clarify the EBA's scope of responsibilities and powers.

7.2.3.5 European Systemic Risk Board

The ESRB[103] is the pan-European body responsible for macroprudential oversight.[104] It is responsible for collecting and analysing information in order to identify signals of risk in EU financial systems and markets, so as to determine if appropriate warnings and recommendations should be issued in view of these risks.[105]

The ESRB is directed by a General Board[106] comprising of the President and Vice-President of the ECB, governors of national central banks, the Chairpersons of the three European Supervisory Authorities, a member of the European Commission, and the Chairs and Vice-Chairs of the ESRB's Advisory Scientific Committee and the Chair of the ESRB's Advisory Technical Committee. The ESRB's work is assisted by an Advisory Scientific Committee,[107] which comprises of experts from across a wide range of fields and skills, and the Advisory Technical Committee,[108] which consists of representatives from national central banks and EU-level representation.

The General Board is assisted by a smaller Steering Committee[109] made up of an even spread of representatives from the ESRB itself, the General Board, the ECB, the ESMA, EBA and EIOPA, the European Commission, the Economic and Financial Committee of the European Council, and the two advisory committees of the ESRB. This composition seeks to address the balance of member state representation in the ESRB while maintaining a decision-making organ that is not overly crowded and risks becoming inefficient.

In order to fulfil its monitoring and policy functions, the ESRB has the power to collect and request information from the three European Supervisory Authorities, from national central banks, and from member state regulators.[110] It also provides information to the three European Supervisory Authorities where appropriate.[111] The collection of information by the ESRB must be in aggregate form and may not identify any particular financial institution.[112] Although this may be understandable in terms of protecting financial institutions from being prematurely identified and affecting public perception,

---

[103] European Parliament and Council Regulation (EU) 1092/2010 of 24 November 2010 on European Union macro-prudential oversight of the financial system and establishing a European Systemic Risk Board [2010] OJ L331/1 (ESRB Regulation 2010).

[104] See discussion of what this means in Chapter 6, section 6.4.

[105] ESRB Regulation, Article 3.   [106] ESRB Regulation, Article 6.   [107] ESRB Regulation, Article 12.

[108] ESRB Regulation, Article 13.   [109] ESRB Regulation, Article 11.   [110] ESRB Regulation, Article 15.

[111] ESRB Regulation, Article 15.   [112] ESRB Regulation, Article 15(3).

the ESRB is arguably prevented from making a judgment on whether an individual institution is particularly important for systemic risk. The ESRB may also consult private sector stakeholders for advice, contributing to its capabilities for analysis.[113]

In 2012, the ESRB set out in its mandate document[114] that member states should designate macroprudential supervisors and that the ESRB should maintain information sharing and coordination relationships with them. This mandate ensures that macroprudential supervision is not only centralised in the ESRB, and perhaps highlights that fears of over-centralisation at the EU level are unwarranted. Further, the mandate also reflects the lack of capacity of institutions at the EU level to undertake comprehensive and thorough forms of monitoring and policymaking.

However, in order to maintain regulatory and supervisory convergence, the ESRB voluntarily undertakes to assess member state's national macroprudential frameworks, against its optimal recommended benchmarks, in order to nudge member states towards convergence.[115] The ESRB has also issued a policy document to guide national macroprudential supervisors so that convergence can be achieved in relation to macroprudential policy objectives.[116] The ESRB recommends that macroprudential supervision be focused on 'intermediate term' objectives and these are defined in Table 7.1. Further, the key policy instruments for achieving such intermediate term objectives are also recommended. This guidance fosters market expectations of predictability and convergent practices in member states, although the ESRB acknowledges that other objectives and policy strategies could be introduced based on country-specific needs or Union needs. The objectives and tools for macroprudential regulation are set out in Table 7.1.

The ESRB monitors the application of macroprudential policy in its yearly stock-take,[117] that is, surveying the application of macroprudential tools by national regulators. It also issues overall frameworks for specific macroprudential tools in order to provide guidance for national regulators.[118] In its 2018 review of the application of the *systemic risk buffer* by national regulators, the ESRB acknowledges country differences that result in different applications but calls for more information sharing and compatibility in approaches for the future.[119]

---

[113] ESRB Regulation, Article 14.

[114] 'ESRB Publishes Recommendation on Macroprudential Mandate of National Authorities' (16 January 2012) at https://www.esrb.europa.eu/news/pr/date/2012/html/pr120116.en.html.

[115] ESRB, *ESRB Recommendation on the Macro-Prudential Mandate of National Authorities* (ESRB/2011/3): Follow Up Report (June 2014) at https://www.esrb.europa.eu/pub/pdf/recommendations/2014/ESRB_2014.en .pdf?600ec3fed1d5300e6a16ef0767b75cc5.

[116] ESRB, *Recommendation of the European Systemic Risk Board of 4 April 2013 on Intermediate Objectives and Instruments of Macro-Prudential Policy* (ESRB/2013/1) at https://www.esrb.europa.eu/pub/pdf/recommendations/2013/ESRB_2013_1.en.pdf?ad6bc3424dd7690e2f818db264c03299.

[117] Yearly *Review of Macroprudential Policy* available on the ESRB's website at https://www.esrb.europa.eu.

[118] Such as the ESRB, *The Macroprudential Use of Margins and Haircuts* (February 2017) at https://www. esrb.europa.eu/pub/pdf/reports/170216_macroprudential_use_of_margins_and_haircuts.en.pdf?b9eeb2de6 5fa0f48d8d2dfd775026912.

[119] IWG Expert Group to the ESRB, *Final Report on the Use of Structural Macroprudential Instruments in the EU* (December 2017).

Table 7.1 Objectives and tools for macroprudential supervision

---

(a) to mitigate and prevent excessive credit growth and leverage;
Key Policy Instruments:
- Counter-cyclical capital buffer
- Sectoral capital requirements (including intra-financial system)
- Macroprudential leverage ratio
- Loan-to-value requirements (LTV)
- Loan-to-income/debt (service)-to-income requirements (LTI)
(see Chapter 6, section 6.4 and Chapter 8, sections 8.4 and 8.5)

(b) to mitigate and prevent excessive maturity mismatch and market illiquidity;
Key Policy Instruments:
- Macroprudential adjustment to *liquidity coverage ratio*
- Macroprudential restrictions on funding sources (e.g. *net stable funding ratio*)
- Macroprudential guidance on loan-to-deposit ratio
- Margin and *haircut* requirements (such as for collateral-based funding) (Chapter 9, sections 9.2 and 9.4)

(c) to limit direct and indirect exposure concentrations:
Key Policy Instruments:
- Large exposure restrictions (See Chapter 9, section 9.3)
- Central counterparty clearing requirement (clearing houses are to stand as counterparties to certain derivatives trades so as to guarantee their fulfilment. This prevents defaults in markets for relatively riskier trading instruments)

(d) to limit the systemic impact of misaligned incentives and moral hazard:
Key Policy Instruments:
- Extra capital charges for systemically important financial institutions (see Chapter 9, section 9.5)

(e) to strengthen the resilience of financial infrastructures:
Key Policy Instruments:
- Margin and haircut requirements on central counterparty clearing (clearing houses are to impose adequate conditions on their participants so that they are adequately financed against the risks of default by their participants trading in relatively riskier instruments.)
- Increased disclosure
- Structural systemic risk buffer (discussed in Chapter 8, section 8.5.3)

One of the ESRB's distinct powers is to recommend the counter-cyclical buffer rate applicable to microprudential regulation of banks (discussed in Chapter 8, section 8.5.3). The ESRB in 2014[120] has set out comprehensive guidance to national authorities

---

[120] ESRB, *Recommendation of the European Systemic Risk Board of 18 June 2014 on Guidance for Setting Countercyclical Buffer Rates* (ESRB/2014/1) at https://www.esrb.europa.eu/pub/pdf/recommendations/2014/140630_ESRB_Recommendation.en.pdf?83075f19bd8f21d8a3b8e6afe7bea49b.

in setting their national counter-cyclical buffer rates. The national counter-cyclical buffer rate should be set according to a benchmark recommended by the ESRB.[121]

The ESRB's role is to issue warnings and/or recommendations to the EU as a whole or to individual member states regulators.[122] These warnings and recommendations are to be contemporaneously transmitted to the Council and Commission. The ESRB may follow up with the addressees as to what actions are taken in respect of the warnings or recommendations, but the general enforcement procedure for breach of Union law under the Treaty does not apply.[123] In other words, the ESRB's warnings and recommendations are soft law and member states are expected to comply or otherwise explain.

The ESRB has carried out considerable work in monitoring European financial markets developments. Its recommendations have included urging national regulators to monitor banks in terms of their foreign currency denominated funding needs (2012), monitoring aspects of shadow banking risks, as such activities that give rise to risks like banks but may not be as tightly regulated as traditional banking activity (2016) and monitoring risks in real estate markets (2016). Although its recommendations are soft law, the ESRB has developed a methodology for assessing the extent of member state compliance.[124] The ESRB requires member states to periodically make information returns on their states of adoption of ESRB recommendations, as against compliance criteria set out accompanying each recommendation. The ESRB scores the degrees of implementation by each member state against an implementation progress grid in order to determine if a member state is 'fully compliant', 'largely compliant', 'partially compliant', 'materially non-compliant', or 'non-compliant'. Further the ESRB determines if any non-compliance is 'sufficiently' or 'insufficiently' explained by member states. The ESRB aims to communicate all results to member states and engage in continuing dialogue with them. These formalised procedures ramp up the persuasive effect of the ESRB's work vis-à-vis member states.

Where appropriate, the General Board may make its warnings or recommendations public, once the Council and addressees have been informed and a two-thirds majority vote is obtained in the meeting of the General Board.[125] The power to issue warnings has been sparingly used, and the only instance to date is the issue of eight warnings to eight member state countries in terms of the need to monitor the systemic risk build-up in relation to their real estate sectors. In particular the concerns revolve around excessive bank lending in relation to residential mortgages and households borrowing too much and being overstretched.[126] A number of

---

[121] member state macro-prudential supervisors are asked to consider the ratio of credit in the economy to its GDP in order to determine if lending by banks should be constrained by a certain level of counter-cyclical buffer.

[122] ESRB Regulation, Article 16.   [123] ESRB Regulation, Article 17.

[124] ESRB, *Handbook on the Assessment of Compliance with ESRB Recommendations* (April 2016) at https://www.esrb.europa.eu/pub/pdf/other/160502_handbook.en.pdf?ad3639a90ee362a34bdc71e2faa56e2a.

[125] ESRB Regulation, Article 18.

[126] ESRB, *Vulnerabilities in the EU Residential Real Estate Sector* (November 2016) at https://www.esrb.europa.eu/pub/pdf/reports/161128_vulnerabilities_eu_residential_real_estate_sector.en.pdf.

commentators[127] have noted that although warnings are 'soft law', these measures are unlikely to be ignored. As discussed in Chapter 6, section 6.4.2, the Financial Policy Committee (FPC) in the UK has responded to the warning and considered in detail the state at play in the UK's residential mortgage sector. Although the FPC has not introduced any macroprudential measure, it has committed to keep the situation under review. This may highlight the different risk appetites in each jurisdiction, which are ultimately tied to each country's economic policies.

7.2.4 Institutional structure and centralisation of financial regulation

The ESFS has established a structure that centralises much of policy and law-making for financial services and markets at the EU level. Is the ESFS indeed a centralised 'regulator' in the EU for financial services as a whole?

The ESFS comprises of multiple bodies and does not represent a monolithic centralised structure. Before the advent of the Banking Union, it may be argued that the European Supervisory Authorities working together in the Joint Committee may slowly develop into a centralised architecture. However, the Authorities' decision-making organs are fundamentally *intergovernmental* (i.e. providing for equal representation from each member state) and they have evolved from informal committees in the 2000s as platforms for member state regulators to network. The conferment of top-down powers for the Authorities vis-à-vis member state regulators could gradually result in the consolidation of the Authorities' distinct identities and purposes from member state regulators. There could be potential for the evolution of the ESFS into a centralised regulatory architecture at the EU. However, we think the advent of the Banking Union has disrupted this trajectory. This point is returned to shortly.

We do not see legal harmonisation and supervisory convergence rendering the ESFS as a centralised 'regulator' in the EU. The levels of rule-making in the EU percolate multiple levels of binding legislation and rules. This structure leaves little room for national regulators to introduce rules different from or in addition to the rules emanating from the EU. However, crucially, national regulators are still at the frontlines for approving and supervising their regulated entities. This even remains the case for much of the Banking Union as will be shortly discussed. ESMA's direct powers over the clearinghouses and credit rating agency industries are the exception and not the norm. Besides, it may be argued that the size of the industries that ESMA oversees is manageable for ESMA. As at mid-2018, ESMA oversees less than 20 clearinghouses[128] and less than 50 credit rating agencies, a number of them are subsidiaries of the same group, such as Fitch and Moody's.[129] It could be a totally different matter for ESMA to assume

---

[127] Eilis Ferran and Kern Alexander, 'Can Soft Law Bodies Be Effective? Soft Systemic Risk Oversight Bodies and The Special Case Of The European Systemic Risk Board' (2010) *European Law Review* 751; Alexandra Hennessy, 'Redesigning Financial Supervision in the European Union' (EUSA conference, Boston, 3–6 March 2011).

[128] https://www.esma.europa.eu/sites/default/files/library/ccps_authorised_under_emir.pdf.

[129] https://www.esma.europa.eu/supervision/credit-rating-agencies/risk.

authorisation, supervisory, and enforcement powers over industries that are substantial, such as over pan-European companies that wish to list their securities on European markets or over investment funds.

In spite of the lack of rule-making space for national regulators, commentators[130] point out how the UK in particular has developed its own regimes, usually 'gold-plating' over EU rules where there is a lack of EU legislation or rules to meet the UK's own needs, such as in financial stability and consumer protection. The UK continues to maintain a more stringent approval regime than the EU as individual approval for senior management functions is required (Chapter 11) and the PRA and FCA enjoy a wide suite of nationally legislated enforcement powers.

Legal harmonisation and supervisory convergence may not be the answer to meeting all of member states' regulatory goals. Indeed, the development of the Banking Union is a reflection of the need to carve out unique 'supervisory' spaces from the overall convergence agenda. It may be argued that the Banking Union does not compromise the Single Rulebook, as the EBA has oversight of the ECB's role in applying the Single Rulebook rigorously across the Union. However, the objectives for the Banking Union may differ from non-Union member states' objectives (see discussion in section 7.3).

We turn to the Banking Union, its objectives and architecture, and its interface with the ESFS.

➜ Key takeaways

- The de Larosière Report is instrumental to the institutionalisation of the ESFS in 2010 after the global financial crisis.

- Institutionalisation is justified for continued regulatory and supervisory convergence to deal with multiple objectives in financial regulation including protecting financial stability and consumer protection.

- The ESFS comprises the European Banking Authority, ESMA, EIOPA, Joint Committee of the three Authorities and the ESRB.

- The EBA's roles and powers are discussed in greatest detail, but it is noted that ESMA and EIOPA have mirror roles and powers.

- The Joint Committee focuses on cross-sectoral issues and represent a form of joined-up EU-level rule-making and oversight that is not limited by sectoral differences.

- The ESRB is the macroprudential supervisor for the EU as a whole and it has powers to make recommendations and warnings. These are subject to a comply or explain regime by member states and are regarded as 'soft law'.

- The institutional architecture of the ESFS does not amount to a centralised or single regulator at the EU level as the institutions interact mainly with national regulators. Moreover, there are distinct spaces for national rule-making or supervisory divergence.

---

[130] Andenas and Chiu, 'Financial Stability and Legal Integration in Financial Regulation' 335.

Key bibliography

Case law

UK v Parliament and Council Case C-270/12 (22 January 2014) at http://curia.europa.eu/juris/document/document_print.jsf?doclang=EN&docid=146621

Legislation

European Parliament and Council Regulation (EU) 1093/2010 of 24 November 2010 establishing a European Supervisory Authority (European Banking Authority), amending Decision No 716/2009/EC and repealing Commission Decision 2009/78/EC [2010] OJ L331/12 (EBA Regulation 2010).

European Parliament and Council Regulation (EU) 1095/2010 of 24 November 2010 establishing a European Supervisory Authority (European Securities and Markets Authority), amending Decision No 716/2009/EC and repealing Commission Decision 2009/77/EC [2010] OJ L331/84 (ESMA Regulation 2010).

European Parliament and Council Regulation (EU) 1094/2010 of 24 November 2010 establishing a European Supervisory Authority (European Insurance and Occupational Pensions Authority), amending Decision No 716/2009/EC and repealing Commission Decision 2009/79/EC [2010] OJ L331/48 (EIOPA Regulation 2010).

European Parliament and Council Regulation (EU) 1092/2010 of 24 November 2010 on European Union macroprudential oversight of the financial system and establishing a European Systemic Risk Board [2010] OJ L331/1 (ESRB Regulation 2010)

Official Papers or Reports

Final Report of the Committee of Wise Men on the Regulation of European Securities Markets (2001) at http://ec.europa.eu/internal_market/securities/docs/lamfalussy/wisemen/final-report-wise-men_en.pdf

Jacques de Larosière and others, *Report by the High Level Group on Financial Supervision in the EU* (Brussels, 25 February 2009) http://ec.europa.eu/internal_market/finances/docs/de_larosiere_report_en.pdf

EBA, *Single Rulebook* at http://www.eba.europa.eu/regulation-and-policy/single-rulebook

ESRB, *Recommendation of the European Systemic Risk Board of 4 April 2013 on Intermediate Objectives and Instruments of Macro-Prudential Policy* (ESRB/2013/1) at https://www.esrb.europa.eu/pub/pdf/recommendations/2013/ESRB_2013_1.en.pdf?ad6bc3424dd7690e2f818db264c03299

ESRB, *Handbook on the Assessment of Compliance with ESRB Recommendations* (April 2016) at https://www.esrb.europa.eu/pub/pdf/other/160502_handbook.en.pdf?ad3639a90ee362a34bdc71e2faa56e2a

Articles

Chiu, IH-Y 'Power and Accountability in the EU Financial Regulatory Architecture: Examining Inter-Agency Relations, Agency Independence and Accountability' (2015) 7 *European Journal of Legal Studies* 68

Ferran, E and Alexander, K, 'Can Soft Law Bodies Be Effective? Soft Systemic Risk Oversight Bodies and The Special Case of The European Systemic Risk Board' (2010) 37 *European Law Review* 751

Lehmann, M and Zetzsche, D, 'Brexit and the Consequences for Commercial and Financial Relations between the EU and the UK' (2016) 27 *European Business Law Review* 113

Moloney, N, 'Financial Market Regulation in the post Financial Services Action Plan Era' (2006) 55 (4) *International and Comparative Law Quarterly* 982–92

Moloney, N, 'EU Financial Market Regulation after the Global Financial Crisis: "More Europe" or more Risks?' (2010) 47 (5) *Common Market Law Review* 1317

Moloney, N, 'Reform or Revolution? The Financial Crisis, EU Financial Markets Law and the European Securities and Markets Authority' (2011) 60 (2) *International and Comparative Law Quarterly* 521

Moloney, N, 'The European Securities and Markets Authority and Institutional Design for the EU Financial Market—A Tale of Two Competences: Parts 1 and 2' (2011) 12 *European Business Organisation Review* 43 and 178 respectively

7.3 The Banking Union

7.3.1 Introduction and background: sovereign debt crisis

After the global financial crisis, many European banks continued to remain weak as they had lent enormous amounts to fund their national governments. Sovereign debt in some euro-area countries (i.e. countries that have adopted the euro as their currency) was astronomically high due to years of uncontrolled fiscal policies maintained by these governments, making these countries ill-prepared for the economic downturn following the crisis. In Ireland, already high levels of sovereign debt were accelerated because the government committed to bank bailouts and exerted more pressure on the country's national budget. Ireland and Portugal received bailouts from the IMF in 2010 and 2011 respectively, while Greece, still deep in austerity, received IMF and EU loans in 2010, 2015, and 2017. Concern has been mounting not only in regard to national banks in troubled countries that lend to their governments, but also other European banks such as in Germany and the UK that have significant exposures too.[131] Further, with economic downturn following the global financial crisis, the weaknesses at European banks that were over-extended to the private sector would also become apparent. Weak banks affected market confidence and economic recovery in the EU, and policymakers decided to address the situation by introducing the Banking Union for euro-area banks. The Banking Union reforms have in fact taken place just ahead of a spate of revelations of failing banks, such as in Cyprus, then Portugal, Spain, Italy, and Latvia.

7.3.2 The two pillars of the Banking Union: SSM and SRM

The Banking Union is a policy that introduces a new supervisory architecture for euro-area banks. Euro-area banks are supervised directly by the ECB, independent of its monetary policy functions.[132] This supervisory mechanism is called the ***Single***

---

[131] 'Who has Europe's Loans?' *New York Times* (6 June 2010) at https://www.nytimes.com/2010/06/06/business/global/06toxic.html?pagewanted=all.

[132] Guido Ferranini and Luigi Chiarella, 'Common Banking Supervision in the Eurozone: Strengths and Weaknesses' (2013) at http://ssrn.com/abstract_id=2309897.

Supervisory Mechanism **(SSM)**.[133] Policymakers are of the view that if the SSM takes over supervision of euro-area banks from member state regulators, those euro-area banks would no longer be perceived to be 'weakly supervised' by their national regulators who may be sympathetic to national economic needs. High levels of lending by euro-area banks to their national governments ought to have been monitored by national regulators as such concentrations of risk are sub-optimal for the safety and soundness of banks. However, national regulators could be seen to be susceptible to being sympathetic to national economic needs and are therefore uncritical of the levels of domestic bank lending to the government. The SSM therefore intends to 'sever the links between weak governments and domestic banks' so that member state governments may become more responsible for their budgets and euro-area banks are less likely to be dragged down by their national governments.

It is, however, argued[134] that the policy decision for the SSM is misplaced as the SSM's attention would be focused on the weakest disciplined banks to rectify their problems. In other words, the institution of the SSM is created not for reasons of coherence in regulatory ideology or architecture but for fire-fighting immediate problems. In this way, the SSM may be founded on a sub-optimal basis for centralised supervision by the ECB.

Further, in order to 'complete' the SSM, another mechanism, the *Single Resolution Mechanism* **(SRM)** is introduced. The SRM is purposed towards dealing with crisis management of SSM-supervised banks. This is necessary, as, without the SRM, SSM-supervised banks would by default have to revert to member state regulators for crisis management.[135] National regulators may defer to their governments' needs in determining how to manage the bank crisis, and may tend to 'bail out' or 'prop up' banks even if this is sub-optimal. These measures could damage confidence in the European banking sector as a whole. Hence, a crisis management mechanism independent of national regulators is also needed, in order to complement the SSM.[136] The SRM has been finalised in July 2014,[137] and together with the SSM forms the Banking Union for euro-area banks. The Banking Union is envisaged to complement the economic and monetary union in the EU, and also endorses the Single Rulebook and the progress towards a common deposit guarantee scheme. The SRM and the EU deposit guarantee scheme are discussed in Chapter 13.[138]

[133] Council Regulation (EU) No 1024/2013 of 15 October 2013 conferring specific tasks on the European Central Bank concerning policies relating to the prudential supervision of credit institutions ('SSM Regulation').

[134] Tobias H Troeger, 'The Single Supervisory Mechanism – Panacea or Quack Banking Regulation?' (2013) at http://ssrn.com/abstract=2311353.

[135] Eilis Ferran, 'European Banking Union: Imperfect but it can Work' (2014) at http://ssrn.com/abstract=2426247.

[136] Kern Alexander, 'Bank Resolution and Recovery in the EU: Enhancing Banking Union?' (2013) 14 *ERA Forum* 81; Daniel Gros and Dirk Schoenmaker, 'European Deposit Insurance and Resolution in Banking Union' (2014) 52(3) *Journal of Common Market Studies* 529–46.

[137] Regulation (EU) No 806/2014 of the European Parliament and of the Council of 15 July 2014 establishing uniform rules and a uniform procedure for the resolution of credit institutions and certain investment firms in the framework of a Single Resolution Mechanism and a Single Resolution Fund and amending Regulation (EU) No 1093/2010 ('SRM Regulation').

[138] Critique of the early workings of the SRM are also discussed.

7.3.2.1 Single Supervisory Mechanism

The ECB now assumes the responsibility for microprudential supervision of banks that are 'not less significant'[139] in the euro-area and in non-euro-area countries that have entered into close cooperation with the SSM.[140] The ECB's responsibilities include authorisation of banks, ensuring compliance with microprudential legislation and rules,[141] stress testing[142] and supervisory review, and to oversee recovery plans and carry out early intervention.[143]

The ECB does not have capacity to supervise *all* banks in the euro-area. It selects two only the most significant banks in the euro-area for direct supervision. All other euro-area banks continue to be subject to national regulators' supervision. However, as national regulators are acting as 'delegates' of the ECB's supervisory authority, they are subject to a reporting duty to the ECB.[144] Hence, the SSM refers to the system of supervision that the ECB and its delegate national regulators together administer. By mid-2018, the ECB reports direct supervisory governance over 118 banks in the euro-area, which represents 18 per cent of the population of regulated banks in the area. National regulators remain responsible for over 3,500 less significant banks.

The SSM is independent of the ECB's monetary function.[145] The governing body for the tasks of the SSM is the Board of Supervisors[146] comprising a Chair and Vice-Chair, four ECB representatives and a representative of each national regulator in euro-area member states. The Chairperson is to be appointed by open selection, and such appointment is to be informed to the European Parliament and Council. The Vice-Chair is to be appointed from the Board of Supervisors. The appointments are not particularly subject to political control, as the ECB is protected under Treaty to be independent. Due to Treaty constraints however, the Board of Supervisors is not able to adopt decisions for the SSM as such. This is because the SSM is not framed as a distinct institution although operationally independent of the ECB's monetary functions. Treating the SSM as a distinct institution with powers to make decisions would require a Treaty amendment. Hence, the Board of Supervisors is asked to send draft decisions to be adopted by the Governing Council of the ECB. Such decisions are deemed to have been accepted if no objection is raised in a maximum of 10 days.[147]

---

[139] That is, banks with assets totalling €30 billion or more, or ratio of total assets over the GDP of the relevant member state exceeds 20 per cent, unless the total value of its assets is below €5 billion, an institution regarded by the national regulator as significant, an institution regarded by the ECB on its own initiative as significant, any institution receiving public financial assistance, and at least the three key banks in every euro area jurisdiction or member state in close cooperation. SSM Regulation, Article 6.   [140] SSM Regulation, Article 7.

[141] The same rules that apply to all European banks whether supervised by the SSM or otherwise, discussed in Chapters 8 and 9.

[142] Discussed in Chapter 9, section 9.6.   [143] See Chapter 13, section 13.2.

[144] This seems to be a balanced form of necessary centralisation according to what may be most efficient and proportionate, see Jean-Edouard Colliard, 'Monitoring the Supervisors: Optimal Regulatory Architecture in a Banking Union' (2014) at http://ssrn.com/abstract=2274164; SSM Regulation, Article 6.

[145] SSM Regulation, Articles 19 and 25.   [146] SSM Regulation, Article 26.

[147] SSM Regulation, Article 26. Ferran and Babis argues that this is adverse to non-euro area member states in close cooperation as those member states would not have a representative in the Governing Council, see Eilis Ferran and Valia SG Babis, 'The European Single Supervisory Mechanism' (2013) 13 *Journal of Corporate Law Studies* 255.

The ECB is a member of the EBA and is in principle subject to the Single Rulebook and supervisory convergence. However, the creation of the SSM could create divergences in policy pursuits between Banking Union and non-Union member states. Further, the different accountability mechanisms applicable to the ESFS and ECB could exacerbate diverging tendencies.

The ECB is subject to no discernible *ex ante* political controls in its capacity for the SSM. For example, the Commission is not able to appoint a representative to the Board of Supervisors. This is different from the composition of decision-making organs of ESFS institutions, discussed earlier. The ESFS institutions are also not represented in the SSM, highlighting the fact that the SSM is distinct from the ESFS. The accountability mechanisms for the SSM are largely *ex post* in nature. The ECB is accountable to the Council and Parliament[148] via annual reporting of the SSM's activities and the Chairperson may be asked to appear before the Council[149] or committees of the Parliament. The annual reports are also to be laid before national parliaments[150] of the euro-area member states, and national parliaments may request for the ECB's written explanations on matters raised by them.

The ECB is also subject to accountability to regulated entities to whom it addresses its decisions. It has established an Administrative Board of Review[151] to deal with requests to review its decisions, to comprise of five independent banking and finance experts appointed by the ECB. The Board's decisions also need to be adopted by the Governing Council in the same manner mentioned earlier. The Board of Review is an internal ECB mechanism and involves no participation from ESFS institutions. The Board of Review's decisions can be appealed to the ECJ. For example, Crédit Mutuel Arkéa[152] has challenged the decision of the ECB to exercise direct supervisory authority over it, as it is a central body over a confederation of local cooperative financial services companies, and sees itself as not a bank, and the confederation as not having a corporate group structure to justify the ECB's supervisory oversight. The ECJ clarifies that it is not necessary for a central body to be a bank under the SSM legislation. Further, the ECJ takes a purposive approach to interpret the objective of the ECB's supervision as relating to identifying prudential risks within a group. As long as the structures within the confederation allow for some form of sharing of risks that may affect their prudential position as a whole, the confederation should be regarded as a group.

In sum, the distinctness of the SSM from ESFS institutions and the largely *ex post* mechanisms of accountability for the SSM highlight the extent of the ECB's independence in the discharge of its tasks.

---

[148] SSM Regulation, Article 20.
[149] i.e. before the groups of Heads of State of euro-area countries in the Council.
[150] SSM Regulation, Article 21.   [151] SSM Regulation, Article 24.
[152] *Crédit Mutuel Arkéa v ECB* (supported by European Commission) Case T-52/16 [13 December 2017] at http://curia.europa.eu/juris/document/document.jsf?text=&docid=197785&pageIndex=0&doclang=en&mode=lst&dir=&occ=first&=1&cid=610579.

A question that can be raised is to what extent the SSM may exert a differentiating or even disintegrating pressure for the legal harmonisation and supervisory convergence agendas the EU has been pursuing. To date, the SSM has not diverged from the EBA's single rulebook and supervisory convergence. The EBA's SREP template (discussed in section 7.2) is adopted in the SSM in terms of supervisory evaluation of banks and communicating findings. Common themes in supervisory policy are also pursued in the SSM, such as monitoring the differences between banks' application of internal models in measuring credit risk (discussed in Chapter 8, section 8.5.8). The ECB has also been fairly transparent about its supervisory priorities, such as monitoring the level of non-performing loans on banks' balance sheets,[153] and coordinates with the EBA in terms of pursuing a supervisory convergence agenda.

The EBA has adopted new decision-making processes so that Banking Union interests will not dominate policy and rule-making in the EBA, and that EU-wide convergence objectives remain paramount. The new decision-making mechanisms[154] distinguish Banking Union members as a voting class distinct from non-Union members. Decision-making at the EBA will be based on majority votes taken at both classes of members. This has also been earlier mentioned in section 7.2.

Although the SSM is purposed to sever the links between weak banks and their national regulators and governments, the ECB continues to face challenge in terms of exerting effective supervisory control of the banks it directly supervises. Such banks remain in close ties with national regulators and governments, and it remains uncertain if the ECB could adopt direct supervisory decisions without consulting national authorities.[155] One controversy that has arisen for the SSM is its supervision of Monte Dei Paschi, the oldest bank in Italy. Since late 2016, Monte Dei Paschi has faced enormous problems in terms of non-performing (or bad and defaulting) loans and tethers on the brink of insolvency. The Italian authorities favour a tax-payer funded recapitalisation of the bank and not one of the crisis resolution mechanisms established in the EU Bank Recovery and Resolution Directive 2014 discussed in Chapter 13. The Directive's resolution options involve bringing in bank creditors and shareholders to absorb the bank's losses as it is restructured, so that the 'private sector' absorbs losses before the state is asked to step in and bail out. As many of the banks' creditors are in fact retail customers who have bought the bank's securities instruments, Italian authorities are unwilling to utilise the Directive's resolution options that would seem punishing to retail customers. The ECB, however, disagrees and is of the view that Monte Dei Paschi should be resolved in accordance with the Directive's provisions. This difference

---

[153] ECB, *Guidance to Banks on Non-Performing Loans* (March 2017) at https://www.bankingsupervision. europa.eu/ecb/pub/pdf/guidance_on_npl.en.pdf.

[154] Eilis Ferran, 'European Banking Union and the EU Single Financial Market: More Differentiated Integration, or Disintegration?' (2014) at https://papers.ssrn.com/sol3/papers.cfm?abstract_id=2426580.

[155] Emilios Avgouleas and Douglas Arner, 'The Eurozone Debt Crisis and the European Banking Union: A Cautionary Tale of Failure and Reform' (2013) at https://papers.ssrn.com/sol3/papers.cfm?abstract_id=2347937 warns of potential fragmentary actions that national authorities would take to undermine the integrated crisis management framework.

brought decision-making on Monte Dei Paschi to a protracted stalemate, creating great uncertainty for investors and markets.[156] The stalemate has finally been resolved in favour of the Italian authorities' preference to rescue Monte Dei Paschi with government funds.[157] This episode highlights the difficulties in practically severing the links between weak banks and their governments. But it can also be argued that without the involvement of the Italian regulator and government, the Banking Union mechanisms could determine Monte Dei Paschi's fate in a manner oblivious to national needs. This can also cause domestic financial instability.

As discussed in Chapter 13, the Monte Dei Paschi episode also highlights the sidelining of the SRM. The SRM is in principle the mechanism by which the resolution tool for banks subject to the SSM would be determined. However, in reality, the SSM and SRM, which have been created to rebalance the stranglehold of national authorities over banks, may themselves be marginalised in view of the political realities in the EU. The perceived disengagement of the SSM and SRM from national regulators and governments may entail significant levels of challenge against powers exercised under the mechanisms. In contrast, the more intergovernmental nature of the ESFS may be more acceptable to member states who see opportunities to influence policymaking from within the ESFS instead of directly challenging it.

7.3.2.2 **Single Resolution Mechanism**

The SRM is the mechanism for determining how banks subject to the SSM are to be resolved. It is administered by the Single Resolution Board (SRB), which is independent of and distinct from the ECB. The SRB's responsibilities and composition are discussed at length in Chapter 13, section 13.1.

There are significant coordination needs between the SRM and SSM. For example, the SRM and SSM need to coordinate with each other in monitoring the signs of bank crisis and to determine how and when a bank is to transition to the stage of crisis management and resolution. [158] The stages of development of bank crises are not clear-cut and predictable, hence the SRM and SSM would need to develop frameworks for coordination, and clarity as to thresholds for transition and the sharing of responsibility. It remains open as to how such coordination would work out[159] and which institution would dominate in making decisions on crisis management and resolution. A commentator[160] warns that boundary uncertainties may contribute towards the ineffectiveness of the Banking

---

[156] 'Brussels and ECB split on Monte dei Paschi's capital proposals', *Financial Times* (25 February 2017) at https://www.ft.com/content/9635b04c-f923-11e6-bd4e-68d53499ed71.

[157] 'The rescue of Italian lender will not end banking woes', *Financial Times* (1 June 2017).

[158] SRM Regulation, Article 13.

[159] Remarks by Rosa Lastra on Charles Goodhart and M Sevagiano, 'The Determination of Bank Recovery' at the 'Law and Monetary Policy' Conference, University of Sheffield, 10 September 2014.

[160] Concetta Brescia Morra, 'From the Single Supervisory Mechanism to the Banking Union. The Role of the ECB and the EBA' (2014) at https://papers.ssrn.com/sol3/papers.cfm?abstract_id=2448913.

Union, preventing decisive actions from being taken. The landscape is further compli-
cated by national regulators' and governments' involvement in crisis resolution, as a
bank crisis within a member state's territory is likely to be of great importance.

The SRM's first resolution decision in 2017 has occurred in relation to Banco
Popular,[161] and it may be argued that the SRM has only adopted this decision as all
relevant authorities have come to agreement, that is, the Spanish authorities, ECB, and
the private sector rescuer of Banco Popular, which is Santander.[162] The SRM seems to
have become a platform for brokering such agreements instead of being a distinct and
independent mechanism that is purported to sever the links between weak banks and
their governments.

The Banking Union has been touted to be a necessary complement to economic and
monetary union, but its real independence seems to be in doubt. National authorities'
interests may collide with the Banking Union's competencies and raise future existen-
tial challenges for the Union. Further, although the SSM purports to follow the Single
Rulebook, its supervisory priorities are centred upon the banks in the euro-area and
these can in time create divergences in terms of supervisory objectives and styles from
non-Banking Union member states. It is queried how the EBA can continue to maintain
supervisory convergence in the abstract for all member states. One may also argue that
the SSM is itself an example of supervisory divergence, as it acknowledges the unique
needs of euro-area banks. In sum, the ESFS and the Banking Union are attempts at pan-
European and centralised regulatory mechanisms for the 'European banking sector', but
in reality, the banking sectors in different European markets present different needs and
problems and exist alongside certain pan-European elements. Hence, regulatory tasks
and solutions cannot practically be over-centralised at the EU level. Intergovernmental
forces will continue to shape bank regulation in the EU, as banks are central to economic
and market policies pursued by national governments and regulators. Box 7.3 highlights
a number of bank crisis episodes from 2013 to 2017, the majority of which have ultimately been dealt with by the national authorities although the passages to resolution
have been fraught with tensions between the SSM/SRM and national authorities. The
limited scope of action for the SRM seems to suggest that not much has been achieved in
relation to 'severing the links' between national governments and their banks.

7.3.3 European Central Bank

The ECB is the central bank of the 19 EU countries that have adopted the euro. Its main
task is to maintain price stability in the euro-area and so preserve the purchasing power
of the single currency. Price stability is regarded as essential for economic growth and

---

[161] 'Single Resolution Board Adopts Resolution of Banco Poplular' (7 June 2017) at https://srb.europa.eu/
en/node/315.
[162] Banco Popular was transferred to Santander for 1 euro, and all necessary transfers are effected by the
Spanish authority in order to keep the continuity of business at Banco Popular under Santander's ownership.
This episode is discussed in greater detail in Chapter 13, section 13.1.

Box 7.3 Episodes on bank crises

Cyprus

Two of its largest banks, Bank of Cyprus and Laiki Bank, tethered on insolvency in April 2013 after being over-extended to a falling property market in commercial real estate. The Cypriot authorities fumbled in applying **bail-in** as a resolution tool, and disagreements occurred between EU-level bodies and Cypriot authorities.

Portugal

Banco Espirito Santo was resolved in 2014 by the Portuguese authorities after years of over-extension of loans and guarantees to companies owned by its founding family.

Spain

Banco Popular, over-extended in relation to the construction sector, was resolved in 2017 by the SRB and Spanish regulator.

Italy

A number of Venetian banks were over-extended to the private sector and weighed under non-performing commercial loans. The Italian authorities preferred to bail out the banks, a policy opposed to by the SRB. Monte Dei Paschi was ultimately bailed out in mid-2017 by the Italian government, while Venetian banks Veneto Banca and Banca Popolare di Vicenza had their good assets sold in mid-2017 and the government bore the cost of winding then down. Although the SRB was of the view that the Italian authorities appropriately took charge in relation to Veneto Banca and Populare di Vicenza as they were not systemically important, the divergence of approach from the Bank Recovery and Resolution Directive 2014 (see Chapter 13) signalled continuing difficulties for the Banking Union in terms of its mandate and prowess, as well as the substantive application of bank crisis resolution frameworks as discussed in Chapter 13.

Latvia

The third largest bank in Latvia, ABLV, was declared by the ECB as failing or likely to fail in February 2018 after the bank came under the US authorities' investigations for extensive money laundering allegations. The Latvian and Luxembourg authorities will resolve the bank as the SRM determined that they did not pose systemic risk to the European financial system. This episode seems again to signal that the SRM will operate within a highly limited scope and puts into question to what extent centralised bank crisis management or resolution that 'severs the links between national governments and weak banks' has been achieved.

Further details on the application of the legal frameworks for resolution and crisis management is to be found in Chapter 13.

job creation and thus the ECB's monetary mandate is nested within the greater public economic interests of the EU. Further, it can be argued that the ECB is regarded as playing a key role in the maintenance of financial stability overall in the EU's financial sectors and markets. The creation of the ESRB, though as an independent outfit under the ECB, as well as the assumption of the SSM by the ECB are important indicators of the 'wider' responsibility and expectations placed on the ECB. This reflects El-Erian's argument[163] that increasingly governments (or supranational 'governing bodies' such as in the EU) are relying on the economic expertise of central banks more generally and not just for monetary stability. Central banks are being looked to for the employment of a variety of instruments in relation to maintaining financial stability as well as promoting the government's economic goals such as economic growth.

The ECB is established as an independent decision-making body in respect of its tasks.[164] The ECB's decisions are made by a Governing Council that comprises its Executive Board and the governors of national central banks whose currency is the euro. The Executive Board is made up of a President, Vice-President, and four other members, all appointed by the European Council by qualified majority. The terms of each Executive Board member last for 8 years and are not renewable, in order to ensure freshness and objectivity in decision-making. The President of the European Council and a member of the European Commission may participate in Governing Council proceedings at the ECB but enjoy no voting rights, in order to prevent any form of political intervention.

The accountability of the ECB is secured by its annual report to the European Parliament, Council, and Commission, and its President may be required to attend before the committees of the European Parliament.

As the ECB, in its monetary policy capacity, supports the promotion of European economic growth, it has applied its monetary policy in such a way as to ensure that lines of financing remain available to the private sector, despite bank financing becoming more constrained. Bank financing has always been a dominant source of credit in many European jurisdictions, and credit extended by banks has become more constrained due to the need for banks to recover from the global financial crisis and attain prudent capital levels.

The ECB has expanded its monetary policy instruments to include some rather controversial measures. We discuss here a couple of initiatives from the ECB to appreciate how the bank supervision agenda and the ECB's new monetary instruments are different parts of the overall mosaic, in order to secure the overall objective of promoting European economic recovery.

7.3.3.1 The ECB's asset purchase programmes and outright monetary transactions regimes

From 2009, the ECB has been engaged in asset purchase programmes.[165] These programmes allow the ECB to buy debt issued by the corporate sector (called the 'corporate sector asset purchase programme'); debt issued by local and national governments (called the 'public sector programme'); and other assets such as asset-backed

---

[163] Mohammed El-Erian, *The Only Game in Town: Central Banks, Instability, and Avoiding the Next Collapse* (Conn: Yale University Press 2016).
[164] Chapter 6, Articles 282–4, TFEU.
[165] See https://www.ecb.europa.eu/mopo/implement/html/index.en.html.

securities[166] and covered bonds.[167] These programmes allow the ECB to participate in financing entities and sectors that otherwise would need to rely on bank financing. As banks need to recover from losses from non-performing loans and years of imprudent lending, bank financing has become constricted. From 2016 the ECB's asset purchase programmes are at about €60 billion on a monthly basis. The asset purchase programme is regarded to be in line with the ECB's monetary policy mandate.[168]

The ECB in 2012 has also adopted a new monetary policy instrument, called Outright Monetary Transactions (OMT), that allows it to purchase sovereign debt of short maturities in potentially unlimited quantities from the secondary market. This ensures that the market for debt issued by European member state governments is protected and remains liquid. If investors for some reason sell-off huge quantities of certain European government bonds or if there is a lack of demand to buy any particular European government's bonds, these market situations could result in the collapsing of prices or demand for such bonds, with adverse economic impact upon the member states in question. The ECB's power to intervene in order to 'prop up' the price or demand for such bonds is a controversial measure as it can be seen as directly providing financial assistance to a member state government in infringement of the TFEU.

The OMT programme has been challenged to be in violation of the Treaty before the German constitutional court, which has referred to the ECJ for a preliminary ruling. The ECJ[169] has ultimately found support for the OMT programme as it is expressly pursuant to maintaining price stability and therefore within the powers of the ECB.[170] The German constitutional court has adopted the same position but articulates the need for the OMT to be carried out under clear and specific conditions.[171] The OMT has to date not been used, but its illegality is no longer in question.

The ECB remains the lender of the last resort for euro-area banks, which refers to its provision of emergency liquidity assistance to banks. The ECB has provided such assistance during the global financial crisis, as well as to Greek banks during the 'sovereign

---

[166] Chapter 1 discusses these securities in relation to the global financial crisis of 2007–9.

[167] These are corporate bonds that are backed by collateral.

[168] The programmes arguably prevent asset price collapse, that is, the collapse of corporate bond prices, for example, and deflation, therefore maintaining an environment of stable but low inflation. See support in Marco Gross and Willi Semmler, 'Mind the Output Gap: The Disconnect of Growth and Inflation During Recessions and Convex Phillips Curves in the Euro Area' (ECB Working Paper 2017) at https://papers.ssrn.com/sol3/papers.cfm?abstract_id=2910934.

[169] Judgment of the Court (Grand Chamber) of 16 June 2015 (request for a preliminary ruling from the Bundesverfassungsgericht – Germany) – *Peter Gauweiler and Others v Deutscher Bundestag* (Case C-62/14).

[170] Support also found in Carsten Gerner-Buerle et al, 'Law Meets Economics in the German Federal Constitutional Court: Outright Monetary Transactions on Trial' (2014) 15 *German Law Journal* 281, which argued that the ECB's measure is targeted at uncoordinated market reactions that would have an adverse impact, and thus the measure is essentially an economic one directed at behavioural sub-optimalities in markets.

[171] 'German high court backs ECB on crisis-fighting tool', *Financial Times* (21 June 2016) at https://www.ft.com/content/0a036094-379d-11e6-9a05-82a9b15a8ee7.

debt' crisis in Greece – that is, the potential default of the Greek government in repaying its debt.[172] The ECB has even made its conditions for assistance more accessible, by accepting a wide range of collateral that can be offered by banks that need access to such facilities. The ECB has also developed longer-term refinancing options for banks, so that liquidity facilities are not necessarily to be repaid in the short term, but banks may have up to four years in refinancing. Such support is provided so that banks can increase their lending through access to these facilities and continue to support member states' economies.

Since the crisis, the ECB has developed new and non-traditional initiatives in order to continue funding economic activities pending the return to health by the banking sector. The ECB's role in supervising euro-area banks and its role in stepping into funding gaps in the name of monetary policy are complementary in nature, and together constitute part of a wider economic policy to protect the EU's economic growth and stability. However, a question can be raised as to whether the ECB's need to 'prop up' the banking sector conflicts with its SSM role in supervising banks' prudential health robustly.

7.3.4 **The European Stability Mechanism**

Since the global financial crisis, mechanisms have also been instituted at the European level to financially assist governments and banks directly. Although not formally a part of 'bank regulation' as such, the discussion of the mechanisms provide a more complete picture of the policy and law at the EU with respect to protecting economic and financial health and stability. We turn to discuss the European Stability Mechanism (ESM).

The ESM is a pan-European funding facility for governments and banks. It first evolved out of the European Financial Stability Facility (EFSF), which was instituted in 2010 in the wake of the global financial crisis. The Council agreed that express financial assistance to euro-area member states in economic difficulty was needed for the objective of preserving financial stability in EU generally. The Facility was an independent body based in Luxembourg, and was initially conceived to have borrowing powers up to about €440 billion, via the issuance of its own bonds. The EFSF would borrow on the basis of the collective economic strength of the EU and lend directly to governments in need. The EFSF was also in part capitalised by Germany, France and Italy as the first contributors to the Facility, but their contributions were treated as capital for loss absorption (in case the EFSF's investments suffered losses) and not as funds for lending. EU member states were in total liable for a capital guarantee in favour of the EFSF of up to €780 billion.

---

[172] Greek government and public sector borrowing is extremely high, see Philip Lane, 'The European Sovereign Debt Crisis' (2012) 26 *Journal of Economic Perspectives* 49. Episodes of potential default surfaced in 2012 and 2015.

The Facility would lend directly to member state governments only upon an agreed programme of reforms, budgetary discipline and repayment schedule. Although initially seen as a measure that would bail out profligate member state governments that lacked budgetary discipline, the EFSF had become widely supported as it met pragmatic financial needs and preserved the solidarity of the EU.[173]

The EFSF (which initially focused on member state governments) has now been absorbed into the expanded ESM.[174] The ESM can also lend directly to recapitalise banks, also upon an agreed programme for restructuring and recovery. The lending limit of the ESM stands at €500 billion.

The ESM has thus far been successful in raising funds from international capital markets and applying such funds to lending programmes. Its current borrowers are member state governments including Greece, Cyprus, Spain, Portugal and Ireland.[175] These governments have been subject to different conditions in their lending programmes, but conditions such as austerity programmes have been controversial in terms of their impact upon social welfare.[176] The ESM also makes investments out of its capital on a prudential basis and establishes governance and control mechanisms comparable to the standards required under bank regulation for banks.

Although the ESM is seen to be necessary as a European facility of financial assistance, like the IMF, the moral hazard effects are rather pronounced for investors in European sovereign and bank debt. Empirical research has found that investors are willing to lend to European governments and banks at a relatively low cost, as the ESM is seen as a public backstop for them if they should threaten to default.[177]

Although the EU has time and again stemmed catastrophic economic declines and failures in the wake of the global financial crisis, the collection of initiatives from the ECB's unusual monetary instruments to the ESM have arguably become crutches for European governments and banks. The 'sympathetic discretion' in EU economic policy that supports initiatives that 'prop up' or 'rescue' governments and banks to an extent conflicts with the policy need to maintain robust and consistent bank regulation and supervision. The latter regime demands that banks lend in an objectively prudent manner and not be captured by political interests. EU bank regulation has started to address this but in a slow manner. In the meantime, the availability of 'crutch' mechanisms may undermine the rigour of regulatory efforts.

---

[173] Carlos Closa and Aleksandra Maatsch, 'In a Spirit of Solidarity? Justifying the European Financial Stability Facility (EFSF) in National Parliamentary Debates' (2014) 52 *Journal of Common Market Studies* 826.

[174] https://www.esm.europa.eu/about-us.

[175] Andrew Martin, 'Eurozone Economic Governance' in Jon Erik Delvik and Andrew Martin (eds), *European Social Models from Crisis to Crisis: Employment and Inequality in the Era of Monetary Integration* (Oxford: OUP 2017) ch 2.

[176] Spyridon N Litsas and Aristotle Tziampiris (eds), *Foreign Policy Under Austerity: Greece's Return to Normality?* (London: Palgrave Macmillan 2016).

[177] Bálint L Horvárth and Henry Huizinga, 'Does the European Financial Stability Facility Bail Out Sovereigns or Banks? An Event Study' (2011) at https://papers.ssrn.com/sol3/papers.cfm?abstract_id=1964148.

→ Key takeaways

- The Banking Union is a policy response to address weak euro-area governments that have been excessively financed by national banks, causing banks to be over-exposed and financially weak.

- The Banking Union comprises the SSM, the SRM, the Single Rulebook, and ultimately a common deposit guarantee scheme that is work in progress (see Chapter 13, section 13.3).

- The SSM is undertaken by the ECB that acts as microprudential supervisor to the key banks in the euro-area. Although all euro-area banks come under the SSM, most are delegated by the ECB to be supervised by national authorities.

- The SSM is supported by the SRM that provides a centralised resolution authority for euro-area banks so that crisis management is not effectively defaulted to national regulators.

- The SRM is administered by the Single Resolution Board, which is separate and independent from the ECB.

- The SSM and SRM are currently challenged by the continued dominance of national interests in bank resolution as well as their relationship with each other and with the ESFS. Bank crises in the EU that have unfolded after the advent of the SRM have largely been dealt with by national regulators.

- The SRM's explicit non-interference rationale is based on the failed banks not being systemically important in the majority of instances. This, however, raises the question of whether the limits of the SRM's scope of action are desirable and in line with the original intentions behind the Banking Union.

- The SSM and SRM are best seen as part of wider EU economic policy. We discuss monetary instruments of the ECB and the role of the ESM to form the larger picture of EU economic policy.

- The ECB's new monetary instruments such as asset purchase programmes and OMT have been the subject of controversy.

- The ESM may be viewed as the ultimate public sector backstop for failing governments or banks.

- The EU continues to face tensions between its need to maintain existing stability, which requires propping up weak governments and banks, and the need to ensure the long-term prudential health of its banking sector.

Key bibliography

Legislation

Council Regulation (EU) No 1024/2013 of 15 October 2013 conferring specific tasks on the European Central Bank concerning policies relating to the prudential supervision of credit institutions ('SSM Regulation').

Regulation (EU) No 806/2014 of the European Parliament and of the Council of 15 July 2014 establishing uniform rules and a uniform procedure for the resolution of credit institutions and certain investment firms in the framework of a Single Resolution Mechanism and a Single Resolution Fund and amending Regulation (EU) No 1093/2010 ('SRM Regulation').

Articles

Avgouleas, E and Arner, D, 'The Eurozone Debt Crisis and the European Banking Union: A Cautionary Tale of Failure and Reform' (2013) at https://papers.ssrn.com/sol3/papers.cfm?abstract_id=2347937

Brescia Morra, C, 'From the Single Supervisory Mechanism to the Banking Union. The Role of the ECB and the EBA' (2014) at https://papers.ssrn.com/sol3/papers.cfm?abstract_id=2448913

Ferran, E, 'European Banking Union: Imperfect but it can Work' (2014) at http://ssrn.com/abstract=2426247

Ferran, E and Babis, VSG, 'The European Single Supervisory Mechanism' (2013) 13 *Journal of Corporate Law Studies* 255.

Gerner-Buerle et al, C, 'Law Meets Economics in the German Federal Constitutional Court: Outright Monetary Transactions on Trial' (2014) 15 *German Law Journal* 281

Books

Busch, D and Ferranini, G (eds), *European Banking Union* (Oxford: OUP 2015)

Howarth, D and Quaglia, L, *The Political Economy of European Banking Union* (Oxford: OUP 2016)

Questions

1. **Critically evaluate the EU's achievements in securing regulatory convergence. Is this a realistic pursuit?**

   Answer tips You should explain the rationale for regulatory convergence in relation to securing the single market for financial services and the key strategy of legal integration. You should discuss how legal integration is carried out and what such integration achieves. In particular, you should question if legal integration meets other regulatory goals such as financial stability and consumer protection. You should discuss the EBA's work in securing legal harmonisation and supervisory convergence. In particular, does the EBA represent a centralised institution in order to secure regulatory convergence?

2. **Does the Banking Union undermine regulatory convergence in the EU?**

   Answer tips You should explain the raison d'etre for the Banking Union and what it comprises. You should examine to what extent the Banking Union may cause divergence from supervisory convergence and whether that has indeed been observed. You should critically place the Banking Union policy within the context of the wider economic policies of the EU and question if the Banking Union may endure. Ultimately it would also be ideal if you could comment on whether regulatory policy should be based on more fundamental ideologies or the topical political and economic needs of the time.

3. **Does the European System of Financial Supervision amount to a form of centralised regulation of financial services at the EU level?**

> **Answer tipss** *You should discuss the rationale for instituting the ESFS and its components. You should critically review the roles and powers of the European Supervisory Authorities, ESRB and Joint Committee in order to flesh out the nature of the ESFS. You should consider to what extent there is indeed the creation of a centralised or pan-European regulator- looking at the intensity of legal and supervisory convergence, but bearing in mind enforcement remains in the hands of national authorities. Does the ESFS substitute national authorities or carry out direct powers of supervision or enforcement? What is the role of pan-European macroprudential supervision reposed in the ESRB?*

8

Micro-prudential regulation I

Capital adequacy

8.1 Introduction to capital adequacy

Banks perform the important economic role of maturity transformation, by 'borrowing short' and 'lending long'. As Chapter 1 explained, this means banks assume short-term liabilities to those they borrow from – that is, depositors and other financial institutions – while using the borrowed monies to create longer-term loan assets in order to generate income. Such longer-term loans can be made to corporations and to individuals such as for the purposes of residential mortgages, personal loans, student loans, and so on. This service that banks perform is often referred to as 'full intermediation' as explained in Chapter 1.

The full intermediation service provided by banks between their depositors and their longer-term borrowers is economically beneficial, potentially very profitable, but highly risky for banks. Banks may engage in excessive or poor lending due to the lure of short-term profits or the exercise of inadequate lending judgment. Hence, there is public interest in ensuring that banks manage their risks well, remain viable, and that failure is prevented, as the social cost of economic disruption that results from bank failure could be significant.

Hence, banks are subject to regulation so that their risks in lending can be kept under control. In order to regulate banks in terms of their risk management, regulatory standards have to strike a balance – to introduce standards so that banks' business decision-making can actually be shaped by the need to adhere to risk control, yet not to be so intrusive that banks' business becomes impossible. This balance has changed over the years of regulatory development, from 'top-down' standards in the 1980s, to more flexible standards negotiated with the banking industry in the early 2000s, and then back again to prescriptive standards and tighter control after the 2007–9 global financial crisis. Further, over the years of regulatory development, the standards for controlling bank risk-taking have expanded in scope and methodology, as banks' business has, as discussed in Chapter 1, expanded in scope and complexity. The theoretical context for micro-prudential regulation is outlined in Box 8.1.

In this chapter, we focus on capital adequacy regulation, a regulatory technique developed since the 1980s. Chapter 9 focuses on other regulatory techniques to control bank risk-taking, many of them developed since the global financial crisis of 2007–9.

Box 8.1 Theoretical context for micro-prudential regulation

Chapters 8 and 9 deal with the regulatory standards that aim to control bank risk-taking. These standards are 'micro-prudential' in nature, which means that they relate to 'prudent' risk-taking by individual banking institutions at the level of each transaction. The standards are by nature **economic tools**, expressed as regulatory standards. Therefore, an understanding of the legal compliance in micro-prudential regulation has to be based on the **economic outworking** of each micro-prudential regulatory tool.

Micro-prudential regulation is very much a study to be guided by the approach in **law and economics**, where economic methods are applied to determine how behaviour can be calibrated, and tools are used to create incentives to align with the desired behaviour.[1]

In relation to the rationale for capital adequacy regulation, Scott[2] explains that:

The primary objective of bank regulation is to avoid bank failure. A key technique in achieving this objective is to ensure that banks hold adequate capital. Capital provides a cushion for losses, increases the exposure of shareholders thereby lessening excessive risk-taking due to moral hazard, and provides a buffer for the deposit insurance fund.

Capital adequacy regulation prescribes that banks can only take certain levels of risk that are supported by adequate levels of capital. In this way, capital adequacy rules provide a form of assurance that banks with adequate levels of capital are likely able to withstand losses that may result from their risk-taking, such as where the bank has made a loan and its borrower defaults. Further, banks can be prevented from over-extension in their risk-taking, such as lending to customers, if their capital levels do not support such excessive lending. Capital adequacy rules are, however, not an exact science, as maintaining adequate levels of capital against risk-taking does not mean that the banks' risk of loss will not materialise, nor does it mean that the bank will certainly be able to withstand the loss that materialises. The adequate levels of capital are an estimated 'safe level' of 'cushioning' for banks only. One should note that if regulatory standards attempt to make this estimate as precisely accurate as possible, regulatory standards would be prescriptive and restricting for banks in their conduct of business. However, poor and inaccurate estimates may be criticised for being worthless. The balance that regulatory standards need to strike is essentially challenging and remains so over the years of regulatory development.

---

[1] See Martin Cave and Robert Baldwin *Understanding Regulation* (Oxford: OUP 2013); Robert Cooter and Thomas Ulen, *Law and Economic Analysis* (6th edition) ch 1, now freely available at https://scholarship.law.berkeley.edu/cgi/viewcontent.cgi?article=1001&context=books; Katja Lagenbucher, *Economic Transplants: On Lawmaking for Corporations and Capital Markets* (Cambridge: Cambridge University Press 2017).

[2] Hal S Scott, 'Models-Based Regulation of Bank Capital' in ch 16, R Cranston ed, *Making Commercial Law* (Clarendon Press 1997) 378.

8.1.2 **Roadmap of regulatory standards development in capital adequacy**

Capital adequacy rules have been developed largely at an international level, under the auspices of the Basel Committee for Banking Supervision, part of the Bank for International Settlements.[3] The international development of such rules is very useful as they are the product of expert deliberations across the most developed financial jurisdictions represented in the Committee.[4] They provide a form of international harmonisation that discourages fragmented national approaches that could promote pockets of low standards and regulatory arbitrage.

The Basel Committee developed its first set of capital adequacy standards in the Basel I Capital Accord of 1988. The Accord was well-received and has been transposed into EU Directives since 1989. The Accord was amended in 1996 to take into account new banking risks that have developed due to changes in banks' business models (see Chapter 1 for an overview of modern banking development). It was subsequently overhauled into the Basel II Capital Accord in 2003. Basel II effectively overtook Basel I, although the framework in Basel I provided important foundations for the development of Basel II. The EU responded to this change by comprehensive regulatory reform, introducing the Basel II Accord standards into law in 2006.[5]

After the global financial crisis of 2007–9 (discussed in Chapter 1), the Basel II Accord's shortcomings were extensively discussed and the Basel Committee introduced a package of reforms starting with Basel 2.5 to Basel III, in order to plug the gaps in Basel II. However, many of the 'baseline' approaches in Basel II remain the starting point to understand Basel III. The Basel III package is the most extensive suite of micro-prudential regulation reforms seen to date, as they deal with capital adequacy and a range of other micro-prudential standards (many of them will be discussed in Chapter 9). The Basel III reforms took place in several phases[6] in order to overwrite a significant number of standards in Basel II, towards becoming more prescriptive and comprehensive in character. The Basel III reforms in the 2011 version have been implemented by the EU in the Capital Requirements Regulation and Directive 2013.[7] In fact the EU's legislative reform has exceeded the Basel III Accord's requirements. The European banking sector was revealed to be rather weak in the global financial crisis and European policymakers have therefore opted for more comprehensive regulation to strengthen confidence in European banks.

The UK has transposed all relevant European legislation since the 1980s, therefore implementing the Basel I and II Accords accordingly. The UK has also completed transposition of the European legislation of 2013,[8] and is responsive to the completion of the

---

[3] See its website at https://www.bis.org/bcbs/. Discussed in detail in Chapter 5.

[4] Mostly central bankers.   [5] EU Capital Requirements Directive 2006/48/EC.

[6] Basel Committee, *Basel III: A Global Regulatory Framework for More Resilient Banks and Banking Systems* (2010) and updated in 2011; and added to by liquidity reforms (Chapter 9) in 2013 and 2014, as well as consultation on amendments to operational risk (see discussion later in this chapter) in 2015. The completion of Basel III was finalised in December 2017 with the issue of *Finalising Post-crisis Reforms* (2017) at https://www.bis.org/bcbs/publ/d424.pdf.

[7] EU Capital Requirements Regulation No. 575/2013; EU Capital Requirements Directive 2013/36/EU.

[8] Much of this is found in the Prudential Regulation Authority's (PRA) Rulebook online.

Basel III Accord as of December 2017. The UK's exit from EU membership is unlikely to water down regulatory requirements as these are seen to be important for preserving confidence in the UK banking sector and maintaining as much equivalence as possible with the EU regime so that favourable trade relations in banking and financial services can continue.

We discuss the development of capital adequacy standards from the 'Standardised and Simple' approach in the Basel I Accord that promoted universalism and easy global adoption, to the 'Flexible and Negotiated' approach in Basel II that represented an era of strong industry influence on regulators. This approach was heavily criticised in the wake of the 2007–9 global financial crisis, and we are now in the 'post-crisis' approach, which tends towards increased prescription, expansion in scope and methodology in regulatory standards, and precautionary treatment of risk-taking in certain areas.

Key takeaways

Micro-prudential regulation refers to a suite of economic tools aimed at measuring risk and changing behaviour at banks so as to prevent them from mis-managing risks and leading to solvency problems.

Micro-prudential regulation has from an early stage been developed as a set of internationally harmonising standards by the Basel Committee and has been adopted by the EU and UK in legislation.

Key bibliography

Books

Armour, J et al, *Principles of Financial Regulation* (Oxford: OUP 2016) chs 2, 3, 4, 13, 14, and 15

Lagenbucher, K, *Economic Transplants: On Lawmaking for Corporations and Capital Markets* (Cambridge: Cambridge University Press 2017)

Mülbert, PO, 'Managing Risk in the Financial System' in Niamh Moloney, Eilís Ferran, and Jennifer Payne (eds), *The Oxford Handbook on Financial Regulation* (Oxford: OUP 2015)

8.2　Standardised and simple capital adequacy regulation (Basel I Capital Accord)

8.2.1　Background to the Basel I Capital Accord

The 1988 Basel Accord, which became known as Basel I, sought to harmonise the rules relating to the capital held by banks conducting significant international business.[9] Such a move towards international convergence of capital adequacy rules was first prompted

---

[9] Basel Committee on Banking Supervision *International Convergence of Capital Measurement and Capital Standards* (July 1988) at http://www.bis.org/publ/bcbs04a.pdf.

by the failure of the German Bankhaus Herstatt in 1974. The bank's foreign exchange exposures amounted to three times its capital and the German regulator withdrew Herstatt's licence to operate.[10] As a result of the abrupt closure, banks outside Germany took heavy losses on their unsettled trades with Herstatt, resulting in the near collapse of the US clearing and international banking systems.[11] While this episode related to the structure of the foreign exchange and settlement markets, it simultaneously exposed the fragility of the emerging international banking industry. This led to the imposition of political pressure on the G10 central bank governors to put in place mechanisms and procedures to bolster the stability of the international financial system.[12] The newly formed Basel Committee on Banking Supervision[13] was therefore tasked to look into how the structure and supervision of individual banking institutions could be improved.

Capital adequacy was on the Basel Committee's agenda from an early stage[14] but the pace towards an international agreement only accelerated following the Latin American debt crisis in the early 1980s. In essence, a rise in oil prices in the early 1970s led to an inflow of funds to commercial banks, some of which was lent to countries such as Mexico, Argentina, and Brazil. Eight US commercial banks had exposures of up to $37 billion to the above countries. The debt constituted 147 per cent of their capital at the time,[15] which meant that the banks would become insolvent if these countries were to default on their debt. In 1982, Mexico was the first to default as it could not afford to pay both capital and interest payments on its debt and requested financial assistance from the International Monetary Fund. This episode revealed that many banks had been taking on too much risk in lending while being supported by thin capital levels. The Basel Committee saw a need to improve capital adequacy levels across international banks.[16] However, because of the disparate views of several of the major countries, the search for an international agreement on capital adequacy standards proved difficult.[17] As such, a bilateral agreement on the issue was reached between the US and UK in 1986, which had the intended effect of putting pressure on the Basel Committee to reach a compromise.[18] The Basel I Accord was eventually published in 1988.

---

[10] For a detailed discussion of this failure see Chapter 5, section 5.2.

[11] George Walker, *International Banking Regulation: Law Policy and Practice* (Kluwer Law International 2001) 29.

[12] Charles Goodhart, *The Basel Committee on Banking Supervision: A History of the Early Years* (Cambridge University Press 2011) 4.

[13] For a detailed discussion of the establishment of this committee see Chapter 5, section 5.2.

[14] In fact, some of the very first papers that were circulated by the Committee concerned the 'Rules and practices to protect the banks' solvency and liquidity' and they included a report by several countries on their capital adequacy requirements. Goodhart, *The Basel Committee on Banking Supervision* 146.

[15] Federal Deposit Insurance Corporation 'The LDC Debt Crisis' in *History of the Eighties: Lessons for the Future, Vol.1: An Examination of the Banking Crises of the 1980s and early 1990's*, ch 5 at http://www.fdic.gov/bank/historical/history/191_210.pdf.

[16] Basel Committee on Banking Supervision *A Brief History of the Basel Committee* (October 2014) 2 at http://www.bis.org/bcbs/history.pdf.

[17] For a detailed discussion of this see Goodhart, *The Basel Committee on Banking Supervision* ch 6.

[18] See Bank of England, *Convergence of Capital Adequacy in the UK and US* (January 1987) at http://www.bankofengland.co.uk/archive/Documents/historicpubs/qb/1987/qb87q18586.pdf.

According to the Basel Committee, there were two fundamental objectives that lay at the heart of their work on regulatory convergence in this area. These were, firstly, that the regulatory standards should serve to strengthen the soundness and stability of the international banking system; and, secondly, that it should establish a fair and a consistent international banking system in order to decrease competitive inequality amongst international banks.[19] There was concern that the capital ratios of the main international banks were deteriorating at a time of growing international risk, reflecting a 'race to the bottom' in global banking competition.[20] As such, the move towards global harmonisation of capital adequacy standards sought to mitigate that trend. As Basel I was intended to set only the minimum requirements, countries would be free to impose higher standards, and demonstrate a 'race to the top'. Moreover, even if countries stuck to the minimum Basel I standards, a landscape of fragmented and low regulatory standards would have been prevented.

Fundamentally, capital adequacy requirements 'act as a road hump to slow down the moral hazard of excessive risk taking'.[21] Linking capital requirements to the risks associated with bank lending acts as a form of control upon banks' taking on of excessive risks in creating credit. As banks benefit from the lender-of-last resort facilities (discussed in Chapter 6, section 6.1) and deposit insurance (discussed in Chapter 13, section 13.3), these may cause moral hazard on the part of banks in determining the level of their risk-taking. Capital regulation prevents banks from succumbing excessively to such moral hazard. Further, capital regulation may achieve the effect of reassuring depositors and thereby preventing bank runs that have a detrimental impact on a bank's liquidity.[22] It is argued that higher capital requirements help to convince the public that the value of a bank's assets minus any liquidation costs will not fall below the value of deposits, so depositors will be less likely to withdraw their deposits.[23]

The Basel I Accord focuses on risk control upon the lending activities of banks, as that was the main area of business concern at the time. The Accord achieves the following:

(a) defines and calibrates the risk in lending for banks, that is, ***credit risk***;

(b) sets a standard for the level of capital that must be maintained against the level of credit risk; and

(c) defines what capital means.

---

[19] Basel Committee on Banking Supervision, *International Convergence of Capital Measurement and Capital Standards* 1.

[20] Basel Committee on Banking Supervision, *A Brief History of the Basel Committee* (October 2014) at http://www.bis.org/bcbs/history.pdf.

[21] Razeen Sappideen, 'The Regulation of Credit, Market and Operational Risk Management under the Basel Accords' (2004) 59 *Journal of Business Law* 70.   [22] Ibid.

[23] Arnoud Boot and Stuart Greenbaum, 'Bank Regulation, Reputation and Rents: Theory and Policy Implications' in Colin Mayer and Xavier Vives *Capital Markets and Financial Intermediation* (Cambridge: Cambridge University Press 1995) 267.

8.2.2 **Credit risk**

Credit risk is the risk that a counterparty that the bank has lent to will be unable to meet its payment obligations.

Basel I recognised that while there were a variety of risks that a bank needed to safeguard itself against including investment risk, *interest rate risk*, and *foreign exchange rate risk* (discussed in section 8.1), the most important consideration for a bank's management (at that time) was credit risk.[24] First it was important for banks to be able to *measure* their credit risk. The Accord developed a methodology for *risk-weighting* the loans made by the bank, that is, *assets* created by the bank. The lending made by banks is referred to as 'assets', as banks expect to generate income and profits from such lending. A standardised and simple-to-use *risk-weighting* methodology helps banks to measure their credit risks consistently and perhaps more accurately, as banks tend to play down a borrower's risk because it is incentivised by the expected income and profits from the loan. In this respect, where a borrower is more likely to default, or is of *higher risk*, banks are likely to generate more income and profit from lending to such a borrower as interest rate charges on these loans are generally higher. Hence, banks are fundamentally incentivised to pursue risk in lending due to the expected 'rewards'. A standardised risk-weighting framework overcomes banks' own incentives towards (less prudent) risk control.

8.2.3 **Risk-weighted assets**

The Accord categorised the assets and off-balance sheet exposures held by a bank and weighed them according to their relative riskiness. Five categories of *risk-weights* were created and bank assets were categorised into one of the five risk-weighted categories. The risk-weighted categories were: 0, 10, 20, 50, and 100 per cent.

Table 8.1 sets out examples of the assets that were placed in the risk-weight categories established in the Basel I Accord. The Accord set out a prescriptive approach in its treatment of the riskiness of loans (or assets) so that banks had no discretion to deviate from the Accord's measurement. The rationale for the Accord's treatment of different types of assets will be explained in greater detail shortly.

In risk-weighting assets, the gross value of the loan (or asset) would be multiplied by the risk-weight, that is, the percentage specified in the risk-weighting category, to derive the risk-weighted value of the asset. Hence the value of every asset would be measured according to its riskiness, which referred to the risk of default and loss. For example, if a bank extended £100,000 in a loan to a couple to purchase a home that would be fully mortgaged to the bank for the value of the loan, the risk-weight of this loan asset would be 50 per cent of the gross value of the loan, that is, £50,000. The Accord would have measured the riskiness of the asset to the bank at £50,000 representing its likely loss if the couple were to have defaulted during the course of the loan.

---

[24] Basel Committee on Banking Supervision, *International Convergence of Capital Measurement and Capital Standards* 9.

Table 8.1 Risk-weighted categories and examples of assets in each category

0%	Cash.
	Claims on central governments and central banks denominated in national currency and funded in that currency.
	Other claims on OECD central governments and central banks.
	Claims collateralised by cash or OECD central government securities or guaranteed by OECD central governments.
0, 10, 20, or 50% (at national discretion)	Claims on domestic public-sector entities, excluding central government, and loans guaranteed by such entities.
20%	Claims on multilateral development banks and claims guaranteed by, or collateralised by securities issued by such banks.
	Claims on banks incorporated in the OECD and loans guaranteed by OECD incorporated banks.
	Claims on banks incorporated in countries outside the OECD with a residual maturity of up to one year and loans with a residual maturity of up to one year guaranteed by banks incorporated in countries outside the OECD.
	Claims on non-domestic OECD public-sector entities, excluding central government, and loans guaranteed by such entities.
50%	Loans fully secured by mortgage on residential property that is or will be occupied by the borrower or that is rented.
100%	Claims on the private sector.
	Claims on banks incorporated outside the OECD with a residual maturity of more than one year.
	Claims on central governments outside the OECD (unless denominated in national currency – and funded in that currency –).
	Claims on commercial companies owned by the public sector.

Risk-weighting each asset provided a global picture of how much risk a bank was incurring and not just how much it was lending. The minimum required amount of capital needed to support the bank's credit risk activities was prescribed at 8 per cent of its total risk-weighted assets as determined by the risk–asset ratio, discussed in section 8.2.5.

We turn to discuss why the Accord gave certain risk treatments to certain assets, that is, why were some assets put into the 0 per cent or 20 per cent risk-weight categories while others were put into increasing levels of risk-weights.

8.2.3.1 Sovereign debt

Many banks would hold assets in the form of sovereign debt and debt issued by public institutions of various countries. Such debt could be issued by a bank's domestic government, by foreign governments, or by domestic or foreign public institutions.

The Basel Committee adopted an approach that measured the riskiness of sovereign debt by grouping countries together according to their credit standing.[25]

A 'club approach' was proposed, whereby the EC and G10 countries were treated as low risk and all other countries as higher risk.[26] However, as highlighted by Goodhart, the problem with utilising this dividing line was the difficulty in justifying the exclusion of a country such as Australia or New Zealand from the 'club' when similar countries such as Canada were included.[27] As such, the Committee concluded that the defining line that would form the basis for applying different risk-weights would be membership of the Organisation for Economic Cooperation and Development (OECD). Full members of the OECD have concluded special lending arrangements with the IMF associated with the fund's General Arrangements to Borrow (known collectively as the OECD countries).[28] They would therefore be regarded as less likely to default and have better credit standing. The sovereign debt and debt issued by the public institutions of such countries would be accorded a lower risk-weight than the debt issued by other countries.

This meant that claims on central governments within the OECD would attract a zero risk-weight and claims on debt issued by other public institutions in OECD member countries would attract a low risk-weight. Furthermore, claims on central governments and central banks outside the OECD would also attract a zero risk-weight provided they were denominated in the national currency and funded by liabilities in the same currency. This was an important and welcomed aspect of the framework, reflecting the reality that the risks associated with the availability and transfer of foreign exchange would be absent on such claims.

Furthermore, the framework encouraged the preservation of short-term lending on the international interbank market. A 20 per cent risk-weight was applied to all banks, regardless of incorporation, that engaged in lending with a residual maturity of up to and including one year. Longer-term claims in excess of this would be weighted at 20 per cent in relation to OECD incorporated banks, and 100 per cent in relation to non-OECD banks. These standards drew a distinction between short-term transactions, which were an important method of managing liquidity and were perceived to carry a low risk, and longer-term cross-border transactions, which, rather than relating to liquidity, often related to particular transactions, and therefore carried greater transfer and credit risk.

8.2.3.2 Debt issued by other public sector institutions

In a domestic context it would be at the discretion of each national supervisory authority to determine the appropriate risk-weight to apply to public sector

---

[25] Basel Committee on Banking Supervision, *International Convergence of Capital Measurement and Capital Standards* 9.

[26] See, for example, the remarks made by the Chairman of the Basel Committee at their Brussels meeting in June 1987, available at BS/87/80.   [27] Goodhart, *The Basel Committee on Banking Supervision* 177.

[28] Basel Committee on Banking Supervision, *International Convergence of Capital Measurement and Capital Standards* 10.

institutions within their country. This reflected the special character and vary-ing creditworthiness of public sector institutions below central government level. Hence, the Committee was unable to decide on a single common risk-weight that could be applied to claims on these entities. In order to preserve a degree of conver-gence the framework stipulated that the risk-weights to be ascribed to such assets should be 0, 10, 20, or 50 per cent for domestic public sector institutions, with a standard 20 per cent weight being applicable to claims on non-domestic public sec-tor institutions in OECD member countries. Claims on non-OECD public sector entities attracted a risk-weight of 100 per cent. Furthermore, the framework pro-vided a blanket 100 per cent risk-weight for claims on commercial companies owned by the public sector 'in order to avoid inequality vis-à-vis similar private-sector com-mercial enterprises.'[29] The risk-weight category for private sector corporations is discussed below.

8.2.3.3 Collateral and guarantees

The risk-weight framework recognised the importance of collateral and guarantees in mitigating credit risk.

Hence collateralised loans attracted a lower risk-weighting. Where loans were secured against cash or against securities issued by OECD governments and specified multilateral development banks, these assets would attract the risk-weight of the col-lateral, either at a zero or 20 per cent risk-weight.

In relation to guarantees, loans guaranteed by sovereigns attracted the respective sovereign's risk-weighting applicable to sovereign debt. Loans guaranteed by OECD central governments, OECD public-sector institutions, or OECD incorporated banks, attracted that risk-weight as if a direct claim were being made on the guarantor, that is, 0 per cent, the risk-weight assigned to OECD sovereign debt. Loans guaranteed by non-OECD incorporated banks also attracted a lower risk-weight of 20 per cent, but only where the transaction had a residual maturity of less than one year.[30]

8.2.3.4 Mortgages

Residential mortgages created by banks were assigned a risk-weight of 50 per cent. This is because the Accord sought to give effect to the low level of loss that had been recorded in the context of loans secured by mortgages on occupied residential property thus far. In applying this 50 per cent risk-weight the national supervisor should have been satis-fied that this rate was applied restrictively for residential purposes and in accordance with strict prudential criteria. The 50 per cent risk-weight only held where there were strict valuation rules in a country that ensured a margin of additional security over the value of the loan made.

---

[29] Ibid, 11.
[30] See section 8.2.3.2, in relation to the perceived risks of short-term transactions that preserve the efficiency of the international interbank market, in contrast with longer-term cross-border loans that carry greater risks.

8.2.3.5 **Private sector credit**

The Accord assigned a 100 per cent risk-weight to all private sector borrowing from banks. This included debt instruments issued by private sector corporations. In this particular category, a one-size-fits-all approach was taken such that all private sector credit was regarded as 100 per cent risky and capable of loss. This approach lacked subtlety and assumed that all private sector corporations were equally likely to default. Why were all corporate loans grouped into a 100 per cent risk-weight? Why not 60, 80, or even 150 per cent, depending on how sound and stable the corporation was? It made no difference to the calculation of capital adequacy whether a bank lent to a company with the highest credit rating,[31] or one that had a poor, or even no, credit rating – according to the framework the risk involved was perceived to be the same.[32] In general, the risk-weighting framework seemed too over-inclusive and crude. The Accord was intent on achieving a standardised and simple-to-use framework and had ridden roughshod over risk differences between assets within the same category. One could question whether all OECD sovereign debt should really be treated as equally risky.

8.2.3.6 **Off-balance sheet transactions**

The discussion so far has centred on the framework for loan-based assets (also known as 'balance sheet' assets). Moreover, the Accord also sought to incorporate certain exposures such as in trade financing that were not loan-based but entailed risk for the bank. Such transactions were collectively known as 'off-balance sheet' transactions. The Basel Committee wished to capture off-balance-sheet transactions within the capital adequacy framework, so that bank exposures not categorised as loans would also be accounted for in terms of their riskiness. The Accord introduced an approach to convert all categories of off-balance sheet exposures to 'credit risk equivalents' by multiplying the nominal principal amounts by a credit conversion factor.[33] The instruments in question were divided into five categories:

1. Direct credit substitutes (including general guarantees of indebtedness, bank acceptance credits, and standby letters of credit serving as guarantees for loans and securities). These assets carried a 100 per cent *credit risk conversion* factor.

2. Certain transaction-related contingent items (including performance bonds and bid bonds). These assets carried a 50 per cent credit risk conversion factor,

---

[31] Such as 'AAA' awarded by S&P.

[32] See Goodhart, *The Basel Committee on Banking Supervision* 195: 'the risk-weights to be applied to the various groups of assets were ad hoc and broad-brush, based on subjective (and political) judgement, not on any empirical studies.'

[33] These credit conversion factors are derived from the estimated size and likely occurrence of the credit exposure, as well as the relative degree of credit risk identified in an earlier paper of the Committee's. Basel Committee on Banking Supervision, *The Management of Banks' Off-Balance Sheet Exposures: A Supervisory Perspective* (Basel, BIS 1986) at http://www.bis.org/publ/bcbsc134.pdf.

3. Short-term, self-liquidating trade-related contingent liabilities arising from
    the movement of goods (including documentary credits collateralised by the
    underlying shipments). These assets carried a 20 per cent credit risk conversion
    factor,

4. Commitments with an original maturity exceeding one year and all note issu-
    ance facilities and revolving underwriting facilities carried a 50 per cent credit
    risk conversion factor. Shorter-term commitments or commitments that could be
    cancelled at any time were regarded as relatively low risk and carried a 0 per cent
    credit risk conversion factor.

5. Interest and exchange rate related transactions (including swaps, options, and
    futures). Special treatment was provided for these items because banks would
    not be exposed to credit risk for the full face-value of their contracts, but only
    the cost of replacing the cash flow should the counterparty default. Credit risk
    was assessed by calculating the current replacement cost and adding a factor to
    represent potential exposure during the remaining life of the contract (the cur-
    rent exposure method). An alternative calculation was offered by the framework,
    which could be applied at the discretion of national authorities. The alternative
    method consisted of conversion factors based on the nominal principal sum un-
    derlying each contract according to its type and maturity (the original exposure
    method). The alternative method did not refer to the current market price of the
    instruments.[34]

Once the bank had calculated the credit risk equivalent amounts in relation to the off-
balance sheet exposures, they would be risk-weighted according to the category of
counterparty in the same way as the main framework that applied to on-balance sheet
assets, as discussed earlier.

8.2.4 Achievements and drawbacks of the risk-weighting model

The model employed by the Basel I Accord in assigning risk-weights to certain categories of assets to calculate credit risk is remarkable in its simplicity. This made the
model ready for immediate adoption, not only by international banks from the Basel

---

[34] For more detailed discussion of these calculations see Basel Committee on Banking Supervision,
International Convergence of Capital Measurement and Capital Standards Annex 3. Note, the Basel Committee
issued a document amending the treatment of off-balance-sheet items in order to (a) recognise netting effects
in the calculation of the 'add-ons' for potential future exposure associated with certain off-balance-sheet items
and (b) enlarge the matrix of add-ons to capture more accurately the potential future exposure associated with
longer maturities and a broader range of transactions not explicitly covered in the original Accord. The amendment was effective from the end of 1995. See Basel Committee on Banking Supervision, *Basel Capital Accord: Treatment of Potential Exposure for Off-Balance Sheet Items* (Basel, BIS 1995) at http://www.bis.org/publ/
bcbs18.pdf. A further document was issued in April 1996 that explained how Committee members intended
to recognise the effects of multilateral netting. See Basel Committee on Banking Supervision, *Interpretation of
the Capital Accord for the Multilateral Netting of Forward Value Foreign Exchange Transactions* (April 1996) at
http://www.bis.org/publ/bcbs25.pdf.

Committee member countries,[35] but also by non-international banks and banks from non-member countries.[36]

There were three principal advantages in adopting the capital adequacy standards in the Accord:[37]

1. It provided a fairer basis for making international comparisons between banking systems whose structures would differ.

2. It allowed off-balance sheet exposures to be incorporated more easily into the measure.

3. It did not deter banks from holding liquid or other assets, which carried low risk.[38]

However, there were a number of issues with the risk-weight approach.

First, it lacked subtlety and was detached from reality in assessing the quality of different types of assets such as in relation to private sector credit (section 8.2.3.5).[39]

Secondly, while the Basel Committee recognised the merit of the framework in not deterring banks from holding liquid or other assets that carried a low risk, conversely, it could be argued that the framework encouraged banks to invest in those assets that carry lower risk-weights, rather than those assets with a higher risk-weight such as corporate loans. This could have broader ramifications for the economy by making it more difficult for companies to borrow.[40]

Thirdly, the risk-weight approach failed to recognise the benefits of risk mitigation in terms of diversified lending. Under the Basel I Accord, a bank that lent £10 million to one company in the UK would be subject to exactly the same capital requirements as one that lent £1 million each to ten different companies operating in different industries.

8.2.5 Risk-asset ratio

The purpose of the previously discussed risk-weighting assets is for the risk–asset ratio to be applied. This refers to the ratio of capital that needs to be maintained against the level of risk-weighted assets.

---

[35] For information on member countries see Chapter 5, section 5.2.
[36] Basel Committee on Banking Supervision *A Brief History of the Basel Committee* 2.
[37] A gearing ratio is a measure of financial leverage that calculates risk exposure by measuring the proportion of a company's borrowed funds to its equity.
[38] Basel Committee on Banking Supervision, *International Convergence of Capital Measurement and Capital Standards* 8.
[39] Indeed, the Committee itself recognises that there are 'inevitably some broad-brush judgments in deciding which weight should apply to different types of assets.' Ibid.
[40] Hal Scott and Philip Wellons, *International Finance, Transactions, Policies and Regulations* (Foundation Press 2002) 254; Sappideen, 'The Regulation of Credit, Market and Operational Risk Management under the Basel Accords' (2004) 72. See also Goodhart, *The Basel Committee on Banking Supervision* 195. He highlights that the application of the Basel I risk-weights 'soon led to serious distortions in bank assets portfolios that undermined Basel I. There was little or no discussion at the time about the impact the Accord might or should have on bank behaviour.'

After extensive debate and discussion,[41] the Basel Committee finally agreed to set the ratio of capital to risk-weighted assets at 8 per cent, a minimum level that they determined was 'consistent with the objective of securing over time soundly-based and consistent capital ratios for all international banks'.[42] Hence, the minimum required amount of capital needed to support a bank's credit risk activities would be 8 per cent of its risk-weighted assets, represented in the following calculation:

$$\text{Risk–asset Ratio (8\%)} = \frac{\text{Capital}}{\text{Risk-Weighted Assets}}$$

Box 8.2 provides a practical example, to demonstrate how the risk–asset ratio worked. The example assumes that we have a bank with a simple loan portfolio. It highlights the different types of assets the bank creates and the risk-weights they attract, and then how much capital is required to support these assets.

Under the Basel I Accord, the capital requirements imposed on banks would only be a fraction of banks' total credit exposures. In the worked example in Box 8.2, the capital requirement of £472,000 is a fraction of the bank's £9 million gross exposure (not risk-weighted). Hence, one may be cautious of how far capital adequacy regulation really moderates bank risk-taking and ensures their soundness and safety. For example,

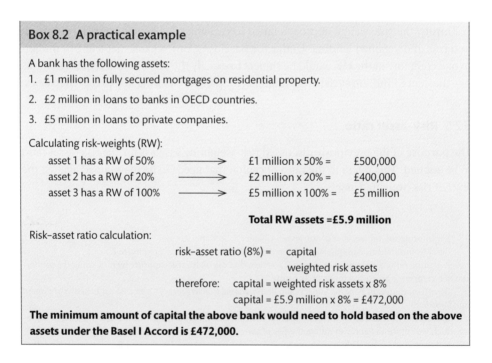

Box 8.2 A practical example

A bank has the following assets:
1. £1 million in fully secured mortgages on residential property.
2. £2 million in loans to banks in OECD countries.
3. £5 million in loans to private companies.

Calculating risk-weights (RW):

asset 1 has a RW of 50% ⟶	£1 million x 50% =	£500,000
asset 2 has a RW of 20% ⟶	£2 million x 20% =	£400,000
asset 3 has a RW of 100% ⟶	£5 million x 100% =	£5 million

Total RW assets =£5.9 million

Risk–asset ratio calculation:

$$\text{risk–asset ratio (8\%)} = \frac{\text{capital}}{\text{weighted risk assets}}$$

therefore: capital = weighted risk assets x 8%

capital = £5.9 million x 8% = £472,000

The minimum amount of capital the above bank would need to hold based on the above assets under the Basel I Accord is £472,000.

[41] A good summary of which is provided by Goodhart, *The Basel Committee on Banking Supervision* ch 6.

[42] Basel Committee on Banking Supervision, *International Convergence of Capital Measurement and Capital Standards* 14.

Northern Rock, the British bank that was taken into state ownership in February 2008, reported a pre-crash risk–asset ratio of 17.5 per cent. Similarly, Kaupthing, the Icelandic bank that was taken over by the Icelandic Financial Supervisory Authority in October 2008, and Lehman Brothers, the US investment bank that collapsed in September 2008, reported pre-crash risk–asset ratios of 11.2 per cent and 16.1 per cent respectively.[43] These were higher than the 8 per cent minimum but did not prevent the above-mentioned banks from failing.

Furthermore, the 8 per cent risk–asset ratio was arrived at as a matter of convenient international banking practice, rather than as a result of rigorous risk management research. During negotiations, information was collected that revealed that the levels of capital held by Basel member countries were within a 7–10 per cent range. The figure of 8 per cent therefore 'emerged naturally' when Peter Cooke – then Chairman of the Basel Committee – proposed it to the Committee, which accepted it.[44] Accordingly there was no empirical analysis to determine what the optimal capital ratio should have been, rather, the figure that emerged largely reflected practice at the time and the aim of bolstering capital reserves without making it inordinately difficult for international banks to comply.

8.2.6 What constitutes capital?

Having discussed risk-weighted assets and the risk–asset ratio, we now turn to consider what constituted capital under the Basel I framework.

Capital was defined according to two different tiers, and at least 50 per cent of a bank's capital base (i.e. 4 per cent of the risk–asset ratio) consisted of *tier one capital*. This tier of capital comprised of equity capital and published reserves, also regarded as good quality capital as being retained in banks, and capable of supporting business and absorbing risks. The rest of a bank's capital base comprised of weaker quality capital, known as *tier two capital*.

8.2.6.1 Tier one capital

Tier one capital was regarded as 'core capital' and consisted of equity capital, that is, issued and fully paid ordinary shares/common stock and non-cumulative perpetual preferred stock, and disclosed reserves (i.e. the retained earnings of the bank). The importance of these types of capital lay in their visibility and permanence. They would be wholly visible in the published accounts of the banking institution and they would form the basis on which most market judgments of capital adequacy were made. Further, such capital would be regarded as stable, as they would ordinarily be retained in banks (i.e. not redeemable and buyback of shares would presumably not be a frequent phenomenon). The emphasis on these particular types of core capital 'reflect[ed]

---

[43] See James Ferguson 'What Went Wrong?' in Patrick Young *The Gathering Storm* (Derivatives Vision Publishing 2010) 10–38.　　　　　[44] Goodhart, *The Basel Committee on Banking Supervision* 178.

the importance the Committee attache[d] to securing a progressive enhancement in the quality, as well as the level, of the total capital resources maintained by major banks.'[45]

8.2.6.2 Tier two capital

The remaining, tier two capital, limited to a maximum of 100 per cent of tier 1 capital (i.e. comprising 4 per cent of the risk–asset ratio), consisted of a variety of 'poorer' quality capital. These related to reserves of the bank that had not been published, therefore lacking in transparency, as well as debt instruments with less priority in insolvency and therefore could act as loss-absorbing devices. The types of tier two capital are set out in Box 8.3.

Box 8.3 Tier two capital instruments

Undisclosed reserves

Undisclosed or hidden reserves that, although unpublished, had been passed through the profit and loss account of a bank. While the intrinsic quality of this asset could be the same as published retained profits, their lack of transparency, and the fact that many countries did not recognise undisclosed reserves as a legitimate form of capital, meant that they were excluded from comprising part of tier one capital.

Revaluation reserves

These arose when the value of an asset, for example, the bank's business premises, became greater than the value that was previously recorded on the balance sheet. Some countries allowed these assets to be revalued, and the balance sheet amended, to reflect their current market value. The resulting revaluation reserves could be included in the tier two capital base. According to the Accord:

> Such reserves may be included within supplementary capital provided that the assets are considered by the supervisory authority to be prudently valued, fully reflecting the possibility of price fluctuation and forced sale.[46]

General provisions or general loan-loss reserves

These reserves were created to address the possibility of future loss generally and not assigned to an identified asset, therefore not reflecting a reduction in the risk-weighted value of an identified asset. They qualified for the purposes of tier two capital. As these provisions had not been ascribed to a particular asset, they would be freely available to meet unidentified losses that could arise elsewhere.[47]

---

[45] Basel Committee on Banking Supervision, *International Convergence of Capital Measurement and Capital Standards* 4.   [46] Ibid, 5. Ibid, 5.

[47] Note, the Accord was amended in 1991 to give greater precision to the definition of general provisions or general loan-loss reserves that could be included in the capital adequacy calculation: Basel committee on Banking Supervision, *Amendment of the Basle Capital Accord in Respect of the Inclusion of General Provisions/ General Loan-Loss Reserves in Capital* (November 1991) at http://www.bis.org/publ/bcbs09.pdf.

Hybrid debt capital instruments

These included capital instruments with characteristics of both equity and debt. Where these instruments were closely aligned to equity, they could be utilised to support losses on an ongoing basis, so could be included in tier 2 capital. These instruments had to meet the following requirements:

> they are unsecured, subordinated and fully paid up; they are not redeemable at the initiative of the holder or without the prior consent of the supervisory authority; they are available to participate in losses without the bank being obliged to cease trading (unlike conventional subordinated debt); although the capital instrument may carry an obligation to pay interest that cannot permanently be reduced or waived (unlike dividends on ordinary shareholders' equity), it should allow service obligations to be deferred (as with cumulative preference shares) where the profitability of the bank would not support payment.[48]

Instruments such as cumulative preference shares[49] and perpetual subordinated debt[50] had these characteristics and were therefore eligible for inclusion within this category of capital.

Subordinated term debt

These included unsecured subordinated debt capital instruments with a minimum 5-year maturity and limited life redeemable preference shares. These enjoyed low insolvency priority and were likely to be written off and hence regarded as loss-absorbing in nature. But they could be deficient as constituents of capital because of their mixed maturity and their inability to absorb losses except in liquidation. These assets would also be subject to an amortisation arrangement whereby, during the last 5 years to maturity, a cumulative discount of 20 per cent per year would be applied to reflect the weakened ability of those instruments to absorb losses. As a relatively poorer capital instrument, the amount of subordinated term debt that could be included as tier 2 capital was restricted to a maximum of 50 per cent of tier one capital (i.e. 2 per cent of the risk–asset ratio).

8.2.6.3 Deductions from capital

The Accord provided for two categories of deductions to be made for the purpose of calculating the bank's capital resources (Box 8.4 shows a brief overview of what constitutes capital). These deductions would prevent the repeated use of the same capital resources in different parts of a banking group. The deductions consisted of goodwill

---

[48] Basel Committee on Banking Supervision, *International Convergence of Capital Measurement and Capital Standards* Annex 1.

[49] Cumulative preference shares are a type of preferred stock where missed dividend payments accrue until they can be paid. What this means is that, if a bank runs into financial difficulty and suspends dividend payments as a result, it will have to pay back all the missed dividends that it owes to the cumulative preference shareholders when it resumes making payments. In contrast, non-cumulative preference shareholders would not be entitled to the missed dividend payments.

[50] An example of perpetual subordinated debt is a bond (a form of loan) with no maturity date, which means that it can be treated as equity rather than debt. When a bank issues a perpetual bond it pays interest (known as coupons) continually, and it doesn't have to redeem the principal.

Box 8.4 Constituents of capital at a glance

Tier one: core capital	Tier two: supplementary capital
- Equity capital: issued and fully paid shares/common stock and non-cumulative perpetual preferred stock	- Undisclosed reserves
	- Revaluation reserves
	- General provisions/general loan loss reserves
- Disclosed reserves	- Hybrid debt capital instruments
	- Subordinated term debt

At least 50 per cent of a bank's capital must comprise tier one core capital.

---

as a deduction from tier one capital,[51] and investments in unconsolidated financial subsidiary companies, that is, subsidiary companies whose accounts were not consolidated with the banks. Accordingly, the Accord stated that 'the assets representing the investments in subsidiary companies whose capital had been deducted from that of the parent would not be included in total assets for the purposes of computing the ratio.'[52] National regulators had the discretion to introduce other deductions in relation to investments in the capital of other banks and financial institutions.

8.2.7 Implementation in the UK and EU

The Basel I Accord was introduced not only in Basel Committee member countries, but also in all other countries with internationally active banks. The UK had already introduced a skeletal set of prudential regulation principles in its Banking Act 1987, but fully transposed the Accord into national law following the enactment of the relevant Directives for the European Economic Area (EEA).[53] The Accord was adopted by the EEA by virtue of the now-obsolete Own Funds Directive,[54] which defined the constituents of capital, and the repealed Solvency Ratio Directive,[55] which specified the rules for estimating the banks' risk-weighted assets. Unsurprisingly, given the fact that the Basel Committee included representatives from seven member countries of the EU, the rules of the 1988 Basel Capital Accord and the two directives were very similar. They differed slightly, for example, in relation to the scope of coverage, as the EU regime applied to all credit institutions, whether or not they engaged in cross-border activity.

---

[51] Goodwill typically reflects the value of intangible assets such as a strong brand name, good customer relations, good employee relations, and patents or proprietary technology. It arises when a company acquires another business and it relates to the difference in value between the purchase price of a business and the value of its identifiable (including intangible) assets.

[52] Basel Committee on Banking Supervision, *International Convergence of Capital Measurement and Capital Standards* 7.   [53] These are discussed in Chapter 7, section 7.1.

[54] Own Funds Directive (1989/229/EC).   [55] Solvency Ratio Directive (89/647/EEC).

> ### Key takeaways

- The 1988 Basel Accord introduced a harmonised framework for the regulatory standards of capital adequacy.
- The central focus of the Accord was the exposure of a bank to credit risk.
- Bank assets were placed into five categories and risk-weighted according to their relative riskiness.
- A minimum ratio of capital to risk-weighted assets of 8 per cent was to be maintained by banks.
- Banks could use two tiers of capital to meet the risk–asset ratio. Tier one and tier two capital were defined and at least 50 per cent of the risk–asset ratio had to be maintained by tier one capital.
- The UK absorbed the Accord into national legislation first under the Banking Act 1987 and then by virtue of transposing the relevant EEA Directives.
- The EU transposed the Basel I Accord by virtue of the Own Funds Directive, 1989 and the Solvency Ratio Directive, 1989.

Key bibliography

Legislation

Own Funds Directive (1989/229/EC)
Solvency Ratio Directive (89/647/EEC)

Reports and recommendations

Basel Committee on Banking Supervision, *Amendment of the Basel Capital Accord in Respect of the Inclusion of General Provisions/General Loan-Loss Reserves in Capital* (November 1991) At http://www.bis.org/publ/bcbs09.pdf

Basel Committee on Banking Supervision, *Basel Capital Accord: Treatment of Potential Exposure for Off-Balance Sheet Items* (Basel, BIS 1995) at http://www.bis.org/publ/bcbs18.pdf

Basel Committee on Banking Supervision, *A Brief History of the Basel Committee* (Oct 2014) at http://www.bis.org/bcbs/history.pdf

Basel Committee on Banking Supervision, *International Convergence of Capital Measurement and Capital Standards* (July 1988) at http://www.bis.org/publ/bcbs04a.pdf

Basel Committee on Banking Supervision, *Interpretation of the Capital Accord for the Multilateral Netting of Forward Value Foreign Exchange Transactions* (April 1996) at http://www.bis.org/publ/bcbs25.pdf

Basel Committee on Banking Supervision, *The management of Banks' Off-Balance Sheet Exposures: A Supervisory Perspective* (Basel, BIS 1986) at http://www.bis.org/publ/bcbsc134.pdf

Articles

Sappideen, R, 'The regulation of credit, market and operational risk management under the Basel Accords' (2004) *Journal of Business Law* 59

Books

Goodhart, C, *The Basel Committee on Banking Supervision: A History of the Early Years* (Cambridge: Cambridge University Press 2011) ch 6

8.3 Pre-development of the Basel II Capital Accord

The Basel I Accord provided a simple, standardised but prescriptive means of working out the required levels of capital to support banks' lending activities. However, its critics were concerned that the overall risk–asset ratio of 8 per cent had been set too low, as this was achieved as a matter of compromise considering the state of international banking practice at the time, and not as a scientific measure of 'bank safety'. Starting at a low level of 8 per cent also entailed a 'norming' effect, making it difficult for more stringent levels of risk–asset ratio to be introduced.[56] Moreover, international banking practice was changing rapidly, and the Accord's focus on credit risk was becoming too limited to capture the variety of bank risks in new activities that banks started to undertake.

By the 1990s, it was recognised by the Basel Committee that banks were exposed to considerable risk of losses from interest rate and foreign currency movements. These risks were not considered in the Basel I Accord. Many bank loans were extended on the basis of variable rates of interest that could change in accordance with the central bank's base rate and other factors affecting banks' cost of borrowing. Banks involved in international payments and financing of international trade were exposed to foreign currency fluctuation risk, which could cause banks loss. The suite of risks affecting bank costs were risks emanating from the market, and they had not been reflected in the capital adequacy standards which only focused on credit risk.

Further, as mentioned in Chapter 1, banks in the US in particular started to move into investment banking aggressively in the 1990s after a law that prevented such consolidation of activities was repealed.[57] Although European banks had never faced such restrictions and always embraced a 'universal banking' model that allowed banks to conduct a variety of financial intermediation services, the newly competitive forces coming from the US were crucial in European and UK banks' expansion into investment activities. Thus, many international banks started to undertake activities such as securities underwriting,[58] corporate finance in restructuring and mergers and acquisitions,[59] proprietary trading,[60] collective investment schemes,[61] and advisory[62] and

---

[56] Eric A Posner, 'How Do Bank Regulators Determine Capital Adequacy Requirements?' (2014) at http://papers.ssrn.com/sol3/papers.cfm?abstract-id=2493968.

[57] The Gramm-Leach Bliley Act 1993 that repealed the restrictions under the Glass–Steagall Act.

[58] Defined as the role of guaranteeing the issue of commercial paper, such as securities. Investment banks guarantee to take up a corporation's public offer of securities, such an activity generating both income from under-writing as well as market gains in the under-writer's subsequent market-making positions in the security concerned. See *Oxford Dictionary of Finance and Banking* (5th edition, Oxford: OUP 2014).

[59] Banks often act as adviser and arranger of corporate finance needs in restructurings or mergers and acquisitions, generating huge fees and income.

[60] Defined as 'trading in which a bank or financial institution buys and sells instruments on its own account rather than on behalf of a customer', see *Oxford Dictionary of Finance and Banking*.

[61] Defined in s235, UK Financial Services and Markets Act as a pooled arrangement for the management of any property as a scheme as a whole, with a view to profit, where investor participants part with day to day control.   [62] That is, investment advice that can be provided to retail or sophisticated investors.

broker services.[63] As banks became exposed to investment activities, the nature of their business risks changed too. Hence it became important to consider how capital adequacy rules should compel banks to make provision for market risks.

8.3.1 **Market Risk Amendment 1996**

In 1996, the Basel Committee developed the 'Market Risk Amendment'[64] to address the market risks that banks faced in relation to the aforementioned activities. The Market Risk Amendment also introduced for the first time the possibility of non-standard models for banks in measuring market risks, in addition to a standardised approach akin to the Basel I Accord for credit risk.

The Market Risk Amendment sought to introduce standards for measuring bank assets that incurred 'market risk' and to ensure that market risk would be supported by bank capital, thus incorporating market risk provision into capital adequacy standards.

Market risk would be measured using either a standardised approach, illustrated later, or a 'model' approach developed by banks. Using either approach, market risk was measured in relation to the range of different market-based activities discussed earlier. The total measure of market risk would then be risk-weighted at 12.5 per cent, that is, only 12.5 per cent of the total measurement of market risk set out in this section would 'count' for the application of the risk–asset ratio. In other words, banks added the risk-weighted market risk measured according to the Amendment to the measurement of risk-weighted assets for credit risk, and the 8 per cent risk–asset ratio would be applied to the global measure of both credit and market risk to determine the capital levels needed to support banks' credit and market risk activities (See Box 8.5 for the relevant calculations).

Box 8.5

Recall that for capital adequacy in relation to credit risk:
 Risk–asset ratio calculation:

$$\text{risk–asset ratio (8\%)} = \frac{\text{capital}}{\text{weighted risk assets}}$$

Post-Market Risk Amendment:
 Risk–asset ratio calculation:

$$\text{risk–asset ratio (8\%)} = \frac{\text{capital}}{\text{weighted risk assets + risk-weighted market risk measurement}}$$

---

[63] An agency service that brings two parties to a contract together, such as in buying and selling of securities. Broker services sometimes include dealer services where the broker trades on its own account as well, in order to make a liquid market in the relevant securities. See *Oxford Dictionary of Finance and Banking*.

[64] Basel Committee, *Amendment to the Capital Accord to Incorporate Market Risks* (1996) at http://www.bis.org/publ/bcbs24.pdf?noframes=1.

We turn now to discuss how market risk measurement was carried out. Market risk measurement was made by standardised approaches in relation to different types of market risk activity, as well as by 'internal model' approaches. The standardised approaches were highly technical, and reflected the challenges the Committee faced in designing measures for risk in transactions shaped by many factors. The riskiness of these transactions would depend on factors such as the nature of the markets they took place in and the bank's portfolio composition (i.e. what mixture of market-based assets it held), making it difficult to introduce simple methodology to capture the nuances of risk. Although the standardised approaches became highly technical, they were still rather crude in nature, unable to distinguish between the granularity of different market transactions. 'Internal model' approaches, however, allowed banks to apply certain models to determine market risk measurement in a more 'tailor-made' manner and could be regarded as more sophisticated and risk-sensitive. However, allowing the use of such models would mean that banks could start introducing their own 'standards' that could undermine the success in standardisation achieved so far.

8.3.2 Standardised approaches to measuring market risk

The Market Risk Amendment prescribed standardised measurements for interest rate risk, foreign currency risk, equities, derivatives and options trading risks, and commodities risk. These are individually discussed below. These standardised measures were not envisaged to be a form of international harmonisation, rather as a rough guideline to help banks towards fashioning more precise risk-measurement systems internally, that could then be used to supersede the standardised measurements.

Such an approach on the part of the Basel Committee seemed contradictory to its international harmonisation efforts for measuring credit risk discussed in section 8.2. It seemed that the Committee was mindful of criticisms that in the Basel I Accord, it had provided a one-size-fits-all model which was insensitive to precise differences in risk profiles between different assets. Hence, in embarking on the Market Risk Amendment, the Committee stressed the importance of banks developing more precise and meaningful risk-measurement models for themselves, departing from the need for international harmonisation, and relying much more on national regulators' supervision of banks to ensure the soundness of banks' risk management overall. A brief overview of the standardised approaches to measuring market risk follows.

8.3.2.1 Interest rate risk

Interest rates are the cost of borrowing. Where a bank is concerned, interest rate risk refers to the possibility that the price at which banks lend fluctuates over the term of the loan, and thus affects its profitability or may even cause loss.

The Market Risk Amendment prescribed that different types of loans were to be risk-weighted for interest rate risk first according to their 'specific risk' and then according to their 'general' risk, which referred to the loan duration. Specific risk was measured in relation to the type of borrower. For example, government and other 'qualifying'

Table 8.2 Market-risk-weighting for different types of bank borrowers in relation to interest rate risk

Government	0%
OECD country or local government borrowing with 6 months' or less maturity	0.25%
Above, with 6–24 months' maturity	1%
Above, with more than 24 months' maturity	1.6%
Other borrowing	8%

borrowing in Table 8.2 would be risk-weighted relatively lightly, while all other borrowing would attract a much higher risk-weighting. The cost of lending to government and 'qualifying' borrowers was seen as less likely to fluctuate compared to other private sector borrowing. Qualifying borrowing was defined as debt securities issued by public sector entities and multilateral development banks, and other securities rated investment-grade by at least two credit rating agencies, that is, at least Baa by Moody's or BBB by S&P.

In terms of measuring general risk, the bank's long and short positions in each debt security they held would be netted,[65] and prescribed risk-weights were applied depending on the time horizon of maturity and the yield promised on the face of the security (referred to as coupon rate). Higher yielding debt securities maturing over a shorter period of time attracted lower market risk-weights compared to lower yielding debt securities over a longer maturity.[66]

The sum of the specific risk measurement for each type of debt security and the general risk measurement applied to that security would be the market risk measurement for the specific debt security in question. The same approach applied to all the banks' debt securities in order to attain a total measurement of interest rate risk for the banks' holding of debt securities.

8.3.2.2 Market risk in equities trading

As banks embarked on investment banking, they became more exposed to risks in relation to trading securities (i.e. corporate shares and debenture products) and derivatives of those securities. Hence banks could incur risks due to the price fluctuations of securities and derivatives in the market.

---

[65] The long positions refer to the debt securities the bank has purchased. The short positions refer to the debt securities the bank promises to sell in advance of purchase as it expects the purchase price to be lower than the selling price. The precise methodology is highly technical as netting is carried out for debt securities across different maturity horizons and then prescribed percentages of 'disallowances' from netting are added back to reflect the risks incurred across different time horizons. Details are not necessary at this level.

[66] Details can be found in Table 1, p 12 of the Market Risk Amendment at http://www.bis.org/publ/bcbs24.pdf?noframes=1.

The Market Risk Amendment prescribed that the 'specific' market risk of the bank's portfolio had to be measured and provisioned for, as well as the 'general' risk of trading in securities and derivatives markets.

First, a bank was required to measure its specific portfolio risk by aggregating all its long and short equities and derivatives positions.[67] A bank's equity positions would be marked to the market prices of those equities. As for derivatives and options,[68] the bank had to measure their market values by converting into positions in the relevant underlying securities. If the bank's portfolio was highly diversified and liquid, it would be imposed with a 4 per cent capital charge, meaning that 4 per cent of the marked to market aggregate value of net positions would need to be provisioned for in capital adequacy. If the portfolio was not as diversified and liquid, then an 8 per cent capital charge would be applied.

The general market risk capital charge was set at 8 per cent, although it was not explained as to why 8 per cent of a bank's portfolio was regarded to be a reliable measure of typical price fluctuations.

In sum, the market risk measurement for equities and derivatives on the banks' trading book was the sum of specific portfolio risk (i.e. 4 per cent or 8 per cent (plus optional 2 per cent if index contracts were involved)) and general market risk (8 per cent).

8.3.2.3 Foreign exchange risk

Banks incur foreign exchange risk due to currency fluctuations in their holdings. Further, their holdings in gold also had to be risk-weighted for in a similar fashion as for currency risk.

The Market Risk Amendment prescribed a standardised approach called the 'shorthand' approach for measuring foreign currency risk. All foreign currencies were assumed to be equal, and the bank's net long and short positions in each currency were worked out according to the spot price of the day. The capital charge would be 8 per cent of the higher of either the net long currency positions or the net short currency positions and of the net position in gold.

8.3.2.4 Commodities risk

Banks have become involved in trading in commodities contracts as part of their services to commercial customers who wished to hedge their positions in commodity trading or as part of market-making on commodity trading exchanges. Commodities contracts can be highly volatile and illiquid.

[67] The long positions refer to the securities the bank has purchased. The short positions refer to the securities the bank promises to sell in advance of purchase as it expects the purchase price to be lower than the selling price.

[68] The market risk measurement for options is based on the method for equities and derivatives, but more sophisticated methods that consider underlying debt securities and interest rate risk can be used in 'delta' methodology, which the chapter will not go into detail. See http://www.bis.org/publ/bcbs24.pdf?noframes=1 p 33.

The market risk for commodities contracts were prescribed on the basis of banks' 'net position' in each commodity. First, banks needed to work out a standard unit of measurement of each commodity holding, and then its net position, long or short in such commodity, even if the commodity contracts in question were of different time horizons. The net position of each commodity would be converted into its spot rate. As commodity contracts would be of different time horizons, the ones nearer to maturity could be used to offset the risks of the ones further off, although such offsetting would be imprecise. After such further offsetting, a capital charge of 0.6 per cent would be applied to the net position.

The Market Risk Amendment then prescribed that the market risk measurement of banks' commodity contract holdings would be 15 per cent of its net position, as already calculated. Further, in order to provision for any basis risk (i.e. that the offsetting discussed above inherently contained imperfect correlations), interest rate risk, or other market risks, a capital charge of 3 per cent of all banks' gross long and short positions would be applied. In sum, the market risk measurement of banks' commodities risk would be 15 per cent of its net position in each commodity plus 3 per cent of its gross long and short positions in each commodity. See Box 8.6 for the standardised measure of market risk.

The standardised approaches were technical but not difficult to apply. They, however, did not distinguish many nuances in market risk incurred by banks. For example, applying an 8 per cent measure as general market risk for equity and derivatives trading completely ignored conditions such as whether the securities and derivatives traded in liquid markets, the quantities held by the bank, and so on; all factors that could play a part in determining potential market losses. The approaches to foreign exchange and

---

Box 8.6 At a glance the standardised measure of market risk

Interest rate risk, that is, the sum of specific debt security risk plus general market risk for that debt security (depending on yield and maturity)

+

Trading book risk, that is, the sum of 4 or 8 per cent specific portfolio risk plus 8 per cent general market risk

+

Foreign exchange risk, that is, 8 per cent of the net long or short position of every foreign currency holding plus net position in gold

+

Commodities risk, that is, 15 per cent of the net long or short position of each commodity plus 3 per cent of all gross positions.

The total measurement of market risk would be risk-weighted at 12.5 per cent. This risk-weighted measure had to be added to risk-weighted assets, for the risk–asset ratio to be applied.

commodities risk assumed that all currencies and commodities were equal and such assumption would not bear out in real markets. Hence, the Market Risk Amendment introduced for the first time the possibility of banks using internal models for measuring their market risk in a more sensitive manner.

8.3.3 Internal models approach to measuring market risk

Banks could disapply one or more of the standardised approaches to measuring market risk discussed above if they were approved by regulators to use internal models to measure interest rate, trading book (equities, derivatives, and options), foreign exchange, and commodities risk. To be eligible to disapply the standardised approaches, banks had to satisfy regulators of qualitative and quantitative robustness in their internal models.

8.3.3.1 Qualitative criteria

The qualitative criteria that banks had to meet related to the quality of their internal risk management systems, for example, by credible and regular stress testing.[69]

Banks had to show that they had independent departments of risk management to determine policies of risk measurement and management, and such departments regularly evaluated the banks' adherence to risk management policies and received daily reports. Such departments would be directly accountable to senior management. The risk management department had to be staffed with persons of adequate skills and training, and the Board of Directors needed to have ultimate oversight of risk management, reviewing daily reports by risk management at a sufficiently senior and knowledgeable level.

Banks also had to show that their risk management was integrated into business operations across all business lines, and there was an integral process for planning, monitoring, and controlling the bank's market risk profile. Banks also needed to have an across-the-board integral policy of compelling compliance with risk management policies and limits at all levels.

Further, banks needed to carry out regular stress testing and back-testing of their risk management systems. They had to put their systems through hypothetical threatening scenarios in order to ascertain if their models were sufficiently robust. They had to regularly review their stress testing and back-testing systems and methodologies, and take prompt action to address any vulnerabilities revealed in such tests. In this regard, regulators paid attention to banks' proven track record of reliability or accuracy in measuring market risks, before granting approval for the use of internal models.

Finally, banks were required to independently review their risk management and stress testing systems, preferably by external audit, such review carried out on a yearly basis.

---

[69] This means putting banks' internal models through hypothetical scenarios of near-failure to see if they remain viable and robust. Stress-testing is discussed extensively in Chapter 9.

8.3.3.2 Quantitative criteria

Banks also had to satisfy regulators that their internal models were credible on the basis of the use of risk factors that were meaningful and sufficient in capturing the risks related to measuring interest rate, foreign exchange, trading book and commodities risks.

The Basel Committee spelt out certain well-established risk factors sensitive to movements in interest rate, foreign exchange, commodities, and equities (and derivatives and options), as guidelines for regulators to look for in evaluating banks' internal models submitted for approval. For example, risk factors relating to individual foreign currencies such as the country's political risk had to be specified in internal models for measuring foreign exchange risk.

However, it is now with the benefit of hindsight that empirical research reveals not many regulators were actually well-versed in risk management technicalities or equipped to evaluate banks' internal models critically.[70] The lack of critical monitoring by regulators was a crucial missing link in the relatively unchecked but gradual augmentation of banks' discretion in rolling out internal models for risk measurement, culminating in the Basel II Capital Accord as will be explored. Regulators would however take another decade or so until after the global financial crisis of 2007–9 to come to grips with monitoring and controlling banks' discretionary risk management.

8.3.3.3 Value-at-Risk methodology

Where banks were permitted to use their internal models for measuring market risk, they employed a value-at-risk methodology. *Value-at-Risk* (VaR), a statistical technique, was used to compute the maximum amount of loss a bank could incur in its portfolio over certain periods like daily or weekly. This 'maximum' amount of loss would be worked out by applying mathematical assumptions to sets of historical data for similar transactions in the market.

The Market Risk Amendment prescribed that the VaR methodology should only include historical market or price information over the previous year, and should be based on a 10-day holding period of the relevant trading instrument concerned (whether equity or debt securities, currency, or commodities) including a range of fluctuations in prices at 'shock' level over 10 days. The methodology was used to estimate daily maximum loss over a narrow band of historical price information and volatility. This approach is perhaps now regarded as overly optimistic, given the benefit of hindsight after the 2007–9 global financial crisis.

By using the VaR methodology, banks worked out a measure of maximum market loss over a regular period, and this amount was then risk-weighted at 12.5 per cent, in order to derive the risk-weighted market risk measure to be added to risk-weighted assets in order to determine adequate capital levels according to the risk–asset ratio.

---

[70] For example, see André Lucas, 'Evaluating the Basle Guidelines for Backtesting Banks' Internal Risk Management Models' (2001) 33 *Journal of Money, Credit and Banking* 826.

8.3.4 **Constituents of capital for market risk**

As discussed earlier in section 8.2, tier one and two capital were required to support the risk–asset ratio. The Basel Committee was of the view that market risk could be supported by even slightly lower quality capital and introduced tier three capital into the mix.

Tier three capital referred to short-term subordinated debt instruments that could be used fully to absorb losses by the bank. Short-term subordinated debt would have very low priority in insolvency and could be written off to absorb bank losses in the event of insolvency. However, as distinguished from subordinated debt that qualified for tier two capital, short-term subordinated debt was poorer in quality as capital as they would mature slightly over 2 years and 'extinguish' sooner. In order to qualify as tier three capital, these debt instruments had at least the following characteristics:

(i)   be unsecured, subordinated and fully paid up;

(ii) had an original maturity of at least two years;

(iii) not be repayable before the agreed repayment date unless the supervisory authority agrees; and

(iv) be subjected to a lock-in clause which stipulated that neither interest nor principal may be paid (even at maturity) if such payment meant that the bank could be in breach of its minimum capital requirement.

The poorer quality of tier three capital also meant that more of it would be needed to 'count towards' meeting the bank's capital adequacy requirements. Tier three capital counted for 2.5 times less than tier one or two capital instruments, and there was a limit to how much of it could be used. The limit was that the sum total of tier two and three capital used to support market risk could not exceed 4 per cent of the risk–asset ratio of 8 per cent.

In sum, the Market Risk Amendment 1996 allowed the Basel Committee to explore into non-credit activities and non-standardised approaches to risk-weighting developed by banks. It signalled the beginning of an approach to adopt a more 'permissive approach' to the capital quality held by banks. This was not surprising as the 1990s represented an era of bank conglomeration and growth as discussed in Chapter 1, and the Committee saw some of its rather crude and one-size-fits-all capital adequacy standards as being unnecessarily obstructive for bank activities. Co-opting banks to design more precise and sophisticated risk measurement systems and tools became a trend that culminated in the Basel II Capital Accord in the 2000s. Banks started to have greater discretion in risk measurement and ultimately 'gamed' the rules by systematically under-estimating their risks, hence under-provisioning for capital adequacy. This had far-reaching consequences culminating in the global financial crisis of 2007–9.

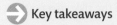 **Key takeaways**

- The 1996 Market Risk Amendment was introduced to require banks to provide adequate capital against 'market risk'.

- Market risk refers to interest rate risk, foreign exchange risk, trading risks in securities, derivatives and options, and commodities trading risk.

- Standardised Approaches were used to measure each component of market risk but these approaches, although not difficult to apply, were rather crude in character and did not reflect the nuances of risk really incurred by banks.

- Banks were also allowed to use internal models to measure market risk if certain qualitative and quantitative criteria were met, in place of the standardised approaches. Regulatory approval was needed to use internal models and regulators needed to be able to competently evaluate banks' internal models in a qualitative and quantitative manner. Regulators often fell short of making precise and competent and assessment.

- Banks were allowed to use short-term subordinated debt capital as 'tier three' capital to make provision for market risk.

Key bibliography

Reports

Basel Committee, *Amendment to the Capital Accord to Incorporate Market Risks* (1996) http://www.bis.org/publ/bcbs24.pdf?noframes=1

Articles

Posner, EA, 'How Do Bank Regulators Determine Capital Adequacy Requirements?' (2014) at http://papers.ssrn.com/sol3/papers.cfm?abstract-id=2493968

8.4 Flexible and negotiated capital adequacy regime (Basel II Capital Accord)

The Market Risk Amendment 1996 was the pre-cursor to new thinking at the Basel Committee in relation to international capital adequacy standards. The Committee was keen to develop an international framework for capital adequacy, and not just a set of easy-to-use standards that increasingly looked simplistic and unable to factor in precise bank risk management techniques. The Committee also believed that a new framework would encourage banks to develop more sophisticated and robust internal risk management models, and this would ultimately be in the interests of bank safety and stability. The 1996 Amendment paved the way for the development of a 'flexible and negotiated' capital adequacy regime in the 2000s in the Basel II Capital Accord (Basel II).[71] Basel II

---

[71] Basel Committee on Banking Supervision, *International Convergence of Capital Measurement and Capital Standards: A Revised Framework – Comprehensive Version* (June 2006) at http://www.bis.org/publ/bcbs128.htm.

was envisaged to provide for more sophisticated standardised approaches that replaced the Basel I Accord and also encouraged banks to develop appropriate internal models. It retained the same risk–asset ratio of 8 per cent and the same requirements for constituents of capital.

We regard Basel II as culminating in a 'flexible and negotiated' framework for capital adequacy, as Basel II moved away from intensely standardised approaches and started to offer menus of options, even where standardised approaches were still being recommended. Further, the option for banks to use internal models showed regulators' willingness to be flexible on how capital adequacy was attained. Flexible regulatory approaches needed to be underpinned by national bank regulators' engagement with their regulated industry, in order to assess their needs and risk profiles accurately and carry out supervisory dialogue and guidance. Hence, such engagement entailed much more 'negotiation' between the industry and regulators, ultimately influencing the regulatory standards as well as supervisory styles.

8.4.1 **The three pillars of Basel II**

Basel II comprised three pillars. The first pillar (*Pillar 1*) provided the capital adequacy framework for banks, which the Committee regarded as *minimum* capital requirements. The second pillar (*Pillar 2*) referred to bank regulators' supervisory role and review of banks' compliance with the capital adequacy framework. The third pillar (*Pillar 3*) referred to market discipline, which imposed mandatory disclosure on banks to their investors in the securities markets, in order to allow investors to assess key pieces of information on the capital, risk exposures, risk assessment processes, and hence the capital adequacy of the bank. As Basel II allowed internal models to be used in risk measurement, Pillars 2 and 3 were intended to ensure that banks' internal models would be subject to appropriate transparency to regulators and investors and scrutinised by them.

We turn to **Pillar 1**, the capital adequacy framework. In this framework, the Committee addressed a wider scope of risk that banks had to make capital provision for– credit risk, market risk and a new category of risk known as operational risk.

8.4.1.1 **Pillar 1: credit risk**

Capital provision for credit risk remained a key part of Basel II as bank lending continued to be a mainstay of the banking business model. However, Basel II moved away from the standardised and one-size-fits-all approach in Basel I, and introduced three alternative frameworks for banks to determine the risk-weighting of its assets.

Standardised approach

First, a standardised approach offered a minimum set of harmonising measures. This approach was modernised so that assets became more differentiated in their risk profiles instead of having to fit within one of five categories as before. The risk-weights of bank assets would be determined according to a choice of standardised frameworks. Three types of frameworks were offered- one based on the credit ratings of securities issued by external credit rating agencies, the second based on the risk scores issued by export credit agencies and the third based on risk-weightings set by the Committee. In practice, there was an overwhelming amount of reliance on credit ratings of securities issued by external credit rating agencies.

The risk-weight for securities issued by sovereigns would now depend on the external credit ratings issued for the sovereign. For example, if S&P's rated a particular sovereign's debt as between AA- and AAA, then a 0 per cent risk-weight was applied to such sovereign debt (see Table 8.3).

This approach of risk-weighting sovereign debt avoided the assumptions made about the creditworthiness of OECD countries in the Basel I Accord, and would allow risk-weights to be adjusted if the sovereign's credit rating changed. Further risk-weights in excess of 100 per cent were provided as reflective of possible losses for the lender in excess of the capital amounts lent, such as in episodes of sovereign default, like the Argentine default in 2001 (and many times thereafter). If the alternative risk-weighting system based on export credit agencies' risk scores were used, a 0 per cent risk-weight would be attached to countries with a score of 0-1, and the highest scoring (most risky) sovereigns attracted a 150 per cent risk-weight. The alternative approaches allowed flexibility in adoption by national regulators.

Risk-weighting based on external credit ratings was adopted extensively for securities issued by financial institutions and private sector corporations. Securities issued by financial institutions would be risk-weighted in close relation to the risk-weight applied to the relevant sovereign. For corporate securities, Basel II moved away from assuming that they were equally risky (as risk-weighted at 100 per cent for all under the Basel I Accord), and distinguished their creditworthiness according to their external credit ratings. Well-rated corporate debt such as at AAA to AA- by Standard & Poor's would enjoy a risk-weighting of 20 per cent, while the worst-rated corporate debt below BB- would be risk-weighted at 150 per cent. Hence, well-rated corporations could find easier access to bank financing as compared to the regime under the Basel I Accord (see Table 8.4).

The standardised approaches also captured risk-weightings in excess of 100 per cent to reflect commercial realities. For example, past due loans for more than 90 days were risk-weighted at 150 per cent, as well as riskier assets such as venture capital or private

Table 8.3 Risk-weighting of sovereign debt based on external credit ratings, derived from the Basel II Capital Accord, http://www.bis.org/publ/bcbs128b.pdf

Credit Rating (e.g. S & P's)	AA- to AAA	A+ to A-	BBB+ to BBB-	B+ to B-	Below B-	Unrated
Risk-weight	0%	20%	50%	100%	150%	100%

Table 8.4 Risk-weighting of corporate debt based on external credit ratings, derived from the Basel II Capital Accord, http://www.bis.org/publ/bcbs128b.pdf

Credit Rating (by Standard & Poor's)	AAA to AA-	A+ to A-	BBB+ to BB-	Below BB-	Unrated
Risk-weight	20%	50%	100%	150%	100%

equity investments. Securitised assets rated between BB+ and BB- were risk-weighted at 350 per cent. Securitised assets involved the packaging or bundling of usually loan assets into securities based on their underlying income streams, to be sold to investors in the market such as institutional investors.[72] Banks also traded and held securitised assets between themselves. However, the introduction of punitive risk-weights, although they could have captured more accurately certain risk profiles of highly risky assets, also shaped banks' incentives to 'game the system'. Banks could structure highly complex securitisation transactions with credit rating agencies' help so as to avoid the punitive risk weights prescribed. This has unfortunately resulted in a systemic failure on the part of credit rating agencies to rate many securitised assets accurately, resulting in their implosion in the global financial crisis of 2007–9.[73]

Although standardised risk-weightings became modernised and less crude, there remained areas of standardisation that proved to be based on inadequate assumptions. For example, Basel II risk-weighted all residential mortgages at 35 per cent. This was due to the assumption that the rates of default for home-owners had been low as they tended to preserve the safety of their homes. However, in the global financial crisis of 2007–9, this assumption was found to be flawed as different types of residential mortgagors adopted different forms of financial management behaviour, with sub-prime mortgage borrowers[74] more likely to default than prime borrowers.

The standardised approach continued in the tradition of the Basel I Accord in recognising risk mitigation techniques applied by banks in order to reduce banks' credit exposures. The risk mitigation techniques recognised by Basel II included the value of collateral (which were themselves risk-weighted by reference to their credit ratings), guarantees, netting and credit derivatives. However, Basel II recommended that a 'haircut' be applied to credit risk mitigation techniques, that is, a discount from face value be applied so that banks would treat the mitigation techniques as worth less than face

---

[72] Such as pension and mutual funds and other collective investment management vehicles.

[73] Aldo Caliari, 'Assessing Global Regulatory Impacts of The U.S. Subprime Mortgage Meltdown: International Banking Supervision and The Regulation of Credit Rating Agencies' (2010) 19 *Transnat'l L. & Contemp. Probs.* 145; Harry McVea, 'Credit Rating Agencies, The Subprime Mortgage Debacle and Global Governance: The EU Strikes Back' (2010) 59 *ICLQ* 701.

[74] Mortgage borrowers who have a less reliable track record of regular income, or assets or debt servicing in general.

value. This was a prudent approach in case the risk mitigation did not fully materialise to reduce losses. Basel II did not provide prescriptive levels of haircuts to be applied to the risk mitigation techniques and encouraged national bank regulators to develop their own frameworks.

Compared to the Basel I Accord, the standardised approach in Basel II seemed more sensitive to peculiar credit features of different credit assets, and utilised well-accepted industry standards such as external credit ratings. Basel II seemed less simplistic and one-size-fits-all than before. However, the Committee did not envisage the standardised approach to be the gold standard, as this was a ready-made framework for banks that had yet to develop more risk-sensitive and sophisticated risk assessment and management models. The Committee envisaged that banks would develop and use their own internal models that would be more risk-sensitive, subject to regulatory approval. Two frameworks for internal models were offered: the Foundation Internal Ratings-Based Approach and the Advanced Internal Ratings-Based Approach.

Internal ratings-based approach

Internal ratings-based (IRB) approaches referred to banks' internal models for assessing the riskiness of their exposures. Internal models were regarded as superior to the standardised approach discussed above as they catered to a wider range of exposures that could be uncommon amongst banks, such as project finance, object finance (aircraft or ship finance), and so on. Further, internal models could incorporate proprietary information that banks held about their borrowers, and entail a more precise assessment of their credit risk.

Banks required supervisory approval from their national regulator to use an IRB approach, which could be the Foundation or the Advanced approach. Depending on how sophisticated banks' internal models were, banks could be approved to use the Foundation IRB approach or the Advanced IRB approach.

If approved, a bank could rely on their own internal estimates of risk components in determining the credit risk of the borrower. The risk components of every credit exposure comprise of: the probability of default (PD), loss given default (LGD), the exposure at default (EAD), and effective maturity (M) (see Box 8.7).

Box 8.7

Under the internal ratings-based approaches, the credit risk of a bank's exposure is measured as follows:

total loss = expected loss + unexpected loss

expected loss = PD X LGD X EAD (including adjustment for M)

Unexpected loss is calculated using a prescribed mathematical formula including PD, LGD, EAD, and M.

The total loss figure indicates the credit risk of the exposure and provides its risk-weight.

Where banks were approved to use the Foundation IRB approach, they would supply their own estimate of the PD measure, while the other risk components were determined as supervisory values by their national regulator.

Where banks were permitted to use the Advanced IRB approach, such banks would have developed convincing systems to generate measures for PD, LGD, EAD, and M. Banks using this approach would supply all of the risk component estimates for credit risk. Only banks that had demonstrated a consistent track record of capturing and using borrower information and default rates, and had a consistent internal evaluation system for credit risk would be permitted to use the Advanced IRB approach. Further, national regulators would need to be satisfied that there was consistent senior management knowledge and oversight of such internal systems and models.

8.4.1.2 Pillar 1: market risk

The Market Risk Amendment 1996 was consolidated into Basel II, with minor tweaks. This allowed Basel II to be a comprehensive framework in one document dealing with banks' key risks: credit and market risks. The introduction of operational risk will be discussed shortly.

Minor adjustment to market risk amendment

The most significant tweak made by Basel II to the Market Risk Amendment 1996 was the incorporation of external credit ratings to determine the market risk-weighting of different types of securities. In the Market Risk Amendment, external credit ratings had already been used to distinguish the riskiness of corporate securities in the trading book. However sovereign securities in the trading book were still being distinguished on the basis of cruder classifications such as OECD membership. Hence, the adoption of external credit ratings as the guide to measuring the risk of all trading book securities was seen as a step towards consistency, and towards an increasingly well-accepted industry standard. See Table 8.5.

The risk assessment measures for interest rate, foreign exchange and commodities risk remained the same as discussed in Section C.

8.4.1.3 Pillar 1: operational risk

The Basel Committee introduced a new category of risk that banks had to make capital provision for, that is, operational risk. Operational risk is defined as the risk of loss resulting from inadequate or failed internal processes, people and systems, or from external events. This definition includes many sources of risk that can cause loss to banks such as litigation expenses, losses caused by the failure of IT systems, or by rogue individuals. For example, rogue traders such as Jerome Kerviel[75] or Kweku Adeboli[76] made huge

---

[75] Previously of Société Générale, see 'Société Générale uncovers £3.7bn fraud by rogue trader', *The Guardian* (24 January 2008) at https://www.theguardian.com/business/2008/jan/24/creditcrunch.banking.

[76] Previously of UBS, see 'Kweku Adoboli: a rogue trader's tale', *Financial Times* (22 October 2015) at http://www.ft.com/cms/s/2/0fa0b42a-783a-11e5-a95a-27d368e1ddf7.html.

Table 8.5 (Amended) market-risk profile for different types of securities in the trading book under Basel II

Government	0%
AAA to AA	0.25% (residual term to final maturity 6 months or less)
A+ to BBB	1.00% (residual term to final maturity greater than 6 and up
BB+ to B	to and including 24 months)
Below B	1.60% (residual term to final maturity exceeding 24 months)
Unrated	8%
	12%
Qualifying corporate borrowing with 6 months' or less maturity	0.25%
Above, with 6-24 months' maturity	1%
Above, with more than 24 months' maturity	1.6%
Other borrowing	8%
BB+ to BB-	12%
Below BB-	8%
Unrated	

and unchecked losses that were passed onto their banks, and such 'personnel' risk could be regarded as part of operational risk faced by banks. Other areas of operational risk would be litigation expenses and regulatory fines, some of which could be very large.[77] Operational risk would include legal risk, but not strategic and reputational risk, as the latter relate to business decisions which generate credit or market risk that would be provisioned for as discussed earlier.

Basel II introduced three approaches to measuring operational risk: the Basic Indicator Approach, Standardised Approach, and Advanced Measurement Approach.

[77] For example, the massive fine of levied by the US SEC upon BNP Paribas for breach of US economic sanctions against Sudan, Iran and Cuba, see 'BNP Paribas to pay $9 billion to settle sanctions violations' (1 July 2014) at http://www.bbc.co.uk/news/business-28099694; the UK FCA's massive fines levied against banks for manipulating the benchmark 'London Interbank Offered Rate' or 'LIBOR' – UBS fined in £940 million, RBS fined in £390 million and Barclays fined in £250 million, see 'Libor-rigging fines: a timeline', *The Guardian* (23 April 2015) at https://www.theguardian.com/business/2015/apr/23/libor-rigging-fines-a-timeline; the UK FCA's fine of £72 million levied upon Barclays for failure to comply with anti-money laundering laws, see 'FCA fines Barclays £72 million for poor handling of financial crime risks' (26 November 2015) at https://www.fca.org.uk/news/fca-fines-barclays-72-million-for-poor-handling-of-financial-crime-risks; and massive fines against banks for mis-selling of financial products such as payment protection insurance, see, for example, the £117 million against Lloyds, 'Lloyds hit by record £117 million fine over PPI handling', *BBC news* (5 June 2015) at http://www.bbc.co.uk/news/business-33018200, and Eilis Ferran, 'Regulatory Lessons from the Payment Protection Insurance Mis-selling Scandal in the UK' (2012) 13 *European Business Organization Law Review* 247–70.

The first two were standardised and prescriptive approaches to measuring operational risk based on banks' gross revenue, the final would measure operational risk based on banks' internal models.

Basic Indicator Approach

The Basic Indicator Approach estimated that a certain percentage of a bank's income would reflect its 'operational loss'. Such an estimate was not based on scientific correlations but was rather a ballpark figure set by the Committee based on reasonableness and perhaps anecdotal observations. This estimate was set at ***15 per cent of the average gross revenue of the bank over the previous three years***. In other words, the above figure represented the 'risk-weighted' operational loss that a bank could suffer.

The 'risk-weighted' operational loss figure would then be added to the risk-weighted assets and risk-weighted market-risk measurements (risk-weighted at 12.5 per cent) in order to work out the total risk-weighted assets of the bank. The 8 per cent risk–asset ratio would be applied to determine the level of capital needed to sustain the banks' credit and market activities as well as their operations. See Box 8.8 for the mathematical representation.

Standardised Approach

The Basic Indicator approach was suitable for banks with few and simple lines of business. Where banks had more lines of business, their risk exposures and income streams from each line could be different. Hence, the Standardised Approach provided a slightly refined approach for such banks to apply instead of the single 15 per cent risk measure of gross revenue.

The Standardised Approach differentiated the business lines of banks into up to eight standard categories. These were: corporate finance, trading & sales, retail banking, commercial banking, payment & settlement, agency services, asset management, and

---

Box 8.8

Recall that under the Basel I Accord:
Risk–asset ratio calculation:

$$\frac{\text{risk–asset ratio (8\%) = capital}}{\text{risk-weighted assets}}$$

Post-Market Risk Amendment 1996:
Risk–asset ratio calculation:

$$\frac{\text{risk–asset ratio (8\%) = capital}}{\text{risk-weighted assets + risk-weighted market risk measurement}}$$

Basel II:
Risk–asset ratio calculation:

$$\frac{\text{risk–asset ratio (8\%) = capital}}{\text{risk-weighted assets + risk-weighted market risk + operational risk measurements}}$$

retail brokerage. A standardised risk-weight of 12, 15, or 18 per cent would be applied according to the average gross revenue from that business line over the previous three years, in order to derive an estimated operational loss figure. See Table 8.6.

Advanced Measurement Approach (AMA)

This approach allowed banks to use internal models in order to work out their operational risk measurement. Again, banks would need to satisfy their national regulator that they met certain qualitative and quantitative criteria as discussed below in order to apply the AMA. Banks using the AMA would not have to apply the Basic Indicator or Standardised approaches discussed above, and would derive their operational loss figure purely using their internal models. Only the most sophisticated banks would have been approved to use the AMA.

Qualitative criteria

At a minimum, banks needed to show that:

(a) its Board of Directors and senior management were actively involved in the oversight of the operational risk management framework;

(b) it had an operational risk management system that was conceptually sound and implemented with integrity; and

(c) it had sufficient resources in the use of the approach in the major business lines as well as the control and audit areas.

With regard to the bank's internal risk management system, it had to be designed and implemented by an independent risk management function with responsibility for overseeing and reviewing regularly. Such a function had to be integrated into day-to-day operations in all business lines and received regular reports on loss experiences. The function's procedures and policies had to be well-documented and cascaded, and

Table 8.6

Business line	Risk-weight
Corporate finance	18%
Trading and sales	18%
Retail banking	12%
Commercial banking	15%
Retail brokerage	12%
Payment and settlement	18%
Asset management	12%
Agency services	15%

had capacity to capture all data flows and relevant information which needed to be recorded. The internal risk management system also had to be subject to internal and external audit and validation.

Quantitative criteria

Banks using the AMA had to show their regulators that they had put in place reliable and sophisticated systems of internal data collection, at a granular level for operational risk factors and loss experiences. The internal data had to be comprehensive, containing accurate information on details of loss experiences and gross amounts. The internal models had to incorporate sound and reliable risk criteria, although regulators need not be too prescriptive. The internal models used to generate risk measurements should also be based on at least 5 years' worth of such data.

Further, banks had to show that they use relevant external data especially when there would be reason to believe that the bank could be exposed to infrequent, yet potentially severe, losses. The use of external data included reference to expert opinion on the likelihood of loss events occurring and their severity.

Finally, banks had to adopt a forward-looking approach to determining their operational risk profile based on their business environment and quality of internal control.

The AMA also permitted banks to factor in the use of insurance policies as a key risk mitigation technique, as long as such policies met certain criteria of robustness such as the insurer having a certain claims-paying ability and that terms and conditions in the policy did not affect the prospects of payout.

The AMA, in the same vein as the internal-ratings-based approaches for credit risk and the internal models for market risk, allowed banks that have developed more sophisticated and 'proven' systems of internal risk management to provide risk-weighting measures instead of using the regulator's standardised and prescribed measures. However, the use of internal models could introduce perverse incentives relating to banks manipulating their own models to suit their own purposes. Hence, Basel II had to be underpinned by a system of monitoring, in Pillars 2 and 3.

8.4.1.4 Pillar 2

Pillar 2 of Basel II supported Pillar 1 by introducing requirements and standards for supervisory review. Whether banks had to adhere to standardised and prescriptive approaches to measuring credit, market, or operational risk, or developed internal models to do so, supervisory engagement with bank compliance was crucial to ensure that such compliance was meaningful and indeed made banks 'safer'.

Basel II set out four principles for national bank regulators in terms of regulatory review and monitoring. These are in Box 8.9.

In terms of Principle 1, national bank regulators had to ensure that bank Boards and senior management were responsible for setting the bank's risk appetite and had effective oversight of risk management policies and implementation in the bank. Bank regulators also needed to be satisfied that banks had comprehensive methodologies

---

Box 8.9

Principles of Pillar 2:

Principle 1: Banks should have a process for assessing their overall capital adequacy in relation to their risk profile and a strategy for maintaining their capital levels.

Principle 2: Supervisors should review and evaluate banks' internal capital adequacy assessments and strategies, as well as their ability to monitor and ensure their compliance with regulatory capital ratios. Supervisors should take appropriate supervisory action if they are not satisfied with the result of this process.

Principle 3: Supervisors should expect banks to operate above the minimum regulatory capital ratios and should have the ability to require banks to hold capital in excess of the minimum.

Principle 4: Supervisors should seek to intervene at an early stage to prevent capital from falling below the minimum levels required to support the risk characteristics of a particular bank and should require rapid remedial action if capital is not maintained or restored.

---

and processes for the capture of risk information and assessment of risk, in relation to the risks required to be managed in Basel II, that is, credit, market, interest rate, liquidity, operational and other risks, and that there was a robust system to assess capital adequacy levels. Banks also had to put in place monitoring and reporting procedures for risk information, changes, and capital levels, and to ensure that their internal control structures were subject to regular review. Internal control structures (discussed in Chapter 12) would need to be reviewed for their ability to identify risk concentrations, stress test (discussed in Chapter 9) and capture complete and accurate data and information.

As for Principle 2, national bank regulators needed to regularly review the processes by which a bank assessed its capital adequacy. In particular, bank regulators could require regular reporting by senior management, carry out on site or off-site inspections of bank systems and records with respect to the bank's management and compliance with capital adequacy requirements, review external audit reports pertaining to the bank's capital adequacy and hold discussions with senior management.

Principle 3 expected national bank regulators to set national capital adequacy standards above the Basel II minimum in order to encourage prudent behaviour on the part of banks. The imposition of more severe standards could then allow bank regulators more flexibility in setting capital adequacy requirements to respond to changing markets, needs and times.

Principle 4 then required national bank regulators to take a forward-looking and hands-on approach to intervene early if any bank under their supervision risked falling below minimum levels of capital adequacy. Of course, this had been premised upon bank regulators having a regular and comprehensive oversight of each bank's capital positions and risk management profiles as envisaged in Principles 1 and 2.

As will be discussed shortly in section 8.4.1.5, the implementation of Pillars 2 and 3 fell far short of expectations. Many national regulators, including the UK regulator, the

FSA (2000–13, discussed in Chapter 6, section 6.1.3) could not be said to have met the standards of being satisfied as to banks' senior management, internal control and risk management processes and oversight, or adhered to the approach of treating the Basel II standards as a minimum or a forward-looking approach to appraise bank risk-taking levels and prevent them from falling below their capital adequacy levels. Crucially, national regulators were ill-equipped to adequate judge and approve banks' use of internal models and subject these to continuing supervision and review. Inadequate supervision was at least contributory to the era that led to the 2007–9 global financial crisis.

8.4.1.5 Pillar 3

In order to complement Pillar 2, Basel II provided that banks had to make public disclosure of their risk exposures, risk assessment processes and capital adequacy levels so that their investors could also assess banks' capital positions and provide market discipline. Banks were required to disclose quantitative and qualitative information of a material nature, subject to protection from disclosure of proprietary and confidential information. Lists of quantitative and qualitative disclosures were prescribed in Basel II.[78]

It was thought that banks, particularly those that were publicly traded companies, needed to account to their shareholders, and shareholders should have been interested in banks' business and financial performance, as well as how prudently they managed risks and complied with capital adequacy requirements. Again, this trust in markets was somewhat misplaced as investors did not place much emphasis on such disclosures, or were unable to assess their meaningfulness in relation to financial performance. If a bank performed well in a quarter by taking high risks, warning signs from capital adequacy disclosures could be under-estimated as investors would welcome the good financial performance.[79] Pillar 3 overall failed to act as a monitoring mechanism for bank capital adequacy.

8.4.1.6 Implementation in the UK and EU

The UK transposed Basel II into national legislation by virtue of the European Directives that adopted it in 2006. The Capital Requirements Directive for credit institutions repealed former Directives related to Basel I, that is, the Solvency and Own Funds Directives discussed in Section 8.B and introduced Basel II provisions into law.[80] Basel II was so heartily endorsed that the EU not only applied it to banks but also extended the requirements of capital adequacy for other financial institutions such as investment firms.[81]

---

[78] P229, http://www.bis.org/publ/bcbs128c.pdf.

[79] The perverse incentives of shareholders are discussed further in Chapter 12.C.

[80] Directive 2006/48/EC of the European Parliament and of the Council of 14 June 2006 relating to the taking up and pursuit of the business of credit institutions (recast).

[81] Directive 2006/49/EC of the European Parliament and of the Council of 14 June 2006 on the capital adequacy of investment firms and credit institutions (recast).

The EU Directives, however, introduced a few requirements that were more stringent and in addition to Basel II. For example, banks were required to have an initial *own funds* amount of at least €5 million in order to be authorised to operate as banks,[82] or in an appropriate case where a lower amount of own funds was more applicable, at least €1 million of own funds should be required.[83] Further, the EU has since 1992 introduced harmonising legislation on large exposures, which will be discussed in Chapter 9. The Directives also made compliance with capital adequacy requirements a condition for the freedom of establishment or provision of banking and financial services by the banks and financial institutions across EEA member states within the scope of the Directives.[84]

Critical assessment of the 'flexible and negotiated' capital adequacy regime

Did Basel II result in stronger banks and more developed forms of risk management towards enhanced bank safety? With the benefit of hindsight in the light of the 2007–9 global financial crisis, Basel II's approach of co-opting banks to develop internal models for risk management turned out to a hazardous approach. Banks, in a fiercely competitive international landscape, chose to engage in high levels of risk-taking that brought immediate rewards, while developing internal models that would minimise their need to keep capital adequacy levels high. Empirical evidence[85] on the application of internal approaches developed by banks for credit and operational risk under Basel II showed that the internal models encouraged banks to set aside less capital than otherwise would have been the case applying standardised Basel II approaches. Further, as risk management and internal control were not centres of revenue generation for banks, some banks marginalised their risk management functions in order not to interfere with business decisions.[86]

Where banks have used internal models merely to avoid regulatory burdens, it could be argued that Pillars 2 and 3 should have been able to keep such manoeuvres in check. In reality, regulators were operating at a meta-level of supervision, as risk management had become devolved to banks' internal models, and regulators found it hard to make judgments on the technical robustness of banks' internal models. Hence, the use of

---

[82] Article 9, Directive 2006/48/EC of the European Parliament and of the Council of 14 June 2006 relating to the taking up and pursuit of the business of credit institutions (recast).   [83] Ibid, Article 10.

[84] Ibid, Articles 23 and 24.

[85] Paul H Kupiec, 'Financial Stability and Basel II' (September 2006) FDIC Center for Financial Research Working Paper No. 2006-10 http://papers.ssrn.com/sol3/papers.cfm?abstract_id=942297; Michael Jacobs Jnr, 'An Empirical Study of the Returns on Defaulted Debt and the Discount Rate for Loss-Given-Default' (September 2009) http://papers.ssrn.com/sol3/papers.cfm?abstract_id=1425146; Jukka Vauhkonen, 'Bank Safety under Basel II Capital Requirements' (November 2009) Bank of Finland Research Paper No. 29-2009 http://papers.ssrn.com/sol3/papers.cfm?abstract_id=1513239.

[86] Michael McAleer, Juan-Angel Jiménez-Martin, and Teodosio Pérez-Amaral, 'What Happened to Risk Management during the 2008–2009 Financial Crisis?' in Robert W Kolb (ed), *Lessons from the Financial Crisis* (New Jersey: John Wiley 2010). House of Commons and House of Lords, Parliamentary Commission on Banking Standards, *An Accident Waiting to Happen: The Failure of HBOS* (4 April 2013).

internal models by approved banks devolved into a form of self-regulation in banks, and they were effectively left unchecked.[87]

In relation to Pillar 3, it could be argued that market discipline was exercised not to the effect of making banks more prudent in risk management, but more competitive in risk-taking. Investors would scrutinise banks' short-term profitability quarter to quarter as banks reported their financial performance to investors, so banks were under tremendous pressure to generate earnings and profits. Hence, being able to increase risk-taking and growing market share were important to bank strategy and some of this was achieved at the expense of maintaining high capital adequacy levels or prudent risk management.[88] Some commentators[89] opined that bank shareholders had indeed driven excessive risk-taking by banks instead of acting as the checking and moderating influence wrongly assumed in Basel II. For example, the Halifax Bank of Scotland embarked on aggressive market growth in lending, and generated significant bad debts in corporate lending that ultimately led to its £45 billion deficit. At its worst, it relied on a £25 billion liquidity assistance line from the central bank to keep it going until it was bought and merged into Lloyds in September 2008.

Basel II had not been fully implemented internationally before the onset of the 2007–9 global financial crisis. However, in the wake of the crisis, the approach of devolving to banks to develop stringent internal models that could achieve responsible risk management became severely doubted. Nevertheless, the banking business had become complex and not easily susceptible to prescriptive standards of micro-prudential regulation.

In response, the Basel Committee rather quickly introduced the Basel III Capital Accord (Basel III) from 2010 to address certain weaknesses in Basel II but not to completely overhaul it. Basel III also introduced a suite of other micro-prudential regulatory tools besides capital adequacy in order to strengthen the overall micro-prudential regulation of banks. The Basel III project took a number of years of refinement, and ultimately completed in 2017. The rest of this Chapter turns to the capital adequacy revisions introduced in Basel III while Chapter 9 deals with other micro-prudential regulatory tools.

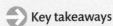 **Key takeaways**

- Basel II was introduced in recognition of banks' changing business and risk profiles.
- Basel II introduced capital adequacy standards for credit, market, and operational risk.

[87] The internal review of the UK FSA in the wake of the Northern Rock failure showed that the FSA department dealing with prudential supervision were not equipped to critically understand banks' models and processes and did not raise relevant queries. See FSA, *The Supervision of Northern Rock: A Lessons Learnt Review* (March 2008) at http://www.fsa.gov.uk/pubs/other/nr_report.pdf.

[88] Such as in HBOS. House of Commons and House of Lords, Parliamentary Commission on Banking Standards, *An Accident Waiting to Happen: The Failure of HBOS* (4 April 2013).

[89] Peter O Mülbert, 'Corporate Governance of Banks after the Financial Crisis – Theory, Evidence, Reforms' (April 2010) ECGI Law Working Paper No. 130/2009 http://ssrn.com/abstract=1448118.

- Standardised approaches to measuring credit, market and operational risks were provided but banks were encouraged to develop more precise and sophisticated internal models to measure such risks.

- Banks could be approved to use internal models, subject to supervisory oversight (known as Pillar 2 of Basel II).

- Banks were also expected to make public disclosure of various risk assessment and capital adequacy information so as to be subject to market discipline (Pillar 3 of Basel II).

- The EU implemented Basel II in the Capital Requirements Directives 2006. The UK, then a member of the EU, transposed the EU legislation into its national law, chiefly via the implementation of subsidiary legislation in the then FSA's Handbook.

Key bibliography

Legislation

Directive 2006/48/EC of the European Parliament and of the Council of 14 June 2006 relating to the taking up and pursuit of the business of credit institutions (recast)

Reports and Recommendations

Basel II Capital Accord 2006, at http://www.bis.org/publ/bcbs128.htm

FSA, *The Supervision of Northern Rock: A Lessons Learnt Review* (March 2008) at http://www.fsa.gov.uk/pubs/other/nr-report.pdf

House of Commons and House of Lords, Parliamentary Commission on Banking Standards, *An Accident Waiting to Happen: The Failure of HBOS* (4 April 2013) at http://www.publications.parliament.uk/pa/jt201213/jtselect/jtpcbs/144/144.pdf

Books

Andenas, M and Chiu, IH-Y, *The Foundations and Future of Financial Regulation* (Oxford: Routledge 2014) ch 12.

Kolb, RW (ed), *Lessons from the Financial Crisis* (New Jersey: John Wiley 2010)

8.5 Post-crisis capital adequacy regulation (The Basel III Accord)

The global financial crisis of 2007–9 brought about a turning point in micro-prudential regulation. The level of regulatory capital established under Basel II proved to be insufficient, particularly for large global banks using internal models which were inadequately checked by national regulators. Banks had gamed the regulatory capital requirements in order to take on excessive risks while appearing to be compliant and safe. For example, banks under-estimated the risk profiles of their assets, such as securitised assets which they pressured credit rating agencies into assigning favourable ratings, so that their risk-weighted assets would look modest, therefore requiring support of only thin levels of capital. The use of internal models further pandered to banks' incentives to under-estimate risks, as documented in empirical research.[90]

Further, it would appear that the baseline 8 per cent risk–asset ratio was also fundamentally inadequate to ensure that a bank was sufficiently capitalised for its risk-taking. Lehman Brothers, the US investment bank that became insolvent in September 2008, had been reporting a healthy risk–asset ratio in excess of the 8 per cent discussed above.[91] National regulators had in effect not been willing to impose in excess of the international minimum of 8 per cent, crucially deviating from Basel Committee's exhortation to treat the 8 per cent risk–asset ratio as a minimum.

Third, it could be argued that the capital adequacy regulatory regime is itself an imperfect tool to control banking sector risks. The regulatory regime narrowly focused on individual bank assets in order to manage individual banks' behaviours in relation to risk-taking. This methodology failed to take into account the aggregate picture of risks in the sector and collective behaviour by banks.

Shortly after the onset of the 2007–9 global financial crisis, the Basel Committee quickly responded to the perceived inadequacies of Basel II by issuing Basel 2.5,[92] which dealt with market risk (explored in section 8.4.1.5) and then introduced the Basel III Accord in phases from 2010.[93]

8.5.1 The corrective approach of Basel III: A bird's eye view

The Basel III Accord bears many features that attempt to correct the perceived weaknesses in Basel II. It addresses the low baseline of the 8 per cent risk–asset ratio as well as the excessive discretion that had devolved to banks allowing them to under-provision for capital adequacy. In the first phases of Basel III in 2010 and 2011, the regulatory tool of 'capital buffers' is introduced to compel banks to meet higher levels of capital adequacy, by adding 'capital buffers' to the baseline 8 per cent risk–asset ratio. We turn to these shortly. Further, we see a return to refining standardised approaches

---

[90] Paul H Kupiec, 'Financial Stability and Basel II' (September 2006) FDIC Center for Financial Research Working Paper No. 2006-10 http://papers.ssrn.com/sol3/papers.cfm?abstract_id=942297; Michael Jacobs Jnr, 'An Empirical Study of the Returns on Defaulted Debt and the Discount Rate for Loss-Given-Default' (September 2009) http://papers.ssrn.com/sol3/papers.cfm?abstract_id=1425146; Jukka Vauhkonen, 'Bank Safety under Basel II Capital Requirements' (November 2009) Bank of Finland Research Paper No. 29-2009.

[91] Some economists argue that capital adequacy ratios have been completely inadequate since their inception, see Anat Admati and Martin Hellwig, *The Bankers' New Clothes: What's Wrong with Banking and What to Do about It* (NJ: Princeton University Press 2014).

[92] Basel Committee of Banking Supervision, *Revisions to the Basel II Market Risk Framework* (Feb 2011) at http://www.bis.org/publ/bcbs193.htm.

[93] Basel Committee on Banking Supervision, *Basel III: A Global Regulatory Framework for More Resilient Banks and Banking Systems* (rev June 2011, Basel: BIS 2010) <http://www.bis.org/publ/bcbs189.pdf. The final completion of Basel III was achieved in December 2017, see *Finalising Post-crisis Reforms* (2017) at https://www.bis.org/bcbs/publ/d424.pdf.

to risk measurement in order to make them more risk-sensitive and robust in light of the lessons learnt in the global financial crisis; and the introduction of standards in controlling how internal models may be used so that their scope for abuse is reduced. It may be queried why the 8 per cent baseline is not simply increased, instead of adopting a patchwork of 'capital buffers' to be added to the risk–asset ratio. The buffers serve precise purposes and allow regulators to adjust them upwards or downwards in order to meet changing regulatory needs. Further, EU policymakers, fearful that European banks remain financially weak, have introduced more buffers in excess of the Basel III Accord to strengthen banks' capital positions.

The Basel III reforms also take on the development of special standards for banks that are regarded as globally systemically important financial institutions (G-SIBs, see discussion section 8.5.5), as they are perceived to pose different types and extents of risks and require different regulatory treatment. Finally, in 2017, the completion of the Basel III reforms sees the introduction of new standardised approaches to measuring risk across credit, market and operational risks, the eclipse of internal models for operational risk measurement, and much tighter control over the use of internal models in credit and market risk. Indeed, banks using internal models cannot deviate from an *output floor* of risk measurement as if they had applied the standardised approaches.

8.5.2 **Introduction of capital buffers**

A key measure under Basel III is to introduce additional regulatory capital requirements on top of the risk–asset ratio. These are called capital buffers. There are two types of capital buffers. One type is 'absolute' in the sense that these are imposed on banks across the board regardless of their risk profile. The **capital conservation buffer** and the **counter-cyclical buffer** introduced by Basel III fall within this category. The **systemic risk buffer** introduced by the EU's Capital Requirements IV Directive 2013[94] (CRD IV Directive) and its UK equivalent, which will be discussed shortly, also falls within this category. These capital buffers are intended to improve a bank's resilience by acting as increased controls on risk-taking behaviour.

Another type of capital buffers would be institution-specific. These are imposed on banks in order to reflect their individual risk profiles. An example would be the **institution-specific counter-cyclical buffer** introduced in the CRD IV Directive 2013. The requirements for **global systemically important banks** (G-SIBs) introduced by the Financial Stability Board (FSB) is another example. Further, the UK regulator may, after supervisory review of individual institutions, impose additional requirements tailored to the bank's risk profile, called the **Pillar 2 buffer**. The buffers are explained in section 8.5.4.

---

[94] Directive 2013/36/EU of the European Parliament and of the Council of 26 June 2013 on access to the activity of credit institutions and the prudential supervision of credit institutions and investment firms, amending Directive 2002/87/EC and repealing Directives 2006/48/EC and 2006/49/EC (CRD IV Directive).

8.5.3 **Capital buffers that apply across the board to the banking sector**

8.5.3.1 Capital conservation buffer

The capital conservation buffer is a regulatory capital requirement that applies across the board to all banks. Banks are required to set aside an extra 2.5 per cent of risk-weighted assets as a mandatory capital conservation buffer, effectively raising the risk–asset ratio from 8 to 10.5 per cent, in order to address criticisms of the 8 per cent being perceived as too low. The capital conservation buffer is phased in between 1 January 2016 and year end 2018 becoming fully effective on 1 January 2019. Its implementation has begun at 0.625 per cent of risk-weighted assets on 1 January 2016 and has increased each subsequent year by an additional 0.625 percentage points, to reach its final level of 2.5 per cent of risk-weighted assets on 1 January 2019. As banks need time to ensure that they have the requisite level of capital to support their activities, a gentle phasing-in of the capital conservation buffer has been provided.

The capital conservation buffer has been implemented in the EU by the CRD IV Directive.[95] The UK has also transposed this requirement into its subsidiary legislation.[96] As this requirement originates from the international standards that the Basel Committee has introduced, it is unlikely to be affected by the UK's EU Referendum vote. This buffer has to be maintained at all times. If a bank fails to meet the capital conservation buffer, it is given an opportunity to submit a plan of remediation to its national regulator within 5 working days. The regulator will approve the plan or require further actions to be taken. Further, during the period of remediation by the bank, the regulator has the power to restrict banks from taking any action that may diminish its capital, such as restricting distributions to shareholders.[97]

8.5.3.2 Counter-cyclical buffer

Next, Basel III provides that where national regulators determine it to be necessary, a counter-cyclical buffer may be imposed on the banking sector in that jurisdiction. The objective of the counter-cyclical buffer is to allow national regulators to compel banks to control risk-taking in times of market exuberance, so that banks can be more prepared and resilient in challenging times.

Banks may be required to provision for up to 2.5 per cent of risk-weighted assets in addition to the risk–asset ratio of 8 per cent and the capital conservation buffer of 2.5 per cent. The counter-cyclical buffer regime is phased-in in parallel with the capital conservation buffer between 1 January 2016 and year end 2018 becoming fully effective on 1 January 2019.

In the EU, this has been implemented in the CRD IV Directive.[98] The Directive envisages that each national regulator is responsible for setting the appropriate level

---

[95] Article 129 CRD IV Directive.
[96] UK Capital Requirements (Capital Buffers and Macro-prudential Measures) Regulations 2014, Regulation 5.
[97] Article 141 CRD IV Directive.   [98] Article 135 CRD IV Directive.

of counter-cyclical buffer. However, the European Systemic Risk Board has the role of making a recommendation that is applicable to all member states. The Directive recommends the buffer to be set between zero and 2.5 per cent, in incremental steps of 0.25 per cent.[99] In relation to the counter-cyclical buffer, commentators sound early warnings that determining an appropriate counter-cyclical buffer is a novel and challenging task. This is because the models for determining the buffer are emerging in nature, and commentators are not certain how well the matrix of broad economic indicators such as gross domestic product (GDP) and bank-specific indicators used in the models will work.[100] Some critics are of the view that contrary to its role, the use of certain indicators in the models for the counter-cyclical buffer will indeed make the buffer pro-cyclical.[101]

The UK has appointed the Financial Policy Committee (discussed in Chapter 6) to be responsible for determining if a counter-cyclical buffer needs to be set and at what level.[102] The Financial Policy Committee has been tasked to make a suitable determination on a quarterly basis. The Committee's approach[103] to setting the counter-cyclical buffer is based on balancing the need to secure a resilient financial sector that can withstand stress and the need to ensure that banks continue to perform their economically useful role of supplying credit to the economy. The Committee will study three core indicators in reaching any decision to impose a counter-cyclical buffer rate, *viz* (i) the likelihood and severity of potential future adverse 'shocks' to the UK economic outlook; (ii) the characteristics of households' and companies' balance sheets that would determine how macroeconomic and financial shocks could translate into defaults and losses; and (iii) the sensitivity of banks' balance sheets to losses on their UK exposures, meaning how severely affected banks would be in relation to defaults and losses suffered in relation to UK borrowers. In June 2017, the Committee determined that a counter-cyclical buffer rate of 0.5 per cent was appropriate as levels of household borrowing seemed too high, and has raised this to 1 per cent. In sum banks in the UK need to maintain the baseline 8 per cent risk–asset ratio, the 2.5 per cent capital conservation buffer fully implemented by 1 Jan 2019 and the 1 per cent counter-cyclical buffer rate currently in application, raising regulatory capitals to 11.5 per cent.

---

[99] Article 136 CRD IV Directive.

[100] Mathias Drehmann, Claudio EV Borio, Leonardo Gambacorta, Gabriel Jimenez and Carlos Trucharte, 'Countercyclical Capital Buffers: Exploring Options' (BIS Working Paper 2010) at http://papers.ssrn.com/sol3/papers.cfm?abstract_id=1648946.

[101] Rafael Repullo and Jesus Saurina Salas, 'The Countercyclical Capital Buffer of Basel III: A Critical Assessment' (March 2011) at http://www.cepr.org.

[102] UK Capital Requirements (Capital Buffers and Macro-prudential Measures) Regulations 2014, Regulation 4, 10–12.

[103] Bank of England, 'The Financial Policy Committee's Approach to Setting the Countercyclical Capital Buffer' (April 2016) at https://www.bankofengland.co.uk/-/media/boe/files/statement/2016/the-financial-policy-committees-approach-to-setting-the-countercyclical-capital-buffer.pdf?la=en&hash=DE1BDDDA9A8628694A5881D6559DE782AFF3A7B1.

The introduction of the capital conservation and counter-cyclical buffers addresses the perception that the 8 per cent risk–asset ratio is too low.[104] However, critics warn that just as banks could systematically under-estimate risk-weighted assets before the reforms, the additional capital buffers, which are still measured in accordance with risk-weighted assets, will suffer from the same flaw.[105] Hence in tandem with these reforms, the Basel Committee and the European Banking Authority are undertaking reforms to close down discretionary treatment of risk-weighting so that the weaknesses with risk-weighted assets may be mitigated in the future. This discussion is taken up in section 8.5.8 of this chapter.

8.5.3.3 Systemic risk buffer

The EU CRD IV Directive introduces a concept called the 'systemic risk buffer',[106] which allows national regulators to impose an additional buffer on the financial sector or one or more subsets of the sector, in order to address long term non-cyclical and macro-prudential risks. In other words, the Directive permits member states to allow their regulators to introduce an additional forward-looking buffer based on the outlook of general economic conditions. The systemic risk buffer is to be set at least 1 per cent of risk-weighted assets held in the member state and beyond. This requirement is in excess of the recommendations made under Basel III.

It is uncertain what the difference is between the systemic risk and counter-cyclical buffers as they appear to both deal with wider economic conditions, and are intended to encourage prudent risk management in order to improve bank resilience in challenging times. A possible distinct role of the systemic risk buffer is that it applies to certain sections of the banking sector whose risks are amplified in certain economic conditions. For example, the ring-fenced banks in the UK discussed in Chapter 10 are susceptible to a special systemic risk buffer in addition to the other requirements. The ring-fenced banks in the UK are important high street banks that provide extensive services to UK households and corporations and pose more danger of damaging the economy if they should become stricken or fail. The UK Financial Policy Committee[107] recommends that ring-fenced banks with more than £175 billion in assets should be required to meet a systemic risk buffer of up to an extra 3 per cent of risk-weighted assets. However, the systemic risk buffer is set at tiered levels according to banks' asset volumes, with banks having in excess of £755 billion in assets attracting the top systemic risk buffer of 3 per cent. The UK PRA will adhere to the FPC's recommendations unless there are

---

[104] Commentators, however, may still take the view that the improvements introduced by the buffers are insufficient, see Admati and Hellwig, *The Emperor's New Clothes*.

[105] R Ayadi, E Arbak and WP de Groen, 'Implementing Basel III in Europe: Diagnosis and Avenues for Improvement' CEPS Policy Brief No 275 (27 June 2012); Alessio Pacces, 'Consequences of Uncertainty for Regulation: Law and Economics of the Financial Crisis' (2010) 7 *European Company and Financial Law Review* 479.

[106] Article 133 CRD IV Directive.

[107] Bank of England, *The Financial Policy Committee's Framework for the Systemic Risk Buffer* (May 2016) at https://www.bankofengland.co.uk/-/media/boe/files/paper/2016/the-financial-policy-committees-framework-for-the-systemic-risk-buffer.pdf?la=en&hash=B354CE2068CD5B965DA07E15F6F10EFC80668B5F.

exceptional circumstances that warrant deviation from the FPC's recommendations,[108] allowing the PRA to apply a full extent of flexible micro-prudential supervisory oversight over UK banks.

8.5.4 Capital buffers according to banks' risk profiles

8.5.4.1 Institution-specific counter-cyclical buffer

The EU CRD IV Directive 2013 requires that for European banks that have credit exposures in a number of jurisdictions, a further institution-specific counter-cyclical buffer be applied.[109] The UK has implemented this requirement in its national transposition[110] but has the discretion to exempt small and medium sized financial institutions from having to comply with it.

This buffer is arguably intended to ensure that banking conglomerates with cross-border footprints are compelled to consider of the economic conditions of other jurisdictions that may affect their risk profiles.

This buffer is calculated by obtaining a weighted average of the counter-cyclical buffers set in each jurisdiction where the bank has exposures,[111] including both EU and non-EU jurisdictions. However, where non-EU jurisdictions set a counter-cyclical buffer rate in excess of 2.5 per cent, the Directive provides that the excess above such 2.5 per cent be ignored and is treated as capped at 2.5 per cent. By capping the upper counter-cyclical buffer rate at 2.5 per cent, this measure ensures that banks subject to this requirement are not prejudiced from expanding their businesses into non-EU jurisdictions.

8.5.4.2 The PRA's Pillar 2A capital

Basel III's introduction of additional capital requirements is not a new concept. Even before the onset of the global financial crisis, the UK implemented a regime of extra regulatory capital known as Pillar 2 capital.[112] Pillar 2 capital refers to additional regulatory capital requirements that the then-regulator, the Financial Services Authority, could impose on banks following supervisory scrutiny and review of a bank's risk profile. Such requirements could be imposed on banks to provision for risks not specified under the Basel Accords, such as interest rate and pension obligation risks. Pillar 2 capital requirements are not part of the international or European harmonised standards for capital adequacy. They may be regarded as 'gold-plating' in regulatory requirements introduced by the UK to meet its policy goals and interests.

---

[108] PRA, *The PRA's Approach to the Implementation of the Systemic Risk Buffer* (December 2016) at https://www.bankofengland.co.uk/-/media/boe/files/prudential-regulation/statement-of-policy/2016/the-pras-approach-to-the-implementation-of-the-systemic-risk-buffer-sop.pdf?la=en&hash=6954AC9765597EB5598414171D90C25982A144CE.   [109] Article 130 CRD IV Directive.

[110] Regulation 19, The Capital Requirements (Capital Buffers and Macro-prudential Measures) Regulations 2014

[111] Article 140 CRD IV Directive, PRA Rulebook, *Capital Buffers*.

[112] Financial Services Authority, *Strengthening Capital Standards 2* (February 2006) 37ff, at http://www.fsa.gov.uk/pubs/cp/cp06_03.pdf.

The Pillar 2 capital requirement continues to be applicable even after the suite of reforms in Basel III and the EU CRD IV Directive, as national regulators continue to be able to exercise supervisory judgment to strengthen banks' own funds.[113] Pillar 2 capital comprises of two components, that is, Pillar 2A and 2B. Pillar 2A relates to a suite of credit, market, operational and other financial risks that are not taken into account of in the modelling for standardised approaches or internal models. Pillar 2B, used to be known as the Capital Planning Buffer, and now the PRA Buffer, is discussed below, and is a discretionary category of extra regulatory capital. We turn first to Pillar 2A which applies to most banks as determined by supervisory judgment. The PRA clarifies[114] for example that Pillar 2A regulatory capital relates to:

- Shortfalls in the measurement of credit risk with regard to bank assets when the PRA applies an approach to compare measurements made using the standardised approach and those made using internal models.

- Shortfalls in credit risk measurement if banks hold significant levels of assets that are risky, such as sovereign debt, mortgages with a high loan-to-value ratio, commercial real estate, and personal credit cards.

- Shortfalls in credit risk measurement where there is credit concentration risk such as extension of loans to businesses in the same sector or geographical areas.

- Shortfalls in the measurement of market risk due to standardised approaches or internal models not adequately accounting for illiquidity, concentration, or one-way risks.

- Shortfalls in the measurement of counterparty risk in certain markets such as derivatives trading, securities financing transactions, in relation to settlement risk or inadequate collateral.

- Shortfalls in the measurement of operational risk such as those that emanate from conduct risk leading to civil litigation compensation or regulatory fines.

- Shortfalls in measuring interest rate risks across different instruments and durations;

- Shortfalls in measuring pension obligation risks.

- Shortfalls in measuring the risk of how institutions may be affected by others in the financial group that suffer stresses, especially in relation to ring-fenced banks (see Chapter 10).

Where the PRA is of the view that shortfalls in credit, market or operational risk measurement is due to inadequacies in internal models, these are treated as requirements to remedy the relevant model instead of being 'compensated' for by Pillar 2A capital.

---

[113] Article 104, CRD IV Directive. The PRA defends its ability to impose Pillar 2A capital in PRA, *Refining the PRA's Pillar 2A Capital Framework* (October 2017) at https://www.bankofengland.co.uk/prudential-regulation/publication/2017/refining-the-pra-pillar-2a-capital-framework.

[114] PRA, *The PRA's Methodologies for Setting Pillar 2 Capital* (December 2017) at https://www.bankofengland.co.uk/-/media/boe/files/prudential-regulation/statement-of-policy/2017/the-pras-methodologies-for-setting-pillar-2a-capital-december-2017.pdf?la=en&hash=A157541ACACD7EC18CEA8C8695CDD5F30E5D1B53.

In sum, the PRA will determine a suitable level of Pillar 2A capital as a definite figure for each individual bank subject to the PRA's supervisory jurisdiction, on a yearly basis. This means that the Pillar 2A capital requirement imposed on each bank may be different, and is in addition to the 8 per cent risk–asset ratio and all regulatory capital buffers discussed above. The PRA will make a Pillar 2A capital determination for each bank by the 15 December of each year and banks are given until the 1 January of the year following the next calendar year in order to implement the requirements. Changes to the PRA's determination may take place more frequently if warranted by supervisory findings of adverse and changed circumstances in the bank.

8.5.4.3　The PRA's capital planning buffer (PRA buffer)

Before the onset of the global financial crisis, it is mentioned earlier that the UK regulator (then Financial Services Authority) had already introduced Pillar 2 capital. One of the features of the Pillar 2 capital requirements was the capital planning buffer.[115] The capital planning buffer was intended to be forward-looking in nature, providing a conservative brake on banks' risk-taking, in order to prepare for the absorption of losses and/or to cover increasing capital requirements in adverse circumstances that are outside the firm's normal and direct control. The level of this buffer was determined by the regulator after considering certain 'worst case scenarios' for the bank. The bank would then be compelled to ensure that the specific level required by the regulator is met. In the event of stress, the regulator envisaged that the capital planning buffer can be drawn down.

In a way, the capital planning buffer has been performing functions similar to the capital conservation and counter-cyclical buffers before the introduction of the Basel III Accord. However, the capital planning buffer is different in that it can be drawn down, unlike the capital conservation and counter-cyclical buffers which are requirements that need to be strictly maintained. Falling below the capital conservation and counter-cyclical buffers is a breach of regulatory capital that can attract the consequences of recovery and resolution discussed in Chapter 13.

After the global financial crisis, reforms to Pillar 2 capital were made. The Prudential Regulatory Authority introduced Pillars 2A and 2B as different components of Pillar 2 capital in 2012, and the capital planning buffer constituted the Pillar 2B requirement. Pillar 2B served a distinctive purpose of imposing additional regulatory capital for banks if the regulator was of the view that the bank's risk management and internal control were inadequate or deficient, after exercising supervisory judgment based on the bank's reporting, stress test results and the regulator's supervisory information. The PRA continued to impose the Pillar 2B buffer,[116] and regarded it as capable of being drawn down in times of stress but would require banks doing so to submit remediation plans for the eventual recovery of the buffer.

---

[115] Financial Services Authority, *Capital Planning Buffers: Feedback on CP09/30 and Final Rules* (September 2010) at http://www.fca.org.uk/static/pubs/policy/ps10_14.pdf.

[116] The Bank of England, Prudential Regulation Authority, *The PRA's Approach to Banking Supervision* (October 2012) 25, para 124, at http://www.fsa.gov.uk/static/pubs/other/pra-approach-banking.pdf.

However, with the introduction of Basel III and the EU CRD IV Directive require-ments, the Pillar 2B buffer has now come to be regarded as excessive.[117] There is still a point to the Pillar 2B buffer, but it may be argued that the regulatory capital buffers introduced in Basel III and the EU CRD IV Directive would be adequate to shape and control risk-taking at banks. The PRA has therefore renamed the buffer as the 'PRA buffer' and not as part of Pillar 2 capital so that its discretionary nature can be distin-guished from the Pillar 2A capital requirements which are mandatory.[118] The PRA will maintain the PRA buffer as a distinct and separate capital requirement, to be deter-mined after supervisory assessment is applied to each individual bank. However, the PRA can exercise the discretion of not imposing any PRA buffer if the other regulatory buffers are adequate.[119] If any PRA buffer on top of the regulatory buffers is imposed, it should only be for the purposes of addressing risks not already addressed under the regulatory buffers.[120] In this way, the PRA buffer remains alive as a concept and poten-tial regulatory tool but is now seldom imposed.

However, the wisdom of the PRA's determination above may be queried, as the PRA buffer is different from other regulatory capital requirements. It can be drawn down in times of stress, and can be regarded as a form of contingency planning for UK banks in order to help them smooth out difficulties without having to trigger crisis management and resolution thresholds (discussed in Chapter 13).

The change in nature of the PRA buffer is represented in Figure 8.1.

8.5.4.4 Leverage ratio buffer

The PRA[121] has led the way in imposing an additional capital buffer upon a group of banks in order to moderate their risk-taking. UK banks that accept over £50 billion in

Figure 8.1 The Evolution of the PRA Buffer

[117] Bank of England, *The Pillar 2 Framework Background* (July 2015) at http://www.bankofengland.co.uk/pra/Documents/pillar2framework.pdf.

[118] PRA, *The PRA's Methodologies for Setting Pillar 2 Capital* (Dec 2017) at https://www.bankofengland.co.uk/-/media/boe/files/prudential-regulation/statement-of-policy/2017/the-pras-methodologies-for-set-ting-pillar-2a-capital-december-2017.pdf?la=en&hash=A157541ACACD7EC18CEA8C8695CDD5F30E5D1B53.

[119] PRA, *The PRA's Methodologies for Setting Pillar 2 Capital* (July 2015) Section II, at http://www.bankofeng-land.co.uk/pra/Documents/publications/sop/2015/p2methodologies.pdf; *Assessing Capital Adequacy under Pillar 2* (July 2015) at http://www.bankofengland.co.uk/pra/Documents/publications/ps/2015/ps1715.pdf.

[120] Ibid.

[121] PRA, *Supervisory Statement: The UK Leverage Ratio Framework* (December 2015) at http://www.bankofengland.co.uk/pra/Pages/publications/ss/2015/ss4515.aspx.

deposits from individuals and households are to maintain a counter-cyclical leverage ratio buffer (CLRB).

The CLRB is different from other capital buffers as its calculation is not based on risk-weighted assets but on 'total exposure', which is the bank's gross lending. 'Total exposure' is defined and explained in Chapter 9, section 9.4. The *leverage ratio buffer* is intended to act as a complementary tool alongside capital adequacy buffers in order to exert restraining forces against excessive lending by banks that have such important retail footprint in the UK.

The CLRB is explained and worked out in Chapter 9, section 4 in conjunction with the discussion of the leverage ratio as a regulatory tool.

Box 8.10 summaries the list of extra capital adequacy requirements that banks have to meet in addition to the 8 per cent risk–asset ratio under the Basel Accords. These requirements are cumulative except for the PRA buffer.

8.5.5 Additional regulatory capital requirements for systemically important banks

The global financial crisis saw the crippling of a number of large global banks (see overview in Chapter 1). These banks were more susceptible to magnified impact due to their exposures in many inter-related markets.[122] Policymakers thus perceived it to be necessary to impose more regulatory capital measures on large global banks in order to moderate their risk-taking. These reforms took place in two stages. Shortly after the onset of the crisis, the Basel Committee and FSB took leadership to identify 'systemically important global banks' that is, global banks whose difficulties or failure would likely cause

---

Box 8.10

The additional capital adequacy requirements (on top of the risk–asset ratio of 8 per cent) for ALL banks are at a glance:

1. Capital conservation buffer of 2.5 per cent (Basel III).

2. Counter-cyclical buffer of up to 2.5 per cent (Basel III, EU, UK – applying 1 per cent).

3. Institution-specific counter-cyclical buffer (EU).

4. Systemic risk buffer of at least 1 per cent (EU, UK applying 0.5–3 per cent on ring-fenced banks holding different levels of assets).

5. National measures, for example, UK's Pillar 2A Capital.

The above requirements are cumulative except the PRA buffer, which has become discretionary. Banks accepting over £50 billion deposits from individuals and households need to meet a counter-cyclical leverage ratio buffer as explained in Chapter 9, section 9.4.

---

[122] The nature of these institutions is further discussed in Chapter 10.

reverberating impact across the financial sectors and economies of many countries. These were to be subject to additional regulatory capital requirements on top of those discussed above. However, it was increasingly recognised that it may not be possible to prevent failure, even with the most stringently-designed capital requirements regimes. Hence, there is a need to ensure that if a systemically important bank fails, it can do so in an orderly manner with least disruption to other parts of the financial sector and the economies of countries affected by the bank concerned. The first stage of reforms has produced an additional capital buffer requirement, which is discussed below. The second stage of reforms deal with introducing a novel form of regulatory capital that provisions for crisis management and resolution. These are discussed in Chapter 9, section 9.5.4 and Chapter 13.

The Basel Committee and FSB have developed a methodology for identifying those banks that have such an important global footprint that their potential failure may cause severe global economic disruption, or the materialisation of 'systemic risk'. This methodology will be discussed in Chapter 9, section 9.5. Based on this methodology, a number of 'global systemically important banks' or G-SIBs are identified by the FSB.[123] This methodology has also been adapted to assist national regulators in identifying other banks that have important national footprint (and may cause severe national disruption in the event of failure) but may not necessarily cause global economic disruption if they fail. Such *domestic systemically important banks* **(D-SIBs)** are not prescribed by international bodies, but are determined by national regulators applying the methodology of identification for D-SIBs. *Global systemically important banks* (G-SIBs) and D-SIBs may be imposed with additional regulatory capital requirements due to their systemic risk profile.

8.5.5.1 Global systemically important banks (G-SIBs) buffer

The FSB publishes in November every year, starting from November 2013, a list of G-SIBs. The Board uses publicly available and regulatory data to analyse the systemic risk profile of globally active banks. Applying the Basel Committee's indicator approach[124] (see discussion in Chapter 9), the Board will identify G-SIBs that fall into one of five risk 'buckets'. Each risk bucket corresponds to a requirement to hold extra capital. The risk buckets are:

- Bucket 1: G-SIBs that are required to an extra 1 per cent of loss absorbent capital on top of the required regulatory capital.

---

[123] The FSB identifies a list of 30 G-SIBs or so every year in November, and publishes its determination at http://www.fsb.org/wp-content/uploads/2015-update-of-list-of-global-systemically-important-banks-G-SIBs.pdf.

[124] Basel Committee, *Globally Systemically Important Banks: Assessment Methodologies and the Higher Loss Absorbency Requirements* (November 2011) at http://www.bis.org/publ/bcbs207.pdf; Basel Committee, *Globally Systemically Important Banks: Updated Assessment Methodologies and the Higher Loss Absorbency Requirements* (July 2013), at http://www.bis.org/publ/bcbs255.pdf.

- Bucket 2: G-SIBs that are required to hold an extra 1.5 per cent of loss absorbent capital on top of the required regulatory capital.

- Bucket 3: G-SIBs that are required to hold an extra 2 per cent of loss absorbent capital on top of the required regulatory capital.

- Bucket 4: G-SIBs that are required to hold an extra 2.5 per cent of loss absorbent capital on top of the required regulatory capital.

- Bucket 5: G-SIBs that are required to hold an extra 3.5 per cent of loss absorbent capital on top of the required regulatory capital.

The Board has identified about 30 global banks that fall into the different risk buckets. For example, in 2017, JP Morgan, an American bank that has a tremendous global footprint is in Bucket 4, which is just short of the top bucket. In the European continent, Deutsche Bank and HSBC are put in Bucket 3. The UK's Barclays bank falls into Bucket 2 of the Board's classification. Buckets 1 and 2 are the most heavily populated, including significant Chinese, Japanese, European, and American banks. No bank has been identified as a G-SIB falling within Bucket 5, the top bucket, to date. In fact, the Board regards Bucket 5 as a deterrent category for banks.[125] The high level of extra capital needed for Bucket 5 G-SIBs is intended to deter banks from expanding their businesses in such a way as to fall within that profile.

The Board has left it open to develop more buckets that correspond to extra capital requirements exceeding 3.5 per cent if Bucket 5 should be populated in the future.

The EU has implemented the above requirements for G-SIBs in the CRD IV Directive, calling them 'Globally Systemically Important Institution' or the 'GSII' buffer.[126] This is transposed in the UK.[127] The Directive allows national regulators to designate all globally systemically important institutions whether banks or other institutions, in a manner not dissimilar from the risk bucket approach adopted by the FSB. In practice national regulators are likely to adhere to the Board's determination although this is not formally endorsed in the Directive.

Where G-SIBs that are headquartered outside of the UK have extensive operations in the UK, the PRA may designate them as Other Systemically Important Institutions for monitoring purposes but not for extra compliance purposes.[128]

One may argue that the risk buckets are modest and do little to make systemically important banks more resilient and less risky for society as a whole. However, the additional capital adequacy requirement has to be seen in context, with the other capital requirement reforms discussed earlier.

---

[125] Para 47, Basel Committee, *Globally Systemically Important Banks: Updated Assessment Methodologies and the Higher Loss Absorbency Requirements* (July 2013), at http://www.bis.org/publ/bcbs255.pdf.

[126] Article 131(4) CRD IV Directive.

[127] Regulations 19, 21–27 UK Capital Requirements (Capital Buffers and Macro-prudential Measures) Regulations 2014.

[128] Regulations 29–34, UK Capital Requirements (Capital Buffers and Macro-prudential Measures) Regulations 2014.

8.5.5.2 **Domestic systemically important banks (D-SIBs) Buffer**

The Basel Committee regards D-SIBs as a category of banks whose failure may cause an adverse systemic impact upon a local economy. As such, national regulators are in a better position to determine which banks under their supervision have such a profile.[129]

Nevertheless, the Basel Committee views it as useful to develop a set of minimum consistent principles for national regulators to apply in determining D-SIBs, as this ensures that opportunities for regulatory arbitrage do not arise due to different approaches taken by national regulators.

Further, D-SIBs may not be confined to a national economy and may have a cross-border footprint. Thus, by setting minimum standards for identifying D-SIBs and principles for applying higher capital requirements, the Basel Committee hopes to minimise negative cross-border spillover effects. For example, in the global financial crisis, Icelandic bank Kaupthing Singer Friedlander, which was the largest bank in Iceland and would be considered a D-SIB in today's terms, was also a significant deposit taker in the UK and Germany. The failure of Kaupthing severely affected Iceland but had tremendous ripple effects upon UK and Germany. By requiring such D-SIBs to hold higher levels of capital, the regulatory benefit of improving such D-SIBs' safety would not only be extended to Iceland, but would be extended to the UK and Germany as well. Although enhanced micro-prudential regulation cannot guarantee zero failure,[130] such requirements may go some way towards moderating risk-taking and improving the safety of banks.

The Basel Committee envisages the same bank should not be liable for both the G-SIB and D-SIB regulatory capital requirements. The higher of either the G-SIB requirement or the combined D-SIB and systemic risk buffer will apply. However, national regulators could regard a bank subsidiary as a D-SIB, while its parent banking group may be identified as a G-SIB. The Committee supports higher capital requirements to be imposed on the subsidiary on a stand-alone basis, but urges that regulators responsible for the parent banking group and the subsidiary work together so as to ensure that the requirement imposed on the D-SIB does not result in the undermining of the capital position of the G-SIB parent. Further, a level playing field should be maintained in the national context for both the parent banking group and the subsidiary bank.

The UK has initially been reluctant to impose additional requirements on D-SIBs. This is because many D-SIBs are subject to structural reforms, a unique UK regulatory regime discussed in Chapter 10, and it is important to allow the impact of structural regulation to be observed before deciding if additional capital requirements are indeed necessary to ensure the safety and soundness of D-SIBs.[131] However, the PRA has now

---

[129] Para 5, Basel Committee, *A Framework for Dealing with Domestic Systemically Important Banks* (October 2012) at http://www.bis.org/publ/bcbs233.pdf.

[130] Now that bank regulators are able to exercise more extensive powers in imposing regulatory capital requirements and have the opportunity to scrutinise banks' risk profiles on a regular basis, it will be questioned to what extent regulators have become more responsible for ensuring that capital adequacy is effective. This issue is discussed in section 8.1.

[131] Financial Policy Committee, *Record of the Financial Policy Committee Meeting* (September 2014) at para 73.

dovetailed its interpretation of D-SIBs with the banks that are subject to the structural reforms (discussed in Chapter 10). These banks are subject to the systemic risk buffer discussed above, which is indeed the PRA's equivalent of the 'D-SIB' buffer.

The EU has implemented the Basel Committee's recommendations on D-SIBs by conferring on national regulators the power to designate 'Other Systemically Important Institutions' or 'OSIIs'.[132] The criteria for determining which institutions to designate as OSIIs is harmonised by the European Banking Authority in consultation with the European Systemic Risk Board to designate banks other than G-SIBs as OSIIs. National regulators have the discretion to impose additional capital requirements on OSIIs based on this framework, up to 2 per cent of risk-weighted assets on top of required regulatory capital.[133] In practice the EBA has applied its harmonised criteria and issues a yearly determination of which are OSIIs in each member state.[134]

Box 8.11 summarises the additional regulatory capital requirements for banks that are G-SIBs or D-SIBs. These are in addition to the requirement of 8 per cent risk asset ratio and the capital buffers specified in Box 8.10.

8.5.5.3 Leverage ratio buffer

The PRA[135] has also introduced an additional capital buffer for UK banks that are G-SIBs or subsidiaries in the UK of an EU G-SIB. This additional capital buffer, known as the Additional Leverage Ratio Buffer (ALRB) is a capital buffer different in nature from the other capital adequacy requirements discussed. The ALRB is not based on risk-weighted assets but based on the bank's 'total exposure' measure, that is, its gross level of lending, defined and measured in accordance with the discussion in Chapter 9, section 9.4.

The ALRB complements the other capital adequacy measures in exerting restraint upon banks in relation to their lending activities so as to encourage them to be more

---

Box 8.11

At a glance, banks with a systemic risk profile may be subject to:

- G-SIB capital requirements of 1–3.5 per cent of risk-weighted assets; OR

- D-SIB capital requirements of up to 2 per cent determined by the EBA (or national regulator).

These requirements do not simultaneously apply for an institution that has both profiles of a G-SIB and D-SIB. The higher of either the G-SIB requirement or the combined D-SIB and systemic risk buffer will apply.

---

[132] Article 131 CRD IV Directive. [133] Article 131(5) CRD IV Directive.

[134] See, for example, the EBA's list in 2016 at http://www.eba.europa.eu/risk-analysis-and-data/other-systemically-important-institutions-o-siis-/2016.

[135] PRA, *Additional Leverage Ratio Buffer Model Requirements for G-SIIs* (2015) at https://www.bankofengland.co.uk/-/media/boe/files/prudential-regulation/supervisory-statement/2015/ss4515-vreq.pdf?la=en&hash=6C23E2FC69A86C381506AE0AAECD140DD89BB8DF.

conservative in view of their systemically important profile. The Basel Committee[136] proposes that such a measure should be made internationally convergent, that is, that all G-SIBs should be imposed with the ALRB by January 2022. The ALRB is discussed in detail in Chapter 9, section 9.4 in conjunction with the discussion on the leverage ratio as a regulatory tool.

8.5.6 Types of capital to support capital adequacy requirements

In section 8.2, we discussed the types of capital required to support regulatory capital requirements in the Basel I Accord. In Section 8.3, we observed that the Market Risk Amendment 1996 and Basel II introduced eligible capital of a lower quality to meet market and operational risk requirements. Basel III now moves away from capital of lower quality and recommends that capital of higher quality should be increased in proportion. Indeed, tier three capital as discussed earlier is abolished. Further, all new regulatory capital buffers introduced in Basel III and in the CRD IV Directive, as well as the leverage ratio buffers, are to be met by the highest quality capital – that is, common equity tier one capital.

First, tier one capital (discussed in section 8.2.4) is to be increased from forming 4 per cent of the risk–asset ratio to 6 per cent by 2015. An incremental approach has been taken to encourage banks to increase their proportion of tier one capital, from an increase to 4.5 per cent in 2013 and thereafter gradually rising to meet the requirement of 6 per cent. Further, the common equity component of tier one capital is to rise from 2 per cent to 3.5 per cent by 2013, and then to 4.5 per cent by 2015. The common equity component of tier one capital is regarded as the highest quality form of capital as it is stable in nature. The rest of tier one capital is known as 'Additional Tier one', such as retained earnings mentioned earlier. In the EU, a list of acceptable common equity tier one capital in each member state is published and updated regularly by the European Banking Authority.[137] The list includes a variety of classes of share capital including non-voting shares and capital in non-corporate business vehicles such as limited liability partnerships in the UK. Basel III prescribes that the all capital buffers are to be met by common equity tier one capital. This is also extended to the capital buffers introduced under the EU CRD IV Directive.

It is noted, however, that under certain circumstances national regulators have often voluntarily exceeded the Basel Committee recommendations. For example, from 2011, the European Banking Authority required all banks in the EU to maintain a tier one capital ratio of 9 per cent of risk-weighted assets, in order to address the loss in value or 'haircut' on banks' holding of sovereign bonds issued by troubled member states such as

---

[136] Basel Committee, *Finalising Post-crisis Reforms* (December 2017) at https://www.bis.org/bcbs/publ/d424.pdf.

[137] See, for example, Updated List of CET 1 Instruments 2014, at https://www.eba.europa.eu/-/eba-updates-list-of-common-equity-tier-1-cet1-capital-instruments.

Greece. The Basel Accord methodology of risk-weighting assets could not have adapted to the rapidly changing circumstances in Greece and would under-estimate the risk profile of Greek sovereign bonds. Hence, the unique compensating measure introduced by the European Banking Authority was intended to shore up the capital strength of European banks, in order to prevent them from being perceived by the market as being weak in light of their sovereign bond holdings.

As for the UK PRA's Pillar 2A capital, it is to be met by 56 per cent common equity tier one capital from January 2015, culminating in being fully met by such high quality capital by January 2016.[138] If a PRA buffer is applied (where a bank's risks are in the PRA's view, not fully addressed by other capital buffers), the PRA will apply a scalar to the common equity tier one capital required to meet the risk–asset ratio. Such a scalar will be in the region of 10–40 per cent depending on the severity of weakness determined by the PRA.[139]

Further, as will be discussed in Chapter 9, common equity tier one capital can also be required to meet leverage ratio requirements.

The new demands placed on banks in ensuring that they have sufficient high-quality capital to meet the new regulatory capital requirements have the following ramifications. Banks may indeed strengthen their capital position by raising equity finance. However, raising equity finance is costly and banks may prefer the easier approach of creating less assets (such as by lending less). There are fears of **deleveraging** at a global level, such deleveraging having the potential to adversely affect economic growth as less credit is available. [140] On the other hand, other commentators are of the view that there is net economic benefit achieved with higher regulatory capital requirements that mitigate the losses and cost of bank crises.[141] Further, it may be argued that high levels of credit are not socially optimal and banks' moderation of credit extension to comply with the new regulatory requirements may indeed be more socially optimal in the long run.[142] Box 8.12 provides a list of what common equity tier one capital is required for.

---

[138] See news release, at http://www.bankofengland.co.uk/publications/Pages/news/2013/181.aspx.

[139] PRA, *The PRA's Methodologies for Setting Pillar 2 Capital* (July 2015) 29, at http://www.bankofengland.co.uk/pra/Documents/publications/sop/2015/p2methodologies.pdf.

[140] See Deloitte & Touche survey 2012, at https://www2.deloitte.com/content/dam/Deloitte/uk/Documents/financial-services/deloitte-uk-fs-european-bank-deleveraging.pdf; Thomas F Cosimano and Dalia Hakura, 'Bank Behaviour in Response to Basel III: A Cross-country Analysis' (2011) at https://www.imf.org/external/pubs/cat/longres.aspx?sk=24870.0. Paolo Angelini et al., 'Basel III: Long-Term Impact on Economic Performance and Fluctuations' (BIS Working Paper 2011) at http://www.bis.org/publ/work338.htm, argue that the Basel III reforms will likely result in a gradual decline in economic output.

[141] Meilan Yan, Maximilian JB Hall, and Paul Turner, 'A Cost-Benefit Analysis of Basel III: Some Evidence from the UK' (2011) at http://www.lboro.ac.uk/departments/sbe/RePEc/lbo/lbowps/Yan_Hall_TurnerWP5.pdf.

[142] Anat R. Admati, Peter M. DeMarzo, Martin Hellwig, and Paul Pfleiderer, 'Fallacies, Irrelevant Facts, and Myths in the Discussion of Capital Regulation: Why Bank Equity is Not Expensive' (2013) at https://www.gsb.stanford.edu/faculty-research/working-papers/fallacies-irrelevant-facts-myths-discussion-capital-regulation-why;

Box 8.12

Common equity tier one capital is required for:

- 6 per cent out of the (8 per cent) risk–asset ratio
- Capital conservation buffer
- Counter-cyclical buffer
- Institution-specific counter-cyclical buffer
- Systemic risk buffer
- PRA Pillar 2A capital (from 2016)
- PRA Buffer (at scalar of 10–40 per cent only determined by the PRA)
- The G-SIB or D-SIB buffer where applicable
- Leverage ratio buffers (i.e. the CLRB and ALRB)

8.5.7 Minimum Requirement for Own Funds and Eligible Liabilities (MREL) in the EU and UK

The FSB and the EU is concerned that capital adequacy requirements are insufficient to address the risks posed by G-SIBs and D-SIBs. This is because capital adequacy, which is an *ex ante* measure to control risk-taking, does not provide practically for absorbing loss or recapitalising a bank (i.e. returning it to a position which allows it to meet regulatory capital requirements) when it becomes crisis-stricken.

The EU has introduced the concept of the ***Minimum Requirement for Own Funds and Eligible Liabilities*** (MREL) for all banks in order to address the *ex post* needs of capital in banks should they need to be resolved or recover from a crisis.[143] However, MREL is defined in such a way as to encompass the default regulatory capital requirements discussed above. The difference is that the default capital requirements are imposed on a 'going concern' basis while MREL deals with a 'gone-concern' basis. Subsequently, the FSB started to develop the 'Total Loss Absorbing Capacity' (TLAC) requirements that focus on gone-concern capital requirements only for G-SIBs.[144] As systemically important banks should not be easily allowed to fail, emphasis must be placed on recovering them, by recapitalising them. As the objectives of MREL and TLAC are similar, the application of MREL and TLAC will be dovetailed to an extent. MREL and TLAC will most likely converge in relation to G-SIBs and D-SIBs, but MREL is a wider concept applying to all banks in the UK and EU.

8.5.7.1 Components of MREL

MREL is defined to comprise of three components.[145] The three components comprise one 'minimum' component, which is set at the level of the default regulatory capital

---

[143] Article 45, BRRD 2014.   [144] See discussion in Chapter 9, section 9.5.

[145] Commission Delegated Regulation (EU) 2016/1450 of 23 May 2016 supplementing Directive 2014/59/EU of the European Parliament and of the Council with regard to regulatory technical standards specifying the criteria relating to the methodology for setting the minimum requirement for own funds and eligible liabilities.

requirements discussed above, and two discretionary 'additional' components. The 'minimum' component is called the 'Loss Absorption Amount' which is basically defined to be the same as the default regulatory capital requirements, that is, the sum of the risk–asset ratio (8 per cent), the Pillar 2A capital applied to a bank and all capital buffers discussed in this Section.[146] However, national regulators are given the discretion to set higher or lower amounts of MREL depending on whether they envisage that loss absorption would be effective and that resolution of the bank is not likely to be impeded.

Next, the two discretionary components of MREL apply largely to banks that should best be prepared to avoid failure and for recapitalisation, in the public interest of avoiding financial stability risks. The 'recapitalisation' component[147] of MREL is defined as the sum of the risk–asset ratio (8 per cent), the Pillar 2A capital applied to a bank and the leverage ratio applicable. National regulators have the discretion to determine that the recapitalisation amount is zero if they are of the view that a bank can be liquidated in an orderly manner. Further, national regulators can require banks to provide for an additional 'market confidence charge' if it is necessary to restore market confidence in the bank upon recapitalisation. This market confidence charge is based on the sum of all regulatory buffers applicable to the bank. The two components are discretionary in terms of whether they apply and to what extent to each bank, as determined by the relevant authority for the bank. As banks subject to the Single Supervisory Mechanism (Chapter 7, section 7.3) will come under the resolution authority of the Single Resolution Board, the SRB prescribes the MREL policy applicable to banks subject to the SSM, working in cooperation with national resolution authorities. For a financial institution group, the lead resolution authority of the resolution college (whether it is the SRB, to be discussed in Chapter 13, section 13.4 or another national authority) will propose the level of MREL in consultation with other concerned resolution authorities and should attempt to reach a joint decision.[148] In the absence of a joint decision, the resolution authorities for subsidiaries within the group are free to impose MREL as they deem appropriate and to communicate it to the lead resolution authority.[149]

The MREL is essentially regarded to be Pillar 2 capital.[150] The minimum level of MREL in effect compels banks to hold an amount of capital on top of the going concern capital adequacy requirements for recapitalisation purposes. Box 8.13 summarises how MREL is computed.

---

[146] Ibid, Article 1.   [147] Ibid, Article 2.

[148] Articles 86–93, Commission Delegated Regulation (EU) 2016/1075 of 23 March 2016 supplementing Directive 2014/59/EU of the European Parliament and of the Council with regard to regulatory technical standards specifying the content of recovery plans, resolution plans and group resolution plans, the minimum criteria that the competent authority is to assess as regards recovery plans and group recovery plans, the conditions for group financial support, the requirements for independent valuers, the contractual recognition of write-down and conversion powers, the procedures and contents of notification requirements and of notice of suspension and the operational functioning of the resolution colleges.   [149] Ibid, Articles 94–6.

[150] Commission Delegated Regulation 2016.

> **Box 8.13 MREL computation**
>
> Loss Absorption Amount (Mandatory) + Recapitalisation Amount (Discretionary)
> + Market Confidence Charge (Discretionary) =
> (Pillar 1 + Pillar 2 + all regulatory capital buffers) + (Pillar 1 + Pillar 2)
> + (All regulatory capital buffers)

8.5.7.2 Implementation of MREL

In the UK, the MREL will be implemented to be consistent with the resolution tools relevant to the scale, size, and nature of the banking business.[151] For small institutions, it is
envisaged that resolution may be by way of insolvency and payouts under the deposit guarantee scheme and so in effect, small institutions are unlikely to need to hold MREL beyond
their compliance with capital adequacy requirements as a going concern. For institutions
that are likely to be resolved by partial transfer of business, the MREL would also be calibrated according to those resolution prospects and would unlikely be one-size fits-all.[152]

However, for systemically important G-SIBs and D-SIBs where private sector bail-
in (discussed in Chapter 13) is likely to be utilised, the MREL is crucial for realising
the effectiveness of bail-in. The UK's MREL regime will be phased in over three stages
between 2019 and 2022, in order to allow banks sufficient time to organise the raising
of capital to meet MREL requirements. The EU and UK are also envisaged to dovetail
the MREL for G-SIBs in line with the TLAC recommendations.[153]

Between January 2019 and January 2020, globally systemically important banks
regulated in the UK would be expected to meet the TLAC requirement of 16 per cent
risk–asset ratio or 6 per cent leverage ratio (discussed in detail in Chapter 9). Between
January 2020 and January 2022, G-SIBs and D-SIBs regulated by the PRA would be
expected to meet an MREL of twice their Pillar 1 Capital (which is the baseline 8 per
cent risk–asset ratio) and one times their Pillar 2A capital requirement, or twice their
leverage ratio requirement. This could be effectively higher than the FSB's TLAC standard to be discussed in Chapter 9. From January 2022, G-SIBs and D-SIBs regulated
by the PRA would need to meet an MREL of twice the sum of Pillar 1 and 2A capital,

---

[151] All resolution tools are discussed in Chapter 13.

[152] PRA, *The Bank of England's Approach to Setting A Minimum Requirement for Own Funds and Eligible
Liabilities (MREL)* (November 2016, updated as of June 2018) at https://www.bankofengland.co.uk/-/media/
boe/files/paper/2018/statement-of-policy-boes-approach-to-setting-mrel-2018.pdf?la=en&hash=BC4499AF
9CF063A3D8024BE5C050CB1F39E2EBC1.

[153] The banking reform package put out by the Commission at the end of 2016, which is undergoing legislative finalisation, see http://ec.europa.eu/finance/bank/docs/regcapital/crr-crd-review/161123-proposal-
amending-regulation_en.pdf.

or twice the leverage ratio applicable.[154] G-SIBs and D-SIBs must continue to meet its going concern capital requirements with instruments that cannot be double-counted towards MREL[155] MREL instruments are however of a wider range.

MREL Eligible Instruments

The range of MREL capital instruments is defined in the Bank Recovery and Resolution Directive 2014 in conjunction with the provision of the bail-in regime (see Chapter 13). The scope of eligible liabilities is wide, including all fully paid up instruments not financed or guaranteed by the issuing institution, unsecured, fully subordinated to other claims, and ranking equally with the lowest claims in insolvency, not based on a derivative or deposit, and has a maturity of at least a year.[156] The SRB has further clarified that it considers the following items excluded from the MREL even if they may in principle meet the characteristics above:

(a) Unprotected deposits, that is, deposits not protected under the Deposit Guarantee Scheme of the member state (discussed in Chapter 13, section 13.3) unless they cannot be withdrawn for a year.

(b) Liabilities issued by banking entities located within the EU.

(c) Liabilities that are not governed by the laws of any EU member state.

(d) Structured notes.

A question arises whether MREL held by the retail sector such as households or individuals should be excluded as they can pose problems to impede resolution. These impediments occur when national authorities are reluctant to bail-in such MREL for fear of the adverse impact caused to confidence in the retail markets, and are wary of the hardship caused to individuals and households. The SRB is not prepared to exclude these but they present real issues at the point in time of bail-in (Chapter 13, section 13.2).

Internal MREL

Further, the EU and UK are concerned about the robustness of bank subsidiaries, whether they are overseas subsidiaries of a banking group regulated by the national regulator or the subsidiaries of a foreign bank operating within their markets. There is a concern that subsidiaries should themselves hold adequate MREL as the resolution of a banking group could take place along the lines of multiple-points of entry (discussed in Chapter 13, section 13.4), where subsidiaries are resolved in their operating jurisdictions separately from the resolution of each other and the parent holding company. In

---

[154] PRA, *The Bank of England's Approach to Setting A Minimum Requirement for Own Funds and Eligible Liabilities (MREL)* (November 2016) at (November 2016, updated as of June 2018) at https://bankofengland.co.uk/-/media/boe/files/paper/2018/statement-of-policy-boes-approach-to-setting-mrel-2018.pdf?la=en&hash=BC4499AF9CF063A3D8024BE5C050CB1F39E2EBC1.

[155] The Bank's 2017 update to the Policy Statement above, at https://www.bankofengland.co.uk/-/media/boe/files/prudential-regulation/supervisory-statement/2017/ss1616update.pdf?la=en&hash=EE48E560E732C247821BBD03CE3B5BFD03465060.   [156] Article 45, BRRD 2014.

such a case it would be important to ascertain if there is sufficient loss absorption capital within such a subsidiary in order not to cause negative spillover effects to the jurisdiction it is based. Such MREL requirements are known as 'internal MREL'. The EU and UK envisage that internal MREL would be calibrated for 'material subsidiaries' that hold at least 5 per cent of the group's risk-weighted assets, operating income or leverage exposures. Internal MREL is calibrated according to the structure of the material subsidiary's holdings, the distribution of loss absorption resources within the group and can be at 75–90 percent of the external MREL applicable to the group or even at 100 percent. Further, the EU is considering requiring foreign branches that are 'material' to be incorporated as subsidiaries in order to apply internal MREL requirements to them.[157]

Implications of MREL compliance

It is expensive for banks to comply with MREL. Banks have to raise further capital even if MREL eligible instruments are of a wider scope. These instruments are usually convertible instruments, which have to pay out relatively high interest rates to investors in view of the risk that they would be used to absorb banks' losses. However, the introduction of MREL provides market discipline for banks, so that the price for banks' risk-taking may be set by and also paid for by investors. One may argue that investors would not set 'right' market prices for bank risk-taking as investors are overly optimistic. They are likely to be attracted by the high interest rate MREL instruments pay and continue to allow banks to take on high levels of risk. However, the actual use of MREL to absorb bank losses may cause investors to revise the price they are willing to pay for such instruments and hence introduce discipline for banks. Nevertheless, in such cases, investors may become overly risk averse and the market for MREL may be adversely impacted. In other words, the effectiveness of using MREL to stimulate market discipline is not necessarily optimal as investors' behaviour may be adjusted disproportionately when the risks underlying the MREL materialise. But in view of the need to compel the private sector to be prepared to contribute towards resolving banks, so that bank crisis and resolution would not always inflict tremendous fiscal cost, the MREL regime should be supported for its risk-sharing ethos. This point will be returned to in Chapter 13 when bail-in is discussed.

Another hazard of the MREL regime has been revealed in the case of *BNY Mellon Corporate Trustee Services Ltd v LBG Capital No 1 plc and another*.[158] In that case, Lloyds Bank Plc incorporated a couple of subsidiaries to issue convertible debt instruments in 2009, the conversion event defined with reference to the trigger set by the PRA in its previous stress test which Lloyds had failed. The instruments, called 'enhanced capital

---

[157] These are pending in nature, for the EU refer to the banking reform package (November 2016) above, and the PRA, *The Bank of England's Approach to Setting a Minimum Requirement for Own Funds and Eligible Liabilities (MREL)* (November 2016, updated as of June 2018) at https://bankofengland.co.uk/-/media/boe/files/paper/2018/statement-of-policy-boes-approach-to-setting-mrel-2018.pdf?la=en&hash=BC4499AF9CF063A3D8024BE5C050CB1F39E2EBC1.

[158] [2016] UKSC 29.

notes' paid a high interest rate of over 10 per cent per annum and could be redeemed in 10–33 years, or be converted into equity if the trigger event occurred. The notes could also be redeemed if there were a capital disqualification event, that is, where the regulator ceases to take into account the notes for stress testing. Indeed, the stress test threshold changed as regulatory capital requirements were still being developed during that period and became more demanding. Hence the conversion threshold stipulated for the notes became too low in view of the new regulatory requirements. Lloyd's proceeded to redeem the notes on the basis of the occurrence of the capital disqualification event, but the investors, represented by their custodian BNY Mellon resisted this and challenged this in court.

At first instance the court held that the notes did not cease to be considered in stress testing, but they were less useful as they would only convert at a very low threshold. The Court of Appeal overturned the high court's ruling and found for Lloyd's as the nature of the capital disqualification event had to be understood in light of the surrounding regulatory capital context, and clearly the notes had lost their main purpose as bail-inable debt (see Chapter 13) for the purposes of stress testing and resolution as they could not be converted at the new thresholds introduced by the PRA. The Supreme Court agreed with the Court of Appeal. Although the result is a relief to Lloyds which will not have to pay out on highly expensive debt instruments that have become for most purposes redundant, this case illustrates the difficulty in issuing MREL that would meet its purposes in an environment of changing regulatory goal-posts.

Finally, a concern that can be raised is that bank regulators may have too much confidence in MREL in absorbing losses, and MREL can engender a false sense of security. Sir John Vickers[159] warned in mid-2018 that capital buffers can be kept low or not imposed as regulators overly rely on MREL's effectiveness. It remains to be seen if there is a trade-off effect between MREL's perceived *ex post* usefulness and the use of *ex ante* or going concern levers in capital adequacy.

8.5.8 Addressing the weaknesses of capital adequacy regulation

Although Basel III has dealt quickly with the low baseline of the 8 per cent risk–asset ratio and its relative inability to effectively induce banks to control their risks prudently, an essential part of reforms to capital adequacy regulation must address weaknesses in measuring the risk-weights of assets, whether in the standardised approaches to credit, market and operational risk or the internal models approaches.

The Basel Committee and European Banking Authority have identified variations within the banking sector in the application of risk-weighting methodologies. The Basel Committee carries out yearly regulatory consistency assessments (RCAP) of jurisdictions in their implementation of the Basel III reforms.[160] These assessments are peer reviews that are intended to monitor states' overall progress in implementing the

---

[159] 'John Vickers warns of 'dangerously high' levels of bank leverage', *Financial Times* (3 May 2018).
[160] Basel Committee, *Basel III Regulatory Consistency Assessment Programme*, from 2013 to date.

reforms as well as the extent of their compliance with the reforms. The RCAPs to date have shown that there is significant variation in bank risk-weighting methodologies.[161]

The European Banking Authority also carries out yearly reviews of the consistency of risk-weighted assets measured by banks and continues to find significant variations.[162] These studies may be carried out at rather granular levels of selected asset classes, such as residential mortgages in 2014.[163]

The initiatives taken to improve consistency in risk-weightings and to mitigate poor risk measurements include: (a) greater use of standardisation across the measurements for credit, market, and operational risk; (b) controls on the parameters of discretion where internal models are used; and (c) subjecting the use of internal models to greater supervision and scrutiny.

8.5.8.1 Refinements to standardised approaches

The Basel Committee has from 2014 suggested greater harmonisation in its standardised approach to credit risk.[164] In this respect, more granular prescription of risk-weightings for assets has taken place, such as under the EU's Capital Requirements Regulation 2013, in order to ensure that a convergent and conservative risk-weighting approach is carried out for banks adopting the standardised approach. For example, commercial mortgages are risk-weighted at 50 per cent only if various conditions are satisfied, or else the risk-weighting to be applied is 100 per cent.[165] Another example is that the EBA has the power to prescribe which assets are 'high risk' in order for them to attract a 150 per cent risk-weighting, including investments in venture capital or private equity firms.[166]

Next, the Basel Committee perceives a need to make more robust the risk-weightings of the standardised approaches in credit and market risk that rely heavily on external credit ratings. This is because external credit ratings may be unreliable[167] or outdated. External credit ratings for structured products in particular were severely discredited during the 2007–9 global financial crisis as it emerged that credit rating agencies gave more favourable ratings than warranted due to the huge fees they would receive for such ratings. Credit rating agencies thus have suffered the taint of inaccuracy affected by their conflicts of interest. Further, external credit ratings may be unresponsive to rapid market changes and do not reflect changes in the creditworthiness of borrowers

---

[161] Basel Committee, *Reducing Excessive Variability in Banks' Regulatory Capital Ratios: A Report to the G20* (November 2014) at para 2.

[162] See http://www.eba.europa.eu/risk-analysis-and-data/review-of-consistency-of-risk-weighted-assets.

[163] EBA, *Fourth Report on the Consistency of Risk-weighted Assets* (11 June 2014) at http://www.eba.europa.eu/documents/10180/15947/20140611+Fourth+interim+report+on+the+consistency+of+risk-weighted+asset.pdf.

[164] Basel Committee, *Reducing Excessive Variability in Banks' Regulatory Capital Ratios: A Report to the G20* (November 2014) 2–3.   [165] Articles 123 and 125.

[166] Article 128.

[167] There have been copious commentaries on the weaknesses and deficiencies of credit ratings for structured products in the pre-crisis era, see, for example, Claire A Hill, 'Why Did Rating Agencies Do such a Bad Job Rating Subprime Securities?' (2010) 71 *University of Pittsburgh Law Review* 585.

and assets.[168] Hence, the Basel Committee encourages that the bank must conduct sufficient due diligence and not mechanistically rely on external ratings. In some asset classes, alternative measures of assessing risk may be available, such as the loan-to-value ratio in residential mortgage loans. Indeed, the Basel Committee has refined the risk-weights applicable to residential mortgages under the standardised approach, so that such mortgages are not treated at a 35 per cent blanket risk-weighting (as in Basel II). Refined levels of risk-weighting will now apply to residential mortgages depending on its loan-to-value ratio.[169] It has also been suggested that in assessing the creditworthiness of corporate borrowers, their revenue and levels of leverage should be taken into account.[170]

Although the move away from relying excessively on external credit ratings is sound, alternative approaches are not easy to apply like the shorthand of external credit ratings. Further, considering these other characteristics may import of banks applying their evaluation and discretion inconsistently from each other. Hence, it remains a challenging task for the Committee to maintain a standardised approach as a baseline for risk-weighting that is accurate, robust, and easy to apply. In view of these difficulties, the Basel Committee remains unable to endorse a wholesale move away from relying on external credit ratings but to encourage non-mechanistic use and to urge alternative measures to be developed such as the loan-to-value ratio for residential mortgages.[171]

Another area where risk-weightings have been made more robust is in relation to securitised assets. Securitisation involves the repackaging of loan assets held by a bank into financial instruments that can be offered for sale as securities to investors. However, information about underlying assets that are securitised is not always transparent and such opacity can cause asset prices to be highly volatile when market confidence is adversely impacted, such as in the 2007–9 global financial crisis.

The post-crisis approach to securitisation now introduces more standardisation that compels banks to adopt a conservative approach to risk-weighting securitised assets. It also introduces more regulatory supervision into how banks treat securitised assets.

First, all securitised assets are recommended to be subject to a floor risk-weighting of 15 per cent,[172] although the EU legislation has implemented a floor of 20 per cent.[173] Banks may risk-weight the securitised assets using the standard approach or internal ratings-based approaches. Where the former is used, certain prescribed criteria must be met, or a standard risk-weighting of 1,250 per cent must be applied.[174] Internal ratings-based approaches are subject to supervisory scrutiny and certain criteria are

---

[168] For example, see *Joint Consultation Paper on Mechanistic References to Credit Ratings* (November 2013), *Final Report* (Feb 2014).

[169] Basel Committee, *Finalising Post-crisis Reforms* (Dec 2017) at https://www.bis.org/bcbs/publ/d424.pdf.

[170] Ibid.

[171] See second consultation document to Ibid, in December 2015 at http://www.bis.org/bcbs/publ/d347.htm, *Finalising Post-crisis Reforms* (December 2017) at https://www.bis.org/bcbs/publ/d424.pdf.

[172] See Basel Committee, *Basel III Document: Revisions to the Securitisation Framework* (July 2014) at http://www.bis.org/bcbs/publ/d303.pdf.   [173] EU Capital Requirements Regulation 2013, Article 251.

[174] Ibid.

now prescribed. The maximum risk-weighting to be applied under the internal ratings-based approach is 1,250 per cent.[175]

Further, the UK has tightened up its criteria for when assets may be treated as having been securitised and cease to count as the bank's 'asset' on its balance sheet. Where banks are of the view that they meet the criteria, they must notify the regulator within one month of the date of the transfer. [176] It has been opined that the regulator may nevertheless challenge the view after supervisory review and recharacterise the transaction.[177] Regulatory capital requirements for the assets in question would need to be complied with.

8.5.8.2 Reducing the scope for flexible approaches

Further, we see that there is a general move towards narrowing down banks' discretion in calculating risk-weighting, in relation to market and operational risks. In particular, the internal models approach of the 'AMA' discussed in section 8.4 for operational risk has been superseded, and operational risk must now be measured in accordance with a standardised approach. In relation to market risk, greater prescription now features even in the use of internal models.

Operational risk reforms

The Basel Committee is of the view that setting aside a proportion of total income by the bank does not really reflect the extent of operational risk incurred. The standardised approaches in Basel II for operational risk were too broad-brush while the internal model approach leaves banks with too much discretion to measure their operational risk.

Drawing from more contemporary research, the Committee introduces a new way of measuring operational risk, using only a standardised approach that is regarded as risk-sensitive.[178] The standardised approach requires that a certain percentage of a bank's 'Business Indicator' be worked out as its operational risk measure. This measure then forms part of risk-weighted assets for the application of capital adequacy requirements.

A bank's Business Indicator (BI)[179] is a composite measure that comprises of the bank's income from loans, other services and different sources of profit and loss. The BI is based on the three key components of a bank's income statement: the 'interest component', the 'services component', and the 'financial component'. The 'interest component' refers to interest income from credit assets after deducting expenses. The 'services component' refers to fee and other operating income net of expenses. The 'financial component' refers to the bank's profitability. These components are aggregated into a BI

---

[175] EU Capital Requirements Regulation 2013, Article 259.   [176] PRA Rulebook, *Credit Risk* para 3.1.

[177] Allen & Overy, *CRD IV Framework: The Securitisation Framework* (2014) 10 at http://www.allenovery.com/SiteCollectionDocuments/Capital%20Requirements%20Directive%20IV%20Framework/The%20securitisation%20framework.pdf.

[178] Basel Committee, *Finalising Post-crisis Reforms* (December 2017) at https://www.bis.org/bcbs/publ/d424.pdf, building on work in 2014 and 2016.

[179] Basel Committee, *Operational Risk – Revisions to the Simpler Approaches* (Consultative Document, October 2014) at http://www.bis.org/publ/bcbs291.pdf and revised as of 2016 at http://www.bis.org/bcbs/publ/d355.htm.

Table 8.7 BI ranges for applying a BIC

Business Indicator ranges	Business Indicator component
Less than 1 billion euros	12%
Between 1 and 30 billion euros	15%
More than 30 billion euros	18%

for each bank. The Committee regarded that the BI is more holistic than gross revenues in capturing banks' exposures to operational risk, and there is a tendency that operational risks increase as business footprint increases, hence the BI is more risk-sensitive to banks' business profiles.

The Committee has developed three BI ranges in order to apply a Business Indicator Component (BIC) against each range (see Table 8.7). The BIC is a percentage of the BI, and represents an estimate of the level of operational loss that may emanate from the scale and nature of banks' business activities.

The BIC will then be multiplied by an 'Internal Loss Multiplier' that is derived from banks' own records of operational loss data. Such data has to be based on previous 10 years' information, although exceptionally 5 years' worth of information may be permitted to be used. It will be assumed that 15 times the average annual operational losses over the previous 10 years would represent a sound estimate of internal loss going forward (Loss Component). The Loss Component is then taken as a percentage of the bank's BI to derive the Internal Loss Multiplier (ILM). If the ILM is equal to the BIC, then the BIC is taken as the risk-weighted operational loss for the purposes of applying capital adequacy requirements. If the ILM exceeds or is below the BIC, it is multiplied to the BIC in order to raise or reduce the BIC accordingly, resulting in a composite 'operational risk capital' (ORC). The ORC is then applied to the BI to derive the operational loss measure for the bank (see Box 8.14).

The operational risk reforms compel larger banks with many business lines to make provision for operational risk to a greater extent than compared to smaller banks. This reflects reality better as larger banks have been at risk of misconduct and regulatory liability to a greater extent than smaller outfits. The reforms also represent more joined up thinking in designing policy for G-SIBs and D-SIBs whose conduct footprint, exposure to digital glitches and problems and business exposure in different geographical locations way exceed those of smaller banks.

Box 8.14 ORC = (BIC × ILM) × BI

Where BIC is prescribed in Table 8.7, ILM is the actual ratio of Loss Component, based on actual loss data to the Business Indicator. Where BIC= ILM, ILM is =1 in the equation above.

Increasing prescription within internal models: market risk

In the immediate aftermath of the global financial crisis, the Basel Committee recommended changes to how banks measure market risk, in order to address gaps and weaknesses in the application of models such as VaR that are now regarded as too optimistic

The Committee recommends that the use of internal models for market risk must be approved in advance by national regulators and must be premised upon the soundness and quality of the bank's own risk management, governance, and internal control systems. The Committee has also made more prescription for the list of factors that banks need to consider in their models pertaining to qualitative[180] as well as the quantitative factors. [181]

Further, banks are asked not only to calculate VaR of their trading portfolios on a daily basis, but to work out a stressed VaR measure[182] on a weekly basis. Such a measure takes into account longer cycles of trade data and mitigates over-optimism and short termism in the VaR measure. The stressed VaR measure will be used in preference over average daily VaR measures for the preceding 60 days if it turns out to be higher. This allows market risk to be measured in a more conservative manner than under the previous approach under Basel II. The Basel Committee is also considering moving away from VaR, which is considered to be too dependent on short-term market pricing and not robust enough to capture stressed situations and unlikely but severe events. The Basel Committee is implementing an alternative measure of 'Expected Shortfall',[183] which captures stressed and severe situations, forcing greater conservatism even where internal models by banks are applied to measure market risk.

8.5.8.3 Internal models

A major weakness identified in relation to banks' risk management during the 2007–9 global financial crisis was the use of internal models to derive low risk-weightings of bank risk in order to minimise regulatory capital compliance. Hence, the use of internal models has to be subject to more robust standards and regulatory scrutiny. Under the EU CRD IV Directive, regulators are compelled to review banks' internal models at least every three years even if approval has been given for their use.[184]

First, the use of internal models has become more prescriptive. The Basel Committee envisages that internal models can be used for more unusual assets such as project,

---

[180] Articles 286–91, 293–4, Capital Requirements Regulation 2013 on the quality of risk control units at banks, the engagement of senior management, the soundness of stress-testing systems, and the integration and quality of internal control functions.

[181] See Capital Requirements Regulation 2013, Articles 282, 292, 295–9, 300–10 on market risk factors pertaining to different trading instruments such as interest-rate based trading instruments, commodities, equities etc.

[182] Basel II.5, see Basel Committee, *Revisions to the Basel II Market Risk Framework* (July 2009) at http://www.bis.org/publ/bcbs158.pdf, p 14.

[183] Basel Committee, *Minimum Requirements for Market Risk* (January 2016) at http://www.bis.org/bcbs/publ/d352.pdf.

[184] Article 101, Directive 2013/36/EU of the European Parliament and of the Council of 26 June 2013 on access to the activity of credit institutions and the prudential supervision of credit institutions and investment firms, amending Directive 2002/87/EC and repealing Directives 2006/48/EC and 2006/49/EC.

object finance, higher-risk real estate, sovereign exposures etc but they need to be classified into different classes for specific risk treatment, in accordance with the loan characteristics prescribed. Further, internal models could be excluded from use in relation to certain asset classes such as financial institution exposures, exposures to certain large corporate and to equities.[185] The reason for this is that there may be a relative lack of historical default information with respect to these exposures to support the use of these models in providing estimates in relation to default. Only the standardised approach will be used to determine the risk-weightings of these exposures.

Regulators need to be robust in ensuring that internal models are based on banks' internal rating systems that are sound. The Basel Committee envisages that such rating systems must process customer-specific information as well as transaction-specific factors both of which affect the risk profile of the asset. The burden is on banks to convince regulators that their internal models are robust, that is, having good predictive power, information input and subject to appropriate human judgment and review. The use of internal models must be subject to robust risk systems and controls and senior management oversight. The European Banking Authority requires IRB models to be internally validated and sequentially implemented according to a roll-out plan that requires each stage of implementation to be subject to regulatory approval. [186] The enhanced scrutiny of the IRB model addresses the potential for banks to design such models in their favour and compromise compliance with capital adequacy requirements, as discussed earlier.

In relation to credit risk, previously banks using internal models are allowed to estimate the PD, EAD and LGD to different degrees depending on whether they are using foundation or advanced internal ratings-based models. The discretion to work out own estimates has been narrowed as banks may, subject to supervisory assessment, be required to use supervisory estimates instead for certain assets. Further, where banks' own estimates may be derived, they are required to do so in a conservative manner.

Further, regulators have also moved in to address the consistency of IRB models amongst banks, as well as compared to the application of standardised approaches. The robustness of IRB models is put to the test by industry-wide comparison exercises that regulators engage in. The Basel Committee advocates the use of 'hypothetical portfolio exercises' to detect where the variations in risk-weighting lie as a result of using IRB models, and the drivers for such variations.[187] Hypothetical portfolio exercises involve small samples of bank portfolios for comparative study in order to chart variations in approaches. These cannot be conclusive as they are small samples, but they would

---

[185] Basel Committee, *Finalising Post-crisis Reforms* (December 2017) at https://www.bis.org/bcbs/publ/d424.pdf, 59.

[186] EBA, *Final Draft Regulatory Technical Standards on the specification of the assessment methodology for competent authorities regarding compliance of an institution with the requirements to use the IRB Approach in accordance with Articles 144(2), 173(3) and 180(3)(b) of Regulation (EU) No 575/2013* (July 2016) at https://www.eba.europa.eu/documents/10180/1525916/Final+Draft+RTS+on+Assessment+Methodology+for+IRB.pdf/e8373cbc-cc4b-4dd9-83b5-93c9657a39f0.

[187] Basel Committee, *Reducing Excessive Variability in Banks' Regulatory Capital Ratios: A Report to the G20* (November 2014).

provide indicative directions for investigating into the nature and drivers of variations in risk-weighting methodologies.

In the EU, national regulators are required to collect information in order to assess whether and to what extent the applications of internal models by banks within their jurisdictions generate different risk-weighting results.[188] National regulators are to conduct yearly assessments and benchmarking exercises of banks' IRB approaches to credit risk and its internal models for market risk.[189] These assessments reach into extensive detail into banks' models in relation to their design, assumptions, use of comparative, industry-wide, and macroeconomic information and their robustness to stressed situations. Benchmarking is carried out in comparing the use of internal models with what risk-weighting results would be derived under standardised approaches. These findings are to be shared with the EBA. The EBA can also conduct benchmarking exercises for banks based on hypothetical portfolio exercises.[190]

Ultimately, both the Basel Committee[191] and European Banking Authority[192] have converged on a prescriptive means of reducing regulatory arbitrage in the application of internal models by banks. In order to achieve a certain level of consistency in applying internal models and to prevent banks from severely under-estimating risk-weightings, there would be 'floors' imposed on the results of using internal models so as to limit the room for deviation from the application of standardised approaches.[193] This addresses the problem discussed earlier in relation to empirical research findings that banks have used IRB approaches in the pre-crisis years to support less capital adequacy requirements for their risk-taking.

Reform has been recommended by the Basel Committee to make banks publicly disclose, and not just to regulators, the risk-weighting measures as derived from internal models, and the risk-weighting measures that would apply to the same assets if a standardised approach had been taken. An 'output floor' is set at a prescribed level of the risk-weighting derived from standardised approaches. If the risk-weighting derived from internal models exceeds this level, then the measure from internal models will apply. If the risk-weighting from internal models is below the output floor, then the output floor applies. The output floors are set and to be phased in as shown in Table 8.8.

---

[188] Article 78, CRD IV Directive 2013.

[189] Commission Delegated Regulation (EU) 2017/180 of 24 October 2016 supplementing Directive 2013/36/EU of the European Parliament and of the Council with regard to regulatory technical standards for benchmarking portfolio assessment standards and assessment-sharing procedures. Also see PRA Rulebook, *Benchmarking of Internal Approaches.*

[190] See, for example, EBA, *Counterparty Credit Risk (Internal Model Method and Credit Valuation Adjustment) Benchmarking Exercise* (2014).

[191] Basel Committee, *Consultative Document: Reducing Variation in Credit Risk-Weighted Assets—Constraints on the Use of Internal Model Approaches* (March 2016) at http://www.bis.org/bcbs/publ/d362.pdf; culminating in *Finalising Post-Crisis Reforms* (December 2017) at https://www.bis.org/bcbs/publ/d424.pdf.

[192] See, for example, EBA, *Guidelines on PD Estimation, LGD Estimation and Treatment of Defaulted Assets* (November 2017) at https://www.eba.europa.eu/regulation-and-policy/model-validation/guidelines-on-pd-lgd-estimation-and-treatment-of-defaulted-assets.

[193] Basel Committee, *Finalising Post-crisis Reforms* (2017) at https://www.bis.org/bcbs/publ/d424.pdf.

Table 8.8 Output floor calibration

Date	Output floor calibration
1 Jan 2022	50% (of risk-weighting as if standardised approaches apply)
1 Jan 2023	55%
1 Jan 2024	60%
1 Jan 2025	65%
1 Jan 2026	70%
1 Jan 2027	72.5%

8.5.9 Implementation in the UK and EU

The EU has adopted the Basel III Accord with alacrity. These have been implemented in the EU Capital Requirements Regulation 2013, which deals with the technical aspects of risk-weighting and computation, and the Capital Requirements Directive 2013, which provides for the standards that require national transposition. The UK has transposed these into national legislation.[194]

As discussed throughout this section, the UK and EU have introduced more stringent requirements in addition to the Basel III Accord, such as the institution-specific counter-cyclical buffer, the systemic risk buffer, and more comprehensive and prescriptive provisions. The more stringent micro-prudential regime embraced by the EU is related to EU policymakers' needs to preserve market confidence in the banking sectors of many member states during turbulent times of sovereign debt and domestic banking crises in the Baltic States (2008–10), Cyprus (2013), Greece (ongoing from 2010), Portugal (2014), Ireland (2012–13), and Spain (2014). member states in central and eastern Europe also risk being affected by the general lack of market confidence in European banks.[195] As many European banks hold significant amounts of sovereign debt issued by their government, and by the governments of other member states, fiscal and general economic weaknesses in these member states would affect the perception of European banks, making them look weak in the market. Hence, the regulatory capital reforms are intended to shore up market confidence in European banks in general.

The UK has transposed EU regulatory requirements into an overall framework of 'Internal Capital Adequacy Assessment' applied to banks.[196] The Assessment

---

[194] UK Capital Requirements (Capital Buffers and Macro-prudential Measures) Regulations 2014; PRA Rulebook, *Capital Buffers, Credit Risk* and *Market Risk*.

[195] See 'Crisis hits central and Eastern Europe', *Financial Times* (22 November 2011).

[196] PRA Rulebook, *Internal Capital Adequacy Assessment*.

framework evaluates all the risks dealt with by the Basel Committee and EU legislation, that is, credit, market, and operational risks, as well as risks that are identified in the Pillar 2A assessment. In sum, the Assessment framework encompasses the following risks:

(a) credit and counterparty risk;

(b) market risk;

(c) liquidity risk;

(d) operational risk;

(e) concentration risk;

(f) residual risk;

(g) securitisation risk, including the risk that the own funds held by a firm in respect of assets that it has securitised are inadequate having regard to the economic substance of the transaction including the degree of risk transfer achieved;

(h) business risk;

(i) interest rate risk in the non-trading book;

(j) risk of excessive leverage;

(k) pension obligation risk; and

(l) group risk.

The Internal Capital Adequacy Assessment requires firms to assess and maintain on an ongoing basis the compliance with capital adequacy standards and to ensure sound processes, systems, and governance exist in the firm for the purposes of achieving such compliance. Firms need to maintain records of identified risks and their risk management on an individual basis for each bank and on a consolidated basis for groups. The sources of their own funds and other tiers one and two capital must also be identified. These will feed into regulatory reporting as well as stress testing (Chapter 9).

The EU's and UK's MREL reforms also intend to ensure greater robustness of banks that need to be resolved. The MREL regime implements but exceeds international standards on the TLAC (further explored in Chapter 9, section 9.5).

The European Banking Authority plays the critical role of ensuring implementation consistency of capital adequacy standards so that the markets will be confident in bank implementation. The European Central Bank's Single Supervisory Mechanism for key euro-area banks, as discussed in Chapter 7 ensures that the capital strength of European banks is overseen by an independent regulator, thus severing any perceived unhealthy links between banks and weak member states.

The near failure of the Halifax Bank of Scotland[197] and the Royal Bank of Scotland[198] created adverse market perception for UK banks and it was thus necessary to ensure that capital adequacy reforms achieve the effect of enhancing the banks' resilience in the aftermath of the crisis. Although the UK has voted to leave EU membership, we do not see the UK as moving away from the capital adequacy reforms, that is, capital buffers and MREL reforms in light of its need to strengthen its banking sector.

Key takeaways

- The Basel III Capital Accord introduces additional capital buffers to enhance the low risk-asset ratio of Basel II.

- The EU and UK have largely transposed the Basel III Accord and imposed further capital buffers on banks.

- The quality of capital required to support the new regulatory capital regime has been improved, focusing on common equity tier one capital.

- G-SIBs and D-SIBs in particular have to meet enhanced regulatory capital requirements due to their systemic risk profile. These reforms, known as TLAC at the international level, have been adopted more universally by the EU, known as MREL.

- MREL ensures that banks hold adequate loss absorption and recapitalising capital instruments, of a wider range than those that support capital adequacy.

- The EU and UK regulatory bodies are continuing to address weaknesses in the capital adequacy regulatory regime, in the variations in risk-weighting methodologies adopted by banks and sub-optimalities in internal models used by banks.

Key bibliography

Legislation

Regulation (EU) No 575/2013 of the European Parliament and of the Council of 26 June 2013 on prudential requirements for credit institutions and investment firms and amending Regulation (EU) No 648/2012 (Capital Requirements Regulation 2013)

UK Capital Requirements (Capital Buffers and Macro-prudential Measures) Regulations 2014

Commission Delegated Regulation (EU) 2016/1450 of 23 May 2016 supplementing Directive 2014/59/EU of the European Parliament and of the Council with regard to regulatory technical standards specifying the criteria relating to the methodology for setting the minimum requirement for own funds and eligible liabilities.

Directive 2013/36/EU of the European Parliament and of the Council of 26 June 2013 on access to the activity of credit institutions and the prudential supervision of credit institutions and investment firms, amending Directive 2002/87/EC and repealing Directives 2006/48/EC and 2006/49/EC (Capital Requirements IV Directive 2013)

---

[197] House of Commons and House of Lords, Parliamentary Commission on Banking Standards, *An Accident Waiting to Happen: The Failure of HBOS* (4 April 2013).

[198] FSA Board, Report on The Failure of the Royal Bank of Scotland (December 2011)

Reports and recommendations

Bank of England, 'The Financial Policy Committee's Approach to Setting the Countercyclical Capital Buffer' (April 2016) at https://www.bankofengland.co.uk/-/media/boe/files/statement/2016/the-financial-policy-committees-approach-to-setting-the-countercyclical-capital-buffer.pdf

Basel Committee, *Finalising Post-crisis Reforms* (2017) at https://www.bis.org/bcbs/publ/d424.pdf

Basel Committee, *Reducing Excessive Variability in Banks' Regulatory Capital Ratios: A Report to the G20* (Nov 2014)

Basel Committee on Banking Supervision, *Basel III: A Global Regulatory Framework for More Resilient Banks and Banking Systems* (rev June 2011, Basel: BIS 2010) <http://www.bis.org/publ/bcbs189.pdf.

PRA, *The Bank of England's Approach to Setting A Minimum Requirement for Own Funds and Eligible Liabilities (MREL)* (November 2016) at http://www.bankofengland.co.uk/financialstability/Documents/resolution/mrelpolicy2016.pdf

PRA, *Refining the PRA's Pillar 2A Capital Framework* (Oct 2017) at https://www.bankofengland.co.uk/-

PRA, *The PRA's Methodologies for Setting Pillar 2 Capital* (Dec 2017) at https://www.bankofengland.co.uk/-/media/boe/files/prudential-regulation/statement-of-policy/2017/the-pras-methodologies-for-setting-pillar-2a-capital-december-2017.pdf

Books

Admati, A and Hellwig, M, *The Bankers' New Clothes: What's Wrong with Banking and What to Do about It* (NJ: Princeton University Press 2014)

Questions

1. 'International harmonisation in the standards of capital adequacy is a great achievement in banking regulation'. Do you agree?

    Answer tips You may wish to consider what capital adequacy standards are for and what harmonisation for international banks achieves. You could take into account the extent of harmonisation achieved under Basel I, Basel II, and Basel III, and seek to elucidate what each stage of harmonisation has done for the development of banking regulation.

2. Has Basel III addressed the weaknesses of earlier capital adequacy Accords?

    Answer tips You should consider in a balanced way what Basel I and II have achieved. Although Basel II was built upon critique of Basel I, Basel II may have swung too far to cater for banks' desire to introduce internal models which they thought were more precise in risk management. You need to consider what the weaknesses of Basel II are and in what respects have Basel III sought to address them. Further, Basel III does not address all the weaknesses of capital adequacy accords. You should explain why, perhaps referring to inter alia, the limitations of prescriptive risk-weighting. Risk-weighting depends heavily on external credit ratings and is not an exact science; risk-weightings in market and operational risk continue to be works in development. A balanced approach in evaluating these efforts in micro-prudential regulation is needed.

3. 'It is impossible to comply with the EU's and UK's additional burdens in capital adequacy regulation to the Basel III Accord. The EU and UK regulatory regimes are too onerous.' Do you agree?

> **Answer tips** *You should explain what the EU and UK have legislated beyond the Basel III Accord and what is the total picture of the regulatory compliance for banks. Do you think these are too onerous for banks, would these hamper banks' socially useful functions in creating credit and lending to the real economy? Is legislation a knee-jerk reaction to the financial crisis and therefore over-done?*

9

Micro-prudential regulation II

Other measures

9.1 Introduction to other measures of micro-prudential regulation

Capital adequacy, as discussed in Chapter 8, has been the dominant tool in the micro-prudential regulation of banks. However, after the 2007–9 global financial crisis, other micro-prudential measures have been developed internationally to support capital adequacy rules, as these rules are not able to capture certain aspects of bank risks. For example, capital adequacy rules do not deal with liquidity risk, that is, the risk that banks may not meet immediate demands (such as withdrawal of deposits) that fall due as their assets may not be realised in time, or can only be realised at a major loss. Liquidity pressures can force banks to suffer more impairment to their assets than necessary and could even result in bank insolvency. Hence, banks need to manage their liquidity needs and this area is now subject to international regulatory harmonisation. Different national regulators may already have in place liquidity rules but these were largely unharmonised at the international level prior to the global financial crisis. The Basel Committee now recommends convergent and high standards for bank liquidity management to be applied to all banks across the globe.

Besides liquidity management rules, this chapter will discuss other measures of micro-prudential regulation developed or enhanced after the crisis. One is the leverage ratio, which sets an absolute amount of lending banks can engage in, regardless of risk-weighting. Large exposures regulation in the EU, which has existed prior to the crisis, deals with controlling the over-concentration by banks in lending to certain customers. This area is also reformed after the 2007–9 global financial crisis.

Although in Chapter 8 we discussed how capital adequacy rules have evolved for all banks, we have already indicated special treatment of systemically important financial institutions. In this chapter, we will devote a section to systemically important financial institutions that are global banks with such an international footprint that their vulnerabilities may threaten financial systems and economies more acutely than other banks. The regulatory needs for such institutions are increasingly regarded as special and therefore entailing an increasingly distinct regime in micro-prudential regulation from that applicable to other banks.

Finally, we address an important new aspect of micro-prudential regulation that is 'supervisory' in nature. Micro-prudential regulation comprises a body of rather technical standards that banks have to comply with, but such compliance is only meaningful if it is regularly monitored by the regulator. As Chapter 8 has discussed, the regulatory role in Pillar 2, which has been lacklustre and inadequate prior to the global financial crisis of 2007–9, is now enhanced after the crisis, in particular by the use of the 'stress testing' tool that feeds into regulatory reporting and supervision. A Section is devoted to discussing the frameworks for stress testing.

9.2 **Liquidity ratios**

As the Basel Committee has explained:

> During the early ... phase of the financial crisis, many banks – despite adequate capital levels – still experienced difficulties because they did not manage their liquidity in a prudent manner. The crisis again drove home the importance of liquidity to the proper functioning of financial markets and the banking sector. Prior to the crisis, asset markets were buoyant and funding was readily available at low cost. The rapid reversal in market conditions illustrated how quickly liquidity can evaporate and that illiquidity can last for an extended period of time. The banking system came under severe stress, which necessitated central bank action to support both the functioning of money markets and, in some cases, individual institutions.[1]

This statement highlights the importance of liquidity management to banks. Liquid markets ensure that banks can sell assets when cash realisation is needed to pay on banks' liabilities, for example, to depositors when they make withdrawal demands. However, liquid conditions cannot always be assumed, as market activities can plummet to very low levels in stressed times. In these times, banks may not be able to sell assets quickly enough or at an optimal value in order to realise cash to meet immediate demands. Banks need to manage their liquidity needs prudently in order to ride out challenges in market conditions.

The Basel Committee has now introduced two liquidity standards for banks as internationally harmonising measures.[2] One is the liquidity coverage ratio, which refers to immediate term liquidity management by banks to meet present demands. The compliance with the liquidity coverage ratio is intended to be a prudent measure to ensure that banks have sufficient liquid assets to meet immediate demands for the next 30 days. The second is the Net Stable Funding Ratio (NSFR), which deals with the longer-term

---

[1] Basel Committee, *Basel III: A Global Regulatory Framework for More Resilient Banks and Banking Systems* (December 2010, rev June 2011) para 34, at http://www.bis.org/publ/bcbs189.pdf.

[2] Basel Committee, *Principles for Sound Liquidity Risk Management and Supervision—Final Document* (September 2008) at http://www.bis.org/publ/bcbs144.htm superseded by *Basel III: The Liquidity Coverage Ratio and Liquidity Risk Monitoring Tools* (January 2013) at http://www.bis.org/publ/bcbs238.pdf and *Basel III; The Net Stable Funding Ratio* (October 2014) at http://www.bis.org/bcbs/publ/d295.pdf.

liquidity profile for bank assets, requiring banks to ensure that they have different assets and types of funding sources to call upon in order to meet their liabilities over the longer term of one year. These have been accepted in the EU[3] and apply to the UK.

9.2.1 Liquidity coverage ratio

The introduction of the liquidity coverage ratio (LCR) is to ensure that a bank has an adequate stock of sufficiently liquid assets in order to meet short-term pressures and demands in the next 30 days. An adequate stock of sufficiently liquid assets refers to cash or assets that can be converted into cash quickly, and at no or little loss of value in the markets. Such assets are known as 'high-quality liquid assets' that would help banks meet immediate demands such as deposit withdrawals and other borrowing liabilities of the bank. High-quality liquid assets also need to be unencumbered, that is, that there are no further claims on them that diminish their value or reliability.

The LCR is intended to ensure that banks can meet their outflows within a 30-day period. Banks need to ensure that their total stock of high-quality liquid assets exceed their total net cash outflows over a 30-day period, therefore maintaining a ratio exceeding 100 per cent.

The EU defines 'high quality liquid assets' as the 'liquidity buffer'.[4] Box 9.1 illustrates how the LCR works.

The LCR is implemented in the EU via the binding Capital Requirements 'IV' Regulation 2013.[5] This is directly binding upon the UK, but would have to be separately provided for in UK legislation when the UK leaves EU membership.[6] The Basel Committee has prescribed the standards applicable for maintaining the LCR, which are largely transposed in an EU Commission Delegated Regulation.[7]

9.2.1.1 High-quality liquid assets

High-quality liquid assets are defined as assets of a low risk profile, with relatively stable market valuation, and easily realisable in an active and sizable market such as a

---

Box 9.1

$$\text{LCR (100)\%} \geq \frac{\text{High quality liquid assets ('liquidity buffer')}}{\text{total net cash outflows for next 30 days}}$$

---

[3] Articles 412–14, Capital Requirements IV Regulation 2013.

[4] Article 6, Commission Delegated Regulation (EU) 2015/61 of 10 October 2014 to supplement Regulation (EU) No 575/2013 of the European Parliament and the Council with regard to liquidity coverage requirement for Credit Institutions (Commission Delegated Regulation 2015).

[5] Article 412.

[6] Note that the PRA Rulebook refers to provisions in the Commission Delegated Regulation of 2015 in relation to the LCR, see Commission Delegated Regulation 2015.

[7] Commission Delegated Regulation 2015.

recognised securities exchange. They should not suffer from excessive volatility in price and should not be correlated with risky assets.

The Basel Committee prescribes a list of three categories of high-quality liquid assets: Level 1 and Level 2, which consists of subsets Levels 2A and 2B. A bank can use Level 1 assets to support the LCR to any amount, but Level 2 assets are limited to 40 per cent overall in their use to support the LCR. There is also a cap of 15 per cent to which Level 2B assets can be used to support the LCR. This is because Level 2 assets are regarded as slightly poorer in liquidity characteristics than Level 1 assets.[8] Level 1 assets are treated at face value, while Level 2 assets are subject to 'haircuts', which means a discount at face value is applied, in order to reflect the possibility of market price decline due to their slightly poorer liquidity quality. Level 2A assets are applied with a 15 per cent haircut, while Level 2B assets are applied at steeper haircuts, from 25 to 50 per cent.

As Level 1 assets are usually 'as good as cash', it would be impracticable to expect banks to hold excessive amounts of Level 1 assets. Such constraints would restrict banks' ability to carry out essential financial intermediation for economic needs, which involve making illiquid loans. Hence the LCR has to be calibrated to take into account the balance between the needs for liquidity risk management and allowing banks to carry on economically useful functions.

Table 9.1 Level 1 assets

- Coins and banknotes.
- Exposures to the European Central Bank (ECB), member state central banks, or other central banks rated at 0 per cent risk.
- Central banks reserves (in the jurisdictions referred to above).
- Zero per cent risk-weighted securities issued or guaranteed by sovereigns referred to above, or borrowing by their regional governments or public sector entities that can be treated as exposures to the sovereign.
- Zero per cent risk-weighted securities issued by the Bank for International Settlements (BIS), the International Monetary Fund (IMF) and other multilateral development banks
- EU only: assets issued by credit institutions that are state-owned in a member state, or a 'promotional lender' promoting public policy objectives at the EU level or in member states enjoying at least a 90 per cent guarantee on its loans by Member state governments.
- EU only: high-quality covered bonds that banks invest in that are given a 10 per cent risk weight but subject to a 7 per cent haircut.

  The above are to be traded in large and deep markets, have a proven track record as a reliable source of liquidity, and do not represent an obligation on the part of a financial institution.

- Banks' investments in collective investment undertakings that invests in equivalent liquid assets can be counted as Level 1 assets subject to haircuts (5–12 per cent for extremely high-quality covered bonds)

---

[8] Transposed in Article 17, Commission Delegated Regulation 2015.

Tables 9.1–9.3 provide key highlights of the lists of Level 1,[9] 2A,[10] and 2B[11] assets. We see that highly liquid assets are also assumed to be of low credit risk. Such an assumption is not likely mistaken but the needs of the LCR and capital adequacy as a whole compel banks to seek 'safe' assets, which may distort their lending behaviour. This point will be further elaborated.

The EU has expanded on the Basel Committee's list of acceptable assets at all levels, as indicated in the boxes above, providing special treatment for member state central banks and sovereigns, and admits of a wider range of assets than that recommended by the Basel Committee. This may be in response to the needs of member state banks in terms of what is already on their balance sheets.

9.2.1.2 Total net cash outflows

The term total net cash outflows is defined as the total expected cash outflows minus total expected cash inflows in the next 30 calendar days. These are set against the context of stressful scenarios, which will be discussed shortly.

Total expected cash outflows are calculated by multiplying the outstanding balances of various types of liabilities and off-balance sheet commitments by the rates at which they are expected to run-off or be drawn down (see Box 9.2). Total expected cash inflows are calculated by multiplying the outstanding balances of various categories of contractual receivables by the rates at which they are expected to flow in, but capping at 75 per cent of total expected cash outflows, in order to provide a prudent estimate of inflows.

Table 9.2 Level 2A assets

---

15 % haircut applied to all of the following

- A 20 per cent risk-weighted securities issued by central banks, member state governments, regional authorities or public sector entities, or the equivalent in other countries.

- Covered bonds risk-weighted at 20 per cent and part of a €250 million issue at least.

- Covered bonds issued by financial institutions risk-weighted at 10 per cent, both categories of covered bonds to be supported by collateral values of at least 7 per cent in excess of the value of the claims.

- Corporate debt securities that are not issued by financial institutions, and risk-weighted at 20 per cent, part of a €250 million issue at least and with at least a 10-year maturity.

These are to be traded in large and deep markets, have a proven track record as a reliable source of liquidity, and not represent an obligation on the part of a financial institution (see exception for covered bonds above).

- Banks' investments in collective investment undertakings with highly liquid assets can also count as Level 2A subject to a higher haircut (20 per cent).

---

[9] Largely transposed by Articles 7 and 10, Commission Delegated Regulation 2015.
[10] Articles 11 and 15, Commission Delegated Regulation 2015.
[11] Articles 12, 13, 15, and 16, Commission Delegated Regulation 2015.

Table 9.3 Level 2B assets

25–50% haircut applied to the following

- Asset backed securities risk-weighted at 20 per cent or better, that are based on good loan assets not re-securitised or synthetic in nature. These should be in senior tranches, representing the best loan quality in underlying assets, be part of an issue size of at least €100 million, and have at least 5 years to maturity. A 25 per cent haircut is applied where the underlying assets are good residential mortgages and a 35 per cent haircut is applied for other loans such as commercial leases and auto loans.

- Corporate debt securities that are risk-weighted at 100 per cent or better in an issue size of at least 250 million and have at least 10 years in maturity (50 per cent haircut applied),

- Corporate equity securities not issued by a financial institution that are exchange-traded and centrally cleared, denominated in the currency of the bank's home jurisdiction, forms part of a major stock exchange index (50 per cent haircut applied),

- Restricted use and committed liquidity facilities from the ECB or central bank in member state,

- Covered bonds that are risk-weighted at 35 per cent or better, in an issue size at least €250 million and to be supported by collateral values of at least 10 per cent in excess of the value of the claims. (haircut of 30 per cent applied).

- Deposits in institutional protection schemes that banks have access to within 30 days (subject to a 25 per cent haircut).

Tradeable assets must be traded in large and deep markets and have a proven track record as a reliable source of liquidity.

> **Box 9.2**
>
> Total net cash outflows over the next 30 calendar days = Total expected cash outflows − (75 per cent of total expected cash inflows)

Expected cash outflows in a stressed scenario include: deposit outflows, secured whole-sale borrowing by the bank where collateral value has diminished and the bank is required to 'top up', funds held by central counterparties or settlement and clearing agents, drawdowns on agreed lending facilities, and other contractual and contingent liabilities. However, some outflows are more likely severe than others and hence they are assigned different rates of 'stability' that will be applied to work out the expected outflow figure. This area is highly technical and has been extensively covered in the EU Commission Delegated Regulation 2015.[12] A couple of examples will be provided in Box 9.3 to illustrate how the different rates of 'stability' work.

---

[12] Articles 22–31, Commission Delegated Regulation 2015.

Box 9.3 Application of different rates of stability to different outflows

Deposits

A key expected outflow in stressed times would be deposits. However different deposits are susceptible to different probabilities of 'flight'. Deposits that are regular salary pay-ins, and protected by a well-established deposit guarantee scheme in a jurisdiction may be regarded as more 'stable' (rated at 3 per cent likelihood of outflow by the Basel Committee but at 5 per cent by the EU Commission Delegated Regulation 2015), compared to deposits not fully covered by a deposit guarantee scheme or denominated in foreign currency (rated at 10 per cent likelihood of outflow).[13]

Draw-down of agreed loan amounts

Another example is, where banks have committed to lend and draw-down by the borrower has yet to occur, some borrowers are likelier than others to draw-down to greater extents. Small businesses and retail customers are regarded as less likely to draw-down fully in stressed situations as they would likely refrain from increasing their borrowing in troubled times (rated at 5 per cent likelihood of outflow). Lending to other financial institutions or structured investment vehicles would likely attract a rapid draw-down (rated at 40-100 per cent of the likelihood of outflow).

The calculation of total expected outflows makes assumptions about different types of behaviour on the part of different bank counterparties, and these assumptions are yet untested. It is therefore to be noted that the maintenance of an LCR does not necessarily guarantee that banks will prevent liquidity crises.

Expected cash inflows include loan interest payments from borrowers, collateral that can be realised from wholesale market lending (subject to a relevant haircut according to collateral quality), business and retail customer inflows and other wholesale inflows. The likelihood of inflows is also rated according to the type of inflow. For example, wholesale inflows committed by financial institutions or central counterparties are rated at 100 per cent, that is, they are regarded as highly certain, while retail and business inflows during a bank's stressed scenario are rated at 50 per cent, representing the uncertainty that consumer trust will be maintained. The EU Commission Delegated Regulation 2015 prescribes in detail different types of inflows and their rates of certainty.[14] The total inflows are however capped at 75 per cent to represent a conservative estimate.[15]

Although the LCR is a ratio maintained for a forward-looking period of 30 days, the PRA has adopted a more conservative supervisory approach. The PRA will monitor for supervisory benchmark purposes inflow and outflow rates of supervised financial

---

[13] For example, see Articles 24 and 25, Commission Delegated Regulation 2015.
[14] Articles 32 and 34, Commission Delegated Regulation 2015.
[15] Article 33, Commission Delegated Regulation 2015.

institutions over a period of 90 days.[16] The PRA does not require the LCR to be maintained over 90 days but it may be regarded as prudent to take a slightly longer view over
30 days in order to assess the resilience of a bank's liquidity position.

9.2.1.3 Maintenance of LCR under stressed conditions

The LCR is expected to be maintained at or above 100 per cent during normal times.
When the LCR was first proposed in 2008, the maintenance of the LCR at 100 per cent
was regarded to be a severe requirement for banks to meet as they were recovering
after the global financial crisis. Hence the Basel Committee adjusted its expectations of
adherence to the LCR, recommending a gradual increase in banks' obligations to maintain the LCR. Banks are expected to maintain a 60 per cent LCR as of January 2015,
increasing by 10 per cent every year until a 100 per cent is reached on 1st January 2019.
The EU Commission Delegated Regulation 2015 expects the LCR to be maintained at
60 per cent as of 1 October 2015, but increasing up to 100 per cent by 1 January 2018.[17]
Deviating from the Basel Committee's and the EU's timeline for the implementation of
the LCR, the PRA requires banks to meet 80 per cent LCR by January 2015, 90 per cent
by January 2017 and 100 per cent by January 2018, a year ahead of the Basel Committee's
slightly more generous timeline, but consistent with the EU's position.

Although a generous timeframe has been provided to allow banks to comply with
the LCR, the Basel Committee's regular surveys of international banks across different jurisdictions shows that on average most developed and emerging countries' banks
maintain LCR at exceeding 100 per cent.[18]

Where stressed conditions occur, such stressed conditions as will be defined here,
the Basel Committee and national regulators expect banks to use their high-quality
liquid assets to meet the demands of outflows. As such, depletion pressures would force
banks to be likely unable to maintain the 100 per cent LCR. The PRA agrees that falling below the LCR in stressed conditions is normal but supervisors need to keep the
situation under review in terms of flexibly adjusting to what can be expected of banks
to comply with, while dealing with the challenge of recovering towards normality. The
PRA expects that banks should have a reasonable amount of time to recover.[19]

Stressed conditions are defined in the following list,[20] they refer to a non-exhaustive
but key list of events that would trigger the outflows already described:

(a) the run-off of a proportion of retail deposits;

(b) a partial loss of the bank's ability to borrow in unsecured wholesale markets;

---

[16] PRA, *Statement of Policy: Pillar 2 Liquidity* (February 2018) at https://www.bankofengland.co.uk/-/me-
dia/boe/files/prudential-regulation/statement-of-policy/2018/pillar-2-liquidity-sop.pdf?la=en&hash=296346
6309B077C9E5FFD64EC4BBAABE26699FD7.

[17] Article 38, Commission Delegated Regulation 2015.

[18] See, for example, the March 2016 survey at http://www.bis.org/bcbs/publ/d354.htm.

[19] PRA, *The PRA's Approach to Supervising Liquidity and Funding Risks* (February 2018) at https://www.
bankofengland.co.uk/-/media/boe/files/prudential-regulation/supervisory-statement/2018/ss2415update.pdf
?la=en&hash=930A502E9DC04EB0BDD6A0A2405C05A846946EEB.

[20] Also see Article 5, Commission Delegated Regulation 2015.

(c) a partial loss of the bank's ability to borrow in secured, short-term financing markets;

(d) additional contractual outflows that would arise from a downgrade in the bank's public credit rating by up to and including three notches;

(e) increases in market volatilities that impact the quality of collateral provided by the bank in its borrowing or other liquidity needs;

(f) unscheduled draws on committed but unused' credit and liquidity facilities that the bank has provided to its clients; and

(g) the potential need for the bank to buy back debt or honour non-contractual obligations in the interest of mitigating reputational risk.

It is to be noted that stressed conditions are framed as relating to individual banks. However, as we have observed from the events leading up to the 2007–9 global financial crisis, liquidity challenges can also be systemic, such as the 2007 'credit crunch'. The 'credit crunch' in 2007 refers to a period of lack of availability of wholesale funding, such that banks have found it much more difficult or expensive to borrow from wholesale institutions (financial institutions, investment funds, money market funds etc) by posting collateral.

Prior to the global financial crisis of 2007–9, many banks had been using securitised assets ('toxic assets', discussed in Chapter 1) as collateral to borrow in wholesale markets, so when the quality of these assets became questionable after underlying subprime mortgage loans in the US were defaulted upon in huge numbers, wholesale market lending seized up due to distrust and lack of confidence in the quality of collateral. The credit crunch affected many banks that relied heavily on wholesale market funding, one example of which was Northern Rock, whose failure, discussed in Chapters 1 and 13, could be traced to the severe liquidity reduction in wholesale markets.

If a widespread systemic liquidity condition such as the credit crunch of 2007 occurs, it remains uncertain whether the LCR and its underlying assumptions of asset quality, outflows and inflows would be reliable and robust enough to safeguard banks. It would be somewhat dangerous to have a false sense of security based on regulatory compliance alone. Empirical researchers have found that in relatively stable times, the maintenance of the LCR does indeed lull banks into a false sense of security and has heightened risk-taking behaviour in those banks.[21]

9.2.1.4 Critically reflecting on the LCR

Further, it has been commented[22] that the LCR may encourage banks to hold excessively safe and liquid assets in order to meet regulatory compliance needs. Safe and

---

[21] Muhammad Saifuddin Khan, Harald Schuele and Eliza Wu, 'The Impact of Bank Liquidity on Bank Risk Taking: Do High Capital Buffers and Big Banks Help or Hinder?' (2015) at http://papers.ssrn.com/sol3/papers.cfm?abstract_id=2481887.

[22] Andrew W Hartlage, 'The Basel III Liquidity Coverage Ratio and Financial Stability' (2012) 111 *Michigan Law Review* 453.

liquid assets both satisfy low risk-weightings for capital adequacy and compliance with the LCR. The requirements of capital adequacy and LCR reinforce each other, creating narrow categories of assets that banks would invest in, potentially neglecting other economic needs. For example, banks could concentrate on holding government securities that are highly rated, therefore distorting the fiscal policies of some borrower countries, or banks could be less willing to lend very long-term to businesses and commercial enterprises, affecting real economic needs. There is thus a need to consider the interactions of various micro-prudential regulatory tools and their side effects.

Finally, the measurement of liquidity risk according to the LCR's high-quality liquidity assets is based on certain assumptions that affect its accuracy. The classification of assets assigned by the Basel Committee and EU is based on the predictability of market characteristics including demand for high-quality liquid assets. Although the market characteristics can be based on historical information and observation, it is also queried whether those assumptions will hold when market and economic conditions change.

The above-mentioned criticisms may be mitigated by the regulator's discretion in giving individual banks guidance on the quality of high-quality liquid assets they hold, the diversity of their portfolio and other qualitative matters. The PRA provides 'Individual Liquidity Guidance'[23] to individual banks. This allows banks to ensure that their liquidity profile is sound while perhaps avoiding a mechanistic approach to complying with liquidity requirements.

9.2.2 Net stable funding ratio

The NSFR[24] requires banks to maintain a stable funding profile, that is, a balance of liabilities of different maturity or materialisation profiles, over a longer term, that is, one year. This would ensure that a bank is not exposed to too many liabilities that it has to meet at short notice. Further, in maintaining the NSFR, banks would not rely excessively on sources of short-term funding. In the pre-crisis era, banks have been increasingly relying on short-term funding in the wholesale markets, financed by collateral, as funding via traditional channels such as deposits is too limited to enable banks to meet their increasing business needs in credit creation and financial intermediation. However, during the 'credit crunch' (discussed earlier), banks that have been excessively reliant on such avenues of funding suffered severely, such as in the case of British bank Northern Rock, as these sources of funding quickly evaporated under conditions of market stress. Hence, a sustainable funding structure for banks will mitigate stresses caused by disruptions to a bank's regular sources of funding and the demands placed on banks as short-term liabilities materialise.

---

[23] PRA, *The PRA's Approach to Supervising Liquidity and Funding Risks* (February 2018) at https://www.bankofengland.co.uk/-/media/boe/files/prudential-regulation/supervisory-statement/2018/ss2415update.pdf?la=en&hash=930A502E9DC04EB0BDD6A0A2405C05A846946EEB.

[24] Basel Committee, *Basel III- The Net Stable Funding Ratio* (October 2014) at http://www.bis.org/bcbs/publ/d295.pdf.

Box 9.4

$$\text{NSFR (100)\%} \geq \frac{\text{Available amount of stable funding}}{\text{Required amount of stable funding}}$$

In sum, the NSFR requires banks to finance themselves using a diverse range of short and long-term funding options, and banks need to maintain the NSFR according to Box 9.4. Banks should maintain a ratio of **available stable funding** over **required stable funding** of over 100 per cent.

The EU has accepted the NSFR in the Capital Requirements IV Regulation 2013.[25] However, there are concerns that the NSFR could have adverse impact upon banks' credit creation for real economy needs, and the NSFR has thus not been implemented immediately. The European Banking Authority (EBA), however, supports the NSFR and calls for EU implementation to be aligned with the Basel Committee recommendations. After some consideration, the EU will finally introduce a binding NSFR for all member states. [26] This is expected to be in line with the Basel Committee's provisions discussed below.

9.2.2.1 Available stable funding

Stable funding refers to funding options that are relatively longer-term and therefore likely to remain available to the bank. Stability is dependent not just on maturity (i.e. when the liability to repay materialises) but on the nature of the source of funding and counterparty.

First, banks' 'available stable funding' (ASF) has to be taken stock of. This means that all sources of banks' funding are examined, and each source of funding is assigned a stability factor, as prescribed by the Basel Committee. The Basel Committee regards funding sources that are of a year's maturity or more as most 'stable', and hence all tier one capital instruments, other capital instruments and secured and unsecured borrowing over a year's maturity are regarded as 'stable' as they cannot be called upon within a year. Deposits are however regarded as more flighty, although certain fixed deposits over a year can be regarded as relatively 'stable'.

Table 9.4 sets out the prescribed stability factors assigned by the Basel Committee to banks' available sources of funding, ranging from 100 per cent stability to 0 per cent stability (meaning that such funding could immediately be withdrawn from the bank).

The NSFR emphasises the importance of tier one capital, which, consistent with Basel III, compels banks to ensure that they are adequately capitalised with good quality

---

[25] Article 414.

[26] Recommended in Commission Proposal to amend the CRD IV Regulation 2013, as of 26 Nov 2016, see http://ec.europa.eu/finance/bank/docs/regcapital/crr-crd-review/161123-proposal-amending-regulation_en.pdf.

Table 9.4 Summary of liability categories and associated ASF factors

ASF factor	Components of ASF category
100%	• Total regulatory capital (excluding Tier 2 instruments with residual maturity of less than 1 year)
	• Other capital instruments and liabilities with effective residual maturity of 1 year or more
95%	• Stable non-maturity (demand) deposits and term deposits with residual maturity of less than 1 year provided by retail and small business customers
90%	• Less stable non-maturity deposits and term deposits with residual maturity of less than 1 year provided by retail and small business customers
50%	• Funding with residual maturity of less than 1 year provided by non-financial corporate customers
	• Operational deposits
	• Funding with residual maturity of less than 1 year from sovereigns, public sector bodies, and multilateral and national development banks
	• Other funding with residual maturity between 6 months and less than 1 year not included in the above categories, including funding provided by central banks and financial institutions
0%	• All other liabilities and equity not included in the above categories, including liabilities without a stated maturity
	• Trade date' payables arising from purchases of financial instruments, foreign currencies and commodities

capital that can absorb the risks of banks' lending and investment activities. However, it would be expensive for banks to secure funding with longer maturities and greater 'stability' to the bank, such as paying higher interest rates for fixed deposits by retail customers of over a year.

9.2.2.2 Required stable funding

Required stable funding (RSF) refers to the needs of the bank to be able to meet its lending commitments. For example, a secured loan given to a customer by the bank over a year is required to be supported by a source of stable funding for the bank over that year. The Basel Committee prescribes for each type of bank asset, its RSF factor, based on the characteristics of the asset such as encumbrances and inherent liquidity. Regulators are to work out the RSF of a bank depending on the profile of its assets.

In sum, banks must ensure that ASF exceeds its RSF. This means that banks need to have a diverse range of funding sources to fund different types of lending the bank has committed to, in a manner not likely to be disrupted. Table 9.5 sets out the Basel Committee's prescribed application of RSF factors to the different assets that banks hold.

To explain Table 9.5, let us consider a few examples.

The Basel Committee assigns a 0 per cent 'RSF factor' to coins, banknotes or central bank reserves held by a bank as these are not commitments that the bank needs to meet, and indeed can be readily realised to support the banks' needs. Hence, they are assigned at 0 per cent because they do *not* require the bank to provision for funding them.

Table 9.5 Summary of asset categories and associated RSF factors

RSF factor	Components of RSF category
0%	• Coins and banknotes • All central bank reserves • All claims on central banks with residual maturities of less than 6months • Trade date' receivables arising from sales of financial instruments, foreign currencies and commodities.
5%	• Unencumbered Level 1 HQLA assets (see section 9.2.1), excluding coins, banknotes, and central bank reserves
10%	• Unencumbered loans to financial institutions with residual maturities of less than 6 months, where the loan is secured against HQLA Level 1 assets and where the bank has the ability to freely rehypothecate* the received collateral for the life of the loan
15%	• All other unencumbered loans to financial institutions with residual maturities of less than 6 months not included in the above categories • Unencumbered HQLA Level 2A assets (see section 9.2.1)
50%	• Unencumbered HQLA Level 2B assets (see section 9.2.1) • All HQLA assets encumbered for a period of 6 months or more and less than 1 year • Loans to financial institutions and central banks with residual maturities between 6 months and less than 1 year • Deposits held at other financial institutions for operational purposes • All other assets not included in the above categories with residual maturity of less than 1 year, including loans to non-financial corporate clients, loans to retail and small business customers, and loans to sovereigns and public sector bodies
65%	• Unencumbered residential mortgages with a residual maturity of 1 year or more and with a risk weight of less than or equal to 35% under the Standardised Approach (see Chapter 8, sections 8.4 and 8.5) • Other unencumbered loans not included in the above categories, excluding loans to financial institutions, with a residual maturity of 1 year or more and with a risk weight of less than or equal to 35% under the standardised approach

RSF factor	Components of RSF category
85%	• Cash, securities, or other assets posted as initial margin** for derivative contracts and cash or other assets provided to contribute to the default fund of a central counterparty
	• Other unencumbered performing loans with risk-weights greater than 35% under the standardised approach and residual maturities of 1 year or more, excluding loans to financial institutions
	• Unencumbered securities that are not in default and do not qualify as HQLA with a remaining maturity of 1 year or more and exchange-traded equities
	• Physical traded commodities, including gold
100%	• All assets that are encumbered for a period of 1 year or more
	• All other assets not included in the above categories, including non-performing loans,*** loans to financial institutions with a residual maturity of 1 year or more, non-exchange-traded**** equities, fixed assets, items deducted from regulatory capital, retained interest, insurance assets, subsidiary interests, and defaulted securities
	* **rehypothecate** means to re-use as collateral in further borrowing by the bank ** **margin** means an initial cash amount that is held in 'deposit' before trading in derivatives contracts can commence *** **non-performing loans** are loans whose repayment has stalled in relation to principal and/or interest for 90 days **** **exchange-traded** means financial instruments that are tradeable on an open market for financial instruments such as a listed market for corporate securities

Short-term secured lending to financial institutions of maturities less than 6 months is also assigned a relatively low RSF factor in the region of 5 to 10 per cent. These demands expire quickly, and do not exert too much demand on the bank to meet them. In contrast riskier long-term loans such as risk-weighted at 35 per cent or more (e.g. residential mortgages) make greater demands on banks to ensure that banks are adequately funded to meet their lending commitments. Hence these assets are assigned an 85 per cent RSF factor.

The RSF factors are prescribed with greater precision than ASF factors as they intend to capture as comprehensively as possible the nature of banks assets, in order to ascertain what demands they place upon banks. However, a pitfall in this approach is that where bank lending has non-standard characteristics, their RSF may not be accurately reflected in the prescriptions above.

In sum, we see that to maintain the NSFR, banks need to work out their RSF according to the profiles of their assets. Banks then match the RSF with their ASF, which, as discussed above, is worked out by assigning stability factors to banks' existing liabilities. Banks need to ensure that there is more ASF than RSF, that is, the ratio of ASF over RSF must exceed 100 per cent.

9.2.2.3 Critically reflecting on the NSFR

To summarise our critical reflections on the NSFR, we can see that a number of the Basel Committee's assumptions need to be sound. First, as mentioned earlier, the assumptions underlying the measurement of stability in the ASF are dependent on counterparty behaviour, and it remains to be seen if these are as predicted under different market conditions. Next, the assumptions underlying the measurement of stability in the RSF are dependent on the nature of assets and interpretation of standardised terms in loan contracts. Non-standard contracts may raise issues for applying the assumptions. The assumptions of 'stability' would need to be reviewed if new jurisprudence emerges to determine the nature of contractual rights in relation to certain assets, and what demands such rights, as interpreted, would exert on a bank's RSF.

For example, in the *LBG v BNY Mellon* case,[27] Lloyds Banking Group (LBG) issued contingent convertible bonds in 2009 to investors paying an interest rate of 10.33 per cent APR. These bonds were to be converted into equity if LBG's tier one capital ratio fell below 5 per cent. The redemption periods were set as 2019–32 on the bonds. On the face of it, this seemed to be a long-term source of funding for the bank. However, as the minimum level of tier one capital was increased to 6 per cent by the Basel Committee in 2015, LBG wished to redeem the bonds early in order to avoid the high expenses of interest payments on instruments that would now only serve their purposes in a limited manner. The bondholders challenged the redemption but failed. The Court of Appeal and Supreme Court interpreted the contractual arrangement as being no longer useful for its intended regulatory compliance purposes, and hence allowed LBG to redeem them. Although this is a case where LBG would benefit from terminating this source of funding, and hence this case is not one that illustrates funding difficulties for the bank, this case nevertheless shows that the durability of a source of funding is subject to *ex post* contractual interpretation in the courts, and hence making excessive assumptions on an *ex ante* basis regarding the 'stability' of any source of funding can be misplaced.

Despite our concerns above, the Basel Committee has been receiving reassuring signs of NSFR compliance from global banks. The Basel Committee has been monitoring global banks' adherence to NSFR, and reports that most global banks meet the NSFR in excess, of up to 10 per cent above the required NSFR.[28]

9.2.3 Implementation in the UK and EU

The EU has introduced the LCR and NSFR by way of a direct regulation binding on all member states without further national transposition.[29] The LCR has been

---

[27] [2015] EWCA Civ 1257, upheld on appeal to the Supreme Court, [2016] UKSC 29.

[28] See, for example, *Basel Committee Monitoring Report 2016* (2016) at http://www.bis.org/bcbs/publ/d354.htm.

[29] Articles 412, 413, Regulation (EU) No 575/2013 of the European Parliament and of the Council of 26 June 2013 on prudential requirements for credit institutions and investment firms and amending Regulation (EU) No 648/2012.

implemented in the EU via a Commission Regulation (Level Two legislation, see Chapter 7, section 7.2) in 2015 but the NSFR has been left to further deliberation. The EU has now proposed a 'banking reform package' in late 2016[30] to implement the NSFR by legislative amendment to the Capital Requirements IV Regulation in order to make it binding.[31]

The UK PRA has absorbed the relevant EU legislation in its 'overall liquidity adequacy rule', which refers to the EU legislation,[32] and extends the LCR to designated investment firms too.[33] This is because the UK has always imposed its own national liquidity rules before harmonisation at the Basel Committee and European levels. Hence the framework for evaluating 'liquidity adequacy' continues to be maintained by the PRA.

In general, banks need to implement an Internal Liquidity Adequacy Assessment Programme (ILAAP) to be reviewed on a yearly basis.[34] This programme consists of several aspects. First, banks have to ensure that they are able to monitor their intraday liquidity positions to ensure that day to day matters such as settlement risk (the risk that transactions they enter into may not be settled due to counterparty default or problems with the settlement system) and collateral risk (the risk that collateral given to or by the bank may suffer a deterioration in value) would be mitigated.[35] Next, banks have to make reporting to the PRA on a regular basis in order for regulators to evaluate the liquidity risk profiles of banks to determine if any remedial or pre-emptive actions need to be taken.[36] The LCR is to be reported monthly, with the option of regulators demanding more frequent reporting if stressed situations occur for a bank. The NSFR has not yet been implemented at the EU level and has also not been implemented in the UK. It is anticipated that with the EU's introduction of the binding NSFR after the banking reform package is successfully passed in legislation, the reporting of the NSFR would likely be based on the EBA's standard of requiring it to be reported quarterly.[37] The PRA prescribes certain procedural requirements for banks to manage their liquidity risk profiles, in particular the LCR. The EBA has prescribed standardised reporting

---

[30] http://www.europarl.europa.eu/legislative-train/theme-deeper-and-fairer-internal-market-with-a-strengthened-industrial-base-financial-services/package-banking-reform-package.

[31] This process is still in progress as the banking reform package needs to respond to the Basel Committee's final micro-prudential regulatory recommendations in December 2017, at https://www.bis.org/bcbs/publ/d424.htm.

[32] PRA Rulebook, *Internal Liquidity Adequacy Assessment* at http://www.prarulebook.co.uk/rulebook/Content/Part/292099/04-07-2016.

[33] PRA Rulebook, *Liquidity Coverage Requirement: UK Designated Investment Firms.*

[34] See PRA Rulebook, *Internal Liquidity Adequacy Assessment* at http://www.prarulebook.co.uk/rulebook/Content/Part/292099/09-05-2016.

[35] PRA, *Statement of Policy: Pillar 2 Liquidity* (February 2018) at https://www.bankofengland.co.uk/-/media/boe/files/prudential-regulation/policy-statement/2018/february/ps218.pdf?la=en&hash=1B058B3B76ED E73D8C2A520698D19297323C3E9F.

[36] Articles 415 and 427, Regulation (EU) No 575/2013 of the European Parliament and of the Council of 26 June 2013 on prudential requirements for credit institutions and investment firms and amending Regulation (EU) No 648/2012.

[37] Articles 15 and 16, Implementing Technical Standards Amending Commission Implementing Regulation (EU) No 680/2014 on Supervisory Reporting of institutions (EBA, 2014) at https://www.eba.europa.eu/documents/10180/1028653/ITS+on+Supervisory+reporting.pdf/9212b4e7-37a1-4bbf-8409-2cc450d8513e.

formats for member states' banks in order to regularise the intervals of reporting and to make reporting information comparable.

Third, the PRA requires that banks need to have a liquidity contingency plan that deals with unexpected stressed situations such as a ratings downgrade applied to the bank that may affect its funding position. One of the facets of a contingency plan would be a liquidity buffer that is in excess of the requirements of the LCR. Finally, banks need to maintain a prudent funding profile overall, by having relevant governance in place. The liquidity appetite and risk profiles of the bank must be designated at the highest senior management levels, implemented via a robust firm-wide process adequately monitored by senior management and regularly stress-tested (this is further discussed at end of this chapter). The UK's requirements for the ILAAP are applied on an individual as well as consolidated basis for a banking group.

Key takeaways

- Basel III introduces harmonised liquidity ratios to help banks manage their liquidity risks in a convergent manner.

- The short-term liquidity ratio is known as the LCR, which ensures that banks have sufficiently high-quality liquid assets that can be sold without significant loss in value to quickly meet liabilities in the next 30 calendar days.

- The types and liquidity quality of bank assets are prescribed by EU regulation in broad adherence to the Basel Committee's recommendations.

- The longer-term liquidity ratio is known as the NSFR, which ensures that banks have a diversity of funding sources of different maturity and characteristics so that banks do not rely too much on short-term funding to meet their lending commitments.

- The EU and UK have implemented the LCR and NSFR.

- The UK has further implemented the ILAAP so that banks are given procedural rules and guidance to comply with the LCR and NSFR.

Key bibliography

Legislation

Regulation (EU) No 575/2013 of the European Parliament and of the Council of 26 June 2013 on prudential requirements for credit institutions and investment firms and amending Regulation (EU) No 648/2012

Commission Delegated Regulation (EU) 2015/61 of 10 October 2014 to supplement Regulation (EU) No 575/2013 of the European Parliament and the Council with regard to liquidity coverage requirement for Credit Institutions

PRA Rulebook, Internal Liquidity Adequacy Assessment at http://www.prarulebook.co.uk/rulebook/Content/Part/292099/09-05-2016

PRA, *Statement of Policy: Pillar 2 Liquidity* (February 2018) at https://www.bankofengland.co.uk/-/media/boe/files/prudential-regulation/policy-statement/2018/february/ps218.pdf?la=en&hash=1B058B3B76EDE73D8C2A520698D19297323C3E9F

Reports and Guidelines

Basel Committee, *Basel III- The Net Stable Funding Ratio* (October 2014) at http://www.bis.org/bcbs/publ/d295.pdf

Basel Committee, *Principles for Sound Liquidity Risk Management and Supervision* (Sep 2008) at http://www.bis.org/publ/bcbs144.htm

9.3 Large exposures

One aspect of micro-prudential regulation that has existed prior to the post-crisis reforms in international standards and in the EU, is the control of large exposures by banks. Large exposures refer to significant extensions of credit to a single client or a group of **connected clients**. Banks' large exposures have been subject to regulation before the 2007–9 global financial crisis. The purpose of such regulation is to allow regulators to monitor the credit risk of banks' significant lending to certain clients,[38] as the materialisation of such risk could pose dangers to banks' safety and soundness. This area has now seen post-crisis reforms in international harmonising standards led by the Basel Committee with which EU regulation is increasingly aligned.

Large exposures are defined as exposures (in terms of lending or trading) to a client or a connected group of clients in excess of 10 per cent of the bank's 'eligible capital', which is the sum of its tier one capital and a third of its tier two capital.[39] The concern with large exposures is that a bank has a high and perhaps concentrated exposure to a particular client or group of clients, heightening the bank's credit risk if the client or group of clients defaults or becomes insolvent.

The EU's regulatory regime is found in the Capital Requirements Regulation 2013 (recast). This regime applies directly to the UK although a few exemptions have been made by the PRA in respect of certain intra-group exposures and sovereign debt exposures.[40] The Capital Requirements Regulation regime consists of guidance for the calculation of large exposures, reporting and monitoring requirements and absolute prohibitions and penalties for exceeding certain limits of large exposures.

9.3.1 Calculating large exposures

Banks are required to calculate their exposures based on both the trading book and the bank's assets on its balance sheet (i.e. bank lending). Exposures are calculated on a

---

[38] Since the superseded Capital Requirements Directive of 2006.

[39] Article 392, Regulation (EU) No 575/2013 of the European Parliament and of the Council of 26 June 2013 on prudential requirements for credit institutions and investment firms and amending Regulation (EU) No 648/2012. [40] PRA Rulebook, *Large Exposures*.

net basis, that is, the bank's long positions net of short ones. For example, if the bank holds equity instruments issued by a client on a long basis but has also sold short, then only the net position counts as the 'exposure'. For certain complex exposures such as repurchase transactions and secured lending, banks may be permitted to use internal models to calculate 'net' exposures subject to supervisory approval and monitoring. Credit risk mitigation or protection techniques are recognised under the regulation of large exposures as these can go towards reducing the overall exposure level.[41] Credit protection includes, for example, the use of credit derivatives that pass credit risk onto an underwriter that takes all or part of the bank's credit risk for a fee arrangement. However, the excessive underwriting of credit derivatives almost cost the American Insurance Group its survival in 2008, resulting in the US government bailout of the Group. The American Insurance Group was active in writing credit default swaps, a form of insurance sold to investment banks to protect them against non-performance in the collateralised debt obligations held by these investment banks. The collateralised debt obligations were securitised assets based on underlying loans such as mortgages, commercial credit etc. The swap entitled AIG to the revenue streams from the collateralised debt obligations, that is, the repayments made on the underlying loans. This instrument allowed AIG an insurance company to invest in such investment assets in an indirect manner. However, if defaults occur in the underlying loans and the revenue streams become disrupted, AIG would stand to lose as they would have to pay out on the protection extended to the investment banks (who remain holders of the securitised assets) for their losses. As AIG had over-extended itself by selling over $500 million worth of such protection to investment banks, there was too much to pay out when the collateralised debt obligations market collapsed in the global financial crisis. Although the Regulation still allows credit derivatives to be taken into account in mitigating the calculation of large exposures, banks must have already been permitted to use internal models for credit risk measurement and such internal models are capable of taking into account the effect of credit derivatives. Such supervisory approval would likely be sensitive to whether credit derivatives themselves are exposed to concentration risk, such as in the case with AIG above.

Some assets are exempt from the large exposures regulation such as sovereign debt risk-weighted at 0 per cent or claims on central banks. These are regarded as relatively risk-free and hence do not need to be limited by large exposures regulation.[42] This means that banks are not circumscribed in terms of how much they hold of such assets. However, it may be questionable as to whether this assumption of absolute safety holds, as sovereign debt can be downgraded, and banks holding excessive amounts of presumably 'safe' debt may find itself in breach of large exposures limits.

---

[41] Article 399, Regulation (EU) No 575/2013 of the European Parliament and of the Council of 26 June 2013 on prudential requirements for credit institutions and investment firms and amending Regulation (EU) No 648/2012.

[42] Article 400, Regulation (EU) No 575/2013 of the European Parliament and of the Council of 26 June 2013 on prudential requirements for credit institutions and investment firms and amending Regulation (EU) No 648/2012.

9.3.2 Reporting of large exposures

All large exposures must be reported to banks' national regulators at least twice yearly.[43] Certain information about these exposures are to be reported, and this assists regulators in monitoring banks' credit risk profiles in a more pro-active manner, in line with the forward-looking or judgment-based approach to supervision, which is now adopted by the PRA[44] and approved internationally.[45] Regulators also provide banks with a standardised reporting template to assess and manage their large exposures. In essence, banks need to report on:

- Value of exposure before *and* after taking into account credit risk mitigation techniques.
- The credit risk mitigation technique used.
- The identity of the client or group of connected clients.
- The expected run-off of the exposure,[46] expressed in monthly 'buckets' over a year and quarterly 'buckets' over 3 years and after.

The PRA monitors UK banks' large exposures, with the additional requirement that any bank that is about to exceed its absolute limit of 25 per cent of eligible capital[47] or becomes aware that the limit has been exceeded must without delay inform the PRA by written notice in order for the PRA to work with the bank under supervision to remedy the situation.[48]

9.3.3 Limits on large exposures

A bank should not have a large exposure that exceeds 25 per cent of its eligible capital[49] or €150 million, whichever is higher.[50] Although EU legislation permits member states' national bank regulators to set a lower absolute limit if they wish to, the UK has adopted the limits set out in the EU Regulation.

If banks breach the absolute large exposures limit for exceeding 10 days, a punitive ladder of increased capital adequacy requirements will be imposed to compel banks

---

[43] Article 394, Regulation (EU) No 575/2013 of the European Parliament and of the Council of 26 June 2013 on prudential requirements for credit institutions and investment firms and amending Regulation (EU) No 648/2012.

[44] PRA, *Our Approach to Banking Supervision* (October 2012) at http://www.fsa.gov.uk/static/pubs/other/pra-approach-banking.pdf.

[45] BIS, *Core Principles for Effective Banking Supervision* (2012) at http://www.bis.org/publ/bcbs230.html, Principle 8.

[46] The repayment of the loan in question. As loans are repaid, the repayments are called the 'run-off' of the exposure. This requirement relates to how quickly the loan is repaid and expected to be repaid over 1 year and 3 years respectively.   [47] Discussed further in section 9.3.3.

[48] Prudential Regulation Authority, *PRA Rulebook: Large Exposures* at http://www.prarulebook.co.uk/rulebook/Content/Part/211538/09-05-2016.   [49] Defined earlier.

[50] Article 395, Regulation (EU) No 575/2013 of the European Parliament and of the Council of 26 June 2013 on prudential requirements for credit institutions and investment firms and amending Regulation (EU) No 648/2012.

Table 9.6 Excess over large exposures limit as a percentage of eligible capital

Factor to be multiplied to risk–asset ratio	expressed as a percentage
40%	200%
40–60%	300%
60–80%	400%
80–100%	500%
100–250%	600%
Over 250%	900%

to remedy the situation.[51] For example, where banks breach the absolute limit for large exposures but such a breach is under 40 per cent of eligible capital, then a bank may be penalised by being required to satisfy double the capital adequacy ratio applicable to the bank. The ladder of punitive capital adequacy requirements penalises the bank with increased capital adequacy requirements the higher the level of excess over the large exposures limit. The ladder of punitive capital adequacy requirements acts as a deterrent to breach of the large exposures limit, as failure to meet capital adequacy thresholds can trigger crisis management and resolution powers to be exercised against banks, as Chapter 13 will discuss. Table 9.6 illustrates the punitive ladder of capital adequacy requirements.

9.3.4 **Limits on large exposures for G-SIBs**

The Basel Committee affirmed the importance of large exposures limitations as a means to control banks' credit risk. It has issued a final standard in 2014[52] to encourage harmonised regulation of large exposures, generally affirming the above-mentioned EU's approach while introducing some updating and refinement.

The Basel Committee has generally adopted the EU Regulation's approach to measuring large exposures and taking into account credit risk mitigation techniques. It also calls for the development of absolute limits of exposure to central counterparties. Central counterparties are institutions that stand between buyers and sellers of financial instruments, guaranteeing settlement but usually at risk of default from a counterparty. Central counterparties are vital for predictability and certainty in market settlement and they provision for the risks they bear by holding contributions from

---

[51] Article 396, Regulation (EU) No 575/2013 of the European Parliament and of the Council of 26 June 2013 on prudential requirements for credit institutions and investment firms and amending Regulation (EU) No 648/2012.

[52] Basel Committee, *Supervisory Framework for Measuring and Controlling Large Exposures* (2014) at http://www.bis.org/publ/bcbs283.pdf.

members, requiring margins, deposits for transactions or collateral. Although central counterparties have been shown to be robust and there has not been a failure or scandal, increased volumes of trades passing through them can cause pressure, and the Committee therefore calls for exposures to central counterparties to be moderated by regulatory monitoring and control.

The Committee also suggests a different large exposures limitation regime for systemically important financial institutions (G-SIBs as discussed in Chapter 8). Such institutions may cause more system-wide shock and upheaval due to their solvency and viability risks, and hence it may be prudent to impose more stringent regulation upon them.

The Committee proposes that systemically important financial institutions should be subject to an absolute limit of large exposures at 15 per cent of tier one capital, instead of the 25 per cent of eligible capital imposed on other banks. This is because such financial institutions are already highly interconnected with other global banks and are more likely to transmit contagion effects upon others. Hence, a more prudent approach of limiting the credit risk exposures of such institutions may be seen to be proportionate to the systemic risks they pose. The Committee also suggests that domestically important financial institutions (D-SIBs as discussed in Chapter 8) should also be subject to more stringent large exposures limits to be determined by national regulators.

The Committee proposes that the new harmonised standards be fully operational for all banks by January 2019. As part of the EU's banking reform package, the EU is planning to implement the Basel Committee's proposal to lower the large exposures limits for G-SIBs.[53]

9.3.5 **Connected clients**

As the large exposures limits relate not only to single clients but to groups of connected clients, the definition of 'connected clients' is important in ascertaining the scope of the large exposures regulation. The EU Capital Requirements Regulation IV 2013 provides that 'connected clients' are:

(a) two or more legal or natural persons that constitute a 'single risk' due to one having direct or indirect **control** over the others; or

(b) two or more legal persons that constitute a 'single risk' not due to control factors but due to *financial interconnectedness* in such a way that if one were to experience financial difficulties, the others would also experience similar difficulties.[54]

The EU's approach to 'connected clients' is a broad one and comes in the wake of the 2007–9 global financial crisis, which made policymakers prefer a more conservative approach to assessing credit risk. The scope of who may be regarded as 'connected clients' for the purposes of implementing large exposures limits, has been broadened in reforms after the crisis. This area has also been subject to international harmonisation

---

[53] Commission Proposal to amend the Capital Requirements IV Regulation 2013, as of 26 November 2016, at http://ec.europa.eu/finance/bank/docs/regcapital/crr-crd-review/161123-proposal-amending-regulation_en.pdf.   [54] Article 4(39), Capital Requirements IV Regulation 2013.

as the Basel Committee issued a report in 2014 to provide guidance on large exposures limits, monitoring and how connected clients are to be determined.[55]

The EBA, in the form of its predecessor, issued Guidelines in 2009[56] to clarify who are 'connected clients'. These guidelines have now been updated in 2017[57] after considering the Basel Committee's recommendations in 2014. The Basel Committee recommended the importance of determining connected clients based on factors of 'control' and 'economic interdependencies'. The EBA now defines 'connected clients' as a group of legal or natural persons where control and financial/economic interdependencies subsist. These interdependencies can result in a 'domino effect'[58] for the group if one were to suffer stress. For connected clients by 'control', the 'domino' effect could be in the form of the experience of financial problems by the controlling entity being transferred to the controlled entity, therefore posing a 'single risk'. For connected clients by financial or economic interdependencies, the 'domino' effect could be in the form of financial difficulties for one entity resulting in an idiosyncratic risk that the other would find it difficult to make full or timely repayment of liabilities.

'Control' is not only defined as legal control such as being in a corporate group structure, but as actual forms of control, such as the actual exercise of voting rights, rights of appointing management, dominant influence such strategic influence, and the rights to coordinate to pursue common objectives.[59] Such a wide approach avoids narrowly construed definitions of control that are designed to avert large exposures regulation, which banks may be tempted to do in order to preserve the goodwill of certain important clients. The EBA guidelines presume that 'control' exists if:

(a) one entity holds the majority of the shareholders' or members' voting rights in another entity;

(b) one entity has the right or ability to appoint or remove a majority of the members of the administrative, management or supervisory body of another entity; or

(c) one entity has the right or ability to exercise a dominant influence over another entity pursuant to a contract, or provisions in memoranda or articles of association.

In all other cases, relevant indicators of control include:

(a) whether one entity has the power to decide on the strategy or direct the activities of an entity;

---

[55] Basel Committee, *Supervisory Framework for Measuring and Controlling Large Exposures* (2014) at http://www.bis.org/publ/bcbs283.pdf.

[56] Committee of European Banking Regulators, *Guidelines on the Revised Large Exposures Regime* (2009) at https://www.eba.europa.eu/regulation-and-policy/large-exposures/guidelines-on-the-revised-large-exposures-regime.

[57] EBA, *Guidelines on Connected Clients under Article 4(1)(39) of Regulation (EU) No 575/2013* (November 2017) at http://www.eba.europa.eu/documents/10180/2025808/Final+Guidelines+on+connected+clients+%28EBA-GL-2017-15%29.pdf. [58] Ibid.

[59] Basel Committee, *Supervisory Framework for Measuring and Controlling Large Exposures* (2014) at http://www.bis.org/publ/bcbs283.pdf.

(b) whether one entity has the power to decide on crucial transactions, such as the transfer of profit or loss;

(c) whether one entity has the right or ability to coordinate the management of an entity with that of other entities in pursuit of a common objective (e.g. where the same natural persons are involved in the management or board of two or more entities); or

(d) whether one entity holds more than 50 per cent of the shares of capital of another related, affiliated, or other relevant entity.

Next, the financial or economic interconnectedness of a group of clients is important in presenting a real picture of the group's credit risk. If a bank is exposed to two clients, one of whom is highly dependent on funding from the other, then the other's insolvency may affect the credit risk of both clients.

The Basel Committee recommended a non-exhaustive list of indicators for the interpretation of economic dependencies. For example, where one party is dependent on at least 50 per cent or more receipts from the other to be economically viable, in relationships of guarantee, or sharing in common sources of funding. The EBA in its consultation paper initially set out three categories of financial/economic connectedness that were adapted from the Basel Committee's approach in 2014. The first category referred to financial interdependency relationships that should give rise to a presumption of 'connected client'. The second category referred to financial interdependency relationships in relation to other factors that would be important though not necessarily conclusive. The third referred to financial interdependency that could arise out of 'control' as already discussed. The first category contained many economic relationships such as receivables, supply, customer, credit, and guarantee relationships, some of which were defined very prescriptively, such as where one entity's output was sold at 50 per cent or more to another entity, or where at least 50 per cent or more of one entity's assets were invested in another entity. These have now been regarded as too rigid and prescriptive and the EBA has reverted to a more broadly-worded and non-exhaustive list of indicators for determining financial/economic interconnectedness.

There are four major 'groups' of indicators as Table 9.7 sets out.

The EBA expects banks to engage in thorough due diligence in order to ascertain sufficient information from clients and their economic and business relationships. It is envisaged that there may be more public information as well as information that can be obtained from clients regarding control relationships. The ascertainment of a web of clients' economic interdependencies is more tricky, and banks are asked to use their best endeavours to do so, their efforts to be reasonably proportionate to the size of the exposure in question. Banks are asked to conduct extensive research including into 'soft' types of information that may not be publicly held or available.[60]

---

[60] Section 8, EBA, *Guidelines on Connected Clients under Article 4(1)(39) of Regulation (EU) No 575/2013* (November 2017) at http://www.eba.europa.eu/documents/10180/2025808/Final+Guidelines+on+connected+clients+%28EBA-GL-2017-15%29.pdf.

Table 9.7 Indicators of financial/economic interconnectedness to determine connected clients

---

Exposure of liability of another entity

- Where a client has fully or partly guaranteed the exposure of another client and the exposure is so significant for the guarantor that the guarantor is likely to experience financial problems if a claim occurs.

- Where a client is liable in accordance with his or her legal status as a member in an entity, for example a general partner in a limited partnership, and the exposure is so significant for the client that the client is likely to experience financial problems if a claim against the entity occurs.

- Other situations where clients are legally or contractually jointly liable for obligations to the institution (e.g. a debtor and his or her co-borrower, or a debtor and his or her spouse/partner).

Significant economic dependency

- Where a significant part of a client's gross receipts or gross expenditures (on an annual basis) is derived from transactions with another client (e.g. the owner of a residential/commercial property the tenant of which pays a significant part of the rent) that cannot be easily replaced.

- Where a significant part of a client's production/output is sold to another client of the institution, and the production/output cannot be easily sold to other customers.

- Where a significant part of the receivables or liabilities of a client is to another client.

Control factors

- Where clients have common owners, shareholders, or managers. For example, horizontal groups where an undertaking is related to one or more other undertakings because they all have the same shareholder structure without a single controlling shareholder or because they are managed on a unified basis. This management may be pursuant to a contract concluded between the undertakings, or to provisions in the memoranda or articles of association of those undertakings, or if the administrative management or supervisory bodies of the undertaking and of one or more other undertakings consist for the major part of the same persons.

Sharing in major funding sources

- Where the expected source of funds to repay the loans of two or more clients is the same and none of the clients has another independent source of income from which the loan may be serviced and fully repaid.

9.4 Leverage ratio

Basel III includes the introduction of the leverage ratio,[61] which restricts the total level of bank lending to bank capital without applying risk-weighting. In sum, this means

---

[61] Basel Committee, *Basel III Leverage Ratio Framework and Disclosure Requirements* (January 2014) at http://www.bis.org/publ/bcbs270.pdf.

→ Key takeaways

- The EU and UK has imposed large exposures limitations on banks before the 2007–9 global financial crisis.

- A large exposure is defined as an exposure to a client or a connected group of clients at 10 per cent or more of eligible capital (tier one plus a third of their two capital).

- Large exposures are calculated based on both the banking and trading books and on a net basis. Credit mitigation techniques can be considered.

- Some large exposures are exempted, for example, sovereign debt weighted at 0 per cent.

- Large exposures have to be reported to national regulators and monitored regularly for credit risk.

- Banks are prohibited from committing to a large exposure in excess of 25 per cent of eligible capital or €150 million, whichever is higher.

- Connected clients are defined widely in accordance with control and financial economic connectedness relationships. These definitions are provided by the EBA in 2017 adapted from the Basel Committee's recommendations in 2014.

- The Basel Committee proposes that large exposures be restricted to 15 per cent of tier one capital for G-SIBs and similar consideration for D-SIBs. This reform is to be implemented in the EU's banking reform package.

Key bibliography

Legislation

Regulation (EU) No 575/2013 of the European Parliament and of the Council of 26 June 2013 on prudential requirements for credit institutions and investment firms and amending Regulation (EU) No 648/2012

Prudential Regulation Authority, PRA Rulebook: Large Exposures at http://www.prarulebook.co.uk/rulebook/Content/Part/211538/09-05-2016

Reports and Guidelines

Basel Committee, Supervisory Framework for Measuring and Controlling Large Exposures (2014) at http://www.bis.org/publ/bcbs283.pdf

EBA, Guidelines on Connected Clients under Article 4(1)(39) of Regulation (EU) No 575/2013 (Nov 2017) at http://www.eba.europa.eu/documents/10180/2025808/Final+Guidelines+on+connected+clients+%28EBA-GL-2017-15%29.pdf.

that the leverage ratio would cap bank lending at an absolute level proportionate to their capital, whether such lending is extended to 0 per cent risk-weighted governments or to residential mortgages. The Basel Committee regards the leverage ratio as 'a simple, transparent, non-risk based leverage ratio to act as a credible supplementary measure to the risk-based capital requirements'.

The functions of the leverage ratio are to:

- restrict the build-up of leverage in the banking sector to avoid the prospect of banks having to de-leverage significantly under stressed conditions. This is because rapid de-leveraging has the potential to damage the broader financial system and the economy; and

- reinforce the risk-based capital adequacy requirements with a simple, non-risk based 'backstop' measure.

The leverage ratio forces banks to measure their 'gross' or absolute levels of credit creation and to ensure that such levels are maintained in proportion to their capital. This information, at a sectoral level, can then feed into policy discussions and thinking, bank risk management and public debate about optimal levels of debt in the economy and created by banks.

9.4.1 **Measuring leverage**

The creation of credit by banks is also known as: debt creation (from the perspective of the borrower, as it is 'credit' from the perspective of the lender), asset creation (as credit creation results in 'assets' for banks), or leverage. In the UK, households, corporations and governments have been increasing their borrowing steadily,[62] and a key source of lending is banks. One of the lessons from the 2007–9 global financial crisis is that lending can become indiscriminate,[63] such as sub-prime mortgage lending in the US that has taken off in the last decade. Banks, in competition with each other to create more assets, are susceptible to lowering their standards in lending, such as in the case of corporate lending carried out by HBOS prior to the global financial crisis, criticised in the aftermath of HBOS' near failure.[64] Increased volumes of leverage increase default risk at the individual bank level, but there is also a wider issue of the sustainability of such levels of debt for the economy as a whole.[65]

---

[62] For household debt, see Centre for Social Justice, *Restoring the Balance: Tackling Problem Debt* (2014); *Maxed Out: Serious Personal Debt in Britain* (2007) at http://www.centreforsocialjustice.org.uk/publications/restoring-the-balance-tackling-problem-debt and cited in 'Levels of UK Household Debt at Record High, Says Think Tank', *The Independent* (3 June 2015) at http://www.independent.co.uk/news/uk/home-news/levels-of-uk-household-debt-at-record-high-says-think-tank-10295579.html. For corporate debt levels, see 'The \$29 Trillion Corporate Debt Hangover That Could Spark a Recession', *Bloomberg News* (28 January 2016) at http://www.bloomberg.com/news/articles/2016-01-28/some-29-trillion-later-the-corporate-debt-boom-looks-exhausted; on global levels of corporate debt outstripping GDP growth, see McKinsey Global Institute (MGI), *Debt and (not much) Deleveraging* (2014) at http://www.mckinsey.com/global-themes/employment-and-growth/debt-and-not-much-deleveraging.

[63] See Howard Davies, *The Financial Crisis: Who is to Blame?* (London: Polity 2010) chs 5 and 6.

[64] House of Commons and House of Lords, Parliamentary Commission on Banking Standards, *An Accident Waiting to Happen: The Failure of HBOS* (4 April 2013) at http://www.publications.parliament.uk/pa/jt201213/jtselect/jtpcbs/144/144.pdf.

[65] Adair Turner, *Between Debt and the Devil* (NJ: Princeton University Press 2015). Increased levels of debt also correspond to increasing systemic risk (see Chapter 1), and Blaise Gadanecz and Kaushik Jayaram, 'Measures of Financial Stability – A Review' (2010) 31 *IFC Bulletin* 365.

Box 9.5

$$\text{Leverage ratio} = \frac{\text{Capital measure}}{\text{Exposure measure}}$$

In order to measure leverage, the Basel Committee proposes that banks' individual levels of leverage be expressed as a ratio in terms of their capital. This is because banks' gross levels of leverage may not be a meaningful figure unless looked at in terms of the bank's capital position to support its leverage. Hence, the leverage ratio is defined as its capital measure over its exposure measure, see Box 9.5.

The capital measure of a bank is its tier one capital. The exposure measure is the bank's gross level of leverage. The Basel Committee sets out rather prescriptive guidance as to how the gross level of leverage is to be measured, in order to capture as comprehensively a picture of the bank's credit creation activities, hence its risk-taking.

A bank's exposure measure comprises of its on-balance sheet items (i.e. the loans it creates and not transferred away), its off-balance sheet items (such as securitised assets where risk may be partially transferred[66]), its derivatives exposures and its securities financing transactions (i.e. its borrowing from wholesale markets backed by collateral). The Committee takes a conservative approach to measuring a bank's exposure. Some principles of such a conservative approach include the ignoring of netting arrangements, collateral and credit risk mitigation, and the treatment of contingent liabilities as equivalent to exposures.

For example, netting arrangements are not to be taken into account unless specifically provided for in the Committee's prescriptions. In particular, for on-balance sheet items, deposits and loans are not to be netted. This means that if a bank's depositor is also a borrower, the loan asset is treated as 'gross' regardless of the amount of deposit in the bank that can be perceived to 'offset' the loan amount. Further, collateral or other credit risk mitigation is not taken into account, so that the integrity of the 'gross level' information is maintained. This is the position for on-balance sheet items, derivatives exposures, and securities financing transactions. Even where a securities financing transaction is structured as sale and repurchase, the bank should conservatively treat such a transaction as collateralised only. For off-balance sheet items, banks are to treat contingent liabilities as converted into liabilities for the purposes of measuring gross levels of leverage. For example, off-balance sheet items include certain commitments to pay, whether such commitments are cancellable, such as on letters of credit for trade finance. These letters are issued by banks so that commercial entities in international trade can be paid on the basis of certain conforming shipping documents.[67] For the purposes of measuring leverage, the liability to pay on the letters is treated as certain before they are actually called upon.

---

[66] Taking into account the fact that the bank may be open to guarantee liability and retention of risk.

[67] A detailed account of the function and law relating to letters of credit, much of whose terms are standardised under the Uniform Customs and Practice for Documentary Credits 600, can be found in Christopher Hare, *Documentary Credits: Law and Practice* (Oxford: Routledge 2016).

9.4.2 Maintaining the ratio

The Basel Committee recommends that a 3 per cent leverage ratio be maintained, meaning that banks' tier one capital should be at a level of 3 per cent or more of its total exposures. Like the risk–asset ratio and various measures of risk-weighting that the Committee has developed, the leverage ratio is not an exact science and does not represent absolute 'safe' levels of lending. In fact, at first blush, it is rather low as gross leverage supported by as low as 3 per cent tier one capital does not seem to be a substantial cushion for losses. Hence as will be discussed below, the UK has already adopted regulatory requirements in excess of the 3 per cent leverage ratio.

For globally systemically important banks, the Financial Stability Board (FSB) recommends the maintenance of a higher leverage ratio, that is, 6 per cent, to be discussed in section 9.5. This ratio, as discussed in Chapter 8, section 8.5, may be applied[68] to the systemically important banks designated in the UK from January 2019.

9.4.3 Implementation in the EU

The EU requires banks to calculate their leverage ratio in the same way as recommended by the Basel Committee.[69] The EU Regulation has further prescribed conversion factors for contingent liabilities to be treated as equivalents to exposures, refining the Basel Committee's recommendation. For example, undrawn credit facilities that can be withdrawn with immediate notice attracts a conversion factor of 10 per cent, while commitments to pay on trade finance facilities convert at between 20 per cent to 50 per cent depending on their likelihood of being called upon. All other off-balance sheet items are converted at 100 per cent.[70]

Initially, the EU's implementation of the leverage ratio is only based on measurement and reporting. The Basel Committee envisages that all banks must compute their leverage ratio for the purposes of public disclosure from January 2015, such disclosure to be made on a consolidated basis for a banking group. This is implemented in the EU by way of a Commission Regulation that requires banks to report their leverage ratio on both an individual and consolidated basis.[71] Banks need to report in quarterly periods, and based on standard information templates in order to assist regulators and

[68] In the alternative vis a vis the maintenance of a 16–18 per cent MREL capital adequacy standard, see discussion in Chapter 8, section 8.5.7.

[69] Articles 429 and 430, Regulation (EU) No 575/2013 of the European Parliament and of the Council of 26 June 2013 on prudential requirements for credit institutions and investment firms and amending Regulation (EU) No 648/2012.

[70] Article 429, Regulation (EU) No 575/2013 of the European Parliament and of the Council of 26 June 2013 on prudential requirements for credit institutions and investment firms and amending Regulation (EU) No 648/2012.

[71] Article 14, Commission Implementing Regulation (EU) No 680/2014 of 16 April 2014 laying down implementing technical standards with regard to supervisory reporting of institutions according to Regulation (EU) No 575/2013 of the European Parliament and of the Council.

their investors to assess the gross levels of bank leverage compared to its financial statements. Such disclosure is intended to stimulate Pillar 3 market discipline (as discussed in Chapter 8, section 8.4).

The Regulation has initially refrained from setting a minimum leverage ratio and recommends that national regulators monitor the needs of their domestic banking sectors and perhaps settle for ranges and thresholds rather than a one-size-fits-all standard.[72] However, at end 2016, reform is underway to adopt the 3 per cent leverage ratio firmly.[73]

The firm adoption of the 3 per cent leverage ratio is in part due to the EBA's[74] empirical research on the benefits of the leverage ratio. The EBA finds that a 3 per cent leverage ratio complements capital adequacy requirements well in terms of controlling risk-taking while not having an excessively significant impact on banks' credit creation to support economic activities. Further, the 3 per cent leverage ratio is observed to produce a counter-cyclical effect, that is, causing banks to be more restrained in lending during times of perceived safety and low risk, and encourages banks to diversify their loan portfolios.

9.4.4 Implementation in the UK

The Prudential Regulation Authority is concerned that excessive levels of bank leverage need to be controlled and monitored and has thus implemented the leverage ratio ahead of the EU and in excess of the Basel Committee's requirements.

The UK has implemented a 3 per cent minimum leverage ratio for all banks that accept deposits in the UK exceeding £50 billion. This was nudged higher to 3.25 per cent following a recommendation by the Financial Policy Committee in October 2017. UK banks and building societies need to meet the leverage ratio on an individual basis, and where the bank is part of an EU group, on a consolidated basis.[75] Further, the leverage ratio of 3 per cent has now formed the basis for calculating and applying additional leverage ratio buffers to certain banks. A leverage ratio buffer is an additional regulatory capital buffer that adds to the capital adequacy requirements that banks need to comply with, as discussed in Chapter 8, section 8.5. As this buffer is worked out using the bank's total exposure measure, and not risk-weighted assets, this buffer exerts a

---

[72] Preambles 94 and 95, Regulation (EU) No 575/2013 of the European Parliament and of the Council of 26 June 2013 on prudential requirements for credit institutions and investment firms and amending Regulation (EU) No 648/2012.

[73] Commission proposal to amend the Capital Requirements IV Regulation 2013, as of 26 November 2016, at http://ec.europa.eu/finance/bank/docs/regcapital/crr-crd-review/161123-proposal-amending-regulation_en.pdf.

[74] EBA, *EBA Report on the Leverage Ratio Requirements Under Article 511 of the CRR* (3 August 2016) at http://www.eba.europa.eu/documents/10180/1360107/EBA-Op-2016-13+%28Leverage+ratio+report%29.pdf.

[75] PRA, *Implementing a UK Leverage Ratio Framework: Policy Statement* (December 2015) at http://www.bankofengland.co.uk/pra/Pages/publications/ps/2015/ps2715.aspx; PRA Rulebook, *CRR Firms: Reporting Leverage Ratio Instrument 2015* (2015).

> **Box 9.6**
>
> CLRB = counter-cyclical buffer (1%) x 35%= 0.35%
>
> Rounding off to the nearest tenth, we get 0.4%
>
> The CLRB is 0.4% x bank's total exposure (as measured in Section 9.4.1) and needs to be supported by common equity tier one capital.

complementary restraint to bank risk-taking as applied by the capital adequacy measures based on risk-weighting assets (covered in Chapter 8, section 8.5).

Banks that accept deposits in the UK exceeding £50 billion have to meet an additional Counter-cyclical Leverage Ratio Buffer (CLRB). The CLRB is currently set at the bank's institution-specific counter-cyclical capital buffer rate multiplied by 35 per cent, with the product expressed as a percentage rounded to its nearest tenth; multiplied by the firm's total exposure measure.[76] This needs to be supported by common equity tier one capital that is not counted towards meeting other capital adequacy requirements. Box 9.6 shows a worked example of the CLRB.

As the CLRB is tied to the counter-cyclical buffer rate set for banks in the UK (discussed in Chapter 8, section 8.5), the CLRB complements the counter-cyclical buffer in exerting restraint upon bank lending in times when banks perceive risks to be low and tend to increase their lending activity. Both the counter-cyclical buffer and its leverage ratio companion are intended to inject a greater dose of conservatism precisely when boom times occur so that banks are less at risk and better prepared for shocks or downturns.

For banks that are globally systemically important financial institutions, the PRA requires them to hold an Additional Leverage Ratio Buffer (ALRB) in addition to meeting the minimum leverage ratio.[77] For such banks, the ALRB is imposed on top of the minimum leverage ratio of 3 per cent and the CLRB. The ALRB is currently set at [an amount to be specified for the individual bank by the PRA expressed as a per cent] multiplied by 35 per cent then multiplied by the firm's total exposure measure. For example, Barclays disclosed at the end quarter of 2017 that its ALRB rate is 0.35 per cent. This means that the PRA has set the buffer rate specific to Barclays at 1 per cent, multiplied by 35 per cent, in order to derive 0.35 per cent. By setting the buffer rate specific to Barclays at 1 per cent, the PRA seems to be using the buffer rate applicable to G-SIBs discussed in Chapter 8, section 8.5. It may be expected that the ALRB is therefore tied to the G-SIB or D-SIB additional capital buffers imposed on these banks (discussed in Chapter 8, section 8.5), so that the ALRB complements the restraining effect exerted by these buffers on bank lending. Common equity tier one capital is to be used to support the ALRB.

Box 9.7 shows how the ALRB is worked out.

---

[76] PRA Rulebook, *CRR Firms: Reporting Leverage Ratio Instrument 2015* (2015).

[77] PRA, *Additional Leverage Ratio Buffer Model Requirements for G-SIIs* (2015) and PRA, *Supervisory Statement: The UK Leverage Ratio Framework* (December 2015) at http://www.bankofengland.co.uk/pra/Pages/publications/ss/2015/ss4515.aspx.

> **Box 9.7**
>
> **ALRB = (G-SIB/D-SIB capital buffer rate in %) x 35%**
> **For example, Barclays having a G-SIB buffer rate of 1% between Nov 2017–18,**
> **ALRB = 1% x 35% = 0.35% of the bank's total exposure. This amount needs to be supported by common equity tier one capital.**

This also means that G-SIBs and D-SIBs are effectively imposed with two leverage ratio buffers in addition to all other risk-weighted capital adequacy requirements discussed in Chapter 8, section 8.5, while also meeting the minimum leverage ratio. The leverage ratio buffers are calibrated according to economic conditions (i.e. counter-cyclical buffer) and the systemic risk profile of the bank (G-SIB and D-SIB buffer).

At the end of 2017, the Basel Committee proposes that G-SIBs must meet a leverage ratio buffer of 50 per cent of the G-SIB buffer rate applicable to the bank.[78] For example, as Deutsche Bank is imposed with a 2 per cent G-SIB buffer rate at the end of 2017, the leverage ratio buffer rate would be 1 per cent. This leverage ratio buffer is recommended to apply from January 2022. It remains to be seen if the UK will revise the ALRB in this light, that is, to apply 50 per cent instead of 35 per cent to the G-SIB or D-SIB buffer rate, in order to align with the Basel Committee's recommendation.

In sum, Table 9.8 shows the regulatory framework for the leverage ratio applied to UK banks.

The UK has also implemented more stringent measures than under the EU Regulation for calculating the leverage ratio for the purposes of quarterly reporting. The EU

Table 9.8 The UK PRA's leverage ratio framework

All Banks with deposits of £50 billion and above	• Minimum leverage ratio of 3% • Counter-cyclical leverage ratio buffer which is: (Counter-cyclical buffer rate % x 35%) x bank total exposure to work out the level of common equity tier one capital needed
All G-SIBs	• Minimum leverage ratio of 3% • Counter-cyclical Leverage Ratio Buffer which is: (Counter-cyclical buffer rate % x 35%) • ALRB which is: (specified % requirement [e.g. 1% for Barclays] x 35%) x bank total exposure to work out the level of common equity tier one capital needed NOTE: common equity tier one capital used to meet leverage ratio buffers cannot be counted towards other capital adequacy requirements.

[78] Basel Committee, *Finalising Post-crisis Reforms* (December 2017) at https://www.bis.org/bcbs/publ/d424.pdf.

Regulation requires banks to calculate their monthly leverage ratios and obtain an average of the monthly ratios for the purposes of quarterly reporting.[79] The reference date for calculations is the last calendar day of each month.[80] However, the UK requires that all on-balance sheet items be calculated daily for the purposes of obtaining a quarterly average exposure figure.[81] Other exposure items are calculated on a monthly basis according to the EU Regulation. Besides making disclosure of the required leverage ratio components on standardised information templates, UK banks also have to disclose every quarter on an individual and/or consolidated basis their leverage ratio, average exposure measure over the quarter, the CLRB and ALRB where applicable.[82]

From January 2019, systemically important banks in the UK may have to either meet a risk–asset ratio of 16 per cent (MREL requirements discussed in Chapter 8, section 8.5) or a leverage ratio of 6 per cent. The PRA envisages that very few banks will fall in the category applying the 6 per cent leverage ratio. It is anticipated that Nationwide Building Society, the largest building society in the UK, which is a mutual, an organisation based on membership, would have the 6 per cent leverage ratio applied to it. The MREL requirements based on capital instruments are not applicable as Nationwide is not a company with a share capital.

In sum, the package of comprehensive measures on capital (discussed in Chapter 8), liquidity, large exposures, and leverage (this chapter) are designed to make banks more robust so that the markets can continue to have confidence in their intermediation. Banks are the key financial intermediaries in Europe, although other jurisdictions such as the US may be more diversified. However, a significant impact of enhanced micro-prudential regulation is that banks reduce lending or make credit creation more expensive and hence inaccessible to its borrowers.[83] Further, there are significant increases in banks' cost of funding,[84] as they need to raise more capital. In cutting down bank risk-taking, there is a concomitant adverse impact on lending activities that are important for the economy and development. These are wider policy dilemmas in the introduction of significantly enhanced micro-prudential regulation.

---

[79] Article 430, Regulation (EU) No 575/2013 of the European Parliament and of the Council of 26 June 2013 on prudential requirements for credit institutions and investment firms and amending Regulation (EU) No 648/2012.

[80] Commission Implementing Regulation (EU) 2016/200 of 15 February 2016 laying down implementing technical standards with regard to disclosure of the leverage ratio for institutions, according to Regulation (EU) No 575/2013 of the European Parliament and of the Council, Annex 1.

[81] PRA Rulebook, *CRR Firms: Public Disclosure (Leverage Ratio Amendment) Instrument 2015* (2015).

[82] PRA Rulebook, *CRR Firms: Public Disclosure (Leverage Ratio Amendment) Instrument 2015* (2015).

[83] Patrick Slovik and Boris Cournede, 'Macroeconomic Impact of Basel III' (OECD Economics Working Paper 2011) at http://papers.ssrn.com/sol3/papers.cfm?abstract_id=2650033.

[84] Artus Galiay and Laurent Maurin, 'Drivers of Banks' Cost of Debt and Long-Term Benefits of Regulation – An Empirical Analysis Based on EU Banks' (ECB Working Paper, 2015) at http://papers.ssrn.com/sol3/papers.cfm?abstract_id=2664171.

Key takeaways

- The Basel Committee recommends a 3 per cent minimum leverage ratio for banks.

- The Basel Committee prescribes how gross levels of bank leverage is to be measured, by calculating total exposure. Total exposure is the sum of all on and off-balance sheet items, derivatives exposures, and securities financing transactions.

- The leverage ratio is expressed as the bank's tier one capital over its total exposure.

- The EU has initially only required banks to measure their leverage ratio to report the ratio to regulators and to the public on a quarterly basis. Banks are to report their leverage ratio in standardised information formats prescribed by the EBA.

- The EU has refrained from setting in stone the maintenance of the minimum 3 per cent leverage ratio as a standard, but reform is underway to introduce a binding 3 per cent leverage ratio as a minimum.

- The UK has implemented the minimum 3 per cent leverage ratio for all banks with deposits of £50 billion or above, which has since risen to 3.25 per cent at the end of 2017.

- The UK has imposed an extra counter-CLRB for the banks above.

- G-SIBs need to maintain the minimum leverage ratio, the CLRB and an ALRB.

- The CLRB and ALRB are additional capital buffers based on total exposure, and not risk-weighted assets and complement the roles of other capital adequacy measures based on risk-weighted assets. They are intended to constrain bank lending during times when banks are susceptible to increasing lending activity in periods of perceived low risk and where banks have a systemically important profile and should be therefore more conservative in risk-taking.

Key bibliography

Legislation

Regulation (EU) No 575/2013 of the European Parliament and of the Council of 26 June 2013 on prudential requirements for credit institutions and investment firms and amending Regulation (EU) No 648/2012

Commission Implementing Regulation (EU) 2016/200 of 15 February 2016 laying down implementing technical standards with regard to disclosure of the leverage ratio for institutions, according to Regulation (EU) No 575/2013 of the European Parliament and of the Council

PRA Rulebook, *CRR Firms: Reporting Leverage Ratio Instrument 2015* (2015)

PRA Rulebook, *CRR Firms: Public Disclosure (Leverage Ratio Amendment) Instrument 2015* (2015)

Reports and Guidelines

Basel Committee, *Basel III Leverage Ratio Framework and Disclosure Requirements* (Jan 2014) at http://www.bis.org/publ/bcbs270.pdf

Basel Committee, *Finalising Post-crisis Reforms* (Dec 2017) at https://www.bis.org/bcbs/publ/d424.pdf

> PRA, *Supervisory Statement: The UK Leverage Ratio Framework* (Dec 2015) at http://www.
> bankofengland.co.uk/pra/Pages/publications/ss/2015/ss4515.aspx
>
> **Books**
>
> Davies, H, *The Financial Crisis: Who is to Blame?* (London: Polity Press 2010)
> Turner, A, *Between Debt and the Devil* (NJ: Princeton University Press 2015)

9.5 Systemically important financial institutions

Systemically important financial institutions (SIFIs)[85] are financial institutions or groups usually characterised as large financial empires with a global footprint. They participate in many markets, carry on a wide range of bank business and is often at the forefront of financial innovation and complex transactions.[86] They are also often highly interconnected with other financial institutions. If a part of a SIFI becomes crisis-stricken, its adversities may infect the entire SIFI group and may also affect other financial institutions through contagion, resulting in systemic effects.[87]

The global financial crisis in 2008 has led to countless bank bailouts in the US and EU precisely because the banks concerned had SIFI profiles, as Chapter 1 has discussed. Post-crisis, banks that are SIFIs have been singled out for special and enhanced regulatory treatment due to their potential systemic impact on the global financial sector and economies. They are called the G-SIBs and D-SIBs, but SIFIs can also apply to other financial institutions. This Section is devoted to the micro-prudential regulation regime for G-SIBs and D-SIBs as a whole. It will recapitulate some earlier discussions in relation to the specific regulatory standards of capital adequacy, liquidity, large exposures, and leverage. Its purpose is to assemble a whole picture of the regulatory regime for G-SIBs and D-SIBs and to show where it is distinguished from micro-prudential regulation that more generally applies to banks.

In order to identify a SIFI, the Basel Committee and the FSB have taken leadership to develop internationally convergent approaches. The internationally convergent approaches have to a large extent been adopted by the EBA in its role of categorising G-SIBs and D-SIBs.

9.5.1 Identification of a SIFI

The Basel Committee and its sister institution, the FSB have developed international standards to identify SIFIs. The leadership of international institutions is important in

---

[85] Rosa Lastra, 'Systemic Risk, SIFIs and Financial Stability' (2011) 6 *Capital Markets Law Journal* 197; Nassim Nicholas Taleb and Charles S Tapiero, 'The Risk Externalities of Too Big to Fail' (November 2009) NYU Poly Research Paper at http://papers.ssrn.com/sol3/papers.cfm?abstract_id=1497973, accessed 4 December 2012.

[86] For example, see L Fischer, 'Major Risks of International Banking', University of St Gallen Law & Economics Working Papers No. 2008–20 at http://papers.ssrn.com/sol3/papers.cfm?abstract_id=1138253.

[87] Tom CW Lin, 'Too Big to Fail, Too Blind to See' (2010) 80 *Mississippi Law Journal* 355.

this regard in order to achieve an internationally convergent approach that is objective and removed from domestic political interests.

9.5.1.1 Basel Committee's Indicator Approach

The Committee, with the benefit of empirical research input,[88] identifies that five factors are especially relevant to the systemic impact of banks. These are: size of the banking group, the global scope of the group's operations, substitutability of services, complexity of structures within the group, and interconnectedness with other financial institutions.[89] An Indicator Approach is used to score banks against each indicator of size, cross-jurisdictional activity, complexity, substitutability and interconnectedness. The scores would then translate into a single systemic risk 'bucket' score that corresponds with the FSB's recommendation for the application of the G-SIB buffer as discussed in Chapter 8, section 8.5.5.

Each of the five indicators is given a 20 per cent weighting in order to add up to a score of 100 per cent. However, national regulators may determine that 'substitutability' deserves a higher weighting, in which case the other weightings need to be adjusted accordingly.[90] Empirical research has discovered that, relative to the other categories that make up the SIFI framework, the substitutability category has a greater impact on the assessment of systemic importance where banks are dominant in the provision of payment, underwriting and asset custody services. Therefore, the Committee has decided to remove the cap to the substitutability category score. Each of the five indicators, except for size, comprises further sub-indicators that are given their respective weightings in their category. The Committee applies the scoring methodology described above to three years of data supplied by banks.

Table 9.9 shows the five main indicators and their sub-indicators in each category, and the score weighting applied to each indicator and sub-indicator.

As we can see, some sub-indicators are rather comprehensive in nature, while some are 'proxy' measures for the indicator category concerned. For example, where

---

[88] See, for example, Jan Lorenz, Stefano Battiston and Frank Schweitzer, 'Systemic Risk in a Unifying Framework for Cascading Processes on Networks' (2010) CCSS Working Paper Series CCSS-09-011 at http://ssrn.com/abstract=1596045; Monica Billio and others, 'Measuring Systemic Risk in the Finance and Insurance Sectors' (March 2010) at http://web.mit.edu/alo/www/Papers/billio_etal.pdf; Rosa Lastra, 'Systemic Risk, SIFIs and Financial Stability' (2011) 6 *Capital Markets Law Journal* 197; Nassim Nicholas Taleb and Charles S Tapiero, 'The Risk Externalities of Too Big to Fail' (November 2009) NYU Poly Research Paper http://papers.ssrn.com/sol3/papers.cfm?abstract_id=1497973; Tao Sun, 'Identifying Vulnerabilities in Systemically-Important Financial Institutions in a Macro-financial Linkages Framework' (May 2011) IMF Working Paper W11/111 http://www.imf.org/external/pubs/ft/wp/2011/wp11111.pdf; Gianni De Nicolo and Myron L Kwast, 'Systemic Risk and Financial Consolidation: Are they Related?' (2002) 26 *Journal of Banking and Finance* 861.

[89] Basel Committee, *Global Systemically Important Banks: Updated Assessment Methodology and the Higher Loss Absorbency Requirement* (July 2013) at http://www.bis.org/publ/bcbs255.pdf.

[90] This cap may be removed from 2019 if reforms to the assessment framework are finalised, see Basel Committee, *Globally Systemically Important Banks: Revised Assessment Framework, A Consultative Document* (March 2017) at http://www.bis.org/bcbs/publ/d402.pdf. In which case the weightings of each component in the framework will have to be recalibrated accordingly.

Table 9.9 Indicator-based Measurement Approach

Category/indicator	Sub-indicator	Weighting
Cross-jurisdictional activity (20%)	Cross-jurisdictional claims	10%
	Cross Jurisdictional liabilities	10%
Size (20%)	Total Exposures defined under the Basel III leverage ratio, see section 9.	20%
Interconnectedness (20%)	Intra-financial[91] system assets	6.67%
	Intra-financial system liabilities	6.67%
	Securities outstanding	6.67%
Substitutability (20%)* *note that the cap of 20% can be increased at national regulators' discretion. All other measures would have to be recalibrated according to national regulators' discretion	Assets under custody	6.67%
	Payments activity	6.67%
	Underwritten transactions in debt and equity markets	6.67% (until Jan 2021) 3.33% (after Jan 2021)
	Trading volume[92]	3.33%
Complexity (20%)	Notional amount of over-the-counter derivatives	6.67%
	'Level 3' (or highly illiquid) assets	6.67%
	Trading and available for sale securities	6.67%

cross-jurisdictional activity is concerned, the measurement of **all** cross-jurisdictional claims and liabilities can be comprehensive in nature. Where interconnectedness is concerned, the measurement of intra-financial sector assets and liabilities, plus all securities used in rehypothecation[93] transactions in the wholesale markets, is also a rather comprehensive measure. However, in the substitutability and complexity categories,

---

[91] Meaning created between financial institutions and not between financial institutions and corporations in other sectors.

[92] Reform proposed in see Basel Committee, *Globally Systemically Important Banks: Revised Assessment Framework, A Consultative Document* (March 2017) at http://www.bis.org/bcbs/publ/d402.pdf.

[93] Short-term borrowing in wholesale markets supported by collateral, usually highly liquid securities.

the Committee has selected key activities as indicative of banks' substitutability and complexity risks, so that these activities form a 'proxy' measure for the qualities of substitutability and complexity.

The Committee found, on the basis of data surveys of banks over previous 3 years, that the following areas of services are difficult to substitute if a bank falls into adversity. These services are in the areas of payments, securities underwriting and custodial services of money and assets. It is not difficult to see why. Payment services are dominated by a cluster of global banks.[94] Securities underwriting takes place in a relational paradigm, that is, based on the cultivation of relationships between corporations that intend to offer securities and their underwriting banks, and hence not easy to substitute. The risks of failure in custodial services are likely to generate market panic. Hence, the footprint of banks in these service areas would be crucial to determine their 'substitutability' score.

On complexity, the Committee regards the engagement by banks in over-the-counter derivative transactions, securitisations, and trading book activities as representative of entanglement in complex financial innovations whose markets may generate unexpected adversities. Although these may be good proxy measures based on current market trends, this category may require updating if new financial innovations start to become popular. The Committee foresees that the Indicator Approach will be refined in due course as national regulators gather more information and data surveys. In order to make more information about SIFIs available not only to regulators but to the public, the Committee recommends that financial institutions with a total exposure measure exceeding EUR 200 billion (total exposure as defined in section 9.4.1; using the exchange rate applicable at the financial year-end) should be required by national authorities to report their profiles based on the 12 indicators used in the assessment methodology. Such reporting is to be made publicly available on an annual basis from 31 December 2013.

9.5.1.2 Financial Stability Board's annual lists

The Basel Committee's Indicator Approach is used to calculate total scores for G-SIBs out of 100 per cent, and the Committee recommends that ranges of scores be set up so that G-SIBs falling within certain ranges would be considered to be at a certain level of 'systemic riskiness' to warrant the imposition of additional capital buffers.[95] Each range of score constitutes a 'systemic risk bucket' in which certain G-SIBs would fall into. The systemic risk bucket applicable to a SIFI would correspond to a recommended percentage of additional capital buffer to be applied, as discussed in Chapter 8, section 8.5.5. Table 9.10 illustrates this.

Where G-SIBs score highly on the five indicators and hit a range between D and E, they are placed into Bucket 5, which attracts an additional capital buffer of 3.5 per cent

---

[94] See, for example, Carol Clark, Victor Lubasi and Gozde Yazar, 'Global Payment Systems' (2005–6) 1 *Journal of Payment Systems Law* 25.   [95] Discussed in Chapter 8.

Table 9.10 Systemic Risk Score Bucketing Approach

Bucket	Score range	Additional capital buffer requirement
5	D–E	3.5%
4	C–D	2.5%
3	B–C	2.0%
2	A–B	1.5%
1	Cut-off point–A	1.0%

of risk-weighted assets. This bucket is however deterrent as discussed earlier in Chapter 8, and no G-SIB has been placed there yet. However, the Committee envisages that there could be a need to introduce more buckets in the future and to move the deterrent bucket upwards. The lowest scoring G-SIBs would be placed in range 0–A or Bucket 1, which attracts an additional capital buffer of 1 per cent risk-weighted assets.

This methodology has been applied by the FSB to assess global banks since its inception in 2013. The Board produces an annual list of G-SIBs in their respective buckets since November 2013, to assist national regulators in determining the rate of additional capital buffers that should apply to these institutions. For example, in the FSB's list updated in November 2017,[96] JP Morgan was placed in Bucket 4. Where UK banks are concerned, HSBC was placed in Bucket 3, Barclays in Bucket 2, and Royal Bank of Scotland (RBS) in Bucket 1. Bucket 1 is the most largely populated bucket with slightly over half of the total number of G-SIBs identified.

The designation of G-SIBs in their respective buckets helps policymakers to determine specific risk-mitigating measures in regulation that should apply. As discussed in Chapter 8, section 8.5, the G-SIB buffer, ALRB and the Total Loss-Absorbing Capacity (TLAC)/MREL measures are highly sensitive to G-SIBs' 'bucket' classification.

9.5.2 Implementation in the UK and EU

The Basel Committee's Indicator Approach has been adopted into legislation by the EU[97]. Level 2 legislation adopted by the Commission[98] now provides for a standardised information provision template for banks so that information can be collected on the Basel committee's indicators in order for regulators to determine if a bank is a G-SIB.

---

[96] http://www.fsb.org/wp-content/uploads/2016-update-of-list-of-global-systemically-important-banks-G-SIBs.pdf.

[97] EBA, *Final Report: Final Draft Implementing Technical Standards Amending the Commission Implementing Regulation (EU) No 1030/2014 on the Uniform Formats and Date for the Disclosure of the Values Used to Identify Global Systemically Important Institutions* (January 2016) at https://www.eba.europa.eu/documents/10180/1333778/EBA-ITS-2016-01+%28Final+draft+ITS+on+G-SII+identification%29.pdf.

The Indicator Approach applies to all EU banks that have a total exposure measure (explained in section 9.4) of €200 billion and above. The Indicator Approach will be used to score banks based on their previous year's data, on an annual basis, to determine if they should be regarded as a G-SIB. The EBA has also set out comprehensive disclosure templates for G-SIBs and requires disclosure of 'ancillary matters' above and beyond the Basel Committee's requirements, in order for regulators to build up a fuller picture of the bank's global footprint. Ancillary matters include funding sources, revenue breakdown, payments made in various currencies and insurance arrangements.[99]

The Indicator Approach is important as it forms the basis for identifying suitable banks that should be subject to enhanced micro-prudential regulatory measures especially targeted at them. Further, applying the Indicator Approach is also an opportunity for regulators to collect much more data about these banks and their risk profiles, in order to feed into judgment-based regulation and macro-prudential supervision (discussed in Chapter 6, section 6.2 and Chapter 7, section 7.2). One of the regulatory breakthroughs achieved after the 2007–9 global financial crisis is the explosion of transparency requirements for banks in order to be more accountable to regulators. Regulators can now require much more disclosure from banks and such information equips regulators with a sounder basis for accurate supervisory activity. In this respect, G-SIBs are subject to the most intense levels of regulatory change in mandatory disclosure requirements to both regulators and to the public.[100]

9.5.3 Domestic systemically important financial institutions

Although the Basel Committee has not intervened prescriptively into how financial institutions that have a significant impact at the domestic level of financial and economic systems ought to be identified, it has urged national regulators to identify them. These financial institutions, which are domestic SIFIs (D-SIBs discussed

---

[98] Commission Implementing Regulation (EU) 818/2016 of 17 May 2016 amending Implementing Regulation (EU) No 1030/2014 laying down implementing technical standards with regard to the uniform formats and date for the disclosure of the values used to identify global systemically important institutions according to Regulation (EU) No 575/2013 of the European Parliament and of the Council.

[99] EBA, *Final Report Revised Guidelines on the Further Specification of the Indicators of Global Systemic Importance and Their Disclosure* (January 2016), at https://www.eba.europa.eu/documents/10180/1388592/Guidelines+on+G-Sll+identification; Commission Implementing Regulation (EU) No 1030/2014 of 29 September 2014 laying down implementing technical standards with regard to the uniform formats and date for the disclosure of the values used to identify global systemically important institutions according to Regulation (EU) No 575/2013 of the European Parliament and of the Council.

[100] Iris H-Y Chiu, 'Corporate Transparency and Reporting in Banks and Financial Institutions' in Iris H-Y Chiu and M McKee (consulting editor) (eds), *The Law on Corporate Governance in Banks* (Cheltenham: Edward Elgar 2015); Iris H-Y Chiu, 'Transparency Regulation in Financial Markets – Moving into the Surveillance Age?' (2011) 3 *European Journal of Risk and Regulation* 303.

in Chapter 8, section 8.5.5) may generate systemic risks that could affect a national economy adversely.

In this respect the Basel Committee has produced a list of Principles[101] to assist national regulators, encouraging domestic regulators to adopt a modified version of the Indicator Approach discussed above. The modified version would include four indicators of size, complexity, interconnectedness, and substitutability, with the possibility that national regulators may add to this their own indicators depending on domestic industry structure, and adapt the sub-indicators established for the four indicators mentioned above.

The 12 Principles are illustrated in Table 9.11.

National regulators are ultimately responsible for developing a consistent and publicly disclosed methodology that is backed up by their assessment of D-SIBs' systemic risk profile. It is also explicitly stated that the point of identifying D-SIBs is to impose additional capital adequacy requirements, but such is left to national regulators to determine.

The EBA has taken its cue from the Basel Committee's Principles to develop a consistent methodology based on the four indicators mentioned above. The EBA's guidelines for D-SIBs are highly persuasive for national regulators though not literally binding (discussed in Chapter 7, section 7.2).

In the EBA's D-SIB guidelines, the four indicators size, complexity, substitutability, and interconnectedness are equally weighted at 25 per cent, and the EBA adopts sub-indicators for the four indicators, each also equally weighted.[102] Table 9.12 illustrates the EBA's D-SIBs Indicator Approach.

The EBA has started evaluating D-SIBs on a yearly basis since 2015 and published a list of D-SIBs across the EU for national regulators to consider applying appropriate regulatory treatment.[103] The list is based on each bank scoring at least 350 basis points on the Indicator Approach illustrated in Table 9.12, with discretion to apply a lower threshold of 275 basis points or raising the threshold to 425 basis points.

The PRA was initially concerned about the impact of identifying D-SIBs in the UK. In particular, D-SIBs may suffer adverse competitive disadvantages and such identification may have unfairly discriminatory consequences.[104] However, upon consultation, the PRA has decided to align its D-SIB identification methodology with the EBA's approach above.[105] The PRA will exclude firms that hold less than 0.02 per cent of the total assets of credit institutions and investment firms authorised in the UK.

---

[101] Basel Committee, *A Framework for Dealing with Domestic Systemically Important Banks* (October 2012) at http://www.bis.org/publ/bcbs233.pdf.

[102] EBA, *Guidelines on the Criteria to Determine the Conditions of Application of Article 131(3) of Directive 2013/36/EU (CRD) in Relation to the Assessment of Other Systemically Important Institutions (O-SIIs)* (December 2014) at http://www.eba.europa.eu/documents/10180/930752/EBA-GL-2014-10+%28Guidelines+on+O-SIIs+Assessment%29.pdf/964fa8c7-6f7c-431a-8c34-82d42d112d91.

[103] See http://www.eba.europa.eu/risk-analysis-and-data/other-systemically-important-institutions-o-siis-/2015.

[104] PRA, *Consultation Paper: The PRA's Approach to Identifying Other Systemically Important Institutions (O-SIIs)* (October 2015) at http://www.bankofengland.co.uk/pra/Documents/publications/cp/2015/cp3915.pdf.

[105] PRA, *Statement of Policy: The PRA's Approach to Identifying Other Systemically Important Institutions (O-SIIs)* (February 2016) at https://www.bankofengland.co.uk/-/media/boe/files/prudential-regulation/policy-statement/2016/ps616.pdf?la=en&hash=07F6BF8B8283A9E6E3080FFCE86DA22E8AEEE977.

Table 9.11 Principles of guidance for national regulators in developing a D-SIBs framework

Principle 1: National authorities should establish a methodology for assessing the degree to which banks are systemically important in a domestic context.

Principle 2: The assessment methodology for a D-SIB should reflect the potential impact of, or wider economic and social cost of a bank's failure.

Principle 3: The reference system for assessing the impact of failure of a D-SIB should be the domestic economy.

Principle 4: Home authorities should assess banks for their degree of systemic importance at the consolidated group level, while host authorities should assess subsidiaries in their jurisdictions, (consolidated to include any of further subsidiaries), for their degree of systemic importance.

Principle 5: The impact of a D-SIB's failure on the domestic economy should, in principle, be assessed having regard to bank-specific factors such as size; inter-connectedness; substitutability/financial institution infrastructure; and complexity. In addition, national authorities can consider other measures/data that would inform these bank-specific indicators within each of the above factors, such as size of the domestic economy.

Principle 6: National authorities should undertake regular assessments of the systemic importance of the banks in their jurisdictions to ensure that their assessment reflects the current state of the relevant financial systems. The interval between D-SIB assessments should not be significantly longer than the G-SIB assessment frequency.

Principle 7: National authorities should publicly disclose information that provides an outline of the methodology employed to assess the systemic importance of banks in their domestic economy.

Principles 8 and 9: National authorities should impose higher capital adequacy requirements on D-SIBs relative to other domestic banks commensurate with their systemic risk profile.

Principle 10: Where a bank is both a G-SIB and D-SIB, National regulators should ensure that additional capital buffers imposed on the bank are coordinated.

Principle 11: Where a D-SIB may be a subsidiary of a foreign bank, the national regulator must coordinate with the regulator of the parent bank in respect of imposition of capital buffer requirements.

Principle 12: Additional capital buffer requirements imposed for the purposes of addressing D-SIB risk should be met out of common equity tier one capital.

It is to be queried why the EBA has chosen to adopt a prescriptive approach to identifying D-SIBs as national regulators may be better placed to exercise their discretion on the factors that matter for determining a bank's domestic impact. However, it may be argued that the EBA's approach prevents a race to the bottom approach by national

Table 9.12

Category/indicator	Sub-indicator	Weighting
Size (25%)	Total assets	25%
Interconnectedness (25%)	Intra-financial system assets	8.33%
	Intra-financial system liabilities	8.33%
	Debt Securities outstanding	8.33%
Importance/ substitutability (25%)	Value of domestic payment transactions	8.33%
	Private sector deposits from depositors in the EU	8.33%
	Private sector loans to recipients in the EU	8.33%
Complexity (25%)	Value of over-the-counter derivatives (notional)	8.33%
	Cross-jurisdictional claims	8.33%
	Cross-jurisdictional liabilities	8.33%

regulators and provides a level of consistency. National regulators may be more likely captured by their domestic banking industry's interests and refrain from imposing stringent requirements upon significant or large banks. Nevertheless, the EBA Guidelines are only of a highly persuasive nature, and member states can choose to adopt more tailor-made arrangements.

We next turn to take stock of the targeted micro-prudential regulatory regime for G-SIBs and D-SIBs. This is a consolidation of various measures we have discussed in Chapter 8 and the foregoing in the current chapter, in order to present the synthesised information in one location for ease of reference, and to point out the distinguishing features from the generally applicable micro-prudential regulatory regime.

9.5.4 Micro-prudential regulatory regime targeted at G-SIBs and D-SIBs

G-SIBs and D-SIBs have systemic risk profiles, meaning that they have the potential to cause widespread disruption to the financial system and potentially more widely to the economy if they fail or become crisis-stricken. Hence, the micro-prudential regulatory regime for them introduces a gone-concern aspect requiring them to hold levels of 'loss-absorbing' capital that can help them absorb losses and recapitalise after a stressful onset. This is in addition to going concern capital requirements discussed in Chapter 8. The EU first developed this concept as MREL, discussed in Chapter 8, section 8.5, but the FSB has refined this concept specifically for application to G-SIBs.

9.5.4.1 Total loss-absorbing capacity reforms

The FSB is of the view that the safety of G-SIBs lies very much in their resolvability if any G-SIB should encounter a crisis. As the objective is to prevent G-SIBs from failing and entailing a cascade of global systemic risks, the adequate capitalisation of G-SIBs should not merely relate to *ex ante* controls on risk-taking effected by capital adequacy regulation which applies on a going concern basis but by the holding of capital instruments by banks that can actually be used to absorb losses and recapitalise the bank if a crisis should occur. Hence, the thinking is that the adequate capitalisation of a G-SIB should tie in with what is required for a G-SIB to absorb losses, recapitalise, and recover, or else be resolved in an orderly manner with least disruption to the wider financial and economic systems.

G-SIBs should therefore hold loss-absorbing capital in a sufficient quantity so that they are able to absorb losses should these occur. Banks therefore need to hold 'loss-absorbing' instruments, which are issued to investors willing to incur the risk of these instruments being used for 'loss absorption'. Loss-absorbing instruments will be priced by markets, and it is arguable that the price banks have to pay will act as a form of *ex ante* control upon their risk-taking.

The FSB has developed the TLAC reforms[106] that require banks to hold sufficient loss-absorbing instruments so that private sector creditors and shareholders will take much of the hit of a bank crisis rather than the public sector (as seen in the 2007–9 global financial crisis, discussed in Chapter 1). In this way, TLAC is related to the importance of bail-in (discussed in Chapter 13, section 13.2.5) as a crisis management and resolution tool for banks.

The FSB's TLAC recommendations are that banks must hold loss-absorbing instruments equivalent to 16–18 per cent of the bank's risk-weighted assets. This figure which is roughly twice the amount of the risk-asset ratio excluding all buffers would correspond to absorbing the losses of the failing bank and providing an amount to recapitalise the bank. It is to be noted that the Independent Commission on Banking in the UK[107] recommended that G-SIBs with risk-weighted assets at more than 3 per cent of the UK's GDP should hold a total of loss-absorbing level of capital at 17 per cent or more. This figure, which the Commission empirically tested, is in line with the TLAC reforms.

9.5.4.2 What is TLAC and internal TLAC?

The FSB envisages that a prescriptive minimum should be set for the TLAC, which will be applied to a G-SIB banking group as a whole. Although it recognises that TLAC should be worked out by each national regulator with its regulated G-SIB in view of each G-SIB's profile, the prescriptive minimum prevents a race to the bottom, and is set at 16 per cent of risk-weighted assets. The minimum of 16 per cent of risk-weighted assets is

---

[106] FSB, *Principles on Loss-absorbing and Recapitalisation Capacity of G-SIBs in Resolution Total Loss-absorbing Capacity (TLAC) Term Sheet* (Nov 2015) at http://www.fsb.org/wp-content/uploads/TLAC-Principles-and-Term-Sheet-for-publication-final.pdf.

[107] Independent Commission on Banking, *Final Report: Recommendations* (September 2011) at http://webarchive.nationalarchives.gov.uk/20131003105424/https:/hmt-sanctions.s3.amazonaws.com/ICB%20final%20report/ICB%2520Final%2520Report%5B1%5D.pdf, ch 4.

to phase in from January 2019. Further in order to prevent banks from gaming the system and manipulating risk-weights of assets, the 16 per cent risk-weighted assets ratio is supported by an absolute minimum 6 per cent leverage ratio, to be phased in at the same time as the minimum of 16 per cent risk-weighted assets. The FSB expects the minimum to be elevated to 18 per cent risk-weighted assets by January 2022, with the minimum leverage ratio set at 6.75 per cent. The FSB expects that national regulators have the discretion to exceed the minimum amounts depending on what they discover in relation to G-SIBs' risk profiles, and the potential adverse impact of G-SIB failure. The EU's and UK's position on the TLAC is that the TLAC will be implemented for G-SIBs and D-SIBs as part of the more broadly framed MREL reforms (discussed in Chapter 8, section 8.5).

Further, although the TLAC is imposed at group level for each G-SIB, it is expected that subsidiaries of a group that may be of importance to their respective local jurisdictions should maintain an internal TLAC. This is to ensure that the resolution of the group, which may involve key subsidiaries elsewhere in the world, can take place at a jurisdictional level (multiple point-of-entry, discussed in Chapter 13, section 13.4). An internal TLAC should be worked out between home and host regulators in co-ordination, and should only apply to 'material sub-groups' within the G-SIB. This means that an internal TLAC is not required for every subsidiary but only for material subsidiaries. 'Material sub-group' is defined as:

(a) having more than 5 per cent of the consolidated risk-weighted assets of the G-SIB group; or

(b) generating more than 5 per cent of the total operating income of the G-SIB group; or

(c) having a total leverage exposure measure larger than 5 per cent of the G-SIB group's consolidated leverage exposure measure; or

(d) having been identified by the firm's group of coordinated regulators as material to the exercise of the firm's critical functions (irrespective of whether any other criteria are met).

Such material sub-group is expected to maintain an internal TLAC of 75 per cent to 90 per cent of the external TLAC requirement imposed on the group as a whole. The UK is set to implement the internal TLAC according to the FSB's approach, while the EU proposes to set the internal TLAC at 90 per cent of the external TLAC requirement.[108]

B-SIBs have since the global financial crisis been subject to increased going concern capital requirements and now substantial levels of gone-concern capital requirements. However, one may argue that imposing a minimum 18 per cent risk–asset ratio is not necessarily challenging if the quality of capital that supports such a ratio is changed to include a more generous range of instruments. Further,

---

[108]   Chapter 8, section 8.5.

several economists are of the view that the capital requirements must fully incentivise bank shareholders to monitor its risk-taking and at low levels, they are not motivated to do so. It is arguably warranted to make risk-taking by banks much more expensive even if this means that bank activity may shrink, and bank funding becomes much more expensive. These economists recommend that the risk–asset ratio should be elevated to between 20 per cent to 30 per cent.[109] In this light, the TLAC reforms may only be seen as a middle ground between the increasingly discredited 8 per cent risk–asset ratio for G-SIBs and 30 per cent ratio suggested by several economists as mentioned above.

9.5.4.3 Eligible instruments and exclusions

TLAC eligible instruments include capital instruments now currently supporting the risk–asset ratio, except that capital instruments issued by subsidiaries, material subgroups and other entities within the potential resolution group within the G-SIB should not count, as those would count as internal TLAC that these entities need to maintain. TLAC eligible instruments also include a wider range of instruments that have 'loss-absorbing' capability as long as the following criteria are satisfied. The TLAC eligible instrument must:

(a) be paid in;

(b) be unsecured;

(c) not be subject to set off or netting rights that would undermine their loss-absorbing capacity in resolution;

(d) have a minimum remaining contractual maturity of at least one year or be perpetual (no maturity date);

(e) not be redeemable by the holder prior to maturity; and

(f) not be funded directly or indirectly by the G-SIB or a related party of the G-SIB, except where the relevant home and host authorities agree to allow such instruments to count towards external TLAC of the G-SIB.

Instruments such as convertible bonds with long-dated maturities issued by banks would count towards TLAC eligible instruments (discussed in Chapter 8 under MREL, see section 8.5.7). However, TLAC eligible instruments should not be redeemable at will by the bank itself. The nature of TLAC eligible instruments closely resembles the liabilities that may be subject to bail-in if a financial institution needs to be recapitalised and resolved (discussed in Chapter 13, section 13.2).

Instruments or liabilities excluded from TLAC also resemble those excluded from bail-in, and they are:

(a) insured deposits;

---

[109] Anat Admati and Martin Hellwig, *The Bankers' New Clothes: What's Wrong with Banking and What to Do about It* (NJ: Princeton University Press 2014).

(b) sight deposits and short-term deposits (deposits with original maturity of less than one year);

(c) liabilities arising from derivatives;

(d) debt instruments with derivative-linked features, such as structured notes;

(e) liabilities arising other than through a contract, such as tax liabilities;

(f) liabilities that are preferred to senior unsecured creditors under the relevant insolvency law; or

(g) any liabilities that, under the laws governing the issuing entity, are excluded from bail-in or cannot be written down or converted into equity by the relevant resolution authority without giving rise to material risk of successful legal challenge or valid compensation claims.

TLAC complements bail-in as it requires banks to raise sufficient loss-absorbing capital in the form of debt and/or equity instruments, therefore putting in place a process to allow the markets to price these instruments appropriately in view of banks' global risks. Purchasers of TLAC eligible instruments are therefore voluntary financiers who exercise market discipline by pricing banks' risk-taking profiles, thereby exerting control upon banks' risk-taking activities, and are also prepared to absorb bank losses when bail-in is implemented in a crisis.[110] The TLAC reforms arguably introduce a market mechanism to prepare for the application of bail-in, in order to avoid some of the unexpected market disruptions and panics that can occur if bail-in is implemented by resolution authorities.[111] However, more sceptical commentators may see TLAC eligible instruments as likely unpopular with major investors, such as institutions, and so funding cost will increase for banks. If banks do not manage to obtain the high level of private sector support for its activities, taxpayers could still be at risk of bailing out failed banks.[112]

9.5.4.4 Relationship with the EU's and UK's MREL reforms

As discussed in Chapter 8, the EU has ahead of the FSB's TLAC recommendations introduced a regime for MREL that serves the same purposes as TLAC but for all EU

---

[110] Although some commentators doubt that the market will be 'educated and prepared' for bail-in, as they will be attracted to the short-term high interest rates paid on these TLAC eligible instruments, see Amitai Aviram, 'Bail-ins: Cyclical Effects of a Common Response to Financial Crises' (2011) *University of Illinois Law Review* 1633.

[111] Iris H-Y Chiu, 'Corporate Governance- The Missing Paradigm in the Mandatory Bail-in Regime for Creditors of Banks and Financial Institutions' (2014) *Journal of Business Law* 611.

[112] Arthur J Wilmarth Jnr, 'SPOE Plus TLAC = More Bailouts for Wall Street' (35 Banking & Financial Services Policy Report No. 3, at 1–14 (Mar. 2016)) at http://papers.ssrn.com/sol3/papers.cfm?abstract_id=2767116.

[113] EBA, *Interim Report on MREL: Report on the Implementation and Design of the MREL Framework* (July 2016) at http://www.eba.europa.eu/documents/10180/1360107/EBA+Interim+report+on+MREL.

[114] Proposed Article 92a, Commission Proposal to amend the Capital Requirements IV Regulation 2013, as of 26 November 2016.

banks generally. The EBA[113] has however recommended minimising the deviation between the MREL and TLAC and the EU's banking reform package as at the end of 2016 is set to implement MREL in a manner that distinguishes G-SIBs and D-SIBs from other banks. The EU will[114] dovetail MREL requirements for G-SIBs in the EU with the upper requirements of TLAC. This means G-SIBs must hold at least 18 per cent risk-weighted assets in eligible recapitalising instruments and meet a leverage ratio of 6.75 per cent. The MREL requirements for other banks in the EU, including D-SIBs, would be imposed based on the Single Resolution Board's and national regulators' discretion (whichever is applicable), as discussed in Chapter 8, section 8.5. The PRA will, however, largely implement the same MREL for G-SIBs *and* D-SIBs (see Chapter 8, section 8.5), and leave the implementation of MREL for other banks to discretionary assessment of whether recapitalising capital is needed for each bank and to what extent. In sum, the FSB's TLAC standards are able to pave the way for the creation of distinct gone-concern regulatory capital regimes for G-SIBs and D-SIBs.

Table 9.13 sets out the key points of comparison between the implementation of MREL generally and the implementation of TLAC as MREL for G-SIBs and D-SIBs.

It is to be noted that the US has implemented the TLAC according to the FSB's timeframe, in a way that subjects G-SIBs whose home jurisdiction is the US to a minimum 18 per cent risk–asset ratio requirement supported by a minimum of 9.5 per cent leverage ratio. For foreign banks operating in the US that are G-SIBs, the TLAC would apply at 16 per cent risk–asset ratio supported by a minimum 6 per cent leverage ratio.[115] It remains to be seen if the different approaches in the EU, UK, and US would result in competitive advantages or disadvantages. Further, it of course remains to be seen which regime may promote more resilient and resolvable

Table 9.13 Comparing the MREL regime for EU banks generally and the MREL/TLAC regime for G-SIBs and D-SIBs

	G-SIBs (and D-SIBs in the UK)	Other banks
Nature of application computation	Mandatory as Pillar 1 as gone concern capital requirements in addition to going concern capital requirements discussed in Chapter 8.	Discretionary as Pillar 2
Nature of capital instruments	MREL eligible instruments are narrower than TLAC as they require full subordination	same
Implementation timeframe	TLAC minimum from 2019 MREL from 2020	From 2019

banks, while allowing banks to function and create credit effectively in normal times.

9.5.4.5 Piecing together with other micro-prudential measures

This section does not introduce anything new but intends to consolidate into one location the specific measures targeted at G-SIBs and D-SIBs, in order for us to appreciate the whole micro-prudential regulatory regime applicable to G-SIBs and D-SIBs. In sum, G-SIBs and D-SIBs are subject to gone-concern capital requirements in addition to going concern capital requirements.

Boxes 9.8 and 9.9 sum up the specific micro-prudential regulatory measures applicable to G-SIBs and D-SIBs. These Boxes show the going concern capital requirements, that is, the basic risk–asset ratio and across-the-board buffers such as capital conservation and counter-cyclical buffers, the liquidity and leverage ratios and large exposures controls. Boxes 9.8 and 9.9 also show the extra or modified regulatory measures applicable to G-SIBs and D-SIBs.

Box 9.8 Micro-prudential regulatory measures for G-SIBs (summary and bird's eye view)

- risk–asset ratio +
- capital conservation buffer +
- counter-cyclical buffer +
- institution-specific counter-cyclical buffer (affects G-SIBs as they are likely to operate in various jurisdictions, and hence exposed to a range of national counter-cyclical buffers beyond EU Member state) +
- systemic risk buffer+
- G-SIB buffer +
- Pillar 2A capital requirements +
- leverage ratio (6.75 per cent) +
- CLRB (as discussed earlier in section 9.4.4) +
- ALRB +
- MREL as gone concern capital
- lower limits for large exposures
- *ring-fencing* measures in the UK (Chapter 10)

---

[115] Federal Reserve of New York Press Release, 30 October 2015 at https://www.federalreserve.gov/newsevents/press/bcreg/20151030a.htm.

Box 9.9 Micro-prudential regulatory measures for D-SIBs (UK only, summary and bird's eye view)

- risk–asset ratio +
- capital conservation buffer +
- counter-cyclical buffer +
- institution-specific counter-cyclical buffer (affects G-SIBs as they are likely to operate in various jurisdictions, and hence exposed to a range of national counter-cyclical buffers beyond EU Member state) +
- systemic risk buffer +
- D-SIB buffer (if any) +
- Pillar 2A capital requirements +
- CLRB (as discussed earlier in section 9.4.4) +
- MREL as gone concern capital computed in the same manner as MREL for G-SIBs
- leverage ratio of twice the amount of leverage ratio applicable to all banks at that time +
- ring-fencing measures (Chapter 10)

It may be queried as to why reduced large exposure limits and the ALRB should only apply to G-SIBs and not D-SIBs as D-SIBs can also cause potentially hazardous impact on the domestic financial system and economy. However, D-SIBs are likely to be more exposed to lending to the domestic sovereign, local corporations, and households compared to G-SIBs, so absolute curbs on lending imposed by reduced large exposures limits and the ALRB may be adverse to local economic needs. Moreover, D-SIBs are subject to regulation to manage risks and to safeguard their retail operations through ring-fencing requirements (discussed in Chapter 10), mitigating the need to further restrain their lending. G-SIBs may be perceived to be more difficult to govern and control as their international profiles dwarf national economies, so stricter limits applied to their lending may be seen as more effective.

Finally, we turn to a supervisory measure for ensuring that micro-prudential regulation is complied with and works effectively for banks.

Key takeaways

- International and national regulators identify the need to develop a methodology to identify SIFIs that have the most potential to cause damage to the financial and economic systems if they fail.
- The Basel Committee developed an Indicator Approach to identify G-SIBs.

- The Indicator Approach is based on five indicators size, complexity, substitutability, interconnectedness, and global footprint, with sub-indicators in each indicator category except size.

- Banks are scored against each sub-indicator to obtain a total score over 10,000 basis points. Score ranges correspond to 5 buckets of systemic importance and banks are placed in those buckets.

- The FSB has drawn up lists of G-SIBs for each of the five buckets, with the top bucket left empty for deterrent purposes.

- The Basel Committee has also developed Principles and a similar Indicator Approach to help national regulators identify D-SIBs but national regulators have more discretion to adapt the Indicator Approach.

- The EBA recommended and the Commission has enacted into legislation the adapted four-Indicator Approach for D-SIBs in the EU.

- The micro-prudential regulatory regimes for G-SIBs and D-SIBs are increasingly more refined and distinguished from the generally applicable micro-prudential regulatory measures for all banks.

- The creation of a special micro-prudential regulatory regime for G-SIBs and D-SIBs has been spurred by the FSB's development of the TLAC regime as Pillar 1 capital for G-SIBs.

- The special TLAC regime is to be implemented within the UK's and EU's MREL regimes.

Key bibliography

Legislation

Commission Implementing Regulation (EU) No 1030/2014 of 29 September 2014 laying down implementing technical standards with regard to the uniform formats and date for the disclosure of the values used to identify global systemically important institutions according to Regulation (EU) No 575/2013 of the European Parliament and of the Council.

Reports and Guidelines

Basel Committee, *A Framework for Dealing with Domestic Systemically Important Banks* (Oct 2012) at http://www.bis.org/publ/bcbs233.pdf

Basel Committee, *Global Systemically Important Banks: Updated Assessment Methodology and the Higher Loss Absorbency Requirement* (July 2013) at http://www.bis.org/publ/bcbs255.pdf

EBA, *Guidelines on the Criteria to Determine the Conditions of Application of Article 131(3) of Directive 2013/36/EU (CRD) in Relation to the Assessment of Other Systemically Important Institutions (O-SIIs)* (Dec 2014) at http://www.eba.europa.eu/documents/10180/930752/EBA-GL-2014-10+%28Guidelines+on+O-SIIs+Assessment%29.pdf/964fa8c7-6f7c-431a-8c34-82d42d112d91

EBA, *Final Report Revised Guidelines on the Further Specification of the Indicators of Global Systemic Importance and Their Disclosure* (Jan 2016), at https://www.eba.europa.eu/documents/10180/1388592/Guidelines+on+G-SII+identification

FSB, *Principles on Loss-absorbing and Recapitalisation Capacity of G-SIBs in Resolution Total Loss-absorbing Capacity (TLAC) Term Sheet* (Nov 2015) at http://www.fsb.org/wp-content/uploads/TLAC-Principles-and-Term-Sheet-for-publication-final.pdf

Articles

Gracie, L, 'TLAC and MREL; From Design to Implementation', speech at the British Bankers' Association (23 July 2015) at http://www.bankofengland.co.uk/publications/Pages/speeches/2015/834.aspx

Lastra, R, 'Systemic Risk, SIFIs and Financial Stability' (2011) 6 *Capital Markets Law Journal* 197

Books

Admati, A and Hellwig, M, *The Bankers' New Clothes: What's Wrong with Banking and What to Do about It* (NJ: Princeton University Press 2014)

9.6 Stress testing

The micro-prudential regulation regimes discussed earlier are designed to control bank risk-taking and intended to help them avert crises and failure. However, they do not guarantee safety and soundness as they are fundamentally based on estimations of market behaviour. For example, the requirement under the LCR in section 9.1 will only work if the assets bank are required to hold *will really be liquid* in markets. For example, the successful recovery of a G-SIB using loss-absorbing TLAC instruments will only work if the prescribed level, that is, 18 per cent of risk-weighted assets, *actually turns out to be sufficient.*

Hence, in order to ensure that banks are complying with their micro-prudential requirements and that these requirements *are likely to work* in situations of stress, a new regulatory framework for stress testing has been introduced. Stress testing refers to the regular testing of banks' capital and liquidity positions in order to take stock of their resilience. There are two types of stress testing: one that banks are to regularly perform themselves and account to regulators for doing so; second is that regulators would carry out such tests across the banks they supervise. Both are forms of health checks for banks, one internally administered according to regulatory frameworks, and the other externally administered. These 'health checks' produce vital information for both banks and regulators as will be explained.

Stress testing carried out by banks is a means of taking stock as well as forward-planning. In taking stock of various aspects of its profile and positions, the bank produces information for senior management to assess and evaluate. As the regulatory framework demands that stress testing adhere to certain standards of rigour and consistency, senior management may have comparable information over periods to assess the overall resilience of their banks. Stress testing also enables banks to identify early signs of nearing regulatory infringements and to take prompt remedial actions. As discussed in Chapter 12, bank senior management have been found to be ignorant of their institutions' risk profiles and weaknesses prior to the 2007–9 global financial crisis. [116] The internal production of vital information by stress testing now provides a more robust information context for senior management and forces senior management to take greater responsibility for risk management.[117]

Next, bank stress testing produces information for regulators. As regulatory frameworks compel stress testing methodologies and results to be documented and reported to regulators, regulators are able to gain insights into banks' risk profiles and what banks think of their risk profiles. This feeds into all the supervisory information that regulators are collecting from banks and enables cross-checking and verification. Further, stress testing results may raise implications for regulatory action such as requiring banks to consider actions in relation to their recovery and resolution planning (discussed in Chapter 13, section 13.2) or in relation to their micro-prudential compliance. The Basel Committee sees the regulatory framework for bank stress testing and accountability as being integral to Pillar 2.[118] Poor stress testing results could put banks at risk of being imposed with increased capital requirements such as under the PRA Pillar 2A capital buffer (Chapter 8, section 8.5). This could create an incentive for banks to manage their risks more prudently to avoid being 'penalised' by increased buffers. However, the threat of regulatory enforcement could arguably create a disincentive for banks to conduct stress testing rigorously, in order to pass under the regulator's radar. Hence, bank stress testing must be supported by further independent stress testing that is externally-led, such as regulator's stress testing discussed below.

Bank stress testing can be seen as a form of comprehensive internal audit, with a forward-planning purpose, and being reportable and accountable to regulators. It has however not developed to the point of requiring the extra verification of an external auditor. Perhaps it is because bank stress testing is not exactly a form of external assurance to be issued to the markets and attracting Pillar 3 discipline. It is primarily seen as feeding into Pillar 2 and for supervisory purposes. Further, such results are for the purposes of preventive monitoring and early remediation and perhaps should not be released to markets for fear of creating unduly adverse market impressions and reactions.

---

[116] Hans J Blommestein, Lex Hoogduin, and JJW Peeters, 'Uncertainty and Risk Management after the Great Moderation: The Role of Risk (Mis)Management by Financial Institutions' (28th SUERF Colloquium, Utrecht, The Netherlands, 3–4 September 2009) http://papers.ssrn.com/sol3/papers.cfm?abstract_id=1489826; Donald C Langevoort, 'Chasing the Greased Pig Down Wall Street: A Gatekeeper's Guide to the Psychology, Culture and Ethics of Financial Risk-taking' (2011) 96 *Cornell Law Review* 1209; Michel Crouhy, 'Risk Management Failures During the Financial Crisis' in Robert W Kolb (ed), *Lessons from the Financial Crisis* (NJ: John Wiley 2010); Elizabeth Sheedy, 'The Future of Risk Modelling' in Robert W Kolb (ed), *Lessons from the Financial Crisis* (NJ: John Wiley 2010).

[117] See more detail in Iris H-Y Chiu, *Regulating from the Inside: The Legal Framework for Internal Control in Banks and Financial Institutions* (Oxford: Hart 2015) ch 3.

[118] Basel Committee, *Stress-testing Principles* (2018) at https://www.bis.org/bcbs/publ/d450.htm.

9.6.1 **The framework for bank stress testing**

Stress testing is ultimately useful for banks' own risk management, and it should be performed with integrity, supported by high levels of relevance, materiality, and a governance and IT infrastructure that meet its needs. The EU Capital Requirements Regulation 2013 establishes certain mandatory stress tests that banks need to carry out, but much of the prescriptive detail is left to be developed by the EBA and in Commission 'Level 2' legislation. The EBA's guidelines[119] intend to achieve a level of convergence for banks across the EU as stress testing has not been highly developed before in bank practices. Banks need to put in place a policy for stress testing themselves (referred to as bottom-up stress testing) with the following elements in Box 9.10.

This section proceeds to deal with the scope and types of stress testing, scenarios for stress testing, the methodologies for stress testing, the governance framework, the data infrastructure, reporting and use of information related to stress testing results and the supervisory response to bank stress testing results.

9.6.1.1 **Scope and types of stress testing**

Banks must carry out mandatory stress tests at least quarterly for the purposes of determining the resilience of banks' capital adequacy.[120] This is implemented as part of the

---

Box 9.10 The elements of the bottom-up stress testing policies banks must maintain

(a) the types of stress testing and their main objectives and application;

(b) the frequency of the different stress testing exercises;

(c) the internal governance regime with clear responsibilities and procedures;

(d) in case of a group, the scope of the entities included and the coverage (e.g. risk types and portfolios) of the stress tests;

(e) the methodological details, including models used and possible links between liquidity stress tests and solvency stress tests, namely the respective magnitude of such dynamic interaction and capture of feedback effects;

(f) the range of assumptions, including business and managerial, and remedial actions envisaged for each stress test; and

(g) the relevant data infrastructure.

---

[119] EBA, *Final Report on Guidelines for Institution Stress Testing* (2018) at https://www.eba.europa.eu/documents/10180/2282644/Guidelines+on+institutions+stress+testing+%28EBA-GL-2018-04%29.pdf/2b604bc8-fd08-4b17-ac4a-cdd5e662b802.

[120] Article 177, Regulation (EU) No 575/2013 of the European Parliament and of the Council of 26 June 2013 on prudential requirements for credit institutions and investment firms and amending Regulation (EU) No 648/2012.

'Internal Capital Adequacy Assessment' framework that the PRA applies to UK banks, discussed in Chapter 8, section 8.5.[121]

Financial institutions are categorised into four types in relation to the extent of stress testing they are required to carry out. Category 1 referring to systemically important institutions (G-SIBs and D-SIBs), Category 2 refers to less systemic but important institutions and Categories 3 and 4 refer to small and medium sized institutions. Although the EBA guidelines are extensive, national regulators would prescribe stress testing frameworks that apply proportionately to the different categories of financial institutions. The PRA applies the same standard of stress testing for the firms subject to its jurisdiction, as they are largely banks, insurers and investment firms that are systemically significant. The FCA applies stress testing requirements to other financial institutions within its supervisory remit in a manner consistent with the nature, size, scale, and complexity of the firms' businesses.[122]

On types of stress testing, banks need in particular to regularly stress test counterparty credit risk across all manners of transactions.[123] The EBA has also produced comprehensive guidelines.[124] It is suggested in the Guidelines that all on- and off-balance sheet risks in terms of solvency and liquidity should be stress-tested. Stress testing should be carried out in terms of individual-level risks in portfolios as well as institution-wide stresses.

Banks permitted to use internal models should subject them to regular stress testing too.[125] The frequency of the latter areas of stress testing is not prescribed, and can be a matter for supervisory discretion. Regulators can determine that stress testing frequency be increased in uncertain times or dependent on bank characteristics. Banks must also carry out liquidity stress testing on at least an annual basis.[126]

Further, both the Basel Committee and EBA regard it as best practice that banks engage in regular reverse stress testing. Reverse stress testing in the Basel Committee's view is a key pillar of forward-looking stress testing,[127] now a mandatory requirement adopted by the PRA.[128]

---

[121] PRA, *Internal Capital Adequacy Assessment* and *Internal Liquidity Adequacy Assessment*.

[122] FCA Handbook, SYSC 20.2.5.

[123] Articles 287 and 290, Regulation (EU) No 575/2013 of the European Parliament and of the Council of 26 June 2013 on prudential requirements for credit institutions and investment firms and amending Regulation (EU) No 648/2012.

[124] EBA, *Final Report on Guidelines for Institution Stress Testing* (2018) at https://www.eba.europa.eu/documents/10180/2282644/Guidelines+on+institutions+stress+testing+%28EBA-GL-2018-04%29.pdf/2b604bc8-fd08-4b17-ac4a-cdd5e662b802.

[125] Article 368, Regulation (EU) No 575/2013 of the European Parliament and of the Council of 26 June 2013 on prudential requirements for credit institutions and investment firms and amending Regulation (EU) No 648/2012.

[126] Article 86(11), Directive 2013/36/EU of the European Parliament and of the Council of 26 June 2013 on access to the activity of credit institutions and the prudential supervision of credit institutions and investment firms, amending Directive 2002/87/EC and repealing Directives 2006/48/EC and 2006/49/EC.

[127] Basel Committee, *Stress-testing Principles* (2018) at https://www.bis.org/bcbs/publ/d450.htm.

[128] PRA Rulebook, *Internal Capital Adequacy Assessment: Reverse Stress-testing* at http://www.prarulebook.co.uk/rulebook/Content/Chapter/302501/13-05-2016.

Reverse stress testing requires banks to first adopt particular adverse end outcomes and then test the bank's resilience against the outcomes. The PRA sets out clearly that the failure or unviability of the bank, due to a range of possible adverse factors, must be reverse stress-tested. Reverse stress testing is mandatory for UK banks on a yearly basis.

9.6.1.2 Scenarios

Stress testing is based on possible adverse scenarios for banks and they should develop historical, non-historical and hypothetical scenarios to test their resilience. The emphasis on forward-looking scenarios is now more pronounced as a lesson learnt since the global financial crisis.[129] Exact scenarios cannot be overly-prescribed or micro-managed, but the EBA and PRA provide some guidance on the nature of scenarios to be selected so that banks do not adopt overly lenient ones. The EBA recommends[130] that the range of scenarios should address all material risk factors, institution-specific vulnerabilities, the correlations between different risk factors, consider innovation and technological development, take into account wider economic contexts and regional factors, system-wide considerations such as market conditions and form a coherent narrative overall. These scenarios should be designed at sufficiently severe yet plausible levels. [131] The PRA requires banks to use scenarios that are of single or a combination of events, which may be protracted or sudden and severe. Banks should take into account dynamic interdependencies between the materialisation of risk factors,[132] so that consequential effects and wider systemic impact can be considered.

The Basel Committee has for example identified several specific areas of complexity or high risks that stress testing ought to give attention to, some of which have been taken up in the EBA's guidelines. Box 9.11 provides such examples of adverse scenarios. The PRA's regime addresses credit and counterparty risk, especially concentrated risks, securitisation, market, operational and liquidity risks, interest rate risk from non-trading activities, foreign exchange lending risk and conduct risk, and potential litigation costs.[133] However, guidance on what aspects are to be considered in scenario framing is useful only to an extent. Firms still have to design the exact parameters of the hypothetical stressful situation, such as if there is a default on a specific large exposure. Firms remain ultimately responsible for putting forward these specific scenarios and it may remain unclear to the regulator whether the scenarios are sufficiently robust

---

[129] Basel Committee, *Stress-testing Principles* (2018) at https://www.bis.org/bcbs/publ/d450.htm.
[130] EBA, *Final Report on Guidelines for Institution Stress Testing* (2018) at https://www.eba.europa.eu/documents/10180/2282644/Guidelines+on+institutions+stress+testing+%28EBA-GL-2018-04%29.pdf/2b604bc8-fd08-4b17-ac4a-cdd5e662b802.
[131] Mario Quagliariello (ed), *Stress-testing the Banking System: Methodologies and Applications* (Cambridge: Cambridge University Press 2011).
[132] The PRA Rulebook, *Stress-testing and Scenario Analysis* also states that connected risk effects and non-linear or contingent effects must be taken into account of in carrying out bank stress testing.
[133] PRA Rulebook, *Internal Capital Adequacy Assessment*. The *Internal Liquidity Adequacy Assessment* chapter identifies 14 specific areas of funding risk that require stress testing.

> ## Box 9.11 Examples of adverse scenarios to be used in stress testing
>
> - Counterparty and credit risks.
> - Cessation of banks' wholesale funding sources.
> - Illiquidity in asset markets.
> - Challenging conditions in relation to complex and bespoke products such as securitised exposures, underwriting activities, off-balance sheet activities and highly-leveraged counterparties, commodities, foreign exchange markets, and so on.
> - Sceptical assessment of the usefulness of risk mitigation techniques (such as fall in the value of collateral pledged to or by the bank).
> - Risk concentrations.
> - Operational risk such as reputation risks from operating certain businesses/in certain regions and vulnerabilities to IT problems.
> - Conduct risks in respect of litigation costs and regulatory fines.
> - Non-trading interest rate risk.

and whether all vital scenarios have been considered. Scenario framing in stress testing is also usually done with the benefit of hindsight, and can be limited and backward-looking. Scenario-framing for SIFIs can be particularly problematic as they have complex and voluminous cross-border operations. The scenarios for such institutions are likely varied, complex, and wide-ranging. It is uncertain if regulators are able to check the comprehensiveness and credibility of scenario-planning across such varied international businesses.

Regulators need to be vigilant against perverse incentives in the designing of scenarios by firms that may be geared towards future regulatory evasion. Regulators need to be keenly aware of the persistent divergence in incentives between the regulator and regulated[134] and develop more familiarity with the business operations of the regulated entities in order to check for cosmetic compliance behaviour. In this respect, we will shortly examine the 'monitoring' mechanisms in the form of bank accountability accompanying stress testing and the framework for regulators' stress testing of banks (i.e. 'top-down stress testing' as termed by the EBA).

9.6.1.3 Methodologies in stress testing

Methodologies in stress testing cannot be overly prescribed or micro-managed, but broad principles have been recommended by regulators in order to prevent minimalist practices.

---

[134] DN Ghosh, 'Quirks of the Market Regulator' (2004) 39 *Economic and Political Weekly* 1550; Onnig H Dombalagian, 'Requiem for the Bulge Bracket? Revisiting Investment Bank Regulation' (2010) 85 *Indiana Law Journal* 777.

The EBA Guidelines urge that stress testing models should be developed to be appropriate to the bank's business and complexity and take account of wider factors in the economic cycle. Stress testing models should also be designed with conservatism and where expert judgment is used, these should be clearly articulated.[135] Models should be developed with appropriate developer responsibility, internal control oversight and senior management approval, and banks should maintain an inventory of models so that they are constantly updated and reviewed.[136]

There is a heavy reliance on quantitative modelling in stress testing, as stress testing measures quantitative matters such as asset values, risk-weighted assets, regulatory capital, liquidity, and profitability. An emphasis on quantitative measures can provide room for manipulation in order to 'fix' the figures and tick the right boxes. It is important that stress testing by firms also becomes qualitative and are able to evaluate risk management processes, systems, and principles.[137] Although the EBA emphasises the importance of both quantitative and qualitative information that is obtained in the processes of reverse stress testing, qualitative aspects are highly undefined at the moment. It would benefit banks to have at least a framework of guidance, as qualitative aspects can relate to governance and culture issues, reputational issues, social responsibility issues[138] and so on, having an important impact on the bank's risk profile and future viability.

9.6.1.4 Governance framework

The Basel Committee and EBA are of the view that the governance framework for bank stress testing is important in ensuring that stress testing is developed robustly, holistically, and that its results feed into strategic decision-making and internal control at banks (see further discussion in Chapter 12).

In particular, the Board and senior management should be responsible for approving stress testing programmes and should engage with discussions of the programmes and be able to challenge key assumptions in the models. Stress testing programmes should be implemented within a framework of internal policies, and should be documented, communicated, and feed into management decision-making and senior management's setting of the risk appetite and limits for the bank.[139] The Basel Committee opines that

---

[135] EBA, *Final Report on Guidelines for Institution Stress Testing* (2018) at https://www.eba.europa.eu/documents/10180/2282644/Guidelines+on+institutions+stress+testing+%28EBA-GL-2018-04%29.pdf/2b604bc8-fd08-4b17-ac4a-cdd5e662b802.

[136] PRA, *Model Risk Management Principles for Stress Testing* (April 2018) at https://www.bankofengland.co.uk/-/media/boe/files/prudential-regulation/policy-statement/2018/ps718.pdf?la=en&hash=B03FD20700A5C1A83A46C89AC1144FF5F0058C0F.

[137] Hans J Blommestein, 'Risk Management after the Great Crash' (2010) 28 *Journal of Financial Transformation* 131.

[138] For example, UK Bank of England Governor and Chairman of the FSB has emphasised the importance of climate risks for banks, see Mark Carney, 'Breaking the Tragedy of the Horizon—Climate Change and Financial Stability', speech at Lloyd's of London (28 September 2015).

[139] EBA, *Final Report on Guidelines for Institution Stress Testing* (2018) at https://www.eba.europa.eu/documents/10180/2282644/Guidelines+on+institutions+stress+testing+%28EBA-GL-2018-04%29.pdf/2b604bc8-fd08-4b17-ac4a-cdd5e662b802.

stress-testing must be developed, carried out and reviewed within a framework that involves multiple units and internal control in the bank, therefore governed by an integated 'enterprise' approach. It is envisaged that such an integrated and holistic approach to implementing stress testing in the firm would also result in better internal communications, feedback, and review of risk information, in order to raise awareness and instigate discussions within the bank more widely.

9.6.1.5 Data and documentation

The EBA emphasises the importance of a comprehensive and credible data environment and infrastructure for robust stress testing. This is because stress testing is based on the bank's gathering of pertinent risk information about itself, and data completeness and integrity is therefore crucial in order to achieve credible stress testing outputs for both the bank and regulators.

Banks should institute a data infrastructure that is adequately resourced and supported, particularly by information technology, in order to capture accurate, timely, and complete data. It is recommended that dedicated resources should be responsible for data collection and aggregation, and automation in data systems is encouraged in order to minimise error.[140] This is consistent with wider recommendations made by the Basel Committee on overhauling the data infrastructure in banks (in order to prepare for more comprehensive and credible internal and regulatory reporting) in general.[141]

Stress test results should also be documented in order for banks to systemically undertake review of business and risk decisions, and for supervisors to monitor the quality of internal control in banks. In particular, management should be prepared to review risk limits and risk mitigation techniques, or even consider more intense actions such as restricting distributions to shareholders, raising capital or changing business strategies. In this respect, the PRA requires that banks keep written records for at least 3 years. These records must identify the major sources of risk that may affect capital and liquidity positions, how the bank intends to deal with those risks, details of the stress tests and scenario analyses carried out, including any assumptions made in relation to scenario framing, and the resulting financial resources needed for any action taken by the bank as a result of the stress test outcome.

9.6.1.6 Supervisory monitoring and review: Pillar 2

As already mentioned, stress testing forms part of banks' internal capital adequacy and liquidity assessments, which are to be regularly reported to regulators.[142] Stress test results not only provides banks with insight as to how resilient they are (or not) but also regulators with crucial information for supervisory monitoring. This includes supervisory insight into near-breaches by banks or risky positions taken by banks that may require supervisory intervention.

---

[140] Ibid.

[141] Basel Committee, *Principles for Effective Risk Data Aggregation and Risk Reporting* (January 2013) at http://www.bis.org/publ/bcbs239.pdf.

[142] PRA Rulebook, *Internal Liquidity Adequacy Assessment* at para 11.8; *Internal Capital Adequacy Assessment* at paras 2 and 3.

Regulators may use such insights as part of supervisory dialogue with banks, but banks should not perceive such transparency as being liable to result in punitive regulatory burdens or consequences. Otherwise banks may be inclined towards perverse incentives to manipulate what needs to be reported to regulators and quality of transparency may become a problem. It remains important for regulators to take a responsive approach to regulation, in the spirit of Ayres' and Braithwaite's pyramid of enforcement[143] so that severe and visible enforcement are reserved for truly non-cooperative and unresponsive behaviour.

The EBA envisages that stress test results could feed into recovery and resolution planning by banks. As will be discussed in Chapter 13, banks need to submit plans to regulators to show how they intend to recover, or otherwise be resolved in an orderly manner if they descend into a crisis. Stress test results could provide insights to challenge the assumptions made in recovery and resolution plans, as well as identify the feasibilities and vulnerabilities in recovery/resolution options. Banks should use such information to adjust their plans accordingly.

The Basel Committee also envisages that national regulators should critically review banks' stress testing procedures and policies, their methodologies and assumptions and implementation. This is an area that requires national regulators to build up quantitative and qualitative expertise over time.

9.6.2 Regulators' stress testing in the UK

We turn now to discuss externally-administered stress testing that is carried out at two levels, one at the national level implemented by the PRA, and the other at the EU level by the EBA across all EU banks and not just those in the single currency area. It remains uncertain if UK banks will be excluded from the EBA's stress tests upon the UK's departure from the EU. If material subsidiaries of UK banks operate in EU member states, it is envisaged that they can still be part of the EBA's stress testing operations and those results can have implications for subsidiaries' capital levels as well as the parent holding company in the UK.

Externally-administered stress testing or top-down stress tests, allows regulators to subject all banks to supervisory health checks periodically, so that regulators do not only rely on bank-reported information for their supervisory decisions and actions. In the absence of external auditing to verify banks' stress test procedures and results, regulators' stress tests are an essential check on banks under Pillar 2. They also provide a fair and transparent level playing field against which to test all banks, so that supervisory relationships may not be regarded as too arbitrary. Supervisory stress test results, which are publicly communicated to all, may be useful for market discipline under Pillar 3. However, supervisory stress tests are not to be taken as a warranty of assurance for markets or the public.

---

[143] Ian Ayres and John Braithwaite, *Responsive Regulation: Transcending the Deregulation Debate* (Oxford: OUP 1992); Robert Baldwin and Julia Black, 'Really Responsive Regulation' (LSE Working Papers 2007) at https://www.lse.ac.uk/collections/law/wps/WPS15-2007BlackandBaldwin.pdf.

Regular stress testing carried out by regulators of a section of banks across their regulatory jurisdiction would be a good compliment to the mandatory requirements for banks to stress test themselves. Regulatory stress testing can better take account of wider macro-economy developments and feed into the development of macro-prudential supervision (undertaken by the Financial Policy Committee in the UK, discussed in Chapter 6).

The PRA has set out clearly its stress testing strategies until 2018, after which this would be reviewed in light of the ring-fencing reforms (discussed in Chapter 10) that are implemented from January 2019.

The PRA's strategy for stress testing is a 'concurrent stress testing' programme,[144] that is, that the regulator is stress testing using similar scenarios as banks themselves, therefore creating a 'concurrent' regime that can check on bank's approaches and results. The concurrent stress testing programme consists of an annual cyclical stress testing aspect and a biennial 'exploratory' or forward-looking stress testing aspect. The annual cyclical stress testing aspect tests banks against predictable and foreseeable challenges within the economic cycle. However, the biennial aspect tests banks against upcoming and emerging trends and challenges, in order to measure banks' resilience against them.

The PRA also sets out its objectives to measure quantitative elements of banks' capital strength, qualitative elements of its governance and to obtain supervisory information to feed into recovery and resolution planning and macro-prudential supervision.

The PRA has started its stress testing programme in 2014. One of the most notable episodes was that the Co-operative Bank was judged to fail in its capital adequacy under stress testing.[145] Box 9.12 illustrates this.

Box 9.12 Co-operative Bank, 2014

Eight major banks in the UK were subject to the PRA's stress test in 2014, which included scenarios of a 35 per cent fall in house prices and a 30 per cent drop in the value of the pound, among other factors. The Co-operative Bank did not pass the stress test, meaning that it was judged not to have capital and liquidity positions sufficiently resilient against those scenarios. The Co-operative Bank therefore had to submit a remediation plan to the PRA as a response to the stress test results. It proposed to bail-in its shareholders and junior bondholders, and that at first met with strong opposition from the junior bondholders, many of whom were hedge funds. The parties ultimately agreed that the major shareholder of the Bank, the Co-operative group would be bailed in up to 30 per cent of its shareholdings while junior bondholders were converted into equity. This restructuring amounted to £1.5 billion recapitalisation for the Co-operative Bank.[146]

---

[144] PRA, 'The Bank of England's Approach to Stress-testing the UK Banking System' (October 2015) at http://www.bankofengland.co.uk/financialstability/Documents/stresstesting/2015/approach.pdf.

[145] PRA, 'Stress-testing the UK Banking System: 2014 Results' (December 2014) at http://www.bankofeng-land.co.uk/financialstability/documents/fpc/results161214.pdf.

[146] 'Co-op Bank's Bondholders Give Go-ahead to Recapitalisation' *Financial Times* (17 December 2013).

Other banks that had been put on a watch list included RBS and Lloyds in 2014 (also in 2015). Standard Chartered was also asked to submit a remediation plan after lacklustre stress test results in 2015.[147] In 2016, the RBS was judged to need more capital after failing the PRA stress test and planned to reduce its volume of lending and risk-taking.[148] In 2017 however, all UK banks subject to the PRA's stress testing passed the test.

Although stress testing is seen as part of rigorous Pillar 2 supervisory monitoring, a number of commentators are concerned that regular stress testing would become predictable and banks could become motivated to do the minimal to 'pass the test'. Such aggressive and boundary-pushing behaviour has been observed in US banks[149] as they have become less conservative over years of stress testing in view of the normalising environment. Hence it is important to monitor not just stress testing results but also the behavioural impact upon both banks and regulators.

9.6.3 Regulators' stress testing in the EU

The EU Capital Requirements Directive 2013 makes it mandatory for regulators in EU member states to develop stress tests for the banks they oversee, at least on an annual basis.[150] To this end, the EBA monitors national regulators in carrying out their stress tests in order to ensure transparency, fairness, and effectiveness.

The EBA emphasises the importance that national regulators should be sufficiently resourced and equipped to carry out effective stress tests, based on systemic and macro-prudential scenarios, assumptions and data, in order to compare banks' positions in broader economic contexts.[151]

The EBA, as meta-level supervisor over member state regulators further carries out EU-wide stress tests in addition to member state regulators' tests. The EBA's stress testing is distinguished on the basis of its general powers to identify, measure, and monitor systemic risks.[152] The EBA carried out yearly stress tests from 2009 to 2011, partly in response to the euro-area debt crisis as sovereigns such as Greece and Ireland looked

---

[147] PRA, 'Stress-testing the UK Banking System: 2015 Results' (December 2015) at http://www.bankofengland.co.uk/financialstability/Documents/fpc/results011215.pdf.

[148] PRA, 'Stress-testing the UK Banking System: 2016 Results' (November 2016) at http://www.bankofengland.co.uk/publications/Pages/news/2016/stresstesting.aspx; RBS, 'Statement on the publication of the 2016 Bank of England stress test results' at http://www.rbs.com/news/2016/november/statement-on-the-publication-of-the-2016-bank-of-england-stress-test-results.html#rY98rTY7qqpQE0Vg.99.

[149] German Gutierrez Gallardo, Til Schuermann and Michael Douane, 'Stress-testing Convergence' (2015) at http://papers.ssrn.com/sol3/papers.cfm?abstract_id=2636984.

[150] Article 100, Directive 2013/36/EU of the European Parliament and of the Council of 26 June 2013 on access to the activity of credit institutions and the prudential supervision of credit institutions and investment firms, amending Directive 2002/87/EC and repealing Directives 2006/48/EC and 2006/49/EC.

[151] EBA, *Final Report on Guidelines for Institution Stress Testing* (2018) at https://www.eba.europa.eu/documents/10180/2282644/Guidelines+on+institutions+stress+testing+%28EBA-GL-2018-04%29.pdf/2b604bc8-fd08-4b17-ac4a-cdd5e662b802.

close to default. It has resumed biennial stress testing from 2014. Although there is no particular legal framework that governs the EBA's carrying out of stress testing, over the years, the EBA has developed a more predictable and transparent programme for its stress tests and communications to banks.

In the 2011 stress testing round, the EBA published its intention to stress test four months ahead of the publication of its scenarios. The scenarios were based on topical macro-economic concerns at the time, that is, decline in growth generally, asset price declines such as housing price declines and sovereign stress. Subsequently the EBA announced the methodologies for stress testing, the key benchmark measurement of common equity tier one capital and the sample of banks selected for stress testing. The EBA published its stress testing results publicly in July 2011, giving individual reports of how each sampled bank's common equity tier one position would be affected under each scenario of the stress test, and addressing to national regulators where individual banks may require remedial action.[153] Some commentators doubted, however, that the stress tests were robust enough to uncover the desperate capital situation in many European banks that were highly leveraged, and the stress tests could be seen to be a way of managing adverse market impression of weak European banks.[154]

In 2014, the EBA adopted a similar procedure, first announcing the intention to stress test, then publishing the scenarios, methodologies, and the sample size, before effecting the stress testing. The scenarios selected again reflected topical macro-economic issues of concern. They were: (i) withdrawal from emerging market economies perceived to be highly risky; (ii) a further deterioration of credit quality in countries with feeble demand; (iii) stalling policy reforms in the public finances of many European countries jeopardising market confidence; and (iv) the weakness of bank balance sheets, for example, in terms of non-performing loans. The results published were in relation to common equity tier one capital levels and showed severe impairment to Greek, Portuguese, and some Spanish and Austrian banks' positions under the stress scenarios. This was partly because many of these banks invested too heavily in their own sovereigns and sovereign risk in these countries remained relatively high. These results were also useful for micro-prudential supervision of these banks by the ECB and by national regulators. However, the EBA did not provide any further guidance as to how these results may be used.

---

[152] Articles 23, 24 and 33, Regulation (EU) No 1093/2010 of the European Parliament and of the Council of 24 November 2010 establishing a European Supervisory Authority (EBA), amending Decision No 716/2009/EC and repealing Commission Decision 2009/78/EC.

[153] See EBA, *European Banking Authority 2011 EU-Wide Stress Test Aggregate Report* (2011) at http://www.eba.europa.eu/documents/10180/15935/EBA_ST_2011_Summary_Report_v6.pdf/54a9ec8e-3a44-449f-9a5f-e820cc2c2f0a.

[154] Viral Acharya and Sascha Steffen, 'Falling Short of Expectations? Stress-Testing the European Banking System' (2013) at http://papers.ssrn.com/sol3/papers.cfm?abstract_id=2370484.

In preparation for the 2016 stress test however, the EBA issued guidance on how stress test results could be used. This move could have been pursuant to the concern that the EBA's stress test results have had little impact on micro-prudential supervision carried out by national regulators or the ECB (where the ECB directly supervises as the SSM, discussed in section 7.3). Hence, the EBA clarified that the banks' relevant micro-prudential regulator may, on the basis of the results, impose 'capital guidance'.[155] Such capital guidance may be in the form of Pillar 2A capital. The 2016 stress tests highlighted Italian bank Monte Dei Paschi as being in particular need of recapitalisation. However, this was *after* news of Monte Dei Paschi's troubles had featured in the news,[156] thus casting doubt on how useful the EBA's stress test results were in general to supervisors and markets.

The EBA's stress testing is arguably important as individual bank stress testing may be limited in taking account of wider macro-economy situations (although they are asked to do so) and the European financial sector as a whole. Further, national regulator's stress testing can be influenced by national issues and preferences and so the EBA's across-the-board stress testing can be regarded as an objective exercise at a higher level. However, it may be argued that the EBA's stress test results lack 'teeth', and it has taken up to 2016 for the EBA to suggest that the results may be useful for capital guidance. Moreover, the 2016 stress testing framework saw the EBA dropping a pass/fail threshold for banks[157] in favour of 'supporting ongoing supervisory' efforts over banks. The EBA's endeavours at stress testing may be seen as providing a backstop to fragmentary or inadequate practices at member states, but yet the EBA needs to be cognisant of member states' concerns and the perception that it may be taking too much direct control over supervision.[158]

> ### ⮑ Key takeaways
>
> - Banks are required to conduct regular stress testing in order to monitor their own risk management and provide information on their resilience to regulators
> - Stress testing is largely a quantitative exercise based on capital adequacy and liquidity but qualitative elements such as governance and internal control are being developed.
> - Stress testing is based on plausible scenarios of stress that may cause banks to fall below their capital thresholds or become unviable.

---

[155] 'EBA clarifies use of 2016 EU-wide stress test results in the SREP process' (1 July 2016) at http://www.eba.europa.eu/-/eba-clarifies-use-of-2016-eu-wide-stress-test-results-in-the-srep-process.

[156] 'Monte dei Paschi mulls rescue bids as EU banks await stress-test results', *The Guardian* (29 July 2016).

[157] EBA, *2016 EU-Wide Stress Test Results* (29 July 2016) at https://www.eba.europa.eu/documents/10180/1532819/2016-EU-wide-stress-test-Results.pdf.

[158] 'Stress tests do little to restore faith in European banks', *Financial Times* (30 July 2016).

- Stress testing needs to be based on holistic and conservative methodology, a robust data infrastructure at banks that has integrity and a responsible and documented governance structure at banks.

- EU regulators are mandated to develop annual stress testing for the banks they oversee.

- The UK PRA has developed an annual cyclical stress testing and a biennial exploratory stress testing framework.

- Stress testing feeds into immediate remediation, such as the UK Co-operative Bank's remediation episode in 2014, and recovery and resolution planning, micro- and macro-prudential supervision.

- The EBA takes on EU-wide bank stress tests although this is completely voluntary. The EBA stress test results have uncovered bank weaknesses, and should be used towards regulators' 'capital guidance'. However, they may also be seen to be for the purposes of assuaging market confidence and lack teeth.

Key bibliography

Legislation

Directive 2013/36/EU of the European Parliament and of the Council of 26 June 2013 on access to the activity of credit institutions and the prudential supervision of credit institutions and investment firms, amending Directive 2002/87/EC and repealing Directives 2006/48/EC and 2006/49/EC

PRA Rulebook, *Internal Capital Adequacy Assessment: Stress Testing and Scenario Analysis* and *Reverse Stress Testing*

Reports and Guidelines

Basel Committee, *Principles for Sound Stress testing Practices and Supervision* (May 2009) at http://www.bis.org/publ/bcbs155.pdf

EBA, *Consultation Paper on Draft Guidelines for Institution Stress-testing* (Oct 2017) at https://www.eba.europa.eu/documents/10180/2006781/Consultation+Paper+on+Guidelines+on+institution%27s+stress+testing+%28EBA-CP-2017-17%29.pdf/0c4ac326-1330-4799-850c-632510f26ed1

EBA, *Consultation Paper: Guidelines on Stress-Testing and Supervisory Stress-Testing* (Dec 2015) at https://www.eba.europa.eu/documents/10180/1314203/EBA-CP-2015-28+(%20CP+on+the+GL+on+stress+testing+and+supervisory+stress+testing).pdf

PRA, 'The Bank of England's Approach to Stress testing the UK Banking System' (Oct 2015) at http://www.bankofengland.co.uk/financialstability/Documents/stresstesting/2015/approach.pdf

Books

Mario Quagliariello (ed), *Stress-Testing the Banking System: Methodologies and Applications* (Cambridge: Cambridge University Press 2011)

Questions

1. Discuss how capital adequacy regulation is supported by the development of other micro-prudential regulatory tools.

   Answer tips You may wish to provide a brief overview of the other tools, namely liquidity standards, leverage ratio, large exposures and discuss their objectives. Are there any complimentary features between them, such as between large exposures and capital adequacy, leverage ratio and capital adequacy? Do the LCR and NSFR complement each other?

2. Do you think the micro-prudential regulation of SIFIs is necessary or an overkill?

   Answer tips You could explain what concerns there are with SIFIs and why regulating them for safety and soundness is a challenge. You may wish to introduce the Basel Committee's and EU's definition of a SIFI before introducing the various aspects of extra regulation imposed on them. Critically discuss the extra measures such as extra capital buffers and ALRB, and consider if these hamper their social usefulness in credit creation or limit their otherwise unchecked behaviour. You should also discuss the developing TLAC reforms and the EU and UK's implementation of the MREL.

3. 'The mandatory requirements for bank and regulator stress testing ensures that the key aspects of information and governance are soundly instituted for the purposes of ensuring that bank resilience is maintained.' Do you agree?

   Answer tips You may wish to discuss what the requirements of bank stress testing are and what purposes stress testing serve, viz how they improve information flows and how governance of bank risk management is secured. You should consider how the information environment is improved or otherwise by stress testing and how this helps banks and regulators. You should discuss how regulators use stress testing results reported by banks. You should then consider what regulatory stress testing is for and how it is carried out. Finally, you may consider if the governance of banks and regulators can indeed improve as a result of imposing stress testing requirements.

10

Structural regulation

10.1 Structural regulation in the UK

Sweeping reforms for its banking sector have been developed by UK policymakers after the 2007–9 global financial crisis. Although many of these reforms emanated from the Basel Committee and the EU, a unique area pioneered in the UK is that of structural reforms.

Structural reforms refer to direct regulatory intervention into a bank's business structure. This applies particularly to large banking groups in the UK. In brief, large banking groups in the UK may be compelled by regulation to restructure themselves for the purposes of preserving key economic functions that are socially important while maintaining their competitive edge.[1] Structural reforms involve the ring-fencing of UK banking groups' retail operations from other operations, in order to preserve the socially important aspects for consumers if the banking group goes under stress. In this way, the other risky operations of the UK banking group will not adversely affect the retail operations and can be resolved much more easily. Operations outside of the ring-fence can also pursue appropriate levels of risk-taking commensurate with their competitive needs.

Although structural reforms are aimed first and foremost at containing systemic risk and improving the resolvability of banks, these reforms may also go some way towards changing the culture of banks, especially retail banks, so that the conduct of retail banks may be more aligned with the public interest in their social utility functions.[2] It may be argued that the merger of investment banking into retail banking, which was facilitated in the UK after the Big Bang of 1986, has introduced a competitive, predatory and toxic culture into banks in general.[3] Structural reforms could go some way towards unravelling those effects.

---

[1] Independent Commission on Banking, *Final Report: Recommendations* (September 2011) at http://webarchive.nationalarchives.gov.uk/20131003105424/https:/hmt-sanctions.s3.amazonaws.com/ICB%20final%20report/ICB%2520Final%2520Report%5B1%5D.pdf.

[2] Luigi Zingales, *Capitalism for the People: Recapturing the Lost Genius of American Capitalism* (New York: Basic Books 2012).

[3] See Chapter 12; see Karen Ho, 'Situating Global Capitalisms: A View from Wall Street Investment Banks' (2005) 20 *Cultural Anthropology* 68–96; Jerome Want, *Corporate Culture* (London: St Martin's Press 2006).

Structural regulation was first recommended by the Independent Commission on Banking led by Sir John Vickers. The Commission was tasked to look into reforms for the UK banking sector in order to mitigate systemic risk effects, and produced a 363-page report in September 2011. The final report, known as the Vickers Report hereinafter, has been adopted in many key respects by the government. The resulting Financial Services (Banking Reform) Act 2013 and the UK Prudential Regulation Authority's implementation are discussed below.

10.1.1 **Vickers Report**

The Independent Commission on Banking (the Commission) was established by the Government in June 2010 to consider structural and related non-structural reforms to the UK banking sector to promote financial stability and competition. The Commission was asked to report to the Cabinet Committee on Banking Reform by the end of September 2011 and did so on time.

The Commission set out its aims towards:

(a) reducing the probability and impact of systemic financial crises in the future;

(b) maintaining the efficient flow of credit to the real economy and the ability of households and businesses to manage their risks and financial needs over time; and

(c) preserving the functioning of the payments system and guaranteed capital certainty and liquidity for small savers including small and medium-sized enterprises (SMEs).

The main proposal of the Vickers Report is the ring-fencing of UK retail banks from their parent banking groups. This measure is regarded as necessary to curb incentives for excessive risk-taking by banks that benefit from the implicit public sector support for its retail operations, and to mitigate the prospects of systemic risk caused by the failure of such banks. The focus of the Report is on large UK banking groups as these groups have the greatest potential to inflict systemic risk on the UK financial system and economy. Indeed, the near-failure of HBOS and Royal Bank of Scotland (RBS) in 2008[4] have led to state bailouts and consequent damaging effects on the UK economy. Hence, it seems sensible and proportionate to require these groups to restructure themselves to limit the damage to financial stability and to make themselves more resolvable.[5]

Ring-fencing also attempts to insulate the state protection of retail banks (which amounts to a subsidy for bank risk-taking) from the banking groups' other operations such as in investment banking, which are perceived as riskier. It is hoped that the risk-taking levels at these banking groups may be moderated if they cannot rely on the implicit subsidy derived from retail banking protection. These banking groups also enjoy a competitive advantage over other banks and financial services institutions as the implicit subsidy derived from retail banking can cost-effectively support their

[4] Discussed in Chapters 1 and 7.   [5] See Chapter 13 on resolution of banks.

riskier operations, resulting in their risk-taking not being appropriately priced by their counterparties and investors. The imposition of ring-fencing may play a part towards dismantling this false competitive advantage.

10.1.1.1 Scope of ring-fencing

Ring-fencing refers to a form of structural separation of the retail banking operations from other operations of the banking group, but it is not *total separation*. Total separation would mean that retail banking operations cannot be carried out by the banking group and the group would have to establish a completely separate and insulated entity for retail activities. The Vickers Report was of the view that total separation would not be practicable or efficient. Retail banking activities now involve forms of risk-taking and hedging in wholesale markets, and hence it may be impracticable and inefficient to sever them from such markets. The needs of financial stability can equally be achieved under the ring-fencing approach so it is not warranted to pursue the more draconian and costly measure of total separation.

Ring-fencing would involve **structural separation** based on banking activities. The entities housing the ring-fenced activities should be separated from the banking group along the lines of ownership, governance, economic, legal, and operational separation. Such separation limits rather than fully prohibits any connection between the retail banking operations and its banking group. The limits determine the 'height' of the ring-fence (discussed below), which the Vickers Report prefers to be substantial rather than minimal.

Ring-fencing is based on the principles of mandated and prohibited activities. The Vickers Report defines mandated activities narrowly as these should be activities that cannot afford to be even temporarily interrupted as consumers would be ill-prepared and significant economic costs would ensue. The Report is of the view that they include only customer deposits and overdrafts from retail customers[6] and SMEs as defined under the Companies Act 2006.[7] Retail credit is not regarded as part of 'mandated activities' as the Commission is of the view that alternative providers are available. Under this proposal, a UK-authorised financial institution cannot provide mandated activities unless it is 'ring-fenced'.

Ring-fenced banks can also provide 'permitted' activities that are essential intermediation for the real economy such as the provision of retail credit and corporate loans, and payment services. However, the Vickers Report does not set out exhaustively what is permitted. It, however, sets out prohibited services so as to establish the boundary of the scope of services ring-fenced banks can provide.

Prohibited activities refer to risk-taking activities that do not achieve economic intermediation in the real economy, and expose banks to risks in markets (whether

---

[6] This excludes high-net-worth customers who are better equipped to plan for financial disruptions and risks.

[7] The Companies Act defines SMEs as satisfying two or more of the following requirements: a turnover of less than £25.9 million; a balance sheet of less than £12.9 million; and fewer than 250 employees.

> **Box 10.1 Vickers report**
>
> Prohibited activities include:
>
> (a) any service that is not provided to customers within the European Economic Area (EEA);
>
> (b) any service which results in an exposure to a non-ring-fenced bank or a non-bank financial organisation, except those associated with the provision of payments services where the regulator has deemed this appropriate;
>
> (c) any service which would result in a trading book asset;
>
> (d) any service which would result in a requirement to hold regulatory capital against market risk;
>
> (e) the purchase or origination of derivatives or other contracts which would result in a requirement to hold regulatory capital against counterparty credit risk; and
>
> (f) services relating to secondary markets activity including the purchase of loans or securities.

global or otherwise) unconnected with real economic intermediation. Box 10.1 sets out the principles for defining prohibited activities, and they would likely include investment banking activities such as underwriting securities, structuring and arranging derivative transactions, investing in securities, bonds, derivatives, and securitisation activities.

However, the Vickers Report recognises that ring-fenced banks, although focusing on real economic intermediation, may need to engage in financial activities in markets for purposes of risk management. As such a list of ancillary activities permitted for ring-fenced banks should be adopted although they expose such banks to certain market risks. For example, ring-fenced banks may purchase interest rate derivatives to hedge their own interest rate exposures in retail and corporate lending. However, limits should be placed on such ancillary activities so that they do not become dominant and raise considerable market risks for ring-fenced banks.

10.1.1.2 Height of ring-fence

As ring-fencing does not require total separation of the ring-fenced bank from the banking group, the height of the ring-fence, which defines the types and extents of separation, becomes crucial to ensure that ring-fenced banks do not provide an implicit subsidy for non-ring-fenced operations and do not suffer from contagion.

The aspects of the height of the ring-fence considered in the Vickers Report are: ownership, governance, legal, economic, and operational separation. Figure 10.1 illustrates the five parameters of the height of the ring-fence.

On ownership, the Vickers Report does not frown upon common ownership between ring-fenced and non-ring-fenced entities, as there are benefits and drawbacks. Common ownership fosters greater economic dependencies between the ring-fenced bank and the rest of the banking group, and reinforces the implicit subsidy for the group. But the rest of the banking group could equally be incentivised to rescue the ring-fenced bank due to the reputational implications of connection. Hence, it is not necessary for

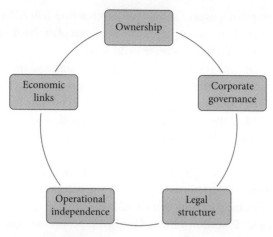

Figure 10.1 Aspects of height of the ring-fence

a ring-fenced bank to have a separate ownership structure. The Commission was more concerned that the ring-fenced bank should be managed and risk-managed separately from the rest of the banking group in order to achieve the objectives set out earlier on ring-fencing.

As such, the Commission places more emphasis on governance separation, exhorting that ring-fenced banks should not be dependent on the rest of the banking group for their solvency, liquidity, or capital management, and should be directed by a Board of sufficient independence from the rest of the banking group. Independence of the Board ensures that financial decisions such as dividend payments are made on an independent basis and that the Board can focus on maintaining the integrity of the ring-fence without being compromised by the group's other aims.

On legal links, the Commission is of the view that ring-fenced banks should be separately incorporated subsidiaries. This also means that ring-fenced entities should meet all regulatory requirements on an individual basis. However, this does not mean that ring-fenced banks are able to be self-contained in terms of operations and support. Even if ring-fenced banks are separate subsidiaries, they could still rely on the banking group's centralised operational and support services such as human resources, information technology, and so on. Hence, it is perhaps more important to ensure that ring-fenced banks have a certain degree of operational independence, although the complete duplication of certain centralised services provided at group level is not practicable. The Report recommends that the banking group should be required to put in place arrangements to ensure that the ring-fenced bank has continuous access to essential operations, staff, data, and services required to continue its activities, irrespective of the financial health of the rest of the group. Such services can be provided by the group to the ring-fenced bank through service agreements, or by third parties directly to the ring-fenced bank. Further the ring-fenced bank should either be a direct member of all the payments systems that it uses or should use another ring-fenced bank as an agent. In this way the ring-fenced bank is not prejudiced if the rest of the banking group is unable to provide services or if third parties cease to do so for it.

Finally, the economic links between the ring-fenced bank and the rest of the banking group should be regulated so that the ring-fenced bank is economically independent to a sufficient degree. The Commission recommends that economic transactions between the ring-fenced bank and the rest of the banking group, that is, intra-group economic relations should be on a third-party commercial basis, with comparable terms and price agreed up front. This principle prevents risk transfers from non-ring-fenced entities to the ring-fenced bank, and safeguards the retail banking operations from contagion. Such intra-group economic relations include intra-group asset transfers that should be at market value, intra-group lending that should be limited to regulatory limits on large exposures (see Chapter 9, section 9.3), and limited exposures via guarantees, as well as the absence of any inordinate reliance by the ring-fenced bank on the group for whole-sale market funding. Ring-fenced banks should be required to disclose all intra-group transactions and exposures regularly and to demonstrate that these are taking place on a commercial and arm's length basis.

10.1.1.3 Implications of ring-fence

First, ring-fencing allows different regulatory requirements to be applied to the ring-fenced bank. This is not unwarranted as ring-fenced banks conduct mandated services close to being social utilities and have different regulatory needs.

The Vickers Report envisages that one of the key regulatory implications for ring-fenced banks lies in the application of different capital adequacy requirements. Ring-fenced banks can be made to be subject to more stringent capital adequacy requirements so that their risk-taking can be strictly moderated. The Commission suggests that ring-fenced banks with a ratio of risk-weighted assets to UK GDP of 3 per cent or more should be required to have an equity—risk-weighted-asset ratio of at least 10 per cent.[8] Further, lending by ring-fenced banks can be controlled by stricter leverage ratios (see Chapter 9).[9]

The implementation of the Vickers Report has indeed resulted in the application of micro-prudential regulation to ring-fenced banks that reflects the public interest importance of their safety and soundness. Ring-fenced banks are either G-SIBs or D-SIBs and are imposed with micro-prudential requirements tailored to their profiles (see Chapter 9, section 9.5).

---

[8] Ring-fenced banks with a ratio of risk-weighted assets to UK GDP in between 1 per cent and 3 per cent should be required to have a minimum equity–risk-weighted-assets ratio set by a sliding scale from 7 per cent to 10 per cent.

[9] The Report suggests that all UK-headquartered banks and all ring-fenced banks should maintain a Tier 1 leverage ratio of at least 3 per cent. All ring-fenced banks with a risk-weighted-assets–UK GDP ratio of 1 per cent or more should have their minimum leverage ratio increased on a sliding scale (to a maximum of 4.06 per cent.

10.1.2 **The Financial Services (Banking Reform) Act 2013 and implementation**

Although the government has largely endorsed the Vickers Report, it has deviated from some proposals as explained in its White Paper in June 2012.[10]

The White Paper accepts the framework of mandated activities providing the scope for ring-fencing, and agrees with the Vickers Report that deposit acceptance from UK retail customers and SMEs is the key mandated activity, leaving secondary legislation to develop more mandated activities if this becomes necessary. The government also supports the scope of prohibited and ancillary activities, proposing to develop specific lists in secondary legislation. Primary legislation provides that ring-fenced banks are not to engage in investment as principal.

The government also supports the Vickers Report's proposals on the height of the ring-fence in respect of ownership, governance, legal, and operational links, but thinks that operational sharing should not be subject to excessive prescription. On economic links, the government accepts most of the Commission's suggestions except limits to intra-group funding. The government perceives advantages that intra-group funding can provide to ring-fenced banks and does not wish to introduce limits. Further, ring-fenced banks should also bear their own pensions liabilities on an individual basis and not be made to share the group's liabilities.

The Financial Services (Banking Reform) Act 2013 has been passed to enact the ring-fencing reforms. These reforms will be implemented by the UK Prudential Regulation Authority.

10.1.2.1 **Application of ring-fence**

Ring-fencing applies to UK deposit-takers having an average of £25 billion in deposits. Large UK High Street banks such as Barclays, HSBC, Lloyd's, RBS, and Santander UK will be captured within its scope. This threshold also ensures that smaller retail banks and new entrants such as Metro Bank would not be disproportionately affected by ring-fencing rules. This average is calculated yearly by averaging out quarterly totals.[11] However, building societies, industrial and provident societies in Northern Ireland, credit unions, housing associations, and investment firms generally are exempted from the ring-fencing regime.[12] Many of these are also not comparable in size and scale as major High Street banks some of whom have significant national and international footprints.

In order to prepare for ring-fencing, affected banks submitted their plans for ring-fencing by 29 January 2016 to the Prudential Regulation Authority (PRA). The PRA is

---

[10] HM Treasury and Department of Business, Skills and Innovation, *Banking Reform: Delivering Stability and Supporting a Sustainable Economy* (June 2012) at https://www.gov.uk/government/uploads/system/uploads/attachment_data/file/32556/whitepaper_banking_reform_140512.pdf.

[11] Section 12, Financial Services and Markets Act 2000 (Ring-fenced Bodies and Core Activities) Order 2014.

[12] Section 11, Financial Services and Markets Act 2000 (Ring-fenced Bodies and Core Activities) Order 2014 and s2, Financial Services and Markets Act 2000 (Excluded Activities and Prohibitions) Order 2014.

able to grant waivers and exemptions in the implementation of each bank's ring-fencing plans.[13] Ring-fencing comes into force in January 2019, but Barclays and HSBC, for example, have already gained approval and carried out their plans.

10.1.2.2 Scope of ring-fence

The Act adopts the approach of the Vickers Report by defining a ring-fenced bank as an entity that is authorised to carry out defined 'core activities'.[14] Core activities are defined as deposit acceptance, and any other activities that the Treasury may by Order prescribe. The core activity of deposit acceptance[15] is defined as:

(a) facilities for the accepting of deposits or other payments into an account which is provided in the course of carrying on the core activity of accepting deposits;

(b) facilities for withdrawing money or making payments from such an account; and

(c) overdraft facilities in connection with such an account.

In other words, essential current account activity would fall within the scope of 'core activities'. This definition is over-inclusive and one has to turn to the Treasury Order to see that the scope of 'core activities' only refers to retail customers' and SMEs' current account services.

The Financial Services and Markets Act 2000 (Ring-fenced Bodies and Core Activities) Order 2014 provides that 'core activities' only means 'core deposits' from which there are a number of exclusions. 'Core deposits' exclude those deposits not made in a branch in the European Economic Area, as only citizens of the EEA are protected in the ring-fencing regulatory regime. This position could be changed to be limited to deposits in the UK after the UK leaves EU membership. Further, bodies or partnerships with a turnover of more than £6.5 million, a balance sheet total of more than £3.26 million and with more than 50 employees (whether full or part-time) are not to be regarded as making 'core deposits'. Charities or other organisations with a gross income of more than £6.5 million a year are also not regarded as making 'core deposits'. Individuals of high net-worth[16] defined as holding at least £250,000 in assets in a year are also excluded from 'core deposits'. These exclusions are largely in line with the Vickers Report and can be amended in due course by secondary legislation.

Ring-fenced banks are not allowed to engage in investment as principal, which is the key 'excluded activity'.[17] The Financial Services and Markets Act 2000 (Excluded

---

[13] See 'Barclays joins list of banks seeking ring-fencing waiver', *Financial Times* (15 October 2015).

[14] Section 142B, Financial Services and Markets Act 2000 as amended by the Financial Services (Banking Reform) Act 2013.

[15] Section 142C, Financial Services and Markets Act 2000 as amended by the Financial Services (Banking Reform) Act 2013.

[16] High net-worth individuals need to be certified by a professional accountant and confirmed by their financial institutions.

[17] Section 142D, Financial Services and Markets Act 2000 as amended by the Financial Services (Banking Reform) Act 2013.

Activities and Prohibitions) Order 2014 prescribes what falls within the scope of excluded activities. The Order may be regarded as 'watering down' some of the rather absolute boundaries set out earlier in the Vickers Report. The Order is clear on prohibiting proprietary trading and trading in commodities (unless involved as collateral to a transaction or as part of a title transfer security transaction). The Order is also clear that the ring-fenced bank cannot own any subsidiaries operating outside of the EEA that may allow it to arbitrage away the ring-fencing requirements. However, many other aspects of market exposure or financial institution exposure have been significantly nuanced in order not to disrupt modern banking activities.

The Order does not prevent ring-fenced banks from incurring market exposures if the purpose is to manage changes in interest rates, exchange rates or commodity prices, changes in any index of retail prices or of residential or commercial property prices; or changes in any index of the price of shares in order to manage credit and liquidity risk. The Order also allows ring-fenced banks to incur financial institution exposures for risk management purposes as long as such transactions are on a commercial arms-length basis. Ring-fenced banks may, pursuant to the above-mentioned purposes, deal in investment and derivative instruments[18] subject to certain position limits.

The Order provides a rather generous berth of permissions for ring-fenced banks, acknowledging the mechanics of modern banking and retail banks' deep interconnections with wholesale money and investment markets. But does this approach compromise the nature of the ring-fence? A number of commentators are of the view that ring-fencing is impracticable to implement, as the boundaries between different types of banking activities are difficult to draw. Banks may innovate to challenge the boundaries of authorised and unauthorised activities. [19] Although it may be argued that the Order leaves much of modern banking business as it is, there are two benefits from the generous approach taken in the Order. One is that banks do not need to engage in excessive innovation and arbitrage to avoid overly stringent or rigid ring-fencing rules, and the second is that the implementation of ring-fencing still confronts banks with the importance of protecting their socially-facing retail functions.

It is noted that that the Treasury has a residual power to prescribe by Order[20] prohibitions for ring-fenced banks from engaging in specific transactions. Where specific developments require the attention of regulators to protect the stability of ring-fenced banks, such an Order can be issued. Hence, it may not be necessary to take an unduly strict approach to define excluded activities. Further, the PRA has a general power to grant waivers or exemptions from ring-fencing requirements. The legislative framework

---

[18] Such as interest rate or currency swaps and forward contracts relating to currencies or commodities

[19] Julian TS Chow and Jay Surti, 'Making Banks Safer: Can Volcker and Vickers do it?' (November 2011) IMF Working Paper WP/11/236 http://www.imf.org/external/pubs/ft/wp/2011/wp11236.pdf. Jan Kregel, 'Can a Return to Glass-Steagall Provide Financial Stability in the US Financial System' (2010) 63 *PSL Quarterly Review* 37.

[20] Section 142E, Financial Services and Markets Act 2000 as amended by the Financial Services (Banking Reform) Act 2013.

has built in many elements of flexibility to keep pace with banking needs. However, it remains imperative that the regulator remains vigilant of the objectives of ring-fencing.

10.1.2.3 Height of ring-fence

The Act delegates to the PRA to make rules for the height of the ring-fence, that is, exactly how ring-fencing is to be achieved via the five aspects of ownership, corporate governance, economic links, legal, and operational structures.[21]

In terms of *ownership*, the ring-fenced bank can be owned by a parent entity that carries out excluded activities or owns entities that do so. In a wider banking group, the ring-fenced bank must be *legally structured* as a subsidiary. The PRA is willing to consider allowing ring-fenced banks to hold stakes in entities that carry out excluded activities, but this is to be a discretionary judgment exercised on an individual basis. We caution against this approach as allowing ring-fenced banks to own entities that can carry out excluded activities can allow regulatory arbitrage, and undermine the purpose of the ring-fence, which is to mitigate interconnections with investment banking business.

On *corporate governance* arrangements, the PRA sets out certain standards that ought to be maintained for key personnel independence, but allows banks to apply for waivers and exemptions. At the Board level, at least half of the Board members should be independent non-executive directors. The definition of independence is borrowed from the UK Corporate Governance Code,[22] but includes a modification. The Code does not consider a director who has received remuneration from the company in the form of employee share options or participated in a pension scheme to be independent. Former employees would only be considered independent 5 years after the employment relationship has ended. The PRA has amended the remuneration criterion so that the receipt of pensions and fixed or variable remuneration (apart from a director's fee) would not be a factor disqualifying a director from being considered independent, as long as the entitlement to the remuneration in question is attributed to a period of employment that concluded 5 years before his or her appointment as a director. However, in order to ensure that there are sufficient 'outsiders' on the Board, the PRA mandates that a third of the Board must be drawn from outside of the wider banking group. Further, vacancies for non-executive directors must be openly advertised.

The PRA also provides that the Chairman of the Board, and Chairs of the risk, audit, nomination, and remuneration committees must be independent and not concurrently engaged in a similar position elsewhere in the banking group. The risk, audit, nomination, and remuneration committees should also be adequately resourced and functionally independent to determine policy and maintain the ring-fence.

---

[21] PRA, *The Implementation of Ring-Fencing: Legal Structure, Governance and the Continuity of Services and Facilities* (May 2015) at http://www.bankofengland.co.uk/pra/Pages/publications/ps/2015/ps1015.aspx.

[22] https://frc.org.uk/Our-Work/Codes-Standards/Corporate-governance/UK-Corporate-Governance-Code.aspx.

In terms of *operational structures*, the PRA is mindful of the economies of scale and practicalities of shared operational services, but standards are set in order to bolster the ring-fenced bank's independent capacity. The PRA does not prevent employees in the ring-fenced bank from carrying out other functions in the wider group, but there should not be 'personnel dependency' so that the ring-fenced bank becomes vulnerable to the availability of such personnel. Ring-fenced bank employees are not prohibited from receiving remuneration in connection with the wider group, such as being compensated in the form of the parent bank's shares. However, the ring-fenced bank must ensure that the remuneration committee sets out policies that support sound and effective risk management and the long-term interests of the ring-fenced bank.

Further, in order to ensure continuity of services to the ring-fenced bank at times of stress, suppliers of services to the ring-fenced bank must be designated as 'permitted suppliers' who are not able to terminate services to the ring-fenced bank due to circumstances with the wider group, even if separate contractual arrangements are not in place. However, where the above is not possible, the ring-fenced bank must ensure that the permitted supplier and the ring-fenced bank enter into arrangements to protect continuity of services to the ring-fenced bank.

In terms of *economic links*, there are two aspects, one relates to the financial resources of the ring-fenced bank, and the other to intra-group exposures and transactions.[23]

On financial resources, it is consistent for the objective of maintaining the resilience of the ring-fenced bank that it should comply with regulatory requirements as an independent entity. The PRA expects the ring-fenced bank to meet capital adequacy standards as an individual entity, and also to carry out stress testing and make regular reporting to the regulator on an individual basis. Moreover, the large exposures limit applies to ring-fenced banks so that their exposures to entities in the wider banking group must be capped at 25 per cent without exemptions. However, the PRA recognises that in terms of liquidity management, the banking group is highly interconnected as liquidity support for each other often comes from within the group. Hence, liquidity compliance would not be imposed on an individual basis but will be considered for the group as a whole. Nevertheless, the ring-fenced bank is to have its own liquidity management function and policies. The PRA also envisages that the ring-fenced bank should be able to access the Bank of England's liquidity facilities on a stand-alone basis. This is consistent with the objective of preserving the stability of the ring-fenced bank.

In terms of intra-group transactions and exposures, first it is to be pointed out that the ring-fenced bank must be provided with stand-alone capacity in important respects such as payments, settlement and clearing in order not to become forced to rely on intra-group arrangements to carry those out. The PRA requires ring-fenced banks to

---

[23] PRA, *The Implementation of Ring-Fencing: Prudential Requirements, Intragroup Arrangements and Use of Financial Market Infrastructures: Consultation Paper* (October 2015) at http://www.bankofengland.co.uk/pra/Documents/publications/cp/2015/cp3715.pdf, final rules in PRA, *The Implementation of Ring-Fencing: Prudential Requirements, Intragroup Arrangements and Use of Financial Market Infrastructures: Policy Statement* (July 2016) at http://www.bankofengland.co.uk/pra/Documents/publications/ps/2016/ps2016.pdf.

be direct participants of the payments and clearing systems or with the PRA's approval use an agent intermediary.

The ring-fenced bank is expected to apply general principles in ensuring that its intra-group transactions and exposures are managed on an arms-length basis. Due to representations from the industry, the PRA has watered down its requirement for all intra-group transactions to be on an arms-length basis, to only requiring such a basis between the ring-fenced bank and entities in the group that do not belong to a ring-fenced sub-group.[24] The PRA expects the ring-fenced bank to institute a governance framework to determine and review such transactions. The governance framework must establish robust processes to identify intra-group transactions, policies for entering into them, processes to review their pricing and dispute resolution procedures, and to subject these to Board approval and internal audit oversight (see Chapter 12).

In particular, certain areas are highlighted. The ring-fenced bank should assume its pensions liabilities separately from the wider banking group.[25] Further, it should not pay out dividends to the parent bank without seeking the PRA's approval. The PRA will determine if such dividend payment is appropriate based on consideration for the ring-fenced bank's financial resources adequacy. The ring-fenced bank must not enter into netting arrangements that permit a counterparty to offset liabilities to the bank with claims that counterparty has on other group members. In any transaction with or exposure to entities in the wider banking group that involves the taking of collateral, the ring-fenced bank must ensure that the quality of the collateral is sound and equivalent to what would have been demanded of third parties. Finally, the ring-fenced bank must ensure that it does not become income-dependent on the generation of revenues by lines of businesses in the wider banking group.

The PRA has attempted to strike a balance between preserving the spirit of the ring-fence while allowing certain commercial practicalities subsisting in the banking sector to continue. This area is likely to be tested by the extent of exemptions and waivers that may be granted, as well as the PRA's supervisory monitoring of how ring-fenced banks conduct themselves.

However, the PRA has a general power to order 'group restructuring' if the ring-fence is being undermined.[26] There are four conditions for the exercise of such a draconian power so as to ensure that it is properly accountable and if necessary, subject to judicial review. Box 10.2 sets out the four conditions.

One can see that the PRA's general power to order group restructuring is a means for intervention where a banking group has not adhered to ring-fencing rules or their

[24] PRA, *The Implementation of Ring-Fencing: Prudential Requirements, Intragroup Arrangements and Use of Financial Market Infrastructures: Policy Statement* (July 2016) at http://www.bankofengland.co.uk/pra/Documents/publications/ps/2016/ps2016.pdf. The ring-fenced sub-group comprises other members in the group that are crucial to the ring-fenced bank's business and usually in the same corporate group structure.
[25] Section 142W, Financial Services and Markets Act 2000 as amended by the Financial Services (Banking Reform) Act 2013.
[26] Section 142K, Financial Services and Markets Act 2000 as amended by the Financial Services (Banking Reform) Act 2013.

Box 10.2 PRA conditions for the exercise of group restructuring

The four conditions for the exercise of 'group restructuring' powers by the PRA are:

- Condition A is that the carrying on of core activities by the ring-fenced body is being adversely affected by the acts or omissions of other members of its group.

- Condition B is that in carrying on its business the ring-fenced body:

    (a) is unable to take decisions independently of other members of its group, or

    (b) depends on resources that are provided by a member of its group and which would cease to be available in the event of the insolvency of the other member.

- Condition C is that in the event of the insolvency of one or more other members of its group the ring-fenced body would be unable to continue to carry on the core activities carried on by it.

- Condition D is that the ring-fenced body or another member of its group has engaged, or is engaged, in conduct that would be likely to have an adverse effect on the financial stability or the continuity of critical services objectives advanced by the PRA or FCA.

---

spirit. The group restructuring powers are subject to two further safeguards. One is that it should not be concurrently ordered by the PRA and its counterpart, the Financial Conduct Authority. Second, such a power can only be exercised by either regulator upon the expiry of at least 2 years after either has made such an order against the banking group. This requirement prevents banks from being subject to constant calls for restructuring which can be a very costly exercise, and ensures that regulators only undertake such powers after having considered the situation thoroughly.

10.1.2.4 Implementation of ring-fence

The ring-fence is implemented by transfers of businesses, such as for core activities to be transferred by the parent bank to a subsidiary, or for certain excluded activities to be transferred out of the entity identified as the ring-fenced bank. In order to ensure that such transfers genuinely meet the purposes of ring-fencing and are financially sound, such transfers, known as ring-fencing transfer schemes are subject to appropriate procedural safeguards.[27]

The PRA sets out a process for ring-fencing transfer schemes to be scrutinised and approved,[28] involving both regulatory and judicial approval.

---

[27] Section 106B; Part 2B inserted into Schedule 12, Financial Services and Markets Act 2000 as amended by the Financial Services (Banking Reform) Act 2013.

[28] PRA, *The Implementation of Ring-Fencing: The PRA's Approach to Ring-Fencing Transfer Schemes: Statement of Policy* (March 2016) and *Policy Statement* (March 2016) at http://www.bankofengland.co.uk/pra/Documents/publications/sop/2016/rftssop.pdf and http://www.bankofengland.co.uk/pra/Documents/publications/ps/2016/ps1016.pdf respectively.

First, the banking group nominates a 'skilled person' to prepare a scheme report for the transfer. The skilled person is a person of adequate knowledge, expertise, and independence and the banking group must provide the PRA with adequate information regarding the nominee's qualifications and experience, the nominee's previous commercial dealings with the banking group, remuneration for the appointment, and any possible conflicts of interest on the nominee's part. The PRA, in consultation with the FCA then determines if the skilled person should be approved.

Once approved, the skilled person prepares a scheme report for the PRA to address the statutory question of '(a) whether persons other than the transferor concerned are likely to be adversely affected by the scheme, and (b) if so, whether the adverse effect is likely to be greater than is reasonably necessary in order to achieve whichever of the purposes [of ring-fencing]'. The PRA sets out the particulars which should be contained in the scheme report, including the impact of the transfer on depositors, the resulting capital and liquidity positions, governance arrangements, business viability, resolvability for the ring-fenced and non-ring-fenced parts of the banking group, and the impact on any third parties such as creditors.

The PRA determines whether the scheme can be supported. Upon approving the scheme, the PRA issues two certificates, one relating to approving the scheme report, and the other in relation to the adequacy of financial resources on the part of the transferee. Where the transferee is authorised in another member state in the EEA, the PRA issues a third certificate to confirm that the home state regulator of the transferee has been notified and at least 3 months have elapsed since the notification. At that point, the transfer scheme is submitted for judicial approval. Judicial proceedings provide an opportunity for all relevant persons interested in the transfer to be represented and heard, so that the transfer scheme can be finalised.

Judicial proceedings were not envisaged in the Act but this additional step introduces an element of objectivity in scrutinising ring-fencing transfer schemes so that they are seen as credible, and not merely negotiated behind closed doors between the PRA and banking groups. It would be highly unlikely that the court would reject a transfer scheme that is already subject to PRA and FCA approval, and could therefore be seen as a rubber-stamping process. But that conclusion should not be too quickly drawn. The judicial proceedings provide a safeguard for third parties' interests.

One pertinent query could be whether banks were likely to transfer core activities away from the parent group and form possibly private limited subsidiaries to house such core activities, or transfer out excluded activities away from the parent group. It maybe surmised that the latter approach looked favourable as core activities revolving around retail and SME deposits are protected by the deposit guarantee scheme and implicit public sector support. The parent bank, which is likely a listed company, benefits from keeping the core activities and the implicit public sector support for such activities, in order to keep its equity markets funding cost low. If investors were to appraise the market value of bank securities on the basis of risky, complex, and international investment banking activities alone, the funding cost for such banks would likely rise significantly. Further, credit rating agencies could also downgrade the listed parent bank that only carries on investment banking activities in view of its changed risk profile. However, in practice, the major High Street banks Barclays, Lloyds and HSBC have all transferred the ring-fenced bank out of the parent entity without suffering market disruptions.

➔ Key takeaways

- The UK pioneered reforms in ring-fencing certain banks in order to protect socially important retail institutions from being contaminated by systemic risk.

- Ring-fencing reforms are proposed by the Vickers Report and implemented largely by the government via legislation in 2013 and 2014. Banks submitted ring-fencing plans by end January 2016 for implementation by January 2019.

- Ring-fencing ensures that only approved banks carry out the core services of deposit-taking, payments, and overdrafts for retail individual customers and SMEs. Ring-fenced banks are not permitted to carry out 'excluded activities' unless within the excepted parameters.

- Ring-fencing involves extents of separation in legal structuring, ownership, corporate governance arrangements, operational structures, and economic links. The PRA sets standards but may apply exemptions and waivers.

- Banks implement ring-fencing through ring-fencing transfer schemes approved by the PRA, FCA and the court.

Key bibliography

Legislation

Financial Services and Markets Act 2000 as amended by the Financial Services (Banking Reform) Act 2013.

PRA, *The Implementation of Ring-Fencing: Legal Structure, Governance and the Continuity of Services and Facilities* (May 2015) at http://www.bankofengland.co.uk/pra/Pages/publications/ps/2015/ps1015.aspx

PRA, *The Implementation of Ring-Fencing: The PRA's Approach to Ring-Fencing Transfer Schemes: Statement of Policy* (March 2016) and *Policy Statement* (March 2016) at http://www.bankofengland.co.uk/pra/Documents/publications/sop/2016/rftssop.pdf and http://www.bankofengland.co.uk/pra/Documents/publications/ps/2016/ps1016.pdf respectively

PRA, *The Implementation of Ring-Fencing: Prudential Requirements, Intragroup Arrangements and Use of Financial Market Infrastructures: Policy Statement* (July 2016) at http://www.bankofengland.co.uk/pra/Documents/publications/ps/2016/ps2016.pdf.

Reports and Guidelines

HM Treasury and Department of Business, Skills and Innovation, *Banking Reform: Delivering Stability and Supporting a Sustainable Economy* (June 2012) at https://www.gov.uk/government/uploads/system/uploads/attachment_data/file/32556/whitepaper_banking_reform_140512.pdf

Independent Commission on Banking, *Final Report: Recommendations* (September 2011) at http://webarchive.nationalarchives.gov.uk/20131003105424/https:/hmt-sanctions.s3.amazonaws.com/ICB%20final%20report/ICB%2520Final%2520Report%5B1%5D.pdf

PRA, *The Implementation of Ring-Fencing: Prudential Requirements, Intragroup Arrangements and Use of Financial Market Infrastructures: Consultation Paper* (October 2015) at http://www.bankofengland.co.uk/pra/Documents/publications/cp/2015/cp3715.pdf

Papers

Chow, JTS and Surti, J, 'Making Banks Safer: Can Volcker and Vickers do it?' (November 2011) IMF Working Paper WP/11/236 http://www.imf.org/external/pubs/ft/wp/2011/wp11236.pdf

10.2 What do structural reforms achieve?

Ring-fencing reforms are unique to the UK although it has been queried whether such reforms, not internationally harmonised, would have traction or pose competitive disadvantages to UK banks that are also global conglomerates. That said, structural reforms are not exclusive to the UK as the broader idea of structural reforms has been more widely accepted. In particular, the US has implemented its own type of structural reform in the 'Volcker Rule' that will be discussed in section 10.3, and many commentators have mooted different versions of structural reform. This section critically considers the objectives of structural reforms and what they may achieve or otherwise.

Structural reforms are seen as key to limiting systemic risk as:

(a) structural reform forces the scale and size of both the retail and parent entities to shrink, thus making either less difficult or perhaps less expensive to resolve (less impact of failure); and/or

(b) the inter-connectedness between the retail and parent entities is reduced and therefore losses occasioned by one entity are less likely to infect the other resulting in a cascade of losses[29] (lower probability of failure);

(c) in particular, with the reduction of inter-connectedness, critical functions of banks such as retail deposits and payment services are protected and prevents disruption to the real economy or adverse perceptions of confidence.

Systemic risk is perceived to be limited as structural reforms could make banks less susceptible to 'too big' or 'too complex' to fail, or in any case achieves clarity as to which parts of the banking group need resolution, making resolution less costly and more manageable. Further, the insulation of critical functions may protect them from contagion, if other parts of the banking group fail.

---

[29] Iris H-Y Chiu, 'The Vickers Independent Banking Commission Report—Does the Ring-fencing of Retail Banks Mitigate Systemic Risk Concerns in the Banking Sector?' (2012) 9 *International Corporate Rescue* 79.

10.2.1 **Do structural reforms reduce systemically important profiles?**

Thinking back on the indicators of systemic importance in Chapter 9, section 9.5, a bank that participates in extensive lines of business across many jurisdictions would likely give rise to the characteristics of size, inter-connectedness, complexity, lack of substitutability, and cross-jurisdictional footprint. Thus, in order to reduce the systemic profile of a bank, structural reforms aimed at limiting the lines of banking business may be the most effective, as such hard limits could prevent complexity and inter-connectedness from arising. This measure was imposed in the US until 1999, discussed in section 10.3. Such limitations are likely regarded as interference with banks' business freedoms and entail loss of economies of scale. Further, they do not necessarily deal with the size, substitutability, and cross-jurisdictional features, as a bank with limited activities could still become a major market player in limited areas and attain systemically important profiles. The US has continued with a more nuanced form of activity limitation in implementing its Volcker Rule. Section 10.3 will discuss the limited achievements in this approach, as well as the susceptibility of such an approach to political lobbying for change, which has been stepped up by banks in the Trump Presidency.

It is important to remember that the UK's ring-fencing approach does not impose limitations on activities, and is therefore less draconian in nature. Ring-fencing results in 'separation' not limitation of activities, and would unlikely have the effect of reducing banks' systemic risk profiles. It could be argued that the ring-fenced bank as well as its parent conglomerate are less likely to become so important that government bailout is needed in the event of failure, as being separated, neither the ring-fenced nor non-ring-fenced entities would become 'too big' or 'too complex' to fail. However, the structural separation may not reduce the systemic importance of either the retail operations or the investment banking operations. For example, a retail bank like Lloyds TSB has a major share of the residential mortgage market and, even if the retail arm of the bank is structurally separate, the significance of the bank in relation to its retail market share could still pose systemic risk. On the other hand, it may be argued that even if a bailout may be in the public interest where a ring-fenced bank fails, the social cost may be more manageable compared to the cost of bailing out a financial conglomerate such as the RBS in 2009.

Further, the structural separation of the retail bank does not mean that the remainder of the parent banking group, which may be involved in investment banking activities, is no longer entitled to ask for state rescue. A wholesale sector financial institution could require rescue as a result of wholesale sector activities, such as American Insurance Group (AIG) in the US during the global financial crisis of 2007–9. The Group had guaranteed many of the underlying mortgage payments in sub-prime mortgage-backed securities, and was adversely affected by defaults on those mortgages. A significant amount of real commercial activity depended on AIG's viability as an insurer, such as the operation of commercial flights and shipping routes. Hence, a financial institution operating only in the wholesale sector may still be systemically important and call upon the state for rescue.

10.2.2 **Do structural reforms protect critical functions?**

'Separation' may be perceived to achieve protection for critical functions as their separateness renders less susceptibility to contagion from losses in other riskier banking activities. Separateness may also achieve clarity as to how different parts of troubled banking groups may be resolved, ensuring that critical functions are protected or 'bailed out'.

The first perception is a myth as it assumes that losses and risk emanate from non-retail financial activities and hence the retail bank must be protected from such contagion. Implicit in the misperception is the assumption that retail banks are less likely to fail by virtue of their more utility-based activities. These assumptions are misplaced. Investment banks are exposed to credit, market, and operational risks and retail banks are likely to be exposed only to credit and operational risks. Retail banks are as likely to fail for taking on high levels of credit risk in lending to the retail sector[30] or as a result of operational failures. Structural reform is not able to deal with bad business decisions and business failure.[31] For example, the failure of Dunfermline Building Society in the UK is largely due to poorly performing domestic commercial loans.[32] The removal of the connection between retail and investment banks in a group may only mean that retail deposits no longer form the capital base for investment banking activities that expose the institution to market risk. However, this does not mean that retail deposits cannot form the capital base for other retail sector related risks, such as credit card lending and small business lending. Further, it may also be queried whether structural separation will have the effect of concentrating certain domestic credit risks in the ring-fenced banks. This could have the effect of augmenting systemic risk in the ring-fenced sector.

Structural reforms such as ring-fencing may mitigate risk contagion between different parts of a banking group but does not necessarily make any part less susceptible to failure. That said, structural reforms may be able to achieve clarity for regulators in terms of the banking group's structure so that different parts of banking groups that are stricken can be dealt with differently, depending on how critical they are for the real economy and society. This also means that any need for public sector support can be more clearly discerned and limited.

If the aim is indeed to achieve total protection of critical functions then alternative options such as 100 per cent reserve banking or narrow banking is likely to be far more effective. However, these options, discussed later, constrain banks' ability to create credit and support the real economy.

---

[30] Such as the US Savings and Loans crisis in the 1980s and 1990s. Peter Wallison, 'Did the "Repeal" of Glass-Steagall Have any Role in the Financial Crisis? Not Guilty. Not Even Close' (2009) 106 *Public Lawyer* 102.

[31] Just as in the secondary banking crisis in the UK in the 1970s, see Margaret Reid, *The Secondary Banking Crisis, 1973–5* (London: Macmillan 1982). Also see Peter Wallison, 'Did the "Repeal" of Glass-Steagall Have any Role in the Financial Crisis? Not Guilty. Not Even Close' (2009) 106 *Public Lawyer* 102.

[32] Bank of England, 'Report under Section 80(1) of the Banking Act 2009 on the Dunfermline Building Society (DBS) Bridge Bank' (July 2010) at http://www.bankofengland.co.uk/financialstability/Documents/role/risk_reduction/srr/resolutions/dbsreport.pdf.

10.2.3 **Benefits of structural reform**

Unless structural reforms are draconian and fundamentally change banks' business models, the systemically important financial institution that threatens financial risk that adversely affects the real economy and society cannot be ruled out. Hence, structural reforms can only mitigate such risks by clarifying that banks' critical functions that enjoy an implicit public sector guarantee cannot be used to subsidise other risky activities. This does not prevent banks that carry out critical functions from failing from risks they incur in their activities, which explains the PRA's determination to subject such banks, largely D-SIBs, to enhanced micro-prudential regulation as discussed in Chapter 8, section 8.5 and Chapter 9, section 9.5.

Other commentators see certain longer-term beneficial effects from structural reform. Weber[33] argues that excessive complexity already exists in the financial sector. Structural simplification contributes towards reducing excessive complexity and could entail general risk moderation in the financial sector.[34] A number of commentators also regard structural reforms as upholding of the social utility aspects of banking as being 'special'.[35] The protection of the social utility core of banking gives the public confidence and could prevent damaging behaviour such as runs on banks.

Zingales also argues that structural separation achieves a couple of other important purposes,[36] promoting competition and shrinking the lobbying power of the banking and financial sector. However, where structural reforms are not draconian, that is, limiting activities, and only take the approach as in the UK to require separation of activities, the landscape for banking is not necessarily rendered more competitive. Indeed, it is the PRA's efforts at nurturing 'new banks' in its pro-innovation 'New Bank Start-up Unit' initiative that is actively helping new banks to enter the market as fully-authorised outfits.[37]

In sum, although there is huge upfront cost to implement structural reform, and it remains uncertain how this may mitigate systemic risk in due course, there are hopes for general changes in the banking sector in terms of de-complexification, more forward-looking planning for crisis resolution and management, and a stronger retail

---

[33] Robert F Weber, 'Structural Regulation as Antidote to Complexity Capture' (2012) *American Business Law Journal* 643.

[34] Robert F Weber, 'Structural Regulation as Antidote to Complexity Capture' (2012) *American Business Law Journal* 643: 'By ramping back the complexity of those elements of the financial system that regulation is designed to protect, … lawmakers can give regulators concrete and achievable mandates' 646.

[35] Ingo Walter, 'The New Case for Functional Separation in Wholesale Financial Services' (July 2009) NYU Working Paper No FIN-09-017 http://ssrn.com/abstract=1442148; Jean-Charles Rochet, 'Systemic Risk: Changing the Regulatory Perspective' (2010) 6 *International Journal of Central Banking* 259. In the words of Sheng, 'Glass–Steagall set up firewalls between networks to prevent contagion between them. Repeal of the act in 1999 set the stage for complete network integration and therefore massive contagion.' Andrew Sheng, *From Asian to Global Financial Crisis* (Cambridge: Cambridge University Press 2009) 326.

[36] Luigi Zingales, *Capitalism for the People: Recapturing the Lost Genius of American Capitalism* (New York: Basic Books 2012). [37] Such as Metro Bank, Atom and Monzo banks that are entirely online.

banking culture, which can be differentiated from the oft-criticised culture in investment banking.[38]

Section 10.3 turns to alternative versions of structural reforms, some of which have been implemented in other jurisdictions.

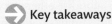 **Key takeaways**

- It is important to determine what objectives structural reforms intend to meet and critically address any misperceptions.

- Structural reforms in the UK are unlikely to reduce the systemic risk profile of large banking groups as they do not impose limitations on activities.

- Structural reforms are likely to mitigate a banking group's use of their retail profile and the implicit public sector support it enjoys to subsidise its risky non-retail activities.

- It is critically queried whether structural reforms can effectively protect critical functions of banks, although one must also bear in mind reforms discussed in Chapter 13.

Key bibliography

Articles

Chiu, IH-Y 'The Vickers Independent Banking Commission Report—Does the Ring-fencing of Retail Banks Mitigate Systemic Risk Concerns in the Banking Sector?' (2012) 9 *International Corporate Rescue* 79

Walter, I 'The New Case for Functional Separation in Wholesale Financial Services' (July 2009) NYU Working Paper No FIN-09-017 http://ssrn.com/abstract=1442148

Weber, RF, 'Structural Regulation as Antidote to Complexity Capture' (2012) 50 *American Business Law Journal* 643

10.3 Options in structural reforms

This section turns to other options in structural reforms. These include the Volcker Rule implemented in the US, as well as the superseded Glass–Steagall Act. We also explore 'moot' options targeted at meeting certain objectives such as protection of critical functions.

---

[38]   Chapter 11; and see House of Lords and House of Commons, *Changing Banking for Good* (Report of the Parliamentary Commission on Banking Standards) (12 June 2013) at Vol 1, para 138ff and Vol II, ch 7; Michael A Santoro and Ronald J Strauss, *Wall Street Values: Business Ethics and the Global Financial Crisis* (Cambridge: Cambridge University Press 2012); Jeanne L. Schroeder, 'Mad Money: Wall Street's Bonus Obsession' (2012) 33 *Cardozo Law Review* 2307; Donald C Langevoort, 'Chasing the Greased Pig Down Wall Street: A Gatekeeper's Guide to the Psychology, Culture and Ethics of Financial Risk-taking' (2011) 96 *Cornell Law Review* 1209.

10.3.1 **Limitations on activities: from Glass–Steagall to the Volcker Rule**

In the US, the Dodd-Frank Act 2011 introduced a form of structural reform that focuses on risky activity limitation. The Volcker Rule[39] limits proprietary trading[40] for banks to 3 per cent of its tier one capital and caps any investment that banks may make in hedge or private equity funds at 3 per cent of its tier one capital too. It also prohibits banks from entering into transactions where there may be 'material conflicts of interest' with investors, such as where the bank has incentives to profit from their clients' investment losses. There are a number of exceptions[41] to the Volcker Rule in order not to adversely affect important risk management activities such as hedging. The Volcker Rule in essence imposes limits on activities that banks can carry out, such limitations may be seen as 'safety' limits in relation to risky activities.

The Volcker Rule[42] does not impose *prohibitions* on activities, unlike the superseded Glass-Steagall Act which was effective in the US until its repeal in 1999. The limitations placed on proprietary trading and alternative investment fund investment do not necessarily entail structural consequences like business separation, unless those business lines are so significant for a bank that they should be rehoused in order to achieve compliance. [43] It is questionable whether the limits imposed bear any real relation to banks' 'safety' from incurring losses in relation to proprietary trading or investments in hedge and private equity funds. The Volcker Rule can be seen as achieving strong and indeed *total* separation where banking groups decide to separate significant levels of such activities. However, such separation is only meaningful from the point of view of containing risk if the activities of proprietary trading or investments in hedge and private equity funds are indeed so hazardous. One doubts that those activities can be so labelled, especially when securitised assets were under the spotlight in the global financial crisis.[44] It seems odd that a measure aimed at limiting banks' risky activities says nothing about securitised assets. Scott[45] argues that investments in alternative investment funds have nothing to do with the financial crisis of 2007–9 and that such arbitrary limitations will only hamper banks' competitiveness.

[39] Dodd-Frank Wall Street Reform and Consumer Protection Act 2011 (Dodd-Frank Act), Pub.L. 111–203, § 619.   [40] See Chapter 1 under 'Modern Banking'.

[41] Market-making and hedging activities are exempted. However, market-making activities could be substantial and hedging activities, while designed to manage the bank's credit, market or liquidity risks could still be undertaken in substantial amounts via derivative contracts.

[42] Matthias Lehmann, 'Volcker Rule, Ring-Fencing or Separation of Bank Activities: Comparison of Structural Reform Acts Around the World' (2015) at http://ssrn.com/abstract=251993.

[43] Andrew F Tuch, 'Conflicted Gatekeepers and Goldman Sachs' (April 2011) Washington University in St Louis Legal Studies Research Paper No 12-12-1 <http://ssrn.com/abstract=1809271>.

[44] See Chapter 1.

[45] Hal Scott, 'A General Evaluation of the Dodd-Frank US Financial Reform Legislation' (2010) 25 *Journal of International Banking Law and Regulation* 477.

Harding[46] argues that the Volcker Rule should not be treated as having 'structural' consequences as it does not deal with interconnections between and within financial institutions and contagion possibilities. Limits placed on proprietary trading and requirements to address conflicts of interest are indeed more relevant to client protection, and not to mitigating systemic risk.

The US used to impose a form of structural regulation based on prohibiting banks from being involved in or owning companies that engage in certain financial activities. The Glass–Steagall Act of 1932 prohibited investment banks from taking deposits and commercial banks from undertaking significant securities and investment activities. This was in response to the 1929 Wall Street crash followed by the 1930s depression, an episode involving banks' exposure to undesirably high levels of market risk through highly risky investments in securities. As a consequence, financial institutions developed different business lines and the Act fostered the growth of a diverse financial sector. However, due to the economies of scale and efficiencies of cross-fertilisation in financial services,[47] the growing US banking lobby had been pressing for exemptions and watering down of the Glass–Steagall prohibitions[48] to the point that by 1999, the government thought it no longer meaningful to maintain the prohibition.

It is highly debatable whether the abolition of the Glass–Steagall regime[49] was key to the global financial crisis. US banks grew exponentially into conglomerates, and amplified the risks of being complex, interconnected and cross-jurisdictional.[50] Securitisation of sub-prime mortgage assets crucially linked retail banks with investment banks in new ways that would not have been possible if the prohibitions under Glass-Steagall were in place. Although the abolition of Glass-Steagall provided an environment for systemic risk to grow in the financial sector, it is not certainly the case that preserving Glass–Steagall would have definitely contained systemic risk. This is because retail banks can take on excessive levels of risk in their limited activities and risk failure. Moreover, the

---

[46] Ted Harding, 'Under the "Volcker Rule" in the United States, It Is proposed that Banks Will No Longer Be Allowed to Own, Invest in, or Sponsor Hedge Funds, Private Equity Funds, or Proprietary Trading Operations for Their Own Profit, Unrelated to Serving Their Customers. Can This Be an Effective Regulatory Response to Risk Issues Exposed During the Financial Crisis that Commenced in the Autumn of 2008?' (August 2010) UCD Working Papers in Law, Criminology & Socio-Legal Studies Research Paper No 37/2010 http://ssrn.com/abstract=1653971. Also see Alessio M Pacces, 'Consequences of Uncertainty for Regulation: Law and Economics of the Financial Crisis' (2010) 7 *European Company and Financial Law Review* 479.

[47] Such as securities and mutual fund firms wishing to access local clientele via a bank's branch service.

[48] These pressures came from securities firms which wanted to access local clientele via banks' vast branch networks and local banks that wanted a slice of the investment market pie, see Douglas Branson, 'A Return to Old-Time Religion? The Glass–Steagall Act, the Volcker Rule, Limits on Proprietary Trading, and Sustainability' (2014) at http://ssrn.com/abstract=2509958.

[49] The Gramm–Leach–Bliley Act (GLBA), also known as the Financial Services Modernization Act of 1999 (Pub.L. 106–102, 113 Stat. 1338, enacted November 12, 1999).

[50] Arthur E Wilmarth Jnr, 'The Transformation of the Financial Services Industry: 1975-2000, Competition, Consolidation and Increased Risks' (2002) University of Illinois Law Rev 215; 'The Dark Side of Universal Banking: Financial Conglomerates and the Origins of the Subprime Financial Crisis' (2009) 41 *Connecticut Law Review* 963; Suzanne McGee, *Chasing Goldman Sachs: How the Masters of the Universe Melted Wall Street Down… And Why They'll Take Us to the Brink Again* (New York: Crown Business 2010).

liberalisation of modern banking should not per se be regarded as an evil to avoid as the economies of scale are immense and finance is made more available generally. It can be regarded as more important to ensure that micro-prudential regulation that effectively contains risk-taking behaviour is in place rather than forcing blanket prohibitions on financial activities that benefit from cross-fertilisation and scale.

10.3.2 Other structural options

We proceed to discuss structural options that have been mooted but not implemented. We turn first to structural options aimed specifically at protecting the critical functions of banks in relation to retail deposits and payments. These options ensure that critical functions are protected because the banks that carry these out are prohibited from carrying out any other activity. Such risk averse approaches would achieve the guarantee of protection but potentially marginalises the benefits of bank risk-taking in lending and investment. The range of structural options we survey here represent perspectives on the 'trade-off' between guaranteed deposit safety and allowing banks to engage in risk-taking that is acknowledged to serve economic needs.

10.3.2.1 One hundred per cent reserve banking

In order to protect retail deposits and critical functions like payments, a 100 per cent reserve banking regime would provide that level of absolute safety. Banks that accept retail deposits would only act as safe-keepers of such deposits and facilitate payment services, but they would not be allowed to lend the deposits, maintaining only a fraction of deposits at any one time. This proposal was made in the 1930s after the Great Depression by a group of eminent economists, known as the 'Chicago Plan'.[51] However, the plan was jettisoned as its draconian approach to banking business was seen as unnecessary when economic recovery began in the US.

In the aftermath of the global financial crisis, Levitin[52] argued again for a 100 per cent reserve banking regime to be introduced. In his view, fractional reserve banking, which allows banks to lend on most if not all of their deposits, has only led banks to excessive risk-taking and credit creation. Such credit creation has also increased money supply exponentially and in an unsustainable manner. If deposit and lending were separated, deposits would be safe, and lending would be carried out only by institutions that receive investors' capital to do so. This limits lending to actual funded levels and mitigates unsustainable levels of credit. There is much to be said for the objectives of prudent financial intermediation and safe deposit-keeping. However, reality is that households, corporations, and states have come to depend on certain levels of borrowing. Further,

---

[51] See, for example, R Phillips, 'The Chicago Plan and New Deal Banking Reform' in D Papadimitriou (ed), *Stability in the Financial Syste* (New York: Macmillan 1996); J Tobin 'The Case for Preserving Regulatory Distinctions' (1974) 30 *Challenge* 10–7.

[52] Adam J Levitin, 'Safe Banking: Finance and Democracy' (2016) 83 *University of Chicago Law Review* 357.

no jurisdiction is likely to introduce this regime, which disadvantages its financial sector relative to global competition.

10.3.2.2 Narrow banking

Moving away from 100 per cent reserve banking, we explore alternatives that infuse its spirit into more moderate proposals.

Kay[53] proposes that consumer deposit-taking and payments business be structurally separated as a 'module' from other financial business and only such services can be called 'banking', so that banking itself becomes a narrow concept, with other business' treated as financial business' generally. Narrow banks may engage in consumer and small business lending as well as residential mortgages, but would not enjoy a monopoly of these functions. They should be regulated for safety and soundness, with consumer protection being a top priority. Kay also suggests that in order to ensure robust consumer protection, deposits should be 100 per cent liquid and invested only in government bonds. This proposal is less restrictive[54] than the Chicago Plan but ensures greater safety for deposits than under the ring-fencing approach. This approach achieves deposit safety but also implies that deposits cannot form the basis of lending. Narrow banks' lending would likely have to come from other sources and their capacity to lend may be naturally limited in this manner. Indeed, narrow banks may ironically have to incur significant risks in other forms of borrowing in order to lend.

Pennachi's[55] version of 'narrow banking' supports deposit safety too but limits the lending of deposits to assets that have little or no nominal interest rate and credit risk, so that these assets can be liquidated easily to meet deposit liabilities. Pennachi's approach shows certainly that a trade-off has to be made between protecting deposits and engaging in a wider range of asset creation to benefit real economic needs. Under this approach, long-term illiquid lending such as residential mortgages is not possible.

The analysis provided by narrow banking commentators shows the dilemmas in designing a regulatory regime that achieves deposit safety while ensuring sufficient investment or lending for longer-term purposes that are illiquid and riskier. But it could equally be counter-argued that the price for lending and investment has been artificially low where deposits have been used to finance risky, long-term, or illiquid assets.[56] Next, we turn to Avgouleas' tiered banking licence proposal that introduces a new balance to protecting deposits while ensuring that financial activities are not unduly restricted.

---

[53] John Kay, 'Narrow Banking: The Reform of Banking Regulation' (2009) at http://www.johnkay.com/wp-content/uploads/2009/12/JK-Narrow-Banking.pdf.

[54] See also L Bryan, *Breaking Up the Bank: Rethinking an Industry under Seige.* (Homewood, IL: Dow Jones Irwin 1998); R Litan, *What Should Banks Do?* (Washington, DC: Brookings Inst 1997).

[55] George Pennachi, 'Narrow Banking' (2012) 4 *Annual Review of Financial Economics* 141.

[56] *Foley v Hill* (1848) 2 HLC 28; 9 ER 1002, discussed in Chapter 2.

10.3.2.3 Tiered banking licence/reorganisation of financial sector

This proposal allows the financial sector to be reorganised in such a way that critical functions are protected while useful risk-taking activity is legitimised and proportionately governed according to the levels of risk that are to be assumed. This proposal benefits from recognising the importance of risk aversion while not excessively focusing on it and losing sight of the utility of banking as a risk-taking business after all.

Avgouleas[57] proposes a three-tier classification of the banking business. He suggests that banks should be licensed *ex ante* only in respect of certain activities, so that we are served by a diverse range of financial services according to our risk needs. The bottom tier comprises retail banks that function like narrow banks focusing on deposit protection. This tier of banks serves staple current account and retail financial needs. An intermediate tier would be banks that take deposits and participate in some capital markets activities but limited by regulatory licence. It is envisaged that these banks would be able to modify their traditional deposit-taking terms such as withdrawal limits and suspensions in times of stress. The relatively reduced 'safety' in these banks correspond with higher risk and returns and it is up to customers to diversify their savings options. These banks should however have limited access to lender of last resort and government support channels, and savers should be aware upfront that the risk–return trade-off is different for this category of institutions than narrow banks. By managing savers' expectations, the fear of depositor runs and retail market panic could be mitigated. Finally, a third tier of banks engaging in investment banking should operate without a deposit-taking licence and with no guarantee of lender of last resort or government support. This would pave the way for the banking sector to become more diversified, so that homogenous risk-taking patterns are avoided. Consumer choice and customer service could also be improved with specialist financial institutions offering a menu of risk choices commensurate with their needs. The need for regulatory oversight and intervention may also become more manageable.

Avgouleas' proposal would compel regulators to be much more involved in shaping the business models and structure of the financial sector, a role that regulators have not played so far. As Chapter 1 has discussed, regulation has been reactive to financial crises and scandals, and bank business models have been left free to be developed according to market needs until the post-crisis reforms.[58] Indeed the post-crisis reforms are arguably the first stab at a comprehensive regime to govern bank behaviour. The UK's structural reforms, and to an extent the Volcker Rule, play a part in taking regulatory control to reorganise banking business, but regulation is far from taking the leadership in organising banking business and structures overall. It may be argued that regulation should not play such a role and financial institutions are better placed to develop and organise themselves to meet customers' needs.

---

[57] Emilios Avgouleas, 'The Reform of "Too-Big-To-Fail" Bank: A New Regulatory Model for the Institutional Separation of "Casino" from "Utility" Banking' (February 2010) at http://ssrn.com/abstract=1552970.
[58] Discussed in Chapters 8, 9, 11, 12, and 13.

However, the global financial crisis taught us that financial sector organisations and structures are not always for meeting genuine market needs, but for meeting the empire-building and profitability needs of individual institutions and well-remunerated bankers. Nevertheless, regulatory intervention into reorganising banking business and structures is challenging as regulators may not 'get it right', and this is likely resisted by the financial sector.

In sum, structural reforms are controversial and face contrary objectives in their design and implementation. Table 10.1 compares to what extent different reforms meet certain objectives and the severity of regulatory intervention required.

Table 10.1

Characteristics	Ring-fencing in the UK	Volcker Rule/ limitations on activities	Narrow banking/ deposit protection services	Tiered banking licence/ reorganisation by regulation
Meeting objective of reducing systemic risk	Not necessarily	Not necessarily	Not necessarily	Yes
Meeting objective of protecting critical functions	Likely	No	Yes	Yes
100% backing for short-term deposits	No, general deposit guarantee, discussed in Chapter 13, applies to all deposit institutions	No, general deposit guarantee in US applies	Yes	Yes, for the right licenced category
Consumer protection and choice	No real impact	No real impact	Yes	Yes
Substantive business change (e.g. limits on activities)	No, activities are separated not prohibited	Yes	Yes	Yes, as banks need to organise themselves to fit pre-determined regulatory categories
Subjection to tailor-made regulatory design	To some extent	No	Yes	Yes

Structural reforms which essentially intervene into banking business freedoms and structures are not easy to justify and calibrate. This may explain why the EU ultimately could not secure agreement to introduce such reforms as a harmonising measure.

10.3.3 Developments in the EU

The EU considered structural reforms over a number of years but ultimately jettisoned the Commission's proposal to harmonise such reforms across Europe. Some of the largest universal banks in the world are European banks and member states are naturally averse to any negative impact structural reforms could cause to their 'national champions' in the banking industry. Further, as European banks are highly connected to their sovereigns,[59] the cost and other adverse impact of structural reforms for banks may affect sovereign borrowing and finances.

We chart the progress of European discussions below.

10.3.3.1 Liikanen Report

The European Commission established an independent committee to look into structural reforms under the leadership of Erkki Liikanen who reported in 2012. The Liikanen Report[60] was of the view that structural reforms were not the only means to deal with the financial stability concerns of the EU, which revolved around ensuring that retail deposit institutions do not suffer contagion from riskier market-based activities, and that systemically important financial institutions are made more robust and can be resolved in an orderly manner. The Report saw structural reforms as only one facet of a package of essential micro-prudential and crisis resolution reforms.[61] However it was of the view that structural reforms were useful for limiting contagion, in the following ways:

(a) a structurally reformed banking group would be unable to take excessive risks with insured deposits, such as to cover trading losses;

(b) a structurally reformed banking group is unable to allow excessive allocation of lending from the deposit bank to other financial activities in the group; and

(c) the interconnectedness between structurally reformed banking groups and the shadow banking system can be reduced, as the shadow banking system is a source of contagion for systemic risk.

---

[59] MK Brunnermeier et al, *European Safe Bonds* (2011) at ESBies.www.euronomics.com; L Reichlin, 'The ECB and the Banks: The Tale of Two Crises', Discussion Paper 964 (London: Centre for Economic Policy Research 2013).

[60] *High-level Expert Group on Reforming the Structure of the EU Banking Sector* (2 October 2012) at http://ec.europa.eu/finance/bank/docs/high-level_expert_group/report_en.pdf.

[61] Discussed in Chapters 8, 9, 11, 12, and 13.

The report proposed that if banks held a significant proportion of their assets for trading, such as 15–20 per cent, or if such assets amounted to at least €100 billion, the national regulator should have the power to examine to what extent there is contagion risk between the bank's trading activities and its deposit-taking functions, and determine what activities ought to be restructured into a separate legal entity. The legally-separate deposit-taking bank and trading entity could operate within a bank holding company structure. However, the deposit-taking bank should be sufficiently insulated from the risks of the trading entity. The separate entities should also comply with regulatory requirements such as capital adequacy on a stand-alone basis. The thresholds in the Report were minimum levels. National regulators could require banks to restructure themselves beyond the scope under the mandatory separation outlined above, if the national authorities determined it necessary to improve a bank's resolvability and protection of critical functions.

The EU and UK dealt with the same objectives of reducing systemic risk and protecting critical functions in considering structural reforms. Whereas the UK took the view that ring-fencing significant deposit-taking banks was the correct move, the Liikanen Report could not be so prescriptive as the nature of banks in the EU differed greatly in their systemic risk impacts in national jurisdictions and the needs to protect critical functions. The UK's ring-fencing approach is arguably appropriate to the market structure, which comprises for or five High Street banks with disproportionately large retail footprint, a highly concentrated market. Some jurisdictions in the EU and in the US, for example, have a much more diverse retail banking landscape with regional and local banks. In the UK, it can be argued that systemic risk limitation and protection of critical functions are objectives that should be concurrently pursued in respect of those banks, such as HSBC, Barclays, Santander UK, Lloyd's, and RBS. In this manner, the affected banks are few and clearly determined. But in many European jurisdictions, systemic risk limitation would apply to banks such as Deutsche Bank or ING whose focus is on investment banking, while protection of critical functions relates to a host of regional and local banks who may face an avalanche of costly implementation from structural reforms. In other words, a one-size-fits-all structural approach is inappropriate in the EU.

Nevertheless, the Liikanen Report made a basic start by identifying the principles of risk separation and the need to ensure that riskier investment banking activities are not subsidised by retail deposits. These could be taken up in more tailor-made regimes by member states.

10.3.3.2 Progress in the EU

The European Commission took a couple of years to respond to the Liikanen Report, and issued a proposal in 2014 that proposed to impose more stringent structural limitations than the Report.[62]

---

[62] European Commission, *Proposal for a Regulation of the European Parliament and of the Council on Structural Measures Improving the Resilience of EU Credit Institutions* (29 January 2014) at *http://eur-lex.europa.eu/legal-content/EN/ALL/?uri=CELEX:52014PC0043*.

The Commission proposed to apply structural reforms to banks considered to be globally systemically important and that exceeded the following thresholds for three consecutive years: (a) the bank's total assets exceeded €30 billion; and (b) the bank's total trading assets and liabilities exceeded €70 billion or 10 per cent of their total assets. The Commission was of the view that a complete ban on proprietary trading was desirable, as such activities generated high levels of market risks and undesirable conflicts of interests. Further, other risky market-based activities would need to be considered for structural separation if the national regulator were of the view that contagion risks had to be limited. National regulators would have the ultimate discretion to require separation of activities or sub-sets of activities into separate legal entities, such risky activities including market-making, securitisation product development and trading, investments in alternative funds, trading in derivatives, and so on. The separate legal entities would be subject to limitations on their economic and governance links and interdependencies, and would have to comply with regulatory requirements such as capital adequacy separately. Further, there would be a ban placed on the trading entities to carry out deposit-taking or retail payment services.

The Commission's proposal introduced thresholds for structural reforms that were lower than the Liikanen Report's and so would affect a greater scope of banks. The complete ban on proprietary trading also went further than the Volcker Rule.

The Commission's proposal was substantially amended by the Council of Finance Ministers in the EU (ECOFIN)[63] in mid-2015. The amended proposal watered down the Commission's approach in some respects while considering the UK's reforms in ring-fencing. The ECOFIN accepted the Commission's proposed scope of application of structural reforms, and added that banks with deposits less than 3 per cent of their total assets or less than €35 billion absolutely should not fall within the scope of structural reforms. The clarification of negative scope would likely relieve investment banks and medium sized deposit-takers operationally largely as national businesses. The ECOFIN rejected the absolute ban on proprietary trading, and preferred that proprietary trading be separated into a distinct legal entity. The ECOFIN also wished to give member states the choice of approaching structural reforms from the point of view of separating proprietary trading and other risky trading activities out of the banking group, or separating the deposit and retail services in order to ring-fence them. Trading entities would be prohibited from taking retail deposits or conducting retail payments. Under this approach, national regulators would also be given a fair amount of discretion to meet their diverse national interests in relation to their banking industry structure.

Since the ECOFIN amendments in mid-2015, discussions have not progressed amidst member state disagreements. In October 2017, the Commission withdrew the

---

[63] General Secretariat of Council, *Proposal for a Regulation of the European Parliament and of the Council on Structural Measures Improving the Resilience of EU Credit Institutions – General Approach* (19 June 2015) at http://data.consilium.europa.eu/doc/document/ST-10150-2015-INIT/en/pdf.

proposal for structural reforms,[64] citing the lack of foreseeable agreement in this initiative. As has already been discussed, structural reforms deal with dilemmas in meeting public interest objectives such as protecting deposit-taking institutions while determining a suitable level of intervention into banks' business freedoms. Further, it is uncertain if any of the variants of structural reforms we have discussed deal adequately with preventing systemic risk. The uncertainty of benefits that such reforms can yield makes it difficult to justify this as a harmonising measure across the EU. Further, as national resolution authorities can require business structure changes on a case-by-case basis under the powers in relation to recovery and resolution planning (Chapter 13, section 13.2), structural reforms can seem too overarching and insensitive.

Although structural reforms for EU banking groups remain unharmonised, a limited type of 'structural' requirement is to be introduced for third country banking groups that have European subsidiaries, in order to ensure that European depositors and constituencies are protected from the risks that may afflict these banking groups.

10.3.3.3 Special structural requirements for material subsidiaries of non-EU G-SIBs

The EU is introducing an important structural requirement that relates to third country G-SIBs with subsidiaries operating in the EU. This reform intends to pre-empt resolution problems that such subsidiaries may pose for EU regulators if the parent G-SIB should need resolution. Subsidiaries of third country G-SIBs may operate in different member states and could become a burden to each member state if the parent G-SIB fails. Hence, the Commission proposes to require third country G-SIBs to set up an EU-based 'Intermediate EU Parent Undertaking' for all their subsidiaries operating in the EU, if their total assets exceed €30 billion.[65] The Intermediate EU Parent Undertaking will be separately authorised in the EU and will be subject to resolution procedures in the EU if the group falls into crisis. This measure may be regarded as tit for tat for the US equivalent of requiring non-US G-SIBs to set up intermediate holding companies if their subsidiary assets are at least $50 billion.

This reform poses significant inconvenience for non-EU G-SIBs as the consolidated Intermediate Parent Undertaking would likely attract D-SIB treatment and enhanced micro-prudential regulation in each member state or under the European Central Bank (ECB). Upon the UK's cessation of EU membership, UK G-SIBs with subsidiaries in Europe may have to comply with this requirement, potentially diluting the powers that UK resolution authorities would be able to exercise if a UK G-SIB needs to be resolved.

---

[64] European Commission Communication, at https://ec.europa.eu/info/sites/info/files/cwp_2018_annex_iv_en.pdf.

[65] Article 21b, Commission Proposal to amend the Capital Requirements IV Regulation 2013, as of 26 November 2016 at http://ec.europa.eu/finance/bank/docs/regcapital/crr-crd-review/161123-proposal-amending-regulation_en.pdf or the 'banking reform package' as discussed in Chapters 8 and 9.

➡ Key takeaways

- Other structural options are explored and critically discussed in terms of the objectives they may achieve and their limitations.

- The Volcker Rule in the US introduces limits on proprietary trading and alternative investment fund investment, arguably achieving total structural separation for banks that conduct high volumes of those activities.

- The Volcker Rule's potential to introduce total activity separation is however modest compared to the superseded Glass–Steagall Act before whose repeal in 1999 enforced a regime of activity limitation for commercial and investment banks. This fostered diversity in the US financial sector although it remains uncertain if activity limitations are key to preventing systemic risk.

- Where protection of deposits is the key objective, 100 per cent reserve banking or forms of narrow banking have been proposed.

- This section highlights Avgouleas' tiered banking licence as a radical proposal to reorganise banking business structures by regulatory leadership, but such levels of regulation are likely to be regarded as high-handed and unlikely to be adopted in reality.

- Structural reforms vary in nature, scope, and design due to the different and often conflicting objectives sought to be achieved.

- The EU considered structural reforms but has ultimately jettisoned these as member state interests are too diverse for such a harmonising measure.

Key bibliography

Legislation

Dodd-Frank Wall Street Reform and Consumer Protection Act 2011 (Dodd–Frank Act), Pub.L. 111–203, § 619

Reports and Guidelines

European Commission, *Proposal for a Regulation of the European Parliament and of the Council on structural measures improving the resilience of EU credit institutions* (29 January 2014) at http://eur-lex.europa.eu/legal-content/EN/ALL/?uri=CELEX:52014PC0043

General Secretariat of Council, *Proposal for a Regulation of the European Parliament and of the Council on structural measures improving the resilience of EU credit institutions—General Approach* (19 June 2015) at http://data.consilium.europa.eu/doc/document/ST-10150-2015-INIT/en/pdf

High-level Expert Group on Reforming the Structure of the EU Banking Sector (2 October 2012) at http://ec.europa.eu/finance/bank/docs/high-level_expert_group/report_en.pdf.

Articles

Avgouleas, E, 'The Reform of "Too-Big-To-Fail" Bank: A New Regulatory Model for the Institutional Separation of "Casino" from "Utility" Banking' (February 2010) http://ssrn.com/abstract=1552970

Kay, J, 'Narrow Banking: The Reform of Banking Regulation' (2009) http://www.johnkay.com/wp-content/uploads/2009/12/JK-Narrow-Banking.pdf

Lehmann, M, 'Volcker Rule, Ring-Fencing or Separation of Bank Activities: Comparison of Structural Reform Acts around the World' (2015) at http://ssrn.com/abstract=251993

Levitin, AJ, 'Safe Banking: Finance and Democracy' (2016) 83 *University of Chicago Law Review* 357

Questions

1. Compare at least 2 different approaches to the structural reforms for banks. Critically discuss what objectives are likely to be achieved.

   Answer tips *You may discuss the UK's ring-fencing framework, the US Volcker Rule, and/or academic commentators' approaches not adopted in policy such as narrow banking and the EU's framework in development. For each approach, you should discuss the key elements and what objectives are connected to them, such as systemic risk mitigation, consumer protection, and so on, and come to an appraisal of the achievements and limitations of the approaches you have chosen to discuss.*

2. The lack of international harmonisation in structural reforms is likely to cause regulatory arbitrage. Do you agree?

   Answer tips *The question expects you to highlight the disparate frameworks for structural reforms that exist between the US, UK, and EU, and point out the key features of their differences. You should analyse the differences in terms of which regulatory features may be regarded as imposing more or less costly regulatory burdens and whether these may cause banks to exploit the differences. You should also critically consider whether there are any pros and cons to a more internationally convergent framework for structural reforms.*

3. Are national structural reforms the pre-cursor to threatening the viability of or ending the international banking business model?

   Answer tips *You should discuss the disparate nature of national structural reform frameworks, highlighting the differences between the US Volcker Rule, the UK ring-fencing approach, and the EU's lack of harmonisation. You should consider what difficulties the disparate frameworks pose for an international bank, whether these difficulties are surmountable or not, and the beneficial effects and disadvantages that flow from having to comply with disparate requirements. You may also consider if there are any imaginative solutions to the issues you raise.*

11

The regulatory framework for bank culture and conduct

11.1 The importance of bank culture

The organisational culture of a bank is often regarded to be the 'software' of the organisation, reflecting the actual practices adopted by the people who run or operate the bank.[1] Bank culture is 'of utmost importance'[2] to regulators as bank culture profoundly affects the outcomes that regulators are concerned with: the prudential safety of banks and banks' conduct in the marketplace.[3] Such culture is forged by individual decision-making and behaviour at banks, as well as the collective ethos and environment at the organisation. The relationship between regulation and bank culture cannot be one of prescription as regulation cannot amount to micro-management of banks. However, regulation can introduce frameworks and incentives for both individual behaviour as well as organisational structures, which together can shape culture. This chapter focuses on individual responsibility, and significant attention will be devoted to the UK's unique 'senior and certified persons regime', while Chapter 12 deals with organisational and governance aspects.

As discussed in Chapter 1, the 2007–9 global financial crisis revealed excessive risk-taking on the part of banks. The banks in the UK that failed or teetered on the brink of failure, that is, Northern Rock,[4] Halifax Bank of Scotland,[5] and the Royal Bank of Scotland[6] all took excessive risks that materialised into severe backlashes. These banks

---

[1] G-30, *Towards Effective Governance in Financial Institutions* (2012) at http://www.group30.org/rpt_64.shtml.

[2] Andrew Bailey, 'Culture in Financial Services: A Regulator's Perspective' (Cityweek Conference 2016, 9 May 2016) at http://www.bankofengland.co.uk/publications/Pages/speeches/2016/901.aspx.

[3] PRA, *The Use of PRA Powers To Address Serious Failings in the Culture of Firms* (Statement of Policy, June 2014) at http://www.bankofengland.co.uk/pra/Documents/publications/policy/2014/powersculture.pdf.

[4] FSA Internal Audit, *The Supervision of Northern Rock: A Lessons Learnt Review* (March 2008) at http://www.fsa.gov.uk/pubs/other/nr_report.pdf.

[5] House of Commons and House of Lords, *Parliamentary Commission on Banking Standards, An Accident Waiting to Happen: The Failure of HBOS* (4 April 2013).

[6] FSA Board Report, *The Failure of the Royal Bank of Scotland* (Dec 2011) at http://www.fsa.gov.uk/pubs/other/rbs.pdf.

have also been found to suffer from poor 'risk cultures' although they were not in breach of prudential regulation. As Chapters 8 and 9 have outlined, prudential regulation does not guarantee zero failure although it seeks to mitigate such possibilities. Hence, there is a 'grey' area of hazardous practices in a bank that can ultimately drive a bank towards prudential and corporate failure. It is imperative for regulators, learning the lessons from the global financial crisis, to engage pro-actively with these signs,[7] as they could indicate culture failings in terms of banks' ability to exercise self-control over their risk-taking tendencies. Mere adherence to the technicalities of prudential regulatory compliance is not enough.

Many commentators explain how the aggressive profit-chasing and growth cultures at banks before the global financial crisis have persistently undervalued[8] the importance of 'risk' or control cultures.[9] In its scathing review, the UK Houses of Parliament Commission[10] demanded regulatory reform to promote sounder cultures at banks, consistent with international opinion.[11]

'Risk culture' is defined as 'an internal sensibility, reflected in the daily thoughts and actions of all of an institution's employees, that reflects knowledge of and respect for risk.'[12] Risk culture is more than just the processes of the risk management framework.[13] Empirical research has found that in a bank where the culture is predominantly 'competitive',[14] the bank attracts employees that are disposed towards higher risk-taking behaviour and the bank itself is also associated with a higher credit risk profile.[15] Risk culture is thus highly relevant to the ultimate safety and soundness of a bank, the key objective in prudential regulation.

Further, a wave of conduct scandals also hit global banks from 2010. These range from consumer mis-selling,[16] the manipulation of interest rate benchmarks and other

---

[7]   G30, *Bank Conduct and Culture: A Call for Sustained and Comprehensive Reform* (2015) at http://group30.org/publications/detail/166.

[8]   Donald C Langevoort, 'Chasing the Greased Pig Down Wall Street: A Gatekeeper's Guide to the Psychology, Culture and Ethics of Financial Risk-taking' (2011) 96 *Cornell Law Review* 1209.

[9]   Michel Crouhy, 'Risk Management Failures During the Financial Crisis' in Robert W Kolb (ed), *Lessons from the Financial Crisis* (NJ: John Wiley 2010); Elizabeth Sheedy, 'The Future of Risk Modelling' in Robert W Kolb (ed), *Lessons from the Financial Crisis* (NJ: John Wiley 2010).

[10]   House of Lords and House of Commons, *Changing Banking for Good* (2013), op cit at Vol II, paras 141–2.

[11]   See FSB, *Guidance on Supervisory Interaction with Financial Institutions on Risk Culture: A Framework for Assessing Risk Culture* (2014) at http://www.fsb.org/2014/04/140407/.

[12]   Erik Banks, *Risk Culture* (Basingstoke: Palgrave Macmillan, 2012) 23. also see Annetta Cortez, *Winning at Risk* (Chichester: John Wiley & Sons, 2011) 145.

[13]   See Chapter 12.   [14]   See section 11.1.1.

[15]   Andreas Barth, 'The Role of Corporate Culture in the Financial Industry' (2016) at http://papers.ssrn.com/sol3/papers.cfm?abstract_id=2707078.

[16]   For example, in payment protection insurance, see FSA, 'The Assessment and Redress of Payment Protection Insurance Complaints: Feedback on the further consultation in CP10/6 and final Handbook text' (August 2010) PS10/12 http://www.fsa.gov.uk/pubs/policy/ps10_12.pdf, accessed 8 January 2013. See Eilis Ferran, 'Regulatory Lessons from the Payment Protection Insurance Mis-Selling Scandal in the UK' (2012) *European Business Organisation Law Review* 248. For the Arch Cru funds, see FSA, *Consumer Redress Scheme in Respect of Unsuitable Advice to Invest in Arch Cru Funds* (December 2012).

Figure 11.1 the Competing Values framework for bank culture

benchmarks by banks to further their short-term trading interests,[17] engagement in money laundering in clear violation of the law.[18] Such behaviour is not easily explained by the indictment of rogue individuals,[19] but seems to be pervasive in bank culture.[20] In this light, there is now a greater need to understand how bank culture relates to socially important goals such as financial stability and regulatory compliance with standards that protect stakeholders such as customers.

11.1.1 **What is bank culture?**

Organisational culture refers to the shared values of an organisation as practised by its people,[21] an informal and unspoken language that binds the organisational personnel together in day-to-day practices and solving problems in an efficient and consistent manner.[22] In studying organisational culture at banks, the 'Competing Values Framework'[23]

---

[17] See Martin Wheatley, *The Wheatley Review of LIBOR* (Sep 2012); 'Citigroup forex trader fired amid global probe', *Financial Times* (10 January 2014); 'Deutsche Bank braced for fines in forex probes: sources', *Reuters* (28 May 2014); 'Barclays suspends six foreign exchange traders', *Financial Times* (1 November 2013); 'UBS First to Report FX Rigging Shows EU Immunity Flaws', *Bloomberg* (2 April 2014).

[18] 'HSBC to Pay £1.2bn over Mexico Scandal', *The Guardian* (11 December 2012); 'Standard Chartered Hit by $3m in Iran Fines', BBCNews (10 December 2012); 'HSBC Helped Clients Dodge Millions in Tax', BBC-News (10 February 2015).

[19] Such as Jerome Kerviel, see Eric Pichet, 'What Governance Lessons Should Be Learnt from The Société Générale's Kerviel Affair' (2008) 3 *La revue Française de Gouvernance d'Entreprise* 117; and the UK's Kweku Adoboli, 'Kweku Adoboli: A Rogue Trader's Tale', *Financial Times* (22 October 2015).

[20] Suggested in Adoboli's interview after release from prison, see 'What Kweku Adoboli and Fellow Fraudsters Can Teach Banks', *Financial Times* (2 August 2016).

[21] Edgar H Schein, *Organizational Culture and Leadership* (NY: Jossey Bass, 2010); Joanne Martin, *Organisational Cultures: Mapping the Terrain* (London: Sage 2001); Peter T Van den Berg and Celeste PM Wilderom, 'Defining, Measuring, and Comparing Organisational Cultures' (2004) 53 *Applied Psychology: An International Review* 570.

[22] Eric van den Steen, Eric, 'On the Origin of Shared Belief (and Corporate Culture)' (2010) 41 *Ran Journal of Economics* 617–48.

[23] Anjan Thakor, 'Corporate Culture in Banking' (ECGI Working Paper 2015) at http://ssrn.com/abstract=2565514.

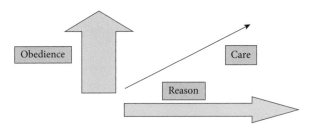

Figure 11.2 Moral DNA framework for bank culture

has been applied to categorise four leading types of bank culture. These types are not exclusive of one another but banks falling within one type show dominant characteristics in that type. Figure 11.1 illustrates the four types of bank culture in the quadrants.

The ***collaborate* culture** emphasises team-work, consensual and collaborative processes, and accountability. The ***create* culture** encourages freedom of thought among employees, entrepreneurial vision and 'rule-breaking' if necessary. The ***control* culture** focuses on achieving organisational effectiveness associated with capable processes, measurement, and control, for example, by subscribing to quality control and assurance processes. The ***compete* culture** emphasises being aggressive and forceful in competitive pursuits, keenly monitoring market signals and interaction with external stakeholders such as customers and competitors. The ***control*** and ***compete*** cultures have been found to be dominant in many financial institutions including retail and investment banks and insurers.[24]

Another framework for studying culture is Steare's MoralDNA,[25] which explores culture along the three axes of obedience, reason, and care (see Figure 11.2). ***Obedience*** refers to rule-based behaviour, such as directed by regulation and other formal rules. ***Reason*** alludes to behaviour on the basis of principles, reflecting beliefs and values. ***Care*** refers to behaviour on the basis of sympathy and understanding for others' concerns and outcomes. Researchers have used this framework to find that ***care*** is generally weak in banks, with ***obedience*** being the dominant determinant of behaviour. This may also refer to behaviour that seeks only to minimally or superficially comply with regulation.

In large global banking groups, sub-cultures can arise in local groupings that may not be entirely consistent with other parts of the group.[26] It is imperative for banks to take stock of their own cultures, in terms of understanding individual and group behaviour, business practices, processes, and decision-making.

---

[24] Although based on another framework, the findings of Ernst & Young, *The Challenges of Risk, Culture, Behaviour and Corporate Integrity in Financial Services: Findings from the MoralDNA™ of Culture and Conduct in Global Financial Services* (2015) at http://www.ey.com/Publication/vwLUAssets/EY-moral-dna-in-fs/$FILE/EY-moral-dna-in-fs.pdf seem to indicate the existence of these dominant cultures.   [25] Ibid.
[26] Anjan Thakor, 'Corporate Culture in Banking' (ECGI Working Paper 2015) at http://ssrn.com/abstract=2565514; Anthony Salz, *The Salz Review: An Independent Review of Barclays' Business Practices* (April 2013) at http://online.wsj.com/public/resources/documents/SalzReview04032013.pdf on the different investment banking culture at Barclays.

The similarity in many bank organisational cultures has also given rise to a perception of sectoral culture. This perception underlies policymakers' and regulators' concerns for banking sector practices and conduct, culminating in international calls for bank culture to be reformed.[27]

11.1.2 **The regulator's approach to bank culture**

Many factors within an organisation shape organisational culture (see Figure 11.3). In particular, regulators consider the following to be salient, which explains why regulation has been extended over these areas:

(a) Senior management leadership and responsibility.

(b) Individual behaviour and responsibility.

(c) Decision-making processes in the bank, especially corporate governance.

(d) The role of internal control functions, especially compliance, risk management, and internal audit.

There is recognition for both 'rotten apples' (i.e. individuals) and 'rotten orchards' (i.e. organisations) in poor bank culture.

This chapter focuses on the individual level, as it is envisaged that improvement at the level of senior management and individual behaviour will have a significant impact on bank culture.[28] Chapter 12 moves onto the 'organisational' aspects in relation to corporate governance, internal control, and remuneration policies.

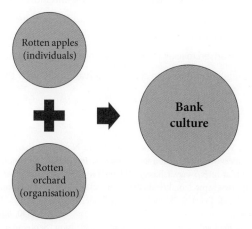

Figure 11.3 Regulatory approach to bank culture

---

[27] G30, *Bank Conduct and Culture*.

[28] See FCA, *Transforming Culture in Financial Services* (March 2018) at https://www.fca.org.uk/publication/discussion/dp18-02.pdf.

Policymakers, regulators, and consultants all converge on the necessity of banks to reform their cultures from within.[29] The G30[30] favours an approach that allows regulators to act on 'culture' findings, that is, regulators should be able to intervene when they discern 'culture' signs that tend to lead the bank into excessive risk-taking or poor conduct. Consistent with the judgment-based forward-looking supervisory approach that many regulators now practice as a result of international consensus after the global financial crisis,[31] regulators integrate culture observations into their supervisory exchanges with banks. The first UK Prudential Regulation Authority (PRA) Chief Andrew Bailey, who is now the Chief Executive of the Financial Conduct Authority (FCA), also seems to favour a more proactive regulatory approach towards making 'culture' findings.[32]

Policymakers and regulators also welcome the banking industry to form trade associations responsible for setting industry standards and encouraging best practices. In the UK, the Banking Standards Board and the Financial Markets Standards Board have been set up for this purpose.[33] These bodies are not wholly voluntary initiatives on the part of the financial sector, as they are the products of reviews commissioned by policymakers, hence owing their existence to policy leadership. However, not being top-down in nature, they serve as a forum for peer level discussion for financial institutions to forge optimal practices as a sector.

> ### ➔ Key takeaways
>
> - Regulators are concerned about bank culture, as culture affects regulatory outcomes in prudential safety and conduct of business.
> - Modern bank culture has been studied in a number of organisational culture frameworks.
> - Regulation cannot micro-manage bank culture but can be introduced to shape individual behaviour and organisational policies and environments.
> - New trade bodies have arisen to look into encouraging better bank culture.
> - We increasingly see regulators integrate culture observations in order to make judgment calls on regulating banks.

---

[29] Ibid; John R Childress, 'Why Banks Should Focus on Culture: Now More than Ever' (The Principia Group, 2011); FSB, *Guidance on Supervisory Interaction with Financial Institutions on Risk Culture: A Framework for Assessing Risk Culture* (2014) at http://www.fsb.org/2014/04/140407/; PwC, *Targeted Change: Making Culture Actionable* (2014) at http://www.pwc.co.uk/industries/financial-services/regulation/other/targeted-change-making-culture-actionable.html; Ernst & Young, *The Challenges of Risk, Culture, Behaviour and Corporate Integrity in Financial Services.*   [30] G30, *Bank Conduct and Culture.*

[31] Basel Committee, *Core Principles for Effective Banking Supervision* (September 2012) at http://www.bis.org/publ/bcbs230.htm, Principle 8. To be discussed further in Chapter 5.

[32] The UK PRA envisages that culture failings should be detected early in their supervisory work and pre-emptive supervisory action could be taken to address culture failings and sub-optimalities. PRA, *The Use of PRA Powers to Address Serious Failings in the Culture of Firms* (Statement of Policy, June 2014) at http://www.bankofengland.co.uk/pra/Documents/publications/policy/2014/powersculture.pdf.

[33] Discussed further in section 11.3.

Key bibliography

Reports and guidelines

G30, Bank Conduct and Culture: A Call for Sustained and Comprehensive Reform (2015) at http://group30.org/publications/detail/166

FCA, Transforming Culture in Financial Services (March 2018) at https://www.fca.org.uk/publication/discussion/dp8-02.pdf

FSB, *Guidance on Supervisory Interaction with Financial Institutions on Risk Culture: A Framework for Assessing Risk Culture* (2014) at http://www.fsb.org/2014/04/140407/

House of Lords and House of Commons, *Changing Banking for Good* (Report of the Parliamentary Commission on Banking Standards) (12 June 2013) at https://www.parliament.uk/documents/banking-commission/Banking-final-report-volume-i.pdf and https://www.parliament.uk/documents/banking-commission/Banking-final-report-vol-ii.pdf

PRA, *The Use of PRA Powers to Address Serious Failings in the Culture of Firms* (Statement of Policy, June 2014) at http://www.bankofengland.co.uk/pra/Documents/publications/policy/2014/powersculture.pdf

Articles

Ernst & Young, *The Challenges of Risk, Culture, Behaviour and Corporate Integrity in Financial Services: Findings from the MoralDNA™ of Culture and Conduct in Global Financial Services* (2015) at http://www.ey.com/Publication/vwLUAssets/EY-moral-dna-in-fs/$FILE/EY-moral-dna-in-fs.pdf

Langevoort, DC, 'Chasing the Greased Pig Down Wall Street: A Gatekeeper's Guide to the Psychology, Culture and Ethics of Financial Risk-taking' (2011) 96 *Cornell Law Review* 1209

Thakor, A, 'Corporate Culture in Banking' (ECGI Working Paper 2015) at http://ssrn.com/abstract=2565514

11.2 Individual responsibility

The behaviour of individuals is regarded as key to forging bank culture, especially 'tone at the top', which refers to senior management behaviour.[34] Regulating individuals is however not new. Since the early 2000s, the Financial Services Authority (FSA) has introduced individual approval and conduct rules for key functions in banks and financial institutions. In the aftermath of the global financial crisis and the subsequent conduct scandals, this regime has been considerably strengthened.[35]

In 2012, the UK instituted a Parliamentary Commission comprised of both Houses to inquire into how banking culture could be changed for good. The Parliamentary

---

[34] Andrew Bailey, 'Culture in Financial Services: A Regulator's Perspective' (Cityweek Conference 2016, 9 May 2016) at http://www.bankofengland.co.uk/publications/Pages/speeches/2016/901.aspx.

[35] Previously the FIT and APER modules of the FSA Handbook.

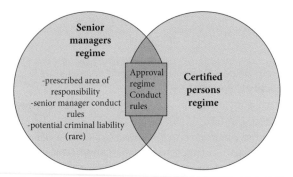

Figure 11.4 The regulatory regime for senior managers and certified persons

Commission took the view that individual responsibility would be key to enhancing banking culture and individuals must be regulated more stringently to change banking for good.[36] This has been implemented in the Financial Services (Banking Reform) Act 2013 and the PRA's and FCA's subsidiary legislation.[37]

The regulation of individuals comprises of two regimes, a more stringent one for 'senior managers' as compared to 'certified persons'. These two regimes broadly comprise the following elements. First, only appropriate individuals can be appointed to specified functions as prescribed by the PRA or FCA.[38] Next, these individuals are subject to individual conduct rules that set out broad standards for their behaviour.[39] In addition, senior managers are subject to enhanced responsibilities, as they are approved with prescribed responsibilities in banks and can incur personal liability for failures in their areas of responsibility (see Figure 11.4).[40] They are also subject to additional senior managers conduct rules. Finally, there is also a new criminal offence for certain individuals who mismanage banks but this is likely to be applied in a limited manner.[41]

---

[36] House of Lords and House of Commons, *Changing Banking for Good* (Report of the Parliamentary Commission on Banking Standards) (12 June 2013) at Vol I, para 116.

[37] The PRA Rulebook deals with the banking sector and extension to the insurance sector, see PRA and FCA, *Strengthening Accountability in Banking and Insurance* (February 2016) at https://www.fca.org.uk/news/ps16-05-accountability-implementation-and-regulatory-references; while the FCA Rulebook deals with investment firms generally, with extension to other wholesale sector activities after the Fixed Income, Commodities and Currencies Markets Review undertaken by the Bank of England, to be discussed in section 11.3, see FCA, *Strengthening Accountability in Banking: Final Rules (Including Feedback on CP14/31 And CP15/5) and Consultation on Extending the Certification Regime to Wholesale Market Activities* (July 2015) at https://www.fca.org.uk/your-fca/documents/consultation-papers/cp15-22.

[38] Section 59 (6) for certified persons and s59ZA for senior managers, Financial Services and Markets Act 2000 as amended by the Financial Services (Banking Reform) Act 2013.

[39] Section 64A, Financial Services and Markets Act 2000 as amended by the Financial Services (Banking Reform) Act 2013.

[40] Sections 60(2A), 66A, and 66B, Financial Services and Markets Act 2000 as amended by the Financial Services (Banking Reform) Act 2013.

[41] Section 36, Financial Services (Banking Reform) Act 2013.

11.2.1 **Approval and certification**

'Senior managers' in banks need to be approved by the PRA,[42] while bank personnel in 'certified functions' are to be certified by banks themselves on the basis of regulatory criteria.[43]

Before the global financial crisis, the UK regulator has always required *ex ante* approval for 'approved persons', individuals who carry out certain prescribed functions such as senior management, internal control, business leadership, and customer-facing roles. [44] The individual approval regime is in excess of international and European standards.

Reforms introduced after Parliamentary report (above) have further adjusted the UK's regime in the following ways:

(a) To introduce more focused and stringent approval for senior managers.

(b) To expand the scope of other persons required for certification.

(c) To delegate to firms to carry out certification of persons in (b).

In other words, regulatory vetting is now focused upon senior managers only, although banks have to adhere to the regulator's criteria of fitness and propriety in certifying other personnel.[45]

11.2.1.1 **Who are senior managers?**

Compared to the EU regulatory regime, the UK's regulation of senior managers is broader in scope. The EU Capital Requirements Directive 2013 deals with Board appointments but not an extensive suite of bank executives and personnel. The European Banking Authority, in its non-binding but persuasive Guidelines, extends the regulation of Board appointments to those delegated with senior management functions such as the Chief Executive Officer, and considers senior executives to be part of the management body as a whole. Further the EBA recommends that 'key function holders' such as heads of business lines and internal control functions to also be subject to regulatory criteria for appointment and ongoing conduct, extending individual regulation to beyond what the Directive provides. [46] We observe a certain

---

[42] S61, Financial Services and Markets Act 2000 as amended by the Financial Services (Banking Reform) Act 2013.

[43] S63E, Financial Services and Markets Act 2000 as amended by the Financial Services (Banking Reform) Act 2013.

[44] S59 of the Financial Services and Markets Act 2000.

[45] See PRA Rulebook, *Fitness and Propriety* at http://www.prarulebook.co.uk/rulebook/Content/Part/303750/31-08-2016.

[46] EBA and ESMA, *Joint ESMA and EBA Guidelines on the assessment of the suitability of members of the management body and key function holders under Directive 2013/36/EU and Directive 2014/65/EU* (Sep 2017) at https://www.eba.europa.eu/documents/10180/1972984/Joint+ESMA+and+EBA+Guidelines+on+the+assessment+of+suitability+of+members+of+the+management+body+and+key+function+holders+%28EBA-GL-2017-12%29.pdf.

Table 11.1 Senior management functions at banks

Executive functions	Chief Executive
	Chief of Finance
	Chief of Risk
	Head of Internal Audit
	Head of Key Business Area where person is ultimately (or intermediately) responsible for a business area managing more than £10 billion of assets or generating at least 20% of the firm's or group's gross revenues
	Head of Compliance (FCA only)
	Significant Responsibility Management Function (FCA only)
	Money-laundering Oversight and Reporting (FCA only)
Board functions	Chairman
	Chairman of Risk Committee
	Chairman of Audit Committee
	Chairman of Remuneration Committee
	Senior Independent Director
	Chairman of Nomination Committee (FCA only)
	All Executive and Non-Executive Directors (FCA only)
Group-level functions	Group entity senior manager (having significant influence upon one or more aspects of regulated activities across the group)
Other functions	Credit Union Senior Manager
	Head of Overseas Branch in the UK

extent of convergence between the EBA's appointment criteria and the UK PRA's criteria for approval of senior appointments. The UK's regime may be regarded as the leading regime for regulating senior managers and individuals.

The list of 'senior managers' is prescribed in Table 11.1.

The designation of senior managers has been finalised after extensive consultation with the banking industry, in order to strike a balance between holding key persons to higher standards of approval and responsibility and avoiding the situation where talented persons are dis-incentivised from taking a top job at a bank.[47]

Senior managers are approved based on a (a) 'statement of responsibility' attached to their application for approval,[48] and (b) satisfying 'fitness and propriety' criteria.

---

[47] PRA, *Strengthening Individual Accountability in Banking: Responses to CP14/14, CP28/14 and CP7/15* (July 2015) at http://www.bankofengland.co.uk/pra/Documents/publications/ps/2015/ps1615.pdf.

[48] Section 60(2A), Financial Services and Markets Act 2000 as amended by the Financial Services (Banking Reform) Act 2013.

11.2.1.2 Senior managers' statement of responsibility

The PRA and FCA have drawn up comprehensive maps of responsibilities for certain roles in all financial firms. This is to ensure that firms allocate all prescribed responsibilities to individuals and it is clear to regulators who is responsible for overseeing a certain area or areas. Firms cannot omit allocating areas of responsibility nor can they institute structures that make it difficult to ascertain 'who is ultimately responsible'.

The list of prescribed responsibilities for banks overseen by the PRA is in Box 11.1. In addition, the FCA prescribes a list of responsibilities[49] for investment firms that are somewhat different from the PRA's list, but we focus on the PRA's list for banks. Further, small firms and overseas bank branches are required by the PRA to designate other responsibilities peculiar to their situation. An individual may be able to perform more than one of the prescribed responsibilities as long as that is clearly identified in the individual's statement of responsibilities.[50]

Box 11.1 List of prescribed responsibilities (PRA)

- The firm's adherence to senior managers' approval and conduct rules.

- The firm's adherence to rules regarding certification of other individuals.

- Maintaining an up-to-date and comprehensive list of individuals with their respective statements of responsibility.

- The firm's adherence to regulatory rules on Fitness and Propriety in respect of its non-executive directors.

- Monitoring effective implementation of policies and procedures for the induction, training, and professional development of senior management, other than Board members.

- Overseeing the adoption of the firm's culture in day-to-day management

- managing the allocation and maintenance of the firm's capital, funding, and liquidity.

- The firm's treasury management functions.

- Production and integrity of the firm's financial information and its regulatory reporting.

- Developing and maintaining the firm's recovery plan and resolution pack[51] and for overseeing the internal processes regarding their governance.

- Managing internal stress tests[52] and ensuring the accuracy and timeliness of information provided to regulators.

- Development and maintenance of the firm's business model by the Board.

- Leading the development and effective implementation of policies and procedures for the induction, training, and professional development of all Board members.

---

[49] FCA Handbook, SYSC 24.2.

[50] With exceptions defined in PRA Rulebook, *Allocation of Responsibilities* at http://www.prarulebook.co.uk/rulebook/Content/Part/215574/31-08-2016.

[51] See Chapter 13.   [52] See Chapter 9.

- Leading the development of the firm's culture by the Board.
- Safeguarding the independence of, and overseeing the performance of, the internal audit function, including the Head of Internal Audit.[53]
- Safeguarding the independence of, and overseeing the performance of, the compliance function, including the person performing the compliance oversight function.[54]
- Safeguarding the independence of, and overseeing the performance of, the risk function, including the Chief Risk function.[55]
- Overseeing the development and implementation of the firm's remuneration policies and practices in accordance with regulation.[56]
- Instituting the independence, autonomy and effectiveness of the firm's policies and procedures on whistleblowing[57] and protection of staff.
- In respect of ring-fenced banks,[58] ensuring compliance with the ring-fencing requirements (from January 2019).
- Responsibility for the allocation of all prescribed responsibilities.
- Specific Board member responsibility below.

Box 11.2 Prescribed responsibilities for Board-level functions

The Chairman function (SMF9) as having responsibility for chairing, and overseeing the performance of the Board.

The Chairman of Risk Committee function (SMF10) as having responsibility for chairing, and overseeing the performance of any committee responsible for the oversight of the risk management systems, policies, and procedures of the bank.

The Chairman of Audit Committee function (SMF11) as having responsibility for chairing, and overseeing the performance of any committee responsible for the oversight of the internal audit system of the bank.

The Chairman of Remuneration Committee function (SMF12) as having responsibility for chairing, and overseeing the performance of any committee responsible for the oversight of the design and implementation of the remuneration policies of the bank.

The prescribed responsibilities for Board members are set out in Box 11.2.

The list of prescribed responsibilities ensures that at least one individual can be called to account for failures in the prescribed area. In this exercise, regulators have also taken the opportunity to define new roles that they would like introduced in banks in order to shape culture. For example, if firms did not have a developed system for whistleblowing before, they are now compelled to develop this substantively since regulators prescribe

---

[53] See Chapter 12.   [54] Ibid.   [55] Ibid.
[56] Ibid.   [57] Ibid.   [58] See Chapter 10.

that a senior person must take the lead and oversee such development. The prescribed responsibility that deals with developing firm culture is another example that forces banks to take culture seriously.

11.2.1.3 Certified persons

We said earlier that certain other bank employees have to be certified in accordance with regulatory rules of fitness and propriety,[59] although not requiring regulatory approval like for senior managers. This means that the regulator does not approve of them as such but banks need to be satisfied that the individuals meet the regulatory criteria. Indeed, a senior manager is specifically identified to be responsible for proper certification.

Certified individuals are defined in Box 11.3.

Where a function falls within both the definitions for senior managers and certified persons, the senior managers regime will apply. Firms need to undertake reviews of all certified persons annually to ensure that they continue to meet the thresholds for certification. We now turn to the criteria for approval, that is, fitness and propriety that apply to *both* senior managers and certified individuals.

11.2.1.4 Fitness and propriety

Both senior managers and certified persons have to meet the criteria for fitness and propriety on a continuing basis. The failure to meet these thresholds on a continuing basis can result in the disqualification of the individual from working in the relevant capacity in the financial services sector.

Box 11.3 List of certified functions

An employee whose professional activities have a material impact on the firm's risk profile – *material risk-takers* – in accordance with criteria set out in Articles 3–5 of the EU Material Risk Takers Regulation.[60]

An employee of a credit union who is part of the Board or senior management, or responsible for the compliance, internal audit and/or risk management functions, or heads a function responsible for legal affairs, finance including taxation and budgeting, human resources, remuneration policy, information technology or economic analysis.

An employee of a third country firm with a UK branch whose profile is such that his or her professional activities have a material impact on the firm's risk profile in accordance with criteria set out in Articles 3–5 of the EU Material Risk Takers Regulation.

---

[59] Sections 63E and 63F, Financial Services and Markets Act 2000 as amended by the Financial Services (Banking Reform) Act 2013. The rules of fitness and propriety also apply to senior managers and will be discussed as a whole shortly.

[60] Includes persons in certain offices, for example, heads of material business units, head of legal affairs, taxation, finance, and so on, as well as persons whose remuneration thresholds take them quantitatively beyond certain levels egg over €500,000 per year and within a certain percentage (0.3 per cent) of the highest paid individuals. This will further be explored in Chapter 12 in relation to regulation of bankers' remuneration.

'Fit and proper' is defined in relation to personal characteristics: reputation and integrity, level of competence, knowledge and experience, and level of qualifications and ongoing training necessary for the function concerned. 'Reputation and integrity' is broadly framed, and the regulator looks for evidence of any previous offences especially in relation to honesty, or incidences that may cast doubt on the financial integrity (such as default in debt, financial embarrassment on a personal basis or in relation to businesses owned or directed) or the character of the individual (such as professional misconduct, disqualifications etc).[61] We also look to FCA enforcement decisions to gain more precise understanding of what the criteria mean.

In 2014, the FCA disqualified Burrows[62] for dishonesty. Burrows was Managing Director at Blackrock Asset Management Investor Services Limited. On several occasions, he deliberately avoided paying his full train fare while commuting to work, but was ultimately caught by the train company's revenue protection officer. Although his conduct was not in relation to his professional capacity, the demonstration of dishonesty in personal life culminated in the FCA's decision to disqualify him from the financial services sector.

In relation to 'competence, knowledge and expertise', some banking roles such as investment advice require specific training qualifications and evidence of such can be objectively perceived. For bank Board members and senior executive officers, the EBA recommends that the educational and professional qualifications of a person, as well as practical experience in previous roles should be collectively considered.[63] The EBA also sets out broadly useful skills that regulators should look out for, but these entail ultimately discretionary judgments to be made of a person's 'leadership' skills or persuasiveness in communication, 'sense of responsibility' or strategic acumen.[64] The regulator is able to mete out punishment against individuals who have failed to obtain the prescribed qualifications for carrying out the function concerned. In September 2016, the FCA disqualified and fined Elizabeth Perry for conducting investment and mortgage business, which required an investment advice qualification that she failed to obtain and in respect of which she fabricated certificates to deceive the FCA.[65]

Although a number of commentators opine that the lack of Board competence or expertise has been correlated with failures and adverse performance at banks and

---

[61] EBA and ESMA, *Joint ESMA and EBA Guidelines on the assessment of the suitability of members of the management body and key function holders under Directive 2013/36/EU and Directive 2014/65/EU* (September 2017) at http://www.eba.europa.eu/documents/10180/1972984/Joint+ESMA+and+EBA+Guidelines+on+the +assessment+of+suitability+of+members+of+the+management+body+and+key+function+holders+%28EB A-GL-2017-12%29.pdf (EBA Suitability Guidelines) at paras 73–78.

[62] FCA Final Notice: Jonathan Paul Burrows, at https://www.fca.org.uk/your-fca/documents/final-notices/2014/jonathan-paul-burrows.

[63] EBA Suitability Guidelines at paras 58–66.   [64] EBA Suitability Guidelines at Annex II.

[65] FCA, 'The FCA fines and prohibits financial adviser for failing to act with integrity and for failing to be open and honest with the regulator' (1 September 2016) and 'Final Notice: Elizabeth Anne Perry' (1 September 2016) at ww.fca.org.uk/your-fca/documents/final-notices/2016/elizabeth-anne-parry.

financial institutions,[66] there is no general prescription provided in EU or UK legislation as to what qualifications may be required for senior managers.[67] However, banking comprises of many diverse financial intermediation activities and it could be said that there is no overall 'banking' professional qualification,[68] and so the regulator should avoid endorsing particular industry standards such as the Chartered Banker or Chartered Financial Analyst. Further, the regulator's endorsement of any particular qualifications may distort the market for professional education, or may indeed risk introducing standards that would in due course not be compatible with the fast-moving needs of the banking industry. Besides, endorsing any particular qualifications would result in bank's Boards having to be populated with individuals with homogenous qualifications or backgrounds.

Banks' certification processes are evidence-based. In order to ascertain an individual's reputation and integrity, the PRA requires banks to obtain previous evidence of probity such as criminal convictions and professional disqualifications.[69] Where false information has been provided by the individual, such as in the case of *Cordle v FSA*[70] (where a previous investigation that was required to be disclosed was withheld) the individual could subsequently be subject to disqualification for being dishonest. Banks must also obtain employee references relating to the individual within the last 6 years in order to assist in their certification process. The references, now known as 'statutory references'[71] are subject to rather prescriptive requirements.

The statutory references must be on a standard template and must include information on:

1. All previous breaches of an individual conduct requirement.

2. Any previous findings that the individual was not fit and proper.

3. Any disciplinary action associated with either of the above.

4. Details of all roles held, including a summary of responsibilities.

---

[66] For example, Hau and Thum's empirical study finds correlations between the lack of financial expertise and experience on the part of supervisory boards in German financial institutions and larger losses suffered by those institutions in the global financial crisis. Harald Hau and Marcel P Thum, 'Subprime Crisis and Board (In-)Competence: Private vs. Public Banks in Germany' (2009) 24 *Economic Policy* 701. Note, however, that Mehran warns that directors with financial expertise and experience may also favour greater risk-taking and hence could exacerbate risk-taking tendencies in banks and financial institutions. See Hamid Mehran, Alan Morrison, and Joel Shapiro, 'Corporate Governance and Banks: What Have We Learned from the Financial Crisis?' (June 2011) Federal Reserve Bank of New York Staff Report No. 502 <http://ssrn.com/abstract=1880009.

[67] PRA Rulebook, *Skills, Knowledge and Expertise* at http://www.prarulebook.co.uk/rulebook/Content/Part/214144/31-08-2016.

[68] 'There is no such thing as the banking profession', *Financial Times* (12 February 2014).

[69] For example, *Rajiv Khungar v FSA* (Case 016, Financial Services and Markets Tribunal); *Allen Philip Elliot* (Case 017, Financial Services and Markets Tribunal).

[70] *Cordle & Scott Briscoe Limited v FSA* [2013] UKUT B1.

[71] FCA, *Strengthening Accountability in Banking and Insurance: Regulatory References Final Rules* (September 2016) at https://www.fca.org.uk/sites/default/files/ps16-22.pdf.

The PRA also envisages that firms should carry out criminal records checks on individuals pending certification.[72]

The Banking Standards Board[73] has provided 11 principles as best practices for banks in carrying out their certification processes. These 11 principles include making certification processes systematic and adequately supervised, having an ongoing and sufficiently frequent review of individuals' fitness and propriety and the information required to be furnished, and ensuring that banks document their processes and reviews appropriately. Banks are encouraged to have group-level processes to be consistent within the group, and also put in place an appeal process for individuals affected by reviews of fitness and propriety.[74]

All individuals approved under the previous 'approved persons' regime[75] prior to the reforms in the Senior Managers and Certified Persons regimes discussed earlier would be grandfathered onto the new regimes without the need for further approval.

11.2.2 Senior managers' Code of Conduct and enforcement

Bank misconduct is often driven by individuals and groups, but wrongdoers may lack a sense of personal responsibility as the bank is made the subject of enforcement. Although an individual responsibility regime existed prior to the global financial crisis, the UK decided to enhance the individual responsibility of senior managers.[76]

First, as senior managers are approved with statements of responsibility, regulatory contraventions that occur within their areas of responsibility could entail personal liability if certain conditions are satisfied.[77] A senior person may be personally liable if the regulator proves that the senior person has not taken such steps as *a person in the senior manager's position could reasonably be expected to take* to avoid the bank's regulatory contravention.[78] In terms of ascertaining whether a senior person has such 'responsibility', the FCA's guidance states[79] that responsibility is ascertained with reference to, *inter*

---

[72] PRA, *Strengthening Individual Accountability in Banking and Insurance – Responses to CP14/14 and CP26/14* (March 2015) at http://www.bankofengland.co.uk/pra/Documents/publications/ps/2015/ps315.pdf.

[73] A voluntary trade association dedicated to improving bank conduct and culture, see section 11.3.

[74] Banking Standards Board, *Standards of Good Practice 1: Certification Regime: Fitness and Propriety* (February 2017) at https://www.bankingstandardsboard.org.uk/pdf/Assessing-F&P-Statement-of-Good-Practice.pdf.

[75] Section 59, Financial Services and Markets Act 2000.

[76] This was first highlighted in House of Lords and House of Commons, *Changing Banking for Good* (Report of the Parliamentary Commission on Banking Standards) (12 June 2013) at Vol 1, para 110ff; Vol II, para 1170; and brought about the Financial Services (Banking Reform) Act 2013 amending Financial Services and Markets Act 2000 by inserting ss64Aff.

[77] Sections 66A(5) and 66B(5) of the Financial Services and Markets Act 2000 amended by the Financial Services (Banking Reform) Act 2013 and subsequently by the Bank of England and Financial Services Act 2016.

[78] Note that this is an adjustment from the position under the Financial Services (Banking Reform) Act 2013, which treated senior managers as strictly liable if a regulatory contravention occurred in their area of responsibility, subject to them being able to prove to the regulator that they had taken all reasonable steps to prevent the contravention.   [79] FCA Handbook DEPP 6.2.9C.

alia, the senior manager's statement of responsibilities, the firm's management responsibilities map, how the firm operates in fact, how responsibilities have been allocated by the firm in practice and the senior manager's actual role and responsibilities in the firm. The evidence for the above-mentioned matters may be drawn from, among other things, minutes of meetings, emails, regulatory interviews, telephone recordings, and actual organisational practice.

11.2.2.1 Reasonable steps to prevent contravention in area of responsibility

The 'reasonable steps' that a senior manager ought to have taken to prevent the bank's regulatory contravention is judged according to 'a senior manager in the position of the manager in question'. The FCA guidance provides a list of non-exhaustive considerations,[80] to construct the standard of the hypothetical senior manager in the same position as the manager in question. The regulator is asked to consider the senior manager's knowledge and information, the reasonableness of his or her conclusion, the timeliness and appropriateness of his or her response, the context of delegation, communications within the firm, the relevant structures of governance and whether joint decision-making is involved.

What standard of care is expected of the hypothetical senior manager in preventing the firm's regulatory contravention? One approach is to adopt the general standard of care applied to professional negligence, that is, a standard of care judged according to a reasonable body of professional opinion by persons assuming similar responsibilities to the senior manager.[81] This is not particularly easy for regulators as banking functions are varied and many of them have not been subject to the same extent of professionalisation[82] as applied to established professions such as law, accountancy, and medicine. In other words, there may not be a 'reasonable body of professional opinion' to draw upon in determining if a particular senior manager falls below the standard of reasonableness. It can also be argued that the standard of care in professional negligence is inapplicable as we are asked to judge the reasonableness of the senior manager's conduct in accordance with a *hypothetical manager in his or her position*. Hence an a-contextualised approach that relies on a professional body of opinion seems contrary to the regulatory position.

Another approach is to regard the standard of conduct expected of senior managers as a distinct regulatory standard from general law.[83] For example, the FCA regards senior managers as subject to a 'duty of responsibility', a *suis generis* regulatory duty. This regulatory duty is framed according to regulators' *expectations of what is considered reasonable conduct on the part of the senior manager.* The FCA Guidance sets out, *inter alia*, what may be regarded as examples of failures or 'unreasonable conduct', such as inadequate seeking of information, inadequate understanding about a delegated

---

[80] FCA Handbook DEPP 6.2.9D and 6.2.9E. See background in FCA, *Guidance on the Duty of Responsibility* (Sep 2016) at https://www.fca.org.uk/sites/default/files/cp16-26.pdf.

[81] The classic test in *Bolam v Friern Hospital Management Committee* [1957] 1 WLR 582.

[82] 'There is no such thing as the banking profession', *Financial Times* (12 February 2014).

[83] Section 66, Financial Services and Markets Act 2000. The enforcement powers of the financial regulators are discussed in Chapter 5.

issue or responsibility, lack of obtaining expert opinion where appropriate, risk-taking in expanding or structuring business without reasonably assessing potential risks, inadequacy in monitoring highly profitable or unusual transactions or highly performing individuals or groups. However, the regulator's expectations cannot be comprehensively prescribed and we can only expect there to be discrepancies between what firms and managers think is reasonable and what the PRA and FCA think. An example of a case in point is case involving John Pottage, discussed in section 11.2.2.2.

The development of regulatory duties for individuals in the banking sector is becoming a regime bifurcated from general law. Such a development is not unwarranted as regulatory duties are owed with a public interest element in mind and should not necessarily be the same as private law duties in negligence. However, overlaps are inevitable and the differences between reasonableness in regulation and reasonableness in general law need to be clarified. Our discussion of cases below highlight the challenges in clarifying the regulatory duties and their relationship with general law.

11.2.2.2 Conduct rules

We turn first to the Rules of Conduct introduced by the PRA and FCA for senior managers.[84] In the PRA Rulebook, senior managers are subject to two sets of rules, the individual conduct rules and the specifically applicable senior manager conduct rules.[85] The individual conduct rules apply to all certified persons and senior managers, and will be discussed in greater detail shortly. The senior manager conduct rules are in Box 11.4.

Enforcement of conduct rules against an individual, whether in relation to individual or senior manager conduct, can culminate in personal fines and/or disqualification.

The two sets of rules to be discussed have been modified from a previous Code of Conduct, APER, applied by the FSA, predecessor to the PRA and FCA. As previous

---

Box 11.4 Senior manager conduct rules

Rule 1: You must take reasonable steps to ensure that the business of the firm for which you are responsible is controlled effectively.

Rule 2: You must take reasonable steps to ensure that the business of the firm for which you are responsible complies with the relevant requirements and standards of the regulatory system.

Rule 3: You must take reasonable steps to ensure that any delegation of your responsibilities is to an appropriate person and that you oversee the discharge of the delegated responsibility effectively.

Rule 4: You must disclose appropriately any information of which the FCA or PRA would reasonably expect notice.

---

[84] Sections 64A and 64B, Financial Services and Markets Act 2000 amended by the Financial Services (Banking Reform) Act 2013.

[85] PRA Rulebook, *Conduct Rules* at http://www.prarulebook.co.uk/rulebook/Content/Part/302382/02-09-2016.

enforcement under APER sheds some light on how the current conduct rules would be interpreted, we discuss enforcement examples based on APER and the current conduct rules. The regulator's enforcement decisions do not always clearly articulate legal reasoning and content. In this respect, legal interpretation from the Upper Tribunal is extremely useful where cases proceed to challenge the regulators' decisions.

Rule 1

In terms of Rule 1, the requirement of 'effective control' likely refers to the institution of systems and processes for the senior manager's area of responsibility for regulatory compliance. 'Control' is a term associated with the notion of 'internal control', which as discussed in Chapter 12, deals with firms' organisational capacity to protect themselves from internal and external wrong-doing. Internal wrong-doing involves non-compliance with internal rules, misuse of corporate assets while external wrong-doing generally involves non-compliance with external regulations or worse, crimes. This conduct rule imposes personal responsibility on senior managers to implement effective internal control and flanks the regulatory requirement for banks to implement effective firm-wide internal control (Chapter 12, section 12.2). Examples of enforcement under the equivalent of this Rule follow.

In 2012, a high-profile enforcement action was carried out against the director of corporate finance at Halifax Bank of Scotland (HBOS), Peter Cummings.[86] Cummings[87] was the director of the Corporate Division of HBOS that needed government rescue in the global financial crisis. In late 2008, HBOS had suffered losses due to impaired loans up to £7 billion out of which £4.7 billion were incurred by the Corporate Division. The massive losses were due to excessive risk-taking in lending. Cummings pursued an aggressive growth strategy for the Corporate Division and would have needed to institute and oversee a robust risk control and management system commensurate with such strategy. The then-FSA alleged that Cummings was in breach of Principle 6 of APER, that is, discharging his functions without due care, skill, or diligence (an individual conduct rule to be discussed shortly). The then-FSA meted out a fine of £500,000 and banned Cummings for life from taking on senior management or certified functions in the financial services sector.

Mapping onto the senior manager conduct rules, Cummings' liability would likely be framed under senior manager conduct rule 1 for failing to ensure that the business area of his responsibility is effectively controlled, in terms of prudential risk management, which is an aspect of internal control. Cummings' strategy was oblivious to firm-wide risk management principles, although in HBOS' case, its firm-wide risk management was almost non-existent at that time.[88] The FSA relied excessively on the individual conduct rule of due care, skill and diligence in pursuing Cummings. In this way it can be argued that regulatory enforcement actions often lack the precision and rigour in legal

---

[86] http://www.fsa.gov.uk/static/pubs/final/peter-cummings.pdf.

[87] http://www.fsa.gov.uk/static/pubs/final/peter-cummings.pdf.

[88] House of Commons and House of Lords, Parliamentary Commission on Banking Standards, *An Accident Waiting to Happen: The Failure of HBOS* (4 April 2013).

reasoning. If cases are referred to the Upper Tribunal,[89] more clarity can be developed in legal interpretation of the conduct rules. Referral does not take place in many enforcement actions as early settlement with the regulator entails a discount in fines applicable to individuals, who may not wish to run the risk of failing at the Upper Tribunal. In a later case of *Palmer v FCA,*[90] Palmer, Chief Executive of a firm that oversaw a network of appointed representatives to provide consumer financial advice and products, was found to be oblivious to heightened levels of consumer mis-selling risk due to his business strategy of giving appointed representatives more autonomy. The FCA framed its case based on Palmer's failure to act with due care, skill, and diligence (an individual conduct rule shortly discussed), but was criticised by the Upper Tribunal, as the specific problems in Palmer's conduct related more precisely to failure to ensure that business models and risk were effectively controlled and overseen. The Tribunal allowed the FCA's case, which may unfortunately conflate the interpretation of senior manager conduct rule 1 with the individual conduct rule below. However, the case illustrates that senior managers are expected to ensure that their business risks are effectively controlled, and that the levels of control are expected to be more intensive the higher the levels of business risk.

Rule 2

Rule 2 imposes personal responsibility for failure to take reasonable steps to ensure that regulatory compliance is achieved in the senior manager's area of responsibility. This conduct rule reflects the above-mentioned duty discussed in relation to senior managers' duty to prevent regulatory contravention in his or her area of responsibility.

In November 2014, the FCA took disciplinary action against three executives- the Chief Executive Peter Halpin, finance director Anthony Clare and director Nicholas Bowyer of Swinton Group Ltd.[91] The firm provided basic insurance products for retail customers such as accidental personal injury insurance, home insurance and motor vehicle cover. The FCA found that there was a persistent sales culture of pushing add-on products to retail customers, such as vehicle recovery cover, accidental injury cover for partners and dependents, and home emergency repair cover. The add-on products were often offered to retail customers with free premiums for a few initial months before additional premiums would become payable. The firm was fined in July 2013 by the FCA for failing to ensure that the add-on products were sold fairly to customers.

Halpin and Clare were alleged to have breached Principle 7 of APER, which is the same as senior manager conduct rule 2 on taking reasonable steps to ensure that business is conducted in a manner compliant with regulations. Halpin was fined in the region of over £400,000 and banned from carrying on significant functions in any other financial institution. He was held to have failed to ensure that compliance programmes such as call monitoring were carried out. Clare was fined £206,000 and similarly banned for the failure to ensure adequate compliance oversight of the sales processes while being in the

---

[89] Discussed in Chapter 6.
[90] Case dated 22–4 February 2017, at https://assets.publishing.service.gov.uk/media/598abd3ae5274a7377b7a1b7/Palmer_v_FCA.pdf.
[91] http://fca.org.uk/news/former-swinton-executives-fined-and-banned-misselling.

position of having oversight of compliance, risk management and finance. Bowyer was fined and disqualified for failure of due care, skill, and diligence (an individual conduct rule discussed shortly), by instituting a predatory sales culture. This case suggests that the senior manager for compliance and internal control oversight incurs a significant level of legal risk as having to meet the regulator's expectations of having adequate systems of internal control. Further, the Chief Executive of an infringing firm is also likely to incur a broad scope of legal risk for any matter that requires strategic oversight.

Rule 3

Rule 3 requires senior managers to delegate to appropriate persons and to undertake effective oversight of delegates. This may not be too different from the application of the director's duty to exercise due care, skill, and diligence under the UK Companies Act.[92] Case law interpretation of this director's duty has explained what is required of directors when they delegate functions to other executives. Directors should have systems and procedures of oversight,[93] and be vigilant to signs of wrong-doing.[94] These lessons can usefully be applied to interpreting the senior manager's duty of oversight. The case below from the Upper Tribunal usefully clarifies the extent of oversight expected, and prevents regulators from having undue expectations.

John Pottage, Chief Executive of UBS, was alleged to have failed to ensure that the business of the firm was organised in a controlled and compliant manner under Principle 7 of APER, equivalent to both senior manager conduct rules 1 and 2, referring to the responsibility to ensure effective control, as well as taking reasonable steps to ensure regulatory compliance in one's area of responsibility.

Pottage assumed position as Chief Executive at a time when he was aware of risk management and control deficiencies at UBS, particularly in relation to the conduct of client money handling. Pottage was of the view that he had instituted a comprehensive review, made new appointments, and installed new systems, and had personal engagement with these issues via frequent meetings. However, the then-FSA alleged that UBS' continued failings were to be attributed to Pottage's inadequate oversight. The Upper Tribunal agreed with Pottage that he had done sufficiently as was required to address the problems brought to his attention. The failure of ground implementation could not fully be attributed to Pottage, and not every defect could be discovered easily. The then-FSA had also relied excessively on an expert opinion report that pointed out what Pottage ought to have done, and the Tribunal disagreed with many aspects, considering the demands excessive. Pottage's case shows that the regulator may be prone to excessive expectations and therefore interpret what is required of 'reasonable conduct' and compliance with conduct rules in a manner that is unrealistic.

On the contrary, in the aforementioned case of *Palmer*, Palmer had been fined and warned by the FSA in 2010 prior to the disqualification action in 2017. Although

---

[92] Section 174, Companies Act 2006.   [93] *Re Barings plc* (No.5) [1999] 1 BCLC 433.
[94] *Lexi Holdings plc (in admin) v Luqman* [2008] WLR (D) 1; *Weavering Capital (UK) Ltd (in liquidation) and others v Peterson and others* [2012] EWHC 1480 (Ch).

Palmer also made governance changes in 2010 on his firm's Board, instituted audit, and risk committees, and made new appointments, he did not effectively implement the job specification for internal control for his new appointments. As his response to the initial discipline was superficial and non-committal, Palmer's efforts were criticised by the Upper Tribunal, which upheld the FCA's disqualification order.

Rule 4

Rule 4 requires senior managers to make disclosure of information to regulators as would be reasonably expected by the regulators. This applies to mandatory informa-tion returns and supervisory information required by regulators. The FCA has taken enforcement action against Perry[95] and Macris[96] on this basis. The enforcement action against Perry is in relation to her fabricated returns to the FCA concerning her pro-fessional qualifications in investment advice. Macris was fined and disqualified for failing to make comprehensive and candid disclosure of JP Morgan's losses when the FCA began investigation of the matter.[97] It is uncertain if senior managers are expected under this conduct rule to make voluntary reports of information, such as reporting the firm's regulatory contravention, as a form of whistleblowing. We are of the view that although the conduct rule is worded widely and could encompass such reporting, the regulator has specific rules on how whistleblowing should be instituted (see Chapter 12, section 12.2). Hence, there should not be an expectation that senior managers should first report their suspicions to the regulator, but should adhere to the whistleblowing framework.

11.2.2.3 Criminal liability

Senior managers could be criminally liable for knowingly taking a risk that causes the failure of a bank.[98] Regulatory reforms now allow the PRA, FCA, Secretary of State, or

---

[95] FCA Final Notice: Elizabeth Anne Perry (1 September 2016) at ww.fca.org.uk/your-fca/documents/final-notices/2016/elizabeth-anne-parry.

[96] FCA Final Notice: Achilles Macris, at https://www.fca.org.uk/your-fca/documents/final-notices/2016/achilles-macris.

[97] See 'JP Morgan makes $920m London Whale payout to regulators', *BBCNews* (19 Sep 2013). The bank lost £6.2 billion in risky derivatives trades overseen by a small coterie in the London office, hiding the losses from regulators until too late.

[98] Section 36, Financial Services (Banking Reform) Act 2013. This is derived from the Parliamentary Com-mission's recommendation that an offence be instituted for the reckless mismanagement of a bank. House of Lords and House of Commons, *Changing Banking for Good* (Report of the Parliamentary Commission on Banking Standards) (12 June 2013) at Vol II, paras 1174–86. This is intended to reflect the need for a severe and credible public interest position in bank safety and soundness, but such prosecution would likely only be undertaken rarely only in the most severe of cases and not likely to be used to punish directors of small institutions. The Parliamentary Commission believed that requiring the mens rea of recklessness is apt as strict criminal liability would be overly-inclusive. An individual must be proved beyond a reasonable doubt to be in a mental state of 'recklessness' in managing the bank, the definition of such a mental state being well-established in general criminal law jurisprudence. The offence of reckless mismanagement of a bank would only be alleged against an individual under such circumstances as bank failure with substantial costs to the taxpayer, lasting consequences for the financial system, or failures that have caused serious harm to customers.

Director of Crown Prosecutions to institute criminal proceedings against senior managers who have knowingly taken a decision for the business, being aware that a risk of failure could ensue, and in so doing has fallen below the standard of a reasonable person in his or her shoes. Such a decision must also have caused the failure of the financial institution. The elements of proof are not easy to satisfy and this action will likely be rare.

In order for this action to succeed, it is surmised that proof must be made of the accused's subjective state of knowledge of the risk. Will the courts require that the accused subjectively knows of the risk *and* its likely consequence to cause the failure of the bank? This is because subjective knowledge as to the risk *and* its outcome, is similar to that applicable to 'recklessness', [99] a standard suggested by the Parliamentary Commission's recommendation but explicitly rejected. As this offence is not intended to be framed as one based on recklessness, the courts could arguably apply an interpretation that is distinguished from 'recklessness' so that a subjective appreciation of the consequences of risk materialisation is not required. Risk materialisation in financial transactions is not easy to discern, as the global financial crisis is often attributed to 'tail risks', meaning risks that are low in probability but could be of serious magnitude if they materialise. If required to prove that senior managers know subjectively both the risk *and* its outcome, the criminal liability provision could prove largely futile in holding senior managers to account.

Further, the failure of the bank should be a 'but-for' cause of the risk decision above.[100] Modern banking as discussed in Chapter 1 is increasingly complex and multi-faceted. There may be combinations of risk decisions taken by the bank and wider sectoral and economic factors that culminate in bank failure. It may be difficult to attribute to any particular senior manager's risk decision as the cause of failure. [101]

Finally, senior managers are not liable for taking on risks that are not fatal for the bank. The criminal offence is premised upon the outcome of bank failure. The section does not extend to situations of widespread externalities or where financial consumers are significantly and adversely affected. In this manner the offence is highly limited and may not redress other severe harms that poor decision-making in banks can entail.

11.2.3 Certified persons' code of conduct and enforcement

The senior managers regime exposes senior managers to enhanced responsibilities, in relation to (a) prescribed areas of responsibility and (b) the senior managers conduct rules (see Figure 11.4). However, a wide range of persons, including senior managers are caught under the individual conduct regime. This regime, which encompasses senior managers and certified persons, form the baseline of governing individual responsibility.

---

[99] *R v G* [2004] 1 A.C. 1034 at 1057.   [100] *R v White* [1910] 2 KB 124.
[101] Douglas O Edwards, 'An Unfortunate "Tail": Reconsidering Risk Management Incentives after the Financial Crisis of 2007–2009' (2010) 81 *University of Colorado Law Review* 247.

> **Box 11.5 Individual conduct rules**
>
> **Rule 1**: You must act with integrity.
>
> **Rule 2**: You must act with due skill, care, and diligence.
>
> **Rule 3**: You must be open and cooperative with the FCA, the PRA, and other regulators.

A curious issue is that the PRA has not designated non-executive directors to be either subject to the senior managers or the certified persons regime, although non-executive directors should be notified to the PRA. The FCA has decided[102] to extend to non-executive directors of banks, building societies, credit unions the individual Code of Conduct (COCON) that applies to certified individuals in investment firms. The basis for such an extension is that the FCA perceives the need to hold non-executive directors to an appropriate level of personal responsibility.

First, senior managers and certified persons are to adhere to the thresholds of fitness and propriety according to which they were approved, on a continuing basis. They can be disqualified for failing to meet these thresholds.[103] Second, both senior managers and certified persons are subject to a set of individual conduct rules[104] in Box 11.5. The individual conduct rules have formed a much more significant basis of enforcement against individuals, whether senior managers or certified persons, than the senior managers conduct rules as such. This may be due to the availability of precedent for conduct rule interpretation as the regime had been in force since the time of the FSA.

11.2.3.1 Individual conduct rules

Rule 1

Individual conduct rule 1 has been drawn from the previous APER regime implemented by the FSA. 'Integrity' seems to be interpreted with reference to the absence of dishonesty and impropriety, such as misleading disclosures, but also includes reckless behaviour, knowingly allowing wrong-doing to take place. [105] The width of 'integrity' is observed in *Hoodless & Blackwell v FSA*[106] as '[connoting the lack of] moral soundness, rectitude and steady adherence to an ethical code. A person lacks integrity if unable to appreciate the distinction between what is honest or dishonest by ordinary standards.'

---

[102] FCA, *Applying our Conduct Rules to All Non-Executive Directors in the Banking and Insurance Sectors* (Sep 2016) at https://www.fca.org.uk/sites/default/files/cp16-27.pdf.

[103] For example, the *Burrows* case, discussed in section 11.1.1.

[104] Section 64A, Financial Services and Markets Act 2000 amended by the Financial Services (Banking Reform) Act 2013; PRA Rulebook, *Conduct Rules* at 2, http://www.prarulebook.co.uk/rulebook/Content/Part/302382/05-09-2016.

[105] The definition of integrity would encompass a few states of conduct and is not limited to dishonesty. See *First Financial Advisors Limited v FSA* [2012] 5 UKUT B16 (TCC).

[106] *Hoodless and Blackwell v FSA* (2003), cited with approval in *Carrimjee v FCA* [2015] UKUT 79.

Cases that deal with an individual's lack of integrity can concurrently be framed as a failure of the threshold conditions of 'fitness and propriety'. Such lack of integrity can relate to dealing in the course of business, such as in *Jeffrey v FCA*[107] where the insurance broker forged documents to obtain cover for clients and also failed to inform clients if cover was indeed not obtained.[108] In *Allen v FCA*,[109] the FCA sought to disqualify an insurance broker who had been involved in civil litigation against his business partner and had produced forged documents during the trial. The lack of integrity was regarded as sufficiently severe by the Upper Tribunal that upheld the FCA's decision. Individuals who were successfully disciplined or convicted of 'integrity-related' offences such as market abuse,[110] or fraud[111] would also likely be permanently disqualified on the basis on the lack of integrity.

On the lack of integrity based on 'recklessness', the FSA's case against Robert Addison[112] provides an illustration. Addison was partner, compliance officer, and held a regulated function for customer-facing duties in Arch Financial LLP, an investment management firm. Arch Financial LLP was responsible for four transactions that gave rise to obvious conflicts of interest, allowing Arch Financial and its related entities to make gains at the expense of investors. As compliance officer, Addison was alleged to have acted without integrity and recklessly in failing to manage the conflicts of interest issues in the four transactions. 'Recklessness'[113] is defined as the taking of an unacceptable risk, being aware of the risk or circumstances that entail awareness of certain risks. The awareness of risk is a subjective test, while the acceptability of the risk is based on an objective test of what a reasonable person would regard as an unacceptable risk. The Upper Tribunal held that Addison had been reckless as the transactions posed real and severe conflicts of interest and he did not put in place adequate systems to manage them.

---

[107] [2013] UKUT B4.

[108] Forging customer documents to obtain insurance cover was also the basis of the FSA's enforcement in *Ainley v FSA* UT [2012] UKUT B17. Mortgage fraud was the basis for enforcement in *Curren v FSA* [2011] UKUT B19.

[109] [2014] UKUT 0348.

[110] *Chaligne, Sejean, Diallo v FSA* [2012] UKUT B21; *Hobbs v FCA* [2013] UKUT B8; *Geddis v FSA* [2011] UKUT 344; *Visser and Fagbulu v FSA* [2011] UKUT B37.

[111] For example, 'FCA decides to ban Tom Hayes' (8 November 2017) at https://www.fca.org.uk/news/press-releases/fca-decides-ban-tom-hayes; involving the convicted trader formerly at UBS and Citigroup who had manipulated the Yen-London inter-bank offered rate. This decision is subject to a reference to the Upper Tribunal. See also *Razzaq v FSA* [2013] UKUT 0140; *Wright v FSA* (2012) FS/2011/0008, both cases involving wrongful misappropriation of moneys proved in other proceedings such as criminal or disciplinary proceedings. In *Karpe v FSA* [2012] UKUT B7, the individual has executed unauthorised trades and transfers of client money to his personal bank account and abused his authority in his private wealth management role at UBS. He was disciplined internally by UBS and then disqualified by the FSA for lack of integrity and therefore failing to meet fitness and propriety threshold conditions.

[112] *Arch Financial Products LLP & Ors v The Financial Conduct Authority* [2015] UKUT 13 (TCC) (19 January 2015).

[113] *Vukelic v FSA* [2009]; *Amir Khan v The Financial Conduct Authority* FS 2013/002 (January 2014); *Arch Financial Products LLP & Ors v The Financial Conduct Authority* [2015] UKUT 13 (TCC) (19 January 2015).

Integrity failings can also occur in relation to individuals who did not 'mastermind' wrong-doing but who facilitated and executed such wrong-doing. In *Betton v FSA*,[114] Betton was a director at broker and market-maker Winterflood Securities. The other director Eagle had orchestrated trades in an AIM-listed company in such a manner to deliberately inflate the share price in the company so that he could use the company as an acquisition vehicle for other companies. Such conduct falls within the prohibition against market manipulation.[115] Betton was responsible for executing the trades and although he insisted that he knew nothing of Eagle's scheme, the FSA was unconvinced that he could not reasonably foresee the impact of the trades on the company's share price. The Upper Tribunal accepted that Betton's senior position entailed greater responsibility over conduct and the failure to report Eagle's trades was therefore dishonest and lacking in integrity. In another case, a bank subordinate who knew of her superior's suspicious and fraudulent activities with client money and allowed such activities to persist for 5 months was held by the Upper Tribunal to lack integrity as she had not merely 'shut her eyes' to wrong-doing but facilitated it by signing relevant authorisations and documents.[116] Although a number of cases treated turning a blind eye to wrong-doing as acting without integrity,[117] it is uncertain to what extent such obliviousness is negligent rather than reckless. The cases of *Carrimjee*, which was determined at the Upper Tribunal, and the FSA's enforcement decision against Ten-Holter (discussed later) illustrate where the fine line is to be drawn.

Rule 2

Regulatory guidance provides examples of falling below due care, skill and diligence, such as carrying out transactions without a full apprehension of risks and information, general failure to obtain an adequate understanding of the business and its risks, and delegation without due monitoring and supervision.[118] However, in regulatory enforcement decisions, the failure of care, skill and diligence may reflect the regulator's expectations, which can be rather demanding, and clarification of what can reasonably be expected can only be obtained if a decision is referred to the Upper Tribunal for clarification. For example, in Pottage's case discussed earlier, the Upper Tribunal took the view that excessive demands in relation to oversight was placed on Pottage. In *Palmer's* case discussed earlier, the Upper Tribunal stated that the standard of due care, skill and diligence is 'a straightforward and well-known standard of acting with reasonable care; that is performing the functions to the standard to be expected of a person in his position, and also taking account of his own particular skills and experience.' This seems consistent with the standard applicable to the directors' duty of care, skill, and diligence.[119]

---

[114] FS/2008/0011.   [115] Then s397, Financial Services and Markets Act 2000.
[116] *Karan v FSA* [2012] UKUT B8 related to *Karpe v FSA*, above.
[117] *Vukelic v FSA* (2009); *Khan v The Financial Conduct Authority* FS 2013/002 (January 2014).
[118] FCA Handbook APER 4.6.
[119] *Re D'Jan of London Ltd* [1994] 1 BCLC 561; *Re Simmon Box (Diamonds) Ltd* [2002] All ER (D) 75; also *Re Barings* (2005).

Where individuals fail to ensure that what is reasonably expected within their job scope is performed, such would be a failure in due care, skill, and diligence.[120] Such job scope includes the obligations of compliance attached to the job scope, such as client money handling rules. In *Joint v FSA*,[121] a director of a commercial and retail insurance broker firm was held to have fallen below the standard of due care and diligence for failing to understand the requirements for setting up compliance systems for client money handling and appointing inappropriate persons to undertake these responsibilities without being adequately supervised.

In a number of cases where failure of due care, skill and diligence was found, there may be ambiguity in relation to whether the individual should be regarded as lacking in integrity as well. These cases concerned individuals that were acting in intermediary capacity, such as brokers that executed trades who may be exposed to their client's wrong-doing, or compliance officers within firms where borderline activities are carried out. Often, with experience and seniority, financial intermediaries are the first lines of defence in gatekeeping against wrong-doing and the failure to do so can render the individual falling below the regulators' expectations of conduct. However, where the illegitimacy or impact of a client's instructions is not 'clear or obvious',[122] the financial intermediary may be held liable for failing to enquire further or raise internal alerts within the firm, rather than 'recklessly' or 'dishonestly' for assisting in or facilitating those schemes.

In *Carrimjee v FCA*,[123] a long-time broker and investment adviser of a client was tasked to execute trades very near to the close of auction for certain financial instruments of an overseas company in the international order book of the London Stock Exchange. Carrimjee needed another broker to execute the trades and introduced Parikh to his client. Both were aware that the client was excessively concerned about the closing price but not precisely why. The client intended to 'bang the close', that is, to enter a volume of orders just before the close of the trading day in order to secure an artificially inflated price that would benefit his other investments. The FCA imposed a fine and partial prohibition on Parikh for failing in due care, skill, and diligence to inquire into the client's scheme and purposes. However, the FCA decided to impose a full prohibition on Carrimjee for lacking in integrity and facilitating the client's manipulative trades. The Upper Tribunal pointed out the inconsistency, and that the client's scheme was equally obscure to Carrimjee and Parikh. The court did not uphold the FCA's basis for enforcement but was of the view that in reference proceedings, the court was not limited in being able to make its own finding. Carrimjee was held to have fallen below the standard of due care, skill, and diligence for not inquiring further and relied excessively on Parikh to initiate that process.

A similar decision was reached by the FSA in relation to a compliance officer at a hedge fund that admitted to insider trading. Ten-Holter[124] was money laundering reporting

---

[120] *Palmer.*   [121] *Joint v The Financial Conduct Authority* [2015] UKUT 636.

[122] *Carrimjee v Financial Conduct Authority* [2015] UKUT 79.

[123] *Carrimjee v Financial Conduct Authority.*

[124] FSA Final Notice: Alexander Edward Ten-Holter (26 Jan 2012) at https://www.fca.org.uk/publication/final-notices/ten-holter-greenlight.pdf.

officer and compliance officer at Greenlight Capital UK (LLP), a hedge fund management firm. Greenlight was a significant shareholder in a UK listed company Punch Taverns. On 8 June 2009, the President of Greenlight, David Einhorn was contacted by Merrill Lynch in relation to a possible share issue by Punch Taverns and was asked if he would be prepared to enter into discussions that involved inside information. Einhorn declined but nevertheless entered into a conversation in which he was hinted at 'secret bad things' that could be revealed. Einhorn did not sign a non-disclosure agreement, but gave orders to Ten-Holter on the same day to dispose of all of Greenlight's shares in Punch Taverns. Between 9 and 12 June 2009, Ten-Holter effected sales of up to a third of Greenlight's holdings in Punch Taverns.

The FSA took enforcement action against Greenlight, Einhorn, Ten-Holter and Greenlight's broker Agnew at JP Morgan for insider dealing. Further, the FSA was of the view that Ten-Holter failed to exercise due care and skill in his compliance function to secure compliance with anti- market abuse regulation. Ten-Holter was aware of the conversation between Punch Taverns and Einhorn, and although Einhorn ultimately declined to receive inside information, he had sufficient confidential signals regarding Punch Taverns' possibly adverse financial position. Ten-Holter should have been alert to the dangers of insider trading if Punch Taverns' shares were traded immediately following the telephone conversation. None of the parties in this series of enforcement actions challenged the decisions in the Upper Tribunal. However, if Ten-Holter genuinely thought that the refusal of Einhorn to receive inside information meant that Greenlight was 'safe' to trade, such an impression could be a legitimate one in industry practice. What is not discussed is whether a reasonable body of skilled opinion in Ten-Holter's position would have considered this to fall short of reasonably expected conduct.[125]

Regulators tend to rely on the breach of this individual conduct rule to discipline individuals in cases where full prohibition or permanent disqualification may not be deserved. This basis for enforcement may also be agreed upon by regulators and individuals in the process of settlement in place of a more precise and alternative basis that is more severe.[126] We surmise that the dynamics of the settlement process in the high-profile enforcement against James Staley, Chief Executive of Barclays Plc in May 2018,[127] was the reason for the enforcement based on a failure to exercise due care, skill, and diligence. In that case, Staley was fined as he tried to uncover a whistleblower who sent a damaging letter involving him to the whistleblowing channels in the bank. In settling for a fine of £642,230 and not subjecting Staley to a prohibition order, the PRA and FCA issued a joint statement explaining that Staley had failed to take care in matters of conflict of interest. However, such conduct would also raise questions in relation

---

[125] *Bolam v Friern Hospital Management Committee* [1957] 1 WLR 582.

[126] Noted in *Palmer* and discussed earlier.

[127] 'FCA and PRA jointly fine Mr James Staley £642,430 and announce special requirements regarding whistleblowing systems and controls at Barclays' (11 May 2018) at https://www.fca.org.uk/news/press-releases/fca-and-pra-jointly-fine-mr-james-staley-announce-special-requirements.

to abuse of power and undermining independent functions within Barclays, a potential breach of senior managers conduct rules 1 and 2 (on ensuring effective control and compliance by the firm with regulatory requirements) and even individual conduct rule 1 (on integrity). There may be a case against punishing Staley too harshly for fear of the adverse impact on Barclays, a systemically important bank in the UK. However, the authorities should beware of enforcing conduct rules in a manner more prejudicial to individuals managing smaller businesses.

Rule 3

This rule relates to an individual's open-ness and co-operation with regulators. Where an individual has been uncooperative with the Authority, signalling contempt for the importance of regulatory supervision, or where expected disclosures were withheld, an individual can be held to breach this rule and suffer from full or partial prohibition.

In *Perman v FCA*,[128] the individual who ran a small mortgage advisory company made every effort to thwart the FCA's supervisory process. After an initial assessment by the FCA that the company's compliance with treating customers fairly needed more scrutiny, Perman received requests for information and the arrangement of a supervisory visit by the FCA. Over a period of 7 months, Perman refused to accept the initial assessment, delayed the supervisory visit, and refused to agree with the FCA on the date and terms of the visit. The Upper Tribunal agreed that the FCA had established its case to disqualify Perman as being not fit and proper to carry on his business.

The enforcement against Macris[129] illustrates the application of the rule to the lack of full disclosure as expected by the regulators. Macris was Head of 'Chief Investment Office International' for JPMorgan Chase Bank, responsible for managing a number of 'synthetic credit portfolios'. The Bank had since 2010 been under close supervision by the FSA. Between end of March and end of April 2012, the portfolios had recorded phenomenal losses and breached certain risk limits set by the Bank. Macris knew the severity of the positions and had taken steps to instruct halting to trading since 23 March 2012 and the production of daily risk reports for him. However, on 28 March 2012, at a supervisory meeting Macris attended with the FSA, he mentioned to the FSA that the portfolio was suffering some losses and efforts were made to rebalance it, without highlighting the real severity.

The stressed portfolio finally broke the news in the media. A 'London whale loss' was highlighted in newspapers of about £412 million. On 12 April 2012 the FSA arranged for a call with Macris to explain the matter. Macris then misled the FSA by informing them that the levels of market risk had decreased (due to a change in the model used to measure risk) and that no material change had taken place since the March meeting.

---

[128] *Perman v FSA* [2011] UKUT B39.
[129] FCA Final Notice: Achilles Othon Macris (9 February 2016) at https://www.fca.org.uk/publication/final-notices/achilles-macris.pdf.

Macris failed to inform the FSA that new risk limits had been breached and that losses had continued to ensue. By the end of April 2012, JP Morgan had suffered losses of about £2 billion and Macris was terminated by the Bank on 12 July 2012. Macris was fined £792,900 for failing to be open and cooperative with the FSA but was surprisingly not disqualified.

Individual conduct rules represent a deterrent threat to individuals in the banking and financial sector, and can support the prevention or gatekeeping of wrong-doing. It is criticised that personal liability regimes are over-inclusive[130] as the non-compliance or harm is occasioned by the firm as a whole. Individual responsibility is now seen as crucially important to the overall culture of the firm, which can render the firm susceptible to wrong-doing.[131] The Upper Tribunal is not willing to accept that the promotion of bad culture by an individual is itself actionable under the conduct rules, but that actions entailing from poor culture would most likely breach the rules.[132] There is international interest[133] in emulating this UK-pioneered regime in the push towards repairing bank culture after the global financial crisis.

 Key takeaways

- New regulatory regimes for senior managers and certified persons have been introduced in 2013 to replace the previous approval regime for 'controlled functions'.

- Senior managers' personal responsibilities and liability have been enhanced via their prescribed statements of responsibility and senior manager conduct rules.

- Senior managers may in appropriate cases be criminally liable for risk decisions taken that cause the failure of a bank.

- Senior managers and certified persons are approved according to fitness and propriety criteria and their approval can be revoked for failing to meet these criteria on a continuing basis.

- They are also subject to an individual code of conduct and can be personally liable, subject to fines and/or full or partial prohibition from working in the financial sector.

Key bibliography

Legislation

Financial Services (Banking Reform) Act 2013

---

[130] Lawrence Cunningham, 'Beyond Liability; Rewarding Effective Gatekeepers' (2007) 92 *Minnesota Law Review* 323.

[131] FCA, *Transforming Culture in Financial Services* (March 2018) at https://www.fca.org.uk/publication/discussion/dp18-02.pdf.   [132] *Palmer.*

[133] FSB, *Strengthening Governance Frameworks to Mitigate Misconduct Risk: A Toolkit for Firms and Supervisors* (April 2018) at http://www.fsb.org/2018/04/strengthening-governance-frameworks-to-mitigate-misconduct-risk-a-toolkit-for-firms-and-supervisors/.

Reports and guidelines

House of Lords and House of Commons, *Changing Banking for Good* (Report of the Parliamentary Commission on Banking Standards) (12 June 2013

PRA Rulebook, *Conduct Rules*

PRA, *Strengthening Individual Accountability in Banking: Responses to CP14/14, CP28/14 and CP7/15* (July 2015) at http://www.bankofengland.co.uk/pra/Documents/publications/ps/2015/ps1615.pdf

Additional reading

FCA, 'Transforming Culture in Financial Services' (March 2018) at https://www.fca.org.uk/publication/discussion/dp18-02.pdf

FSB, 'Strengthening Governance Frameworks to Mitigate Misconduct Risk: A Toolkit for Firms and Supervisors' (April 2018) at http://www.fsb.org/2018/04/strengthening-governance-frameworks-to-mitigate-misconduct-risk-a-toolkit-for-firms-and-supervisors/

11.3 Soft law in banking culture and ethics

In view of the public appetite for bank conduct to be improved, policymakers also encourage the development of soft law in terms of voluntary industry standards in banking ethics. A review of bank industry standards was undertaken by Sir Richard Lambert who reported in 2014 recommending the establishment of a Banking Standards Council to champion the development of good practices for banks. Further, following bank misconduct in relation to manipulation of interest-rate benchmarks and foreign exchange trading reported from 2012-2016, the Bank of England has also instituted a review of wholesale market activities and conduct, the Fair and Effective Markets Review. The outcome of the Review is the Fixed Income Currency and Commodities (FICC) Markets Board established in June 2016 to develop standards for bankers' activities in wholesale markets.

11.3.1 Banking Standards Board

Sir Richard Lambert was tasked in September 2013 to develop thinking on a professional body that will improve banking standards. This initiative was a response to the Parliamentary report on the state of banking scandals in the UK up to 2013.[134] A final report[135] was published in May 2014 outlining the role of a new Banking Standards Council, its organisational structure, and its relationship with the industry.

The new body, ultimately named the Banking Standards Board, is an independent champion of better banking standards in the UK. It is a professional body for

---

[134] House of Lords and House of Commons, *Changing Banking for Good* (Report of the Parliamentary Commission on Banking Standards) (12 June 2013).

[135] Richard Lambert, *Banking Standards Review* (May 2014) at http://1984london.com/_banking-standards/pdf/banking-standards-review.pdf.

institutions, not for individuals and is not envisaged to carry out individual training and standards accreditation.[136] The Board will however look to align its work with regulatory standards while providing a consultation platform to engage extensively with the industry and stakeholder groups. The Board is funded by the industry, but its appointments are to be independently made. The first Chair of the Board, Dame Colette Bowe, has been selected by the Governor of the Bank of England and an independent panel.

The Board plays the part of monitoring the actual state of bank culture, as seen in its comprehensive yearly surveys.[137] Its survey includes employee and Board interviews and focus group discussions in order to take stock of and report the state of bank culture. Its work in identifying good and poor practices could play a part in encouraging behavioural and cultural change in banks, as a form of 'peer pressure' is applied by virtue of the transparency in the surveys. The information on bank culture can also feed into regulators' thinking in regulatory policy and supervision.

The Board has also produced a General Statement of Good Practice for certification, which contains 11 principles as to how firms should undertake certification. This supports firms in complying with the certification regime discussed in section 11.2.[138]

The 11 principles deal with ensuring that firms use an adequate variety of information sources, establish a systematic frequency of review, put in place a structured framework for applying fitness and propriety criteria, institute proper training and governance processes for certification, put in place adequate record keeping of certification processes and provide channels of review and appeal for the individuals affected by the firm's decision.[139] The Statement is supported by Supporting Guidance,[140] which deals with two issues in particular. One, the Supporting Guidance specifies the types of information source required to support the application of fit and proper criteria at different stages of certification, whether it be entry or ongoing review. Two, the Guidance provides an assessment template for certification so that the process, outcome, and reasons can be clearly recorded in a universal format. This template can help firms make consistent certification decisions and ensure that certification governance is sound.

It remains open to question whether the application of the Statement will be recognised by regulators as being sufficient to demonstrate compliance with regulatory standards. It is not unheard of for regulators to endorse the soft law produced by voluntary bodies as meeting regulatory standards, such as in the case of the Joint Money

---

[136] Individual training and accreditation is carried out by a number of different accreditation bodies such as the Chartered Banker Institute.

[137] Banking Standards Board, *Banking Standards Board Annual Review 2015–6* at http://www.bankingstandardsboard.org.uk/annual-review-2015-2016/ and *Banking Standards Board Annual Review 2016–17* at http://www.bankingstandardsboard.org.uk/annual-review-2016-2017/assessment/.

[138] Banking Standards Board, *Certification Regime: Fitness and Propriety* (Consultation Paper, June 2016) at http://www.bankingstandardsboard.org.uk/wp-content/uploads/2016/06/FP-Consultation-Paper-BSB-June-2016.pdf and *Consultation Report* (28 February 2017) at http://www.bankingstandardsboard.org.uk/pdf/Assessing-F&P-Consultation-Report.pdf.

[139] Banking Standards Board, *Statement of Good Practice* (2017) at http://www.bankingstandardsboard.org.uk/pdf/Assessing-F&P-Statement-of-Good-Practice.pdf.

[140] Banking Standards Board, *Supporting Guidance to Statement of Good Practice* (2017) at http://www.bankingstandardsboard.org.uk/pdf/Assessing-F&P-Supporting-Guidance.pdf.

Laundering Steering Committee's guidelines for banks in their due diligence and anti-money laundering systems and procedures (see Chapter 14, section 14.3). However, such juridification of soft law may entail hazards, as the content of legal standards becomes determined by non-legal fori, and may become captured by the industry.[141]

11.3.2 FICC Markets Board

The FICC Markets Board is an industry body established at the recommendation of the Fair and Effective Markets Review initiated by the Treasury and Bank of England in June 2014.[142] The context prompting the review was the uncovering of systemic misconduct on the part of bankers in relation to manipulating key benchmarks such as interest rate benchmarks, foreign currency benchmarks and commodities trading price benchmarks.[143]

The Review recognised that legislative reforms have been carried out in benchmarks regulation[144] and punishing market misconduct,[145] but it identified remaining gaps.

First, it proposed that the senior managers and individual certification regimes should be extended to persons engaged in FICC markets. Next, it proposed that an industry body be set up to take responsibility and leadership in setting standards for best practices and acceptable behaviour in FICC markets. Finally, it proposes that international convergence under the auspices the International Organization of Securities Commissions (IOSCO) should be pursued.

The FICC Markets Board is an industry-led body supported by about 30 banks and investment firms.[146] It is established as an independent body staffed by a Board supported by three working committees dedicated to developing best practices, codes, and standards. Its members are represented in an advisory council that holds the Board to account. The Board will also engage with international organisations and regulators.

The FICC Markets Board has issued standards for the conduct of FICC transactions, and a Statements of Good Practice in relation to FICC market participants, that is, firms.[147] The standards of conduct for transactions focus on known risks such as managing conflicts of interest and clarifies how market participants should behave.

---

[141] For example, see Lauren B Edelman, Christopher Uggen and Howard S Erlanger, 'The Endogeneity of Legal Regulation: Grievance Procedures as Rational Myth' (1999) 105 *American Journal of Sociology* 406.

[142] HM Treasury and Bank of England, *Fair and Effective Markets Review: Final Report* (June 2015) at http://www.bankofengland.co.uk/markets/Documents/femrjun15.pdf.

[143] See, for example, *Libor Scandal: Indepth News* at http://www.ft.com/indepth/libor-scandal?ft_site=falcon&desktop=true; Philip Augar, 'How the forex scandal happened', *BBC News* (20 May 2015) at http://www.bbc.co.uk/news/business-30003693.

[144] See, for example, critical appraisal in Iris H-Y Chiu, 'Regulating Financial Benchmarks by 'Proprietisation': A Critical Discussion' (2016) 11 *Capital Markets Law Journal* 191.

[145] Introducing enhanced civil and criminal penalties for market misconduct.

[146] See http://www.fmsb.com/mpp-members/.

[147] FICC Markets Board, *Surveillance Core Principles for FICC Market Participants: Statement of Good Practice for Surveillance in Foreign Exchange Markets* (December 2016) at http://fmsb.com/wp-content/uploads/2017/01/16-12-08-SoGP_Surveillance-in-FX-Markets_FINAL.pdf; http://fmsb.com/wp-content/uploads/2017/01/16-12-08-SoGP_Surveillance-in-FX-Markets_FINAL.pdf; *Statement of Good Practice for FICC Market Participants: Conduct Training* (December 2016) at http://fmsb.com/wp-content/uploads/2017/01/16-12-08-SoGP-Conduct-Training_FINAL.pdf.

The Statement of Good Practice covers more general matters such as good internal control and governance, record keeping, risk management and staff training. Firms should develop effective internal surveillance systems to detect potential instances of market abuse and ensure that there is proper governance and oversight of the systems. There should also be complete and robust retention of records based on surveillance.[148] Firms should also conduct compliance training for all relevant personnel,[149] and engage in identifying areas of conduct risk.

Further, the Board has played a part in forging international standards of conduct for global foreign currency markets. A Global foreign exchange (FX) Code[150] has been introduced under the auspices of the Bank for International Settlements to ensure that traders behave appropriately and firms that trade in foreign currency have appropriate governance and control systems. The Board will oversee the adoption and implementation of the Code in member firms.

 Key takeaways

- Policymakers support the establishment of industry-led bodies to develop best practices and standards (soft law) for the banking sector.
- The Banking Standards Board surveys bank culture and issues best practice guidance to assist regulatory compliance by banks.
- The FICC Markets Board issues standards and oversees bank and financial sector firms and personnel involved in FICC markets activity.

Key bibliography

Reports and Guidelines

HM Treasury and Bank of England, *Fair and Effective Markets Review: Final Report* (June 2015) at http://www.bankofengland.co.uk/markets/Documents/femrjun15.pdf

Lambert, R, *Banking Standards Review* (May 2014) at http://1984london.com/_banking-standards/pdf/banking-standards-review.pdf

Additional Reading

Iain MacNeil, 'Rethinking Conduct Regulation' (2015) at http://eprints.gla.ac.uk/120459/1/120459.pdf

---

[148] FICC Markets Board, *Surveillance Core Principles for FICC Market Participants*.

[149] FICC Markets Board, *Statement of Good Practice for FICC Market Participants: Conduct Training* (December 2016) at http://fmsb.com/wp-content/uploads/2017/01/16-12-08-SoGP-Conduct-Training_FINAL.pdf.

[150] See https://www.bis.org/mktc/fxwg/gc_may16.pdf.

Questions

1. 'Bank misconduct ultimately boils down to individual irresponsibility.' Do you agree and how do you think regulators can address this?

   > **Answer tips** *You may wish to provide a brief overview of the episodes of bank misconduct, and examples of individual and group behaviour that are insufficiently accountable and penalised. You should then discuss the reforms in the UK in the form of the senior managers and certified persons regimes. You should critically appraise these regimes in terms of what you think they achieve and if any gaps remain.*

2. 'Industry self-regulation is unlikely to play a significant part in changing poor systemic bank behaviour.' Do you agree?

   > **Answer tips** *You may wish to explain industry self-regulation in relation to the era of no formal regulation discussed in Chapter 6, section 6.1, and compare to the contemporary developments as being led by policymakers and supporting regulatory regimes. You may wish to explain the evolution of the Banking Standards Board and the FICC Markets Board, their remits, roles and critically discuss what they have achieved so far.*

12

Regulating the governance, structures, and incentives at banks

12.1 Internal control and corporate governance

Bank regulation does not intuitively deal with how each bank is organised and governed, as these are matters best left to banks and regulation can amount to micro-management. However, since the global financial crisis of 2007–9, regulators have first uncovered excessive risk-taking behaviour at banks, followed by misconduct such as mis-selling and manipulative behaviour in markets (see discussion in Chapter 11). These problems reflected poor culture at banks, an issue discussed in Chapter 11, section 11.1. Culture is not merely a culmination of behaviour at individual level or groups of individuals (as discussed in Chapter 11), but is also intricately affected by how the bank is organised and governed. Chapter 11 has discussed how regulatory reforms target individual responsibility and behaviour, but at a more 'collective' level, policymakers have also become sceptical of banks' ability to institute sound organisational governance in order to bring about a thorough cultural and behavioural change. This chapter now turns to how regulation addresses sub-optimal internal organisation and governance at banks in order to change behaviour. These regulatory frameworks have particularly been introduced in post-crisis reforms.

First, this chapter examines regulatory reforms to enhance **internal control** at banks. The Basel Committee[1] defines the role of internal control at banks to be for three purposes: to assist in achieving profitability and performance, to ensure the reliability and integrity of financial information relating to the bank and to assist in external compliance with regulations. Internal control may be regarded as an internal

---

[1] 'A system of strong internal control can help to ensure that the goals and objectives of a banking organisation will be met, that the bank will achieve long-term profitability targets, and maintain reliable financial and managerial reporting. Such a system can also help to ensure that the bank will comply with laws and regulations as well as policies, plans, internal rules and procedures, and decrease the risk of unexpected losses or damage to the bank's reputation.' See Basel Committee on Banking Supervision, *Framework for Internal Control in Banking Organisations* (1998) at http://www.bis.org/publ/bcbs40.pdf.

form of gatekeeping[2] to prevent businesses from succumbing to wrong-doing, and to ensure that business objectives and accountability requirements are met. Regulators have increasingly come to regard internal control at banks and financial institutions as crucial to securing regulatory objectives. This is because internal control functions are well-placed to monitor the firm from the inside, and reaches where regulatory supervision and enforcement may not.

In the post-crisis environment, the roles of internal control at financial sector firms are subject to enhanced regulatory expectations in the EU and UK.[3] This trend is consistent with a wider international movement, in terms of the Basel Committee's leadership in articulating best practices and calls for internal control to be strengthened in US banks.[4] The need for strengthening banks' internal control, and arguably regulating these functions, has sharpened since the scandal of Wells Fargo where staff systemically fabricated bank accounts in order to earn performance-based remuneration.

Next, this chapter discusses regulatory reforms into the ***corporate governance*** dimension of banks and financial institutions. Corporate governance may be defined as 'a system by which companies are directed or controlled'.[5] As a framework for determining exercise of power, decision-making, and accountability, corporate governance is important in the shaping of an overall organisational culture, but is not the only factor for the development of organisational culture or organisational change.[6]

As the corporate governance of publicly listed banks is also subject to corporate governance rules and standards of their listing jurisdictions, the regulatory reforms to bank corporate governance are more precise and limited in nature. These reforms do not replace the corporate governance rules or standards for listed banks as those deal largely with governance practices that hold Boards accountable to shareholders and ensure that Boards are effective for the purposes of strategic management and overseeing

---

[2] The role to monitor and provide reasonable assurance to management that business objectives are being met could be described as a form of gatekeeping. The role of gatekeeping is, however, not only the premise of a particular department in the firm, but is increasingly a part of all employees' job descriptions as a front line of defense, so that specific internal control departments act as second and third lines of defenses, see COSO, *Internal Control: Integrated Framework* (December 2011) paras 11 and 21 at http://www.coso.org/documents/coso_framework_body_v6.pdf.

[3] G30, *Banking Conduct and Culture: A Call for Sustained and Comprehensive Reform* (July 2015) 14, at http://group30.org/publications/detail/166.

[4] Independent Directors of Wells Fargo, *Sales Practices Investigation Report* (10 April 2017) at https://www.wellsfargo.com/about/press/2017/independent-investigation-findings_0410/.

[5] Adrian Cadbury, *Report of the Committee on the Financial Aspects of Corporate Governance* (Dec 1992) (Cadbury Report) para 2.5.

[6] Thomas G Cummings & Christopher G Worley, *Organization Development and Change* (8th edition, South-Western College Pub 2004).

executive management.[7] Indeed the chief difference between such corporate governance rules and regulatory reforms is that the former is not mandatory. Corporate governance rules and standards are in the form of a Code in the UK, subject to a 'comply-or-explain' basis for all listed corporations. They extend to a wider scope than banks, and companies subject to them should comply or else explain to shareholders why they deviate from them and what alternative arrangements they have in place to ensure good corporate governance.

The regulatory reforms for bank corporate governance are targeted towards specific aspects of bank corporate governance that relate to regulatory objectives, such as how bank corporate governance affects 'risk management' or 'compliance' cultures that affect banks' safety and soundness.[8]

What is the relationship between regulatory standards for banks and the general corporate governance rules and standards in their listed markets? The two bodies of standards co-exist for banks that are listed companies, but they do not just exist in the parallel, and are sometimes aligned with and sometimes challenge each other. More detailed discussion on the relationship between the two bodies of standards can be found elsewhere,[9] but two main points can be made here. One is that the elevated importance of risk management for bank Boards has become a useful standard for corporate governance *generally*, and has to an extent been absorbed into general corporate governance rules and standards.[10] However, there is resistance from the general corporate sector in accepting regulatory standards in corporate governance, preferring for them to remain in the form of a Code subject to comply-or-explain.[12] Second, the focus on accountability to and scrutiny by shareholders in general corporate governance rules and standards is to an extent contradictory to the type of corporate governance that would promote prudent risk-taking consistent with regulatory objectives.[12] Regulatory reforms in bank corporate governance have struggled to grapple with this satisfactorily.[13]

Finally, the chapter discusses ***regulation of bankers' remuneration***, in order to moderate the incentives in remuneration structures towards hazardous forms of risk-taking. Although such regulation affects bankers individually, there are aspects of 'collective' policy in remuneration regulation that seek to control organisational freedom in giving rewards, as well as aspects that affect individual incentives.

---

[7] See the UK Corporate Governance Code for listed companies, at https://www.frc.org.uk/directors/corporate-governance-and-stewardship/uk-corporate-governance-code.

[8] These become clearer in section 12.2.

[9] Iris H-Y Chiu, 'Financial Corporations and Corporate Governance' in T Baums and Helmut Anheir (eds), *Advances in Corporate Governance* (Oxford: OUP forthcoming).

[10] Para C.2, UK Corporate Governance Code; Marc Moore, 'The Evolving Contours of the Board's Risk Management Function in UK Corporate Governance' (2010) 10 *Journal of Corporate Law Studies* 279.

[11] Peter O Mülbert, 'Corporate Governance of Banks after the Financial Crisis – Theory, Evidence, Reforms' (April 2010) ECGI Law Working Paper No. 130/2009 http://ssrn.com/abstract=1448118.

[12] Discussed in section 12.3.   [13] Ibid.

> ➲ **Key takeaways**
>
> - Bank misconduct and poor culture could be attributed in part to weaknesses in its internal control frameworks and corporate governance.
> - Regulatory reforms have been introduced post-crisis to enhance the powers, responsibilities, organisational profile, and positioning of internal control functions.
> - Regulatory reforms have also been introduced for certain aspects of corporate governance and remuneration structures for bankers.

> **Key bibliography**
>
> **Additional Reading**
>
> Brunnermeier, M, Crockett, A, Goodhart, C, Persaud, AD, and Shin, H, 'The Fundamental Principles of Financial Regulation' 11 *Geneva Reports on the World Economy* (2009)
> Ferranini, G, 'Understanding the Role of Corporate Governance in Financial Institutions: A Research Agenda' (2017) at https://papers.ssrn.com/sol3/papers.cfm?abstract_id=2925721
> Mülbert, PO, 'Corporate Governance of Banks after the Financial Crisis – Theory, Evidence, Reforms' (April 2010) ECGI Law Working Paper No. 130/2009 http://ssrn.com/abstract=1448118

12.2 Regulation of internal control functions

Internal control is more broadly understood as a firm-wide system of gatekeeping against aberrant behaviour, but there are three departments in banks that particularly deal with this: the Compliance, Risk Management, and Internal Audit departments.[14] The regulatory attention given to internal control is based on their gatekeeping capacity. The post-crisis regulatory framework now empowers and enhances the three functions but also prescribes specific responsibilities, as set out in Box 12.1.

The regulatory framework for internal control is developed in the UK's PRA Rulebook and FCA Handbook. These are drawn from recommendations from the Review of Corporate Governance in Banks and Financial Institutions that the Treasury commissioned Sir David Walker to undertake in 2009 (hereinafter the 'Walker Review 2009'),[15] as well as Guidelines from the European Banking Authority.[16] We also discuss where relevant inspiration is drawn from recommendations from the Basel Committee.

---

[14] Paras 154, 417, COSO, *Internal Control: Integrated Framework* (December 2011) at http://www.coso.org/documents/coso_framework_body_v6.pdf accessed 15 February 2013.

[15] David Walker, 'A Review of Corporate Governance in UK Banks and Other Financial Industry Entities: Final Recommendations' (26 November 2009) at http://webarchive.nationalarchives.gov.uk/+/http://www.hm-treasury.gov.uk/d/walker_review_261109.pdf.

[16] EBA, *Guidelines on Internal Governance under Directive 2013/36/EU* (2017) at https://www.eba.europa.eu/documents/10180/1972987/Final+Guidelines+on+Internal+Governance+%28EBA-GL-2017-11%29.pdf (hereinafter 'EBA Guidelines').

> ## Box 12.1 The regulatory framework for internal control
>
> The Framework comprises of the following:
>
> (a) the Risk Management function;
>
> (b) the Compliance function;
>
> (c) the Internal Audit function;
>
> (d) the whistleblowing procedures; and
>
> (e) firm-wide systems, policies, and procedures that are meant to enhance the awareness and need for internal control across all of the firm's lines of business and operations
>
> This section focuses on (a)–(d) as specialist functions in a bank.

This regulatory approach may more generally be regarded as a new form of corporate regulation seeking to change firm behaviour by targeting organisational constituents from the 'inside' of the organisation.[17]

12.2.1 Regulation of risk management

The Walker Review 2009 was key to pointing out the need for organisational reform of a bank's risk management function and leadership. It recommended that risk management should be separately instituted, be independent and empowered as a distinct function, and led by a sufficiently senior person. This ensures the importance of risk management is not marginalised in favour of business functions.[18] This resulted in the then Financial Services Authority (FSA) adopting regulatory rules instituting the office of the Chief Risk Officer and the Risk Committee of the Board for firms of a certain scale, size, and business complexity. European-wide initiatives then followed, in the form of guidelines articulated by the European Banking Authority (EBA Guidelines),[19] which now supports the primary legislative framework in the Capital Requirements Directive and Regulation of 2013.[20] The European regime, consolidated with the UK's initial reforms, are now found in the PRA Rulebook on Risk Control.[21]

---

[17] Iris H-Y Chiu, *Regulating (from) the Inside: The Legal Framework for Internal Control at Banks and Financial Institutions* (Oxford: Hart 2015).

[18] As the post-crisis diagnoses of some banks have revealed, see UBS AG, *Shareholder Report on UBS's Write-Downs* (18 April 2008), available at http://www.ubs.com/1/ShowMedia/investors/share_information/shareholderreport? contentId=140333&name=080418ShareholderReport.pdf, discussed in Paul Rose, 'Regulating Risk by "Strengthening Corporate Governance" (2010) 17 Connecticut Insurance Law Journal 1; House of Commons and House of Lords, *Parliamentary Commission on Banking Standards, An Accident Waiting to Happen: The Failure of HBOS* (4 April 2013), paras 19 and 50.　　　　　　　　　　　　[19] EBA Guidelines.

[20] Regulation (EU) No 575/2013 of the European Parliament and of the Council of 26 June 2013 on prudential requirements for credit institutions and investment firms and amending Regulation (EU) No 648/2012 and Directive 2013/36/EU of the European Parliament and of the Council of 26 June 2013 on access to the activity of credit institutions and the prudential supervision of credit institutions and investment firms, amending Directive 2002/87/EC and repealing Directives 2006/48/EC and 2006/49/EC.　　　　[21] PRA Rulebook, *Risk Control*.

12.2.1.1 Chief Risk Officer

In the pre-crisis years, uneven levels of importance had been given to the function of risk management in different banks. The banks that failed had been observed to suffer from weak risk management.[22] Hence, the UK mandates that banks of a certain size and scale should appoint Chief Risk Officers, who should be provided with sufficient authority and stature.[23] This has been quickly echoed in the Capital Requirements Directive 2013[24] and international recommendations. The stature of the Chief Risk Officer (or 'Head of Risk Management' as referred to in the EBA Guidelines) should be ensured in terms of organisational positioning, and this appointment is at a peer level to senior management executives.[25] The Chief Risk Officer is envisaged to report directly to the Board,[26] such a reporting line reinforcing the Chief Risk Officer's seniority as well as independence, an important characteristic of the risk management function discussed later. The Chief Risk Officer is not to be removeable by senior executive officers, only by the Board.[27] The seniority required of the Chief Risk Officer means that appointments should only be made in relation to persons with sufficient expertise and experience.[28]

The Chief Risk Officer is a senior management function,[29] subject to a statement of responsibility approved by the PRA and to the senior managers regime discussed in chapter 11. The EBA Guidelines, supported by the Financial Stability Board's (FSB) recommendation, suggests that the Head of Risk Management should perform a key advisory role to the Board[30] in relation to the Board's overall responsibility in risk management (see section 12.3) and crucially be prepared to challenge an institution's decisions on exposure to risk.[31] In addition, the PRA sets out some specific responsibilities for the Chief Risk Officer, including overseeing the adoption of the firm's risk culture in day-to-day operations, the carrying out of internal stress tests, and the maintenance of the firm's funding, capital and liquidity positions.[32]

12.2.1.2 Risk Committee of the Board

The Walker Review 2009 proposed that listed FTSE100 banks and insurers institute Board-level risk committees staffed by independent directors in order to have oversight of a firm's risk management and provide advice to the Board.[33] This is now reflected in

---

[22] For example, see House of Commons and House of Lords, *Parliamentary Commission on Banking Standards, An Accident Waiting to Happen: The Failure of HBOS* (4 April 2013);

[23] The then-FSA Handbook SYSC 21.1.2. Now see PRA Rulebook, *Risk Control* at 3.4 and 3.5.

[24] Article 76, and supported by EBA Guidelines.   [26] EBA Guidelines, para 155.

[26] PRA Rulebook, Risk Control at 3.4; EBA Guidelines, para 184; Basel Committee, Guidelines: Corporate Governance Principles for Banks (July 2015) at Principle 6.

[27] The CRD IV Directive ensures access to the Board, and removal only by the Board, see Article 76(5).

[28] Ibid.   [29] PRA Rulebook, *Senior Management Functions*, at 3.4.   [30] EBA Guidelines para 183.

[31] EBA Guidelines para 185. The FSB also recommends core responsibilities for the Chief Risk Officer especially for systemically important financial institutions, see FSB, *Principles for an Effective Risk Appetite Framework* (17 July 2013) para 4.3. Also see Basel Committee, *Guidelines: Corporate Governance Principles for Banks* (July 2015) at Principle 6.   [32] PRA Rulebook, *Allocation of Responsibilities* para 4.1.

[33] Walker, 'A Review of Corporate Governance in UK Banks and Other Financial Industry Entities'.

[34] EU Capital Requirements Directive 2013, Article 76(3).   [35] PRA Rulebook, *Risk Control* para 3.1.

European legislation.[34] In implementing this, the PRA requires that banks are to institute a Board-level risk committee where it is 'significant'.[35] Although 'significant' is not defined in the PRA Rulebook, we consider it highly likely that the interpretation will dovetail with the systemic importance of the bank in relation to its 'G-SIB' or 'D-SIB' status (see Chapter 9, section 9.5). However, 'significant' can be more widely applied, that is, to subsidiaries that on a stand-alone basis is regarded by the regulator as 'significant'. Rules on the risk committee's composition and responsibilities are supported by the EBA Guidelines. Smaller and less complex banks may not have to institute a risk committee as such, as the EBA Guidelines leave it open ended as to its proportionate application to such banks.[36]

The risk committee should be composed of at least three members (a requirement applicable to other Board committees discussed in section 12.3).[37] All members of the risk committee should be non-executive.[38] In G-SIBs and D-SIBs, a majority of members on the risk committee need to be independent, and the Chair should also be independent. [39] These members should not sit on other Board committees although it is envisaged that all Board committees should be engaged with each other and observe each other's meetings.[40] The Basel Committee recommendations stipulate specifically that the risk committee should be distinct from the audit committee and have members that have risk management knowledge and expertise.[41]

The risk committee has the responsibilities of identifying, measuring, and reporting all material risks in the firm, advising the management body on overall risk appetite and strategy, and overseeing their implementation.[42] The committee has overall oversight of the firm's capital and liquidity positions and reviewing scenarios for stress testing (Chapter 9, section 9.6). The risk committee must also review whether prices of liabilities and assets offered to clients take fully into account the firm's business model and risk strategy. Where prices do not properly reflect risks in accordance with the business model and risk strategy, the risk committee must present a remedy plan to the management body. These responsibilities of the risk committee are now transposed into subsidiary legislation by the PRA.[43] The risk committee should have regular and adequate communication with the risk management function and Chief Risk Officer, provide input into the setting of remuneration policies and review the appointment of any external consultants by the Board in overseeing executive management functions, and any findings from internal and external auditors.[44] It is also envisaged to provide advice and input for the benefit of the audit committee and the remuneration committee with respect to the setting of remuneration policies of the firm.[45] These roles are consistent with international standards. [46]

---

[36] EBA Guidelines para 18.   [37] EBA Guidelines para 47.
[38] PRA Rulebook, *Risk Control* para 3.1; EBA Guidelines para 50.
[39] EBA Guidelines para 53.   [40] EBA Guidelines paras 48, 56, and 61.
[41] Basel Committee, *Guidelines: Corporate Governance Principles for Banks* (July 2015) at Principle 3.
[42] PRA Rulebook, *Risk Control* at 3.1-3.5; EBA Guidelines para 60.   [43] Ibid.
[44] EBA Guidelines para 60; PRA Rulebook, *Risk Control* para 3.3.
[45] PRA Rulebook, *Risk Control* para 3.3.
[46] Basel Committee, *Guidelines: Corporate Governance Principles for Banks* (July 2015) at Principle 3.
[47] EU Capital Requirements Directive 2013, Article 76(3) and PRA Rulebook, *Risk Control* para3.2.

In order to assist the risk committee in its functions, the risk committee should have adequate access to relevant information and data within the firm.[47] The EBA Guidelines envisage regular reporting to be made by the risk management function to the risk committee. The risk committee should also be supported by having adequate resources to appoint an external adviser for assistance.[48]

It is to be noted that the Chairman of the Risk Committee is designated as a senior manager by the PRA to be subject to personal responsibility and liability under the senior managers regime discussed in Chapter 11. Is the Chairman of the Risk Committee therefore personally responsible for overseeing the performance of the risk function and of the Chief Risk Officer, and ensuring their independence?[49] It may, however, be argued that such a scope of personal responsibility is too wide- that is the remit of the collective responsibility of the committee. The Chairman's personal responsibility only relates to 'chairing and overseeing' the Committee as stated in the PRA Rulebook.[50] However, it may be argued that the point of prescribing responsibilities is for them to attach to an individual, so the PRA cannot be regarded as designating collective responsibility that would result in no particular person being called to account. It is thus queried whether the Chairman of the Risk Committee would effectively be susceptible to personal liability for the substantive performance of the committee's functions.

12.2.1.3 Risk management function

Besides leadership reforms in the form of the Chief Risk Officer and the risk committee of the Board, regulatory rules have in general become more prescriptive in order to protect and enhance the effectiveness of the risk management function.

First, the risk management function is to be a separate and specialist function and not to be embedded in different business lines.[51] The EBA Guidelines[52] clarify that risk officers can be assigned to material business lines but there should be a central function for such officers to report to so that they are not subordinate to the business lines they are monitoring. This prevents the risk management function from being narrowly confined and marginalised in favour of business operations. Next, post-crisis reforms emphasise the independence of the risk management function.[53] There are many factors that shape the quality of independence- the accountability channel, the setting of remuneration for the Chief Risk Officer and risk managers and the appointment and removal of the Chief Risk Officer.

The independence of the risk management function may be protected in the following manner in addition to being 'separate' from other business lines as already mentioned. These measures ensure that the risk management function is independent of business considerations:

---

[48] EBA Guidelines para 59.   [49] PRA Rulebook, *Allocation of Responsibilities* para 4.1.

[50] *Senior Managers' Functions*, at para 4.3.

[51] Capital Requirements Directive 2013, Article 76(3) and PRA Rulebook, *Risk Control* para 3.4.

[52] Paras 162–8.   [53] Article 76(5), CRD IV Directive, PRA Rulebook, *Risk Control* para 3.2.

[54] EBA Guidelines, para 158.

(i) The function does not perform any operational tasks that are performed by the business lines it is intended to monitor and control.

(ii) The Chief Risk Officer or Head of Risk Management should not be subordinate to a person responsible for the business line that the risk management function monitors or controls.

(iii) The remuneration of the risk management function's staff should not be linked to the performance of the activities it monitors and controls, so as not to compromise staffs' objectivity. [54]

One of the weaknesses of the risk management function in the pre-crisis era was that there were no specific regulatory responsibilities for the function. Hence, the function could be entirely subject to organisational manipulation in terms of the needs it serves. However, these cannot be over-prescribed as regulation cannot capture all organisational needs. Regulation now provides for a core of risk management responsibilities so that the function can effectively monitor risk-taking decisions. Table 12.1 sets out the core responsibilities and their regulatory sources in UK and European legislation as well as international standards.

The specified responsibilities in regulation reflect lessons learnt from the global financial crisis. The involvement of risk management in product governance is seen as necessary to mitigate prudential and conduct risks. Novel products can heighten prudential risks. The global financial crisis was in part due to the retention by banks of excessive levels[55] of novel and untested securitised products.[56] Further, the involvement of risk management in material changes such as mergers and acquisitions may prevent episodes such as the RBS acquisition of ABN-AMRO in early 2009, which proved to be a disaster due to the latter's excessive holdings of toxic securitised assets.

The PRA Rulebook has taken a more principles-based approach, articulating its expectations of risk management in more general terms, viz to establish adequate risk management policies and procedures to identify, assess, monitor, and mitigate the firms' risks.[57] On the one hand, such an approach does not foray into micro-managing banking businesses, but on the other hand may not provide sufficient guidance for the regulatory expectations of risk management. Further, a certain extent of non-exhaustive prescription could safeguard the authority of the risk management function over certain matters in the bank. For example, the Basel Committee's principles, which contain specifications of risk management's tasks could provide a template for adoption. [58]

---

[55] Gilles Bénéplanc and Jean-Charles Rochet, *Risk Management in Turbulent Times* (New York: OUP 2011) 7ff.

[56] Richard E Mendales, 'Collateralized Explosive Devices: Why Securities Regulation Failed to Prevent the CDO Meltdown, and How to Fix it' [2009] *University of Illinois Law Review* 1359.

[57] PRA Rulebook, *Risk Control* paras 2.3. This is similar to the European subsidiary legislation for regulating investment firms, Article 22; MiFID Commission Delegated Regulation (EU) 2017/565. For investment firms, the lack of prescriptive detail may reflect the relative lack of clear historical lessons unlike in the banking sector after the global financial crisis.

[58] Basel Committee, *Guidelines: Corporate Governance Principles for Banks* (July 2015) at Principles 6–8.

Table 12.1 Core responsibilities and their regulatory sources

Regulatory responsibilities for risk management function	Regulatory source
Policies: establish policies for continuous identification and management of risks across the whole enterprise, implying comprehensive capture of risks across all business lines	PRA Rulebook, *Risk Control*, para 2.3 EBA Guidelines paras 136–7; Basel Committee, Guidelines: Corporate Governance Principles for Banks (July 2015) paras 174–80, Principle 7
Advice: providing advice at an early stage for strategic risk decisions, risk appetite setting and risk strategies for all business lines; as well as ongoing risk guidance for all business lines	EBA Guidelines paras 170–1 Basel Committee Guidelines Principle 7
Limits: establishing, monitoring and follow-up procedures in relation to internal risk limits and breaches of those	EBA Guidelines paras 138, 181–2 Basel Committee Guidelines Principle 7
Tools: development of appropriate quantitative and qualitative tools for risk management and review, stress-testing models and the review of such models and limitations, and review of any external assessment such as credit ratings and their limitations	EBA Guidelines paras 140–4 Basel Committee Guidelines Principle 7
New products: establishing procedures for decision-making before development of new products in relation to their market and business risks and impact on the risk profile of the firm	EBA Guidelines, paras 147; 150–2 Basel Committee Guidelines, Principle 7[59]
Material changes: involvement in evaluating the impact of material changes on risk profile of firm, such as mergers and acquisitions, setting up of new structures, new geographical markets, material changes to business generally	EBA Guidelines paras 148; 172–3

Finally, the organisational positioning, powers and responsibilities of the risk management function have to be supported by an adequate resourcing of the risk management function. The resources for an effective risk management function include information resources that should be comprehensive and prompt, information technological resources and equipment, and human resources in terms of adequate staff count and skilled expertise.[60]

---

[59] See also Basel Committee, *Principles for Enhancing Corporate Governance* (October 2010) 21, para 88; CRM Policy Group, 'Containing Systemic Risk: The Road to Reform – The Report of the CRMPG III' in Melvin R Turley (ed), *Reforming Risk in Financial Markets* (New York: NovaScience Publishers, 2009) 1.

[60] Basel Committee, *Guidelines: Corporate Governance Principles for Banks* (July 2015) at Principle 6; EBA Guidelines paras 145–6; 160–1.

12.2.1.4 Risk culture

The articulation of regulatory responsibilities for the risk management function and leadership can entail the perverse effect of banks 'offloading' these responsibilities to the specialist function while business lines are disengaged from the ethos of risk management. In order to prevent this from happening, the bank is tasked with the regulatory responsibility of ensuring that risk culture is the responsibility of everyone and every business line in the firm. Senior management has the responsibility of setting the tone from the top, but the risk culture framework should be enterprise-wide and all business lines and personnel should embed risk principles in their operations and decision-making.[61] In particular, there should be a firm-wide appreciation of how the firm is structured, especially in a group context, so that any complex structures can be fully understood for their economic purposes. Such structures should prevent the shielding of risks especially money laundering or other financial crime risks.[62]

12.2.2 Regulation of the Compliance function

The Compliance function may be seen as a key gatekeeper to prevent banks from overstepping regulatory requirements, whether in terms of prudential regulation or regulation that relates to banks' conduct of business. Hence, European legislation and international standards have already addressed the role of the Compliance function before the onset of the 2007–9 global financial crisis.

EU legislation has since 2004 required the institution of a compliance function in all financial institutions that conduct investment business.[63] This requirement is applicable to banks too where they conduct investment business. EU legislation sets out certain attributes that need to be instituted in firms' organisation,[64] one of which is the establishment of a permanent and effective compliance function.[65] The UK regulator (then FSA, 1997–2013) applied the requirement to all regulated firms including banking and credit institutions.[66] This is consistent with international standards as the Basel Committee has since 2005 identified the importance of the compliance function in banks.

---

[61] EBA Guidelines, paras 94–8.

[62] EBA Guidelines, paras 75–81; 82–93, including clarity and governance of outsourcing arrangements.

[63] European Parliament and Council Directive 2004/39/EC of 21 April 2004 on markets in financial instruments amending Council Directives 85/611/EEC and 93/6/EEC and Directive 2000/12/EC of the European Parliament and of the Council and repealing Council Directive 93/22/EEC [2004] OJ L145/1 (Markets in Financial Instruments Directive, Article 13. (MiFID); Commission Directive 2006/73/EC of 10 August 2006 implementing Directive 2004/39/EC of the European Parliament and of the Council as regards organisational requirements and operating conditions for investment firms and defined terms for the purposes of that Directive OJ 2006 L241/26 (MiFID Commission Directive 2006), Article 6. Although the 2004 Directive is now superseded by the MiFID II Directive 2014, the compliance function continues to be enshrined in subsidiary legislation, Commission Delegated Regulation (EU) 2017/565 Article 22.

[64] Article 13, MiFID, now Article 16, MiFID II Directive 2014.

[65] MiFID Commission Delegated Regulation (EU) 2017/565 Article 22.

[66] FSA Handbook, SYSC 3.2.7 and 6.1.3.

The Basel Committee defined the Compliance function as having a role that assists senior management to monitor and manage compliance risk. Compliance risk was defined as 'the risk of legal or regulatory sanctions, material financial loss, or loss to reputation a bank may suffer as a result of its failure to comply with laws, regulations, rules, related self-regulatory organisation standards, and codes of conduct applicable to its banking activities'.[67] The objectives of securing compliance therefore revolve around the avoidance of financial loss and the management of reputational risk. The Basel Committee's recommendations in 2005 provided considerable detail[68] as to *how* the compliance function would carry out its responsibilities, [69] many of which continue to be endorsed in post-crisis reforms.[70]

Post-crisis reforms now provide more guidance on specific aspects of the compliance function across a range of financial institutions,[71] including banks.[72] The PRA has adopted the European subsidiary legislation provisions for the compliance function in investment firms and extended them to banks.[73]

12.2.2.1 Post-crisis reforms

Two key aspects relating to the Compliance function have been enhanced since 2009. First, the Compliance function is more overtly protected in its authority and independence from business lines. Second, regulation has become more prescriptive as to the core responsibilities of the Compliance function.[74]

As to the first aspect, the Compliance function continues to be 'permanent' and 'independent' and should have the necessary authority, expertise, access to resources and information in carrying out its responsibilities.[75] Permanence is explained in relation to instituting a dedicated compliance function and having arrangements in place to ensure that such permanence is ongoing.[76] 'Independence' is explained in terms of

---

[67] Basel Committee on Banking Supervision, *Compliance and the Compliance Function in Banks* (April, 2005) 7, para 3.

[68] Basel Committee, *Guidelines: Corporate Governance Principles for Banks* (July 2015) at Principle 9. The Basel Committee envisaged that the compliance function would develop firm-wide written guidance and policies on how compliance risk is to be managed, and undertake advisory and educational responsibilities to senior management and all staff. The compliance function should develop measures to assess compliance risk in the firm, and assess the appropriateness of firm procedures and systems by monitoring and testing such procedures and systems. The compliance function should develop a compliance programme for its workplan and report to senior management as to its assessment of how the firm is managing its compliance risk.

[69] Basel Committee on Banking Supervision, *Compliance and the Compliance Function in Banks* (April, 2005) 13–14, paras 34–41, at Principle 7.   [70] See section 12.2.2.1.

[71] ESMA, *Guidelines on Certain Aspects of the Mifid Compliance Function Requirements* (6 July 2012); MiFID Commission Delegated Regulation (EU) 2017/565 Article 22.   [72] EBA Guidelines, paras 187–96.

[73] PRA Rulebook, *Compliance and Internal Audit* at http://www.prarulebook.co.uk/rulebook/Content/Part/214145/13-09-2016, at para 2, reflecting adoption of MiFID Commission Delegated Regulation (EU) 2017/565 Article 22.

[74] MiFID Commission Delegated Regulation (EU) 2017/565 Article 22; EBA Guidelines paras 187.

[75] Ibid and EBA Guidelines paras 189–90.

[76] ESMA, *Guidelines on Certain Aspects of the MiFID Compliance Function Requirements* (6 July 2012) at Annex II, paras 53–54.

the non-interference by senior management and business units and the safeguarding of tenure for compliance officers.[77] The authority and independence of the function is protected by the appointment and removal of officers only by the Board; reporting directly to the Board, methods of remuneration setting that do not compromise their objectivity and non-involvement in the activities the function is to monitor.[78] These are not dissimilar to the conditions that protect the independence and authority of the risk management function discussed earlier. The UK regulators indicate that the head of compliance is to be regarded as a senior manager for the purposes of the application of the senior managers regime discussed in Chapter 11. This person's role can be combined with another role if warranted by the nature, scale, and complexity of the business of the bank.

Further, there are specific prescriptions for the compliance function to enjoy certain powers such as access to information on a firm-wide basis, [79] and access to staff for the purposes of interviewing and monitoring. The compliance function is to have access to all relevant databases. Further, in order to have a permanent overview of the areas of the investment firm where sensitive or relevant information might arise, the compliance function will have access to all relevant information systems within the investment firm as well as any internal or external audit reports or other reporting to senior management or the supervisory function. Where relevant, compliance officers should also be able to attend meetings of senior management or the supervisory function. Where this right is not granted, the compliance function should document this in writing. The compliance function should also be empowered to have in-depth knowledge of the firm's organisation, corporate culture, and decision-making processes in order to be able to identify which meetings are important to attend. Further, the enhanced powers of the compliance function would be supported by increased resources.[80]

Next, the specification of regulatory responsibilities of the Compliance function can to some extent protect compliance officers in their authority and in the effective discharge of gatekeeping functions. This is because if regulators prescribe that the Compliance function must monitor a certain activity, there is less scope for banks to undermine or manipulate the Compliance function. Table 12.2 sets out the core regulatory responsibilities for the Compliance function.

Although not prescribed as a core responsibility, the Compliance function is often involved in educating the firm in relation to matters beyond compliance policies and

---

[77] ESMA, *Guidelines on Certain Aspects of the MiFID Compliance Function Requirements* (6 July 2012) at Annex II, para 60.

[78] MiFID Commission Delegated Regulation (EU) 2017/565 Article 22.

[79] ESMA, *Guidelines on Certain Aspects of the MiFID Compliance Function Requirements* (6 July 2012) at Annex II, para 48.

[80] Annex II, *Guidelines on Certain Aspects of the MiFID Compliance Function Requirements* (6 July 2012) paras 45–7.

Table 12.2 Core regulatory responsibilities for the Compliance function

Regulatory responsibilities for compliance function	Regulatory sources
Policy: establishing compliance policies and procedures for entire enterprise and advising all relevant business decisions and providing guidance	MiFID Commission Regulation 2017/565, Article 22 (incorporated in PRA Rulebook, *Compliance and Internal Audit,* para 2) EBA Guidelines para 191-192
Advice: providing half-yearly reporting to Board on the internal control environment. Including being consulted on material non-routine decisions and changes in business.[81]	MiFID Commission Regulation 2017/565, Article 22 EBA Guidelines para 192-193
Monitoring: establishing an enterprise-wide monitoring programme to educate, monitor compliance with laws and regulations	MiFID Commission Regulation 2017/565, Article 22 EBA Guidelines para 193
Complaints-handling: monitoring the complaints-handling processes and allow such information to feed into determination of firms' compliance risks	MiFID Commission Regulation 2017/565, Article 22
New products: advising at early stage the development of new products, compliance risks, and coherence with existing legal frameworks, in conjunction with the work of the risk management function.[82]	EBA Guidelines para 194 para 41, Annex II, ESMA Guidelines on Certain Aspects of the MiFID Compliance Function Requirements (6 July 2012)
Detection: detecting and reporting instances of internal, external fraud or breaches or wrong-doing	MiFID Commission Regulation 2017/565, Article 22 EBA Guidelines para 195

procedures- such as adherence to ethical conduct, especially in accordance with corporate codes of ethics. One of the recommendations in the EBA Guidelines for banks is that banks should institute firm-wide codes of ethical conduct[83] in order to guide individuals towards 'good behaviour' and not merely legalistic or cosmetically compliant behaviour. The Compliance function may often be tasked with development of such codes and monitoring the adherence to them.

---

[81] Annex II, *Guidelines on Certain Aspects of the MiFID Compliance Function Requirements* (6 July 2012) paras 40–2.

[82] ESMA, *Final Report: ESMA's Technical Advice to the Commission on MiFID II and MiFIR* (December 2014) 19.

[83] EBA Guidelines paras 99–116 including conflicts of interest management policies and procedures.

12.2.3 **Regulation of internal audit**

The Internal Audit function may be regarded as a 'third line of defence',[84] in the infrastructure of internal control at banks and financial institutions. The Internal Audit department is envisaged to have residual oversight of internal control generally and acts as gatekeeper for business operations and management, as well as compliance and risk management. This perspective has recently been endorsed as part of the international[85] and EU regulatory frameworks.[86]

Pre-crisis, European legislation required all investment firms to establish a separate and independent Internal Audit function that is able to review the effectiveness of the firm's internal control framework.[87] This is a minimal regulatory provision as no further prescription on the organisational positioning, powers and responsibilities of the Internal Audit department are specified. The requirement to institute separate and independent internal audit has since been applied to all banks and investment firms in the UK.[88] Post-crisis regulatory reforms continue to maintain the importance of the Internal Audit function and have enhanced its core responsibilities.

12.2.3.1 **Post-crisis reforms**

In the wake of the global financial crisis 2007–9, the Basel Committee has issued more specific standards and expectations for the internal audit function in order to address perceived shortcomings revealed in the crisis.[89] These are regarded as professional standards and have been supported and fleshed out further by the internal auditors' professional body, the UK Chartered Institute of Internal Auditors. The Institute has issued guidance for their members in the form of a Code for internal audit in the financial sector.[90] European and UK regulators have adopted these initiatives to an extent but not all of the prescriptive detail.[91] This may be because the professional stature of internal auditors means that they are being governed by their professional body making it unnecessary for regulation to be overly prescriptive.

In order to protect the Internal Audit department's authority and independence, the function should not be combined with other functions or be involved in designing

---

[84] Peter Hughes, 'Bank Internal Audit – Third Line of Defence or First Line of Attack?' *Interim Management* (ICAEW, August 2011).

[85] Basel Committee on Banking Supervision, *The Internal Audit Function in Banks* (Final Report) (Basel: BIS, June 2012) at Principle 13, para 60ff.   [86] EBA Guidelines at 3.

[87] Commission Directive 2006/73/EC of 10 August 2006 implementing Directive 2004/39/EC of the European Parliament and of the Council as regards organisational requirements and operating conditions for investment firms and defined terms for the purposes of that Directive OJ 2006 L241/26 (MiFID Commission Directive 2006), Article 8.   [88] The former FSA Handbook, SYSC 6.2.

[89] Basel Committee, *The Internal Audit Function* (2012) at http://www.bis.org/publ/bcbs223.htm.

[90] Chartered Institute of Internal Auditors, *Effective Internal Audit in the Financial Services Sector* (July 2013) at https://www.iia.org.uk/media/1558662/Effective-internal-audit-in-Financial-Services-sector.pdf.

[91] PRA Rulebook, *Compliance and Internal Audit* at para 3 incorporating MiFID Commission Delegated Regulation (EU) 2017/565 Article 24, which is not excessively detailed; EBA Guidelines para 197–207.

Table 12.3 Key regulatory responsibilities of the Internal Audit function

Regulatory responsibilities of Internal audit function	Regulatory sources
Audit plan: Establishing and implementing an audit plan approved by the Board on a yearly basis	MiFID Commission Regulation 2017/565 Article 24 incorporated into PRA Rulebook, *Compliance and Internal Audit,* para 3. EBA Guidelines paras 205 and 206
Assurance/verifying role: objectively review all compliance, governance, internal control systems and policies in the firm, outsourcing policies, the robustness of their methodologies and assumptions, providing advice and recommendations upon review and reporting to the Board	MiFID Commission Regulation 2017/565 Article 24 EBA Guidelines paras 201–2
Remedial issues: Identifying and addressing all issues that require remediation and reporting them to the Board	MiFID Commission Regulation 2017/565 Article 24 EBA Guidelines para 207.

internal control policies.[92] It should also be staffed by persons of adequate skills and expertise, be adequately resourced and have unfettered access to firm-wide information and records.[93] The function reports directly to the Board or the audit committee of the Board.[94] The PRA ensures that Internal Audit has a sufficiently important profile by defining the Head of Internal Audit to be a senior manager. The Head of Internal Audit has responsibility for leading and safeguarding the independence of, and overseeing the performance of, the Internal Audit function as specified in the PRA's map of responsibilities for senior managers discussed in Chapter 11.[95] The PRA envisages that the Head of Internal Audit reports to the Chairman of the Audit Committee of the Board, and not directly to senior management.

Both the EBA and PRA regard the Internal Audit function as the ultimate assurance provider of the firm's internal control systems. Table 12.3 sets out the key regulatory responsibilities of the Internal Audit function.

Two matters should be noted. One is that although regulation has kept the prescription of Internal Audit functions' conduct and responsibilities to the minimum, in practice Internal Audit functions can be subject to many responsibilities from ensuring the integrity of financial reporting in firms to overseeing the whole range of internal adherence such as to compliance and risk management systems and policies. The expansion of the Internal Audit function's remit has resulted in significant burdening of the function.[96] Second, the increasing enhancement of professionalism on the part of the

---

[92]   EBA Guidelines paras 198 and 200.   [93]   EBA Guidelines paras 197–199 and 203.

[94]   Article 25(2), MiFID Commission Delegated Regulation (EU) 2017/565.

[95]   PRA Rulebook, *Allocation of Responsibilities* para 4.1 and *Senior Manager Functions* para 3.5.

[96]   Iris H-Y Chiu, *Regulating (from) the Inside: The Legal Framework for Internal Control at Banks and Financial Institutions* (Oxford: Hart 2015) ch 4.

compliance and risk management professions may in time lead to less regulatory pre-scription for their conduct and responsibilities, as is shown in the case of the Internal Audit function. The compliance and risk management professions are fast emerging under the leadership of their respective professional bodies.[97]

12.2.4 The institution of whistleblowing at banks

An important institution is now required in the organisational framework of banks and financial institutions- whistleblowing. This institution allows deviant behaviour to be reported confidentially within the firm and helps to support internal control functions. Even if regulators provide a wide range of regulatory standards and preventive regula-tory frameworks, non-compliance and wrong-doing may still occur. Individuals may deviate from internal norms and processes, as well as regulatory rules and standards. An internal reporting system is necessary especially in a large organisation where pano-pticon transparency cannot practically be achieved.

An important story that occurred in the unfolding of the 2007–9 global financial crisis was in relation to former Head of Risk Management, Paul Moore at Halifax Bank of Scotland (HBOS). The story is summarised in Box 12.2.

Box 12.2 Paul Moore and HBOS

Moore was appointed as Head of Risk in the Insurance and Investment Division at HBOS in 2002, subsequently moving up to Head of Group Regulatory Risk in 2003. In 2004, Moore uncovered dubious sales practices and mis-selling while conducting a review of the bank's sales culture and practices. He informed the Board that there was aggressive risk-taking in sales practices and a sub-optimal sales culture of unfair mis-selling, which were out of step with the systems and con-trols for the firm. He was promptly fired by HBOS in November 2004, which claimed that they had no longer any need for his role. Moore then contacted the FSA with his concerns, and the FSA appointed audit firm KPMG to investigate Moore's concerns. KPMG concluded that HBOS had adequate risk control systems in place and the FSA closed the matter. Subsequently, HBOS almost failed during the episode of the global financial crisis as it had suffered excessive losses from its highly risky sales strategies and uncontrolled expansion.

The near-failure of HBOS vindicated Moore's concerns, and Moore provided evidence to the Treasury Select Committee as well as the Parliamentary Commission that looked into the near-failures of UK banks during that period. Moore's revelations brought into sharp focus the weak-nesses of internal control at banks and a prevalent and toxic culture of fear and suppression of wrong-doing.[98]

---

[97] Such as the Institute of Compliance Association; Institute of Risk Management; Professional Risk Manag-ers' International Association; and so on. The professionalism developments and implications are discussed in Iris H-Y Chiu, *Regulating (from) the Inside: The Legal Framework for Internal Control at Banks and Financial Institutions* (Oxford: Hart 2015) chs 2, 3, and 7.

[98] See 'Whistle-blowing almost Killed Me', *The Financial Times* (London, 5 June 2013), Paul Moore, Mike Haworth and Guy Mankowski, *Crash Bank Wallop* (New Wilberforce Media Ltd 2015), which is the memoirs of Moore's episode at HBOS.

In the UK, the importance of ensuring that banks have sound whistleblowing regimes is partly in response to the Moore episode. The Parliamentary Commission on Banking Standards is of the view that banks need to institute robust systems of whistleblowing in order to encourage employees to come forward to report wrong-doing, driving out the 'fear' culture in banks where many remain silent about questionable practices for fear that they may suffer retaliation.[99] Whistleblowing can form an important plank of the internal governance of banks and financial institutions, encouraging information flows and due oversight of business practices.

12.2.4.1 Regulatory framework

The UK has instituted a whistleblower protection regime since 1998[100] in order to encourage legitimate whistleblowing in the public and corporate sectors. The UK whistleblowing regime is not based on incentivising such behaviour by rewards, but rather on *ex post* protection of a person if a legitimate disclosure has been made. The persons seeking protection has to be a 'worker' defined in legislation, and the 'protected disclosure' is confined to information[101] defined in Box 12.3.

The whistleblower may report internally to higher levels of the employer or externally to certain prescribed persons, and the Act confers protection on such a person against suffering detriment for having made a report.[102] A protected person who has suffered detriment may bring a complaint to the Employment Tribunal.[103] The Department of Business has consulted upon the design of a regime with a wider scope of protection,[104]

Box 12.3 Definition of 'protected disclosure'

(a) the commission or likely commission of a criminal offence;

(b) information that a person has failed, is failing or is likely to fail to comply with any legal obligation to which he is subject;

(c) a miscarriage of justice has occurred, is occurring or is likely to occur;

(d) the health or safety of any individual has been, is being or is likely to be endangered;

(e) the environment has been, is being, or is likely to be damaged; or

(f) information tending to show any matter falling within any one of the preceding paragraphs has been, is being or is likely to be deliberately concealed.

---

[99] House of Lords and House of Commons, *Changing Banking for Good* (Report of the Parliamentary Commission on Banking Standards) (12 June 2013) at Vol I, para 142ff.

[100] Public Interest Disclosure Act 1998.

[101] Section 43B, Public Interest Disclosure Act 1998 amending the Employment Rights Act 1996.

[102] Section 47B, Public Interest Disclosure Act 1998 amending the Employment Rights Act 1996.

[103] Section 48(1A), Public Interest Disclosure Act 1998 amending the Employment Rights Act 1996.

[104] BIS, *The Whistleblowing Framework: Call for Evidence* (July 2013).

and in 2013, the Enterprise and Regulatory Reform Act has extended the definition of 'worker'[105] for the purposes of protected disclosures but the scope of protected disclosures remains the same. Further, whistleblowers have to reasonably believe in the public interest[106] in carrying out whistleblowing. This measure seems intended at ensuring that any protection offered to whistleblowers is based on socially-acceptable justifications rather than more liberally incentivising such behaviour.

The PRA has extended the scope of the national whistleblowing regime in its application to certain firms in the financial sector. Firms supervised by the PRA with total average gross assets over £250 million[107] must institute proper whistleblowing procedures in excess of the scope of 'protected disclosures' defined under the national legislative framework. They must put in place and maintain a whistleblowing procedure within the firm that is specific, independent, and autonomous, in order for any person, including the firm's employees, to make a protected disclosure. The EBA also supports whistleblowing frameworks, which are called 'internal alert procedures'. Such reporting channels may be outside of an employee's regular reporting channels.[108] The PRA initially provided for reportable matters beyond the scope of protected disclosure, including failure to comply with the firm's policy and procedures and behaviour that has or is likely to have an adverse effect on the firm's reputation or financial well-being. This has since been amended to align with the scope of protected disclosure.

A firm has the duty to inform all workers of such a whistleblowing channel, and that they may also make a protected disclosure directly to the PRA or FCA. The firm is prohibited from discouraging employees to use the internal whistleblowing procedure or preventing them from making a protected disclosure to the PRA or FCA.[109] The PRA extends these rules to overseas banks' subsidiaries and branches in the UK, that their UK-based employees of branch must be informed of access to the subsidiary's whistleblowing arrangement.[110] The Parliamentary Commission recommends that a senior person be made responsible for overseeing whistleblowing systems, preferably the Chairman of the Board.[111] The PRA has now prescribed that the oversight of an independent, autonomous and specific whistleblowing procedure is a responsibility that a firm must designate a senior person to undertake, and such a senior manager is subject to the senior managers regime discussed in Chapter 11.[112]

---

[105] Section 20, Enterprise and Regulatory Reform Act 2013 amending section 43K of the Employment Rights Act 1996.

[106] Section 17, Enterprise and Regulatory Reform Act 2013 amending section 43B of the Employment Rights Act 1996.

[107] Determined on the basis of the annual average amount of gross assets calculated across a rolling period of five years or, if it has been in existence for less than five years, across the period during which it has existed, see PRA Rulebook, *General Organisational Requirements: Whistleblowing* at para 2A.1, at http://www.prarulebook.co.uk/rulebook/Content/Chapter/307285/13-09-2016.

[108] EBA Guidelines para 118.   [109] EBA Guidelines paras 2A.4–6.

[110] FCA, *Whistleblowing in UK Branches of Overseas Banks* (CP 2016) at https://www.fca.org.uk/sites/default/files/cp16-25.pdf; enacted in PRA Rulebook, *General Organisation Requirements: Whistleblowing*.

[111] House of Lords and House of Commons, *Changing Banking for Good* (Report of the Parliamentary Commission on Banking Standards) (12 June 2013) at Vol II, ch 6 generally at 787, 791.

[112] PRA Rulebook, *Allocation of Responsibilities* para 4.1 (19).

The EBA Guidelines further provide that whistleblowing procedures must be documented, and that whistleblowing instances must be dealt with and escalated where appropriate. Firms must also ensure that employees actually receive protection from unfair or victimisation treatment.[113]

The effective implementation of whistleblowing channels and whistleblower protection is important for the promotion of a strong compliant culture in UK banks. A high-profile episode on whistleblowing occurred culminating in disciplinary action in 2018 for the Chief Executive of Barclays Bank, James Staley. Letters were sent to Barclay's internal security unit, the channel set up for whistleblowers to address their concerns, in 2016. One of the letters raised queries about a former banker at JP Morgan hired by Barclays in 2016. The banker in question was a friend of Staley who suffered from alcohol problems. After seeing the content of the letter, Staley was of the view that the writer was vindictive and tried to smear his friend who had gone through rehabilitation. He attempted to uncover the whistleblower whose identity was kept from him. He compelled internal security staff to reveal to him and was told that the writer was not an employee but a former colleague of the banker in question. He was warned that his conduct was not appropriate and the Board withheld his bonus that year. However, he came under investigation by the PRA and FCA for his conduct in the matter and was ultimately fined over £600,000. There was some criticism of the PRA and FCA for jointly fining Staley and not disqualifying him for breach of personal conduct rules (see Chapter 11), but the decision may have considered the Board's views as well as the systemic implications for Barclays. Further, as Staley had threatened to undermine Barclay's 'internal security procedures', which is the whistleblowing channel, Barclays was put into 'special measures' by the regulators to overhaul its whistleblowing channels under regulatory supervision.

The US whistleblowing regime for the financial sector also provides an interesting comparison with the UK regime. The US Dodd–Frank Act 2010 now provides for positive incentives for whistleblowers to report directly to regulators such as the Securities Exchange Commission with original information about a violation of the securities laws. Such whistleblowers are then entitled to share in part of the penalties recovered by the regulator in the proportion of 10–30 per cent in a successful enforcement action against the firm concerned, if monetary sanctions exceeding $1 million is recovered.

Commentators[114] acknowledge that bounties could incentivise intelligence provision to regulators. Further, bounties could also act as a form of protection for financial sector whistleblowers who may find themselves at a disadvantage in seeking future employment. However, concerns can be raised with regard to implications of such incentivises in adversely affecting trust in the organisation. Further it can be questioned if selfish

---

[113]   EBA Guidelines para 123.
[114]   Ibid and Geoffrey Christopher Rapp, 'Mutiny by The Bounties? The Attempt to Reform Wall Street by The New Whistleblower Provisions of The Dodd-Frank Act' (2012) *Brigham Young University Law Review* 73.

motivations on the part of whistleblowers would adversely affect the quantity and quality of intelligence received. The UK does not appear to be introducing similar reforms.

 Key takeaways

- European and UK regulation introduced reforms to internal control functions at banks in order to boost their gatekeeping roles and capacity.

- Such reforms include the institution of the Chief Risk Officer and the Risk Committee of the Board for banks of a certain scale, size, and complexity; and the institution of a more effective and powerful risk management function.

- Further, regulatory reforms in the EU and UK have provided for a more powerful, responsible, and effective compliance function.

- International guidelines have influenced the enhancement of professional standards for internal auditors at banks, and these serve to support a broadly-framed regulatory framework in the EU and UK to ensure the effectiveness of the Internal Audit function.

- European and UK regulation now provide for the institution of whistleblowing channels within banks for the internal reporting of wrong-doing.

Key bibliography

Legislation

Directive 2013/36/EU of the European Parliament and of the Council of 26 June 2013 on access to the activity of credit institutions and the prudential supervision of credit institutions and investment firms, amending Directive 2002/87/EC and repealing Directives 2006/48/EC and 2006/49/EC (CRD IV Directive 2013)

MiFID Commission Delegated Regulation (EU) 2017/565

PRA Rulebook, *Allocation of Responsibilities, Compliance and Internal Audit, Risk Control, Senior Management Functions, General Organisational Requirements*

Reports and Guidelines

Basel Committee on Banking Supervision, *Compliance and the Compliance Function in Banks* (Basel, April, 2005) at http://www.bis.org/publ/bcbs113.pdf

Basel Committee, *The Internal Audit Function* (2012) at http://www.bis.org/publ/bcbs223.htm

Chartered Institute of Internal Auditors, *Effective Internal Audit in the Financial Services Sector* (July 2013) at https://www.iia.org.uk/media/1558662/Effective-internal-audit-in-Financial-Services-sector.pdf

EBA, *EBA Guidelines on Internal Governance* (28 September 2017) at https://www.eba.europa.eu/documents/10180/1972987/Final+Guidelines+on+Internal+Governance+%28EBA-GL-2017-11%29.pdf

ESMA, *Guidelines On Certain Aspects of the Mifid Compliance Function Requirements* (6 July 2012) at https://www.esma.europa.eu/sites/default/files/library/2015/11/2012-388_en.pdf

---

Articles

Ferran, E, 'Regulatory Lessons from the Payment Protection Insurance Mis-Selling Scandal in the UK' (2012) *European Business Organisation Law Review* 248

Books

Chiu, IH-Y, *Regulating (from) the Inside: The Legal Framework for Internal Control at Banks and Financial Institutions* (Oxford: Hart 2015)

12.3 Regulating aspects of corporate governance

Where there are corporate failures in the UK, it has become almost customary to look into the governance of the firms concerned to discern if corporate governance failures have contributed to firm failure.[115] This approach was also taken in the wake of the global financial crisis and post-mortem examinations of the corporate governance of banks were commissioned in the UK and at the international level.[116]

The Walker Review of Corporate Governance in Banks and Financial Institutions, which reported in 2009, formed the basis of much of the regulatory reforms in bank corporate governance. The momentum was carried on in the European Capital Requirements IV Directive 2013, which gave a legislative foundation for regulating bank corporate governance. In this section we discuss the regulatory reforms to Board responsibilities, Board composition, specific Board -level functions such as committees of the Board and the Chairman and aspects of directors' commitments. The Walker Review has also recommended that shareholders' monitoring roles should be made more effective and this has been taken up in soft law in the UK,[117] and to an extent in European legislation.[118]

Adams[119] and Cheffins[120] conducted empirical research on the corporate governance of US financial institutions and US and UK financial firms respectively, in the

---

[115] For example, in relation to the failure of Barings Plc in 1995, several directors were disqualified for not having instituted sufficient oversight systems and controls throughout the banking group. See *Re Barings plc* (No.5) [1999] 1 BCLC 433. In relation to the Equitable Life scandal of failure to pay out on guaranteed annuities, see Lord Penrose's report, which criticised the governance and the role of directors in the mutual, see http://news.bbc.co.uk/1/hi/business/3543549.stm, where the report is available in full.

[116] David Walker, 'A Review of Corporate Governance in UK Banks and other Financial industry Entities: Final Recommendations' (26 November 2009) (The Walker Review); Basel Committee, *Principles for Enhancing Corporate Governance* (October 2010); OECD, *Corporate Governance and the Financial Crisis: Key Findings and Main Messages* (June 2009).

[117] UK Stewardship Code, at https://www.frc.org.uk/Our-Work/Codes-Standards/Corporate-governance/UK-Stewardship-Code.aspx.

[118] Directive (EU) 2017/828 of the European Parliament and of the Council of 17 May 2017 amending Directive 2007/36/EC as regards the encouragement of long-term shareholder engagement.

[119] Renee Adams, 'Governance and the Financial Crisis' (ECGI Working Paper in Finance 2009).

[120] Brian R Cheffins, 'Did Corporate Governance "Fail" During the 2008 Stock Market Meltdown? The Case of the S&P 500' (ECGI Law Working Paper 2009).

years leading up to the global financial crisis 2007-9. They found that well-accepted corporate governance best practices were reasonably robust in financial institutions. Therefore, it seemed that there were no marked 'corporate governance failures' at many banks and financial institutions. However, certain mainstream corporate governance best practices such as shareholder engagement[121] could be adverse to the public interest of financial stability. The most salient cause of financial institution failure in the global financial crisis was the high level of risk-taking that those institutions engaged in. A number of commentators drew the connection between excessive risk-taking in certain financial institutions and their objective to maximise shareholder value. For example, empirical researchers[122] found that shareholder-friendly Boards were correlated with worse financial performance. Hence, the corporate governance reforms for banks should be treated differently from conventional corporate governance standards that seek to enhance Board accountability to shareholders.[123] These reforms relate to governing sound decision-making in banks that affect the public interest in maintaining financial stability.

12.3.1 **Board responsibilities**

The functions of the Board of regulated credit institutions[124] and investment firms[125] in the EU are articulated to include (a) the overall responsibility for strategic objectives, risk strategy and internal governance; (b) the responsibility to ensure integrity in accounting and financial reporting; (c) the responsibility to ensure compliance with laws and regulations; (d) the oversight of disclosure and communications in the firm; (e) the responsibility to provide effective oversight of senior management; and (f) periodic review of strategic objectives, regulatory compliance and governance arrangements. These explicit Board responsibilities are now transposed by the PRA.[126]

Of particular note is that risk governance has now been raised in profile to sit alongside the Board's usual role in strategic management and this reflects the public interest in the prudential management of banks.[127] Boards in the pre-crisis years have been

---

[121] For example, see Christopher M Bruner, 'Conceptions of Corporate Purpose in Post-Crisis Financial Firms' (2012) 36 Seattle University Law Review 527.

[122] Andrea Beltratti and René M Stultz, 'Why Did Some Banks Perform Better during the Credit Crisis? A Cross-Country Study of the Impact of Governance and Regulation' (July 2009) NBER Working Paper No. 15180 http://papers.ssrn.com/sol3/papers.cfm?abstract_id=1433502. Reint Gropp and Matthias Köhler, 'Bank Owners or Bank Managers: Who is keen on Risk? Evidence from the Financial Crisis' (January 2010) European Business School Research Paper No 10–02 http://ssrn.com/abstract=1555663. Hanna Westman, 'The Role of Ownership Structure and Regulatory Environment in Bank Corporate Governance' (January 2010) http://ssrn.com/abstract=1435041 accessed 18 March 2013.

Marc van Essen, Peter-Jan Engelen, and Michael Carney, 'Does "Good" Corporate Governance.

[123] Discussed in section 12.1.   [124] CRD IV Directive, Article 88(1).

[125] MiFID II Directive, Article 9 contains similar provisions on oversight of effective and prudent management and the Board's responsibility to set an appropriate remuneration policy.

[126] PRA Rulebook, *General Organisational Requirements: Management Body* paras 5.1 and 5.1A.

[127] CRD IV Directive, Article 76.

roundly criticised not to have prioritised the monitoring of risk-taking and management.[128] Boards are expected to devote more direct attention to risk management, capital and liquidity compliance, internal control arrangements and remuneration policies that have an impact on risk profile.[129] In the wake of conduct scandals involving banks such as mis-selling and the manipulation of interest rate benchmarks (see Chapter 11, section 11.1), Boards are also now expected to take leadership for fostering an ethical culture in banks.[130] In this way, the regulatory prescriptions for Board responsibilities now infuse elements of public interest and are not merely framed towards being accountable to shareholders.

The regulatory reforms in the EU and UK are consistent with international standards, as the Basel Committee's recommendations for optimal corporate governance at banks very much echo the above-mentioned suite of Board responsibilities, emphasising Board responsibility and oversight of internal and risk control, strategy, compliance, and culture.[131] The EBA Guidelines take the approach of specifying that the 'management' function of the Board, that is, executive directors and officers are responsible for strategy and constructively challenging strategic and business decisions, while the 'supervisory' function of the Board is responsible for the oversight, monitoring and constructive challenge of various aspects of business, governance, internal control, and so on.[132] This approach is not taken by the PRA, but it can be argued that the senior managers regime (Chapter 11, section 11.2) with its clear delineation of individual responsibilities of key members of the Board, that is, the Chairman, Senior Independent Director, Chairmen of the Audit, Risk and Remuneration Committees, provides greater specification in terms of responsibility and liability for particular individuals.[133]

One may argue that prescribing Board responsibilities is merely a rhetorical exercise. This is because the Board is collectively responsible and it would be difficult to impeach the Board as a whole or any individual director for failure to discharge responsibilities.[134] The individual liability of Board members is indeed not addressed in EU legislation. In the UK, the senior managers regime can crucially affect individual directorial conduct towards securing regulatory objectives and the public interest. It may be queried whether the directors' duties in company law would also secure the conduct of bank directors to manage banks prudently and properly. Although directors' duties

---

[128] OECD, *Principles for Enhancing Corporate Governance* (2010) at p.38; Deepa Govindarajan, 'Corporate Risk Appetite: Ensuring Board and Senior Management Accountability for Risk' (2011) at http://ssrn.com/abstract=1962126; Klaus Hopt, 'Better Governance of Financial Institutions' (2012), op cit. David Larcker and Brian Tayan, *Corporate Governance Matters: Closer Look at Organisational Choices and Their Consequences* (NJ: Pearson 2011), ch 6.

[129] EBA Guidelines para 23.   [130] Ibid.

[131] Basel Committee, *Guidelines: Corporate Governance Principles for Banks* (July 2015) at http://www.bis.org/bcbs/publ/d328.pdf.

[132] EBA Guidelines, paras 28–33.

[133] The FCA's senior managers regime is wider as it covers all executive and non-executive directors and the Chair of the Nomination Committee, see Chapter 11.

[134] Mark Bovens, *The Quest for Responsibility: Accountability and Citizenship in Complex Organisations* (Cambridge: Cambridge University Press 1998) 45ff.

such as in the UK Companies Act 2006 provides for general duties such as loyalty and due care, skill, and diligence,[135] these duties are largely to be enforced in private proceedings, such as by liquidators or shareholder derivative actions. These duties are not oriented towards meeting public interest or regulatory objectives and there have not been successful enforcement actions against directors of banks affected during the global financial crisis.[136]

12.3.2 Board composition

Certain aspects of Board composition are now prescribed in EU legislation,[137] and transposed into UK law by the PRA.[138] It may be argued that such regulatory intervention is rather intrusive into an essentially private matter in terms of determining banks' internal leadership. However, the public interest in bank leadership may be justified based on revelations in the global financial crisis in relation to bank Board deficiencies, such as the lack of any financial expertise on the part of zoologist Chairman Matt Ridley at Northern Rock, the tendency of Boards to be deferential and subject to groupthink where a dominant CEO exists such as in the Royal Bank of Scotland and in Lehman Brothers.[139] Hence regulation has moved in to ensure that Boards are 'fit for purpose'.

First, Board members are to be assessed for suitability for their appointment 'as a whole'. [140] This means that individual qualities, skills and experience are looked at in order to ascertain fit for the Board as a whole.[141] The EBA suggests that all members of the Board should collectively be able to contribute to the needs of the Board in relation to each material area of business, financial competence and accounting, risk management, information technology and security, legal and regulatory environment, managerial skills and experience, strategic abilities, group management skills, and expertise in particular geographical locations where the group operates.[142] This is consistent with international standards recommended by the Basel Committee.[143] The Basel Committee sees the diversity and balance of skills and expertise as necessary so that different views and critical discussion can be promoted on the Board. The need to

---

[135] For example, ss171, 172, and 174.

[136] Iris H-Y Chiu, 'Regulatory Duties for Directors in the Financial Services Sector and Directors' Duties in Company Law- Bifurcation and Interfaces' (2016) *Journal of Business Law* 465.

[137] CRD IV Directive, Article 91(7), MiFID II Directive 2014, Article 45(4)ff for market operators.

[138] PRA Rulebook, *General Organisational Requirements: Management Body* paras 5.2–5.8.

[139] Fred Goodwin of RBS and Richard Fuld of Lehman Brothers.

[140] EBA and ESMA, *Joint ESMA and EBA Guidelines on the assessment of the suitability of members of the management body and key function holders under Directive 2013/36/EU and Directive 2014/65/EU* (September 2017) at http://www.eba.europa.eu/documents/10180/1972984/Joint+ESMA+and+EBA+Guidelines+on+the +assessment+of+suitability+of+members+of+the+management+body+and+key+function+holders+%28EB A-GL-2017-12%29.pdf (EBA Suitability Guidelines) paras 31–6.

[141] PRA Rulebook, *General Organisational Requirements* para 5.2.

[142] EBA Suitability Guidelines para 71.

[143] Principle 2, Basel Committee, *Guidelines: Corporate Governance Principles for Banks* (July 2015) at http://www.bis.org/bcbs/publ/d328.pdf.

ensure diverse and balanced Board may run counter to the perceived need for prescribing qualifications. Collective suitability is to be assessed in accordance with a consistent methodology adopted by the Board and a default matrix recommended by the EBA Suitability Guidelines can be utilised.[144]

Individual suitability is also assessed in relation to skills and competence as well as fitness and propriety (discussed in Chapter 11, section 11.2). Although as mentioned in Chapter 11, section 11.2, the regulators have avoided prescribing precise qualifications or skills for Board members and senior persons, there are some specific exceptions. The PRA requires that at least one member of the audit committee must have accounting expertise, and all the members of the audit committee must have competence in relation to the sector the financial firm is operating.[145] Further, all members of the risk committee are required to have relevant knowledge, skills, and expertise to fully understand and oversee the firm's risk strategy and risk appetite.[146]

The Board has overall responsibility for ensuring that it sets out a suitability policy for criteria for appointments, selection processes and succession planning.[147] These roles may be specifically undertaken by the nomination committee of the Board.[148] In particular the suitability policy for appointments must include a diversity policy. EU legislation supports the introduction of more gender diversity on bank Boards.[149] The move towards increasing the number of female directors on corporate Boards is not limited to the financial sector, as there is a broader movement in the EU to champion this cause.[150] However, in the financial sector, research on the effect of the male hormone testosterone on risk-taking on trading floors[151] may have become rather important to the cause of championing for diversity. Perhaps the 'moderating' influences of female directors on bank and financial institution Boards would be necessary for overall risk governance. Further, it is believed that gender diversity on Boards would enhance critical and constructive challenge in Board discussions.[152]

---

[144] EBA Suitability Guidelines para 151, Annex I.   [145] PRA Rulebook, *Audit Committee* para 2.2.
[146] PRA Rulebook, *Risk Control* para 3.1.   [147] EBA Suitability Guidelines, paras 110–28.
[148] Discussed later.   [149] CRD IV Directive, Article 88(2)(a); MiFID II Directive 2014, Article 45(4)(a).
[150] European Commission, *Proposal for a Directive of the European Parliament and of the Council on improving the gender balance among non-executive directors of companies listed on stock exchanges and related measures* (Nov 2012). See further proposal to increase quantitative representation to 40 per cent of the Board, see European Commission, 'Improving the Gender Balance in Company Boardrooms' (2014) at http://ec.europa.eu/justice/gender-equality/files/gender_balance_decision_making/boardroom_factsheet_en.pdf.
[151] John M Coates, Mark Gurnell, and Zoltan Sarnyai, 'From Molecule to Market: Steroid Hormones and Financial Risk-Taking' (2010) 365 *Philosophical Transactions of the Royal Society B: Biological Sciences* 331; John M Coates and Joe Herbert, 'Endogenous Steroids and Financial Risk Taking on a London Trading Floor' (2008) 105 *Proceedings of the National Academy of Science* 6167; John Coates, *The Hour Between Dog and Wolf. Risk Taking, Gut Feelings, and the Biology of Boom and Bust* (New York: Penguin Press 2012).
[152] Melsa Ararat, Mine H Aksu, and Ayse Tansel Cetin, 'The Impact of Board Diversity on Boards' Monitoring Intensity and Firm Performance: Evidence from the Istanbul Stock Exchange' (April 2010), at http://papers.ssrn.com/sol3/papers.cfm?abstract_id=1572283 on Turkish banks; MA Gulamhussen and Silva Maria Santos, 'Women in Bank Boardrooms and Their Influence on Performance and Risk-Taking' (April, 2010) at http://papers.ssrn.com/sol3/papers.cfm?abstract_id=1615663 argues that gender diversity on bank Boards improves risk moderation.

A number of commentators,[153] however, caution against viewing the issue of gender diversity on Boards as a merely instrumental issue towards improving efficacy on bank Boards. This is because empirical results on proving such efficacy may be elusive,[154] and may in due course undermine a rather important social cause. Viewed in this light, the regulation of Board composition in terms of gender diversity on financial sector Boards is part of a broader movement to introduce socially motivated regulation into corporate governance. [155] Nevertheless, the EBA seems to be moving away from promoting merely gender diversity to wider forms of diversity including educational and professional background, gender, age, and, in particular for institutions that are active internationally, geographical provenance.[156]

Collective and individual suitability are to be assessed at the time of recruitment as well as on an ongoing basis, at least annually by the Board or by the nomination committee of the Board delegated with this responsibility.

Further, it may be argued that there is no need for regulation to prescribe qualifications for bank Board members as regulation makes it mandatory for them to be trained in the bank's specific business needs. EU legislation now makes it mandatory for Board members to acquire firm-specific knowledge by due induction and training to ensure that they understand and are able to oversee the firm's businesses.[157] This has been transposed in the UK.[158] The UK supports the mandatory requirement for Board members' training by prescribing that a senior manager must have personal responsibility for ensuring the due training and induction of Board members.[159] General educational qualifications do not necessarily contribute to the individual's firm-specific competence and abilities. Ensuring that bank Board members familiarise themselves with the firms' specific businesses is more important to ensure that they are adequately informed and prepared to manage the businesses.

Finally, one of the key qualities of a bank Board member, especially for the purposes of monitoring and overseeing senior management, is that of objectivity. Such objectivity is termed as 'independence of mind' by the EBA. 'Independence' of mind is sometimes associated with 'formal independence', which is the lack of formal or financial connections between an individual and the firm. 'Formal independence' is explained for example in the UK Corporate Governance Code relating to formal existing or

---

[153] John M Conley, Lissa L Broome, and Kimberley D Krawiec, 'Dangerous Categories: Narratives of Corporate Board Diversity' (2010) 89 *North Carolina Law Review* 760 and at http://papers.ssrn.com/sol3/papers.cfm?abstract_id=1679775; James A Fanto, Lawrence M Solan, and John M Darley, 'Justifying Board Diversity' (2011) 89 *North Carolina Law Review* 901.

[154] Renee B Adams and Daniel Ferreira, 'Women in the Boardroom and Their Impact on Governance and Performance' (2012) at http://papers.ssrn.com/sol3/papers.cfm?abstract_id=1107721; Deborah Rhode and Amanda K Packel, 'Diversity on Corporate Boards: How Much Difference Does Difference Make?' (2010) at http://papers.ssrn.com/sol3/papers.cfm?abstract_id=1685615.

[155] See Laura Horn, 'Corporate Governance in Crisis? The Politics of EU Corporate Governance Regulation' (2012) 18 *European Law Journal* 83.

[156] EBA Suitability Guidelines paras 104–9.   [157] Article 91(9), CRD IV Directive 2013.

[158] PRA Rulebook, *General Organisational Requirements: Management Body* para 5.3.

[159] PRA Rulebook, *Allocation of Responsibilities* para 4.1.

previous relationships[160] with the company that may cloud the objectivity of the director concerned. The independence quality required of a bank director is 'substantive independence', which relates to a personal ability to be objective and uninfluenced, offering critical observations and comments on the Board, being able to resist group-think and having the courage to speak up.[161] However, focusing on the substantive quality of an independent mind may also be regarded as less stringent than formal independence, as this may become a flexible requirement not requiring the maintenance of formal independence. The EBA and Basel Committee[162] seem to have converged on a balanced approach where potential conflicts of interest on the part of a director should be screened in order to determine if substantive independence is affected. Evidence of such potential conflicts of interest could be found in existing or past employment or professional relationships with the bank.[163] Hence, formal independence criteria would still be used to an extent to consider if a director indeed can act objectively and with independence of mind.

Further, in order to improve 'independence of mind' on the part of Board committees, the importance of whose roles will be discussed further, committee members and Chairs may be rotated from time to time to keep their perspectives 'fresh'.[164]

Box 12.4 summarises the regulatory criteria for appointment to bank Boards.

We now turn to discuss regulatory provisions for committees of the Board. As a matter of best practice, establishing committees of the Board may be seen to be a way of effective division of labour, as well as ensuring that certain Board responsibilities are carried out by a group of non-executive or independent directors who can principally undertake a monitoring role in the specific areas reserved to committees. The EBA envisages that committees should interact with each other and cross-participate in each other's meetings.[165] Such processes can encourage more holistic deliberations in each committee.

Box 12.4 Regulatory criteria for bank Board members

(a) good repute and integrity;

(b) adequate educational qualifications;

(c) sufficient experience;

(d) part of the balanced slate of skills, expertise, and experience needed for the bank; and

(e) independence for some of the Board members, see in relation to discussions on Board committees.

---

[160] See UK Corporate Governance Code 2018, Provision 10 at https://www.frc.org.uk/getattachment/88bd8c45-50ea-4841-95b0-d2f4f48069a2/2018-UK-Corporate-Governance-Code-FINAL.PDF.

[161] EBA Suitability Guidelines para 82. For example, see Donald C Langevoort, 'Human Nature of Corporate Boards: Law, Norms, and the Unintended Consequences of Independence and Accountability' (2000) 89 *Georgetown Law Journal* 797.

[162] Principle 2, Basel Committee, *Guidelines: Corporate Governance Principles for Banks* (July 2015) at http://www.bis.org/bcbs/publ/d328.pdf.   [163] EBA Suitability Guidelines paras 84–7.

[164] EBA Guidelines para 49.   [165] EBA Guidelines para 56.

12.3.2.1 Nomination committee

The PRA requires a bank that is 'significant' must institute a nomination committee of the Board. 'Significance' is not statutorily defined, but likely relates to the nature, scale, size, and complexity of the business.[166] As already mentioned, 'significance' likely dovetails with the definition for G-SIBs and D-SIBs but may be of wider import. For example, subsidiaries of a G-SIB or D-SIB can be significant on a stand-alone basis too. The nomination committee must comprise fully of non-executive members and the Chairman of the nomination committee selected by its members.[167]

There is some prescription as to the responsibilities of the nomination committee. The PRA prescribes one of the nomination committee's responsibilities as identifying and selecting suitable as well as diverse qualities for Board and senior management appointments, including having targets to improve the balance of the under-represented gender on the Board. Further, the nomination should keep under review the structure, size, composition, and performance of the Board and the knowledge, skills, and experience of individual members. The nomination committee should ensure that the time commitment required for the Board's needs can be met by appointments to the Board, and that Board dynamics are healthy and not dominated by certain groups or individuals.[168]

12.3.2.2 Audit committee

The PRA stipulates that all banks must have an audit committee on the Board whose members must be non-executive and a majority of them independent in terms of formal independence.[169] If the bank is 'significant',[170] then all the members of the audit committee must be independent.[171] As mentioned earlier, specific prescriptions as to members' competence are introduced in relation to at least one member having accounting expertise and that all members should have relevant experience in the sector that the bank is operating.[172] If the bank is not significant, the audit committee could be combined with the risk committee.[173]

The responsibilities of the audit committee are prescribed and key aspects[174] include oversight of the financial reporting mechanisms within the bank in order to comply with statutory audit and reporting requirements, oversight of the bank's internal control functions, systems and processes and responsibility for appointment and review of

---

[166] Article 76(3), CRD IV Directive 2013.

[167] PRA Rulebook, *General Organisational Requirements: Nomination Committee* para 6.1.

[168] PRA Rulebook, *General Organisation Requirements: Nomination Committee* para 6.2. These are drawn from and broadly consistent with Basel Committee, *Guidelines: Corporate Governance Principles for Banks* (July 2015) at http://www.bis.org/bcbs/publ/d328.pdf, at Principle 3.

[169] PRA Rulebook, *Audit Committee* para 2.2.

[170] See earlier explanations of 'significant' in relation to risk and nomination committees.

[171] PRA Rulebook, *Audit Committee* para 2.2.   [172] Ibid.

[173] PRA Rulebook, *Audit Committee* para 2.3 transposing CRD IV Directive 2013 Article 76(3).

[174] Ibid; see also EBA Guidelines para 63.

tenure of the external auditor. These responsibilities are by and large endorsed by the Basel Committee.[175]

It should be noted that the PRA designates the Chairman of the Audit Committee to be a senior manager subject to personal liability for failure to discharge his or her responsibilities. It is queried whether the Chairman of the Audit Committee would be personally responsible for the due discharge by the committee its functions. For example, one of the prescribed responsibilities for the committee is that of ensuring the production and integrity of financial information and its reporting for regulatory purposes. Would misreporting by the bank then implicate the Chairman's personal liability? On the other hand, it could be argued that the function of the Chairman of the Audit Committee is expressly spelt out as 'having responsibility for chairing, and overseeing the performance of any committee responsible for the oversight of the internal audit system of a firm'.[176] Hence, the personal responsibility is arguably related to managing and overseeing the committee only, and not to the substantive performance of the collective responsibility of the committee. In which case it may be queried whether there would still be gaps in the personal liability regime for senior persons discussed in Chapter 11. Would regulators be unable to hold individuals to account for regulatory and other infringements where 'collective responsibility' is involved?

12.3.2.3 Risk committee

As discussed in section 12.2, the importance of risk management has risen high on policymakers' agenda after the global financial crisis of 2007–9 and many organisational reforms have been introduced to boost risk management in banks. A key reform is to ensure that there is Board-level attention to risk management, including establishing a Board risk committee to oversee this. Section 12.2 has detailed the organisational set-up of the committee and its prescribed responsibilities.

12.3.2.4 Remuneration committee

EU legislation provides that a bank that is significant [177] in terms of size, internal organisation and in relation to the nature, scope and the complexity of its activities must establish a remuneration committee in order to determine remuneration policies that are consistent with the bank's capital, liquidity, and funding risk profiles.[178] This is consistent with the earlier recommendations of the Walker Review of 2009,[179] and has been transposed into the UK.[180]

The remuneration committee must comprise of a Chairman and members who are non-executive. The committee is responsible for ensuring that bank remuneration

---

[175] Basel Committee, *Guidelines: Corporate Governance Principles for Banks* (July 2015) at http://www.bis.org/bcbs/publ/d328.pdf, Principle 3.

[176] PRA Rulebook, *Senior Manager Functions* para 4.4.

[177] See earlier explanations in relation to risk and nomination committees.

[178] Article 95, CRD IV Directive 2013.   [179] Recommendations 30, 35, the Walker Review 2009.

[180] PRA Rulebook, *Remuneration* para 7.4.

policies are consistent with sound risk management and consider the interests of shareholders, stakeholders, and the public.[181] The emphasis on remuneration being aligned with sound risk management is designed to meet public interest in banks' prudent risk-taking.[182] It may be queried if such responsibilities would create anomalies, as how would a remuneration committee be able to judge if remuneration policies at one bank affects 'public interest' more widely? However, we suggest that the committee's responsibilities should be interpreted as meaning that bank remuneration policies should be compliant with the remuneration regulation that has been introduced in the public interest and discussed in section 12.4. This approach creates greater clarity and manageability in terms of the committee's prescribed responsibilities.

The Basel Committee also expressly recommends that the remuneration committee works and coordinates with the risk committee as to the implications of remuneration policies for the bank's risk profile and culture.[183]

12.3.2.5 Other committees

The Basel Committee recommends that there should be an ethical and compliance committee on the Board to drive proper decision-making, due consideration of the risks to the bank's reputation, and compliance with laws, regulations, and internal rules.[184] Such a committee would likely be seen as the ethical champion or the leadership body for firm culture in the bank. Such a prescription has not been adopted in EU legislation. However, as discussed in Chapter 11, the PRA has prescribed that a senior manager must be designated to have 'responsibility for overseeing the 'adoption of the firm's culture in the day-to-day management of the firm and responsibility for leading the development of the firm's culture by the governing body as a whole'. It is queried as to which senior manager may be held personally responsible for these- the Chief Risk Officer, Head of Internal Audit, and Chairman of Risk Committee may be possible candidates, and so is the Chairman whose overall responsibility remit may well include developing and leading the culture of the bank. Hence, although responsibility for overall bank culture and ethics is not regulated by means of a corporate governance reform into Board composition, the PRA's senior managers' regime is likely to capture aspects of this, making personal responsibility and liability an important means to drive behavioural change at firms.

Table 12.4 sets out in summary the obligations for banks to institute Board committees at a glance, according to the PRA Rulebook and EBA Guidelines.

---

[181] Ibid.   [182] Will be discussed in detail shortly.

[183] Basel Committee, *Guidelines: Corporate Governance Principles for Banks* (July 2015) at http://www.bis.org/bcbs/publ/d328.pdf, Principle 3, EBA Guidelines.

[184] Basel Committee, *Guidelines: Corporate Governance Principles for Banks* (July 2015) at http://www.bis.org/bcbs/publ/d328.pdf, Principle 3.

[185] Recommendations 6 and 11, The Walker Review 2009.

Table 12.4 Obligations for banks to institute Board committees

Board committee	Significant bank	Non-significant bank
Audit committee	Mandatory	Mandatory
Risk committee	Mandatory	No, and can be combined with audit committee or nomination committee (EBA Guidelines)
Nomination committee	Mandatory	No, and can be combined with risk committee (EBA Guidelines)
Remuneration committee	Mandatory	No, potential combination not proposed

12.3.3 Directors' commitments and obligations

The Walker Review of 2009 highlighted certain members of the Board, in particular the Chairman and non-executive directors to undertake certain roles and responsibilities in order to ensure that the Board can effectively discharge its responsibilities as a whole. The Review focused on the Chairman's leadership and expertise attributes, and the roles and attributes of non-executive directors in order to improve Board effectiveness. In particular, non-executive directors were called to step up to challenging the Board while the senior independent director is to act as a sounding Board for the Chairman and liaise with shareholders where relevant.[185]

The Review's perception of non-executive directors as being able to take distinctly critical roles on the Board is not unfounded, and is aligned with the perspectives in UK corporate governance generally.[186] This view is endorsed by the G30 recommendations[187] for improving corporate governance in banks and financial institutions. Moore[188] argues that non-executive directors in the UK are expected to play a role in risk moderation in particular challenging executive decisions on risk management. Thus, the Walker Review has also paid particular attention to beefing up non-executive directors' knowledge of the business, time commitment and access to advice,[189] and has expressly articulated expectations for non-executive directors to 'to challenge and test proposals on strategy put forward by the executive. They should satisfy themselves that Board discussion and decision-taking on risk matters is based on accurate and appropriately comprehensive information.'[190]

---

[186] UK Corporate Governance Code, which highlights the distinction between executive and non-executive directors, at https://www.frc.org.uk/Our-Work/Codes-Standards/Corporate-governance/UK-Corporate-Governance-Code.aspx.

[187] G30, *Towards Effective Governance in Financial Institutions* (2012) at http://www.group30.org/rpt_64.shtml.

[188] Marc T Moore, 'The Evolving Contours of the Board's Risk Management Function in UK Corporate Governance' (2010) 10 *Journal of Corporate Law Studies* 279.

[189] Walker Review 2009, Recommendations 1–3 and 5–6.

[190] Walker Review 2009, Recommendation 6.

Although the European and UK legislation have not imposed special responsibilities for non-executive directors as such, the membership requirements of Board committees would engage non-executive directors in particular roles in those committees. All directors, however, are encouraged to act with 'independence of mind', as has been discussed, and would be individually assessed for possessing such quality on an ongoing basis.

The Walker Review has also suggested special responsibility on the part of the Chairman to provide leadership and to facilitate meaningful and adequate Board discussions between executive and non-executive directors for decision-making on strategy and risk.[191] This has been generally adopted in the UK Corporate Governance Code,[192] but has not found its way into distinct regulation. That said, it may be queried whether the senior managers regime has in effect implemented the Review's proposals on the Chairman's role. The PRA defines the Chairman's function as 'chairing and overseeing the performance of the governing body of the firm'.[193] The EBA Suitability Guidelines have also adopted specific responsibilities for the Chairman in order to ensure effective agenda-setting and information flows and discussion at Board meetings. The Chairman has the specific role of promoting open and critical discussions on the Board.[194]

As the Chairman is a senior person with potential to incur personal liability for failure to discharge his functions, we query what s/he may be liable for. Does the Chairman's function extend to ensuring the effective substantive discharge of Board-level duties? A number of the prescribed responsibilities by the PRA relate to Board-level functions, such as 'responsibility for the development and maintenance of the firm's business model by the governing body', 'responsibility for leading the development of the firm's culture by the governing body as a whole' and 'responsibility for the allocation of all prescribed responsibilities'.[195] As these responsibilities are to be attached individually to a senior manager (see Chapter 11, section 11.2), senior persons tasked for these prescribed responsibilities would likely be personally liable for these. But would the Chairman incur any form of personal liability in relation to oversight if an executive director should fall short? As the Chairman has general oversight responsibility for the performance of the Board in general, it remains uncertain if secondary liability attaches to the Chairman for primary failures by executive members of the Board tasked with prescribed responsibilities. This approach could make the Chairman's personal responsibility a rather onerous burden. The PRA initially provided for the Chairman's office to be supported by adequate resources,[196] implying certain expectations for the Chairman's responsibilities. This provision has been repealed and may signal a moderation of expectations on the part of the regulator.

---

[191] The Chairman's leadership role is also highlighted in the Basel Committee, *Principles for Enhancing Corporate Governance* (October 2010) at Principle 3, paras 44–5.

[192] Section 12.1.3.   [193] PRA Rulebook, *Senior Managers Functions* para 4.1.

[194] EBA Guidelines paras 34–8.   [195] PRA Rulebook, *Allocation of Responsibilities* para 4.1.

[196] PRA Rulebook, *General Organisational Requirements* on the now-abolished section on *Chairman's Office* para 8.

[197] Walker Review 2009, Recommendation 7.

12.3.3.1 Time commitment

The Walker Review of 2009 was of the view that bank Boards, especially of large and complex global banks based in the UK, did not spend sufficient time overseeing the business of the bank. Banking business can be inordinately complex, having many lines of financial intermediation business across the globe. Thus, the Review proposed that bank Board members, especially the Chairman and non-executive directors, should increase their time dedication to a bank Board. In particular, the Review recommended that the Chairman of the Board should devote at least two-thirds of his time to the management of the relevant bank or financial institution.[197] Further, the Review recommended that non-executive directors should be prepared to spend 30–6 weeks in a year dedicated to the bank Board's business.[198]

Although the UK regulators did not take up the prescriptions recommended, EU legislation[199] has overtaken these proposals. The EU's approach contains a mixture of prescription and principled application. Board members are now prohibited from taking on too many commitments so that they are in a position to dedicate themselves adequately to the bank Board's business. Such prohibition may be crude but the hard limits for directors taking on too many directorships work as a 'proxy' to determine the director's availability for commitment to the bank directorship. The prescription is balanced against the Board's ability to exercise its discretion in determining if a director can provide sufficient 'time commitment' at the point of recruitment, and on an ongoing basis.

It is arguable that with the UK's senior managers' regime, there is no need for overprescription on time commitments, as the relevant senior manager has to weigh up for herself what it takes in order to discharge the relevant personal responsibilities effectively.

On the hard limits prescribed in regulation for bank directors' commitments, executive directors are now prohibited from holding another executive directorship elsewhere and not more than two other non-executive directorships.[200] Non-executive directors on the other hand are allowed to hold up to four other non-executive directorships elsewhere.[201] The scope of 'executive' and 'non-executive' directorships excludes directorships at not-for-profit organisations such as charities.[202] This presumably allays fears that suitable governors, trustees or directors in the charitable sector or other nonprofit outfits such as schools would have to step down in view of their bank Board obligations. Further, directorships held in different entities within the same group count as

---

[198] Walker Review 2009, Recommendation 3.   [199] CRD IV Directive, Article 91(3).

[200] CRD IV Directive, Article 91(3)(a), also applied to investment firms in Article 9, MiFID II Directive. Market operators are also subject to the same corporate governance prescriptions, see Article 45, MiFID II Directive.

[201] CRD IV Directive, Article 91(3)(b), also applied to investment firms in Article 9, MiFID II Directive. Market operators are also subject to the same corporate governance prescriptions, see Article 45, MiFID II Directive.

[202] PRA Rulebook, *General Organisational Requirements; Management Body* paras 5.5 and 5.6; EBA Suitability Guidelines paras 56–7.

'one directorship',[203] presumably because multiple directorships in the same group may benefit from the economies of scale in relation to the director's knowledge and understanding of the group and hence each directorship may not be as demanding in relation to the director's time. These requirements have been transposed in the UK.

The Board is required to assess upon recruitment and on an ongoing basis that individual directors are able to dedicate 'sufficient' time commitment to the needs of the Board. 'Sufficient' time commitment is determined according to the bank's needs, for example, the nature, complexity and scale of the bank's business, periods of increased activity such as mergers and acquisitions or crisis management, the geographical foot print of the bank's business and any specific roles undertaken by the director, such as membership in Board committees.[204] 'Sufficient' time commitment is also determined according to the profile of the director concerned, such as the director's level of induction and training, the director's other commitments, including professional and political activities, periods of absences required etc.[205] The EBA intends to carry out yearly benchmarking exercises to survey the extent of multiple directorships undertaken by bank directors, as well as substantive time commitment to the bank's affairs, expressed as a percentage of the individual's time commitments. The results of the benchmarking exercises also provide guidance for Boards in assessing 'sufficient' time commitment by directors.[206]

Next, we turn to discuss corporate governance reforms in relation to shareholder conduct. This area is not underpinned by regulatory prescriptions in financial regulation but in general corporate law and soft law, and so to an extent applies generally to the corporate sector. However, the genesis of these initiatives is the global financial crisis and the Walker Review's recommendations.

12.3.4 Shareholders' roles

In the wake of the global financial crisis, institutional shareholders were accused of having been 'asleep'.[207] The critique is that institutional shareholders have been uncritical of risky business practices in their investee banks and should have monitored Board risk management. Expectations are placed on institutional shareholders, largely on the basis that they are investment funds that would monitor their investee companies as part of their accountability regimes to their investors.

The Walker Review advocates that institutional shareholders should be more engaged with their investee companies, as this is not only in their private interests but is also a basis for their 'social legitimacy' as managers of many ordinary citizens' savings.[208] In

---

[203] EBA Suitability Guidelines paras 49–55.   [204] EBA Suitability Guidelines paras 41–8.
[205] Ibid.   [206] EBA Suitability Guidelines para 43.
[207] Jennifer Hughes, 'FSA Chief Lambasts Uncritical Investors' *Financial Times* (London, 11 March 2009); Kate Burgess, 'Myners Lashes out at Landlord Institutional shareholders' *Financial Times* (London, 21 April 2009). Also see Helia Ebrahimi, 'Institutional Institutional shareholders Admit Oversight Failure on Banks' *The Daily Telegraph* (London, 27 January 2009).   [208] Walker Review (2009) para 5.7.

Box 12.5   Principles of the UK Stewardship Code

1. Institutions should publicly disclose their policy on how they will discharge their steward-ship responsibilities.

2. Institutions should have a robust policy on managing conflicts of interest in relation to stewardship, which should be publicly disclosed.

3. Institutions should monitor their investee companies.

4. Institutions should establish clear guidelines on when and how they will escalate their stewardship activities.

5. Institutions should be willing to act collectively with other investors where appropriate.

6. Institutions should have a clear policy on voting and disclosure of voting activity.

7. Institutions should report periodically on their stewardship and voting activities.

---

particular, the Review calls for shareholder engagement to be carried out in the spirit of 'stewardship'. The Institutional Shareholder Committee, which is a trade body for institutional investors, swiftly developed a Statement of Shareholder Responsibilities in order to demonstrate responsiveness to the call to engage with their investee companies. The Financial Reporting Council then established a Stewardship Code[209] based on the Committee's Code, which applies as soft law for those institutions and asset managers that voluntarily sign up to the Code.[210]

The Stewardship Code now provides seven principles for shareholder engagement with companies, in order to facilitate shareholders' roles in 'monitoring' their investee companies. Box 12.5 sets out the seven principles.

The Stewardship Code applies only to voluntary signatories, on a comply-or-explain basis. This means that institutions who choose to adhere to the Code need not fully comply with the principles as long as they explain how they would achieve 'stewardship' objectives in their relationship with their investee companies.

The Principles in the Code largely require institutions to **establish policies**, **carry out engagement**, and **make disclosure**. Institutions are asked specifically to establish policies on stewardship, voting activities and the management of conflicts of interest. Conflicts of interest can exist, where for example, institutions are retained by corporations to manage their pension schemes. These institutions may feel beholden to management, and at the same time ought to act as 'monitoring' shareholders in the same corporation. [211] Institutions are asked to regularly monitor their investee companies

---

[209]   https://www.frc.org.uk/Our-Work/Publications/Corporate-Governance/UK-Stewardship-Code-September-2012.pdf.

[210]   Walker Review 2009, Recommendations 16–20.

[211]   For example, see Jennifer S Taub, 'Able but Not Willing: The Failure of Mutual Fund Advisers to Advocate for Shareholders' Rights' (2009) 34 *Journal of Corporation Law* 102.

and if concerned, they should engage in informal dialogue and 'escalate' matters to the Board. Further, institutions should collectively bring their pressure to bear on Boards if there is wider public interest to do so.

It may, however, be argued that asking shareholders to engage actively with investee banks is highly misplaced. This is because where banks are concerned, it is only economically rational for bank shareholders to prefer risk-taking,[212] as risk-taking bolsters profits for them, while losses are borne by a range of stakeholders including depositors and creditors.[213] Institutions' influence upon banks in that manner can be contrary to the public policy objectives of financial stability. It remains puzzling why policymakers are convinced that institutions should be more engaged in monitoring banks. The assumptions they make about the beneficial nature of such engagement seem superficial and oblivious to the concerns pointed out about the dangers of institutional shareholder influence.[214] However, the reliance on shareholders to 'monitor' is consistent with the assumptions underlying general corporate governance standards for listed companies. The lack of policy articulation to address shareholders' possibly adverse influences on banks reflects the challenge in deviating from established corporate governance standards for the corporate sector generally. Hence, regulatory reforms to corporate governance, as has already been discussed, relate to specific matters in relation to the Board and avoid being contrary to general corporate governance standards.

In general, encouraging shareholders of banks to be engaged is only a minor part of the governance framework for banks. Much more is entrusted in the hands of the regulator after the global financial crisis to supervise banks and compel them to comply with an enhanced suite of regulation.[215] The influence of the Stewardship Code in general continues to be significant in the UK investment sector and internationally too but this will not be discussed in detail here.[216]

---

[212] See earlier discussion and Chapter 1.

[213] Simon Deakin, 'Corporate Governance and Financial Crisis in the Long Run' in Cynthia A Williams and Peer Zumbansen (eds), *The Embedded Firm: Corporate Governance, Labor and Finance Capitalism* (New York: Cambridge University Press 2011); Peter O Mülbert, 'Corporate Governance of Banks after the Financial Crisis – Theory, Evidence, Reforms' (April 2010) ECGI Law Working Paper No. 130/2009 http://ssrn.com/abstract=1448118.

[214] Iris H-Y Chiu, 'Institutional Shareholders as Stewards: Toward a New Conception of Corporate Governance' (2012) 6 *Brooklyn Journal of Corporate, Financial and Commercial Law* 387; 'Turning Institutional Investors into "Stewards"- Exploring the Meaning and Objectives in "Stewardship"' (2013) *Current Legal Problems* 1.

[215] In relation to micro-prudential regulation (Chapters 8 and 9), macro-prudential regulation (Chapters 6 and 7), crisis management rules (Chapter 13), and structural reforms (Chapter 10). Avgouleas and Cullen argue that regulatory reforms to corporate governance are only ancillary to and do not deal with the heart of the problems that surfaced during the global financial crisis, see Emilios Avgouleas and Jay Cullen, 'Market Discipline and EU Corporate Governance Reform in the Banking Sector: Merits, Fallacies, and Cognitive Boundaries' (2014) 41 *Journal of Law and Society* 28.

[216] For an account of why the Stewardship Code appeals internationally, see Iris H-Y Chiu, 'Learning from the UK in the Proposed Shareholders' Rights Directive 2014? European Corporate Governance Regulation from a UK Perspective' (2015) 114 *ZVgIRWiss* 1.

Key takeaways

- Bank regulation has extended into bank corporate governance in order to ensure that certain aspects relating to Boards and shareholder roles serve the public interest of bank safety and proper conduct.
- The UK instituted the Walker Review in 2009 to make recommendations into corporate governance regulation. This is followed by formal legislation in the EU transposed by the PRA.
- Board responsibilities are now expressly articulated in regulation.
- Board composition is also regulated in relation to collectively suitable appointments, the recruitment of directors with 'independence' of mind and able to give 'sufficient time commitment'.
- Board committees are to be instituted for significant banks, with lighter requirements for non-significant banks. They are regulated in terms of their composition and specific responsibilities.
- Shareholders are asked to monitor management more actively although it is doubtful as to why shareholder engagement should be regarded as an unequivocal good for banks.
- The UK Stewardship Code has developed to set out best practices for shareholder engagement and applies on a comply-or-explain basis to voluntary signatories.

Key bibliography

Legislation

CRD IV Directive 2013

PRA Rulebook, *Allocation of Responsibilities, Audit Committee, Senior Manager Functions, Remuneration, General Organisational Requirements*

Reports and Guidelines

G-30, *Towards Effective Governance in Financial Institutions* (2012) at http://www.group30.org/rpt_64.shtml

Basel Committee, *Guidelines: Corporate Governance Principles for Banks* (July 2015) at http://www.bis.org/bcbs/publ/d328.pdf

EBA and ESMA, *Joint ESMA and EBA Guidelines on the assessment of the suitability of members of the management body and key function holders under Directive 2013/36/EU and Directive 2014/65/EU* (September 2017) at http://www.eba.europa.eu/documents/10180/1972984/Joint+ESMA+and+EBA+Guidelines+on+the+assessment+of+suitability+of+members+of+the+management+body+and+key+function+holders+%28EBA-GL-2017-12%29.pdf (EBA Suitability Guidelines)

David Walker, 'A Review of Corporate Governance in UK Banks and other Financial industry Entities: Final Recommendations' (26 November 2009) at http://webarchive.nationalarchives.gov.uk/+/http:/www.hm-treasury.gov.uk/d/walker_review_261109.pdf

Additional Reading

Avgouleas, E and Cullen, J, 'Market Discipline and EU Corporate Governance Reform in the Banking Sector: Merits, Fallacies, and Cognitive Boundaries' (2014) 41 *Journal of Law and Society* 28

Hopt, KJ, 'Corporate Governance of Banks after the Global Financial Crisis' in E Wymeersch, KJ Hopt, and G Ferrarini (eds), *Financial Regulation and Supervision, A Post-Crisis Analysis* (Oxford: OUP 2012) 337–67

Horn, L, 'Corporate Governance in Crisis? The Politics of EU Corporate Governance Regulation' (2012) 18 *European Law Journal* 83

Mehran, H, Morrison, A, and Shapiro, J, 'Corporate Governance and Banks: What Have We Learned from the Financial Crisis?' (June 2011) Federal Reserve Bank of New York Staff Report No. 502 <http://ssrn.com/abstract=1880009

12.4 Regulation of bankers' remuneration

A major initiative that attempts to change incentives for risk-taking behaviour has been introduced in the form of financial sector remuneration regulation.[217] The structure of financial sector remuneration has arguably given rise to a number of perverse incentives[218] on the part of financial sector employees and management, including short-termism and excessive risk-taking. This is because bank remuneration is structured in such a way as to include a variable remuneration component that is a significant part of the total remuneration composition. The level of variable remuneration is usually tied to performance metrics that are short-termist in nature, such as volumes of sales of financial products, without having due regard for the long-term performance of the product to meet customers' needs. Indeed, financial products can be structured in complex, albeit innovative manners, in order to attract investors, even if their investment performance is highly speculative and their social utility limited.[219] In this manner, bank employees can be incentivised to pursue performance strategies that would entitle them to receive high levels of variable remuneration even if such strategies may be linked to mis-selling and other forms of adverse conduct.[220]

---

[217] Also see Basel Committee, *Guidelines: Corporate Governance Principles for Banks* (July 2015) at http://www.bis.org/bcbs/publ/d328.pdf, Principle 11.

[218] Markus K Brunnermeier et al., 'The Fundamental Principles of Financial Regulation' *Geneva Reports on the World Economy* (London: Centre for Economic Policy Research 2009); FSB, 'Thematic Review on Compensation: Peer Review Report' (30 March 2010) http://www.financialstabilityboard.org/publications/r_100330a.pdf; Bernard S Sharfman, 'How the Strong Negotiating Position of Wall Street Employees Impacts the Corporate Governance of Financial Firms' (2011) 5 *Virginia Business and Law Review* 350.

[219] Emilios Avgouleas, 'Regulating Financial Innovation' in Niamh Moloney, Eilís Ferran, and Jennifer Payne (eds), *The Oxford Handbook of Financial Regulation* (Oxford: OUP 2015); Dan Awrey, 'Complexity, Innovation, and the Regulation of Modern Financial Markets' (2012) 2 *Harvard Business Law Review* 236.

[220] For example, see findings in FCA, *Commercial Insurance Intermediaries – Conflicts of Interest and Intermediary Remuneration: Report on the Thematic Project* (May 2014) 6ff; FCA, *Risks to Customers from Financial Incentives: Final Guidance* (January 2013) 13ff.

The regulation of bankers' remuneration arguably makes inroads into the freedom of contract between bank employers and employees, not only at individual levels but at an organisational and sectoral level. The raison d'etre for such regulation is to ensure the compatibility of pay policies overall with the financial stability of the bank and the systemic stability of the financial system.

The Walker Review of 2009 also devoted significant attention to reforming bankers' remuneration, these recommendations constituting a quarter of the Report's total recommendations.[221] These recommendations include: (a) regulating a range of bankers' remuneration beyond Board-level personnel; (b) compelling disclosure of remuneration composition and levels; and (c) ensuring that the remuneration committee puts in place more holistic considerations in designing remuneration policy. These recommendations have largely been overtaken by EU legislation[222] that the UK has transposed,[223] but legislation nevertheless features provisions that deal with similar issues. The remuneration regulatory regime is relatively prescriptive in nature and applies to all banks. However, the EBA supports more flexible and proportionate application to small and non-complex banks.[224]

12.4.1 Scope of regulation

The range of bank employees affected by the regulatory regime are 'categories of staff including senior management, staff engaged in control functions and any employee receiving total remuneration that takes them into the same remuneration bracket as senior management and risk-takers, whose professional activities have a material impact on their risk profile' (i.e., ***material risk-takers***, to be discussed later).[225]

In other words, bank staff subject to the remuneration regime are senior personnel and staff involved in significant risk-taking decisions. The range of individuals goes beyond Board-level personnel, unlike in general corporate governance norms,[226] as there are many decision-makers in various business units in banks that can generate significant risks and affect the bank's fate. For example, the synthetic derivatives

---

[221] Walker Review 2009, Recommendations 28–39.   [222] CRD IV Directive, Articles 92–95.

[223] PRA Rulebook, *Remuneration*; also FCA has implemented these to an extent for significant investment firms in FCA Handbook SYSC 19A while watering down the requirements for smaller firms see SYSC 19B and 19C.

[224] EBA, 'Opinion of the European Banking Authority on the application of the principle of proportionality to the remuneration provisions in Directive 2013/36/EU' (December 2015) at http://www.eba.europa.eu/documents/10180/983359/EBA-Op-2015-25+Opinion+on+the+Application+of+Proportionality.pdf.

[225] CRD IV Directive 2013, Article 92(1).

[226] Mainstream corporate governance see executive pay as problematic as levels of pay are determined by executives who have a vested interest in augmenting their package. This essential agency problem has spawned much literature in corporate governance best practices, see Lucian Bebchuk, *Pay without Performance: The Unfulfiled Promise of Executive Compensation* (Cambridge, MA: Harvard University Press 2012); Randall S Thomas and Jennifer G Hill (eds), *Research Handbook on Executive Pay* (Cheltenham: Edward Elgar 2016); Jay Cullen, *Executive Compensation in Imperfect Financial Markets* (Cheltenham: Edward Elgar 2014).

division in the London office of JP Morgan lost over £6 billion in 2012 due to adverse synthetic credit derivatives trades undertaken by one business unit. [227]

The UK has transposed remuneration regulation for bankers based on the Capital Requirements Directive 2013 and its secondary legislation, the Material Risk-Takers Regulation 2014.[228] The UK has initially opposed the introduction of this regime in a particular aspect known as the 'bankers' bonus cap', discussed in section 12.4.2, because UK policymakers see the regime as unduly restrictive for contractual freedoms and could affect London's position as a global financial centre able to attract global financial talent. Hence, upon departure from the EU, the PRA has the freedom not to retain it. On the other hand, the entire regime is part of the EU's prudential regulatory regime and any move away from this may render the UK's regulatory framework as not being equivalent for the purposes of third country treatment by the EU.[229]

'Material risk-takers' are defined with reference to qualitative and quantitative criteria. Qualitative criteria refer to an individual's office or nature of responsibility, while quantitative criteria refer to the numerical level of earnings of the individual. These criteria apply on a disjunctive basis, meaning that individuals falling within either set of criteria would be caught within the scope of 'material risk-takers' subject to the regulatory regime.

Box 12.6 sets out the list of individuals defined to be 'material risk-takers' by virtue of Article 3 of the 2014 Regulation.

The qualitative criteria capture many bank employees who have some form of decision-making or oversight authority in risk-taking, internal control, business strategy and key support, and affect at least many middle management employees. However, the UK applies a 'proportionality' rule that regards individuals who are not remunerated in excess of €500,000 in the preceding year *and* whose variable remuneration is not more than a third of total remuneration to be exempt from the remuneration regulation.[230]

The quantitative criteria presume that an employee earning above a certain threshold is a 'material risk taker' unless the bank determines, on the basis of objective criteria set out in the Regulation, that the individual makes no material impact upon the bank's risk profile.[231] The quantitative criteria cover the following individuals: an individual otherwise earning €500,000 or more in the preceding financial year, **or** being in the top 0.3 per cent remunerated of the number of staff; **or** being a staff member

---

[227] The investment decisions were not overseen at Board level and became sharply highlighted to Board level executives only much later. US Senate Permanent Subcommittee on Investigations Committee on Homeland Security and Governmental Affairs, *JP Morgan Chase Whale Trades: A Case History of Derivatives Risks and Abuses: Majority and Minority Staff Report* (2012).

[228] Commission Delegated Regulation (EU) No. 604/2014 of 4 March 2014 supplementing Directive 2013/36/EU of the European Parliament and of the Council with regard to regulatory technical standards with respect to qualitative and appropriate quantitative criteria to identify categories of staff whose professional activities have a material impact on an institution's risk profile.

[229] See Longjie Lu, 'The End of Bankers Bonus Cap: How Will the UK Regulate Bankers Remuneration after Brexit?' (2016) 27 *European Business Law Review* 1091.

[230] Also known as the 'Remuneration Code', FCA Handbook SYSC 19D.3.35.

[231] Article 4, Material Risk Takers Regulation 2014.

Box 12.6 Qualitative criteria for material risk-takers

(a) Board member.

(b) Senior management member (such as C-suite officers like the Chief Executive, Chief Financial Officer, etc.).

(c) The Chief Risk Officer (or equivalent), Head of Internal Audit, or Head of Compliance.

(d) Any staff member responsible for risk management in a material business unit, defined as carrying out activities that attracts capital adequacy requirements.

(e) The head of a material business unit.

(f) Managerial level staff members in internal control functions or material business units

(g) The head of a function relating to legal affairs, finance including taxation and budgeting, human resources, remuneration policy, information technology, or economic analysis.

(h) Staff member responsible for the management of operational risk, liquidity risk, leverage risk, interest rate risk, concentration risk, securitisation risk, or residual risk.

(i) Staff member responsible for lending decisions or structuring credit where the credit exposure exceeds €5 million and is at least represented by 0.5 per cent of the bank's capital.

(j) Staff member responsible for trading decisions that would incur market risk represented by at least 0.5 per cent of the bank's capital or the equivalent under the application of an internal-based ratings approach.

(k) Staff member with managerial responsibility over staff members in (i) or (j).

(l) Staff member who has the authority to make decisions for or veto new products.

(m) Any staff member with managerial responsibility for any individual identified in (a) to (l).

---

with managerial responsibility or key decision-making in material business units and awarded an amount of remuneration equal to the lowest total amount of remuneration awarded to a member of senior management in the preceding financial year.

However, if such an individual earns above a total amount of €750,000, and a bank wishes to exempt the individual from the regulatory regime, the bank must seek regulatory approval before doing so. Where such an individual earns above €1 million, the relevant bank's regulator must notify the EBA before giving its approval to the bank.

The UK has transposed the Material Risk-Takers Regulation 2014 into its rules.[232] It also extends the application of this remuneration regulation regime to foreign non-EEA firms in the UK but in a limited manner. The qualitative criteria in Box 12.6 would not apply, and only individuals earning €750,000 and above in the preceding financial year or otherwise meeting the above-mentioned quantitative criteria would fall within the scope of 'material risk-takers'.[233]

---

[232] PRA Rulebook, *Remuneration* and FCA Handbook SYSC 19D that applies to dual-regulated firms, that is, UK banks subject to both PRA and FCA oversight. The two pieces of subsidiary legislation contain some duplicative provisions.   [233] Ibid para 3.2.

The identification of 'material risk-takers' in each bank is essentially a self-assessment exercise based on the criteria set out in Box 12.6. However, the EBA recommends that each firm follows a rigorous process[234] of documenting how material risk-takers are identified.[235] The documentation processes and system should also be subject to appropriate governance such as the oversight of the remuneration committee of the Board.[236]

12.4.2 Controlling remuneration

The regulatory regime purports to control bankers' remuneration using the three pronged approach as follows:

1. Regulatory provisions designed to improve the ***governance*** of remuneration decisions.

2. Regulatory provisions that intervene into ***remuneration principles and policies***, these being drawn from the EU Capital Requirements Directive 2013[237] and the FSB's Sound Compensation Principles.[238]

3. Regulatory provisions that ***prescribe precise controls*** on the use of variable remuneration, as a response to the misuse of variable remuneration in the years leading up to the global financial crisis.

These are further flanked by regulatory provisions on ***malus*** and ***clawback***, which incentivise long-term decision-making by material risk-takers and other individuals within the scope of the regulatory regime.

12.4.2.1 Governance

First, on regulatory provisions designed to improve the governance of remuneration decisions, each bank must institute remuneration policies 'consistent with and promote sound and effective risk management.'[239] The Capital Requirements Regulation 2013 provides the template banks must use to report their remuneration policies and practices to regulators. Hence, it is likely that banks will dovetail their remuneration policies with the reporting template.[240] The EBA further recommends that remuneration

---

[234] Being clear, consistent, properly documented, and periodically updated.

[235] EBA, *Guidelines on Sound Remuneration Policies under Articles 74(3) and 75(2) of Directive 2013/36/EU and Disclosures under Article 450 of Regulation (EU) No 575/2013* (2015) (EBA Remuneration Guidelines) at https://www.eba.europa.eu/documents/10180/1314839/EBA-GL-2015-22+Guidelines+on+Sound+Remuneration+Policies.pdf/1b0f3f99-f913-461a-b3e9-fa0064b1946b, 41.

[236] Ibid 43.   [237] Article 92.

[238] Financial Stability Forum, *FSF Principles for Sound Compensation Practices* (2009) (FSB Principles 2009) and the Financial Stability Board's *Implementing Standards* (2009) at http://www.fsb.org/what-we-do/policy-development/building-resilience-of-financial-institutions/compensation/, and the FSB's update to these Principles urging banks to include misconduct risk in remuneration policies and the application of malus and clawback (see later), FSB, *Supplementary Guidance to the FSB Principles and Standards on Sound Compensation Practices* (March 2018) at http://www.fsb.org/wp-content/uploads/P090318-1.pdf.

[239] CRD IV Directive 2013, Article 74(1).

[240] Article 450, Capital Requirements Regulation No570/2013. The template is provided in Box 12.12.

policies must comprehensively set out all components of remuneration and the pension policy, including, where relevant, the framework for early retirements.[241]

Responsibility is reposed in the Board to ensure that bank remuneration policies are comprehensive and compliant. The Board (or the remuneration committee of the Board) has the responsibility to periodically review the remuneration policies,[242] including commissioning independent internal reviews (such as by the Internal Audit function) on a yearly basis. In particular the risk management and compliance functions should be able to provide advisory input into remuneration design.[243] Where banks are sufficiently significant, they must establish a remuneration committee on the Board, whose responsibilities are as discussed in section 12.3. The remuneration and risk committees of the Board are encouraged to work together on remuneration policies.[244]

Banks must also ensure that staff in internal control functions are adequately remunerated and independently from the business areas they control so that business objectives do not affect their independence.[245]

Principles and policies

Next, the regulatory regime articulates optimal principles to guide the bank's discretion in designing remuneration policies. The EBA defines remuneration as capable of being structured only as fixed or variable remuneration. Fixed remuneration[246] is defined as remuneration with the characteristics in Box 12.7.

Box 12.7 Definition of fixed remuneration

(a) Remuneration that is based on predetermined criteria.

(b) Remuneration that is non-discretionary reflecting the level of professional experience and seniority of staff.

(c) Remuneration that is transparent with respect to the individual amount awarded to the individual staff member.

(d) Remuneration that is permanent, that is, maintained over a period tied to the specific role and organisational responsibilities.

(e) Remuneration that is non-revocable; the permanent amount is only changed via collective bargaining or following renegotiation in line with national criteria on wage setting.

(f) Remuneration that cannot be reduced, suspended, or cancelled by the institution.

(g) Remuneration that does not provide incentives for risk assumption.

(h) Remuneration that does not depend on performance.

---

[241] EBA Remuneration Guidelines p25.
[242] PRA Rulebook, *Remuneration* paras 7.2 and 7.3, transposing Article 92, CRD IV Directive 2013, and consistent with the FSB Principles 2009 at Principle 1; FCA Handbook, SYSC 19D.3.10–12.
[243] EBA Remuneration Guidelines p27.   [244] Ibid.
[245] PRA Rulebook, *Remuneration* para 8.1, transposing Article 92, CRD IV Directive 2013 and consistent with the FSB Principles 2009 at Principle1; FCA Handbook SYSC 19D.3.15–17.
[246] EBA Remuneration Guidelines p47.

Variable remuneration is defined as being not fixed remuneration, and therefore captures a wide scope of payments. The EBA recognises that ***allowances*** are sometimes paid to staff such as expatriate staff in terms of living expenses. Allowances that satisfy the fixed remuneration criteria in Box 12.7 should count as fixed remuneration or otherwise be regarded as part of variable remuneration.[247] There is no scope for treating allowances as outside of the scope of remuneration altogether or else banks would have a clear means to avoid complying with the remuneration rules. Further, the EBA clarifies that retention bonuses, discretionary pension benefits and severance pay all count towards variable remuneration.[248]

Remuneration regulation deals with principles that intend to align the design of remuneration, especially variable remuneration towards serving the bank's longer-term and prudent objectives, as well as ethical and complaint behaviour. Box 12.8 provides

---

Box 12.8 Regulatory policies and principles for bankers' remuneration

- Remuneration policies including pensions must be consistent with and promote sound and effective risk management and does not encourage risk-taking beyond the tolerated risk-taking level of the firm (PRA Rulebook, *Remuneration* para 6.2, 12.1, FCA Handbook SYSC 19D.3.7, CRD IV Directive 2013, Article 92).

- Remuneration policies including pensions must be in line with the business strategy, objectives, values, and long-term interests of the firm (PRA Rulebook, *Remuneration*, para 6.3, 12.1, FCA Handbook, SYSC 19D.3.8; 31, CRD IV Directive 2013, Article 92).

- Remuneration policies must include measures that avoid conflicts of interest (PRA Rulebook, *Remuneration*, para 6.4, FCA Handbook SYSC 19D.3.9, CRD IV Directive 2013, Article 92).

- Remuneration policies must be designed to promote ethical behaviour and compliance with laws, regulations, and internal conduct standards (FSB, *Supplementary Guidance to the FSB Principles and Standards on Sound Compensation Practices* (March 2018) at Principle 1, p7).

- Remuneration policies, practices, and procedures, including performance appraisal processes and decisions, must be clear and documented (PRA Rulebook, *Remuneration*, para 6.5).

- Remuneration regulation is to be applied by firms in proportion to their size, internal organisation, and the nature, the scope, and the complexity of its activities (PRA Rulebook, *Remuneration*, para 5.1).

- Early termination payments must reflect performance achieved over time and are designed in a way that does not reward failure or misconduct (PRA Rulebook, *Remuneration*, para 15.14, FCA Handbook SYSC 19D.3.54, CRD V Directive Article 94, FSB, Principles for Sound Compensation Practices: Implementing Standards (2009) at Standard 12. Failure is defined by the EBA Remuneration Guidelines 2015 to include bank insolvency, receipt of government aid and significant business losses).

---

[247] EBA Remuneration Guidelines p48.   [248] Ibid 52.

the regulatory principles and policies to be applied in remuneration design; Box 12.9 shows policies and principles relevant to variable remuneration only.

The Principles in Boxes 12.8 and 12.9 are broadly-framed to guide banks and their remuneration committees in designing appropriate remuneration policies. Several of the policies and principles are directed at the design of variable remuneration only as the flawed design of variable remuneration continues to be blamed for contributing to excessive risk-taking at banks leading up to the global financial crisis of 2007–9.

The general principles such as referring to 'risk-adjusted' pay or applying a multi-year performance framework are open-textured in nature. The bank is able to determine its level of risk tolerance in remuneration design, as well as the time-frame for

---

Box 12.9 Policies and principles relevant to variable remuneration only

- Levels of variable remuneration must not jeopardise the bank's capital base (PRA Rulebook, *Remuneration*, para 9.1, FCA Handbook SYSC 19D.3.19, CRD IV Directive 2013, Article 94, and drawn from the FSB, *Principles of Sound Compensation Practices: Implementation Standards* (2009) at Standard 3).

- Variable remuneration must be risk-adjusted by taking into account all types of current and future risks (PRA Rulebook, *Remuneration*, para 11.1, FCA Handbook SYSC 19D.3.23-24, FSB, *Principles of Sound Compensation Practices* (2009) at Principle 2).

- Performance-related variable remuneration must be based on profits-based measures that are risk-adjusted and not revenue-based measures (PRA Rulebook, *Remuneration*, para 11.2-11.5, FCA Handbook SYSC 19D.3.27-29).

- Performance-related variable remuneration must be based on performance of the individual, business unit and overall bank performance (PRA Rulebook, *Remuneration*, para 15.4, FCA Handbook SYSC 19D.3.39, CRD IV Directive 2013 at Article 94, FSB, *Principles for Sound Compensation Practices: Implementing Standards* (2009) at Standard 4).

- Performance-related variable remuneration must be based on performance assessed over a multi-year framework in the interests of the bank's long-term performance (PRA Rulebook, *Remuneration*, para 15.6, CRD IV Directive 2013, Article 94).

- Performance-related variable remuneration must include assessment of performance in relation to non-financial metrics that address a full spectrum of misconduct risks over a sufficiently long time-frame (for misconduct risk to materialise) (FCA Handbook SYSC 19D.3.40-41, FSB, *Supplementary Guidance to the FSB Principles and Standards on Sound Compensation Practices* (March 2018) at Principle 5, 9).

- Variable remuneration cannot be structured in a way that allows employees to hedge their risks in remuneration arrangements or in any way non-compliant with regulation (PRA Rulebook, *Remuneration*, paras 13.1, 14.1, FCA Handbook SYSC 19D.3.34, CRD IV Directive, Article 94, FSB, *Principles for Sound Compensation Practices: Implementing Standards* (2009) at Standard 14).

consideration. The EBA attempts to define[249] the parameters of bank discretion by setting out acceptable performance criteria relating to risk management and operational efficiency. However, these cannot be over-prescribed. In relation to the use of performance metrics, the FCA clarifies that performance metrics must include non-financial metrics such as adherence to risk management policies and systems, compliance with laws and regulations and metrics relating to conduct. Indeed, non-financial metrics such as relating to conduct should override financial ones where appropriate.[250]

Prescriptive controls

Next, we turn to the somewhat prescriptive regulatory regime that targets only controls on variable remuneration. Variable remuneration in theory could work as a way to manage bank costs in proportion to their performance. As long as variable remuneration is truly adjusted to reflect lean times/performance as well as good times/performance, they could provide the right incentives for employees to drive performance.[251] The flawed use of variable remuneration by banks leading up to the crisis is that variable remuneration has been used unabashedly to inflate pay using metrics that favoured employees' short-term interests and disregarded the banks' and stakeholders' long-term interests. This is why regulatory focus has in response been turned to controlling variable remuneration. However, some of these specific prescriptions can be regarded as highly constrictive for remuneration design.

Guaranteed variable remuneration

Guaranteed variable remuneration is discouraged unless justified by 'exceptional' conditions. Guaranteed variable remuneration can only be paid out when hiring new staff and where the institution has a sound and strong capital base and is limited to the first year of employment.[252] Such remuneration must also adhere to the overall principles of consistency with risk management, and pay for performance.[253] The control on guaranteed variable remuneration prevents banks from sidestepping remuneration rules by the power of private contracts.

Prohibitions on paying variable remuneration

It is also to be noted that there are a few prescriptive prohibitions in relation to paying variable remuneration. One is that non-executive directors of the bank cannot be paid variable remuneration.[254] The other is that for banks benefiting from government intervention, that is, banks bailed out by tax-payers' money, they must not pay variable

---

[249] EBA Guidelines 2015 65.
[250] FCA Handbook, SYSC 19D.3.40, and FCA, *Remuneration in CRD IV Firms: New Guidance and Changes to Handbook* (May 2017) at https://www.fca.org.uk/publication/policy/ps17-10.pdf.
[251] John Thannasoulis, 'The Case for Intervening in Bankers' Pay' (2012) 67 *The Journal of Finance* 849.
[252] PRA Rulebook, *Remuneration* para 15.7; CRD IV Directive 2013, Article 94, FSB, *Principles for Sound Compensation Practices: Implementing Standards* (2009) at Standard 11.
[253] Ibid.   [254] PRA Rulebook, *Remuneration* para 15.3; FCA Handbook SYSC 19D.3.38.

remuneration to members of the management body,[255] although variable remuneration may be paid to other staff as long as such is limited to a percentage of net revenues and does not affect the bank's capital base.[256] One can understand the need for restraint in remuneration if a bank has been bailed out by tax-payers. However, such a bank also needs talented executives to turn it around and may find itself unable to reward executives competitively.

These contests of perception were played out in relation to Stephen Hester, the first Chief Executive appointed to bailed-out UK bank Royal Bank of Scotland. Hester was awarded pay of over £1 million every year between 2010 and 2013 during his tenure.[257] These awards were offered amidst often hostile scrutiny from the media although the level of remuneration, compared to CEO pay of other banks at the same time, could be regarded as relatively modest. Hester also declined his bonus in the year that RBS suffered a severe computer outage. Hester dealt with many legacy issues including the bank's misconduct that continued to attract regulatory fines after his departure. Hester's successor Ross McEwan continued to battle public disapproval of his bonuses and in 2013 and 2014 declared upfront that he would take no bonus so that RBS' performance would not be distracted by media scrutiny over executive pay. In 2015, he also handed back part of his first awarded bonus by the bank (£1 million).[258]

Ratio between fixed and variable remuneration

One of the areas of extensive prescription is in the area of remuneration composition, that is, the structure and balance of fixed and variable components in total remuneration. It is prescribed that the fixed portion must be sufficiently high[259] to allow the operation of a fully flexible policy on variable remuneration components, including the possibility to pay no variable remuneration. This prescription is clearly in response to the flawed use of variable remuneration design by banks prior to the global financial crisis where only ratcheting up was observed.

Variable remuneration is to be capped at 100 per cent of the fixed component of remuneration,[260] and can only increase to 200 per cent of the fixed component if shareholder approval in general meeting is obtained.[261] The value of the variable component of remuneration can, however, be discounted by 25 per cent if it is paid in deferred instruments for more than 5 years.[262]

---

[255] PRA Rulebook, *Remuneration* para 10.1, FCA Handbook SYSC 19D.3.21, CRD IV Directive 2013, Article 93, *Principles for Sound Compensation Practices: Implementing Standards* (2009) at Standard 10.

[256] FCA Handbook SYSC 19D.3.21.

[257] 'New RBS row over £1 m payout to ex-chief Stephen Hester', *The Guardian* (16 November 2014).

[258] 'New RBS chief Ross McEwan to receive no bonus this year or next', *BBCNews* (2 August 2013); 'RBS chief Ross McEwan declines £1m of his pay', *Financial Times* (25 February 2015).

[259] PRA Rulebook, *Remuneration* para 15.9; CRD IV Directive 2013, Article 94.

[260] PRA Rulebook, *Remuneration* para 15.10, CRD IV Directive 2013, Article 94; FCA Handbook SYSC 19D.3.48–51.   [261] PRA Rulebook, *Remuneration* para 15.11, CRD IV Directive 2013, Article 94.

[262] PRA Rulebook, *Remuneration* para 15.13, Article 94, CRD V Directive 2013, EBA, *Guidelines on the Applicable Notional Discount Rate for Variable Remuneration* (2014) at http://www.eba.europa.eu/documents/10180/643987/EBA-GL-2014-01+%28Final+Guidelines+on+the+discount+rate+for+remuneration%29.pdf.

The prescription on variable remuneration limits, known popularly as the banker's bonus cap, was particularly unsupported by the UK. The UK viewed the cap as a crude measure to regulate remuneration and that it ignored the potential benefits of a flexible variable remuneration policy for supporting the competitiveness of the UK financial sector. The UK commenced legal challenge[263] against the bankers' bonus cap, alleging that the bonus cap was not a measure designed to safeguard financial stability but instead related to employment and working conditions, that it was not supported by the proportionality principle in the Treaty for the European Union. However, the Advocate-General delivered an opinion that dismissed the UK's challenge and in November 2014 the legal challenge was withdrawn.[264]

Banks are attempting to avoid succumbing to the restrictive remuneration ratio in legislation by inventing new forms of pay that they interpret to be 'fixed remuneration'. This is because 'fixed remuneration' is not subject to a cap, and only guided by general principles such as having to reflect the individual's professional experience and organisational responsibility.[265] An example is that of 'role-based allowances'. Role-based allowances have been used to retain staff, and they are structured in such a way as to be not dependent on performance and hence interpreted as 'fixed remuneration'. However, such allowances are not included in basic salary, not pensionable and usually subject to review and can be adjusted or terminated with notice. They are in fact discretionary and function like variable remuneration except not based on performance criteria. The UK did not clamp down on these allowances but the EBA has issued a report[266] that treats role-based allowances as variable remuneration intending to circumvent regulation. The EBA is of the view that remuneration can only be characterised as fixed or variable, and since role-based allowances are not numerically certain and are awarded by discretion, they are in fact variable remuneration and should be subject to the legislative cap. That said the EBA does not have direct enforcement power against banks. The EBA may be able to take enforcement action against the PRA for failing to implement EU legislation,[267] but such a prospect may be overtaken by the UK's departure from the EU.

Further, as the bonus cap compels banks to change their pay structures, banks have tended to do so without causing great disruption to the financial expectations of their employees and executives.[268] For example, banks are now awarding additional fixed remuneration to executives in shares in order to rebalance the disadvantages executives

---

[263] Case C-507/13 *United Kingdom v Parliament and Council*, ECLI:EU:C:2014:2481.

[264] Michael Randall and Longjie Lu, 'Capping of Bankers' Bonuses? *Case C-507/13 UK v. Parliament and Council*' (2015) 42(2) *Legal Issues of Economic Integration* 383 and 385.

[265] PRA Rulebook, *Remuneration*, para 15.2, CRD IV Directive 2013, Article 92(2).

[266] http://www.eba.europa.eu/documents/10180/534414/EBA+Report+on+the+principles+on+remuneration+policies+and+the+use+of+allowances.pdf.

[267] Article 17, Regulation (EU) No. 1093/2010 of the European Parliament and of the Council of 24 November 2010 establishing a European Supervisory Authority (European Banking Authority), amending Decision No. 716/2009/EC and repealing Commission Decision 2009/78/EC.

[268] Andreas Kokkinis, 'Exploring the Effects of the 'Bonus Cap' Rule: The Impact of Remuneration Structure on Risk-Taking by Bank Managers' (2018) 18 *Journal of Corporate Law Studies* forthcoming.

would suffer from the forced restructuring of their pay packages to comply with the bonus cap. It is important to examine the behavioural implications of the bonus cap in order to ascertain if the larger objectives, such as prudent decision-making and risk-taking at banks and their impact on systemic stability, may be adversely affected.

Structure of variable remuneration

The regulatory regime prescribes certain structures for variable remuneration so that the incentives of employees can be controlled towards the long-term interests of the bank. These are largely derived from the Financial Stability Board's recommendations for sound compensation practices,[269] such international standards providing legitimacy for these rather controversial standards.

The prescribed structures for variable remuneration are listed in Box 12.10. They refer to proportions of variable remuneration to be paid in share-based instruments or tier one or two capital-eligible instruments, so as to align employees' interests with the performance and prudential safety of the bank. The prescribed structures also include deferral of payment, so that employees are forced to consider the long-term consequences of their actions.[270] However, the award may vest in the employee during the course of the deferral period, on a *pro rata* basis as prescribed in EU legislation and the PRA Rulebook (see Box 12.9). The EBA recommends that there should be an absolute period of 12 months from the date of the award that vesting cannot occur,[271] so that banks do not minimise compliance with deferral rules by rapid vesting of the award.

The rules on the structure of variable remuneration in the UK go further than the EU legislation or the FSB's standards, where senior managers are concerned. Senior managers are required to subject remuneration in excess of £500,000 to deferral for at least 7 years and not to vest until at least 3 years after the award. The stringent requirements placed on senior managers are explained by the PRA as necessary to ensure long-term accountability of senior managers' decisions.[272]

Proportionality of application

The bonus cap and certain other prescriptions on the structure of variable remuneration here are subject to proportionate application.[273] This means that certain banks do not have to apply the full range of remuneration principles and prescriptive controls. In the FCA's guidance to dual-regulated firms (i.e. UK banks regulated by both the PRA

---

[269] FSB, *Principles for Sound Compensation Practices: Implementing Standards* (2009) at Standards 6–9.

[270] CRD IV Directive Article 94, consistent with the above-mentioned FSB standards. The PRA Rulebook citations are in Box 12.10.

[271] EBA Remuneration Guidelines 70.

[272] PRA and FCA, *Strengthening the Alignment of Risk and Reward: New Remuneration Rules* (July 2014) at http://www.bankofengland.co.uk/pra/Pages/publications/ps/2015/ps1215.aspx.

[273] FCA, *General Guidance on Proportionality: The Dual-Regulated Firms Remuneration Code (SYSC 19D)* (May 2017) at https://www.fca.org.uk/publication/finalised-guidance/guidance-dual-regulated-firms-remuneration-code.pdf.

Box 12.10 Prescribed structures of variable remuneration

(a) Fifty per cent of variable remuneration is to be paid in the form of shares, share-linked instruments or other instruments that are eligible as tier one or two capital instruments discussed in Chapter 8.

(b) The above must be subject to an appropriate retention policy, one year as recommended by the EBA Remuneration Guidelines 2015, pp73–4.

(c) The above applies to deferred and non-deferred remuneration in accordance with the deferral prescriptions below (PRA Rulebook, *Remuneration* paras 15.15 and 15.16; FCA Handbook SYSC 19D.3.56). But where the remuneration is deferred, then the minimum retention policy for staff members not senior management should be 6 months, while the retention policy for senior management members should be 1 year, see EBA Remuneration Guidelines 2015, p74.

(d) At least 40 per cent of variable remuneration must be deferred, and in the case of director's remuneration received from a bank that is significant in terms of its size, internal organisation, and the nature, scope, and complexity of its activities, at least 60 per cent of variable remuneration exceeding £500,000 must be deferred (PRA Rulebook, *Remuneration* paras 15.17 and 15.18; FCA Handbook SYSC 19D.3.59-60).

(e) The 40 per cent deferral rule applies to different individuals over different periods of time:

   (i) A material risk taker not falling within (ii) or (iii) below, a period of deferral of 3 years.

   (ii) A material risk taker who satisfies the qualitative criteria in Box 12.6 but does not perform a senior management function, a period of deferral of 5 years.

   (iii) A material risk taker performing a senior management function, a period of deferral of 7 years. (PRA Rulebook, *Remuneration* paras 15.17 and 15.18).

(f) Upon the completion of the deferral period, the award does not vest in individuals in (e)(i) and (ii) unless on a pro rata basis and the award does not vest in individuals in (e)(iii) until at least 3 years of the award. (PRA Rulebook, *Remuneration* paras 15.17 and 15.18).

(g) The deferral periods above can be regarded as the minimum, and any longer periods adopted by the firm must be consistent with business cycle, the nature of the business, its risks, and the activities of the employee in question (PRA Rulebook, *Remuneration*, para 15.19).

and FCA, as discussed in Chapter 6, section 6.2), the FCA provides for three proportionality levels set out in Box 12.11.

Banks falling within proportionality level three can disapply the bankers' bonus cap and prescriptive controls such as deferral and payment in retained shares, as well as the malus and clawback rules, to be discussed in section12.4.3. Banks falling within proportionality level one must apply the full suite of remuneration regulation discussed in this section. Banks falling within proportionality level two may determine at their discretion which rules to disapply, but they must be able to explain to the FCA's satisfaction how their remuneration policies remain risk-aligned and encourage incentives towards prudent risk management and ethical and compliant conduct. The proportionality

---

Box 12.11 The FCA's three proportionality levels

Proportionality of application of remuneration regulation	Thresholds for bank
Proportionality level one	UK Banks, building societies with assets exceeding £50 billion
Proportionality level two	UK Banks, building societies with assets exceeding £15 billion but not exceeding £50 billion
Proportionality level three	UK Banks, building societies with assets below £15 billion

---

rules can mitigate the regulators' and industry's perception of the restrictive nature of the remuneration regulation, so that talented individuals may not be dis-incentivised to work for banks, especially the smaller or medium-sized banks.

12.4.3 Malus and clawback

The remuneration regulation regime is supported by mandatory malus and clawback, which allow firms not to pay out or indeed recover variable remuneration that is no longer justified.[274] The power to do this is expressly provided in regulation as contractual power may be limited. Banks are likely not incentivised to impair their relations with individual members of staff and may not provide for strong malus or clawback provisions of their own accord. Further, the regulatory basis for banks to vary their contracts in relation to remuneration is an important one, as the private law of contract has made it extremely difficult for banks to do so on their own, for example, by introducing material adverse change clauses.

In *Dresdner Kleinwort Limited and Commerzbank AG v Richard Attrill & Ors and Fahmi Anar & Ors*,[275] a case that predates the EU legislation on malus and clawbacks, 104 employees of Dresdner Kleinwort Limited, which was acquired by Commerzbank AG, sued to recover alleged remuneration entitlements of over €50 million. The alleged remuneration entitlements arose due to an oral promise in August 2008 by the then CEO of Dresdner that a minimum bonus pool had been set aside for employees and would be paid out 'no matter what'. The promise was made in order to maintain employee stability pending Commerzbank AG's takeover of Dresdner, which was agreed and announced on 31 August 2008. However, on 19 December 2008, employees were informed that a material adverse change clause would be inserted in their bonus letters to qualify their bonus entitlement to be in line with the financial performance of Dresdner. Following a review of Dresdner's financial performance, the decision was taken by the Board to invoke the material adverse change clause and employees were informed in February 2009 that

---

[274] Based on the FSB, *Sound Principles for Compensation Practices: Implementing Standards* (2009) at Standard 5.   [275] [2013] EWCA Civ 394.

bonus awards would be reduced by 90 per cent. Claims were brought against Dresdner and its acquirer Commerzbank AG by 104 employees for the unpaid balance of the amounts stated in their respective bonus letters and against Commerzbank for inducing breach of contract. The claimants succeeded in the High Court but on appeal, the Court of Appeal dismissed the banks' appeal. It reasoned that the oral promise was a valid variation of employees' contracts and therefore provided a guaranteed minimum bonus pool. Hence the material adverse change clause later introduced was invalid and in breach of the implied contractual duty of mutual trust and confidence in employment contracts. Despite the fact that Dresdner's financial circumstances had deteriorated significantly and Commerzbank was in receipt of state bailout, the court was of the view that the claimants' case succeeded on the application of contract law principles.

The Dresdner case may highlight the disengagement between the application of private law concepts and the reality of public interest. Regulatory provisions that now put contractual variation on a firmer basis can be seen as being consistent with the post-crisis approach of subjecting rights, freedoms, and entitlements in private law (see Chapter 13 in particular) to the countervailing considerations of public interest. Regulators see malus and clawback as providing crucial incentives to govern risk decisions on the part of individuals as they would likely think of the long-term prospects of their decisions since there is 'skin in the game'.

The regulatory provisions for malus and clawback produce two ramifications. One is that they provide a basis for specific material adverse change clauses to be introduced into contracts to vary them. The contractual status of malus and clawback are thus made firmer with regulatory mandates, and the bank can enforce such contractual variations without suffering breach allegations. Second, the regulatory provisions provide a continuing basis for bank enforcement against former employees in the situations of malus and clawback specified. Where former employees are concerned, variation of contract is no longer an option, and it is important to ensure that there is a statutory basis to take enforcement action or else bank staff would be incentivised towards low job loyalty in order to avoid the enforcement of remuneration adjustment rules. Under both sets of circumstances, banks are the parties with standing to sue for enforcement purposes although the basis to sue in the second scenario cannot arguably be based on contract. In the second situation, the enforcement carried out by the bank would be on the basis of a duty to comply with regulation that compels it to act, rather like an action on behalf of the regulator.

The regulatory regime allows banks to adjust their remuneration obligations in the following manner:

(a) Reduction of unvested deferred remuneration in some circumstances.

(b) Ensuring that conditions of vesting are appropriate.

(c) Recovery of vested but not yet paid remuneration through the application of malus in certain circumstances.

(d) Recovering awarded remuneration through clawback extending to a certain number of years under certain circumstances.

The Capital Requirements Directive 2013 requires that malus or clawback should be based on at least one of two conditions, that is, the employee concerned participated in or was responsible for conduct that resulted in significant losses to the institution or failed to meet appropriate standards of fitness and propriety.[276] The EBA Guidelines explain 'significant losses to the institution' as meaning specific criteria such as material downturn in business, material failure in risk management or attraction of regulatory sanctions.[277] The PRA and FCA now provide that banks may reduce unvested deferred remuneration where there is reasonable evidence of employee misbehaviour or material error; where the firm or the relevant business unit suffers a material downturn in its financial performance; or the firm or the relevant business unit suffers a material failure of risk management. Where the reduction pertains to shares or non-cash instruments, the numbers of such shares or instruments to be awarded may be reduced.[278]

The specific criteria for 'material' error, 'material downturn' in business, or 'material failure in risk management' must be set out[279] although it can be envisaged that such granularity is hard to achieve with certainty and that contractual disputes could well arise. The FSB[280] recommends that where remuneration adjustment is made on the basis of misconduct, it is important to set out specific criteria relating to the level of involvement in the misconduct, the level of culpability, any relevant history of misconduct and root causes. As misconduct entails implications of disciplinary issues, the establishment of misconduct needs to be subject to clear and documented procedures for reporting, investigation, and decision-making.

Next, variable remuneration is only paid or vested if it is sustainable according to the financial situation of the firm as a whole, and justified on the basis of the performance of the firm, the business unit and the individual concerned.[281] This could mean that the conditions of vesting and payment can be subject to material adverse change clauses. In light of the general obligation for banks to make specific their criteria for malus or clawback,[282] material adverse change clauses would likely have to be introduced in specific terms, minimising the bank's discretion of opportunistic use.

Where variable remuneration has vested but not yet paid out or realised, such as in the case of shares that are awarded but subject to a retention period, banks must make all efforts to recover an appropriate amount of remuneration where any of the above-mentioned conditions are met.[283]

Finally, where variable remuneration has already been paid out, banks are entitled to take action to clawback an appropriate amount of such remuneration where there

---

[276] CRD IV Directive 2013, Article 94. [277] EBA Remuneration Guidelines 75.

[278] PRA Rulebook, *Remuneration* para 15.22.

[279] PRA Rulebook, *Remuneration* para 15.21; FCA Handbook SYSC 19D.3.63.

[280] FSB, *Supplementary Guidance to the FSB Principles and Standards on Sound Compensation Practices* (March 2018) at http://www.fsb.org/wp-content/uploads/P090318-1.pdf.

[281] PRA Rulebook, *Remuneration*, para 15.20(1), FCA Handbook SYSC 19D.3.61, CRD IV Directive 2013, Article 94.

[282] PRA Rulebook, *Remuneration* para 15.21; FCA Handbook SYSC 19D.3.62.

[283] PRA Rulebook, *Remuneration* para 15.23, FCA Handbook SYSC 19D.3.64.

is reasonable evidence of employee misbehaviour or material error; the firm or the relevant business unit suffers a material downturn in its financial performance; or the firm or the relevant business unit suffers a material failure of risk management.[284] These are the same conditions that can prevent unvested deferred remuneration from vesting.

The potential clawback period is 7 years from the date the variable remuneration is awarded. Where the remuneration awarded concerns a senior manager, clawback can potentially take place over a longer period. Banks can give notice to such an employee no later than the end of the 7 years, that the clawback period is extended to 10 years. The extension of the clawback period can be on the basis that the firm has commenced an investigation into facts or events that it considers could potentially lead to the application of clawback were it not for the expiry of the clawback period; or the firm has been notified by a regulatory authority (including an overseas regulatory authority) that an investigation has been commenced into facts or events that the firm considers could potentially lead to the application of clawback.[285]

It is set out clearly that up to 100 per cent of the variable remuneration in question[286] can be subject to malus or clawback. The extent of malus or clawback is essentially discretionary at the point in time of application, and it is envisaged the level of remuneration subject to malus or clawback can potentially be a contentious issue. Employees could argue that the extent of malus or clawback is not proportionate to the operation of the relevant condition. Future litigation may provide more guidance on the judicial interpretation of how malus and clawback should work.

Banks may find dis-vesting, malus, and clawback provisions useful as they help to adjust the bank's liability to pay remuneration in times of difficulties or where the circumstances no longer justify the payment to the employee concerned. However, the effectiveness of these powers may be questioned if regulation has, as earlier discussed, made variable remuneration a less significant component of an individual's remuneration. An individual's incentives may be less sensitive to the risk of malus or clawback if the malus or clawback is not going to apply to a significant amount of variable remuneration. In this manner, the bonus cap may undercut the potential incentive effects of the adjustment powers on the part of the bank. Further, the application of adjustment powers depends on the specific conditions stipulated by banks in relation to what 'material error', 'material downturn', and 'material failure in risk management' mean. Higher levels of specificity may mean less legal uncertainty in the application of malus or clawback but such could also result in narrower future applications of malus and clawback. We surmise that banks are unlikely to capitalise on their powers to introduce adjustment powers in employment contracts as they may become unattractive employers for a pool of transient talent. Further, the application of adjustment powers remains open to legal challenge, and regulatory compliance can give rise to increased legal risk for banks in this area.

---

[284] PRA Rulebook, *Remuneration* para 15.19, FCA Handbook SYSC 19D.3.64.
[285] PRA Rulebook, *Remuneration* para 15.20; FCA Handbook SYSC 19D.3.61.
[286] CRD IV Directive 2013, Article 94.

12.4.4 **Reporting requirements**

Banks are required to report their remuneration policies to the regulator in order to demonstrate compliance (or shortfalls) with the regulatory regime.[287] Further, they are asked to highlight 'high earners' and report specific matters in relation to these.[288] The EBA is also entitled to require specific remuneration information from national regulators in order to perform an annual benchmarking exercise of pay levels across the EU.[289] The information returns are intended to allow the national regulator as well as the EBA to have a bird's eye view of pay levels and their relationship with regulatory objectives such as financial stability.[290]

First, banks need to report their compliance with remuneration regulation, via the disclosure of their remuneration policies and practices. The disclosure points are highly prescribed. This may be intended to prevent banks from qualitatively 'massaging' the nature of their disclosure, and also provides a comparative template for regulators to assess remuneration policies and practices across banks. The downside of such prescription is that a box-ticking approach may be applied to information disclosure. Further, banks may enlist the help of remuneration advisers or consultants to manage their mandatory disclosure. This could have the effect of encouraging similar remuneration policies across the industry.

Box 12.12 sets out the prescribed elements of disclosure. These are based on Article 450 of the Capital Requirements Regulation 2013 and are to be reported on a yearly basis (EBA Remuneration Guidelines 2015 p77).

Next, banks have to provide specific remuneration information in respect of particularly 'high earners' to their regulator.[291] A 'high earner' is defined as any member of staff earning €1 million and above. Banks need to submit a 'high earner's report' that sets out the number of natural persons who are high earners, and their job responsibilities, the business area involved and the main elements of salary, bonus, long-term award and pension contribution.[292] The EBA further clarifies that the scope of coverage would include all banking group entities, that is, subsidiaries and branches, and only staff whose job responsibilities are predominantly in relation to the EEA.[293] The EBA

---

[287] CRR IV Regulation 2013, Article 450.

[288] CRD IV Directive Article 75, and CRR iv Regulation 2013, Article 450.

[289] CRD IV Directive 2013, Article 75.

[290] On the general explosion of mandatory transparency to the regulator after the global financial crisis and the rise of the surveillance regulatory state, see Iris H-Y Chiu, 'Transparency Regulation in Financial Markets- Moving into the Surveillance Age?' (2011) 3 *European Journal of Risk and Regulation* 303. The EBA provides guidance to regulators as to what to look out for in reviewing banks' disclosures, see EBA Remuneration Guidelines 83–6.

[291] PRA Rulebook, *Remuneration* para 18.1; Article 75, CRD IV Directive 2013, and Article 450, CRR IV Regulation 2013.   [292] Ibid.

[293] EBA, *Guidelines on the Data Collection Exercise regarding High Earners* (July 2014) at https://www.eba.europa.eu/documents/10180/757283/EBA-GL-2014-07+%28GLs+on+high+earners+data+collection%29.pdf/da42488f-09c1-4558-ae4e-6258e11b8345.

Box 12.12 Reporting requirements for remuneration policies and practices

(a) The decision-making process used for determining the remuneration policy, and the governance structure for determining the policy.

(b) Identification of staff (more detail in EBA Remuneration Guidelines 2015, p79).

(c) Information on link between pay and performance.

(d) The most important design characteristics of the remuneration system, including the criteria used for performance measurement and risk adjustment, deferral policy and vesting criteria (elaborated on in the EBA Remuneration Guidelines 2015, p80).

(e) The ratios between fixed and variable remuneration (in tabular format, per EBA Remuneration Guidelines 2015, p81), including shareholder vote details if the level of variable remuneration exceeds 100 per cent of fixed remuneration and was subject to shareholder approval.

(f) The performance criteria on which the entitlement to shares, options or variable components of remuneration is based.

(g) The main parameters and rationale for any variable component scheme and any other non-cash benefits.

(h) Aggregate quantitative information on remuneration, broken down by business area.

(i) Aggregate quantitative information on remuneration, broken down by senior management and material risk-takers in terms of fixed and variable remuneration, variable remuneration split into cash, shares and other instruments, amounts of outstanding deferred amounts split into vested and unvested portions, amounts of paid out deferred remuneration and amounts reduced by malus, new sign-on and severance payments made during the financial year, and the number of beneficiaries of such payments; the amounts of severance payments awarded during the financial year, number of beneficiaries and highest such award to a single person.

---

prescribes templates for the high earner's report and requires national regulators to submit these reports to the EBA annually.[294]

Finally national regulators are required under EU legislation to submit remuneration information to the EBA for benchmarking exercises conducted on a yearly basis.[295] Hence, the PRA requires banks to submit a yearly Remuneration Benchmarking Information Report that covers largely the information regarding fixed and variable remuneration ratios and structures in (g), (h), and (i) in Box12.12.[296] The EBA also provides templates for national regulators to return the relevant information for benchmarking, and clarifies that such information must relate to all full-time equivalent staff and pertain to all banking group entities, that is, subsidiaries and branches.[297]

---

[294] Ibid.   [295] CRD IV Directive 2013, Article 75.   [296] PRA Rulebook, *Remuneration*, para 17.
[297] EBA, *Guidelines on Remuneration Benchmarking Exercise* (July 2014) at https://www.eba.europa.eu/documents/10180/757286/EBA-GL-2014-08+%28GLs+on+remuneration+benchmarking+%29.pdf/9d87c18b-ed79-4ceb-a3f6-64928cc26065.

12.4.5 **Breach of remuneration rules**

Where banks are in breach of the remuneration rules, that is, that remuneration practices are not compliant with the regulatory regime, there are three sets of consequences. One is that the PRA can, pursuant to its general enforcement powers, fine and discipline the bank for non-compliance. Two, the Chairman of the Remuneration Committee and any senior manager responsible for developing and implementing remuneration policies (as defined under the PRA's prescribed responsibilities discussed in Chapter 11) may incur personal liability if they did not take reasonable steps to prevent the contravention. Third, a special regime is instituted that compels banks to recover sums pursuant to the contravention.[298]

Mandatory civil recovery by banks only applies if the bank or its group has total assets exceeding £50 billion, and the concerned individual's total remuneration exceeds £500,000 of which 33 per cent or more is variable remuneration.[299] Such mandatory civil recovery is on the basis that the regulators provide for the statutory voiding of remuneration contractual provisions that contravene the regulatory regime.[300]

The statutory voiding does not apply to a 'pre-existing provision', that is, a contractual provision for remuneration that was made when the bank did not satisfy the above-mentioned asset threshold or when the individual did not meet the remuneration thresholds. Even if the bank's asset threshold subsequently changes to exceed £50 billion or if the individual's remuneration amount and structure meets the threshold, the 'pre-existing' provision is not invalidated. However, if a contravening provision is made void and the application thresholds no longer apply (i.e. the bank subsequently falls below the £50 billion asset threshold or the individual's remuneration amounts and structure subsequently falls below the stipulated threshold), the bank remains liable to undertake mandatory civil recovery pursuant to the contravening provision.[301]

Banks compelled to undertake civil recovery may do so in terms of recovery of payments made or property transferred.[302] It is likely that pursuant to general law, the recovery of illegally obtained payments or property transferred can be traced into other property bought or held on constructive trust for the individual concerned.[303] This is because it is arguable that the illegally paid amounts can be regarded as held on trust

---

[298] PRA Rulebook, *Remuneration* para 16 generally; FCA Handbook SYSC 19D.3.67.
[399] PRA Rulebook, *Remuneration* paras 16.2–16.7; FCA Handbook SYSC 19D.3.67.
[300] PRA Rulebook, *Remuneration* para 16.9; FCA Handbook SYSC 19D.3.68.
[301] PRA Rulebook, *Remuneration* paras 16.10–12 and 16.15; FCA Handbook SYSC 19D.3 Annex I.
[302] PRA Rulebook, *Remuneration* para 16.14; FCA Handbook SYSC 19D.3 Annex I.
[303] *Attorney-General for Hong Kong v Reid* [1993] UKPC 36;

for the bank that made the payment.[304] Although case law in this area concerns largely bribe moneys illegally paid, a similar case can be made for remuneration illegally paid in contravention of the regulatory rules. [305] There may also be implications of third-party liability,[306] such as companies formed to hold the payments or property.

Finally, a bank is prohibited from paying variable remuneration to an employee who has received remuneration in contravention of the rules until civil recovery is made and resolved. Perhaps the PRA intends to penalise both the bank and individual concerned by abrogating the individual's entitlement to variable remuneration if payments received in contravention have not been resolved. However, this is a crude penalty as banks still have existing contractual obligations to meet. To mitigate the difficult position banks may be put in, a bank may seek an appropriately qualified, independent, and properly reasoned legal opinion to justify payment of such variable remuneration pending civil recovery.[307]

Key takeaways

- The regulatory regime for bankers' remuneration is in response to flawed remuneration structures that encouraged excessive risk-taking behaviour up to the global financial crisis of 2007–9.
- The regulatory regime is supported at the international level by the FSB, legislated in the EU and transposed by the PRA.
- The regulatory regime covers material risk-takers defined by quantitative and qualitative criteria.
- The regulatory regime provides for due governance over remuneration policies and practices.
- The regulatory regime provides for general principles in remuneration design such as longer-term performance metrics, non-financial metrics for evaluating performance, risk adjustment, and consistency with sound risk management principles and principles for compliant and ethical conduct.
- The regulatory regime provides prescriptive rules on guaranteed remuneration, the structure of variable remuneration and its ratio to fixed remuneration.
- Taxpayer bailed-out banks need to comply with stricter limits in remuneration practices.
- The regulatory regime also provides for pay adjustments through vesting adjustments, malus, and clawback.
- The PRA can compel banks to take civil recovery of remuneration paid in contravention of the remuneration regulatory rules on the basis of statutory voiding of the relevant contractual provision.

[304] Analogy with *FHR European Ventures LLP v Cedar Capital Partners LLC* [2014] UKSC 45.
[305] Ibid.
[306] *Royal Brunei Airlines Sdn Bhd v Tan* [1995] UKPC 4; *Barlow Clowes International Ltd v Eurotrust International Ltd* [2005] UKPC 37.
[307] PRA Rulebook, *Remuneration* para 16.16; FCA Handbook SYSC 19D.3 Annex I.

- Mandatory civil recovery will only be imposed on banks with a certain asset size threshold and where the amount of remuneration to be recovered exceeds a certain prescribed threshold.

Key bibliography

Legislation

Capital Requirements Directive and Regulation 2013, mentioned earlier
PRA Rulebook, *Remuneration*
FCA Handbook SYSC 19D

Guidelines and Reports

EBA, *Guidelines on Sound Remuneration Policies under Article s 74(3) and 75(2) of Directive 2013/36/EU and Disclosures under Article 450 of Regulation (EU) No 575/2013* (2015) at https://www.eba.europa.eu/documents/10180/1314839/EBA-GL-2015-22+Guidelines+on+Sound+Remuneration+Policies.pdf/1b0f3f99-f913-461a-b3e9-fa0064b1946b . Note that the UK notified that it does not intend to comply with these and this remains the position post-Brexit.
Financial Stability Forum, *FSF Principles for Sound Compensation Practices* (2009) (FSB Principles 2009) and the *Financial Stability Board's Implementing Standards* (2009) at http://www.fsb.org/what-we-do/policy-development/building-resilience-of-financial-institutions/compensation/
FSB, *Supplementary Guidance to the FSB Principles and Standards on Sound Compensation Practices* (March 2018) at http://www.fsb.org/wp-content/uploads/P090318-1.pdf

Articles

Bebchuk, LA, Cohen, A, and Spamann, H, 'The Wages of Failure: Executive Compensation at Bear Stearns and Lehman 2000–2008' (2010) 27 *Yale Journal on Regulation and Public Policy* 25
Bebchuk, LA and Spamann, H, 'Regulating Bankers' Pay' (2010) 98 *Georgetown Law Journal* 247
Thannasoulis, J, 'The Case for Intervening in Bankers' Pay' (2012) 67 *The Journal of Finance* 849

Questions

1. **Why should regulators intervene in banks' organisational matters such as internal control?**

   Answer tips *You may wish to provide a brief discussion of the weaknesses of internal control, such as risk management and compliance in the global financial crisis and bank misconduct episodes, to set the context. You should highlight the regulatory provisions for empowering internal control functions, such as making them more independent and effective, and critically discuss what they intend to achieve. You should also discuss the need for and the UK's regime in respect of a whistleblowing framework in banks. You should critically weigh the pros and cons of such a regulatory framework in terms of its ability to affect organisational behaviour and the risks of over-prescription.*

2. Will the regulation of bank corporate governance meet regulatory objectives?

> ***Answer tips*** *You may wish to provide the brief context of international attention to bank corporate governance and in the UK (e.g. Walker Review). You should discuss the key elements of corporate governance regulation and how they relate to regulatory objectives. Does Board composition reforms ensure that banks are better and more prudently managed? Do the individual Board members' criteria and their duties go far enough? Further you should critically consider whether shareholder engagement can indeed be effective towards bank prudential management or is counter-productive.*

3. 'The regulation of bankers' remuneration goes too far and unduly interferes with contractual freedom.' Do you agree?

> ***Answer tips*** *You may wish to critically discuss the scope of interference with contractual freedom in bankers' remuneration by critically discussing the key elements of regulation: the scope of persons affected, the policies for remuneration design, the prescriptions relating to composition of fixed and variable remuneration, and variable remuneration structures. You should critically consider what those elements can achieve in terms of changing individual incentives. Further consider how malus and clawback provisions interfere with contractual freedom.*

13

Crisis management and resolution

13.1 The development of a regulatory regime for crisis management and resolution

Prior to the global financial crisis of 2007–9, leading financial jurisdictions in the world did not have a special regime or *lex specialis* to deal with bank crises. Banks that face a liquidity stress may request emergency facilities from their central bank, an arrangement that is bilateral in nature.[1] However, if banks become insolvent and fail, processes of corporate insolvency would take over (such as in the case of Herstatt in 1974[2] and BCCI in 1991[3]). Corporate insolvency laws are not the most appropriate[4] in a bank crisis situation as these laws are principally focused on private interests, seeking to achieve maximum and fair realisation of assets for all creditors. Corporate insolvency would involve the liquidation of bank assets to meet liabilities, which is essentially very tricky.

Many bank assets are loans that may not have matured, and may not have a ready market value, so liquidating them and realising their value may cause significant deterioration in their value. Further bank liabilities are all financial, such as liabilities to depositors and other financial institutions that lend to them. The financial liabilities of banks are part of the money and credit creation system for the wider economy and the threat that they may not be repaid would result in severe adverse impact on the financial system and the wider economy generally. In a bank crisis, the interests of financial stability may conflict with and indeed trump the private interests of creditors. This is because the bank may provide vital services such as payments, and insolvency will bring about disruption that can be very chaotic and costly (such as in the case of Herstatt in 1974). A regulator-led and managed process of resolution could better address the needs of financial stability and preserve critical continuities for customers.

Where bank failures are rare and ad hoc in nature, there may be no need for a formal *lex specialis* to manage bank failures. However, the UK, faced with Northern Rock's near-failure in September 2007, realised that there was no adequate regulatory policy in place to (a) manage crisis-stricken banks and mitigate damaging action from the

---

[1] If the bank is publicly listed or traded, then the market may need to be notified of the receipt of emergency liquidity assistance from the central bank, and such news may itself become reputationally jeopardising for the bank.

[2] Discussed in Chapter 1, section 1.3.   [3] Discussed in Chapter 6, section 6.1.   [4] Ibid.

markets (such as a depositor run on the bank); and (b) resolve a bank in an orderly manner that avoids adverse consequences to financial stability.

13.1.1 **Northern Rock and UK Banking Act 2009**

Northern Rock, a UK building society that became a publicly listed company, was an aggressive competitor in the UK household lending market, and engaged in rapid growth of its mortgage business. It was lending up to 95 per cent of the value of properties, a highly risky strategy. It was also heavily reliant on short-term funding from the wholesale markets[5] as it did not have a large enough deposit base to provide the level of funding needed for its ambitious loan targets. Its risky business model was highlighted to the then Financial Services Authority (FSA), but the Authority took little action to supervise Northern Rock closely. This was despite Northern Rock's profit warning after its lending book started to experience defaults, and when its capital requirement fell below the regulatory threshold.[6] On 14 September 2007, Northern Rock requested emergency liquidity facilities from the Bank of England, which was only acceded to 3 days later. In the meantime, the share price of Northern Rock plummeted and depositors rushed to withdraw their deposits from the bank. Failing to stem the run on the bank, the government stepped in to guarantee all deposits in order to calm the panic, exposing one of the fault lines in bank regulation, which is an inadequate deposit guarantee system to prevent bank runs.[7] It then dawned on the government that there was a need to take over the coordination of Northern Rock's crisis management in order to prevent further adverse market reaction or knock-on effects upon other lenders.[8] Parts of Northern Rock's business were sold to JP Morgan Chase in order to repay the Bank of England's loan. However, in February 2008 the government ultimately raised the national debt and nationalised significant parts of Northern Rock that were not sufficiently viable for sale. Northern Rock was run by the government in a manner designed to stabilise it and preserve its assets, and ultimately sold at a loss to Virgin Money in 2011.[9]

The Northern Rock episode made UK policymakers realise that there was a need for a *lex specialis* for resolving crisis-stricken banks. This is because there are immense financial system stability implications from a crisis-stricken bank. Bank assets and liabilities can be opaque and hard to value, and such information asymmetry causes market panic at the whiff of a possible bank crisis. Bank creditors and depositors could bring collective pressure to bear, exacerbating a bank's situation, while market sentiment may

---

[5] Discussed under 'shadow banking' in Chapter 1, section 1.2.

[6] FSA, 'The Supervision of Northern Rock: A lessons learned review' (March 2008) http://www.fsa.gov.uk/pubs/other/nr_report.pdf.   [7] This issue is addressed in section 13.3.

[8] 'The Rise and Fall of Northern Rock', *The Telegraph* (14 August 2014) at http://www.telegraph.co.uk/finance/newsbysector/banksandfinance/11032772/The-rise-and-fall-of-Northern-Rock.html.

[9] See 'Northern Rock sold to Virgin Money' BBC News (17 November 2011) http://www.bbc.co.uk/news/business-15769886.

plummet, causing further implications such as rating downgrades, triggering more panic reaction from counterparties. Such financial stability implications are far more pronounced for banks than companies in other sectors, hence there is a strong case for regulatory governance to step in for an orderly management of the situation.[10]

In 2008, as other UK banks became embroiled in the global financial crisis, the UK Houses of Parliament passed the Banking Act 2009, which provided a statutory framework for resolving banks. This framework was important in giving designated authorities, that is, the then-FSA, Bank of England, and the Treasury extensive powers to manage and coordinate in bank crisis management and resolution, with certain safeguards for creditors', shareholders' and third-party rights. The UK Banking Act 2009 became the pioneering piece of legislation on bank crisis management and resolution followed by the US Dodd–Frank Act 2010, which gave the Federal Deposit Insurance Corporation extensive powers to resolve and liquidate banks. The UK's template fed into international and European developments so that bank crisis management and resolution frameworks became internationally harmonised to some extent. This convergence also helps to facilitate better cross-border coordination in resolving global banks that have multi-jurisdictional footprint.

The substantive law on crisis management and resolution will be discussed in detail shortly. In particular, the UK Banking Act 2009 has evolved from a domestic piece of legislation to be convergent with the European Bank Recovery and Resolution Directive 2014. These are convergent to a large extent with international standards such as the Financial Stability Board's (FSB) work in this area, to which we will now turn.

13.1.2 International and European harmonisation of crisis management and resolution

During the 2007–9 global financial crisis, the failure of a number of international banks and cross-border banking groups exposed the fault lines in a global financial system that lacked a systematic and coordinated approach to resolving bank failures and stemming adverse impacts on financial stability.

The failure of US investment bank Lehman Brothers is a case in point. Lehman Brothers had an extensive global footprint, operating with many branches worldwide. The parent company in the US had, however, been hiding severe cash flow problems[11] that had built up over several years due to Lehman's aggressive growth and investment in highly risky and illiquid assets such as commercial property, hedge funds and securitised assets. The investment bank was also highly leveraged (had borrowed excessively) and had been making steady losses, culminating in a loss announcement on

---

[10] Rosa Lastra, 'Northern Rock and Banking Law Reform in the UK' in Franco Bruni and David T Llewellyn (eds), *The Failure Of Northern Rock: A Multi-Dimensional Case Study* (2009) at 131 at www.suerf.org/download/studies/study20091.pdf.

[11] Amirsaleh Azadinamin, 'The Bankruptcy of Lehman Brothers: Causes of Failure & Recommendations Going Forward' (2012) at http://ssrn.com/abstract=2016892.

10 September 2008, which was followed by a severe stock price decline. By 13 September 2008, the Federal Reserve Bank of New York was in talks with Lehman about resolving its precarious state but there emerged no ready buyer to rescue Lehman. Lehman filed for bankruptcy on 15 September 2008 and thereafter a wave of litigation in the US and in many other jurisdictions,[12] including London, commenced as the bank's customers, creditors and other counterparties scrambled to recover their monies or assets. The liquidation and litigation processes were drawn out over 8 years before Lehman Brothers International (Europe) was wound down and all creditors paid. This experience highlights the difficulties in relying on corporate insolvency laws to resolve a failed bank. Although the courts resolved complex issues in the enforcement of contesting private rights, the liquidation of Lehman was costly and arguably relatively inefficient. Regulators therefore prefer to look into a more coordinated form of resolution between authorities at the international level if a global bank fails.

At the EU level, policymakers came to realise that the Internal Market in banking needed to be supported by a crisis resolution framework for cross-border banking. During the global financial crisis, several Icelandic banks that had extensive deposit-taking business in the UK, Germany, and the Netherlands failed as a result of severe losses from high leverage (their excessive levels of borrowing) and holdings of 'toxic' securitised assets.[13] Due to a lack of a pan-European framework for resolving banks, national regulators did not work with each other but instead took unilateral actions to protect their own depositors.[14] The Icelandic authorities did not give undertakings that they would make good their obligations to protect all depositors under the Deposit Guarantee Directive. Hence, the UK seized all the available assets of the banks in the UK utilising terror laws, a highly individualistic solution.[15] The saga was a setback for the Internal Market and the respect for EU law.[16] The resolution of Fortis by the Netherlands, Belgium, and Luxembourg was also not straightforward although a memorandum of understanding had been in place between the Benelux countries pre-crisis. The resolution of Fortis initially proceeded in a coordinated manner, but the Netherlands was the first to move away from a multilateral resolution of Fortis and nationalised the Dutch operations of Fortis. The unilateral action started by the Dutch was due to insufficient commitment to a multilateral solution and the perceived lower cost of national resolution. Belgium and Luxembourg then arranged for the rest of Fortis operations in their respective countries to be sold to the BNP Paribas Group.

---

[12] Anna Cox, 'The Liquidation of Lehman Brothers', speech at *Bank Resolution Regimes: What Next?* University College London, London, 9 November 2016.

[13] Names such as Kaupthing SF and Icesave, the online bank outfit of Landsbanki.

[14] Zdenek Kudrna, 'Cross-Border Resolution of Failed Banks in the European Union after the Crisis: Business as Usual' (2012) 50 *Journal of Common Market Studies* 283.

[15] Michael Waibel, 'Iceland's Financial Crisis—Quo Vadis International Law' (2010) 14 ASIL Insight at http://www.asil.org/insights100301.cfm.

[16] Eyvindur G. Gunnarsson, 'The Icelandic Regulatory Response to the Financial Crisis' (2011) *European Business Organisation Law Review* 2.

Policymakers in the EU and international bodies perceived the need to put in place legal frameworks for coordinated efforts. First, the FSB undertook to introduce a set of international best practices for harmonising national resolution processes and to promote cross-border coordination in resolution processes. The Board introduced the ***Key Attributes of Effective Resolution Regimes*** in 2011,[17] in order to encourage a systematic and internationally convergent approach towards resolution, so that resolution could be timely and efficient, any disruptions to services and to the financial system may be mitigated, and that international cooperation can be promoted. The Key Attributes are reflected in the EU regulatory initiatives the Bank Recovery and Resolution Directive 2014 and Single Resolution Mechanism Regulation 2015.[18]

13.1.2.1 The *Key Attributes of Effective Resolution Regimes*

The 2011 Key Attributes, updated in 2014, first require states to establish a resolution authority that can carry out resolution processes with the overall objective of financial stability in mind. Such authorities need to be operationally independent from government but be adequately empowered and resourced. The Attributes set out the key powers for such an authority.[19] The common adoption of an independent resolution authority with similar key powers is crucial to facilitating globally consistent approaches and international coordination, as resolution processes can then be framed within similar institutional frameworks even if they are established by different states.

Resolution authorities should oversee banks in planning for resolution in 'normal times', so that banks can be prepared for crises. Resolution authorities should require banks to first prepare plans for 'recovery', that is, to overcome a stressful onset in order to return to normal. Second, they should require banks to make plans for appropriate 'resolution', which would involve more intrusive action to deal with the bank and mitigate financial stability implications, if the bank cannot recover. These plans are discussed in detail in section 13.2. Besides the benefit of early planning, these plans contain useful information about the bank's business, structures, and interdependencies so that the bank and regulators can become better aware of how they can provide for contingencies and resolve a bank effectively if that is called for.[20] Resolution authorities should regularly assess the ease of resolving a bank based on the information provided in their plans.[21]

In the event of resolution, resolution authorities should be able to carry out a similar set of resolution powers including effecting sales of the bank or parts of its business,

---

[17] http://www.fsb.org/wp-content/uploads/r_111104cc.pdf updated in 2014.

[18] These are discussed in section 13.3, but also see Chapter 7, section 7.3 for the Single Resolution Mechanism.

[19] Key Attribute 1 of the 2014 version at http://www.fsb.org/what-we-do/policy-development/effective-reso-lution-regimes-and-policies/key-attributes-of-effective-resolution-regimes-for-financial-institutions/#1scope.

[20] Key Attribute 11 of the 2014 version at http://www.fsb.org/what-we-do/policy-development/effective-resolution-regimes-and-policies/key-attributes-of-effective-resolution-regimes-for-financial-institutions/#1scope.

[21] Key Attribute 10 of the 2014 version at http://www.fsb.org/what-we-do/policy-development/effective-resolution-regimes-and-policies/key-attributes-of-effective-resolution-regimes-for-financial-institutions/#1scope.

imposing on certain creditors and shareholders to absorb losses (***bail-in*** as discussed in section 13.3) and creating temporary institutions to take over bank management in order to stabilise the bank for future action—such as a ***bridge institution***, discussed in section 13.3. In order to give effect to any of the above resolution strategies, a resolution authority needs extensive powers such as to: remove senior management and appoint administrators, transfer assets and liabilities, terminate or vary contracts, stay termination rights of private contracting parties and enjoy immunity and protection in the exercise of its powers.[22] The Key Attributes also provide that each jurisdiction should ensure that contractual provisions such as set-off, netting, collateral, and early contractual termination, as well as legal regimes such as client money protection should be clear and not impede effective resolution.[23] These extensive powers seek to mitigate the disruption that any pursuit of individual contractual or property rights may entail. In this manner, the resolution regime for banks prioritises collective objectives such as financial stability and necessarily involves trade-offs in the enforcement of individual rights. These dilemmas are fleshed out in section 13.3. Private parties are, however, assured that overall, they would be no worse off than under the application of corporate insolvency laws. Resolution authorities should also provide for affected parties in the resolution process to bring claims for compensation.[24]

The Key Attributes also address the situation of poor international coordination in cross-border resolution, and attempt to dissuade national authorities from unilateral or competitive actions. The Attributes encourage early development of cooperation and trust between national authorities. National authorities should in 'normal times' form groups to supervise globally systemically important banks and put in place crisis management groups and the procedures to be applied in order to coordinate cross-border resolution.[25] In order to improve the prospects of effective and smooth cross-border resolution, resolution authorities are also asked to put in place laws that respect and recognise foreign resolution measures and to assist each other by sharing information.[26]

Finally, resolution authorities are required to put in place funding arrangements in anticipation of the expenditures required for resolution. Even without nationalising a bank, centrally managed resolution may be costly and it is warranted to plan ahead as to how resolution should be financed. The industry should contribute to such cost on

---

[22] See Key Attributes 2 and 3 of the 2014 version at http://www.fsb.org/what-we-do/policy-development/effective-resolution-regimes-and-policies/key-attributes-of-effective-resolution-regimes-for-financial-institutions/#1scope.

[23] Key Attribute 4 of the 2014 version, at http://www.fsb.org/what-we-do/policy-development/effective-resolution-regimes-and-policies/key-attributes-of-effective-resolution-regimes-for-financial-institutions/#1scope.

[24] Key Attribute 5 of the 2014 version, at http://www.fsb.org/what-we-do/policy-development/effective-resolution-regimes-and-policies/key-attributes-of-effective-resolution-regimes-for-financial-institutions/#1scope.

[25] Key Attributes 8 and 9 of the 2014 version at http://www.fsb.org/what-we-do/policy-development/effective-resolution-regimes-and-policies/key-attributes-of-effective-resolution-regimes-for-financial-institutions/#1scope.

[26] Key Attribute 7 of the 2014 version, at http://www.fsb.org/what-we-do/policy-development/effective-resolution-regimes-and-policies/key-attributes-of-effective-resolution-regimes-for-financial-institutions/#1scope.

an *ex ante* or *ex post* basis, such as via privately financed deposit guarantee schemes and resolution funds.[27]

The Key Attributes are intended to form the basis for substantive law to be adopted in states, and the FSB has put in place a mechanism to chart the progress of international convergence on the basis of the Key Attributes.[28] The Key Attributes are indeed the foundational template for the EU's Bank Recovery and Resolution Directive 2014,[29] which establishes for all member states a harmonised framework for establishing national resolution authorities, providing for resolution powers and intra-European coordination for the resolution of cross-border banks. The UK has transposed the Directive by amending the Banking Act 2009 and issuing relevant secondary legislation.

Besides the establishment of standards for bank crisis management and resolution in the Key Attributes, there is substantial work at the international level to facilitate better *ex ante* and *ex post* coordination of bank crisis management and resolution involving cross-border banks. These are fleshed out in section 13.4.

13.1.2.2 Bank Recovery and Resolution Directive 2014

There was broad policy consensus to adopt the Bank Recovery and Resolution Directive 2014[30] (BRRD 2014) at the EU level. The global financial crisis resulted in many EU member states using taxpayers' receipts to bail-out stricken banks,[31] and EU policymakers perceived such actions as ad hoc and unprincipled, likely to entail moral hazard. State bailouts are seen to promote a form of 'lemon socialism'.[32] 'Lemon socialism' is a term that refers to the phenomenon of governmental nationalisation or **bail-out** of weak enterprises that should have been allowed to fail in the natural working of market capitalist forces. The adverse effects of 'lemon socialism' are social cost in supporting weak and uncompetitive enterprises and the consequent distortions in the competitive

---

[27] Key Attribute 6 of the 2014 version, at http://www.fsb.org/what-we-do/policy-development/effective-resolution-regimes-and-policies/key-attributes-of-effective-resolution-regimes-for-financial-institutions/#1scope.

[28] FSB, *Key Attributes Assessment Methodology for the Banking Sector* (19 Oct 2016) at http://www.fsb.org/2016/10/fsb-publishes-methodology-for-assessing-the-implementation-of-the-key-attributes-of-effective-resolution-regimes-in-the-banking-sector/, which provides the criteria and methodology for self and third-party assessment with regard to compliance with the Key Attributes.

[29] European Commission's proposal to introduce the Bank Recovery and Resolution Directive, 2012, at http://eur-lex.europa.eu/legal-content/EN/TXT/?uri=CELEX:52012PC0280.

[30] Directive 2014/59/EU of the European Parliament and of the Council of 15 May 2014 establishing a framework for the recovery and resolution of credit institutions and investment firms and amending Council Directive 82/891/EEC, and Directives 2001/24/EC, 2002/47/EC, 2004/25/EC, 2005/56/EC, 2007/36/EC, 2011/35/EU, 2012/30/EU and 2013/36/EU, and Regulations (EU) No 1093/2010 and (EU) No 648/2012, of the European Parliament and of the Council.

[31] In the UK, taxpayers' money was used to bail out Northern Rock, the Royal Bank of Scotland and then Lloyd's after its purchase of stricken Halifax Bank of Scotland. The German government rescued Hypo Real Estate in an amount of close to €50 billion, the Netherlands nationalised the Dutch operations of Fortis as discussed above. Ireland bailed out its banks up to €85 billion, including taking a loan from the IMF. Even Switzerland bailed out UBS in 2008.

[32] See, for example, Robert Reich, 'How America Embraced Lemon Socialism' (23 January 2009) at http://robertreich.org/post/257310131.

Box 13.1 Coverage of the BRRD 2014

- Appointment of national resolution authority
- Recovery planning
- Resolution planning
- Early Intervention measures
- Resolution objectives, tools, and powers to support the resolution tools
- Safeguards for affected shareholders, creditors and third parties
- Procedures/tools for resolution
- Accountability/challenge of resolution authority's exercise of powers
- Coordination of member state resolution authorities within the EU
- Relations with third-country resolution authorities and effects of third-country resolutions
- Establishment of financing arrangements in each member state to fund resolution, including use of the deposit guarantee schemes

---

landscape. Further, state bailouts are often financed by national debt, and the long-term effects of fiscal cost drag the economy into the doldrums for at least five to seven years. Ireland for example had to finance part of its state bail-out using an International Monetary Fund (IMF) loan and was obliged to impose terms of austerity that affected citizens' welfare adversely in the ensuing years. State bailouts generally leave a bad impression of moral hazard as the financial sector would seem insulated from learning its lessons.[33]

The BRRD 2014 deals with the aspects of resolution shown in Box 13.1, to be substantively fleshed out in section 13.2.

The BRRD 2014 has already to an extent been addressed by the UK's antecedent resolution regime in the Banking Act 2009. However, amendments to the Act were made in 2012 to extend its scope to financial institutions beyond banks. In 2014, the UK Bank Recovery and Resolution Order 2014 implemented the BRRD 2014 into the Banking Act 2009.

13.1.2.3 **EU Single Resolution Mechanism**

The EU has arguably taken the international convergence of resolution frameworks to a new level of integration, in the form of the Single Resolution Mechanism (SRM) introduced in 2014. The SRM is a pan-European resolution authority that will administer resolution-related matters such as recovery and resolution planning, and the making and implementation of resolution decisions. The SRM applies only to banks subject to the Single Supervisory Mechanism (SSM) discussed in Chapter 7, section 7.3. The SRM

---

[33] Niall Ferguson, 'The Rule of Law and its Enemies' (BBC Reith Lectures, London, June–July 2012) part 2.

is established by Regulation[34] and its objectives, scope, powers, and tools are convergent with the BRRD 2014. The SRM sits above national authorities and is in a position to implement an integrated and consistent resolution framework for all euro-area banks subject to the SSM.

The SSM, as discussed in Chapter 7, has been established in order to de-link weak sovereigns from banks, in order to prevent a prolonged and deep banking crisis in the EU. Many euro-area banks lend extensively to their national governments and the sovereign-bank link proved to be a weak link in the aftermath of the global financial crisis. In the wake of many bank failures during that time, markets have become much more sensitive to banks' health and many European banks came under critical scrutiny for their heavy lending to European sovereigns who are already heavily in debt and put under further stress after the crisis. In particular, fiscally flagrant sovereigns are supported by their national banks such as in Greece, Cyprus, Portugal, Italy, and Spain. Even Western European banks such as German, Dutch, UK and French banks have tremendous exposure to most European sovereigns. In 2013, two Cyprus banks failed: the Bank of Cyprus and Cyprus Popular Bank. Both held a tremendous amount of Greek sovereign debt, which lost almost three-quarters of its value when Greek sovereign debt was written down in a deal in 2011 after the Greek government neared default. In attempting to resolve the crisis, the Cypriot authorities mishandled the crisis. The authorities intended to apply 'bail-in' as a resolution tool, that is, require private parties to absorb their banks' losses, but this policy would apply indiscriminately to all depositors, including those protected by the national deposit guarantee scheme. This resulted in riots and public outcry forcing the Cypriot government to seek alternative methods of resolution, with input and advice from the IMF and European Central Bank (ECB). The Cypriot government ultimately nationalised Bank of Cyprus and wound down Popular Bank, protecting all guaranteed deposits but forcing all other junior creditors to absorb losses, a majority of which were wealthy depositors who had unguaranteed deposits. This episode preceded the introduction of the SSM and showed acutely the needs in the European financial sector for some form of predictability and consistency in bank crisis management and resolution.

In 2014, the ECB commenced taking on the pan-European supervisory role of micro-prudential compliance by euro-area banks, in its independently constituted capacity of the SSM.[35] Troeger,[36] however, argues that the SSM has come about in order

---

[34] Regulation (EU) No 806/2014 of the European Parliament and of the Council of 15 July 2014 establishing uniform rules and a uniform procedure for the resolution of credit institutions and certain investment firms in the framework of a Single Resolution Mechanism and a Single Resolution Fund and amending Regulation (EU) No 1093/2010.

[35] Guido Ferranini and Luigi Chiarella, 'Common Banking Supervision in the Eurozone: Strengths and Weaknesses' (2013) at http://ssrn.com/abstract_id=2309897.

[36] Tobias H Troeger, 'The Single Supervisory Mechanism—Panacea or Quack Banking Regulation?' (2013) at http://ssrn.com/abstract=2311353.

to institute oversight and discipline over the weakest banks. The SSM and SRM seem to be fire-fighting measures rather than representing the development of coherent regulatory ideology. Bank regulation reforms are nevertheless often in response to crises and scandals (e.g. see discussion in Chapters 6 and 7) and this appears to be an inevitable path for the development of bank regulation.

The SRM is arguably a 'necessary' element that completes the SSM[37] as the same rationale for delinking banks and sovereigns applies in resolution measures. If it is appropriate to remove national micro-prudential supervision powers to the European level in order to strengthen banks' credibility, then national authorities should not be responsible for exercising resolution powers or this may compromise the purpose of pan-European supervision. However, the SRM should be independent of the SSM or else the ECB would have too much power or may become involved in politically charged issues in resolving any particular member state's bank. Hence, the SRM is established to be a mechanism essentially controlled by and accountable to the European Commission and Parliament. Commentators have urged the importance of coordination and cooperation between these institutions in order to secure coherent but balanced decision-making in resolution decisions.[38]

The SRM is directed by a Board (SRB), which is an independent agency with separate legal personality independent of the ECB.[39] The SRB has the responsibility for drafting resolution plans, adopting early intervention measures imposed under the SSM, adopting resolution decisions, and carrying out the administration of resolution.[40] The SRB comprises a Chair, Vice-Chair, and four other full-time members. These members are appointed by the Parliament based on a shortlist recommended by the Commission and the representatives of the national resolution authorities of participating member states.[41] At the plenary[42] and executive sessions of the SRB, a representative each of the ECB and Commission may be in attendance as permanent observers.[43] The SRB works in close cooperation with national resolution authorities,[44] but decision-making involves another set of institutions that will be discussed here.

[37] Eilis Ferran, 'European Banking Union: Imperfect but it can Work' (2014) at http://ssrn.com/abstract=2426247; Kern Alexander, 'Bank Resolution and Recovery in the EU: Enhancing Banking Union?' (2013) 14 ERA Forum 81; Daniel Gros and Dirk Schoenmaker, 'European Deposit Insurance and Resolution in Banking Union' (2014) 52 *JCMS CHK*.

[38] See Eddy Wymeersch, 'Banking Union: Aspects of the Single Supervisory Mechanism and the Single Resolution Mechanism Compared' (2015) at https://papers.ssrn.com/sol3/papers.cfm?abstract_id=2599502; Iris H-Y Chiu, 'Power and Accountability in the EU Financial Regulatory Architecture: Examining Inter-agency Relations, Agency Independence and Accountability' (2015) *European Journal of Legal Studies* 68.

[39] SRM Regulation, Article 42.　　[40] SRM Regulation, Article 7.

[41] SRM Regulation, Articles 43 and 53.

[42] The plenary sessions are annual in nature and deal with important issues such as adoption of work programme and budget, SRM Regulation, Articles 46–8. The executive sessions are relevant to the Chair, Vice-Chair and four full-time members only and deal with the executive management of the Board's tasks including preparatory work for the plenary sessions, SRM Regulation, Articles 51–2.

[43] SRM Regulation, Article 43.　　[44] SRM Regulation, Article 31.

The SRB carries out dialogue with the ECB and national regulators in order to draw up resolution plans for the banks subject to the SSM,[45] and determines if a bank faces impediments to resolvability.[46] The resolution plans adopted by the SRB are implemented by the SSM and banks' impediments to resolvability have to be accordingly addressed.

The SRB is responsible for proposing a resolution decision for a bank, in accordance with the objectives and principles governing resolution.[47] However, decisions are made at a political level. The SRB notifies the Commission,[48] which is responsible for adopting of the resolution decision within 24 hours. The Commission then notifies the Council for joint adoption of the decision in 12 hours from the Commission notification.[49] Political control of resolution decisions may be necessary as resolution of banks is a matter of key national interest in many bank-based economies in the EU.[50] The SRB has exclusive power to determine if the Single Resolution Fund[51] needs to be called upon to financially assist a bank in crisis. This power is concurrently checked by the Commission, which assesses the appropriateness of state aid if the Fund should be used.[52] Dermine[53] argues that the perception of financial strength in EU-level institutions is crucial to maintaining positive market perceptions in a bank crisis.

The SRM represents an institutionally integrated and pan-European approach to bank resolution, which is especially useful for cross-border bank resolutions. Indeed, the EBA supports the SRB's role by instituting a resolution database to communicate all national resolution decisions in order to facilitate learning and 'soft' convergence.[54]

However, in bank crises, many contesting interests would emerge that need to be both politically and technocratically resolved between member states and EU institutions. Although the legal framework places the SRB at the forefront of deciding and implementing bank resolution, experience is that bank resolution is deeply entangled with national interests and national resolution authorities remain very powerful and are not 'subjects' of the SRB. This is not unexpected as the fate of a bank is an issue close to the hearts of national politicians and citizenry.

The first SRM decision was made on 28 November 2017 concerning Spanish bank Banco Popular, which had suffered extensive losses after a decade of extending risky

[45] SRM Regulation, Article 8.   [46] SRM Regulation, Article 10.
[47] SRM Regulation, Articles 14 and 15.   [48] SRM Regulation, Article 18.   [49] Ibid.
[50] This means many European economies rely on banks as being the main source of credit creation or support or economic activities.
[51] Funding mechanisms for resolution will be discussed in the chapter shortly.
[52] SRM Regulation, Article 19.
[53] Jean Dermine, 'The Single Resolution Mechanism in the European Union: Good Intentions and Unintended Evil' (2016) at https://papers.ssrn.com/sol3/papers.cfm?abstract_id=2838793.
[54] See https://www.eba.europa.eu/regulation-and-policy/recovery-and-resolution/notifications-on-resolution-cases-and-use-of-dgs-funds.

home loans during the Spanish property bubble just prior to the global financial crisis. After Deloitte had been commissioned to value Popular's assets at negative €2 billion, the ECB announced on 7 June 2017 that Popular was 'failing or likely to fail', triggering the resolution threshold provided in the Bank Recovery and Resolution Directive (see section 13.3). On the following day the SRB adopted a resolution decision to transfer Popular to Santander for 1 euro, and effectively made all subordinated creditors absorb the bank's losses (bail-in, see section 13.3). In order for these decisions to have been made by the ECB and SRB in quick succession, extensive background liaison had taken place between the Spanish regulator, the ECB, SRB and Santander the intended purchaser. Although the SRM seems to be a centralised platform intended to support the de-linking of European banks from their governments, the SRB's actions fundamentally need support from both European and national institutions. Indeed, the lack of action on the part of the SRB in a number of other bank failures in member states indicates the challenges for it to take leadership in bank resolution.

The SRB clarifies that it does not need to act if the institution is not systemically important and can be dealt with by national resolution authorities.[55] This has been the case with the failure of Venetian banks Veneto Banca and Banca Popolare di Vicenza, which have been wound up by the Italian resolution authority in mid-2017, episodes involving the government sustaining the losses of the banks' bad debts. The failure of the Latvian Bank ABLV in February 2018 was also handled by the national resolution authority, not the SRB for the same reason. In both cases, however, the ECB made the determination that the banks were 'failing or likely to fail' and they were wound up by national resolution authorities.

The near-failure of Italian bank Monte Dei Paschi, however, highlights the challenges the SRB faces in rebalancing the stranglehold national authorities have over bank resolution. The bank is the third-largest in Italy and the world's oldest bank but has been suffering losses from non-performing loans on its balance sheet. The ECB and Italian authorities have clashed openly on their preferred ways ahead for Monte Dei Paschi as the latter wish to avoid having the ECB declare the bank as 'failing or likely to fail' but the former lacks confidence in the capital-raising measures that the Italian authorities support.[56] The Italian authorities do not wish to have to resolve the bank as the resolution implications are politically unappealing. The bank's shareholders and creditors would have to absorb the bank's losses and many of these are retail investors. After protracted negotiations, the Commission agreed to allow the Italian government to bail the bank out at over €5 billion, taking an excess of 68 per cent equity stake in the

---

[55] 'The SRB will not take resolution action in relation to Banca Popolare di Vicenza and Veneto Banca', press release 23 June 2017 at https://srb.europa.eu/en/node/341; 'The Single Resolution Board does not take resolution action in relation to ABLV Bank, AS and its subsidiary ABLV Bank Luxembourg S.A.', press release 24 February 2018 at https://srb.europa.eu/en/node/495.

[56] 'The Problem with the Monte Dei Paschi Problem is That it Doesn't Have a Solution—not a good one', *Forbes.com* on 10 December 2016.

bank.[57] The bank was significantly restructured under majority government ownership and raised new capital in early 2018.[58] This episode highlights the inevitable entanglement between the ECB, SRB, and national regulators in bank crisis management and resolution, and we anticipate continuing implementational challenges to the intended institutional framework laid down in EU legislation enshrining the leadership of the SSM and SRB.[59]

In sum, although EU legislation has achieved a substantive regulatory framework and institutional architecture for implementing bank crisis management and resolution, there are many difficulties in practice. There are disagreements between institutions, especially between member state institutions and European level institutions, as discussed earlier, and resolution actions face legal challenges by affected private parties. Banco Popular's creditors have raised legal challenges against the SRB especially in respect of the valuation report that formed the basis of the SRB's recommendation, and the perceived failure to pursue other resolution strategies. The shareholders of the failed Latvian bank ABLV have also asked the ECJ to rule on the legality of the ECB's decision on its meeting the threshold of 'failing or likely to fail'. The efforts at making cross-border bank crisis management and resolution clear, predictable, and efficient do not go unopposed. It remains to be seen if they offer superior solutions to seemingly 'messy' corporate insolvency proceedings.

 Key takeaways

- The lack of a coherent policy toolkit to deal with bank failures and cross-border bank failure implications in the 2007–9 global financial crisis sets the context for policy reform in bank crisis management and resolution.

- The UK introduced the pioneering piece of legislation on bank resolution followed by international standards introduced by the FSB. The EU introduced the Bank Recovery and Resolution Directive 2014 based on the FSB's Key Attributes for Effective Resolution Regimes.

- The EU's unique problems of weak sovereigns linked to weak banks prompted major policy overhaul in centralising the micro-prudential supervision of euro-area banks under the ECB. This is completed by a centralised resolution mechanism for the banks subject to ECB supervision, the SRM.

- Difficulties in implementing cross-border and integrated bank resolution at the EU level have been experienced and highlight the unique challenges in this area.

---

[57] 'EU Approves Monte dei Paschi Bailout—as it had to, really' *Forbes.com* 4 July 2017.

[58] 'Monte dei Paschi plots first bond deal since government rescue', *Financial Times* (4 January 2018).

[59] It has been argued that a Treaty basis is needed to strengthen the centralisation of powers in the SRM, see Kern Alexander, 'European Banking Union: a Legal and Institutional Analysis of the Single Supervisory Mechanism and the Single Resolution Mechanism' (2015) *European Law Review* 154.

Key bibliography

Legislation

UK Banking Act 2009

UK Bank Recovery and Resolution Order 2014

Directive 2014/59/EU of the European Parliament and of the Council of 15 May 2014 establishing a framework for the recovery and resolution of credit institutions and investment firms and amending Council Directive 82/891/EEC, and Directives 2001/24/EC, 2002/47/EC, 2004/25/EC, 2005/56/EC, 2007/36/EC, 2011/35/EU, 2012/30/EU and 2013/36/EU, and Regulations (EU) No 1093/2010 and (EU) No 648/2012, of the European Parliament and of the Council

Regulation (EU) No 806/2014 of the European Parliament and of the Council of 15 July 2014 establishing uniform rules and a uniform procedure for the resolution of credit institutions and certain investment firms in the framework of a Single Resolution Mechanism and a Single Resolution Fund and amending Regulation (EU) No 1093/2010

Reports and Recommendations

FSB, *Key Attributes of Effective Resolution Regimes* (2011) at http://www.fsb.org/wp-content/uploads/r_111104cc.pdf updated in 2014 at http://www.fsb.org/what-we-do/policy-development/effective-resolution-regimes-and-policies/key-attributes-of-effective-resolution-regimes-for-financial-institutions/#1scope

Additional Reading

Alexander, K, 'Bank Resolution and Recovery in the EU: Enhancing Banking Union?' (2013) 14 *ERA Forum* 81

Chiu, IH-Y., 'Power and Accountability in the EU Financial Regulatory Architecture: Examining Inter-agency Relations, Agency Independence and Accountability' (2015) *European Journal of Legal Studies* 68.

Lastra, R, 'Northern Rock and Banking Law Reform in the UK' in Franco Bruni and David T Llewellyn (eds), *The Failure Of Northern Rock: A Multi-Dimensional Case Study* (2009) at 131 at www.suerf.org/download/studies/study20091.pdf

Wymeersch, E, 'Banking Union: Aspects of the Single Supervisory Mechanism and the Single Resolution Mechanism Compared' (2015) at https://papers.ssrn.com/sol3/papers.cfm?abstract_id=2599502

13.2 Crisis prevention, management, and resolution

The regime for bank crisis management and resolution in the UK is found in the Bank Recovery and Resolution Order 2016 (amending the Banking Act 2009) and the PRA Rulebook, transposing the European Bank Recovery and Resolution Directive 2014. This regime is convergent with the international standards in the *Key Attributes*, covering crisis prevention, which refers to advance planning by banks, early intervention by resolution authorities short of resolution, the processes and powers in resolution, safeguards and accountability in resolution and funding for resolution. Section 13.3 deals specifically with cross-border resolution.

In the UK, the Bank of England, the PRA, and the Treasury are all involved in bank resolution at different points, as we shall see shortly. However, the Bank is the designated resolution authority.[60]

First, we turn to *crisis prevention measures* that require banks to plan ahead as to how they would deal with challenging situations. The key crisis prevention measure is recovery planning. Banks are also asked to plan for resolution, and such plans inevitably feed into recovery planning too.

13.2.1 Recovery plans

Financial institutions are required to submit recovery plans to their resolution authorities. This applies to parent institutions of a financial group, subsidiaries of banks and investment firms authorised in the European Economic Area, and any significant branches of EEA banks in a host member state. Recovery plans contain 'measures to be taken by the institution to restore its financial position following a significant deterioration of its financial situation'.[61] Where a group of financial institutions is concerned, a group recovery plan may be drawn up (which would be assessed differently from individual institutions, as will be discussed below).[62] The purpose of the recovery plan, defined in UK legislation is: 'to achieve the stabilisation of the group as a whole, or any institution within the group, where the group or institution is in a situation of financial stress, in order to address or remove the causes of the financial stress and restore the financial position of the group or the institution'.[63]

The recovery plan should be reviewed annually, and updates must be filed with the resolution authority.[64] In the UK, the Bank has the power to exempt or modify the application of this obligation to smaller firms where not all of the information prescribed needs to be submitted.[65]

13.2.1.1 Recovery plan indicators

The recovery plan is intended to stimulate forward-looking thinking by banks to plan for contingencies of stress and challenges ahead. The PRA envisages that banks should plan for scenarios of severe macroeconomic and financial stress that are firm-specific as well as system wide.[66] In recovery plans, banks need to specify the recovery triggers that bring in the operation of the plan. These need to be clear and predictable, so that

---

[60] Article 4, Bank Recovery and Resolution Order (No 2) 2014 at http://www.legislation.gov.uk/uksi/2014/3348/pdfs/uksi_20143348_en.pdf.

[61] Article 5, BRRD 2014; PRA Rulebook, *Recovery Plans* paras 2 and 3.

[62] Article 7, BRRD 2014; PRA Rulebook, *Recovery Plans* para 3.

[63] Section 192JB(f)(1A), Bank Recovery and Resolution Order 2014, amending the Financial Services and Markets Act 2000.

[64] Para 4, PRA Rulebook, *Recovery Plans*, para 33, Bank Recovery and Resolution Order No 2, 2014 at http://www.legislation.gov.uk/uksi/2014/3348/pdfs/uksi_20143348_en.pdf.

[65] Sections 7–8, Bank Recovery and Resolution Order No 2, 2014 at http://www.legislation.gov.uk/uksi/2014/3348/pdfs/uksi_20143348_en.pdf.   [66] Paras 2.10 and 3.9, PRA Rulebook, *Recovery Plans*.

recovery plans can be carried out not too early and not too late. These recovery triggers are known as recovery 'indicators'.[67] Recovery indicators refer to signals of situations that tell the bank that a certain stress or challenging threshold has been reached so that the bank can consider its actions. The bank is responsible for drawing up the indicators, and it is expected that such indicators should be integrated with contingency planning such as liquidity contingency planning by the bank (see Chapter 9, section 9.2).[68]

The PRA Rulebook specifies that indicators can be quantitative or qualitative.[69] This has been further fleshed out in the European Banking Authority's guidelines.[70] The EBA has focused on largely quantitative indicators and recommend that at a minimum, firms should include *capital and liquidity indicators*, as consistent with the firm's micro-prudential compliance (discussed in Chapters 8 and 9); *profitability indicators* that relate to the firm's income and operational risks; *asset quality indicators* that relate to non-performing assets on and off the firm's balance sheet; *market indicators* that relate to equity prices, debt-market conditions such as debt or default swap spreads and credit rating movements; and *macroeconomic indicators* that relate to a range of metrics that measure the performance of sectors and economies.[71]

Goodhart[72] predicts that recovery plans may be triggered only when they are too late in time to apply. This is because banks may succumb to the common behavioural trait of over-confidence, and therefore underestimate the importance of the onset of a recovery indicator. Banks may also wish to avoid any unnecessary adverse reaction between counterparties and in the markets. The application of quantitative indicators is able to mitigate the problem of bank management triggering recovery plans too late in the day if left to their complete discretion to do so. However, such an application may also introduce 'automatic' triggers in perhaps temporary situations. Hence, the Directive has provided for bank management to have the discretion to override the application of the triggers in either bringing about recovery in advance of the quantitative triggers or not to do so in spite of the triggers being met, as long as such a decision is notified to the resolution authority without delay.[73] The PRA encourages banks to use indicators that provide an early warning signal so that the bank can be prompted to look into the impending challenge. Banks should not be made to see recovery indicators as triggers for certain pre-defined management actions or as necessarily entailing drastic measures as such, and should maintain flexibility in their response to recovery indicators.

---

[67] Article 9, BRRD 2014; PRA Rulebook, *Recovery Plans* para 6.

[68] PRA, *Recovery Planning* (December 2017) at https://www.bankofengland.co.uk/-/media/boe/files/prudential-regulation/supervisory-statement/2017/ss917.pdf?la=en&hash=D5317FDD3B9858CF1ADA8FD6B6BB69E459762D03.

[69] Ibid, para 6.2.   [70] Chapter 7 contains a discussion of this.

[71] EBA, *Final Guidelines on the Minimum List of Qualitative and Quantitative Recovery Plan Indicators* (May 2015) at https://www.eba.europa.eu/documents/10180/1064487/EBA-GL-2015-02+GL+on+recovery+plan+indicators.pdf/4bf18728-e836-408f-a583-b22ebaf59181.

[72] Charles Goodhart, 'Basel on wrong path to tackle systemic risk' *Financial Times* (8 July 2011).

[73] Article 9, BRRD 2014.

13.2.1.2 Contents of a recovery plan

The contents of a recovery plan are highly prescribed by the European Commission in the form of a delegated Regulation that is directly binding upon all member states. The PRA has provided supplemental guidance to these rules.[74]

The recovery plan must contain[75] a strategic analysis of the recovery options and a description and number of the entities that would be involved. The recovery plan must set out the overall business strategies, business model and scope of business entities that are covered within the plan, and the structural, legal, business, and economic connections and material exposures of each entity to each other, so that a comprehensive picture is constructed as to the interconnections and overall structure of the institution or group of institutions concerned.[76] The plan must then provide a range of recovery options, including extraordinary measures that may be pursued, including but not limiting to capital and liquidity measures, structural measures (such as disposing of certain business units) and measures aimed to reduce liabilities.[77] The PRA also envisages that recovery options include the possibility of disposals and wind-downs,[78] and banks' access to emergency lending facilities by the Bank of England as well as how banks intend to repay those loans.[79] The range of recovery options should be wide and capable of timely implementation.[80]

The recovery plan must also set out how continuity of operations is to be preserved, including ensuring access to relevant financial market infrastructures.[81] It is envisaged that clearing and settlement houses or payment systems may impose punitive requirements for access if an ailing bank 'loses trust and confidence' with infrastructure operators. However, it is crucial that recovering banks should not be penalised in the process of recovery and there is a need to consider if reforms need to be made to ensure that financial market infrastructures remain prudent but do not impose exacerbating conditions to impede a bank's recovery.[82]

Recovery options should be 'scenario-tested' to ensure that they are credible. This means that banks should design scenarios of stress relevant to their business model and are sufficiently severe to test the plan, and explain which recovery option would be used in what scenario.

---

[74] PRA, *Recovery Planning*.

[75] Article 4, Commission Delegated Regulation (EU) 2016/1075 of 23 March 2016 supplementing Directive 2014/59/EU of the European Parliament and of the Council with regard to regulatory technical standards specifying the content of recovery plans, resolution plans and group resolution plans, the minimum criteria that the competent authority is to assess as regards recovery plans and group recovery plans, the conditions for group financial support, the requirements for independent valuers, the contractual recognition of write-down and conversion powers, the procedures and contents of notification requirements and of notice of suspension and the operational functioning of the resolution colleges (Commission Regulation 2016) at http://eur-lex.europa.eu/legal-content/EN/TXT/PDF/?uri=CELEX:32016R1075&from=EN.

[76] Article 7, Commission Regulation 2016.   [77] Articles 8–9, Commission Regulation 2016.

[78] PRA, *Recovery Planning*.   [79] PRA Rulebook, *Recovery Plans* para 2.6.

[80] Para 2.9, PRA Rulebook, *Recovery Plans*.   [81] Article 12, Commission Regulation 2016.

[82] Remarks by Geoffrey Davies, Bank of England, at the Bank Resolution Regimes Conference, University College London, 9 November 2016.

The recovery plan should also provide a formal impact assessment and feasibility assessment, such as considering any impediment to implementing recovery options.[83] The PRA further explains that banks should explain the 'recovery capacity' of recovery options, and this means a form of cost-benefit analysis of each recovery option. The plan must also contain information on the preparatory measures for carrying out recovery options and carry out preparatory measures[84] to remove impediments in order to facilitate recovery actions if they need to be carried out. The plan also includes the governance aspects of the recovery plan, a communication and disclosure plan if recovery were to be carried out, and a summary of all of the above aspects. The plan should in the PRA's words read like a 'playbook' so that it is clear, easy to navigate and gives rise to effective implementation. The rather prescriptive template compels banks to provide meaningful information as required by resolution authorities, and in a comparable manner with other recovery plans so that resolution authorities can more meaningfully assess their quality and viability (to be discussed shortly). It is to be noted that the BRRD allows national authorities to apply the recovery plan requirements proportionately so that they are not so demanding for smaller and less complex banks.[85]

13.2.1.3 Governance of recovery plans

The recovery plan has to be appropriately administered within the bank to ensure that it remains relevant if recovery options should be carried out. The bank also needs to ensure that recovery plans can be implemented in an effective and timely manner. Hence, adequate governance measures must be established in order to draw up, update and review as well as implement the recovery plan.[86] The PRA has implemented these governance arrangements by requiring that the Board as a whole oversees, assesses and approves the recovery plan before submission to the resolution authority, but the audit committee of the Board has the responsibility of regularly reviewing the relevance of the plan and for suggesting updates. An executive director of the bank must also be personally responsible for overseeing the internal processes relating to the governance of the plan. The recovery plan must also set out the governance arrangements regarding escalation and decision-making in relation to the recovery plan at a sufficiently senior level. These requirements apply similarly to the group recovery plan.[87]

Communication and disclosure

It is also envisaged that recovery planning includes the bank's communications regarding recovery. Recovery options need to be implemented effectively without attracting unintended and adverse consequences from stakeholders and the markets. Hence banks are to specify[88] how they would carry out their internal communications for

---

[83] Articles 10–11, Commission Regulation 2016.   [84] Article 15, Commission Regulation 2016.
[85] Preamble 21, BRRD 2014.   [86] Article 5, Commission Regulation 2016.
[87] Paras 5.2 and 5.3, PRA Rulebook, *Recovery Plans*.   [88] Article 14, Commission Regulation 2016.

recovery implementation, such as to employees and to entities within a group context, as well as their external communications such as to shareholders, counterparties etc. Further, the bank needs to ensure that they consider how their communications to the market should be carried out in order to prevent or mitigate adverse reactions and consequences.

Frequency of submission

The PRA will determine for each bank the frequency for submission of recovery plans. However, larger firms can expect an annual submission to be required.[89] The BRRD 2014 leaves room for national authorities to require even more frequent submissions of recovery plans if necessary.[90] The PRA may require that a bank performs a 'fire drill' on its recovery plan prior to submission so that the robustness of the plan can be tested. A 'fire drill' is a 'live' simulation exercise where a bank acts out key parts of a recovery plan in response to a designed scenario. Banks are expected to conduct a fire drill in this manner at a minimum of once every three years.

Assessment of recovery plans—criteria and actions

Resolution authorities are to assess recovery plans chiefly in terms of their likelihood in maintaining or restoring the viability of the bank, as well as the likelihood of their timely implementation.[91] The Bank of England in the UK has the responsibility to consider if the bank's preparatory measures are adequate, whether there are any impediments to achieving recovery, given the bank's complexity in organisational and business structures.[92]

Resolution authorities must assess the comprehensiveness of the plan, the quality of the plan in terms of its level of explanation, internal consistency and details provided, issues in implementation and whether the plan is likely to achieve its objectives and whether there are circumstances that countervail this, such as conflicts with other objectives or unfriendly external/market situations.[93] Where a recovery plan refers to an entire group, the group recovery plan should be assessed in terms of the likelihood of maintaining stability and restoring viability to the group as a whole and whether there are any consistency challenges or impediments to achieving this objective.[94]

Where banks' recovery plans may be deficient, resolution authorities should direct banks to address these deficiencies such as removing impediments to recovery and to resubmit plans.[95] UK legislation[96] sets out a non-exhaustive list of directions the Bank of England can give to banks in amending their recovery plans, such as:

---

[89] PRA, *Recovery Planning.*   [90] Preamble 21, BRRD 2014.   [91] Articles 6, 8 BRRD 2014.
[92] Section 13, Bank Recovery and Resolution Order No 2, 2014 at http://www.legislation.gov.uk/uksi/2014/3348/pdfs/uksi_20143348_en.pdf.   [93] Articles 16–19, Commission Regulation 2016.
[94] Article 20, Commission Regulation 2016.   [95] Article 6, BRRD 2014.
[96] Section 11, Bank Recovery and Resolution Order No 2, 2014 at http://www.legislation.gov.uk/uksi/2014/3348/pdfs/uksi_20143348_en.pdf.

(a) reduction of risk profile, including liquidity risk profile;

(b) review of structure and strategy;

(c) timely recapitalisation;

(d) changes to funding strategy in order to improve the resilience of core business lines and critical functions; and

(e) changes to governance structure.

The preparation and submission of a recovery plan provides an opportunity for banks to take stock of their position and their long-term viability. In particular, systemically important banks can take the opportunity to rethink their structures so that they are more easily be recovered or resolved.[97] Indeed, the resolution authorities' assessment of such institutions' recovery plans gives rise to an opportunity to order the simplification of their structures in order to mitigate resolution problems.

Assessment of group recovery plans: special issues

Where a group of financial institutions is concerned, a group recovery plan is envisaged to be submitted to the 'consolidating supervisor' in the EEA. –The consolidating supervisor is usually the 'home supervisor' discussed in Chapter 7 for cross-border banks in the EEA or the lead supervisor if so appointed. However, in view of other member state's interest in the group's cross-border banking operations, the consolidating supervisors must circulate the group recovery plan to all concerned national resolution authorities.[98] The consolidating supervisor must also endeavour to reach a joint decision with all concerned national resolution authorities on whether to approve the group recovery plan, what actions to recommend, including whether recovery plans for any individual institutions or branches need to be drawn up.[99] A consensus-led decision should be aimed to be achieved in four months from the submission of the group recovery plan.[100]

Where the concerned resolution authorities cannot reach a consensus in relation to the group recovery plan, the BRRD envisages that they would refer the matter to the European Banking Authority, which has a general power to effect conciliation for disagreements among national regulators, and in the event of complete deadlock, to effect a decision.[101] The UK has implemented this provision by requiring that where the consolidating supervisor is the PRA or FCA, the dissenting authority that wishes to refer a disagreement to the EBA must refrain from imposing any decision on branches in its territory until at least a month after reference to the EBA and that the EBA has

---

[97] Emilios Avgouleas, Charles Goodhart and Dirk Schoenmaker, 'Living Wills as a Catalyst for Action' (2013) 9 *Journal of Financial Stability* 210.
[98] Article 7, BRRD 2014, reflected in s13, Bank Recovery and Resolution Order No 2, 2014 at http://www.legislation.gov.uk/uksi/2014/3348/pdfs/uksi_20143348_en.pdf.
[99] Article 8, BRRD 2014, reflected in s 21, Bank Recovery and Resolution Order No 2, 2014 at http://www.legislation.gov.uk/uksi/2014/3348/pdfs/uksi_20143348_en.pdf.
[100] Article 8, BRRD 2014, reflected in s20, Bank Recovery and Resolution Order No 2, 2014 at http://www.legislation.gov.uk/uksi/2014/3348/pdfs/uksi_20143348_en.pdf.   [101] Article 8, BRRD 2014.

made its decision.[102] A similar position is to apply to the PRA or FCA where either is not the consolidating supervisor but may be in a position to raise dissent to the EBA.[103]

Upon the UK's departure from the EU, it is envisaged that the UK resolution authority would not be able to assert a right to have group recovery plans of EEA banks shared with it. Such sharing would have to take place under the auspices of wider international coordination principles such as the Basel Committee's recommended supervisory colleges and resolution colleges, discussed in Chapter 5. Further, the international arrangements do not give the UK authority a right of dissent and a procedure for formalising and resolving such dissent. This could be rather disadvantageous for the UK as many EEA banks have branch presence in the UK.

However, it may be argued that the UK may be able to mitigate the systemic impact of foreign branches through its enhanced supervision scheme introduced in 2014.[104] The PRA would only allow foreign branches to operate if their economic activity is *de minimis*, defined as attracting less than £100m in deposits, not having more than 5000 customers, and generally not having an impact upon critical services in UK financial markets. The PRA also needs to be satisfied with their recovery and resolution plans. This unilateral power could mitigate the authority's perceived lack of 'control' over the impact of foreign branching and is arguably consistent with the cautionary notes in the 1983 and 1992 Concordats (discussed in Chapter 5).[105]

13.2.2 Resolution plans

A resolution plan is a document that sets out circumstances of failure or near-failure for financial institutions, and the options for resolving the institution.[106] The plan is to be drawn up and maintained by resolution authorities, in order to provide them with blueprints going forward if resolution should become necessary.[107] Where the bank concerned is subject to the SSM, the SRB is the relevant resolution authority and should draw up resolution plans in consultation with the ECB and national resolution authorities.[108] Resolution authorities are to review their resolution plans on an annual basis.[109]

---

[102] Sections 25 and 26, Bank Recovery and Resolution Order No 2, 2014 at http://www.legislation.gov.uk/uksi/2014/3348/pdfs/uksi_20143348_en.pdf.

[103] Sections 31 and 32, Bank Recovery and Resolution Order No 2, 2014 at http://www.legislation.gov.uk/uksi/2014/3348/pdfs/uksi_20143348_en.pdf.

[104] PRA, *Supervising International Banks: The PRA's Approach to Branch Supervision* (September 2014) at http://www.bankofengland.co.uk/pra/Pages/publications/ss/2014/ss1014.aspx.

[105] Bank for International Settlements, *Principles for the Supervision of Banks' Foreign Establishments* (1983) http://www.bis.org/publ/bcbsc312.pdf; Bank for International Settlements, *Minimum Standards for the Supervision of International Banking Groups and Their Cross-Border Establishments* (1992): http://www.bis.org/publ/bcbsc314.pdf caution that home and host authorities of cross-border banks should be cautious of each other's capacity to coordinate supervision, and in cases of doubt should perhaps prevent the cross-border establishment from taking place. [106] PRA Rulebook, *Resolution Pack* para 2.5.

[107] Article 10, BRRD 2014; s37, Bank Recovery and Resolution Order No 2, 2014 at http://www.legislation.gov.uk/uksi/2014/3348/pdfs/uksi_20143348_en.pdf.

[108] Article 8, SRM Regulation.   [109] Article 10, BRRD 2014.

Although it is the resolution authorities' responsibility to draw up and maintain the resolution plan, financial institutions are required to assist authorities with relevant information.[110] Indeed the PRA sets out in its Rulebook that financial institutions are to be responsible for submitting their resolution packs[111] in order to assist the resolution authority in firming up its plans. Where a financial institution group has the PRA as its consolidating supervisor, a group resolution pack must be submitted to the PRA.[112] In order to ensure that the provision of information by financial institutions is credible and up-to-date, the PRA imposes an obligation upon financial institutions to ensure the sufficiency of information and that the pack is up-to-date and reflects all material developments in the institution's business.[113] Further, financial institutions must be supported by adequate governance arrangements to ensure that the institution or group resolution pack is prepared with due oversight: the Board's oversight is required for the preparation of the resolution pack, similar to the governance arrangements for a firm or group's preparation of the recovery plan. An executive director must have personal responsibility for overseeing the internal processes for the preparation of the resolution pack, and the pack should be periodically reviewed by the audit committee of the Board.[114]

13.2.2.1 Prescribed content for resolution plans

The contents of resolution plans are highly prescribed.[115] This is arguably in response to regulators' bad experience of having to cope, without much preparation at all, with the fallout from the global financial crisis of 2007–9. The resolution plan is now intended to arm regulators with sufficient information and antecedent planning so that resolution would be less unprepared, more considered and also publicly accountable. One can see value in the prescription of plan content in order to achieve comprehensiveness and comparability for resolution authorities' forward-looking work.

What if, however, a scenario of failure should occur that is not captured in the resolution plan? Resolution authorities are not spared from having to think on their feet in those circumstances. What if a resolution plan measure does not work out in a predictable manner in the event of a failure or crisis? Resolution authorities would still have to adapt or respond to the changing situation at hand. We need to be cautious against 'over-planning' in resolution plans, as resolution authorities should keep in mind the broader objectives in resolution (which will be discussed shortly).

The BRRD 2014, complemented by the Commission delegated Regulation 2016 provides for a comprehensive list of matters that must be contained in a resolution plan. The categories of information that must be contained in the resolution plan are set out in Box 13.2.

---

[110] Article 11, BRRD; s37(3), Bank Recovery and Resolution Order No 2, 2014 at http://www.legislation.gov.uk/uksi/2014/3348/pdfs/uksi_20143348_en.pdf.

[111] PRA, *PRA Rulebook, Resolution Pack*, paras 2.3–2.5.   [112] PRA, *PRA Rulebook, Resolution Pack*, paras 3.3–3.5.

[113] PRA, *PRA Rulebook, Resolution Pack*, paras 2.5, 3.6, 4.1, and 4.2.   [114] PRA, *PRA Rulebook, Resolution Pack*, paras 5.1 and 5.2.

[115] Article 10, BRRD 2014; s22, Commission Delegated Regulation 2016.

> ### Box 13.2 Information in a resolution plan
>
> 1. A range of resolution strategies and options, including the processes needed for effecting them, and likely timeframe for implementation.
>
> 2. Arrangements to ensure operational continuity of critical functions including the firm's internal and external interdependencies, critical shared operations, and access to external infrastructure such as clearing and settlement facilities.
>
> 3. Information that supports the credibility of the above (1) and (2) and whether such information is up to date. Such information is primarily obtained from the financial institutions in question, but in the UK, the Bank is given power to obtain information on financial contracts/transactions from other relevant third parties and to require them to maintain records (s58 of the Bank Recovery and Resolution Order No 2, 2014).
>
> 4. The financing of the resolution without assuming extraordinary assistance from the central bank or state.
>
> 5. Communication plan to stakeholders, depositors, creditors, counterparties, financial market infrastructures and the media etc, in particular, an impact assessment with regard to employees.
>
> 6. A determination of resolvability and any measures taken to remove impediments to resolvability.
>
> 7. How and whether the institution may return to regulatory levels of capital and liquidity.
>
> 8. Any opinions offered by the institution in question.

How resolution authorities should arrive at the prescribed contents

Resolution authorities are required to perform stages of assessment before finalising the information in the resolution plans. These stages may be seen to be procedural best practices, and secures consistency in approach by resolution authorities. They may also perform a function of vindicating resolution authorities if the resolution plan ultimately does not work in a real crisis.

The stages of assessment are found in the Commission Delegated Regulation 2016.

First, resolution authorities must determine the feasibility of normal insolvency procedures for the financial institution concerned, including its wider market implications and the interests of financial stability.[116] Only where a resolution authority has determined that normal insolvency procedures will not be feasible, or not meet resolution objectives or the needs of the wider public interest will it identify a preferred resolution strategy or its variants.[117] The Regulation sets out in detail how resolution authorities are to consider the feasibility of its preferred resolution strategy, including considerations regarding its structure and operations, financial resources, the capability of the institution or group to

---

[116] Sections 23–4, Commission Delegated Regulation 2016.
[117] Section 25, Commission Delegated Regulation 2016.

provide accurate information to the resolution authorities in carrying out resolution, any cross-border impediments and coordination difficulties, and whether regulatory obstacles or contractual documentation impediments exist that may affect resolution.[118]

Next, resolution authorities are to determine the credibility of the preferred resolution strategy in terms of: the wider market impact of resolution, impact on confidence, access to financial market infrastructures, and potential contagion effects upon other financial market institutions and the wider economy.[119]

The highly prescriptive procedural approach ensures that each resolution plan may as far as is possible, be justified. However, there are hidden hazards in such elaborate processes. Does the institution of such an elaborate process mean that resolution decisions have to be undertaken following a similar approach? As will be discussed later, decision-making in resolution is not framed this way, and can be highly discretionary. This is especially the case since resolution is envisaged to take place over the weekend when markets are closed. If actual resolution is carried out in a more discretionary manner, then a sharp contrast would exist between the highly regulated nature of resolution planning and the relatively discretionary nature of resolution in practice. This discrepancy could call into question resolution decisions and measures seen as discretionary or not in adherence to the resolution plan.

Assessment of resolvability

Part of the resolution planning process by resolution authorities is identifying impediments to resolvability and requiring financial institutions to address those impediments. It must be appreciated that this is a very forward-looking approach to regulatory intervention, requiring a financial institution to make changes in advance of a possible hypothetical failure. The thresholds for an impediment to resolvability would be where the *feasibility* or *credibility* of a resolution is affected.[120] However, a resolution authority should not make that determination unless it has consulted with the relevant financial institution's regulator.[121] Where the UK is concerned, the resolution authority, that is, the Bank of England must have considered all relevant matters, the wider systemic implications and the absence of extraordinary support before determining that a bank needs to remove an impediment to resolvability.[122]

The resolution authority's determination must be communicated to the financial institution, which should be provided with a four-month period to address the impediment/s. The authority must then assess the adequacy of the financial institution's measures. If the authority finds them inadequate, the authority has the power to instruct the removal of impediment/s within one month of the written notice of remedial measures given to the

---

[118] Sections 26–31, Commission Delegated Regulation 2016.
[119] Section 32, Commission Delegated Regulation 2016.
[120] Articles 15, 16, BRRD 2014.   [121] Article 17, BRRD 2014.
[122] Section 60 for institutions, and 62 for groups where the PRA or FCA is consolidating supervisor, Bank Recovery and Resolution Order No 2, 2014 at http://www.legislation.gov.uk/uksi/2014/3348/pdfs/uksi_20143348_en.pdf.

financial institution. In the UK, the Bank of England as resolution authority must consult the Financial Policy Committee (see Chapter 6) on the imposition of the remedial measures, before giving the financial institution a reasoned and written notice of such measures.[123] This is because the imposition of such remedial measures must be in the interests of wider financial stability of the UK. UK legislation has not prescribed what the remedial measures may be, but the BRRD 2014[124] has set out a non-exhaustive list including:

(a) the revision or provision of any intra-group financing agreements;

(b) requiring the institution to limit its maximum individual and aggregate exposures;

(c) imposing specific or regular additional information requirements relevant for resolution purposes;

(d) requiring the institution to divest specific assets;

(e) requiring the institution to limit or cease specific existing or proposed activities;

(f) restricting or preventing the development of new or existing business lines or sale of new or existing products;

(g) requiring changes to legal or operational structures of the institution or any group entity, either directly or indirectly under its control, so as to reduce complexity, and in order to ensure that critical functions may be legally and operationally separated from other functions;

(h) requiring an institution or a parent undertaking to set up a parent financial holding company in a member state or a Union parent financial holding company;

(i) requiring an institution to issue eligible liabilities for the purposes of bail-in (see discussion later);

(j) requiring an institution to take other steps to meet the minimum capital adequacy requirements;

(k) where an institution is the subsidiary of financial group, requiring that the holding company set up a separate financial holding company to control the institution, in order to facilitate the resolution of the institution and to avoid the application of the resolution tools and powers having an adverse effect on the non-financial part of the group.

The affected financial institution has a right of appeal to the Upper Tribunal, which as Chapter 6 has discussed, is an independent specialist judicial body considering references to it relating to the financial regulators' decisions in the UK. The Upper Tribunal may confirm the authority's decision or else disagree and remit back to the authority for an appropriate revised decision.[125]

[123] Section 66, Bank Recovery and Resolution Order No 2, 2014 at http://www.legislation.gov.uk/uksi/2014/3348/pdfs/uksi_20143348_en.pdf. [124] Article 17.
[125] Section 67, Bank Recovery and Resolution Order No 2, 2014 at http://www.legislation.gov.uk/uksi/2014/3348/pdfs/uksi_20143348_en.pdf.

It is envisaged that the Tribunal would be able to review whether the resolution authority's is acting reasonably in its decision-making process determining the feasibility and credibility of resolution planning. This can be a procedural approach whereby the court assesses whether the Bank of England has performed the staged assessments in the Commission Regulation. It is questioned whether more substantive queries can be raised, such as whether the impediment identified is material, and the cost–benefit of requiring its removal by the financial institution concerned. The Tribunal is empowered to hear all matters of evidence afresh and hence it is surmised that the Tribunal can have substantive scrutiny of the resolvability matters raised.

Group resolution plans: special issues

As with group recovery plans, group resolution plans raise special issues of coordination between concerned resolution authorities. It is envisaged that all concerned resolution authorities would work together towards achieving a joint decision, and the Commission Delegated Regulation[126] sets out in detail the procedures for doing so. Concerned resolution authorities of a cross-border financial group should work together including consultation on drafts, meeting with the parent financial group, putting together the agreed decision and communicating to all and to the parent financial group. UK legislation has transposed this. Where the PRA or FCA is the consolidating supervisor for a group, the Bank is the authority responsible for drawing up the group resolution plan. The plan will provide for resolution options in the group context bearing in mind wider interests of financial stability and should not occasion any disproportionate impact upon any member state.[127] The Bank is to consult all other relevant resolution authorities for the group and endeavour to reach a joint decision for the plan.

Resolution authorities who do not agree have the option of opting out of the plan,[128] in which case it assumes the responsibility for planning for the resolution of those institutions within its territory, or refer the matter to the EBA to resolve disagreement in the same manner as discussed above in relation to group recovery plans.[129] The EBA has the power to make a determination after conciliation processes are carried out and the final resolution plan must be adopted within one month of the EBA's decision.[130]

Where the PRA or FCA is not the consolidating supervisor for a group, and the Bank of England is one of the relevant resolution authorities for the group, the group resolution plan will be led by another member state. If the Bank does not agree with the group

---

[126] Articles 66-72, Commission Delegated Regulation 2016.

[127] Article 12, BRRD 2014; s40, Bank Recovery and Resolution Order No 2, 2014 at http://www.legislation.gov.uk/uksi/2014/3348/pdfs/uksi_20143348_en.pdf.

[128] Section 42, Bank Recovery and Resolution Order No 2, 2014 at http://www.legislation.gov.uk/uksi/2014/3348/pdfs/uksi_20143348_en.pdf. This is pursuant to Article 13 BRRD 2014, which allows resolution authorities for subsidiaries to draw up their own resolution plans as long as they are clearly reasoned and communicated, and for resolution authorities that do not agree with the group plan to opt out.

[129] Section 43, Bank Recovery and Resolution Order No 2, 2014 at http://www.legislation.gov.uk/uksi/2014/3348/pdfs/uksi_20143348_en.pdf. 　　[130] Ibid.

plan or there is no consensus reached on the group plan, the Bank will draw up its own resolution plan for the relevant institutions in the UK and provide a reasoned notice to the group for its decision.[131] A reference to the EBA can also be made in order to effect a conciliation process for the settlement of disagreements, in which case the EBA is in a position to make a decision for the group.[132] The EBA can also be invited to play an earlier role of facilitating agreement within the group before any formalised process for conciliation is activated.[133]

Where the EBA has not been referred to, the default situation in the absence of agreement would be that each resolution authority would adopt its own reasoned plan and communicate their individual decisions to each other.[134] Although the scheme of things envisages that the EBA would make a decision in cases of disagreement, the first case submitted to the EBA between the SRB and Romanian resolution authority was not definitively 'decided' by the EBA. Rather the EBA took the view that a certain procedure had not been exhausted (i.e. resolution authorities' need to determine the material impediments to resolvability and consider how they should be dealt with), and directed the disagreeing authorities to undertake that step and coordinate as best as possible thereafter to reach a consensus.[135] This case perhaps highlights the EBA's somewhat awkward position in arbitrating disputes and its support for promoting a cooperative and 'peer-level' interactive spirit amongst regulators.

We can see that although the processes of coordination aim to achieve agreement, leeway is also provided in case of disagreements that may not ultimately be resolved, as each member state has its financial stability interests to protect.[136] However, it is queried what would happen to a member state that wishes to opt out of agreement but is outdone by a request made to the EBA by another member state to resolve differences? Any resolution authority has such a right within four months of the endeavours to agree a joint plan, and in such a case, it would seem that everyone must put their decisions on hold until the EBA decides. However, as the EBA has shown its willingness to foster continuing cooperation among member states to achieve understanding and consensus, it seems unlikely that reference to the EBA can be used 'strategically' by disagreeing member states against each other.

---

[131] Sections 47–9, Bank Recovery and Resolution Order No 2, 2014 at http://www.legislation.gov.uk/uksi/2014/3348/pdfs/uksi_20143348_en.pdf.

[132] Section 51, Bank Recovery and Resolution Order No 2, 2014 at http://www.legislation.gov.uk/uksi/2014/3348/pdfs/uksi_20143348_en.pdf.

[133] Article 13, BRRD 2014, ss44 and 52, Bank Recovery and Resolution Order No 2, 2014 at http://www.legislation.gov.uk/uksi/2014/3348/pdfs/uksi_20143348_en.pdf.

[134] Sections 73–5, Commission Delegated Regulation 2016.

[135] 'Decision of the EBA on the settlement of a disagreement' (27 April 2018) at https://www.eba.europa.eu/documents/10180/16082/EBA+decision+on+the+settlement+of+a+disagreement++between+the+SRB+and+the+NBR+-+EN.pdf.

[136] Mads Andenas and Iris H-Y Chiu, 'Financial Stability and Legal Integration in Financial Regulation' (2013) *European Law Review* 335, discussing how different needs of financial stability can lead to divergent approaches that conflict with the legal harmonisation and integration agendas pursued in the EU.

Another issue that arises with group resolution plans is where the assessment of resolvability by the lead resolution authority results in disagreement between resolution authorities concerned. Again, it is envisaged that resolution authorities would consult each other and agree on the identification of impediments of resolvability and the action plan to redress those. The action plan must be drafted after consultation within the group and with the group financial institution as well, and must be communicated to all concerned resolution authorities.[137] UK legislation has transposed this. Where the PRA or FCA is the consolidating supervisor of the group, the Bank is the lead resolution authority responsible for assessing any impediments to resolvability. It will, working with other relevant resolution authorities, attempt to make a joint decision so that a reasoned determination in the manner discussed above can be communicated by written notice to the affected financial institution as to remedial measures that are needed. As the affected financial institution is given four months to respond, its response needs to be considered jointly by the group of resolution authorities again over a period of four months in order to reach a joint decision on whether the financial institution's proposals are adequate. At each stage, where such a joint decision cannot be made, the Bank may decide the matter and leave dissenting authorities to opt out, who would then be responsible for dealing with the financial institution's branches in their territory. This is unless before the end of each four-month period a resolution authority submits to the EBA for conciliation and possible decision-making.[138] Where the EBA is not referred to, the default position is that in the absence of consensus, resolution authorities will each have individual decisions vis a vis the entities in their territories, but they would need to communicate all individual decisions to each other.[139]

In the matter of addressing remedial measures to a financial institution group, it can be appreciated that having one decision, either by the group of resolution authorities jointly or by the EBA, is likely preferred by the financial institution. One set of remedial measures can be implemented consistently across the group. Unilateral actions taken by different member states may result in cumbersome, costly, and even conflicting obligations for financial institutions.

Where the PRA or FCA is not the consolidating supervisor of a group but the Bank of England is a concerned resolution authority, the Bank is required to use its best endeavours to participate in a joint decision with the rest of the group of resolution authorities. Where it is unable to agree, after considering financial stability concerns relevant to the UK and EEA as a whole, it will proceed to impose remedial measures upon the institution within the UK. Such measures are finalised by the Bank only after consulting with the relevant regulator (PRA or FCA) and the Financial Policy Committee. However, if one of the resolution authorities in the group refers the matter for conciliation and

---

[137] Sections 77–83, Commission Delegated Regulation 2016.
[138] Article 18, BRRD 2014 read with ss68–73, Bank Recovery and Resolution Order No 2, 2014 at http://www.legislation.gov.uk/uksi/2014/3348/pdfs/uksi_20143348_en.pdf.
[139] Articles 84 and 85, Commission Delegated Regulation 2016.

decision-making by the EBA, the EBA's final decision will apply in relation to the remedial measures imposed on the financial institution concerned.[140] The BRRD and UK legislation provide for a formalised approach to overseeing group resolution planning, which may be important for avoiding coordination pitfalls when resolution actually occurs. The EBA is likely to play a key role in fostering coordination between resolution authorities on such an *ex ante* basis. In the event of the UK's cessation of EU membership, the UK would unlikely have the benefit of such deep engagement in resolution planning and would have to default to the looser arrangements at the international level of colleges.

Where the SRB is involved in group resolution plans, it is envisaged to take leadership as it has primary responsibility for approving the plan, although the group resolution authority has responsibility for drafting after consultation with other national resolution authorities and the ECB.[141] The SRB's aim would be to achieve an equitable and balanced plan that does not impose disproportionate impact on any member state and that would adhere to. In this manner the SRB may play the role for facilitating and arriving at an agreed plan for the group, although it can be questioned whether the SRB's power is 'unequally' weighted compared to other group contexts discussed above which allow peer level authorities to disagree with each other.

In relation to resolution planning relating to groups that involve non-EEA banks, the PRA's position is that it would work with the resolution college[142] that is instituted under the auspices of the Bank for International Settlements in order to reach joint decisions annually on resolution planning for the group. However, although the UK would work together with crisis management groups for each G-SIB[143] at the international level in the event of a resolution that involves cross-border entities, the UK reserves the right to take independent action on the UK branches of non-EEA firms in the interests of preserving financial stability.[144] These procedures are not dissimilar in spirit to the ones above except that at the international level where authorities are all peers, there is no equivalent of an EBA to offer a top-down solution for reconciliation of differences. The coordination mechanisms at the international level are further fleshed out in section 13.4.

13.2.3 Intra-group financial support: early crisis management

Moving onto the scenario that banks may experience early signs of difficulties, we would expect that recovery plans should kick in. However, the BRRD 2014 has also provided that if an institution within a larger banking group experiences early signs of trouble, a banking group may arrange to help itself by intra-group financial support

---

[140] Sections 76–81, Bank Recovery and Resolution Order No 2, 2014 at http://www.legislation.gov.uk/uksi/2014/3348/pdfs/uksi_20143348_en.pdf.

[141] Article 8, SRM Regulation.   [142] See section 13.4.   [143] See section 13.4.

[144] PRA, *The Bank of England's Approach to Resolution* (October 2017) at https://www.bankofengland.co.uk/-/media/boe/files/news/2017/october/the-bank-of-england-approach-to-resolution.pdf?la=en&hash=FC806900972DDE7246AD8CD1DF8B8C324BE7652F at paras 3.18 and 3.19.

arrangements. Such arrangements can be useful as they are a self-help device, therefore reducing the burden and cost for resolution authorities. However, there is also the danger that intra-group financial group could be based on short-termist 'fire-fighting' instincts and are thus poorly planned and excessive. If so the carrying out of such support could have an adverse knock-on effect on the entire group, resulting in a worse situation for resolution authorities to deal with.

The EU and UK therefore seek to control the use of intra-group financial support arrangements while recognising their usefulness. In principle, member states should not prohibit them.[145] As for application in the UK, intra-group financial support may run counter to its structural reforms discussed in Chapter 10 to insulate retail banks from their wider banking group, or may perhaps be made subject to the 'arms-length' requirements relevant to intra-group transactions discussed in Chapter 10, section 10.2.

Intra-group financial support arrangements cover parent and subsidiary financial institutions within the group, and could be in the form of parent-subsidiary assistance or vice versa. Such arrangements need to be approved by the relevant regulator of the group concerned or they cannot be validly applied. We turn now to the conditions for a valid intra-group financial arrangement and the approval processes.

13.2.3.1 Conditions for valid intra-group financial arrangements

In order to ensure that intra-group financial arrangements can work and would not jeopardise the group in turn, stringent conditions are imposed to help regulators determine if such arrangements can be approved. These conditions ensure that the financial assistance offered to a stricken member of the group would be effective and meets its objectives, would likely be repaid by the stricken member and would not in any way threaten the financial viability and regulatory obligations of the group. Further, these arrangements must be duly considered and entered into freely by all parties. Regulatory supervision over these arrangements may resolve any inconsistency with the application of ring-fencing discussed in Chapter 10. Box 13.3 summarises the conditions and the relevant regulatory sources.

Approval by regulators

All intra-group financial arrangements have to be formalised, transmitted to the relevant regulator, and approved based on the criteria above. Where the UK is concerned, such arrangements would be valid if the PRA expressly approved them (or subject to modifications) or if the PRA does not express a view after the lapse of 5 business days.[146] The PRA has the power to prohibit or restrict certain parts of the arrangements if it does not so agree.[147] However, as most intra-group financial arrangements concern a group of resolution authorities too, the BRRD 2014 and the implementing UK

---

[145] Article 19, BRRD 2014.   [146] PRA Rulebook, *Group Financial Support* para 7.
[147] Section 102, Bank Recovery and Resolution Order No 2, 2014 at http://www.legislation.gov.uk/uksi/2014/3348/pdfs/uksi_20143348_en.pdf.

Box 13.3 Conditions for valid intra-group financial support

1. Each party is informed, acting freely, and out of its best interests (BRRD 2014, Article 19(7)).

2. The support is provided on the basis of contractual consideration and has contractual en-forceability. (BRRD 2014, Article 19(7), 23(1), PRA Rulebook, *Group Financial Support*, para 4.1)

3. The support will result in likely effectiveness in redressing the financial difficulties of the stricken member and preserve the financial stability of the group. (BRRD 2014, Article 23(1), PRA Rulebook, *Group Financial Support*, para 4.1). In assessing this, the group needs to clearly articulate the capital and liquidity needs of the supported entity, an analysis of the financial difficulties, underlying assumptions and how the difficulties developed, the expected default risk of the supported entity and the group's expected loss, and an action plan going forward to redress the supported entity's financial situation (Commission Delegated Regulation 2016, Articles 33–4).

4. The support will not jeopardise the group or the parent entity in terms of its financial viability or capital and liquidity obligations, or the resolvability of the supporting entity or the group (BRRD 2014, Article 23(1), Commission Delegated Regulation 2016 at Articles 34-35, PRA Rulebook, *Group Financial Support* para 4.1).

5. The support will not entail a threat to wider systemic financial stability in the UK. (PRA Rulebook, *Group Financial Support* para 4.1)

6. The decision to enter into such arrangements is made by the Board of the group hold-ing company, supported by shareholders' resolution (BRRD 2014, Articles 21, 24, PRA Rulebook, *Group Financial Support* para 5). Such a resolution is an ordinary resolution (i.e. simple majority of the shareholders present at the general meeting) where the proposal for the resolution is made available for inspection by the members at least 15 days before the meeting at the group's registered office. The resolution can be revoked by shareholders by ordinary resolution as well, and shareholders are to be kept apprised of the performance or implementation of such arrangements by annual reporting by directors. (see ss 98–100, Bank Recovery and Resolution Order No 2, 2014).

---

legislation provide for how such coordination between resolution authorities should be formalised.

Where the PRA or FCA is the consolidating supervisor for the banking group, it must attempt to reach a joint decision with other concerned regulators for the group, with the possibility of inviting the EBA at this early stage to facilitate a joint decision.[148] Regulators may not all agree, in which case opposing regulators may object with rea-soned notification.[149] The consolidating supervisor must review the plan again[150] or

---

[148] Article 20, BRRD 2014, ss86 and 88, Bank Recovery and Resolution Order No 2, 2014 at http://www.legislation.gov.uk/uksi/2014/3348/pdfs/uksi_20143348_en.pdf.

[149] Article 25, BRRD 2014.

[150] Sections 103 and 104, Bank Recovery and Resolution Order No 2, 2014 at http://www.legislation.gov.uk/uksi/2014/3348/pdfs/uksi_20143348_en.pdf.

opposing regulators may refer the situation to the EBA within two days of notifying opposition, in order to start the EBA's conciliation processes.[151] Where there is no express opposition but the group does not agree, the consolidating supervisor may make its own decision,[152] unless within a four month period of the application by the group, one of the regulators concerned refers to the EBA for conciliation processes to commence, similar to the procedures discussed above in relation to recovery and resolution plans. In that case the EBA may facilitate conciliation or determine a decision if conciliation fails.[153]

Where the PRA or FCA is not the consolidating supervisor of the banking group, it must review and endeavour to reach a joint decision with the consolidating supervisor.[154] However, it remains open for the PRA or FCA to raise an objection to the EBA within two days of notifying the consolidating supervisor or within four months of the banking group's application, in order to invite the EBA to start the conciliation process or else determine the situation.[155] In essence the EBA will play significant roles in finalising decisions such as joint recovery and resolution plans and in relation to a banking group's application to use intra-group financial support.

Where an approved intra-group financial arrangement is to be amended, it must be re-authorised based on the same criteria and in the same manner as above, and cannot be applied unless approved.[156] All finalised arrangements must be transmitted to resolution colleges in order to share vital information.[157]

Upon the UK's cessation of EU membership, the coordination arrangements for approval of intra-group financial support applications by banking groups may become uncertain, as there may be no hard and fast obligation for the UK regulator to work with other EEA regulators and vice versa. It is arguably in the best interests of all relevant regulators to coordinate a view on whether a banking group's application can be supported, as diverging decisions by the UK and EU regulators or the EBA can result in inconsistency, inconvenience, and extra regulatory cost for banking groups.

13.2.4 Early intervention regime: early crisis management

Regulators are keen to establish a ladder of options to manage crisis-stricken banks without necessarily resolving or dissolving them. One such range of options is the 'early intervention' measures provided in the BRRD 2014, which the Key Attributes

---

[151] Article 25, BRRD 2014.   [152] Article 20(6), BRRD 2014.

[153] Section 87, Bank Recovery and Resolution Order No 2, 2014 at http://www.legislation.gov.uk/uksi/2014/3348/pdfs/uksi_20143348_en.pdf.

[154] Sections 92–3, Bank Recovery and Resolution Order No 2, 2014 at http://www.legislation.gov.uk/uksi/2014/3348/pdfs/uksi_20143348_en.pdf.

[155] Section 94, Bank Recovery and Resolution Order No 2, 2014 at http://www.legislation.gov.uk/uksi/2014/3348/pdfs/uksi_20143348_en.pdf.

[156] Section 96, Bank Recovery and Resolution Order No 2, 2014 at http://www.legislation.gov.uk/uksi/2014/3348/pdfs/uksi_20143348_en.pdf.   [157] Article 25, BRRD 2014.

Box 13.4 Early intervention measures

1. Requiring the bank to implement one or more measures in its recovery plan. It may be argued that the triggers in the recovery plan ought to have been set-off by then. However, as discussed earlier, bank management may be slow to respond to recovery triggers. Early intervention measures therefore provide an option for regulators to force the recovery plan to be carried out in the appropriate time. (Article 27, BRRD 2014)

2. Requiring the bank's Board to draw up an action plan to address the situation, including convening shareholders' meetings where necessary. (Article 27, BRRD 2014)

3. Requiring the removal of some members of the Board in order to put into effect an action plan to redress the situation. This power can extend to the removal of the entire Board and senior management where the financial situation of the bank is sufficiently dire or where infringements of regulation are implicated. (Articles 27 and 28, BRRD 2014)

4. Requiring the bank's Board to convene creditors' meetings in order to restructure debt. (Article 27, BRRD 2014)

5. Requiring the bank's Board to effect changes to business strategy and/or to operational and structural aspects of the bank. (Article 27, BRRD 2014)

6. Where the bank's Board and senior management are removed, the regulator can appoint one or more temporary administrators to manage the bank, in accordance with the regulator's specified roles, functions and powers. Such an appointment may be notified to shareholders via the convention of a meeting and should not last beyond a year. (Article 29, BRRD 2014)

---

established by the FSB also recognise as being useful.[158] Early intervention measures are led by the bank regulator, not the resolution authority, as these measures take place pre-resolution, and are an attempt to turn the bank around. They, however, involve a significant amount of intervention in the ordinary course of bank management.

The BRRD 2014 sets out the criteria for triggering early intervention measures, viz: where a financial institution is in a rapidly deteriorating financial condition, and is likely in the near future to fall below the regulatory thresholds in relation to capital, liquidity, and leverage.[159] Indicators of 'rapidly deteriorating condition' include deteriorating liquidity, increasing levels of leverage, non-performing loans, or concentration of exposures. These criteria have been adopted in UK legislation.[160]

Early intervention measures include the following in Box 13.4. The list is non-exhaustive.

---

[158] See para 3.2, at http://www.fsb.org/what-we-do/policy-development/effective-resolution-regimes-and-policies/key-attributes-of-effective-resolution-regimes-for-financial-institutions/#3resolutionpowers.

[159] Article 27, BRRD 2014.

[160] Section 107, Bank Recovery and Resolution Order No 2, 2014 at http://www.legislation.gov.uk/uksi/2014/3348/pdfs/uksi_20143348_en.pdf.

Early intervention measures are also flanked by on-site inspection by regulators where the bank management is retained to give effect to the measures.[161]

It is envisaged that when early intervention measures kick in, such measures border on the horizon of resolution, and hence resolution authorities should be kept informed of the measures and their progress.[162] This is an area where the regulator and resolution authority should work closely together. In the UK, it would be the PRA working with the resolution department in the Bank. The advantage of both the regulator and resolution authority being situated within the Bank of England is that there may be efficiencies in working together and communications. However, their interactions and decision-making may become opaque and inscrutable. Where the EU is concerned, the SSM would be responsible for pre-resolution situations such as early intervention and would have to work closely with the SRB.[163] As the SRB is a separate outfit from the ECB acting as the SSM, there may be more opportunities for inter-agency differences to arise. However, such opportunities may also provide a form of inter-agency check and balance in decision-making.

Early intervention measures also raise another concern in terms of cross-border coordination for financial groups. How should the PRA or FCA proceed if it were to decide on early intervention on a UK-based entity that has a cross-border footprint? We turn now to consider how EU legislation has provided for coordination amongst EEA regulators in relation to early intervention measures.

13.2.4.1 Coordination for early intervention measures in groups

Where a regulator who is consolidating supervisor of a financial group is of the view that the criteria for early intervention are satisfied, it must consult other concerned regulators over a period of three days. The regulator must assess the impact of such measures upon the group as reflected in feedback obtained from consulting concerned regulators. However, the regulator has the right to make a decision and after which must notify all concerned regulators and the EBA. This also applies to a regulator that is the competent authority for a subsidiary of a group established in its jurisdiction.[164]

There may be a situation where the consolidating supervisor for the group wishes to carry out early intervention, and other regulators for the same group's subsidiaries have the same desire. In such a case, regulators are urged to coordinate towards a joint decision, as it may be more efficient and consistent to have the same set of early intervention measures across the group (such as appointing the same temporary administrator).[165]

---

[161] Article 27, BRRD 2014.   [162] Ibid.

[163] The potential for checks and balances between these two relatively powerful bodies could provide a sound framework for decision-making, although it will be queried if decisions can be timely and efficient. See Iris H-Y Chiu, 'Power and Accountability in the EU Financial Regulatory Architecture: Examining Inter-agency Relations, Agency Independence and Accountability' (2015) *European Journal of Legal Studies* 68.

[164] Article 30, BRRD 2014; s111, Bank Recovery and Resolution Order No 2, 2014 at http://www.legislation.gov.uk/uksi/2014/3348/pdfs/uksi_20143348_en.pdf. Section 112 further provides the reciprocal right for the PRA or FCA to be consulted where another consolidating supervisor decides to take early intervention measures against a group entity that the PRA or FCA are not supervisor of but are concerned, as there may be cross-border branches within the UK.   [165] Article 30, BRRD 2014.

UK legislation prescribes that the consolidating supervisor must begin the process of facilitating a joint decision within five days of receiving the most recent notification from another regulator as to the intention to carry out early intervention measures.[166]

Where there is a lack of a joint decision or there is disagreement among the relevant regulators as to whether and what early intervention measures to take, any of the concerned regulators can refer the matter to the EBA for it to decide within three days.[167]

The formalised coordination measures are useful for the PRA or FCA to be part of an early dialogue process with fellow EEA regulators before early intervention measures are carried out. Upon the UK's cessation of EU membership, it could be envisaged that the PRA or FCA would not be privy to such early dialogue and coordination, unless such a practice is maintained among supervisory colleges at the international level under the auspices of the Bank for International Settlements (see discussion in section 13.3). Further, recourse to the EBA for resolution of differences would not be available.

13.2.5 Precautionary recapitalisation

A grey area exists between early intervention or pre-resolution measures and the commencement of resolution. Article 32(4) of the BRRD provides that where extraordinary public financial support (i.e. bail-out by state) is required, a financial institution should be regarded as triggering the resolution condition of 'failing or likely to fail' (discussed below in detail). However, there may be exceptional cases where resolution is not regarded as triggered, and such a financial institution may indeed receive state support, even though state support is highly frowned upon in the BRRD's scheme of things.[168]

In this grey area, it seems that certain banks could, under specific conditions, receive state support and stave off the drastic actions of resolution. The conditions are that:

(a) There is a serious disturbance in the economy of a member state.

(b) The member state sees state support as necessary to preserve financial stability.

(c) State support is structured in one of three ways, that is, a state guarantee to back the bank's borrowing from the central bank's emergency liquidity facilities, a state guarantee of newly issued liabilities or recapitalisation using state funds on terms that do not confer an advantage to the bank.

(d) Such state support can only be used for solvent banks.

---

[166] Sections 113 and 118, Bank Recovery and Resolution Order No 2, 2014 at http://www.legislation.gov.uk/uksi/2014/3348/pdfs/uksi_20143348_en.pdf. section 113 and 118 are mirror provisions, the former applying where the PRA of FCA is the consolidating supervisor and the latter where another regulator is the consolidating supervisor.

[167] Article 30, BRRD 2014, ss114 and 119, Bank Recovery and Resolution Order No 2, 2014 at http://www.legislation.gov.uk/uksi/2014/3348/pdfs/uksi_20143348_en.pdf. Sections 114 and 119 are mirror provisions, with the former applying where the PRA or FCA is the consolidating supervisor and the latter where another regulator is the consolidating supervisor.

[168] As will be discussed in relation to temporary nationalisation later.

(e) Such state support must be precautionary and temporary in nature and proportionate to remedy the consequences of the serious disturbance and shall not be used to offset losses incurred by the bank.

(f) Such support must be approved by the EU state Aid framework.

This power is known as ***precautionary recapitalisation*** and has come to be used in cases where a bank facing stronger capitalisation pressures, usually after a poor or failed stress test result, has failed to raise adequate capital from private investors. This is understandable as a bank does not inspire investors' confidence after a poor stress test result, and investors may avoid investing in such a bank even though a bank desperately needs fresh equity capital at such a time. In 2015, the Greek government sought to recapitalise two banks, Piraeus Bank and National Bank of Greece that faced a shortfall after a poor response to its capital raising exercise. The Hellenic Stability Facility was given approval to purchase €2.7 billion of contingent capital instruments issued by the two banks.[169]

Although the conditions for precautionary recapitalisation are highly prescribed, it would be hard to argue against a member state that perceives a 'serious disturbance' to its economy or its needs for financial stability, especially where it is not entirely clear whether a bank is indeed 'solvent'. Bank assets are hard to value and illiquid, and valuing non-performing loans is far from standardised.[170] In 2017, the Italian government sought to bail-out Monte Dei Paschi under the provision for precautionary recapitalisation although there had already been debate and disagreement between the Italian and EU level authorities on whether Monte Dei Paschi should have entered resolution. The success of the Italian authorities in activating this power in favour of Monte Dei Paschi was critically queried[171] in terms of how this could undermine the resolution regime and the coordination of bank crisis management with the EU. Indeed, this power opens a back door to state bail-out, which is one of the undesirable avenues sought to be minimised by the introduction of internationally convergent, prescribed, and hopefully predictable resolution regimes.

13.2.6 Resolution

If a stricken bank enters into a phase of vulnerability that is beyond early crisis management, resolution options would have to be considered. Leaving banks to be wound up under corporate insolvency laws may be highly undesirable if systemic consequences

---

[169] European Parliament Briefing, 'Precautionary recapitalisations under the Bank Recovery and Resolution Directive: conditionality and case practice' (2017) at http://www.europarl.europa.eu/RegData/etudes/BRIE/2017/602084/IPOL_BRI(2017)602084_EN.pdf.

[170] The EBA has only started consulting on standards for managing non-performing loans in banks, see 'The EBA launches consultation on how to manage non-performing exposures' (8 March 2018) at https://www.eba.europa.eu/documents/10180/2150622/Consultation+Paper+on+Guidelines+on+management+of+non-performing+and+forborne+exposures+%28EBA-CP-2018-01%29.pdf.

[171] Christos Hadjiemmanuil, 'Monte dei Paschi: A Test for the European Policy Against Bank Bailouts' (2 May 2017) at https://www.law.ox.ac.uk/business-law-blog/blog/2017/05/monte-dei-paschi-test-european-policy-against-bank-bailouts.

Box 13.5 Resolution objectives

1. Ensuring the continuity of UK banking services and critical functions (e.g. payments systems).

2. Enhancing and protecting the UK's financial system in terms of preventing contagion and maintaining market discipline.

3. Protecting and enhancing public confidence in the UK financial system.

4. Protecting public funds from being used for bail-out.

5. Protecting investors and depositors in accordance with the statutory schemes of guarantee and protection.

6. Protecting client assets and money in accordance with regulatory duties.

7. Avoiding interference with property rights contrary to the Human Rights Act 1998.

---

entail. Hence, resolution regimes are developed as a *'lex specialis'* for banks, and these inevitably require action led by authorities and involve funding implications. However, where banks are unlikely to cause systemic consequences, it may not be necessary to trigger a resolution process,[172] and such banks can be wound up.

The UK resolution authority is the Bank of England, whose objectives in resolution are seven-fold as set out in the Banking Act 2009 (amended in 2014 by the Bank Recovery and Resolution Order). The Bank of England may appoint a resolution administrator to exercise its powers.[173] Resolution objectives are set out in Box 13.5.

It is questionable how resolution authorities are to keep in balance the multiple objectives.[174] They are not listed in order of priority and so are equally imperative. However, during a resolution, it is inevitable that certain trade-offs would have to be made,[175] and individual property rights may not be protected for example, if there is a need to minimise them in order to achieve a resolution package in the interests of overall financial stability. It would also be uncertain how maintaining market discipline can be balanced against resolution measures that are in the interests of achieving financial stability and public confidence. Resolution objectives may be regarded as statements of principle,

---

[172] Bank of England, *The Bank's Approach to Resolution* (Oct 2017) at https://www.bankofengland.co.uk/-/media/boe/files/news/2017/october/the-bank-of-england-approach-to-resolution.pdf?la=en&hash=FC806900972DDE7246AD8CD1DF8B8C324BE7652F, p7; see discussion in section 13.1.2.3 on the SRB's refrain from resolving a number of Venetian banks and the Latvian Bank ABLV where no systemic consequences were expected.

[173] Sections 62B–E, Banking Act 2009 amended by the Bank Recovery and Resolution Order 2014.

[174] Section 4, Banking Act 2009, amended by the Bank Recovery and Resolution Order 2014. Relevant BBRD 2014 provision is Article 31.

[175] The Bank of England expressly reserves discretion to prioritise objectives, see para 1.15, Bank of England, *The Bank's Approach to Resolution* (2017) at https://www.bankofengland.co.uk/-/media/boe/files/news/2017/october/the-bank-of-england-approach-to-resolution.pdf?la=en&hash=FC806900972DDE7246AD8CD1DF8B8C324BE7652F.

> ### Box 13.6 Resolution tools at a glance
>
> 1. Private sector purchase
> 2. Bridge bank
> 3. Asset management vehicle
> 4. Bail-in by shareholders and creditors
> 5. Public sector financing support

but they would go towards the examination of a resolution authority's discretion in the event of judicial review. The ECB is currently facing such review actions from the shareholders and junior creditors of Banco Popular,[176] which has been resolved by sale in 2017 to Santander for 1 euro after the ECB has determined it 'failing or likely to fail' and triggered resolution.

The Bank of England has at its disposal the following resolution tools set out in the Box above. When the pioneering regime for resolution was introduced in the Banking Act 2009, the only resolution tools were private sector purchase, bridge bank and temporary nationalisation, all of which could involve significant public sector intervention and cost. The fiscal cost of the bank resolutions carried out during the 2007–9 global financial crisis made policymakers keen to avoid this again, and they called for the private sector to bear a greater share of responsibility for resolution. Shareholders and creditors of banks who benefit when the bank is a going concern should be prepared to absorb more losses under the development of the 'bail-in' tool. The bail-in tool was endorsed in the FSB's Key Attributes and given legislative footing in the BRRD 2014 and the UK transposition in the Bank Recovery and Resolution Order 2014. Further, recognising that depositor runs on banks could gravely exacerbate a crisis, deposit guarantee is regarded as a key part of crisis management and this area has been reformed by the UK and the EU in successive steps since the global financial crisis. The resolution tools (see Box 13.6) are to be used by the resolution authority in accordance with a Treasury Code of Conduct.[177]

Resolution tools can only be activated upon the meeting of certain thresholds. First, the PRA must be satisfied that the ailing bank (or other financial institution) is failing or likely to fail.

13.2.6.1 Failing or likely to fail

'Failure' refers to breach of authorisation conditions, that is, capital adequacy thresholds established in regulation, or that the bank is insolvent according to either the balance sheet test (i.e. the bank's liabilities exceed its assets) or if the bank fails to pay liabilities as

---

[176] 'Investors file 51 lawsuits against EU for shutting Banco Popular', *Reuters.com* (30 August 2017).

[177] Section 5, Banking Act 2009, amended by the Bank Recovery and Resolution Order 2014.

they fall due.[178] It may be argued that as a bank reaches insolvency thresholds, it would likely already have fallen below the capital adequacy threshold conditions. As capital adequacy thresholds are set to rise, as discussed in Chapter 8, banks face increased pressure to stay above these thresholds, and only the most robust banks would be fit to survive.

Next, the Bank of England must be satisfied that no other measures including private sector measures or early intervention measures would reasonably likely prevent such failure from taking place, and that resolution is necessary in the public interest to achieve one or more of the special resolution objectives. In this respect the Bank needs to work with the PRA, which is responsible for recovery and early intervention measures, in order to ensure that resolution is timed appropriately upon the certainty that recovery and early intervention are unlikely to be effective. The Bank must also be convinced that the special resolution objectives discussed above are unlikely to be achieved by the application of corporate insolvency procedures to the bank. In the UK, express coordination is stipulated between the PRA, Bank of England, and the Treasury in determining that resolution is appropriate. This formalised arrangement seeks to overcome the criticisms of the former 'tripartite' arrangement that did not work well in the 2007–9 global financial crisis.[179]

The BRRD sets out certain general principles for the practice of resolution. These seek to ensure that throughout the EU, convergent practices can be carried out. Convergence in resolution practice are aimed at preventing national authorities from being tempted to resort to public financing and at treating affected private sector parties as equally and as fairly as possible, so that challenges to resolution, which may add to the already stressful situation, may be minimised.[180]

The BRRD compels resolution authorities to ensure that shareholders and creditors bear losses first, and that the management body is replaced (or otherwise made to give effect to the resolution measures) and members of the management body may be open to personal liability for their part in causing the bank crisis. Further, resolution must not make any creditor worse off than under liquidation and creditors should be treated as equally as possible. Finally, the resolution authority must adhere to the obligations to protect covered deposits (which we will discuss under deposit guarantee) and adhere to the safeguards in the Directive.

The BRRD's principles are in response to the lessons learnt in the last crisis and clearly denounce quick resort to public sector financing, which can introduce moral hazard as well as 'beggar thy neighbour' effects. An example on point is that when Ireland was faced with the potential failure of a few of its banks in the global financial crisis of 2007–9, it unilaterally guaranteed all deposits in Irish banks, beyond the maximum amount stipulated under law. This caused an outflow of deposits to Ireland from other member state countries, notably the UK. Thus, general principles for the practice of

---

[178] Article 32, BRRD 2014, s7, Banking Act 2009 amended by the Bank Recovery and Resolution Order 2014.
[179] Discussed in Chapter 6, section 6.1.   [180] Article 34, BRRD 2014.

resolution by authorities seek to restrain unilateral behaviour that may have adverse impact upon others. It is now clear that any form of public financing resolution tool such as nationalisation must take a back seat. The bail-in tool is therefore of prominent importance in resolution.

Where a resolution power is to be exercised over a UK entity that is a financial group with impact in other jurisdictions, the Bank of England must also have regard to any adverse impact on the group as a whole, and on the financial stability of other jurisdictions in the EEA and third countries.[181] We turn now to the resolution powers or 'tools' that are available to resolution authorities. The tools are likely to be used in combination in order to stabilise and restructure a bank during the resolution process.[182]

13.2.6.2 Bail-in

The 'bail-in' tool[183] is envisaged to be utilised if a stricken bank can indeed be recapitalised over the resolution weekend and then continue to carry on its critical functions until such time that it completely recovers without any further participation from resolution authorities.[184] The PRA envisages that bail-in is to be used for larger and more complex banks.[185]

'Bail-in' is in essence a form of private sector 'burden sharing' in absorbing bank losses, as well as having the prospect of recapitalising a bank. In other words, bail-in, which involves the absorption of bank losses by its shareholders first and then a range of junior and unsecured creditors, is regarded as the necessary policy to countervail the prospects of bail-out by states, which entail moral hazard and are costly for taxpayers. Bail-in is supported on the basis of empirical evidence[186] that shows that many of the banks that neared failure in the 2007–9 global financial crisis would have been perfectly recapitalised if bail-in had taken place.

The application of bail-in is in reality complex and varied. This is because its perceived usefulness has entailed its application in a wider scope of situations than in resolution alone. First, bail-in can be 'voluntary', in the sense that the bank can issue certain instruments that help it to carry out recapitalisation on a voluntary basis if it should be close to breaching capital adequacy requirements. These instruments are known as 'contingent convertible capital instruments' (CoCos) that allow a bank to treat the

---

[181] Article 33, BRRD 2014; s7A, Banking Act 2009 as inserted by the Bank Recovery and Resolution Order 2014.

[182] The Bank of England expressly reserves discretion to prioritise objectives, see Part 2, 21, Bank of England, *The Bank's Approach to Resolution* (2017) at https://www.bankofengland.co.uk/-/media/boe/files/news/2017/october/the-bank-of-england-approach-to-resolution.pdf?la=en&hash=FC806900972DDE7246AD8CD1DF 8B8C324BE7652F

[183] Section 48B, Banking Act 2009 amended by the Bank Recovery and Resolution Order 2014; Article 43, BRRD 2014.

[184] Bank of England, *The Bank's Approach to Resolution* (2017) at https://www.bankofengland.co.uk/-/media/boe/files/news/2017/october/the-bank-of-england-approach-to-resolution.pdf?la=en&hash=FC8069009 72DDE7246AD8CD1DF8B8C324BE7652F, para 2.10ff.   [185] Ibid.

[186] Thomas Conlon and John Cotter, 'The Anatomy of a Bail-in' (2013) at http://ssrn.com/abstract=2294100.

instrument as debt upon which the bank would pay a favourable interest return to the holder, until such time that certain trigger conditions occur and allows the bank to convert the debt to equity in order for it to function as recapitalising capital. Investors can be attracted to the high interest rates that CoCos pay, as illustrated in the case of *BNY Mellon Corporate Trustee Services Ltd v LBG Capital No 1 plc and another*[187] discussed in Chapter 8, section 8.5.

Bail-in that is not applied by the bank voluntarily but imposed by regulators would be 'mandatory'. Mandatory bail-in has been used as a resolution tool but also beyond the scope of resolution. For example, the bail-in tool can be used ***not*** as part of resolution,[188] such as in remedial actions to be carried out after adverse stress-testing results. This was implemented in the case of the Co-operative Bank.[189] Bail-in can also be implemented alongside other resolution tools. For example, in the resolution of Banco Popular discussed in section 13.1, bail-in was carried out prior to the sale to Santander. Bail-in can also be carried out alongside temporary public sector ownership in order to minimise the level of loss absorption that may be inflicted upon the public sector.[190]

It has been criticised that the wide possibilities for the use of bail-in creates uncertainty for private sector investors who are subject to the potential of bail-in. This can cause two problems.[191] One is that the private sector investors are unable to price adverse possibilities correctly in the market and thus bail-in instruments are not able to act as instruments of market discipline. The cost to banks of issuing bail-inable instruments acts as a form of market discipline for banks' risk-taking. If investors are able to perceive their risks accurately and price the instruments appropriately, this acts as a form of market discipline for banks' strategic decisions in risk-taking. However, the uncertainties as to when bail-in would happen can create market distortions, as investors may be too optimistic or pessimistic about the prospect of bail-in and price these instruments incorrectly. The practice of bail-in by regulators has not helped as they are responsible for the discretionary onset of bail-in and have not clarified the predictability of when bail-in should occur. For example, in the case of Monte Dei Paschi, bail-in has not occurred although the bank has failed a stress test and has been recapitalised by the government through precautionary recapitalisation instead. On the contrary, the Co-operative Bank was subject to bail-in after failing a stress test although not yet pronounced to be in resolution.

Second, the uncertainty as to the application of bail-in and its processes would cause investors to scrutinise the exercise of discretion by resolution authorities very carefully, as their rights would be affected. This can entail costly litigation against resolution

---

[187] [2016] UKSC 29.

[188] Articles 59, 60, BRRD 2014, s6B, Banking Act 2009, inserted by the Bank Recovery and Resolution Order 2014.

[189] Discussed in Chapter 9, section 9.6.

[190] Section 6A, Banking Act 2009, inserted by the Bank Recovery and Resolution Order 2014.

[191] Tobias Troeger, 'Too Complex to Work: A Critical Assessment of the Bail-In Tool Under the European Bank Recovery and Resolution Regime' (2018) at https://papers.ssrn.com/sol3/papers.cfm?abstract_id=3023184.

authorities and complicate the process of bail-in. This point is being proved as the principles of bail-in are widely-worded concerning affected shareholders' and creditors' rights, and litigation relating to bailed-in episodes are being carried out.[192] It is suggested that bail-in should be used not as a resolution tool, but as a pre-resolution or early intervention tool, since its main purpose is to recapitalise the bank and allow it to carry on its business albeit after some restructuring and reorganisation. This would allow bail-in to be used with earlier triggers, and in a more predictable manner.[193]

We turn now to examine bail-in as a resolution tool, in recognition of its varied and complex uses.

How bail-in works

The bail-in tool is used to write-down or convert the rights of share and bondholders in order to return the bank to meeting capital adequacy thresholds.[194] The bank should then be re-organised in order to be turned around. The PRA envisages that holders of MREL instruments, as discussed in Chapter 8, section 8.5, are to be subject to bail-in, and the order of bail-in would proceed as follows.[195]

Shareholders should first be made to write-down their capital, that is, to be diluted or cancelled to the extent that is needed to recapitalise the bank. If a bank's net asset value is negative or zero, as determined by valuation (discussed in section 13.2.6.6), shareholders' rights should be cancelled not diluted. Dilution should only take place where the bank has a positive net asset value, according to the 'conversion principles' to be discussed below.[196]

Next, holders of other capital instruments known as 'additional tier one instruments' are to be converted into ordinary equity. Additional tier one instruments refer to all instruments that are fully paid, perpetual, not secured or subject to claims or guarantees, and contain conversion triggers at stressful points that are pre-liquidation (the conversion factors for such instruments are clearly prescribed), such as where the common equity tier one capital of institutions fall below 5.125 per cent.[197] These instruments are also subject to deductions in specifically prescribed circumstances,[198] meaning that they count for less than their face value according to regulatory prescriptions. These instruments are a form of convertible and subordinated debt and the EBA has introduced various standardised templates for banks to use in issuing them so that they can be used for bail-in as intended.[199] Next in line would be holders of Tier 2 instruments

---

[192] Such as in relation to Banco Popular, discussed in section 13.1.

[193] Tobias Troeger, 'Too Complex to Work: A Critical Assessment of the Bail-In Tool Under the European Bank Recovery and Resolution Regime' (2018) at https://papers.ssrn.com/sol3/papers.cfm?abstract_id=3023184.

[194] Article 46, BRRD 2014, s12A, Banking Act 2009, inserted by the Bank Recovery and Resolution Order 2014.

[195] Article 48, BRRD 2014, s12AA, Banking Act 2009, inserted by the Bank Recovery and Resolution Order 2014.

[196] EBA, *Final Guidelines on the treatment of shareholders in bail-in or the write-down and conversion of capital instruments* (April 2017) at https://www.eba.europa.eu/documents/10180/1807527/Guidelines+on+the+treatment+of+shareholders+in+bail-in+%28EBA-GL-2017-04%29.pdf.

[197] Article 54, CRR 2013.   [198] Articles 56–60, CRR 2013.

[199] EBA, *EBA Standardised Templates for Additional Tier 1 Instruments* (July 2016) at https://www.eba.europa.eu/documents/10180/1360107/EBA+draft+AT1+templates+-+2016.pdf.

who would be converted into ordinary equity. These are subordinated debt that are fully paid-up, not subject to security or guarantees, have a maturity date of at least 5 years and not subject to accelerated payment.[200] They are also subject to express amortisation provisions close to maturity and deductions in certain circumstances,[201] meaning that they count for much less closer to maturity.

Where the cancellation or dilution of shares or conversion of the above instruments is not sufficient to recapitalise the bank, that is, to meet its capital adequacy thresholds, then other 'eligible liabilities' may be converted.[202] These are all fully-paid-up instruments not financed or guaranteed by the issuing institution, unsecured and not based on a derivative or deposit, and has a maturity of at least a year.[203] The sequence of bail-in is mandatory and reflects normal insolvency principles.

Box 13.7 below sets out the order of bail-in.[204]

Resolution authorities have the discretion as to the extent of bail-in that is needed in relation to the hierarchy set out above. The Bank of England envisages that it will set out a resolution instrument[205] for bail-in to specify those affected over the resolution weekend. However, processes for valuation and conversion (below) will take longer to be effected.

Conversion principles

Where liabilities are to be converted to equity in bail-in, such conversion should adhere to three principles.[206] First, the conversion must not make the creditor worse off than under normal insolvency proceedings, second the conversion rates and processes must

---

Box 13.7 Order of bail-in

(a) Common equity tier one

(b) Additional tier one instruments

(c) Tier two instruments

(d) Other subordinated debt, in accordance with the normal insolvency hierarchy

(e) Other eligible liabilities, in accordance with the normal insolvency hierarchy

---

[200] Article 63, CRR 2013.   [201] Articles 64-70, CRR 2013.

[202] Article 48, BRRD 2014, s12 AA, https://www.eba.europa.eu/documents/10180/1360107/EBA+draft+AT1+templates+-+2016.pdf; Bank of England, *The Bank's Approach to Resolution* (2017) at https://www.bankofengland.co.uk/-/media/boe/files/news/2017/october/the-bank-of-england-approach-to-resolution.pdf?la=en&hash=FC806900972DDE7246AD8CD1DF8B8C324BE7652F, para 2.13.   [203] Article 45, BRRD 2014.

[204] EBA, *Final Guidelines concerning the interrelationship between the BRRD sequence of writedown and conversion and CRR/CRD* (April 2017) at https://www.eba.europa.eu/documents/10180/1807502/Guidelines+on+the+interrelationship+BRRD_CRR+%28EBA-GL-2017-02%29.pdf.

[205] Bank of England, *The Bank's Approach to Resolution* (2017) at https://www.bankofengland.co.uk/-/media/boe/files/news/2017/october/the-bank-of-england-approach-to-resolution.pdf?la=en&hash=FC806900972DDE7246AD8CD1DF8B8C324BE7652F, paras 2.11–2.13.

[206] Sections 48E and 48G, Banking Act 2009 amended by the Financial Services (Banking Reform) Act 2013; Article 48, BRRD 2014.

adhere to the hierarchy of creditors under insolvency laws, and third, creditors in the same class should be treated in a similar and equitable manner.

Resolution authorities would determine and apply conversion rates from debt to level of equity, and this is an area of significant exercise of discretion by them.[207] The operation of bail-in is underpinned by valuation procedures for the relevant equity and debt instruments, which as discussed shortly, are an overarching requirement that underpins all of the resolution tools. Legislation also provides for supportive powers to complete the bail-in process such as the amendment of relevant registers of interests, such as share registers and/or delisting or relisting where appropriate.[208] The valuation process would assist authorities in arriving at the values of debt and equity instruments as if normal insolvency procedures had been applied, so that authorities have a starting point for conversion to take place. Debt-holders who are bailed-in should receive a conversion to equity level that is equal to or greater than the value of their claims.

Resolution authorities have the discretion to apply different rates of conversion to different classes of creditors as long as the principle of 'no creditor worse off than under insolvency' is met. It is envisaged that senior debt-holders may be converted to a lesser proportion or on better terms to reflect their status in the insolvency hierarchy, but this should not disproportionately affect junior debt-holders adversely.

The Bank of England has to provide a copy of each resolution instrument pursuant to the exercise of its bail-in powers to the FCA, Treasury, PRA, the bank, and other concerned persons, and to report on the exercise of the powers and their effects to the Chancellor of the Exchequer, ensuring that the highest level of ministerial attention is given to the impact of bail-in.[209]

Expressly excluded liabilities

Certain liabilities are excluded or protected from the bail-in regime in order to protect certain social expectations as well as to inflict minimal damage to holders of property rights.

Covered depositors (those protected by a deposit guarantee scheme, see section 13.3), tax and social security liabilities and remuneration (except bonuses) owing to employees and pension liabilities should be excluded in line with the protection of social interests. Secured lenders, client assets and monies and other assets arising out of a fiduciary relationship are also excluded, in order to uphold property rights protected under one of the resolution objectives discussed earlier. Inter-bank liabilities with a maturity of under seven days are excluded in order not to totally disrupt the short-term money

---

[207] EBA, *Final Guidelines on the rate of conversion of debt to equity in bail-in* (April 2017) at https://www.eba. europa.eu/documents/10180/1807514/Guidelines+on+the+rate+of+conversion+of+debt+to+equity+in+bail -in+%28EBA-GL-2017-03%29.pdf.

[208] Article 53, BRRD 2014, s48L, Banking Act 2009 amended by the Bank Recovery and Resolution Order 2014.

[209] Sections 48E and 48T, Banking Act 2009 amended by the Financial Services (Banking Reform) Act 2013.

markets. Liabilities owing to infrastructure providers with a maturity under seven days are also to be excluded, perhaps in order to ensure critical access to services.[210] The UK Treasury may amend or add to this list by Order if it sees fit.[211]

The resolution authorities may also seek to exclude liabilities where the bail-in cannot be implemented in a timely manner or that the value of those liabilities would deteriorate beyond a worthwhile point for bail-in, or where contagion and systemic risk, or critical continuity may be adversely affected.[212] The UK has provided for a procedure whereby such exclusions can only be effected if the Bank of England notifies the European Commission upon reasoned grounds for such exclusion taking into account to need to treat liability holders of the same class equally. Where the UK ceases EU membership, this layer of check and balance would be lost and it would be imperative to institute a measure of accountability for the Bank of England if it should wish to implement exclusions to bail-in.

Another mechanism that 'checks' a resolution authority's discretion to exclude certain liabilities for bail-in is the BRRD 2014 provision that requires the authority to top up the recapitalisation of the stricken bank as if the liabilities in question had not been excluded. However, it is uncertain if the contribution is a requirement or an option, as the Directive's terms are drafted as follows: 'resolution authorities *may* make a contribution to the institution'. Such financing contribution can be advanced from the national resolution financing arrangements. However, such contribution is limited to not exceeding 5 per cent of the institution's total liabilities, and where the bailed-in amounts have already met at least 8 per cent of the total liabilities of the institution.[213] The Bank of England has not transposed this provision.

The 'excluded liabilities' provision does not provide for the converse situation, that is, to create exceptions to the exclusion of liabilities. This means that excluded liabilities are protected and there is no room to consider exceptional circumstances to bail them in. It is arguable that such a provision functions in a distributive manner- to establish as a matter of principle where bank losses fall, sparing stakeholders who are not in a position to bargain for their protections or those that come with social implications. The distributive framework connects the needs of financial stability with protecting certain social expectations, as the severe disruption of the latter can have dampening effects upon market and economic confidence and affect financial stability objectives. A notorious episode is recalled where in 2013, the Bank of Cyprus and the Cypriot Popular Bank were nearing failure for having held excessive amounts of Greek debt that lost much of their face value after a near Greek default. The Cypriot government proposed to bail-in covered depositors in order to spare high net worth foreign depositors from the worst of the bail-in procedures. This resulted in a severe backlash and social

---

[210] Article 44, BRRD 2014, s48B(7A), Banking Act 2009 amended by the Bank Recovery and Resolution Order 2014.

[211] Section 48F, Banking Act 2009 amended by the Financial Services (Banking Reform) Act 2013.

[212] Ibid.   [213] Article 44, BRRD 2014.

outcry, leading to a reversal of that position. The distributive framework also achieves efficiency, as certain creditors and financial instrument investors who have voluntarily assumed those positions, are better placed to bear losses (such as pursuant to the purchase of MREL instruments, as discussed in Chapters 8 and 9, which reward them with usually high rates of interest). These voluntary risk-bearers are arguably better prepared to have *ex ante* risk management mechanisms in place.

Contractual recognition

It is imperative that mandatory bail-in achieves its intended effects in private law between the bank and its creditors and investors, so that it is not thwarted or avoided by contractual provisions. Hence the BRRD 2014 specifically provides that member states must ensure that contractual recognition of bail-in is carried out so that the bailed-in effects cannot be questioned by private litigation.[214] The UK has implemented this in the PRA Rulebook.[215] The PRA imposes the obligation on all banks and banking groups to ensure that all liabilities created are to contain clauses that recognise the exercise of the mandatory bail-in power by the Bank of England and its effects other than in relation to deposits, excluded liabilities and those governed by the law of a third country outside of the EEA.[216] The UK applies this obligation to all debt instruments created after 19 February 2015 and other eligible non-debt instruments created after 31 December 2015, unless these instruments created before the respective dates above have been materially amended since 31 July 2016.[217]

The EBA has provided guidelines on how such contractual clauses should be drafted, short of issuing a template clause. It is, however, understood that private trade bodies such as the Association for Financial Markets in Europe are leading the creation of master clauses that can be adapted by parties.[218] Recognition clauses must at least include:

(a) the acknowledgement and acceptance by counterparty that the liability may be subject to the exercise of write-down and conversion powers by a resolution authority;

(b) a description of the write-down and conversion powers of each resolution authority that is relevant;

(c) the acknowledgement and acceptance by the entity's counterparty:

(1) that it is bound by the effect of an application of the powers referred to in (a) including:

(i) any reduction in the principal amount or outstanding amount due, including any accrued but unpaid interest, in respect of the liability under the relevant agreement;

---

[214] Article 55, BRRD 2014.   [215] *Contractual Recognition of Bail-in.*
[216] Ibid para 2.1.   [217] Ibid para 2.3.
[218] See https://www.afme.eu/globalassets/downloads/standard-forms-and-documents/afme-model-clauses-for-contractual-recognition-of-bail-in.pdf; http://www.drsllp.com/blog/bail-in-2/bail-amendments-now-available/.

      (ii) the conversion of that liability into ordinary shares or other instruments of ownership;

  (2) that the terms of the relevant agreement may be varied as necessary to give effect to the exercise by a resolution authority of its write-down and conversion powers and such variations will be binding on the entity's counterparty; and

  (3) that ordinary shares or other instruments of ownership may be issued to or conferred on the counterparty as a result of the exercise of the write-down and conversion powers.[219]

This standardisation is also part of wider international harmonisation encouraged by the FSB[220] urging all national regulators to give mandatory effect to contractual recognition of resolution actions in general, so that cross-border resolution may be more coherent and coordinated (a point we return to in section 13.4).

The regime for the TLAC/MREL mitigates the potential problems posed by contractual recognition as those instruments would clearly have to be capable of writing down and conversion. However, the PRA also requires that MREL instruments be certified by a properly reasoned independent legal opinion so that they can be effectively bailed-in.[221] It is uncertain what consequences for the drafter of the legal opinion there may be if MREL instruments are subsequently challenged in private litigation or litigation against the resolution authority. The resolution authority could presumably sue the drafter of the legal opinion for losses if it incurs problems with enforcing MREL. A relationship of reliance and proximity would likely be met for either an action in negligence[222] or misrepresentation.

Business reorganisation

As bail-in is intended to recapitalise a bank so that it can return to normal business operations, resolution authorities have the power to oversee the period of bank reorganisation after the onset of bail-in to ensure that return to normality can take place successfully. The Bank of England envisages that it will appoint a resolution administrator[223] to oversee the bank's reorganisation and restructuring right at the commencement of bail-in. Within a month, the bank must produce a reorganisation plan in order to plan for return to normal.

The reorganisation plan reflects the bank's full understanding of the reasons that caused it to need resolution and must propose changes that are to be made to its structure

---

[219] EBA, *Draft Regulatory Technical Standards on the contractual recognition of write-down and conversion powers under Article 55(3) of Directive 2014/59/EU* (July 2015) at Article 3, at https://www.eba.europa.eu/documents/10180/1132911/EBA-RTS-2015-06+RTS+on+Contractual+Recognition+of+Bail-in.pdf/c66aa9cb-e2ff-4896-85e6-dca7ba5cba65. This is implemented in Art 44, Commission Delegated Regulation 2016/1075, referred to earlier.

[220] FSB, *Cross-Border Recognition of Resolution Actions* (3 Nov 2015) at http://www.fsb.org/wp-content/uploads/Cross-Border-Recognition-of-Resolution-Actions.pdf.

[221] PRA Rulebook, *Contractual Recognition of Bail-In* para 2.2.

[222] The test in *Caparo Industries plc v Dickman* [1990] 2 AC 605.

[223] Bank of England, *The Bank's Approach to Resolution* (2017) at https://www.bankofengland.co.uk/-/media/boe/files/news/2017/october/the-bank-of-england-approach-to-resolution.pdf?la=en&hash=FC806900972DDE7246AD8CD1DF8B8C324BE7652F, para 2.17.

or business going forward.[224] The BRRD 2014 is somewhat prescriptive about reorganisation plans having to include changes to structures and operations, sales of business lines, withdrawal from uncompetitive activities etc. The UK transposition[225] has, however, avoided the prescriptive approach, leaving it open-ended to meet the needs of addressing long-term viability. The reorganisation plan needs to provide a timeframe for implementation and banks are to submit progress reports every 6 months to the resolution authorities as they implement the plan.

The EBA has developed standards and guidelines[226] for the minimum contents of the reorganisation plan and abovementioned progress reports. Initially the EBA's proposals are highly prescriptive, for example a bank is asked to include predictions of the financial performance of the bank after reorganisation, as well as sufficient information to enable resolution authorities to make a viability assessment, such as projected profit and loss figures and wider macroeconomic factors. Such prescriptions are likely impractical as they require a fair amount of guesswork on the part of the bank based on assumptions that may change. We are sceptical of over-prescription in business reorganisation plans although we see it as an important measure for accountability to bank resolution authorities, regulators, and stakeholders. The sacrifice of many private law rights to give effect to bail-in should be followed by the achievement of the public interest of bank recovery and return to financial viability. The business reorganisation plan is a roadmap towards that.

The final EBA Guidelines have opted for a more sensible approach, urging banks to produce plans that are credible and viable, including content prescriptions only as guidance. Emphasis is placed on timely implementation of the plan, and the coordinated scrutiny of such implementation by both the resolution authority and the regulator of the bank concerned.

The EBA's approach is an improvement over the primary Directive provision as it recognises the important balance between flexibility and commitment on the part of the recovering bank. Further it recognises the important involvement of the bank regulator in scrutinising implementation progress as the bank returns to health.

Cross-border application

The application of mandatory bail-in for cross-border banking groups can be challenging as regimes of bail-in may not be consistent in different jurisdictions, especially outside of the EU. The FSB has issued a set of 21 principles[227] to guide consistent implementation and cooperation amongst resolution authorities. The lack of consistent implementation

---

[224] Article 52, BRRD 2014.

[225] Section 48H, Financial Services and Markets Act 2000 amended by the Financial Services (Bank Reform) Act 2013.

[226] EBA, *Final Guidelines on the minimum criteria to be fulfilled by a business reorganisation plan* (19 June 2016) at https://www.eba.europa.eu/documents/10180/1312845/EBA-GL-2015-21+GLs+on+Business+Reorg anisation+Plans.pdf.

[227] FSB, *Principles on Bail-in Execution* (June 2018) at http://www.fsb.org/wp-content/uploads/P210618-1.pdf.

can potentially give rise to affected private parties' challenge in litigation, and impede the smooth implementation of bail-in. The Principles urge regulators to be transparent on an *ex ante* basis as to instruments that are included within the scope of bail-in so that the holders of such instruments and markets generally are better prepared. Regulatory oversight of the valuation process and transparency of the valuation framework are also regarded as fundamentally important to how private parties perceive their rights have been treated. There is also a need for prompt and effective implementation of exchange where debt is converted into equity and for there to be a clear and transparent process with regard to compliance with securities registration and listing requirements, for the purposes of transferring the financial institution into new ownership after bail-in has been effected. Although the UK and EU's regulatory regime meet the requirements of the FSB principles, international convergence in this area remains a work in progress.

Next, we turn to resolution tools that involve options to transfer all or part of the bank's business.

13.2.6.3 Private sector purchase

If it is possible for a stricken bank to be taken over by a private sector purchaser, this could be ideal, as continuity for the supply of services can be assured. If a private sector purchaser emerges for the bank's business as a whole, the Bank of England can give effect to this resolution tool, upon satisfaction that the tool is necessary for the public interest of financial stability. The Bank of England needs to consult the Treasury and achieve Treasury approval to activate this tool.[228]

It is anticipated that normal takeover or sale of business procedures arguably cannot apply under these extraordinary circumstances as such procedures are designed for market transactions. In a private sector purchase of a stricken bank, the purchase has to be carried out swiftly to meet objectives that are not confined to commercial ones. Although the BRRD urges that any sale should take place consistent with commercial terms,[229] the circumstances of the resolution are highly 'non-commercial' in nature. The resolution authority plays a significant role in brokering the private sector purchase in the public interest of achieving resolution objectives and protecting the UK's financial stability. Further, the resolution authority is conferred with legislative powers to give effect to the private sector purchase through share and property transfer instruments.[230] In brokering the private sector purchase, the Bank of England has the exclusive power to make all transfer instruments.

In relation to share transfers,[231] these instruments are made by the Bank of England who must send a copy within a reasonable time to the PRA and Treasury and publish them for public viewing.[232] The instruments are given effect to by Treasury Order,

---

[228] Section 8, Banking Act 2009, amended by the Bank Recovery and Resolution Order 2014.
[229] Article 38(2) and (3), BRRD 2014.
[230] Section 11, Banking Act 2009 and Articles 38–9, BRRD 2014.
[231] Sections 15 and 16, Banking Act 2009.   [232] Section 24, Banking Act 2009.

which provides the backing of legislative authority to rewrite private parties' rights.[233] Share transfers can be made to achieve the immediate cessation of current shareholders' rights, and vest the rights in shares such as voting rights in the purchaser immediately.[234] Such transfers can be made free from any encumbrances or liability,[235] and seek to allow the purchaser to step into the shoes of the seller immediately to ensure continuity in the exercise of any related rights.[236] The Treasury Order may also provide for the mandatory reduction of shares if appropriate.[237] In order to give effect to these transfers without resulting in undue turbulence in securities markets, the Treasury Order may provide for the conversion of classes of shares, the suspension of share trading or the delisting of the shares of the bank to be sold.[238]

Sale of business can also be carried out by way of sale of assets, and in such a case property transfer instruments will be made by the Bank of England,[239] which has to be sent to the PRA and Treasury reasonably quickly and be publicly published.[240] The property transfer instrument can relate to any rights or liabilities, in whole or in part, and can have effect notwithstanding any contractual limitations or encumbrances.[241] It can provide for the continuity of certain arrangements or its termination, such as in relation to licences,[242] contracts of employment,[243] as well as contracts with directors and senior management.[244] The transfer instrument can also relate to foreign property, in which case the transferor and transferee must engage with best endeavours to give effect to the transfer. The transferee would bear the related expenses for this process. If despite these best endeavours it is not possible for the transfer to be made effective, the Bank of England may cease to apply that aspect of the transfer instrument.[245]

The Bank of England is, however, prevented from partial property transfers that may allow it to 'cherry pick' favourable aspects of rights to be transferred while ignoring other related aspects to those rights.[246] It is clarified in subsidiary legislation that the Bank of England is not to transfer away rights that are subject to set-off or netting, or liabilities without their attached collateral, or to interfere with financial markets contracts in such a way that would cause disruption to standard market rules provided by trade or clearing bodies.[247]

As property transfers will effectively strip out the original entity, the Bank of England may provide for the suspension or delisting of the transferee bank's shares.[248] This route

---

[233] Section 25, Banking Act 2009.
[234] Article 38, BRRD 2014, s17, Banking Act 2009.
[235] Section 17, Banking Act 2009.   [236] Section 18, Banking Act 2009.
[237] Section 18, Banking Act 2009 as amended by Bank Recovery and Resolution Order 2014.
[238] Section 19, Banking Act 2009 as amended by Bank Recovery and Resolution Order 2014.
[239] Section 33, Banking Act 2009.   [240] Section 41, Banking Act 2009.
[241] Section 34, Banking Act 2009.   [242] Section 37, Banking Act 2009.
[243] Section 35, 36, Banking Act 2009.   [244] Section 20, Banking Act 2009.
[245] Section 39, Banking Act 2009, amended by Bank Recovery and Resolution Order 2014.
[246] Section 47, Banking Act 2009.
[247] Sections 3–7, The Banking Act 2009 (Restriction of Partial Property Transfers) Order 2009.
[248] Section 39B, Banking Act 2009 as amended by Bank Recovery and Resolution Order 2014.

is likely to hurt shareholders without a commensurate share transfer instrument/order. However, it may be possible for them to claim some form of compensation as will be discussed below.

The extensive and draconian interventions that can be achieved in the Bank of England's role in effecting a private sector purchase are based on certain fundamental premises: principles of best practice laid down in the BRRD, a robust valuation process and the accountability mechanisms underlying the Bank of England's exercise of power (to be discussed shortly).

The BRRD provides certain overarching principles in the 'sale of business' tool. These principles include the transparency of the sale process, non-discriminatory treatment of potential purchasers, freedom from conflicts of interest, non-conferment of advantage to any potential purchaser, the need to achieve a rapid resolution and the maximisation where possible of the sale price under the various instruments.[249]

However, the EBA[250] recognises that the strict application of them can undermine the resolution authority's discretion to achieve a good result. Hence it recommends that where the resolution authority perceives a material threat to financial stability, it may apply the principles in a more nuanced manner. For example, transparency of the sale process may jeopardise the sale altogether and there must be discretion to consider how transparency should accommodate the objectives in achieving the sale. A rapid and effective resolution may also mean that maximising sale price may not necessarily be achieved. Further, it is difficult for the resolution authority to ascertain comprehensively that freedom from conflicts of interest is achieved in the interests to arrive at a rapid resolution. Non-discriminatory treatment between the potential purchasers may also not be practicable if some potential purchasers are more likely to contribute positively to financial stability than others.[251] The Bank of England, however, prefers an auction process for sale or partial sale wherever possible unless financial stability objectives are jeopardised.[252]

There are several safeguards that seek to assuage affected parties, and these apply to all resolution tools and will be discussed shortly. Share and property transfers pursuant to a private sector purchase must be premised upon appropriate valuation of the rights, liabilities, assets, and securities to be transferred, a point that we will return to shortly. Further, a range of accountability measures apply, viz the requirements imposed on the Bank of England to publish publicly the share and/or property transfer instruments as

---

[249] Article 39, BRRD 2014.

[250] EBA, *Guidelines on factual circumstances amounting to a material threat to financial stability and on the elements related to the effectiveness of the sale of business tool under Article 39(4) of Directive 2014/59/EU* (August 2015) at https://www.eba.europa.eu/documents/10180/1080767/EBA-GL-2015-04_EN_Guidelines+on+the+sale+of+business+tool.pdf/6c15f73e-7557-48a6-b9f2-a70fda290149.

[251] Such as a potential purchaser who is more likely to maintain its own regulatory threshold conditions in capital adequacy and liquidity after absorbing the stricken bank.

[252] Bank of England, *The Bank's Approach to Resolution* (2017) at https://www.bankofengland.co.uk/-/media/boe/files/news/2017/october/the-bank-of-england-approach-to-resolution.pdf?la=en&hash=FC806900972DDE7246AD8CD1DF8B8C324BE7652F, at para 2.19.

well as to coordinate with the PRA and Treasury. Finally, the exercise of transfer powers is subject to the availability of compensation for affected counterparties and third parties, to be discussed shortly.

The achievement of a private sector purchase inevitably means that shareholders' and creditors' rights would be disrupted. Private sector purchase brings to great test the balancing objectives of protecting private property interests and maintaining the overall financial stability objective. Shareholders and creditors in the bank for sale could feel undermined, but equally could the shareholders of the purchaser. In the UK, Lloyds was the private sector purchaser of stricken bank Halifax Bank of Scotland in 2008. The deal was clearly brokered very quickly by the authorities. Shareholders of Lloyds were asked to attend a general meeting where they approved of the deal, but they subsequently alleged that the deal was made on poorer terms that they would have agreed to if the full facts of HBOS' financial situation came to light. The Lloyds shareholders commenced group litigation[253] against Lloyds for personal compensation but the case has been struck out as Lloyds' directors do not owe them fiduciary duties to secure the best deal for them. The duty is owed to the company as a whole.[254] The derivative claim by the shareholders on behalf of the company has been heard in February 2018 by the High Court but at the time of writing the judgment has not yet been handed down.

A challenge also arose in the European Court of Justice to challenge the validity of bank resolution powers that affect the application of property and company law rights, but the Court has affirmatively stated that such powers are valid in face of the extraordinary circumstances and needs of public interest.[255]

13.2.6.4 Bridge institution

Where a private sector purchase cannot be rapidly finalised in the immediate hours of resolution, it may be necessary for a bridge institution to be formed to take over the ailing bank, pending an eventual private sector purchase of all or parts of the business or indeed a gradual wind-down.[256] The removal of the ailing bank to a bridge institution would have the effect of insulating it from disorderly private claims or insolvency procedures, while it is given time to be resolved.

A bridge institution must be formed as a wholly or partly-owned institution by public authorities.[257] In the UK, the Bank of England is responsible for incorporating and

[253] 'Lloyds shareholders launch £350m HBOS lawsuit', *The Telegraph* (22 July 2015).
[254] Unreported, see Brickcourt Chambers News that provides a summary, at http://www.brickcourt.co.uk/news/detail/lloyds-hbos-group-litigation-high-court-strikes-out-allegation-that-directors-of-lloyds-owed-broad-fiduciary-duties-to-its-shareholders.
[255] Case C-526/14, REQUEST for a preliminary ruling under Article 267 TFEU from the Ustavno sodišče (Constitutional Court, Slovenia), made by decision of 6 November 2014, received at the Court on 20 November 2014 and decided on 19 July 2016. http://curia.europa.eu/juris/document/document.jsf?text=&docid=181842&pageIndex=0&doclang=EN&mode=req&dir=&occ=first&part=1&cid=91508.
[256] Bank of England, *The Bank's Approach to Resolution* (2017) at https://www.bankofengland.co.uk/-/media/boe/files/news/2017/october/the-bank-of-england-approach-to-resolution.pdf?la=en&hash=FC806900972DDE7246AD8CD1DF8B8C324BE7652.   [257] Article 40, BRRD 2014.

managing the bridge institution.[258] This power can only be exercised if the Bank of England is of the view that the tool is necessary for the public interest of financial stability and obtains Treasury approval to carry this out.[259]

In order for the bridge institution to step into the shoes of the ailing bank, the Bank of England would effect share and property transfer instruments.[260] These are subject to the same powers and safeguards as discussed above in relation to private sector purchase. The bridge institution is to pay appropriate consideration for those transfers, and provides continuity in the arrangements and roles of the transferee bank.[261] The bridge institution, however, owes no duties to the shareholders of the transferee bank pending resolution.[262]

The BRRD 2014 expressly provides for the bridge institution to exercise certain powers in managing the transferee bank, such as determining its strategy and risk profile, approving its constitution, management body and remuneration of the management body.[263] Further, bridge institutions are to be recognised as authorised financial institutions and they should meet regulatory obligations such as the threshold conditions for capital adequacy and liquidity as far as is possible.[264] A bridge institution is likely to be managed in a conservative manner, that is, to be stabilised and for its assets to be preserved in value while the institution is managed with a view to exit. It is not likely to be run as a for-profit organisation.

In 2009, the Bank of England applied the bridge institution tool to resolve the failure of Dunfermline Building Society. Dunfermline made ambitious and excessive commercial property lending and suffered severe damage to its balance sheet when many defaults occurred. It was close to failure in March 2009. A private sector purchaser Nationwide Building Society was immediately found to purchase certain healthy parts of Dunfermline's business, including deposits and residential mortgages. However, its social housing loan book was not part of the purchase and was transferred to a bridge bank formed as a company in Scotland by the Bank of England. The bridge bank managed the remaining business conservatively with a view to providing continuity while finalising a private sector purchase deal. After 6 months, the remaining business was eventually transferred to Nationwide Building Society.[265] The bridge bank was wound up following the final sale. As this example illustrates, the bridge institution is a useful tool to stem panic and insulate an ailing bank from potentially disruptive private sector actions pending the realisation of a resolution strategy that may take longer to materialise. Nationwide possibly did not agree to take on the perceived riskier assets until it had conducted all relevant due diligence.

It is important for the bridge institution not to become a nationalisation measure by the back door. One of the implicit roles or even duties of the bridge institution would be to seek an exit through merger, sale of whole or part of the business on terms that

---

[258] Section 12, Banking Act 2009, as amended by Bank Recovery and Resolution Order 2014.
[259] Section 8, Banking Act 2009.   [260] Above, and Article 40, BRRD 2014.
[261] Article 40, BRRD 2014.   [262] Ibid.   [263] Article 41, BRRD 2014.   [264] Ibid.
[265] Bank of England, *Report under Section 80(1) of the Banking Act 2009 on the Dunfermline Building Society (DBS) Bridge Bank* (July 2010).

are as commercial as possible.[266] Hence the BRRD 2014 stipulates clearly that a bridge institution must be managed with a view to eventual winding down within a maximum period of 2 years unless an extension can be justified.[267]

The bridge institution tool is also underpinned by independent valuation that will shortly be discussed, as well as the availability of compensation redress for affected counterparties and third parties, to be discussed shortly. These safeguards also underpin the private purchase resolution tool.

13.2.6.5 Asset separation/management vehicle

A bridge institution may not be the most appropriate tool when a stricken bank has a mixture of good and 'bad' or non-performing assets, in which case the removal of 'bad' assets may be sufficient to allow the rest of the bank to recover. In this case, an appropriate resolution tool would be the establishment of a separate asset management vehicle that purchases the 'bad' assets in order to manage them to the point of eventual sale or winding down.[268]

Resolution authorities can establish one or more asset management vehicles to manage groups of impaired assets.[269] In the UK, the Bank of England is responsible for determining that the tool is appropriate in the interests of financial stability and that the normal liquidation of those assets would result in adverse impact.[270] The Bank may after consultation with the PRA and Treasury, establish such institutions where appropriate.[271] The EBA has issued guidelines[272] in order to ensure that asset management vehicles are legitimately set up, to relieve otherwise 'good' banks of genuinely bad assets, and not perform a role of bail-out by the back door. The EBA requires resolution authorities to assess the assets in question thoroughly with reference to: their market liquidity, market value in comparable asset classes, forward-looking market prospects for comparable asset classes, volatility in the market, impairments to other institutions holding similar assets (such as downward revision of credit ratings), and the general market conditions for disposal of such assets in terms of whether systemic risk or contagion may entail.

The Bank of England would be required to carry out the above diligence before implementing an asset management vehicle.[273] The asset management vehicle will manage the impaired assets, with similar management powers as stated for the bridge

[266] Above and s12, Banking Act 2009, amended by the Bank Recovery and Resolution Order 2014.

[267] Article 41, BRRD 2014. The Bank of England may extend this period for up to a year in the interests of financial stability or to preserve continuity of services, s12, Banking Act 2009 as amended by the Bank Recovery and Resolution Order 2014.

[268] Bank of England, *Report under Section 80(1) of the Banking Act 2009 on the Dunfermline Building Society (DBS) Bridge Bank* (July 2010).   [269] Article 42, BRRD 2014.

[270] Section 8ZA, Banking Act 2009, inserted by the Bank Recovery and Resolution Order 2014.

[271] Sections 8ZA and 12ZA, Banking Act 2009, inserted by the Bank Recovery and Resolution Order 2014.

[272] EBA, *Guidelines on the determination of when the liquidation of assets or liabilities under normal insolvency proceedings could have an adverse effect on one or more financial markets under Article 42(14) of Directive 2014/59/EU* (May 2015) at https://www.eba.europa.eu/documents/10180/1080779/EBA-GL-2015-05+Guidelines+on+the+asset+separation+tool.pdf/6441452a-d464-4618-9296-d71549a4f2c2.   [273] Above.

institution,[274] with a view to eventual sale or winding down. The asset management vehicle being a separate legal personality may issue its own debt in order to fund the purchase.[275] It is to be noted that the asset management vehicle is not regarded as a bank and therefore does not need to meet regulatory capital thresholds applied to a bank. This, however, also means that its functions are limited to asset management and it, unlike a bridge institution, is not placed in a position to provide continuity for a range of services that a bank provides. However, it is envisaged that the 'good' bank would provide continuity of services for customers.

There is no provision for a limited timeframe in which the 'bad' asset management vehicle must be wound down. This may be because such a vehicle can be partly financed by the private sector, if the asset management vehicle issues debt, and hence it can be managed as commercially as is possible for eventual realisation of value. The asset management vehicle is able to manage the 'bad assets' in its own time, and aims to time the selling off of those assets as the markets for them recover.

An example of a successful asset management vehicle is the National Assets Management Agency (NAMA) set up by the Irish government at the height of the Irish banking crisis during the global financial crisis. Many Irish banks had over-extended themselves in the pre-crisis years lending to property developers on the basis of rising residential and commercial real estate prices. However, during the Irish bank crisis, asset values plummeted by almost 50 per cent while non-performing loans sky-rocketed. The NAMA was set up to take the largest developer loans (exceeding €20 million) out of bank balance sheets in order for them to recover. In order to do so, banks needed to recognise losses early and many loans were sold to NAMA at an almost 57 per cent discount. However, this process allowed banks to recover quicker. NAMA has since been able to sell off many of the loans as markets recovered in order to mitigate the losses suffered by the taxpayer at the height of the crisis.[276]

The asset management vehicle tool is subject to the same fundamental valuation processes that underpin the private sector purchase and bridge institution tools. It is also subject to the availability of compensation redress for affected counterparties and third parties in the UK. However, it does not seem that the Bank of England is required to make public publication although it is subject to the same coordination frameworks as applied to the private sector purchase and bridge institution tools.

It may be thought that the asset management vehicle tool is confined to holding impaired assets. The story of Banco Espirito Santo, formerly the largest Portuguese bank, illustrates that the asset management vehicle can be used to constitute both 'good' and 'bad' banks, with certain unexpected practical ramifications. On balance this story perhaps warns against using the asset management vehicle for *both* good and bad assets, and it may be argued that a bridge institution with its safeguards is a more

---

[274] Article 42, BRRD 2014, s1ZA, inserted by the Bank Recovery and Resolution Order 2014.
[275] Article 42, BRRD 2014.
[276] Dirk Schoenmaker, 'Stabilising and Healing the Irish Banking System: Policy Lessons' (2015) at https://www.imf.org/external/np/seminars/eng/2014/ireland/pdf/schoenmaker_irishbanking.pdf.

appropriate crisis management tool if resolution authorities in fact wish to intervene in *all* of the bank's assets in question.

Banco Espirito Santo, formerly Portugal's largest bank was largely owned and controlled by the Espirito Santo family. In August 2014, investors started to become concerned that the bank was stricken as it was highly exposed to other companies controlled by the Espirito Santo family, and many of those loans were not performing. The Portuguese authorities decided to resolve the bank, by utilising the asset management vehicle and hiving off the 'bad assets', that is, the non-performing corporate loans in question. However, it was impracticable to retain the bank under its original brand and the Portuguese resolution authority therefore created another 'good bank' Novo Banco to manage the 'good' assets of the bank, effectively splitting the bank into two asset management vehicles.

There is no legislative blueprint for a 'good' asset management vehicle, which should ideally not be run in the same way as for impaired assets. The Portuguese resolution fund that became the sole shareholder of Novo Banco was managing it towards an eventual sale. It, however, struggled to find a suitable buyer and in mid-2016 embarked on a second round of looking for a potential buyer. The value of Novo Banco had of course been tarnished by the split of the original bank and investors were not willing to pay a high price for it. Hence, there are serious hazards in using the asset management vehicle for 'good' banks as their commercial prospects and value may be damaged by the application of the tool. Moreover, the use of an asset management vehicle for a 'good' bank' may be questioned in terms of not adhering to the BRRD 2014. The separation of 'bad' assets is appropriate to allow the rest of the bank to move forward. Implementing a 'good' bank managed by the resolution authority is anomalous and is no different from a bridge institution. However, it could be said that the troubles experienced by Novo Banco are not universally applicable and could come down to the management suboptimalities of the Portuguese resolution authority.

First, the resolution authority had a stormy relationship with the first appointed chief executive of Novo Banco resulting in the latter's swift departure. This entailed a certain amount of disruption and adverse market perception. Further, the resolution authority, being responsible for both asset management vehicles, tried to mitigate the cost of managing Novo Banco by transferring liabilities between the 'good' and 'bad' banks, a move that was opposed by affected bondholders. The use of the asset management vehicle tool by the Portuguese resolution authorities was arguably confused as the 'good bank' was not able to move forward in a commercial manner and cease to be interfered with by the resolution authority. The ECB did not intervene in this episode as the resolution started before the SRB's role officially commenced.[277] This precedent is arguably not to be followed and a bridge institution that would manage the entire stricken bank could have been more appropriate.

---

[277] 'ECB under fire as Portugal hits Novo Banco bondholders', *Financial Times* (7 Jan 2016) in which it is reported that the Portuguese resolution authority had taken its own actions in resolution and the ECB declined to comment.

13.2.6.6 Valuation

As resolution actions involve valuing assets and liabilities in order to effect cancellation, dilution, conversion or transfers, resolution authorities' decisions are underpinned by valuation principles and mechanisms. Resolution authorities are to appoint an independent valuer for the purpose of effecting any of the resolution tools. In the interests of expediency, the resolution authority may need to carry out a provisional valuation before an independent valuer is properly appointed. This, however, cannot be regarded as final and would need to be replaced by an independent valuation as quickly as possible, and adjustments between the provisional and final independent valuation would have to be made.[278]

The independent valuation should be carried out based on prudential assumptions of asset values and default rates, and ignore any extraordinary public sector financing support.[279] It should be 'fair, prudent and realistic'[280] and produce as far as is possible a prudently and conservatively valued balance sheet and list of assets for the bank under resolution.[281]

The independent valuer is also required to be a qualified and experienced person who is structurally and legally separate from relevant public authorities concerned in the resolution (i.e. the resolution authority and the regulator) as well as from the bank concerned.[282] S/he must not be subject to any material conflicts of interest, such as having any common interest with management, shareholders or creditors of the bank, or any personal, financial, investment, or other business or service relationships with the bank concerned.[283]

Valuation in resolution is not an easy exercise of judgment and can entail litigation risk for the resolution authority. The EBA is cognisant of the harshness of wiping out shareholders in the event of an unfavourable valuation, and has issued guidelines[284] to prevent expropriation of shareholders as long as there is some positive net asset value determined by the independent valuer. In the UK, the valuation of Northern Rock shares was an issue in contention between shareholders who were wiped out and the UK government that nationalised the bank in early 2008. At the point of nationalisation, the valuer appointed by the Treasury valued Northern Rock shares at 0 in terms of value, and so shareholders were completely expropriated. They argued that the valuation was

---

[278] Article 36, BRRD; ss6E and 48X on the provisional valuer and 62A on the appointment of an independent valuer, Banking Act 2009 as amended by the Bank Recovery and Resolution Order 2014.

[279] Article 36, BRRD; s62A, Banking Act 2009 as amended by the Bank Recovery and Resolution Order 2014.

[280] See, for example, EBA, *Final Guidelines on the rate of conversion of debt to equity in bail-in* (April 2017) at https://www.eba.europa.eu/documents/10180/1807514/Guidelines+on+the+rate+of+conversion+of+debt+to+equity+in+bail-in+%28EBA-GL-2017-03%29.pdf.

[281] Article 36, BRRD; s62A, Banking Act 2009 as amended by the Bank Recovery and Resolution Order 2014.

[282] Article 38, Commission Delegated Regulation 2006.

[283] Articles 39-41, Commission Delegated Regulation 2006.

[284] EBA, *Final Guidelines on the Treatment of Shareholders in Bail-in or the Write-down and Conversion of Capital Instruments* (April 2017) at http://www.eba.europa.eu/documents/10180/1807527/Guidelines+on+the+treatment+of+shareholders+in+bail-in+%28EBA-GL-2017-04%29.pdf.

incorrect as Virgin Money had made some indication of interest to purchase at that time and so the shares were not completely worthless. However, the Treasury argued that Northern Rock shares would be nil if not for public sector financing, as it would inevitably have become insolvent. The Treasury's argument was upheld in the Upper Tribunal.[285] An appeal was then lodged but dismissed.[286]

13.2.6.7 Contractual default references

Next, in order that any early intervention measures or resolution can be carried out in an orderly and effective manner, certain private law rights in contractual termination and enforcement would have to be forcibly suspended.

For example, financial contracts may refer to 'events of default' that allow the bank's counterparty to terminate its contract with the bank or carry out private enforcement rights. Such events of default often include the onset of insolvency or administration proceedings so that counterparties are no longer bound to incur expenses that are unlikely to be repaid. However, if all counterparties of a bank in resolution were to terminate their contracts in view of early crisis intervention or resolution, then the bank's chances of recovering would be gravely reduced. Hence, legislation has provided that crisis intervention and resolution measures would not constitute events of default or otherwise give rise to termination rights even if drafted in other ways.[287] Further, cross-default clauses that allow counterparties of bank subsidiaries to treat an event that occurs to the parent company as an event of default would also be suspended.[288] This suspension of termination rights applies not only to the actions of the national resolution authority but to third country intervention and resolution actions carried out.[289]

At a broader theoretical level, this is referred to by Pistor in the 'legal theory of finance', which argues that: although private law rights often underpin financial transactions in normal market conditions, such as rights in contract and property giving certainty to enforcement and protection of value in financial contracts, these rights are likely to result in individualistic actions that undermine financial stability in abnormal times.[290] Hence, in extraordinary situations such as early intervention or resolution, the suspension of such rights may become necessary in the public interest.

However, the PRA has created an exception to protect a UK bank that may be entitled to enforce security interests against a counterparty in accordance with a third country resolution regime,[291] except where mandatory bail-in has occurred. As the UK prepares to leave EU membership, the potential scope of such enforcement could be extended to EEA countries. Such actions seem to undermine the objective of orderly crisis management

---

[285] *NR Applicants vs Caldwell and the HM Treasury* [2011] UKUT 408 (TCC).

[286] *CA Harbinger Capital Partners v Caldwell (As the Independent Valuer of Northern Rock Plc) & Anor (Rev 1)* [2013] EWCA Civ 492.

[287] Article 68, BRRD 2014; s48Z, Banking Act 2009 amended by the Bank Recovery and Resolution Order 2014.

[288] Article 68, BRRD 2014.

[289] Section 48Z, Banking Act 2009 amended by the Bank Recovery and Resolution Order 2014.

[290] Katharina Pistor, 'A Legal Theory of Finance' (2013) *41 Journal of Comparative Economics* CHK.

[291] PRA Rulebook, *Stay in Resolution* para 2.2.

and resolution, but there is scope for coordinated action for cross-border resolution under *resolution colleges* (see section 13.4) to exert control over unilateral actions.

13.2.6.8 Compensation

One of the fundamental principles of resolution is that shareholders and creditors of a bank that has been resolved should fare no worse than if the bank underwent corporate insolvency procedures. Hence, where they may be 'worse off', the resolution authority should compensate them for the difference, which would be established by independent valuation.[292] In the UK, the Treasury is responsible for making the relevant *compensation scheme* orders for counterparties affected by transfers or bail-in.[293] Counterparties affected by transfer orders may also be paid proceeds of sale where relevant, after considering any public sector financial support. The Treasury may set up a *resolution fund* to carry this out, supported by independent valuation.[294] Third parties who are affected by resolution actions may also be compensated under discretionary *third-party compensation schemes*, or mandatory compensation schemes if they have been affected by partial property transfers (which are in fact prohibited, as discussed earlier).[295]

13.2.6.9 Financing resolution

The BRRD 2014 provides that member states should establish resolution financing arrangements in order to be able to administer resolution measures.[296] For example, the resolution authority needs to be able to purchase the stricken bank's assets and liabilities if a bridge bank were utilised, and it needs to contribute towards recapitalising a bank if certain liabilities were excluded from bail-in. These financing arrangements are separate from the deposit guarantee scheme (see section 13.4). The target level for resolution financing arrangements is set at 1 per cent of the guaranteed deposits in each member state[297] but the EBA disagrees that this is a suitable measure. The EBA is of the view that a bank liabilities-based measure is more suitable as those provide an indication of what is required for recapitalising and recovering the bank.[298] As resolution financing arrangements are to be fully implemented by 2024, there is yet time to consider how they should be designed.

Resolution financing arrangements are funded by *ex ante* contributions by banks, and where resolution funds have been used, *ex post* contributions may be called for. The *ex ante* contributions for banks are determined on a pro rata basis, depending on the risk profile of the bank and the level of banks' 'non-excluded' liabilities.[299] The risk

---

[292] Article 75, BRRD 2014.   [293] Sections 49–52A, Banking Act 2009.

[294] Section 58, Banking Act 2009.   [295] Sections 59 and 60, Banking Act 2009.

[296] Article 100, 101, BRRD 2014.   [297] Article 102, BRRD 2014.

[298] EBA, *Report on the Appropriate Target Level Basis for Resolution Financing Arrangements* (October 2016) at https://www.eba.europa.eu/documents/10180/1360107/Report+on+the+appropriate+target+level+basis+for+resolution+financing+arrangements+%28EBA-OP-2016-18%29.pdf/6540edd9-b339-4bca-97fe-57167d34c587.

[299] Articles 103, 104, BRRD 2014 and the excluded liabilities are specified in Commission Delegated Regulation (EU) 2015/63 of 21 October 2014 supplementing Directive 2014/59/EU of the European Parliament and of the Council with regard to ex ante contributions to resolution financing arrangements.

profile of the bank is determined in a prescribed and technical manner, in relation to the bank's level of capital adequacy and assets, its liquidity profile, its systemic importance and other risk factors such as membership of a deposit guarantee scheme and its trading activities.[300] These indicators are used in such a way as to ensure that the banks that are highly exposed or have systemically important footprints contribute the most to the *ex ante* financing of resolution schemes. Indeed, small banks such as those with total liabilities below €100 million would contribute a fixed sum of €1,000 annually, and fixed annual contributions are prescribed for banks with liabilities up to €1 billion.[301]

As major banks in the euro-area are directly overseen by the Single Supervisory Mechanism discussed in Chapter 7,[302] they are also subject to the SRM that seeks to support the SSM. The SRM is funded by the Single Resolution Fund to which euro-area member states contribute. This Fund is to be funded by at least an amount equivalent of 1 per cent of guaranteed deposits in euro-area member states. However, as member states also manage liquidations and resolutions of non-systemically important financial institutions, it is yet uncertain if they continue to maintain a national resolution fund, or pool all resolution financing at the Single Resolution Fund level.

Even if the UK leaves EU membership, having a resolution financing arrangement in place is sound as this avoids having to rely on the deposit guarantee scheme, which may be stretched during a bank crisis. The benefit of continuing EU membership would be that resolution financing arrangements can borrow from each other. Although the terms of such borrowing cannot be standardised and have to be approved by national authorities and governments, they may be on reasonably friendly terms.[303] Further, where a European banking group is resolved, a formal arrangement is put in place in the BRRD 2014 for all affected resolution authorities to share in the cost, via a mutualised financing plan for their resolution financing arrangements.[304] This promotes more orderly coordination and arguably fairer burden sharing for cross-border resolutions within the EU.

13.2.7 **Public sector financing**

After the state bailouts in the global financial crisis of 2007–9 (see Chapter 1), public sector authorities are anxious not to repeat these in view of the massive fiscal cost and social discontent that ensued. Hence, public sector financial support for a stricken bank should be seen as a last resort, only when no other resolution tools are likely to work effectively.[305] In the UK, the 'temporary public ownership' tool was introduced in the Banking Act 2009, and can only be used if the Bank of England has already provided emergency liquidity facilities to the bank. To resort to this tool, the Treasury needs to be satisfied that it is in the public interest to resolve a serious threat to the UK's financial

---

[300] Commission Delegated Regulation above, Articles 6-9.
[301] Commission Delegated Regulation above, Article 10.
[302] See Chapter 7, section 7.3.   [303] Article 106, BRRD 2014.
[304] Article 107, BRRD 2014.   [305] Article 56, BRRD 2014.

stability.[306] This determination of 'necessity' in the public interest and the perceived 'seriousness' of the threat to financial stability can only be made by the Treasury upon consultation with the Bank of England and PRA. The BRRD 2014 requires that such public sector support must be consistent with state aid principles under competition law. This is usually a determination to be made by the EU's Competition Commission.

The BRRD 2014 envisages that public sector financial support can be provided by the injection of recapitalising capital using taxpayers' funds or in the form of nationalising the bank using a company wholly owned by the state.[307] The Banking Act 2009 only refers to temporary public ownership,[308] but it is envisaged that such 'public ownership' could also mean a minority stake in a bank, for the purposes of recapitalising the bank, as in the case of Lloyds TSB in 2008.

In the UK, three key episodes of 'temporary public ownership' occurred during the global financial crisis of 2007–9. The first was Northern Rock, which was taken into complete public ownership in February 2008 after a deposit run on the bank precipitated its failure in late 2008. The next was the Royal Bank of Scotland into which the Treasury injected in 2007 about £20 billion in exchange for a 58 per cent stake in a mixture of ordinary and preference shares. When the preference shares were converted in 2009, the government's stake ballooned to 84.4 per cent. The third was Lloyds TSB, which had been brokered into a private sector purchase of Halifax Bank of Scotland at the height of HBOS' crisis. Lloyds had underestimated the extent of non-performing assets at HBOS and suffered a massive loss after the acquisition. The government took a 43 per cent stake in Lloyds in order to provide crucial capital and to stabilise the bank.

The main challenge for public sector financial support is that it should remain temporary so that a bank can be recovered and participate normally in market mechanisms again. However, the exit from public sector financial support is not always achieved in a timely manner and may indeed create a loss for taxpayers. The FSB calls for public sector authorities to develop best practices in exiting from public sector support, such as having a credible plan, and creating certainty by appropriate public disclosures. However, governments need to have flexibility in how exit is carried out after balancing various objectives such as minimising fiscal cost and bringing stability to the financial sector.[309] The keen-ness of the state in selling its bank stake may indeed depress the price a purchaser may be willing to pay. Holding onto the stake, however, may create moral hazard. The UK government eventually sold the nationalised Northern Rock to Virgin Money at a loss in 2011.[310] However, the Irish government, which nationalised Anglo-Irish Bank in 2008, eventually wound down the bank in 2013. In a happier case, the UK government has been able to reduce its stake in Lloyds to about 9 per cent by 2016 and

---

[306] Section 9, Banking Act 2009.
[307] Articles 57 and 58, BRRD 2014.   [308] Section 13, Banking Act 2009.
[309] FSB, *Exit from Extraordinary Financial Sector Support Measures* (March 2009) at http://www.fsb.org/2009/11/r_091107b/.
[310] 'Northern Rock sold to Virgin Money', *BBC News* (17 November 2011).

finally disposed of its entire stake in May 2017, making a profit of £900 million.[311] The Swiss government did better by selling its stake in UBS a year after the bail-out, making a profit of USD$1 bn. As for RBS, the UK government, which owns close to 72 per cent of RBS, has only begun to sell some of its stake in early 2018, almost 10 years after bailing out the bank.

The varied outcomes of the cases above show that public sector financial support is not per se a bad decision, as it can achieve a quick stabilisation of a bank in turbulent times and some banks are better placed to recover than others. However, as we have now established early intervention and resolution regimes, the bail-out seems to be confined to cases where resolution regimes may not work. In those cases, there may be little to be optimistic about the outcomes for the bank or the government. Nevertheless, the powerful stabilisation effect of a bail-out is an easy antidote that governments are attracted to, and this may explain why member states in the EU have ultimately bargained for the existence of the precautionary recapitalisation power in the BRRD 2014, which, as discussed, can bring in state bail-out by the back door.

13.2.8 Liquidation

The PRA envisages that smaller banks that do not entail financial stability concerns can be liquidated instead of being put through a resolution scheme.[312] This is similar to the SRB's approach in relation to its decision not to intervene in the Italian authorities' winding down of Veneto Banca and Banca Popolare di Vicenza in September 2017.[313]

However, bank liquidation is not left in the hands of creditors like in the private commercial sector. The Bank of England or Secretary of State of the Treasury are reserved the powers to apply for a bank liquidation order in court.[314] Such an order can only be applied for if the bank is unable to pay its debts (as consistent with the threshold for general insolvency proceedings), it is in the public interest to wind the bank up and there are depositors protected under the Deposit Guarantee Scheme.[315] The Treasury can apply for such an order on the other grounds even if a bank is not insolvent.[316] For example, a liquidation order can be sought against a bank in order for national authorities to seek control over the bank's assets, if the bank becomes subject to asset freezing elsewhere due to investigations in connection with criminal activity such as fraud or money laundering. The national liquidation order would allow national authorities to take leadership over the processes of asset disposal and realisation in order to protect national constituents such as depositors and other creditors. This has happened in

---

[311] 'Lloyds returns to full private ownership after Government sells down remaining shares', *The Telegraph* (17 May 2017).
[312] Bank of England, The Bank of England's Approach to Resolution (2017) at https://www.bankofengland.co.uk/-/media/boe/files/news/2017/october/the-bank-of-england-approach-to-resolution.pdf?la=en&hash=FC806900972DDE7246AD8CD1DF8B8C324BE7652F.
[313] Discussed in section 13.1.   [314] Section 95, Banking Act 2009.
[315] Section 96, Banking Act 2009.   [316] Ibid.

relation to ABLV, the Latvian bank alleged to be involved in money laundering by the US Treasury's Financial Crimes Enforcement Department, as well as to Caledonian Bank, a Cayman Islands bank accused by the US Securities and Exchange Commission for facilitating fraud.

A bank liquidator, who is a professional insolvency practitioner, is to be appointed in order to ensure that protected depositors realise their guarantee and that the creditors of the bank achieve a best possible result.[317] The bank liquidator is to report regularly to the liquidation committee that oversees the bank liquidator, comprising of the Bank of England and Financial Services Compensation Services.[318]

The bank liquidator enjoys most of the general powers under the Insolvency Act, except where specified.[319] These powers generally involve making disposals of assets to realise value for creditors, but in a manner that is underpinned by duties of care, skill, and diligence. The bank liquidator must prioritise the transfer of protected depositors successfully to another financial institution and/or to realise their protected deposits,[320] and upon achieving this, the liquidator may propose a voluntary arrangement among creditors in settlement of their claims,[321] or seek an administration order[322] if the bank has prospects of returning to health, or seek an order to dissolve the bank.[323] These may be sought in court unless the Bank of England determines that it would seek a bank insolvency order.

13.3 Deposit guarantee schemes

One of the key lessons learnt in the deposit run on Northern Rock in 2008 (discussed in section 13.1) is that a sufficiently robust depositor protection scheme is necessary to support the objectives of financial stability. A deposit run on a bank creates massive liquidity pressures, in addition to other pressures on liquidity and capital a stressed bank faces. If the potential for a deposit run can be mitigated, this goes some way towards maintaining stability and order in bank crisis management and resolution.

> **⊙ Key takeaways**
>
> • Crisis management and resolution comprises a framework from planning to early crisis intervention to resolution.
>
> • The planning aspects relate to recovery plans and resolution plans. Banks are to put in place credible recovery plans capable of timely implementation. Resolution authorities are to maintain resolution plans based on information returns and dialogue with banks.

---

[317] Section 99, Banking Act 2009.   [318] Section 100, Banking Act 2009.
[319] Sections 103–4, Banking Act 2009.   [320] Section 99(4), Banking Act 2009.
[321] Section 113, Banking Act 2009.   [322] Section 114, Banking Act 2009.
[323] Section 115, Banking Act 2009.

- Early crisis intervention measures may be implemented with a view to recovering a stressed bank. They include temporary management by a manager appointed by the bank's regulator and precautionary recapitalisation.

- Resolution can only be introduced to meet certain public interest objectives and where a bank fails its threshold conditions or is insolvent.

- The resolution authority in the UK is the Bank of England, which is obliged to consult the PRA and Treasury in the exercise of its powers.

- A key resolution power to be exercised is bail-in that ensures that bank shareholders and creditors absorb losses and recapitalise the bank. If necessary however, resolution tools involving a partial or full transfer of the bank would be effected. These include private sector purchase, the establishment of a bridge institution, and the use of asset management vehicles to purchase the bad loans of a bank.

- The exercise of resolution powers inevitably affects the private property rights of bank shareholders and creditors and safeguard principles are provided such as 'no creditor worse off' and the adherence to priority principles under insolvency laws, the use of independent valuation and institution of compensation regimes.

- Temporary public sector financing can be used as a last resort and under certain conditions, but exit from such support remains a challenge for states.

- Bank liquidation is envisaged as appropriate for smaller banks that do not give rise to financial stability concerns. The liquidation process is started and overseen by the resolution authority and is broadly similar to general liquidation procedures.

Key bibliography

Legislation

Bank Recovery and Resolution Directive 2014

Commission Delegated Regulation (EU) 2015/63 of 21 October 2014 supplementing Directive 2014/59/EU of the European Parliament and of the Council with regard to *ex ante* contributions to resolution financing arrangements

Commission Delegated Regulation (EU) 2016/1075 of 23 March 2016 supplementing Directive 2014/59/EU

Banking Act 2009

Financial Services (Bank Reform) Act 2013

Bank Recovery and Resolution Order and (No 2) Order 2014

PRA Rulebook, *Recovery Plans, Resolution Pack, Contractual Recognition of Bail-in, Group Financial Support*

Reports and Recommendations

Bank of England, *The Bank of England's Approach to Resolution* (2017) at https://www.bankofengland.co.uk/-/media/boe/files/news/2017/october/the-bank-of-england-approach-to-resolution.pdf?la=en&hash=FC806900972DDE7246AD8CD1DF8B8C324BE7652F

EBA, *Guidelines on the determination of when the liquidation of assets or liabilities under normal insolvency proceedings could have an adverse effect on one or more financial markets under Article 42(14) of Directive 2014/59/EU* (May 2015) at https://www.eba.europa.eu/documents/10180/1080779/EBA-GL-2015-05+Guidelines+on+the+asset+separation+tool.pdf/6441452a-d464-4618-9296-d71549a4f2c2

EBA, *Guidelines on factual circumstances amounting to a material threat to financial stability and on the elements related to the effectiveness of the sale of business tool under Article 39(4) of Directive 2014/59/EU* (Aug 2015) at https://www.eba.europa.eu/documents/10180/1080767/EBA-GL-2015-04_EN_Guidelines+on+the+sale+of+business+tool.pdf/6c15f73e-7557-48a6-b9f2-a70fda290149

EBA, *Final Guidelines on the Minimum List of Qualitative and Quantitative Recovery Plan Indicators* (May 2015) at https://www.eba.europa.eu/documents/10180/1064487/EBA-GL-2015-02+GL+on+recovery+plan+indicators.pdf/4bf18728-e836-408f-a583-b22ebaf59181

EBA, *Final Guidelines on the rate of conversion of debt to equity in bail-in* (April 2017) at https://www.eba.europa.eu/documents/10180/1807514/Guidelines+on+the+rate+of+conversion+of+debt+to+equity+in+bail-in+%28EBA-GL-2017-03%29.pdf

EBA, *Final Guidelines on the treatment of shareholders in bail-in or the write-down and conversion of capital instruments* (April 2017) at https://www.eba.europa.eu/documents/10180/1807527/Guidelines+on+the+treatment+of+shareholders+in+bail-in+%28EBA-GL-2017-04%29.pdf

FSA, 'The Supervision of Northern Rock: A lessons learned review' (March 2008) http://www.fsa.gov.uk/pubs/other/nr_report.pdf

PRA, *Supervisory Statement: Recovery Planning* (January 2015) at http://www.bankofengland.co.uk/pra/Documents/publications/ss/2015/ss1813update.pdf

Additional Reading

Gleeson, S and Guynn, R, *Bank Resolution and Crisis Management* Oxford: OUP 2016

Schillig, M, *Resolution and Insolvency of Banks and Financial Institutions* Oxford: OUP 2016

Troeger, T, 'Too Complex to Work: A Critical Assessment of the Bail-In Tool Under the European Bank Recovery and Resolution Regime' (2018) at https://papers.ssrn.com/sol3/papers.cfm?abstract_id=3023184

13.3.1 The development towards robust depositor protection

Since 1994, the EU maintained a minimum harmonised framework for deposit guarantee in all EEA Member States. The guaranteed amount was set at €20,000 for each depositor per credit institution. The UK, however, maintained a higher protection level than the EU, that is, at 100 per cent of the first £20,000 and up to 90 per cent of a maximum of £33,000 for each depositor per credit institution. The level of deposit guarantee, however, proved to be inadequate in 2007 when the deposit run occurred in light of Northern Rock's revelation that it needed emergency liquidity facilities from the Bank of England. The spectre of depositor queues outside all of Northern Rock's branches was testament to the loss of confidence depositors experienced. The UK immediately raised deposit protection to £50,000 for each depositor per credit institution.

As the global financial crisis of 2007–9 unfolded across the EU, European policymakers embarked on reforms to deposit protection, now seen as an important pillar for the purposes of maintaining financial stability. The EU's minimal deposit guarantee scheme was quickly revised in 2010 to protect each eligible deposit account up to €100,000, and in 2014, further reforms were introduced to make such schemes more credible by introducing efficient payout schedules and by providing how they should be funded.[324] These reforms have now been transposed in the UK.[325] The UK initially set its deposit guarantee at £85,000, but after the plunge of the sterling after the EU Referendum vote of June 2016, the deposit guarantee level temporarily readjusted to £75,000 as equivalent to €100,000. The UK has since raised its deposit guarantee level to £85,000 as of 30 January 2017.[326]

The raising of deposit protection levels and the credibility of such protection is now seen as a key pillar of financial stability. This is based on the theoretical work of Diamond and Dybvig[327] in relation to why bank runs occur and how they can be mitigated. They show that even for healthy banks, depositors may rush to withdraw their deposits if they perceive the likelihood of other depositors' withdrawals. Deposit guarantee may be the only way to minimise panicked and competitive withdrawal instincts by depositors. Although it may be argued that the deposit guarantee creates moral hazard for depositors who would not undertake any diligence in screening or monitoring the safety of banks, such screening or monitoring is inherently difficult anyway given the information opacity and complexity of bank assets and liabilities to the ordinary depositor. The deposit guarantee may be seen as a public good that underlies state support for the economically useful functions of banking institutions.

Deposit guarantee is at the moment provided as national schemes. The EU sees potential in consolidating deposit protection into a pan-European scheme in the future for the euro-area subject to the SSM,[328] in order to boost depositor confidence. Such a prospect may create a competitive advantage for banks subject to the SSM as they are perceived to be supported by a pan-European, perhaps stronger safety net, than nationally-administered schemes. However, national schemes have to adhere to the same standards harmonised under the Deposit Guarantee Directive 2014.

13.3.2 **Scope of protected deposits**

The UK has established the Financial Services Compensation Scheme (FSCS), an independent body, to be overseen by the PRA and FCA. The deposit guarantee scheme is a part of and administered by the FSCS.

---

[324] Directive 2014/49/EU of the European Parliament and of the Council of 16 April 2014 on deposit guarantee schemes (DGS Directive 2014). [325] PRA Rulebook, *Depositor Protection*.

[326] PRA, *Deposit Protection Limit* (Consultation paper, 21 November 2016) at http://www.bankofengland.co.uk/pra/Documents/publications/cp/2016/cp4116.pdf.

[327] DW Diamond and PH Dybvig PH, 'Bank Runs, Deposit Insurance, and Liquidity' (1983) 91 *Journal of Political Economy* 401–19.

[328] The European Deposit Insurance Scheme, see https://ec.europa.eu/info/business-economy-euro/banking-and-finance/banking-union/european-deposit-insurance-scheme_en.

The scope of protected deposits is defined by reference to excluded deposits. Further deposits would only be protected if placed in a UK bank that is a member of the UK's deposit guarantee scheme or an EEA bank that is a member of a deposit guarantee scheme established in the relevant EEA member state. The scope of deposit guarantee may require revisiting when the UK ceases membership of the EU.

Excluded deposits are:[329]

(a) a deposit made by another credit institution;

(b) own funds (which is defined as the sum of tier one and two capital, see Chapter 8 for relevant definitions);

(c) a deposit arising out of a transaction in connection with which there has been a criminal conviction for money laundering;

(d) a deposit by a financial institution;

(e) a deposit by an investment firm;

(f) a deposit made but the identity of the holder or any beneficial owner (as defined in Regulations 5 and 6 of the Money Laundering, Terrorist Financing and Transfer of Funds (Information on the Payer) Regulations 2017) has not yet been verified in accordance with Regulation 28 of the Money Laundering, Terrorist Financing and Transfer of Funds (Information on the Payer) Regulations 2017.[330]

(g) a deposit by an insurance undertaking or a reinsurance undertaking;

(h) a deposit by a collective investment undertaking;

(i) a deposit by a pension or retirement fund (but excluding deposits by personal pension schemes, stakeholder pension schemes and occupational pension schemes of micro, SMEs);

(j) a deposit by a public authority, unless it is a small local authority;

(k) a debt security issued by the bank and any liabilities arising out of own acceptances and promissory notes.

The exclusions relate largely to financial institutions, thereby ensuring that they do not take advantage of the deposit guarantee scheme to manage their liquidity risks. These exclusions also reflect the public policy position of not extending protection to deposits that may have been the subject of money laundering.

The EU and UK are cognisant that depositors may have temporarily high balances such as receipt of proceeds from the sale of a house pending purchase of another. In such situations, if a depositor were to encounter the misfortune of a bank crisis in relation to where the temporary balance is held, such a depositor would technically be left without protection for any amounts in excess of the guaranteed level. The EU thus provides that member states should provide for higher protection levels up to 12 months for such temporarily high balances.[331] The PRA has transposed this to protect the temporary high imbalances shown in Box 13.8.

[329] Article 5, DGS Directive 2014; para 2.2, PRA Rulebook, *Depositor Protection.*
[330] See further discussion in Chapter 14.   [331] Article 6, DGS Directive 2014.

Box 13.8 Protected temporary high balances

- monies deposited in preparation for the purchase of a private residential property (or an interest in a private residential property) by the depositor;

- monies that represent the proceeds of sale of a private residential property (or an interest in a private residential property) of the depositor;

- monies that represent the proceeds of an equity release by the depositor in a private residential property;

- benefits payable to the depositor under an insurance policy;

- sum payable to the depositor in respect of a claim for compensation for personal (including criminal) injury;

- state benefits paid in respect of a disability or incapacity;

- sum payable to the depositor in respect of a claim for compensation for wrongful conviction;

- sum payable to the depositor in respect of a claim for compensation for unfair dismissal;

- sum payable to the depositor in respect of their redundancy (whether voluntary or compulsory);

- sum payable to the depositor in respect of the dissolution of marriage or civil partnership;

- benefits payable to the depositor on retirement;

- benefits payable to the depositor in respect of another's death

- sum payable to the depositor in respect of a claim for compensation in respect of another's death

- a legacy or other distribution to the depositor from the estate of a deceased person;

- sums held in an account on behalf of the personal representatives of a deceased person for the purpose of realising and administering the deceased's estate

- sums otherwise serving a social purpose provided for in law, which is linked to the marriage, civil partnership, divorce, dissolution of civil partnership, retirement, incapacity, death of an individual, or to the buying or selling of a depositor's only or main residence that is not freehold, heritable, or leasehold property.

The FSCS has the responsibility to contact all depositors who appear to be holding eligible temporary high balances in order to prove their eligibility.

13.3.3 Mechanics and funding of scheme

In order to assure depositors of the credibility of deposit guarantee, the mechanics of the scheme are prescribed in relation to when the scheme applies and the payout schedules.

The deposit guarantee scheme is activated once a bank is unable to allow deposit withdrawal normally, or 'in default' as defined by the PRA, which usually means that the bank has entered into resolution, administration or insolvency.[332] Payouts to depositors

---

[332] Article 2(1), DGS Directive 2014, para 3.2, PRA Rulebook, *Depositor Protection*.

should be made as soon as possible as depriving depositors of their balances for a time could be seen as equivalent to the lack of protection, and could result in potential suits against the scheme for depositors' financial losses.[333] Hence the EU has led the way in prescribing an efficient payout schedule of seven working days from the date of the abovementioned 'default'.[334] However, in order to prepare the Scheme to administer payouts at this level of efficiency, the Scheme is given time to bolster its administrative capacity. Existing schemes need to meet a schedule of 20 working days from default to payout until 31 December 2018. Thereafter, schemes need to pay out within 15 working days between 1 January 2019 to 31 December 2020, and then within 10 working days between 1 January 2021 to 31 December 2023. From 1 January 2024, the Scheme must meet the desired payout schedule of seven working days.

The PRA has also prescribed that payouts can only be made to other deposit accounts of entitled individuals, trustees of relevant small pension schemes and specific persons directed by the entitled depositor.[335] The FSCS may, however, refrain from paying out if such sums are subject to legal dispute, restrictive measures such as sanctions imposed by a third country or if subject to offences in relation to money laundering.[336]

The Scheme is subrogated to the rights of the depositor in relation to relevant claims that may be made against the bank under resolution, administration, or liquidation.[337]

13.3.3.1 Scheme funding

The EU Directive envisages that member states' deposit guarantee schemes should be funded to the level of 0.8 per cent of guaranteed deposits in each member state by 2024, unless express approval is obtained from the Commission to lower it to not less than 0.5 per cent of the member state's guaranteed deposits.[338]

The PRA also envisages that its deposit guarantee scheme will be funded by its regulated credit institutions, which include banks, building societies, credit unions, and foreign bank subsidiaries authorised in the UK. These are designated as members of the scheme.[339] UK banks may from time to time be asked to contribute to the scheme in respect of a 'compensation costs levy', 'management expenses levy' or a 'legacy costs' levy.

The compensation cost levy is the main instrument for raising finance from the regulated firms to cover the Scheme's incurred and expected expenditures on a yearly basis, unless the Scheme is adequately funded already for expenses incurred and expected expenditure for the next 12 months.[340] A management expenses levy[341] can be imposed if the Scheme is unlikely to meet the expenses incurred, for example due to supporting resolution. Further, if the deposit guarantee scheme has been used to pay out, or has

---

[333] Although this possibility is constrained by immunity legislation that supports the exercise of these public powers, see Chapter 6 in relation to the UK's accountability regime.
[334] Article 8, DGS Directive 2014, para 9.3, PRA Rulebook, *Depositor Protection*.
[335] Paras 6.2, 6.3, PRA Rulebook, *Depositor Protection*.   [336] Para 9.3, PRA Rulebook, *Depositor Protection*.
[337] Article 9, DGS Directive 2014, para 28, PRA Rulebook, *Depositor Protection*.
[338] Article 10, DGS Directive 2014.   [339] Para 1.1, PRA Rulebook, *Depositor Protection*.
[340] Para 34, PRA Rulebook, *Depositor Protection*.   [341] Para 35, PRA Rulebook, *Depositor Protection*.

incurred cost in borrowing from other schemes (from other EEA Member States, as will be discussed shortly), a legacy cost levy[342] may be imposed on Scheme members on a pro rata basis according to the level of guaranteed deposits held by them. The EBA further provides that schemes should vigilantly enforce their members' payment commitments and should enter into financial collateral arrangements with their members so that low risk collateral free from encumbrances can be posted with the Scheme. Such collateral can be liquidated in case Scheme members do not meet their mandatory contributions.[343]

The maximum amount that can be levied each year must not exceed £150 million and the maximum amount of compensation cost levy imposed must not exceed 0.5 per cent of the guaranteed deposits in the UK.

The EU Directive envisages that deposit guarantee schemes can borrow from each other within the EEA area. Although such loans will be arranged on a bilateral basis, there is some oversight by the EBA in terms of being informed of the reasons for borrowing and ensuring that the loan can be repaid over 5 years and are not excessive, that is, does not exceed 0.5 per cent of the member state's guaranteed deposits. The loan rate is tracked to the ECB's marginal lending facility, therefore ensuring that it is fairly set and unlikely to be exorbitant or too low.[344] The UK's exit from EU membership may mean that the UK is unable to access such financing arrangements or participate in lending to other schemes, similar to the position with respect to resolution financing. The closure of such opportunities and relationships with the EU could increase the financial stability risk in the UK.

⬅ Key takeaways

- Depositor protection is a key pillar in protecting financial stability by mitigating the potential of deposit run on banks.

- The level of deposit protection in the EU is harmonised at €100,000 for each depositor in a credit institution authorised to operate in any EEA member state. The UK's level is set at £85,000 (from 1 January 2017).

- Deposit protection excludes liabilities owed to most financial, investment and central government institutions, as well as monies subject to money laundering offences.

- The UK's FSCS administers the deposit guarantee scheme and is financed by different types of mandatory contributions from PRA-regulated credit institutions who are designated its members.

- EU legislative reforms have increasingly shortened payout schedules, to be limited to seven working days from 1 January 2024.

---

[342] Para 36, PRA Rulebook, *Depositor Protection*.

[343] EBA, *Guidelines on payment commitments under Directive 2014/49/EU on deposit guarantee schemes* (May 2015) at https://www.eba.europa.eu/documents/10180/1089310/EBA-GL-2015-09+Guidelines+on+DGS+payment+commitments.pdf.   [344] Article 12, DGS Directive 2014.

Key bibliography

Legislation

Directive 2014/49/EU of the European Parliament and of the Council of 16 April 2014 on deposit guarantee schemes

PRA Rulebook, *Depositor Protection*

Reports and Guidelines

EBA, *Guidelines on payment commitments under Directive 2014/49/EU on deposit guarantee schemes* (May 2015) at https://www.eba.europa.eu/documents/10180/1089310/EBA-GL-2015-09+Guidelines+on+DGS+payment+commitments.pdf

Additional Reading

Kleftouri, N, *Deposit Protection and Bank Resolution* Oxford: OUP 2015

13.4 Cross-border crisis management and resolution

In section 13.1 we discussed the need for a *lex specialis* for resolving banks and efforts made at international harmonisation of resolution regimes. International harmonisation is particularly relevant to the problems experienced in resolving banks with cross-border or indeed a global footprint. Former Bank of England Governor Mervyn King opined that 'banks are global in life but national in death'. This encapsulates much of the challenges in cross-border resolution and crisis management- often the home authority of the global bank has to deal with a scale and cost of bank fallout beyond its expectations or indeed its capacity, and may choose to take little care of the bank's foreign operations. The host authorities may take defensive actions in return to protect their constituents' interests. The Icelandic resolution of its three failed banks Kaupthing, Glitnir and Landsbanki was a key example of putting the protection for national interests above achieving a coherent cross-border resolution for those banks that had significant deposit-taking businesses in the UK and the Netherlands.[345] Iceland protected its own depositors and refused to extend its deposit guarantee to foreign depositors of the failed banks.[346] The UK in response seized all the available assets of the banks within its jurisdiction.

---

[345] Michael Waibel, 'Iceland's Financial Crisis—Quo Vadis International Law' (2010) 14 *ASIL Insight* at http://www.asil.org/insights100301.cfm. The Icelandic authorities did not give undertakings that they would make good their obligations under the Deposit Guarantee Directive. EU law on the other hand does not allow the seizing of assets as UK authorities undertook in response. The whole saga was a set-back for the Internal Market and the respect for EU law, and similarly the emerging principles of universality in the handling of insolvencies. Eyvindur G Gunnarsson, 'The Icelandic Regulatory Response to the Financial Crisis' (2011) *European Business Organisation Law Review* 2.

[346] However, see *EFTA Surveillance Authority with the European Commission v Iceland* Case E-16/11 (28 January 2013), which vindicated Iceland's decision.

If cross-border crisis management and resolution becomes disorderly, this could have an adverse impact on financial market confidence and stability in many jurisdictions. It is thus beneficial for resolution authorities to work with each other.

13.4.1 Formalisation of cross-border coordination

Since 2009, the FSB and Basel Committee have promoted more formalisation of 'groupings' of bank regulators and resolution authorities in order to coordinate with each other in supervisory processes as well as crisis management. The framework for *supervisory colleges* discussed in Chapter 5 led by the Basel Committee helps bank regulators to share information, knowledge and to develop a coherent supervisory strategy for global banks. Similarly, the FSB advocates more coordination and cooperation among national regulators in crisis management,[347] and has developed a formal recommendation for 'crisis management groups' to be formed for global banks.[348]

13.4.1.1 Crisis management groups

These groups should comprise of the relevant national bank regulators, national resolution authorities, central banks, and finance ministries where relevant. It is envisaged that crisis management groups should coordinate on an *ex ante* basis in relation to the global bank's recovery and resolution planning and assessment of resolvability. It is also envisaged that the Group may enter into 'institution-specific' cross-border arrangements,[349] that specify Group member obligations *vis a vis* each other to share information regularly, to coordinate with each other in managing a crisis, such as by setting out procedures to be taken and responsibilities for each member in carrying out procedures. Group members should also consult each other before unilateral actions are taken. It is hoped that the benefit of orderliness and reduction of adverse impact on financial stability in all jurisdictions concerned will motivate crisis management groups to work together coherently, even if they are likely to bring different interests to the table.

The FSB also envisages that coordination and cooperation within such groups can further promote the streamlining of laws and regulations. This is necessary in order to support each jurisdiction's resolution action so that cross-border legal recognition of resolution measures can be achieved. This area remains a challenging work in progress,[350] as the FSB calls for more convergence in the substantive law on crisis management to be placed on statutory footing.

---

[347] FSB, *Principles for Cross-border Cooperation on Crisis Management* (April 2009) at www.financialstabilityboard.org/publications/r_0904c.pdf.

[348] Key Attribute 8 of the 2014 version at http://www.fsb.org/what-we-do/policy-development/effective-resolution-regimes-and-policies/key-attributes-of-effective-resolution-regimes-for-financial-institutions/#8crisismanagementgroups.

[349] Key Attribute 9 of the 2014 version at http://www.fsb.org/what-we-do/policy-development/effective-resolution-regimes-and-policies/key-attributes-of-effective-resolution-regimes-for-financial-institutions/#8crisismanagementgroups.

[350] FSB, *Principles for Cross-border Effectiveness of Resolution Actions* (Nov 2015) at http://www.fsb.org/wp-content/uploads/Principles-for-Cross-border-Effectiveness-of-Resolution-Actions.pdf.

13.4.1.2 Resolution colleges in the EU

The EU has also provided for more formalisation of 'crisis management groups' for European banks in the form of 'resolution colleges'. Resolution authorities responsible for a banking group have to establish resolution colleges in order to ensure that any resolution is carried out in a coordinated manner under the college's agreed 'resolution scheme'.[351] Further, European resolution colleges may also be established for third country banks operating significant subsidiaries or branches in the EU.[352] These colleges could involve the SRB (as taking the place of national authorities in relation to banks subject to the SSM)[353] and national resolution authorities of banks not subject to the SSM.

Resolution colleges are mandated to coordinate and work with each other in respect of assessing recovery plans, resolution plans and assessing impediments to resolvability, as discussed in section 13.2. Default provisions are also provided in case agreements are not reached within the college. The EBA is invited to all resolution college meetings and thus is in a position to exert informal influence to promote consensus.[354]

In crisis management, a resolution college is expected to develop a 'resolution scheme' for the bank group concerned before any resolution authority takes action. It is envisaged that the bank group's resolution authority will take the lead in drafting a resolution scheme to set out proposed resolution measures for the bank, considering the group resolution plan. The 'resolution scheme' also outlines the needs for coordination in the college and provides a draft financing plan.[355] All members of the college are to be consulted upon and the group resolution authority must take into account all views, including divergent views to arrive at a finalised joint decision in as timely a manner as possible.[356] The group resolution authority must then make reasoned explanation to the college.[357] Dissenting college members could in the appropriate case, embark on a divergent process as long as the same procedures are followed to achieve a joint decision within a sub-group in the college.[358]

European resolution colleges may be established for significant third country subsidiaries or branches in the EU, but such colleges may not include the third country home authority. In crisis management involving a third country authority, the European resolution college may be able to present a 'united front' for the purposes of constructive cooperation, but also for the purposes of making demands or choosing not to recognise third country actions in order to protect the EU's interests in financial stability.[359] Further, such colleges can initiate resolution action against a third country subsidiary

---

[351] Articles 88, 91 and 92, BRRD 2014.

[352] Article 89, BRRD 2014.   [353] Preamble 91, SRM Regulation 2015.

[354] Article 88, BRRD, also pursuant to the EBA's statutory objective, see Preamble 40, Regulation (EU) No 1093/2010 of the European Parliament and of the Council of 24 November 2010 establishing a European Supervisory Authority (European Banking Authority), amending Decision No 716/2009/EC and repealing Commission Decision 2009/78/EC.

[355] Articles 91 and 92, BRRD 2014.   [356] Articles 91 and 92, BRRD 2014.

[357] Articles 104–7, Commission Delegated Regulation 2016.

[358] Articles 108–9, Commission Delegated Regulation 2016.   [359] Articles 94 and 95, BRRD 2014.

or branch under the BRRD 2014 irrespective of whether resolution actions are taking place in the third country.[360] These powers can be important in creating negotiating power between the EU and third countries if thorny issues in cross-border resolution emerge. The exit of the UK from EU membership may weaken the UK's negotiating position in cross-border coordination with third countries, but it is noted that the UK has a bilateral memorandum of understanding with the US Federal Deposit Insurance Corporation, the resolution authority in the US.[361] The memorandum sets out both authorities' willingness to share information, cooperate and coordinate in giving assistance in effecting orderly resolution. As many globally significant banks operating in the UK are US banks, the securing of this memorandum may largely safeguard the UK's position in cross-border cooperation. The terms of cooperation are, however, polite and remain vague, so their credibility can only be tested by actual outworking.

13.4.2 Single and multiple points of entry in cross-border resolution

In order to assist crisis management groups and resolution colleges in their coordination under stressful conditions,[362] the FSB has proposed two substantive options in cross-border resolution, the single point of entry (SPE) and multiple point of entry (MPE) approaches.[363] These approaches provide a standardised menu of options for crisis management groups and resolution colleges, so that decisions can be more efficiently and predictably taken.

The SPE allows a bank group to be resolved, usually at the level of the parent undertaking overseen by its home resolution authority. This approach is appropriate if the parent undertaking is likely to have sufficient loss-absorbent capital, making the approach credible and unlikely to create adverse impact for foreign subsidiaries and branches. Further, this approach is also suitable where high levels of mutual trust and cooperation exist between the home resolution authority and other concerned authorities so that the latter would refrain from taking independent actions.

The MPE is suitable where the bank group is structurally amenable to be resolved in different jurisdictions by different resolution authorities, and where there may be sufficient levels of loss-absorbing capital in each key jurisdiction the bank group operates. In such resolution it is important to ascertain that the bank group can be 'divided' along jurisdictional lines in terms of legal and operational structures. The 'division' of the bank group for resolution should, however, not jeopardise its critical activities such as in payments clearing and settlement. Even in an MPE approach the crisis

---

[360] Article 96, BRRD 2014.

[361] At http://www.bankofengland.co.uk/publications/Documents/other/financialstability/srrmou.pdf.

[362] Jens Hinrich Binder, 'Cross-Border Coordination of Bank Resolution in the EU: All Problems Resolved?' (2016) at https://papers.ssrn.com/sol3/papers.cfm?abstract_id=2659158.

[363] FSB, *Recovery and Resolution Planning for Systemically Important Financial Institutions: Guidance on Developing Effective Resolution Strategies* (July 2013) at http://www.fsb.org/wp-content/uploads/r_130716b.pdf?page_moved=1.

management group or resolution college should ensure that adequate cooperation and coordination takes place to ensure orderly resolution as a whole. Overall if a bank's operations are highly interdependent, an SPE approach may be more efficient than an MPE approach, which is likely to work well for banking groups that are relatively more decentralised.[364]

With the underpinning of international convergence in resolution regimes and the development of formal groupings to resolve bank crises, we may be closer to ending fear and uncertainty surrounding international bank crisis management and resolution. This chapter does not deal with cross-border insolvency recognition and enforcement, as it is envisaged that cross-border groups should be subject to the resolution processes and coordination mechanisms discussed above. However, we recall that Lehman Brothers was the subject of protracted cross-border insolvency procedures and litigation, and policymakers may wish to avoid a similar experience with the reforms discussed in this chapter. Further bank insolvency is likely to apply to small banks whose failure is unlikely to cause financial stability implications, and these banks may have limited cross-border footprint.

 Key takeaways

- Cross-border resolution of banks raises unique problems of contests of interests that can result in disorderly resolution.

- Formalised coordination mechanisms are now introduced by the Financial Stability Board and in the EU to compel resolution authorities to work together in a cooperative and accountable manner to each other.

- The FSB proposes two key resolution strategies, the SPE and Multiple Points of Entry to guide resolution authority groups in finalising an appropriate resolution scheme.

Key bibliography

Reports and guidelines

FSB, *Principles for Cross-border Effectiveness of Resolution Actions* (November 2015) at http://www.fsb.org/wp-content/uploads/Principles-for-Cross-border-Effectiveness-of-Resolution-Actions.pdf

FSB, *Recovery and Resolution Planning for Systemically Important Financial Institutions: Guidance on Developing Effective Resolution Strategies* (July 2013) at http://www.fsb.org/wp-content/uploads/r_130716b.pdf?page_moved=1

---

[364] Patrick Bolton and Martin Oehmke, 'Bank Resolution and the Structure of Global Banks' (2016) at https://www0.gsb.columbia.edu/faculty/moehmke/papers/BoltonOehmke_BankResolution.pdf.

Additional Reading

Binder, JH, 'Cross-Border Coordination of Bank Resolution in the EU: All Problems Resolved?' (2016) at https://papers.ssrn.com/sol3/papers.cfm?abstract_id=2659158

Čihák, M and Nier, E, 'The Need for Special Resolution Regimes for Financial Institutions—The Case of the European Union' (September 2009) IMF Working Paper No WP/09/200 http://www.imf.org/external/pubs/ft/wp/2009/wp09200.pdf

Hupkes, E, '"Form Follows Function"—A New Architecture for Regulating and Resolving Global Financial Institutions' (2009) 10 European Business Organisation Law Review 369

Schillig, M, *Resolution and Insolvency of Banks and Financial Institutions* Oxford: OUP 2016) ch 16

Singh, D, 'The UK Banking Act 2009, Pre-Insolvency and Early Intervention: Policy and Practice' (2011) Journal of Business Law 20

Questions

1. Discuss the effectiveness of preventive measures (except micro-prudential regulation) in avoiding bank crises.

   Answer tips You should identify what are preventive measures. Recovery plans is a good starting point and you should appraise the regulatory regime and the likely achievements and limitations. You should also discuss resolution planning in particular the regulator's power to order the removal of impediments to resolvability and whether that may help prevent a future bank crisis. Early intervention measures are also relevant but they may be too close to resolution to be of preventive effect.

2. Bank resolution measures do not necessarily outlaw the state bail-out for systemically important banks. Do you agree?

   Answer tips You should critically appraise the resolution tools and give examples of how they have worked. You should pay attention to bail-in as being a key measure to first shift losses onto the private sector, and critically discuss if that is likely to be effective. You should also note the higher threshold conditions for temporary public sector support and the context of lessons learnt in the global financial crisis of 2007–9.

3. 'Work is in progress to end fears and uncertainty over the failure of globally systemically important banks with large cross-border footprints.' Do you agree?

   Answer tips You should provide context as to the difficulties in resolving banks with cross-border operations. You should discuss what work in progress has been made, in formal coordination procedures, as well as in substantive strategies for cross-border resolution. You should critically appraise work led by the Basel Committee, FSB, and EU policymakers and also provide discussion on the remaining gaps and progress that needs to be made.

14

Combatting financial crime

14.1 Introduction to regulation in anti-money laundering and terrorist financing

Banks and financial institutions are at the heart of money transmission. They process transactions for perfectly legitimate purposes, such as my purchase of a sofa using a debit card, or the payment of salary from employers' accounts to their employees' accounts. However, banks and financial institutions are also used by criminals to transfer illegally obtained monies or proceeds of crime. Further, the financing of terrorism also involves banks and financial institutions, as monies are transmitted, oftentimes internationally, for organising terrorist activities. Hence, regulation now compels banks and financial institutions to play an active part in combatting financial crime.

Regulation takes two approaches, one is to enforce anti-money laundering laws *through* banks and financial institutions; and the other approach is to enforce anti-money laundering laws *against* them if they should be found to be complicit in transferring proceeds of crime. Under the first approach, regulation imposes duties on banks and financial institutions to act as gatekeepers to prevent money laundering from taking place and to identify such incidents so as to help regulators carry out enforcement. Under the second approach, banks and financial institutions may be punished for sometimes inadvertently becoming complicit in money laundering, and this provides a strong incentive for them to treat their gatekeeper roles seriously.

Money laundering is a process by which monies of an illegal origin (either they have been obtained illegally or are the proceeds of other criminal activity, also known as 'dirty money') are made to appear legitimate or 'clean'. Leong[1] describes how money laundering is carried out in three stages: placing, layering and integration. 'Placing' involves putting monies of an illegal origin into the financial system, for example, by depositing into a bank account, by investment in financial instruments etc. Thereafter, such monies are 'layered', that is, moved, usually through a series of transactions involving different entities, different assets, and different jurisdictions, so as to sever any audit trail and hence make tracing their origins harder. Finally, the criminal is able to resume control of the monies free from any link to their criminal source, arriving at the point

---

[1] AVM Leong, 'Anti-money Laundering Measures in the UK' (2007) *Company Lawyer* 35.

of 'integration'. If dirty money is successfully placed and layered through the financial system, its legitimacy is considerably strengthened at the point of integration.

Anti-money laundering legislation is targeted at the processes of 'placing' and 'layering' in order to disrupt the money laundering process and apprehend the criminals concerned. It may be appreciated that the criminals involved in laundering dirty money may not be the same as the criminals involved in the crimes that give rise to the dirty money. However, money laundering is itself an offence, predicated upon the money or 'proceeds' involved being 'proceeds of crime'. The crime of money laundering is set out in the UK Proceeds of Crime Act 2002.

14.1.1 **The criminal offence of money laundering**

It is stipulated to be a criminal offence for a person to *conceal, have control of* or *facilitate another to have control of* 'criminal property'.[2] If a person *acquires, uses,* or *has possession* of criminal property,[3] such a person would commit the offence of money laundering. The above *actus reus* relates to control of criminal property and corresponds to the 'placement' stage above. Any person who facilitates the placement stage would commit the money laundering offence, that is, if a person becomes involved in or makes an arrangement to facilitate another to *acquire, use, control* or *retain* criminal property.[4] The *actus reus* of 'concealing' includes all forms of attempt to hide the nature, source, location of or rights to the criminal property, such as *disguising, converting, transferring* and *removing,*[5] which correspond to the layering stage.

First, for money laundering to be proved, one needs to establish that the property subject to the alleged *actus reus* above is indeed 'criminal property'. In *R v Loizou,*[6] the police descended on a group exchanging money in the sum of £80,000 in a car park. The individuals involved were charged with the offence of money laundering under s327 of the Proceeds of Crime Act involving the 'transfer' of criminal property. The defendants argued that the offence could only be proved if the property was indeed criminal property, which meant that the property was either illegally obtained or constituted the proceeds of crime. It turned out that the money was to be used for payment for illegally imported cigarettes, but the illegal importation had not happened when the police disrupted the exchange in the car park. Hence there was no primary offence of illegal importation of cigarettes for the relevant money laundering offence to be based upon. The defendants were found not guilty as at the point of exchange, no criminal property was transferred.

However, this does not mean that a money laundering offence can only be made out if it were incontrovertibly proved that the property involved is 'criminal property'. This is because s328 can be used to impose liability upon a person for being involved in the

---

[2] Sections 327–9, Proceeds of Crime Act 2002.   [3] Section 329, Proceeds of Crime Act 2002.
[4] Section 328, Proceeds of Crime Act 2002.   [5] Section 327, Proceeds of Crime Act 2002.
[6] [2005] 2 Cr. App. R. 37.

actus reus despite having a 'suspicion' of money laundering. In other words, a person can become criminally liable for failing to deal with 'suspicion' of money laundering (in the manner permitted under law as will be elaborated upon below) and becoming involved in the *actus reus*. This position may be attributed to the public interest in preventing and dis-incentivising people from assisting the processes of money laundering. Further, the need to prove that a crime in relation to the property has already occurred may be unduly onerous. Hence, the Terrorism Act 2000 takes a wider approach towards criminalising individuals involved in arrangements that facilitate the *control* or *retention* of terrorist property by *concealment, transfer, removal,* or other forms of transactions.[7] 'Terrorist property' includes monies or property *likely to be used for* acts of terrorism.[8] In this manner, terrorist financing is criminalised whether or not acts of terrorism are indeed carried out.

The raison d'etre for combatting money laundering lies in 'taking the profit out of the crime'. If criminal activity is penalised in terms of the removal of profits associated with it, the incentives to commit crimes, especially organised crimes such as illegal drug dealing or systemic corruption, may be reduced. Targeting the proceeds of crime may also reduce the financing of further crimes, especially terrorist activities. Besides its deterrent purposes, policymakers support anti-money laundering laws as they contribute to the perception of integrity in financial systems and markets, that they are not used for the purposes of placement and layering by criminals. The maintenance of sound reputation in a country's financial systems and markets helps to promote genuine financial flows for economic activity. Further, the reduction of money laundering activity in an economy helps to reduce distortions in an economy. If dirty money is used to finance activities such as the purchase of residential property, then property prices may inflate to the disadvantage of genuine buyers due to the flooding in and purchasing power of 'dirty money'. Stemming 'dirty money' reduces distortions in the prices of real estate and luxury goods, and sustains an economy for legitimate activities that can be properly financed.

Although the Act targets all persons involved in money laundering, such as criminal associates of the predicate offender, the width of the *actus reus* scope captures banks and financial institutions if they become involved in the placement or layering processes. Banks' potential liability is dealt with under section 14.4.

We turn next to regulatory development. Money laundering and terrorist financing spans many jurisdictions as the cross-border nature of financial transfers assists in the layering process and makes it more difficult to track the trail of 'dirty money'. Hence, regulation can only be effective if it is applied to the international banking and financial system and achieves a level of standardisation and universal application. Section 14.2 discusses the development of international standards and how these have been adopted in EU and UK legislation. In sections 14.3 and 14.4, we consider the substantive regulation applied to banks and financial institutions, which largely deal with *preventing*

---

[7] Section 18, Terrorism Act 2000.   [8] Section 14, Terrorism Act 2000.

money laundering. Banks treat this area of regulation very seriously, and 'anti-money laundering' compliance has become a recognised professional practice.

 Key takeaways

- This section introduces the legal definitions of the offence of money laundering found in the UK Proceeds of Crime Act 2002.

- The offence of money laundering can include the financing of yet-to-be-committed crimes such as terrorist financing.

- Banks and financial institutions are highly exposed to money laundering risk due to the inherent processes needed to make 'dirty' money appear 'clean'.

Key bibliography

Legislation

Proceeds of Crime Act 2002 (including subsequent amendments)
Terrorism Act 2000 (including subsequent amendments)

Additional Reading

Alexander, RCH, *Insider Dealing and Money Laundering in the EU: Law and Regulation* (Ashgate 2007)
Leong, AVM, 'Anti-money Laundering Measures in the UK' (2007) *Company Lawyer* 35
Ryder, N, *Money Laundering—An Endless Cycle?: A Comparative Analysis of the Anti-Money Laundering Policies in the United States of America, the United Kingdom, Australia and Canada* (Oxford: Routledge 2012)

14.2 Development of anti-money laundering regulation internationally, in the EU, and nationally

Anti-money laundering laws have been developed at an international level before percolating down to national governments. This is largely due to international concerns for organised illegal drug trafficking, which is highly profitable, resulting in the need to launder the proceeds of crime. A Global Programme led by the United Nations (UN) Office on Drugs and Crime was established since 1997 after the introduction of the UN Convention against Illicit Traffic in Narcotic Drugs and Psychotropic Substances of 1988. This Programme has initially focused on combatting money laundering of the proceeds of drug crime, but has now extended to wider money laundering issues such as corruption, human trafficking, and terrorist financing. These extensions are as a result of international agreement secured in the International Convention for the Suppression of the Financing of Terrorism (1999), the UN Convention against Transnational Organized

Crime (2000) and the UN Convention against Corruption (2003). The Financial Action Task Force was established in 1989 to support the Programme by taking leadership in developing principles to fight money laundering, terrorist financing and financial crime. These have largely been implemented in the UK. EU legislation has also been introduced to harmonise anti-money laundering regimes across the EEA and to lift standards across the bloc, also transposed in the UK.

14.2.1 International standards and the Financial Action Task Force

The Financial Action Task Force (FATF) is an international body formed by ministerial representatives in various countries in 1989, in order to explore international standards, as well as secure international cooperation in combatting money laundering, terrorist financing and other related threats to the integrity of the international financial system.[9] The FATF currently has 36 member countries and is chaired by a rotating presidency amongst its members. Each presidency has a tenure of a year. FATF meetings occur twice yearly in order to determine strategic directions pursuant to its objectives above.

The FATF introduced its pioneering 40 recommendations for combatting money laundering in 1990. These have since become the starting point for many countries' anti-money laundering laws, including the UK. The recommendations include the setting up of new institutions and regulatory regimes, and the imposition of new regulatory responsibilities, duties, and obligations on entities likely to come into contact with 'dirty money'. They include:[10] (a) criminalising the offence of money laundering; (b) establishing enforcement agencies in member states to investigate and enforce against criminal property; (c) establishing financial intelligence units in all member countries that may receive reports on transactions and monitor money laundering; (d) imposing on businesses, financial institutions and professional services that may risk coming into contact with laundered money the obligations to detect signs of money laundering; (e) imposing on financial institutions extensive duties in relation to preventing money laundering or reporting suspicious transactions; and (f) compelling all member countries to render to each other mutual legal assistance and other forms of international cooperation such as information assistance in enforcement against money launderers.

The 40 recommendations form the backbones of an anti-money laundering regime that includes *prevention* and *enforcement*. *Preventive* monitoring is carried out by gatekeepers of 'placement' and 'layering' activities, now designated under regulation. These are banks, financial institutions, professional services, and other businesses such as casinos and real estate agencies. In particular banks and financial institutions are imposed with the most extensive gatekeeping obligations that involve customer due diligence, monitoring and reporting, all of which will be discussed in sections 14.3 and 14.4. In terms of enforcement, specialist agencies are required to be set up in member countries to have extensive powers of intelligence, investigations, and enforcement,

---

[9] http://www.fatf-gafi.org/about/whoweare/.   [10] Box 14.1 sets out the latest standards.

and to render each other mutual legal assistance where cross-border elements are involved.

In 2001, the FATF supplemented the 40 recommendations with nine special recommendations on terrorist financing.[11] These require member countries to ratify and to implement fully the 1999 UN International Convention for the Suppression of the Financing of Terrorism, to criminalise the financing of terrorist activities, to introduce a suite of extensive investigative and enforcement powers against terrorist finance and assets, and to impose on banks and financial institutions, as well as other businesses involved in transferring money (such as cash couriers, wire transfer services etc) monitoring and reporting obligations in order to perform a gatekeeping role in disrupting terrorist financing.

The FATF standards have since been revised and updated[12] and the consolidated version of the standards is set out in Box 14.1. There are now 40 standards that deal with both anti-money laundering and countermeasures to terrorist financing.

Box 14.1 FATF Standards (Consolidated) as of 2012

1. Member countries should assess their exposure to money laundering and terrorist financing risks and adopt a risk-based approach in designing policies and dedicating resources to combat these.

2. Member countries should ensure that their national agencies in intelligence and enforcement are able to coordinate with each other in combatting money laundering and terrorist financing.

3. Member countries should criminalise money laundering.

4. Member countries should introduce extensive enforcement powers to freeze, seize and confiscate criminal property.

5. Member countries should criminalise terrorist financing, whether directed at acts, individuals, or terrorist organisations.

6. Member countries should apply financial sanctions in order to prevent or suppress terrorism and terrorist financing.

7. Financial sanctions should be extended to the proliferation of weapons of mass destruction and its financing.

8. Member countries should apply proportionate but targeted measures at non-profit organisations that may be vulnerable to terrorist financing. (This may include enforcement against assets directed at or transferred via organisations such as charities and religious organisations).

---

[11] At http://www.fatf-gafi.org/media/fatf/documents/reports/FATF%20Standards%20-%20IX%20Special%20Recommendations%20and%20IN%20rc.pdf.

[12] FATF, *International Standards on Combatting Money Laundering and the Financing of Terrorism and Profliferation* (2012) at http://www.fatf-gafi.org/media/fatf/documents/recommendations/pdfs/FATF_Recommendations.pdf.

9. Member countries should ensure that financial institution secrecy laws do not inhibit implementation of anti-money laundering and counter-terrorist financing regulations.

10. Financial institutions must undertake customer due diligence including the identities of beneficial owners of interests, in the establishment of business relationships and on an ongoing basis.

11. Financial institutions must maintain customer and transaction records for at least 5 years.

12. Financial institutions must conduct enhanced due diligence and ongoing monitoring of politically exposed persons.

13. Financial institutions should ensure that correspondent banks are able to perform customer due diligence and institute adequate internal controls to combat money laundering.

14. Member countries should ensure that all money transfer services operating in their jurisdictions are licensed and subject to regulatory compliance and supervision in relation to anti-money laundering.

15. Member countries should constantly assess money laundering or terrorist financing risks that may arise due to the development of new products, services, and technology.

16. Member countries must implement common standards to ensure that all wire transfers are carried out based on accurate originator and beneficiary information.

17. Financial institutions may outsource their customer due diligence processes but must monitor and ensure that such outsourcees are able to comply with regulatory requirements.

18. Financial institutions are to apply internal control programmes in anti-money laundering and terrorist financing across the entire international financial group.

19. Financial institutions are to apply enhanced due diligence measures in all business relationships with countries identified as 'higher risk' by the FATF.

20. Financial institutions must report suspicious transactions.

21. Financial institutions and their employees are protected in civil immunity in relation to the reporting above but must not disclose such reporting ('tipping off').

22 and 23. Designated customer due diligence and reporting obligations are imposed on other businesses exposed to money laundering and terrorist financing risk such as casinos, real estate agents and professional services.

24 and 25. Legal and beneficial ownership of legal persons and other legal arrangements such as trusts are to be made available to authorities in a timely fashion.

26. Financial institutions are to be subject to adequate regulation and supervision in anti-money laundering and counter-terrorist financing.

27, 31 and 35. National supervisors and enforcement agencies should have extensive investigative and supervisory powers, and a range of sanctions should be available in enforcement.

28. Designated non-financial businesses exposed to money laundering and terrorist financing risks should be authorised, regulated, and supervised.

29. Member countries should establish financial intelligence units to receive and analyse suspicious transaction reports and other information relating to money laundering.

30. Law enforcement agencies should act in a pro-active manner in investigations and render assistance as well as cooperate with each other across member countries.

32. Member countries should establish a system for declarations by cash couriers and have the powers to stop and detain the transportation of such cash.

33. Member countries must maintain statistical records of the efficiency and efficacy of their anti-money laundering and counter-terrorist-financing systems.

34. Member country intelligence, regulatory and enforcement agencies should establish guidelines and feedback channels to assist financial institutions and designated non-financial businesses in their regulatory compliance.

36. Member countries should ratify and fully implement the listed international conventions on corruption, money laundering, terrorism, and cybercrime.

37 and 38. Member countries should render each other mutual legal assistance in investigations and enforcement.

39. Member countries should constructively and effectively execute extradition requests in relation to money laundering and terrorist financing, without undue delay to avoid providing a safe haven for indicted persons.

40. Member countries should engage in other forms of international cooperation in relation to anti-money laundering and counter-terrorist-financing including formalising such arrangements in Memoranda of Understanding.

The FATF carries out 'mutual evaluations' that are peer reviews of member countries' anti-money laundering and counter-terrorist financing systems. Such evaluations are a form of internationally persuasive peer pressure for member countries in order to ensure that they effectively implement the Recommendations. Mutual evaluations are carried out on the basis of the latest standards (in this case the 2012 standards in Box 14.1) and clearly communicated to the relevant member countries. Such evaluations are carried out after on-site visits and inspections by the FATF. The procedures that the FATF will apply in relation to its on-site visits and inspections are detailed in its evaluation template.[13] The results of each mutual evaluation are published for public transparency.

The FATF also carries out reviews of all countries whether member countries or otherwise three times a year in order to highlight 'high-risk' jurisdictions where anti-money laundering and counter-terrorist financing laws and compliance are weak.[14] Such reviews are carried out by examining publicly available information in terms of published laws, institutional architecture, and enforcement information. As 'high-risk' jurisdictions can be subject to member countries' financial sanctions according to the FATF standards, identified jurisdictions may be incentivised to improve on their anti-money laundering and counter-terrorist financing measures.

---

[13] FATF, *Procedures for the FATF Fourth Round of AML/CFT Mutual Evaluations* (October 2013) at http://www.fatf-gafi.org/media/fatf/documents/methodology/FATF-4th-Round-Procedures.pdf.

[14] See http://www.fatf-gafi.org/publications/high-riskandnon-cooperativejurisdictions/?hf=10&b=0&s=desc(fatf_releasedate).

The FATF's 'soft law' has largely achieved success in the legalisation of anti-money laundering and counter-terrorist financing regulations in member countries and around the world. Further, its 'soft supervision' in mutual and high-risk evaluations has created pressures and incentives for national governments to take legalisation and enforcement seriously.

Further, where countries are in receipt of aid from the International Monetary Fund, these countries are subject to a yearly Financial Sector Assessment Plan, which includes a peer review of the countries' implementation of the Recommendations. The effective implementation of these Recommendations often forms a basis for eligibility in continuing to receive aid.

Other international organisations also support the FATF's efforts at anti-money laundering and counter-terrorist financing. For example, the Financial Stability Board (FSB) has led efforts to develop a common standard in the form of the 'Unique Transaction Identifier[15]' for all financial transactions so that financial transaction records can be standardised. The Identifier contains information on the identities and interests of transacting parties and facilitates tracing of financial transactions trails, so as to disrupt the layering processes in money laundering. Although the development of the Identifier is aimed at a variety of regulatory objectives including surveillance for macro-prudential regulation (see Chapters 6 and 7), it can be used for surveillance in relation to financial crime. Further, international agencies such as Interpol and the OECD carry out leadership in developing standards for combatting various forms of financial crime such as cybercrime, bribery/corruption, and tax evasion.[16]

14.2.2 Harmonising legislation in the EU

The international standards issued by the FATF were promptly implemented in the European Economic Area (EEA) in the first Anti-money Laundering Directive in 1991. This has since been superseded by the second and third Anti-money Laundering Directives in 2001 and 2005 respectively that incorporated counter-terrorist financing standards and standards of gatekeeping imposed on a wider scope of businesses and services exposed to money laundering risk. The 2005 Directive also dealt specifically with the making of payments or carrying of cash as these can be made by entities that are not regulated banks and financial institutions.[17]

---

[15] The Unique Transaction Identifier is a technical standard developed by CPMI and IOSCO jointly, see CPMI and IOSCO, *Technical Guidance: Harmonisation of the Unique Transaction Identifier* (2017) and the FSB's supporting framework for this in *Governance Arrangements for the Unique Transaction Identifier* (Dec 2017) at http://www.fsb.org/2018/01/fsb-publishes-governance-arrangements-and-implementation-plan-for-the-unique-transaction-identifier-uti/.

[16] The substantive law in relation to these will not be covered in this book but students should be aware of the wider scope of financial crime in general, where corporations are the main agents involved. See https://www.interpol.int/Crime-areas/Cybercrime/Research; OECD, *OECD Convention on Combatting Bribery of Foreign Public Officials in International Business Transactions* (2009); *Implementing the Tax Transparency Standards: A Handbook for Assessors and Jurisdictions* (2010) and *Convention on Mutual Administrative Assistance in Tax Matters* (2017).

[17] Commission Directive on Money Laundering 2006; Wire Transfer Regulations 2006 (Regulation (EC) No 1781/2006 of the European Parliament and of the Council of 15 November 2006 and Cash Control Regulations 2005 (Regulation (EC) No 1889/2005. These have now been consolidated and superseded.

Following the revision of the FATF standards in 2012, the EU introduced the fourth Anti-money Laundering Directive 2015, consolidating the 2005 Directive and secondary legislation.[18] In recognition of the payment services industry that may be different from the banking and finance sector, a regulation[19] is also introduced to accompany the 2015 Directive that now consolidates and adds to the previous requirements in secondary legislation relating to wire transfers. The 2015 Directive provides harmonising principles for all member states in relation to the institutional architecture, policies and regulatory frameworks against money laundering and terrorist financing. The 2015 Directive has since been amended[20] by policymakers to include new payment services providers such as virtual currency exchange providers within the scope of anti-money laundering regulation, so that loopholes can be closed in relation to the migration of money laundering activities through unregulated virtual currency (such as bitcoin) transactions.

Further, European authorities perform the role of assessing their member states' implementation of anti-money laundering regulations in order to adhere to the FATF's Recommendations. Member States are asked to assess the effectiveness of their policies, regulation, and implementation according to a risk-based approach, that is, to show that the highest risks are given emphasis and that regulatory efforts are proportionate to the level of money laundering risk posed. National assessments are reported to EU authorities who may conduct separate EU-wide risk assessments. The EU-wide assessment is carried out by the Joint Committee of the European Banking Authority (EBA), European Securities and Markets Authority and European Insurance and Occupational Pensions Authority (discussed in Chapter 7). The Joint Committee has produced a template of issues to consider and reflective questions for regulators in order to help them develop risk assessment frameworks and the development of policies in response.[21] The Joint Committee further surveys the EU's financial sector regularly in order to highlight key risks.[22]

---

[18] Directive (EU) 2015/849 of the European Parliament and of the Council of 20 May 2015 on the prevention of the use of the financial system for the purposes of money laundering or terrorist financing, amending Regulation (EU) No 648/2012 of the European Parliament and of the Council, and repealing Directive 2005/60/EC of the European Parliament and of the Council and Commission Directive 2006/70/EC.

[19] Regulation (EU) 2015/847 of the European Parliament and of the Council of 20 May 2015 on information accompanying transfers of funds and repealing Regulation (EC) No 1781/2006.

[20] See 'Statement by First Vice-President Timmermans, Vice-President Dombrovskis and Commissioner Jourovà on the adoption by the European Parliament of the 5th Anti-Money Laundering Directive' (19 April 2018), pending publication in the Official Journal.

[21] Joint Committee, *Preliminary Report on Anti-Money Laundering and Counter Financing of Terrorism Risk Based Supervision* (October 2013) at https://www.eba.europa.eu/documents/10180/16145/JC-2013-72+%28Report+on+Risk+Based+Supervision%29.pdf.

[22] For example, see Joint Committee, *Joint Opinion on the Risks of Money Laundering and Terrorist Financing Affecting the Union's Financial Sector* (20 February 2017) at https://www.eba.europa.eu/documents/10180/1759750/ESAS+Joint+Opinion+on+the+risks+of+money+laundering+and+terrorist+financing+affecting+the+Union%E2%80%99s+financial+sector+%28JC-2017-07%29.pdf.

The EBA has a specific role in providing technical standards[23] and guidelines[24] to banks and financial institutions so that they can effectively comply with regulations in anti-money laundering and counter-terrorist financing. National authorities are to regularly review their supervisory plans and these are subject to guidance from the EBA so as to achieve convergent supervisory approaches across the EU (see Chapter 7, section 7.2).

14.2.3 Implementation in the UK

The key piece of UK legislation that implements the relevant FATF standards and EU legislation is the Proceeds of Crime Act 2002, which has been amended in 2005, 2007, 2009, 2011, 2013, 2014, 2015, and 2017. It is supported by the Money Laundering, Terrorist Financing and Transfer of Funds (Information on the Payer) Regulations 2017, which implements the EU's 2015 Directive. The Terrorism Act 2000 deals with counter-terrorist financing measures and liability, and the Act has been amended by subsidiary legislation introduced in 2010, 2012, 2013, 2014, and 2016. As sections 14.3–14.5 highlight, this chapter will focus on the substantive issues relating to the banks and financial institutions' gatekeeping duties and liabilities. Institutions whose financial activities are limited or ancillary, such as amounting to less than £100,000 on a yearly basis or less than 5 per cent of their annual turnover (as long as they are not carrying out payment or remittance services) are exempted from the scope of these obligations.[25] A financial transaction that is less than €1,000 in value is also exempted from the regulatory regime.[26]

The institutional architecture in the UK for combatting money laundering and terrorist financing comprises of government and statutory agencies. At the government level, the Home Office and Treasury have led policy making in anti-money laundering and counter-terrorist financing.[27] The key regulatory, supervisory and enforcement authorities are the National Crime Agency (NCA), Financial Conduct Authority (FCA) in supervising banks and financial institutions' gatekeeping roles and other regulators. The Proceeds of Crime Act 2002 initially set up an Assets Recovery Agency to be

---

[23] Such as the development of technical standards for central counterparties in combatting financial crime risks, see https://www.eba.europa.eu/regulation-and-policy/anti-money-laundering-and-e-money/rts-on-ccp-to-strengthen-fight-against-financial-crime.

[24] See EBA, *Joint Guidelines under Articles 17 and 18(4) of Directive (EU) 2015/849 on simplified and enhanced customer due diligence and the factors credit and financial institutions should consider when assessing the money laundering and terrorist financing risk associated with individual business relationships and occasional transactions* (June 2017) at https://www.eba.europa.eu/documents/10180/1890686/Final+Guidelines+on+Risk+Factors+%28JC+2017+37%29.pdf. Substantive issues will be discussed in section 14.3.

[25] HM Treasury, *Money Laundering Regulations 2017: A Consultation* (15 March 2017) at https://www.gov.uk/government/consultations/money-laundering-regulations-2017. Section 15(3) of the Money Laundering Regulations 2017.   [26] S15(3), Money Laundering Regulations 2017.

[27] See, for example, Home Office and HM Treasury, *Action Plan for Anti-Money Laundering and Counter-Terrorist Finance* (April 2016) at https://www.gov.uk/government/uploads/system/uploads/attachment_data/file/517993/6-2118-Action_Plan_for_Anti-Money_Laundering__print_.pdf.

dedicated to investigations, enforcement, and confiscation of criminal property. The Agency, however, failed to achieve its recovery targets, and its underperformance was highlighted in the National Audit Office report in 2007, which warned that the Agency would unlikely become self-financing.[28] The Agency suffered from various problems including inefficiencies in case management and high expenditures in training. It was closed and merged with the agency in the UK responsible for serious organised crime, the Serious Organised Crime Agency. However, the Serious Organised Crime Agency itself was dissolved to form the NCA in 2013, absorbing a number of units for combatting various crimes including child exploitation, wildlife crime, cybercrime etc. We now turn to the architecture of the regulatory, supervisory and enforcement authorities in the UK.

14.2.3.1 National Crime Agency

The NCA is the UK's primary agency in assessing money laundering and terrorist financing risks overall.[29] The NCA is the authority envisaged in the FATF standards to undertake risk assessments and to take a risk-based approach to combatting money laundering and terrorist financing. The EBA has issued a guidance on how national authorities should undertake risk assessments in their jurisdictions of money laundering and terrorist financing risks, promoting a convergent approach in the EU overall.[30]

The NCA is tasked with investigatory and enforcement powers over serious organised crime in the UK. For the purposes of this chapter, the NCA has responsibilities for pursuing money launderers and those involved in terrorist financing, asset recovery of criminal property, and receiving suspicious transaction reports as the Financial Intelligence Unit (in accordance with the FATF standards). It has other responsibilities in relation to pursuing organised crime such as drug dealing, corruption cases and cybercrime.

The NCA coordinates with police forces across the UK and intelligence units in order to discharge its responsibilities in combatting serious organised crime.[31] The NCA's intelligence and enforcement powers are significantly enhanced in the Criminal Finances Act 2017 amending the Proceeds of Crime Act 2002. In particular, the NCA is able to request the court to make 'unexplained wealth orders' against persons in relation to suspect property valued at least £100,000 in order to gather more intelligence

---

[28] NAO, *The Assets Recovery Agency* (21 February 2007) at https://www.nao.org.uk/wp-content/uploads/2007/02/0607253.pdf.

[29] For example, see NCA, *High End Money Laundering: Strategy and Action Plan* (October 2014) at http://www.nationalcrimeagency.gov.uk/publications/625-high-end-money-laundering-strategy/file.

[30] EBA, *On the Characteristics of a Risk-Based Approach to Anti-Money Laundering and Terrorist Financing Supervision, and the Steps to be Taken When Conducting Supervision on a Risk-Sensitive Basis* (16 November 2016) at https://www.eba.europa.eu/documents/10180/1663861/Joint+Guidelines+on+Risk-Based+Supervision+%28ESAS+2016+72%29.pdf/7159758d-8337-499e-8b12-e34911f9b4b6.

[31] NCA, *The NCA Commitment to Working in Partnership with UK Operational Partners* (August 2015) at http://www.nationalcrimeagency.gov.uk/publications/178-the-nca-commitment-to-working-in-partnership-with-uk-operational-partners/file, esp. at Annex A.

on potential criminal property. The NCA's enhanced enforcement powers include the seeking of interim freezing orders for unexplained wealth, account freezing orders against accounts in banks and financial institutions, and longer periods for the completion of investigations where customers' payment transactions have been interrupted (to be discussed below in section 14.5).

It may be curious to note that it is the American Department of Justice and not the NCA that has levied significant fines upon key UK bank groups in relation to money laundering offences. HSBC was fined $2 billion for the part played by its Mexico outfit in facilitating money laundering by customers involved in drug dealing offences and in significant sums.[32] Standard Chartered was accused of facilitating money laundering in relation to Iran and settled with the Department of Justice at $340 million. It was required to establish anti-money laundering controls and be monitored by the Department for 2 years at least.[33] In addition the US Department of Justice meted out a $630 million fine to Deutsche Bank for money laundering failings in relation to its Russian and London offices,[34] and continues to remain on the offensive in policing money laundering with global implications.[35]

14.2.3.2 Financial Conduct Authority

The FCA regulates banks and financial institutions in terms of duties imposed on them for preventing and detecting money laundering and terrorist financing. These duties in relation to anti-money laundering compliance are discussed in sections 14.3 and 14.5. The FCA's supervisory remit includes banks' and financial institutions' customer due diligence and procedures, and banks' and financial institutions' systems and controls for combatting money laundering and terrorist financing and the governance of such systems (see later).[36] The FCA regularly surveys its regulated entities in order to build up perspectives of the risk factors in various parts of the financial sector, such as in trade finance,[37] asset management[38] and banks.[39]

---

[32] 'HSBC money laundering report: Key findings' *BBC News* (11 December 2012).

[33] 'StanChart faces extension of U.S. money-laundering vigilance' *Reuters* (2 September 2016).

[34] 'Deutsche Bank fined $630 million over Russia money laundering claims' *The Guardian* (31 January 2017).

[35] See mandate of the Money Laundering and Asset Recovery Section of the Department of Justice to be committed to pursuing multi-district, international money laundering offences, at https://www.justice.gov/criminal-mlars.

[36] These are covered in s338, Proceeds of Crime Act 2002; s21A Terrorism Act 2000 in relation to reporting. In relation to internal control procedures, see FCA Handbook SYSC 6 and the Joint Money Laundering Steering Committee Guidelines, both to be discussed in section 14.5; and in relation to due diligence see Articles 11–20 of the Fourth Anti-money Laundering Directive 2015.

[37] FCA, *Thematic Review: Banks' Control of Financial Crime Risks in Trade Finance* (July 2013) at https://www.fca.org.uk/publications/thematic-reviews/tr13-3-banks%E2%80%99-control-financial-crime-risks-trade-finance.

[38] FCA, *Report: Banks' Management of High Money Laundering Risks* (June 2011) at http://www.fsa.gov.uk/pubs/other/aml_final_report.pdf.

[39] FCA, *Thematic Review: Anti-Money Laundering and Anti-Bribery and Corruption Systems and Controls: Asset Management and Platform Firms* (Aug 2015), at https://www.fca.org.uk/publications/thematic-reviews/tr13-9-anti-money-laundering-and-anti-bribery-and-corruption-systems.

Further, the FCA is also designated the Payment Services Regulator, and performs the role of authorising payment services providers (consistent with the requirements of EU legislation discussed above)[40] as well as supervising their compliance with similar duties in anti-money laundering compliance.[41]

The FCA is able to take enforcement action against its regulated entities if it is of the view that banks and financial institutions have failed to conduct procedures or maintain systems and controls appropriate for monitoring money laundering and terrorist financing. These enforcement actions can take place even if the money laundering or terrorist financing offences have not been established as such against banks, financial institutions, or their customers. Individuals responsible for anti-money laundering control under the Senior Managers Regime (discussed in section 14.5) can also be held personally responsible for breach of duties. Enforcement can be carried out by public censure, fine of the institution as well as public censure, fine and/or disqualification of the individual concerned.[42]

It is queried why the FCA is not given a share of the NCA's intelligence role in receiving and analysing suspicious transaction reports (see section 14.4). This would potentially spread the workload in monitoring suspicious transactions and 'giving consent' (discussed in section 14.4) so that the NCA is not overwhelmed.[43]

Box 14.2 provides two examples of the FCA's enforcement actions against banks in the UK for failing to implement adequate customer due diligence procedures and anti-money laundering controls therefore in breach of regulatory duties. These incidents are themselves enforceable even if the money laundering offence has not been established against the banks concerned or their customers. The regulatory enforcement therefore provides a deterrent signal to banks to take their regulatory duties seriously as part of their gatekeeping roles against financial crime.

Box 14.2 FCA enforcement examples

Enforcement Action by the FCA, 15 May 2012: Habib Bank AG Zurich was fined £525,000 for generally failing to put in place adequate policies for carrying out a duty of enhanced due diligence (see section 14.3) for customers that warranted that treatment. The Money Laundering Reporting Officer (MLRO) of the bank was also individually fined £17,500.

Enforcement Action by the FCA, 23 January 2014: Standard Bank was fined £7.6 million for failing to conduct enhanced due diligence for customers that are connected to politically-exposed persons (see section 14.3), exposing the bank to serious risk of money laundering in high-risk African jurisdictions.

---

[40] Discussed also in Chapter 3.
[41] Payment Services Regulations 2017, transposing the EU Payment Services Directive 2 (2015). These require the existence of appropriate internal control to form part of the basis for authorisation.
[42] General powers of the FCA discussed in Chapter 6.
[43] 'NCA warns on company abuse of money-laundering checks' *Financial Times* (12 October 2015).

14.2.3.3 **Other regulators**

Other regulators within the scope of anti-money laundering and counter-terrorist financing regulation are also expected to regulate and oversee their regulated entities' compliance with the regulatory duties to gate-keep money laundering and terrorist financing. For example, the Gambling Commission, which licenses gambling services providers (such as casinos), makes the prevention of financial crime a condition of licensing. Further a code of practice is issued for adherence by all licensed gambling providers to gate-keep against financial crime.[44]

In light of the 2016 Action Plan[45] that is intended to strengthen supervisory endeavours and coordination across various sectors in order to foster an intolerant and hostile environment for financial crime, the Treasury has established a new regulatory body for membership associations or bodies for professional services, the Office for Professional Body Anti-Money Laundering Supervision (OPBAS).

This Office, established in January 2018, oversees membership associations or bodies for professional services providers such as lawyers, accountants, tax advisors, insolvency practitioners and book-keepers. Professional services providers may in the course of business come across signals or information of money laundering or terrorist financing, and it is the duty of their membership associations or bodies to provide guidance and supervision on how professional services providers should gate-keep money laundering and terrorist financing activities. OPBAS requires professional services membership associations or bodies to provide industry-wide as well as specific guidance to firms based on a risk-based approach, and to effectively supervise their members by carrying out inspections, audits, thematic reviews, interviews with senior management, surveys, and questionnaires. Professional services membership associations or bodies must also be prepared to share information and intelligence with the authorities.[46]

The OPBAS functions as a meta-regulator as it does not directly regulate professional services providers. These remain overseen by their membership associations and bodies, but OPBAS' role is to ensure that these membership associations and bodies are robustly assisting and overseeing their members in gatekeeping money laundering and terrorist financing. Membership associations and bodies are respected by their members, but they may also be beholden to their members as they are funded by their members. For example, accountants' audit conduct is no longer subject to the membership body's supervision as a regulatory body, the Financial Reporting Council is regarded

---

[44] Discussed in HM Treasury, *Money Laundering Regulations 2017: A Consultation* (15 March 2017) at https://www.gov.uk/government/consultations/money-laundering-regulations-2017.

[45] Home Office and HM Treasury, *Action Plan for Anti-Money Laundering and Counter-Terrorist Finance* (April 2016) at https://www.gov.uk/government/uploads/system/uploads/attachment_data/file/517993/6-2118-Action_Plan_for_Anti-Money_Laundering__print_.pdf.

[46] OPBAS Sourcebook, at https://fca.org.uk/publication/opbas/opbas-sourcebook.pdf.

as more effectual and credible. Perhaps the meta-regulatory role of OPBAS is a signal that more direct supervision can be introduced for professional services firms if their membership associations or bodies fail to undertake supervision effectively.

Key takeaways

- The FATF provides leadership at the international level for the development of anti-money laundering and counter-terrorist financing architecture, standards, and powers in member countries and the rest of the world.

- The FATF issues Standards by which to evaluate member countries. It also evaluates non-member countries in order to identify 'high-risk' countries. 'High-risk' countries are pressured to elevate their anti-money laundering standards in order not to suffer from constraints in dealings with member countries.

- EU legislation has comprehensively implemented the FATF standards.

- The Joint Committee of EU agencies (EBA, ESMA, and EIOPA) is tasked with the responsibility of evaluating EU-wide money laundering and terrorist financing risks on a regular basis.

- The UK has also implemented the FATF standards in transposing EU legislation in its Proceeds of Crime Act 2002 and in subsequent amendments, and the Terrorism Act 2000 with subsequent amendments.

- EU legislation has been implemented in the Money Laundering Regulations 2017 in the UK.

- The UK government takes leadership on anti-money laundering and counter-terrorist financing policies.

- The architecture of regulatory, supervisory and enforcement agencies comprises the NCA, the FCA and other regulators such as the Gambling Commission, Office of Professional Body Anti-Money Laundering Supervision.

Key bibliography

Legislation

Proceeds of Crime Act 2002

Terrorism Act 2000

Money Laundering Regulations 2017

Directive (EU) 2015/849 of the European Parliament and of the Council of 20 May 2015 on the prevention of the use of the financial system for the purposes of money laundering or terrorist financing, amending Regulation (EU) No 648/2012 of the European Parliament and of the Council, and repealing Directive 2005/60/EC of the European Parliament and of the Council and Commission Directive 2006/70/EC

Amending Directive 2018 TBC

Regulation (EU) 2015/847 of the European Parliament and of the Council of 20 May 2015 on information accompanying transfers of funds and repealing Regulation (EC) No 1781/2006

Reports and official papers

FATF, *International Standards on Combatting Money Laundering and the Financing of Terrorism and Profliferation* (2012) at http://www.fatf-gafi.org/media/fatf/documents/recommendations/pdfs/FATF_Recommendations.pdf

Joint Committee, *Preliminary Report on Anti-Money Laundering and Counter Financing of Terrorism Risk Based Supervision* (October 2013) at https://www.eba.europa.eu/documents/10180/16145/JC-2013-72+%28Report+on+Risk+Based+Supervision%29.pdf.

EBA, *On the Characteristics of a Risk-Based Approach to Anti-Money Laundering and Terrorist Financing Supervision, and the Steps to be Taken When Conducting Supervision on a Risk-Sensitive Basis* (16 November 2016) at https://www.eba.europa.eu/documents/10180/1663861/Joint+Guidelines+on+Risk-Based+Supervision+%28ESAS+2016+72%29.pdf/7159758d-8337-499e-8b12-e34911f9b4b6

NCA, *The NCA Commitment to Working in Partnership with UK Operational Partners* (August 2015) at http://www.nationalcrimeagency.gov.uk/publications/178-the-nca-commitment-to-working-in-partnership-with-uk-operational-partners/file

14.3 Due diligence

The regulatory duty of due diligence imposed on banks, financial institutions, and other entities within the scope of the Money Laundering Regulations 2017 is key to preventing and identifying potential money laundering. In essence due diligence refers to banks gaining adequate knowledge about their customers in order to ascertain that their transactions do not infringe anti-money laundering laws. What this entails will be explored below. The EU 2015 Directive, transposed in the UK Money Laundering Regulations 2017, imposes due diligence obligations for a range of businesses including payment services providers such as pre-paid electronic money instruments, money remitters, trade finance providers, real estate agents, casinos, and of course, banks and financial institutions. The standards of due diligence in the UK are also further extrapolated by a voluntary association established by UK banks, the Joint Money Laundering Steering Group (JMLSG).

The Steering Group is a trade body comprising of industry representatives working with the Bank of England to produce guidance for the industry to comply with anti-money laundering and counter-terrorist financing regulation.[47] The Guidance is endorsed as part of the regulatory framework as it is recognised as guidance issued by a trade body capable of being used to determine if a bank has breached its anti-money laundering obligations.[48] Such guidance needs to be approved by the Treasury and published in order to be used as the basis for enforcement.[49] The Guidance is aimed

---

[47] http://www.jmlsg.org.uk/.

[48] Regulations 19, 21, 24, 35, 48, 76 and 86, Money Laundering Terrorist Financing and Transfer of Funds (Information on the Payer) Regulations 2017.

[49] See http://www.jmlsg.org.uk/industry-guidance/article/jmlsg-guidance-current on the most recent approved version.

> **Box 14.3 When banks need to conduct customer due diligence (Article 11, AML Directive 2015, s27, Money Laundering Regulations 2017)**
>
> (a) establishing a business relationship;
>
> (b) carrying out an occasional transaction that:
>
>   (i)   amounts to EUR 15 000 or more, whether that transaction is carried out in a single operation or in several operations which appear to be linked; or
>
>   (ii) constitutes a transfer of funds exceeding EUR 1 000;
>
> (c) in the case of persons trading in goods, when carrying out occasional transactions in cash amounting to EUR 10 000 or more, whether the transaction is carried out in a single operation or in several operations which appear to be linked;
>
> (d) for providers of gambling services, upon the collection of winnings, the wagering of a stake, or both, when carrying out transactions amounting to EUR 2 000 or more, whether the transaction is carried out in a single operation or in several operations which appear to be linked;
>
> (e) upon suspicion of money laundering or terrorist financing, regardless of any derogation, exemption or threshold;
>
> (f) when there are doubts about the veracity or adequacy of previously obtained customer identification data.

at giving banks concrete directions for compliance, a prescriptive task that, if not delegated successfully to the JMLSG, would have to be undertaken by the FCA.

Banks are required to conduct customer due diligence in the circumstances listed in Box 14.3. These in essence prevent banks from servicing anonymous accounts.[50]

A 'business relationship' is defined as a business, professional or commercial relationship that arises in the course of business of the bank or financial institution, and is expected to have an element of duration after contact is established.[51] An 'occasional transaction' is defined as a transaction that is not part of a 'business relationship' as defined above.[52] A 'beneficial owner' in relation to a body corporate (including a limited liability partnership), is defined as an individual who ultimately controls the body corporate or who holds at least 25 per cent of the shares or voting rights in the body corporate.[53] A beneficial owner in relation to a trust refers to an individual who is able to control the trust (to exercise specified powers in the Money Laundering Regulations 2017) or benefits from the trust, including the settlor, trustees, beneficiaries and any other individual able to control the trust.[54]

---

[50] Article 10 of the AML Directive 2015 prohibits anonymous accounts from being opened or serviced.

[51] Section 4, Money Laundering, Terrorist Financing and Transfer of Funds (Information on the Payer) Regulations 2017 (Money Laundering Regulations 2017).

[52] Section 3, Money Laundering Regulations 2017.   [53] Section 5, Money Laundering Regulations 2017.

[54] Section 6, Money Laundering Regulations 2017.

Customer due diligence applies to the establishment of a business relationship as well as ongoing business carried on in that relationship as long as any of the thresholds above are met. Banks are prohibited from carrying out any transaction for the customer until due diligence is completed,[55] but in certain cases this prohibition is qualified.

A bank account can be opened pending the completion of customer due diligence as long as transactions are not carried out on the account.[56] In cases of 'low risk' (to be discussed shortly), the customer's transaction can be uninterrupted 'for the purposes of the normal course of business' as due diligence is being completed.[57] Where payment service providers issue a customer with electronic money instruments, they can be exempted from customer due diligence at very low thresholds, such as where the payment instrument is not loaded beyond €250 or cannot be made to make payments above €250 per month, and where the instrument is not anonymous and subject to adequate safeguards and conditions.[58] The UK will apply the higher permitted threshold of €500 instead.[59] Banks need to monitor and review their customer relationships generally, especially if any changes are detected to the customer's risk profile.[60]

14.3.1 What is required in customer due diligence?

Banks are required to carry out several key tasks in customer due diligence in order to assess the risk of money laundering. The key tasks are:

(a) Identifying and verifying the customer's identity on the basis of information or documentation from an independent and reliable source.

(b) Identifying and verifying a body corporate's identity and ley information such as the identities of senior management.

(c) Identifying and verifying the identity of any beneficial owner.

(d) Establishing the intended nature and purpose of the business relationship or occasional transaction.

(e) Construct a risk profile for each customer by assessing the level of risk posed by each customer, such as in relation to the intended purpose or nature of the business relationship, the level of assets deposited by the customer or size of

---

[55] Section 30(2), Money Laundering Regulations 2017.

[56] Article 14(3) AML Directive 2015, s30(4), Money Laundering Regulations 2017.

[57] Article 14(2), AML Directive 2015, s30(3), Money Laundering Regulations 2017.

[58] Article 12, AML Directive 2015. Member States can increase the maximum payment instrument threshold to €500.

[59] HM Treasury, *Money Laundering Regulations 2017: A Consultation* (15 March 2017) at https://www.gov.uk/government/consultations/money-laundering-regulations-2017, s38, Money Laundering Regulations 2017.

[60] Article 14(5), AML Directive 2015 and para 108, EBA, *Joint Guidelines under Articles 17 and 18(4) of Directive (EU) 2015/849 on simplified and enhanced customer due diligence and the factors credit and financial institutions should consider when assessing the money laundering and terrorist financing risk associated with individual business relationships and occasional transactions* (June 2017) at https://www.eba.europa.eu/documents/10180/1890686/Final+Guidelines+on+Risk+Factors+%28JC+2017+37%29.pdf. (Joint Guidelines 2017.)

transactions the customer wishes to carry out, and the regularity and duration of the business relationship.

(f) Conducting ongoing monitoring of the business relationship to ensure that transactions are consistent with the bank's knowledge of the customer's risk profile.

(g) Reviewing the existing records of customer due diligence and ensure that they are kept up-to-date.[61]

14.3.1.1 Identity establishment and verification

First, in terms of verifying an individual's identity, the bank must use 'reliable' and 'independent' sources of information, such as passports and driving licences issued by public authorities.[62] Increasingly as customers' identity information may be held by electronic sources of information, banks may have to verify with such sources. The above information should as far as is possible be obtained from public sector, governmental or regulated bodies,[63] but commercial sources may also be used as long as banks are satisfied of the extensiveness, reliability, and credibility of such commercial sources. Even social media sources may be used for corroborating effect. The public and reliable sources of information that banks are encouraged to consult by the EBA include the European Commission's supranational risk assessment, information from governments, regulators, intelligence and enforcement agencies, information from professionals and experts, trade and industry bodies, international standard-setting bodies, civil society, media sources, commercial organisations that provide risk and intelligence information, statistical organisations and academia.[64] The lack of provision of relevant expected documentation may not necessarily stop banks from conducting business with the customer if a risk-based approach is taken in assessing particular customers such as financially excluded customers, young customers, customers whose gender assignment is non-standard, customers lacking in capacity to manage own financial affairs, and international students.[65]

In relation to a body corporate, a bank must verify identity information in relation to the name and registration number of the body corporate, its registered office, the law to which the body corporate is subject (or the law of its incorporation), the body corporate's constitution, the full names of its Board of directors and senior management.[66]

In relation to verifying the identity of a beneficial owner, the bank must establish the identity of the natural person who is the beneficial owner, or where the beneficial owner is a legal person, to establish the structure involving the beneficial owner. Such verification goes beyond checking the register of persons with significant control in company or partnership registers.[67] It is envisaged that banks may use commercial sources that

---

[61] Article 13, AML Directive 2015, s28, Money Laundering Regulations 2017.
[62] Para 5.3.31, JMLSG Guidance.   [63] Paras 5.3.39–53, JMLSG Guidance.
[64] Paras 15–16, Joint Guidelines 2017.   [65] Paras 5.3.108–125, JMLSG Guidance.
[66] Section 28, Money Laundering Regulations 2017.   [67] Ibid.

provide electronic means of verification, but banks need to understand the sources of information checked by such commercial providers and the basis for any scoring or rating system used by such commercial providers in order to rely on their verification.[68]

14.3.1.2 Constructing a risk profile of each customer

Next, banks need to construct a risk profile for each customer. The risk factors are in relation to 'customer risk factors', 'geographical risk factors', 'product and services risk factors', 'transaction risk factors' and 'delivery channel risk factors'.[69] The EBA has developed detailed guidelines to elaborate on elements of each risk factor,[70] and to assist banks to 'risk-weight' elements in each risk factor in order to arrive at an appropriate risk profile for the customer.[71] This approach is methodical and compels the bank to give an informed and intelligent consideration to each customer.

Customer risk factors include the customer's or beneficial owner's business or professional activities, reputation, and behaviour. These are ascertained against a non-exhaustive checklist of questions that banks should obtain satisfaction, such as whether any previous media report or suspicious reporting activities affects the customer's reputation, whether the customer has complex business structures or behaviour in secrecy that may give an indication of the customer's behaviour, and so on. Banks may wish to gather information on the following:[72]

- nature and details of the business/occupation/employment;
- record of changes of address;
- the expected source and origin of the funds to be used in the relationship;
- the origin of the initial and ongoing source(s) of wealth and funds (particularly within a private banking or wealth management relationship);
- copies of recent and current financial statements;
- the various relationships between signatories and with underlying beneficial owners; and
- the anticipated level and nature of the activity that is to be undertaken through the relationship.

Box 14.4 sums up the categories of risk factors banks need to consider in assessing customers and will be elaborated further.

Customer risk factors include the customer's or beneficial owner's business or professional activities, reputation, and behaviour. These are ascertained against a non-exhaustive checklist of questions that banks should obtain satisfaction, such as whether any previous media report or suspicious reporting activities affects the customer's

---

[68] Paras 5.3.79–84, JMLSG Guidance.
[69] Section 18, Money Laundering Regulations 2017.
[70] Paras 18–33, Joint Guidelines 2017.
[71] Paras 36–9, Joint Guidelines 2017.
[72] Para 5.3.24, JMLSG Guidance.

Box 14.4 Categories of risk factors

- Customer
- Geographical
- Products and services
- Transactions
- Delivery channels

---

reputation, whether the customer has complex business structures or behaviour in secrecy that may give an indication of the customer's behaviour, and so on.

'Geographical risk factors' relate to the customer's main locations of business and locations with which the customer has personal links. Banks need to ascertain whether the customer is associated with 'high-risk' countries. A Commission Regulation[73] flanks the 2015 Directive by setting out 'high-risk' countries where anti-money laundering and counter-terrorist financing controls and regulation are weak. There are currently 11 countries on the list. Banks also need to assess whether customers' identified geographical links are in jurisdictions of equivalent anti-money laundering regulation comparable to the EU, and whether these jurisdictions may be of dubious reputation, such as in relation to providing tax or secrecy havens, or are politically unstable.

'Product, services and transactions risk factors' include the transparency, complexity and value/size of the financial product, service or transaction to be undertaken by the customer. Banks may ascertain these risk factors by finding out about the structures involved, whether multiple parties or jurisdictions are involved, whether there are high value and/or cash intensive components, and whether there are innovative aspects such as involving new technology.

'Delivery channel risk factors' refer to whether the bank's relationship is conducted on a face-to-face basis or otherwise, and whether other intermediaries or third parties may interpose in the relationship. Banks need to ascertain if the customer is physically present for identification purposes and whether the customer has been introduced via intermediary or regulated channels.

Where banks conduct business with their customers in specific contexts, additional elements of risk factors may be prescribed. The following provides some examples but these are not exhaustive.

---

[73] Commission Delegated Regulation (EU) 2016/1675 of 14 July 2016 supplementing Directive (EU) 2015/849 of the European Parliament and of the Council by identifying high-risk third countries with strategic deficiencies.

Issuing electronic money

Where banks issue electronic money, for example, in pre-paid cards, specific elements in risk factors are further prescribed by the EBA. For example, banks need to consider the number of transactions that can be carried out and limits on transactions (under 'product, services or transactions risk factors') and whether the customer's address or online IP address has changed (in relation to 'customer risk factors').

Remittance or wire transfer

In terms of money remittance or transfer services, banks are subject to an EU Regulation that supports the 2015 Directive. The Regulation applies more widely to all payment transfer intermediaries, recognising that not only banks and financial institutions are payment service providers.[74] The Regulation deals with standardising the information needed for payment transfers to be made within and from any member state, and the right of payment intermediaries to reject or suspend payments in the event of missing information, such as related to the payee.[75] Standardised information goes some way to assisting banks in their due diligence compliance. The EBA has identified that in funds transfers where payment information is incomplete, higher risk entails and banks need to carry out real-time monitoring and robust back-testing of samples of transactions.[76] Moreover, the EBA prescribes that banks need to pay attention to specific elements in risk factors, such as the reputation and nature of receiving agents (under 'delivery channel risk') and the reputation of the receiving jurisdiction in relation to organised crime levels and the establishment of formal banking systems (under geographical risk factors).

Private wealth management

For private wealth management, banks are asked to ascertain specific elements of 'customer risk factors' in relation to source of wealth in particular whether any connection is made to arms or extractive industries and whether the customer has connections with secrecy havens.

Trade finance

Where banks conduct trade finance, specific elements of customer risk factors include whether the buyer and seller of purported goods are the same legal or beneficial person. Banks need to ascertain whether any unusual features exist in the proposed transaction compared to the customer's previous ones (under product, service, or transactions risk factors).

---

[74] The widening of payment services is permitted in the Payment Services Directive 2, Directive (EU) 2015/2366 of the European Parliament and of the Council of 25 November 2015 on payment services in the internal market, amending Directives 2002/65/EC, 2009/110/EC and 2013/36/EU and Regulation (EU) No 1093/2010, and repealing Directive 2007/64/EC.

[75] Payments under €1,000 may be exempted from the stringent requirement to comply with obtaining all payor and payee information prescribed. [76] Joint Guidelines 2017.

Asset management

Where banks carry out investment or asset management, particular elements of customer risk factors include whether the customer is an unregulated or offshore entity. Banks should also be mindful of the size and purported redemption by the customer (in relation to 'product, services or transaction risk factors').

The requirements of due diligence in terms of information gathering and assessing information against risk factors may be an arduous task, and in pursuing efficiency, technological systems can be deployed in facilitating or carrying out customer due diligence. Technological or automated systems can engage in rapid data collection, efficient alert management and prioritisation, advanced case management, ad hoc investigation, integrated research tools, and comprehensive centralised audit trails and reporting.[77] Although much importance is placed on banks complying with their customer due diligence obligations, exceptional policies are to be put in place for possibly financially excluded customers who may be unreasonably denied access to financial services.[78]

14.3.2 Simplified due diligence

Banks may conduct simplified due diligence in areas of 'lower risk' but subject to ongoing monitoring.[79] Simplified due diligence means that banks may be able to adjust the extent, timing or type of due diligence carried out,[80] while maintaining the normal standards of due diligence as a starting point. This may mean that banks may be able to carry out due diligence less intensely or at later points in time, although no specific guidance is prescribed. Banks may treat the existence of certain elements of risk factors (as discussed above) as indicating the appropriateness of applying simplified due diligence. These elements are set out in Table 14.1.

Where banks consider it appropriate to carry out simplified due diligence for customers, based on one or more of the elements above, banks should recognise that the existence of such elements are not conclusive evidence of 'low risk' and should exercise their discretion with care. The elements listed above are also not comprehensive.[81] Further, banks should keep under review the use of simplified due diligence measures and continue to monitor the customer's activities for any unusual signs. Where banks doubt the veracity of any information supplied by the customer, or the risk assessment of the customer changes, or the conditions for enhanced due diligence (below) are met or money laundering or terrorist financing is suspected, banks must cease to apply simplified due diligence.

---

[77] Angela SM Irwin and Kim-Kwang Raymond Choo, 'The Future of Technology in Customer Identification & Relationship Risk' (2014) at https://papers.ssrn.com/sol3/papers.cfm?abstract_id=2431944. Distributed ledger technology is discussed in José Parra-Moyano and Omri Ross, 'KYC Optimization Using Distributed Ledger Technology' (2017) at https://papers.ssrn.com/sol3/papers.cfm?abstract_id=2897788.

[78] FCA Handbook, SYSC 6.3.7.   [79] Article 15, AML Directive 2015.

[80] Section 37, Money Laundering Regulations 2017.

[81] Section 37(4), Money Laundering Regulations 2017.

Table 14.1 Risk Factors for 'Lower Risk' Areas Qualifying for Simplified Due Diligence

Customer risk factors

- public companies listed on a stock exchange and subject to adequate rules of the exchange, such as disclosure requirements that ensure adequate transparency of beneficial ownership
- a credit or financial institution subject to the EU 2015 Directive and supervised for compliance with the Directive's requirements
- public administration, or a publicly-owned enterprise
- individual resident in a geographical area of lower risk (read with geographical risk factors below)

Product, Service, Transaction or Delivery Channel risk factors:

- life insurance policies for which the premium is low (for example small regular premiums paid by direct debit or for policies with no investment value)
- insurance policies for pension schemes if there is no early surrender option and the policy cannot be used as collateral
- a pension, superannuation or similar scheme that provides retirement benefits to employees, where contributions are made by way of deduction from wages, and the scheme rules do not permit the assignment of a member's interest under the scheme
- financial products or services that provide appropriately defined and limited services to certain types of customers, so as to increase access for financial inclusion purposes
- products where the risks of money laundering and terrorist financing are managed by other factors such as purse limits or transparency of ownership
- Child trust funds and junior ISAs as defined under relevant legislation

Geographical risk factors

- An EEA member state
- third countries that have effective anti-money laundering and counter-terrorist financing systems
- third countries identified by credible sources as having a low level of corruption or other criminal activity such as terrorism (within the meaning of s1 of the Terrorism Act 2000(94)), money laundering, and the production and supply of illicit drugs
- third countries that, on the basis of credible sources, such as evaluations, detailed assessment reports or published follow-up reports published by the FATF, the International Monetary Fund, the World Bank, the Organisation for Economic Co-operation and Development or other international bodies or non-governmental organisations, have in place effective systems to implement the requirements of the FATF Recommendations of 2012 updated as of 2016

14.3.3 **Enhanced due diligence**

In some cases, banks are obliged to carry out enhanced due diligence. These are situations where a relatively higher risk of money laundering or terrorist financing may be involved. The FCA is in particular keen on monitoring banks' compliance with enhanced due diligence obligations as the enforcement examples we discussed in section 14.2 show. In these cases, banks had failed to ensure that systems were established for identifying cases for enhanced due diligence and to carry out such due diligence.

Enhanced due diligence is to be carried out by banks in the following situations:[82]

(a) where high risk is identified after the bank has constructed a risk profile in normal due diligence procedures already discussed;

(b) a business relationship or transaction involves a person established in a high-risk jurisdiction;[83]

(c) where the transaction is unusually large, complex or has no apparent legal or economic purpose;

(d) where correspondent banking relationships are established in non-EEA countries;

(e) where politically exposed persons[84] are involved (see definition in Box 14.5);[85]

(f) where the customer has provided false or stolen identification; or

(g) where the transaction by its nature gives rise to a higher risk of money laundering or terrorist financing.

Box 14.5 PEPs (Article 3, AML Directive 2015)

- heads of state, heads of government, ministers, and deputy or assistant ministers;
- members of parliament or of similar legislative bodies;
- members of the governing bodies of political parties;
- members of supreme courts, of constitutional courts or of other high-level judicial bodies, the decisions of which are not subject to further appeal, except in exceptional circumstances;
- members of courts of auditors or of the boards of central banks;
- ambassadors, chargés d'affaires, and high-ranking officers in the armed forces;
- members of the administrative, management or supervisory bodies of state-owned enterprises;
- directors, deputy directors and members of the Board or equivalent function of an international organisation.

---

[82] Section 33, Money Laundering Regulations 2017.

[83] Defined in Commission Delegated Regulation (EU) 2016/1675 of 14 July 2016 supplementing Directive (EU) 2015/849 of the European Parliament and of the Council by identifying high-risk third countries with strategic deficiencies.

[84] This includes family members and known associates of the politically exposed person, Article 23, AML Directive 2015; and for at least 12 months after a politically exposed person has ceased political office, Article 22, AML Directive 2015. [85] Articles 18–23, AML Directive 2015.

Table 14.2 sets out the indicative elements in risk factors that give rise to one of the above seven thresholds for conducting enhanced due diligence.

Table 14.2 Risk Factors for Higher Risk Triggering Obligations to Conduct Enhanced Due Diligence

---

Customer risk factors

- the business relationship is conducted in unusual circumstances
- the customer is resident in a geographical area of high risk
- the customer is a legal person or legal arrangement that is a vehicle for holding personal assets
- the customer is a company that has nominee shareholders or shares in bearer form
- the customer is a business that is cash intensive
- the corporate structure of the customer is unusual or excessively complex given the nature of the company's business

Geographical risk factors

- countries identified by credible sources as not having effective systems to counter money laundering or terrorist financing
- countries identified by credible sources as having significant levels of corruption or other criminal activity, such as terrorism (within the meaning of s1 of the Terrorism Act 2000), money laundering, and the production and supply of illicit drugs
- countries subject to sanctions, embargos or similar measures issued by, for example, the EU or the UN
- countries providing funding or support for terrorism
- countries that have organisations operating within their territory that are designated as proscribed under the UK Terrorism Act, or as terrorist organisations by the EU or UN
- countries identified by credible sources as not implementing requirements to counter money laundering and terrorist financing that are consistent with the recommendations published by the FATF's most recent recommendations.

NOTE in all cases credible sources refer to official evaluations and assessments such as by the EU, UN, OECD, IMF, World Bank

Product, services, and delivery channel risk factors

- product involves private banking
- the product or transaction is one which might favour anonymity
- the situation involves non-face-to-face business relationships or transactions, without certain safeguards, such as electronic signatures
- payments will be received from unknown or unassociated third parties
- new products and new business practices are involved, including new delivery mechanisms, and the use of new or developing technologies for both new and pre-existing products
- the service involves the provision of nominee directors, nominee shareholders or shadow directors, or the formation of companies in a third country

---

In relation to points above, enhanced due diligence involves:[86]

1. Taking additional steps to obtain independent and reliable sources to verify the customer and/or beneficial owner's identity.[87]

2. Taking additional measures to understand better the background, ownership and financial situation of the customer, and other parties to the transaction, as well as the intended purpose and nature of the business relationship and/or transaction.

3. Taking further steps to be satisfied that the transaction is consistent with the purpose and intended nature of the business relationship. For example, banks are required to put in place mechanisms to detect unusual transactions compared to the customer's normal profile, and to require more information on the purpose of the transaction, the nature of the customer's business.[88]

4. To subject the business relationship to greater degree and nature of monitoring, including greater scrutiny over transactions and to detect suspicious transactions.

Special steps in enhanced due diligence are applicable to (d) where correspondent banking relationships are established in third countries outside the EEA. Banks are prohibited from establishing correspondent relationships with 'shell' banks, that is, an institution carrying out banking services that is incorporated in a jurisdiction in which it has no physical presence, nor involving meaningful mind and management, and that is unaffiliated with a regulated financial group.[89]

In terms of the steps for enhanced due diligence, banks are required to gather sufficient information, such as from publicly available and credible sources, about the correspondent institution to understand fully the nature of the respondent's business, reputation, and quality of supervision in relation to the correspondent institution. Banks also need to assess the correspondent institution's controls in anti-money laundering and counter-terrorist financing. In particular, banks need to ascertain that if customers have direct access to the correspondent institution's accounts ('payable-through accounts'), that the correspondent institution has put in place customer due diligence and ongoing monitoring, and is able to supply the bank with such information if requested. The bank is required to obtain approval from senior management before establishing a new correspondent relationship, and to document clearly the respective responsibilities of each institution.[90]

Senior management is defined as 'officer or employee with sufficient knowledge of the institution's money laundering and terrorist financing risk exposure and sufficient seniority to take decisions affecting its risk exposure, and need not, in all cases, be a member of the Board of directors.'[91] The relevant person could be the designated MLRO (discussed in section 14.5) or a senior employee of equivalent stature.

---

[86] Section 33(4) and (5), Money Laundering Regulations 2017.
[87] Para 107, Joint Guidelines 2017.   [88] Para 56, Joint Guidelines 2017.
[89] Articles 3 and 24, AML Directive 2015; s34, Money Laundering Regulations 2017.
[90] Article 19, AML Directive 2015, s34, Money Laundering Regulations 2017.
[91] Article 3, AML Directive 2015.

The implementation of enhanced due diligence for correspondent banks has over the years resulted in many banks from Western jurisdictions terminating their correspondent relationships on risk-averse grounds, therefore making it difficult to facilitate even legitimate international flows of finance.[92] This can result in practical impossibility for individuals working in the UK for example to send money home to a country that is listed as high-risk in the Commission Regulation mentioned above. The FATF and FSB are both concerned with regard to the overall decline in correspondent banking relationships. The FATF has now provided guidance to assist banks in more intelligently assessing correspondent banking risks and to manage risks by clear lines of responsibility and ongoing dialogue and monitoring.[93] The FSB further undertakes to provide clearer regulatory guidance for correspondent relationships, supports public and private sector initiatives to build up the capacity of correspondent banks to meet anti-money laundering and counter-terrorist financing regulation.[94] Such initiatives include standardisation of the due diligence items for banks.[95]

In relation to (e), enhanced due diligence is needed whenever a business relationship or transaction is carried out with a politically exposed person (PEP). PEPs are defined in Box 14.5.[96] The family and known associates of PEPs are defined in Box 14.6.

Box 14.6

Family members of politically exposed persons (Article 3, AML Directive 2015)

(a) the spouse, or a person considered to be equivalent to a spouse, of a politically exposed person;

(b) the children and their spouses, or persons considered to be equivalent to a spouse, of a politically exposed person;

(c) the parents of a politically exposed person.

Persons known to be close associates of a politically exposed person

(a) natural persons who are known to have joint beneficial ownership of legal entities or legal arrangements, or any other close business relations, with a politically exposed person;

(b) natural persons who have sole beneficial ownership of a legal entity or legal arrangement which is known to have been set up for the de facto benefit of a politically exposed person.

---

[92] 'Poor Correspondents', *The Economist* (14 June 2014).

[93] FATF, *FATF Guidance on Correspondent Banking Services* (October 2016) at http://www.fatf-gafi.org/media/fatf/documents/reports/Guidance-Correspondent-Banking-Services.pdf.

[94] FSB, *Action Plan to Assess and Address the Decline in Correspondent Banking* (December 2016) at http://www.fsb.org/wp-content/uploads/FSB-action-plan-to-assess-and-address-the-decline-in-correspondent-banking.pdf.

[95] Such as the Correspondent Banking Due Diligence Questionnaire introduced in early 2018, see http://www.fsb.org/2018/03/bcbs-cpmi-fatf-and-fsb-welcome-industry-initiative-facilitating-correspondent-banking/.

[96] The UK government's initial proposal to include senior members of international sporting federations in the list was not supported and ultimately ditched. See HM Treasury, *Money Laundering Regulations 2017: A Consultation* (15 March 2017) at https://www.gov.uk/government/consultations/money-laundering-regulations-2017.

No public function referred to in points (a)–(h) shall be understood as covering middle-ranking or more junior officials.

If a person has ceased to be a PEP, banks are to continue to apply enhanced due diligence to such a person for up to 12 months of the cessation of the person's PEP functions or role.

Banks are required to adopt appropriate risk management procedures and systems to ascertain whether a customer or beneficial owner is a PEP, including whether the beneficiary of a life insurance policy or investment-related insurance policy is a PEP or a legal person whose beneficial owner is a PEP.[97] Enhanced due diligence in relation to such persons includes the determination of the risk profile of such persons upon the conduct of normal due diligence procedures as discussed above, and taking appropriate enhanced due diligence procedures in accordance with such risk profile. Enhanced due diligence steps include the taking of adequate measures to establish the source of wealth and funds and carrying out of enhanced ongoing monitoring of the business relationship.[98] Further, the establishment of any business relationship with a PEP must be subject to obtaining the approval of senior management. The UK will also institute a redress procedure for PEPs who wish to complain against their financial institutions by allowing them to access the services of the Financial Ombudsman's Office.[99]

> ### Key takeaways
>
> - Banks are required to carry out customer due diligence at the establishment of business relationships with customers or for the carrying out of transactions.
>
> - Customer due diligence involves the verification of customers' identities, including those of a beneficial owner, from reliable and credible sources of information that may be public or commercial, or even on social media.
>
> - Due diligence also involves the construction of a risk profile for customers based on the fivefold categories of customer risk, geographical risk, product or services risk, transactions risk, and delivery channels risk.
>
> - Due diligence is an ongoing obligation for banks as they are required to keep customers' risk profiles under review and respond to changes in the risk profile.
>
> - Simplified customer due diligence may be warranted in specified situations.
>
> - Enhanced customer due diligence is required in areas of higher risk such as where a high-risk jurisdiction, as defined by an EU Commission Regulation, is involved, or where the nature of the transaction or the customer, such as being a politically-exposed person indicates signals of relatively higher risk.

---

[97] Articles 20, 21, AML Directive 2015, s34, Money Laundering Regulations 2017.

[98] Article 20, AML Directive 2015; s34, Money Laundering Regulations 2017.

[99] HM Treasury, *Money Laundering Regulations 2017: A Consultation* (15 March 2017) at https://www.gov.uk/government/consultations/money-laundering-regulations-2017; Schedule 3, s7, Money Laundering Regulations 2017.

- Non-exhaustive elements of risk factors under the five-fold categories are introduced to guide banks as to when simplified or enhanced due diligence may be appropriate. However, the determination of whether to apply such due diligence procedures remains to an extent discretionary, depending on the bank's construction of the customer's risk profile.

Key bibliography

Legislation

Anti-Money Laundering Directive (EU) 2015/849
Money Laundering Regulations 2017

Other reports or papers

EBA, *Joint Guidelines Under Article 17 And 18(4) of Directive (EU) 2015/849 on Simplified and Enhanced Customer Due Diligence and the Factors Credit and Financial Institutions Should Consider When Assessing the Money Laundering and Terrorist Financing Risk Associated with Individual Business Relationships and Occasional Transactions (The Risk Factors Guidelines)* (21 Oct 2015) at https://www.eba.europa.eu/documents/10180/1240374/JC+2015+061+%28Joint+Draft+Guidelines+on+AML_CFT+RFWG+Art+17+and+18%29.pdf
Joint Money Laundering Steering Group Guidance (January 2018) at http://www.jmlsg.org.uk/industry-guidance/article/jmlsg-guidance-current

Articles

Philip J Ruce, 'Anti-Money Laundering: The Challenges of Know Your Customer Legislation for Private Bankers and the Hidden Benefits for Relationship Management ("The Bright Side of Knowing Your Customer")' (2011) 128 *Banking Law Journal* 548

14.4 Financial intelligence reporting

The UK has established the NCA to be the Financial Intelligence Unit responsible for receiving reports from banks, financial institutions and other designated businesses of suspicious transactions in relation to money laundering and terrorist financing.[100] The UK Proceeds of Crime Act 2002 (and subsequent amendments) provide for the obligation to report suspicious transactions, on pain of criminal liability.[101] This is discussed shortly in this section and in section 14.4.1.

The EU 2015 Directive clearly provides that persons who make a suspicious transaction report should not be exposed to liability in contract or under law, nor be treated in a hostile, adverse, or discriminatory manner.[102] Persons who make such reports are

---

[100] Consistent with the FATF Standards and Article 32, AML Directive 2015.
[101] Articles 33 and 34, AML Directive 2015, s330, Proceeds of Crime Act 2002.
[102] Articles 36 and 37, AML Directive.

protected under the Public Interest Disclosure and Employment Rights Acts. Such reporting can also be contrary to the bank's duty of confidentiality to its customers (discussed in Chapter 2, section 2.4), and the Proceeds of Crime Act expressly provides for such disclosures not to be treated as in breach of restrictions, however, imposed on such information, as long as the disclosure adheres the Act's suspicious transaction reporting regime.[103]

In *K v National Westminster Bank Plc*,[104] the customer instructed the bank to pay £235,000 to its supplier for mobile phones. The mobile phones were to be sold to a Swiss company after which the customer would reclaim VAT that represented £20,000, his business profit. The bank made a suspicious transaction report to the Serious Organised Crime Agency and thus was suspended from carrying out the payment, which caused the customer losses. The customer challenged the bank's action but the bank could not be made liable for failing to make the customer's payment under contractual mandate, as the bank had acted lawfully in compliance with anti-money laundering regulation.

In *Shah v HSBC Plc*,[105] Shah was a private bank customer of HSBC who was subject to significant delays in his payment instructions on at least four occasions, including paying into his own Swiss bank account in a sum over £28 million and paying his former employee in Zimbabwe in a sum of over $7 million. Shah was not aware that the bank had raised suspicious transaction reports in relation to those payment instructions. Nevertheless, the transactions were allowed to proceed after investigations by the Serious Organised Crime Agency, and hence there was no implication of money laundering liability. However, the former employee reported to Zimbabwean police suspicions that Shah was involved in money laundering that led to Shah being questioned by the Reserve Bank of Zimbabwe. Subsequently the anti-money laundering authorities froze Shah's assets in Zimbabwe, causing him a loss of over $300 million. At first instance, the High Court dismissed Shah's challenge against the bank's failure to execute his transactions, holding that the bank was protected in complying with anti-money laundering regulation. Shah appealed against the summary judgment and the Court of Appeal[106] then overturned the summary judgment and allowed a full trial on whether the bank would still have owed contractual duties in informing Shah of the suspicious transaction report and Serious Organised Crime Agency investigations.

In the full trial before the High Court, Shah argued that the bank owed him duties to account for the bank's conduct in suspicious transaction reporting and their procedures. He argued that contractual terms should be implied to provide him with a wide range of information relating to the suspicious transaction reporting thresholds, procedures, and identities of officers, as well as investigation information. Shah argued that such information was owed to him as customer and would be relevant to clearing his name in Zimbabwe towards the release of his assets by authorities there. The High Court, however, dismissed Shah's case and stated that such terms regarding disclosure

---

[103] Section 337.   [104] [2006] EWCA Civ 1039.   [105] [2012] EWHC 1283 (QB).
[106] [2010] EWCA Civ 31.

of information cannot be implied as the Serious Organised Crime Agency and police would not have allowed it, being likely prejudicial to the exercise of their investigative powers.[107] Indeed, implied terms should be inserted in banking contracts that allow banks to suspend their contractual duties to perform transactions when complying with anti-money laundering regulations. Shah's case may have been looked at unfavourably due to the widely framed duty of accountability sought, and his demonstrated hostility against several named employees in HSBC plc. Further, the non-disclosure of information by the bank was judged not to have caused Shah's losses as the losses were directly caused by the Zimbabwean authorities' actions that were unrelated to the bank's conduct. It is queried whether disclosure duties of a narrower nature could find favour with courts.

In sum, the protection of bank employees for raising a suspicious transaction report is comprehensive as compliance with regulation overrode contractual duties and the court has not been willing to imply duties of disclosure to the customer afterward. We now turn to the nature of the obligation to make suspicious transaction reports.

14.4.1 Suspicious transactions reports/authorised disclosures

Persons in the regulated sector (banks, financial institutions, payment services providers) who come across information or any matter within the course of business that raises knowledge, suspicion or reasonable grounds for knowledge or suspicion of money laundering, must make disclosure to a nominated officer or directly to the NCA.[108] The nominated officer refers to the MLRO discussed in section 14.5.

Upon receipt of a suspicious transaction report made internally, the nominated officer must consider each report, the grounds for the report, and access all relevant information within the bank or financial institution in order to make a judgment of whether the transaction is reportable to the NCA. To this end a bank or financial institution must ensure that the nominated officer has such access. Where the nominated officer is of the view that a suspicious transaction has occurred, an external report should be made to the NCA[109] via a prescribed online system.[110] The external report should contain as much useful information relating to the identity of the potential money launderer and the suspected laundered proceeds as far as is possible.[111] Where the nominated officer decides not to make the external report, the decision must be documented with reasons.[112] Failure to make such reports as soon as is practicable may render the persons above liable for a criminal offence under s330-332 of the Proceeds of Crime Act regime.

Further, any person who may be involved in 'concealing' or 'acquiring, retaining, using or controlling' criminal property, or involved in arrangements that facilitate the above could avoid liability if such a person made an 'authorised disclosure'.[113]

---

[107] See discussion on s333, in section 14.4.3.   [108] Section 330, Proceeds of Crime Act 2002.
[109] Sections 331–2, Proceeds of Crime Act 2002.   [110] Para 6.35, JMLSG Guidance.
[111] Paras 3.21–27, 6.3 JMLSG Guidance.   [112] Para 6.32, JMLSG Guidance.
[113] Sections 327–9, Proceeds of Crime Act 2002.

Authorised disclosures are made to a constable, customs officer, NCA or nominated officer in a regulated institution.[114]

14.4.1.1 Meaning of knowledge and suspicion

As suspicious transaction reports and authorised disclosures are made on the basis of 'knowledge', 'suspicion' or 'reasonable grounds for raising suspicion', it is queried whether the bank's exercise of discretion to report can be challenged.

'Knowledge' is explained as actual knowledge of facts or inferred from facts that bank or financial institutions staff come across in the course of business.[115] Suspicion is more subjective in quality and falls short of firm evidence.[116] However, suspicion is not mere speculation and needs to be founded on some basis, but such basis need not be objectively required to be reasonable or firm.

In *K v National Westminster Bank Plc* above, the aggrieved customer challenged the bank's basis for 'suspicion' but the court held that suspicion is a subjective state of mind, and that the bank's suspicion, as long as it is more than a fanciful supposition, is a valid one and cannot be questioned. This position was affirmed in *Shah v HSBC Plc*,[117] adding that any previous case law that demanded that 'suspicion' had to be 'settled' is undue.

Certain persons are exempted from the obligation to make suspicious transaction reports, largely due to their obligations as professionals or circumstances of privilege. These are lawyers, accountants, auditors, and tax advisers.[118]

14.4.2 The need for NCA's 'consent' to proceed if a suspicious transaction report is made

After a suspicious transaction report has been made, the bank is unable to proceed with the customer's transaction unless 'appropriate consent' under ss335 and 336 of the Proceeds of Crime Act 2002 has been obtained. 'Appropriate consent' can be obtained expressly, or be presumed after the lapse of 7 working days from the date of the report, and the NCA has not refused consent. If the NCA refuses consent within the 7 working days from the date of report, then the transaction is held for a moratorium period of 31 working days. The moratorium period is the period in which the NCA carries out its investigations. Before the expiry of the period, the NCA may raise the need to extend the moratorium if the preceding 31 days have not provided sufficient time for the NCA to complete its investigations. The Criminal Finances Act 2017[119] now permits a senior officer from the NCA to request the court for an extension of the moratorium period. The court may make multiple extension orders, but each one should only be for 31 working days from when the moratorium period ought to have ended. The court's power to extend the moratorium periods is, however, capped at a total of 186 working

---

[114] Section 338, Proceeds of Crime Act 2002.   [115] Para 6.10, JMLSG Guidance.
[116] Para 6.11, JMLSG Guidance.   [117] [2012] EWHC 1283 (QB).
[118] Section 330 Proceeds of Crime Act 2002 amended as of 2006, and Article 34(2), AML Directive 2015.
[119] Section 336A–D, Proceeds of Crime Act 2002 amended by the Criminal Finances Act 2017.

days for the moratorium period. In the absence of the NCA's request for extension and at the lapse of a 31-day period, the bank may presume that 'appropriate consent' is achieved and proceed with the transaction.

Where the NCA refuses consent for the customer's transaction to proceed, it can be envisaged that the customer is held in suspense, and such situations can cause the customer great inconvenience as personal or business accounts may be frozen. In *UMBS Online v SOCA*,[120] UMBS carried on a money remittance business through a number of international currency transfer institutions one of which was the now defunct Laiki Bank of Cyprus. Laiki Bank made a suspicious transaction report against UMBS that caused UMBS' transfers to be suspended. Within 7 working days, SOCA refused consent to proceed, which was very damaging to UMBS' business. UMBS requested SOCA to review the decision but SOCA refused, citing that the moratorium period would last 31 days. UMBS then challenged SOCA's refusal to review under judicial review proceedings. These failed as the High Court held that SOCA's decision was not reviewable under legislation. On appeal, the Court of Appeal disagreed that SOCA's decision was not reviewable and remitted back to the High Court to hear the review. It, however, opined that SOCA needed to keep records of their reasons in refusing consent and should give consent where there is no longer any good reason to hold the transaction.[121]

Now that the moratorium period is raised in favour of the NCA, it is hoped that the NCA would also put in place formal complaint and review mechanisms for individuals and businesses affected. The Court of Appeal's stance in holding that the agency's decisions have to be reasoned and documented and may be subject to review, is a welcome safeguard against the vast powers of the NCA.

14.4.3 Tipping off offence

The NCA's powers to effectively investigate suspicious transactions is further protected by secrecy duties imposed under the Proceeds of Crime Act 2002. If a bank is unable to carry out a transaction within its normal promptness, this may highlight to the customer concerned that a suspicious transaction report has been made. If customers have such knowledge and take steps to re-arrange their financial affairs in such a way as to obstruct the NCA's investigations, the NCA's investigations would be prejudiced. Hence, the UK and EU have maintained a regime that prohibits 'tipping off' by persons where suspicious transaction reports have been made.[122] The Proceeds of Crime Act 2002 makes it an offence for any person to disclose to another that either a suspicious transaction report has been made or that investigations into money laundering are contemplated or underway,[123] if the information is obtained in the course of business in the regulated sector and disclosure is likely to prejudice any investigation into the matter.

---

[120] [2007] Bus LR 1317.　　[121] *UMBS Online Ltd v SOCA* [2007] EWCA Civ 406.
[122] Section 333, Proceeds of Crime act 2002 and Article 39, AML Directive 2015.
[123] Section 333A, Proceeds of Crime Act 2002 amended in 2007.

The tipping off offence often puts banks in a difficult position after they have initiated a suspicious transaction report. This is because the bank's client would presumably be anxious as to the delay in the execution of the transaction, but the bank is unable to inform the client what the cause is for the delay. In *Squirrell Ltd v National Westminster Bank Plc and HM Customs & Excise (Intervenor)*,[124] a case related to the same facts in *K v National Westminster Bank Plc* discussed earlier, the customer whose account was frozen while the bank waited for the lapse of 7 working days or for SOCA to refuse consent challenged the bank for failure to explain why the transactions were being held. The court held that the bank had to comply with the reporting obligations upon suspicion of money laundering and were also prohibited from disclosing to their client the state of affairs. The bank was in an unenviable position but such conduct could not be impeached.

However, the 2007 amendments to the UK regime provided for a white list of disclosures that would not be regarded as tipping off. The provisions clarified that disclosures within the same firm or group are not to be treated as tipping off.[125] This is necessary to enable different personnel in the firm to deal with internal control, advice, or training. Further, disclosures made between financial institutions and between professional advisers are also protected from the tipping off offence[126] if made for the purpose of preventing a money laundering or terrorist financing offence, and the relevant institution or adviser is situated in an EEA country and is subject to equivalent duties in confidentiality and personal data protection. Disclosures made to authorities for the purposes of assisting investigation or enforcement are also protected.[127]

➜ Key takeaways

- Banks are required to carry out suspicious transactions reports if there is knowledge, suspicion, or reasonable grounds to suspect money laundering.

- Knowledge refers to actual knowledge of facts or knowledge inferred from facts but suspicion is more subjective in nature and requires some form of a basis although such basis need not be objectively ascertained.

- Suspicious transaction reports are first carried out internally to the MLRO discussed in section 14.5. The Officer may then externally report this to the NCA.

- If a suspicious transaction report is made, the transaction may proceed after a lapse of 7 working days if the NCA does not refuse consent to its proceeding.

- The NCA may refuse consent within 7 working days in which case a moratorium period of up to 31 days applies for the NCA to carry out investigations while the transaction is suspended.

---

[124] [2005] EWHC 664 (Ch).   [125] Section 333B, Proceeds of Crime Act 2002 amended in 2007.
[126] Section 333C, Proceeds of Crime Act 2002 amended in 2007.
[127] Section 333D, Proceeds of Crime Act 2002 amended in 2007.

- The moratorium period can be extended upon request made to the court by the NCA for further periods of 31 days up to a maximum of 186 days, during which time a customer's account would be frozen.

- Customers are unlikely to successfully seek redress from banks for failing to carry out transactions.

- Further, banks are prohibited from disclosing to customers the nature of the delay in their executions in order not to prejudice NCA investigations. This is the essence of the offence of 'tipping off'.

- Judicial review may be sought for the NCA's decisions.

Key bibliography

Legislation

Criminal Finances Act 2017 amending the Proceeds of Crime Act 2002

Additional reading

Issacs, M, 'Money Laundering: Further Guidance for Banks on What to Do When Faced with Conflicting Duties Following a Suspicious Transaction Report: The N2J Case' (2006) *Journal of International Banking Law and Regulation* 431

Ryder, N, *Money Laundering—An Endless Cycle?: A Comparative Analysis of the Anti-Money Laundering Policies in the United States of America, the United Kingdom, Australia and Canada* (Oxford: Routledge 2012)

14.5 Internal control and governance

Banks and financial institutions need to ensure that they have in place systems and procedures to consistently and effectively implement the duties of due diligence and suspicious transaction reporting discussed above. Overall, banks and financial institutions are required to install and maintain an organisational framework or architecture for such compliance. To this end, the FCA[128] has established procedural and governance rules for banks. In general, banks and financial institutions are to put in place adequate policies and systems proportionate to the nature, scale, size, and complexity of their businesses and in accordance with the nature and range of financial products and services it engages in.[129] We turn first to the governance requirements imposed by the FCA, followed by the procedural requirements. The governance requirements relate to the organisation of responsibility for implementing, overseeing, and reviewing compliance policies and procedures within the bank or financial institution.

---

[128] Largely to be found in FCA Handbook SYSC 6. The need for adequate policies and control is also stated in Article 46, AML Directive 2015.   [129] FCA Handbook SYSC 6.1.2.

14.5.1 **Governance**

The FCA mandates that a director or senior manager of the bank or financial institution[130] has overall responsibility for maintaining the policies and systems for compliance with anti-money laundering and counter-terrorist financing regulation. Where a bank or financial institution group is concerned, anti-money laundering and counter-terrorist financing policies are to be maintained on a group-wide basis. The policies must be documented, as this will ensure due dissemination to the rest of the firm for effective and consistent implementation, and for training and awareness purposes.[131]

Reposing the ultimate responsibility for maintaining compliance systems and procedures in a director or senior manager ensures that the need for compliance and its implementation is directed at the highest levels of authority in the bank or financial institution, and that oversight is carried out at such levels. As putting in place compliance systems and procedures are necessarily costly and they would inevitably interfere with business, banks and financial institutions may not be motivated to implement such systems and procedures effectively. The imposition of potential personal liability on a director or senior manager for failure to implement effective systems and procedures is arguably a compelling incentive for directors and senior managers tasked with this responsibility. The personal liability regime for senior managers is discussed in Chapter 12, and the earlier example of FCA enforcement against Bank Habib AG Zurich mentioned in section 14.2 shows that the FCA is willing to punish individuals, in that case the Money Laundering Reporting Officer, for failures to effectively implement compliance systems and procedures.

Further, a specific MLRO must be designated in the bank or financial institution unless the firm is a sole trader. The MLRO acts as a focal point for the anti-money laundering and counter-terrorist financing compliance in the firm and has oversight for effective implementation of systems and procedures.[132] The MLRO is also likely to be the one carrying out the functions of 'nominated officer' discussed above in relation to receiving internal suspicious transaction reports and to making the judgment call of whether to make an external report to the NCA or otherwise. This person may be the same as or different from the responsible 'director or senior manager' mentioned above, and where the MLRO is a different person, there would likely be a line of accountability to the director or senior manager so that the MLRO's roles and functions can be overseen.

The MLRO is to be given sufficient stature in the firm, and protected in his/her independence. S/he is also to be adequately resourced.[133] Further, the MLRO is responsible for preparing an annual report of the oversight of compliance to senior management, in order for review and improvement to be implemented.[134] We turn to discuss the regulatory requirements for systems and procedures for compliance and their effectiveness.

---

[130] FCA Handbook SYSC 6.3.8.   [131] FCA Handbook SYSC 6.3.7.   [132] FCA Handbook SYSC 6.3.9.
[133] FCA Handbook SYSC 6.3.9.   [134] FCA Handbook SYSC 6.3.7.

14.5.2 **Systems and procedures**

Compliance systems and procedures in relation to anti-money laundering and counter-terrorist financing involve data collection, analysis and processing systems, alerting for action, reporting and review. Banks and financial institutions are imposed with extensive record-keeping duties, the information in records forming the basis for compliance systems and procedures. Banks and financial institutions are required to maintain the following records:

(a) Information for conducting customer due diligence including deviations from normal due diligence procedures such as for financially excluded customers.[135]

(b) Supporting information for customer transactions that are the subject of customer due diligence or ongoing monitoring.[136]

(c) All actions taken to identify beneficial owners of bodies corporate.[137]

(d) All internal reports made to the MLRO whether or not acted upon to be reported to the NCA, with reasons documented for not acting upon the internal report.[138]

(e) All external reports made to the NCA. [139]

(f) All MLRO annual reports on oversight of compliance systems and procedures.[140]

(g) All internal records of training for compliance with systems and procedures for staff.[141]

Due diligence and transaction records are to be maintained for 5 years from the completion of transaction or end of business relationship.[142] Other records such as internal and external reports or internal records of annual reports or training records should be maintained for 5 years from the date of each record.[143] Records can be kept in paper copies or in electronic form,[144] but the overriding factor that may assist in determining how and where records are to be kept is whether such records can be accessed without undue delay in order for banks and financial institutions to perform due diligence, ongoing review, or transaction reporting.[145]

The use of automated systems may to an extent be important in assisting banks and financial institutions in meeting their compliance requirements.

First, banks and financial institutions are required to keep customer information up-to-date as part of ongoing customer due diligence. The use of automation can assist banks and financial institutions in identifying significant points in time for seeking new customer information or evidence, such as the establishment of a new business relationship or opening of new accounts.[146]

---

[135] Section 40, Money Laundering Regulations 2017; para 8.9, JMLSG Guidance.   [136] Ibid.
[137] Section 28, Money Laundering Regulations 2017.   [138] Para 8.21, JMLSG Guidance.
[139] Para 8.22, JMLSG Guidance.   [140] Para 8.24, JMLSG Guidance.   [141] Ibid.
[142] Section 40, Money Laundering Regulations 2017, which specify that records are not required to be kept in any case exceeding 10 years.   [143] Para 8.23, JMLSG Guidance.
[144] Para 8.26, JMLSG Guidance.   [145] Paras 8.29–33, JMLSG Guidance.
[146] Paras 5.3.27–28, JMLSG Guidance.

Next, banks and financial institutions are to maintain systems and procedures for monitoring customers. Such monitoring is for the purpose of ensuring that transactions fit the risk profiles of customers, and for detecting unusual or suspicious transactions so that appropriate determination can be made as to internal and external reporting. Monitoring systems should be capable of both real-time monitoring as well as periodic reviews after customer transactions have taken place. Both types of monitoring should be capable of leading to the flagging up of suspicious transactions.[147] Monitoring should not be a mechanical process and banks should adopt indicators for review that are based on customers' risk profiles, up-to-date information and adopting a risk-based approach.

Further, banks and financial institutions should explore both manual and automated systems in different combinations in order to carry out monitoring. Where banks and financial institutions process a significant volume of transactions, some extent of automation in applying monitoring procedures would likely be necessary.[148] Automated systems may be simple or sophisticated along a spectrum of artificial intelligence, and they may be input with parameters for the bank's needs in order to flag up suspicions or unusual transactions. Banks and financial institutions need to ensure that where they purchase such automated systems from commercial suppliers, the suppliers are able to calibrate the systems according to the bank's needs. Banks and financial institutions that procure and use automated systems should also understand how the systems work in terms of the assumptions and parameters they implement and whether they may be intelligent enough to learn from past experience.[149] Manual processes can be more effective when human judgment is needed such as 'staff intuition, direct exposure to a customer face-to-face or on the telephone, and the ability, through practical experience, to recognise transactions that do not seem to make sense for that customer.'[150] Hence it is important for banks and financial institutions to maintain appropriate compliance training[151] for relevant staff in order to sustain staff alertness to suspicious transactions. Such compliance training should also be subject to a systematic approach to ensure that all relevant staff are adequately equipped to manage money laundering and terrorist financing risks and comply with the duties imposed on banks and financial institutions.

Systems and procedures in relation to anti-money laundering and counter-terrorist financing are subject to review by internal audit according to the latter's role and responsibility discussed in Chapter 12, as well as by senior management, as earlier discussed.

14.5.3 FCA enforcement

Although the requirements in relation to systems and procedures sound highly procedural, they have formed the basis of much of the FCA's enforcement against banks and financial institutions. The FCA can carry out enforcement against banks and financial

---

[147] Paras 5.7.4–8, JMLSG Guidance. [148] Para 5.7.16, JMLSG Guidance.
[149] Paras 5.7.15–19, JMLSG Guidance. [150] Para 5.7.14, JMLSG Guidance.
[151] FCA Handbook SYSC 6.3.7.

institutions for failing to put in place adequate governance, systems, or procedures even if there is no substantive finding of money laundering or support for terrorist financing. This is because the failure to maintain adequate systems and procedures could result in significantly increased risk that money laundering is facilitated and undetected. The failure to maintain such systems and procedures often entails a breach of the duty to conduct customer due diligence or to make a transaction report, as the ability to conduct customer due diligence or make transaction reports is highly dependent on the effectiveness of systems and procedures.

The FCA has fined several banks in relation to adequate systems and controls in relation to customer due diligence, especially in relation to enhanced due diligence, identification, and risk-monitoring of high-risk customers and PEPs. The private bank Coutts was fined £8.75 million[152] in 2010 for failings in this regard, and Standard Bank Plc[153] was fined in 2014 in the sum of £7.6 million for similar types of failings. Lesser fines of over £500,000 were levied on Habib Bank AG Zurich[154] in 2012 and Guaranty Trust Bank (UK) in 2013[155] for similar failings. In 2016, the FCA levied a £3.2 million fine on Sonali Bank (UK) for failures in governance such as adequate senior management oversight, failings in the MLRO's functions and overall weak systems for customer due diligence and monitoring.[156] The MLRO was personally fined in the sum of £17,900 under the personal liability regime discussed in Chapter 11. The largest fine to date was, however, levied on Deutsche Bank in 2017 in the sum of £163 million.[157] Box 14.7 encapsulates the enforcement case.

Box 14.7 FCA fine against Deutsche Bank for failings in anti-money laundering compliance

The Deutsche Bank's Corporate Banking and Securities division (CB&S) in the UK were alleged to have:

(a) performed inadequate customer due diligence;

(b) failed to ensure that its front office took responsibility for the due diligence obligations;

---

[152] See http://www.fsa.gov.uk/library/communication/pr/2012/032.shtml.

[153] https://www.fca.org.uk/news/press-releases/standard-bank-plc-fined-£76m-failures-its-anti-money-laundering-controls.

[154] https://www.fca.org.uk/publication/final-notices/habib-bank.pdf.

[155] https://www.fca.org.uk/news/press-releases/fca-fines-guaranty-trust-bank-uk-ltd-£525000-failures-its-anti-money-laundering.

[156] 'The FCA found serious and systemic weaknesses affected almost all levels of its AML control and governance structure, including its senior management team, its money laundering reporting function, the oversight of its branches and its AML policies and procedures. This meant that the firm failed to comply with its operational obligations in respect of customer due diligence, the identification and treatment of politically exposed persons, transaction and customer monitoring and making suspicious activity reports.' See https://www.fca.org.uk/news/press-releases/fca-imposes-penalties-sonali-bank-uk-limited-money-laundering.

[157] https://www.fca.org.uk/news/press-releases/fca-fines-deutsche-bank-163-million-anti-money-laundering-controls-failure.

(c)   used flawed customer and country risk rating methodologies in assessing money launder-
      ing risk;

(d)   deficient anti-money laundering policies and procedures;

(e)   an inadequate anti-money laundering IT infrastructure;

(f)   lacked automated anti-money laundering systems for detecting suspicious trades; and

(g)   failed to provide adequate oversight of trades booked in the UK by traders in non-UK
      jurisdictions.

As a result of these failings the FCA took the view that:

Deutsche Bank failed to obtain sufficient information about its customers to inform the risk assessment process and to provide a basis for transaction monitoring. The failings allowed the front office of
Deutsche Bank's Russia-based subsidiary (DB Moscow) to execute more than 2,400 pairs of trades that
mirrored each other (mirror trades) between April 2012 and October 2014. The mirror trades were used
by customers of Deutsche Bank and DB Moscow to transfer more than $6 billion from Russia, through
Deutsche Bank in the UK, to overseas bank accounts, including in Cyprus, Estonia, and Latvia. The customers on the Moscow and London sides of the mirror trades were connected to each other and the
volume and value of the securities was the same on both sides. The purpose of the mirror trades was the
conversion of Roubles into US Dollars and the covert transfer of those funds out of Russia, which is highly
suggestive of financial crime.

 Key takeaways

- Banks are to ensure that anti-money laundering and counter-terrorist financing policies are
  maintained at the level of a director or senior manager who has personal responsibility in the
  terms discussed in Chapter 11.

- Banks are to appoint a MLRO for oversight of the implementation of effective anti-money
  laundering and counter-terrorist financing systems and procedures.

- Banks must put in place adequate systems and procedures for dealing with the duties in customer due diligence, monitoring and review, transaction reporting, training, and education of
  staff, generating reports to senior management, record retention, and day-to-day operations
  where money laundering risks feature.

- These systems and procedures should be able to perform both real-time and periodic post-
  transactions review, and should be a combination of automated and manual systems and
  procedures where appropriate. The fine against Deutsche Bank seems to suggest that where
  automated systems may be useful, not installing them can be regarded as a failure to implement effective systems and procedures, attracting FCA enforcement.

- The FCA is the principal enforcer of breaches of duties in customer due diligence, monitoring
  and review, and transaction reporting, as well as failures to implement and maintain adequate
  systems and procedures. The FCA has fined a number of banks, including Deutsche Bank to
  date.

Key bibliography

Legislation

FCA Handbook SYSC 6

Additional reading

Angela SM Irwin and Kim-Kwang Raymond Choo, 'The Future of Technology in Customer Identification & Relationship Risk' (2014) at https://papers.ssrn.com/sol3/papers.cfm?abstract_id=2431944

Questions

1. Critically evaluate the obligations imposed on banks in respect of their role in financial intelligence relating to money laundering. Are bank customers adequately protected when a bank makes a suspicious transaction report?

   Answer tips *You may wish to discuss the obligations for a bank under ss330–2 and the effect of suspension of customer transactions pending appropriate consent under ss335–6 Proceeds of Crime Act 2002. You should discuss to what extent customers can challenge bank decisions or call banks to accountability, in light of the s333 tipping off offence. You should also assess if judicial review is available against the NCA. You should refer to key case law in this area.*

2. Should banks be fined heavily for breaches of procedural requirements that are preventive in nature, whether or not money laundering has indeed occurred?

   Answer tips *You may wish to provide an overview of the procedural requirements in due diligence, reporting of suspicious transactions and the implementation of systems and procedures. While bearing in mind the high-level nature of this question and the need to be succinct with selective detail, you should discuss what you consider to be the spirit of such preventive measures and how they relate to disrupting the money laundering process. You may also discuss key enforcement cases such as the Deutsche Bank fine.*

Glossary

ACCOUNT INFORMATION SERVICE PROVIDER An online service to provide consolidated information on one or more payment accounts held by a payment service user with either another payment service provider or with more than one payment service provider.

ACCOUNT SERVICING PAYMENT SERVICES PROVIDER The provider (normally a bank) where a customer's payment account is held.

ASSET MANAGEMENT VEHICLE In the context of resolution, this means the establishment of an asset management vehicle by the state that purchases 'bad' or non-performing assets from a bank that is in crisis, in order to manage them to the point of eventual sale or winding down.

ASSIGNMENT (LOANS) The transfer of the original lending bank's (the assignor) rights to all or part of its interest in the loan to the other participating banks (the assignees).

AVAILABLE STABLE FUNDING The funding resources that banks have that 'stay' with them across different time horizons. This is required for measuring banks' compliance with the net stable funding ratio.

BAIL-IN This involves writing down or cancelling the rights of shareholders first and then a range of junior and unsecured creditors in order to provide for loss absorption by a bank.

BAIL-OUT When an individual, a business or a government offers money (loans, bonds, stocks, or cash) to a failing business to prevent the consequences of its downfall.

BANKING UNION Comprising of the Single Supervisory Mechanism and the Single Resolution Mechanism that ensures a form of centralised supervision and crisis management for euro-area banks. These are discussed in Chapter 7.

BRIDGE INSTITUTION An institution set up by the State to take over ownership of bank shares and/or assets in order to insulate it from disorderly private claims or insolvency procedures, while it is given time to be resolved.

CAPITAL Instruments held by the bank that were capable of retention and seen as capable of absorbing businesses losses made by banks. Tier one capital, the preferred forms of capital are largely in the form of the shareholders' equity capital invested in banks and banks' retained earnings. Weaker forms of capital, that is, tier two capital are less permanent in nature such as redeemable shares or long-term subordinated debt.

CAPITAL ADEQUACY Regulatory standards that prescribe that banks can only take certain levels of risk that are supported by adequate levels of capital, extensively discussed in Chapter 8.

CAPITAL CONSERVATION BUFFER A regulatory capital requirement stipulated in the Basel III Accord and EU CRD IV Directive 2013 that requires banks to hold an extra 2.5 per cent of risk-weighted assets as regulatory capital by 1 January 2019. This that applies across the board to all banks.

CHARGE A form of security which gives the lending bank the power to apply to court to realise the property subject to the charge in priority to other creditors.

CHEQUE A written instruction to a bank from an account holder requesting the bank to pay a sum of money to a third party.

COLLECTIVE INVESTMENT SCHEME Means an investment vehicle such as a trust or a company that is established to manage contributions of investment from investors in a centralised manner so that investors do not have day-to-day control over the management of the pooled investment capital, but expect to share in financial gain in the outcomes of the investment management, see also s235, Financial Services and Markets Act 2000.

CONDITIONS PRECEDENT Terms that must be complied with before a borrower can draw down the funds from the bank in relation to a loan facility.

CONNECTED CLIENTS Clients of a bank that are economically connected to each other or structurally part of the same corporate group, as defined in the manner in Chapter 9.

CONTRA PROFERENTUM A doctrine of contractual interpretation which provides that any ambiguity in the wording of a clause will be construed against the party seeking to rely on it.

CONVERSION Conversion is a tortious action which occurs when one person interferes with the property rights of another.

COUNTER-CYCLICAL BUFFER A regulatory capital requirement stipulated in the Basel III Accord and EU CRD IV Directive 2013 to allow national regulators to compel banks to hold additional capital in order to control risk-taking so that banks can be more prepared and resilient in challenging times.

COUNTERMAND The revocation of a previously given instruction.

COVENANTS Undertakings given in the context of a loan facility by a borrower to a bank which give the bank a degree of control over the conduct of the borrower's business to ensure that the borrower preserves his financial standing.

CREDIT RISK The risk that a counterparty that the bank has lent to will be unable to meet its payment obligations.

CREDIT RISK CONVERSION Applying a method to treat off-balance sheet exposures as equivalent to a loan so as to apply credit risk-weighting to such off-balance sheet exposures.

CREDIT TRANSFER A push of funds from the payer to the payee, a credit transfer involves a communication from the payer to his bank, instructing it to credit the account of the payee.

CREDITOR A person or corporation to whom money is owed.

D-SIB Domestically systemically important bank, a bank whose failure may create severe impact for the financial sector and local economy (also included in the scope of 'Other Systemically Important Institutions or OSIIs' under the EU CRD IV Directive 2013).

DEBIT TRANSFER A pull of funds by the payee from the payer, a debit transfer involves a communication from the payee to the payer's bank, instructing it to transfer funds from the payees account.

DEBTOR A person or corporation who owes money to another.

DEFERRED NET SETTLEMENT CLEARING SYSTEM A net settlement system where final settlements occur between participating banks at the end of a predefined settlement cycle (e.g. once a day at a particular time) when the net obligations between participants are calculated and presented to the settlement agent (e.g. the Bank of England) for settlement.

DELEVERAGE (ING) Rapid reduction of debt levels, for example by selling off assets, not committing to new lending.

DIRECT DEBIT A payment instruction initiated directly by the payee pursuant to the payer's authority.

DRAWER (OF A CHEQUE) The party who writes and signs the cheque.

DUAL-REGULATED Referring to banks that are regulated by both the Prudential Regulation Authority (PRA) and Financial Conduct Authority (FCA) in the UK. These entities are discussed in Chapter 6.

EUROPEAN SYSTEM OF FINANCIAL SUPER-
VISION (ESFS) Regulatory architecture
at EU level for overseeing member state
regulators and sometimes regulated entities
directly, comprising of the European Banking Authority (EBA), European Securities
and Markets Authority (ESMA), European
Insurance and Occupational Pensions Authority (EIOPA), a Joint Committee of these
authorities and the European Systemic Risk
Board (ESRB). These entities are discussed
in Chapter 7.

FIXED-TERM LOAN A loan made to an individual or business for a fixed period of time.

FOREIGN EXCHANGE RISK The risk of currency fluctuations in banks' holdings.

FREEZING INJUNCTION An order issued pursuant to Rule 25.1(f) of the Civil Procedure
Rules 1998 which freezes the customer's
assets with the aim of preventing him from
otherwise dispersing the proceeds of the
account in order to avoid the execution of a
judgement that has been made against him.

G-SIBs Globally systemically important
banks, determined by the Financial Stability
Board in November each year in order to
apply additional regulatory capital buffers
to them.

GENERAL GOOD Exceptions that can be
imposed in national law on incoming EEA
goods, services or branches, in order to
protect legitimate public interest in that
Member State. This is discussed in the case
of *Alpine Investments BV v Minister van
Financiën* (1995) C-384/93.

GIRO SYSTEM Traditionally, a paper-based
fund transfer system initiated by the Post
Office in the 1960s. In recent years we have
seen the development of electronic fund
transfer systems, the main ones being BACS
or CHAPS transfers.

HAIRCUT Discount applied to face value
of a financial instrument for purposes of
conservative valuation.

HIGH-QUALITY LIQUIDITY ASSETS Defined
by the Basel Committee and EU legislation
to be held by banks in certain proportions
in order to meet the Liquidity Coverage
Ratio.

HOLDER (OF A CHEQUE) The recipient of
a cheque i.e. the person in whose favour a
cheque is drawn.

HOME COUNTRY CONTROL The home mem-
ber state that authorises a financial services
firm remains responsible for supervising it
even in relation to foreign branches.

INSTITUTION-SPECIFIC COUNTER-CYCLICAL
BUFFER The buffer, stipulated in the EU
Capital Requirements IV Directive 2013, is
calculated by obtaining a weighted average
of the counter-cyclical buffers set in each
jurisdiction where the bank has exposures,
including both EU and non-EU jurisdictions.

INTEREST RATE RISK Interest rates are
the cost of borrowing. Where a bank is
concerned, interest rate risk refers to the
possibility that the price at which banks
lend fluctuates over the term of the loan,
and thus affects its profitability or may even
cause loss.

INTERNAL CONTROL The functions of compliance, risk management and internal audit
as defined and explained in Chapter 12.

LARGE EXPOSURES Lending by banks to
a single customer or a group of connected
customers in excess of 10 per cent of the
bank's 'eligible capital', which is the sum of
its tier one capital and a third of its tier two
capital.

LENDER OF LAST RESORT The role of the
central bank in providing emergency lending facilities to banks against a wide range
of collateral if banks encounter short-term
funding problems.

LEVERAGE RATIO A regulatory ratio that restricts the total level of bank lending to bank
capital without applying risk-weighting. This
is discussed in Chapter 9, section 9.4.

LEVERAGE RATIO BUFFER A capital buffer that is measured using the bank's total exposure measure and not risk-weighted assets. There are two types of leverage ratio buffers, the Counter-cyclical leverage ratio buffer and the Additional leverage ratio buffer. They provides restraining forces to moderate total levels of lending by banks.

LIQUIDITY COVERAGE RATIO A ratio of liquid assets to be maintained by banks in order to ensure that it can meet its net outflows (net of inflows and outflows) for a forward-looking period of 30 days. This is discussed in Chapter 9, section 9.2.

MACRO-PRUDENTIAL REGULATION/SUPER-VISION Regulatory responsibility reposed in a body that undertakes a bird's eye view of the financial sector and markets and makes recommendations to deal with problems or risks in a manner intended to prevent financial crises. The Financial Policy Committee of the Bank of England performs this role in the UK (discussed in Chapter 6, section 6.4) and the European Systemic Risk Board performs this role at the EU level (discussed in Chapter 7).

MANDATE An instruction from a customer to its bank.

MARKET RISK Risk incurred by banks in relation to 'market-based' activities which may cause loss. These activities include securities underwriting, corporate finance in restructuring and mergers and acquisitions, proprietary trading, collective investment schemes and advisory and broker services, see footnotes in Chapter 8, section 8.3. Market risk is a collective term used to refer to *foreign exchange risk, interest rate risk, commodities risk* and *trading book risk*.

MATERIAL RISK-TAKERS Categories of staff including senior management, staff engaged in control functions and any employee receiving total remuneration that takes them into the same remuneration bracket as senior management and risk takers, whose professional activities have a material impact on their risk profile, defined in the Material Risk Takers Regulation 2014.

MICRO-PRUDENTIAL REGULATION Capital adequacy regulation as well as other regulatory techniques such as liquidity regulation, leverage ratio, the MREL/TLAC regulatory standards and stress-testing, covered in Chapters 8 and 9.

MINIMUM REQUIREMENT FOR OWN FUNDS AND ELIGIBLE LIABILITIES (MREL) Loss absorption and recapitalising capital as defined in Commission Delegated Regulation (EU) 2016/1450 of 23 May 2016.

NET STABLE FUNDING RATIO A longer term liquidity ratio to be maintained by banks to ensure that they have a range of funding resources that match their funding needs over different horizons. This is discussed in Chapter 9, section 9.2.

NOVATION (LOANS) A device where the original loan contract is cancelled and replaced with a new contract on the same terms (except with a new lender). Allows the transfer of both the rights that the bank has against the borrower, and the obligations that the bank owes the borrower.

OPERATIONAL RISK The risk of loss resulting from inadequate or failed internal processes, people and systems or from external events.

OUTPUT FLOOR A prescribed level set by the Basel Committee of risk-weighting measurements that are derived from standardised approaches, in order to compare with risk-weightings derived from internal models and to provide a minimum level of risk-weighting measurements in case of internal model measurements being lower.

OVERDRAFT An extension of credit from a bank to a customer when an account reaches zero. When an account becomes overdrawn the bank becomes the creditor and the customer becomes the debtor.

OWN FUNDS Defined under the EU Capital legislation and refers to the sum of tier one and two capital.

PAYING BANK (CHEQUES) The bank at which the drawer of a cheque holds an account.

PAYMENT INITIATION SERVICE PROVIDERS A service provider that initiates a payment order at the request of the payment service user with respect to a payment account held at another payment service provider. For example, Apple Pay allows users to initiate a payment through their mobile phone interface, which stores their credit or debit card information in its digital wallet.

PILLAR 2 BUFFER Additional regulatory capital requirements that may be imposed by the UK PRA, following supervisory scrutiny and review of a bank's risk profile.

PRECAUTIONARY RECAPITALISATION State injection of funds into a solvent bank that is not subject to resolution, under Article 32(4) of the Bank Recovery and Resolution Directive 2014 discussed in Chapter 13.

POSSESSORY SECURITY Arrangements where the lender acquires possession of property that serves as collateral in respect of a loan or overdraft facility.

PROPRIETARY SECURITY Arrangements where the borrower grants to the bank a proprietary right in the relevant property which gives the bank the right to seize the property in the event of default or the insolvency of the borrower.

REAL TIME GROSS SETTLEMENT SYSTEM The continuous process of settling payments in real time without netting debits with credits across the participants' account with the Bank of England.

RECOVERY PLANS Mandatory plans required to be maintained by banks containing measures to be taken by the institution to restore its financial position following a significant deterioration of its financial situation.

REQUIRED STABLE FUNDING The funding needs that banks have in order to meet their contractual commitments to lend. This is needed for measuring banks' compliance with the net stable funding ratio.

RESOLUTION A suite of tools for dealing with a bank crisis, to be applied by a resolution authority after determining that a bank is 'failing or likely to fail'.

RESOLUTION COLLEGE A group of resolution authorities that are concerned with a cross-border banking group have to establish a resolution college in order to ensure that any resolution is carried out in a coordinated manner, under mandatory EU legislation or under best practices recommended by the Financial Stability Board.

RESOLUTION PLAN Plans for each bank's resolution options as drawn up by resolution authorities subject to input from banks, and other resolution authorities where a banking group is concerned.

REVERSE STRESS TESTING A regulatory requirement for banks to put in processes to adopt particular adverse end outcomes and then test the bank's resilience against the outcomes.

RING-FENCING To structure a UK bank that accepts in excess of £25 billion in retail deposits in accordance with the The Financial Services and Markets Act 2000 (Ring-fenced Bodies and Core Activities) Order 2014 and Financial Services and Markets Act 2000 (Excluded Activities and Prohibitions) Order 2014 discussed in Chapter 10, section 10.1.

RISK-WEIGHTING Applying a risk factor to the value of exposure by the bank, in order to determine the riskiness of that exposure. The 'risk factor' framework has been subject to prescriptive, standardised as well as flexible approaches in the years of developing capital adequacy regulation discussed in Chapter 8.

SECONDARY BANKS The banking sector that existed in the UK since the 1950s extending household and business credit to riskier borrowers who could not have borrowed from more established High Street banks. This sector was almost wiped out in the secondary banking crisis that occurred between 1973–5.

SECURITISATION (OR SECURITISED ASSETS) The packaging or bundling of usually loan assets into securities based on their underlying income streams, to be sold to investors in the market such as institutional investors.

SECURITY Gives the bank some form of proprietary or possessory right in the borrower's (or a third party's) property that it can exercise in order to enforce repayment of a loan or overdraft facility.

SENIOR MANAGERS REGIME A regime for prescribing responsibilities and conduct rules for individuals that are responsible for defined 'senior' or executive functions in a bank, which can entail personal liability imposed by the UK regulators, the PRA or FCA. This is discussed in Chapter 11.

SINGLE RESOLUTION MECHANISM (SRM) The mechanism for carrying out resolution powers in relation to banks supervised under the SSM.

SINGLE SUPERVISORY MECHANISM (SSM) The supervisory role played by the European Central Bank, as an independent function, over banks in the euro-area designated to be directly supervised by it.

STANDING ORDER An instruction given by a payer to his bank for the bank to make regular fixed payments to a payee.

STRONG CUSTOMER AUTHENTICATION A method of authenticating online payments or verifying customer's identity before accepting an online payment. Authentication is based on the use of two or more elements that are independent.

SUB-PARTICIPATION (LOANS) Creates separate contracts between the original lending bank and the participants which transfers the credit risk from the lending bank (known as the grantor or seller) to a third party (known as the grantee or buyer).

SUPERVISORY COLLEGE Multilateral working groups of relevant supervisors that are formed for the collective purpose of enhancing effective consolidated supervision of an international banking group on an ongoing basis.

SYNDICATED LOAN A loan where two or more banks who each contribute towards making a single loan to a borrower.

SYSTEMIC RISK BUFFER Stipulated in the EU CRD IV Directive that allows national regulators to impose an additional buffer on the financial sector or one or more subsets of the sector, in order to address long term non-cyclical and macro-prudential risks.

THIRD-PARTY DEBT ORDER An order issued pursuant to Part 72 of the Civil Procedure Rules 1998 which allows the court to grant to a judgement creditor of the customer, an order which attaches to funds held by a third party (i.e. a bank).

TRADING BOOK RISK Risks incurred by banks in relation to trading in securities and derivatives, discussed in Chapter 8, section 8.3.

TRANSFER OF FUNDS The movement of a credit balance from one account to another.

VALUE-AT-RISK A methodology for measuring maximum loss in market risk which used to focus on narrow time horizons of historical data and is now required, in post-crisis reforms, to incorporate greater stress boundaries and to be more conservative.

Index

NB Boxes, tables and figures are located by a prefix B,T and F respectively before the page number

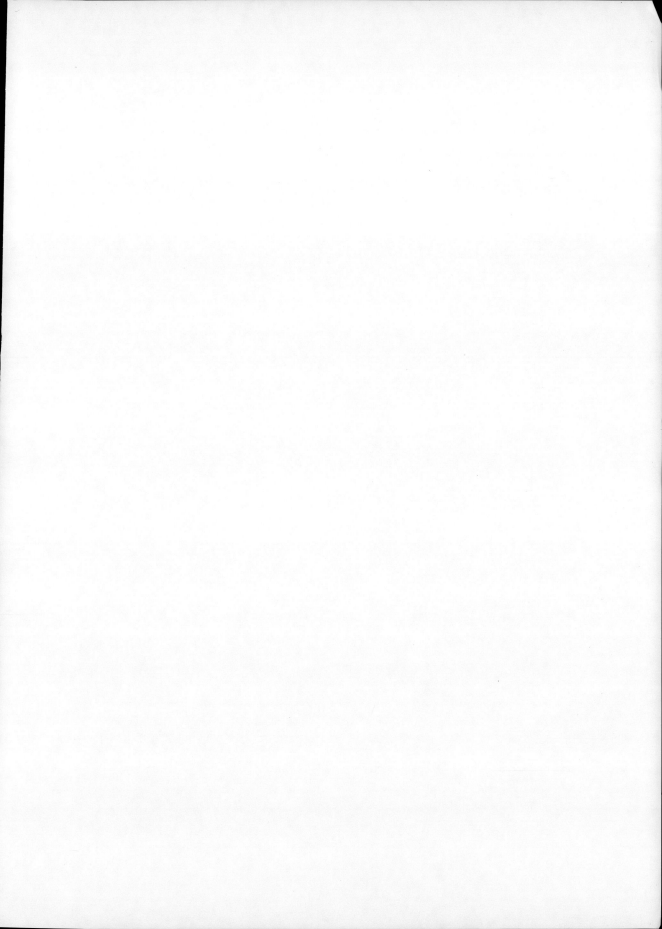